1 MONTH OF
FREE
READING

at

www.ForgottenBooks.com

By purchasing this book you are eligible for one month membership to ForgottenBooks.com, giving you unlimited access to our entire collection of over 1,000,000 titles via our web site and mobile apps.

To claim your free month visit:

www.forgottenbooks.com/free916620

ISBN 978-0-265-96544-3
PIBN 10916620

7-8 EDWARD VII.   SESSIONAL PAPER No. 29a   A. 1908

CIVIL SERVICE COMMISSION
1908

MINUTES OF EVIDENCE

VOL. I

BOARD OF CIVIL SERVICE EXAMINERS.
DEPARTMENT OF SECRETARY OF STATE.
DEPARTMENT OF AGRICULTURE.
DEPARTMENT OF CUSTOMS.
DEPARTMENT OF FINANCE.
GEOLOGICAL SURVEY.
DEPARTMENT OF INDIAN AFFAIRS.
DEPARTMENT OF INLAND REVENUE.
DEPARTMENT OF THE INTERIOR.
DEPARTMENT OF JUSTICE.
DEPARTMENT OF PUBLIC PRINTING AND STATIONERY.
DEPARTMENT OF LABOUR.
DEPARTMENT OF MARINE AND FISHERIES.
DEPARTMENT OF MILITIA AND DEFENCE.
ROYAL NORTHWEST MOUNTED POLICE.

Pages 1 to 768

PRINTED BY ORDER OF PARLIAMENT

OTTAWA
PRINTED BY S. E. DAWSON, PRINTER TO THE KING'S MOST
EXCELLENT MAJESTY
1908

[No. 29a—Vol. I—1908]

TABLE OF CONTENTS.

CIVIL SERVICE COMMISSION.

MINUTES OF EVIDENCE.

Witnesses who Appeared before the Commission, and were Examined; also Memorials and Statements Submitted by Witnesses.

CIVIL SERVICE COMMISSION.

NAMES OF WITNESSES ARRANGED ALPHABETICALLY

NAMES OF WITNESSES ARRANGED ALPHABETICALLY—*Concluded.*

ROYAL COMMISSION ON THE CIVIL SERVICE.

OTTAWA, WEDNESDAY, May 15, 1907.

The Royal Commission on the Civil Service met this morning at 10.30 o'clock.

Present:—Mr. J. M. COURTNEY, C.M.G., Chairman.

Mr. THOMAS FYSHE, Montreal, and

Mr. P. J. BAZIN, Quebec.

Dr. A. D. DeCELLES, General Librarian of Parliament, called and sworn and examined.

By the Chairman:

. You are one of the Board of Civil Service Examiners ?—A. Yes.

Q. And you have been since 1882 ?—A. Since 1882, since the board was started.

Q. You and Dr. Thorburn are the survivors of the original board ?—A. Yes.

Q. And you have been holding examinations more or less since 1882 ?—A. Twice a year—the two examinations, the Entrance Examinations and the Promotion Examinations.

Q. The Entrance Examinations are held in November?—A. Each year.

Q. Each year. And the Promotion Examinations in May of each year ?—A. In May, yes.

By Mr. Fyshe:

Q. Have you any rigid method of conducting your examinations ?—A. What do you mean by 'rigid method?'

Q. I mean have you a regular fixed system ?—A. We have a fixed system. It was established when the board was organized and our regulations are submitted to the Government who approved of them.

Q. Were your recommendations generally accepted ?—A. Yes.

By the Chairman:

Q. What is your remuneration for the examinations you conduct?—A. $500 a year is the remuneration.

By Mr. Fyshe:

Q. To begin with ?—A. It is a fixed salary not subject to increase as in the Civil Service.

By the Chairman:

Q. In addition to your salary as librarian?—A. Yes, in addition to my salary as librarian.

By Mr. Fyshe:

Q. I suppose your duties as a Civil Service Examiner take up a good deal of time ?—A. Yes, the duties take up a great deal of time. The examinations are held

29a—1

NAMES OF WITNESSES ARRANGED ALPHABETICALLY—*Concluded.*

ROYAL COMMISSION ON THE CIVIL SERVICE.

OTTAWA, WEDNESDAY, May 15, 1907.

The Royal Commission on the Civil Service met this morning at 10.30 o'clock.

Present:—Mr. J. M. COURTNEY, C.M.G., Chairman.

Mr. THOMAS FYSHE, Montreal, and

Mr. P. J. BAZIN, Quebec.

Dr. A. D. DECELLES, General Librarian of Parliament, called and sworn and examined.

By the Chairman:

Q. You are one of the Board of Civil Service Examiners ?—A. Yes.

Q. And you have been since 1882 ?—A. Since 1882, since the board was started.

Q. You and Dr. Thorburn are the survivors of the original board ?—A. Yes.

Q. And you have been holding examinations more or less since 1882 ?—A. Twice a year—the two examinations, the Entrance Examinations and the Promotion Examinations.

Q. The Entrance Examinations are held in November ?—A. Each year.

Q. Each year. And the Promotion Examinations in May of each year ?—A. In May, yes.

By Mr. Fyshe:

Q. Have you any rigid method of conducting your examinations ?—A. What do you mean by 'rigid method?'

Q. I mean have you a regular fixed system ?—A. We have a fixed system. It was established when the board was organized and our regulations are submitted to the Government who approved of them.

Q. Were your recommendations generally accepted ?—A. Yes.

By the Chairman:

Q. What is your remuneration for the examinations you conduct?—A. $500 a year is the remuneration.

By Mr. Fyshe:

Q. To begin with ?—A. It is a fixed salary not subject to increase as in the Civil Service.

By the Chairman:

Q. In addition to your salary as librarian?—A. Yes, in addition to my salary as librarian.

By Mr. Fyshe:

Q. I suppose your duties as a Civil Service Examiner take up a good deal of time ?—A. Yes, the duties take up a great deal of time. The examinations are held

29a—1

7-8 EDWARD VII., A. 1908

twice a year but we have to supply information all the year round in answer to applicants.

Q. There is a regular office for the Board then?—A. Yes, there is now an office and a secretary.

By the Chairman:

Q. On the occasion of the last investigation in 1892, you stated that you did not approve altogether of competitive examinations?—A. Yes.

Q. Are you still of that opinion?—A. Yes, after examining and studying the system in England and in the United States. I saw that they were opposed to it to some extent although they kept it up. It was supposed that the candidate coming out of the competitive examination with the highest number of marks would generally take the place offered to him but his success as a rule would give him ambition and a successful candidate would not accept the office offered to him when the salary was small, and then they would have to omit the best qualified man and fall back on another person.

By Mr. Fyshe:

Q. And in that case the man rejecting the situation, was he given something better?—A. No, he was dropped from the list.

Q. He was dropped altogether?—A. Yes.

Q. Would that not result in the selecting of inferior men?—A. It would give, I suppose, a second-class man, an average man.

Q. Then any man who declined what he was offered, was dropped altogether from the lists?—A. He was dropped from the lists.

By the Chairman:

Q. Do you believe in examinations to some extent?—A. Yes, to some extent.

By Mr. Fyshe:

Q. Would not there be a possibility of the appointers having the power to shelve a man whom they disliked, even if he had higher marks?—A. I do not think so.

Q. That would be in their power you know?—A. I could not say.

Q. Unless the offices were fixed in advance, in rotation? If they were fixed in advance, the contestants would have what they looked for.—A. Of course, what I say is not true of every case. Some will probably accept the offer. But I regard that as one argument against competitive examinations. On the other hand, I hold that a man coming out best at an examination is not always the best fitted.

Q. It does not follow that he is superior in a particular thing?—A. Of course the Government have to look for a certain rule.

By the Chairman:

Q. Do candidates repeatedly try now?—A. Yes.

Q. They do still, do they?—A. Yes.

Q. They come back and back again to the Entrance Examination?—A. Yes.

By Mr. Fyshe:

Q. They are allowed to do that?—A. Yes.

By Mr. Bazin:

. Q. At any time?—A. At any time. If they have failed in one subject only, they are allowed to come up again for examination in that subject alone.

By Mr. Fyshe:

Q. Just as they are allowed to do sometimes in the University examinations?—A. If they fail in more than one subject, they have to undergo the whole examination again.

By the Chairman:

Q. Does it often happen now that people come up again ?—A. Yes, I suppose I might say one-fourth of them come back again.

Q. You go to Montreal do you ?—A. Yes.

Q. You superintend the examinations in Montreal ?—A. Yes.

By Mr. Fyshe:

Q. Do the candidates as a rule come from any special class ?—A. No, they come from all classes of society. I do not think they are the best of the young men in any case.

Q. They are not ?—A. No.

By the Chairman:

Q. I see there were 17 points at which examinations were held last November ?—A. Yes, we have increased the number.

Q. And there are only three examiners ? Where does Dr. Thorburn preside over the examinations ?—A. He presides over the examination in Toronto.

Q. And where does Dr. Glashan preside ?—A. Over the examination here in Ottawa.

Q. And you go to Montreal?—A. To Montreal. Of course we have sub-examiners at other points. There are only three examiners composing the Board. One of them presides in Montreal—that is myself; a second in Toronto—that is Dr. Thorburn; and Dr. Glashan presides here. The board is represented by sub-examiners at other points.

By the Chairman:

Q. Halifax, Charlottetown and other places ?—A. Yes. I might mention here that six years ago there were more candidates in Ottawa than the rest of the Dominion put together.

By Mr. Fyshe:

Q. How is that ?—A. Perhaps it is because of the view of the buildings.

Q. They are in a better position to realize the advantages?—A. To realize the advantages, and they don't hear the grumbling of those who are in the service. Another fact I might mention here is, that for the last five years the number of lady candidates has been superior to that of the men.

Q. Are you generally employing women now ?—A. Some departments have a very large number.

Q. What is your experience in regard to them; is it satisfactory ?—A. I would not express any opinion on this point because in my department there are only three.

By the Chairman:

Q. In the Library there are only three lady employees and you do not know what the experience is in other departments after they pass the examinations and receive appointments ? Do you think there is much copying now in these examinations ?—A. Not much, no.

Q. There is not much, you say, but still there is a little copying?—A. Not much, the great danger in the examinations now is the personation of candidates.

Q. I was coming to that. There is still personation going on ?—A. There are a few cases, but the number has diminished because they are invariably caught after they are appointed. The cases of copying have diminished but there are still some cases of personation. We had three cases of the latter during the last two years.

By Mr. Fyshe:

Q. Where was that?—A. One was detected at Montreal. The candidate was a man who had been up before and who had passed and of course we turned him out.

29a—1½

7-8 EDWARD VII., A. 1908

In the case of two other candidates, they had been appointed on the strength of their examination but they were found to be so weak that the chief of the department where they were employed wrote to the Board asking how it happened that two men so utterly bad——

Q. Should pass the examination ?—A. Should pass the examination. We said that we had no explanation to give, but we examined the papers of the two individuals in question and we found that their writing did not tally. They had exchanged numbers with personators.

By Mr. Bazin:

Q. Is every candidate who wishes to become an employee of the government subjected to examination ?—A. Yes.

Q. He has to pass an examination ?—A. That is the law.

Q. Before getting his appointment ?—A. That is the law. There are a few exempt.

Q. I mean any class ?—A. Those that hold a certificate from the Royal Military College, Kingston, and those that hold the certificate of Bachelors of Universities are exempt.

By Mr. Fyshe:

Q. They are not required to pass an examination ?—A. No.

By the Chairman:

Q. Reverting to the subject of personation, section 14 of the Civil Service Act reads as follows:—

'Every person, who, at any examining held under this Act, personates any candidate or employs, induces or allows any person to personate him, is guilty of an offence against this Act, and liable, on summary conviction, to imprisonment to a term not exceeding six months, or to a fine not exceeding two hundred dollars, and, if he is employed in the Civil Service, to be dismissed therefrom.'

Did you ever exact that fine ?—A. Yes.

Q. Did you ever get it ?—A. Yes. There was some years ago a professional man who was fined $50.

Q. Why did you compromise ? When the fine is $200 why did you compromise on $50 ?—A. It is within the discretion of the magistrate to fix the fine.

Mr. Fyshe.—The section says the fine shall not exceed two hundred dollars.

By the Chairman:

Q. Is that the only occasion when criminal proceedings were taken during your experience of 25 years as an examiner ?—A. No, there were several instances. A large number of candidates—not a large number but a certain number of candidates—who were copying or being personated were dismissed from the service in Montreal and in different other places. The trouble is we cannot always get the personator. We tried to do so in the last investigation we made in Montreal, and we found that one personator had gone to the States and of the other there was no trace at all.

Q. Have you ever got a hint that it is desirable you should give, say, Mademoiselle Dubois, for illustration, the benefit of every doubt ?—A. No, we never have any doubts.

Q. I would not like to contradict you in that. Possibly it is done in the case of English speaking people ?—A. It would not be of any use going to Dr. Thorburn at all.

Q. You have nothing to do with the selection for employment of passed candidates ?—A. No, although I have been asked sometimes to point out from the list of successful candidates a man I would consider well up in a certain branch of the examination. For example to find out if a man is well up in literature and mathe-

SESSIONAL PAPER No. 29a

matics. I would glance at the record and say ' this man '—without knowing who he was—' seems to be competent.'

Q. Here is a list of the candidates that passed successfully last November. There are 349 altogether, of whom 193 live in Ottawa. They are not published in order of merit are they, after passing ? A. No, not at all.

Q. The list published is simply the names of the passed candidates ?—A. Yes.

By Mr. Fyshe:

Q. Are they published in alphabetical order ?—A. Yes, in alphabetical order. The government gets a list of the candidates with the number of marks gained by each.

By the Chairman:

Q. The Secretary of State gets that ?—A. Yes.

By Mr. Fyshe:

Q. Do you not arrange the successful candidates in order of merit ?—A. No.

Q. You never do ?—A. No.

Q. That is not wanted ?—A. That is not asked for. We have not been asked to place the list of candidates in that manner. The Government have before them the list of candidates with the number of marks secured by each. If they want to consult that list they are able to do so

Q. The list is not put before them in such a way as to carry its maximum of effect ?—A. No.

Q. And that is not wanted because they desire to introduce the political way ? No answer.

By the Chairman:

Q. Do you find the candidates that are coming up now are equal to those of 20 years ago ? Is there an equally strong desire to compete at the examinations ?— A. I find that these examinations cause the young men to study more than they formerly did. They now prepare for the examinations.

By Mr. Fyshe:

Q. Do you think they have improved ?—A. They have improved. They have more advantages than the earlier candidates enjoyed.

Q. The same thing gets more systematized ?—A. The questions prepared every year are subsequently published in pamphlet form and those who desire to enter for examination have the advantage of studying those questions.

Q. Of course you do not have the same questions ?—A. No, but after an interval of 25 years we have been obliged to go back. Candidates have to study history for example and if they consult the published questions they have to open up their text books and study all around.

Q. Are the questions recorded every year ?—A. Yes.

Q. Is that desirable, do you think ?—A. I think so.

The CHAIRMAN.—They do that in the Annual Report of the Civil Service Examinations in England.

The WITNESS.—I think it is important. If a man studies each of these questions, he will certainly go through the history of England, the United States and Canada.

By Mr. Fyshe:

Q. Of course an examination of that kind in history is more or less a test of memory, but with mathematics it is different. When women are employed what do you give them to do ?—A. Copying.

7-8 EDWARD VII., A. 1908

Q. And typewriting ?—A. Typewriting and shorthand writing.

Q. Are they good shorthand writers ?—A. Yes. That is their best point, as a rule, in my experience, although my experience is very limited; we have only three ladies in the Library.

By the Chairman:

Q. When examinations are held do you get testimonials as to character from the candidates ?—A. Yes, as to character—in the examinations.

Q. How many testimonials do you get as to character?—A. One from a clergyman. We generally get a testimonial as to the character of the candidate.

Q. In the competitive examinations in England the candidates get three testimonials ?—A. We exact three, one as to the character as I have just stated, one as to health——

Q. Apart from that, the candidates at the competitive examinations in England get three testimonials as to character ?—A. Three ?

Q. One from a clergyman, and two from friends, justices of the peace and similar persons. You only get one testimonial as to character ?—A. We only get one.

Q. Does that not help the persons interested ? An individual, for instance, like the one you spoke of, that personated, might write out the character himself ?—A. Yes, he might but how can we find out?

Q. If you had a greater number of testimonials ?—A. Yes, I think we might increase the number.

Q. Is that in your power ?—A. Yes.

Q. You would have to get an order in council ?—A. We would have to get the sanction of the Government.

By Mr. Fyshe:

Q. Does the applicant as a rule, provide recommendations from members of parliament and so on ?—A. No, not from members of parliament.

Q. From whom then?—Very often from clergymen or a well known person in the locality to which the candidate belongs.

Q. People of local influence ?—A. Yes.

Q. But often are they not members of parliament?—A. No, I have not seen any from members of parliament.

Q. The members of parliament come in afterwards? The political influence comes in after the candidate has passed? Are these testimonials as to character obtained perfunctorily and just filed away?—A. They are examined.

Q. What do you call ' examined ?'—A. The Board takes cognizance of these certificates of course.

Q. In addition to a testimonial as to character, you have a medical certificate in each case?—A. A medical certificate, yes.

By Mr. Bazin:

Q. In the case of both sexes the law is the same?—A. Yes.

By the Chairman:

Q. Then we ought to have in the public service, as the result of the examinations, candidates of good moral character and good physical ability?—A. Well their testimonial carries that.

Q. Although frequently they obtain leave of absence almost immediately after appointment on the ground of sickness?—A. That has not been my experience.

Q. In the matter of health, although for the examinations they get certificates from their doctor that they were in sound health successful candidates have often got leave of absence, on the ground of sickness, after having been appointed only 12 months?—A. That does not mean always that they are sick.

Q. What other testimonials do you require besides testimonials as to character and health?—A. As to age.

Q. You get a certificate of age?—A. Yes.

By Mr. Fyshe:

Q. Have you any restriction as to age?—A. Yes, they cannot go through the entrance examination before they are 18.

Q. Will you take anybody into the service after they are 25?—A. The age limit is up to 35 for the inside service.

Q. Do they have to have special qualifications?—A. No.

Q. They do not?—A. No.

Q. Are you familiar with, or have you any knowledge of, the kind of examination that is required in a bank for instance?—A. No.

Q. I was going to ask you how your examinations compare with those of a bank?—A. I have no knowledge at all, of the examinations of clerks in banks.

Q. The subjects at your examinations would be Grammar, Arithmetic and History?—A. Yes, and Composition.

Q. Yes, Composition?—A. English or French, and Arithmetic.

Q. Geography?—A. Geography, Writing and Orthography.

Q. It is practically the three R's? According to my experience our educational system is terribly deficient in the commoner things?—A. Yes.

Q. It is getting to be almost impossible now to obtain a man who writes a decent hand. In this connection I find the French are far better writers than the English?—A. My experience is not the same.

Q. Is it not?—A. No, I find that in the province of Quebec, the writing is not as good as in the other Provinces.

Q. That is not my impression. I think the French are well taught?—A. You must have come across some very good candidates, or very good men.

Q. I do not mean to say that they are generally superior, but they seem to write a good hand?—A. The writing has improved during the last few years.

By the Chairman:

Q. There are also optional subjects at the examinations?—A. Yes.

Q. How many are allowed to count?—A. They do not count for anything now. The candidate before the regular curriculum may take some optional subjects.

By Mr. Fyshe:

Q. That he has made a specialty of?—A. Yes.

By the Chairman:

Q. But that does not count now?—A. It does not count. Formerly the Government would give some advantage to those passing in optional subjects.

By Mr. Fyshe:

Q. I think in the schools they try to teach them too much and do not succeed?—A. No.

By the Chairman:

Q. Do you know whether there is much coaching for the Civil Service?—A. In Ottawa there is a great deal of coaching—a great deal.

Q. Cramming?—A. Through retired school teachers, and some that are in active teaching, who open schools.

7-8 EDWARD VII., A. 1908

By Mr. Fyshe:

Q. They may be very effective?—A. Yes. Of course those teachers have a great deal of experience in the way the questions are put, and I should fancy they are of great help to the candidates.

Mr. Fyshe.—It develops a kind of experts, you know. In the United States they have regular expert coachers.

The Chairman.—What are called in England 'crammers.' There are men in Ottawa who cram up for the civil service. It is like cramming a turkey. Now do these candidates who come from the 'crammer' and pass the Civil Service Examination, remember, in subsequent life, what they learned?

The Witness.—Not much.

Mr. Fyshe.—I do not think the cramming system develops the thinking faculties.

By the Chairman:

Q. That is just what I was trying to get at; I have not looked at your questions for some years, but I have heard it is rather a favourite form of amusement to give what are called 'catch questions'?—A. I have heard that same objection, but my experience is that for quite a number of years large questions have been given.

Q. The larger and broader questions?—A. Questions of a very general character, I know that at the start such a question was asked as 'Who was the first Mayor of Toronto' was given, but I objected to it.

By Mr. Fyshe:

Q. There is nothing in that?—A. That is not history.

By the Chairman:

Q. But it is gaining so many marks, you know?—A. Well that was done.

Q. The board prepared the different examination papers for the different departments?—A. For promotion?

Q. No, for entrance?—A. Yes.

Q. You would not want a man in the Finance Department to be a literary character, but you might want such a qualification in the Department of the Secretary of State?—A. We suggested, a few months ago, a re-arrangement to the Government. Experience has shown us defects in the existing system of examinations. For example, it is not fair to subject men who are to be employed as railway mail clerks to the same examination as in the case of candidates who will have to attend to correspondence, or duties of that kind, or of a higher character. We have therefore suggested to the Government to let us arrange three scales of examinations according to the work of the department in which the candidate intends to enter.

By Mr. Fyshe:

Q. You do not want them to be the same?—A. The questions would be the same but the board would not exact the same number of marks to qualify for employment in the different branches. For example thirty per cent should qualify a railway mail clerk, and fifty per cent, a clerk in the inside service.

By the Chairman:

Q. Do you know whether any examination papers ever get out of the Printing Bureau now. You formulate your examination papers and send them to the Printing Bureau to be printed?—A. Yes.

Q. It has been stated that some examination papers get out. Has anything of that kind happened?—A. No. We take the greatest precautions to have the papers printed on the same date. We count the number of papers that are sent to the Bureau and those papers and even the type set out are put under lock and key.

SESSIONAL PAPER No. 29a

Q. And the number of sheets, are they counted?—A. They are counted.

Q. Of course the examination papers are printed in both languages?—A. In either language.

By Mr. Fyshe:

Q. It goes without saying that you do not get any applicants from the class of people who go in for college courses?—A. Oh, yes. We have lawyers sometimes and we get candidates from all classes.

Q. I should have thought that people who had ambition enough to take a college course with a view to following a professional career would not want to join the Civil Service?—A. Several of them come every year; lawyers and students-at-law.

Q. Is it not the fact, in those cases, that they are what you might call 'failures?'— A. Well, some of the professions are over crowded now and people often get discouraged and pass our examinations in the hope of getting employment. Of course it is seldom that we find first-class subjects. We even have to give certificates to men who hold University degrees as Bachelor of Science.

Q. You would pass such candidates without examination, would you not?—A. Of course.

By the Chairman:

Q. That is laid down in the Civil Service Act?—A. That is laid down in the Civil Service Act.

Q. In the promotion examination, a candidate, if he is a French Canadian may request the papers to be printed in his own language?—A. Yes.

Q. That is to say if it were the Department of Finance for example, to take a concrete case, where there is an English deputy who prepares the papers, the candidate for examination if he happened to be a French Canadian, might require the papers to be translated into French?—A. Yes. As a rule we provide for that. If we find from the list there are no French candidates we have the papers printed in English only.

Q. But if there are French candidates you have the papers printed in French?— A. Yes.

Q. Is there any method by which the candidate could get hold of these papers during the process of translation?—A. No.

Q. I see that the same question was asked by the Commission in 1892?—A. It would be desirable if as the candidates from the different departments passed a promotion examination on the same subjects. The same subjects ought to be required from all and ought to form part of the regular examination. Because in some departments, candidates get through by being examined simply in one or two subjects whilst in other departments they have to take the whole course. The deputy heads can dispense with the examination in certain subjects.

Q. I was coming to that. That is to say, a deputy head, in response to political pressure and his own desire to pass candidates for examination, might simply examine them in the duties of their office, the papers being prepared by himself?—A. Yes, barring political pressure.

Q. And that contracts the thing out of the Civil Service Board of Examiners altogether?—A. It annuls our examinations altogether. The paper on efficiency and on the duties are prepared by the deputy head and he can annul our examinations altogether.

By Mr. Fyshe:

Q. You have nothing to do, I understand, with Engineers?—A. No, nothing to do with them. They come before a special board.

Q. I thought they were not examined at all?—A. Yes, they are examined. They have to have certificates, I understand, from some board of examiners.

7-8 EDWARD VII., A. 1908.

By the Chairman:

Q. They do not come before you, those who are exempt from examinations ?—A. They come under the Special Qualification Clause.

By Mr. Fyshe:

Q. They are what is called 'experts'?—A. Yes.
Q. They do not belong to the Civil Service?—A. Yes, they do.
Q. They do belong to the Civil Service?—A. They do.
Q. And are they under Civil Service rules ?—A. The requirements are not the same.

By the Chairman:

Q. In the case of the promotion examinations, some departments take it in the fullest extent, while with respect to others it is narrowed down to examination in the subject of efficiency and duties which are prepared by the deputy head?—A. Yes, and they might simply ask the candidates to conform themselves to the smallest extent to the wishes of the Board.
Q. Has that habit grown?—A. It has not changed. It is not growing; it could not grow any more.

By Mr. Fyshe:

Q. There is a large amount of discretion given, I suppose, in regard to appointing people?—A. In regard to appointing people?
Q. I mean to those who have authority to make the appointment?—A. The Government have it altogether in their hands, I suppose. We pass the candidates but we have nothing to do with their appointment. After we pass the candidates our duty ends; we have nothing further to do with them.
Q. You have nothing further to do with them?—A. Oh, no.
Q. Who has the appointing power afterwards, the Deputy Minister?—A. No. I suppose the Minister on the recommendation of the deputy head.

By the Chairman:

Q. It is practically the minister?—A. Yes, the minister.

The CHAIRMAN.—In England, a department when a vacancy occurs, applies to the Civil Service Board, and the latter sends the most meritorious candidate.

Mr. FYSHE.—The department has nothing to do with it?

The CHAIRMAN.—The department has nothing to do with it.

Mr. FYSHE.—And the sub-head of the department has nothing to do with it?

The CHAIRMAN.—He has nothing to do with it.

Mr. FYSHE.—That system might be abused, because you might not be able to get exactly the kind of man who is wanted.

The CHAIRMAN.—There is of course a period of probation. That is always six months, and if the man is not suitable he is sent back and another appointment made.

The WITNESS.—There is a period of probation also here.

The CHAIRMAN.—There is a period of probation here.

The WITNESS.—But it always establishes that the man is all right.

By the Chairman:

Q. The Canadian Board of Civil Service Examiners simply forwards to the Secretary of State the list of successful candidates with their respective marks?—A. Yes.
Q. And they have nothing to do afterwards with the appointment?—A. Nothing at all.

Q. And in point of fact, as long as the candidates pass, the selection of the man for office may be made without reference to the candidate who has the greatest number of marks?—A. Certainly. All the candidates are eligible in the same degree.

By Mr. Fyshe:

Q. Of course it would be too much to ask whether there is any consideration in such cases?—A. Oh, no.

Q. That would be too much to ask?—A. Yes.

Q. Whether it was a matter of prejudice—whether the minister really thought that the appointee had special qualifications or whether it was just because he was a friend of his?—A. Of course I have nothing to do with that whatever.

Witness discharged.

The Commission rose.

OTTAWA, May 15, 1907.

The Commission resumed at 2 o'clock p.m., Mr. Courtney, Chairman, presiding.

Dr. JOHN THORBURN called and sworn and examined.

By the Chairman:

Q. Have you any other occupation in the public serivce of Canada than that of Chairman of the Board of Civil Service Examiners? Have you left the Geological Survey?—A. Yes.

Q. What are you paid as a member of the Board?—A. $500 per annum, the same as the other examiners.

Q. Were you an examiner for the Royal Military College?—A. I was for seventeen years, till the examinations were given to the Professors of the College.

Q. Is this your sole emolument in the public service now?—A. At present it is, but the Militia Department is organizing a system of examinations for officers who do not go through the Military College, and I was applied to by Col. Fiset, Deputy of the Department, to see if the Civil Service Examination Board would do that work.

Q. But in the meantime your stipend as a Civil Service Examiner is the only emolument you enjoy?—Yes.

Q. You have been Chairman of the Board since its inception in 1882?—A. Yes.

Q. And you have had 25 years' experience of practical work in that connection? —A. Yes.

Q. The Entrance Examinations take place in November and the Promotion Examinations in May?—A. Yes.

Q. You occasionally have had, I suppose, an intimation that in the case of certain candidates it would be desirable to give them the benefit of every doubt?—A. No, not before the examination.

Q. Or has it been done afterwards in computing the marks?—A. Yes.

Q. Afterwards you have had occasional hints?—A. When the candidates failed.

By Mr. Fyshe:

Q. You have been asked if you could not modify somewhat your judgment?—A. Yes.

Q. So that candidates would pass?—A. Yes, repeatedly. I could give you the names of some of the candidates and on my refusal on some occasions I have been threatened to have the matter brought up in the House of Commons.

7-8 EDWARD VII., A. 1908

Q. Have you ever done so?—A. Done what?

By Mr. Chairman:

Q. You have never strained your conscience?—A. I will give you an instance of the danger of conferring a favour on a candidate. Immediately after the initiation of the system of Civil Service Examinations, a lady applicant failed to pass by a few marks. I forget what subject it was in now, because the instance occurred away back in 1883 or 1884. She came to my house, and begged of me to give her the few marks necessary to pass; she told me she had a young family dependent upon her. She said to me 'Of course no one will know except myself and yourself' as if that made any difference to me. In my good heartedness, I gave her the few marks necessary to pass, and next day, two ladies came and demanded the same privilege. So I made up my mind there and then, that that was a very unsafe course to pursue. It was a lesson to me for the rest of my life.

Q. Then, Doctor, you have nothing to do, as I understand, with the candidates after they have passed, you have nothing to do with their appointment?—A. Oh, no.

Q. The candidates who passed the Civil Service Examination last November numbered 375?—A. I presume so, but I have not counted them.

Q. They are not published in order of merit but alphabetically?—A. Yes, alphabetically.

Q. Would it not be desirable to publish them in order of merit?—A. I think very likely it would.

Q. It never struck you that way?

Mr. Fyshe.—I have no doubt it struck him.

A. You know I have been in favour of competitive examinations, but I cannot say, in connection with the Civil Service Examinations, as at present conducted, that I ever thought of the point you mention. I never thought of having the names printed in order of merit.

By Mr. Fyshe:

Q. Perhaps you know it was not desired by the powers that be?—A. Well, I have my own ideas in regard to that.

By Mr. Chairman:

Q. At all events, the names of successful candidates are not published in order of merit?—A. No.

Q. And the names of the candidates who made the worst showing may be submitted afterwards for appointment to office?—A. Very frequently these are the persons that have the best chance of getting appointed because they get their friends, also members of parliament, and the Church to which they belong to intervene; whereas a good man, you know, is above that kind of work.

Q. You have been engaged in connection with these examinations since 1882?—A. Yes.

Q. Is there as good a class of candidates coming up for examination now as there was 25 years ago, or has there been a falling off?—A. I do not think that there has been a falling off. I might mention this: Those taking degrees in Canadian Colleges or Universities and the graduates of the Royal Military College, Kingston, are now exempt from examination. They were not so at first. There has been quite a number of them taken into the service.

By Mr. Fyshe:

Q. Is there a larger proportion of them now than there was formerly?—A. Yes, there is.

SESSIONAL PAPER No. 29a

By the Chairman:

Q. But they go up for appointment to some technical position, as an engineer or surveyor, as a rule?—A. I believe so, but of course we have nothing to do with that.

Q. But the ordinary rank and file of the candidates that present themselves, those who go in as copyists, &c., have they as much ability now as they had 25 years ago?—A. I could not say that very definitely. I may state that, as a general rule, now candidates put themselves under a coaching process to prepare for the examination which gives them a better chance of passing.

By Mr. Fyshe:

Q. And of course you do not follow them in their subsequent career, therefore you have no knowledge of how they turn out?—A. Very frequently I do, because there are quite a number of those in the Civil Service that I have known ever since they entered. .

Q. But it was not your business to keep track of them?—A. No.

By the Chairman:

Q. What I am trying to get at, Doctor, is this: Do they compare in point of ability—the class entering now—with the class of 25 years ago?—A. They are no better, anyhow.

Q. They are no better?—A. I do not think they are any better.

By Mr. Fyshe:

Q. Of course the facilities for education in the country are increasing all the time?—A. Yes, that is true.

Q. And, therefore, there ought to be a better class of applicants than you were formerly accustomed to?—A. Yes, there should be, but there is such a large number coming up for examination now.

By the Chairman:

Q. There were 17 points at which examinations took place last November for entrance into the Civil Service. Of this number 206 passed at Ottawa, and one at Sault Ste. Marie. Gradually the whole number of candidates at the Entrance Examinations is being furnished by Ottawa?—A. They are getting more and more numerous here.

By Mr. Fyshe:

Q. How do you account for that?—A. Well, I do not know but such is the case.

Q. Does it appear to the people generally that the public service is a very desirable service?—A. Well, the country is opening up, you know, and there is more demand for public servants. In Winnipeg we have quite a large number of candidates now and other places in the Northwest are coming along.

By the Chairman:

Q. I see that 21 candidates passed in Winnipeg?—A. Originally there would be only one or two.

Q. To have 206 candidates pass in Ottawa, out of 375, is a big proportion?—A. Yes.

Q. Now 121 out of that 206 were probably women, but from some of the names you could not distinguish of what sex the candidates were?—A. We know that at our office.

Q. I take it that 121 out of the 206 are undoubtedly women, but there are a greater number even than the former figures would indicate. The list should give the names in full?—A. We have that information down at the office. Of course they are required to give their *names in full on the* form they fill in.

7-8 EDWARD VII., A. 1908

Q. Such names as K. C. Arnold, J. C. Breton, and E. M. Babin might mean .anything?—A. I fancy those are names of men. I think as a general rule you will find those are names of men.

Q. We do not know. There are more women present themselves now than formerly?—A. Yes.

Q. You superintend the Ottawa examinations?—A. No, I go to Toronto.

By Mr. Fyshe:

Q. You live in Ottawa?—A. Yes, I live in Ottawa.

By the Chairman:

Q. There were only 20 that passed in Toronto?—A. Yes. Those passed the Qualifying or Higher Grade Examination.

Q. Would that be because you had a stricter supervision of the candidates?—A. I do not think so.' I do keep a strict oversight, but the reason more pass in Ottawa is because there are more candidates who write.

Q. Who looks after Ottawa?—A. Dr. Glashan.

Q. And Dr. DeCelles after Montreal?—A. Yes.

Q. Then there are 14 sub-examiners?—A. Yes, we have sub-examiners.

Q. Where is the examination held in Ottawa, in the House of Commons?—A. In the House of Commons generally.

Q. Do you know whether the last examination was held there?—A. Yes.

By Mr. Fyshe:

Q. Why should it be held there?—A. Because there is no other building sufficiently large to accommodate the candidates.

Q. Referring to the large proportion of college graduates applying for appointment in the government service, how do you account for that? One would think that people who are ambitious enough to secure a University degree would be above undertaking the ordinary service of a Government office?—A. If you send for our last report, I mean the last Civil Service report, you will see the number of those that have taken University degrees.

Q. Does it not appear to you that a man who has obtained a University degree should have an ambition higher than that of filling the position of a government clerk?

The CHAIRMAN.—Dr. Thorburn is a University graduate himself.

Mr. FYSHE.—I know, but he is not a Government clerk.

By the Chairman:

Q. In the House of Commons there is seating capacity for about 216. Now as 295 persons presented themselves for examination there could not have been seats enough to go around?—A. I was not present at the Qualifying Examination in Ottawa. I was referring in my last remark to the Promotion Examination recently held.

Q. Then Dr. Glashan had charge in Ottawa?—A. Yes.

Q. Well, 295 persons exhausted the seating capacity of the House of Commons?—A. I think for the Qualifying Examination a number of candidates were sent to the Senate Chamber. I made application for the Senate Chamber in case we would require it at the recent Promotion Examination.

By Mr. Fyshe:

Q. You hold the examinations in the Commons Chamber in order to have all the candidates, as far as possible under the eye of the examiner?—A. Yes. But in some cases the House of Commons was not sufficiently spacious to have the candidates placed at the requisite distance from each other so we used the Senate Chamber as well.

By the Chairman:

Q. Dr. Glashan was the only person who had them under supervision, I suppose? —A. No, he had assistants.

Q. How many assistants had he?—A. I cannot say exactly. He has had two or three and more if required.

Q. In Toronto, where did you hold the examinations?—A. I held them in the Medical Hall till the last examination, which was held in 'Forum Hall,' Yonge street.

Q. There were 20 candidates passed? Do you recollect how many candidates entered?—A. There were 41 according to the report for the Qualifying Examination.

Q. Was the hall sufficiently large to keep the candidates separate from each other?—A. Yes.

Q. There was no chance of copying there?—A. No, I have very reliable assistants in Toronto. (Report of the Board of Civil Service Examiners produced.) In this report you will find a list of the graduates of Canadian universities for each year since 1889.

Q. You only get one testimonial as to the moral character of the candidate?—A. Yes.

Q. In Great Britain the candidates require to have three testimonials. The person who testifies as a rule is the clergyman or curé?—A. Yes.

Q. We heard yesterday of a professional man who personated a Civil Service candidate. Is it not possible that such a personator might give the candidate a testimonial of character?—A. It is possible enough.

Q. Do you not think it would be better to increase the number of testimonials of character as in England, such testimonials being from an old friend of the family or a justice of the peace?—A. It would be safer.

Q. Then as to the candidate's health, a certificate from a doctor is required?—A. Yes.

Q. Does it not occasionally happen, after a candidate has passed and been appointed to the service, that he or she is found to be in weak health?—A. I could not say as to that.

Q. Furthermore a certificate of the candidate's age is required?—A. Yes.

Q. How is that certificate obtained?—From the parish register, the registrar of births and deaths, or from the family Bible?—A. I forget just now. I think it is from the registry of births and baptisms or by a declaration sworn to by the candidate. We require to get their age at any rate.

Q. Dr. De Celles yesterday stated that there is a practice growing up, especially in Ottawa, of having 'coaches' or 'crammers,' like the army 'crammers,' who 'cram' candidates for the examinations?—A. Yes.

Q. Now you have lived in Ottawa for many years and have had the opportunity of seeing the candidates that have passed the examinations. What is the effect of the 'cramming' system? Do not the candidates forget as quickly as they learn?—A. They are apt to.

Q. They are apt to?—A. Yes. Excuse me just for a moment while you are on this subject. A number of years ago, a man, who is dead now, but then was a 'coach', came to me, I remember, and commiserated me upon the amount of work I had to undergo in examining so many papers and he offered to assist me. I thanked him, but told him I could not do that. I found out afterwards that he was. . . . .

By Mr. Fyshe:

Q. He was a 'coach'?—A. Yes, he had been coaching candidates, and, besides that, he was assisting Dr. Glashan in supervising the examinations.

7-8 EDWARD VII., A. 1908

Q That was simply giving him an insight?—A. Yes, it afforded him a chance of helping his pupils.

Q. You did not agree to it?—A. Certainly not, nor do I suppose Dr. Glashan knew of his having pupils writing at the examination.

By the Chairman:

Q. He is too high minded for that?—A. Yes, I am satisfied he is. The arrangement made by this man with the candidates was that, if they passed, they were to pay him. If the candidates failed, they were not to pay him.

Q. The statement is made—I have heard it myself in Ottawa two or three times—that in these examination papers there are occasionally what are called 'catch' questions. For example, question like 'Who was the first mayor of Toronto' and that kind of thing.—A. Our questions are generally of such a character as to test the general knowledge of the candidate.

By Mr. Fyshe:

Q. To test the general intelligence of the candidate, and not question him upon mere insignificant things?—A. Yes, our questions are meant to test the general intelligence of the candidates.

Q. About the question of the number of University graduates presenting themselves, I find that from 1889 to 1906, there has been a pretty steady increase—not so much for the first few years but latterly the number has become more conspicuous. There were three for 1889, two for 1890, one for 1893, five for 1894, three for 1895, six for 1896, four for 1897, three for 1898, seven for 1899, seven for 1900, eight for 1901, ten for 1902, ten for 1903, nine for 1904, eleven for 1905, and seventeen for 1906.

By the Chairman:

Q. I suppose they might not all be appointed for one thing?—A. I should suppose not.

Q. Some of them might go into the transcontinental surveys?—A. I fancy so.

Mr. FYSHE.—That shows the college graduates are gradually getting more numerous.

By the Chairman:

Q. That includes the graduates of the Royal Military College?—A. I should think so. If they applied for positions in the Civil Service their names would be included. The graduates of the Royal Military College as you know are exempt now. The statement is headed 'List of Graduates of Canadian Universities who have exhibited their diplomas to the Board and who, in consequence, are qualified for employment in the public service without examination.' Probably, therefore, none of the Royal Military College graduates are included. Mr. Foran, our secretary, could give you definite information in regard to this.

Q. As to the examination papers, are they quite as stiff as they were in the beginning or have the bars been lowered?—A. I think not. I think they are just about the same, so far as my recollection goes. Of course I can vouch decidedly for my own questions.

Q. Do you set the question for Arithmetic or Grammar?—A. I set the questions for Penmanship, English Grammar, English Composition, and Typewriting.

Q. In what subjects does Dr. Glashan set the questions?—A. He sets the questions for Orthography, Arithmetic, Transcription and Bookkeeping.

Q. And for Geography?—A. No. Dr. DeCelles sets the questions for Geography, History and Stenography.

Q. And French grammar?—A. Yes.

SESSIONAL PAPER No. 29a

By Mr. Fyshe:

Q. The students are examined in History of course?—A. Yes. We have the History of Great Britain, France and Canada.

Q. And Geography?—A. And Geography.

Q. You do not examine them on the sciences I suppose?—A. No.

Q. Nor on Geology?—A. No.

Q. Are the papers about on a level with the entrance papers for high schools and collegiate institutes or are they stiffer?—A. I think they are stiffer. I think they cover more ground. You can see the questions in this report. The questions are printed as you will see. We have special examinations, but you will come to that, I suppose, later. For example here is Penmanship, Orthography, and Arithmetic. This is the Preliminary Examination for the lower grade. The Arithmetic is simple Arithmetic of the first four rules. Then for the Qualifying Examination there is Penmanship, English Composition, Arithmetic, Geography, History, English and French Grammar, Orthography and Transcription. Then there are extra optional subjects. There is Book-keeping for example, Typewriting and Stenography.

By the Chairman:

Q. I was coming to that. There is nothing gained by taking optional subjects?—A. I was not aware of this. There used to be an allowance of $50.

Q. There is nothing about it now?—A. I have not been paying much attention to that matter.

Q. In Great Britain, I know, they have different examinations for the different departments?—A. Yes.

Q. That is to say the examination of a candidate for appointment to the Treasury would be different from that of a candidate for appointment to the Foreign Office. Do you think our plan of having the same papers all around is desirable or could it be changed with advantage?—A. It would entail a very large amount of extra work, preparing papers for different examinations, it would multiply the work indefinitely.

Q. To get at the average intelligence of Canadian candidates you think the qualifying papers are sufficient?—A. I think so for beginners. You might hear some of the questions. Here is Geography for example:—

'Name the principal rivers and chains of mountains of British Columbia?'

'What are the principal rivers and lakes of Manitoba?'

'What are the great districts of Canada which have not yet been formed into provinces?'

'What are the straits, isthmuses and principal bays of the provinces of New Brunswick and Nova Scotia?'

'Name the three principal towns in Prince Edward Island?'

'Name the largest islands in the St. Lawrence river?'

'What are the principal mountains in the province of Quebec?'

'Give the exact situation of the towns of Fort William, Sudbury, and Sault Ste. Marie?'

'Name the great railways of Canada?'

'Name the four largest rivers of the United States?'

'Name Canada's principal seaports?'

A person that can answer all these questions is pretty well informed in regard to the physical features of Canada.

Q. It would indicate a full knowledge, but certainly not a very extensive knowledge?—A. Well, it is a general knowledge.

Q. And that is on one subject?—A. Yes.

Q. Still referring to the Entrance Examination,—we will come to the Promotion Examination later,—you have had experience of personation?—A. Yes, of personation.

29a—2

Q. You know the 14th section of the Civil Service Act deals with personation, and provides for a penalty not exceeding two hundred dollars. We have heard from Dr. DeCelles than a man in Montreal was fined $50 for personation?—A. Yes.

Q Is there any other case of the kind? I do not recollect anybody being prosecuted under that section?—A. I do not think so either. Of course, we report the result of the examinations, and that is all we have to do, I presume. I have recommended repeatedly that cases of that kind be handed over to the Department of Justice.

Q. Was it in your memory that this section of the Civil Service Act existed?—A. Yes, I know it was there. At the last examination, four candidates, whose papers were put aside for copying should have been prevented from coming up at any subsequent examination, as shown by section 41 of 'Regulations,' App. 2, but there was a change made—in the department—that the papers for that examination were to be cancelled, but the candidates were to be allowed to come up again. I am in favour of the guilty parties being kept out of the service altogether after their offence.

Q. Is there very much personation?—A. Yes, there have been too many cases.

Q. Compared with the number of candidates that come up?—A. There are a good many cases, and I am afraid we do not find out all of them. The first case that we had was in Toronto—at least the first that came to my knowledge. My assistant there thought that one of the candidates who was writing had been up at a previous examination and passed. I went to the candidate and asked him, and he said no, that he had not been up at a previous examination.

By Mr. Fyshe:

Q. He said that he had not been at the previous examination?—A. He said that he had not been at the previous examination. Well, I noticed that he kept watching me after that with a suspicious look as if there was something troubling him, so I sent my assistant to examine the names. I thought if the candidate had several initials, and if he were not the right man, he might not be able to give the correct initials. Unfortunately, there was a considerable number of candidates present, and before my assistant got round to him, this particular candidate had finished his paper and handed it to me. Then I touched him on the shoulder, and said I wanted to see him in my private room. He came, and I told him I suspected there was something wrong. He got into a blazing passion and asked me how I came to that conclusion. Finally, he toned down, and said he would come down to the Queen's Hotel and bring a friend to identify him. I took my assistant down to the hotel with me to be a witness. We waited and waited, but the man did not come, and I returned home none the wiser. Well, I do not like to be beaten, so when I came home I looked up the form on which the candidate's application had been written and I found that the handwriting on it was different from the handwriting on the papers the suspected man had handed in. I took the papers and showed them to Col. White, who was then Deputy Minister of the Post Office Department, and he concurred in my view that there was something wrong. Then I wrote to the Postmaster at the place where the man lived who should have written at the examination. I described his appearance, and asked if he, the Postmaster, would be good enough to tell me if that was the man who came from that place. The man who wrote had on a particular kind of coat and he was stylishly dressed. I described his appearance to the Postmaster. The Postmaster wrote back and said he wondered how I suspected there was anything wrong; that this was the man who should have written. I went to Col. White, having found out, as I said, that there was a difference in the handwriting, and asked him to send up the case to the Inspector of the district where the candidate came from. The Deputy Postmaster General did so. The Inspector went around making inquiries, and when the postmaster to whom I had written, found this out, he wrote down to the Postmaster General, regretting that he had misinformed and misled the board in regard to this matter; that this was not the fellow at all. I discovered afterwards that the

SESSIONAL PAPER No. 29a

same person had been in the habit of writing for teachers' certificates and getting $25 or $35 from those whom he personated. That was the first case I found out.

Mr. FYSHE.—I think you gave an account of that in your evidence of 1892?

The CHAIRMAN.—Yes, you gave the circumstances of that case fifteen years ago. —A. I had forgotten that I did so.

By Mr. Fyshe:

Q. You were asked if that postmaster was still in the service and you said yes? —A. I forgot about this.

By the Chairman:

Q. You try to give variety to the papers?—A. Yes.

Q. They are framed to find out a man's general intelligence?—A. Yes.

Q. In regard to the Entrance Examinations at what hour do they begin in the morning?—A. At nine o'clock.

Q. When do they break up, at twelve?—A. We break up generally at twelve and meet again at half past one.

Q. I suppose you give so many sheets of papers to a candidate?—A. We give as many as they require.

Q. Can they take their examination papers out with them?—A. Oh no, they are not allowed to do so.

Q. You could not keep a watch outside on the papers?—A. At Toronto, if any one wants to go out during the examination, one of my assistants goes out along with him.

Q. At twelve o'clock, if the Arithmetic paper had not been completed the candidate could not take the paper out, consult a friend, and come back at one o'clock?—A. No, this would not be allowed.

By Mr. Fyshe:

Q. In connection with the banking system of examinations we had papers prepared on different subjects, Arithmetic, History, Grammar, Geography, and so forth, and each subject was limited to one paper. The applicant only got one paper at a time, and after he got it he could not leave until he had finished that paper and handed it in?— A. It is the same with the Civil Service Examination.

By the Chairman:

Q. There is a blank paper put down before the candidate. Could he take what he had written of the questions and go out with that to a friend?—A. As will be seen from Appendix 2 'Regulations for the governance of the Board, &c.,' no candidate is allowed to leave the room during the treatment of a subject, nor is he allowed to re-enter until the time for the next subject, save in cases of extreme necessity.

By Mr. Fyshe:

Q. Under our banking examinations the applicant had to finish the paper at one sitting. That was the condition we insisted on. He could not take the questions away even in his memory and come back and answer them?—A. Neither can our candidates.

By the Chairman:

Q. So the candidate at twelve could not take anything out with him?—A. Certainly not. That paper on which the candidate had been at work must be handed in before he leaves the room.

Q. There are only a certain number of sheets allowed to each candidate and they have to make a return of that number?—A. We do not give any definite number of sheets. They get as many sheets as they require.

7-8 EDWARD VII., A. 1908

By Mr. Fyshe:

Q. But what check have you in order to see that you get all the papers back?—
A. It makes no difference how many sheets are returned, the only ones we want are
those containing the answers to the questions. In Toronto, for example, the papers are
gone over and counted and we know all the candidates that are present. Before they
break up, if any paper has not been handed in, the candidate possessing it, whose number we have, is applied to.

Q. And he would have to account for it?—A. Yes.

By Mr. Bazin:

Q. You give each candidate a fixed number?—A. Each candidate writes under a
given number but we give them as many sheets of paper as they require.

Q. Have you a means of checking that, when they come back, you can determine
whether you have the same number of papers?—A. We know whether all the written
papers are returned by counting them, but we do not require to count the number of
sheets returned.

By the Chairman:

Q. Take a concrete case: You give questions in Arithmetic?—A. Yes.

Q. Some of the questions would relate to exchange transaction, buying at sixty
days and all that sort of thing?—A. Yes.

Q. Could a candidate write those questions out in duplicate, leave a sheet behind
him and take a copy out to a banker or a financial firm?—A. No, they must be handed
in before they leave.

Q. If you did not know how many papers there were some of them might go
out?—A. Each candidate gets only one copy of each question paper and the candidates
have to suffer if they do not hand in all their papers before they leave.

By Mr. Bazin:

Q. But how can you know that?—A. We find out when we count the papers.
Cases have happened where a candidate came up with a paper and said he had overlooked it. Supposing for example, a candidate was writing before twelve o'clock and
on returning at half past one came to me and said: 'I find I have a sheet that was
not returned. Will you allow me to put it in?' I would say 'No'. So the paper is
not handed in.

By the Chairman:

Q. You would not receive such sheets when returned?—A. No.

By Mr. Fyshe:

Q. You do not check the number of blank sheets? It might be possible to do
that?—A. It would not serve any good purpose.

Q. It would serve this purpose: It would show they did not use the sheets to place
questions on and carry them outside?—A. Supposing they did?

Q. Supposing they did it might not affect their examination but another person's
examination?—A. No, because they are all examined at the same time. If a person
was coming in afterwards to a second examination that might happen.

By the Chairman:

Q. We are still on the subject of the entrance examinations. You, Dr. Glashan,
and Dr. De Celles prepare the papers?—A. Yes.

Q. They are sent down to the Bureau?—A. Yes.

Q. And they are printed there?—A. Yes.

Q. What precautions are taken at the Bureau to see that examination papers do
not go out? There have been such cases have there not?—A. Yes, there was one case

in particular. In former days Mr. Lesueur himself used to go down to supervise the work of safeguarding the examination papers. When Dr. Dawson came to the Printing Bureau he did not approve of that; he thought it was a reflection on his men. Before Dr. Dawson came I think there was a case where examination papers were taken by parties in the Bureau and sold. One of the candidates was examined and he owned up to it.

Q. That he bought the papers?—A. Yes, he bought them and if I recollect aright, he was fined and dismissed from the service.

By Mr. Fyshe:

Q. He got the papers in advance?—A. Yes, down at the Printing Bureau. When this was found out, the guilty party who sold them, decamped, went to the United States and remained there for quite a while and then came back. He was again taken into the Printing Bureau. I heard that this was so and I went down to see if such was the case. Dr. Dawson told me it was so, and said 'It is very wrong.' I went and saw the minister in regard to this. He made a memo. of it, send down to the Bureau and the fellow was dismissed.

By the Chairman:

Q. Then you have no control yourself of the examination papers from the time they are sent to the Bureau until they come back again?—A. No.

Q. But you have no reason to think that any paper is obtained surreptitiously out of the Bureau?—A. There was that Tetreau case for example. That fellow was brought up last year and examined for personation. In his evidence he swore that he knew of parties that had got papers before the examination from the Printing Bureau. I went down and saw Dr. Dawson about it. He called his man who had charge of the papers and he denied that there was anything in it. He said there was no possibility of that being done.

By Mr. Bazin:

Q. I hear a good deal about that. Have no steps been taken to prevent such a practice?—A. These cases have all been reported to the Secretary of State. If everyone were punished who was guilty of such work it would stop the practice, but, unfortunately, the guilty parties are not being punished.

Q. You do not know the names of the candidates when you examine them?—A. No. We examine them by numbers. We do not know the names.

By the Chairman:

Q. But the number corresponds to the applicant?—A. Yes.

By Mr. Bazin:

Q. Is the application signed or simply numbered?

The CHAIRMAN.—The applicant to write at the examination has to apply in his own name?

A. He has to fill out a form. Candidates are required to give their name and age and produce a certificate from some prominent p rson, such as a clergyman, or justice of the peace as to their character.

By Mr. Fyshe:

Q. You must have their names otherwise they cannot be identified?—A. We must have their names. They are kept in a book at our office, but they are not on the papers.

Q. They are not on the papers you handle?—A. No, they are not allowed to appear there.

7-8 EDWARD VII., A. 1908

By the Chairman:

Q. In regard to copying, you have detected it by the answers being the same?—A. Yes.

Q. Is copying pretty prevalent?—A. Unfortunately it is, nor is it confined to the Civil Service. You will find it also in connection with examinations for medical degrees every now and then.

By Mr. Fyshe:

Q. It is a weakness of human nature, disclosed in a great many cases. As a rule I think students taboo any fellow who is found to be guilty of the practice?—A. I would not like to say that.

By the Chairman:

Q. Of course at the Entrance examination it does not matter whether a candidate is French speaking or English speaking. But it is different when you come to the Promotion examination. Take a what you might call an English department like the Post Office Department, or the Finance Department, where there are English deputies and French Canadian clerks, or take a Marine Department where there is a French Canadian deputy and English speaking clerks, the French speaking candidate can demand to have the examination papers set in his own language?—A. Yes.

Q. In the process of translation, is there a chance of a candidate obtaining knowledge of the papers?—A. There should not be.

Q. When I was in the Finance Department, I would write out the papers for the Promotion examination, and they would then go 'to Dr. DeCelles who would set them in French. In the case of the Marine Department Col. Gourdeau would write papers in French and send them to be translated into English. Take the case of a French Canadian deputy is there any chance of the papers getting out?—A. I have no means of knowing it. There should not be. I do not know what Dr. DeCelles does with his papers, when they are being translated.

Q. Are you ever asked to recommend a 'coach' by any candidate?—A. No.

Q. I recollect asking you the question fifteen years ago as to whether you did not think it would be desirable to vary the place at which you conducted the examination so that you might occasionally go to Halifax, for example, and get sub-examiners at Toronto. Do not the candidates begin to expect that Dr. Glashan will have charge in Ottawa, Dr. DeCelles in Montreal and you in Toronto?—A. I think it is possible.

Q. Do you think there would be any weakness they would get on to?

Q. I was coming to that. The sub-examiners are appointed politically?—A. Yes.

Q. I do not know anything about the sub-examiners. But supposing there should be a sub-examiner at Halifax and there was a candidate who was strong politically, the former might be desirous of getting that candidate passed somehow or other?—A. Yes, I remember an example now that you speak of it.

Q. This question suggested itself to my mind?—A. I will refer to a case that happened in Kingston. It was a good many years ago now. It was in 1889. The brother of the sub-examiner there had coached a number of the candidates and what does the sub-examiner do? He wrote out the answers to the questions in his own hand-writing, and instead of the candidates who had taken the lessons from the brother, copying the answers for themselves, they sent in the papers written by the sub-examiner. I went up to Kingston to investigate the case. I swore the sub-examiner, and got the facts. I reported these to the department and he was dismissed. There was another case in St. John. We had representations from there that things were not altogether straight. I went down to St. John and summoned the candidates whose papers were similar and gave evidence of copying. I found out that the sub-examiner had been coaching half a dozen of them, and allowed the questions to be discussed in the hall during the examination. Of course I reported him and he was dismissed.

SESSIONAL PAPER No. 29a

By Mr. Fyshe:

Q. Do you have the same examiners all the time at these places?—A. Yes, if they do their duty.

By the Chairman:

Q. You have no opportunity of knowing this. They simply return the papers from the candidates?—A. Exactly.

By Mr. Fyshe:

Q. Is there no means at these places of having a check on him?—A. No. Of course in a city like Montreal, Toronto, Quebec or Ottawa, there is generally a young man or a couple of young men to assist and to oversee. But unfortunately we cannot always depend upon these. There was a case which happened in Montreal many years ago, I think it was in 1894. At that time I found out that this rascality was going on, so I went down to Montreal, and I discovered that a number of men were in the habit, before the examination began, of being around and offering their services for $25 or $30.

Q. To the applicants?—A. Yes, to any one that would employ them. Well, there were two assistants to our sub-examiner there. One was a medical student and the other a law student.

Q. They were assistants to the examiner?—A. Yes, assistants to the sub-examiner. They were employed to assist him. I found out that one of them demanded $10 from one of the candidates who was personated. I examined, under oath, the man who demanded the $10, the Assistant Postmaster, Mr. Palmer, translating the questions into French. He swore he had not demanded $10 from any one.

Q. You mean the assistant to the sub-examiner?—A. Yes. Well, the one from whom he demanded the $10 was in an adjoining room. I had obtained his evidence before, so I sent for him and placed him under oath. He swore that the assistant had demanded $10 from him. I then turned to the fellow and asked him how he dared to forswear himself thus. He excused himself by saying that he did not understand the question, although the questions had been asked in French.

By the Chairman:

Q. And he claimed that he did not understand the question?—A. Yes.

Q. Do you not think it would be advisable to vary the existing practice and, instead of your going continuously to Toronto, Dr. Glashan remaining continuously in Ottawa, and Dr. DeCelles, continuously having charge in Montreal, to occasionally take charge in other cities such as St. John, Halifax and Quebec?—A. The trouble is, Dr. Glashan could not well get away. He is inspector of Public Schools here. There is the trouble.

Q. But you and Dr. DeCelles could get away?—A. Yes, we could get away.

Q. There are sub-examiners at 14 places. At one place only one candidate passed. That was at Sault Ste. Marie, and the successful candidate was Osmonde Roy Smith. Did you have a sub-examiner in that case?—A. You will find the list of sub-examiners in the report. I think they are given there.

Q. At Sault Ste. Marie the sub-examiner is James Bassingthwaighte?—A. We have had him for a considerable time a sub-examiner there.

Q. Well now, Doctor, take the general question. There is an examination to be passed. As a good citizen do you think that is sufficient or would you advocate a system of competitive examinations?—A. I think it would be more satisfactory for the government.

Q. To have a system of competitive examinations?—A. Yes, I have always had that idea.

Q. You have always been in favour of competitive examinations?—A. Yes.

7-8 EDWARD VII., A. 1908

By Mr. Fyshe:

Q. Do you think it would be desirable to raise the limit and to make such examinations a little more difficult?—A. It is not so much that as having competitive examinations and getting the best men you can for the position. They do that in the United States now largely.

Q. They do it there?—A. Yes. One of my old boys went to the United States and studied at Cornell University. He came out as head man there in his work, and went to Washington where there was a vacancy by competitive examination, and he told me when he came back, that he had been appointed to the position.

By the Chairman:

Q. In the mother country, as you know, Doctor, when a vacancy occurs in a department, the Under Secretary or some other official, applies to the chairman of the Civil Service Board, and a candidate who has passed the necessary examination is sent to the Department in question?—A. Yes.

Q. There is no political interference in one way or the other?—A. Not so far as I know.

Mr. Fyshe.—The official applies for the kind of man he wants.

The Chairman.—The official says he has a vacancy and the Civil Service Board send him a man. That man is taken on probation and if he does not come up to the standard of the department he is returned. That is to say, politics are entirely eliminated in England.

The Witness.—Yes.

Q. Do you think that system could be adopted here with benefit?—A. Not if the ministers retain the power of appointment in their hands.

By Mr. Fyshe:

Q. Do you not think it would be a great relief to the ministers to be relieved from the pertinacity of applicants?—A. Certainly it would. The trouble is, as I said before, that weak candidates frequently get the positions because they induce their friends, members of parliament and the church to which they belong, to back them up. That is the great trouble.

Q. But you know that in giving an appointment like that to a man, who perhaps should not have it, while making one friend the government are as likely as not to make several enemies?—A. I have never noticed that.

Q. But it stands to reason. The applicants cannot all get the appointment, and no doubt the applicant who succeeded did so by influence. It stands to reason that while the successful applicant is satisfied there will be several persons dissatisfied?—A. Possibly.

Q. So it can be shown that it is in the interest of the politicians themselves to have nothing to do with patronage.—A. One would suppose so, but I do not like to sit in judgment upon public men in that way. One knows that when there are aspirants for a position the Government would naturally require to consult their strongest friends.

By the Chairman:

Q. You were until recently Librarian in the Geological Survey?—A. Yes.

Q. Did you have custody of the records of the explorers?—A. No.

Q. You did not have them? Do you know how the records, valuable in case of the opening up of a new country, are preserved? They are in the department, are they not, and are not sent away?—A. No, they are not sent away, they are kept in the department.

Q. Are they carefully guarded?—A. Yes, I think the records to which you allude are incorporated in the reports of exploring parties and are printed.

Q. They could not be lost sight of?—A. No.

Q. The Geological Survey prepares maps?—A. Yes.

Q. And the Post Office Department prepares maps for postal routes as well as the Departments of Public Works, Marine and Fisheries, Militia and Defence, and Interior. Do you not think it would be more economical and efficient if all these maps were prepared as in England, under one system, and not as it is here, scattered among several departments?—A. I would not like to express an opinion because the different departments might want different characteristics given on the maps.

Q. You know the Ordnance Survey prepares all the maps for England?—A. Yes.

Q. You probably know that a very good atlas has been prepared here by Mr. White, Geographer of the Department of the Interior, copies of which have been presented to members of parliament? Have you seen that atlas?—A. No, I have not seen it.

Q. Why should we not establish a mapping department and not have different departments preparing maps?

Mr. FYSHE.—Instead of having separate maps prepared by separate departments?

The CHAIRMAN.—Yes, these are the kind of maps that are prepared: the Geological Survey prepares its own maps of the country explored; the Militia Department prepares maps of military surveys and fortifications; the Marine Department prepares maps for the coast service and hydrographic surveys; the Public Works Department prepares maps for dredging; the Railway Department prepares map for railway lines and canals; and the Post Office Department prepares maps for postal routes.

Mr. FYSHE.—I quite see the point of your suggestion. It would seem to me very reasonable that you should combine the whole of this work.

The WITNESS.—Of course I am not in a position to judge of a matter of that kind, for example, the Geological Survey maps require to show certain sections of country where certain minerals are found.

By the Chairman:

Q. I do not know whether you have seen the atlas I allude to, which has been issued within the last two or three months. This atlas, which has been highly praised, contains geological and other maps.—A. I have not seen it.

Q. Occasionally, when a man failed to pass the examination required for a letter carrier or a messenger, has he not been employed as a 'labourer'?—A. I could not say; not to my knowledge.

Q. You have never heard heard of that kind of thing?—A. No, but individuals are frequently employed by departments before they have undergone the examination.

Q. Have you any suggestions in regard to the dismissal of government employees? It is said that when a change of government takes place a number of employees are dismissed?—A. I am scarcely in a position to say anything in regard to that.

Q. We read in the press that when a new government enters office, there are wholesale dismissals?—A. Of course I get that information the same as you do, but otherwise, I do not know.

By Mr. Fyshe:

Q. You are probably not consulted?—A. No.

Q. Would you advocate an attendance book?—A. I think it is very serviceable in certain cases. Certain men are so derelict in their duty that they take no account of time. For the proper management of the duties of a department it is necessary, because a number of the employees you cannot control in any other way.

Q. Section 105 of the Civil Service Act refers to the matter of attendance. Ought that not to be left to the regulations of a department rather than to be made mandatory in a Public Act?—A. I think I would have the whole thing definitely decided for all the departments alike, because the different deputy ministers might have different views in regard to this and other matters. Let me give you an example of that in connection with the Promotion examination. There were 300 marks assigned at one time for the paper on 'efficiency.' Well, some of the deputies, in every case, gave the full number of marks while others again gave only say 150 or 160,- as the case might be. They did not all estimate the efficiency work alike. Therefore I think it is better to have a definite rule for the whole service in regard to the regulations of each department.

By the Chairman:

Q. I am glad you mentioned the subject of the Promotion examination. There are two subjects in which the candidates must pass, a minimum of two?—A. The deputy ministers have been making changes all the time.

Q. And the deputy ministers have to report the papers on 'efficiency' and 'duties of office'?—A. Yes.

Q. Then practically the deputy minister can take the whole examination in his own hands?—A. We have had cases of that kind. It did not use to be the case at first.

Q. Is the practice growing?—A. Unfortunately it is growing worse.

Q. I think Dr. DeCelles said it had got to a certain point and stopped?—A. It has not stopped, because if you look at the examination list you will see that the candidates in some departments pass with three or four subjects and in others there are only two. I think there ought to be some uniform system.

By Mr. Fyshe:

Q. Have you any knowledge of the discipline maintained in the different departments?—A. No.

Q. I mean when applicants for positions in the Civil Service are accepted and appointed to the different departments: what course of discipline is observed in handling them?—A. I could not say. I have nothing to do with that.

Q. It is probable of course that it differs in accordance with the temperament of the official head?—A. Yes. The fact is, as I stated to you a moment ago, that some deputy ministers assign the full number of marks for efficiency and others do not. They do not discriminate, giving the best men the highest number of marks. It is not at all likely, supposing half a dozen men are going up from a department that they should all get 100 marks for efficiency. It used to be 300 marks, but that was thought too high. We then suggested that the numbers should be 100 and we have found out by experience that some deputy ministers give all candidates the same number of marks, without discrimination. I am giving you my opinion, and it is possible I may have said more than I ought to have stated in regard to this matter.

Q. We want you to say honestly what you think?—A. Exactly.

Q. In regard to the system pursued, at these examinations do you think the existing plan is all that is necessary or can you suggest improvements?—A. I have thought that the competitive system would be far more serviceable and beneficial to the country than that which now prevails.

Q. But even in that case, the result would only be good provided it were honestly followed?—A. Yes, that is certainly the case.

Q. That is that the candidate with the highest marks should get the first chance? —A. Yes, that should be done.

Q. But you do not think that in such examinations, I mean competitive examinations, too much might be allowed for the intellectual evidence and too little to the matter of character—in fact it is difficult to ascertain by any kind of examination what the character of a person is?—A. That is true enough. When the system of competitive examinations was first introduced in connection with the Civil Service of India, the same objection that you are now raising was made ; that a number of bookworms would be introduced into the service. Experience, however, showed that although the system was not in every case perfect, still its general trend was in favour of competitive examinations.

Q. In other words the element of character was apt to follow the candidates' intellectual attainments?—A. When men are put on trial their character can be found out.

By Mr. Bazin:

Q. In the case of a man who is already in the service, has he to go through another examination before he can be promoted?—A. Some deputy ministers allowed a certain percentage gained at the first examination to qualify for chief clerk without undergoing another examination. It may be a dozen or 15 years before a man qualifies for that position, and if he knows that he has no further examinations to undergo he may become careless and indifferent, whereas, if he knows he has to undergo examination for every promotion, he will be on the *qui vive* all the time and keep up to the work.

By Mr. Fyshe:

Q. Is that one of the rules, that officials are to undergo a fresh examination for certain promotion?—A. Not necessarily.

Q. Do you not think it is desirable?—A. Unquestionably.

Q. I am told that in German schools the teachers have to undergo periodical examinations right through the whole course of their lives?—A. Yes.

Q. I suppose the object is to prevent them from getting rusty?—A. So far as my recollection goes I think it was understood at first that there was to be——

Q. A promotion examination at every step?—A. Yes, but somehow or other that was got over.

By the Chairman:

Q. I forget who raised the point. The Department of Justice, was it?—A. We had nothing to do with it, so I cannot say.

Q. The Department of Justice was consulted and gave the opinion that the original examination was supposed to carry them up to the highest step?—A. It is a very undesirable thing that the first examination should govern because it may be an easy examination. I think it is a very undesirable thing that the result of the first examination should carry civil servants up through the various stages to the chief clerkship.

By Mr. Fyshe:

Q. I know it is the custom in some banks to put men through an examination before they are entitled to rank as accountants?—A. The same should be done in the Civil Service, I think, if a man is to be promoted. Possibly you may find it referred to in the evidence taken by the previous commission ?

By the Chairman:

Q. In 1892? I do not think the question was a live one then?—A. Perhaps not. It would certainly be an incentive to the candidates if they knew they had to undergo an examination before being promoted. They would then be on the *qui vive* all the time.

By Mr. Fyshe:

Q. No doubt. In every position in life there is a great deal to learn, and a conscientious person will acquire the necessary learning where a person who is otherwise will not?—A. Exactly. If a candidate knows he has no chance of promotion, unless he gets to be thoroughly proficient in his work, that is an incentive to him. That answers your question, I think.

Witness discharged.

The Commission adjourned.

OTTAWA, THURSDAY, May 16, 1907.

The Commission met at 10.30 a.m.   Present: Mr. Courtney (Chairman), Mr. Fyshe and Mr. Bazin.

Dr. JOHN C. GLASHAN, sworn and examined.

By the Chairman:

Q. You are one of the Board of Civil Service Examiners?—A. Yes.

Q. How long have you been a member?—A. Ten or twelve years.

Q. Have you also examined for the Military College?—A. I did. I do not now.

Q. Have you any other position in the public service at Ottawa?—A. No other.

Q. You are inspector of schools for the city?—A. Yes.

Q. You are a graduate of Toronto University?—A. Yes.

Q. Are you a member of the Senate of the University?—A. No.

Q. You have had a large experience in examinations in connection with the schools?—A. I have had thirty-five years' experience as official examiner in connection with the Ontario Government.

By Mr. Fyshe:

Q. You have been all your life connected with educational matters?—A. Yes. I was at one time for eight years a member of the Central Committee of Examiners.

Q. And you know all about the schools of the country?—A. The schools of Ontario.

By the Chairman:

Q. You have compiled some text books?—Yes, an Arithmetic and Algebra—books published in the United States.

Q. You generally superintend the Civil Service examinations in Ottawa?—A. Yes, both Preliminary and Qualifying and occasionally the Promotion.

Q. The examinations in Ottawa are held in the House of Commons?—A. In the House of Commons and in the Senate.

Q. The desks in the House of Commons are side by side?—A. Yes, but the candidates sit at every second desk.

Q. Of the 349 candidates who passed last November, 193 passed in Ottawa, so that there must have been a great overflow—some were rejected, I presume?—A. The number who passed and the number who were rejected are given in our last report.

Q. If these were all the candidates, they would have to overflow into the Senate?—A. Yes. We can seat only about 120 in the House of Commons, and the last time we used also one of the Committee Rooms. We need a large number of presiding examiners.

Q. You could not be in the three rooms at one time—how did you arrange that?—A. I have an assistant in the same room with me, and two messengers. In the Senate there are two presiding examiners and two assistants; and in the committee room there is one examiner. It is quite close to the House of Commons, and one of my messengers acts there with me.

By Mr. Fyshe:

Q. I suppose it would be difficult to prevent copying and crooked work with such a small number of watchers?—A. It all depends on the watchers.

Q. But some are very expert at crooked work?—A. I do not think we have much crooked work in the House of Commons where I am.

By the Chairman:

Q. In the House of Commons the desks are in pairs, but no person sits beside the candidates?—A. No, that would never do. A candidate who was perfectly honest might see something that his neighbour was writing.

By Mr. Fyshe:

Q. They might have collusion?—A. I had better explain to you the arrangement. One examiner remains near the Speaker's chair or in the space between the two sides of the House. Another examiner remains near the bar of the House. One of the messengers stands at the back of the seats on one side, looking down over the candidates, so that they cannot see him. Another stands at the back on the other side and looks down over the candidates on that side. That explains why we need four.

By the Chairman:

Q. Does the same system prevail in the Senate?—A. We cannot arrange matters so well in the Senate. I am not satisfied with the arrangements we can make there.

Q. Is that because you have no control in the Senate?—A. No, it is because the seats are all single desks, and we cannot put the candidates far enough apart; and further because the Senate does not accommodate a sufficient number of candidates in the seats to enable us to have none sitting on the floor of the House. We have to put some at tables on the floor of the House, and they are seated irregularly.

Q. How is it in the committee room?—A. The committee room is a long room—Room 16 of the House of Commons. We have there small tables, and we keep the candidates quite distant from each other.

Q. I suppose you can detect copying if there is any peculiarity in the answers?—A. That is very easily done. We can easily detect it if the work is wrong. If a candidate makes a mistake, another one who copies from him will make exactly the same mistake. That may occur in one question, but if it occurs in two or three, that fact instantly calls attention to the matter, and immediately the examiner who suspects copying reports to the other examiners and asks them to compare their answer-papers.

Q. Have you had any personation in Ottawa?—A. No, I have never known a case. Nine-tenths of the candidates I know personally; but if I do not know them I require them to be identified. That is our rule.

Q. You have lived here nearly all your life?—A. I have been inspector in Ottawa for thirty years.

Q. You return the number of marks to the Secretary of State, but the names of the candidates are not published in the *Canada Gazette* in the order of merit?—A. No.

Q. They are simply published alphabetically?—A. Alphabetically.

Q. Don't you think it would be desirable to have them published in order of merit—the public would then know who came out at the top?—A. It would if you divided the candidates according to nationality, according to the subjects they write on; because the French candidates and the English candidates do not write on the same Grammar, the same Orthography or the same Composition, nor are their answers read by the same examiners. In my subjects I take both French and English, but Dr. Thorburn in Grammar and Composition takes only English. I think it would be advisable to have the results published in the order of merit, but you might have them divided into classes.

Q. Do you find the candidates that enter now as desirable a lot of candidates as those who entered formerly, or are they tempted to other occupations—comparing to-day with ten years ago?—A. I think on the whole they are just as good, but there is a far greater number of women coming in, and that will affect the answer.

7-8 EDWARD VII., A. 1908

Q. I am speaking of ability?—A. I mean ability.

By Mr. Fyshe:

Q. The machinery of education throughout the country is better than it used to be, is it not?—A. In some respects.

Q. A larger number of people are in a position to get a university degree, for instance, and there are a much larger number of applicants who have a university degree than there used to be?—A. The people with degrees do not come before us.

Q. I was speaking generally on the fact that there are more graduates of colleges applying for positions in the Civil Service than there used to be?—A. There are three reasons for that increase. There has been a very large increase in the number of graduates in the universities.

Q. Are they lowering the bars?—A. No, but there are more going on to higher education. That is the first reason. Consequently there are more to draw from. Second, there are more women passing through the universities. Formerly the universities did not admit women. Third, you have more men doing technical work in the service now than formerly, and they have to be university graduates. Within the last ten years the number of men at the University of Toronto taking the practical side of the scientific course has increased nearly thirtyfold.

By the Chairman:

Q. Are the bars lowered in your examinations?—A. No. I cannot say that they have been raised either.

Q. That is to say they are about the same height?—A. Yes.

By Mr. Fyshe:

Q. When you speak of technical men, you mean engineers?—A. Engineers, surveyors, geographers, and so forth.

By the Chairman:

Q. Out of the 193 successful candidates in Ottawa last November 117 were indubitably women?—A. Yes.

Q. In the case of a great number you cannot tell from their initials what their sex is?—A. If the initials only are given, I would take it that they are men. However, I think that should be stopped—giving only the initials.

By Mr. Fyshe:

Q. The full name should be given?—A. Yes.

By the Chairman:

Q. There are 117 who are indubitably women, and there may be a few more?—A. Yes, there may be more.

Q. That is, considerably more than half of those who passed were women?—A. Yes.

Q. What is the effect on the service of the increased number of women passing and entering the service?—A. I would prefer that the deputy heads should answer that. I have only an opinion on that. But I can state why there is a large increase of women—that the pay of women in the service relatively to the pay outside is much higher than the pay of men in the service relatively to the pay of men outside. That is, there are many more prizes for men outside the service than for women, and men will remain where there are prizes to be won. A woman enters the service knowing that she will not rise very high, but she is contented with that, because she knows that she cannot rise very high out in the world.

By Mr. Fyshe:

Q. The natural qualifications of women would limit them to the mechanical part of the work?—A. Yes; but there are many able and highly educated women in the service, and no distinction is made. A woman who can do simply typewriting has as much advantage as a woman doing translation from half a dozen different languages. In fact, the typewriter is perhaps paid higher.

By the Chairman:

Q. In the service they begin at $500 a year?—A. Yes.

Q. And in ordinary mercantile work their average of pay is from $250 to $300?—A. Yes.

Q. That is one of the reasons for the redundancy in the number of women coming into the service?—A. Yes.

Q. You get only one testimonial as to character from the candidates?—A. That is all.

Q. In the English Civil Service Board they require three?—A. Yes.

Q. Do you think it would be advisable to extend the number of testimonials?—A. I do not think that would meet the case of personation at all. We have had very few cases of personation. The way to meet that is to do as is done in Ontario or as is done in a bank—having some person you know to come and identify the candidate.

Q. In England they commenced at one, but it was found that a good natured friend could easily be got to give his testimonial, and they required to extend the number?—A. I would not require a testimonial of character at all. I would leave the deputy head, when making the appointment, to inquire into the character of the candidate. I do not think an inquiry into the character of the candidates is a part of our duties as examiners because we cannot do it effectually.

Q. Then it comes to this, that the probationary period of a clerk should be strictly lived up to?—A. Yes, and the person recommending that clerk to the deputy head should be held responsible for his recommendation. I must confess that I have never looked at the recommendations.

By Mr. Bazin:

Q. What do you mean by the person recommending being responsible?—A. Responsible to the Minister.

Q. What would be the consequence of that?—A. I would leave that between him and the Minister. I would not make any legal responsibility. I mean a matter of moral responsibility between the deputy head and his Minister.

By the Chairman:

Q. Would not that be adding to the burden of the deputy head?—A. I think he is now the man who has to answer to the head of the department for the appointments, and I do not know that we have ever considered the written testimonial as to the character of the candidates that is sent in to the secretary of the board. I cannot recall a case where the certificate of character has been called for.

Q. Then you have a medical certificate?—A. Yes.

Q. Is that looked into?—A. That is looked into by the secretary of the board.

Q. He receives a certificate from an undoubted medical practitioner?—A. Yes.

Q. You know generally about the health of the people in Ottawa coming before you?—A. Yes.

Q. They are a healthy lot?—A. They are as a whole.

Q. It has happened, I believe, that a candidate not long appointed has had to take an extended leave of absence for his health?—A. Yes, that has happened both to candidates that have been admitted for examination by the Board and candidates admitted on a university degree; but even then it is doubtful if they would have been rejected at the time of their appointment by any medical man. However, the question of

7-8 EDWARD VII., A. 1908

health should also be referred to the deputy head at the time of appointment, because a candidate may not be appointed for five years after he has passed the Board. The medical certificate should be obtained at the time of appointment, not at the time of passing.

Q. Then, rejected candidates come on again and again until they manage to get through?—A. Yes. I know a candidate whom I have rejected four times.

Q. Then, the third certificate you require is the age certificate?—A. Yes.

Q. That comes from some legitimate source?—A. A question has arisen recently as to the interpretation of the statute with regard to age; that is, with regard to the admission of candidates to the qualifying examination in their eighteenth year. We have admitted them on the condition that the certificate did not issue until they have attained the full age of eighteen years. The question of age is connected with the question of the appointment of more men in the Civil Service. There are boys in the schools who can pass the qualifying examination at the age of thirteen. Usually a boy has to leave school at the age of fifteen to do something for himself. His parents may not be well enough off to keep him at school until he is eighteen. He goes out into the world, and in three years he has probably forgotten his technical qualifications to pass that examination. I would recommend that candidates be allowed to write on the Qualifying examination at sixteen years of age, though they might not receive their certificate until say seventeen. I will give the reason that was given to me by two deputy heads for lowering the age for temporary writers from eighteen to seventeen years. They said: We cannot take any of these young men, according to the statute, until they are eighteen; but if we could take them in at seventeen and put them to work on work that they could well do, we could be training them for a permanent appointment, if necessary, at eighteen. They would be on probation until they were eighteen.

By Mr. Fyshe:

Q. When they had reached eighteen, they would be very much better men that they would be if taken in at eighteen?—A. That is it. What is done now in some cases is to bring them in as messengers at sixteen or seventeen, but the deputies say they are not allowed to use them for anything else; and that simply spoils them instead of making them better.

Q. When boys leave school at the age of fifteen, they should go into business; that is the custom in Scotland?—A. Furthermore they are then plastic in mind and habits, and can be trained for the particular work for which the deputy wants them. But if they act as messengers up to the age of eighteen they have got into the wrong way of doing things. Several of the deputies would like the age at which candidates can come up for the Qualifying examination to be lowered. I would prefer that no age should be set for the examination, but that the age should be set for appointment.

Q. Would even that be desirable?—A. It might be, in order to prevent pressure on the deputy. In that case you should consult not the examiners, but the deputy heads as to the age which they would like to have fixed for appointments. I know that many of our candidates in Ottawa would have passed a better examination if they had come up from three to five years before the time they did.

By the Chairman:

Q. This provision about the certificate of character is mandatory on the Board; but you say it is simply perfunctory, and is never examined by the board?—A. Yes. The appointment may not be made until three or five years after the examination. So that this duty is imposed on the wrong body.

Q. It is also mandatory on the Board to see that the candidate 'is free from any physical defect or disease which would be likely to interfere with the proper discharge of his duties?'—A. Yes. Deaf and dumb people have come up for examination, and have been allowed to write and pass and have been appointed. The question of physical defects should also, I think, be left to the deputy. Why the Board of Examiners on academic subjects should also be constituted a board for examining into the character and health and physical condition of the candidates I do not know. That provision should be revised and part of it should be eliminated. Even if it were wholly eliminated, the deputy heads should look into these matters for their own interests.

Q. The preliminary examination for messengers and such like is a less trying examination than the qualifying examination for clerks?—A. Yes. That brings up another matter. We have two standards of examination at present—the Preliminary, which is very simple, and the Qualifying, which is about the same as what we call the entrance to the Collegiate Institute or the fourth book class in our public schools. I would recommend that instead of two there should be three standards of examinations— one for messengers and such like, about the same as the Preliminary—one perhaps somewhat lower than the present Qualifying examination and on different subjects, for temporary writers, copyists and railway mail clerks. There is at present a great difficulty in getting enough railway mail clerks for the rapidly extending service in the Northwest, and in getting those who are able to pass the present Qualifying examination. Then, for the higher appointments, there should be a third examination rather more advanced than the present Qualifying examination, and any person who has passed that should have no other academic examination afterwards. In other words, there should be no academic examination for promotion, as there it at present. If any candidate has passed that higher examination, it should open the whole service to him, apart from anything that the deputy may prescribe.

Q. In the mother country they have different examinations for the different departments?—A. Yes, and for different offices.

Q. That is to say, the candidate for appointment to the Finance Department requires different qualifications from those of a candidate for the Secretary of State's Department?—A. Yes.

Q. But here we have one common examination?—A. Yes.

Q. Do you think it would be advisable to differentiate a bit?—A. I think that the deputy head should have the right to raise the qualifications or to add to the qualifications for any particular branch of his department—to add so much in any particular subject to the general examination.

By Mr. Fyshe:

Q. Would it not be better to have that defined rather than to trust it to any particular individual?—A. Certainly. But the deputy head, I think, should say that such and such shall be required for certain appointments in his department, and he should notify the Board of that; or he might have that special examination at the time of appointment. Perhaps the simplest way would be to leave it to each deputy head to state what special examination he would require for his department in addition to the general examination.

By the Chairman:

Q. Are you not proposing to throw too much on the deputy head?—A. My suggestion is that that should be defined once for all for each department in the Civil Service Act—that you should consult the different deputy heads as to what they would advise should be added for their respective departments, and that that should be added in the Statute. I was speaking of the subject of examinations. The subjects at present are: Penmanship, Orthography, Arithmetic, including interest, vulgar and decimal fractions. That should be commercial transactions, not interest. Then there is Geography, chiefly on the Dominion of Canada; History, British, French and Canadian, chiefly the latter; Grammar and Composition. Now, there is the question of Transcription. I would recommend that that be struck off. It is clean copying. The Composition should include precis making. For the second class there are three subjects—Bookkeeping by double entry, Shorthand and Typewriting. I would strike off Bookkeeping, and for the middle or intermediate examination for clerkships, I think

29a—8

· 7-8 EDWARD VII., A. 1908

that Shorthand and Typewriting might well be made compulsory instead of Transcription; certainly Typewriting should, while Shorthand might be left as the one optional subject.

Q. The optional subjects have practically died out?—A. Yes. Many girls take Typewriting.

Q. But there is no inducement to take them?—A. No inducement.

Q. In former years candidates got $50 for each optional subject?—A. Yes, but that worked unfairly also, I will explain how. There is a rule that they must take that examination at the same time as they take their Qualifying examination. They are not allowed to come up for that one optional subject only. A girl takes her Qualifying examination and passes but does not take her optional. After she enters the service she learns typewriting and Shorthand, but never gets her $50. If you have an optional subject they should be allowed to come up for that at any time.

Q. Do you set any catch questions?—A. The difficulty is in defining what is a catch question. I have the subjects of Arithmetic, Orthography and Transcription. In Arithmetic a candidate is apt to call any question which he cannot answer a catch question.

Q. Do you pay any attention to punctuation?—A. That should come under the subject of Composition.

Q. Under that subject is any attention paid to punctuation?—A. I could not say definitely, not being the examiner, but my impression is that very little attention is paid to it. '

By Mr. Fyshe:

Q. Don't you think that punctuation is more generally honoured in the breach than the observance?—A. Yes. Some writers are very particular about their punctuation. There should be a certain amount of attention paid to it.

By the Chairman:

Q. And the attention to capital letters?—A. I include that in punctuation. There is another matter I would like to call your attention to The law allows a candidate to write his examination in either English or French, but the Board has carried that out in what seems to me to be a peculiar way. It necessitates the candidate choosing one or other language and sending in all his papers in that language. I think a candidate should be allowed to choose on any paper which language he shall write in.

By Mr. Fyshe:

Q. I suppose there are very few who would write in either or both languages?—A. I have every year quite a number of candidates coming to the entrance examination at the Collegiate Institute who write some of their papers in English and some in French, and occasionally I have had on a paper one answer in English and the next one in French. A French candidate, for example, writing in History, if he has not studied History in English, has not merely to write the History, but has to do translation as well. That is doing double work. That is a good reason why he should be allowed to write his history in English or in French. But suppose that candidate preferred to take the English grammar or the English composition, why not allow him to do so if he has studied that subject in that language? Why not allow the candidate perfect liberty to answer in which ever language he pleases? I have met with candidates who would like to have written in English to show their knowledge of that language.

By the Chairman:

Q. The present provision handicaps the French Canadian in some respects at times?—A. At times; but it is not merely that. A man who knows both English and French has no advantage in the examination. So that I would like to add, at least for the higher examination, translation as an optional subject, and there should be something allowed for that. I might explain that in Ontario our options are taken differently from what they are here. A candidate who passes his options here has no advantage after that, whereas in Ontario if a candidate makes more than fifty per cent on an option, the premium is added to his other subjects. That is what I mean by allowing any candidate to write on any subject in either of the two recognized languages of the country. If he chooses one of them as an option and makes more than fifty per cent, give him the excess applied to other subjects, and restore translation from English to French and from French to English.

Q. Coming to the Promotion examination, there is a difference of opinion prevailing as to the number of subjects that should embrace. As a rule two subjects are allowed as the minimum?—A. Yes.

Q. There are a variety of subjects on which the Promotion examination is based originally?—A. Under the rules the obligatory subjects are Penmanship, Orthography, Arithmetic, Composition, duties of office and a report on efficiency. By an order in council that can be changed and be reduced to two. The Minister of Justice decided that there could not be less than two.

Q. Practically that takes the Promotion examination out of the hands of the intended body, and reduces it to promotion by the deputy head on the two subjects of duties of office and efficiency?—A. No, efficiency does not count as one of the two subjects. For example, in the Post Office Department they take duties of office and orthography.

Q. That brings the candidates under the supervision of the Board?—A. Yes.

Q. But suppose they take arithmetic instead of orthography, the nature of the change is determined by the deputy head of the department?—A. Yes.

Q. The deputy head might, by selecting duties of office and arithmetic, have the control of the examination in his own hands?—A. Yes. I may say that I would prefer that these academic subjects were struck out of the Promotion examination entirely, and that the compulsory subjects were reduced to two, duties of office and efficiency, and then let the deputy head be given the right to prescribe any other. Furthermore, I think he should be allowed to set these papers. I allow that in arithmetic now. In one branch three candidates came up for examination, and the head of that branch set the paper. These candidates have to know a certain amount of very technical arithmetic for that branch, and the paper had direct reference to their work. It was a paper that could very well be put under duties of office, and the head of the branch is the proper person to set such a paper.

By Mr. Fyshe:

Q. To what particular branch of the service would that apply?—A. There are several branches. The branch I am speaking of is Printing and Stationery. As an example, one of the questions was as to how many reams of paper would be required for 500 copies of a book of 450 pages demy octavo, and what that paper would cost. Men in that department should be able easily to work out a question like that, while the way of the ordinary arithmetic would send them altogether wrong in their quantities of paper.

By the Chairman:

Q. At the present moment there are divers methods of promotion?—A. Yes. I had four different arithmetic papers sent at the last examination, in four different systems, and I think that is quite right. We might have had six or seven. For example, take the Finance Department; the ordinary paper would be perfectly useless for the Promotion examination. That department should be allowed to set its own paper to suit the candidates coming up. Some of them have a good deal to do with regard to foreign exchange. They should have special papers on that, and these papers should be set either by the deputy head of the department or by a person he appoints.

7-8 EDWARD VII., A. 1908

By Mr. Fyshe:

Q. Have you ever been consulted by any of the banks in regard to their examination papers?—A. Not officially. Unofficially I have been.

By the Chairman:

Q. Would it not be advisable that while the subjects are defined, candidates for promotion should be examined in more than two subjects?—A. No. I would allow each department to prescribe its own subjects; but on a man being transferred from one department to another, it should not be compulsory on the deputy head to receive him unless he has passed the examination of that department or its equivalent. But what is more important, I would like the academic examination to be omitted unless it is prescribed by the deputy head. A man should not be asked to keep up questions in arithmetic if he has not used it for years in his department. For instance, composition may be made an excellent subject of examination, or it may be made one of the worst possible. If composition were a test of writing a letter on some subject in connection with the work of a man's department or a test of whether he can express himself correctly and punctuate correctly, that would in itself be a good examination; but if he were asked about figures of speech, as is sometimes the case, why should a man who has been for a number of years a clerk in a department be required to keep up his knowledge of such things. He would have to cram, and the cramming would interfere with his work during the day, and cause him a lot of worry.

Q. Are there coaches for these examinations?—A. Yes. I am often applied to for recommendations of coaches.

Q. Do coaches coach for Promotion examinations as well as the Preliminary?—A. Yes.

Q. A candidate for promotion can select which language he chooses to have the paper set in?—A. Yes.

Q. The papers are sent to the Board by the deputy head?—A. Yes.

Q. Suppose in an English department there is a French Canadian candidate—there is an interval for the translation of the paper?—A. Yes.

Q. Could that translation get out by any means?—A. That is more than I can answer.

Q. What is the process of the translation?—A. It is sent to Mr. DeCelles.

Q. And Mr. DeCelles is above suspicion?—A. Yes. The only question might be whether the papers were left on a desk where anybody could see them. I may say that I copy my papers out and send them to the secretary, and then I destroy my original. I absolutely keep no copy of my own papers. It might be possible for the papers to get out without the head of the Printing Bureau knowing them to have got out.

Q. Is there any tab kept on the number of blank sheets at the Bureau on which the questions are to be printed?—A. I should expect that the head of the Bureau would look after that sharply.

Q. After you prepare the papers you do not know how far they are treated confidentially down at the Bureau?—A. No.

Q. No account kept of spoiled papers or anything else?—A. No one could answer that but the head of the department or some other person down there.

Q. In your examination in the House of Commons the candidates are numbered?—A. Yes. That brings up another question. From my own experience I can frankly say that I like to have the candidates numbered. Even if I do not know them, I do not like to read the names. Then again, if I know the name, I would know whether the candidate was a man or a woman, and if a woman wished to get a higher position, there might be some feeling in the matter. But with the candidates numbered, my mind is perfectly easy. I may say that Dr. Thorburn and Dr. DeCelles and myself, the three examiners, preside at centres. I do not think the examiners should preside at all. Even though I try to get rid of the knowledge, I know the numbers of quite a number of the candidates. I should not know one candidate from another. If the candidates are going to write by numbers, the examiners who are going to read the papers should not even be allowed in the room. We should not know the names or anything about the candidates until our returns are sent in. I preside in Ottawa, and there may be some candidates that I am interested in whose numbers I cannot help remembering. Then, on account of the date on which the examinations are held, it is extremely difficult to get properly qualified examiners. The examiners should be men who have experience in watching candidates at work. Teachers are the best, but at the time the examinations are held it is almost impossible to get teachers to preside, as they are all at work. If the examination were held during the holidays in the schools, we could get the teachers as presiding examiners. In the next place, we could get better rooms—rooms in the high schools and academies. Next, by having more rooms, we need not put many candidates into one room. In Ontario in the university examinations for matriculation, and in the teachers' examinations, we are not allowed to have more than 25 candidates in one room under one examiner. Here I have over 100.

Q. You had 206 who passed and 89 who were rejected, that is, 295 candidates? A. Yes, and it is getting worse. Again, where there are a great number of candidates coming up, should you not permit the holding of two examinations.

Q. In that case you would have to change your papers?—A. Certainly. In the last examination we had to do that on account of the mail service in the Northwest. In Winnipeg we have two sets of papers. Furthermore, we could not use the chambers here at the right time. We had to use them a week ahead of the standard time set for all the other centres except Winnipeg, so that we had a different set of papers for Ottawa from what we had everywhere also except Winnipeg, and in Winnipeg we had both sets. There were a large number of mail clerks coming up who were temporarily in the service. You could not call them all in on one day, because that would disarrange the whole service for the Northwest, so we called in half of them in one week and the other half in the next week. There should be more liberty given to the Board in regard to the examinations, and they should be held at a more convenient time than they are at present. The time of the Promotion examinations should also be changed. They are held in May. Now that the fiscal year ends on March 31, the promotion examination should be held before that time. They could very well be held during the Christmas holidays.

Q. With the session being called earlier than formerly you will suffer from the disadvantage of not being able to use the House of Commons?—A. If they were held during the Christmas holidays we could get the use of the Collegiate Institute, where there are a large number of rooms where grown up candidates could be seated, with not more than 25 candidates in one room. Then we should have a larger number of examiners at Ottawa.

By Mr. Fyshe:

Q. How does your system of examination compare with that in England?—A. It is quite different. It is much lower, that is in the advanced work. In England the examinations are competitive, and the candidates are allowed to do the best they can. But here the examination is up to a certain standard, and if you set the standard too high you will throw out a certain number of candidates.

Q. Have you ever examined the continental system?—A. No.

Q. I suppose that in Germany the examinations would be very thorough?—A. In Germany military service is recognized in a great many appointments, which are in many cases rewards for military service. Their mail clerks are all ex-military men. I do not know about France.

By the Chairman:

Q. What would you think of the application of the competitive system here?—A. If it could be carried out I believe it would be an excellent thing.

7-8 EDWARD VII., A. 1908

By Mr. Fyshe:

Q. Of course, you would have to give the more successful competitor the particular advantage he should have?—A. That is the meaning of the competitive system.

Q. It would not do to allow the appointing power to ignore the result of the competitive examination?—A. Oh no. Where they have the competitive system, they state that there are so many clerks of a certain class to be appointed, and there are examinations held for those vacancies. There might be an examination every week in the year.

By the Chairman:

Q. Is it not a fact that in so high a service as the Indian Civil Service, as a rule the men appointed solely on account of their intellectual attainments, turn out to be men of high character?—A. Yes. When the system was applied first, there was bitter opposition to the examinations. These men have swept away that prejudice, and it is now recognized that they are the best administrators in England to-day. Many of these men are public school men. They go through a public school, and then get their special training. A man who goes through the Cambridge University may afterwards go to a trainer to get his special training for the Indian Civil Service.

By Mr. Byshe:

Q. Is it not true that this technical thing such as all academic men go through is rather a different thing from making them great business men or administrators or men of the world?—A. The great majority of the successful men in the United States are university men. The statistics show that, and the percentage is increasing.

Q. That is quite a different thing. They are university men, but not specialists; and after they leave the university, they begin where 15 year old boys going into banks begin, and that broadens them out. The point I wish to make is that college education tends to narrow people in their specialty?—A. Rather it gives them an inclination for that specialty if they choose to take it up. I spoke of Cambridge men going to a trainer; but that trainer prepares them in the special subjects of the Indian Civil Service, not in science or anything of that kind. For instance, they must know some of the native languages of India, and the trainer will prepare them in these. Then they go to India prepared for their special work to a certain extent, and they will be able more quickly to learn to speak to the people and get into their way of thinking.

By the Chairman:

Q. You said that you thought a system of competitive examinations would benefit Canada?—A. Yes, although if wrongly applied it would be more mischief. Anything that is good can be made to do more harm than what is merely milk and water.

Q. Will you amplify that—what do you mean when you say that if a system of competitive examinations were wrongly applied?—A. The subjects must be specially selected for the department or the office. Next, the examination papers must be thoroughly practical. One of the troubles with our examination papers in general is that a great deal of the work is of no practical importance.

Q. The logical result of that system was that when a vacancy occurred, application would be made to the Civil Service Commission?—A. Yes.

Q. And politics would be eliminated altogether?—A. Yes. The object is to eliminate politics and get the best trained men into the service. You might hit on a mean between the strictly competitive examination and ours by following the example of the United States and selecting certain branches and certain classes for competitive examination and leaving the general examination for the rest.

Q. The higher men get into the Finance Department or into the railway service? —A. It would be for you to select them. Let all the higher appointments be strictly by competitive examination for entrance, and after that leave all changes within the department.

Q. Of course, you would allow people who had not got into the service to go into competition a second time with other people?—A. Certainly. I remember a case in England of a man who boasted that he had gone up for three of the very highest offices and had come out first each time, and yet for some reason he refused the offices.

Q. Or the top one may not be acceptable to the department?—A. That may be.

Q. So that the logical conclusion of the competitive system would be to eliminate politics?—A. Yes.

Q. And the deputy head might reject a man who is not suitable?—A. Yes. The man might have a temper or disposition that might make him unsuitable. The deputy head would not reject him except for very good reasons.

Q. In England the Under Secretary has to give his reasons when he rejects a candidate who has been passed by the examiners?—A. Yes, or he might reject him after the provisional period.

The Commission adjourned.

Mr. JOSEPH POPE, C.M.G., I.S.O., sworn and examined.

By the Chairman:

Q. You are the Under Secretary of State?—A. Yes.

Q. How long have you occupied that position?—A. Eleven years.

Q. Before that you were Assistant Clerk of the Privy Council?—A. Yes.

Q. How long were you in that position?—A. Seven years.

Q. And you were in the service for some years before that—how long have you been in the service altogether?—A. Upwards of twenty-eight years.

Q. Besides your ordinary duties in connection with the Department of the Secretary of State, you have had a good deal to do with *la haute diplomatie*?—A. Yes.

Q. You were at Paris in connection with the Behring Sea arbitration?—A. Yes.

Q. And in London in connection with the Alaska Boundary question?—A. Yes.

Q. And you prepared the cases?—A. I would not say that I prepared the cases. I have prepared many papers on these subjects.

Q. And you were connected with the Washington business?—A. Yes, the International Commission at Washington in 1898. I was the agent of our government there, and I was the associate secretary of the commission in connection with the Alaska Boundary case, and was attached to the staff of the British agent at Paris in 1893 in the Behring Sea arbitration.

Q. How much are you paid for all this?—A. For the past four years, $4,000 a year.

Q. And no extras?—A. None.

Q. No vote covers extra services of any kind?—A. None. I think I may say that the most important part of my work in the last twenty years has lain outside of what may be called the sphere of my official duties.

Q. You have prepared a statement showing the staff of your department and the work in 1892 and in 1906?—A. Yes.

Q. In 1892 you had a staff of 40?—A. Yes.

Q. In 1906 you had a staff of 31?—A. Yes.

Q. The salaries are about the same?—A. Yes. There is not $400 difference in the vote.

Q. And the revenue of the department increased from $60,700 to over $95,000?—A. Yes, or if you take the calendar year, to $108,000.

By Mr. Fyshe:

Q. From what sources do you get revenues?—A. From fees on charters for joint stock companies principally.

Q. What is the usual percentage of charge based on the capital?—A. We charge $225 on a capital of $100,000, and from that up. A capital of $1,000,000 pays $500, and each additional $1,000,000 pays $100.

Q. How does that compare with the cost of charters granted by the different states of the United States?—A. I have never had occasion to inquire into that, but it is about the same as the cost of charters in the various provinces of Canada.

Q. I presume they make similar charges for chartering companies in England?—A. Yes. They have a system of registration there which amounts to the same thing and they charge something approximating to our fees.

Q. In the United States there are certain states that apparently give more favourable charters than others, notably the State of New Jersey, where an immense number of important companies go for their charters, though they may not do any business in that state?—A. They come here sometimes. We have a clause in our Act under which companies incorporated elsewhere may be reincorporated here.

Q. In New Jersey they charge pretty good fees?—A. Yes. We charge fairly good fees too. I have known a fee of $2,900 paid on a single charter.

By the Chairman:

Q. Your revenue now is about two and a half times your expenditure?—A. Yes. Whereas in 1892 our expenditure was $37,000 and our revenue $6,000, in 1906 our revenue was $109,000 and our expenditure no more than it was before—in fact it is less.

By Mr. Bazin:

Q. These revenues are fluctuating?—A. They are going to be a great deal more this year. The revenue is increasing all the time.

By the Chairman:

Q. In bad times there might be a certain set back?—A. I presume so; but formerly it was never contemplated that what the newspapers call the 'sealing-wax department' and the 'fifth wheel to the coach' would be a revenue producing department. But that is what it has now become. Last year it produced a net result to the good of $70,000, after paying all expenses.

Q. The other adjuncts to the department, such as commissions and applications for parliament have also considerably increased during the period?—A. Yes, and we have had large additions under the Naturalization system. The administration of the Naturalization Act is a most irksome business.

Q. With increased immigration, the work under the Naturalization Act grows more and more in importance?—A. Yes. It involves much work, because the names are mostly unpronounceable and badly written. We keep a record of them, and the deciphering of these foreign names is no easy matter.

Q. The department is divided into two branches—the correspondence branch and the registration branch?—A. Yes.

Q. You have three chief clerks—Pelletier, Colson and Storr?—A. Yes. Mr. Pelletier is head of the correspondence branch and my substitute in my absence. He is a barrister. Mr. Colson is the accountant and au fait of the work generally. Mr. Storr is the head of the register branch.

Q. Beginning with the entrance into the service, have you any idea or suggestion to offer with regard to the Board of Civil Service Examiners?—A. I wish to say that in 1892 or perhaps a few years before that, the Board of Civil Service Examiners had a separate organization, a separate office and a staff of several clerks, costing $1,600 or $1,800 a year. Now the Board of Civil Service Examiners is administered in my department by two of my clerks at a cost of about $300 or $400 a year. That is a subject that should be taken into consideration; we are doing the whole clerical work of the Board. I have no suggestions to make as to the Board itself.

Q. With regard to the appointment to the Civil Service, have you any ideas as between competitive examinations and the present system?—A. Yes.

By Mr. Fyshe:

Q. Considering the difficulty of getting men into the Civil Service, don't you think it would be well to exercise the greatest care possible in making a selection?—A. My experience in the service goes to show that it is not always the most highly educated men who make the best clerks.

Q. Still, in the long run would it not be safer to trust to the Civil Service examination than to the judgment of the appointers?—A. In the beginning, but I would not have competitive examinations for the entrance.

Q. Of course you would have an examination?—A. Yes, I think we should have an examination to see that the youth is grounded in the ordinary requirements—that he can spell and add and that sort of thing; but I do not think I would go further in the initial appointments.

Q. When a man is appointed an ordinary third-class clerk his salary is $500 ? A. Yes.

Q. Have you found any difficulty in filling vacancies?—A. Not in the way of promotion.

Q. Do you favour promotion examinations?—A. Yes.

By the Chairman:

Q. It is stated here that owing to the earnings in other branches of life it is rather difficult getting enterprising young men to come into the service?—A. That is true. There is very great difficulty in getting good young men. When asked that question a moment ago I understood you to refer to promotions within the department. There is difficulty in getting good men from outside.

Q. The consequence of that is an inordinate number of women entering the service?—A. I suppose it is a consequence. It is a very unfortunate thing.

Q. How many women have you in your department?—A. Three.

Q. That is not an inordinate number?—A. No. One of them is assistant private secretary to the Secretary of State, and is a very good clerk.

Q. She has been some years with you?—A. She has been there about 12 years.

By Mr. Fyshe:

Q. Is it usual for these women in the different branches of the Civil Service to get married?—A. Now and again.

Q. You do not raise any objection, do you?—A. They give up their positions when they get married—that is understood.

By Mr. Bazin:

Q. They cannot then stay in the service?—A. No.

By the Chairman:

Q. What is your idea of the employment of women in the public service?—A. Speaking generally, I do not think it desirable, though I know of several exceptions. But I am speaking of the general principle, because I find that as a rule women clerks claim the rights of men and the privileges of their own sex as well.

Q. When a third-class clerk is appointed, he is appointed on probation?—A. He is appointed on probation.

Q. Is that probation ever taken seriously?—A. Not so far as I know.

By Mr. Fyshe:

Q. That is to say, the heads of departments never exercise their right to reject them?—A. I have never done that, and I have never heard of it being done.

Q. There must have been a large number of cases in which it would have been justifiable to have taken action in that way?—A. Quite likely.

By the Chairman:

Q. When the probation expires the clerks have annual increments of $50 a year?— A. Yes.

Q. The deputy head has to recommend those?—A. Yes.

Q. That is done perfunctorily?—A. Absolutely. It is automatic.

By Mr. Fyshe:

Q. Is there no provision in the Act by which special excellence can be rewarded by a larger increase?—A. None in the Act. It would require a special vote of parliament to give a man an increase of $100 a year. For instance, I could not recommend my best clerk for an increase for $100 a year without a special vote by parliament, mentioning his name.

Q. Would you not call that a defect in the regulations?—A. That opens up a large question. If the deputy head stood in the same position as a bank manager I should say, yes.

Q. It makes the service too mechanical?—A. I do not like the system, but some people say it is the only system that can practically be worked.

By the Chairman:

Q. You have to report to the minister within the year that probationary clerk is fitted to remain?—A. Yes.

Q. That is practically perfunctory?—A. Quite so.

Q. You have no political appointments like city postmasters in your department? —A. None. The only appointments we have from time to time are those of examiners in different cities under the Civil Service Act.

Q. They are appointed under patronage?—A. Yes.

By Mr. Fyshe:

Q. Wouldn't it be within the power of your office to change the examiners?—A. I do not as a matter of fact interfere with the Civil Service Examiners at all. The statute says that the Board shall be administered by the Secretary of State, which includes the Under Secretary, but as a matter of fact they go straight to the minister. I never interfere with the Board myself. It is merely, as it were, attached to the department. It is not in practice subordinate to it.

Q. If there was a change decided on in that respect, it could easily be carried out by your office interfering to that extent—I mean, to make a change from time to time, sending these examiners from one place to another?—A. The statute says that the Civil Service Examiners shall be under the direction of the Secretary of State. The practice has always been for the minister to deal directly with the Board and the practice is agreeable to me.

By the Chairman:

Q. You have never re-employed in your department a man who has resigned?— A. No.

Q. You occasionally have promotion examinations in your department?—A. Yes.

Q. How many subjects are your men examined in?—A. It depends. In some cases the test is confined to duties of office.

Q. You have not altogether contracted yourself out of the regulations and the arithmetic and duties?—A. No.

Q. You have allowed the Civil Service Board to have a hand in it?—A. Yes. But I would like to say that I do not believe in the present system of Promotion examinations at all. At present the Government of the day makes the appointments. I think that system will continue for our time; I am not discussing it. But I think that after a man enters the service his promotion should be largely in the hands of the deputy—that the deputy head should apply the tests necessary for promotion. I think he should have the matter pretty much in his own hands, and be able to say to a man, I will promote you or I will not advance you, as the case may be. I think better work would be had.

Q. Section 46 says:—'Except as herein otherwise provided, when any vacancy occurs in one of the higher classes, in either division, the head of the department shall select.' Would it not be better that the head of the department on the report of the deputy head should select?—A. Yes, I think it would.

Q. Then, section 47, subsection 2, says:—'At any time during the first year the head of the department may reject the person promoted.' Would you say that it

7-8 EDWARD VII., A. 1908

should be the head of the department on the report of the deputy head?—A. Yes, I agree with that.

Q. Referring to section 50, have you ever had any transfers to or from your department?—A. Yes, occasionally.

Q. At the desire of the men or at your own desire? —A. Generally both. I generally try to get their concurrence, but I have found it in the public interest to make a transfer. It is generally necessary to secure the concurrence of the ministers of both departments, and I endeavour to meet their wishes.

Q. I am speaking of the men themselves?—A. I have had transfers without the concurrence of the parties chiefly interested.

By Mr. Fyshe:

Q. It seems to me that should also be at the option of the deputy head, not the head of the department?—A. You must remember that under our system the minister is the head of the department, and you cannot give his subordinate greater powers than you give him. The statute does not contemplate that and it would be foreign to our system of government which makes the minister responsible to parliament.

By Mr. Bazin:

Q. As a matter of fact, does it not work that way?—A. I have only served as deputy head under two Ministers, and I have always found both of them ready to adopt my suggestions. You must not give the deputy head too much power, though I think he should have more power than he has. In the advancement of clerks with respect to rank or salaries, I think the deputy should have a greater say than he has at present; it would be conducive to the efficient administration of a department, and it should be well understood by the clerks that the deputy head is the man they have to deal with and satisfy, whereas now they get the automatic increase, and it does not matter whom they please. The practice is that all get the increase who are not undeserving. It should be that no one should get it who is not deserving.

By the Chairman:

Q. Section 56 provides that in all cases the salary of the deputy head shall be limited to $4,000 per annum. I presume you consider that the deputy heads are not sufficiently paid?—A. I do not think they are. If a man is fit to be the head of a department of the public service, I think he is worth more money than that, if he is worth anything.

By Mr. Fyshe:

Q. We think so in the commercial world, but the trouble is that when you do things in a mechanical kind of way, under general rules, it is hard to frame such general rules as will not be abused?—A. Still, there are only twenty deputies, and it seems to me that they should be taken out of the rut and dealt with separately, particularly if you entrust them with larger powers.

Q. And in giving them larger powers you should hold them to greater responsibility—you should hold them to the responsibility of a well administered department?—A. I think, too— I am not extravagant in my ideas—that it is quite impossible for a man in the position of a deputy head to live quietly in Ottawa as a gentleman and to bring up and educate his family, on the present salary. Therefore the salary is inadequate.

By the Chairman:

Q. Section 82 provides that the employment shall commence at the minimum salary. In your opinion is that advantageous to the service, or should a clerk begin at $500 or $600 or $700, according to his competence?—A. The provision is a protection.

SESSIONAL PAPER No. 29a

Q. But it is mandatory?—A. Without that provision influence would be brought on the minister to start every new appointee at a salary higher than the minimum.

By Mr. Fyshe:

Q. It seems to me that everything should be done to eliminate political influence altogether, if it is possible by any arrangement?—A. We of the permanent service are not the ones to discuss that.

Q. But if you think so, you should say so?—A. It is not always prudent to say all one thinks.

By the Chairman:

Q. Suppose there were some clause saying, ' Subject to the approval and concurrence of the deputy head,' don't you think some wider latitude might be given?—A; I think such a provision would be desirable. I think the deputy should have a certain amount of latitude. In the case of an exceptionally clever young fellow, he should be at liberty to start him at $600 or $700 if he so desires.

Q. Under section 86 you can suspend the annual increment for misconduct?—A. Yes.

Q. Are all the men in your department good, or is that carried into effect?—A. I have in rare instances been compelled to advise suspension, and stopped their salary, but I have never taken away any clerk's annual increase. During the period of suspension the pay of the delinquent stops.

Q. Stoppage of salary may be for neglect of duty or misconduct?—A. I have heard of it being done in other departments, but I have never done it.

Q. Don't you think it would be better to enlarge that too, and make it on the report of the deputy?—A. That might bring the deputy into conflict with the minister.

Q. Take section 92—has anybody ever suffered loss of pay in your department for unauthorized absence?—A. I have suspended one or more officials, and suspension stops pay.

Q. But not on account of illness?—A. No, I have never done that.

Q. Section 101 provides for the annual leave of absence. Do you find three weeks sufficient to give to your men gathered here in Ottawa from all parts of the Dominion? —A. No; I have always interpreted that to include twenty-one working days. That is what I have done in all cases with the sanction of my minister.

By Mr. Fyshe:

Q. Is that the universal allowance?—A. No, I do not think so; but the question arose, and the minister, Sir Charles Tupper, decided to interpret the section in that way. I believe in treating my clerks generously so far as it is in my power to do so. If they do their work faithfully for eleven months in the year, I would give them the full three weeks' holiday. I believe they would be all the better for a full month's holidays.

By Mr. Bazin:

Q. Do you not think three weeks is sufficient?—A. That is very well in regard to some of them; but I want you to realize that in the case of many men in the Civil Service their hours are far longer than from 9 to 4. They work very hard and long. There are a certain number not bound by any official hours, but who are at work early and late, and such men need a good rest.

Q. I suppose they can easily get leave of absence for a few days occasionally?— A. Yes, but that is not quite the same thing as a regular vacation.

By the Chairman:

Q. Would you make the holidays compulsory?—A. Yes, I would make clerks take their holidays.

Q. In your department no abuse has occurred in connection with the holidays?—
A. No, no abuse.

Q. You say you have suspended a man under section 103?—A. Yes, though very rarely. With reference to that I would make a suggestion. The statute says: ' The head of a department, and in his absence the deputy head, may suspend.' I think the words, ' and in his absence the deputy head,' should be eliminated for this reason: they were intended to strengthen the hands of the deputy head, but they operate the other way. The Interpretation Act says the head of the department includes the deputy head, and if those words were struck out the deputy head could suspend at any time. Now he can only suspend in the absence of the minister. I think the powers of the deputy should be strengthened, but without derogating from the powers and responsibilities of the minister, who must be supreme.

Q. Coming to section 104, has any clerk been dismissed from the Department of Secretary of State in your time?—A. No.

Q. You have no observation to make as to that, so far as your practical experience goes?—A. No, I think that is right.

Q. I presume that generally speaking you have an idea of whether there should be cause shown for dismissal?—A. Quite so; but for the security of the clerk I would have an order in council for dismissal, because we hold office during pleasure.

By Mr. Bazin:

Q. Was ever any one dismissed without cause?—A. It has happened. Section 52 provides that when a deputy head is removed from his office a statement of the reasons for so doing shall be laid on the table of both Houses of Parliament; but that clause is illusory. The deputy is first dismissed, and then the reasons—any reasons—for his dismissal shall be laid on the table. Our tenure of office is during pleasure.

By the Chairman:

Q. Do all your officers sign the attendance book?—A. Yes, without exception.

Q. What time do you close it?—A. At 10 o'clock.

Q. There are no fixed hours in your department—the officers work till the work is done?—A. They work till the work is done.

Q. In the slack season they get out at four o'clock?—A. Not all. I do my best work after four, and some of my most valuable clerks stay till six o'clock.

Q. How long do you give them for luncheon?—A. I am not very strict as to that. If a man lives at a long distance from the office, I give him an hour and a half—from an hour to an hour and a half. I am generally in my office until half past six. I turn up at 10 o'clock in the morning. Sometimes I come earlier, sometimes a little later, but as a rule my hours are from 10 until 6.30.

Q. The office is always open to the public?—A. Yes, as a rule there is somebody in my department from 9 in the morning till 6 o'clock at night.

Q. Your officers are all in the one building?—A. Yes, all in the one building.

Q. You have no objection to Mr. Bazin and Mr. Fyshe going into your office?—A. None whatever.

Q. Now we come to the question of retiring allowance. You are working under the old Superannuation Act?—A. Yes.

Q. All the officials who are under the old system still go under it?—A. Yes.

Q. But those appointed since 1897 have a deduction made from their salaries?—A. Yes, there is an abatement from their salaries, but they have no superannuation.

Q. What do think of the change of law?—A. I think it is very unfortunate and unjust to those who have come into the service since its operation.

Q. The stability of the service has suffered?—A. Greatly, in my opinion.

Q. And men are now constantly leaving the service, men of intelligence and good position, like Bain, the Assistant Commissioner of Customs, and Stewart, the Commissioner of Forests, and others, because there is no superannuation?—A. Exactly, and many men are being held in the service only for the sake of the Superannuation which they expect, and but for which they would leave the service to-morrow.

Q. Then your idea is that the sooner the Superannuation Act is restored to the statute book the better?—A. I think so, unquestionably, and I think it is particularly hard on the appointees of the present Government who come into the service and find that the old officials have superannuation while they have none. They naturally feel aggrieved. This is detrimental to the efficiency of the service.

Q. Would you like some system of insurance or provision for a widow to be added to the superannuation system?—A. Undoubtedly. I am very much in favour of such a provision. I think that the superannuation system should not only be restored but improved. There are a number of excellent gentlemen in this city who serve the state in a military capacity. If any of these are superannuated they draw their pension; if they die, their widows and each child up to a certain age draw an allowance. The civil servants, who I think serve the state equally well, have no such advantage. If we die after a service, it may be of fifty years, our widows and children derive no advantage from the moneys we have been contributing for half a century it may be to the Superannuation fund.

Q. The Militia Pension Act to which you refer has been enacted since the Superannuation Act was abolished—A. Yes.

DEPARTMENT OF THE SECRETARY OF STATE.

Number of Clerical Staff.

	1892.	1906.
Chief clerks..	2	3
First-class clerks..	6	6
Second-class clerks..	13	8
Junior second-class clerks..	..	8
Third-class clerks..	9	2
Messengers..	4	1
Temporary clerks..	5	..
Temporary messengers..	1	3
	40	31

Salaries of clerical staff..	$37,827 45	$ 38,252 84
Total revenue..	6,725 75	95,754 80
" (calendar year)..	....	108,913 10
Number of charters issued..	71	374
Commissions, bonds, renewals and other documents registered and recorded..	1,104	4,729
Applications for pardon..	288	800
Of which there were granted..	190	469

NOTE.—The Naturalization Act and the Ticket of Leave Act were not in existence in 1892. These Acts are administered by this department.

Under the former Act in the year 1906, 10,778 names of naturalized subjects were registered, classified and indexed, and the returns filed for reference. During the last two years over 70,000 names have been so dealt with. The returns are received from some 400 officers of various law courts throughout the Dominion and necessarily involve considerable correspondence. Payments are made to each returning officer according to a special tariff twice yearly. About one thousand cheques being issued on this account.

Under the Ticket of Leave Act some 600 applications were dealt with in 1906, 294 tickets being granted.

7-8 EDWARD VII. A. 1908

J. M. COURTNEY, Esq., C.M.G., I.S.O.,
460 Wilbrod Street,
Ottawa.

OTTAWA, May 25, 1907.

DEAR MR. COURTNEY.—I inclose a memorandum for the consideration of the Commissioners. If you consider it a subject of which they have cognizance, I should be glad if you will kindly lay it before them. I am up to my eyes in business just now arranging for the visit of the Japanese Prince, but I feel I shall be busier later on, and I want to place this matter before the Commissioners, or somebody who will bring about this much needed reform.

In great haste,

Yours sincerely,

(Sgd.) JOSEPH POPE.

MEMORANDUM FOR CONSIDERATION OF THE CIVIL SERVICE COMMISSIONERS.

I desire, with the permission of the commissioners, to offer a few observations upon a matter akin to the subject of their inquiry in respect of which I had not an opportunity of inviting their attention when recently before them. I refer to the desirableness of establishing a more systematic mode of dealing with what I may term, for want of a better phrase, the *external affairs* of the Dominion.

It is commonly supposed that such matters are now administered by the department of which I am the deputy head, but this is a misapprehension. The Secretary of State is primarily and principally the official mouthpiece of His Excellency the Governor General in respect of *Canadian affairs*; he is the channel of communication between the Dominion Government and those of the Provinces, towards which he occupies somewhat the same relation that the Colonial Secretary does towards the Colonies. All communications which reach the Secretary of State for transmission to England or to a foreign country, are forwarded by him to the Governor General with a recommendation that he would be pleased to transmit the same to their destination. All despatches from the Colonial Office are addressed to the Governor General and by His Excellency are sent, for the most part, to the Privy Council where they are referred to the heads of those departments which they particularly concern. Much of this correspondence relates to domestic matters, and with it I have no concern here. Much, however, bears upon what I have called external affairs, that is to say, questions touching our relations with foreign countries, as the Behring Sea Seal question, the Alaska Boundary, the Atlantic Fisheries, International boundaries, and other pending controversies with the United States; or, it may be, with questions whose scope and bearing, though within the empire, extend beyond the bounds of the Dominion; such for example as the difference with Newfoundland over the boundary in Labrador. Let us say the Imperial government have occasion to communicate with the government of Canada in respect of any one of these subjects: The Colonial Minister addresses a despatch to the Governor General; that despatch is forwarded by command of His Excellency to the Privy Council, which means with us the cabinet. The Privy Council refers it to the minister at the head of the department to which it relates, who causes to be prepared a reply in the form of a report to the Privy Council thus:

'The undersigned to whom was referred a despatch from the Secretary of State for the Colonies dated..........on the subject of...........has the honour to report that............'

That report, when it reaches the Privy Council, is turned into a minute, preserving the sense, and even the phraseology unchanged. It has, as it were, merely been given a head and tail, thus:

'The Committee of the Privy Council have had under consideration a despatch from the Secretary of State for the Colonies dated the...... The Minister of......

to whom the said despatch was referred, reports that (here follows the minister's report verbatim).

' The committee concur in the foregoing observation of the Minister of.........., and advise that a copy of this minute, if approved, be transmitted to the Secretary of State for the Colonies for the information of His Majesty's Government.'

This minute, when approved by the Governor General, is forwarded to England. If it is an important despatch, the policy of the Government in regard to the principle involved is, no doubt, discussed and agreed to in Council; but the terms of the report are almost invariably left to the department to which the despatch was originally referred. Under this mode of dealing with official correspondence there is no uniformity of system or continuity of plan.

The preparation of despatches is a technical acquirement, attained only after special study of the questions involved, and by assiduous practice in drafting. It may happen; it must sometimes happen; that the official to whom these Imperial despatches are referred (for it cannot be expected that a busy minister has time to attend to such matters personally, calling for much study, and a large acquaintance with intricate details) while fully competent to deal with the merits of the question in its present aspect, is not familiar with the past history of the controversy or skilled in the framing of State papers. There are moreover certain questions which relate partly to one department and partly to another, so that it may not be easy to tell at first sight to whom a new despatch should be referred. The earlier communication may have related to cne department, and a later despatch on the same subject to another. Neither department having any knowledge of what has been referred to the other, the consequence is that both departments, *quoad* this particular subject, are working more or less in the dark.

In the early years of Confederation, when these questions were few, the inconvenience of which I speak was not so greatly felt, as the Prime Minister of the day kept them pretty much in his own hands; but with the growth and development of the Dominion this is no longer possible.

The practical result of the system in vogue is that there does not exist to-day in any department a complete record of any of the correspondence to which I have alluded. It has been so scattered, and passed through so many hands that there is no approach to continuity in any of the departmental files. Such knowledge concerning them as is available, is, for the most part, lodged in the memories of a few officials. I fear too that in Downing street, Canadian despatches are noted for diversity rather than for elegance of style. As the Dominion grows this state of things must always be getting worse. If some reform is not soon effected it will be too late. Even now, I am of opinion that it would be an extremely difficult task to construct from our official files anything approaching to a complete record of any of the international questions in which Canada has been concerned during the past fifty years. To give one illustration: Thirty-five years ago the question of ownership of the Island of San Juan, long at issue between Great Britain and the United States, was decided by the Emperor of Germany in favour of the latter. That surely is a matter of important historical concern to the Dominion, yet I should be at a loss to know to-day to what department of the government to turn for any information as to this arbitration. Indeed, I am quite confident that it does not exist in any of them.

My suggestion is, that all despatches relating to external affairs should be referred by the Privy Council to one department, whose staff should contain men trained in the study of these questions, and in the conduct of diplomatic correspondence. These officials should be in close touch with the other departments, from which they could draw all necessary information, the raw material, as it were, of their work; but the digesting of this information and its presentation in diplomatic form should rest with them, through, of course, the same channels as at present; for in this suggestion there is no thought of change in that regard. Every effort should be made to collect from the beginning all papers bearing on the questions I have indicated, from the office of the Governor General, the Privy Council office, the various departments and the Foreign and Colonial offices. I wish most earnestly to impress upon all concerned that if this work is not soon systematically begun it will be too late. The few men throughout the service conversant with these questions are growing old, and must soon disappear. So far as I know they will leave no successors. Much of the early history of these subjects, so far as Canadian records are concerned, will thus be lost.

I recommend that a small staff of young men, well educated and carefully selected, be attached to the department whose creation I have advocated, and that they be specially trained in the knowledge and treatment of these subjects. In this way we shall acquire an organized method of dealing with international questions which at present we wholly lack.

I have spoken of the creation of another department, but I see no reason why this work should not be done under the supervision of the Secretary of State, whose present department might be divided into two sections, one for Canadian, and one for External affairs.

All of which is respectfully submitted.

(Signed)   JOSEPH POPE.

OTTAWA, May 25, 1906.

OTTAWA, THURSDAY, June 6, 1907.

The Royal Commission on the Civil Service met this morning at 10.30 o'clock.

Present:—Mr. J. M. COURTNEY, C.M.G., Chairman.

Mr. THOMAS FYSHE, Montreal, and

Mr. P. J. BAZIN, Quebec.

GEORGE F. O'HALLORAN, sworn and examined.

By the Chairman:

Q. You are the Deputy Minister of Agriculture?—A. Yes.
Q. How long have you been deputy minister?—A. Since May, 1902.
Q. You succeeded Mr. Scarth?—A. I did.
Q. And his predecessor was Mr. Lowe?—A. Yes.
Q. Your department is directly charged with looking after Copyrights?—A. Yes.
Q. Trade marks?—A. Yes.
Q. Patents?—A. Yes. .
Q. In connection with the department there is a bureau of Census and Statistics?
—A. Yes.
. And Experimental Farms?—A. Yes.
. And Quarantine?—A. Yes, both human and animals.
. And also Dairying and Agriculture?—A. Dairying, seed and live stock.
. You also have something to do with the Cow Census?—A. Yes.
. And with Creameries?—A. Yes.
. And Cheese Curing?—A. Yes.
. And Poultry?—A. Yes.
. And Fruit?—A. Yes.
. And Tobacco?—A. Yes.
Q. And Cold Storage in general?—A. Yes.
Q. And Refrigerator cars?—A. Yes; and one important branch which is being
established—the subsidizing of Cold storage warehouses. We are just now organizing
that branch of the service.

By Mr. Fyshe:

Q. Are you going to extend that over the whole country?—A. Yes; under an Act
passed last session under which thirty per cent of the cost is to be paid as a subsidy
for Cold storage warehouses for the preservation of food products.
Q. Will that be reckoned an advantage all over the country—in the west, for instance?—A. I think so. That is the opinion of the Government in passing the measure.
Q. Don't you think there is enough private enterprise in the country to establish
these things if they are called for?—A. Evidently Parliament thought otherwise in
passing the Act. There appeared to be a very general demand for it, especially in
some of the fruit districts. It was represented that there were not adequate facilities.

By the Chairman:

Q. In addition to the other things enumerated, the Archives of the country are
under the control of your department?—A. Yes, the Archives, including the public
records.

29a—4½

Q. You were asked to render a statement—this (showing) is the statement?—A. Yes.

Q. I asked you to bring up a supplementary memorandum?—A. I produced a duplicate of the current pay-list.

Q. On June 30, 1906, you had 59 permanent employees against 53 on June 30, 1902?—A. Yes.

Q. And you had 16 extra clerks in 1892 and 24 in 1906—these are the clerks paid out of civil government contingencies?—A. Yes.

Q. Of the permanent clerks you have 7 chief clerks attached to the department. Mr. Chittick is the accountant?—A. Yes.

Q. And Mr. Doherty?—A. Private secretary.

Q. How did he come to be made a chief clerk?—A. I think it is the general practice of the department now to make a private secretary chief clerk.

Q. Mr. Doughty is the Archivist?—A. Yes. I may say that at present the Archivist has been removed from the operation of the Civil Service Act. That chief clerkship was abolished, and the Archivist is now paid out of the Archives vote.

Q. Then there is Mr. Jarvis, the secretary?—A. Yes.

Q. And Mr. Lynch, of the patent branch?—A. Yes.

Q. What is Mr. Ritchie doing?—A. He is the registrar of trade marks and copyrights.

Q. Mr. Jackson is dead. Has there been a chief clerk appointed to succeed him?—A. Mr. Ritchie has succeeded Mr. Jackson.

Q. Then, there are practically only five chief clerks: Chittick, Doherty, Jarvis, Lynch and Ritchie?—A. Yes.

Q. Mr. Johnson has been superannuated and his position has been merged into the census and statistics branch?—A. Yes.

Q. Are the five chief clerks doing chief clerks' work?—A. Yes, with the exception of the private secretary.

Q. They are doing distinctive work?—A. Each one is the head of a branch.

Q. Coming to the first-class clerks, of whom you seem to have the same number in 1906 that you had in 1892, 10—are these people doing work of a first-class character, or after they were promoted, did they do the same work that they did in the lower class? Mr. Bailey, I know, is a patent examiner?—A. Among the first-class clerks there are six patent examiners. Several of these were promoted from second-class clerkships on my recommendation to the minister.

By Mr. Fyshe:

Q. A man requires special skill to examine patents—a knowledge of mechanics?—A. Under the present rule of the department only graduates in science from Canadian universities are appointed.

Q. And they have to have a special knowledge of mechanics in addition?—A. Yes. We have graduates who have taken the electrical course and graduates who have taken the mechanical course, and so on through all the different branches of science.

Q. You endeavour to get these specialists to take the position of patent examiners?—A. They must be specialists or they could not do the work.

By the Chairman:

Q. Then, six out of the ten first-class clerks are examiners of patents?—A. Yes.

Q. Have you one in Routhier's place?—A. He died recently, within a month.

Q. Are the second-class clerks doing the work they did before they were promoted from the junior second class, and are the junior second-class clerks doing the work they were doing when they were third-class clerks?—A. Generally.

Q. That is, the promotion did not make a difference in the work?—A. No.

Q. Then you have a large number of third-class clerks, some paid out of civil government contingencies, some out of the archives vote, some out of census, and some out of agriculture and dairying. Why have you so many extra clerks paid out of civil government contingencies in proportion to your permanent staff?—A. I found that state of affairs existing when I came into the department, and the Minister has been averse to creating permanent clerkships, and we have gone on in the same way.

By Mr. Fyshe:

Q. Have you got barely enough or too many?—A. We have what I consider simply sufficient for the work of the department.

Q. Where are your offices?—A. Our principal offices are in the Langevin Block.

By the Chairman:

Q. Where else are your offices?—A. In what is known as the Canadian Building—one of the Woods' buildings.

Q. You have no objection to Mr. Fyshe and Mr. Bazin going over your offices?—A. I would be pleased to show them through. We have a separate building, recently erected, for the archives, and we have a building on the corner of Queen and Metcalfe streets used by the exhibition branch of the department.

Q. Then it has been considered politic to have a large number of temporary clerks in proportion to the permanent staff?—A. Yes.

Q. Are these temporary clerks shoved on the department, or do you take them when necessary?—A. They are employed when I recommend to the minister the necessity for their employment.

Q. They are employed only on your recommendation?—A. As a general rule.

Q. And you derive that information, I suppose, from the chiefs of the several branches?—A. Yes.

Q. And the employment of these temporary clerks is not forced on the department, but you ask for them?—A. I ask for them.

Q. Are they political appointments?—A. They are selected from the list of applicants, and they are recommended by supporters of the governement. We generally try to ascertain as far as we can the qualifications of the applicants. We make it a rule to get as good clerks as we can.

By Mr. Fyshe:

Q. Would it not be better to have an automatic selection on the basis of a competitive examination?—A. No. I have very little faith in competitive examinations. I often find that clerks who can pass a very good examination are not satisfactory otherwise.

By the Chairman:

Q. I think all the clerks paid out of civil government contingencies are women?—A. With a few exceptions.

Q. I think with the exception of the messengers they are all women?—A. There is a man named Morgan.

Q. Miss T. Morgan?—A. The 'Miss' is a mistake.

Q. Then, with one exception all the clerks paid out of civil government contingencies—what are called your temporary assistants—are women?—A. Yes.

Q. Is the staff made up of women because men were not procurable at the price?—A. As a rule.

Q. You do not find young men of enterprise and ambition willing to enter the service at $500 a year?—A. No.

Q. But women being content with $500 a year are pushing to enter the service?—A. Yes, that is, in the inside service.

Q. As a matter of fact they are in general permanent?—A. Yes.

Q. Once in they remain in?—A. As a rule.

Q. Although the theory is that you can get rid of them at any time, you never do get rid of them?—A. Except for cause—for misconduct.

Q. Do you ever get rid of any of them for cause?—A. Oh yes.

Q. You have an attendance book in your department?—A. Yes.

Q. One attendance book?—A. One attendance book in what I may term the inside service—for those branches which are located in the Langevin block. There is also an attendance book in each branch in the outside buildings.

Q. I have counted the number of employees, temporary and permanent in this list, charged to civil government; there are 85 of them, and you keep an attendance book for all these?—A. Yes.

Q. Do you keep the attendance book?—A. It is kept under my direction by a first-class clerk who is also my clerk. It is brought to me at intervals for my examination and my initialling. He makes it up daily.

Q. When these people are appointed they are presumed to be fitted in age, health and moral conduct—they are appointed on probation, I suppose?—A. Yes, under the terms of the Act.

Q. Do you ever reject any of them during the period of probation?—A. I do not remember of it ever having been done.

Q. After the period of probation has expired and you have certified that they are fitted to remain in the public service, have you ever had occasion to remove any of them?—A. You are speaking now of the inside service?

Q. The inside service.—A. No.

By Mr. Fyshe:

Q. Whose duty is it to report on the fitness of a man who has been on probation for six months?—A. The Deputy Minister.

Q. But the deputy cannot know from personal observation exactly what the man is fit for—he must depend on somebody else?—A. He must depend on the chief of the branch in which the clerk is serving.

Q. I suppose you have a chief clerk in every branch who exercises some kind of supervision over the work of the others?—A. Yes. Of course the deputy must rely to a great extent on the chiefs of the branches for information in regard to the individual clerks.

By the Chairman:

Q. What is your present salary?—A. $3,900.

Q. Next year it will be $4,000?—A. Yes.

Q. You get the ordinary salary paid to a deputy head?—A. I do.

Q. Before you were appointed you were in practice as a barrister in Montreal?—A. I was.

Q. Do you ever regret coming into the service?—A. I have been too busy to trouble myself with vain regrets.

Q. What leave of absence prevails in your department?—A. The usual statutory leave of three weeks.

Q. And for the temporaries?—A. It is given to the temporaries as well as to the permanents.

Q. What are the hours for luncheon?—A. An hour and a quarter.

Q. Do you all go out to lunch at the same time?—A. No. Our department is peculiar in some respects. There are certain branches that must be kept open all the time. For instance, the patent office must be kept open during the usual business hours.

Q. What are your office hours?—A. From half past nine till four.

Q. At times of emergency, for instance during the session of parliament, do the men go at four?—A. They remain as long as I require them to keep up the work of the department. I have frequently given an order to a branch for all the clerks to remain until five o'clock.

Q. The ordinary hours are from half past nine till four, but when you want any of them to remain longer, you keep them?—A. Yes.

Q. In what state are your records now?—A. They are kept in a very satisfactory way, in charge of Mr. C. W. Bate, a first-class man.

Q. All records pertaining to the history of the Dominion you have turned over to the archivist?—A. Entirely.

Q. There was a Treasury Board minute passed in 1879 forbidding the use of political influence by clerks—did you ever see it?—A. No.

Q. The effect of it was that the use of political influence by any clerk was tantamount to sending in his resignation?—A. I am aware that there is such a rule, though I have never seen it.

Q. Do clerks seeking promotion pass you by and go direct to the Minister?—A. I think they have found that it is well to follow the regular course and come to me.

Q. You have nothing to object to, generally speaking, in the conduct of the staff?—A. No. It is very satisfactory on the whole.

Q. Have you a greater staff than the business ot the department requires?—A. No.

Q. Do you think you are undermanned?—A. No, I think our staff is sufficient. If I thought otherwise, I would recommend to the Minister an increase in the staff and he generally acts on my recommendations.

By Mr. Fyshe:

Q. You could not achieve the same end by putting more work on each?—A. We would have to extend the hours. I think that as a rule the clerks work faithfully in the office hours.

Q. There is a great difference in capacity, even for mechanical work, between one man and another?—A. Certainly.

Q. As a rule clerks who are not kept under a spur all the time are apt to get pretty lazy and do very little work?—A. I must say that I have found that the Civil Service clerks work very much harder than I thought they did before I came into the service.

By the Chairman:

Q. You have been appointed since the Superannuation Act was abolished?—A. Yes.

Q. You know nothing personally of the condition of the service at the time that Act was in existence?—A. I know nothing of the service prior to my coming here.

Q. Do you not think superannuation gives stability to the public service?—A. I do.

Q. Do you think it would be desirable to restore the Superannuation Act or establish some kind of pension system?—A. I do, for the reason that I find that the large industrial and financial institutions generally are adopting the system, and they would not adopt it unless it were wise to do so.

Q. You think the adoption of some kind of pension system would have an economical bearing on the public service?—A. I think that what is good for these private corporations would be good for the Government.

Q. The Archives branch is now by itself?—A. Yes, in a separate building.

Q. Are the employees of the Archives branch appointed without reference to the Civil Service Act—that is to say, do they pass an examination?—A. The Archives vote at present is not subject to the Civil Service Act, but there are some old clerks in the Archives branch who are governed by the Civil Service Act. Incoming clerks are not governed by the Civil Service Act.

Q. Either in point of emolument or in point of examination?—A. No.

Q. They require no examination?—A. They may be admitted without regard to the Civil Service Act; but with one or two exceptions the Minister has insisted that all should have passed the Civil Service examination before being appointed.

Q. The work of compilation, collation, indexing and calendaring in the archives, one would think, would require a technical education?—A. Yes.

Q. Some knowledge of the history of the country?—A. Yes.

7-8 EDWARD VII., A. 1908

Q. Some grasp of state papers?—A. Yes.

Q. Are the people appointed to that branch of your department fitted to carry on the work?—A. The principal clerks in that branch have been selected on account of their special and technical qualifications for the work. Unless one have some taste for the work, it would be so irksome that it would be almost impossible to carry it on.

Q. I see by the papers that a board met the other day, consisting of represntatives from several universities, with Mr. Doughty, the archivist, and yourself, to lay down a scheme?—A. What is known as the Canadian Historical Manuscripts Commission, established by Order in Council a few months ago, composed of the professors of history of the principal Canadian universities—Dr. Colby of McGill, Dr. Wrong of Toronto, Professor Shortt of Queen's, the Reverend Abbé Gosselin and Dr. Edmond Roy of Laval, and also a representative of one of the universities of the maritime provinces and a representative of one of the universities of the west. These gentlemen are to act in an advisory capacity to the minister, determine the broad lines on which the new work of the Archives branch shall be conducted. A meeting for the purpose of organization was held recently and there will be another meeting held in the fall. It is proposed to hold about four meetings of these men.

Q. Were you chairman of the meeting?—A. Yes. Under the Order in Council the deputy minister acts as chairman in the absence of the minister. The minister had left for England.

Q. If the minister were here you would still be on that board?—A. No. It is provided in the Order in Council that I shall act in the absence of the minister.

Q. Do you intend, in connection with the archives, to do any publishing?—A. Yes.

Q. You publish now?—A. Yes, we publish a report. The last one contains what are termed the constitutional papers of Canada. It is a very large volume, taking in about fifty years after the Cession It is proposed from time to time to publish historical papers of interest.

Q. What is Mr. Doughty paid now?—A. $3,000.

Q. He is only attached to the department in this sense, that he has the same minister as yourself?—A. I understand that he is attached to the department the same as any other officer.

Q. He is paid from an outside vote?—A. Yes, the Archives vote.

Q. Coming to another large branch of your department, the Census and Statistics branch, the office of the director of census and statistics is in one of the Woods buildings?—A. Yes, in what is called the Canadian building.

Q. He has a large staff?—A. Yes, some 29 at present.

Q. What salary is paid to the director of census and statistics?—A. $4,000.

Q. He publishes a statistical year book?—A. Yes.

Q. He is engaged from time to time in the collection of special statistics?—A. Yes, and the collection of such statistics as the Minister may direct him to obtain.

Q. You have just published, for instance, a collection of statistics relating to the manufactures of Canada?—A. Yes. Those statistics were obtained with reference to the year 1905. He is now gathering statistics for an agricultural census of the Dominion.

Q. When the work of the compilation of the general consus of the Dominion is about accomplished, the operation of this branch of your department is then turned to other statistics?—A. Yes.

Q. There are more clerks employed in this branch when the work of the census is under way?—A. When a decennial census is being compiled we may have as many as 150 or 200.

By Mr. Fyshe:

Q. Do you discharge all these people after their work is done?—A. Yes.

Q. Have you charge of the census?—A. I have.

SESSIONAL PAPER No. 29a

By the Chairman:

Q. Although it is under the department, there is a special director to look after it!—A. The same as for every other branch of the department.

Q. In your department there are several highly paid officers, paid at the rate of $4,000 a year?—A. Yes.

Q. Mr. Blue is paid $4,000?—A. Yes.

Q. Dr. Montizambert is paid $4,000?—A. Yes, and Dr. Saunders, the director of the experimental farm, is paid $4,000 and the equivalent of $1,000 more—a free house, light and fuel, and a horse and carriage.

By Mr. Fyshe:

Q. Don't you find, in connection with the census, that your work practically extends over the whole ten years?—A. Yes. That work is performed by what we may call our permanent staff—the 29.

Q. I should think it would take five years to complete a census?—A. Yes, pretty nearly.

By the Chairman:

Q. The extra 120 are gradually dropped?—A. Yes.

Q. And they are gradually taken on?—A. They are taken on long in advance of the actual taking of the new census, for preparatory work.

Q. Then, in the Agriculture and Dairy Commissioner's branch you have a large list of clerks?—A. I might explain that that has been divided. When Dr. Robertson was Commissioner of Agriculture and Dairying, the dairying and the seed work and the live stock work were all under the one commissioner. When he retired from the service, his branch was subdivided into three branches—dairying, including fruit and cold storage, seed, and live stock. There is now a commissioner for each one of these branches.

By Mr. Fyshe:

Q. What salary did Dr. Robertson get?—A. $5,000.

By the Chairman:

Q. What salary does Mr. Ruddick get?—A. $3,500.

Q. What does Dr. Rutherford get?—A. $4,000. He occupies the dual position of veterinary director general and live stock commissioner.

Q. Who looks after the seed business?—A. Mr. G. H. Clarke.

Q. What is he paid?—A. $2,600.

Q. Dr. Robertson had all these in his hands, and he broke down from nervous exhaustion, and had to be sent away to where he could not see a paper or a book?—A. Yes, he got an extended leave of absence before he retired. But I must add that Dr. Robertson's retirement did not increase the expense of carrying on the work which was under him. On the contrary, there was a reduction. All these men were working under Dr. Robertson. Mr. Ruddick, who is now dairy commissioner, had charge of the dairy work under Dr. Robertson, and Mr. Clarke, who is seed commissioner, had charge of that work, under him.

By Mr. Fyshe:

Q. The work was specialized and put under practically the same men that it was under before?—A. Yes. Dr. Robertson had charge of these three branches. Now there is no one between the heads of these three branches and the Deputy Minister.

By the Chairman:

Q. And the work under Dr. Robertson got to be so important that it was thought better for these three heads to communicate with the Deputy Minister direct?—A. It was considered advisable.

Q. Dr. Robertson in his zeal for the public service broke down completely?—A. Yes.

Q. He went somewhere where he could see no one or get a book or a paper?—A. Yes. Dr. Robertson was one of the greatest workers I ever saw. He was a most indefatigable worker.

Q. What do you call the cow census?—A. That is a method that has been devised for selecting the profitable animals of a herd and rejecting the unprofitable animals. A man is sent out from the department to visit a certain number of farms in a district. He goes periodically to the farms and takes a sample of milk from each cow. By testing these samples he is able to determine the quality of the milk. After a certain period he makes a report to the farmer, showing which of his animals are profitable, which he should keep, and which are unprofitable and should be got rid of.

Q. Are there any fees attached to the work?—A. The work of cow-testing is done without any expense to the farmer, except that he may be required to purchase a few bottles and a small set of scales, at a very trifling expense.

By Mr. Fyshe:

Q. Do the farmers try to co-operate with these men?—A. They are very anxious to have the work done. They found that it was a great advantage to them, and we continually are having applications for it. It is necessary to a certain number of farmers to unite themselves into an association to get a man sent out.

Q. After a little experience, I suppose, the farmers find it advisable to keep up these operations?—A. Yes, that is what we try to show them.

By the Chairman:

Q. In the year 1906 there was a revenue derived from the inspection of cattle of $11,000?—A. That is the quarantine inspection.

By Mr. Fyshe:

Q. There is an improvement in cattle in Canada from the importation of thoroughbred bulls?—A. Yes.

Q. There is also a large importation of Clydesdale horses, is there not?—A. Yes, that is getting on.

Q. And Shorthorn bulls?—A. Shorthorns are the principal breed imported.

Q. The Polled Angus is not very numerous, is it?—A. It is quite numerous in the west.

Q. It does not seem to be as popular as the Shorthorn?—A. No, the Shorthorn is the popular breed of the country.

By the Chairman:

Q. Dr. Rutherford has in his head office a staff of 17 including himself?—A. That is in his office as Veterinary Director General.

Q. He has an assistant and four travelling inspectors together with about 80 correspondents?—A. Those are resident inspectors.

Q. Does he have daily returns from these people?—A. Not daily.

Q. Constant returns?—A. Constant returns. Every outbreak of disease and every inspection by his inspectors must be at once reported to him.

Q. The greatest possible care is taken with the health of the animals?—A. I think Dr. Rutherford deserves very great credit for the work he has done. It would be almost impossible to improve on the present state of his work.

Q. Who looks after the creameries and the cheese curing?—A. Mr. Ruddick.

Q. Dr. Rutherford simply looks after the health of animals?—A. Yes, and acts as live stock commissioner. The cow testing is carried on for the purpose of determining the value of the cattle for dairy purposes and for that reason it comes under Mr. Ruddick as dairy commissioner.

SESSIONAL PAPER No. 29a

Q. Under the supervision of Dr. Rutherford is there a live stock record kept, showing the pedigrees of animals?—A. That is under the control of the live stock commissioner. We have now what is termed a system of national records kept here. Every association has its secretary and registrar here in Ottawa, and all the animals are registered here. The certificate of registration, if it meets with the approval of the representative of the Minister, is stamped with the departmental seal.

By Mr. Fyshe:

Q. Does that include native born cattle as well as imported?—A. Yes.

Q. You have a registrar for each breed?—A. Yes.

Q. Both cattle and horses?—A. Yes. I think there is one registrar for all breeds of sheep. Any registrar may act for two associations.

Q. But the registers are kept separate?—A. Kept separate.

By the Chairman:

Q. Does the same apply to pigs?—A. Yes.

Q. Under whose division does the poultry work come?—A. All the poultry work is carried on at the experimental farm, in charge of Mr. Gilbert. In Dr. Robertson's time some of the poultry work which was more of a commercial character, was carried on under him; but that is all abandoned, and the whole work is now carried on at the experimental farm.

Q. What are the duties of the seed commissioner?—A. His duties consist largely in enforcing the Seed Control Act, which was passed for the purpose of securing better seed.

By Mr. Fyshe:

Q. Do you follow the American system of distributing free seed?—A. That is done from the experimental farm.

Q. In the United States that is rather farcical, and some agitation has been got up to stop it?—A. I think our system is different. We send out only a few sample pounds of seed, more for the purpose of finding out what varieties are suitable.

Q. I suppose the experimental farm people are careful to send them to men who can handle them properly, and give a good account of the experiment?—A. I think a report is required and a sample of the seed harvested must be returned to the farm. If the report and sample are not received at the farm, I think no second sample will be sent to the farmer.

By the Chairman:

Q. You have a fruit branch?—A. That comes under the dairy commissioner He deals largely with the transportation of fruit and the enforcement of the Fruit Marks Act, which requires fruit to be properly graded. Of course, at the experimental farm, the experimental work with regard to fruit is carried on. The dairy commissioner deals with fruit rather in a commercial way than in the way of culture.

Q. I suppose the same remark will apply to tobacco?—A. Tobacco is in charge of an officer who is not in charge of any branch. He reports direct to me.

Q. I see by the Auditor General's Report, at page D—53 that the dairy commissioner, in order to develop the dairying business in Canada, advanced $218,279, of which he got back in revenue $216,848.65, showing a debit balance of $1,430?—A. That work has been entirely discontinued. That was in the Northwest Territories. When the new provinces were established and organized, the Provincial Governments relieved us of that work.

Q. When the cold storage business comes into operation under the Act of last year, under whose control will that be?—A. Mr. Ruddick's. His title is dairy and cold storage commissioner. I may say that that Act is in force at present.

Q. Since April 1?—A. It was assented to at the date of prorogation. The regulations under the Act have just been passed and the forms furnished.

7-8 EDWARD VII., A. 1908

Q. The director of the experimental farm at Ottawa, you say, gets $4,000 a year？—A. Yes.

Q. And also a house？—A. Yes.

Q. That house and his other privileges are equivalent to $1,000 a year？—A. The house if in the city could easily rent for $1,000 a year. In addition to the house, he gets his fuel and light and a horse and carriage.

By Mr. Fyshe:

Q. What previous experience had Dr. Saunders？—A. He is a chemist by calling or occupation.

By the Chairman:

Q. The purpose of the experimental farm is to diffuse throughout Canada a knowledge of high-class farming？—A. Yes. Experimental work in all the branches of agriculture is carried on at the farm and the results are published in the annual report and in the bulletins published from time to time and distributed free amongst the farmers of the country.

By Mr. Fyshe:

Q. I presume that it is more to obtain fresh knowledge in regard to seeds and agriculture generally rather than to be a model to show the farmers？—A. Entirely. The work is purely experimental. It is not conducted in any hope of a return.

By the Chairman:

Q. Besides the director of the farm, there is a chemist and an assistant chemist？— A. Yes. The chemist is Mr. Shutt. There is also an entomologist and botanist, Dr. Fletcher; an agriculturist, Mr. Grisdale; a horticulturist, Mr. Macoun; and a cerealist, Dr. Charles E. Saunders.

Q. And an assistant to each？—A. Yes. The chemist has two assistants.

By Mr. Fyshe:

Q. Do they all live at the farm？—A. Yes, all the principal officers are provided with residences on the farm.

Q. Are they generally married men？—A. I think they are all married with the exception of two or three of the assistants.

By the Chairman:

Q. There are about 28 of these salaried officials. There is a manager of the poultry department？—A. Yes, Mr. Gilbert. He has an assistant, Mr. Fortier.

Q. Under the director there is a series of specialists？—A. Yes.

Q. Each looking after a particular division there？—A. Yes.

Q. And in addition there are farm labourers？—A. Yes.

Q. Do any of these farm labourers live on the farm？—A. A few—very few.

Q. How are the labourers appointed？—A. Their appointment is largely left to the director. Most of them might be called permanent. They have been working there for years.

Q. Is there any feeling on the part of the labourers, as there is in other parts of the public service, as to the emoluments paid to them？—A. The question of salaries was adjusted by the Minister a short time ago, I think to the satisfaction of the labourers.

Q. They are paid by the week？—A. Yes.

Q. Do you happen to know if there is an undue amount of labour employed there？ —A. I am sure there is not.

Q. How are these labourers appointed—are they put in originally by politics？— A. As a rule their selection is left entirely to the director.

SESSIONAL PAPER No. 29a

Q. The expenditure of the farm, at page D—21 of the Auditor General's Report, is divided carefully into several heads, such as salaries, farm work, care of stock, &c., &c. There is a certain revenue derived from the farm?—A. The products of the farm are sold to the best advantage, but it was never hoped that there could be a revenue derived from the farm. For instance, a wheat field will be divided into plots of half an acre, and the crop of each half acre would have to be harvested with the greatest care to avoid its getting mixed with the product of the adjoining plot.

Q. Do any of the officers of the farm, in addition to their residence, get any of the products of the farm?—A. They have only what they pay for. They are treated the same as the public. The officers and employees of the farm consume the products of the farm to a great extent, but they pay for them just the same as any outsider.

Q. In addition to the Central Experimental Farm you have other experimental farms—at Agassiz, Brandon, Indian Head and Nappan?—A. Yes, and we have recently established one at Lethbridge and another at Lacombe, in Alberta.

Q. In the province to the westward, and at Nappan, in Nova Scotia, you have farms?—A. Yes. We intend to establish another one in northern Saskatchewan, and I think one on Vancouver island.

By Mr. Fyshe:

Q. Is there much good agricultural land on the island of Vancouver?—A. Dr. Saunders tells me that there is a great deal of rock, but that there are also many fertile districts there.

By the Chairman:

Q. In addition to developing and promoting the interests of the Dominion by means of experimental farms and in other ways, you have a staff engaged in showing the resources of Canada at the various exhibitions held in different parts of the world?—A. Yes, by our exhibition branch.

Q. You had exhibits at St. Louis, Pittsburg, London, Liège, Milan and New Zealand?—A. Yes.

Q. There is a chief officer employed?—A. Yes, styled commissioner of exhibitions.

Q. That is Mr. Hutchison?—A. Yes.

Q. When there are several exhibitions going at the same time, how do you manage—there is one in Dublin at present, is there not?—A. Mr. Hutchison has joint secretaries, Mr. Burns and Mr. Brodie. Mr. Brodie has been in Europe with Mr. Hutchison for the last two years. When the New Zealand exhibition came on, Mr. Burns was appointed a joint commissioner with T. H. Race, and they looked after that.

Q. Mr. Hutchison might have a general supervision over both Dublin and Milan?—A. They were not going on at the same time. Dublin is going on now.

Q. Is there any exhibition besides Dublin going on at the present moment?—A. No.

Q. Mr. Hutchison is in Dublin?—A. He is in Dublin at present.

Q. What happens when all the exhibitions are over?—A. They are never over. As soon as one closes we are preparing for another. At the present time we are preparing for the great Franco-British exhibition to be held in London next year to celebrate the *entente cordiale*, in which we hope to participate. So the exhibition work is continuous.

Q. Then, at the Imperial Institute in London, you have a part of the building?—A. Yes, we have a permanent exhibit there.

Q. In which the products of Canada are shown to the public?—A. Yes. That is under the High Commissioner.

Q. But Mr. Hutchison also goes there?—A. Mr. Hutchison has recently rearranged the exhibit and installed new exhibits. There is a Canadian curator, Mr.

Harrison Watson, who reports to the High Commissioner; but Mr. Hutchison, on account of his experience in exhibition work, was charged by the Minister with the rearrangement of the exhibits and the installation of new exhibits.

Q. Dr. Montizambert is head of the Quarantine branch?—A. Yes.

Q. He has by statute the rank of a deputy head?—A. Yes.

Q. The quarantine is a branch of your department?—A. There is no distinction between Dr. Montizambert's branch and any other branch of the department.

Q. Still, an Act of Parliament gives him that rank?—A. He has the rank of a deputy minister, but the Act expressly provides that he has no powers whatever with regard to the administration of the department. His administrative powers are not greater than those of any other officer in charge of a branch, and I would respectfully suggest to the Commission that if Dr. Montizambert is to be called to give evidence the same privilege should be accorded to other chiefs of branches who hold positions of equal responsibility in the department.

Q. The Quarantine branch is charged to look after the health of the people coming into the Dominion?—A. Yes.

Q. And for that reason it has physicians at the ports of entry?—A. Yes.

Q. Do they also look after the public health generally?—A. No. The public health generally is looked after by the several provinces.

Q. I see there is some distribution of vaccine?—A. Yes. The department has occasionally taken charge of an outbreak of small-pox in the Northwest Territories; I think that was before the provinces were organized; but that is the only work of an internal character I have known the department to do. I may add that Dr. Montizambert has also the administration of what is called the Public Works Health Act, that is, the supervision of health on public works, such as the construction of railways and canals.

Q. He has also under his supervision the Tracadie Lazeretto?—A. Yes, and one on Vancouver island, at D'Arcy island.

Q. With the great influx of immigration which is pouring in daily at Quebec, that branch of your department must be extending?—A. Naturally.

Q. Have you physicians enough at Quebec to pass the immigrants as they come along?—A. I am not aware of any request for an increase to the staff. I presume it is adequate.

Q. You have port physicians at Quebec and several other ports?—A. At the quarantine station at Grosse Isle, just below Quebec.

Q. You have port physicians at St. John, Halifax and Charlottetown?—A. Yes, at all the principal ports.

Q. A ship coming up the St. Lawrence would be quarantined at Grosse Isle?—A. She would be inspected and quarantined if any quarantinable disease were found on board.

Q. After she leaves Grosse Isle, on her arrival at Quebec, another physician takes charge and goes through her?—A. Yes.

Q. That physician is not under your department?—A. No. He is under the Immigration Branch of the Department of the Interior.

Q. As the quarantine service is in your department and you are looking after the Public Health Act, and as this is an extra examination of the people coming into the Dominion, would it not be advisable that it should all be under one department?—A. I should certainly say so.

Q. As it is now, there is a divided duty, one part of the work being under the Department of the Interior and another part under your Department?—A. Yes.

Q Now, we will come to the issue of patents, which is exclusively under your department. You are Commissioner of Patents?—A. I am Deputy Commissioner of Patents.

Q. Who is the Commissioner of Patents?—A. The Minister.

Q. Is Mr. Bailey still in your department?—A. Yes, he is a patent examiner.

Q. Mr. Bailey was a witness before the Civil Service Commission in 1892, and he stated then that under the system then in force, before a patent was issued it underwent twenty-five processes. Does a patent going through the department now, from the date of the application to the time it is finished, go through all that number of hands? —A. The application is received by the correspondence clerk. A back is put on the application and it is properly endorsed, and a record is made of it in an entry book. Then the papers are sent to what is called the comparing room.

Q. What is that?—A. All applications have to be in duplicate; all drawings have to be in duplicate. In that room the duplicates are compared to see that they are correct and true duplicates. In that room the application is examined as to its compliance in a general way with the forms and rules of the patent office. There may be an apparent irregularity in the application which may be detected in that room, and it may get no further, but be sent back to the applicant. If the application be found in order, it is sent for classification to a clerk and sent by him to the examiner charged with the examination of the class of patents to which it belongs. If the examiner finds that the application should be granted, he so notes it, and it is then sent to the chief of the engrossing division, where it is engrossed and initialled by the chief of that division and sent to me for signature, and then sent out.

Q. At what stage is a comparison made to see that it infringes on no other patent?—A. That is the work of the patent examiner. That is what his examination is principally for.

Q. The cashier has also to take the fees?—A. The correspondence clerk who finds the remittance with the application, makes out a slip giving the number of the application. This is sent to the accountant, who issues a receipt in duplicate, one receipt being attached to the application and the other is sent to the applicant.

Q. I see that the patent fees in the last year amounted to about $160,000?—A. I asked the accountant to prepare a statement this morning which I thought might be of interest.

Q. According to the statement the fees in 1901-2 amounted to $126,000 and in 1906-7 they had increased to $177,000, an increase in the five years of $50,000. That, I suppose, is to a certain extent another evidence of the progress and development of the Dominion?—A. I think it is the best evidence of the increased industrial activity of the country.

Q. When the last Civil Service Commission sat, it was discovered that there was a caveat clerk, a first-class clerk. Is there still such an official?—A. No. The caveats are prepared by a clerk who is employed generally in connection with the correspondence of the chief clerk of the office. The caveats come to me daily for signature.

Q. There is no officer now employed exclusively on caveats?—A. No.

Q. Are there many caveats now?—A. Hardly a day passes that I do not sign some. There must be some hundreds every year. The exact number is given in our annual report.

Q. Then, since that time the work has been considerably shortened?—A. Yes. Many of the operations stated in the evidence of Mr. Bailey in 1892 should not have been mentioned. Some of them mean simply the passing of the papers from one clerk to another.

Q. The patent business has now come down within proper limit, and there is not an undue number of officials engaged in getting a patent through?—A. No. At intervals since I entered the office, I have required the staff to work over hours in order to keep the work of the patent office up in connection with the examination of applications. That work was very much in arrears when I came into the department.

By Mr. Fyshe:

Q. Of course, that would be strongly objected to by the applicants?—A. Naturally, but by making efforts I have got the work now in fairly satisfactory condition. We receive very few complaints from applicants of delay in the office in getting their applications through.

By the Chairman:

Q. How long does it take as a rule, from the receipt of the application before the patent issues?—A. The average time is about three months. The patent office at Washington is supposed to be the model patent office of the world, and that is the ideal they aim at—to keep their work within three months.

Q. Your staff is not greater than the work requires?—A. No. It is not so great as the staff at Washington in comparison with the work.

Q. You have also jurisdiction over copyrights?—A. Yes. Before we leave the patent office, I would like to make a statement personal to myself, if I may be allowed to do so. Before I entered office there was no one connected with the patent office or the department who had any legal experience. I think that as a consequence the work of the patent office went on in rather a perfunctory way. An attorney having an application rejected by the patent examiner, and knowing that there was no one connected with the department with any legal training or experience, would let it go, and it was rather unsatisfactory to go to the department, as there was no one there who was able to deal with the matter from a legal point of view. As soon as my appointment was known, it was found that the number of attorneys or legal agents coming into the department was greatly increased.

By Mr. Fyshe:

Q. Was that an advantage?—A. I do not know about that, but I know that it increased my work over that of any of my predecessors. Then, shortly after I entered office, in consequence of a judgment of the Supreme Court the whole practice of the office was changed.

By the Chairman:

Q. What was that case?—A. The case of Power *vs.* Griffin.

By Mr. Fyshe:

Q. The judgment was against the office?—A. It was against the practice of the office. Under the Patent Act the patentee is bound to manufacture his invention within two years after the date of the patent. The commissioner is empowered to extend that term. Before the case of Power *vs.* Griffin came up, these extensions were granted indiscriminately without any reason being shown, and during the whole term of the patent one after the other; so that the obligation to manufacture was an absolute nullity. These extensions were granted only for two years, but before the expiration of the two years the patentee would come for a further extension. It was held in the case of Power *vs.* Griffin that that practice was contrary to the law, that the Commissioner could grant only one extension and that for a period not exceeding two years. This brought up the whole matter of the practice of the patent office, and I received my instructions to conform strictly to the law as interpreted by the Supreme Court in that case, and to grant one extension only when it was proven to me that it was an absolute impossibility for the patentee to manufacture within the two years. So that in consequence of this change, each of these applications, which were very numerous and which up to that time had been dealt with in a perfunctory way without any examination at all, had to be dealt with by me judicially, like a case in court. That increased my work and responsibility enormously. Very often these applications were contentious, and both parties would be represented by counsel. The same thing applies to importation. Under the Patent Act the patentee has one year during which he can import the invention after the patent is granted. The Commissioner is empowered to grant one extension of that term; so that my remarks in regard to manufacture apply also to importation. Then shortly afterwards our Patent Act was amended, introducing the British license system.

SESSIONAL PAPER No. 29a

By Mr. Fyshe:

Q. What is that system?—A. The system is this. The patentee is not bound to manufacture his invention, but if any person desires to use his patent and the patentee refuses to give him a license, this person may apply to the patent office, and the patent office may order the license on such terms as it sees fit. If the patentee does not comply with the order, the patent office may cancel the patent. The British system was not introduced absolutely. We left the old law in regard to manufacture as it was, to apply to patents generally; but the patentee was given the option of having his patent brought under the British system if the office considered that the invention was such that it would be unreasonable to compel him to manufacture it. For instance, if a patent were granted for a graving dock it would be absurd to compel the patentee to manufacture his graving dock in the absence of any demand. The Act provided that in a case like that the patentee within six months of the date of this patent might come to the office and say, I do not wish my patent to be governed by the general law in regard to manufacturing. Place me under the British license system. All that increased my duties. The applications came in by the hundreds immediately after the change, as the law was made retroactive and applied to existing patents, until I had over 4,000 applications from patentees to have their patents placed under the licensing system. Every one of these had to be dealt with by myself. I did it only by working from nine o'clock in the morning until half-past six, and going back after my dinner and working till half-past ten. However, it was done, and now I have only a few of these to deal with every day. The work has been caught up, but all that has greatly increased the work of the office, and it gave me a great deal more to do than any holder of the office ever had before.

By the Chairman:

Q. In addition to having a greater number of applications for patents?—A. Yes. I would simply wish to add this that it has been recognized that the professional work done by a deputy minister should receive an additional remuneration. In addition to my work as Deputy Commissioner of Patents, I think I have as much to do as the average deputy minister. I think the duties outside of the patent office are as onerous as those of the average deputy minister.

By Mr. Fyshe:

Q. I suppose the work of all the departments tends to increase with the growth of the country?—A. Naturally. As I was saying, as parliament has established the precedent that professional work should receive extra remuneration, I think I am fairly entitled to ask for something more than the ordinary deputy minister. The Deputy Minister of Railways and the Deputy Minister of Justice have been paid more than the ordinary deputy minister on the ground that they have been doing professional work. From what I have said, I think you will see that there is not only professional work, but professional work of a very high character, to be done in connection with the patent office.

Q. I suppose you have not been long enough at it to draw any inference as to whether your decisions have been appealed against or carried into the courts. I suppose you have had to decide a good many things on your own judgment?—A. Certainly.

By the Chairman:

Q. Your decisions have been governed a good deal by the decision of the Supreme Court in that case?—A. The court deals with the question whether the patent was properly granted or not—whether the examiner made a proper examination.

By Mr. Fyshe:

Q. You sometimes refuse a patent, do you not?—A. Yes.

29a—5

7-8 EDWARD VII., A. 1908

Q. Are not these refusals sometimes appealed against?—A. There is no appeal to the courts against that refusal; there is an appeal to the Governor in Council. That is very rarely taken. There is no appeal from my decision granting or refusing an extension; it is absolute as to that.

Q. How long is the life of a patent?—A. Eighteen years.

By the Chairman:

Q. As to reissues?—A. It frequently occurs during the progress of a trial that the patentee finds that his patent has been improperly issued, that it is too broad, claiming more than he is entitled to. Then he surrenders his patent and applies for a reissue. That is generally a contentious proceeding before me, and in these applications I have had sometimes had my office nearly filled with the leading counsel of Canada and the United States arguing different sides.

By Mr. Fyshe:

Q. And you have to sit and hear them alone?—A. Absolutely alone. What I have said in regard to patents will not apply to the same extent to trade marks.

By the Chairman:

Q. You said just now that it takes about three months from the time the application is received until the patent is issued?—A. Yes.

Q. And the duration of the patent, you say, is eighteen years?—A. Yes.

Q. Occasionally applicants, having received a patent and having allowed the two years to expire without manufacturing, go to parliament to try to get a special Act?—A. Yes. I should say that on the average there are about ten Bills of that character each session.

Q. What is the fee for a patent?—A. $60 for the full term, but the patentee has the option of paying it in instalments of $20.

Q. There are about 3,000 patents issued a year?—A. There are about 6,000. The patentee has the option of paying only one-third of the fee when he gets his patent, that is, $20 for the first six years, another $20 for six years more, and another $20 for six years more. With regard to these special Bills, I may say that it is the practice of the committees of both Houses to call me before them whenever a Patent Bill is up for consideration.

By Mr. Fyshe:

Q. Is the number of patents applied for increasing?—A. Yes, to a great extent.

Q. Rapidly?—A. Yes, rapidly.

By the Chairman:

Q. In consequence of that decision of the Supreme Court, the work of the patent office is becoming more systematized?—A. Yes.

Q. Who is the particular officer in your department who looks after trade marks?—A. Mr. P. E. Ritchie. He is styled the registrar of trade marks and copyrights.

Q. He has both trade marks and copyrights?—A. Yes, and timber marks and industrial designs.

Q. Any other marks?—A. No.

Q. Do canned goods, such as Crosse and Blackwells, have their trade marks registered—A. Their whole labels are registered as trade marks.

Q. Do trade marks on canned fruits and vegetables all have to be registered?—A. Yes.

Q. Is that compulsory?—A. No, they are registered for their own protection.

Q. What is the process? An applicant makes an application to be allowed to use a trade mark—that goes first to the correspondence clerk I suppose?—A. It would go

SESSIONAL PAPER No. 29a

direct to the registrar of trade marks, who deals with all the correspondence himself in the first instance.

Q. What is your position with respect to trade marks?—A. The office of registrar is created only by order in council. There is no deputy registrar. I sign all the certificates of registration of trade marks, copyrights and industrial designs as Deputy Minister of Agriculture.

Q. In 1892, at the inquiry by the last Civil Service Commission, the then registrar of trade marks was examined, and it was found that his wife received money from the public service under the guise of compiling an index. Nothing of that kind occurs now?—A. Nothing at all. No clerk is paid for anything beyond his salary.

Q. Copyright applies to books and music published in the Dominion?—A. Yes.

Q. Do you get a copy of every book published in the Dominion?—A. Every book of which we grant copyright—we get three copies.

Q. Does the same thing apply to music?—A. Yes.

Q. Do any copies go to the Parliamentary Library?—A. One goes to the Parliamentary Library, one to the British Museum and one is kept on record in the department.

Q. That follows pretty much the rule as to copyright in existence in England?—A. Yes, I think so.

Q. How long does a copyright last?—A. Twenty-eight years.

Q. There was some years ago a question of international copyright—is that one of the vexed questions still open?—A. Yes.

Q. At the time of the last Commission it was found that another clerk in the department, since dead, received in the maiden name of his wife, regular remuneration with the sanction of the then deputy. Is any subterfuge of that kind in existence now?—A. Not at all. Everybody in the department renders service for any money he gets.

Q. Then, in the whole range of the department, with all its diversified branches, you do not consider that it is overmanned?—A. No.

Q. You have no redundant staff?—A. No.

Q. The officers as a rule are capable?—A. Yes, very.

Q. You think the present method of appointment under the Civil Service Act and with a Qualifying examination is sufficient?—A. Yes.

Q. You would not prefer competitive examinations?—A. From my experience I would much prefer the present system as opposed to a competitive system.

Q. Would you consider it desirable to extend the jurisdiction of the present Civil Service Examining Board to have them select the candidates for the departments and do away with political patronage?—A. If it were practicable it would be preferable.

Q. What do you think, generally speaking, of the gradations of the clerks into the different classes—first class, second class, third class and so on?—A. I do not see that the classification amounts to a great deal. For instance, we have a third-class clerk, say at $650. I think he is entitled to $100 more, and I recommend the Minister to grant him this increase. To get it he has to be promoted to the junior second class.

Q. Do we understand that you are not altogether in accord with the statutory increase of $50 only, but you think it would be advisable to have some power to give a greater increment?—A. The Minister has that power to a certain extent.

Q. As the law stands a junior second-class clerk can only get an increase of $50 a year?—A. Yes.

Q. Suppose a man were more capable than his fellow, and you thought it advisable to give him an increase of $100 a year?—A. It would be very desirable for the Minister to have that power, to give more than mere statutory increase.

Q. In order to avoid the necessity of giving $50 a year increase, promotions take place?—A. I have no doubt of it.

29a—5½

Q. Consequently there are men in the higher classes who do precisely the same kind of work that they did in the lower classes?—A. You might find that a clerk was doing his work in such a way that he was earning more than he was getting. Without actually changing his duties you might wish to put him into a higher class on account of the efficient way in which he was performing his duties.

Q. For instance, a typist might in a length of time go from the bottom of the third-class to become a first-class clerk?—A. I do not think it would be possible. In our own department the statutory increases go on one might say automatically. I do not know any case since I have been in office where the increase has been withheld; but when the maximum of a class is reached, the clerk would not go any further unless he showed special qualifications. The permanent list of our department will show that. At the top of the junior second class there are a large number of clerks who have been there for some time. I have never felt that I should recommend their promotion to the Minister. I consider that they are amply paid for the work they are doing and should stay where they are.

Q. But is there not constant pressure from friends to promote them?—A. Certainly.

Q. And that you have to struggle against?—A. Certainly.

Q. And very often a promotion takes place although the man promoted does the same work?—A. I would not say very often, but it does happen. Five or six of our patent examiners were senior second-class clerks at a maximum of $1,500. As these men were worth more and could get more, I recommended to the Minister that they should be made first-class clerks, and he acted on my recommendation; but they are doing precisely the same work that they did when they were senior second-class clerks.

Q. You have men at the top of the junior second-class who you think are sufficiently paid?—A. Yes.

Q. Very often pressure is brought on the department to promote these men, and occasionally the pressure is so great that a man does get promoted?—A. I do not know of any instance since I have been in office in which promotion has been due to pressure. Promotion is made on the ground of merit.

Q. If anything further occurs to you, we would be glad to have you send in a supplementary memorandum?—A. Thank you. I understood that you wished me to furnish a list of the clerks of each branch. The registrar of trade marks and copywrights has prepared a short brief, which he asked me to submit to the Commission. I have read it carefully, and I endorse everything Mr. Ritchie says in it. (Paper read and filed.) Mr. Ritchie is a very able man and a very industrious and satisfactory officer.

By Mr. Bazin:

Q. He was appointed four years ago?—A. Yes. He was appointed as an assistant to Mr. Jackson, and it was very fortunate that he was able to take the place when Mr. Jackson died. There is one other thing I should say. We cannot employ a clerk at a lower salary than $500 a year. A girl just fresh from school comes to us and starts at $500 a year for four or five hours work. If she went to an ordinary business office, she would not get more than half that.

By Mr. Fyshe:

Q. Would you suggest a change in that respect? Would you suggest that the entrance salaries for women should be reduced?—A. I think the Minister should have some discretion. Of course, a great many women who come in are entitled to $500. They may have had some experience in office work; but a girl fresh from school who is not a typewriter or stenographer and has no special qualification is different.

By the Chairman:

Q. All these appointments are political and are made from all over the Dominion?—A. Applications are sent in from all over the Dominion, usually supported by the member for the county in which the applicant resides.

Q. And under our system of government the Minister coming from a district has to look to some extent into the appointment of applicants residing in that district?— A. Certainly.

Q. Do you ever take holidays for yourself?—A. I have taken an occasional day, but in my whole five years in office I do not think I have taken three weeks.

Q. Do you think that is right?—A. No. I think it is a great mistake. I think I would do better work if I had a full month of holidays at least every year.

By Mr. Basin:

Q. Why do you not take it?—A. I have been pretty busy since I came into office, and there is a great deal of work there that I have to do myself. If I go away for a holiday the work accumulates, and when I come back I have to attend to it.

The Commission took recess till 2.30 p.m.

DEPARTMENT OF AGRICULTURE,
OTTAWA, June 6, 1907.

MEMO. FOR MR. O'HALLORAN.

I beg to submit the following comparative statement on patent fees and trade marks for the fiscal years 1901-2 and 1906-7:—

Patent fees, 1901-2...................... $126,894 68
"   1906-7...................... 177,881 19
Trade marks, 1901-2...................... 18,088 32
"   1906-7...................... 31,700 90

In five years the patent fees show an increase of $50,986.51, and in the trade marks, $13,612.58.

MEMORANDUM on the Status and duties of the Registrar of Copyrights, Trade Marks, Industrial Designs, and Timber Marks.

The functions of the Registrar involve the administration of three separate Acts,—

(1) The Copyright Act,
(2) The Trade Mark and Design Act,
(3) The Timber Marking Act.

His duties are not only those of a chief clerk, or clerical duties of the highest class, but are to a very large extent, professional and technical; the position of the Registrar in determining what is registerable and in adjudicating upon conflicting claims having been declared by the courts to be of a judicial nature.

For the proper conduct of the business of the branch, the Registrar must have a thorough knowledge of Copyright and Trade Mark law,—two branches which in other countries are separately administered—necessitating the constant study, not only of the leading text books, but also of the current reports of decisions of the courts on these branches of law in Canada, England and the United States.

In order to avoid conflicting registrations, most careful searches of the indexes and registers have to be made, and as, the total number or registrations is steadily increasing, the work of searching grows daily, more arduous and difficult.

That the rights of registrants may be safeguarded and unnecessary litigation avoided, official documents and certificates require to be drawn with absolute clearness and accuracy.

A large portion of the correspondence of the branch, conducted as occasion requires, both in English and in French, is carried on with members of the legal profession, and being frequently of a controversial character, is of a very exacting nature, frequently involving special study and research, which necessitate the attendance of the Registrar at the office at night, in order that the routine business of the branch may not be delayed and congested to the detriment of the public.

The Registrar must also hold himself in readiness to give evidence in copyright and trade mark cases when required to do so by any party to a suit or action.

The responsibility of the Registrar is rendered more onerous owing, first to the complexity of copyright law and secondly to the enormous pecuniary interests involved in Trade Mark rights. The latter may be aptly exemplified by citations from the evidence taken before the Select Committee on Trade Marks Bill. Mr. William Hodge Coats, representing J. and P. Coats, Limited, states that the profits of that Company for over two years have been two and a half million sterling—that the value of a trade mark was what their Board attached the greatest importance to.

Mr. J. E. Trustram, a member of the trade marks' section of the London Chamber of Commerce and a practising solicitor, of some sixteen years' standing, said: 'A trade mark is perhaps the most important thing that there is commercially.'

The industrial activity of the country is reflected in the increased business of the branch comparing the twelve months ended March 31, 1907, with the last complete year ended October 31, 1905, the foolowing increases are to be noter:—

Copyright registration from..	1,130 to	1,228
Trade Mark registration from..	661 to	1,119
Renewals from..	5 to	17
Assignments from..	154 to	282
Letters received from..	3,367 to	5,340
Letters sent from..	3,902 to	5,193
Fees received from..	$23,706.77 to	$33,107.13

DEPARTMENT OF AGRICULTURE,
OTTAWA, June 3, 1907.

THOS. S. HOWE, Esq.,
    Secretary, Civil Service Commission,
        Room 2, the Senate, Ottawa.

SIR,—Adverting to your letter of date May 18, asking for a memorandum showing the number of the staff of this department, permanent and extra, with amount of salaries paid during the years ended June 30, 1892, and June 30, 1906, together which memoranda showing special votes such as relate to census, experimental farms, &c., I now inclose you such memoranda, which I trust contain the information you desire.

Your obedient servant,

A. L. JARVIS,
Secretary.

PERMANENT STAFF, DEPARTMENT OF AGRICULTURE, JUNE 30, 1892.

		$ cts.
1 Deputy head........ .	1 at $3,200.00.........	3,200 00
4 Chief clerks..........	1 at $2,400.00—1 at $2,125.00—1 at $1,850.00—1 at $1,800.00.....	8,175 00
10 First-class clerks	3 at $1,800.00—1 at $1,550.00—2 at $1,500.00—4 at $1,400.00.....	15,550 00
7 Second-class clerks...	2 at $1,450.00—1 at $1,360.00—1 at $1,200.00—3 at $1,100·00....	8,650 00
22 Third-class clerks....	1 at $600.00—1 at $562.50—1 at $550.00—1 at $475.00—2 at $700.00	
	2 at $675.00—2 at $1,000.00—3 at $950.00—1 at $900.00—1 at $475.00	
	1 at $437.50—3 at $400.00—4 at $780.00	15,445 00
3 Messengers .	2 at $330.00—1 at $300.00....	960 00
2 Packers	2 at $500.00.........	1,000 00
1 Model repairer.	1 at $500.00..........	500 00
1 Guardian	1 at $500.00......	500 00
1 Deputy commissionner		
of patents.....	(Statutory)	2,800 00
1 Private secretary	1 at $600.00........	600 00
53		57,380 00

SESSIONAL PAPER No. 29a

PERMANENT STAFF, DEPARTMENT OF AGRICULTURE, JUNE 30, 1906.

		$ cts.
1 Deputy head..........	1 at $3,800.00	3,800 00
7 Chief clerks..........	1 at $2,500.00—1 at $2,412.50—1 at $2,300.00—1 at $2,200.00	
	1 at $2,000.00—2 at $1,900.00....................................	15,212 50
10 First-class clerks	4 at $1,900.00—1 at $1,750.00—1 at $1,650.00—4 at $1,500.00 ..	17,000 00
13 Second-class clerks....	1 at $1,500.00—1 at $1,450.00—4 at $1,400.00—1 at $1,350.00	
	1 at $1,300.00—5 at $1,200.00.......	17,200 00
24 Junior second-class clerks.................	10 at $1,100.00—2 at $1,050.00—1 at $1,000.00—1 at $950.00—	
	7 at $900.00—1 at $850.00—2 at $800.00......................	23,800 00
2 Third class clerks.....	1 at $680.00—1 at $600.00........................	1,280 00
1 Messenger............	1 at $400.00......	400 00
1 Private secretary.....	1 at $600.00...........................	600 00
59		79,292 50

DEPARTMENT OF AGRICULTURE.—TEMPORARY CLERKS PAID FROM CIVIL
GOVERNMENT CONTINGENCIES, JUNE 30, 1892.

		$ c.	$ c.
Extra Clerks..........	1 at	912 50	912 50
"	....	2 at	730 00	1,460 00
"	....	2 at	600 00	1,200 00
"	....	4 at	547 50	2,190 00
"	... .	3 at	456 25	1,368 75
"	....	3 at	400 00	1,200 00
"	....	1 at	365 00	365 00
Total..............	16		8,696 25

TEMPORARY CLERKS PAID FROM CIVIL GOVERNMENT CONTINGENCIES
JUNE 30, 1906.

		$ c.	$ c.	$ c.
Extra Clerks.....	1 at	912 50	912 50	
"	....	4 at	700 00	2,800 00	
"	....	1 at	680 00	680 00	
"	....	1 at	650 00	650 00	
"	....	1 at	620 00	620 00	
"	... .	5 at	600 00	3,000 00	
"	... ...	3 at	550 00	1,650 00	
"	....	4 at	500 00	2,000 00	
				12,312 50	
Messengers..........	1 at	650 00	650 00	
"	....	1 at	600 00	600 00	
"	....	1 at	550 00	550 00	
"	....	1 at	500 00	500 00	
		24		2,300 00	14,612 50

7-8 EDWARD VII., A. 190

DEPARTMENT OF AGRICULTURE :—ARTS, AGRICTLTURE AND STATISTICS.

—	June 30, 1892.	June 30, 1906.
	$ cts.	$ c.
Archives	5,875 40	21,985
Historical data re Acadian Families.	Nil.	1,300
Census and Statistics	269,939 40	6,542
General Statistics	Nil.	14,114
Quinquennial Census of Manitoba, Saskatchewan and Alberta	Nil.	4,462
Criminal Statistics	2,985 56	2,07
Statistical Year Book	Nil.	7,13
Patent Record	7,246 28	27,00
Exhibitions	11,199 98	149,07
Imperial Institute Exhibit	Nil.	20,51
New Westminster Exhibition	Nil.	50,00
Aid to Agricultural Societies	9,367 92	7,00
Experimental Farms	75,000 00	110,45
Compensation for injuries, H. Anderson, Indian Head	Nil.	20
Printing and distributing bulletins, &c., at Farms	Nil.	7,00
Fumigating Stations	Nil.	4,00
Development of the live stock, dairying and fruit industries, &c.	21,080 64	166,292
To promote dairying by advances for milk and cream	Nil.	1,430
Live Stock Records of the Dominion	Nil.	3,003
Health Statistics	4,971 14	Nil.
Adam Brown, honorarium	2,000 00	Nil.
Dominion Dairy at Sherbrooke	10,000 00	Nil.
Haras National Co., Montreal	6,000 00	Nil.
Registration, Quebec	837 00	Nil.
	426,503 32	603,590 34
Immigration	177,604 82	Nil.
Quarantine	53,388 02	624,758 33
MISCELLANEOUS.		
Gratuity of 2 months salary to widow of late J. B. Jackson	Nil.	416
Grant to Canadian Association for the Prevention of Tuberculosis	Nil.	2,000
Compensation to Howard F. Holmes for loss of arm	Nil.	500
Relief of the famine sufferers in Japan	Nil.	24,824
	657,496 16	1,256,120

DEPARTMENT OF AGRICULTURE, REVENUE.

—	1891-92.	1906-07.
	$ cts.	$ cts.
Patent Fees	77,413 58	177,881 19
Trade Marks	8,485 18	31,700 90
	85,898 76	209,582 09

SESSIONAL PAPER No. 29a

DEPARTMENT OF AGRICULTURE.—CIVIL GOVERNMENT SALARIES.

Name.	Rank.	Salary.
		$ cts.
George F. O'Halloran..........	Deputy Minister..........................	3,900 00
A. L. Jarvis............	Secretary................................	2,600 00
W. J. Lynch....	Chief Clerk..............................	2,350 00
F. C. Chittick....................	" and Accountant.......	2,250 00
T. K. Doherty....	"	1,950 00
P. E. Ritchie	"	1,950 00
R. H. St. Denis........	First Class Clerk........................	1,900 00
T. McCabe..................	"	1,900 00
H. H. Bailey....	"	1,900 00
A. E. Caron...............	"	1,700 00
C. E. Mortureaux....	"	1,600 00
C. W. C. Bate.................	"	1,550 00
T. L. Richard	"	1,550 00
T. P. Neville.............	"	1,550 00
M. A. Belanger	"	1,550 00
W. H. T. Megill	"	1,500 00
William Ide	"	1,500 00
M. L. Rush..	"	1,500 00
W. J. Withrow................	"	1,500 00
A. Tache...................	Second Class Clerk....	1,450 00
M. W. Casey.............	"	1,450 00
J. W. D. Verner..........	"	1,400 00
A. E. Powell.....	"	1,350 00
F. J. Audet........	"	1,250 00
C. M. Goddard.............	"	1,250 00
L. G. Bowker....	"	1,250 00
J. A. McKenna...	"	1,250 00
J. F. D. Withrow...	"	1,250 00
James Skead	"	1,200 00
J. Wilkins........	"	1,200 00
E. A. Thomas	"	1,200 00
J. Kilgallin.... .	"	1,200 00
W. A. Fraser.....	"	1,200 00
E. Copping........	Junior Second Class Clerks....	1,100 00
M. J. Morrison..............	"	1,100 00
E. R. Dewhurst.	"	1,100 00
A. Duff	"	1,100 00
C. Steacy.	"	1,100 00
W. J. Walsh.................	"	1,100 00
A. Desjardins...............	"	1,100 00
M. Leyden..	"	1,000 00
A. E. Rodman.....	"	950 00
H. Dubourg..................	"	950 00
A. Archambault................	"	950 00
C. G. Brown............. ..	"	950 00
J. C. O. Dupuis.................	"	950 00
J. P. Beaudoin	"	950 00
R. C. Macpherson	"	950 00
G. Bourret	"	900 00
E. L. Carter..	" ' "	850 00
J. D. Dupuis.	"	850 00
C. P. Grenfell....., ...	"	800 00
M. J. Martineau..	Third Class Clerk.......................	700 00
A. M. Dawson...	" '	650 00
A. G. Monoghan.....	"	600 00
P. Davieau............	Messenger	690 00

7-8 EDWARD VII , A. 1908

DEPARTMENT OF AGRICULTURE.

CIVIL GOVERNMENT CONTINGENCIES.

G. Bowden..	$ 700 00	M. A. Prentiss..	$ 600 00
T. Morgan..	700 00	H. Stark..	600 00
L. A. Kingsmill..	700 00	S. Hunter..	600 00
U. Dorion..	700 00	M. E. McIver..	600 00
F. S. Armstong..	700 00	A. Irwin..	600 00
E. W. Rogers..	700 00	T. M. Dick..	550 00
M. A. Hanlon..	650 00	J. Leafloor..	700 00
M. St. Germain..	650 00	G. O. Gorman..	650 00
A. A. Cook..	650 00	E. Proulx..	650 00
L. B. Brunette..	650 00	D. V. Graziadei..	600 00
L. Braden..	650 00		

HEALTH OF ANIMALS.

J. G. Rutherford, V.D.G..	$4,000 00	B. M. Bayless..	$ 850 00
George Hilton..	2,200 00	A. Mackie..	800 00
A. E. Moore..	1,800 00	B. Drummond..	850 00
C. H. Higgins..	1,800 00	Robert Fee	600 00
G. H. L. Sharman..	1,450 00	Wm Laidlaw..	600 00
S. Hadwen..	1,200 00	M, Dewar	500 00
D. Henderson..	1,200 00	D. St. George..	550 00
E. C. Oliver..	1,200 00	John Hutchingame..	550 00
G. Fitzgerald..	912 50		

LIVE STOCK.

Jas. B. Spencer..	$1,900 00	J. C. Bonneville..	$ 550 00
W. A. Clemons..	1,550 00	L. Brown..	550 00
D. Drummond..	1,100 00	J. F. Grant..	500 00
C. M. Macrae..	1,100 00	M. Macdonald..	500 00
L. Boulet..	650 00		

DAIRYING DIVISION.

J. A. Ruddick, Commissioner..	$3,500 00	Mrs. A. Schingh..	$ 550 00
George H. Barr..	1,800 00	L. Mohr..	550 00
D. Halpin..	850 00	R. E. Armstrong..	600 00
1. L. Henderson..	700 00	A. Long..	500 00
A. H. Hubbell..	650 00		

FRUIT.

A. McNeill, Chief..	$1,900 00	K. B. Robinson..	$ 700 00
M. R. Baker..	1,250 00	A. Keir..	500 00

COW TESTING.

C. F. Whitley..	$1,400 00	A. Laplante..	$780 00
I. Trudel..	850 00	A. B Beauchesne..	750 00
H. H. Sinclair..	800 00	E. Villeneuve..	720 00
J. F. W. Aylmer..	800 00		

MARKETS.

W. W. Moore, Chief..	$1,900 00	M. L. Elliott..	$ 550 00

COLD STORAGE WAREHOUSES.

R. J. Cochrane..	$1,200 00	J. L. Hudon..	$ 600 00
B. I. Langford..	600 00		

SEED

G. H. Clark, Chief..	$2,600 00	S. Kipp..	$ 600 00
T. G. Raynor..	1,500 00	James Hayes..	600 00
J. C. Cote..	1,200 00	R. Ralston..	600 00
G. Michaud..	1,200 00	H. Hill..	600 00
A. Cranston..	800 00	J. Fisher..	600 00
S. Millette..	700 00	J. M. Kilburn..	600 00
A. L. Brown..	700 00	J. Tremblay..	550 00
M. F. Hartley..	700 00	L. Reardon..	550 00
A. M. Bradley..	700 00	W. Winthrop..	550 00

CENSUS AND STATISTICS.

A. Blue, Commissioner..	$4,000 00	M. Jenkins..	$ 590 00
J. C. Macpherson..	1,600 00	G. Kehoe..	590 00
E. S. Macphail..	1,600 00	L. Keir..	590 00
J. R. Munro..	1,200 00	Mrs. F. Lovekin.. .. .. •.. ..	590 00
R. E. Watts..	1,100 00	R. H. Field..	560 00
F. A. Brown..	800 00	B. Drysdale..	540 00
R. C. Marcil..	750 00	E. Bertrand..	540 00
A. J. Pelletier..	750 00	S. Dauray..	540 00
C. Ross..	700 00	A. E. Ogden..	540 00
J. C. H. Pelletier..	700 00	E. Thomson..	540 00
E. Babin..	650 00	Wm. A. Archer..	500 00
Mrs. K. M. Battle..	650 00	O. Gravel..	500 00
E. H. St. Denis..	600 00	Angus McGillivray..	500 00
A. Bradley..	590 00	Mrs. M. S. Weelands..	500 00
A. Bourret..	590 00		

ARCHIVES.

A. G. Doughty, Archivist..	$3,000 00	B. B. Boutet..	$ 600 00
Robert Laidlaw..	1,200 00	F. A. McDonald..	600 00
A. R. Holmden..	1,200 00	M. Greaves..	600 00
L. M. Pelletier..	1,200 00	K. Brown..	575 00
P. P. Gaudet..	1,200 00	L. Shouldis..	500 00
F. Grey..	900 00	J. F. Mackay..	500 00
P. L. Mercure..	900 00	V. Muir..	500 00
D. A. McArthur..	900 00	H. M. Russell..	500 00
M. G. Phelps..	850 00	G. Ogilvy..	500 00
W. Pennington..	804 00	M. Smith..	· 500 00
M. Casey..	800 00	V. Bigras..	500 00
W. D. LeSueur..	780 00	N. Fee..	500 00
D. Poirier..	700 00	K. McCoy..	420 00
M. Robertson..	625 00	J. D. Bradley..	570 00
J. B. Baril..	600 00	Désiré Prot..	260 00

EXHIBITION BRANCH.

Wm. Hutchison, Commissioner.. ..	$3,000 00	H. C. Knowlton..	$1,080 00
James Brodie..	1,700 00	W. D. Gagne..	650 00
W. A. Burns..	1,700 00	George Brown..	650 00
E. Girardot..	1,200 00	A. V. Despard..	300 00
Samuel Anderson..	1,200 00		

QUARANTINE PORTS.

F. Montizambert, M.D..	$4,000 00	C. G. Rogers..	$1,250 00
Arthur Nowlan..	900 00		

EXPERIMENTAL FARM.

Wm. Saunders, Director..	$4,000 00	M. C. O'Hanley..	$1,050 00
Jas Fletcher..	2,450 00	A. McMurray..	1,050 00
F. T. Shutt..	2,450 00	J. F. Watson..	1,050 00
J. H. Grisdale..	2,250 00	D. D. Gray..	1,000 00
W. T. Macoun..	1,950 00	C. T. Brittell..	850 00
C. E. Saunders..	1,750 00	W. T. Ellis..	800 00
A. T. Charron..	1,350 00	H. Holz..	800 00
A. G. Gilbert..	1,250 00	G. O. Morisset..	750 00
J. A. Gingnard..	1,200 00	G. J. Fixter.. .. .. .'	720 00
H. W. Charlton..	1,200 00	G. K. Wetmore..	700 00
T. M. Cramp..	1,150 00	A. Bélanger..	650 00
Eug. Pelletier..	1,150 00	John Nevins..	600 00
A. Gibson..	1,100 00	J. Mailleur..	600 00
V. Fortier..	1,050 00		

MEMO. FROM PATENT OFFICE.

To the Civil Service Commission:

GENTLEMEN,—The Examiners of the Patent Office respectfully ask your consideration of this memorial, which deals briefly with the following topics:—

    I. The importance of patent law and practice.

    II. The nature and importance of the Examiner's work.

    III. The esteem in which like work is held in other countries and the lack in
Canada of proper regard for the Examiners as technical officers doing skilled
work, and of adequate remuneration.

    IV. The sufficiency of the office income to provide for satisfactory remuneration
and for better facilities for work.

    V. Request for improved conditions.

An appendix is also added.

I. All nations advanced in civilization realize to some extent the value and indis-
pensability of a patent system, but comparatively few people fully appreciate its
importance. A good patent law not only encourages invention but stimulates, and in
many instances makes possible, profitable manufacture.

'It is generally recognized by the most profound students of our institutions,
both at home and abroad, that no one thing has contributed more to the preeminence
of this country in industrial arts and in manufactures than the encouragement given
by our constitution and laws to inventors and to investors in patent property.'—
(C. H. Duell, United States Commissioner of Patents, Report for 1900.)

'I assert, without fear of successful contradiction, that we mainly owe to our
patent system such foothold as we have gained during the past fifty years in foreign
lands for our manufactured products.'—(Report United States Commissioner C. H.
Duell, 1898.)

'Patents have been one of the most important factors in the growth of the United
States from a group of poverty-stricken non-manufacturing dependencies to the
greatest manufacturing country in the world. In fact the late Senator O. H. Platt,
of Connecticut, one of the profoundest minds of the United States Senate for the past
thirty years, maintained that the American patent system has been the greatest factor
in the material development of the nation.'—(E. J. Prindle, in *Engineering Magazine*,
September, 1906.)

A cursory examination in connection with other countries having a well developed
patent system will show that they also occupy an advanced position in manufacture
and commerce, and it should be noted that the Canadian system closely resembles
that of the United States.

II. The courts regard a Canadian patent as *prima facie* evidence of novelty and
invention. A valid patent is of value, sometimes of immense value, not only to the
inventor but to the whole country, but even a good patent law may be to a large extent
defeated by the issue of patents that are not valid, and 'the validity of a patent depends primarily on the Examiner in charge of the application.'

Thus it is seen that the Examiner holds no mean position in the scientific and
industrial life of the country. He is a skilled technical workman, who has acquired
a knowledge of the arts and sciences by college training or special study and experience, or both. In his office work he becomes a specialist in certain arts and, granted
proper facilities for search and comparison, is enabled to protect the public against
fraudulent patents and secure for the inventor a valid and reliable document. His
work is equally important whether the application be made by the inventor directly or
through a patent attorney. In most instances the inventor, however skilled in his art,
is unfamiliar with the method of procedure necessary to secure adequate protection.
On the other hand, the attorneys, while versed in the methods of procedure, cannot

SESSIONAL PAPER No. 29a

be expected to know the details of the numerous arts in the broad field covered by their various clients.

Most patent attorneys aim to secure for their clients claims of as broad a scope as the state of the art will allow, and depend on the Examiner to see that no untenable claims are permitted to stand.

The Examiner must be familiar with patent law and practice. He must see that the formal papers of an application conform with legal requirements. He must insist on the specification (and drawings) being such as to set forth fully and clearly the nature of the invention. He must have sufficient insight to determine whether an alleged invention is useful and practicable. He must have keen discriminating power to determine the bearing on a given case of others of a similar nature, to detect novel elements among others that are old and to decide what an applicant has a right to claim as his invention. He must have a good command of language in order to express clearly to an applicant the conclusions arrived at in examination, and to show the bearing of facts that may not be obvious, also to assist the applicant if necessary, or if requested, in framing valid and appropriate claims. The importance of this last item can scarcely be overestimated. The Supreme Court of the United States has said that the claim of a patent is one of the most difficult pieces of composition to write.

'The Patent Office should command the highest order of talent. There is no person, whatever be his abilities or attainments, who would not find, as an Examiner, full exercise for all his talents. A practical sound sense is nowhere more important. All learning connected with the arts and sciences finds here an ample field for exercise; and even questions of law that tax to their utmost the abilities of the most learned jurists frequently present themselves for the decision of the office, and should be rightfully decided by the Examiner.'—(Report United States Commissioner Mason for 1853.)

III. In 1848 the United States Congress considered the value of the Patent Examiner to his country equal to that of a representative to Congress, as is evidenced by their being granted equal salaries of $2,500 a year. Since that time the Commissioner has repeatedly appealed for increased remuneration for his staff, mainly on the ground of its being in the interest of the country to retain skilled and experienced men.

In 1848 the United States office issued 607 patents. The receipts for the year were $67,577. In 1906 the Canadian Patent Office issued 6,026 patents, the receipts being $187,791.

In Great Britain and Germany also the patent examiners have a standing as technical officers approximately equivalent to that accorded to skilled engineers in other branches of Government service. The salary of officers in the British Office doing work similar to that done by the Canadian Examiners is from £550 to £700.

In this country the work of the Examiners is not wholly unappreciated. In July, 1905, Hon. Mr. Fisher, Commissioner of Patents, clearly expressed in the House his estimate of them as technical men:—

Mr. FISHER.—'I have found that it is impossible to keep patent examiners, who are technical officers. . . . I regret to say that within the last year I have had to lose some of the best men because they could not receive more than the ordinary statutory increase. . . . I want to give them increases greater than the ordinary increase in the statutory allowance simply because they are technical officers and I cannot keep them at their present salary. . . .

In answer to a remark referring to men mentioned for increase of salary Mr. Fisher further says 'Certain of them are technical officers and of course they have to be deal with in a different way from the ordinary clerk in the service.'—(Official Report of Debates, 1905. (July 7, pp. 9056-8.)

Nevertheless such appreciation is, throughout the service in general and in the mind of the public, almost entirely wanting. In evidence of this is the fact that the

Civil Service Act makes absolutely no provision for remuneration of Examiners as distinct from clerks.

The United States statement of requisites for 1907 is, in part:—

Commissioner of Patents.. . . . . $5,000
Assistant Commissioner of Patents.. 3,000
  3 Examiners in Chief, each.. 3,000
  1 Examiner of Interference.. 2,500
39 Principal Examiners and 1 to be added, each.. 2,500
44 1st Assistant Examiners and 6 to be added, each.. 1,800
52 2nd Assistant Examiners and 8 to be added, each.. 1,600
63 3rd Assistant Examiners and 7 to be added, each.. 1,400
73 4th Assistant Examiners and 7 to be added, each.. 1,200

The British Patent Office for 1907 provides for:—

Comptroller General.. . . . . £1,800
Chief Examiner.. 1,200
  4 Supervising Examiners... £700 to £800 (yearly increment £25)
20 Examiners.. . . . .   550 to 700 ("   25)
26 Deputy Examiners.... ..   400 to 550 ("   20)
141 Assistant Examiners.. .. 150 to 450 ("   15)

(These latter were known up to 1883 as 'indexing and abridging clerks,' from which the nature of their work may be inferred.)

As to the United States schedule, Commissioner Allen states in his report for the year 1906:—

'It will also be necessary if this service is to be maintained in efficiency to check the frequent resignations of skilled Examiners by increasing their compensation somewhat above the present figures. In the last year resignations from the examining corps of this office amounted to 32, distributed as follows: 2 Principal Examiners, 3 first assistants, 5 second assistants, 15 third assistants, and 7 fourth assistants. It will be seen that the largest number of resignations came in the grade of third assistants, a grade in which an assistant may be supposed to have reached a capacity for effective and independent action in the transaction of the work of examining applications. At the present time the temptation to resign in order to accept employment with practising attorneys or with large manufacturing establishments which have patent departments is not able to be met by any inducements which this office can present in the way of salary. It should not be forgotten that there is wide field of employment for the Examiners of the Patent Office outside of the Government service, and I believe that those outside inducements are more frequently presented to our Examiners than to any other group of technically-trained men in the Government service. In 1848 the salary of a Principal Examiner in this Office was $2,500 at that time equaling the salary of a Representative in Congress. The pay of these Examiners has not been increased from that time to the present, while the cost of living has increased very considerably.'

In Canada each Examiner is in full charge of applications falling under a certain number of industrial arts and hence fully responsible for the condition of patents issued. From this it is manifest that, at least after a few years experience, he should be classed not lower than the United States Principal Examiners or the British Examiners. It is equally evident that the remuneration of the Canadian Examiners is entirely incommensurate with the service they render.

IV. The income of the Canadian Patent Office is amply sufficient to cover suitable remuneration of the employes and a much-needed improvement in facilities for doing effective and economical work. For example, the total income of the office for the year ended October 31, 1905, was $149,341.12; salaries, $44,430; surplus over working expenses, $87,911.12. The total receipts for the calendar year 1906 were $166,968.83; which will evidently leave a very large surplus.

V. In addition to the foregoing facts relating to the Civil Service, it may be stated that a number of fellow-graduates of the Examiners, and others of similar attainments, are receiving in outside occupations remuneration much greater than that given the Examiners. In many instances these positions afford opportunities for rapid advancement to a maximum limited only by the measure of a man's ability; whereas within the Service the yearly increments are small and the maximum definitely fixed.

The special increases granted to some in 1905 are found to be scarcely more than sufficient to offset the rapid increase in the cost of living. Moreover, they did not affect the small annual increment and low maximum salary.

Again, it would be a great gain to the department if there were provided means for enabling the Examiners to consult scientific and legal works of reference and to conduct a search of records more readily and hence more economically. Specific suggestions in this connection will be offered if desired.

In view of all the preceding, the Examiners feel amply justified in respectfully requesting improved conditions as follows:—

1. A definite standing as Technical Officers, and provision in the Civil Service Act for their general recognition as such.

2. Remuneration commensurate with the importance of the work and its value as a national asset, and with that received by skilled technical officers in other departments of the Government service, considering the emolument granted British and United States examiners.

3. Provision for an increased rate of advancement during the early years of service, and still greater after full efficiency has been attained, in order that a rapid rise to the maximum may to some extent compensate for the fact that the maximum is fixed.

4. Better recognition of the value of the Patent Office by Parliament so that the heads and staff of this office may raise its efficiency to a higher standard as is the tendency in the more advanced countries. This we believe would be in the best interests of our country's prosperity.

Respectfully submitted, and signed on behalf of the Examiners.

F. D. WITHROW,

OTTAWA, June 26, 1907.   *Representative.*

Appendix (comprising)—

(1) Letter from British Patent Office.
(2) Letter from United States Patent Office.
(3) Statistical tables referring to United States and Canadian Patent Offices.

THE PATENT OFFICE,
25 SOUTHAMPTON BUILDINGS, CHANCERY LANE,
LONDON, W.C., May 28, 1907.

A. E. CARON, Esq.,
    Department of Agriculture,
        Patent Office,
            Ottawa.

DEAR SIR,—I have to acknowledge the receipt of your letter of the 16th instant, and in reply to furnish you with the following information.

1. The technical work of the Patent Office is dealt with by an Examining Branch.

7-8 EDWARD VII., A. 1908

2. The present organization of the Examining Staff and the scale of their salaries is shown below:—

No.	Title.	Scale of Salaries.		
		£	£	£
1	Chief Examiner	900	by 50 to	1,100
4	Supervising Examiners..	700	„ 25 „	800
25	Examiners..	550	„ 25 „	700
30	Deputy Examiners..	400	„ 20 „	550
165	Assistant Examiners...	150	„ 15 „	450

3. Vacancies in the higher ranks of the staff are filled as they occur by promotion from the ranks below, and such promotion is determined by merit.

4. The assistant examiners are appointed by open competition held under the Regulations of the Civil Service Commissioners. I inclose a copy of the regulations for a recent competition.

5. The duties of the Examining Staff are to examine and report upon the specifications of inventions, to index and abridge them, and to deal with their amendments and the correspondence arising therefrom.

If there are any further points on which you desire information, I shall be happy to supply it to the best of my ability.

Yours truly,

(Sgd.)   P. S. L. Webb,

Chief Clerk.

Department of the Interior,
United States Patent Office,
Washington, D.C., May 21, 1907.

A. E. Caron, Esq.,
   Examiner, Patent Office,
      Department of Agriculture,
         Ottawa, Canada.

Sir,—Your letter of the 16th instant is received, stating that at its last Session of Parliament the Government of Canada appointed a Royal Commission to report and advise as to the re-adjustment of the salaries of the Civil Service, and asking, as a delegate representing the technical staff of the Department of Agriculture, to which the Patent Office is attached, for the following information from this office:—

'Whether or not you have a technical branch in connection with your office; what officers constitute that branch; their duties, their remuneration; the method of appointment and of promotion, and any additional information that may bear on this subject.'

In reply you are informed that the technical corps of this office consists of three hundred examiners and assistant examiners, besides an examiner of interferences and an examiner of trade-marks and designs. The duty of these examiners is to examine applications for patent and decide upon novelty and patentability of the inventions presented therein. Entrance to the examining corps is through competitive examination given by the Civil Service Commission, and the lowest grade is that of fourth assistant examiner, with a salary of $1,200 a year. Promotion from this grade is based upon seniority of service, as vacancies occur, and is made through the grades of third, second, and first assistant examiner, with salaries of $1,400, $1,600, and

SESSIONAL PAPER No. 29a

$1,800. The primary examiners, of whom there are forty, are selected from the first assistant examiners and receive a salary of $2,500 a year.

The examiner of interferences, who receives the same salary as a principal examiner, decides the question of priority of invention, which may be appealed from him to the board of examiners-in-chief, consisting of three members, appointed by the president, at a salary of $3,000 each. Appeals from the primary examiners on the question of merits or patentability may also be taken to this Board, from which a further appeal lies to the Commissioner.

Trusting that this information is what you desire,

I remain,

Yours very truly,

(Sgd.)   E. B. MOORE,

Acting Commissioner.

TABLE OF COST AND WORK, YEAR 1906.

United States Patent Office.	—	Canadian Patent Office.	—
Number of patent examiners..	275	Number of patent examiners	13
Number of patent applications........	55,676	Number of patent applications...... .	6,905
Yearly average per examiner.........	202	Yearly average per examiner..	531
Weekly average per examiner....	3·88	Weekly average per examiner.	10·2
Salary of examiners..	$447,200	Salary of examiners....	$18,590
Amount of examiners' salary per application.........	$8.03	Amount of examiners' salary per application..	2.69

—		Income.	Salaries per cent of income.	Surplus per cent of income.
		$ cts.		
United States Patent Office.	1902..........	1,552,859 08	51	10
	1903	1,642,201 81	50	12
	1904.....	1,657,326 53	50	11
	1905.............	1,806,758 15	47	18
	1906	1,790,921 38	50	13
Canadian Patent Office.....	1901	118,024 67	28	58
	1902........	127,113 71	26	62
	1903	139,037 87	28	59
	1904....	142,962 68	29	58
	1905.....	149,341 12	29	59

The cost of living in Washington, D.C., and in Ottawa is substantially the same, as shown by a comparison of the cost of certain necessities of life made during May and June, 1907.

29a—6

MEMO. FROM CENTRAL EXPERIMENTAL FARM.

CENTRAL EXPERIMENTAL FARM,
OTTAWA, June 12, 1907.

To the Honourable Civil Service Commission,
Ottawa, Ont.

GENTLEMEN,—We the undersigned officers of the staff of the Central Experimental Farm of the Department of Agriculture, at Ottawa, all doing scientific work in agriculture, with the knowledge and approval of the chiefs of the branches affected, take the liberty of presenting our case for the consideration of the Civil Service Commission now in session at Ottawa.

As the Central Experimental Farm is now a permanent branch of the Department of Agriculture at Ottawa, we would respectfully urge the advisability,—

1st. Of making our positions permanent through regular appointment by Order in Council;

2nd. Of granting us distinctive rank in the Civil Service by placing us in the class of technical officers of the Civil Service;

3rd. Of increasing our salaries so as to make them equal to those of technical officers in other branches of the service, who have been employed for a similar number of years.

In conclusion, may we be allowed to point out that in our estimation the fact that we have had to devote a number of years to acquire special qualifications to be in a position to accomplish our work is deserving of special recognition.

For your guidance, we state below the dates of our respective appointments, with our initial and present salaries per annum:—

Name and title.	Date of appointment	Initial salary.	Present salary.
J. A. Guignard, B.A., Assistant Botanist	April, 1892	$ 600 00	$1,200 00
A. T. Charron, M.A., 1st Assistant Chemist. Analytical Chemist qualified for the Dominion........	July, 1898	600 00	1,350 00
Arthur Gibson, Assistant Entomologist.......	April, 1899	600 00	1,100 00
H. W. Charlton, B.A.Sc., 2nd Assistant Chemist.................	Nov. 1899	600 00	1,200 00
A. Gordon Spencer, B.A., M. Sc., 3rd Assistant Chemist..'.......	June, 1907	1,000 00	1,000 00

With the sincere hope that our claims will receive due consideration at your hands, when other technical or professional branches of the service are being considered, we beg to subscribe ourselves.

Yours very respectfully,

J. A. GUIGNARD,
A. T. CHARRON,
ARTHUR GIBSON,
H. W. CHARLTON,
A. GORDON SPENCER.

OTTAWA, FRIDAY, June 7, 1907.

The Royal Commission on the Civil Service met this morning at 10.30 o'clock.

Present:—Mr. J. M. COURTNEY, C.M.G., Chairman.

Mr. THOMAS FYSHE, Montreal, and

Mr. P. J. BAZIN, Quebec.

Mr. JOHN McDOUGALD, Commissioner of Customs, called, and sworn and examined.

By the Chairman:

Q. You are Commissioner of Customs?—A. Yes.

Q. How long have you held that position?—A. Since May 1, 1896.

Q. You were asked to produce a statement. Have you got it with you?—A. This is the statement.

(Statement produced and filed.)

Q. Comparing notes with 1892, you have now 132 Customs ports as against 110 in that year?—A. Yes.

Q. And the outports have increased from 245 to 288?—A. Yes.

Q. And the stations have increased from 173 to 192?—A. Yes.

Q. What is a Customs station?—A. It is a preventive station for protecting the revenue, and in some cases the officers there are allowed to collect duties.

Q. The Customs duties in 1892 amounted to about $20,500,000, and in 1906 they had increased to $46,671,000?—A. Yes.

Q. What is your salary?—A. $4,000 a year.

Q. Is there anybody in the whole Customs service who is paid at a higher rate than you are?—A. Not in the Customs service. The highest salary of a collector is $4,000.

Q. There is in the department now an Assistant Commissioner?—A. Yes, there has been for some time.

Q. In addition to that you have three chief clerks?—A. Yes.

Q. Mr. Bennet, Mr. Farrow and Mr. Morin?—A. Mr. Farrow was promoted to be Assistant Commissioner, and Mr. Frost has taken his place.

Q. Then the chief clerks are Messrs. Bennet, Frost and Morin?—A. Yes.

Q. What are their distinctive duties?—A. Mr. Bennet is chief clerk of statistics. Mr. Frost is the chief clerk and accountant. Mr. Morin was in charge of seizures, but his health failed and just at present he is supervising frontier manifest work.

Q. Your chief clerks are few in number, and they have distinctive duties?—A. All of them.

Q. How many first-class clerks have you got?—A. Eight.

Q. Have they as a rule distinctive duties to perform?—A. Some of them have, but not all. They were first-class clerks, most of them, before I entered the service.

Q. Who have been appointed first-class clerks since you came in?—A. Messrs. Watson and Saunders. They have distinctive duties.

Q. Then some of the others may have been performing the same duties as second-class clerks that they are now doing as first?—A. Yes. Lately Mr. Rorke was made a first-class clerk. He discharges the duties of assistant to the chief accountant.

7-8 EDWARD VII., A. 1908

Q. How many second-class clerks have you got?—A. Fifteen.

Q. Are they doing the same duties that they discharged before they were promoted?—A. I think so.

Q. Then they were promoted as a rule because of lengthy service?—A. Because of lengthy service.

Q. Not because of any distinctive rise in the character of their work?—A. The policy of the department has been to have the routine work done by second-class clerks when they serve long enough.

Q. Although they did it just as effectively when they were junior second-class clerks?—A. Yes.

Q. How many junior second-class clerks have you got?—A. Eighteen.

Q. Were they promoted from third-class clerks or did they come in as junior second-class clerks?—A. Most of them came in as junior second-class clerks. Some have been promoted.

Q. There are only one or two ladies among the junior second-class clerks. Miss Mason and Miss Sixsmith?—A. There are more than that number in the Civil Service list now.

Q. There is Miss Bertram, Miss Cram, and Miss Low?—A. They are all in during the present year as junior second-class clerks.

Q. What does the salary of a junior second-class clerk begin at?—A. $800.

Q. They are all good I presume?—A. Yes, I think they are all very fair.

Q. Is it not a matter of difficulty at present to get good men to enter the service at $500?—A. I do not think we could get them. Most of the junior seconds have come in under the Board of Customs where the limitation of salary for clerks is $1,200 and have been transferred afterwards from the outside to the inside service.

By Mr. Fyshe:

Q. Without examination?—A. They passed the examination.

Q. In the first instance?—A. Yes.

By the Chairman:

Q. You have many applications on behalf of women I suppose, for positions in the service?—A. Quite a number.

Q. They are growing in number every year?—A. Every year. I notice that women compose the majority of the successful candidates who passed the Civil Service Examinations last November.

Q. I presume the reason of so many women applying to enter the service is that they get better pay under the Government than they would outside?—A. I think that is so.

Q. You have also attached to the department now, what you call a Board of Customs and Statistical Staff?—A. Yes.

Q. That scarcely existed fifteen years ago?—A. I do not think so—at least not to the same extent. The compilation of statistics was moved from the ports to Ottawa and we now compile direct from the entries and for that reason we have to employ a larger number of men at Ottawa.

Q. There are a large number of men on the staff here in Ottawa who compile statistics and as a rule they are brought in from the outside service?—A. The majority of them are.

Q. That is to say you found it better to compile the statistics here under your direct supervision than to have the figures compiled at the ports?—A. At the ports we could not get the work done as satisfactorily nor as promptly.

Q. And in addition to that you have a few people employed in the Customs Laboratory?—A. Yes, there are five.

Q. You call them analysts and examining officers?—A. The analyst is Mr. Babbington. The others are qualified for testing sugar and molasses by the polariscope test. The other members of the staff are called examining officers.

By Mr. Fyshe:

Q. Is Mr. Bremner in the Service?—A. He is inspector at Halifax.

Q. Doing the same work that he has been doing all along?—A. Pretty much.

By the Chairman:

Q. All these people that have entered the department at Ottawa have passed the Civil Service Examination?—A. All that appear in the Civil Service list on the inside service have passed the examination.

Q. And I presume also most of the statistical officers that are here?—A. Not altogether. I think the majority have, but there are a number that have not. We could not get the men at the time we made the change who had passed the examination.

Q. Then have the people in the inside service, charged to Civil Government, passed the required standard as to age, health and moral conduct?—A. Yes.

Q. They are appointed on probation?—A. On probation.

Q. You give at the end of the six months a certificate that their services are satisfactory?—A. Yes.

Q. And on that they are continued? You often have pressure put upon you to appoint people to the inside service?—A. Applications are continuously received by the minister.

By Mr. Fyshe:

Q. Is there pressure to put in new men or advance old ones?—A. To put in new men; we are not troubled so much in regard to advancement.

By the Chairman:

Q. When an appointment is made how is the necessity for it discovered, from one of the chief clerks?—A. They report it.

Q. Then you examine the matter yourself?—A. Always.

Q. Have you a greater staff under your own supervision charged to Civil Government, than the needs of the department require?—A. No, not now, we are short handed.

Q. And the staff as a rule is efficient?—A. As a rule it is.

Q. Coming now to the Promotion Examination. Yours is a very important department, are the Promotion Examinations carried on strictly on the rules of the Civil Service Examiners?—A. Yes.

Q. How many sets of papers are prepared? There are your own two?—A. The 'Duties of Office' paper is all I prepare.

Q. But you certify as to their efficiency and punctuality and all that sort of thing?—A. Yes, in addition.

Q. And the Civil Service Examiners set the other papers?—A. Yes.

Q. The members of the staff are examined all round when they come up for promotion?—A. Yes.

By Mr. Fyshe:

Q. There has been a large increase in your staff?—A. Yes. And the work itself has trebled.

Q. Is the tariff more complicated in character than it was 15 years ago?—A. A little.

Q. Has it involved more trouble?—A. More work. There are more entries.

By the Chairman:

Q. Appointments to the grade of third-class clerks are made at $500 a year?—A. Yes.

Q. And if you appoint a second-class clerk how is that done?—A. By promotion; he is at the minimum. If transferred in from the outside service he is transferred in at the salary he is then receiving.

Q. The minimum of a junior second-class clerk is $800?—A. Yes.

Q. But as a third-class clerk only gets $700, you could not make him a junior second-class clerk at $800?—A. Yes, by promotion. A clerk on the outside service could be transferred in at $800 or more.

Q. But I am talking of the inside service. When an official is appointed on the inside service, his salary is the minimum of his class. If a little latitude were allowed the department could you not appoint more third-class clerks and less second-class clerks? That is to say if you were allowed the option instead of appointing at the minimum of $500 to bring clerks in at between $500 and $800?—A. I suppose we could get clerks to begin at between $600 and $800.

Q. If you could do that the carrying on from $800 to $1,100 would cease to some extent?—A. They are doing pretty nearly the same work. I do not think they would remain in the service—the clerks we desire would not remain in the service—without going beyond the $800.

Q. You have no temporary clerks in your department?—A. Not now.

Q. You do not employ men temporarily at any time?—A. Very few, because our work is of a permanent character. There is always a large mass of work to be done.

Q. What leave of absence do you give your clerks?—A. Three weeks.

Q. How often do you take a holiday yourself?—A. Whenever I can get it. I have had very few since I have been in the service.

Q. When did you take a holiday last?—A. I had a fortnight last year, but used principally on public business.

Q. Do you think that is right?—A. I am allowed holidays when I can take them. I do not think work all the time is very good for a man's health, but we had special work on last year.

Q. Would not the appointment of an assistant commissioner help you to take some holidays yourself?—A. I think so. I think he will be an assistance in that way.

Q. Has anybody ever been dismissed from the inside service?—A. I do not recollect it; not during my time.

Q. You keep an attendance book?—A. Yes.

Q. Is that attendance book under your own direction or under the direction of a chief clerk?—A. It is under my own direction.

Q. What are the office hours?—A. From nine till five, with an hour for luncheon.

Q. Do all the officials go to luncheon at the same time?—A. Not the same hour, different hours; we have to keep the office open.

Q. Then you find it a necessity to keep the department continuously open during working hours?—A. We do.

By Mr. Fyshe:

Q. In which building are your offices?—A. In the West Departmental Block.

By the Chairman:

Q. Is your department assembled under one roof or is the staff scattered?—A. The Statistical Branch is housed in the Woods building on Slater street; there are some eighty officers there. The others are together in the West Block.

Q. Have you any objection to Mr. Bazin and Mr. Fyshe going over the department?—A. No objection at all.

Q. They would like to see how the work is performed?—A. We are shifting rooms at present and are not in very good shape, but the Commissioners can see what we are doing.

Q. Every chief and first and second class clerk on your staff comes under the old Superannuation Act as a rule?—A. I think so.

Q. Do you not find it difficult to get good men now to come in on account of the abolition of the Superannuation Act?—A. I have not heard the question raised.

Q. If the Superannuation Act were restored do you think it would add to the stability of the service?—A. I think it would, superannuation in some form or another.

Q. Then you are of opinion that a pension scheme of some form or other would add to the stability of the service?—A. I think so.

Q. And tend to economy?—A. I think so, if it was carefully guarded.

Q. You know that there was a Treasury Board minute adopted in 1879 prohibiting the use of political influence by public employees?—A. Yes.

Q. Are the officers of the Customs Department aware of that?—A. They are.

Q. Both outside and in?—A. Both outside and in.

Q. Do the officials pass you over in endeavouring to get increases of salary or promotions, and go direct to the Minister, or do they appeal to you?—A. The members of the inside service, I think, appeal to me first as a rule.

Q. But the members of the outside service put pressure on the Minister and disregard you?—A. Yes, to a considerable extent.

Q. There was a scale of salaries laid down, I think in 1882, as regards the Customs by the Civil Service Act, providing that the salary of inspectors should be from so and so to so and so, and for collectors from so and so to so and so. That scale of salaries is still in force?—A. I fancy there have been some slight changes since.

Q. I have got the last Civil Service list here?—A. I think the tide surveyors, for instance, had their salaries increased from $1,000 to $1,200, but substantially the list is as laid down in 1882.

Q. Of course when this schedule was laid down the revenue of the Customs Department was not more than about $15,000,000 or $16,000,000?—A. About that amount.

Q. Now it is about three times that sum?—A. Yes, about three times.

Q. And the collector at Montreal who now takes in, I suppose, about $18,000,000 a year——A. We expect to collect that much this year. The customs revenue at Montreal was over $15,000,000 last year.

Q. Well, his salary remains under the same scale as when he was collecting only $5,000,000?—A. Yes.

By Mr. Fyshe:

Q. Do you not think that the salaries paid to the head Customs officials in Montreal are inadequate?—A. I think I will have to let you judge as to that.

By the Chairman:

Q. Collectors are political appointments?—A. Collectors and inspectors. But as a rule inspectors are taken from the service. We are trying to follow that rule, but they do not require to pass the Civil Service Examination.

By Mr. Fyshe:

Q. They are selected from the ranks of business men are they not?—A. The collectors in some cases have formerly been members of Parliament.

By the Chairman:

Q. What about the preventive officers?—A. They do not require any examination. They are of two classes, those for special service and those that are merely guarding the ports.

Q. Appraisers are very frequently appointed on account of their technical qualifications are they not?—A. Yes, but they have to pass an examination.

Q. A departmental examination?—A. A departmental examination. I might say there is a clause in the Customs Act for the appointment of temporary officers, section 6.

Q. I wonder whether in the revision of the statutes that clause has been inserted in the Civil Service Act?—A. No, it is in the Customs Act. As I say the appraisers pass the departmental examination.

Q. Of course with a enormous revenue like that of the Customs and which is increasing it is desirable to have inspectors continually on the road?—A. It is.

Q. What travelling allowance do the inspectors get?—A. Their actual expenses.

Q. An inspector must necessarily be out of pocket every time he goes out?—A. I should think so.

Q. Would it not be more advantageous to the service if he had some kind of per diem allowance rather than being paid his simple out of pocket expenses?—A. The inspectors have not complained.

Q. In the English outside service the tendency rather is to give smaller salaries and higher travelling expenses so as to induce the inspectors to go out constantly on the road?—A. The inspectors are expected to make an examination once a year of each port in their district. That you see requires them to make an inspection and to be around a good deal.

Q. But would it not be better instead of having a minimum requirement that they should be continually on the road?—A. I think under our present system they are on the road constantly. Of course it would be more satisfactory to the inspectors to have a larger allowance I have no doubt.

Q. Your inspectors are now getting to be old men?—A. Most of them.

Q. Mr. Bremner, Mr. Lemieux and others are getting up in years?—A. And Mr. O'Meara is getting up in years too.

Q. Take Mr. Bremner, for instance, he would not have any inducement to go to Barrington, or an outside outport, in Nova Scotia in the middle of the winter?—A. Not in the middle of the winter. He would select his seasons for the difficult points.

Q. And the consequence is that by selecting his seasons for the difficult points the collectors would know almost to a certainty when the inspectors would come around?—A. I think so.

Q. If the collectors know when the inspector is coming around they can always, if there is anything suspicious, cover up their tracks?—A. It would give them a better opportunity but it is difficult for them to cover up their tracks under the system we have in operation.

Q. What are the inspectors' duties, When Mr. Bremner goes to Weymouth, for example, what does he do?—A. The first thing is to count the cash. He then looks over the work of the port, and compares the entries with the manifest. The manifests are not filed in the department, they remain at the port as a record of the goods coming in.

By Mr. Fyshe:

Q. The manifests are kept at the port?—A. Kept at the port. That is the manifest of goods received.

Q. What check has the department at Ottawa that the full duties are being received?—A. We have the entries. The entries are sent to Ottawa when they are passed by the importer.

Q. And these correspond with the manifest?—A. They are supposed to and the inspector checks them to see that they do.

Q. Would the inspector go over all the manifests that have accumulated since the last inspection?—A. At small ports he would, but not at the large ports, it would be impracticable.

Q. You say that in most cases the collector would know that the inspector was coming around?—A. I think he would.

Q. The inspector surely would not notify him?—A. No.

Q. Why should he know then?—A. He may know that he is at a neighbouring port, and that he will likely take other ports in their turn.

Q. Under the system of bank inspection the inspector drops down when he is utterly unexpected, and when there are two or three branches together he does not take them all at once, but goes away and returns again?—A. At the large ports there is a system of check that tends to prevent any fraud by the officers. The danger is at the small ports where there is only one officer. At the other ports one officer is a check upon the other.

Q. Of course wherever you can do that you do it?—A. We do it at all the large ports. Each officer has his distinctive duties.

Q. Have you had much trouble from defalcations?—A. Not any serious trouble, considering the volume of business.

By the Chairman:

Q. The salary of the inspectors runs from $1,600 to $2,500?—A. Yes.

Q. How many inspectors have you got in the province of Quebec?—A. Two.

Q. Then the inspector in such an important position as the Montreal district, with a revenue from Montreal alone of about $20,000,000, can only reach a maximum salary of $2,500 a year?—A. That is all.

Q. You have no system of annual increments such as the Excise Department has? —A. Not in the outside service.

Q. You took a special vote of about $100,000 at the last session of Parliament to increase salaries in the outside Customs service?—A. Yes.

Q. How did you divide that up?—A. There was more than $100,000. Approximately the officers were increased $100 in some cases, and in some cases less; that was about the average.

Q. And of course that increase of $100 was rather to the clerks in the lower divisions?—A. It was used largely to increase salaries which were considered too low.

Q. That is to say the large vote that parliament gave you did not apply to the collectors or inspectors at all?—A. It was applied more largely to those in subordinate positions. All the collectors and inspectors were considered in the vote, except those at the maximum.

Q. What about Mr. Robert White, for instance, Collector of Customs at Montreal?—A. He could not benefit because he was paid at the maximum salary.

Q. The collectors and inspectors in receipt of the maximum salary did not benefit by this arrangement?—A. Mr. O'Meara got nothing, but his assistant was raised to $2,400 from $2,250.

Q. The inspectors, collectors and preventive officers, you stated, are political appointments?—A. They may be appointed without examination.

Q. You never transfer a collector from one port to another?—A. It is very seldom that has been done.

Q. But it has been done. The Collector of Customs at Kingston once went to Montreal under special circumstances?—A. It is very rarely done.

Q. We will take the great port of Montreal. All the appointments in that city are made, after the examination has been passed, at the instance of the members of parliament for the district?—A. The appointments are made upon their nomination.

Q. Of course all the vacancies are filled by people who pass the examination?—A. The acting officers may be taken on without examination. If they are appointed permanently as clerks or examining officers they have to pass the examination. In some cases they may be appointed as preventive officers.

Q. And that also is scheduled, under the Act, as an appointment that can be made without examination?—A. Yes.

Q. The staff at Montreal are retained there from the time they are appointed until they die or retire?—A. As a rule. A few go out on special work temporarily to relieve pressure.

Q. But there are no means of raising the mass of employees in your outside service by transfer to fill vacancies which might occur here and there?—A. No, that would be objected to by the politicians in the locality.

By Mr. Fyshe:

Q. You mean there is no chance of promotion from the outside?—A. No chance of a transfer to an appointment in an outside constituency. That is looked upon as local patronage.

By the Chairman:

Q. If the collectorship of Customs at Ottawa happened to fall vacant there could be no promotion, say by appointing a surveyor at Hamilton to take the place under the existing practice?—A. Under the existing system it would not be practicable.

Q. It would not be practicable under the existing system, however, beneficial it might be?—A. No.

By Mr. Fyshe:

Q. Would it not be practicable to promote the next in seniority in the place where a vacancy occurred?—A. That might be done.

By the Chairman:

Q. But as a rule that it not done even?—A. It may not be. It has been done in cases, but it is not the rule.

Q, The position of collector is looked upon as a piece of political patronage?—A. A piece of patronage. The surveyor of course has to pass an examination.

By Mr. Fyshe:

Q. Why not bring the inspector from a small port to a more important one like Ottawa?—A. The transfer from one district to the other would be objected to by the local men on account of the patronage.

Q. The service should be regarded as a whole?—A. It is not.

By the Chairman:

Q. What prospect has a junior officer appointed to Montreal? Can he get on the service if he is a lucky man?—A. He may get up to an outside chief clerkship.

Q. And at the utmost that would be $2,000 a year salary?—A. Yes, or he may be also a surveyor, but such appointments are very few.

By Mr. Fyshe:

Q. Even if he had a first-class record?—A. He may be a chief clerk or a surveyor. Of course there is only one surveyor and there may be more chief clerks.

By the Chairman:

Q. How many officials have you got in your service?—A. I should think about 2,000; I could not say exactly.

Q. And of these 2,000 persons in the outside service there is no prospect of one person appointed to the junior ranks ever becoming collector?—A. It would not follow as a matter of procedure; it might be done.

Q. But never is done?—A. It is sometimes, but very rarely.

By Mr. Fyshe:

Q. Do you not think that a collector would be a more efficient officer if he knew all the subsidiary duties?—A. Undoubtedly, he has to learn them.

Q. From the bottom to the top of the department?—A. Undoubtedly.

By the Chairman:

Q. Here and there you get men of rare ability like Mr. Robert White, the collector at Montreal?—A. We have got a number of very good collectors and some of rare ability.

Q. But here and there you get a number of collectors who simply do nothing?— A. There are some. I do not think they are the majority.

Q. But to put it plainly, a junior of good ability, fair record and honest character can scarcely hope to attain to the higher positions in the Customs service?—A. They don't as a rule, attain to the highest positions in the outside service.

Q. Do you not find as a consequence, especially in the west, that the young men in your department are leaving?—A. They are leaving on account of the salaries.

Q. If they could see something ahead of them, might not some of them stay?— A. Possibly. There is a spirit of unrest in the west.

By Mr. Fyshe:

Q. What do you mean when you speak of the 'west'?—A. I mean the country west of Ontario. We have to pay our staff better in the west or we could not hold them.

Q. Recently you lost the service of a most capable young man, the Assistant Commissioner?—A. Yes.

Q. There was no higher office that he could attain to except your own?—A. That was all. He had the highest position except that of Commissioner.

Q. The young man in question got $3,000 a year?—A. Yes, $3,000 a year.

Q. You have appraisers in different commodities at the principal ports?—A. At the principal ports they are in divisions. There are the dry goods, the grocery, hardware and drugs, divisions. Of course there are other subsidiary divisions mixed in with these, but these are the leading lines.

Q. And the same system is adopted at all the chief ports?—A. At all the city ports. Montreal, Toronto, Quebec, Winnipeg, Halifax, St. John, London, Hamilton, and Vancouver.

Q. Do you find the smuggling tendency increasing or diminishing?—A. I think the tendency is about the same. We are watching them a little better than formerly.

Q. There is a continual attempt to smuggle?—A. Yes, constantly.

By the Chairman:

Q. Going back to the appraisers, these people have to acquire a knowledge of the kinds of goods that are imported and also their value?—A. That is their duty, to appraise.

By Mr. Fyshe:

Q. An appraiser would not be of much good if he did not have a special knowledge of the goods, would he?—A. Except what he would gather from comparing other goods. The appraiser has a series of invoices before him, and he would gather information very rapidly if he has got fair education and ability.

Q. And especially if he has been in the trade?—A. Yes.

By the Chairman:

Q. These men, of course, having the technical knowledge you have to go outside to get them?—A. As a rule; sometimes they are promoted from the service from among clerks that have had training in that branch as appraisers.

By Mr. Fyshe:

Q. Would it not be more justifiable to appoint appraisers from the outside than any other class of officers?—A. I think so.

Q. So it seems to me, because they are in a measure experts?—A. I think the majority of them are taken from the outside. That is the rule.

By Mr. Bazin:

Q. I know in Quebec we have got four?—A. There they all come from the outside.

By the Chairman:

Q. And the highest salary paid an appraiser is $2,000?—A. $2,000 for a good man; that is too low.

Q. Supposing a man were dishonest, having the technical knowledge could he not largely increase his salary by consenting to a system of undervaluation?—A. Well, possibly. It is not very easy but it might be done. There is a large number of officers with the appraiser in the large ports; he is not alone.

Q. There would be a check upon him?—A. There is a check upon him.

Q. An appraiser would therefore have to be honest?—A. I think as a rule they are.

Q. I do not say they are not, because I know nothing about them. What are the gaugers?—A. They are for measuring and testing the strength of liquids.

Q. What are the office hours in the outside service as a rule?—A. The hours for the outdoor officers are from 8 to 6, but in the Custom-house the hours are from 9 to 4. The office is kept open that long for business, and of course the officers have to finish their business for the day before leaving.

Q. Supposing an Allan Line steamer comes into port at 5 o'clock in the morning, what happens?—A. There are officers present to examine the baggage, who get overtime. There are officers who are always in readiness.

Q. So there is no delay no matter at what hour the steamer gets in port?—A. There is always an officer on duty.

By Mr. Fyshe:

Q. What supervision is there upon the outside officers who have to get at work at 8 o'clock in the morning? Who is there to see?—A. The tide surveyor is over the officers.

By the Chairman:

Q. Do the officers in the outside service who have to meet steamers and work after hours get additional remuneration?—A. They are paid 30 cents an hour for services before 8 o'clock in the morning and after 6 o'clock in the afternoon.

Q. Is there a roster kept of the men engaged in this duty? Do the same men come down to meet the steamers day after day?—A. As a rule during the summer.

Q. Does the increased pay apply to the tide waiters and the ordinary landing waiter?—A. The ordinary landing waiter and the tide waiter.

Q. Both get 30 cents an hour overtime?—A. Yes; they are also paid overtime for holidays—the seven or eight holidays we have in the year—that is the outside service. The inside are not.

Q. Is the working out of the Customs tariff more complicated than it should be? —A. Before you reach that I want to say something about the inspectors.

Q. Very well, you can do so?—A. I think the Customs inspectors should be put on the same scale as the Inland Revenue and the Post Office inspectors in order to avoid friction. Then I think our packers and messengers are paid too low. The scale should be increased to $800 as a maximum, and in the case of the appraisers at large ports the scale ought certainly to be increased.

Q. Would you still have the revenue as a test of a large port?—A. To a large extent.

Q. Then I presume you think that generally speaking this schedule ought to be revised for the large ports?—A. Yes, for the large ports.

Q. You are speaking of the packers and messengers. There would be no packers or messengers at small ports where the collector had only $300 a year salary?—A. No.

SESSIONAL PAPER No. 29a

Q. Do you not think the minimum of $300 is very small?—A. You cannot get men for the price at all. You cannot get suitable men to begin at less than $500 where they are needed all the time.

Q. Do you ever appoint inspectors now, at $1,600?—A. We call them assistant inspectors. I do not think we appoint men at $1,600 and call them inspectors. There is another point: The second-class clerks complain that $1,500 is too low a salary and I think it should be increased by $100 at least.

Q. Do you find that the working out of the present Customs tariff has increased your work as compared with former tariffs?—A. I think so, for this reason: In 1892 there was only one tariff, a general tariff. The present tariff has a general tariff, a preference tariff, a surtax, a special or dumping tariff, and then there is the French treaty. . This year there is a new clause put in to protect the revenue in regard to the drawback for home consumption, which gives a great deal of work, but is good security for the revenue.

Q. Then the work has been much increased under the working of the new tariff?— A. I think it is 50 per cent more.

Q. Is smuggling on the increase?—A. I do not think so. In fact so far as the liquor business is concerned it is nearly wiped out, but not altogether.

Q. By vigilance and close watching down the St. Lawrence do you think the smuggling of liquor has been nearly wiped out?—A. Nearly wiped out. Probably most of the smuggling we have is along the frontier in tobacco and small stuff.

Q. Seizures are made of course under information given to the officers of the department?—A, Or to the officer who makes the seizure.

Q. What rate of pay do you give to the informers as a rule?—A. We now give one-fourth of the gross proceeds, as a rule. It is not to exceed one-third of the net proceeds.

By Mr. Fyshe:

Q. Do you think that is a wise arrangement?—A. It secures information that you would not get otherwise.

By the Chairman:

Q. What proportion does the seizing officer get?—A. The same, one-fourth.

Q. What becomes of the other half?—A. It goes into the revenue.

Q. Could there not be a put up job between the informer and the seizing officer to effect a seizure in a certain class of commodities? It used to be done in liquor on the St. Lawrence?—A. It was said to be done in three or four cases in the St. Lawrence, but it is not done now, I do not think it is practicable.

Q. The seizures that are made now are, if the term can be used, 'honest' seizures? —A. I think so. I do not think there is collusion in the seizures now; I am satisfied there is not.

Q. At one time one of the principal officers in the inside Customs service made money by following up seizure work?—A. That is not allowed now. None of the inside officers can participate in seizures.

Q. It is not permitted now for any officers of the inside service to share in the profit from seizures?—A. No. That is regulated by order in council.

Q. You are going to have probably a Customs revenue of $50,000,000 this fiscal year?—A. I think so.

Q. Entries are made in the several Customs offices by the importers?—A. Yes, by the importers in duplicate.

Q. One copy comes here to the department?—A. With the invoices. That is a change which adds to our work.

Q. The other copy is kept at the Custom-house?—A. Yes, at the Custom-house.

Q. And the inspector can look over it when he makes his round?—A. That is his duty.

Q. When the importers make the entries they deposit the moneys?—A. They deposit the moneys.

Q. These moneys are deposited in banks designated by the Finance Department? —A. Yes.

Q. These moneys are remitted daily?—A. At the large ports they are remitted daily.

Q. There is a limit as to the amount that even a collector can hold, is there not? —A. He is supposed to remit all the moneys received. In the smaller ports remittances are made to the department twice a week, but the moneys should be deposited daily in the bank.

Q. What check is there that you get the whole of the duties in the department? —A. There is a statement which comes with the entries, called 'F—1,' being a list of all the entries. That is added up and compared with the deposit receipts placed to the credit of the Receiver General and balanced. There is an absolute check on that.

By Mr. Fyshe:

Q. Is there a deposit made in the bank?—A. A deposit made in the bank to the credit of the Receiver General. We get all the entries—they are numbered in rotation—and we add them up and compare them against the amounts deposited.

By the Chairman:

Q. When remittances are made the original statement is kept by the collector, the duplicate goes to the Department of Customs, and the triplicate and a draft to the Finance Department?—A. Yes, that is the proceeding.

By Mr. Bazin:

Q. How is it that when we draw a cheque for the Inland Revenue Department we have to make that payable to the order of the Receiver General of Canada, whereas when the transaction is with the Customs we give our cheque simply payable to bearer?—A. There would be so many transactions in the Customs that it would be difficult to keep track of them. There are, I suppose, nearly 1,000 entries a day. For instance, at Montreal——

The CHAIRMAN.—I will have to ask about that, because I do not recollect ever receiving a cheque in that way from the Inland Revenue Department.

Mr. BAZIN.—I know the Excise people will not accept our cheque if it is not made payable to the order of the Receiver General of Canada; in fact we get a stamp made especially for that purpose.   —

By the Chairman:

Q. With all this system of checking in Montreal, it is possible for a defalcation to occur like the Hobbs' defalcation?—A. That was by fraud and falsifying documents.

Q. Tell us all about it?—A. The matter is in the courts, and I have not received the full details yet. Hobbs would take two invoices each representing, say, one car of iron. He typewrote the two cars on the one invoice and suppressed the other. That is the way the most of it happened.

Q. And in that special instance the officer of the Customs with whom he dealt was rather a stupid man, was he not?—A. That is alleged. Then the Canadian Pacific Railway, for whom Hobbs was acting, claim that they gave him cheques to cover the whole amount. He deposited the cheques with the Customs cashier, and got the difference back contrary to the orders of the department.

Q. Was there a superior officer over the Customs clerk who dealt with Hobbs?— A. There was. The entries would be checked up by the clerk in the long room, and after that the invoice would go to the appraiser.

SESSIONAL PAPER No. 29a

Q. Where you have intricate machinery some part of it must continually break down. You do not regard this as a loss to the Government; you are still making claim on the Canadian Pacific Railway?—A. Yes, to recover the amount of unpaid duties.

Q. Has the effect of the Hobbs' defalcation been such that additional safeguards have been imposed?—A. I suppose the officers have got a little experience, but very few changes in the rules have been made. If the cashier had obeyed orders, a portion, at least, of the defalcation would not have happened. The rule is that no money is to be returned without cheque. The collector returns by cheque if there is an overplus.

Q. How long a period was this defalcation spread over?—A. About two years.

Q. Hobbs was the entry clerk for the Canadian Pacific Railway?—A. For the Canadian Pacific Railway.

Q. His duties were to enter the contents of all the cars?—A. Everything that was imported by them.

Q. Steel rails, fastenings, coal and everything else?—A. Everything arriving at Montreal.

Q. The entries he made were made almost daily?—A. Yes.

Q. And yet for two years these manipulations were made without being discovered?—A. The great proportion of the entries were right, these defalcations were only special cases.

Q. What was the amount of the defalcation in round numbers?—A. Over $60,-000 of which about $30,000, I am only speaking from memory, were returned. The Customs claim now is something over $30,000.

Q. Was the officer who had to deal with Hobbs a recent appointment?—A. He was a recent appointment, that is, the cashier who received the money. In passing the entries, Hobbs would not be dealing with one clerk, but with various clerks.

Q. Was this man appointed without examination?—A. Yes.

Q. And at an advanced age?—A. I should suppose he would be about fifty, but I am not quite sure about that.

Q. In fact he was a careless man and was put in because of some political influence?—A. I do not know. The former cashier was superannuated, I think.

Q. He was an old man too?—A. Yes, he was an old man.

Q. What sureties are given by the collectors of Customs? In what form?—A. They are under guarantee bonds.

Q. You have no private bonds at all?—A. None whatever.

Q. Does the department pay the premiums?—A. It has been doing so this year.

Q. There is no limit of age in the outside service? A collector may be appointed at sixty years of age?—A. Yes.

Q. He may be appointed at 70 years of age?—A. He may be, as far as the law is concerned.

Q. Very often, when appointed, they are old men?—A. Say fifty years of age.

Q. They have passed their first youth?—A. In the large ports, as a rule, they are men who have seen other service, before appointment.

Q. Coming to the personal equation: What do you think of the salaries that are paid to deputies now?—A. I think they are low compared with the sums paid for services of the same class outside.

Q. Although the revenue will probably be this year $50,000,000, you are paid only $4,000?—A. Yes, $4,000.

Q. Who has the task of adjudicating cases of seizures?—A. The Minister decides on a report from the Commissioner.

Q. Are you invested with magisterial powers?—A. No, I merely require to report.

Q. You decide on the written evidence, do you?—A. On the written evidence.

Q. And then the Minister approves?—A. Approves, or he can decide otherwise if he does not agree to the recommendation in the report. The party has the right of appeal to the court, if dissatisfied with the decision.

Q. The office of informer is not looked upon with great respect by the community. Do you find, as a rule, that the information you get through the informers might be given on account of spite?—A. In some cases it might be.

Q. In some cases an honest trader might be put to inconvenience through a spiteful informer?—A. Well as a rule the case is investigated before action is taken. The nature of the information is sifted by the seizing officer. I do not remember any cases coming before me of that character. The information has come secretly and of course unless secrecy was maintained it would not come at all. The information has perhaps been vouchsafed by employees in the service of the party.

Q. And you are very sure of your ground before seizures are made?—A. As a rule the Chief Inspector, Mr. McMichael has had supervision over the larger portion of them and he sifts the information before he makes a seizure.

Q. How do you pay these informers?—A. They are paid through the collector or through the inspector. The collector will have the name, or the inspector of the special branch. We do not want the name.

Q. It might not be possible that the seizing officer and the informer, if the informer is paid in this way, might have a kind of tacit agreement together?—A. Well, the department agrees to give them a certain sum. There is a declaration especially made that the money has been paid to the proper parties.

Q. Occasionally seizures are made by the seizing officers themselves without the intervention of informers?—A. In some cases.

Q. That of course is perfectly right and legitimate?—A. Yes, if they have the knowledge themselves.

Q. Do you give any commission to the collectors of the different ports now for seizures?—A. The collectors whose salaries do not exceed $2,000 get 5 per cent for distributing.

Q. That still goes on?—A. That still goes on. When the salary is over $2,000 the collector gets nothing. Mr. McMichael, for instance, distributes the largest share of the seizures, but he gets no commission.

By Mr. Fyshe:

Q. Where is he stationed?—A. In Toronto. Seizures are made under his direction, but he only receives a salary.

Q. Why should there be the largest share of the seizures there?—A. It is his special business to look after seizures.

Q. Is there more smuggling there?—A. The smuggling goes on all over the country, but this is a special division with a special branch.

By the Chairman:

Q. You occasionally have a defalcation amongst the collectors? You have one at St. Hyacinthe, I think?—A. No, at Drummondville. That is where there is only one officer.

Q. How long did that defalcation go on?—A. I suppose some months.

Q. That office was inspected, I presume?—A. Yes.

Q. Did the inspector discover the defalcation?—A. Not at first, for the reason that the manifest was destroyed. It was a manifest from Montreal, and he took the last number for the year. You see we have consecutive numbers. Suppose you had twenty from Montreal, he destroyed No. 20, and there was no record against him in the case—and there is where the greatest danger comes in—there was only one officer at the place.

Q. And that happens by the suppression of vouchers?—A. The suppression of vouchers, and it was discovered in this way: There was a transfer of liquor in bond, and there was some question which arose as to where the liquor was. It was traced up, and then the discovery was made that it had not been accounted for. It was done by the suppression of the manifest used in forwarding the goods from one port to the other.

Q. Are the manifests pasted in books in the Customs?—A. No, they are numbered in succession.

Q. Then if a collector omits to put the number and just suppresses the manifest——A. Well, they are numbered in succession. Montreal would give progressive numbers of manifests on Drummondville, starting with 1 at the beginning of the year. If 1 had been suppressed it would have been discovered that that number was missing.

Q. But in this case it was the last one?—A. It was the last one.

Q. About the transhipment of goods in bond. Of course in a place like Montreal or Quebec, where large cargoes are landed, are the goods after being unloaded entered through the local port?—A. No. Unless they are entered for warehouse. They may be entered for warehouse and warehoused.

Q. Take a concrete case. Supposing goods are sent up to Ottawa addressed to H. N. Bate & Sons that have been landed at Quebec or Montreal. How do those goods get to Ottawa?—A. They are forwarded under a manifest signed by the Customs officer at Quebec and by the steamship agent.

By Mr. Bazin:

Q. They are addressed to Ottawa?—A. They are addressed to Ottawa. There are two manifests. One is left at Quebec and the other one comes with the goods. When they are entered here one of the copies goes back to Quebec to show that the goods have been accounted for.

By the Chairman:

Q. It is strange that one of the questions asked by the Commission in 1892 was what was to hinder a collector at a small port from suppressing an invoice and putting it into the fire. That is really what happened at Drummondville?—A. He suppressed the last manifest of the series for the year. I think that can be checked, but our work has of late been so hard that it is difficult to keep pace with it.

Q. You think on the whole your system of inspection is very careful?—A. I think so—that is our check is very good. Of course if you increase the number of inspectors it will make it still more efficient.

Q. You think you get most of the money the treasury should get under the law? —A. I think we do, the great mass of it.

Q. Is it possible for goods of the same quality to be entered at different prices at different ports?—A. There would be some variation. One merchant will buy the same goods cheaper than another. We depend largely on the invoice.

By Mr. Fyshe:

Q. Do you do nothing to equalize them?—A. If it is the actual transaction there is not much done. If the invoice honestly represents the transaction we do not interfere when the difference in the value is trifling.

Q. I do not see how you could?—A. We would otherwise have friction all the time and it is too large a business to secure absolute uniformity therein.

By Mr. Bazin:

Q. I remember for instance, quantities of gin in cases coming from the same shippers. A certain duty would be paid in Quebec and another duty in Montreal?— A. That is measurement.

Q. But it was actually an identical package containing similar bottles?—A. There would be slight variations.

Q. Now the thing has been equalized, and we pay so much on the goods, that is much better.

29a—7

By the Chairman:.

Q. Does it not occasionally happen that there are vacant collectorships in some ports which are not filled up immediately?—A. Occasionally.

Q. That is to say when there is a general election pending or as a matter of political convenience?—A. I do not think there is much of that. There may be a question about the selection of the man. It may take a little while, but as a rule these positions are not kept open very long.

Q. In your outside ports, especially in the case of tide waiters, where you require men of good physical strength do they pass a certain test?—A. I do not think we ask any more than a medical certificate.

Q. You get a medical certificate?—A. As a rule.

Q. A man may be called upon to be up all night or night after night and you will require a strong man?—A. They should be in good health, but as a rule they are not up all night. As a rule we make six hours the limit.

By Mr. Fyshe:

Q. For what?—A. For overtime, six hours continuously. That is only in a few ports like Montreal, Halifax and Quebec.

Q. Might that not go on very frequently week in and week out?—A. It might go on during the summer, but then in winter there is not so much for them to do.

Q. If you had men on duty for sixteen hours in the summer it would be pretty continuously?—A. There would be very few.

By the Chairman:

Q. Under the English regulations they have to be of a certain height, a certain weight, a certain number of inches around the chest and fulfil other requirements. Do you exact anything of that kind?—A. We have no physical test.

Q. Do you require your men to wear uniforms?—A. The officers meeting the public are uniformed now. They are allowed $35 towards the expense of two suits of uniform a year. That is the first year an allowance has been made to that extent. The officers in the inside service are not uniformed.

Q. You do not, as in the case of letter carriers, give the uniforms to them out and out?—A. Our service is so very scattered we prefer they should get the uniforms in their own locality. We supply the buttons and the bands and they supply the rest.

Q. Do any of the railway companies now refund to you the cost of special services?—A. Any Sunday service has to be refunded—we will not pay for any Sunday work—but the balance is borne by the department now.

By Mr. Fyshe:

Q. Do you consider your service efficient?—A. Our inside service is fairly efficient.

,   *By the Chairman:*

Q. And not over-manned?—A. It is not over-manned but under-manned at present because the work has been going on so rapidly it is difficult to keep up with it.

By Mr. Fyshe:

Q. Is there any efficiency test of the work done by each clerk in the service? Is there any authority in the different offices watching the amount of work that each man does?—A. The chief clerk in each division watches over his men and the work is allotted out to them. That is so far as the Customs Department is concerned.

Q. If Mr. Bazin and I go around to your office and the other offices can we see from the books the amount of work done by each clerk?—A. You will see them working.

Q. Could we examine the books and see what their daily and weekly work is?—A. You could see in the Accountant's office what each man does and then there is the checking of the entries.

Q. I would like to figure out whether each man is doing a man's work?—A. You can only tell that by seeing the work he is doing.

Q. Because I think that is the essential point in administrative affairs not only to see that the work is efficiently done but that a full day's work is expected?—A. If the work is not done in the Customs Department you will very soon hear of it. They are chasing us all the time. It is a business department which comes into contact with the public.

Q. What I would like to get at would be the amount of revenue brought in to the Customs-houses and the cost of each?—A. That is published. The cost of collection is less than four per cent.

By the Chairman:

Q. That cost is decreasing?—A. Yes.

Q. As the revenue gets bigger and bigger it costs less to collect?—A. That is the tendency. I think it would be pretty difficult to get it any lower. There are great complaints that salaries are too low.

By Mr. Fyshe:

Q. Would that four per cent include the whole expenses of the department?—A. Outside but not inside.

By the Chairman:

Q. If it occurs to you to supplement your oral evidence in any way you can embody it in a memorandum, and we will be glad to receive it from you?—A. Very good. I desire to draw the attention of the Commission to this volume which is published monthly. It is a detailed statement of imports and exports for each month up to the end of the financial year, for the nine months ending March. It is one of the heaviest works that the staff has to turn out at Ottawa. There are some eighty men employed on it, and also on the annual report.

Q. This is the work of the Statistical Branch of the department?—A. The information contained in this volume is compiled from the entries made at the ports, item by item.

By Mr. Fyshe:

Q. When I asked you if your staff was efficient and you replied that it was so far as regards the inside service, did you mean to convey the idea that the outside administration is not as efficient?—A. I do not think the clerks in the outside service, on the whole, are as efficient as in the inside service because the latter is the supervising division.

Q. And they are under a better supervision?—A. Certainly, they are all under one head.

Q. There is very much better supervision than there is on the outside?—A. The outside service is scattered.

Q. There is much to be trusted to the conscientiousness of the individual?—A. Yes. The officers are selected more carefully for the inside service—that is to say the pressure of members is not so great as on the outside, the local pressure.

Q. But of course the outside service is infinitely larger than the inside?—A. Yes. I think the salaries paid the inside service amount to only $150,000 a year, whereas our expenditure for salaries is above a million dollars.

Q. I suppose the tendency is not to make the work simpler, or to make the tariff simpler?—A. It has been getting more complex.

29a—7½

Q. That is rather disadvantageous, is it not?—A. Yes, for administrative purposes.

Q. It requires more labour and produces less results?—A. I do not know that it produces less results.

Q. I mean in the way of income?—A. I do not know that it does. It is a pretty good revenue-producing tariff; the results show that.

Witness discharged.

The following suggestions are respectfully submitted:—

Inside Service of the Customs.

1. That employees of the Third Class comprise messengers, packers and employees required to pass the Preliminary Examination only,—the maximum salary to be increased to say $800 a year.

2. The salaries of the Junior Second Class to range from $700 to $1,200 a year for clerks who pass the Qualifying Examination,—clerks possessing special qualifications to enter at $800.

3. The maximum salary in the Second Class to be increased to $1,600.

4. The maximum salary in the First Class to be increased to $2,000.

5. Grade 'A' Chief Clerks to be abolished and the maximum salary of a chief clerk to be raised to $2,800.

6. Annual increase in the Third Class and the Junior Second Class to be $50.

7. Annual increase in the higher classes to be $100.

8. That the salary of the Assistant Commissioner of Customs be not less than that of the Assistant Deputy Postmaster General, or the Assistant Deputy Minister of Finance.

As to the Outside Service of the Customs.

9. That the Schedule be revised, striking out packers, messengers and tide waiters, and classifying them at preventive officers.

10. That in view of the increased cost of living, the maximum salaries be raised at the large ports as follows, viz.:—

Assistant Surveyors	$1,400
Appraisers	2,400
Assistant Appraisers	1,800
Gaugers	1,400
Clerks	1,400
Examining Officers	1,200

11. That Inspectors of Customs be paid at the same rate as Post Office Inspectors and Inspectors of Inland Revenue,—maximum say about $2,800 a year.

DEPARTMENT OF CUSTOMS,
OTTAWA, June 6, 1907.

THOS. S. HOWE, Esq.,
Secretary, Civil Service Commission.

SIR,—Referring to your letter of the 3rd instant I have the honour to inclose Memoranda respecting the Department of Customs in reply to the request of the Civil Service Commission.

I have the honour to be, sir,
Your obedient servant,

(Sgd.)   JOHN McDOUGALD,
Commissioner of Customs.

MEMORANDUM RESPECTING THE DEPARTMENT OF CUSTOMS.

Fiscal Year ended June 30, 1892.

1 Chief clerk,
5 First-class clerks,
11 Second-class clerks,
7 Third-class clerks,
2 Messengers,
1 Packer.

27—Total salaries for year.. .. .. $36,834.81
No extra clerks or messengers in 1892.
   Paid from outside votes—
4 Permanent officers, salaries for the year.. .. ..   2,869.40

       Total for 1892ˈ .. .. ·· $39,704.21

Fiscal Year ended June 30, 1906.

3 Chief clerks,
8 First-class clerks,
15 Second-class clerks,
18 Junior Second-class clerks,
3 Third-class clerks,
1 Messenger.

48—Total salaries for year.. .. .. $57,887.49
   Paid from outside votes—
63 permanent officers,
39 temporary officers.

102—Total salaries for year.. .. ..   *91,769.20

       Total for 1906.. .. .. $149,656.69

80 out of 150 employed on statistics.
There were no special votes for the Department of Customs in either 1892 or 1906.
NOTE.—The above total for 1906 includes the salaries of officers engaged in compiling Customs Statistics at Ottawa as follows: Payable out of vote for Board of Customs.
Officers employed in the Statistical Branch of the Customs Department; 45 permanent and 20 temporary, the salaries paid in 1905-6 amounted to $57,354.25.
The greater part of this work was done at the ports outside in 1892.
A detailed *Monthly* Statement of Imports and Exports has been issued by the Customs Department since 1900, involving a large amount of work not undertaken in 1892.

    Customs duties collected in 1892.. .. .. $20,550,581 53
    Customs duties collected in 1906.. .. ..   46,671,101 20

Dominion of Canada.	1892.	1906.
	No.	No.
Customs Ports	110	132
" Outports..	245	288
" Stations	173	192

MONTREAL, Thursday, September 12, 1907.

The Commission resumed at 2 p.m.

Mr. HENRY McLAUGHLIN, Surveyor, Customs Department, Montreal, called, sworn and examined.

By the Chairman:

Q. You are the Surveyor of the port of Montreal?—A. I am sir,—we have prepared a memorial which I desire to submit to the Commission.

(Memorial of the Customs staff of the Port of Montreal read.)

Q. Next to the collector, you are the chief officer at the port?—A. Yes, sir.

Q. How long have you been in the service?—A. Twenty-six years.

Q. What grades have you passed through?—A. I started on the wharf checking cargoes, and graduated from that to examining packages at the depots and checking that, and from that to a clerkship and finally to accountant, tide surveyor and surveyor.

Q. Is there an accountant now in the department?—A. Well, we have an accountant, but not as such, there is no official appointed, he is appointed as chief clerk, Mr. McKenna, he is chief clerk acting in capacity of accountant.

Q. You served in all capacities until you were appointed to your present position?—A. Yes, sir.

Q. Now, as regards the first thing, which is the question of salaries the Customs Department unlike the Post Office and the Inland Revenue have no fixed statutory increases have they?—A. None whatsoever.

Q. Not in any port of the Dominion?—A. Not in any port of the Dominion so far as I know.

Q. The chief officer has his salary based on the amount of revenue has he not?—Not for the Customs, no. The Post Office are based on a matter of revenue, but not for the Customs.

Q. But there is a limit to this extent that whether the revenue is $2,000,000 or $20,000,000 that the collector and other men could not get over certain amounts?—A. Not in the Customs service. I do not think they give a limit to the salaries so far.

Q. The chief clerk could not get more than $2,000?—A. No.

Q. And the Act limiting the salary to $2,000 was passed in 1892?—A. I could not exactly state the year.

Q. And that has been the limit for fifteen years without revising the amount?—A. Yes.

Q. Now the prices of commodities having increased 40 per cent as you say, although the revenue has trebled you could not get more than $2,000?—A. When I joined the service twenty-six years ago the collector at the port received $4,500 and the surveyor $2,500 and the chief clerk had $2,000. I have a memorandum prepared here dealing with that question showing the number of officers and the average salary of each class.

Q. Will you please put that in?

(Memorandum filed and read.)

Q. I suppose the assistant appraiser does practically the same work as the appraiser?—A. He assists in the examination of the goods and the appraiser deals with the invoices and the Department.

Q. Why are some called examining officers?—A. Some years ago, three years ago, the department created a new office called 'examining officers,' in order to appoint officers to that position who had been more than three years in the service and who were able to pass the examination in the duties of office, and the Government created that position with the name 'examining officer' so that officers heretofore known as 'tide waiters' and 'lockers' could obtain an increase of salary without passing what we call the Qualifying examination, which is rather difficult and includes a lot of things not called for by our duties. By the creation of the grade of examining officers the Department was enabled to relieve those men from the disability imposed upon them by their failure to pass the Qualifying examination, while they were good men for the work of the department.

Q. What are the duties of the tide waiter?—A. Originally they were supposed to be men dealing with the cargo on the docks and at the freight sheds, men who were dealing with the freight entirely. I might explain to you in connection with the small number of 'tide waiters' on the staff that it is owing to the fact that last April the Preventive Officers staff was increased by the addition of nearly all the tide waiters to that staff in order to enable the department to increase the salaries of those men who had been previously graded as tide waiters.

Q. Do collectors at the outside ports have private business to attend to besides acting as collectors?—A. Oh, no, they are entirely in the service of the Customs Department.

Q. What is the extra salary they get?—A. Well, some of them receive a small salary as sub-collectors of the Inland Revenue Department as well as their salary as Customs collectors, but they do not get more than $200 in addition to their salary on that account.

Q. How can you get a responsible man to handle the money and do his duty conscientiously for $500 salary?—A. Apparently they get them.

Q. You know in the Post Office that the salary is increased by annual increments?—A. Yes.

Q. Well, in the outside service of that Department the salaries are increased by annual increases?—A. We understand that.

Q. And in the Inland Revenue men get only increments of 5 per cent?—A. Five per cent according to their class.

Q. Now, with regard to the thirty-one clerks and the seventy preventive officers—the clerks range from $400 to $1,200 per year according to schedule; so, in the Customs service there are no annual increments in between those?—A. None whatever.

Q. The Customs differ from the Inland Revenue and the Post Office Departments in that when you are appointed at the minimum or between the minimum salaries no provision is made for annual increments?—A. None whatever.

Q. And when officers arrive at the maximum laid down there is no increase at all?—A. There is a possibility of being made a chief clerk.

Q. I know, but that is in the way of promotion?—A. Yes.

Q. No clerk can get beyond $1,200?—A. No.

Q. And the collector cannot get beyond $4,000 and the surveyor $2,400?—A. No, and the appraiser cannot receive more than $2,000.

Q. You differ from the Inland Revenue and the Post Office Departments in the fact that within the limits of your class there are no annual increments?—A. I cannot say that there are no annual increments, because a few receive it every year, but there are no fixed annual increments.

Q. To obviate the position of affairs, and try and get some additional remuneration in proportion to the increase in the price of commodities, there have been grants made within the limits of the class within the last twelve months, have there not?—A. Yes.

Q. How much was distributed in Montreal?—A. Roughly speaking, about $25,000.

Q. But none who had come up to the maximum of his class could participate in that distribution?—A. No, sir, the collector of the port could not participate.

Q. And those clerks who have arrived at the maximum of $1,200?—A. No.

Q. There was a distribution of $25,000 to the people in the Customs service at the port of Montreal within the limits of their respective classes?—A. Yes, sir; last April.

Q. Now, with regard to the general increase of salaries, what is your idea about that? You are speaking for the staff generally, are you not?—A. Yes. Well, my idea would be in accordance with the memorial, that there should be statutory increases on the recommendation by the Head of the Department.

Q. Candidly, I think the unsatisfactory condition with regard to increases in the Customs service has been detrimental?—A. It has been most deplorable.

Q. Like the outside services in other departments there should be in the Customs annual increments, you consider?—A. Yes.

Q. In passing from one class to the other, you think it is necessary to go through Promotion examination?—A. Yes, we recommend an examination on duty of office only.

Q. Under whose supervision would you like to have that?—A. Well, it has been done so far under the supervision of the Inspectors here.

Q. Who are your two inspectors?—A. Mr. O'Meara and Mr. Lemieux.

Q. You consider that the present system is rather cumbrous, I suppose?—A. Well, it is awkward because you will find in Montreal men in different classes performing different duties, and they have been unable to get out of doing those different duties owing to the fact that examinations have been obligatory heretofore.

Q. Once a Customs officer always one, and once a Customs officer appointed at the port of Montreal they never can leave that port?—A. We have a few transferred occasionally to Ottawa.

Q. That is in the statistical branch, that is another thing; but if a vacancy should occur in the Customs at Sydney, no man in Montreal could succeed to it?—A. That has never happened, anyway.

Q. You want a change in the classification and statutory increases. All the officers here are appointed by passing the Qualifying examination, are they not as a rule?—A. Most of them.

Q. Appraisers are sometimes appointed for technical knowledge?—A. And on examination under the Customs Act and Orders in Council.

Mr. WILLIAM DRYSDALE.—I would like to say a word on behalf of the appraisers. The appraisers, I might say, are officers who collect the revenue. We collect the revenue and see to it that the people pay the proper rate of duty, preventing fraud as far as possible. The salary paid is quite inadequate for the technical knowledge required to be a good appraiser. I am quite sure Mr. McLaughlin will agree with that, that the appraisers need some special consideration. They are a class mentioned by themselves in the statute, and in other places, in the United States, I find that the salaries paid to appraisers are about three times the amount paid in Canada.

Q. You have not been long in the service, Mr. Drysdale?—A. No, sir, three years.

The examination of Mr. McLAUGHLIN resumed.

Q. There are three chief clerks, did they go through the several stages like yourself, Mr. McLaughlin?—A. They did, all of them, I believe.

Q. Well, now, with reference to the several appraisers, as a rule they are appointed without examination in the beginning?—A. They are appointed temporarily before they are given a permanent appointment by Order in Council.

Q. It is not to be presumed that within the ranks of the Customs Department or any other branch of the Public Service you could select men who know all about silk or cheese and who would be as competent to act as appraisers as persons taken from the outside who were engaged in business?—A. Certainly.

Q. Therefore, usually the appraiser is temporarily appointed?—A. Yes.

Q. After examination?—A. No, he is assigned to duty six months on probation and then is examined on the Customs Act and Orders in Council.

SESSIONAL PAPER No. 29a

Q. The thirty-one clerks have all passed their Qualifying examination, I suppose?
—A. Yes, or they could not be appointed.

Q. The preventive officers are appointed politically?—A. No, they are appointed
from the staff, they are most of them brought up from the tide-waiters, the majority
of them. If you will look at the Civil Service List, you will find last year a great
number of tide-waiters, while an examination of this year's will show that they have
disappeared.

Q. 'Collectors and preventive officers in the Customs Department may be appointed without examination'?—A. Yes, they are appointed without examination.

Q. The seventy preventive officers were appointed without examination?—A. No,
not without examination; about fifty of them passed the Preliminary examination for
tide-waiters and from that went to preventive officers without examination.

Q. Do you find that you have men graded as in one class and doing duty in another class?—A. Yes.

Q. For instance, we find that in the Post Office, postmen or letter carriers were
doing clerks' work and because they were doing clerks' work they lost privilege of wearing uniform and of being carried free on the cars. Have you in the Custom-house
here people that are graded in the lower class and doing the work of a superior class?—
A. Yes.

Q. Does that exist to any extent?—A. Well, a few, probably fifteen or twenty of
them.

Q. What is the reason of that?—A. You take the lower class tide-waiters for instance, they are not able to pass the Qualifying examination, while they are fit to do
the work, their ability is equal to doing the work of a higher grade, although they could
not pass the examination.

Q. They are employed at superior work although they had not passed the examination?—A. That is it.

Q. It was not the fact that you put these men in to do the work dreading that the
politicians would ask you to appoint incompetent men?—A. No.

Q. There was no dread of the politicians in this arrangement?—A. No.

Q. In the supernumerary list you have all sorts of salaries among that total of
seventy-three. Have these men on the supernumerary list passed the examination?—
A. No.

Q. Who nominates them?—A. They are nominated by the department at Ottawa, the Minister of Customs.

Q. I suppose you only have to guess how the Minister of Customs gets their
names?—A. They do not tell us.

Q. The Minister of Customs would not know anything of any man living down
here?—A. Oh, yes, the pay-sheets go to Ottawa from here.

Q. Yes, but the Minister who sends down the name of Mr. So-and-So to be appointed would not know that there was such a man personally?—A. No, he probably
gets the recommendation from somebody else.

Q. The names of those seventy-three temporary men came from Ottawa?—A.
Yes, direct to the collector.

Q. Are those people on the supernumerary list employed all the year around?—
A. Yes, last winter we employed everybody because the collections were equal to those
of the summer.

Q. In the good old days you laid them off in the winter?—A. Yes, about ten or
twelve were laid off.

Q. But you employ everybody now all the year around?—A. Yes, because last
winter our collections were in excess of those of the summer.

Q. You wish that Promotion examinations from class to class should be on the
duties of office only?—A. Yes, sir.

Q. Do you think there is any absolute necessity for a Promotion examination?
—A. Well, Promotion examinations, as we have them now, include duties of office, but
they include other subjects that are foreign to the duties of the office.

7-8 EDWARD VII., A. 1908

Q. In the English Public Service where it is entirely by open competition, after the examinations for the entrance, they have no such thing as Promotion examination afterwards?—A. I am not familiar with the custom there at all.

Q. If efficient men could be got to enter the public service at the beginning after competitive examination, do you think that Promotion examinations would then be necessary?—A. I think so, yes.

Q. How long have these seventy-three people been on the supernumerary list?— They vary, some of them have probably been supernumeraries for ten years, and some of them more than that.

Q. You ask that after three years of that purgatory they should be appointed permanently?—A. Yes.

Q. Despite the fact that they have not passed the other examination?—A. Well, you see in the Customs here we have the examining warehouse where the duties involve more manual labour and an examination of any kind is absolutely useless except that it is necessary that a man should be able to read and write, and in their case it would be a good thing if the examination was abolished or else that it was made simply an examination as to their fitness for the duties they are called upon to perform.

Q. Do you not think that in three years' service a man might not cram up the subjects in order to pass the examination?—A. Some might and others might not.

Q. Do you think if it has been found desirable, and the law lays it down that there shall be an entrance examination, that you would get over it by saying that people should be appointed after three years' temporary service?—A. They get over it now by creating the grade of examining officer, of course, they pass an examination in the duties of office and the simple rules of orthography.

Q. Then there is no particular reason in your recommendation that they should become permanent after three years?—A. Well, they do not always appoint them, some of them are ten years there and have not been made examining officers.

Q. Is it a matter of selecting and appointment of some and the non-appointment of others?—A. Sometimes a man may be there ten years and may be passed over, he may not attempt any examination.

Q. A man who was appointed as temporary officer before 1896 may stay there forever?—A. If they appointed them regularly.

Q. You say they have staid there ten years or over?—A. Nearly all the old ones have been appointed now.

Q. Does it not happen that some of those on the supernumerary list are there because they were appointed by another party?—A. No, not to my knowledge, in fact I think all those who are there now have been appointed by this administration.

Q. You say the cost of living has increased from 40 per cent to 50 per cent?—A. Yes.

Q. Has anybody got the record of their yearly expenditure fifteen years ago as compared with the present time?—A. We know that from our own personal experience.

Q. But it would strengthen us greatly if we were furnished with a budget of that information?—A. We can give you a copy of that statement which was presented to the Minister last winter when we gave a detailed statement of the cost of commodities.

Q. Of course, since then milk has gone up to 10 cents?—A. I can furnish an instance of a house which ten years ago rented at $15 per month and is now $27.50.

Q. You can let us have a copy of that memorial with the prices brought up to date can you?—A. Yes.

Q. How does the staff compare now with what it was when the last Civil Service Commission sat in 1892, has it been largely increased in the last fifteen years?—A. No, our percentage of cost of collection is less.

Q. I meant the staff numerically?—A. In '91 we had 213 in the Port of Montreal, that was sixteen years ago, and we have now 273, that is including the outports.

SESSIONAL PAPER No. 29a

Q. You have increased 60, not quite one-third in that time?—A. Yes, and our revenue is treble, and the port is enlarged, and we have stations four miles from the port where we have four or five men stationed.

Q. You also request that the maximum salaries as allowed by law should be paid to the staff in Montreal which is the chief port?—A. I do.

Q. Do you think it desirable that there should be a difference made between two places?—A. Well, in view of the large collection and the amount of labour involved in collecting it we do.

Q. Although Toronto might not have as large revenue as Montreal, living in Toronto I presume costs as much as it does in Montreal?—A. Well, although not mentioning other ports we meant it to apply to chief ports like Toronto and Montreal.

Q. That part of your memorial does not apply exclusively to Montreal?—A. No.

Q. And, of course, in this revenue you collect here you collect for other ports in the Dominion?—A. Very little.

Q. Is not most of the revenue collected on goods consigned to Montreal which are destined for other places?—A. Nine-tenths of the goods destined for other points go through in bond. Another point I want to emphasize is that while we derive no revenue from these goods that travel through here to the interior and to points in Europe, we have the handling of the manifests, &c., but we get no revenue from those goods, although we have a lot of work to do in connection with them.

Q. You keep no record of them?—A. We keep an absolute record of them.

Q. I am glad you have brought that out, because it would seem on the face of it to the uninitiated that part of this revenue at Montreal was derived from goods that merely passed through en route to other places?—A. We issued 38,000 manifests, which will cover 38,000 cars of goods, upon which we did not receive one cent of revenue; they were distributed all over the Dominion, and that will be greater than any other port in the Dominion by 35,000 cars.

Q. You state in the memorial that the emoluments of some officers are less than the wages paid to corporation labourers. What is the cost of labour here in Montreal? .—A. $2 per day to the corporation labourers.

Q. And some of your clerks get only $500 and $550?—A. Yes.

Q. When one of the Allan ships, or any of those other ships come in, what are office hours?—A. While working in the harbour they come on duty at 7 in the morning and stay until six, but they earn some overtime, and on four nights in the week they remain from 6 until 12.30; that is, on Mondays and Tuesdays; they are off Wednesday, and on Thursday and Friday, for which they receive extra pay at 30c. per hour.

Q. Well, if the *Empress* comes in to-night, for instance, the staff of the Custom house go down to receive her?—A. Yes.

Q. And they are paid extra?—A. Yes, 30c. per hour.

Q. For whatever time it is, day or night?—A. No, in the daytime, of course, it is in their regular hours.

Q. But before seven o'clock in the morning or after six in the evening, whatever time the vessel comes into port, the Customs officer gets extra pay?—A. 30c. an hour.

Q. Have the officers any uniform?—A. Yes, a blue cloth sacque suit, brass buttons and a cap.

Q. And they have winter coats, and some other clothes?—A. Well, that is not provided every year.

Q. Does the extra pay constitute any material addition to the ordinary officer's salary?—A. Some of them, but they are all low grade salaried men who receive these fees.

Q. The clerks would not get any of this extra pay?—A. No, except where you put a clerk to perform the duties of tidewaiter or outside work.

Q. That is in the case we have mentioned where a man may be graded in one class and work in another?—A. And work in another.

7-8 EDWARD VII., A. 1908

Q. In the Montreal Customs Office are there any men who have been brought from other ports; you have sent men to the department at Ottawa?—A. We have exchanged a few with Ottawa, one or two.

Q. Yes, they have gone up to the statistical branch?—A. Yes, they have given us a man in the place of one of them.

Q. But, as a rule, if a man is appointed to the Custom House at Montreal he stays here all the days of his career?—A. Yes.

Q. Do you find that men applying for employment in the Customs now are as efficient as they used to be in the old days?—A. I do not notice any difference.

Q. Do you think that with the present rates of pay efficient men are attracted to the Public Service?—A. I think we would get more efficient men if we had greater emoluments to offer them.

Q. You do not think that the new-comers are less efficient than the men appointed years ago?—A. I think they compare favourably with the average.

Q. Have any men resigned their positions in the Customs House to better their positions?—A. I think about two have in my time.

Q. These supernumerary men, do they stay all the time or do they come in or go out? Do they resign?—A. No.

By Mr. Fyshe :

Q. Do you think you get a fair day's work out of the employees?—A. I do, but the hours are long and the work is hard.

Q. They are not accustomed to loaf?—A. No, not so far as we can see; we have no trouble with them.

By the Chairman :

Q. Coming to the question of the Pension Act, under the old Superannuation scheme there was a deduction of a certain percentage of salary?—A. Yes.

Q. And in the course of time many men have died without receiving a cent back?—A. Yes, I have known of some very sad cases that way.

Q. You suggest that if any pension scheme is re-enacted provision should be made for the widows and others dependent upon men in the service who should be provided for?—A. We haven't made that specific item on the memorial, but we are in sympathy with that proposition. We recommend that Superannuation be re-established.

Q. You are in sympathy rather with the extension of the Superannuation?—A. Yes.

Q. And you think it would add to the stability of the service?—A. Yes.

Q. It would be an inducement to good men to enter the service?—A. Yes.

Q. And to remain in the service?—A. I think so.

Q. And you would expect better service?—A. I think men would give better service if they felt that their families would be provided for.

Q. You ask at the end that we adjust that, and that a period of service be added?—A. We have quite a number who have served ten years on the supernumerary list, and their Superannuation would only date from the Order in Council appointing them permanently.

Q. Rather you would suggest that in calculating their Superannuation they should be given credit for the time during which they were on the supernumerary list?—A. Yes.

Q. Have you any other remark you would like to make?—A. None, except some of the other gentlemen have any ideas to offer.

Witness retired.

Mr. HENRY McLAUGHLIN recalled.

By the Chairman:

Q. Mr. Drysdale mentioned the case of seizures, is there any extensive revenue derived by the officers in the Montreal Custom-house by seizures now?—A. Well, there are some cases. A year ago last May the Department abolished the participation by the port officers in the investigation of seizures where under valuation had passed the thirty days' limit, so that in a case where the under-valuation was three months old it would be sent to Ottawa, so that practically that source of revenue has been cut away.

A. Did that amount to much?—A. Some years it would amount to a few thousand dollars.

Q. And that was distributed among the whole crowd?—A. Yes.

Q. And now that is done away with?—A. Yes, except in the cases of smuggling. If an officer comes across a case of smuggling three years old he can make the seizure and take the benefit.

Q. If a person on the *Victorian* attempts to pass through a lot of goods, what would that officer get?—A. It may be one-fourth, at the discretion of the Minister, but in very few instances, if the case is a large one, have they ever been given the full amount.

Q. Why I was asking this question was that in taking cognizance of the salaries of the different officials, I have asked about extra pay, and I wanted to know whether it was a very large amount in this case?—A. It is very small, you will find, from the Auditor General's Report that it has been very small in Montreal.

Q. Beyond the overtime, and possibly an amount on account of seizures, does any officer at the port of Montreal receive anything directly or indirectly in addition to his salary?—A. Nothing whatsoever.

Witness retired.

CUSTOMS CANADA,
PORT OF MONTREAL, September 11, 1907.

THOS. S. HOWE, Esq.,
Secretary Civil Service Commission.

DEAR SIR,—The following officers of Customs, acting on behalf of the staff of the Port of Montreal, desire to appear before the Commission for the purpose of presenting a memorial, and would respectfully request that an hour be fixed at which they may so appear:—

Henry McLaughlin, A. A. Lantier, W. J. McKenna, A. E. Giroux, J. M. Bessette, L. A. Jacques, Wm. Drysdale, J. Z. Corbeil, H. N. Isaacson.

Yours truly,

(Sgd.) W. J. McKENNA,
Secretary.

Telephone, Main 407.

CUSTOMS CANADA,

PORT OF MONTREAL.

Memorandum Re Staff in month of August, 1907:—

Appointed Officers,—

1 Collector at $4,000 per annum (maximum paid).
1 Surveyor at $2,000 per annum (maximum $2,400). Present Surveyor has over
25 years of service.
3 Chief Clerks at $1,350, $1,400 and $1,600, or average salary of $1,450 (maximum for class, $2,000). Average service, 34 years.
1 Tide Surveyor at $1,200 (maximum paid).
6 Appraisers from $1,500 to $1,800 per annum. Average salary $1,700. (Maximum is $2,000).
15 Assistant Appraisers from $900 to $1,400. Average $1,090. (Maximum fixed at $1,500).
31 Clerks from $600 to $1,200. (Maximum fixed at $1,200). Average salary $970—8 at maximum.
70 Preventive Officers, ranging from $650 to $1,400, acting as tidewaiters, lockers, clerks, chief lockers, warehouse keeper and cashiers. Average salary $743. (No maximum salary fixed for this class).
53 Examining Officers ranging from $650 to $1,000 and averaging $753—acting as clerks, lockers, packers, tidewaiters, &c. (Maximum of this class is $1,000 and four officers are receiving maximum).
2 Assistant Gaugers at $800 and $1,100, respectively. (Maximum for class is $1,200).
3 Tidewaiters—two at $500 and one at $600—two of whom are acting as stampers in Long Room. (Maximum for this class is $600).
6 Landing Waiters ranging $650 to $1,000—and averaging $817 per annum. (Maximum for class is $1,000, at which figure there is one officer).
3 Lockers ranging from $700 to $950 (maximum of class is $1,000). Locker at $900 acting as clerk. Average salary $800.
1 Cheese Inspector at $1,000.
4 Sub-Collectors at Outports—Joliette, $900; St. Jérôme, $600; St. Regis, $500; Dundee, $650.
Making a total of 200 appointed officers on list.

Supernumerary List,—

1 officer at $ 500 per annum.
1   "   550   "
17   "   600   "
35   "   650   "
8   "   700   "
2   "   60 per month.
1 . "   800 per annum.
1   "   900   '
1   "   1,200   "   (Acting Assistant Appraiser.)
1   "   1,600   "   (Acting Appraiser).
3 boys at $22.50, $20 and $30 per month respectively.
1 outport officer (Marieville) at $100.
1   "   (Trout River) at $400.
Making a total of 73 supernumerary or extra officers on list.
Grand total of officers at Montreal and outports, 273.

Total collections of Customs duties during five months of fiscal year 1907-8 (to August 31) were $7,539,539.59.

Cost to government for salaries of permanent officers and extra staff, 1.20 per cent. Total cost of collections, including salaries, cartage of examination packages and general contingencies, 1·35 per cent.

Customs, Canada, Sept. 12, 1907.
Accountant's Branch, Montreal.

CUSTOMS, CANADA, PORT OF MONTREAL, September 12, 1907.

To the Members of the Civil Service Commission:

GENTLEMEN,—The undersigned delegates, duly appointed for the purpose by the officers of Customs at the port of Montreal, beg leave to commend to your favourable consideration the following subjects:—

1. A general increase in salaries.
2. A change in the classification of Customs officers in the outside service, with minimum and maximum salaries attaching to each class, and statutory increases in salary.
3. Promotion from class to class on passing examination on duties of office only.
4. Provision for the permanent appointment of acting officers after three years of supernumerary service.
5. Re-enactment of the Superannuation Act.

Dealing with these points seriatim, we believe it unnecessary to dwell at any length upon the request for a general increase in salaries of Customs officers. The representations already made you by the inside service as to the increased cost of living in Ottawa apply with equal if not greater force in Montreal. It is twenty years since the schedule of salaries of Customs officers was framed, and in that period the cost of living in this city has risen from 40 to 50 per cent. Moreover, the work of the staff has enormously increased. From a total of $6,000,000 twelve years ago, the Customs collections at this port have risen to upwards of $17,000,000 in the current year, or nearly three-fold, while in the same period the numerical strength of the staff has grown less than 30 per cent. The result is to materially enlarge the responsibility and work of individual officers. We beg to submit also that the maximum salaries provided by law should be paid at the chief port of Canada, while as a matter of fact only two or three of the higher officials in the port are so paid. Down to a very recent period the wages of scores of officers at this port holding responsible positions were on a par with, and in some instances lower than those of corporation labourers, and are yet considerably below the wages of the mechanic class and the clerical class in mercantile establishments. In justice to those presently in the service, therefore, we submit that a salary increase is called for, and if such an increase is made a better class of men than now seek entrance to the service will be available as vacancies arise.

Coming to the second point, that of the classification of officers, we may observe that Customs officers in the outside service now consist of collectors, surveyors, chief clerks, chief landing waiters, landing waiters, tide surveyors, tidewaiters, clerks, appraisers, gaugers, chief lockers, lockers and packers, thirteen classes in all. In many instances the designations are misnomers, the rank of the officer having no relation to the character of the work performed. Thus a tidewaiter may perform the duties of a locker, a locker the duties of a landing waiter, a landing waiter the duties of a clerk, and so on. We would recommend that the staff be constituted by statute of the following classes: Collectors, surveyors, chief clerks, appraisers, gaugers, first, second and third class clerks, and packers and truckers. The rank of collector and of his chief executive officer, the surveyor, as well as of the officers possessing technical knowledge, namely, appraisers and gaugers, it is proposed to retain, while all other officers are divided into grades of clerks, save the packers and truckers who perform merely manual labour. A maximum and minimum salary should be attached to each rank, with statutory increase from minimum to maximum of each class, subject to good behaviour and on the favourable report of the collector, concurred in by the commissioner and approved by the Minister.

The promotion from the third-class clerkship to second-class clerkship, and so on, to a chief clerkship, should, in our opinion, be based on an examination on duties of office only, and not on an academic examination on subjects absolutely foreign to the work performed, always, of course, under reservation of good behaviour and the favourable report of the head of the port.

If the staff were so graded and arranged, an incentive to good and faithful service would be held out, officers knowing that promotion in rank and salary would hinge upon merit and not upon influence, and the result could hardly be otherwise than beneficial both to the public and the service.

We have no recommendation to make as respects the manner of obtaining entrance into the Customs service, that being a matter with which we cannot properly concern ourselves.

Finally, we request the re-enactment of the Superannuation system. The principle of a Superannuation law has never, we believe, been seriously opposed, hostile criticism which led to the repeal of the Act a few years ago being based on the considerable annual charge imposed on the country. That, however, is a matter of administration to some extent, and a detail to be dealt with in fixing the annual contribution of officers. When the great corporations of the country, the banks, railways, insurance companies, have deemed it prudent in their own interests to provide a pension system for their employees, and have considered it wise economy to yearly contribute out of their general revenues to the fund, it would seem proper for the government to adopt a similar course towards the Civil Service.

We are prepared to bear our fair share of the cost of a pension system, and if legislation is had in this direction, we would further urge that the Act contain a provision similar to that embodied in the legislation of this province, namely, that the Governor in Council may add to the years of service of an appointed officer, in calculating his superannuation allowance, such period as he may have served as a supernumerary officer. It seems just that the whole period of service should form the basis of superannuation if good conduct through a lengthened period of years produces a pension for old age.

We have the honour to be, sir,

Your obedient servants,

(Signed)	Henry McLaughlin,	Louis A. Jacques,
	A. A. Lantier,	J. Z. Corbeil,
	A. E. Giroux,	J. M. Bessette,
	W. Drysdale,	A. M. Latouche,
	H. N. Isaacson,	W. J. McKenna.

CUSTOMS DEPARTMENT, MONTREAL.

Memo. showing cost of living and increase in price of necessaries of life in ten years.

And now permit us to give a few reasons which we claim entitles us to your consideration.

In the first place: Cost of living for a family of six:—

Rent, per month from $12 to $18, average	$ 15 00
Fuel....................................	4 50
Food....................................	43 00
Furnishings..............................	3 00
Clothing................................	12 00
Schooling...............................	3 00
Medical expense..........................	2 00
Church.................................	2 00
Recreation..............................	3 00
Insurance...............................	4 50
Retiring and guarantee fund...............	2 80
Light and gas...........................	2 00
Help..................................	4 00
Total per month..................	**$100 80**

or $1,209.60 a year. You will observe that the item of food amounts to $43 for a family of six persons for a month. Now, let us see what this means; a family of six with three meals a day equals 540 meals per month. That gives about eight cents per meal per head—not very high living.

We will also quote a few comparisons in prices of market produce, as taken from the leading papers:—

Articles.	1896.	1906.	Percentage of increase.
Pork...............	4-3c. 4c. to 5c.	8c. to 9c.	70
Beef, hind qtrs......	4-3c 4c.	8c.	68
Lamb..............	5c. to 7c.	8c. to 12c.	66
Butter..............	20c.	30c.	50
Eggs..............	14c. to 16c.	30c. to 35c.	106
Potatoes, bag........	40c.	85c. to $1.10	143
Chickens...........	9c.	12c. to 14c.	44
Turkeys............	9c. to 12c.	16c. to 18c.	62
	Average, 76%.		

These are market prices and are lower than store prices. Meats have greatly increased; steaks and roast have risen from 9 and 10 to 16 and 18 cents a pound; lamb and mutton from 10 to 15 and 18 cents; pork about the same; groceries, boots and shoes, dry goods, clothing, in fact everything the officer requires has increased from 10 to 100 per cent in the last ten years.

Mr. WILLIAM DRYSDALE, assistant appraiser, Montreal Customs staff, called, sworn and examined.

By the Chairman:

Q. Well, Mr. Drysdale, what have you to say?—A. I respectfully submit that the appraiser's position is a very responsible one, and that the salary of the chief appraiser is very inadequate for the services rendered.

Q. How long since you were appointed appraiser?—A. Two years.

Q. What was your occupation before that?—A. For thirty-two years I was in the book trade.

Q. You were in the firm of William Drysdale & Company?—A. Yes.

Q. And there being a vacancy here for appraiser in fancy goods, paper of all kinds and books, the government went outside and secured your services?—A. In this connection, I might say that the chief appraiser in our department, Mr. Lunny, has been in the service a long time, and he being a druggist the department thought they would have a man acquainted with the constituent element of the cost of books, and in that way a position became open for myself. They needed a man who had technical knowledge of the book, paper and fancy goods trade, and I having that knowledge, I presume the department thought it was feasible to make the appointment.

Q. What age were you when you came into the service?—A. Fifty-six.

Q. You came in knowing there was no superannuation?—A. I did.

Q. What pay did they give you?—A. I came in on $1,000, and they have since increased it to $1,200, and then by the last increase I got $1,300.

Q. You are one of those happy men who were within the limits, you had not attained the maximum?—A. Yes, I expected when I was appointed that I would get the maximum on account of my technical knowledge, but it seems that was impossible, as I came in and passed the examination.

Q. What is the maximum of the appraisers?—A. The maximum of the assistant appraiser $1,500 and the appraiser $2,000. In former years when the appraiser was appointed and these salaries were no doubt fixed, and while there was no rule in regard to the matter, there was an understanding that they receive some benefit from the seizures. Of course, that was not provided in the statute, but they had it in those days, and they were satisfied with the salary then, because there was a little to be made in that way. But now the appraiser is supposed to know his business so thoroughly that these things are impossible, and therefore he is cut off from what was possible revenue nowadays, and therefore this omission ought to be considered.

Q. You were appointed at $1,000?—A. Yes.

Q. And you have got up to $1,300 and your maximum is $1,500?—A. Yes.

Q. You entered the service with your eyes open?—A. I did.

Q. You are a shrewd Scotchman and knew what was happening?—A. Yes, but, of course, like all others, I had in mind the Scotchman who went into the bank in London as messenger and came out as manager.

Q. And you thought there was an office in which you had a good chance before you?—A. I did not see it in that light, you know.

Q. You thought there was a prospect before you?—A. Yes.

Q. You had evidently not studied the Civil Service. If you, knowing the condition of affairs two years ago, entered the service, you personally have no present reason to complain of the remuneration paid?—A. Well, yes, I can.

Q. One could imagine that because thirty years ago the salaries were fixed, and because the price of commodities has increased and the work has grown that a person who was appointed many years ago might complain, but you were only appointed two years ago?— A. Yes, but at the same time I thought there was a possibility of the matter being put right, and I have great confidence in the gentlemen who have the matter in hand and who have long practical experience in the service, and one of whom is an efficient writer on questions about labour, and I think that the whole staff will get a proper show.

SESSIONAL PAPER No. 29a

Q. You thought when appointed two years ago that things were not right?—A. I thought that the maximum would be paid to the man who had technical knowledge, and having accepted the position, I had retired from the book business, and having a desire to do something—I had no one to succeed me in the book business—this being a nice position and carrying with it some respect, I accepted it.

Q. You did not come in with the intention of doing no work, although you accepted the appointment then when things were not quite satisfactory, you thought they would be made right?—A. I thought it was not possible, when I came in, for Mr. R. J. Lunny, a member of the Pharmaceutical Association, to be working for a salary of $1,200; he was a graduate of the Pharmaceutical Association, a thorough chemist, and had purchased books in connection with his profession, and gone to a good deal of expense qualifying. I found that was all he had when I came in, and he was doing work there for years as chief of that branch and he was only getting $1,200, but since then his position has been improved, though he is still within the maximum, and all the positions, no doubt, will be improved in time. He succeeded Mr. Ambrose.

Q. Is he in the list here?—A. Yes, he is in the Civil Service List.

By Mr. Fyshe :

Q. Do you think your services are of value to the government?—A. Well, yes, I think they have the best of it so far.

Witness retired.

Mr. JOSEPH ZEPHIRIN CORBEIL, Appraiser, Customs Department, port of Montreal, called, sworn and examined.

By the Chairman:

Q. On what point do you desire to address the Commission, Mr. Corbeil?—A. In respect to the superannuation. This (producing document) is the Quebec statute (4 Edward VII., 1904, chapter 10).

Q. Yes, this is a recent statute, I have never looked at that?—A. It says that any employee, after ten years in the service, the government may add to his service the years he may have served as a supernumerary to count for his superannuation. This is the provincial statute for Quebec. I have not much objection to say that instead of ten years, as the Quebec Government says, you should make it fifteen, twenty or even twenty-five years. But if a man has served five, six or seven years as a supernumerary before receiving his permanent appointment then, after whatever period of permanent service the department may think fit to specify, he should be given credit for those years additional which he served as a supernumerary.

By Mr. Fyshe:

Q. Ordinarily would not the years you serve as a supernumerary be taken into account?—A. No, they do not count now.

By the Chairman:

Q. Your idea is that following the Quebec Act whatever term a man serves as temporary or supernumerary officer, should be added to his permanent service?—A. Yes.

Q. If the principle of your proposal is good, why should not the temporary service be counted no matter how long such an officer has been in the permanent service?

29a—8½

—A. That is a matter which, of course, must be left to the Government and this honourable Commission to do what they like.

Q. Do you think the mere fact of putting in a term of years should be taken into consideration—I am only asking in your own case?—A. I think that whatever a man has served should be the basis of his retirement. I might explain my own case. I joined the Custom-house, I entered the service in 1875, under the Mackenzie Government—leaving politics aside of course. And then I was permanently appointed in 1883, that was eight years after I first entered the service. I have only twenty-four years' service to my credit although I have served thirty-two years. Supposing that in three years from this, that will be thirty-five years I have actually served in the employ of the Government, and suppose I feel sick and say, 'well, give me my pension,' they will say you have only twenty-seven years' service. I would say of course that I have been in the service thirty-five years, therefore, I want the regulations made so that those eight years of service on the supernumerary list will count in some way.

By Mr. Fyshe:

Q. What have you done in the matter?—A. We have been up to Ottawa at different times and have offered to pay into the fund what we should have paid during those eight years we were on the temporary staff, and they have said, 'we will take this into consideration.'

Q. The Superannuation Act has been abolished altogether; it has been taken off the statute book. There is no such thing as a Superannuation Act now?—A. I know that.

By the Chairman:

Q. Because there is no Superannuation Act on the statute book we cannot amend it as we desire, we cannot amend that which does not exist?—A. Well, it is in force to a certain extent.

Q. It is only in force to this extent that the people who contribute under that Superannuation Act have not been deprived of their interest, but the principle has been abolished. Your idea is that if the Superannuation Act is re-enacted the whole of a man's time should be calculated when he is leaving the service?—A. Certainly; and in this connection I submit the Order in Council of January 7, 1884, by which the principle we are contending for was recognized.

(Copy of Order in Council filed.)

Witness retired.

Exhibit referred to by Mr. Corbeil.

Montreal sitting. September 12.

Re Superannuation.

Order in Council, January 7, 1884.—The Board has under consideration the fact that several recommendations to place temporary officers on the permanent list has been referred to them for report.

The Board, in compliance with the law, have recommended favourably on the cases submitted to them, but at the same time the Board have to direct the notice of the Council to the fact that the placing of these officers on the permanent list has the effect of bringing them under the operation of the Superannuation Act, and that hitherto no provision has been made for the payment of abatements on the pay of these officers while temporarily employed, although their temporary service counts on retirement.

The Board now recommends to Council that from and after the 1st inst., it shall be optional with temporary officers, on receiving permanent appointments, to place themselves, as regards their temporary services, under the operation of the Superannuation Act; but that in the cases where officers desire to avail themselves of this privilege, the Board are of the opinion that abatements should be paid on their past temporary salaries since the Superannuation Act came into force, when the officers have served so long back; otherwise, from the commencement of their temporary services.

The Board further recommends that, as the immediate' payments of abatements on past salaries would, in many cases, involve considerable hardship, a period of six months be allowed for paying the same, the deduction to be made in six equal parts, to be taken from each monthly pay for the first six months of the permanent appointments.

Certified.   (Signed) JOHN J. McGEE, C.P.C.

Order in Council, February 9. 1893.—That the Order in Council of January 7, 1884, permitting temporary officers on receiving permanent appointments to place themselves as regards their temporary services under the operation of the Superannuation Act, be cancelled.

(Signed) JOHN J. McGEE. C.P.C.

Mr. ROBERT SMEATON WHITE, Collector of Customs, Port of Montreal, called, sworn and examined.

By the Chairman:

Q. We have had a deputation from the Custom-house, you are the collector?—A. Yes.

Q. How long have you been collector?—A. Since December 31, 1895.

Q. That is, you were appointed twelve years ago?—A. Yes.

Q. You were appointed at $4,000?—A. Yes.

Q. And you have had the same salary ever since?—A. The same salary since.

Q. Under the law that salary cannot be increased?—A. It cannot.

Q. During the last few months there has been about $25,000 distributed in salaries to the officers in the Custom-house here?—A. At the port of Montreal, yes.

Q. That is to say, to the people that happened to be within the limits?—A. Yes, every salary has been somewhat increased within the limits.

By Mr. Fyshe:

Q. Was that handed over to you to be distributed on your discretion?—A. Oh, no, that was done by the Minister by Order in Council. The Order was passed upon the recommendation of the Minister.

Q. They did not ask you for your recommendation?—A. I went over the list with the Commissioner of the Department at Ottawa.

Q. Which Commissioner?—A. The Commissioner of Customs, who is the Deputy Head of the department in Ottawa, and I may say that this increase was given without regard particularly either to the merits or the class of work performed by the officers.

Q. But why?—A. Because there was not, as I understand it sufficient money available to do justice all around and the increase was made on the basis of a flat rate. Practically it was $100 a head irrespective of the work or the position held by the officer, or his merits. It was a flat increase of $100 per head.

Q. To about 200 people?—Yes.

By the Chairman:

Q. All those people who, like yourself, were up to the limits got nothing?—A. No.

Q. It was simply given to 200 of those people who happened to be within the limits?—A. A flat rate of $100 each.

Q. This increase was not given to everybody in the service, but only to those who were within the limits of their class?—A. Practically it was a flat rate, I think there was a general increase of $100 as I remember, but in a few cases, or comparatively few cases, somewhat more, $150 was given. But speaking generally of the action of the Minister at that time it was a flat rate, it was known as such by the department, it was treated by the department as a general increase, and the relative merit of the officers was not taken up at all.

Q. And this did not apply to Montreal only, but to the department all over the Dominion?—A. The Minister obtained $200,000 at the last session of Parliament for the purpose of increasing the salaries throughout Canada and of that amount $25,000 was allotted to the Port of Montreal.

Q. But you should have got more than $25,000?—A. If it was based upon the revenue we would be entitled to $60,000, as we collected that proportion at the Port of Montreal, 30 per cent of the entire Customs collections of Canada.

By Mr. Bazin:

Q. This $25,000 was not given as a bonus?—A. No, it was a permanent increase of salary.

By the Chairman:

Q. This increase, although not based on merit, was possible in the Customs service because, in that service, there are no annual increments of salaries like there are in the Inland Revenue and Post Office?—A. Quite so, no statutory increase is provided for in the outside service of the Customs.

By Mr. Fyshe:

Q. But there is for the inside branch of the Customs?—A. Yes.

Q. And there is a statutory enactment for annual increments in the Post Office and Inland Revenue Departments, but in the Customs, neither in practice nor legislation is there provision for annual increments, so the Minister of Customs for the outside service of the Customs alone, got this thing through?—A. Yes.

By the Chairman:

Q. You told Mr. Fyshe that you were consulted and went over the list with the Commissioner?—A. Yes, and with the accountant, the present assistant commissioner.

Q. This, like the rain, went to the just and unjust alike?—A. Very much so.

Q. Were there any people so totally inefficient that they got nothing?—A. I do not think so, I do not recall a case of that kind. I recall a case where a landing waiter received no increase because he was at the maximum of his class, but I do not recall any case where, because of inefficiency standing against an officer, he did not participate in that flat rate increase.

Q. Most of the officers here, through that $25,000, possibly reached the maximum of their grades?—A. No, there are comparatively few officers in this port at their maximum.

By Mr. Fyshe:

Q. Why is that?—A. You will have to ask the Minister on that point.

By the Chairman:

Q. Perhaps they have not served long enough?—A. Some of them have served thirty-three years and yet they are not at their maximum. The view I take personally is this, that when Parliament provides a maximum rate of salary for a Customs officer in the outside service, that rate should be paid at the principal port of Canada presuming that the officer has put in length of service and is efficient. But that principle, so far as I can learn, under no government has ever ben observed.

Q. That difficulty is not traceable to this Government?—A. Not more than to its predecessors. It has always been the case.

By Mr. Fyshe:

Q. Well, you see there is a clear margin evidently allowed by law to somebody in authority, and yet the terms of the law are not complied with, although they have the margin allowed?—A. The salaries in the port of Montreal of the higher officers are lower than they were thirty-five or forty years ago. The salary of the chief clerk forty years ago was $2,000, to-day it is $1,600, and he had only $1,500 last year.

Q. And probably he does four times the work now that was done then?—A. Yes, and the cost of living is much greater as you know.

By the Chairman:

Q. If $25,000 has been distributed this year, if the Minister is in a genial mood he may get another $25,000 next year?—A. Possibly.

Q. And he might widen the limits and yet give the increase in an eleemosynary way?—A. As to a considerable number of the officers I might tell you this, that the minister encountered a practical difficulty in making an increase during the year, for instance, the tide waiting class. By the Civil Service Act, the maximum salary of a tide waiter is $600, and some of them perform quite responsible and somewhat important duties, and it was thought this amount was not an adequate salary. The Minister, under the law, however, could not increase their emoluments beyond $600, so in order to meet the case he appointed all these tide waiters as preventive officers, he changed their rank, as there is no limit put on the salary of a preventive officer by law. If you will look at the memorandum which the accountant submitted to you, you will find that there are very few tide waiters in the port of Montreal, while there are a great many preventive officers. That change was made in order that they might get a higher salary than the law provided for tide waiters. Obviously, the proper way to overcome in future a like difficulty is to amend the law.

Q. It is possible now, having the precedent established, and if Parliament is in a generous mood, this $25,000 grant might be repeated ad infinitum, until every one gets to the limit?—A. That can be done, certainly.

By Mr. Fyshe:

Q. It will soon become an abuse, and what we want to do is to put it on a proper basis.

By the Chairman:

Q. To what extent has the staff increased during your term of office?—A. My recollection is that in the season of navigation of 1896, our staff consisted of 210 officers, that included outports; we have had two outports since established, Marieville and St. Agnes de Dundee, and to-day our staff consists of 273 officers.

Q. That is an increase of something under 30 per cent?—A. Yes.

Q. How do you find out when the necessity exists for getting a new man?—A. The head of the branch in which he is required reports to me.

Q. And then you report to Ottawa?—A. I fill the gap if I can out of the existing staff.

Q. You fill the gap if you can?—A. If I can I do so out of the staff by transferring a man from another branch; if I cannot do so I ask the Minister to give me another man.

Q. You know, as an old Member of Parliament, how things happen, you have no notion what man the Minister may nominate?—A. Not the slightest.

Q. Although you may have a shrewd guess?—A. I know nothing about it until the name comes to me and then I employ Mr. So and so.

Q. Up to the present the Minister has never lived in Montreal, and cannot know anything individually about the individual people here, and he generally takes the man whose name is sent to him?—A. It comes under the political system which has always existed.

By Mr. Fyshe:

Q. Who suggests the name?—A. The member for the district usually.

By the Chairman:

Q. Do you find that owing to the increase in prices of commodities you are not getting as good men now enter the Customs as you used to?—A. I think so far as I can observe there are fewer applications for positions in the Public Service by far than there were ten years ago.

Q. And the people that are appointed now, are they, in comparison, as efficient as were the people appointed ten years ago?—A. I think not, we get a smaller proportion of young men. Our practical difficulty seems to be to get young intelligent men in the service of the class that we require.

Q. The young men of that class do not seek to come in now?—A. Apparently not, because we do not get them.

Q. Have you any women on your staff?—A. None.

Q. You do not want women on your staff, I suppose?—A. I would prefer not.

Q. You want young intelligent men?—A. Particularly young intelligent men.

Q. But you do not get them now, they used to come in?—A. No, we we do not get as many intelligent, capable young men. We suffer mostly in this port from a lack of competent clerks, men who are fairly good and competent men, who know something about figures and have a reasonable amount of intelligence. The staff, in my opinion, is weak in respect to that class of general utility men, men who can be taken out of our office to-day and who can be placed in a new position and who will quickly pick up the new work. They appear to run very much in the groove in which they are working.

By Mr. Fyshe :

Q. And they are bad hand writers?—A. As a rule, they are poor penmen.

By the Chairman :

Q. In looking over the Civil Service List I notice that you have nobody graded as accountant. Have you one in the port of Montreal?—A. Yes, and it is a very important branch in the port.

Q. Who is he?—A. Mr. McKenna.

Q. He is not graded as an accountant?—A. We call him locally the accountant, but there is no such rank in the outside service.

Q. How many men has he in his branch?—A. Only two.

Q. What position did Mr. Meunier occupy?—A. He was cashier.

Q. Have you a cashier now?—A. We have three. we have had three for some years.

Q. Mr. Meunier was appointed on account of a special qualification?—A. I cannot tell you, that is beyond my knowledge.

Q. He was over age when he entered the service? He came in beyond the age at which clerks ordinarily enter the service?—A. We have them come in a great deal older than Meunier was. I do not consider Mr. Meunier to have been too old to do the work.

Q. Mr. Meunier when appointed was appointed as cashier?—A. Yes.

Q. Without being examined or any tests as to his qualification either?—A. He was appointed as cashier.

Q. What was he before he came into the service, do you know?—A. I understand he was connected with the Montreal Turnpike Trust.

Q. He was a trustee there, I believe. He was a trustee, he had no executive duties to perform?—A. I can't tell you.

Q. He entered the Custom House and became cashier. How long was he in the service of the Customs?—A. Speaking off-hand, I should say about three years.

Q. How long was it before he became acquainted with Mr. Hobbs?—A. I should think probably he became acquainted with him almost the day he entered the service.

Q. Mr. Hobbs found him an easy mark?—A. Apparently.

Q. Mr. Meunier became acquainted with Mr. Hobbs, who did the work of clearing goods on behalf of the Canadian Pacific Railway?—A. He was the Canadian Pacific Railway Customs agent.

Q. A deficiency arose in the accounts amounting to $32,000?—A. Thereabouts.

Q. What was the modus operandi adopted by Hobbs to get this?—A. He falsified the invoices in the first instance; the invoices which were given him by the Canadian Pacific Railway, the treasurer's office, were falsified by him. He received with these invoices from the Canadian Pacific Railway a cheque for the duty upon the goods representing the full amount of duty accruable or accruing on the goods. By manipulation of these invoices, by forgery upon the invoices, he was able to clear the goods, as we use the term, and to enter a much larger quantity of goods than he paid duty upon. For instance, there were three carloads of car couplers consigned to the railway and three invoices, each representing one carload. He took the invoice for one car; they were typewritten invoices, and added to that invoice the car numbers of the other two cars, and paid duty, say, on $4,000 instead of $12,000, each carload representing $4,000 worth of goods. He made on this forged invoice an entry for $4,000 worth of car couplers contained in three carloads, the numbers of three cars being given on this invoice by the addition of the numbers of the other two cars, when as a matter of fact that $4,000 was contained in only one car. His cheque from the Canadian Pacific Railway was for, say, $3,000. Now, when the entry had been checked, these forgeries could not, in my opinion, have been easily detected. I can see no responsibility to be thrown upon the check clerks, having examined the documents since, as I have. When Hobbs came there and handed in his cheque for $3,000, his entry only called for $1,000 duty, and Mr. Meunier handed him back the difference in cash, which was in direct violation of his instructions, and when I called him before me, in the presence of Mr. Corbett, the foreign freight agent of the Canadian Pacific Railway—that was before we detected the fraud—and asked him if he ever did such a thing, he denied it—that was in the presence of Mr. Corbett and myself—he denied that he handed out any money in change. He handed out this money to Hobbs instead of retaining this surplus change and having it refunded to the Canadian Pacific Railway by collector's cheque, as directed by the regulations. That is the whole story of the fraud.

By Mr. Fyshe:

Q. How old is this man?—A. Fifty-five or sixty years age, I would think.

By Mr. Bazin:

Q. Is he still there?—A. No, he is not there; Mr. Meunier was suspended the day the fraud was detected. I suspended him, and he is under suspension ever since.

By the Chairman:

Q. He has not been dismissed, and he is not retained?—A. I believe not.

Q. Should he not be disposed of one way or the other?—A. His services have been dispensed with. .

Q. This was a great deal owing to the deficiency on Meunier's part and lack of understanding the regulations?—A. It could not well have been lack of understanding because his instructions had been drummed into him.

By Mr. Fyshe:

Q. Do you think he had any suspiciousness of crookedness on the part of Hobbs?
—A. He did what he ought not to have done.

By Mr. Bazin :

Q. Did you trace several transactions like that?—A. They covered a period of about eighteen months.

By the Chairman:

Q. Nothing has come before the department to show that Meunier participated in the proceeds of the fraud?—A. Not to my knowledge.

By Mr. Fyshe:

Q. Was this man Hobbs an old officer of the Canadian Pacific Railway?—A. No, it was discovered afterwards that he had served a term of seven years in the penitentiary in Scotland.

By the Chairman:

Q. Hobbs is a clever fellow?—A. Very, he is a man who would favourably impress anybody, and he would quickly exicte your confidence, a man of good address and ability.

By Mr. Bazin:

Q. Has the Canadian Pacific Railway made good that amount?—A. The matter is still under consideration in Ottawa. Whether the Government intends to sue the Canadian Pacific Railway or not, I cannot say, but the amount has not been recouped to the revenue.

Q. But they are held responsible?—A. I cannot say what action may be taken.

By Mr. Fyshe:

Q. Have you ever had any difficulty with your book-keeping?—A. With our system?

Q. Yes?—A. No, I do not profess to be an accountant, I am not an expert accountant at all, but I am of the opinion that the system of checking the Customs revenue a most admirable one, and I have never been able to see where any leak could occur. But you cannot, and I think you will bear me out, from your own experience in a bank, you cannot guard against deliberate dishonesty. You can punish, and you can make regulations with a view to preventing, in a measure, dishonest men from being dishonest, but no institution in the world has ever yet been free from thieves in its service. You can punish them after you detect them, but subject to that reservation the check in the Customs is a close, complete and admirable one.

Q. I did not refer to that so much as to what I have noticed in other cases, a tendency to have book-keeping too cumbersome, too redundant, a repeating of the work over and over again?—A. I do not think it is that way with us, we have in the accountant's branch a cash-book and a ledger, and the items are transferred from the cash-book to the ledger.

By the Chairman:

Q. You have no objection to Mr. Fyshe seeing the books in your office?—A. None whatever.

Q. How often are you inspected?—A. Our inspector spends about six months in the year in the port; that is, he has his office in the port.

Q. He can come in and inspect whenever he likes?—A. At any time he chooses.

Q. Who is your inspector?—A. Mr. O'Meara, and Mr. Lemieux assistant inspector.

Q. Those invoices in the Hobbs case were materially altered?—A. Yes.

Q. They are on file in the Custom-house. When the inspector made his inspection could he not see they had been altered?—A. He could not, except by checking the quantities, and that is not a branch of his work.

Q. The reason I ask was that if this went on for eighteen months and the invoices were constantly altered and amended, would not that give rise to suspicion by the inspector?—A. That would not be the inspector's duty to go over that class of work, it is the appraiser does that.

By Mr. Fyshe:

Q. How on earth did this fellow manage to make one car serve for three by the document he had in his possession?—A. The Canadian Pacific Railway made out their own advice notes to begin with, and Hobbs would make out his own advice notes. For instance, there would be advice notes for three cars of car couplers, they come in from the United States at a frontier port, which issues a manifest upon the port of Montreal in duplicate. One of the manifests is kept in the landing waiters' office at the Custom House and the other accompanies the car and is taken up by the the invoices and the department.

Q. But he would not have three invoices for three carloads?—A. He obtained three invoices from the purchasing agent's office, and from the treasurer's office of the Canadian Pacific Railway he obtained a cheque for say, $3,000 representing the duty upon these three car-loads. He takes one of these three invoices, which were typewritten and bears upon it the number of the car and the weight. Say there are three cars, N.Y.C. 10970, N.Y.C. 13480 and N.Y.C. 15061, and there is a separate invoice for each, the number of the car being specified on the invoice. He takes the first invoice and he had typewritten upon it the other two car numbers, leaving the quantity and value of the goods contained in that one car, to which the invoice actually refers. without alteration. The invoice then bore the numbers of three cars, and' the quantity of goods and amount of duty represented the contents of one car only. The check clerk sees upon this invoice when tendered to him three car numbers, and his suspicion is not aroused because the advice note is for three carloads, and the manifest calls for three carloads and the manifests are closed by this one entry for the three cars. The entry goes up to the cashier calling upon the face of it for duty upon $4,000 contents of these cars instead of $12,000.

By the Chairman:

Q. The vouchers would not excite any suspicion in the minds of the landing waiter, the clerks or any other officers?—A. They would not. It is fair to remember this that in dealing with the Canadian Pacific Railway which is a great corporation these entries were treated as above suspicion, we could not see that any individual officer, from the President, Sir Thomas Shaughnessy, down, could profit or have any personal gain in perpetrating a fraud upon the Customs.

Q. The one suspicious thing was the handing back of the money?—A. That was in direct violation of positive instructions. and Mr. Meunier denied having done so when asked if he did such a thing before the fraud was detected. The point has been raised why did not the Inspector discover this, why did not the Inspector walk into Mr. Meunier's cash box, count his cash at the close of the day's work and discover that it was wrong. As a matter of fact the Inspector did count the cash from time to time. What would he find? That the receipts of the day were so much, call it $30,000 as the total revenue of that day, he would count Mr. Meunier's cash and find he had $32,000 that day; he would say naturally to Mr. Meunier: ' You have $2,000 over,' and Mr. Meunier would say: ' Yes, that is Canadian Pacific Railway money for entries that have not gone through, that is surplus change.' The Inspector might have said: ' You put this through the Collector's account and pay it by cheque,' and Mr. Meunier would reply ' Yes,' to the inspector's question. But the money was paid to

Hobbs not to the Collector's account as surplus, was paid over to Hobbs through a boy sent by Hobbs from the Canadian Pacific Railway office. All this came out in the trial that the money was sent through a Canadian Pacific Railway office boy, who was sent up from the Caandian Pacific Railway office by Hobbs late in the afternoon after everyone had left, and the fraud would have gone on in spite of the Inspector's vigilance. I want to point out that no inspection will guard absolutely against dishonesty of that kind.

Q. I asked about this to try and clear up any doubts there might be in the public mind with regard to the method and efficiency of the inspection?—A. I think this is one of those frauds such as occur in banks and other institutions against which it is impossible to guard if you have dishonesty on the one side and stupidity on the other.

By Mr. Fyshe:

. Q. Before passing this entry the check clerk, who fixes the amount of duty, would have his eyes opened would he not by the small amount of duty paid on three carloads of car couplers?—A. The check clerk does not know anything about the dimension of the car.

Q. If I remember aright, the invoice was changed from one car to three cars, according to the number of the cars, but the contents were only those of one car?— A. Yes.

Q. Would not that open the eyes of any employee there? Would the employee who passed the entry not say, ' here is an entry for three cars of car couplers which instead of being $12,000 is only $4,000? Would not that employee know that there was not the proper quantity there for three cars?—A. You have three carloads of car couplers, the duty is 30 per cent, and supposing it is worth $4,000 per car. A check clerk does not know whether a carload of couplers is worth $1,000 or $10,000; he is not an expert, he does not know whether it is the full car or part of a car. He does know that the duty on car couplers is 30 per cent, and on $1,000 worth he collects a duty of $300. He could not possibly tell there was any fraud. The only way in which suspicion might be excited in this case would be if the altering of the invoice was done in a careless or crude kind of way. But Hobbs had it down so fine that he had different kinds of typewriting ink, and he would use ink, in putting on these additional car numbers, that conformed to the original ink used in the genuine invoice. These facts all came out in the court in evidence.

By the Chairman:

Q. You were in the Bank of Montreal?—A. A great many years ago.

Q. How long were you in the bank?—A. Twenty-one months.

Q. You had some experience in accounting?—A. I was a very young man at that time; I went in as a junior.

Q. You were also, I think, in the newspaper business, and had the management of the accounts in the *Gazette*?—A. I was in editorial work.

Q. You had some experience in accounting. Do you think looking at the result of this Hobbs' business that you can suggest any change in the method of bookkeeping?—A. None whatever. I have not suggested any changes, because I could not suggest any, and I will say further that while this matter was doubtless considered by the department officials, no change whatever has been made in our regulations as a result. We are unable to advise or suggest any safeguard which does not at present exist.

By Mr. Fyshe:

Q. How many clerks have you in the Customs here?—A. 273.

Q. Are they all in one building?—A. No.

Q. How many are there in your building?—A. I could not tell you; we have so many different departments, accountants, tide surveyors, landing waiters, long room and so forth.

By the Chairman:

Q. The revenue is now how huch a day?—A. I expect it will be over $17,000,000 this calendar year; the collections run from $55,000 to $60,000 a day.

Q. Is the greater part of the duties paid in cash or in cheque?—A. Not in cash, by cheque.

Q. Are these cheques all stamped good?—A. They are certified good. It is contrary to the regulations to accept other than certified cheques.

By Mr. Fyshe:

Q. Do you keep statistics reaching back thirty or forty years?—A. Of imports and exports?

Q. Yes?—A. These records exist in the department, but we have not kept them in the port for some years.

Q. I would like to have statistics of the cost of collecting?—A. I may tell you offhand that when I came here in the fiscal year '95-6 the cost of collection was 2·10 per cent; that was when I entered the port. This year it will be about 1·35 per cent.

By the Chairman:

Q. You said the daily collections are between $55,000 and $60,000; at what hours do you deposit?—A. All the moneys collected in the department are deposited in the Bank of Montreal the same day.

Q. When do you close?—A. We cease taking money at four o'clock, and the Bank of Montreal makes arrangements by which it keeps two officers there to receive our deposit box every night, and it reaches the bank usually about six, and on heavy days it is 6.30 p.m. or thereabouts.

Q. As a matter of fact no moneys collected from duties are held here in the Custom-house over night?—A. None whatever; but, of course, the money is not counted in the bank until the following morning, nor is the draft obtained until next morning, but it is deposited the same day as collected.

Q. That leads to another thing. You have, I suppose, a system of vaults for your money chests?—A. We have vaults for our books.

Q. For what period do you retain the manifests before sending them away to Ottawa for statistical purposes?—A. We send a copy of every entry to Ottawa daily.

Q. You keep the original here?—A. Yes, and we send a copy; all entries are in duplicate, one copy is retained in the port and the other copy is sent daily on the following day to Ottawa·with the form known as Form F 1, representing the amount of duty collected on each entry.

By Mr. Fyshe :

Q. And you send with these the receipts from the Bank of Montreal?—A. We send a draft in favour of the Receiver General for the amount. Then we have another form we send to the Auditor General's office showing the amount of collections each day.

By the Chairman:

Q. Then practically the only records kept in the Custom-house here are the original entries of which duplicates are sent to Ottawa, and no cash is kept here over night?—A. None whatever.

Q. Are your men under bond?—A. Practically every officer in the port is under bond.

By Mr. Fyshe:

Q. How many of them?—A. Well, the labourers, the mere truckers are not, but speaking generally our officers are all under bond other than the labourers and truckers and the bonds run from $500 in the case of the lower grade officers and tide-waiters, to $10,000 in the case of the collector.

7-8 EDWARD VII., A. 1908

By the Chairman:

Q. I think you yourself handle no money ?—A. No, except that I may handle a little money, such as yesterday, when I had $500 poll-tax on a Chinaman which I took and handed to the accountant.

Q. Does the collector participate in any seizures ?—A. None.

Q. There is no addition whatever to your salary ?—A. No addition. Of course, as far as that goes, like all other officers, I would like to have more money and I base my plea upon the growth of the work, the enormous increase in the business, and upon the fact that the collector of this port is paid less money than he was thirty or forty years ago. Thirty years ago the shipping fees were the emoluments of the collector. To-day there is a separate shipping master who derives a substantial perquisite from the fees. Mr. Simpson, who succeeded Mr. Deslisle as collector enjoyed for a short period the shipping master's fees, until the Mackenize government appointed Col. Smith at a salary and turned the fees into the general revenue. Mr. Simpson, according to our books, was superannuated on the basis of $4,500 salary, and I think he got the extra $500 in lieu of the shipping fees. Then, again, I have no assistant collector since 1897. Previous to that there was an assistant at $2,500.

By Mr. Fyshe:

Q. You are not old enough in the service to come under the superannuation system ?—A. Oh, yes, I am, I have paid nearly $1,700 since I have been collector to the superannuation fund.

By the Chairman :

Q. Under this provision of the Civil Service Act you cannot get any increase to your salary ?—A. Not unless the Act is amended.

Q. Do you find that you are getting good men in the service now?—A. I say we get as good men as we can expect for the salaries paid, but I do not go so far as to say that we have as good men as the character of the service demands.

Q. And there are not as many applications to enter the service as there used to be ?—A. Not from what I can judge. I do not consider that we have as good a staff, speaking of it as a whole as the character and responsibility of the service demands, but we may have as good a staff as we can expect for the money paid.

Q. Have you a sufficient staff ?—A. In numbers? Yes. .

Q. All your staff are employed all the year around, are they not ?—A. Yes, pretty much so.

Q. In the old times there was formerly a portion of the staff that was paid off in the winter ?—A. Yes, and even in my time during the winter we have reduced the staff by eight or ten and we may possibly dispense with the service of half a dozen this winter.

Q. But in the old days a very much greater number were dispensed with in the winter, there was a lesser number of permanent employees ?—A. Thirty, forty or fifty years ago the character of the business was such that there was only about half as much business done in the winter as there was in the summer. To-day we collect as much money on the average during the winter months as we do during the season of open navigation.

By Mr. Fyshe:

Q. Is that due to the fact that the imports come in over the railroads in the winter time ?—A. No, the conditions of business have changed. We get as much money at this port during the winter months as during the season of navigation. If the goods are from Europe they are landed at St. John, Halifax or Portland in bond and are brought on here and the duty is paid on them.

SESSIONAL PAPER No. 29a

By the Chairman:

Q. All the importations twenty-five years ago were made during the summer season?—A. Largely so, and they lessened during the winter season.

Q. Now, the importations go on all through the year?—A. Yes.

Q. I asked you do you think you have sufficient in number to carry on the work of the port?—A. Yes, and I have never had any difficulty in getting an extra man or two if required.

Q. The conditions of the port are such that you require the same staff of employees in the winter as in the summer?—A. Speaking generally, yes, but we are not quite so busy in the winter because we have not the riverside staff employed in transit work.

Q. But you have a railway staff when the steamer comes in from Halifax?—A. Yes, that is true; we transfer the riverside staff to the Dalhousie depot and Point St. Charles where they deal with the Canadian Pacific Railway freight from St. John, and the Grand Trunk Railway from Portland.

Q. That is to say that the passengers and freight come in all the year around, and if the riverside business is not as brisk in the winter then the business is largely transferred to the depots?—A. Quite so.

Q. What do you think about the scheme of promotion in the Customs Office?— Are the people generally in your office stuck at what they entered on when they joined the service? Is there a fair show of promotion?—A. There is no certainty about it and that, of course, I regard, looking at it from an interested standpoint as an executive officer, as one of the weaknesses in the present system, that is in the system as long as I have known anything about it, for many years past. It is largely a matter of luck or pull with an officer whether he gets along or not. His merit may mean promotion, but there is no assurance of it.

By Mr. Fyshe:

Q. Do you not feel a large amount of responsibility for seeing that something like justice is done to the men under you?—A. I have no power, my case is one of responsibility without power. I cannot employ anybody, nor, of course, can I dismiss; I can suspend, that is one of the powers given to the Collector, and enables him to exercise a certain amount of authority.

Q. Now, take for instance, David Tuff, who is called a landing waiter; he entered the service in 1871 at the age of twenty-five years, and has been thirty-six years in the service, and gets $750 a year?—A. He got his $100 last year.

Q. Yes, but don't you think that a man with that long service, if he is at all efficient, should be in a better position. there should be some method of giving him promotion?—A. Yes, Mr. Tuff is a good officer; he is landing waiter at the Dalhousie depot, and does the work exceedingly well and is very satisfactory. Now, the Civil Service, as you must have learned long ago, is honeycombed with anomalies. Take this port, and take this case in point that I am speaking of. We have at Bonaventure depot, the Grand Trunk Railway depot. an officer named James Sherritt, who through political influence in 1896, in the spring of 1896, under the old government, was given a salary of $1,000 and no other landing waiter in the port has been able to reach that point in the eleven years that have since elapsed, although his is not the most important depot nor would I say that Mr. Sherritt is a more efficient officer than four or five others whom we have performing the same class of work; yet no other officer has been able to get the same salary. He was fortunate enough to have a little influence. But these other poor fellows have been struggling along ever since unable to get similar recognition.

By Mr. Fyshe:

Q. Was he a new appointment?—A. No, he was an old officer, but he got a good jump through influence which was exercised on his behalf at that time. I do not say that he is getting too much, but I do say he is either getting too much or the others have not enough.

By the Chairman:

Q. You say that Tuff is a good man?—A. I say that he is a good man in a responsible position, the landing waiter in the Dalhousie depot.

By Mr. Fyshe:

Q. What possible objection could there be to allowing a collector who knows all these men to recommend increases of salary to the men under him with a favourable chance of his recommendation being approved?—A. As a matter of fact I do recommend increases from time to time, but then it is entirely within the discretion of the Minister whether that increase to Council; that is a matter of policy; I have nothing to do with that.

Q. Would it not be a matter of good judgment to say that unless the Minister, who is the official head of the department, could show a very good reason to the contrary, that the Collector's recommendation should carry; that the onus should not rest upon the political head whether this should go or not?—A. I have always thought that we should have a statutory increase, between the maximum and the minimum, and that upon the recommendation or report of the local head, concurred in by the deputy and approved by the Minister, the officer should go to the maximum of his class, and that as vacancies occur and he is found worthy, he might be moved to another class. I know of no other way in which the salary question can be adjusted in a businesslike way except that.

By the Chairman :

Q. Take this comparison of Tuff and Sherritt. Tuff was appointed nineteen years before Sherritt, and Sherritt has got up to $1,000 eleven years ago and he is doing duty at Bonaventure; Mr. Tuff, who was appointed nineteen years before Sherritt and is doing duty at Dalhousie, only gets $750. They are both good men, I suppose?—A. Yes.

Q. There is no reason why one should be discriminated against in comparison with the other?—A. None whatever, so far as the character of the men or their merits are concerned.

Q. They are both doing similar work?—A. The same class of work.

Q. Then it comes to the pass that there is no method in the Customs outside service by which to get an efficient man promoted, or to get him into a higher sphere. Mr. Tuff, for instance, with all his past experience and the record of the good work he has done is unable to get beyond the position of landing waiter?—A. No, in the ordinary gradation Mr. Tuff might move to the position of tide surveyor; that would be about the next step in promotion for a landing waiter.

Q. How many of these tide surveyors have you?—A. Only one, who is the head of the river staff.

Q. Could not a man of great respectability and long service, and all that, be moved in the ordinary course to some other position in the Custom-house?—A. He might, of course, be made chief landing waiter by promotion along that line, or he may be moved to the position of tide surveyor, which is a higher one along the line of promotion, or in course of time he might attain to the rank of surveyor. The present surveyor began in the rank of supernumerary and worked up to his present position.

Q. It is simply a habit of keeping the men to the position that they were first appointed?—A. One cannot ignore, nobody can, the political element which is always present. It is not a question of party, but a question of system. The practical difficulty which is encountered is that when a vacancy occurs in the Customs in the higher positions to which the better salary attaches there is always danger of an outsider coming in to the prejudice of men who are already in the service.

SESSIONAL PAPER No. 29a

By Mr. Fyshe :

Q. That can only be done through political influence?—A. That has always been done under every Government.

Q. That should be eliminated, or an effort should be made to do so. Moreover, something else is necessary in the Government service, which is not like a private service or the service of any of the outside corporations. In any outside corporation, or in the service of the individual, there is always some element in the institution which is available to see that something like justice is done in governing the staff. There is somebody to appeal to, somebody who is responsible for doing justice to the staff, and there is no getting away from it, no pull from the outside can get over it. They may say, ' Well, the directors will not do so and so,' but as a matter of .fact, that is usually got over, and the staff feel there is somebody they can appeal to, and from whom they can demand justice, and, moreover, they are sure to-get it or if they do not they take it as an intimation that their services are not wanted?—A. Not only that, but the moment the manager in a private corporation discovers ability in a junior he avails himself of it.

Q. Certainly, there is nothing more important than to encourage ability and discourage disability. There is nothing to take the place of that element in the Government service. As it exists now the only way I can see to induce a spirit of that kind is to give the Deputy Heads everywhere the same responsibility that the manager of a bank would have or the manager of a big corporation in dealing with his men. He should have the power either to cut down or to promote always with the consent of his Political Head, but the Political Head s hould have no power to stop it unless he can show good reason for interfering with his Deputy.

By the Chairman:

Q. Does it not follow that when a man does the same work for thirty-five years, and has no hope of bettering himself, he becomes perfunctory in the performance of his duty?—A. I think there is no doubt about that.

Q. And these men, however honest or capable they may be, they gradually must deteriorate, owing to the system?—A. Yes, these cases crop up constantly.

Q. Are there many of that class here like Tuff, for instance?—A. Of old service?

Q. Yes?—A. Well, we have a number of old servants, men who have served from twenty to thirty years.

Q. Don't you think that if this was brought to the attention of the Minister of Customs, who is essentially a just man, he might see the injustice to these old servants?—A. Well, I imagine the practical difficulty is that it is a very large department. If the Minister had only one port to deal with, he might be able to .remedy the existing state of things and to rectify the injustice, but he has probably 300 or more ports in Canada scattered all over the country, and not only the cases of the officers to consider, the good and the worthy officers, but he has also the politicians on his back; he may be promoting a worthy officer or he may be promoting a man not so good, and it makes it practically impossible, in my opinion, for any Minister to remedy that state of affairs himself.

By Mr. Fyshe:

Q. Yes, you are putting the work on the wrong shoulders; that work should not be done by the Minister?—A. Very well, then you have to change the system.

By the Chairman:

Q. Under the present system of affairs one-half of the Minister's time is fully occupied on matters of administration and not on matters of politics. In your opinion, would it not be desirable that he should be divested of all that and the administration of affairs left in the hands of the permanent officers?—A. No doubt that would be an advantage. Altogether, too much of the time of the Minister is taken up with officers'

29a—9

petitions, and a great deal of the worry of the Minister arises from the patronage system.

By Mr. Fyshe:

Q. My own experience leads me to the belief that there is no more difficult task for any man than to award proper compensation for the officers under him. Year after year I went through the list of every officer in the bank, it can be done, and with a reasonable degree of success, because you can convince people you are trying to do justice.

By the Chairman:

Q. Probably a man of thirty-five years' service in some position has long ago outgrown the knowledge of people who appointed him, probably they are all gone, and the little influence he had is gone. It does not pay the man or the system to trust to politics, does it?—A. Oh, no.

Q. Mr. Tuff was probably appointed in the days of Sir George Cartier?—A. Yes.

Q. All the men of that time are dead and gone?—A. Yes, I should say as far as the present Minister of Customs is concerned, he has done his utmost to ignore distinction of politics in the Civil Service; he has rightly assumed that a man being in the service he is no longer a politician. Of course, under the political system, the discipline is nothing like what it should be, in my opinion, and nothing like it would be if it were divested of some of the political element. The officers, and you cannot get it out of them, feel that they have a protection and that they can find protection in the politician who appointed them, and if they do misbehave a little or are indifferent to their work even if they are incompetent, they can be held there through influence.

Q. And after a few years the official is left a stranger without any influence?—A. Yes, and we cannot get rid of him after he has been there a number of years, they are like so much dead wood which we have to carry.

Q. We had an instance of a man yesterday being appointed twenty-one years ago, he was appointed at a certain salary at that time, and his sponsors are either all dead or gone out of power. That man has no ability to do very onerous work, has no ability to get any increased emolument; taking this typical instance of Tuff, I presume all his sponsors have long since passed from this world, so that he has no one left to help him. Following this system, after a certain length of time, the political support does not benefit an appointee?—A. No, it does not.

Q. Have you anything to add to that memorial which was presented this morning?—A. No, I think I have nothing. There are three points which the officers of this port would urge upon the Commission as desirable from their standpoint; one is the common one of an increase in salary, the second one is a reclassification with statutory increases and the third one is a revival of superannuation.

By Mr. Fyshe:

Q. With regard to that statutory increase that is not mechanical?

By the Chairman:

Q. That is better than nothing.

By Mr. Fyshe:

Q. Yes, I admit that, but is it not possible to exercise some judgment?—A. What is wanted is a statutory increase which cannot be demanded by an officer, but which may be given to him if he deserves it; he cannot sit on his chair and do nothing for a year and then come and say 'I want my increase.'

By the Chairman:

Q. The problem is that in the case of the Post Office there is a certain amount of amelioration which the Customs has not got?—A. There is to-day no proper in-

SESSIONAL PAPER No. 29a

centive to good work on the part of the Customs officer. There is neither an assurance of their getting more pay through merit, nor of getting higher rank through merit. That is about the position, there is no assurance of advancement and it does seem to me that the public service of the country should be so constituted that merit would tell.

Q. We find that in England, where the Minister is also responsible, and where the work is of a much larger character that the Minister although responsible has practically nothing to do with the adminstration of his department; that is in the hands of his deputy. Wouldn't it be better to come to some system whereby the Minister in this growing country should only deal with questions of policy and the permanent officers should deal with questions of administration?—A. Yes, and with mutual advantage to the staff and to the country.

By Mr. Fyshe:

Q. The Inspectors of the Customs Department report to Ottawa?—A. Yes.

Q. They do not report to you?—A. They are absolutely independent of me. The Inspector's office is in the Custom-house building and he spends about one-half the year in this port.

Witness retired.

Mr. F. ALFRED ST. LAURENT, Express Department of the Customs, Montreal, called, sworn and examined.

By the Chairman:

Q. What position do you occupy?—A. I am in the Express Department of the Customs.

Q. That is to say you are looking after the Express parcels and collecting the duties?—A. Yes, sir.

Q. Did you pass an examination when you were appointed?—A. Certainly, I passed my examination as Appraiser before Mr. O'Meara and understood I was going to be appointed Appraiser, but I never was, and I do not know where it stuck.

By Mr. Fyshe:

Q. In what special line?—A. The special line would be in hardware, because I have been in that line my whole life, and I have been with the firm of Frothingham & Workman.

By the Chairman:

Q. You were brought in as an expert in hardware and passed an examination before the Inspector of the district as Appraiser?—A. Before Mr. O'Meara.

Q. How long ago is that?—A. Three years ago I think.

Q. Did you ever do anything in the way of Appraiser's duties?—A. Oh yes, I have been in the Post Office and they have to appraise there for the Customs duty.

Q. But when you came in as an appraiser, appraisers are not wanted in the Post Office, the appraisers value the invoices as they come in from the ships and railways do they not?—A. Yes.

Q. After you had passed the examination why then were you not kept doing appraisers' duties in the regular way like Mr. Drysdale does for the stationery and somebody else does for other lines? Why were you not kept with the other appraisers in the Custom-house instead of being sent into the Post Office if you were an appraiser?—A. I never was appointed appraiser.

29a—9½

7-8 EDWARD VII., A. 1908

Q. You passed an examination for appraiser?—A. Yes.

Q. But you never were appointed appraiser?—A. No.

Q. Why was that?—A. That is what I would like to find out. I never could find out. I do not know whether it was somebody here or at Ottawa that was against me, because Mr. O'Meara told me he wrote to Ottawa to find out and to give me satisfaction about it, but I never got satisfaction. At last I had to pass another examination as an examining officer, which gives me a salary of $1,000, but I never got the salary which my position allows me.

Q. What salary do you get?—A. I get $700, and it is very little for a man to live on in Montreal with a family.

Q. To recount the various steps if you will allow me, you passed an examination as appraiser but were never appointed as an appraiser; then you passed another examination, and were appointed examining officer?—A. Yes, but it does not give me the full salary of an examining officer.

Q. Did they ever put you to the duties of examining officer?—A. Not an examining officer; they never put me to that.

Q. You were never put to the duties of appraiser or examining officer?—A. I beg pardon, I am appraiser at the Post Office; we have to appraise every parcel that passes there.

By Mr. Bazin:

Q. That is not what you call an appraiser?—A. You have to do the business of an appraiser.

By the Chairman:

Q. That is not an appraiser's duty; there is no hardware coming through the Post Office?—A. Yes, that is where you are mistaken; there are all kinds of goods coming through, and we have to know the duty on the different lines and the value of the articles.

Q. What hardware comes through the Post Office?—A. Samples and tools of different kinds.

Q. You appraise the samples, you do not appraise the goods themselves. In the Post Office if you did any appraiser's work it was simply the appraising of samples? —A. Yes; but those samples are subject to duty.

Q. You do a little appraising of samples in the Post Office, but you never did regular appraiser's work?—A. No.

Q. Then you were examined as an examining officer?—A. Yes.

Q. Did you ever do examining officer's work?—A. No, never so far.

Q. Then you were sent into the Express Department?—A. Yes, sir.

Q. What are your duties there?—A. To deliver parcels there.

Q. Then you are simply a kind of messenger?—A. Well, you might call it that. I go to the appraiser, and say there is a parcel for which there is no invoice; sometimes I have to open the parcel for the appraiser, and I have to tell him sometimes, I know, not to say too much about myself, but I know better than they do the value of the articles, because I have been in the business all my life. I know the value of cutlery, scissors and all those things. The other day they had a sample of scissors to the amount of $12, and they were not sure what it was worth; I could tell them at once that it was worth that amount.

Q. How long have you been in the Customs Department?—A. Ten years.

Q. Who appointed you?—A. The Hon. Mr. Préfontaine and Senator Shehyn.

Q. Mr. Préfontaine got you into the Customs Department?—A. Yes.

Q. How long were you with Frothingham & Workman?—A. Three years, and with Lloyd Philips before that, and with Delisle Brothers and McGill, that was the first house I travelled for in Montreal. I used to be in the hardware with S. J. Shaw in Quebec.

SESSIONAL PAPER No. 29a

Q. Then you were an expert in hardware when you came into the Customs service?—A. Sure. .

Q. If you passed the examination as appraiser and were an expert is there any defect or reason why you should not be made an appraiser?—A. I do not know the reason; that is what I would like to know, if there is any reason. I do not know whether it was stopped here in Montreal or in Ottawa. There was something very suspicious about it.

By Mr. Fyshe:

Q. How old are you?—A. I am sixty.

. You are more than that are you not?—A. Sixty years of age.

Q. Are you not more than that?—A. No.

By the Chairman:

Q. I may assure you that while, of course, this case will be taken down and reported, that neither of the Commissioners know anything about the facts of the case. All that we can do is to report and to make inquiry, and that, of course, will be done in due course?—A. You understand I have sworn to what I have said, and I can prove what I have said. .

Witness retired.

QUEBEC, WEDNESDAY, September 18, 1907.

A deputation appeared on behalf of the customs officers of the port of Quebec, consisting of Captain W. H. Carter, surveyor; E. Beaudet, chief clerk; A. Gaumond, appraiser; J. G. Watters, appraiser; Colonel L. N. Laurin, chief landing-waiter; W. E. Edge, check clerk; L. M. Vallerand, preventive officer; J. A. Belleau, clerk, and J. Fullerton, examining officer.

Captain W. H. CARTER, sworn and examined, said:—The officers of the Customs met yesterday and appointed this deputation to wait upon this commission to-day. The deputation met this morning, and elected me as their chairman. The officers have unanimously came to the conclusion to submit to you a memorial on behalf of the members of the outside Customs Service. (Memorial read and filed.)

By the Chairman :

Q. You are the oldest in point of appointment in the Customs Service ?—A. Very nearly. I have been between thirty-six and thirty-seven years in the service.

Q. You were appointed in 1871 ?—A. In May, 1871. I think Mr. Dugal, the chief locker, was appointed six months before me.

Q. Were you originally appointed surveyor ?—A. No. I was originally appointed as a landing-waiter.

Q. You went through all the grades ?—A. In the beginning of 1884 I became chief clerk, and sixteen years or more ago I became surveyor.

Q. I need not examine you on what may be called the political side of the question, because you have unanimously come to the conclusion that the patronage system should be abolished ?—A. Yes, I think we all agree on that. I might say that during the time of my service and the service of many other officers, there have been hardships on certain men, who have not got on from a pecuniary point of view because they have had nobody to push their claims, while other men of very much less ability have got on much better.

Q. How many temporary officials have you in the Custom-house now ?—A. On what we call the supernumerary list there are thirty-seven.

Q. How many are on the permanent staff ?—A. Forty-five. This number includes the sub-collectors at the outports and one preventive officer.

Q. Where are the sub-collectors?—A. At Chicoutimi, Victoriaville, Magdalen Islands, Beauceville, Rivière du Loup, an acting sub-collector at Murray Bay, and a preventive officer at Trinity Bay. There are five on the permanent list outside of Quebec.

Q. That reduces the number on the permanent list employed at Quebec to forty ? —A. Yes.

Q. Then, practically, you have as many on the non-permanent list at Quebec as on the permanent list—a difference of only three ?—A. Yes.

Q. Why is there such a large number on the non-permanent list as compared with the permanent list ? Are these men on the permanent list shoved on the Customs-house through political influence?—A. They have not been put on the permanent list in many cases, I suppose, because they are not qualified either by examination or otherwise. A great number of them are kept on all the year round.

By Mr. Fyshe :

Q. You do not have work for them all, do you, during the winter months ?—A. We could do without some of them.

By the Chairman :

Q. The thirty-seven on the supernumerary list are there mainly because they have passed no examination?—A. They have been appointed at so much a year or at so much a month, and they have not qualified either by Preliminary examination or Qualifying examination, or by becoming examining officers.

Q. Then the greater number of those on the non-permanent list are there because they have failed to pass the necessary examinations ?—A. Yes, I think that would be a fair way of putting it. A good many of these officers, some at least, are men who could not pass these examinations; they are porters and packers, and do not require to do so.

Q. Packers have to pass a Preliminary examination?—A. I do not know that our packers have passed an examination. I am using the term with reference not to permanent packers, but to individuals employed as packers. One has passed, I think ; that is Murphy, who is housekeeper. He is on the permanent list now.

Q. But the thirty-seven are on the non-permanent list chiefly because they have not passed any examination ?—A. Yes, I do not know any other reason why they should not be on the permanent list.

Q. And all those on the non-permanent list might be appointed permanently if they passed the examinations ?—A. There is nothing to prevent them being appointed.

By Mr. Bazin:

Q. Do these people refuse to pass the examination, or have they not the opportunity of doing so?—A. As the examinations stand now, I do not think they have the necessary education. For instance, we have two or three labouring men, who could not go up even for the Preliminary examination.

By the Chairman:

Q. How long have these men been on the supernumerary list, the majority of them?—A. There are some old men who have been kept there for 50 years. They were originally old boatmen, and they do messenger work.

Q. How many men had you on the supernumerary list, say ten years ago? Had you 37 then?—A. No, I do not think so many.

Q. Had you half that number?—A. I think we must have had.

Q. Has the list been largely increased within the last few years?—A. It has been increased, but I would not say largely increased.

Q. What was the revenue of the port in the last fiscal year?—A. The last fiscal year was only nine months, but adding one-third more, I think it would amount to over $1,700,000.

Q. How much was it ten years ago?—About $650,000.

Q. The revenue has increased in ten years three-fold, but the supernumerary list has not doubled?—A. That is correct.

Q. Among the number who have been put on in the last ten years are there any that you might call inefficient, who have been shoved on you for purposes other than the well-being of the Customs?—A. That is a rather difficult question to answer.

Q. Have useless men been placed on the supernumerary list within the last ten years—men who could not get a living outside and have been put on for political ends?—A. Unless I had the names of the men before me I could not answer that.

Q. With the development of the Dominion and the increased facilities for able men to get on in the world, do as good men now enter the service of the Customs-house at Quebec as did ten years ago?—A. The seven or eight men appointed last year at the Customs-house at Quebec were exceedingly good men, taking them as a whole.

Q. Is that because Quebec is a less expensive place to live in and the salaries are more commensurate with the cost of living than in other places?—A. No; I should say from my experience that Quebec is an exceedingly expensive place now to live in.

Q. Do many men resign from the service of the Customs here?—A. No, very few.

Q. They are contented to stay despite the increase in the cost of living and despite the remuneration being stationary?—A. They do because it is a very difficult matter for a man at a certain time of life to start out in a new direction.

Q. The young men are not leaving you?—A. We have not many young men. We have some quite young, and they push their way along and do well.

Q. How many are discharged in the winter, when the season of navigation ends?—A. Nine.

Q. Would you think it desirable that these men who are redundant in the winter months at Quebec should be sent to Halifax or St. John, where an increased staff is required?—A. Yes.

Q. And they might be brought back to Quebec in the summer?—A. Yes. I believe that is done in the Immigration Department.

Q. In the outside service of the Post Office Department the officials get annual increments?—A. I think so.

Q. That also applies to the officials of the Inland Revenue Department?—A. Yes, and I think they are classified.

Q. Except perhaps the inspectors of Gas?—A. Yes, and the inspectors of Weights and Measures.

Q. In the Customs Department there is no classification of the outside officials??—None whatever.

Q. And no steady annual increment?—A. None whatever.

Q. How much of the special grant distributed in Quebec in the last few months was devoted to the amelioration of salaries?—A. I will send you a memorandum of that. I think about $4,000.

Q. Was it distributed with reference to the length of service of the officials?—A. I do not think so. I think it was done to bring them up to a living wage.

Q. This was done without regard to classification or anything of that kind?—A. I think so.

Q. Those who were at the limit of their class, like yourself, got nothing?—A. I have not reached the limit of my class. If I were to make a complaint, that would be my complaint.

Q. Those supposed to be at the maximum of their class got nothing.

7-8 EDWARD VII., A. 1908

Mr. LAURIN.—I received a reply from my application to the effect that having reached the maximum of my class, I could not get an increase; but some who were at the maximum of their class got increases.

CAPTAIN CARTER.—I think they were made preventive officers.

Q. I presume that, in a rough and ready way, there is a certain scale in force at each port. For instance, the Collector at Montreal gets $4,000, while the Collector here gets $3,000?—A. He got an increase of $200.

Q. Would it follow that the remuneration of all the other officials bears some proportion to the remuneration of the Collector?—A. I do not think so. The Civil Service Act provides that Collectors may have salaries from. a certain amount to a certain amount and surveyors from a certain amount to a certain amount, but there is no provision that a man should get an increase because of length of service or anything else. He would only get it if he had a pull strong enough.

Q. I notice, looking at the scale, that you would have $1,800 instead of $2,000, so that the remuneration of the Collector does not affect that of any of the subordinates?—A. No, it has nothing to do with that.

Q. Does length of service count in the matter of the annual statutory increases? How did you get up to $2,000? Was that always your salary as surveyor?—A. Oh, no. I had to get it done.

Q. When you were first made surveyor in 1891, what did you get?—A. $1,600.

Q. And then?—A. Two years ago, I think it was, I had an increase of $200. I acted as Collector at Sherbrooke for three years in addition to my duties here, and after that I think I was given another $100, and later on another $100. It is an unsatisfactory process, and a humiliating thing also, to have to get your friends to obtain for you what I call justice.

Q. You mention in the memorial that under the present system of no classification some officers in charge of offices are drawing less salaries than their assistants. Would that apply, for instance, to Mr. Belleau and Mr. Hamel?—A. Mr. Belleau is drawing $700 and his assistant $750. Mr. Belleau was put in charge of that office, and Mr. Hamel, being a younger man, was put in as his assistant.

(A letter from Mr. J. A. Belleau to the Commission was read and filed.)

(A letter from Mr. Pierre Hamel was also read and filed.)

Q. In his turn Mr. Hamel complains that, though he is a permanent officer, he gets less remuneration and less increase than temporary officers?—A. That is true in his case. For instance, Mr. Samson, who has come from Levis, gets $900.

Q. I suppose there were special reasons for that?—A. He is an exceedingly good officer.

Q. He should be made permanent?—A. If he passed the examination, I think, without doubt, he would be made permanent.

Q. Is there any reason why people in the same grade and appointed almost at the same time, should have different salaries? I find that an assistant appraiser appointed in 1888 gets $950, while another appointed three years later gets $750?—A. You are referring to the cases of Watters and Hannon. Mr. Watters gets $1,050 now, and Mr. Hannon has only lately been appointed assistant appraiser. He was a packer and had charge of our express office. He has passed the examination.

Q. Here are two other men, one of whom was appointed on the 1st of May, 1904, and gets only $650, while the other, appointed on the 1st of June, one month later, gets $850?—A. They are doing different sorts of work.

Q. They are both graded as clerks?—A. But there are clerks and clerks.

Q. Again, here are two men appointed on the same day, the 1st of October, 1893, one a tidewaiter and the other an assistant tidewaiter, but both get the same salary. Is there not a difference in the duties of a tidewaiter from those of an assistant tidewaiter?—A. The tidewaiter has the maximum salary of his class, but in the other case there is no maximum; the man has been doing the work of a shipping clerk in the long room.

Q. In order to get round the matter you call him a shipping clerk ?—A. He is doing a shipping clerk's work; but I do not see why he should not get $1,000 as an assistant tide surveyor.

Q. Then, the limit of a tide surveyor being $1,000, there is no reason why an assistant tide surveyor should not get $1,000?—A. I think so. Mr. Laurin tells me that the maximum of a tide surveyor is $1,200.

Q. There is nothing in this list about an assistant tide surveyor—is that an innovation?—A. Oh, no. There was an assistant tide surveyor when I came in here thirty-six years ago.

Q. There are only these two who are called tide surveyors?—A. That is all.

Q. I will put another case. One gentleman who was appointed preventive officer on the 13th of October, 1899, is in the enjoyment of $900 per annum, while another, who was appointed on the 17th of August, 1899, is on the list as a preventive officer, drawing $500 per annum?—A. I suppose one man has made better efforts than the other.

Q. Then, it comes to this, that these salaries depend largely on the amount of push and influence the men can get?—A. I think so, and I think it is detrimental to the public service.

By Mr. Bazin :

Q. You do not mean to say that it is more so with the present Government than with others?—A. Not at all. No matter what party is in or out, it is the same thing —you get in by pull and you get on by pull. This has nothing to do with politics; I am no politician.

By Mr. Fyshe:

Q. Has the collector anything to do with increases of salaries?—A. The present collector, I think, has nothing to do with the increases of salaries, except in one case; I know that he did recommend the case of our cashier, a man who has been thirty years in the service and gets $1,200 a year. He handles all the money that is collected, and he is in his cage pretty nearly all day long. There may have been one or two other cases in which increases called for special recommendation; but the collector has never interfered with the question of salary increases.

Q. Was his recommendation acted upon in that case?—A. No, it was not.

By the Chairman :

Q. What is the first step you take to get an additional tide surveyor or an additional landing water appointed?—A. We notify the Department of Customs that we require more help.

Q. What do they do then?—A. They send us somebody.

Q. Somebody from the place?—A. I suppose from the district to which the patronage belongs.

By Mr. Fyshe:

Q. When the department is called upon for assistance, whom do they send for? The local member?—A. I do not know anything about that. They settle that themselves. I would say this, however, that last season Mr. Bain came down here, and he was informed that we wanted six or seven officers, and a number of people were sent to him by the different members who had the patronage, and from them he selected a certain number, and a very good selection they turned out to be.

Q. That was after a personal interview?—A. Yes.

Q. And a kind of sizing up or test of ability?—A. Yes, the sizing up of a man by conversation with him, and so on.

Q. Neither you nor the collector know anything about any of those people entering the service until they come?—A. Nothing at all.

By the Chairman:

Q. What do you think has been the increased cost of living in the last fifteen years?—A. All I know is that it has been enormous. I suppose it must have increased fifty per cent in the last twenty-five years. I could not give an opinion as to the percentage of increase in the last fifteen years.

By Mr. Bazin:

Q. As a matter of fact, you know that it costs much more to live to-day than it did fifteen years ago?—A. Yes, and the cost is going up all the time, as far as I can see.

By the Chairman:

Q. Here is a budget submitted by some of your officers of the actual annual expenses $10; medicine,$15; washing,$60; fuel,$50; dry goods, $200; boots, $40; retirement fund, of a family of eight persons for a year: Rent $144; life insurance, $30; fire insurance, $10; medicine, $15; washing, $60; fuel, $50; dry goods, $200; boots, $40; retirement fund, $38; church, $15; electric light, $20; extra expenses, $24; living, at 5 cents per person for each meal, 40 cents a meal, $1.20 a day, or $438 a year; or an expenditure of $1,084 per annum. Is that a reasonable estimate, and if so, how can a man getting $750 or $650 live? How is the list made up?

Mr. WATTERS.—The men made it up themselves, and some of their friends assisted them.

Q. If that is a reasonable statement, then I ask again, how do the employees make both ends meet?

Mr. LAURIN.—They don't.

Q. Is there a general falling behind in the world of the permanent employees?

Captain CARTER.—I never ask them about their private affairs, and I should not like to say. I know it is a hard struggle to keep clear of debt.

Mr. WATTERS.—There is one thing—I am not able to pay my way.

The CHAIRMAN.—Are there any little extra perquisites earned by the men who go down to meet the steamships?

Captain CARTER.—Yes, but they do not amount to very much in the aggregate. Mr. Belleau gets pay for extra hours sometimes and also Mr. Laurin. How much they make they themselves can tell you.

Mr. BELLEAU.—I do not make more than $50 extra in a year.

The CHAIRMAN.—The average result is that the people who work extra will not get more than $100 the year round?

Captain CARTER.—The average would be less than $100, though some get more.

Q. Then in some cases uniforms are found?—A. Yes.

Q. That would add a little to the emolument?—A. In some cases it does, but not in all cases, because they simply put on the uniform for a particular duty. In other cases, for instance, at a railway station, the officer wears the uniform all the time.

Q. In the old days, all the passengers used to be discharged at Quebec—the first-class, the second-class and the steerage?—A. Yes.

Q. At present the first-class, and the second-class passengers go up to Montreal? —A. Yes, except those of the Empress steamers. According to the law, all the third-class passengers land in Quebec. All the Empress steamers' passengers, first-class, second-class and steerage, land at Quebec, because there is a train waiting for them which takes them to Montreal free.

Q. Has the increased number of first-class passengers going on to Montreal, and the diminution of the number landing at Quebec, had any effect in diminishing the duties of the office here?—A. I do not think so.

Q. On the other hand, the number of immigrants having increased, the number of customs examinations has increased?—A. Oh, yes, and more officers are required. Of course, the examination of immigrants' baggage is not very keen or searching, but the numbers are so great that more officers are required at a time.

Q. Having regard to the fact that many of these immigrants are coming to the country for the first time and are ignorant of either of the languages of the country, are they treated with every consideration and courtesy by the Customs officials?—A. There is no question about that.

Q. The feeling among the Customs officials is that these people are strangers in a strange land, and they extend every attention and courtesy to them?—A. There is no question about that. They are treated with every kindness and consideration by our people as well as by the immigration people.

The CHAIRMAN.—If on consideration you or any of the other gentlemen think of any additional facts which you would like to present to the Commission, we shall be very glad to have you supplement your answers with a further memorandum.

COLONEL JOSEPH B. FORSYTH, sworn and examined.

By the Chairman:

Q. You were appointed on the 17th of April, 1881, as Collector of Customs at Quebec?—A. Yes.

Q. Were you appointed at $3,000 a year?—A. Yes.

Q. And you have remained at that ever since?—A. Until this spring.

Q. When you were given $200 more?—A. Yes.

Q. During those 16 years the revenue has trebled?—A. Yes.

Q. Have you a memorandum which you wish to submit ?—A. Yes.

(Memorandum read and filed.)

Q. Have you had any hand in the appointments to the Custom-house staff at Quebec since you have been collector?—A. No.

Q. When you wanted additional assistance you applied to Ottawa?—A. Yes.

Q. And you were told from Ottawa that somebody was appointed?—A. On one occasion I did recommend a man, and he was appointed, and he is doing remarkably well.

Q. You recommended, we are told, that the salary of that very deserving officer, the cashier, should be increased?—A. Yes.

Q. Did you succeed in that instance?—A. No. They told him that he was getting the highest salary that he could receive, and that unless he passed an examination the matter could not be considered.

Q. That is to say, he is graded as a clerk, and I presume that the idea was that he must become a chief clerk, and pass a Promotion examination ?—A. Yes.

Q. However, the result was that your well meant effort to obtain for him increased remuneration failed?—A. Entirely.

Q. Then, judging by the fact that you have only succeeded in making one appointment, and that you failed utterly in the one attempt that you made to get an officer an increase of salary, it would appear that the department acts on its own motion without any regard or reference to you ?—A. Entirely, I think.

Q. Although yours is a political appointment, do you think that it is desirable that appointments should continue to be made as they are now, or should the patronage system be entirely abolished?—A. I think it would be a very good thing for the service if the patronage system were entirely abolished.

Q. Although you come in as a collector of Customs, the result of your 16 years observation is that in your opinion it would be better for the service if the patronage system were abolished?—A. I think so.

Q. Do you think appointments should be probationary?—A. I think it would be an excellent thing if they were.

7-8 EDWARD VII., A. 1908

Q. You think there should be a limit of time, and if a person appointed served creditably then you would make his appointment permanent?—A. Certainly.

Q. You have now, I understand, about the same number of supernumerary officials as you have permanent officials?—A. Very nearly.

Q. That is to say, you have 37 supernumeraries as against 45 permanents?—A. Yes.

Q. And out of the 45 permanent, six are sub-collectors at outports or preventive officers?—A. Yes.

Q. So that it practically comes to this that there are 37 supernumerary as against 39 permanent?—A. That is about it.

Q. Is that a desirable state of things, that nearly one-half of the staff are not in permanent positions?—A. I think it would be very much better if they were all permanent; but the trouble with us in Quebec is that while we want a great many men in summer to examine baggage coming off the ships and to go on the wharf, we have no work for those men in winter. That is why, I fancy, this system is continued.

Q. Captain Carter said that there were six or seven officers so situated, and it was suggested that those who were redundant here during the winter might be sent to Halifax and St. John, and that when the winter was over they might be sent back to Quebec ?—A. That might be done.

Q. That is done by the Allans and by the immigration people in the government service ?—A. There might be a difficulty about that. The men are located here with their families, and they would consider it a hardship to be sent to Halifax or St. John unless they received extra remuneration. I think it would be an excellent thing if it could be managed.

Q. In the Post Office and in the Inland Revenue Departments the outside officials are classified and they have annual increments of salary ?—A. Yes.

Q. In the Customs that is not so?—A. It does not obtain in the Customs.

Q. You think the outside service of the Customs should be classified?—A. I do.

Q. And that they should be given annual increases until the maximum of their respective classes is attained?—A. Yes, especially with deserving men.

Q. It is stated that under the present system of no classification there are some officers in charge of offices drawing lower salaries than the officers under them ?—A. Yes.

Q. That is not general, I presume?—A. It is not general, but it is the case. The man in charge of the record office, Mr. Belleau, receives $700 and Mr. Hamel who is under him receives $750. I think at any rate they ought to be paid the same.

Q. I want to ask you if Mr. Hamel has extra politicial influence ?—A. It is not exactly that. His father, who was in the Custom-house, and was an exceedingly good officer, died rather suddenly, and the son was appointed to his father's position, and he is a very good young man.

Q. Still, as a matter of right and wrong, it is not desirable that a higher grade officer should draw a lower salary than his assistant ?—A. No, it is not usual.

By Mr. Fyshe:

Q. Practically, I suppose they do the same work ?—A. Very much the same work.

Q. That being the case, why should they call one man the chief and the other the assistant?—A. Mr. Belleau is in charge of the office, and is responsible for what goes on there. If I want anything explained, I call on Mr. Belleau.

By the Chairman :

Q. Mr. Hamel also brings to the notice of the Commission the fact that whilst he gets $750, somebody else who is not a permanent officer, gets more. Is it a fact that temporaries are getting more than permanent officers ?—A. I think not.

Q. What do the examining officers get ?—A. Their salaries have not been increased. I want to call your attention to the case of one of the checking clerks. It

SESSIONAL PAPER No. 29a

is very important in the custom-house to have good checkers. We have three very good checkers, and one of them, Mr. Samson, is simply on the supernumerary list at present.

Q. He ought to be appointed permanently?—A. He certainly ought to be.

Q. The deputation suggested that the minimum salary be fixed at a liberal amount to cover the increased cost of living; do you agree with that?—A. Entirely. I worked the matter out very carefully myself, because in some of the representations made to the Honourable the Minister last winter, it was stated that the increased cost of living amounted to from 60 to 75 per cent. I think that is an exaggeration. I think you may say it amounts to 50 per cent.

Q. Mr. Beaudet writes that in 1901 he was appointed to the customs and that in 1903 he was acting chief clerk. Is he still acting as such ?—A. Yes, he is acting chief clerk.

Q. He is called a preventive officer. Has he failed to pass the Promotion examination ?—A. He never tried. When he was first appointed, he was appointed as an appraiser. He was a man who had great experience in hardware and on the death of Mr. Gouin, who was chief clerk, he was appointed acting chief clerk.

Q. What did Mr. Gouin get ?—A. I think $1,200.

Q. If he passed the examination and were graded a chief clerk, he would get more than he gets now?—A. Certainly.

Q. He did not pass the examination ?—A. I do not think he was ever asked to pass the examination.

Q. Would it not be better for him to go up when the next Promotion examination comes ?—A. Mr. Beaudet is almost as old as I am.

By Mr. Bazin:

Q. What examination did he pass the other day ?—A. He passed an examination to be an appraiser.

Q. And he was not appointed an appraiser ?—A. No.

By the Chairman:

Q. Mr. Beaudet appears to have been appointed in 1903?—A. His first appointment to the Civil Service was on May 1, 1901.

Q. Looking at the openings in other branches of life, do you find the same inducements to young men in Quebec to enter the public service as existed fifteen years ago?—A. I do not think so.

Q. Have you any resignations now of able men in the Customs service at Quebec? —A. No.

Q. Have any of your men resigned?—A. None. One or two have left us, but I might say that they left their country for their country's good.

Q. They did not resign to better themselves?—A. No. They were not the most temperate men, and one man had to go and the other resigned.

Q. But you have not found in Quebec that the public servants are leaving in any number?—A. No.

By Mr. Fyshe:

Q. You have not power to dismiss them?—A. On one occasion I had. A young man was told that unless he behaved better I could either keep him or dismiss him, and I gave him several trials for his own sake or the sake of his family, but finally he had to go. In the Civil Service, when a man will not do his work, but leaves it to others, there is a great deal of grumbling.

Q. Is the work in the Custom-house at Quebec generally up-to-date, or are there any arrears ?—A. It is very much up-to-date.

By the Chairman:

Q. Do you find that the abolition of superannuation has been beneficial to the service?—A. I cannot say.

Q. Do you think that the present system, under which there is an abatement and a retiring fund, adds to the stability of the public service?—A. I think it does.

Q. You think that a retirement fund is better than the old superannuation?—A. Yes.

Q. Then you would not suggest that the old Superannuation Act should be re-enacted?—A. I think not. It is not a matter that I have studied very much, but I think the present is a very good arrangement.

Q. Do you find that the salaries now paid in Quebec are adequate to the needs of the majority of the officials?—A. I think not.

Q. Do you think it probable that many of the officers are getting behind in the world?—A. I am sure that they are either getting behind or are pinching themselves and their families to a very great extent.

Q. Would you think that the statement presented to us by the officers of the Custom-house is an accurate representation of the expenditure of a Customs officer in Quebec?—A. I daresay it is very near it.

Q. You think it is not exaggerated?—A. No. I think that men with families cannot live on less than $100 a month if they pay up everything.

Q. Is it desirable that the state of things should continue in which a man drawing only $750 a year requires from $90 to $100 a month to live?—A. No, I think it is very dangerous.

Q. Does it expose men to temptation?—A. Of course it does.

Q. Is there any means by which a Customs officer, if he relaxed a little in his notions of right and wrong, could increase his income?—A. Not in the Customs.

Q. Then, in this unfortunate case a man has simply to go behind and run absolutely into debt?—A. Yes.

Q. That would interfere with his performance of his daily work?—A. It would, having this constant worry and anxiety.

Q. One gentleman who was appointed a preventive officer at Quebec in 1905 is now a landing waiter and his salary is $700. Do you name the men to fill the places of landing waiters if there are vacancies?—A. Not landing waiters. We have only two in our department, Mr. Laurin and Mr. Boulger; but these men are appointed as tide-waiters or assistant tidewaiters, and I assign their work.` Mr. Pageau is a kind of acting clerk; he is in the landing waiters' room doing a clerk's work.

Q. Then he is graded lower than an ordinary man doing the same duties would be graded?—A. He is graded as a landing waiter or tidewaiter.

Q. Is that lower than a clerk in the scale?—A. Yes.

Q. Has he failed to pass the examination?—A. I am not aware that he has passed any examination.

Q. Because he does the duties he does, his pay should be increased?—A. His salary is fixed at Ottawa without any consultation with me as to whether it is sufficient or not.

Q. Do you, from dread of the politicians or from other causes, have any of your officials doing work of a higher grade than their grade in the Civil Service list?—A. In this very case of Pageau, he is really doing clerk's work, whereas he is called an examining officer, which means anything you like.

Q. I suppose he is about the only man called an examining officer?—A. No, we have about ten other men who passed a sort of nondescript examination which I do not think amounts to very much.

By Mr. Fyshe:

Q. An examination on what?—A. They are examined by the inspector. If they write a little, do a few sums and calculate duties, they are made examining ˙officers, which puts them on the permanent list.

SESSIONAL PAPER No. 29a

By the Chairman :

Q. And then, after they get on the permanent list without departmental examinations, if they are appointed to do higher grade duties, they cannot get the higher grade because they have not passed the examination?—A. No. I never heard of examining officers until two or three years ago.

Q. Do you know anything about the case of Placide Langlois (showing the witness a letter)?—A. Yes, he is a very good clerk.

Q. Do you know if he has passed any examination?—A. I do not think he ever went up for examination.

Q. Then a great deal of friction and difficulty and a certain amount of discontent arises from the want of ability to carry out the regulations laid down by the Civil Service Act?—A. Yes. Of course, young men can pass these examinations; several of them have done so. Langlois, I should think, would be quite able to do so if he tried.

Q. Have you recently had men put on the list who are beyond the age, and whom you employ temporarily?—A. No.

Q. As a whole, are the officials of the Custom-house at Quebec efficient?—A. They are very good men, indeed.

Q. Have they good habits?—A. Oh, yes.

Q. Have you had any occasion to report any of them to Ottawa recently?—A. No, not for a very long time.

Q. When you have had occasion to report to Ottawa on the habits of an officer, was any regard paid to your recommendations?—A. Oh, yes, very promptly. They wrote very severe letters.

Q. You have had, both from the Minister of Customs and the Commissioner, every support that you would want in the exercise of your duties as Collector of Customs?—A. Entirely.

Q. What is your general idea as to the percentage that salaries in Quebec should be increased?—A. We all agree, I think, about the increased cost of living, and, although I do not suppose perhaps that the Government would agree to a fifty per cent increase, I do think that if they gave a twenty-five per cent increase, it would not be too much.

Q. I presume it is desirable that the public official should have a certain position in the community?—A. Certainly.

Q. And now, owing to the increased cost of living, the position of a public servant in the community is less influential than it used to be?—A. Of course it is. He has to be very quiet and keep pretty much to himself.

Q. Then, in point of fact, the public servant, instead of being a citizen who would be looked up to in the community, is now retiring to the background?—A. He has to do it.

Q. He is falling below par?—A. Perhaps he is not doing so in the estimation of his friends, but we know that he has to retire because he has not the means to live as he used to.

Q. After all, looking at the matter from the worldly point of view, does not the world respect men who are rather prominent in the world's eye?—A. I suppose that has always been so.

Q. Then, the public servant, having now to lead a quiet and unostentatious life, however good he may be, cannot mix with the world, and to that extent want of knowledge of the world may be detrimental to the efficient performance of his duties?—A. Yes, there are a good many considerations.

Q. If you wish to supplement your evidence in any way you think desirable, we would be glad to have you do so?—A. There is just one thing I would like to call attention to. In the examining warehouse we have three appraisers. Two of them are called assistant appraisers. Mr. Dion is for dry goods; his salary is $1,500. Mr. Gaumond, also a very good appraiser, is for hardware; he gets $1,150. Then we have Mr. Watters, who gets $1,050; he is put down as assistant appraiser, and I believe he has really more

7-8 EDWARD VII., A. 1908

to do than the other two men. Another man who gets $900 is in charge of the express; his name is Harry Hannon.

By Mr. Fyshe:

Q. Is there any opportunity for receiving perquisites in that office?—A. I do not think so. His books are examined carefully, generally twice every month, and all the parcels are looked into. Harry Hannon is a man I think very highly of. There is no doubt that the office of appraiser is a very important one, and when one has good men, we should try to keep them and do what we can for them. I think Mr. Dion is satisfied with what he gets, but I think Gaumond, Watters and Hannon should be paid more than they are.

Q. In the list there is one preventive officer who was appointed on October 14, 1899, who is stated to have been paid in the year ending June 30, 1906, $950 a year, while another appointed on August 17, 1899, is stated to have been paid in the same year $500 a year?—A. One of them, Mr. Vallerand, is put down as accountant and registrar's clerk. He is one of our best officers. He makes up all the monthly accounts for Ottawa and looks after the registration of all the vessels here. Mr. Lafond, a preventive officer, who only gets $550, is a locker.

Q. An examining officer appointed on September 1, 1905, got $550, another appointed on April 1, 1905, got $550, another appointed April 1, 1905, got $650, another appointed December 1, 1905, got $550, and another appointed on April 1, 1906, got $700. What is the reason for these little discrepancies?—A. We have nothing to do with that in the Customs here. We are told to appoint a man and his salary is so much.

Q. Although he may be a junior and doing exactly the same work, he might have more salary than his senior?—A. It would be quite possible.

J. B. St. Amant, sworn and examined.

By the Chairman:

. What is your position in the Customs Department?—A. I am a clerk.

. Are you on the permanent list?—A. Yes.

Q. When were you appointed to the permanent list?—A. On the 1st of May, 1904.

Q. How long were you in the service before that?—A. Three years.

Q. You passed the Entrance examination.?—A. Yes.

Q. What is your salary now?—A. $750.

Q. Are you one of the men who got $100 increase recently?—A. Yes.

Q. What is it in your case that you think needs rectifying?—A. I think that when we pass an examination like that we should get an increase each year and be paid more than messengers.

Q. How is it that a clerk who was appointed a month after you gets $100 or $150 more than you?—A. He was appointed before me, and we passed our examination together.

Q. Are you doing the same kind of work?—A. I am clerk in the landing waiters' room. My assistant gets $700, only $50 less than I get, although I have been four years in the office and he has been there only one year.

Q. Who nominated you to the public service?—A. Sir Charles Fitzpatrick.

Q. Sir Charles Fitzpatrick having gone out, I suppose you feel rather at a loss?—A. Yes.

Q. And you would like some one else to look after your interests?—A. Yes.

Q. As there is nobody now to look after your interests, you suffer from the want of friendship?—A. Yes.

Q. Does that mean that in the Custom-house at Quebec the only way to get an increase of salary is to be recommended by a member of Parliament or a politician?— A. Sometimes we have to get the name of the Collector or the Inspector.

By Mr. Basin:

Q. Is it necessary absolutely, in order to secure an increase, to get the recommendation of a politician?—A. Yes.

By the Chairman:

Q. Have you ever applied to the Collector to send a recommendation to Ottawa for an increase in your salary?—A. No.

Q. Don't you think that instead of taking the extreme measure of coming here, it would have been better to have taken the official method and to have asked your Collector to forward to the authorities in Ottawa your application for an increase of salary?—A. I have not tried that yet. The past experience is that that has not been successful.

CUSTOMS CANADA.
PORT OF QUEBEC, September 17, 1907.

THOS. S. HOWE, Esq.,
Secretary of Commission.

DEAR SIR,—The following have been selected as a deputation to wait on the Commission to-morrow afternoon at 2 o'clock:—

Capt. W. H. Carter, Surveyor; E. Beaudet, Chief Clerk; A. Gaumond, Appraiser; J. G. Waters, Appraiser; Col. L. N. Laurin, Chief Landing Waiter; W. E. Edge, Check Clerk; L. N. Vallerand, Preventive Officer; J. A. Belleau, Clerk; J. Fullerton, Examining Officer.

Respectfully yours,

J. B. M. FORSYTH,
Collector.

CUSTOMS, CANADA—PORT OF QUEBEC.

Recommendations by the Customs Officers of the Port of Quebec.

1st. That the patronage system be abolished and that all appointments to the Customs service shall be in the hands of a Civil Service Board, by whom such appointments shall be made from those who have passed the required examinations. That before such appointments shall be confirmed by said board, the person so appointed shall serve for a period of three months, and be reported on favourably by the head of the department under whom he has served.

2nd. That all officers shall be appointed on the permanent staff. And inasmuch as more officers are required at such ports as Montreal and Quebec in summer than in winter, and more at Halifax and St. John in winter than in summer, the officers not required at the former ports be transferred to the latter during winter, and in the same way those of Halifax and St. John not wanted, be sent to Quebec and Montreal in summer.

3rd. That the outside service shall be classified ; that in each class there shall be an annual increase of salary to each officer until the maximum salary of such class is reached, provided he is reported favourably on by the head of the department in which he is serving.

29a.—10

4th. There shall be promotion examinations from class to class, and that such examinations shall be on the duties the officer will be called on to perform. Under the present system of no classification, we find some officers in charge of offices drawing less salary than their assistants.

5th. That the minimum scale of salaries be fixed at a liberal amount to cover increased cost of living, it being borne in mind that the present scale of salaries was made twenty-five years ago, and the cost of living has increased by about 50 per cent.

6th. That extra service pay on Sundays be increased from 30 cents to 50 cents an hour.

(Sgd.)   W. H. CARTER,
Surveyor, Chairman of Deputation.

QUEBEC, Sept. 18, 1907.

CUSTOMS, CANADA,
PORT OF QUEBEC, Sept. 17, 1907.

To the Commissioners of Civil Service, Quebec :

GENTLEMEN,—I have been appointed to H. M. Customs in April, 1905, as preventive officer at $550 a year, but two months later I was put in charge of the Record Office, with Mr. Pierre Hamel as assistant at $600 a year.

In the fall of 1905 I passed the qualifying examination with success, and I was appointed permanent as clerk in April, 1906, with an increase of $50, when my assistant got a hundred.

This year I was given $700 and Mr. Hamel $750, yet $50 more. You will surely agree with me that I have a very good reason to come before you and that my case is one that should be considered.

If you desire certificates of my capacities, I am quite sure that you would have the very best from my chief in Quebec.

I am very often called to take other places, when they are sick or absent, specially the cashier; that is one of the most important in the Customs.

All other officers in charge of departments are receiving more salary, specially they are getting more than their assistants, for having the responsibility. Your honourable consideration would oblige,

Your obedient servant,
(Sgd.)   J. A. BELLEAU.

Record Office, H. M. Customs, Quebec.

CUSTOM HOUSE,
QUEBEC, September 18, 1907.

To the Commissioners of the Civil Service, Quebec, P.Q.

GENTLEMEN,—I beg the honour of your attention to the following facts: In May, 1891, I was named acting appraiser at the Custom-house of Quebec, and in February, 1903, I was assigned, by the Commissioners, to the duties of acting chief clerk in place of Mr. Gouin.

I beg respectfully of you, gentlemen, to raise my salary to the maximum which this responsible position demands.

I have the honour to be, gentlemen,
Your obedient servant,
(Signed)   E. BEAUDET,
Acting Chief Clerk.

CUSTOMS, CANADA,
PORT OF QUEBEC, September 17, 1907.

To the Commissioners of Civil Service, Quebec.

GENTLEMEN,—I have been appointed to H.M. Customs in the year 1903 as 'Acting landing waiter, $600,' and in 1904 and 1905 I passed two examinations, the Preliminary and the Qualifying, and in 1906 I was appointed as 'clerk.'

During those four years I received an increase of salary of $150, while some of the officers here who never passed any examinations and being never appointed clerk received $200 and $250 of increase.

I don't see what was the good of passing those two examinations if I should not get a larger salary than the examining officers or the messengers. It is true that I was appointed permanent, but some of those officers mentioned above are also permanent and are getting as high a salary as I am and have not been in the service any longer than I have been.

I would be very thankful to you, gentlemen, if you would investigate my case.

I have worked in different departments, and I gave, I think, satisfaction in each, and I am sure that the collector and inspector could give you a satisfactory report of my work and conduct.

Believe me to be, gentlemen,
Yours respectfully,

(Signed)   PIERRE HAMEL.

PIERRE HAMEL,
Custom House, Quebec.

CUSTOMS, CANADA,
QUEBEC, September 18, 1907.

To J. M. COURTNEY, Esq.,
Chairman, Civil Service Commission.

DEAR SIR,—I inclose statement *re* increases of salary of Customs officers at this port.

Yours truly,

(Signed)   W. H. CARTER,
Surveyor.

CUSTOMS CANADA.

PORT OF QUEBEC.

Increase of Salaries from April 1, 1907.

Permanent Staff—

1 at $200	$ 200
3 at 150	450
25 at 100	2,500
10 at 50	500
	$3,650

Temporary Officers—

```
 1 at $160..............................  $   160
 2 at  110..............................      220
 2 at  100..............................      200
 1 at   50..............................       50
10 at  120..............................    1,200
11 at   70..............................      770
```

$2,600

Permanent Staff........................... $3,650
Temporary Staff...........................   2,600

Total for port....................... $6,250

(Sgd.)   W. H. CARTER, *Surveyor.*

DOUANES, CANADA,
PORT DE QUÉBEC, QUÉ., 17 sept. 1907.

A la Commission d'Enquête, Service Civil, Canada.

MESSIÉURS LES COMMISSAIRES,—Sachant que le but pour lequel vous vous assemblez est de prendre en considération les griefs des employés des Douanes, je m'empresse à vous formuler les miens, étant employé moi-même.

Je suis marié et père de famille et comme tel mon devoir est d'améliorer ma condition le plus possible suivant mon mérite personnel.

Vous n'ignorez pas que la vie est dispendieuse et que le pauvre employé civil est le seul dans la vie sociale qui n'a pas vu une augmentation dans son salaire, mais s'aperçoit fort bien des dépenses augmentées forcément.

Ma nomination comme "Active Preventive Officer" date du 1er septembre 1906, avec un salaire de $550.00 à l'année, non permanent. Plus tard une augmentation générale de $100.00 par année fut allouée à tous les employés et mon salaire actuel est $650.00 par année, soit $54.17 par mois, à retrancher proportionnellement le temps perdu.

Vous pouvez constater que le dit salaire de $650.00 par année est le plus bas payé à un employé des Douanes de Québec.

Depuis le 1er décembre 1906, on m'a mis en charge du département des "Posts and Refunds", c'est-à-dire pour faire amender les entrées erronées. Ce serait suffisant pour occuper un homme consciencieusement vu l'augmentation d'ouvrage dans ce département, ailleurs; mais on m'a confié la charge en plus d'un registre de toutes les entrées du jour avec particularités et à faire la liste des argents collectés par le caissier pour envoyer à Ottawa. Ceci est un surcroît d'ouvrage, mais je ne m'en suis jamais plaint espérant que mon mérite serait reconnu en justice; voilà pourquoi je m'empresse de m'adresser à vous, puisque vous êtes nommés pour nous rendre justice. Est-ce que la charge d'un département comme la mien et la responsabilité qui en découle mérite le plus bas salaire et moins que celui d'un simple messager?

J'ai préparé ma demande pour ma permanence. J'ai fait un cours classique complet et je suis de plus porteur d'un diplôme de bachelier-ès-lettres de l'université Laval, et je puis vous dire que mes chefs ont été forcés parfois de me féliciter de mon ouvrage. Avec tout cela je mériterais d'être moins payé que le plus simple employé sans capacité et responsabilité.

Messieurs les commissaires, j'espère que votre rapport à Ottawa pour moi sera favorable et que votre acte de justice en ce cas-ci, vous acquerra la plus profonde gratitude de

Votre dévoué serviteur,

(Signé)   PLACIDE LANGLOIS,
Douanes, Québec.

CUSTOMS—CANADA.

PORT OF QUEBEC, September 18, 1907.

Memo. from Collector.

It is not necessary for me to refer to the great increase in the present cost of living compared to what it was a few years ago. I think I am within bounds when I place it at 50 per cent *more* than formerly. The memorial presented to the Hon. Wm. Paterson, Minister of Customs, in January last went very fully into these details. I may also remind the Commissioners that the press of Canada was strongly in favour of increasing the salaries of Customs Officers, the Toronto *Globe* of January 18 last declared ' There is no branch of the Civil Service worse paid than the members of the Customs staff.'

A slight increase has been made of $50 to $100 but that has been looked on as of ' temporary assistance only,' pending the final result of your Commission which is looked forward to with great anxiety by all members of the Civil Service.

I may here state that the employees at this port are a well-conducted set of men who do their work in a highly creditable manner, and it is very seldom that I receive any complaints or am obliged to give a reprimand. Our annual receipts have increased from $1.197,669 in 1901-2 to $1,675,523 to year ending June 30, 1907, with a large increase since that time, this of course entails a great deal more work, while the staff has only been increased by three or four *outside men.*

Another matter which I wish to bring before you is the maximum allowance of twenty-five years ago, which should not obtain at present but should be considerably augmented. I will give here the case of our cashier, a most careful and accurate accountant with thirty-four years' service, who is daily at work from 9 or 9.30 to 4 or 4.50. When he applied for an increase he was told to pass a Civil Service examination, a hard thing for a man to do when he arrives at a certain age.

I well remember Mr. Dunscomb, for many years collector at this port, telling me that one man was plucked because he could not tell who the Druids were.

It also seems to me that there should be first, second and third-class clerks the same as in other branches of the Civil Service, that this would stimulate young men to improve and work their way up instead of trusting to their political friends as at present.

I also think that all officers employed in the Customs as clerks or acting clerks should be made permanent, for as the inclosed list shows— one check clerk and several acting clerks are on the supernumerary list.

It would certainly be a great thing for the Civil Service if the pensions earned by officers of the permanent force were continued to their widows, or if a man dies in harness the pension be given to his widow during her life time.

I may state that this port has a great many more outports and preventive stations than elsewhere (twenty-seven in all), which adds greatly to the amount of checking, correspondence, &c., and though our contingent account ($2,025.65) in August looks rather high we are really short of outside men, for it must be remembered that ships discharged all their immigrants and many passengers here, on some occasions three or four steamers arriving in one day.

CUSTOMS—CANADA.

COLLECTOR'S OFFICE, QUEBEC, September 18, 1907.

(Pay-Lists)—Port of Quebec.

Permanent staff list for August........ ... .$			3,416 58
Less superannuation, No. 1..............$	27 47		
Less superannuation, No. 2........... ..	2 04		
Less retired fund................. ..	81 08		
			110 59
			$ 3,305 99
Contingencies—Extra service...........$	1,695 02		
Cartage..............	162 90		
Cleaning.............	40 00		
Postage..	17 20		
Travelling....	75 25		
Sundries..	32 31		
Telegrams..	2 97		
			2,025 65

Revenue.

1907—July... ... .$194,067 74	
August.. .. .. 158,943 27	
September 18... .... 97,908 34	

DOUANES, CANADA,

PORT DE QUÉBEC, 18 septembre 1907.

A Messieurs les Commissaires du Service Civil, Québec.

MESSIEURS,—J'ai l'honneur de vous soumettre:

1° Que j'ai été nommé, en 1905, douanier (examining officer) à Québec;

2° que depuis un an je remplis la charge de commis au bureau du préposé au débarquement (landing waiter);

3° que mon salaire n'est que de $700;

4° que ce salaire est insuffisant pour subvenir aux besoins de ma famille vu l'augmentation des loyers et de tout ce qui est nécessaire à la vie, je demande en conséquence une augmentation de salaire et j'ose espérer que ma requête sera accordée.

Veuillez me croire votre tout devoué,

(Signé)   CHARLES PAGEAU,
Examining officer.

CUSTOMS, CANADA,

PORT OF QUEBEC, September 18, 1907.

Civil Service Commission.

SIRS,—Permit me to profit by this suitable occasion to submit to you a few details regarding my position. I am in the principal office of the Custom-house for nearly five years, as assistant bookkeeper, and all other work concerning the office, such as bookkeeping, checking the entries, signing the orders, examining the goods as is the rule in all the original entries, make the monthly additions. and quarterly (balances) in book No. 1; also the statements, monthly, quarterly, and yearly accounts, and this, sirs, for the small sum of $750 a year.

I have never been able to have obtained for me a reasonable salary to meet the wants of my family, and to recompense the merits of my position. I see no obstacle that should hinder me from obtaining a reasonable and suitable salary in accordance to my position.

As I have already mentioned above, that I am in the principal office of the Custom-house, I passed two examinations (Preliminary and Promotion), and up to the present have given entire satisfaction. I hope, sirs, that on this occasion you will give me all the credit possible.

On the last page I am giving you the amount of absolute expenses for my family, which is composed of eight persons, and I hope you will find my conduct up to the present satisfactory.

Thanking you in advance. I hope this message will prove favourable for the increase in my salary.

Yours very humble,

(Signed)   L. G. FAGUY.

Remarks:—My position, according to my examination,— Ex. Officer.

My position 'since 1903 up to day,—Asst. Bookkeeper.

Absolute Yearly Expenses for my Family, composed of Eight Persons.

Rent, $12 per month	$144 00
Life assurance	30 00
Insurance on household effects	10 00
Doctor	15 00
Washing, $5 per month	60 00
Heating	50 00
Dry goods	200 00
Footwear	40 00
Funds left at Custom-house	38 00
Church pew	15 00
Electric light	20 00
Extra expenses (absolute), $2 per month	24 00
Recreation	......
Food, 5c. per person per meal, 40c.; three meals per day, $1.20; 365 days	438 00
	$1,084 00
Salary	750 00
Deficit	$334 00

QUEBEC, August 14, 1907.

GENTLEMEN,—I have the honour to state that on April 9, 1884, I received a commission as preventive officer in the Customs service with a salary of $600. From this period I acted as a landing waiter and did various other Customs duties till October 1, 1893, when I was appointed assistant tide surveyor at $1,000, which position I filled till 1898, when I was instructed to act as shipping clerk, which I have done ever since; this involves the keeping of the registers of 'ocean-going vessels,' 'coasting trade,' and 'rivers and lakes trading to the United States,' for not only the port of Quebec, but all the outports and preventive stations under the jurisdiction of said port, seeing that sick mariners' dues, 'tonnage and harbour dues,' are collected and paid to the cashier; also all 'export,' 'in transitu entries,' and 'special customs manifests,' issuing of 'coasting licenses,' have charge of steamboat inspection certificates, hospital register, Chinese immigration, International Customs Journal, reports re trade and commerce, establishment book, &c. I also perform the duties of the tide surveyor when, from absence or sickness, that officer is not available.

As a preventive officer, I hold a 'writ of assistance,' covering the whole Dominion, and have made some important seizures in connection with the smuggling of contraband from St. Pierre and Miquelon, &c., all of which are on record.

Now, in view of the fact that any amount can be paid to a preventive officer, and in consideration of my length of service, now in the 24th year, as also the responsible position which I fill, I believe that if this is placed before the honourable the Minister of Customs he will, no doubt, grant me an increase of $200, which I am sure you will admit is not asking too much in these times when living is so expensive.

With reference to the work I do, and how it is performed, I would most respectfully refer the honourable the Commissioners to my Collector, who is the best judge of the same.

I have the honour to be, gentlemen,
Your obedient servant,
(Sgd.   F. WOOD GRAY,
Asst. Tide Surveyor and Preventive Officer.

The Civil Service Commission, Ottawa :

In view of the foregoing, in which I entirely concur, and of the faithful and exceptionally efficient manner in which Colonel Gray's work has always been performed, I shall be greatly pleased if an increase of salary be given to him, and I consider that the amount which he asks is, under the circumstances, quite reasonable.

(Sgd.)   J. BELL FORSYTH.
QUEBEC, August 14, 1907.

TORONTO, September 27, 1907.

The Royal Commission on the Civil Service met this morning at 10.30 o'clock.
Present:—Mr. J. M. COURTNEY, C.M.G., Chairman
Mr. THOMAS FYSHE, Montreal, and
Mr. P. J. BAZIN, Quebec.

Dr. SMITH, Windsor, called, sworn, and examined.

Witness handed in a memorial which was filed.

By the Chairman:

Q. You are the spokesman of the gentlemen present?—A. Yes.

Q. Mr. Patterson, who is also here, was, I believe, the secretary of the committee that waited on the Minister of Customs last January, was he not?—A. Yes.

Q. How long have you been in the service?—A. I was appointed four years ago last June.

Q. The other gentlemen representing various branches of the service have been longer in the service, I suppose, than you have?—A. All these gentlemen have been longer in the service than I have and they are associated with me this morning in case you might ask any questions on points that I am not familiar with. In which event they can answer on behalf of their respective departments.

Q. In the Civil Service Act the departments scheduled as having officers outside are the Inland Revenue, the Post Office, and the Customs Department?—A. Yes.

Q. The Inland Revenue and the Post Office Departments allow their staff annual increments?—A. Yes.

Q. There have been no such increments allowed by the Customs Department? There are only limits placed for the salaries of the officers?—A. That is all. There have not been any for years, with the exception of an occasional case, until this year when an increase was granted as we mentioned in our memorial.

Q. Things got to such a pass that during the last session of parliament the Minister of Customs, Mr. Paterson, tried to cut the Gordian knot by giving to each man within the limits $100 a year increase?—A. Yes. Some with longer service $150 and others $200.

Q. But this increase was confined to men within the limits?—A. Yes.

Q. The inspectors who get $2,500 or the collector who is in receipt of $4,000 could not get any more?—A. He was at the limit and could get nothing.

Q. So that this eleemosynary grant was given to people entirely within the limits?—A. Yes.

Q. In your memorial you refer to the hours of service? What is the average daily service for a Customs official?—A. What grade do you have reference to.

Q. I mean all around? How long is the Custom-house open during the day?—A. The Custom-house proper where the entries are taken, opens at 9 o'clock in the morning and closes at 4 p.m.

Q. Do the officials stay after 4 o'clock, to make up the books?—A. If necessary. If not able to keep up the books they may be there for an hour or two hours after the Custom-house closes. It depends upon the amount of work that has to be done.

Q. At frontier ports where trains or boats continually arrive, some of the Customs officers have to wait to meet them?—A. We have on the frontier, where trains arrive, under regulation a twelve hours' service. That is the regular ten hours in the service of the government and two hours overtime, so that the officers are putting in twelve hours out of every twenty-four.

Q. That two hours overtime is paid by the steamboat or train people is it not?—A. With respect to the railroads they pay for Sunday service only. The steamboats pay for a service from six to eight o'clock in the morning and from twelve at night until two o'clock the next morning or whatever hour the vessels may reach port after that. But they are granted service free of charge from eight o'clock in the morning until midnight each day. The Government pays for that, but the steamboat company pays for the service of the officer between twelve midnight and eight o'clock next morning.

Q. At what hours do people come in from New York pass through Toronto?—A. Of course, trains come in at night and at all hours. They come in at one hour at Bridgeburg and another time at the frontier port. It is not only the passenger trains that have to be met. There is the freight, coming in that is manifested and put in bond. That has to be attended to as the trains come in. An officer's certificate is required, otherwise the trains would have to be held.

Q. Is the baggage of passengers checked at the frontier?—A. If the passenger is with the baggage it is supposed to be examined at the frontier. If not it is manifested in bond, the same as any other merchandise would be, to its point of destination.

Q. A person coming from New York, by way of the Suspension Bridge, with two or three trunks, would have to have those trunks examined?—A. If the passenger accompanies the trunks he is supposed to go forward to the baggage car and have them examined. If he did not come forward, or was not present on the train, the officer would manifest the baggage to its destination.

Q. Some of these trains pass the Suspension Bridge during the night?—A. At all hours.

Q. You do not wake up a passenger to have his baggage examined during the night?—A. He is supposed to be present, but if he does not wish to get out of his berth he simply hands the keys over to the porter, or whoever is in charge of the car, and this man goes forward and attends to the matter.

Q. The baggage of a passenger by train, whether by day or by night, is supposed to be examined at the Suspension Bridge provided the passenger is present, but in the case of freight arriving that is only manifested to its destination, and is not checked there?—A. It is transit freight going through the country; if it is manifested, and goes right on, it is not to be detained any longer than is necessary to make out the papers to bond it. With local freight some of it is examined at the frontier and some is sent through in bond.

Q. What are the hours of the Customs officers at the Suspension Bridge?—A. The regular office hours of the Government service would be from 8 o'clock in the morning until 6 p.m.

Q. But I mean the hours of the officers at the stations?—A. They are there at all hours. For instance, the officer commencing at 8 o'clock in the morning would work until 6 o'clock and he would probably be there until two hours later when the night shift comes on. However, it depends upon the requirements of the different stations. You cannot make a fixed hour because where you have a batch of officers you require more in the daytime than at night and you would arrange the work.

Q. Are the same men always on night duty?—A. As a rule they are on night duty week about or month about. That is left largely to the discretion of the collector and the officers themselves at the port.

Q. Then their hours are shifted about?—A. Yes.

Q. Here in Toronto there is a certain amount of Customs supervision at the Union Station?—A. Yes.

Q. When do the men begin their work there?

Mr. McCaffry.—That would be more in the hands of Mr. Bertram, the Surveyor, but the regular hours are from eight to six o'clock. Any time put in after that is overtime.

Q. But there are people coming in after that time?—A. Yes, but I think 11 o'clock at night is the latest. I do not think they have anybody there from 11 o'clock until the following morning.

Q. Referring to your memorial you consider that this eleemosynary gift of $100 was not the most ideal way of doing things?

Dr. Smith.—We expected at the time that something would be fixed as we asked in our memorial for an annual increase. But the time was limited. It was in January and provision had to be made for it. It was done hurriedly and in view of the appointment of a Royal Commission Mr. Paterson only granted, as he states, temporary relief.

Q. In a short concise sentence you ask, 'Is this plan likely to produce the best results'? You consider it is not such a plan and it has not produced the greatest efficiency?—A. No, it has not. We should have a minimum and a maximum salary and there should be a statutory increase as an encouragement for a man to do his duty.

Q. Are men leaving the Customs service now, attracted by higher rates of pay? Because you state in a pregnant sentence 'We know that this very condition has driven many men from the Government employ'?—A. Yes, we have cases throughout the country like that.

Q. Are they leaving in any numbers?—A. Not in any great numbers, but there are quite a number of them.

Q. That is the case in Toronto I suppose where the opportunities for bettering themselves are numerous?—A. Even in some smaller places it is the case.

Q. In order to fill the vacancies, of course, new men must be appointed?—A. Yes.

Q. Are you getting as good men to come in as you did in the old days?—A. My experience, of course, has been limited to four years, but I should judge comparing the men who are coming in with those that have been in the Government employ for some time that the former will be just as serviceable as the latter when they have had the same period of service. The men coming in now would not be as good as the experienced men who had been in the service for some years, but I think there is just as good a class coming in now as in former days. But there is that difficulty about salaries and a cry is going forth all the time.

Q. Considering that good men are snatched up everywhere do you really think you are getting as good men to come into the service as you did ten years ago?—A. Speaking strictly my own opinion is that I do not think there are. I know men who are applicants for positions in the Customs service and when they have found what the salaries were declined and withdrew their applications.

Q. You are one of the favoured men who entered the service without any examination?—A. Yes.

Q. And you know how appointments are made now?—A. Yes.

Q. That is to say if you, at your large port of Windsor, wanted a new officer you would write to the Department at Ottawa and the Department would sanction it if it was found desirable and they would give you a man?—A. They would ask me to forward the name of a man. I had three appointments last August. I asked for the appointment of three additional men in the service and sent a letter to the Commissioner at Ottawa. He wrote me back asking questions concerning the matter and finally consented. He asked me to forward the names of three men which I had to turn over to the party who has the patronage and he forwarded the names.

Q. You were appointed only four years ago?—A. Yes, four years ago.

Q. And without going into your personal proclivities you are *persona grata* with the people in Ottawa?—A. Exactly.

Q. And naturally they would listen with favour to your recommendations?—A. I presume there may be something in that.

Q. But supposing, Mr. Small, the Collector of Customs here, for instance, wanted new preventive officers appointed. Would they accept his recommendation, or would he find that men would be put in he did not know anything about?—A. I would be inclined to say that the Government would put their friends there. Such has always been the custom, and it was in vogue before I entered the service.

Q. In your case you have this advantage—you can see whether the men are desirable people to enter the service? That is rather a happy condition of affairs?—A. Indeed it is a pleasure, a great satisfaction, because you know something of the men and can recommend them.

Q. You say in your memorial that 'officers who have been in the service for a number of years should be allowed such an increase as will equal the amount they would be entitled to had they entered the service at the minimum salary now proposed.' Mr. McCaffry is a typical case. He entered the service on the Queen's Birthday in 1869?

Mr. McCaffry.—Yes, that is the case.

Q. You entered the service nine days before I did. Then, Dr. Smith, if there was a new minimum and maximum for chief clerks, Mr. McCaffry, taking his as a typical case, should have an increase of salary which would equal the amount he would have been entitled to had he entered the service at the minimum salary?—A. Yes.

Q. That is to say, Mr. McCaffry would have the maximum?—A. He should have it, sir. You will notice in the same paragraph the statement 'This will be granting Customs officers the same treatment which has been accorded the Inland Revenue and other branches of the Civil Service.' These other branches have all enjoyed the benefit of the increase, while Mr. McCaffry, who is doing just as serviceable work to the country, has not been in a position to enjoy the money we claim he is entitled to.

Q. I have asked you before about the day's work of the Customs officer. Sometimes the officers, in a Customs office, work ten or twelve hours, do they not?—A. At the frontier ports they have to work that long, because a continuous Customs service of twenty-four hours is required. In this connection, there is a point to which I would like to draw your attention. The men work their twelve hours, two hours of which is overtime, for which they receive extra pay at the rate of 30 cents an hour. When the extra time is on Sunday the 30 cents is paid by the railways. When the overtime comes to $33 per month or under the department will pay it. Some months, however, the extra pay for overtime amounts to more than that sum. Now, the Government collects the charge from the railway corporations and others, but the men do not receive anything in excess of $33. We claim that as very unfair, and we are engaged in discussing that point at the present time with the department. There is another matter which should be referred to. We have at various points on the frontier what are called ferry landings. For example, there is the ferry running beween Windsor and Detroit, and the service will be from 6 o'clock in the morning until 2 o'clock the next morning. An officer goes on duty in the morning from 6 to 8 o'clock and continues until 6 p.m., that constituting twelve hours' work, and for this he is allowed two hours' overtime; or, a number of men go on relief duty from 6 p.m. to 8 p.m., which is allowed as overtime, they having commenced at 8 o'clock. Now, two of them have to continue from 8 p.m. until 11 p.m. when one is relieved; the other remains on duty until 2 a.m. the following morning. The man retiring at 11 p.m. receives no pay for the service after 8 p.m., as he has already put in his extra time from 6 to 8. The man remaining until 2 a.m. works from 10 to 12, but gets no further overtime, having put in his extra hours from 8 to 10 p.m. on that day; and it must be remembered that these officers are on duty every day at regular hours between 8 a.m. and 6 p.m. Where there are a number of men at the ferries, say three, four or five, as the case may be, they shift daily so that each man put in the long hours every three or four days as may be required, depending upon the number of men employed at that particular point, thus averaging for the month 12 hours daily, or 2 hours overtime.

Q. You told us the watch was shifted about?—A. That is on the railroads where the service is continuous.

Q. What about the ferry boats?—A. They run from 6 a.m. until 2 a.m. the next morning. They stop from 2 a.m. until 6 a.m. each day.

Q. Does one man go on duty at 6 o'clock every morning?—A. Yes.

Q. He does not shift to the other man?—A. He works continually until 6 o'clock at night. His hours are from 6 a.m. to 6 p.m.

Q. Then the other man goes on duty from 6 p.m. until 2 o'clock next morning?—A. No, he goes on duty from 8 a.m. to 8 p.m.

Q. But do you not shift the men about?—A. Yes, they are shifted week about.

Q. You say also in your memorandum, 'We believe that eight hours do constitute a fair day's work for outside officers.' Then at some of the frontier ports where trains are continually arriving some of the officers work twelve hours at a stretch?—A. Yes.

Q. You think that instead of two officers there should be three, so that they could relieve each other?—A. We should have three officers, so that we could arrange three shifts of eight hours each. They do that on the American side. The shifts of the officers there are eight hours each.

Q. Now, we come to the retiring fund. You ask that the Government should give an amount equal to the men's own contribution?—A. Yes.

Q. We have heard from a great many that some kind of pension Act would be desirable. Do you think that such an Act would be desirable in place of the existing retirement fund?—A. The present system only returns a man's own money with something added for interest.

Q. It would be better to have a Superannuation Act or some kind of a pension Act?—A. Personally I like the idea of the retirement fund. As an association we are divided to some extent on that question, and I would like to have the other gentlemen express their own views. Personally I would prefer the retirement fund on the basis that we have outlined in our memorial.

Q. There might be reasons in your case why you personally would prefer the retirement fund?—A. Yes. So on that account I would not like to commit the whole association to my personal views.

Q. Is there anything else you would like to say on your own account?—A. Well, in connection with the superannuation system there is this point: that the family of a person who dies in the service should receive some benefit. As the system stands at present a man who is dependent upon a salary pays in a large amount of money to the fund and yet when he dies his family get nothing. They are deprived of the use of that money during the life of the officer, and we claim that they should have some compensation on his death.

Q. A striking instance of that is offered in Toronto through the death of Mr. Patteson, the late postmaster?—A. I claim that should be remedied. It is not fair to a man's family to take money from him during his life and when he dies to retain that money. There is another point. We claim that in the interest of efficiency and fairness all branches of the service should be placed on equal terms.

Q. There should be no difference between the inside and the outside service?—A. There should be no difference in the matter of appointments into the service. We claim that the Inland Revenue officer has been paid for the same service far in excess of our own officers. The argument may be raised that a man may come back and take an examination. But these men did it in their boyhood days when they left school. It would not be any trouble for me to undergo an examination in my youth, but to put me up against say four years ago I might have some difficulty. I do not think that should detract from a man's ability. The men intended for the Inland Revenue service after passing their examination go in behind counters and do not have to appear before the public to the same extent; there is not the same demand for their services. As years go on they receive their statutory increase, until they stand where they are to-day. And we hope their position will be even better. Now, sir, the Customs officer the moment he enters the service has to walk right out and meet the public. He needs to be a trained and efficient man to do that. I, therefore, think the Customs officers should be entitled to the same remuneration as the man in the Inland Revenue service who has lived to the same age and given the same service. It may be urged that the work in the Inland Revenue Department is of a technical character. Well, gentlemen, I maintain that ours is just as technical. We require to have our appraisers and our gaugers. We have to be posted in the regulations of the Departments of Agriculture, Inland Revenue, Marine and Fisheries and other branches of the public service. On the other hand, the Inland Revenue officers become in a sense specialists, and deal only with the one subject. We claim the system of the past has been an injustice, and has worked against the Customs officer. We ask the whole service should be put on the same footing. If the Government insists upon examinations we would not object to a practical examination. However, Mr. Chairman, we know that we are going to receive justice at your hands, and, therefore, we have no desire to enter into details. You have before you all the statistics that are necessary to enable you to make up your mind except in regard to two articles, water and champagne. Water is a debatable thing. Champagne we as Customs officers know nothing about.

The witness retired.

Mr. J. R. McCaffry was called, sworn, and examined.

By the Chairman :

Q. You are the oldest officer, in point of chronology in the service to-day ?—A. Yes.

Q. The collector of the office here was appointed in 1891 ?—A. Yes.

Q. And the surveyor was appointed in 1901 ?—A. Yes.

Q. The gentleman filling the office of cashier was first appointed in 1872?—A. Yes.

Q. More than three years after yourself ?—A. Yes.

Q. He was promoted to cashier in 1891?—A. Yes, it would be about that year.

Q. The present assistant cashier received his first appointment in 1873?—A. Yes.

Q. And he was appointed as assistant cashier in 1891?—A. Yes.

Q. How much salary does the cashier get now?—A. I think the last increase made his salary $1,700.

Q. And how much do you get now?—A. I got $150 increase this year which gives me a salary of $1,450.

Q. That is to say—we will put to one side the collector and surveyor—the cashier who was your junior receives more salary than you are paid?—A. $250 more than I do.

Q. Is there any explanation of that? You have been a long faithful servant. Did you go in from the bottom and work your way up?—A. I did. It is practically twenty years since I did any routine work. I have been connected with the administration of the port for about that time.

Q. When did you become chief clerk?—A. On the death of my predecessor in the fall of 1894 I passed my Promotion examination. At that time the Government expected a deficit and they held no Promotion examinations in 1895. However, I went up for examination in June, 1896, and I was told by the acting commissioner that I got 100 marks out of a possible 100 but it was ten years before I got my appointment.

Q. Although you have been now for thirty-eight years in the public service?—A. Thirty-eight years last May.

Q. Of course, we cannot go into the question of the distribution of offices. However, it seems to me that if you entered the service as a boy of eighteen you have been through all the grades?—A. Yes.

Q. You would have known the duties of cashier, I suppose?—A. I presume so.

Q. And although you were senior you were passed over when the appointment came to be made and a junior officer was appointed in your place at a higher salary?—A. That appears to be the case.

Q. Was any political influence brought to bear to effect that?—A. I do not know.

Q. Does the assistant cashier get the same salary as you do?—A. I think not. I think his salary is very low, only $1,200.

Q. Then you, although the senior of all the men in the Custom-house here, have been superseded and passed over by others?—A. It looks that way.

Q. How many employees have you got in the Custom-house now?—A. In round figures about 140.

Q. How many of them are temporary employees?—A. I would guess probably about fifty.

Q. Have these temporary men passed the examination?—A. No, not as a rule.

Q. Are they called labourers or how are they designated?—A. Those that have not passed the Qualifying examination are generally employed as preventive officers or acting Customs officers.

Q. Without any examination?—A. They pass an oral examination. After being three years in the service they have the privilege of going before an officer and passing an oral examination.

Q. Are the thirty men called preventive officers?—A. Sometimes the men may be called an acting Customs officer.

Q. But he does not get the appointment?—A. No.

Q. When the man does get the appointment he is called a preventive officer?—A. Preventive officer, sometimes an examining officer.

Q. But the preventive officer would get the appointment without examination?—A. Yes.

Q. You have been for thirty-eight years in the service? You have seen many men pass in and out, and you have a thorough knowledge of the old system and the new system. Do you find there are many resignations of the good men taking place now?—A. I do not think we are getting so many good men in the service now.

Q. I am not asking that. I am asking whether there are any resignations of the younger men?—A. Yes.

Q. Do you think the men that come into the place of those that have resigned are as good men and as efficient? You may as well be frank?—A. I do not think they are. I think the personnel of the service has deteriorated very much in the last twenty or twenty-five years. The deterioration is very decided. I had a young man to act for me as stenographer. I saw by his appearance and manner that he was studious and anxious to improve himself, but when he heard of the salary that I was receiving after so many years of service his jaw dropped and I concluded that he would not stay. He left in the course of a month or two and he is getting a bigger salary to-day than I am. There is another case of a man who left the service who said to me 'I have never worked as hard or been paid as little since.' That man is getting three or four times my salary.

Q. So really and truly there is no inducement for men of good character and ability to enter the service?—A. Of my companions who started life with me there is not one that is not getting at least three times the salary that I am paid. I did not come here to speak of my own case, but if I did not have a little private means of my own and was dependent upon my salary I would be a soured official, I would feel that I could not live respectably in Toronto on my income. I have never done that, and if I had to do so I would be a dissatisfied official and consequently not a competent official. A good business man would not have a dissatisfied official with him under any circumstances. However, I do not expect to be long here now.

Q. I hope so. You are a much younger man than I am. You are on the right side of sixty?—A. I shall be fifty-seven next summer.

Q. You are a young man yet. How many sub-collectors are there in your division now?—A. Port Credit, Barrie, Brampton, Streetsville, Orangeville, Georgetown, Aurora and Newmarket. Orillia and Midland which were outports under Toronto are now ports.

Q. What about Toronto Junction?—A. It is a port now. In the event of Toronto Junction joining the city there would be two ports of entry in Toronto.

Q. Do all these sub-offices account through you?—A. They make their returns through Toronto.

Q. You as chief clerk have a knowledge of this correspondence?—A. It was part of my business for a number of years. I conducted the official correspondence of the port and attended to the registration of shipping.

Q. You do the clerical work Are there any young ladies working for you?—A. One. There are three up in the Post Office Branch.

Q. Are young women pressing to enter the service, do you know?—A. I have heard of a number that are anxious.

Q. What salary do you give your woman clerk?—A. $600 a year.

Q. No doubt she is good and efficient, but what would a lawyer or broker pay a woman clerk in this city?—A. It all depends. I know the Hon S. H. Blake gave his stenographer $25 a week, and I know others who only get $5 a week.

Q. The case of Mr. Blake's stenographer would be a special one. Take the average stenographer in a broker's or lawyer's office, what would she get?—A. $6, $7 or $8 a week.

Q. Then the salary given is an inducement for a woman to enter the service if she can?—A. Yes.

Q. With the prospect of being raised to $1,000 a year?—A. We have not any at that figure.

Q. No doubt with promotion she will get to that figure. A woman clerk in your office is getting $600 now?—A. Yes.

Q. In the Customs Service there are no annual increments?—A. No, not in the outside service.

Q. If there were annual increments no doubt the salary of this lady would go up with the others?—A. Yes.

Q. I do not desire to keep a woman back from earning her living, but do you not think that the prospect in the Government service is better than she would get in outside life ?—A. So much depends upon the nature of the work that women are called upon to do.

Q. You must not take the exception as the rule. The ordinary woman in a broker's or solicitor's office would not get $12 a week ?—A. Not as a rule.

Q. I selected you for examination because of your lengthened service and my own knowledge of your efficiency. Is there anything else you would like to say to us as the result of your long experience ?—A. The trouble is the absence of an annual increase. For instance, the maximum salary of a clerk now is $1,200, but none of them get that amount. I think the highest paid is $1,000 although some have services of twenty-five or thirty years. Take the maximum salary of a chief clerk. There is not a chief clerk in the Dominion who gets $2,000. Take the Bank of Montreal, $1,500 is the lowest salary they will allow their clerks to marry on. Now, if a bank thinks that a man cannot marry, and support a family, and be honest on less than $1,500 I think the Customs clerk should have as much to look forward to as the bank clerk. A Customs clerk is supposed to be an intelligent man. I do not suppose there are any laws so irksome in character and as hard to administer as the Customs laws. The Customs clerk is supposed to be familiar with the Customs Act, the Audit Act, the Merchant Shipping Act, the Chinese Immigration Act, the quarantine regulations and other matters, and his knowledge is supposed to cover a larger area than is required in any other branch of the public service.

Q. May I ask if the appraisers are efficient in the lines of business they are appointed without examination ?—A. I think the Act provides for that.

Q. May I ask if the appraisers are efficient in the lines of business they are brought into contact with ?—A. I suppose most of them are.

The witness retired.

Dr. SMITH.—I think you gentlemen are so well conversant with the whole circumstances that it seems almost a waste of time to detain you any longer. We are perfectly satisfied with the manner in which you are about to deal with the question and we can withdraw feeling that our interests are in safe hands.

By Mr. Fyshe:

Q. I gathered from your evidence that you are in favour of a continuation of the existing Retirement Fund ?—A. Yes, that is my personal opinion.

Q. You do not mean, I presume, that it is to be in any sense a substitute for the Superannuation Fund ?—A. I presume it would have to be a substitute for the Superannuation Fund.

Q. The Retirement Fund is simply dealing with the officer's own money. It might be a prudent thing, but it is not at all in the nature of a bonus or a gift ?—A. In this memorial we say that the Government should double the amount and allow us the interest on the whole.

Q. But even that would hardly provide for the demands usually met by a Superannuation Fund ?—A. Of course, there is only one object in a Superannuation Fund and that is a man must live to enjoy it.

Q. Your remark applies to the old Superannuation Act, but under a proper conception the Superannuation Fund would provide for a good deal more than the old Act did. The chief object I take it, in the establishment of a Superannuation Fund is not to provide so much for the officer himself, but for himself and his possible dependents ?—A. And that is the position I would like to see taken, but we have to deal with the matter as it exists now.

Q. There would be no particular objection to carrying on the Retirement Fund as it exists now provided it was not in any sense to supersede or take the place of a Superannuation fund?—A. I am agreeable to that. The idea had not suggested itself to me or I had not heard any of the officers suggest it. The recommendations contained in the memorial are the results of a discussion on points that were brought up.

The witness retired.

Mr. ALEXANDER PATTERSON, jr., called, sworn, and examined.

By the Chairman:

Q. You represent the appraisers?—A. I represent the appraisers of Toronto.

Q. Well, what have you to say?—A. I am now on the list as an assistant appraiser although I have been acting for a number of years as an appraiser. Unfortunately for me when the increases were being given this last year on account of being down as an assistant appraiser, I could only reach a maximum of $1,500, although I had been for years acting as appraiser, having charge of the department. I was unaware that I was designated at Ottawa as an assistant appraiser, thinking I was either considered acting appraiser or an appraiser. Unfortunately when the increases were granted the department looked over the list and found that I was down as an assistant appraiser with the result that I only got an increase of $100 instead of $200. I have been twenty-six years in the service and men that entered a number of years later are drawing from $200 to $400 more than I am. There are probably three or four men who are drawing four, or five hundred dollars more than I am.

By Mr. Fyshe:

Q. Have you passed the same examination?—A. The same examination and probably a more rigid one, because mine was written while theirs was oral.

Q. Had the people you refer to influence?—A. I think so.

Q. But how could they get more salary in the shape of a statutory increase?—A. They have not got more, they have got the limit. As acting appraiser and in reality appraiser, I am only getting $1,500 while others are drawing $1,700 to $2,000. I have only received $50 increase in a period of ten years.

By the Chairman:

Q. What class of goods does your department appraise?—A. Stationery, fancy goods, drugs and such like.

Q. You were appointed as an assistant appraiser?—A. That was my appointment, yes.

Q. Is there an examination between assistant appraiser and appraiser?—A. I should not think so.

Q. There has not been one to your knowledge?—A. None to my knowledge.

Q. Then it is a case of promotion without examination from assistant appraiser to appraiser?—A. I would think so.

Q. Is there an appraiser for stationery or fancy goods?—A. I am the appraiser.

Q. Is there any one called the appraiser who appraises the same goods as you do?—A. At the port of Montreal, not at this port.

Q. You are the only man that appraises stationery and fancy goods?—A. Yes.

Q. Your contention is that instead of being designated assistant appraiser you should be called appraiser?—A. That is it.

29a—11.

Q. And in consequence of your designation as assistant appraiser you have not got the maximum salary of the appraisers' class?—A. $2,000 is the maximum, but I have not got to that.

Q. You are at the maximum salary of an assistant appraiser?—A. Yes, that is it.

Q. Why not bring to the notice of the Customs Department that while you are the man in charge of the classes of goods stated by you you are still designed simply as assistant appraiser?—A. I was unaware of the fact at the time. I can explain this better by giving you an example. Mr. Davidson, who has charge of the dry goods department, is on the list the same as I am myself as an assistant appraiser. He has never had his appointment made as appraiser, but at Ottawa he was looked upon as acting appraiser. Now, I did not know this. Had I known it I should certainly have brought the matter before the department and asked them to give me the status of an appraiser.

By Mr. Fyshe:

Q. Does the other man get $1,900?—A. Yes, although probably he has been ten years less in the service than I am.

By the Chairman:

Q. Is he designated the same as you are?—A. Yes, as far as the blue book is concerned.

Mr. FYSHE.—Those are things evidently past finding out.

By the Chairman:

Q. The assistant appraiser or acting appraiser, to whom you refer is not getting $1,900 according to the Civil Service list?—A. He was getting the $1,700, as stated in the blue book, but he got an increase of $200 this year which brought his salary up to $1,900.

Q. What is the maximum salary of an assistant appraiser?—A. $1,500.

Q. And you say this Mr. Davidson is getting $1,900, although still an assistant appraiser?—A. Yes.

Q. That is one of those incongruities I cannot understand, but I think, with all due deference, that is a matter you should bring to the notice of your department at once?—A. I do not want to bother them; they have a lot of correspondence.

Q. You are looking out for your own rights, we are here to look after the interests of the Civil Service as a whole?—A. Not to take up individual cases?

Q. Not to look after individual cases or grievances, and I would recommend you—no doubt it is worth looking into—to write to Mr. McDougald—send your communication through the collector in the official form—drawing attention to your case and asking for redress?—A. I must apologize for bringing my case before you. I know the department is very well satisfied with my performance of my duties, because I have had it from more than one source. I went into the service at $600 a year against my will, but I was told that I would be very shortly getting very much more.

The witness retired.

To the Honourable the Royal Commissioners, appointed to inquire into matters pertaining to the Civil Service of the Dominion of Canada:

HONOURABLE SIRS,—The officers of the Customs Service of the province of Ontario, desire to express their satisfaction upon the appointment of a commission, to investigate the condition of the officers of the Civil Service, and the confidence they have, that they will receive justice at the hands of your Honourable Body.

SESSIONAL PAPER No. 29a

No doubt other branches of the Civil Service have gone fully into the position and obligations of the Civil Servants, as to their condition ten years ago and at the present time. We therefore wish to state our position as briefly as possible, as the cost of living, the education of our children, &c., affect all branches of the Civil Service alike.

The fact that the cost of living has increased so materially and persistently during the past ten years, scarcely needs to be again brought to your attention, as it is admitted by all, and borne out by facts, and it is safe to say the average advance would closely approximate 50 per cent, as shown in our memorial presented to the Honourable the Minister of Customs in January last, (copy herewith attached) and appears likely to continue for a long time.

For the past ten years this condition has prevailed, until the Civil Servant, with a fixed salary finds himself relatively at a great disadvantage, with men in other walks of life.

We ask you, Honourable Commissioners, to investigate our statements, believing that your finding will be practically the same as that here presented; as we have endeavoured to be conservative and careful in every instance.

The question of salaries, hours of service, superannuation, and retiring allowances, are matters of grave interest and importance to us.

No doubt you are aware, Customs officers on the outside service (which includes all officers not connected with the department at Ottawa) do not receive an annual statutory increase.

Many officers have been in the service for twenty years and more who never received any increase until the present year, when the Honourable the Minister of Customs kindly advanced our salaries $100 for all lower grade officers.

We ask you, is this just? Is this a plan likely to produce the best results, and secure the greatest efficiency in the service? We know that this very condition has driven good men from the Government employ.

We ask that officers be assured a minimum salary of at least $900 per annum, where their services are fully given to the department, added to this, an assurance of a statutory increase of $50 each and every year until the maximum is reached.

We would further suggest that all superior officers, such as inspectors, collectors, surveyors, appraisers, chief clerks, &c., be paid in proportion to the responsibilities of the various offices; that due consideration be given to officers whose time is not wholly devoted to Customs service, and that all officers, west of Lake Superior, should receive an extra increase consistent with the higher cost of living in the west. We believe this would result in securing service for the Customs Department excelled by none of the various Government services.

That officers who have been in the service for a number of years should be allowed such an increase as would equal the amount they would be entitled to had they entered the service at the minimum salary now proposed, with the annual increase in accord therewith. This will be granting customs officers the same treatment which has been accorded the Inland Revenue and other branches of the Civil Service; which they have enjoyed for a number of years.

We believe that eight hours should constitute a fair day's work for outside officers and seven hours for inside, that health and efficiency considered, we should not be asked to labour beyond this. In cases of emergency, when officers are compelled to work over these hours, and on Sundays, or holidays, he should receive extra remuneration, commensurate with the extra work, but not less than 40 cents per hour. That frontier and other ports, where there is a continuous service, the twenty-four hours should be divided by three shifts of officers, of eight hours each. An eight hour day is now almost universally recognized as fair and just between employer and employe, and officers should receive such remuneration for eight hours as will enable them to live comfortably, educate their families and save something for their declining years.

29a—11½

SUPERANNUATION AND RETIRING FUNDS.

1st. That some provision should be made in the Superannuation Act, whereby officers who have been paying into this fund for years, and who die in the service, a certain sum should go to those depending upon them.

2nd. That the retiring fund is not just to the officer, as 5 per cent of his salary is held, and interest allowed semi-annually at 4 per cent; when the money is worth a great deal more. If he undertakes to build a home, he will have to pay 6 or 7 per cent on the money borrowed. Might we suggest that the government add an equal amount to the officers' retiring fund, and allow 4 per cent interest on the total?

Honourable sirs, we submit, for the sake of efficiency and fairness, all branches of the Civil Service should be placed upon equal terms.

We lay these facts before you, well aware that your knowledge of the questions at issue is such that whatever your decision may be, it will be for the best interests of the Government Service at large.

Thanking you, gentlemen, for hearing our appeal on behalf of the Customs Officers.

We have the honour to be,

Your obedient servants,

(Signed)   F. T. PATTISON,

Secretary.

CANADA CUSTOMS MUTUAL BENEFIT ASSOCIATION.

GENTLEMEN,—I beg to submit the following report of a meeting of the Customs Mutual Benefit Association, held in Ottawa on January 16 and 17, 1907, for the year pose of laying before the Honourable Wm. Paterson, M.P., Minister of Customs, the question of a general increase of salaries for the officers of the Customs Service.

Delegates were present from every part of the Dominion, and every province had one or more delegates present, viz.:—

ONTARIO.

Dr J. A. Smith, Windsor,
W. C. Bushell, Windsor,
F. E. Lloyd, Toronto,
A. G. Elson, Toronto,
Robt. Colvin, Hamilton,
Wm. Peebles, Hamilton,
R. D. Anglin, Kingston,
O. H. Talbot, London,
B. C. McCann, London,
F. T. Pattison, Bridgeburg,
G. A. Clark, Bridgeburg,
J. M. Stephens, Sault Ste. Marie,
Henry Foreman, Collingwood,
J. G. Hess, Stratford,
M. McNamara, Walkerton,

A. S. Valleau, Deseronto,
S. J. Sidey, Port Colborne,
T. Hayne, Sarnia,
J. J. Flynn, Niagara Falls,
J. B. Stephens, Niagara Falls,
F. F. Wood, Niagara Falls,
A. Grey, Niagara Falls,
A. T. Montreuil, Walkerville,
E. A. Myles, Ottawa.
M. F. Kehoe, Ottawa,
S. H. Waggoner, Ottawa,
N. P. Horton, Owen Sound,
M. Schiedel, Berlin,
M. Murphy, Carleton Place,
J. H. Cline, Cornwall.

QUEBEC.

R. S. White, Montreal,
Henry Laughlin, Montreal,
A. Magnan, Montreal,
L. A. Jacques, Montreal,
A. E. Giroux, Montreal,
J. M. Bessett, Montreal,
W. Drysdale, Montreal,
W. J. McKenna, Montreal,
P. M. McGoldrick, Montreal.

Robt. P. Clerk, Montreal,
Lt.-Col. L. N. Laurin, Quebec,
Alphonse Gaumond, Quebec,
C. H. McClinton, Stanstead,
J. Dunn, Abercorn,
G. H. Henshaw, St. Hyacinthe,
O. L. Deseve, Sherbrooke,
J. B. Daly, Coaticooke.

NEW BRUNSWICK.

L. E. Tapley, St. John,   Henry Graham, St. Stephens,
G. J. Green, McAdam Junction,   T. J. Coffey, Moncton.

MANITOBA.

H. M. Sutherland, Winnipeg,   H. C. Graham, Brandon.

NOVA SCOTIA.   BRITISH COLUMBIA.

R. J. Saxton, Halifax.   Wm. Marchant, Victoria.

NORTHWEST TERRITORIES.

A. Allan, Calgary,   F. A. Osborne, Edmonton.

Sessions of the association were first, held at the Grand Union Hotel, Ottawa, when all arrangements were completed for the delegates to interview the Hon. the Minister of Customs, and other routine business conducted.

The delegates supported by the following Senators and Members of Parliament, waited upon the Hon. Wm. Paterson at his office, at 11 a.m., January 17; Senators Dandurand, Gibson, Coffey, Ross and David; Members of Parliament: Hon. R. F. Sutherland, Messrs. German, Harty, Greenway, Fortier, Smith (Nanaimo), Roche, Beland, Clarke, Schell (Glengarry), Schell (Oxford), Stewart, Carney, Pardee, Telford, McKenzie, Parent, Gervais, Archambault, Dubeau, Dr. Cash, Barker, Kemp, Crocket, Ames, Heron, Lancaster, Worthington, Lefurgey, Gergeron, Daniels, Elson, and Tisdale.

The Hon. R. F. Sutherland, Speaker of the House of Commons, presented the Memorial in a most able manner, and spoke very strongly on the question of an increase. He compared the salaries of the Canadian Customs officers with the Customs officers of the United States. He was ably supported by Messrs. German, M.P., Greenway, M.P., Kemp, M.P., Barker, M.P., Roche, M.P., Smith, M.P. Daniels, M.P., Crockett, M.P., and Senators Dandurand, Gibson, Coffey and David, who advanced very strong arguments why the Minister should give a substantial increase to the Customs officers.

Mr. R. S. White, Collector of Customs, for the Port of Montreal, spoke from the officers' standpoint, and also gave strong reasons why some relief should be given.

The following is the Memorial:—

To the Honourable William Paterson,
    Minister of Customs.

Honourable Sir,—The officers of the Custom service of the Dominion of Canada respectfully ask your consideration of their appeal for an increase of salaries consistent with the increases of their work, and the advance in the cost of living.

The enormous advance in Customs receipts is ample proof of the additional work required by the various officers throughout the Dominion, the increase in the past six months amounting to three and one-half millions of dollars.

With the increase of work the cost of living has also increased by leaps and bounds. During these years of great prosperity, rents, fuel, clothing, and almost everything that enters into the cost of living have gone higher and higher, until the man with a fixed salary is compelled to seek relief, or become hopelessly in debt. It has been truly said, 'That the Customs officers, with an almost unchanged salary, were never so poor as now, amidst all this abounding wealth.'

But, Honourable Sir, before going further into this matter, allow us, on behalf of the gentlemen representing the different ports under your department to thank you most heartily for granting us this privilege of laying before you the matter of an increase of salaries; a question which, to us, is of such great importance.

And now, Honourable Sir, permit us to give a few reasons which we claim entitles us to your consideration:

In the first place: Cost of living for a family of six:

Rent, per month from $12 to $18, average..	$ 15 00
Fuel..	4 50
Food..	43 00
Furnishings..	3 00
Clothing..	12 00
Schooling..	3 00
Medical expenses..	2 00
Church..	2 00
Recreation..	3 00
Insurance..	4 50
Retiring and Guarantee fund..	2 80
Light and gas..	2 00
Help..	4 00
Total per month..	$100 80

or $1,209.60 a year. You will observe that the item of food amounts to $43 for a family of six persons for a month. Now, let us see what that means; a family of six with three meals a day equals 540 meals per month. That gives about eight cents per meal per head—not very high living.

We will also quote a few comparisons in prices of market produce, as taken from the leading papers:

Articles.	1896.	1906.	Percentages of increase.
Pork	4-3 4c. to 5c.	8o. to 9c.	70
Beef, hind qtrs..	4-3 4c.	8c.	68
Lamb.. •	5c. to 7c.	8c. to 12c.	66
Butter..	20c.	30c.	50
Eggs..	14c. to 16c.	30c. to 35c.	106
Potatoes, bag.	40c.	85c. to $1.10	143
Chickens..	9c.	12c. to 14c.	44
Turkeys	9c. to 12c.	16c. to 18c.	62
		Average 76 p. c.	

These are market prices and are lower than store prices. Meats have greatly increased; steaks and roasts have risen from 9 and 10 to 16 and 18 cents a pound; lamb and mutton from 10 to 15 and 18 cents; pork about the same; groceries, boots and shoes, dry goods, clothing, in fact everything the officer requires has increased from 10 to 100 per cent, in the last ten years.

Where through illness in the family or other cause, domestic help is required, we may point out that, while servants received $1.50 per week in 1896, to-day we have to pay $3 up.

The Waterous Engine Works Company. of Brantford, between the period of 1890 and 1906, has increased employers' wages as follows, viz.: Machinists, 40 per cent; moulders, 42 per cent; boilermakers, 40 per cent.

The Brantford Carriage Company, and the Buck Stove Company, of Brantford have increased the wages of their employees in the last fifteen years from 50 to 100 per cent. The Canada Southern Railway, in the same length of time, has increased conductors, baggagemen and brakemen 60 per cent, yardmen 100 per cent and clerical force 50 per cent.

Brantford union scale of wages:—

Bricklayers from 25 cents per hour to 40 cents, increase 75 per cent; labourers, from 12½ cents per hour to 22½ cents to 25 cents, increase 84 per cent.

Carpenters, from 17½ cents to 20 cents per hour to 30 to 35 cents, increase 75 per cent.

Painters, from 15 cents to 17½ cents per hour to 25 to 27½ cents, increase 62½ per cent.

The great railway corporations, manufacturing concerns, companies and firms, have voluntarily increased the wages of their employees in sympathy with the advance in the cost of life's necessities.

In coming here we fully recognize the fact that we are subordinate officers. We make no demands we appeal, Honourable Sir, for simple justice only. We ask for a revision of our salaries, because the change in condition has made it, in most cases, impossible to support our families respectably on our present incomes. Under present conditions it is impossible for many of your officers to make both ends meet without having some other source of income, let alone the saving of anything for illness or old age.

We recognize the fact that the Minister of Customs has been liberal with the Civil Service, but we venture to assert that the increase of salary is not commensurate with the increased cost of living.

If we might be permitted to do so, we would suggest that an increase of at least 50 per cent of the present salary be granted, this would bring the minimum salary to $900 in the case of all officers entitled to the same, whose time is wholly taken up in the government service, and should be supplemented with an annual increase of $50 a year until the maximum of each class is reached. We would further suggest that all superior officers, such as inspectors, collectors, surveyors, appraisers, chief clerks, etc., be paid in proportion to the responsibilities of the various offices. We would submit that 50 per cent be added to all present minimum and maximum salaries as scheduled.

We feel that there is no need to enlarge on these conditions. It is admitted that a salary of $800 per annum a few years ago was as satisfactory and had as much purchasing power as a salary of $1 200 would have to-day.

We ask you, Honourable Sir, to give these facts your kind consideration, and we leave the matter in your hands, confident that the justice of our appeal will be recognized, and that we may be granted the relief for which we so earnestly and respectfully pray.

Memorial from the West.

To the Honourable WILLIAM PATERSON,
　　　　Minister of Customs.

HONOURABLE SIR,—The officers of the Customs service west of Lake Superior respectfully desire to express their hearty concurrence in the general statements and prayer of the memorial already presented to you.

We desire, however, specially to call attention to the largely increased cost and more expensive standard of living in the West, and desire therefore (with the full concurrence of the other petitioners throughout the Dominion) to request that a special provisional allowance of at least $15 per month be added to the remuneration of each and all of the officers of that district. To instance one point only, viz.: house rents: an ordinarily well situated six to eight-roomed house in the West costs from $25 to $50 per month.

It is generally admitted that the cost of living west of Lake Superior is now, and always has been, 25 per cent and 40 per cent higher than in the east, and we

7-8 EDWARD VII., A. 1908

therefore respectfully submit that our request for the above special allowance is a moderate one and one that might well be granted.

The Hon. WILLIAM PATERSON, in reply, went fully into the points set forth in the memorial and made some comparisons as to the conditions of the service in 1896 and at the present time. Reverting to the question of salaries he said that he was asking this year for an increased vote of $100,000 for Customs, a large portion of which would be given for salaries and increases, but would not be nearly sufficient to provide for anything like a large augmentation. The whole subject would receive very serious consideration, and a comparison would be made of the salaries of Customs clerks with men in commercial life who performed similar duties.

He was glad to see that the present request was supported by members of both sides, and if, after full consideration, it should appear that a case had been made out a supplementary estimate would be taken to cover the increased amount required. In closing he asked the delegates not to desire to obtain too large a sum in one year, but to be content with an increase by degrees and in a few years they would be in good condition.

CUSTOMS, CANADA.

PORT OF TORONTO, September 25, 1907.

To the Honourable the Civil Service Commission :

GENTLEMEN,—As Assistant Hardware Appraiser, I beg to lay before you my individual case as follows :—

1st. As the senior assistant in the most important department in one of the largest and most important ports in the Dominion, I think my services are entitled to recognition by an increase of salary in view of the length of service (sixteen years) and my proficiency.

2nd. As this is a first-class port and one of the leading ports in Canada, and as more special and important appraisements are made in the Hardware Department than any other, I can see no reason why I should not receive the maximum salary set by law for the position I hold.

3rd. If a proficient senior officer of a great number of years of service cannot obtain the maximum salary set by law, what is the use having a maximum set by law ?

4th. Being, as I believe I am, a competent and proficient officer, making a great many valuable appraisements and residing in a city in which living is very expensive, and rapidly becoming more so, I think you will agree with me that the salary I am now getting is not commensurate with the responsibility and dignity of the office or the efficient service which I render.

5th. That the salary is certainly not anything like equal to that paid by other Governments, or that paid in similar walks of life by commercial houses for like service.

6th. As I am now giving the best years of my life to the service, and as very few live to obtain or enjoy a superannuation, I cannot hope for more than the majority ; therefore in justice to me, I think I should be paid a fair salary commensurate with the service rendered, at the time in life when I am able to live and enjoy it.

I have the honour to be, gentlemen,

Your obedient servant,

(Signed) S. J. WESTMAN,

Asst. Hardware Appraiser.

CUSTOMS CANADA.

PORT OF VANCOUVER, B.C., September 5, 1907.

The Honourable the Civil Service Commission, Ottawa, Ont.:

SIRS,—I have the honour to inclose Memorial from the Ports of **Vancouver,** Victoria, Nanaimo and New Westminster, B.C.

The officers of the above-mentioned ports are gratified to present for your consideration their views on various matters pertaining to the Civil Service.

We submit herewith, the result of their deliberations confident in the justice of their claims and confident, too, in your disposition to give them fair and full consideration.

I have the honour to be, sir,
Your obedient servant,
(Sgd.)   W. J. SPEAR,
Secretary.

Retirement Fund.

The method in force at present is to deduct 5 per cent from the salary of officers known as the 'Permanent Staff,' with interest at the rate of 4 per cent per annum compounded half-yearly.

This system does not appeal to the officers of our ports as being the best arrangement that can be made. For instance, an officer is added to the staff at the age of thirty years, and gives, say, twenty-five years of the best part of his life to the service of the country, at an average salary of $900 per year, 5 per cent of which will, in twenty-five years, amount to $1,125, plus 4 per cent compounded half-yearly. His salary is $855 net per annum. With this amount he is unable to do more than keep body and soul together, no opportunity for investment, or saving; therefore, at the end of twenty-five years service, he has nothing in the world but the $1,125 plus 4 per cent; and finds himself forced to the 'Old Man's Home'; or dependent on the charity of his friends.

What form of relief is best, we are not prepared to say; but if the Retirement Fund is continued the money deducted from officers' salaries should be supplemented by an amount from the Government.

It is self evident, however, in order to keep a good and efficient service, something must be done to keep officers of integrity, sobriety, honesty and ability, otherwise the efficiency of the service will be seriously impaired, and we therefore desire to place on record an earnest desire for a liberal and comprehensive scheme.

Salary Increase.

The Civil Service Act sets forth the amount of salary each officer is to receive, and provides for an annual increase until the maximum is reached.

The minimum and maximum has had little to do with the salary paid to the Customs officer, and the provisions of the Act have not been carried out. The officer who has been in the service for 15 years, is to-day being paid the same salary as a temporary officer who has been in the service only a few days. We earnestly desire that the provisions of the Act be carried out, so that an officer in a reasonable time will attain the maximum according to the provisions of the said Act.

It is the general belief that when the Act became law, the salaries as set forth were found to be sufficient, but we are living under very different conditions now, and the minimum and maximum will need to be advanced by about 50 per cent.

Cost of Living.

The question of the cost of living is, on the whole, the most difficult of all the problems, which we, as Civil Servants are compelled to face. The pronounced advance in prices which has taken place in the last few years, has been the cause of considerable dissatisfaction, discontent, discomfort and embarrassment, and has been, and is, being severely felt by every officer in this Province. Living has increased by leaps and bounds, rents, fuel, clothing, and every article has gone higher and higher until we are compelled to seek relief or go hopelessly in debt; yet, in spite of these conditions the salary remains the same, and the officers find it more and more impossible to make ends meet; and we, as Civil Servants, accept with gratitude your kind invi-

7-8 EDWARD VII., A. 1908

tation to forward data, and do so, with the earnest hope that our claims, which are just and reasonable, will receive due consideration.

We give below a comparison in prices ruling on the 17th day of August, 1900 and 1907 respectively, together with the percentage of increase or decrease.

These comparisons are not mere guesses, but in every case have been obtained from reliable sources; from the books of reliable merchants, from the records of several Trade Unions, and can be verified at any time.

Articles.	1900.	1907.	Increase.	Decrease.
			p. c.	p. c.
Sugar per lb...	5½c.	5¾c.	Slight adv'ce	
Syrup "	7c.	9c.	22	
Hams "	18c.	25c.	39	
Bacon "	20c.	30c.	50	
Lard "	12½c.	20c.	60	
Apples (45 lbs.)...	$1.10	$1.50	36½	
Peaches per lb...	10c.	12½c.	25	
Pears "	10c.	12½c.	25	
Tomatoes "	10c.	15c.	50	
Potatoes (100 lbs.)...	75c.	$1.35	80	
Cabbage per lb...	2c.	3c.	50	
Peanuts "	14c.	20c.	43	
Nuts of all kinds	20c. per lb.	25c.	25	
Flour (Pastry)...	$1.20 (49 lbs.)	$1.50	25	
Bread flour...	$1.15 "	$1.60	39	
Rolled oats...	5c. per lb.	5c.	....	
Cheese...	16c. "	20c.	25	
Eggs (N.L.)...	25c. per doz.	50c.	100	
" (Case)...	20c. "	35c.	75	
Sausage	12½c. per lb.	15c.	20	
Beef...	12c. to 14c. p.lb.	20c. to 23c.	64 to 67	
" seconds	8c. to 10c. "	15c. to 18c.	87½	
Mutton (leg)...	11c. to 13c. "	18c. to 20c.	64	
" (chops)...	10c. to 13c. "	15c. to 20c.	50	
Lamb..	18c. per lb.	30c.	67	
Veal	14c. "	20c.	43	
" (stew)	8c. to 12c. p. lb.	13½c. to 17c.	69	
Butter table...	25c. to 27c. "	45c.	73	
" cooking	20c per lb.	35c.	75	
Fish fresh	6c. "	12c. to 15c.	100	
Milk...	7¾c. "	10c.	37	
Bread...	4c. per loaf.	5c.	25	
Poultry...	20c. per lb.	25c.	25	
Wood (cord)...	$3	$5	67	
Coal (ton)...	$5.50	$7.50	36	
Lighting	15c.	13c.	....	15·4
Lemons ·.	25c. per doz.	30c.	20	
Oranges...	35c. "	50c.	43	
Rent (house of 6 rooms)..	$18 to $20	$35 to $45	94 to 125	
Rent 1 room furnished...	$6 to $8	$10 to $20	66 to 150	
Rent 3 rooms unfurnished apartment house..	... ...	$45	... ...	
Table board	$15 to $17 mo'th	$22.50 to $30	50	
Domestic service Chinese by month	$10 to $14	$35 to $50	250 to 257	
Domestic service per hour	12½c.	25c. to 30c.	100 to 140	
Dressmakers	$1 a day	$2 to $2.50	100 to 150	
Washerwoman...	75c. to $1	$1.50 to $2	100	
Nurse (week)	$10	$17.50 to $20	75 to 100	
Painters (hour)...	33½c.	50c.	53	
Masons "	50c.	62½c.	25	
Bricklayers "	50c.	62½c.	25	
Plasterers "	50c.	75c.	50	
Hod carrier (day)...	$2	$4	100	
Plumbers "	$2.75	$4	45½	
Machinists (hour)...	32½c.	40c.	32	
Carpenters "	35⅜c.	53½c.	50	
Boilermaker "	35c.	43¾c.	25	
	Increase aver-age, 45 p. c.			

SESSIONAL PAPER No. 29a

From the above prices you will see how high the living is in the west, but, it must also be borne in mind, that the above are summer prices. In winter the increase is considerable; potatoes going as high as $3 per sack; apples to $3 per box of 45 lbs.; eggs to 75 cents per dozen; butter to 50 and 55 cents per pound and wood as high as $7 per cord.

From this you will see how impossible it is in strenuous times like the present, to pay our way. This matter is a most serious one to every officer here; in the question of rents alone fifty per cent of the salary is required.

Laundry articles have increased from 30 to 115 per cent; clothing has increased materially, and the cost of lumber has doubled.

We are unfortunate in not being able to supply you with the present prices in the east, as the difference is so great, that on this we base our claim for extra salary.

You will also note that the prices are extremely high on every article, and no place in the Dominion (Yukon excepted) is living as high as on the Pacific coast ; therefore calling for larger salary than is paid to the Eastern officer. Almost everything we use is brought from Eastern Canada, to which must be added a long and costly haul, with extra handling, charged to the cost of the goods; or from the United States, to which must be added freight and duty, and last, but not least, that the new tariff places extra duty on the articles of daily use, thus aggravating the result.

The Customs Department has already recognized that the Western officer is entitled to extra salary, because in 1904 through the efforts and good work of our M.P.'s, the British Columbia staff was given an increase, to partly cover the difficulty, and, therefore, ask that the same policy be maintained.

CONCLUSION.

We would like to emphasize some of the foregoing statements, that we are opposed to the present system of compulsory savings, at such a low rate of interest, and look for a more liberal scheme of retirement fund, or another scheme which has the essence of fairness in it. That the salary of every officer (all things being equal) be increased year by year until the maximum is reached; that the present salaries set forth in the Civil Service Act, are entirely inadequate for present conditions; and that the West shall have increased salaries over and above what is paid to the Eastern officer.

We may also point out that the Customs and Immigration officers of the United States, resident in this port, working side by side with our officers, receive salaries from 58 to 90 per cent more than the Canadian officers ; that the overtime paid to the United States officer is from $5 to $7, while our officers receive 40 cents per hour and are limited to two hours per day.

Signed:—
  C. C. ELDRIDGE, for Vancouver.
  FRED. R. GREER, for Vancouver.
      Chief Clerk.
  ROBERT ALLEN, sub-collector.
  Chemainus and Crofton.

Signed:—
  E. J. LENNIE,
      New Westminster.
  W. TURNBULL,
      New Westminster.

CUSTOMS CANADA.
PORT OF ST. JOHN, N.B., October 11, 1907.

Civil Service Commission, Ottawa.

GENTLEMEN,—I have been elected as representative of the out-door staff of the St. John Customs, to present a memorandum of what they consider should be done to improve conditions in their service.

The undeniably large increase in the cost of living makes it absolutely necessary that our salaries should be increased.

I herewith submit a schedule of what we think these salaries should be at Ports collecting $1,000,000 and upwards annually.

Surveyors.—Should attain present maximum by annual increases.

Gaugers.—From $800 to $1,500 to be attained by annual increases.

Tide Surveyor.—From $800 to $1,500 to be attained by annual increases.

Landing Waiters and Lockers.—From $700 to $1,000, to be attained by annual increases.

Preventive Officer (or Tidewaiter).—From $700 to $1,000 to be attained by annual increases.

No increases to be considered unless recommended by Collector of the Port.

Promotion.

I submit that when a vacancy occurs in any office of the service such position should be filled by the next officer in order. Merit and seniority in service to be considered, and in every case to be contingent upon the recommendation of the Collector of the Port.

Examination.

I believe an examination for promotion should embrace only the subject of 'Duties of Office.'

Sunday Work.

The staff are opposed to Sunday work.

Holidays.

Are satisfactory as at present.

Appointments.

We submit that all appointees should be men of fair education and recognized good standing in the community.

Superannuation.

We are in favour of the 'Superannuation Act' believing it to be in the best interest of the service with such amendments as would secure to relatives of a deceased officer some return, where decease occurred before superannuation.

Respectfully submitted,

(Sgd.)   H. P. ALLINGHAM.

CUSTOMS CANADA.

PORT OF ST. JOHN, N.B., October 10, 1907.

Royal Civil Service Commission, Ottawa:

GENTLEMEN.—I have been requested by the appraisers and clerks of the Customs staff at St. John, N.B., to place before you their views on matters now being considered by the Commission. Statements to show the largely increased cost of living are omitted, as we have been informed that ample evidence on that point has already been laid before you.

Appraisers.

The appraisers consider their salaries should reach a maximum of $2,000, this maximum to be attained by yearly increases.

The examining rooms used by the appraisers are too small and the business now being done requires at least twice as much space as is available.

The business public also have free access to the examining rooms, which is not desirable.

Clerks.

We consider that clerks at ports collecting $1,000,000 and upwards should be classified as First, Second and Third Class clerks and be paid salaries as follows:—

First-class clerks—Minimum, $1,500. Maximum, $2,000.

Second-class clerks—Minimum, $1,200. Maximum, $1,500..

Third-class clerks—Minimum, $600. Maximum, $1,200.

Maximum in all cases to be attained by yearly increases on recommendation of the collector that officers receiving increases are competent and satisfactory.

At present the maximum salary of a clerk is $1,200, but only one clerk at this port has reached that figure. We feel that the salary should be advanced, and that yearly increases should be given to worthy officers.

We do not approve of the employment as clerks of officers holding the rank of tidewaiter, preventive officer, &c., and hope that this practice will be discontinued.

Superannuation.

The clerks and appraisers are unanimously in favour of the Superannuation Act, believing it to be best for the interest of the service and for the men. We strongly recommend a return to the Superannuation Act, with an amendment which would give the legal representative of a deceased officer who had been fifteen years or more in the service a sum equivalent to one year's superannuation.

Hours of Duty.

Satisfactory as at present.

Sanitary Condition of Offices.

Offices all well lighted but poorly ventilated, and not cleaned frequently enough.

Promotions.

We believe that promotions should be made on merit, and examinations for promotion should only be on duties of office.

Holidays.

Satisfactory as at present.

Appointments.

Appointments should be of young men of fair educational ability and good standing in the community.

I have the honour to be, gentlemen,

Your obedient servant,

(Signed)   SAMUEL W. KAIN.

7-8 EDWARD VII., A. 1908

CUSTOMS, CANADA.

PORT OF ST. GEORGE, N.B., May 2, 1907.

J. M. COURTNEY, Esq., C.M.G.,
    Ex-Deputy Minister of Finance,
        Ottawa.

SIR,—I have observed by the newspapers that you have been appointed chairman of a Commission to inquire into the Civil Service of Canada, and I take the liberty of calling your attention to the fact that I was appointed Collector of Customs at this port in September, A.D. 1879, at an annual salary of $600 per annum, less one dollar per month superannuation tax and upon a promise of an increase of salary upon a satisfactory term of service or an increase of revenue at this port. At that time this was an independent or principal port of entry, and there was one preventive officer under the survey of this port; in 1885 said preventive officer was superannuated and his place was never filled, but I was called upon to perform both the inside and outside work of the port, which I have done ever since, but have never received any increase in salary; about 1887 this port was reduced to an outport under survey of St. John, N.B., and two preventive stations erected within what was formerly the port of St. George, and said stations report their collections direct to St. John, and notwithstanding this and also the fact that a large portion of the dutiable goods consumed here are imported at St. John and St. Stephen, N.B., and while the collections at this port are not large, yet during the twenty-seven and a half years that I have served, the average annual collections have been considerably in excess of the average annual sum collected by my predecessor in office during his term, and as to whether my duties have been satisfactorily performed or not, during my tenure of office, I respectfully beg to refer you to the Commissioner of Customs. Therefore, under these circumstances, and also owing to the fact of a large increase in the cost of living during the past quarter of a century, also that the country is now wealthy and prosperous, I feel that I have a fair and reasonable claim for an increase of salary of at least from 30 per cent to 50 per cent upon my original salary, and I sincerely trust and hope that your commission may be able to view my request in a favourable manner and recommend such increase in my salary as is asked for.

When I was appointed I was fortunate enough to possess about $2,000 worth of property, and during the first few years that I held office, by practising strict economy and prudence, I was able to save a little over living expenses each year, but during the last ten years it has been impossible to do so, and as I am now 71 years of age and considerably rheumatic and not likely to perform the duties of my office for many more years, therefore unless I am fortunate enough to receive a substantial increase of salary or a liberal superannuation allowance, my prospects for the future are not bright. Therefore, trusting to the fair and favourable consideration of your commission, I remain,

        Respectfully, your humble and obedient servant,
                (Signed)   JAMES McKAY,
                                      Collector.

OTTAWA, October 23, 1907.

Mr. THOMAS SCOTT, Winnipeg, called and sworn and examined.

By the Chairman:

Q. How long have you been Collector of Customs at Winnipeg?—A. Twenty years.

Q. You were appointed from the House of Commons to the position?—A. Yes.

Q. You had been settled in Winnipeg some time before that?—A. Yes, since 1870.

Q. What is the Customs revenue of Winnipeg?—A. Something over four million dollars.

Q. What salary were you appointed at?—A. $3,000 with free house, fuel, light and so forth.

Q. Now you are getting $4,000?—A. $4,000 without any perquisites.

Q. You could not get any more salary than $4,000 out of the Civil Service Act?—A. I am sorry to say that is so.

Q. You are absolutely limited by the schedule set forth in that Act to a salary of $4,000?—A. Yes.

Q. What was the revenue of Winnipeg when you were appointed collector?—A. It was about $425,000.

Q. If, instead of the revenue being $4,000,000 it amounted to $40,000,000 you could not get any more salary?—A. That is the position.

Q. There are no annual increments for the Customs officers in the outside service?—A. No.

Q. How many officers have you at Winnipeg?—A. Seventy-eight.

Q. How many are permanent?—A. About forty.

Q. You have a very large number of temporary employees?—A. About one-half are temporary.

Q. Are they what is called down here permanent temporaries?—A. Yes, permanent temporaries. They are all there during good behaviour.

Q. Some of them have been there for years, I suppose?—A. Some have been twenty or twenty-five years.

Q. Under what process do they become permanent officers, or do they ever become permanent?—A. A few were placed on the permanent list on account of length of service, last year, some of the old officers. A number have been made permanent officers, after three years in the service, without any examination.

Q. Have you a surveyor in Winnipeg?—A. Yes.

Q. Who is the surveyor?—A. H. M. Sutherland.

Q. When was he appointed to that position?—A. About two years ago.

Q. What is his salary now?—A. $2,000.

Q. He was a preventive officer before that, was he not?—A. He was sub-collector at Killarney.

Q. In the 1906 Civil Service List he is called H. M. Sutherland, preventive officer, $1,600 salary?—A. He was transferred as preventive officer to keep him on the permanent staff.

Q. He was first appointed about three years ago to go to Killarney, was he not?—A. No, he was there about ten or twelve years.

Q. I see that H. M. Sutherland's first appointment is dated January 1, 1904?—A. He was for some eight or ten years at Killarney as sub-collector.

Q. He has been junior to Mr. Thompson, Mr. Allen, and a lot of others?—A. He was junior.

Q. And he was put over their heads?—A. Put over their heads.

7-8 EDWARD VII., A. 1908

Q. He was brought in from a lower grade and put over the heads of all these men?
—A. Right over their heads.

Q. May one ask did he show superior ability?—A. No.

Q. Then the only other reason was that he had a certain amount of pull?—A. That is the only way we can account for it.

Q. Are there any other anomalies, of a similar description in the Winnipeg office?
—A. No.

Q. Who is next to Mr. Sutherland?—A. Mr. Thompson.

Q. He has been there twenty-six years?—A. That is about it.

Q. That is a long period of service for Winnipeg?—A. He has been twenty-six years in the Winnipeg service.

Q. I suppose he was somewhere else in the public service before that?—A. Yes, in Ottawa.

Q. You almost all at that time were newcomers?—A. All.

Q. There were no native born up there then?—A. No.

Q. He had no experience in the Customs service before he joined the Winnipeg office?—A. I understand not.

Q. Now he is chief clerk?—A. He has been for a long period of years, for the last twenty years.

Q. Is he the compendium of all the information?—A. Yes.

Q. He is the man upon whom the whole thing devolves?—A. Yes, he is the principal officer.

Q. He knows everything, and from his past experience can be called upon to do anything?—A. He is acquainted with all the management and the interior working of the port.

Q. Were the appraisers appointed without examination?—A. All our officers have been appointed without examination. We have not an officer in the service there that has ever passed an examination.

Q. How did you manage that?—A. I do not know. They were appointed and we have them at work. Winnipeg is a growing city, and we presume the staff must continually increase.

Q. Who brings to your notice the fact that another appraiser or preventive officer is wanted?—A. I notice when the work is increasing that it is necessary to have another man, and I make application to the Commissioner at Ottawa, and the next thing I hear of it is that a man's name is sent to me, and I notify him and he is put to work.

Q. Does he begin on the temporary list?—A. He begins on the temporary list.

Q. What do you pay your men on the temporary list?—A. $800. They have always been appointed at that figure. It is tantamount to that. They were appointed at $2.50 a day.

Q. That does not include Sundays?—A. No.

Q. Do the temporary employees ever get any annual increment?—A. Yes. During the last two or three years they have been getting an increase every year, but there is no fixed sum. It is arranged each year as decided upon at Ottawa.

Q. It is chiefly a kind of eleemosynary distribution?—A. Yes, in a way.

Q. There is nothing in the Act to give any annual increments to Customs officers in the outside service?—A. No. Unfortunately a good man does not get as much of an increase as the man who does not deserve an increase at all. That is the trouble.

Q. At the last session of Parliament there was an appropriation of $100,000 obtained to provide increases for Customs officers?—A. Yes.

Q. How much of that went to Winnipeg?—A. I do not know, but there was a considerable increase. The average increase, I think, was about $100 an officer, which would give a total of about $8,000.

Q. And this increase was not given, of course, to the men whose salaries were within the limits. That is to say, you could not get anything more, because, under the Act, you could not receive more than $4,000?—A. I was the only unfortunate one.

Q. All the rest were within the limits of the Act?—A. All the others.

Q. They all got the $100 increase?—A. Yes.

Q. It was given to great and small alike, was it?—A. Yes.

Q. How many sub-collectorships have you got now?—A. There are only three.

Q. There are sub-collectors at Gretna and Morden?—A. Gretna has been made a port. We have Morden, Crystal City and Sprague.

Q. Selkirk has been made a port?—A. And Selkirk, yes. It is a very small place.

Q. What about Portage la Prairie?—A. It is a port now. Emerson and Gretna are also ports.

Q. Do you find that men are leaving the service now to better themselves?—A. We lost about three years ago the best men we had. A few of them left on account of the salary question.

Q. They left to better themselves?—A. To better themselves.

Q. Do men leave the service now to better themselves?—Q. No, we have not lost any these last three years.

Q. But before that they went wholesale?—A. Not wholesale. Our staff was not very large then. It has only been increased this last three or four years.

Q. But several men left the service?—A. A few of the good men left on account of the low salary.

Q. You have a new style of officer called an examining officer, now?—A. Yes, they have given the officer that name.

Q. That was to get around the Act, was it not?—A. I do not know what the intention was. There is a preventive officer now and an examining officer.

Q. Your preventive officers, as a rule, are paid how much?—A. They commence at $800.

Q. And what salary do they go to?—A. There is no fixed maximum. There are now quite a number receiving $950.

Q. Who is Mr. Eadie?—A. He is an appraiser appointed about two years ago.

Q. He was called a preventive officer at $1,200?—A. Yes. He was what is known as a preventive officer. Then he was promoted to be an appraiser.

Q. I see in the Civil Service List that preventive officers are receiving such salaries as $900, $950 and $1,200. What is the reason of this haphazard business? —A. I cannot explain that.

Q. In Montreal they have a uniform rate for their preventive officers?—A. The term preventive officer is a misnomer; they are not preventive officers. The preventive officer is engaged on the frontier preventing smuggling. These men were appointed preventive officers, but they are really clerks or landing waiters.

Q. Is there any provisional allowance in the Customs service in the west?—A. None.

Q. The salaries you receive are not supplemented in any way?—A. No.

Q. Is there any other means by which an addition could be made to the emoluments of your officers? Do they attend to any late trains?—A. There is what we call extra service.

Q. For instance, is the baggage of people coming from England examined at the port of arrival or bonded through to Winnipeg?—A. It is generally bonded through. In the case of a passenger coming from England his baggage is bonded to Winnipeg and examined by our officer there and cleared.

Q. And what about passengers coming from the United States?—A. It is bonded at the frontier.

Q. Then your officers may be employed over time?—A. Yes, there are quite a large number of them employed over time every day.

Q. What do you pay these officers for overtime?—A. They get 30 cents an hour overtime.

Q. That is the same payment as is made in the east?—A. In the case of an officer getting $1,000 a year the 30 cents an hour is not equal to what he is receiving in the form of salary. The overtime ought proportionately to be greater than the salary because the work is performed either early in the morning or late at night.

Q. What pay does the ordinary labourer get in Winnipeg?—A. He gets $2.75 a day.

Q. Then in the case of a Customs officer in receipt of $750 or $800 he is only paid for meeting early trains or late trains 30 cents an hour overtime, and the ordinary labourer in the daytime gets more than 30 cents an hour?—A. He does.

Q. So that your officer, for the additional time put in in the morning or at night, gets less than a corporation labourer?—A. He does. The landing waiters have to be on duty at 8 o'clock in the morning. Their hours are from 8 a.m. to 6 p.m. We have some fifteen officers that go on from 7 o'clock to 8 o'clock, and all they get is 30 cents an hour overtime. They have to get up on a winter's morning in order to be on duty at 7 o'clock, and it is pretty hard that they should receive only 30 cents.

Q. What time do trains arrive in Winnipeg?—A. The Customs warehouses are open at 7 o'clock in the morning. Our men are there at 7 o'clock and are paid overtime for the hour until their regular duties commence. At one time the railway companies paid this overtime, but for some reason the department decided that they would make the payments. This amounts to 30 cents for the hour's work, but the men do not feel that it is any emolument at all, especially when they have to turn out on a cold winter's morning and walk a mile to their work.

Q. You have looked at the Civil Service Act, I suppose? Have you any observations to make respecting the classification of inspectors, collectors, surveyors and so forth?—A. No, I have not.

Q. You have no tide-waiters?—A. No, we have no tide-waiters.

Q. The service at Winnipeg is rather overmanned than undermanned?—A. We have a larger staff than is really necessary if we had more competent men.

Q. If you had more competent men you could do with a lesser staff?—A. And do the work better, too.

Q. Then if you have incompetent officials your staff is rather overmanned than otherwise?—A. That is the case.

Q. Do you thoroughly agree with the clause in the memorial presented to us this morning respecting superannuation?—A. Yes.

Q. And you agree with Dr. Barrett in what he has said?—A. Yes.

Q. Does the absence of a retiring allowance deter capable men from entering the service?—A. Well, I do not know. The trouble is that the men who are in the service feel there is nothing to look forward to.

Q. Do you know what initial salary is paid to a boy on entering a bank in Winnipeg?—A. I do not know.

Q. Is there an inspector of Customs for your division?—A. Yes.

Q. An inspector for the province?—A. Inspector Young acts for the province of Manitoba.

Q. I suppose his headquarters are at Winnipeg?—A. Yes.

Q. Is his office in your building?—A. Yes, in the Customs-house.

Q. You know exactly when he is or is not there?—A. Yes.

Q. But he can drop in upon you when he likes?—A. At any time.

Q. If he happens to be in your office, you do not know whether he is going to inspect it?—A. No.

Q. What ports have been established lately?—A. Gretna and Emerson have been made ports lately. Portage la Prairie was made a port some time ago, and Brandon is already a port.

Q. The last report gives Winnipeg, Brandon and Emerson. In addition to that there is Gretna?—A. Yes, Gretna, Portage la Prairie and Brandon.

Q. And Selkirk?—A. Selkirk is an outport of Winnipeg.

Q. How are your officers appointed in the west, by political association or on the nomination of a member?—A. As I understand it, the member exercises the patronage, I suppose, with the consent of the executive committee.

SESSIONAL PAPER No. 29a

Q. I thought you might know, being an old parliamentary hand?—A. Well, I know more than I care to know sometimes.

Q. There is nothing else you would like to say to us?—A. No.

The witness retired.

OTTAWA, May 23, 1907.

Mr. T. C. BOVILLE, called and sworn and examined.

By the Chairman:

Q. You are the Deputy Minister of Finance?—A. Yes.
Q. You have held that position since November 1, last?—A. Since November 1, 1906.
Q. How long have you been in the department?—A. Since January 26, 1883.
Q. That will be 25 years next January?—A. Twenty-five years next January.
Q. What class did you come in at?—A. Third-class.
Q. You worked your way up through every grade by Promotion examination until you became deputy minister?—A. Yes.

By Mr. Fyshe:

Q. Have you passed several Promotion examinations?—A. One was all I had to take.
Q. Simply with regard to the duties of office, I suppose?—A. Other subjects besides; arithmetic, grammar, composition, and possibly one or two other subjects.

By the Chairman:

Q. You are a graduate of Toronto University?—A. Yes, I graduated in 1884.
Q. You need not have passed any other Promotion examination, because you had obtained a sufficient percentage of marks to obviate the rest? Such was the ground taken by the Department of Justice?—A. That was the ground. At the first examination I obtained sufficient marks to qualify me for any grade.
Q. What is your salary now?—A. $4,000 per annum.
Q. Without any prospects, under the Civil Service Act. in your case, of an increase?—A. Not under the Act..
Q. The Act declares that had you been a bank manager you might have got a salary of $5,000?—A. Yes.
Mr. FYSHE.—That is a funny statement.

By the Chairman:

Q. So that although you have had 25 years' experience you could not obtain more than $4,000 salary, unless there was a revision of salaries?—A. $4,000 is the very limit. It seems strange that service under the Government should not qualify for the Government service.
Q. Really in the last fifteen years the financial business of the country has doubled?—A. The revenue has increased, roughly speaking, from 40 millions to 80 millions.
Q. In the same time the permanent staff has only increased from 31 to 39?—A. That is the permanent staff chargeable to Civil Government has increased from 31 to 39 in number.
Q. And the temporary staff, also chargeable to Civil Government, has increased from 1 to 10?—A. One to 10.
Q. The staff employed in connection with charges of management, such as management of the public debt, looking after the note issue, &c., has increased from 11 to 33?—A. The staff has increased from 11 to 33, and within the last month we have had to add four persons additional.

By Mr. Fyshe:

Q. Extra men?—A. Extra women, these are all women.

By the Chairman:

Q. Women are engaged in signing and destroying the currency?—A. Signing the new currency and counting and destroying the old currency.

By Mr. Fyshe:

Q. The old currency business is under your control, is it?—A. Yes.

Q. The controller of currency is one of your officers?—A. He is one of our officers.

By the Chairman:

Q. You have now over $14,000,000 of currency, one's and two's?—A. Yes, according to the last *Gazette*.

Mr. FYSHE.—In circulation?

The CHAIRMAN.—Yes.

By the Chairman:

Q. Can you tell me what it was in 1892?—A. I can not give it to you exactly. It was about seven millions.

Q. I see that in 1899, at its highest point in October, the currency only amounted to $9,000,000?—A. Yes.

Q. In 1892 it was about $7,000,000?—A. Yes.

Q. You will give us the actual figures?—A. Yes.

By Mr. Basin:

Q. That is only for one's and two's?—A. Only for one's and two's.

By Mr. Fyshe:

Q. I suppose that is the principal part of your circulation?—A. One's and two's form the volumes. In amount the large notes are the principal factor.

Q. They are not circulating, they are probably held in banks?—A. We issued ones, twos and fours from our office to the amount of $2,348,000 in the year 1891-2——

Q. That is, you issued that amount?—A. We issued that amount. We cancelled and destroyed besides that $2,500,000. In 1905-6 we issued $12,712,000 and cancelled $11,500,000.

Q. How did you come to increase to that amount? That is an enormous increase? —A. The business of the country demanded it.

By the Chairman:

Q. Then the issue of currency increased sixfold?—A. Yes. In 1892 we redeemed and cancelled ones and twos and fours—to the extent of about $2,500,000. In 1905-6 we redeemed ones, twos and fours to the extent of $11,500,000.

By Mr. Fyshe:

Q. More than five times?—A. Nearly five times.

The CHAIRMAN.—And the staff in that particular branch has only increased from 11 to 33.

By Mr. Fyshe:

Q. There is one thing that you might have been more rigid about and that is as to the quality of the circulation. Some of the banks keep the notes until they are absolutely filthy. Others keep their notes measurably clean. I think, however, we have heard more complaints about the Dominion notes?—A. We have been keeping the circulation, within the last eight or ten years, very clean.

7-8 EDWARD VII., A. 1908

Q. That would tend to increase the amount redeemed, of course?—A. Yes.

By the Chairman:

Q. While the increase in one direction has been sixfold and in the other direction fivefold, the staff has only increased threefold?—A. About threefold.

Q. You receive from the Minister the names of people inquiring for employment, when it is necessary to engage a new clerk?—A. Yes.

Q. Can you get good boys now to enter the service at $500 a year?—A. I am afraid not.

Q. Latterly you have had to give them something more?—A. We have had to give practically $800.

Q. And in that way you have strained the Civil Service Act and have had to get special votes from Parliament?—A. Yes, we have to go beyond the minimum of $500 prescribed by the Civil Service Act.

By Mr. Fyshe:

Q. At what age do you usually engage youths?—A. Generally speaking, I should say about 23 or 24.

Q. You do not take them immediately after they leave school?—A. No, not as a rule.

Q. But they must have had some experience between leaving school and entering the Government service?—A. Some of them have had slight exeprience in banks, some have taught school for a short time, and others have had some slight commercial experience.

Q. If you could get boys at the age of 16 or 17, just after leaving school, such as the banks take, especially in the old country, they would be content with very much less than $800, in fact they would be content with $200?

By the Chairman:

Q. You cannot get them for that kind of work you require?—A. Not for the class of work we have. It requires a good deal of intelligence and a good deal of level-headedness, which you can hardly expect from boys of 17 or 18.

Mr. FYSHE.—Well, perhaps so.

By the Chairman:

Q. But the women you take in at $500?—A. The women we take in at $500?

Q. There is a greater demand on the part of women than on the part of men for employment?—A. Yes.

Q. I know that you have stacks of applications from women?—A. Our applications from women are very much more numerous than from men.

By Mr. Fyshe:

Q. Have you any restrictions as to age in the case of women?—A. There is no restriction in the case of temporary clerks. The only restriction we have is the restriction that one necessarily lays down in trying to get good service.

Q. I mean, would you take them when they come to a certain age?—A. Most of the women we employ are, I should say—one cannot be too curious—between 20 and 30 years of age. Most of the young women coming into the department now are between 20 and 30.

Q. I am surprised at their coming in at so young an age as that?—A. There is one coming in on Monday next and her age is 20.

By the Chairman:

Q. They have all passed the Civil Service examinations?—A. They have all passed.

Q. And there is an age limit under the Civil Service Examination?—A. Yes, 18 to 35 years of age, but one may have passed her examination fifteen years ago. Our aim is to get good, intelligent women, of good character, and women whose health is sufficient to enable them to stand the stress of a good deal of hard work.

Q. As a rule your employees are all healthy?—A. Yes.

Q. And scarcely without exception they are of good character?—A. The employees of the Department of Finance are of the highest character.

By Mr. Fyshe:

Q. Are you more careful in your selection?—A. We are very careful in selection.

Q. And your political head does not give you any trouble?—A. None whatever. He is very reasonable and very careful to give us as good material as he possibly can obtain.

By the Chairman:

Q. Of course they have to pass a probationary period?—A. Yes, the permanent appointments have to pass the probationary period required by the Civil Service Act.

Q. You have been deputy minister so short a time that you could not have had any opportunity of rejecting an unqualified person?—A. We have had no permanent appointments in the Finance Department since I became deputy minister.

Q. The officials of the Finance Department are of exceptionally good character?—A. I can say so without reserve.

Q. They compare well with officials in any branch of commercial or public life outside?—A. So far as my experience is concerned they would compare with those employed on any branch I have had anything to do with.

Q. In consequence of the training they received many former officials of the Finance Department have succeeded in outside life?—A. Yes.

Q. Mr. Ross left the department?—A. Yes, Mr. Chipman left the department.

Q. To become chief factor for the Hudson Bay Company?—A. Mr. Baker left the department in your time, Mr. Courtney.

Mr. FYSHE.—Is that Mr. Baker of the C.P.R.?

The CHAIRMAN.—Yes. The Finance Department has trained up a lot of men.

The WITNESS.—Mr. Tabor is now a lawyer in Dawson.

By the Chairman:

Q. And while men have constantly left the department you have had no applications from any who have retired to come back again?—A. No.

Q. What about Promotion examinations in the Finance Department?—A. The examination papers will speak for themselves, they are published in the report of the Secretary of State.

By Mr. Fyshe:

Q. I suppose they are chiefly concerned with the duties of office?—A. Duties of office and arithmetic largely. The last examination subjects were duties of office and arithmetic.

By the Chairman:

Q. In sections 46 and 47 of the Civil Service Act—this is a stereotype question—it is provided that in case of a vacancy the position shall be filled by the head of the department. There is no mention made of the deputy minister?—A. In case of a promotion a report from the deputy head is not required.

By Mr. Fyshe:

Q. Does the Act not require his comment and concurrence?—A. No, not under the law.

7-8 EDWARD VII., A. 1908

By the Chairman:

Q. In practice the deputy does have something to say?—A. In practice the opinion and advice of the deputy head are taken.

Q. And having had a series of good ministers in the Finance Department, there has been no trouble?—A. No.

Q. For the general good of the service, taking it altogether, would it not be advisable that appointments should be made on the report of the deputy head?—A. I think so.

By Mr. Fyshe:

Q. It seems to me that the initiative should be left to the deputy minister, but the consent of the chief of the department should be had, of course?—A. The consent of the minister should be had. The deputy minister, of course, is the man who is responsible, and knows the value of a man's services in his capacity as clerk.

Q. And he is responsible for preserving discipline and efficiency?—A. Yes.

By the Chairman:

Q. Occasionally there have been transfers, particularly from the Post Office Department, of eligible persons to the Finance Department?—A. Yes, we have had two or three such transfers.

Q. That was to the general benefit of the service?—A. It was to the benefit of the Finance Department, anyway.

Q. The transfer, in such cases, was not made for political purposes?—A. No, I do not think so.

Mr. FYSHE.—But how could the receiving department be thoroughly aware of the capacity of the people they were getting?

The CHAIRMAN.—We subjected them to an examination outside of the Act altogether.

Mr. FYSHE.—But an examination is never sufficient, you know, to test a person's ability.

The CHAIRMAN.—And we had the opinion of the chief officers.

Mr. FYSHE.—Of the department they came from?

The CHAIRMAN.—Yes.

By Mr. Fyshe:

Q. It is practically impossible, in my judgment, to tell what a man is like, if you appoint him from outside. You may get good reports of him, and all that sort of thing, but it is impossible to tell whether he is suited for the position or not?—A. That is why six months' probation is provided for in the Civil Service Act.

Q. But if you once get him, and you find that he does not suit your purposes, you cannot dismiss the man, you simply shunt him?—A. We have the power of dismissing him.

Q. I know, but that is a different thing.—A. Practically when a man is employed on probation it is impossible to get rid of him.

By the Chairman: .

Q. In the case of all classes of clerks the annual increment is $50?—A. Yes, irrespective of the class.

Q. Do you think it would be advisable to change the method?—A. I think some rearrangement of the statutory increase ought to be made. In the case of the first-class clerks an increment of $50 a year is hardly sufficient. Take a good officer who is serving at $1,500 a year, in order to obtain a salary at the maximum of the first-class it would take him six years.

SESSIONAL PAPER No. 29a

By Mr. Fyshe:

Q. To get what?—A. To get a salary of $1,800. If he is a good man he is worth more than $50 a year. If he is a poor man $50 a year is enough.

Q. Have the Government ever taken into consideration one thing, namely, that one of the usual and almost necessary obligations of a man is to marry and raise a family? If so, I do not see how they can expect him to do it satisfactorily on the small salary he receives. It seems to me, especially in a country like this, where population, and that of good quality is required above everything else, that the raising of families should be considered as much as any other thing?—A. I think as between a single man and a man who is married and bringing up a young family, consideration should be given to the latter.

Q. There seems to be no recognition of that in the rules?—A. There is none.

Mr. FYSHE.—Do you not think it is only reasonable?

The CHAIRMAN.—Of course it is.

Mr. FYSHE.—The married man, other things being equal, is decidedly the better citizen. Do you not think so?

The CHAIRMAN.—Yes.

The WITNESS.—I think it sometimes leads to, I should say, misfortune, to give a very high salary to the young man without family ties.

By Mr. Fyshe:

Q. It is easy enough for a single man to live on $1,000 a year, I mean, if he will restrict his wants. I remember when I came out here first, I had $700 a year, and I could save money on that. So that a single man could easily live on a salary of from $1,000 to $1,200, but for a married man it is simply impossible?—A. We have married men in the department with young, growing up families who are drawing only about $1,200 a year. It makes living very hard. I think that the married man should have some consideration.

By the Chairman:

Q. Well, considering the fact that in the Finance Department you have had to break the law by appointing young men at $800 per annum, is it advisable to have the minimum increased or done away with?—A. I think a little elasticity in the limit would be advantageous, leaving the salary discretionary with the appointing officer.

Mr. FYSHE.—It would be necessary, I think, if you were going to make a change of that kind to provide that the salary should not be larger than some officer already in the department is drawing for similar work.

The CHAIRMAN.—The work in the several departments is not analogous. The Finance Department has to do with banking, the Secretary of State's Department, with routine and records, and the Inland Revenue with Excise returns. There is nothing analogous between them. The Finance Department would require a youth who is acquainted with banking methods and the system of cheques, pass-books, and that kind of thing. There is nothing about the work of the Finance Department that would compare with any other department.

By Mr. Fyshe:

Q. It would not be proper to appoint a man at $800 when you already had a man in your department who is doing the same work at $600?—A. That would not be fair.

By the Chairman:

Q. I suppose the trouble would be if you wanted to take a boy, as was done recently from the Bank of Commerce, and pay him $800—if the Civil Service Act were amended as to allow of that, some other youth, having political pressure, might be

7-8 EDWARD VII., A. 1908

appointed to another department at the same salary?—A. That might be a source of trouble. The whole difficulty is that the Act tries to arrange every department on the same basis.

Q. You were practically assistant secretary of the last Civil Service Commission and did a good deal of work?—A. Yes.

Q. And you prepared the analytical index to the report?—A. Yes.

Q. Was there ever a man suspended in the Finance Department?—A. I have no recollection of such a case.

Q. The leave of absence granted is three weeks?—A. Yes, that is the statutory leave.

Q. But you act generously in granting leave?—A. We give the provision of the law an elastic interpretation.

By Mr. Bazin:

Q. When you say three weeks, you mean seven days each week?—A. The ordinary three weeks, from day to day.

By the Chairman:

Q. You keep the attendance book?—A. Yes.

Q. And everybody signs the attendance book?—A. Everybody except the private secretary.

Q. And the attendance book is brought in to you every day at ten o'clock?—A. Every day at ten o'clock.

Q. Your clerks at this time of the year quit work at four o'clock, I suppose?—A. Oh, yes, on the fine days.

Q. But during the season when there are estimates and returns to be submitted to Parliament they have to remain until the work is accomplished?—A. Yes.

By Mr. Fyshe:

Q. When do they arrive in the morning?—A. Between nine and ten o'clock.

Q. When they sign the attendance book do they state the hour they arrive?—A. Not generally. Of course we draw the line at ten o'clock. Our observance of the rule as to attendance is elastic in this way: We have quite a number of employees who during the session of Parliament and during the busy time of the year remain until five o'clock, half-past five, and you often find them there at six o'clock. If these employees report at a quarter or ten minutes to ten in the morning no fault can be found. A certain amount of latitude should be given.

By the Chairman:

Q. And in the session time, owing to the preparation of estimates and the attendance upon the Minister in the House, the work is very arduous? Sometimes a person is required to be in the House almost every night?—A. Yes, and somebody in the department almost every night. In fact, in the Department of Finance the hours of attendance are regulated by the work—and practically by the gentlemen themselves. The staff, without being instructed, will stay three times a month until ten or eleven o'clock at night so as to prepare special balance sheets. The balance sheet is prepared three times a month, at the end of each ten-day period.

By Mr. Fyshe:

Q. All the year around?—A. All the year around. On the tenth day of the month at four o'clock the ten-day period ends, and next morning the balance sheet is on my desk. That is prepared after four o'clock of the previous day.

Q. I should think that is very judicious. You want to keep thoroughly posted as to your funds from week to week?—A. Each month a full statement of the revenue and expenditure, practically the balance sheet, is published in the *Canada Gazette*, and that requires considerable work.

Q. Every calendar month?—A. Every calendar month, and it has to be published very shortly after the end of the month.

By the Chairman:

Q. Coming back to the women employees, they as a rule are employed in the currency branch of the Department of Finance?—A. Yes.

Q. You encourage them to learn typewriting and shorthand?—A. Yes, they are encouraged to do so.

Q. And now and again some of them will leave the currency branch and enter the general work of the department when they are found able?—A. Yes, we have four or five ladies who are employed in that way now.

By Mr. Fyshe:

Q. Do you give them any monetary inducement to do that?—A. No.

The CHAIRMAN.—They get permanent rank, as a rule, instead of being simply temporary clerks.

Mr. FYSHE.—That is not much inducement for the women to work hard to improve themselves.

The WITNESS.—The probable inducement lies in the fact that they like the outside class of work better.

By the Chairman:

Q. Of course, it is deadly monotonous work, merely signing names to bills and destroying them?—A. Yes, it is very monotonous.

Q. And after that time the women do it perfunctorily?—A. It must become mechanical.

Q. You are always keeping an eye on a likely girl with a capacity to enter the department from the currency branch?—A. Yes.

Q. Was there ever any test made as to the amount of work done on the notes? For instance, how many notes they could sign in a day?—A. We have had tests of that kind.

By Mr. Fyshe:

Q. I should think that would be interesting. That is a very good way of testing the mechanical capacity of the clerks?—A. We have done that.

By the Chairman:

Q. That has been done three or four times?—A. Yes, we had tests as to how quickly a very fast writer could sign notes.

By Mr. Fyshe:

Q. Of course, it would depend somewhat upon the length of a name?—A. Yes, but we take a medium name. We have had several tests made and we have a pretty accurate idea of the amount of work that should come from each pen during the week.

Q. I was once in an office where there was keen rivalry between the staff. About one-third of the staff was Scotch and the rest English, and there was so much rivalry between them that the great part of the work of the office was timed. Whenever a new clerk was employed half a dozen watches took note of what he was doing. That is the only office I ever saw it done in. Under such circumstances you get very quick work.—A. No doubt.

By Mr. Bazin:

Q. Have you any means of checking the number of notes you give to the women to destroy?—A. Yes.

7-8 EDWARD VII., A. 1908

By the Chairman:

Q. They are given out in bundles of a thousand?—A. The new Dominion notes come in bundles of a thousand sheets, four notes to a sheet.

By Mr. Fyshe:

Q. They sign them more readily that way, I think?—A. Yes, they come in that state from the printer. Then they are counted and handed to the women, who also count them. The notes are put into a cash box, each women having such a box, and they are counted to see that the thousand sheets are there. Then she signs the notes and returns them to the controller of currency and they are counted again.

Q. The same thing is done, I suppose, when they destroy the old notes? They are counted by the controller?—A. The old notes come to the controller in bundles of a thousand and the bundles are handed over to the women to count and label them, and return them checked with a check mark on them. The notes are then destroyed.

Q. To whom are they handed first, to the controller?—A. The controller hands them to the women.

Q. He does not count them himself?—A. He does not count them, the women count them.

Q. They come from outside offices?—A. From the offices of the Assistant Receivers General.

Q. It seems to me that in a bank there would be joint custody and joint responsibility, and in remittances there should be two officers to count, one overlooking the other?—A. The quantity of notes that are received to be signed is enormous. There is joint custody and responsibility.

By the Chairman:

Q. The old notes come from the offices of the Assistant Receivers General in bundles of a thousand?—A. Yes.

Q. The women have to count them to see whether each bundle contains a thousand, and the next point is the destruction?—A. Yes.

Q. And they are destroyed by officers of the Finance Department and the Audit Office?—A. By officers of both departments.

Q. And the Audit Office checks the number of bundles?—A. Checks the number of bundles, and the officer from that department has the right to take out any bundle and check it.

By Mr. Fyshe:

Q. Do they not check every one?—A. The Audit Office?

Q. Yes?—A. They check by bundles.

Q. Do they not count every note?—A. They would have to duplicate our staff to do so.

Q. Do you keep a note account book?—A. By number?

Q. Yes?—A. Not at all, and I will tell you why.

Q. The banks do?—A. Yes.

The CHAIRMAN.—But they have got nothing under a five-dollar note.

The WITNESS.—If you make a mistake in one number, one mistake in your note-account, it invalidates the whole.

By Mr. Fyshe:

Q. How?—A. Because no account can be verified and sworn to as being absolutely accurate when there are millions and millions of notes going through. The rest of your count is no good.

Q. I would not say that.—A. It is no good as a count.

Q. An absolutely correct system, I think, is that adopted by some of the banks. They do not all do it, but we followed it in the Bank of Nova Scotia. Every single note redeemed was marked off in a note book opposite a number. They are all registered on specifications, in fact the numbers are published on the specification of the notes to be cancelled. So if 5,000 bundles are put on a specification, each note is numbered there and the specifications are generally kept to be marked off in the note-book. The numbers are all filled in in the specification and they have to be counted by an officer—the accountant generally—and initialled, and then they have to be counted by the directors and initialled, and the fact that they were destroyed on such a date is marked on the specification.—A. Our notes run up into the millions, and to adopt such a system would necessitate the employment of an army of people. It would be not only cumbrous but ineffective with such enormous quantities as we have to deal with.

By the Chairman:

Q. The Department of Finance deals only with the Assistant Receivers General?—A. Yes.

Q. The Assistant Receivers General send back these mutilated notes?—A. Yes, the worn and mutilated notes.

Q. They are first checked?—A. Yes, the inspector may go into an Assistant Receiver General's office at any time and check his cancelling.

Q. And the inspector is constantly travelling to count the cash and the notes held by the Assistant Receiver General?—A. Yes.

Q. Then the mutilated notes come to the women at Ottawa, who also count them?—A. Yes.

Q. Then they are destroyed by the officers of the department, not the women?—A. By one of our chief officers.

Q. In conjunction with an officer of the Audit Office?—A. Yes.

Q. And that officer of the Audit Office checks the bundles here, there and everywhere, and counts them?—A. He has a right to do so.

By Mr. Fyshe:

Q. Every bundle should be counted by two officers at the time they are destroyed, and it is all the more necessary if you have not got each number registered and marked off?—A. It would be necessary to greatly increase the staff in order to do that, and the results would not be of value.

By the Chairman:

Q. How could you do that with $11,000,000 worth of notes to be destroyed, millions of ones and twos?—A. A million dollars means a million notes. At the commencement of this business when our circulation was small they did try to keep a note count by number and it was found to be quite impracticable because one mistake or two or three mistakes would nullify the whole.

By Mr. Fyshe:

Q. A mistake is an ugly thing, but you cannot say it nullifies the whole business. If you make mistakes in a number you will find it out when the right figure comes along, but it does not follow that it destroys the whole thing?—A. Well, it invalidates the usefulness of the count.

By the Chairman:

Q. You are, ex officio, Secretary of the Treasury Board?—A. Yes.

Q. The Treasury Board reports to the Privy Council all increases of salary and all promotions, also appointments?—A. Promotions and appointments.

7-8 EDWARD VII., A. 1908

Q. Your office is not only looking to see whether the increases are obtained, but you, as Secretary of the Board, may say something as to the expediency of certain increases?—A. Yes.

Q. The Treasury Board, in addition to its other powers, grants certificates to banks to do banking business under the Bank Act?—A. Yes, and also grants certificates in case of increases of capital.

Q. They also grant certificates to insurance companies?—A. Yes.

Q. The Treasury Board also approves of changes of securities lodged by insurance companies?—A. The exchange and acceptance of securities are subjects for consideration by the board.

By Mr. Fyshe:

Q. Do you mean securities of insurance companies?—A. Yes. And the acceptance of the different classes of securities.

By the Chairman:

Q. The board also deals with all cases of Superannuation?—A. Superannuations are required by law to be approved by the Treasury Board.

Mr. FYSHE.—In all the departments?

The CHAIRMAN.—In all the departments. There are thousands of cases that go through the Treasury Board every year.

The WITNESS.—Yes, there are thousands. The number will probably run from 2,000 to 3,000 cases a year.

By Mr. Fyshe:

Q. Cases of what?—A. Individual reports as to superannuation and increases of salary.

Q. I should think they would receive very summary treatment?—A. No.

By the Chairman:

Q. In the case of the Post Office Department, for example, where there are over 300 employees, the reports as to the annual increment of salary are very numerous?—A. We put through the other day many increases of salary in the Customs Department. Almost every officer of the Customs throughout the country received an increase of salary beginning April 1.

Q. You take care that not only are all these increases, promotions and appointments made within the terms of the Act, but if you know anything with respect to individual cases, you inform the board?—A. As a matter of expediency.

Q. Has there ever been, since the Treasury Board took up that work, any disallowance of an annual increase by it?—A. Not that I am aware of.

Mr. FYSHE.—The Auditor General is supposed to examine every item of every account?

The CHAIRMAN.—He has to see that everything is correct according to the law.

By Mr. Fyshe:

Q. But is not that impossible?—A. It has to be done.

Q. You mean that it is necessary to see that it is done?—A. It is done.

By the Chairman:

Q. The work of the Treasury Board has been of so good a character, that the Auditor General accepts its recommendations, except in the case of contracts and that kind of thing. The board's recommendations have not been disallowed?—A. No.

Q. Or have not met with his opposition?—A. There have been cases where he has questioned increases. There was, for instance, one of my own.

Q. But that recommendation went through afterwards?—A. The Auditor General's objection was over-ruled by the Treasury Board.

Q. That is correct. The Auditor General also raised the question of leave of absence, which is also dealt with by the Treasury Board?—A. Yes, leave of absence to temporary employees.

Q. I was going to say only in the case of temporary employees?—A. Only in the case of temporary employees. I think in some other cases he has absolutely demanded the reasons for the leave being granted.

By Mr. Fyshe:

Q. Supposing a man wanted to have a day's fishing. Could the deputy give him leave of absence right off?—A. Yes. It is easily made up in one day or the other. One of our staff is going fishing to-night, to stay over Saturday and be back Monday morning.

Q. You certainly ought to have power to do that.—A. But the same man very frequently is back in the department at night.

Q. Of course you want a certain amount of give and take?—A. Yes.

By the Chairman:

Q. Since the case of Martineau, the employee of the Militia Department who forged a number of cheques, all the cheques drawn under the credits granted by the Department have been returned to the Department to examine?—A. The cheques paid by the banks under letters of credit with the statements come direct to the Department of Finance.

By Mr. Fyshe:

Q. And form their voucher?—A. No, they are sent to us for the purpose of adjusting the cash balance of the bank.

Q. You have in that way a chance to check the correctness of the payment?—A. Yes, the cheques are every one examined back and front.

By the Chairman:

Q. The Banks return to the Department of Finance the paid cheques at the end of each month?—A. Yes.

Q. The Department drawing the cheques sends a list of the cheques so drawn?—A. Yes.

Q. These cheques are compared one with the other?—A. Yes.

Q. They are carefully looked at as to the matter of endorsation?—A. Yes, and a statement of the outstanding cheques, or rather a list, is taken out.

Mr. FYSHE.—Is there only one account for a number of Departments?

The CHAIRMAN.—No, each Department has its own account.

Mr. FYSHE.—With the Bank?

The CHAIRMAN.—With the Bank.

By Mr. Fyshe.

Q. Then of course it is more easy to check?—A. Each letter of credit has an account with the Bank.

By Mr. Bazin:

Q. The cheques are drawn against the letters of credit?—A. Yes.

Q. That is why you would get the cheques back to establish the balance that may be in the Bank. I mean as regards a certain letter of credit?—A. It is to adjust the letter of credit account.

By the Chairman:

Q. You get a list of the outstanding cheques?—A. These cheques are adjusted once a month. A list of the outstanding cheques is made out and the accounts are adjusted each month.

By Mr. Fyshe:

Q. When you take a note of the outstanding cheques you are careful to see there is good reason for their being outstanding?—A. A great many cheques are issued in the last two or three days of the month.

Q. I know, but if there is anything outstanding for a month you would make inquiries?—A. Probably further back than that, two or three months, and we would find out from the Department.

By the Chairman:

Q. Do you recollect offhand how many cheques are issued yearly under the letter of credit system?—A. Last year we put through about 600,000 cheques.

Mr. FYSHE.—That is a large number.

By the Chairman:

Q. That varies from an immense number in connection with the Intercolonial Railway, for instance, to a small number in the Department of Justice?—A. The number runs from about 13,000 a month for the Intercolonial Railway to probably 25 or 30 for the Department of Justice. The employees of the Intercolonial Railway are all paid by cheque.

Mr. FYSHE.—Do you mean to say the Finance Department has those cheques drawn?

The CHAIRMAN.—No, the credits are granted to the officers of the several Departments.

Mr. FYSHE.—I see. And the Intercolonial Railway people draw against those credits.

By the Chairman:

Q. Then the Banks return to the Finance Department at the end of each month the cheques that are paid and the Department sends in to you a list of the cheques drawn? Since this system began, the Department has been very careful about looking after the endorsations?—A. Yes.

Q. The Finance Department found out in the case of one Department, from the numbers of the cheques being out of order, that wrong-doing had occurred?—A. Yes, that a messenger had stolen a cheque book. That is the case of Corcoran, who stole a cheque book.

Q. Fortunately the amounts were not large?—A. The amounts were small.

Q. How many cheques do you recollect he drew?—A. Four cheques.

By Mr. Fyshe:

Q. Of course forgery was committed?—A. Yes, the man forged the signatures. I think there was one in favour of himself, one or two cheques, and a couple were in favour of trades people.

Q. Are the cheques drawn to order?—A. Every cheque is drawn to order.

By the Chairman:

Q. But as a result of this system you found out immediately at the end of the month that a cheque book had been stolen?—A. Yes, it was found out in a very short time. Supposing a man forges a cheque at the first or second day of the month his account is adjusted at the end of the month within four or five days or perhaps a week after the close of the month.

By Mr. Fyshe:

Q. That is very good?—A. Yes. This is done month after month. Last year, as I said, we put through almost 600,000 cheques. This year the number will be larger. We have several people employed in doing that work.

By the Chairman:

Q. And two or three of the staff are very sharp women?—A. Two of them are sharp women.

Q. You receive from the Customs Department, the Inland Revenue Department, the Post Office Department, the Railway Department, and all the other Departments daily statements of deposits in the several banks to the credit of the Receiver General?—A. Yes, a daily statement of the receipts and revenues generally.

Q. These statements are on special forms? When the Collector of Customs at Prescott, for instance, deposits his collections he is handed three forms and a draft?—A. Three receipts. The original is for himself.

Q. The duplicate he sends to the Department, and the triplicate and the draft on the head office of the Bank are sent to the Finance Department?—A. Yes.

Q. These things come in daily?—A. Daily.

By Mr. Fyshe:

Q. You send these drafts to the several banks where they are credited to the Receiver General?—A. The statements come in the morning and they are deposited in the Bank before three o'clock in the afternoon.

Q. And the receipts are filed?—A. The receipts are filed, of course. They come into us in all sorts of shapes. They will run from $300,000 to $600,000 a day, and we have to deposit them with the Banks.

By Mr. Bazin:

Q. Do you mean to say that you get these receipts from the collector at every port? Does the Collector for the port of Quebec and the Collector for the port of Montreal send these receipts?—A. The Collector of Customs at Quebec will send his receipts to the Customs Department. The department gathers them together and sends them to us day by day.

By the Chairman:

Q. And every day the revenues are got in from the big Departments?—A. Daily.

Q. And daily before three o'clock these drafts are sent to the Banks?—A. Except on Saturday, when the Bank closes at twelve o'clock. In the old days, when the Banks closed at one o'clock on that day, by rushing things we could get the majority of drafts to the Bank before one o'clock. But under the new rule the Banks now close at noon on Saturday.

By Mr. Fyshe:

Q. Do all the branches close at twelve now?—A. Yes. Some of the small branches are open in the evenings.

Mr. FYSHE.—That is a curious thing. Scotland is the only country where I ever heard of it being done, and they are following the same plan here now. In Glasgow the greatest commercial centre next to London, all the banking business is done in two hours every Saturday.

By the Chairman:

Q. In each place there is only one Bank receiving the Government deposits?—A. Except in large cities like Toronto and Montreal. In those cities the deposits are made in different places.

29a—13.

7-8 EDWARD VII., A. 1908

Q. I mean to say where there are branch post offices they may use another Bank? —A. Yes, but the general rule is that in each place our business is conducted with one Bank.

By Mr. Fyshe:

Q. That is only reasonable?—A. It is reasonable.

By the Chairman:

Q. A post office instead of sending its money to a distant office of the Bank of Montreal, would use the Bank next door?—A. For public convenience.

Q. The Finance Department is continually worried by Banks that want to get deposits away from the other Banks?—A. Frequent applications are made of that character.

Q. To receive the deposits on account of the Receiver General in a district gives a Bank a certain amount of prestige?—A. Yes, the fact of the Government transacting business with a Bank carries with it, in the eyes of the public a certain amount of prestige.

The CHAIRMAN.—The Banque Ville Marie, for instance, used to open branches here and there at hamlets where there was a post office and made repeated and insistent applications to obtain the deposits of these local post offices, with the idea of getting deposits from the habitants of the country around?—A. With the idea of using the Government prestige to obtain deposits. As a rule the more urgent the demands are——

By Mr. Fyshe:

Q. The less you are inclined to grant them?—A. The less we are inclined to grant them and the more reason there is for not granting them.

Mr. BAZIN.—Is there any profit to the Bank?

The CHAIRMAN.—Not the slightest.

The WITNESS.—Practically none with the exception of a few thousand dollars we may keep without interest.

By the Chairman:

Q. You are worried in the department by Banks desiring to open accounts?—A. It is a very troublesome class of business.

Q. And I suppose you continue the policy that when a Bank gets insistent and troublesome it is to be watched?—A. Yes.

Q. In the Department of Finance you also keep check of the Superannuation receipts that come in from the Banks?—A. Yes. Our Superannuation payments are made not by cheque from the Department but on an official receipt which the official signs, and the Bank in his immediate locality, on instructions from the Department, cashes for him. These checks are all sent in to us by the Banks, and of course are properly checked.

By Mr. Fyshe:

Q. You deal directly with the persons superannuated and you just give them authority to draw?—A. We give them a supply of these forms each year.

By the Chairman :

Q. Then in addition to that, for the purpose of checking the superannuation payments, you keep an establishment book in the department?

Mr. FYSHE.—A special account with the Finance Department?

The WITNESS.—A service account.

The CHAIRMAN.—It is an establishment book, showing the date of entry in each service, the date of service, the variations in pay and all that kind of thing?

By Mr. Fyshe:

Q. But what check do you keep against the superannuated person drawing two cheques instead of one?—A. The bank is only authorized to pay him so much a month.

Q. But he might go to another bank ?—A. If he does the receipt comes in about two days after it is signed by him, and we do not pay it.

Q. But supposing you do not keep a special account of his payments?—A. We have an account.

The CHAIRMAN.—But that has nothing to do with the establishment book.

Mr. FYSHE.—But supposing a man is allowed superannuation he can come to my office and exchange this cheque or receipt for say $50.

The CHAIRMAN.—It would be at your risk?

The WITNESS.—It would be at your risk, we do not pay it.

By Mr. Bazin:

Q. Supposing a superannuated person who wanted to do wrong came to my office and exchanged another receipt for the same amount?—A. As a rule we do not allow them to transfer these by endorsement.

By the Chairman:

Q. The superannuated official has twelve receipts given to him at the beginning of the year?—A. Yes.

Q. And if he used those before the year expired he would be hard up?—A. The terms of the receipt require him to go before a justice of the peace each month and make a declaration that he is entitled to the money. That declaration is signed by the justice.

By Mr. Fyshe:

Q. That is one of the regulations governing superannuation payments?—A. Yes.

By the Chairman:

Q. Now, in repaying the Banks for the cheques drawn on the letters of credit, paying sums of money to contractors, &c., you draw cheques on the several Banks?—A. Yes.

Q. These cheques are signed by the Auditor General?—A. Yes.

By Mr. Bazin:

Q. The Bank accounts are audited each month by the Auditor General?—A. Yes.

By Mr. Fyshe:

Q. How many Bank accounts have you?—A. Twenty-three now. We dropped one the other day. The Peoples' Bank of New Brunswick was absorbed by the Bank of Montreal.

By the Chairman:

Q. You do not open accounts with new Banks?—A. We have not opened an account with a new Bank since 1886, I think.

Mr. FYSHE.—That is good policy.

By the Chairman:

Q. I am glad to hear that. In England there is only one account. The Imperial Government keeps only an account with the Bank of England, and in Ireland with the Bank of Ireland?—A. I think that is so.

Q. And in France and Germany the governments do business with the Bank of France and the Bank of Germany, respectively?—A. With their respective national banks.

Q. And in India with the Bank of Bengal, the Bank of Madras and the Bank of Bombay?—A. Yes, I believe so.

Q. In Australia there is an association of Banks?—A. Yes.

Q. In this country at one time we had over thirty accounts with Banks?—A. Yes. we had 32 or 33 Bank accounts.

Q. That was an inheritance we derived from a former time, and it has been a matter of the greatest difficulty ever since to resist the pressure of Banks to have accounts opened?—A. Yes.

Q. Until 1886, when an order in council was passed to prevent the opening of further Bank accounts?—A. Yes, the order in.council was passed, I think, in 1886.

By Mr. Fyshe:

Q. And you have not opened one since?—A. Not one since.

Q. I think that is a piece of good administration.

By the Chairman:

Q. Now we will come to another class of work which is peculiar to the Finance Department. There is a good deal of Parliamentary work?—A. Yes, the Parliamentary work is becoming quite onerous.

Q. The Finance Departments not only collects the estimates of the different Departments, but they are printed and laid before the Privy Council and before Parliament?—A. Yes, the estimates are collated and printed by the Department of Finance and put before Council.

Q. These estimates are examined by the Department?—A. Yes.

Q. And submitted to Council afterwards?—A. Yes, properly collated.

Q. In addition to that the Deputy Minister of Finance has to attend all the meetings of the Public Accounts Committee?—A. Yes.

Q. He must be ready to respond when explanations are required?—A. Yes, impromptu.

Q. You also have to attend the meetings of the Banking and Commerce Committee?—A. Yes, the Department has to be represented at the meetings of that committee for the purpose of overlooking the legislation respecting Banking and Commerce.

Q. The Banking and Commerce Committee looks after the incorporation of new Banks?—A. And insurance companies.

Q. You have to see that no undue powers are asked for, and to explain to the committee if undue powers are asked for, that they are in accordance with precedent? —A. Yes.

Q. And in addition there is always a certain amount of legislation prepared by the Department, as for example, the ten years renewal of Bank charters?—A. Yes, there is legislation every year of one kind or another.

Q. The Finance Department prepared the most of the Bounty Acts?—A. Yes.

By Mr. Fyshe:

Q. What is that ?—A. The Acts respecting the payment of iron and steel bounties.

By the Chairman:

Q. What I want to get at is the fact that you have during the session of Parliament a very large amount of work?—A. Yes, the session adds very materially to the amount of work to be done.

SESSIONAL PAPER No. 29a

By Mr. Fyshe:

Q. And it is all of a more or less responsible character?—A. Yes, very responsible. It requires frequent attendance at the House.

By the Chairman:

Q. And in addition to what has been mentioned there are other Acts, such as the granting of extended lending powers to the Montreal harbour works?—A. Yes.

Q. Anything of that nature is also referred to you?—A. Yes. Assistance in the preparation of the Budget Speech is also an important piece of Parliamentary work.

Q. The Department of Finance gathers facts that are expounded in the Budget Speech?—A. Largely.

Q. And in addition to making up the estimates, forecasts the probable total receipts and total expenditure for the year?—A. Yes, that is one of the important duties of the department.

By Mr. Fyshe:

Q. Why does the Government permit the different Provinces to have an inheritance tax?—A. That is a constitutional question.

By the Chairman:

Q. That is within the British North America Act, is it not?—A. Yes. The inheritance tax will never trouble the civil servants.

By Mr. Fyshe:

Q. Perhaps not, but it troubles a good many people. It seems to me to be all wrong. I hear some complaints of the inheritance tax being levied on an estate in two or three different provinces?—A. That may be.

The CHAIRMAN.—The only thing is to get an occasional conference with the Provinces and point out these things to them.

Mr. FYSHE.—It appears to me that it should not be permitted. I think it is wrong to allow a Province to levy such a tax.

By the Chairman:

Q. In order to meet the interest on the public debt, for the purchase of stores, and for other requirements in England, the Department of Finance has to purchase a large amount of exchange during the year?—A. Yes.

By Mr. Fyshe:

Q. In buying that exchange you take competitive offers, do you?—A. Yes. In round numbers about £3,000,000 are purchased during the year.

By the Chairman:

Q. The Finance Department calls upon almost every Bank for an offer when it wants to buy exchange?—A. Yes, by telegram.

By Mr. Fyshe:

Q. In your books the discount is put down as profit?—A. Practically profit. If we remit bills and they are allowed to run out their term of sixty days it is practically profit. If we discount them before the expiry of the sixty days, discount will have to be deducted to show the net profit.

By the Chairman:

Q. The Department practically has to keep a watchful eye when exchange is favourable to find out when the best terms can be made?—A. Yes, we do not speculate in exchange, but we buy when we want it with an eye to the market. A few days may make a difference.

By Mr. Fyshe:

Q. I presume if it is in your power you would buy when exchange is cheap, would you not?—A. Rather.

Mr. FYSHE.—The right time to do that, of course, is when gold is tending towards the importing point.

By the Chairman:

Q. If by delaying a week you can see there will be a probable fall in exchange, you would delay that week, would you not?—A. Certainly.

Q. And you have bought at sixty days under 8?—A. Very considerably under 8.

By Mr. Fyshe:

Q. Not often?—A. We have bought around 7¾.

Q. When?—A. Recently we bought at less than 7¾ and on two or three previous occasions we have bought below 8.

By the Chairman:

Q. They are all prime bills?—A. Everything is prime bills, bankers' bills.

By Mr. Bazin:

Q. You do not buy from merchants?—A. No, the bills we buy are bankers' bills.

By the Chairman:

Q. It is because of the training you have received in the Department of Finance that you are constantly on the look out as to the course of exchange?—A. Yes, we keep track of it day by day. We have kept track of exchange day by day for the last 25 or 30 years. We buy by tender and the lowest tender is accepted. We have the records for each purchase of exchange.

By Mr. Fyshe:

Q. You do not go to the trouble of asking the 20 or 30 banks for offers?—A. Not 20 or 30. We take probably all the banks who deal in exchange.

By the Chairman:

Q. I used to send out to every one of the banks who deal in exchange. I suppose you do the same?—A. There are several banks which do not tender.

Q. But you give them the opportunity of tendering?—A. Always.

By Mr. Fyshe:

Q. I see that the Bank of Nova Scotia is not in your list?—A. We seldom buy from the Bank of Nova Scotia. Some of the banks make a specialty of dealing in exchange.

By the Chairman:

Q. There is no money in it now?—A. Not a very great deal.

Q. There is none at all?—A. I suppose that is why the Bank of Nova Scotia keeps out of it.

Q. In addition to buying exchange you have to arrange in the London market for the renewal of loans?—A. Yes, both temporary and permanent loans.

Q. You issue treasury bills if you want temporary assistance?—A. We issue treasury bills when we require money temporarily.

Q. There are no treasury bills now?—A. There are no treasury bills now outstanding. The last issue of £250,000 fell due on the first of May and was redeemed.

Q. There is great difficulty in the present moment in placing loans?—A. The conditions are extreme. The conditions for placing permanent loans on the market at the present time are exceedingly difficult.

Q. On the first day of May a loan fell due?—A. On the first of May last the four per cent loan of 1874 which fell due in 1904 and part of which was extended for three years to the first of May, 1907, fell due.

Q. And had to be renewed?—A. The amount was about £1,830,000.

Q. Was it renewed at the same rate?—A. Practically at the same rate, a little better.

Q. For a limited term of years?—A. For four years.

Q. It was continued rather than renewed?—A. It was extended at the same rate of interest.

By Mr. Fyshe:

Q. There was nothing else to be done?—A. We could not do anything else.

Mr. FYSHE.—The Government, with its magnificent revenues, ought to be paying off some of its debt.

By the Chairman:

Q. There are large loans falling due in the next few years?—A. Yes, next year there is a large loan falling due in November, and the year after there is the Consolidated Canadian loan of £6,000,000 odd. We have loans falling due practically year by year up to 1910.

Q. And all this work of renewing loans and keeping the credit of Canada up to the highest pitch and providing the funds is a source of constant anxiety to the Department?—A. It is a matter that has constantly to be kept in mind.

By Mr. Fyshe:

Q. Do you keep in constant communication with your financial correspondents in London?—A. Yes.

Q. Who are they principally?—A. The Bank of Montreal, London, is our financial agent.

Q. Have you no direct communication with any big loan houses?—A. No direct connection.

Q. It is through the Bank of Montreal?—A. Yes.

Q. Then you expect the Bank of Montreal to keep in touch with all these big houses?—A. They do and they advise the Department. We get practically weekly general letters from the Bank of Montreal as to the state of the market.

Q. Because of course everything would depend upon the relationship maintained between them and the big borrowers or big lenders?—A. The Bank of Montreal has an extensive clientele and it is through their clientele that we are usually able to negotiate these large amounts of treasury bills.

Mr. FYSHE.—You used to have direct connection or at least if you did not, some Provincial Government did. I remember going over one year to England and meeting Mr. Fielding when he was Premier of Nova Scotia. He had some loans to negotiate, and he did so with the National Provincial Bank.

The CHAIRMAN.—It was in 1891. I was in London then and indirectly helped him.

The WITNESS.—The Bank of Montreal has intimate relations with the National Provincial Bank.

By the Chairman:

Q. You have seven offices of the assistant receivers general?—A. Yes, we have an assistant receiver general at Charlottetown, and at Halifax, one at St. John, one at Montreal, one at Toronto, one at Winnipeg, and one at Victoria.

By Mr. Fyshe:

Q. I see that Mr. Isaac Mather has been appointed at Halifax?—A. Yes, he has been our assistant receiver general for a few years at Halifax.

Q. He is an excellent man?—A. A very good man.

By the Chairman:

Q. The assistant receivers general do not come under the Civil Service Act at all? —A. No, they are not subject to the Civil Service Act.

Q. And although good men have been appointed as a rule, it is because the Minister has been advised on the importance of the post?—A. Yes, the appointments are made on the nomination of the Minister altogether.

By Mr. Fyshe:

Q. What salary does Mr. Mather get?—A. He is now receiving $2,500 a year.

Q. He is a man with an excellent business training?—A. Yes, he is a very methodical man.

Q. He has good judgment and good sense?—A. For business of that kind, of course, we need to have men of the highest capacity, character, and integrity.

By the Chairman:

Q. You have inspectors who are constantly travelling, and call upon the receivers general at any time?—A. We have an inspector, just as a bank has an inspector, who walks into any of these offices and takes possession the moment he enters.

Q. These officers send in weekly returns?—A. Yes.

Q. Showing the cash on hand and the notes issued and redeemed?—A. In these offices are held large amounts of our reserve and specie.

By Mr. Fyshe:

Q. It is held by them?—A. It is held by them. They also hold supplies of silver and copper for the public, and it is through them that the supplies of Dominion notes are issued to the banks.

Q. Supposing a bank wants to draw specie, to the amount of $100,000 or $200,000, down, at Halifax, would it get it there?—A. Yes, we keep a supply at all these places to meet any contingency. We can meet at any of these points any requirements for gold that is presented to us.

By the Chairman:

Q. In fact you watch over it just like a bank watches its own account?—A. Yes.

·Q. And at no time has there been an assistant receiver general who could not meet any demands made upon him?—A. No.

By Mr. Fyshe:

Q. In order to check the Banks from making such demands, is it not the case that you occasionally provide, say in Halifax, that your Dominion notes shall be paid in Toronto?—A. That is all done away with. Dominion notes are now payable at any of these offices, big or little.

By the Chairman:

Q. I suppose you examine the returns coming from the Banks which are published in the *Canada Gazette?*—A. We have to keep track of them.

Q. If the requirements of the Bank Act are not complied with in regard to these returns it involves a penalty?—A. Yes, in some cases.

Q. You see that the Bank does not over-issue, for instance?—A. Yes, that is one of our principal duties.

Q. You have to examine the returns to see that there is no over-circulation of the Banks?—A. Yes.

Q. You have to examine also to see that the cash reserve——?—A. That the Bank holds sufficient Dominion notes. We also examine the returns to compare the averages of Dominion notes, they held during the month with the actual amount they held on the last day of the month. There is a growing tendency to build up for the last day of the month.

By the Chairman:

Q. What is called 'window dressing'?—A. Yes, window dressing. This is revealed in the returns by the average amount of notes they held during the month compared with what they held during the last day.

Q. The Bank of Montreal—we will take a concrete instance—if the amount they held in cash reserve was only $10 and they had a four dollar Dominion note in that——?—A. It would be within the four corners of the Bank Act.

By Mr. Fyshe:

Q. That seems ridiculous, but it does not relieve banks from the necessity of using proper judgment. I do not know what your practice is, but I should think it would help you in making comparisons, if you wanted to criticise the Bank's statements, to have an opening in one of your books for the monthly returns of each Bank by itself?—A. We keep a book for each Bank, and we enter up in each column the different items month by month. So, you can take the bank's statements in this book, and by glancing at the column trace the business of any Bank month by month.

By the Chairman:

Q. And year by year?—A. And year by year.
Mr. Fyshe.—That is a very nice thing to do.

By the Chairman:

Q. Then, of course, you examine the averages as well as the totals?—A. Yes, and the loans to and the loans from Banks. The loans to ought to equal the loans from.

By Mr. Fyshe:

Q. I suppose it is sometimes difficult to distinguish between a loan from a Bank and a deposit from a Bank?—A. Yes, one Bank may treat a loan in one way and another in another way.

Q. There is one item I wanted to draw your attention to which I consider anomalous. The item of liabilities is not included under other heads. All the Banks treat that as a very questionable column, and they only put doubtful items into it; they all keep their figures down to insignificant amounts, except the Bank of British North America. That bank sometimes has 11 or 12 millions in that column, but no other Bank has a tenth part of that amount. That arises from the fact that they go on the principle of putting in that column all the sterling bills of exchange they buy and are current?—A. Yes.

Q. I used to do the same thing in the Bank of Nova Scotia before we opened in Minneapolis and Chicago, and I remember at one of the renewals of the bank charters —Sir Leonard Tilley was then Minister of Finance—the whole day was devoted to discussing the Banking returns. This thing had been apparently utterly forgotten and neglected, and just as the meeting was breaking up I broached the subject. and half a dozen of them nearly jumped on me and assaulted me for raising the question. It was a proper objection. There was no provision made for that. The ordinary Bank, it might be, buying and selling an enormous amount of exchange might have four or five or six millions running and in the report they would place what they drew against what they bought, which is no statement at all. You might simply show nothing of your capital and rest account?—A. That is so.

Q. At the same time, although it is strictly correct, it would be an impossibility to compel the other Banks to do it. It makes the figures so big you know?—A. I think in the course of time we will be able to get a little more uniformity on the part of the Banks in the manner of treating the items about which there might be any doubt.

Q. That, of course, is one very conspicuous item?—A. There are one or two other items, I think, that in the course of time we will be able to get systematized.

By the Chairman:

Q. Although we have nothing to do with it, there seems to have risen a determination on the parts of the Banks generally to have a fixed reserve in cash and a fixed reserve in liquid securities as against their liabilities?—A. Yes. There is no absolutely cash reserve demanded by the Bank Act, but that arrangement is made between themselves.

Q. I believe the Bankers' Association have moved in that direction?—A. Yes.

Q. The Department notices by the returns that there is a tendency to a fixed reserve although there is nothing said about it in the Act?—A. Yes, there has been an improvement in that direction as compared with some years ago.

Q. Just before I left the Department we found in some of the annual returns submitted to the Department, a want of unanimity?—A. Yes, I think that the form of the statement to be submitted to the shareholders should be established in the Bank Act.

By Mr. Fyshe:

Q. Do you think it ought to be in strict harmony with the Government's monthly statement?—A. No, but the form of it should harmonize.

Q. That is a good idea. I know in making my annual statement I was careful to give as complete a statement as I possibly could in order that the shareholders might obtain as clear an idea as possible of what the bank's assets consisted of. There is a clause in the Bank Act setting out in general terms what shall be submitted to the shareholders, but I always went further than that.—A. Yes, and some Banks do not go quite so far.

By the Chairman:

Q. Last year that was found in the case of one Bank particularly?—A. Yes.

Q. The next revision of the Bank charters is in 1910?—A. The charters are carried on until 1911 and Parliament will act the previous year.

Q. In what state are the records of your department now?—A. The records are in very fair shape.

By Mr. Fyshe:

Q. What do you mean by 'records'?—A. The correspondence of years gone by, papers, books, vouchers, ledgers and all that kind of thing. During the last three or four years we have had a man employed wholly on that work, and he has been getting our books, papers, vouchers, &c., in a very good shape.

Q. Where do you keep your records?—A. We have basement rooms.

Q. Will you not have them filled up soon?—A. It is tending in that direction.

By the Chairman:

Q. Are you not taking steps to destroy what might be called the useless records?—A. We are doing a certain amount of weeding out. Documents of no value for purposes of reference, or for historical or other purposes are being culled out and destroyed under the authority of the Governor in Council.

By Mr. Bazin:

Q. After having been preserved for some years?—A. After being held for a number of years.

By Mr. Fyshe:

Q. Are the vaults in which they are kept fireproof?—A. They are not vaults, but simply basement rooms.

By the Chairman:

Q. Have you taken any steps yet to transfer to the archives the documents of historical interest?—A. We have sent nothing to the archives so far.

Q. But you will do so?—A. Yes.

Q. When I was on the commission appointed to consider the custody of state papers and records, we discovered documents relating to the war of 1812?—A. Yes, we have some interesting old documents respecting the early construction of the Welland canal. There are a number of old stock books, and I think the signature of the Duke of Wellington appears in one of them.

Q. All the members of your staff are in the one building? You have no outside offices?—A. We have no outside offices in the city here. The staff of the Finance Department is all housed in the Eastern block.

Q. Some of the officers are crammed with employees?—A. We have in the note room from 30 to 35 women.

By Mr. Fyshe:

Q. That is where Mr. Toller presides?—A. Yes. The other offices are not so very much crowded, but they are not adapted for business purposes. The offices are simply detached rooms and are really not adapted for modern business methods.

Q. It seems to me that all the business relating to currency should be transacted in one big room?—A. The business is practically done in one big room, but that is the only big one we have.

By the Chairman:.

Q. The structural condition is such that you cannot knock the rooms together?—A. Yes.

By Mr. Fyshe:

Q. It seems to me that the handling of the currency should be done in the same way as the Banks do it, by means of telling boxes?—A. Every one of the women, practically, has a telling box under lock and key.

By the Chairman:

Q. The note circulation, I think, now amounts to about $50,000,000?—A. The note circulation throughout April amounted to $57,000,000.

Q. In that branch there is a controller of currency and a chief clerk?—A. A controller of currency, a chief clerk and a first-class clerk.

Q. Those are all the males employed there?—A. Those are all the males. There are three men; two chief clerks and a first-class clerk.

Q. Having supervision over the $57,000,000?—A. Yes.

Q. In addition to that, the controller of currency keeps the securities which the Government compels the insurance companies to deposit?—A. Yes, he has the custody of all the securities that are deposited and held by the Receiver General on account of the various insurance companies.

Q. And it is part of his duty to cut the coupons off the several bonds?—A. Yes, he has to cut the coupons off as they mature month by month, and send them to the different companies.

By Mr. Fyshe:

Q. And in doing that is there any provision for joint custody?—A. Yes. These securities are kept in a vault and the outer door is under the joint custody of two of the officers, while the inner doors are also under joint custody. The amount of securities so held by the controller has practically doubled since 1892.

Q. Those are not all securities of insurance companies?—A. Practically the whole of it is.

By the Chairman:

Q. The offices and the vaults are guarded by police night and day?—A. Yes.

Q. You have an Assistant Deputy Minister of Finance who is also a barrister? —A. Yes.

By Mr. Fyshe:

Q. Who is that officer?—A. Mr. Henry T. Ross.

Q. Is that a new appointment?—A. It was made on November 1, last.

Q. What is the object of making that appointment?—A. It is a growing necessity. Before Mr. Ross' appointment we had a secretary of the department who was a lawyer and a very useful officer indeed, Mr. Treadwell.

Q. What has become of him?—A. He broke down in health and retired in 1905. It was necessary to get some one with legal qualifications to take up the position of secretary, and it was thought wise to make him at the same time Assistant Deputy Minister, so that he could act in all cases when the Deputy was absent.

By the Chairman:

Q. There was an Assistant Deputy previously?—A. Prior to the appointment of Mr. Ross, Mr. Fitzgerald, Superintendent of Insurance, acted as Assistant Deputy.

Q. And that was an incongruous arrangement, because Mr. Fitzgerald could not pay any attention to the department?—A. He was having his hands full with the insurance office, and had no time to devote to the duty of Assistant Deputy Minister of Finance.

Q. Then you also have two chief clerks in the department, one looking after revenues and estimates, and another looking after expenditures?—A. Yes, one man is getting a little over $1,900 a year.

By Mr. Fyshe:

Q. What are his duties?—A. He is a chief clerk and looks after the bank account and has a general oversight over the revenue side of our accounts. The other officer who is a chief clerk has charge of the expenditure.

By the Chairman:

Q. And gets out the public accounts?—A. He prepares the public accounts, the balance sheets and all that class of work.

Q. You have also a first-class clerk who is called accountant of contingencies? —A. Yes.

Q. The accountant of contingencies is a statutory officer?—A. He is not a statutory officer, but the keeping of the contingencies by the Department of Finance is regulated by statute which provides for the appointment.

Q. The accountant of contingencies has to pay the salaries of the temporary clerks?—A. Yes.

Q. The travelling expenses of officials?—A. Yes, of all the different departments, and the petty cash, printing and stationery, and newspaper accounts.

Q. The payments for newspapers subscribed for by the several departments?— A. Yes.

Q. He also, by an accident, has the control and direction of the charwomen ?—
A. All the charwomen and charmen who clean the offices occupied by the Government
in the city are controlled by this officer under the Minister of Finance.

By Mr. Fyshe:

Q. Does that not seem to be an interference with the special duties of each special
department? Surely each special department can look after its own charwomen?—A.
It is anomalous, but it is economical.

By the Chairman :

Q. The greatest pressure is brought by politicians to get charwomen appointed to
the government service ?—A. Yes, I prefer to renew a loan rather than appoint a
charwoman.

By Mr. Fyshe :

Q. Do you mean to say the Deputy Minister of Finance cannot do that ?—A. Yes,
but it is an easier matter to renew a loan than undergo all the trouble connected with
the appointment of charwomen.

By the Chairman :

Q. They wait on you themselves ?—A. Yes.

Q. And their backers wait on you ?—A. Yes.

Q. And they call at your house ?—A. Yes, and they write any quantity of letters.

Q. To avoid political pressure as far as possible a limit has to be placed to the
number of charwomen to be employed ?—A. The limit of the number of people to be
employed is set by order in council.

Q. Without that limit the number would be trebled ?—A. I would not like to say
what it would be.

Q. There would be no holding them ?—A. No.

Q. And if the several Departments had to engage their charwomen, and no limit
was fixed, you would not like to say what would happen ?—A. Such an arrangement
would give a good deal of elasticity.

Q. Having an accountant of contingencies meets a long felt necessity?—A. Yes,
and it has proved a very useful appointment.

Q. There is a limit to the subscriptions to be paid for newspapers by each department ?—A. Yes, but I am afraid it is not very strictly adhered to.

By Mr. Fyshe :

Q. What newspapers are usually allowed to the department ?—A. Anything that
is published. The limit laid down by order in council is about $500 per year per de-
partment. That is the amount it can spend on newspapers.

Q. Is it necessary you should have them at all ?—A. There are certain newspapers
we must have.

The CHAIRMAN.—The financial papers are required by the Department of Finance,
and the railway papers by the Department of Railways. There must be some newspapers in every department.

By Mr. Fyshe :

Q. You must keep abreast of what is going on ?—A. Yes, we have to, but there
are a great many newspapers that are not needed.

By the Chairman :

Q. To carry on all the work that has been enumerated you do not think the department is overmanned ?—A. The department is undermanned.

Q. The department is rather undermanned than overmanned ?—A. Yes.

Q. And the staff of the department is efficient. I cannot speak too highly of the service that is being rendered, as a whole by the staff of the Department of Finance.

By Mr. Fyshe :

Q. Do you not think you would save a good deal of money to the country if you did not take so many newspapers, for which you say $500 is allowed for each department ?—A. We might save a couple of hundred dollars or some such amount.

Q. If you were to save a couple of hundred dollars in each department it would be a good deal. Every dollar saved in that direction might be available for increasing well earned salaries ?—A. Yes.

By the Chairman :

Q. The positions of the other officers are in accordance with the duties they fulfil ?—A. Yes.

Q. The first-class clerks do first-class work and the second-class clerks, second-class work ?—A. As a rule the first-class clerks are doing first-class work, as the Commissioners will see when they visit the department. The second-class clerks are likewise doing good work for that class, the junior second-class clerks the same, and the temporary clerks are giving us very good service. I might say in connection with the women employees who are working on the notes, that we have some who have been in the service since 1877 or 1878.

Q. That is before I was appointed deputy ?—A. Before Mr. Courtney was appointed deputy. Those women, as you will understand, are becoming fairly worn out. They have been a long time in the service and have done good work and the question is, what are we going to do with them? They are getting close to the time when they cannot be regarded as being very efficient. They are temporary employees and their pay ceases the minute they leave the government service. They were not under the old Superannuation Act at all. The question arises, what is to be done. So far I have dealt with them as gently as possible. They always work when they possibly can but they are inclined to be away a great deal and as the time goes on the number of such persons will become very much larger.

Mr. FYSHE.—There is only one way of dealing with them and that is to put every man and woman who is in the Government service under Superannuation.

By the Chairman:

Q. That brings up the whole question of Superannuation. Do you think it is expedient to restore the Superannuation Act ?—A. I think it is an absolute necessity, the restoration of some kind of——

By Mr. Fyshe:

Q. Pension system ?—A. Pension system. You can call it Superannuation or Pension, as you please.

Q. It should be a Pension system, and instead of being abolished it should be considerably extended. It should be extended so as to cover widows and children ?—A. I look upon the Superannuation system, as an economic necessity for the Government.

Q. It is only bare justice to commence with ?—A. I do not look upon it as absolutely in the interest of the service, but as being necessary in the interest of the state.

Q. It is necessary for both ?—A. It is necessary primarily in the interest of the state because this condition I am pointing out to you is one which, in a very few years, will arise all through the service. We have some five or six employees who have been in the department from 20 to 30 years, and whom we have to carry on and pay salary to right along until they die. Practically you have to do that. Very soon the same condition will arise throughout the service generally.

SESSIONAL PAPER No. 29a

Q. It does not seem to me permissible for the Government to plead poverty in dealing with a matter of this kind?—A. I think it is in the interest not merely of the service itself but for the purpose of carrying on the work of the Government efficiently and properly that the Superannuation system or some such system should be restored. I do not regard a Pension altogether in the light of a gratuity. I look upon it as being deferred salary. If the Superanuuation law were on the statute-book at the present minute, I do not think there would be the same demand for increased remuneration. A man would be content with a medium salary if his declining years were provided for.

Q. This is rather a mild basis to put it on?—A. I am trying to tell you what the effect would be, I am not reasoning it out academically. I think, besides, the looking forward to the receipt of a pension in later life has a very steadying effect on a man's service and in a man's integrity.

Q. Undoubtedy?—A. Because he is not going to imperil his future pension by inefficiency or misconduct.

Q. It really is not worth arguing about, the thing has passed that stage altogether ! —A. In the case of temporary employees we have a very large number, as you see, who are women, and there is a constant desire to have their employment made permanent. It has a good side.

Q. You know it is an awful difficult question to deal with?—A. We are pressed on two sides. First of all we do not want to pay any money for the service of the country than the work is worth. Then we are pressed on the other side by the fact that some of these people have been with us for from 20 to 30 years, and they are getting exactly the same remuneration as those who came in during the last three or four years. Now that creates a little bit of unrest.

By the Chairman:

Q. And it is the same work that is done in both instances?—A. It is the same work.

Q. You have been in the department for 25 years and are, therefore, qualified to speak. Is the same standard maintained in the Entrance examination?—A. I think there has been a tendency towards relaxation. I look on the value of the Entrance examination not as indicating the best men for the service, but it is of great value in the elimination of the unfit.

By Mr. Fyshe:

Q. Of the absolutely unfit?—A. Of the absolutely unfit and of the unfit.

Q. It does not provide positively for your getting the best material there is?— A. No, but it eliminates those who should not be appointed under any consideration.

Q. Not the best, but the second best?—A. You may by chance light on the second best. So far as Promotion examinations are concerned, I feel very much like having a Promotion examination whenever Promotions are necessary.

Q. You would leave that to the judgment of the deputy?—A. Yes.

Q. A strong deputy ought to be empowered to promote the people under him as he thinks fit?—A. Well, I think the value of the Promotion examination is in its elimination of the unfit.

Q. It puts a certain check upon a deputy, that is it prevents him from doing a gratuitously unjust thing?—A. Glaringly unjust thing.

By the Chairman:

Q. Whatever opinion we may have as to the Entrance examination for the lower grades in the Finance Department, you have obtained as good results by having strong Ministers as you could have by competitive examination?—A. I think the results would compare very favourably.

Q. But that might not be the case in all the Departments?—A. It depends upon the Minister.

Q. But naturally the Minister of Finance must be a strong man?—A. He usually is.

Q. So far, the Department has been blessed in having strong men, so that they have put in efficient and good clerks into the Department;—A. They have, yes. Reverting again to the subject of Superannuation, with a Superannuation scheme if you get a good man in your Department, he will stay with you; Superannuation will hold him. Now, under the present system, with nothing but the Retirement Act——

' Q. There is nothing to hold him?—A. There is nothing to hold him, and I have practically in my hands to-day the resignations of three of my best officers.

Q. On that account?—A. On that account.

The CHAIRMAN.—You had better send in a memorandum upon the system of superannuation and its effects, also upon the employment of temporary clerks and aged women, and any other matters that you think of.

Witness discharged.

OTTAWA, June 19, 1907.

Mr. THOMAS C. BOVILLE, Deputy Minister of Finance Department, re-called and sworn and examined.

By the Chairman:

Q. Is it true that there has been a forgery discovered within the last day or two in the Inland Revenue Department?—A. Yes.

Q. How did it come about, tell us the whole story —A. I have not been officially notified as yet, but so far as I can ascertain from the Department of Inland Revenue, thirteen blank cheques were stolen out of one of the cheque-books sometime about the beginning of May.

By Mr. Bazin:

Q. Of this year—A. Yes, May, this year. The theft was not discovered until June 13.

By Mr. Fyshe:

Q. Are your cheques numbered?—A. Yes, the cheques are all numbered consecutively.

Q. Should it not have been discovered at once?—A. Well, it would have been very difficult to have discovered it at once, unless one had the curiosity to examine the cheque-books. The cheques were stolen from the end of the cheque-book. On June 13 the Deputy Minister of Inland Revenue advised the manager of the Bank of Montreal that these cheques had been stolen and that he had better notify his branches to be on the lookout for them. One cheque came into the Bank of Ottawa and was paid by the Bank of Ottawa on June 1. The signature to the cheque was forged, of course. (Cheque produced.)

Q. That cheque was paid by the Bank of Ottawa?—A. Yes. The signatures of Mr. Himsworth, Secretary of the Department, and Mr. Campeau, the Accountant, are forgeries. The first cheque was paid by the Bank of Ottawa on June 1; it was paid over the counter. June 1 was a Saturday, a short day, and the second cheque (cheque produced) was paid on June 15.

By the Chairman:

Q. By what Bank?—A. By the same Bank and the same teller.

Q. That was also on a Saturday?—A. Also on Saturday, and a short day. The first cheque is drawn in favour of J. E. Valin, it is dated May 31 and is for the sum of $225.53.

By Mr. Fyshe:

Q. Who is Mr. Valin?—A. Mr. Valin is an employee of the Department of Inland Revenue, and the cheque is endorsed by 'J. E. Valin.'

Q. Is that a forgery?—A. That is also a forgery. The teller asked the man who presented the cheque if he were Mr. Valin, and he replied 'No.' The teller said, 'You had better put your own signature underneath,' and he put his signature underneath, 'L. Leclair.' The second cheque is dated May 15.

By the Chairman:

Q. May 15 or June?—A. May 15. The cheques were stolen at the beginning of May. The other cheque is dated on May 15 and is for the sum of $245.53; it is in favour of R. D. Archambault, and is endorsed by R. D. Archambault.

Q. Also a forgery?—A. Yes. It was paid by the Bank of Ottawa on June 15 on that endorsation.

By the Chairman :

Q. June 15 ?—A. Yes. We do not know who Archambault is.

Q. How many cheques have been stolen ?—A. Thirteen.

Q. How many have been presented ?—A. Two.

Q. Only two ?—A. Yes.

Q. The numbers are known?—A. The numbers are known. Of course, these two cheques came into the Bank of Montreal through the Bank of Ottawa——

By Mr. Fyshe :

Q. They dropped on them ?—A. They dropped on them and threw them out.

By the Chairman :

Q. What steps have the Inland Revenue Department taken——

By Mr. Fyshe :

Q. The Bank of Montreal had paid them also ?—A. Well, apparently the cheques had gone through the cash department of the Bank of Montreal and thence were sent up to the examiner's department.

By Mr. Bazin :

Q. Did you say that the Bank of Montreal perceived the forgery ?—A. On the advice they received from the Department of Inland Revenue.

Q. They had been previously advised ?—A. They had been advised by the Department of Inland Revenue that these blank cheques had been stolen and when the cheques came in they threw them out.

By the Chairman :

Q. What steps have the Inland Revenue people taken to discover these ?—A. They have communicated with the Dominion police.

Q. They have ?—A. Yes, they advised the Dominion police people on Friday last.

29a—14

By Mr. Fyshe :

Q. The theft of the cheques must have been done by one of the staff ?—A. Well, it is difficult to say; apparently the theft of the cheques was by some one who understood the routine of the department thoroughly well because the cheques are dated on the 15th and 31st.

Q. On the pay days ?—A. Yes, the 15th is the pay day for the ordinary civil servant and the 31st is the pay day of the temporaries, and the cheques are drawn on those two days, the 15th and the 31st.

By the Chairman :

Q. Who had the custody of the cheque books ?—A. The accountant.

Q. Mr. Campeau ?—A. Yes.

Q. Are they kept locked up ?—A. Yes, except when required for business purposes during the day ?

By Mr. Fyshe :

Q. I suppose they are kept in a safe ?—A. They are locked up in some secure place during the night.

Q. But during the day they would be accessible ?—A. Yes.

By the Chairman :

Q. In that report on the Martineau defalcation wasn't there some recommendation that these cheque books should be kept in a secure place ?—A. Yes, and the Finance Department has been endeavouring to have the recommendations of the Martineau commission carried out.

Q. With regard to the cheque books ?—A. Yes, with regard to keeping the cheque books in safe custody.

Q. As a matter of fact these cheques should be kept as carefully as bonds, in a bank safe ?—A. Just so, and the Department of Finance have been impressing that on the other departments as much as possible.

Q. They should not be kept locked up at night merely, but all the time ?—A. These cheque books are required constantly during the day, but the man who has charge of them should take just as much care of them as he would of any other security.

By Mr. Bazin :

Q. Are these thirteen cheques numbered consecutively ?—A. The cheques taken from the books bore consecutive numbers; we can tell, of course, the numbers of the cheques that were taken because the cheques are all numbered consecutively.

By the Chairman :

Q. Why wasn't this reported to the Finance Department ?—A. I shall answer that question by saying that it was not reported to the Finance Department.

Q. I will put my question this way: Was this reported to the Finance Department ?—A. No report has yet been received by the Finance Department.

Q. These cheques were stolen early in May ?—A. Yes.

Q. The first cheque was presented on June 1 ?—A. Yes.

Q. They were aware that the cheques had got into circulation, two of them at least, on June 1 and 15 ?—A. Yes.

By Mr. Fyshe :

Q. The Bank of Montreal got notice that the cheques had been stolen before the first one was cashed ?—A. The first cheque was cashed on June 1 before the Bank of Montreal had been advised by the Department of Inland Revenue of the theft of the cheques.

By the Chairman :

Q. Has the Department of Inland Revenue, as yet, advised officially the Department of Finance ?—A. Not yet.

Q. Who placed it in the hands of the Dominion police ?—A. The Department of Inland Revenue.

By Mr. Fyshe:

Q. Does the report of the Martineau Commission advise that cheques should be properly kept?—A. It advises that every blank cheque should be accounted for whether cancelled or issued, and that no unnumbered cheques should be allowed to exist.

By the Chairman:

Q. It is perfectly evident that the person who manipulated these cheques was aware of the system in the Department?—A. Yes.

Q. And he knew where to get hold of the cheque book and where to take the blank cheques?—A. And he understood the routine of the department.

By Mr. Fyshe:

Q. It is hardly conceivable that an outsider stole those cheques?—A. No.

Q. So that you are driven to look in the Department for the offender?—A. It must be either some one in the Department or some one who is very well acquainted with the routine of the Department.

Q. Or who was posted by some one in the Department?—A. Yes.

By the Chairman:

Q. The Commissioner of Dominion Police is away?—A. Yes. Inspector Hogan is looking after it.

Q. The loss so far has been borne by the Bank of Ottawa?—A. So far it has fallen on the Bank of Ottawa.

Q. At all events the Government are no losers?—A. The Government are not the losers. Of course, the teller of a bank will take a Government cheque and cash it through almost without thinking.

By Mr. Bazin:

Q. Do you say that all these blank cheques are numbered in advance?—A. Yes— in the report on the Martineau defalcation it is laid down that the cheques should be all numbered.

By the Chairman:

Q. This matter is in the hands of the Dominion Police?—A. Yes.

Q. And inquiries and researches are being made?—A. Yes.

Q. Are you going to advise the Inland Revenue Department that they ought to have sent you advice at once?—A. They are notifying me at once, I understand. I told Mr. Gerald that we ought to have been notified the first thing of this, that we should be notified immediately anything of this kind is discovered, and I understand he is writing me to-day. In my reply to his letter I will tell him that in future he must notify us immediately of any transaction of this nature.

By Mr. Fyshe:

Q. He should have notified you the moment the cheques were discovered to be stolen?—A. Yes.

Q. Mr. Boville, you were not here when Mr. Fraser was giving us some evidence of the absurdity of the reintroduction of the Paymaster's Branch of the Militia De-

29a—14½

partment, and this trouble of course has some bearing on it also. Would it not be a simplification of matters if the Finance Department made all payments for every department?—A. Theoretically, yes, as an academic proposition, yes, but as our business is so tremendous and is spread over such a wide area it is not practicable.

The CHAIRMAN.—How many of these cheques do you think they pay in a year?

Mr. FYSHE.—I have no idea.

The CHAIRMAN.—Somewhere about 700,000 of all grades. Your idea is that the Finance Department should be Paymaster for the whole Government.

Mr. FYSHE.—Should take charge of the whole thing, of every payment from five cents to five thousand dollars. Of course each department should look after its own expenditure and vouch for its payment, for the amount to be paid, but the Finance Department or the Auditor General's Department should make the payment, they have to go over this thing anyway.

The CHAIRMAN.—The theory governing the Finance Department is that it deals with the finances of the country.

Mr. FYSHE.—Yes, well let them make the payments.

The CHAIRMAN.—You must allow the other departments some latitude in the matter of small change. The Finance Department and the Auditor General's Office do make the big payments now, but if they were required to make all the payments as you suggest it would probably require a staff of a thousand men to do it.

Mr. FYSHE.—You would simply concentrate the staff in one Department instead of having it scattered around?—A. Apart from that, this credit system we have established facilitates very materially the transaction of the Government's business at distant points. Supposing all the payments were concentrated here in Ottawa, you would have constant growling at the delay in making payments.

Q. Not necessarily, if the pay-lists or accounts were properly vouched for and forwarded. It is only a question of drawing the cheque and sending it?—A. Which in the case of a payment in British Columbia would mean two weeks' delay.

Q. Well, you might make an exception in that case?—A. Then Prince Edward Island, it would mean a delay of nine days there.

By Mr. Bazin:

Q. And in winter what would the delay be?—A. In winter it would mean a delay of weeks sometimes.

By the Chairman:

Q. That is all the information we can obtain from you at present, I think, Mr. Boville, you will advise us if there is anything more heard about this?—A. Yes, if anything transpires I will let you know.

Q. Is there anything in this unfortunate transaction that would lead you to suggest any further recommendations in regard to the custody of cheques or any matter in regard to cheques?—A. I think the regulations as they exist at present, if they are fairly carried out, would meet troubles of this kind so far as they can be met.

By Mr. Fyshe:

Q. You know it is quite evident they are not being carried out. It is quite evident that these cheques are kicking about like stationery in the department?—I do not think so, Mr. Fyshe, I think they are being fairly well looked after, but there may be a case, an odd case of oversight or neglect. I think as a whole, and as a rule, the cheque books are being thoroughly well safeguarded.

Q. Well, the feeling I have about anything like that is that somebody is deplorably to blame, and I would find out who he is and punish him for it?—A. That is right.

Witness retired.

FINANCE DEPARTMENT,

OTTAWA, CANADA, June 13, 1907.

T. S. HOWE, Esq.,
Secretary of Civil Service Commission,
The Senate, Room 2, Ottawa.

DEAR SIR,—I send you herewith a statement of the number of officers and the cost
of administration of the Finance Department in 1892 and 1906, respectively.

Yours truly,

(Signed) T. C. BOVILLE,
Deputy Minister of Finance.

FINANCE DEPARTMENT STAFF, 1892 AND 1906.

No. 1892.	No. 1906.	Rank.	Cost. 1892.	1906.
			$ cts.	$ cts.
1	1	Deputy..	4,200 00	5,000 00
4	5	Chief clerks	8,850 05	8,358 32
4	10	First class clerks	6,737 50	17,100 00
18	12	Second class clerks	23,700 00	16,637 50
... ..	9	Junior second class clerks	....	7,985 81
3	0	Third class clerks	2,850 00	....
... .		Private secretary	600 00	....
4	2	Messengers	1,545 00	1,340 00

CONTINGENCIES.

1	8	Temporary clerks	731 06	4,231 66
....	2	Messengers	175 00	1,225 00

CHARGES OF MANAGEMENT.

11	33	Temporary clerks	4,683 50	19,630 19

FINANCIAL INSPECTION.

2	0	Inspectors	2,999 00	....
48	82		57,081 06	82,008 48

1 messenger employed temporarily for a short period afterwards appointed permanently.

MEMORANDUM.

SUPERANNUATION.

In this memorandum I desire to speak from the point of view of the F
Department and its business. One department differs from another, and whi
views herein expressed may have general application they are given with special
ence to the department named.

It is unnecessary to sketch the history of the Civil Service Superannuatic
or trace its workings. By the legislation of 1897 its provisions were repealed,
as those thereafter entering the service were concerned, and in its stead a Retir
Act was enacted. At the present time then, the staff is composed of two clas
men, those who can look forward to retiring upon a decent pension if they liv
enough, and those who have no prospect of a pension, but who, under the terms
Retirement Act, will receive upon leaving the service the product of a savings
account in which is deposited monthly five per cent of their salary. I have w:
with some interest the results of the two systems, and I desire to place befo
Commission briefly the conclusions at which I have arrived.

The business of Government differs somewhat from business of the ordinary
acter. It is conducted on a larger scale, in the interests of the country as a
and not for any individual or corporation. It is of a continuous character, a
carry it on to the best advantage the staff must be possessed of a certain amor
historical acquaintance with the different subjects to be dealt with. To the
departmental training and experience are invaluable. An employee in the cou
a number of years gradually becomes a storehouse of useful departmental know
For that reason the bringing in of young men and the training of them in the d
ment make for efficiency. One of the strong levers to retain under the terms
Civil Service Act men who have proved themselves valuable has been the pe
system. Under the Retirement Act, there being nothing to hold him, if a ma
an opening elsewhere providing for the moment a better wage he leaves the g
ment and takes with him his knowledge and the balance of his savings bank ac
In the interests of a continuous service the Superannuation Act was highly a
tageous.

The fact that an employee has before him an honourable retiring allowand
a steadying influence on his character and conduct. He will refrain from any l
of trust or other act that would endanger the provision for his future.

The most important advantage of any system of retiring annuity is its va
a measure of economy.

A private individual has no compunction about getting rid of an employe
is no longer able to make up his tale of bricks; a corporation likewise frequent
to dispense with the services of the aged, though in a good many large establish
the pension system is being adopted. Without discussing the moral obligation
individual or corporation to provide for the future of those who have grown
their employment, it will be found that a government, in the face of influences
the various and varied kinds that can be brought to bear, simply cannot get
those who, worthy in themselves, and who have given years of honest service,
outgrown their usefulness, and must carry them on at high salaries while yo
men have to be employed to do the work. In other words, in the absence of any
sion or other kindred scheme the staff in its higher branches must be duplicate
is more economical and better in the interests of the work that such persons a
be removed from the active staff.

This difficulty is not an imaginary one. In the case of the so-called temp
employees it has to be faced to-day. Some of these temporary employees have
in the service since the seventies, and have grown gray in the employ of the G

ment. Being the oldest they are at the maximum salary that can be paid. They have done their best, but the infirmities of age impair their ability to carry on their daily toil, and seriously interfere with their attendance. Indeed their spirit and loyalty sometimes carry them beyond what is reasonable in their desire to maintain their former efficiency. What is to be done? It seems to me that some method or system should be adopted to meet such cases.

There has recently been an extensive agitation in the service for higher remuneration. Wonder has often been expressed that the country has been able to get and retain in its service under the scale of wages set forth in the Civil Service Act, men whose abilities were widely acknowledged and who served their country well and long. I am convinced that the Superannuation Act was the means of retaining such men. I believe further that they regarded any allowance under that Act as merely deferred salary, and were willing to serve at a moderate recompense for the present in view of the advantage of a provision for their old age—a provision which they might or might not live to enjoy. I believe that the establishment of some scheme of retiring allowance for honourable service would be in the best interest of the service of the country as well as in the interest of economy.

TEMPORARY CLERKS.

Under the provisions of the Civil Service Act, the salary of a temporary clerk begins at $500 and runs up to $700 by increases of $50 each year. At the present time there are over 40 so-called temporary clerks in the Finance Department. Some of these temporary clerks have been in the service of the department for over thirty years. It would appear reasonable that, after a period of some years' service at work that is of just as permanent a character as any other, the temporary feature should be eliminated and the employment should be elevated to the dignity that attaches to permanency. Take for instance the case of the women employed in counting and signing notes. The work is simple, but to all intents and purposes as permanent as any other. After a term of say three years in the temporary rank, such a clerk might be regarded as permanent, and so designated. For the class of work to be done, I think a third-class clerkship would be sufficient. The advantage to be gained by the clerk from such an arrangement would be derived from any improvement that would be made in the third-class clerkships arising out of any amendments that might be made to the Civil Service Act.

T. C. BOVILLE,
Deputy Minister of Finance.

OTTAWA, November 8, 1907.

TORONTO, September 26, 1907.

Mr. J. G. RIDOUT, Toronto, called and sworn and examined.

The WITNESS.—I beg to produce a memorandum which Mr. Creighton, the Assistant Receiver General, who is at present absent from the country, left with me in order that it might be brought before you.
Statement read and filed as exhibit.

By the Chairman:

Q. Mr. Ridout, you have been in the Assistant Receiver General's office here from the very beginning?—A. It was opened one year before I came. I was appointed in 1872, and the office was opened the year previous.

Q. The first Assistant Receiver General here was Mr. C. S. Ross?—A. Yes.

Q. He was paid a salary of $3,000?—A. Yes.

Q. Is the same salary paid now?—A. The same until last July, when Mr. Creighton got an increase of $300.

Q. Mr. Creighton was appointed in 1895?—A. Yes.

Q. And he has received a ten per cent increase in salary?—A. Yes.

Q. You have been in the office since 1872 and came originally from the Bank of Commerce?—A. Yes, I came out of the Bank of Commerce at $800 salary.

Q. You were selected as a good capable junior, knowing banking?—A. They wanted a teller here. Mr. Grasett, who had been teller, suddenly left. They wanted a teller in his place and telegraphed the offer to Goderich, where I then was, and I came down immediately.

Q. Personal reasons, your parents being then in Toronto, induced you to accept the position?—A. Yes.

Q. The idea that you had was that once in Toronto you would always be in Toronto?—A. To tell you the truth, I did not think very much about it. My people wanted me to come home, and the position I accepted in the Assistant Receiver General's Office gave me an immediate increase of $200 more than I was receiving from the bank.

Q. You were twenty-seven years of age when you entered the service?—A. Yes.

Q. When you entered the service, how many composed the staff?—A. Mr. Ross, Percy Eliot, and myself. There were three.

Q. And the messenger?—A. There was no messenger at that time, but one was appointed later on, when we came into the building that we now occupy. We were formerly on Wellington Street, in a little bit of a place there.

Q. Then you acquired a new place and a messenger was appointed who lives over the building?—A. Yes. By-the-by, I should say that Mr. Orde was sent up, and he made a fourth member of the staff, before we left the Wellington Street place.

Q. At that time, in common with the other Assistant Receiver General's Offices, you had a Savings Bank branch?—A. Yes.

Q. The Savings Bank branch, after many years, was found to be unnecessary and was done away with?—A. It was done away with two years ago.

Q. Your balances were then turned over to the Post Office Savings Bank?—A. Yes.

Q. Now your office is that of the Assistant Receiver General only?—A. That is all.

Q. Who compose the present staff?—A. Mr. Creighton, myself, the teller, a junior clerk, and a messenger.

SESSIONAL PAPER No. 29a

Q. What salary did you come in at?—A. $800.

Q. What are you getting now?—A. $1,700.

Q. Can you tell us how the increases have happened?—A. The last $100 I got in July, 1905, and the one before that was in 1904. My salary was then increased from $1,500 to $1,600, and in 1905 it was made $1,700.

Q. Do you recollect how long you were at the $1,500?—A. A good many years; I could not tell how long. I remember receiving a letter from yourself when I was advanced to $1,400, stating that I could flatter myself that I was a second-class clerk. My first increase, from $800 to $1,000, was at the time Mr. Ross died. That was in order to put me on a level with Mr. Orde, who was nominally the senior.

Q. That would be between 1877 and 1878?—A. That was about 1877 or 1878, or earlier.

Q. Mr. Ross was succeeded by Mr. Fraser?—A. Yes.

Q. Mr. Fraser died?—A. Yes, he died.

Q. Then Mr. C. J. Campbell came in?—A. Yes.

Q. He had been an experienced banker?—A. Yes, he had been.

Q. And it was a great comfort to the department when he was there?—A. Yes, it was.

Q. Mr. Campbell got on in years and was retired?—A. Yes.

Q. And Mr. Creighton was appointed?—A. Yes.

Q. Mr. Creighton has developed into a very capable man?—A. Very.

Q. He has very great capacity?—A. Finance was his hobby. He was a newspaper man and a member of the local Legislature?—A. Yes.

Q. He was the Opposition's financial critic in the local Legislature?—A. Yes.

Q. So he had theoretically a certain knowledge of the subject before he came in?—A. Yes.

Q. There is one Assistant Receiver General's Office in each province?—A. One in each province.

Q. Your position, or rather that of the office, is looked upon as provincial rather than local?—A. I should say so.

Q. You are looked upon as within the province? Just as in the case of a clerk at Ottawa, the appointments are not regarded as a matter of local patronage?—A. In Toronto originally our appointments were not made for political reasons at all.

Q. Originally you were opening a new office, and bankers were looked upon as necessary to carry on the new duties?—A. Mr. Ross, Percy Eliot, and myself were appointed, not from political reasons, but on account of efficiency. The two last appointments to the office of tellers have certainly been political, and they are Toronto men.

Q. There is a young man I noticed in your office yesterday that I had not seen before?—A. Mr. Kane. He comes from Newmarket. I think Mr. Aylesworth was his sponsor, and he is a very good clerk.

Q. Was he in a bank before?—A. He had left school a few months before.

Q. He is a very capable young man?—A. Yes, very capable.

Q. The appointments to staff of the Assistant Receiver General's Office are supposed to be of the nature of appointments from the province rather than appointments from the locality? In addition to this office, there are offices in Halifax, St. John, Charlottetown, Winnipeg and Victoria? There are only five offices besides yours?—A. Yes.

Q. There are only a small number of officials connected with these offices, taken collectively?—A. Yes.

Q. And they have never been graded into a class?—A. No.

Q. And the emoluments differ in each place?—Mr. Creighton gets rather more than the Assistant Reveiver General in Victoria?—A. I did not know that. I thought they were all paid $3,000.

7-8 EDWARD VII , A. 190

Q. Mr. Mathers, Halifax, gets $2,200; Mr. Howard D. McLeod, St. John, N.B gets $2,200; Mr. H. M. Drummond, Winnipeg, gets $2,250; Mr. McLaughlin, Vi toria, $2,400, and Mr. Percy Pope, Charlottetown, $2,200?—A. I was under the ix pression they were all paid the same salary.

Q. It would seem, in view of the fact that some get more than others, that leng of service has been considered in fixing the emolument, except in Toronto?—A. Y

Q. Did this Mr. Kane, who has been recently brought in, pass the Civil Serv examination ?—A. I am not aware of his having been asked to pass an examinatic

Q. You say he had no banking experience ?—A. No.

Q. What do you pay him ?—A. $600.

Q. What does Mr. Tovell, the next man, get now ?—A. He receives $1,000.

Q. How long has he been in the service ?—A. Four years last April.

Q. Supposing Mr. Tovell had entered the Bank of Commerce what would he hav received at the end of four years ?—A. He was in the Ontario Bank previously, bt left there and was doing nothing when our teller was appointed to the Sovereign Ban Then Mr. Tovell obtained the appointment in our office.

Q. What salary would he have been getting had he stuck to banking ?—A. I suppose about the same or a little more.

Q. Of course, in the Assistant Receiver General's offices, unfortunately, there i no chance of promotion like there is in the banks ?—A. There is not.

Q. You think that something should be done to compensate for this lack of pro motion ?—A. Yes, I think the clerks should have their regular increases that they ca count upon. In the office here neither of the young men on the staff can get any pro motion unless I either die or am superannuated. The teller cannot go forward an the junior cannot either unless the teller is promoted. I am simply a stumbling bloc to the progress of these other men.

Q. Unfortunately, although they are doing the same class of work as tellers i banks there are no branch banks to which they can be appointed ? There is only th one office in each province and they have no means of getting out of the teller's box —A. No.

The CHAIRMAN.—And you could hardly destroy the market by paying an inordinat price to a teller.

Mr. FYSHE.—That is one of the conditions that make it easier for big banks t attract men away from the little ones.

By the Chairman :

Q. You cannot well pay a teller more than a teller is worth ?—A. No.

Mr. FYSHE.—Sometimes even in a big bank a teller gets fixed. His mind get stereotyped and he is unfit for promotion. He has made himself a mechanical mar

By the Chairman :

Q. What holidays do you enjoy here?—A. Three weeks a year.

Q. And when you go away who acts for you ?—A. Mr. Creighton does here.

Q. The two higher officers interchange ?—A. Yes.

Q. You have inspectors who come around from Ottawa ?—A. Yes.

Q. They come without giving you any notice ?—A. Yes.

Q. They take possession of the whole place and count everything ?—A. Yes.

Q. Even all the bags of gold ?—A. No, they count the bags and weigh them. The do not count the pieces of gold.

Q. But they empty the bags ?—A. They empty the bags into a scale and weigl the contents.

Q. Then they count the bags of silver ?—A. They count the number of bags o gold and the number of bags of silver.

Q. The bags of silver are just the same as they come from the mint ?—A. Yes.

SESSIONAL PAPER No. 29a

Q. And the copper the same ?—A. Yes.

Q. And they count all the notes ?—A. Yes.

Q. How do you mutilate the notes ? Do you gouge out the signatures with a chisel ?—A. Yes.

Q. Then they are sent to Ottawa ?—A. Yes, we sent to-day $230,000, somewhere about that amount, and we still have as much nearly on hand.

Q. Do you send away the notes as fast as you can ?—A. I suppose as fast as they can take them in Ottawa.

Q. They are all destroyed there ?—A. They are all destroyed there.

Q. Once you consider a note is no longer fit for circulation it is destroyed ?—A. Yes.

Q. When the inspector comes all the gold is weighed and the notes are counted ? —A. The weighing of the gold is a very heavy piece of business and for the last few years the inspectors have tried to alleviate that somewhat by sealing up compartments in some safes. In one case the contents of a whole safe was verified and the safe sealed up. Even so, that will leave us about nearly two-thirds of the amount of gold we have on hand still to be weighed. There is somewhere about one-third under seal.

Q. Then the inspector with his own particular seal seals up the gold ?—A. Yes. It is a very heavy piece of business.

Q. All the $1 and $2 notes, the small currency of the Dominion, are signed at Ottawa before they are sent to you ?—A. Yes.

Q. In the case of the big notes, five hundreds, thousands and five thousands, the officer goes from Ottawa to sign, they are not trusted through the express company ? —A. An officer goes from Ottawa to sign. One signature is signed in Ottawa and an officer goes to sign the other.

Q. In the old time—I am speaking of some years ago— the notes of large dimension were made payable at a particular place, say Halifax or St. John ?—A. Yes.

Q. The notes were inscribed on the back ' Payable at Halifax.' To please the banks that was done away with some years ago?—A. Yes.

Q. And in consequence the reserve had to be increased in order to meet any sudden demand that might be made?—A. You mean the reserve of notes?

Q. The reserve of gold?—A. Yes, that is the fact.

Q. Now there is a movement among the banks in this direction: that the notes being changed say at Winnipeg the gold should be given out in Toronto?—A. We have not had any requests of that kind.

Q. Have you not heard that that is the latest proposition?—A. I have not heard that.

Q. In connection with the removal of the crops?—A. I think I remember that being done between Montreal and Toronto many years ago.

Q. The whole tendency of the currency of the country lately has been to benefit the public and facilitate matters with the banks as far as possible, doing away with the special places of redemption?—A. Yes.

Q. Now in satisfying the demands of branch banks for note circulation of small dimension. A branch at Orangeville, for example, may ask for five hundred on a draft on the head office at Toronto?—A. Yes.

Q. That is $1 notes?—A. Yes.

Q. Who pays the cost on those $1 notes to the banks?—A. We do not pay, the bank pays.

Q. Your work has been greatly enlarged by the multiplication of branch banks?— A. Yes, very much.

Q. Do you find difficulty now with the tellers of the city banks here in making up their bundles of notes for exchanges? An arrangement was arrived at with the Bankers Association?—A. That has not been adhered to at all.

Q. You had better explain that?—A. The idea was that bundles should be sent in in five hundreds or multiples of five hundred, sorted without the necessity of sorting notes for reissue from notes to be cancelled. I do not know whether any bank has made an effort to do it at all. If they have they have dropped it. The larger portion of our work is from notes taken in by the large departmental stores and the railways, put up in hundred notes at a time; sent into the banks and by the banks sent into us without counting at all. The bank clerks say: 'We have not time to count six or eight thousand one dollar notes; you are going to count it anyway.' So they send the notes in to us as they come to them, uncounted. That is the heaviest part of our work. They are responsible for it, but if we report any error they send it on to Eaton, or Simpson, or a railway company, whoever it may be, and say: 'This has come from you.' They ask us to say who the bundle comes from. Sometimes we can and sometimes we cannot. The original idea of the Bankers' Association that notes should be sorted and only sent in to us in multiples of $500 has not been adhered to.

Q. Mr. Ross, formerly of the Bank of Nova Scotia, when he was in the service of the Finance Department, made arrangements with the Bankers' Association that these notes sent in for redemption should be in proper order and in five hundred or multiples of five hundred. This arrangement you say has been departed from?—A. Yes.

Q. And departed from largely?—A. Yes.

Q. And the onus of the work thrown upon the Assistant Receiver General's office?—A. Yes.

By Mr. Fyshe:

Q. You should not allow that. Make them stick to the agreement.—A. We have tried to fight it here, but we do not seem to be able to succeed. The bankers say it is our business to sort notes and we say it is not. We say: 'If you have too many notes for issue that you do not want send them in to us and we will give you large notes for them. If you have a large amount of notes unfit for circulation send them in and we will redeem them. But it is not fair to send in three thousand or four thousand dollars worth of notes and then ask us next day for notes for reissue.'

By the Chairman:

Q. Do any of the banks keep up to the agreement?—A. The Bank of Toronto always sends in an even thousand dollars of notes at a time that are only fit for cancellation. I do not know of any other bank that does so.

Q. Then one bank lives up to the agreement?—A. There is this difference that the business of one bank may permit of their doing it in that way. The business of the Bank of Toronto does but the business of the Bank of Montreal or the Sterling Bank may not permit them to do so. The nature of their business is such that we could hardly expect the clerks to sort them.

Q. Do you find now that with children's savings banks and things of that character the supply of coppers dries up at certain periods of the year?—A. It is marvellous to me what becomes of the coppers. We are very seldom asked to take in ten dollars or twenty dollars worth of coppers. If we were asked we would tell them to go to one of banks; we do not take in any coppers. Where the coppers go is a perfect marvel.

Q. At Christmas time is the great time for the outflow of the coppers?—A. Yes.

Q. And previous to that time a lot of coppers are gradually accumulating in children's savings banks and such like, are they not?—A. Possibly. I do not know about that, but I do know they do not come to us.

Q. The big stores and the street railway company are the people that have the greatest amount of coppers?—A. The big stores take from us a large number of coppers. The street railway people do not take any from us, but they frequently supply the banks.

Q. How is the small change of the country in silver? Is there enough in circulation?—A. There is a shortage of small silver just now, particularly ten cent pieces. That, I suppose, will be rectified very soon.

Q. The five cent pieces disappear like drops of water?—A. Yes. But with the small silver it is different from the coppers. We are very frequently asked to take in the small silver from the banks. They write to us to say 'we have $500 or $800 worth of small silver. Can you relieve us or help us to get rid of it'? We do not take it in, but we send orders from other banks. We may have a bank that sends in for small silver and we want to help out another bank that has it. So we say to the bank that is applying 'Go over to such and such a bank and get it there.'

Q. The duty of your office is to exchange notes for notes, notes for gold, or gold for notes, or to supply silver and coppers?—A. Yes.·

Q. Perhaps you have not studied the question, but is it not a fact that the Government of Canada is coming to be very much like the Bank of England at home: it is the store-house or the reserve of the country?—A. I am certain it must be so.

Q. Do you happen to know what the circulation of the small notes, one's and two's, is? About fourteen millions, is it not?—A. Yes.

Q. About ten years ago it was about four million?—A. I could not give evidence about that.

Q. That is one of the evidences of the increase in the business of the country?— A. Of course, I know of my own knowledge that the quantity of one's and two's we are issuing and getting is vastly on the increase.

Witness retired.

ASSISTANT RECEIVER GENERAL,

TORONTO, August 1, 1907.

Although the Chairman of the Commission will be aware that the business of this office has been increasing rapidly, yet even he will no doubt be surprised when the actual figures are presented.

Taking the date May 10, 1895, when the present Assistant Receiver General took office, as a convenient time for starting comparisons, the number of bank agencies in Ontario have increased from 264 in 1895 to 788 in December 1906, and from the rapid increase recently there will be nearly 1,000 by this time.

Taking the years ending May 10, 1896, and May 10, 1907, the increase of business in the office has been as follows:—

New $1 and $2 notes received from Ottawa: 1895-6, $1,205,000; 1906-7, $5,638,000.

Gross Receipts.

	1895-6.	1906-7.
Notes..	$5,972,029	$28,844,865
Specie..	616,956	8,331,267
	$6,588,985	$37,176,132

Gross Payments.

	1895-6.	1906-7.
Notes..	$5,809,509	$28,486,471
Specie..	441,799	2,388,134
	$6,251,308	$30,874,605

The total business of the office has increased from $12,840,293 in 1896, to $68,050,-737 in 1907.

As showing the comparative importance of the office, of the silver received from the Mint, in the five years ending June 30, 1906, nearly one-half was put out by the Toronto office, or $1,084,000, as against $1,349,000 for all the other offices combined, while for coppers the figures were $72,000 and $73,000, or almost half.

When the present Assistant Receiver General came in, the amount of specie carried in the office was less than one-seventh of the amount now on hand, and the total cash is now more than five times what it then was.

As from all quarters the great increased cost of living will have been urged on the Commission, it will hardly be necessary to touch on that point more than to say that in no place has this increase been greater than in Toronto.

But it might be urged that the remuneration in an office like this should not be based on the mere labour involved (although that is becoming heavy for our limited staff), but should be on a scale commensurate with the importance of the business transacted, and the great responsibility connected with the custody and handling of such large sums of money. The officer in charge and those associated with him should be paid on a scale at least equal to the main office of our leading banks—and this the Government can well afford to do, for although this office is not looked on as revenue collecting in the ordinary sense, yet on the silver and coppers alone put out from it during the past five years, the country has made a profit of $652,284—with this essential difference from ordinary revenue, where our people have to pay every dollar that is collected, that the coins being absorbed in the business of the country, while facilitating it, the Government has a profit of the large sum between the cost and the nominal value without the people being called on to contribute a cent towards it.

Of course the figures herein are for the information of the Commission, and not to be made public.

(Signed)   D. CREIGHTON,
Assistant Receiver General.

OTTAWA, October 16, 1907.

A deputation representing the labourers and charmen employed in connection with the various Government buildings in Ottawa, and consisting of Messrs. R. H. Maveetey, Richard Berthiaume, Jean Savary, Martin Watson and Robert Wimperis, submitted a memorial, which was read and filed.

R. H. MAVEETEY, sworn and examined.

By the Chairman:

Q. You represent the labourers under Mr. Conroy?—A. Yes.

Q. There are about 21 of you now ?—A. Yes.

Q. And you all receive $400 a year, except Gallagher?—A. Yes, and one other—Stack.

Q. Is Stack alive yet?—A. Yes, but he is bedridden. His son does the work in his place.

Q. Stack and Gallagher have been on nearly forty years ?—A. Stack has been on 45 years, and Gallagher about 40 years.

Q. Do you know when the limit of $400 a year was fixed?—A. About twenty-five years ago.

Q. How many buildings are under the control of Conroy?—A. The East Block, the West Block, the Langevin Block, the Museum, the Corry Block, the Woods Blocks, 66 Queen Street, and the building on the corner of Slater and Metcalfe Streets.

Q. What time do you go on in the morning?—A. Between half-past six and seven.

Q. You have to get all the work done before the officials arrive at half-past nine? —A. Yes. We have to have the corridors swept and the water closets cleaned and the fires laid before the men come, and then we have to break up the coal and cut the wood to be ready for the fires the next morning.

Q. In the summer months no coal is wanted?—A. No, but there is more traffic and consequently more dirt, and we have to clean the fire-irons and the fenders and the pan in front. Then, there is more water used, and we have to filter the water.

Q. What people in the outside world do you think you could compare yourselves to?—A. I do not know; but general labourers get from $1.50 to $2 a day now. Living has got so expensive that their pay has been increased.

Q. Then, you consider that the scale, which was laid down about a quarter of a century ago, should be increased in proportion to the higher prices of commodities?— A. Yes.

Q. Have you formed any idea in your own mind as to what you think you should have ?—A. I think, $1.50 a day.

Q. What do the Public Works Department pay their labourers?—A. The least is $1.50 a day, and they go up to about $2.

Q. After the gentlemen come to the offices and you have broken up the coal, and so forth, when does that day's work end?—A. We get through at half-past eleven or twelve o'clock.

Q. What do you do then?—A. We go home.

Q. When do you come back ?—A. Sometimes we have to come back and do messages, and sometimes the urinals overflow, and we have to look after them.

Q. You do not act as messengers?—A. We have to act as messengers for Mr. Conroy, to go for women.

Q. Do you take day and day about to come back in the afternoon ?—A. Yes.

. 7-8 EDWARD VII., A. 1908

Q. The whole staff is engaged practically until dinner time?—A. Yes.

Q. Then in the afternoon you take it watch and watch about.

Q. What do you do on Sundays?—A. Sometimes we have to come back on Sundays. I myself have always to come back on Sunday, when Mr. Fitzpatrick was Minister of Justice, and remain all the time he was in the office.

By Mr. Fyshe:

Q. What work did he give you to do?—A. To keep the fire while he was in his office.

By the Chairman:

Q. There is very little work on Sundays?—A. Very little.

Q. Who is Mr. Conroy's assistant?—A. Mr. Chitty.

Q. Does one or other of them go there every Sunday to see if anything is wanted?—A. Oh, no, I do not think so.

Q. Then practically the regular hours of work are about six hours absolute, and then every other day or so coming back in the afternoon?—A. Yes.

Q. I suppose your work is very dirty?—A. It is very dirty and very hard while it lasts, because it has to be done very rapidly. At the rate we have to work, no man could keep it up all day. When we are through we are wet with perspiration, and after the excitement of the work is over it takes the rest of the day to recover.

Q. How many rooms do you have to attend to?—A. Twenty-two rooms—grates to attend to.

By Mr. Fyshe:

Q. I suppose quite a number find other things to do during the day?—A. I have tried several times to take up something outside, but I always found that it clashed with my work in the buildings. Sometimes I would be detained in the buildings, and people always prefer a man who can come in the morning and can stay the whole day.

By the Chairman:

Q. You are supposed always to be at the beck and call of Mr. Conroy?—A. Yes, whenever he wants us.

Q. Is there anything else you think we should know?—A. The main thing is that it is very hard for us to live on only $400 a year. We are always in debt.

Q. What does the city corporation pay its labourers?—A. It used to pay $1.50. Now it pays from $1.75 to $2.

Q. You have the advantage of stability in your employment?—A. Yes.

Q. And if you get sick, somebody else is allowed to go and do your work and you get the pay?—A. We have to pay somebody to do our work for us.

Q. Still, you can get somebody to do your work?—A. It all depends. If it is a friend, you can; but if it is a stranger, he gets our pay.

Q. How long has Stack been laid up?—A. I think over two years.

Q. And he is still allowed to be on the pay-list and his son does the work?—A. Yes.

Q. The charwomen used to get 50 cents a day?—A. Yes.

Q. Now they get 75 cents?—A. Yes.

Q. When was their pay increased?—A. About two years ago.

Q. You get no extra remuneration of any kind?—A. No.

Q. You could not engage to do any other work, because you are always subject to the call of Conroy or Chitty?—A. Yes, and I have always found that when I did get a little job that that was the day that I was wanted at the buildings. It is all very well to get a little job like taking off or putting on double windows, but it is not every day that one can get that. I do not make $10 a year extra. We can save nothing for old age and there is no superannuation for us, and it is pretty hard to look forward to the Perley Home or the Old Men's Home. I think I would prefer to die rather than do that.

SESSIONAL PAPER No. 29a

To the Chairman and Members of the Civil Service Commission,
Ottawa. .

DEAR SIRS,—The charmen and general labourers working in the different Dominion buildings have the honour to submit their claim for an increase of salary, and beg to submit the following reasons for their increase:—

1. They have to clean out the ashes and relay about eighteen or twenty fires every morning; also attend to the filling and supply of the scuttles with coal for the fires during the day; this coal has to be broken up every morning. as it is very large when it is received from the contractor; also cut the wood for the laying of the fires for the next day.

2. They have to attend to two large corridors, sweeping the floor of same every morning and the side walls. Occasionally sweep some five or six flights of stairs, dusting banisters, &c.

3. They have to attend to the water filters in each department, about five or six to every man, and supply them with ice and clean water for the day.

4. They have to clean some two or three sets of water closets, and attend to the supplying of paper, &c., every morning.

5. Attend to the sweeping of the walls of about thirty or forty rooms, japan the front of the fire places, clean fenders and fire-irons; also take down cobwebs.

6. They have to do all messages wanted by Mr. Conroy for women and carry the supplies for the outlying buildings when required, such as brooms, pails, paper, flannels, &c., &c.

We respectfully submit that we are in receipt of an inadequate salary for this work. We are receiving only $1.09.

This added to the excessive cost of living should be taken into account and we have every reason to hope that your Board will recommend an increase of our salary in your report.

We have the honour to remain, dear sirs,

Your obedient servants,

(Signed) ROBERT MAVEETY, *President.*
Address, 76 Slater St.
R. R. WIMPERIS, *Secretary.*
191 Creighton St.

To the Royal Commission.

The humble petition of the charwomen in the employment of the Dominion Government, showeth,

We the charwomen in the employment of the Dominion Government respectfully solicit the attention of your honourable body to our application for consideration in the matter of an increase of salary.. The present remuneration for services rendered by charwomen is at the rate of seventy-five cents per day, for six days in the week only, notwithstanding that we are obliged to be at the service of our employers for the remaining day without additional pay, whenever they find it necessary to call upon us. Many of our number are obliged to maintain families on the small wages so earned. Aside from the argument of the increased cost of living during recent years, and the difficulty of obtaining a reasonable livelihood from such salary, we submit that considering the arduous character of the work alone we are entitled to more substantial remuneration than the amount we receive.

We would also direct your honourable committee's attention to the fact that the charwomen of the Senate (who are not parties to this petition) are now receiving the sum of one dollar per day for work of an exactly similar character to that which we are called upon to perform for smaller remuneration. For the reasons aforementioned,

29a—15

we would respectfully request your honourable committee to take into your consideration the substance of this petition—which we will be pleased to supplement with such further information as may be required—and to make such report thereon as may be in accordance with the justice of our demands.

And your petitioners will ever pray.

Mrs. LIZZIE WALSH,
President of Committee.
JOSÉPHINE OUIMET,
Secretary.

OTTAWA, May 29, 1907.

Mr. A. P. Low, sworn and examined.

By the Chairman :

Q. You are the director of the Geological Survey ?—A. Yes.

Q. Since the last session of Parliament your department is called?—A. The Department of Mines.

Q. Which includes the old Geological Survey ?—A. Yes, and also Dr. Haanel's branch in the Interior Department.

Q. How long have you been in the survey ?—A. I joined the survey in 1882. I was in the service as a summer assistant in 1881 and was appointed in 1882.

Q. How long have you been director ?—A. Just a year.

Q. Before that you were an explorer ?—A. Yes, and geologist.

Q. The duties of the survey are to explore all over the Dominion ?—A. Yes.

Q. From the Hudson bay to Cape Breton and in the Yukon ?—A. Yes.

Q. What is your salary for looking after all these explorations and all the duties of the survey ?—A. My present salary is $3,600. I started at $3,500.

Q. There are no additional emoluments ?—A. No, none whatever.

Q. These (showing) are the statements you were asked to produce?—A. Yes.

Q. The survey works under two Acts, the Civil Service Act and the Geological Survey Act ?—A. There is no Geological Survey now and no Geological Survey Act.

Q. Until the last session of Parliament and the Bill then passed was assented to you were working under two Acts ?—A. Yes.

Q. In your department there is one chief clerk, two first class, four second class and two juniors; you have not much clerical assistance there?—A. No, we do not require very much of that.

Q. Your department is made up entirely of what are called technical officers ?— A. Yes.

Q. When a new junior second-class clerk is to be appointed, what is done? Does one of your officers apply to you for an assistant?—A. Yes.

Q. Do some of your junior officers say that they want a man?—A. Yes, or I want him myself.

Q. You do not have a man pushed on if you do not want him?—A. Not as a rule. I have had no trouble of that kind.

Q. And a man put on in that way is subject to probation?—A. Yes.

Q. And you certify to his proficiency before he is appointed permanently?—A. Yes.

Q. On your temporary staff, how are taxidermists, museum assistants and photographers appointed—they do not come under the Civil Service Act?—A. No, they are paid out of the ordinary vote for the Survey.

By Mr. Fyshe:

Q. Are these experts specially appointed, or have they risen in the service?—A. Most of them have risen in the service.

By the Chairman:

Q. You are a deputy as well as director?—A. Yes.

Q. Yours is a department, in fact?—A. Yes.

Q. There is no special Minister for the Geological Survey—any Minister may be designated by the Governor in Council?—A. Yes.

29a—15½

7-8 EDWARD VII., A. 1908

Q. The present Minister of Inland Revenue is your minister?—A. Yes.

Q. What leave of absence do you give to the clerks in your department?—A. Three weeks.

Q. Do they get more than three weeks?—A. Not as a rule.

Q. Have you an attendance book?—A. Yes.

Q. Does everybody sign the attendance book?—A. Yes.

Q. Including all the technical officers?—A. Yes, all the technical officers.

Q. Do you continue Dr. Selwyn's plan of requiring them all to sign when they go out to lunch and when they come back?—A. Yes. They sign four times a day.

Q. Is that attendance book really observed?—A. Yes.

Q. Do they all go out to lunch at the same time?—A. No.

Q. What time do you allow for. luncheon?—A. An hour or an hour and a quarter.

Q. What are the office hours?—A. From half-past nine to half-past four.

Q. But I suppose if any of the staff are wanted longer, they remain longer?—A. Most of them remain till after five.

Q. You publish a good many maps?—A. Yes.

Q. Has White taken that over from you now?—A. No, we still publish our own maps.

Q. Would it not be better that there should be a cartographical department in which all maps should be published?—A. Yes, I think it would. We had a committee that met last winter, which drew up a resolution for Council on that subject.

Q. Are all your officers in the one building on Sussex street?—A. Yes. We are very much crowded.

Q. Do your officers know about the Treasury Board minute passed in 1879 in regard to political interference?—A. I expect they do. We do not have any of that, or very little.

Q. Were all the officers under the Superannuation Act prior to 1897?—A. Yes.

Q. What is your idea about the abolition of that Act?—A. I think it was a mistake. We want to get technical men into the service, and if they have no guarantee of superannuation, they have nothing to look forward to, and they can make twice as much outside.

Q. In looking over your statement, I find that since 1892 in the permanent staff Mr. Tyrrell resigned, Mr. Ferrier and Mr. Brumell?—A. Yes.

Q. These men who were there in 1892?—A. Yes.

Q. I suppose others have resigned that came in since?—A. Yes.

Q. In fact, there are continual resignations?—A. Yes.

Q. Is Dr. Daly in your department?—A. No, he is in the Interior Department, on the international boundary.

Q. He has resigned?—A. Yes. He has been working in our department.

Q. Among the temporaries, Mr. Russell resigned and Mr. McEvoy resigned?—A. Yes.

Q. And Mr. Jacob resigned?—A. Yes.

By Mr. Fyshe:

Q. When they resign, do they get any benefit from the superannuation?—A. No. I paid for 18 years into the superannuation fund, and I resigned for fifteen months, and lost my superannuation, and I cannot get back again. During the 18 years I paid in two per cent of my salary.

By the Chairman:

Q. You had occasion to resign, and were absent about fifteen months?—A. Yes.

Q. By so doing you lost the benefit of the Superannuation Act?—A. Yes.

Q. You are not now under the Superannuation Act?—A. No.

By Mr. Fyshe:

Q. Did you know when you resigned that your absence was only to be temporary?—A. I did not know then.

Q. Could you have made it a condition that you could be reinstated under the Superannuation Act if you came back?—A. I did not make it.

By the Chairman:

Q. The Act was abolished in 1897?—A. Yes.
Q. And you resigned in 1901?—A. Yes.
Q. If you had remained on, the Act would have applied to you?—A. Yes.
Q. But having resigned and the Act having been abolished, you cannot now get on again?—A. No.
Q. You think it would add stability to the service if the Superannuation Act were restored?—A. I have not the slightest doubt of it.
Q. You know that by reason of so many officers of your department having left to better themselves?—A. Yes, of course they lost their superannuation by doing so.
Q. Mr. McEvoy went to the Crows Nest Coal Company to become their chief geologist. If there had been something to keep him here, he might have remained?—Yes.
Q. How are all these technical officers appointed—for instance, an assistant chemist or a geologist?—A. Just in the ordinary way.
Q. What do you call the ordinary way—they are not under the Civil Service Act? —A. Yes, by Order in Council. We generally put them on probation for a year before appointing them on the permanent staff.
Q. They are not required to pass the ordinary Civil Service examination under the Civil Service Act?—A. Not at all.
Q. They are appointed on account of their scholastic attainments?—A. Yes. They are nearly all graduates in science of some university, and have also taken field work for at least a year.
Q. Mr. Tyrrell, for instance, went up to the Yukon?—A. Yes.
Q. What did Mr. Ferrier do?—A. He went to a mine in British Columbia. Mr. Tyrrell is with Mackenzie and Mann now. These men got salaries at least double those they were getting in the service. They usually go out for about $4,000 or $5,000 a year. In the Survey they get $1,800 or $2,000.

By Mr. Fyshe:

Q. What work is Tyrrell doing for Mackenzie and Mann?—A. He is their mining engineer and explorer.
Q. He has had a great deal of experience?—A. Yes.
Q. He has travelled practically from the Hudson Bay to the extreme west?—A. Yes.

By the Chairman:

Q. How much did McEvoy get?—A. I think $5,000.
Q. And you were paying him how much?—A. $1,500, I think.
Q. In your department there has been more than the average number of resignations?—A. I think so.
Q. Simply because people outside are ready to take up the men you require?—A. Yes. There is a great demand from the outside for men on our staff.
Q. The highest paid man next to yourself is Dr. Bell?—A. Yes.
Q. He gets $3,000 a year?—A. Yes.
Q. He has been in the service over forty years?—A. I think about fifty years.
Q. And the next highest paid is $2,500 or $2,600?—A. Yes.
Q. There is no prospect of a scientific man coming into the service getting more than $2,500 or $2,600?—A. No, there is not much chance of his getting more than that.
Q. Are your reports printed up to date now?—A. They are a little behind in the Printing Bureau.

7-8 EDWARD VII., A. 1908

Q. Are they all done there?—A. There are a lot of them down there. We cannot print quite up to date, because we have to get our maps made and the reports written, and it is generally a year before a report in some part of the country is issued.

Q. In former years they were ten years behind?—A. Yes, when we had the old volumes, we used to wait to bind them up together.

Q. Except for the exigencies of the department, they are now printed up to date? —A. Yes, when we can get the work done in the Printing Bureau.

Q. The practice of printing them in outside offices is done away with?—A. Yes.

Q. Dr. Selwyn stated in 1892 that the department was divided into branches— Exploration and Surveys, Topography and Photography, Palæontology and Zoology, Botany, Chemistry and Mineralogy, Library, Mines and Statistics. Does that generally prevail now?—A. Yes, it does roughly. We have not heads for these different branches, but we classify the staff in that way.

By Mr. Fyshe:

Q. You are doing practically the same work?—A. Yes.

By the Chairman:

Q. Besides the surveys, you have a museum?—A. Yes.

Q. Are some of your officers delegated to attend to the museum and to collect specimens for it?—A. Yes, nearly all our officers do that.

Q. Is somebody always in charge of the museum to show it to strangers and scientific men?—A. No, we have no curator. Dr. Whiteaves is curator of a part and Dr. Hoffmann of another part.

Q. Do they spend their time in Ottawa?—A. Yes.

Q. They do not go exploring?—A. No.

Q. They are ready to show about any distinguished geologist from the United States or from Paris or London?—A. Yes.

Q. The building is not a very safe one?—A. No, not very.

Q. By and by you will move to the new museum?—A. Yes.

Q. What are you doing now with regard to safety from fire?—A. We have hydrants in the building and night watchmen.

Q. You are a graduate of McGill?—A. Yes.

Q. There was a fire in the museum at one time?—A. Yes, but it did not amount to anything.

Q. Many of your specimens, both mineralogical and geological, could not be replaced?—A. There are a lot of fossils and mineral specimens that could not be replaced.

Q. How long will it be before the new museum will be available?—A. I do not know. It will be two or three years anyway.

Q. Is there a caretaker now living in the old museum?—A. Yes, we have a caretaker.

Q. Does he perambulate the building?—A. Yes. He does not do it at night.

Q. In England assistant geologists and fossil collectors are appointed by competitive examination?—A. Yes. We do not do that here.

Q. But you take good care that they should be scientific men?—A. Oh, yes, and properly qualified.

Q. You try them for twelve months?—A. Yes.

Q. You do not think it would add anything to the betterment of your survey if these men were appointed by competitive examination?—A. I do not think it would be a wise thing to do. We take them on the strength of their college degree.

Q. At this time of the year, do you decide where your exploration parties shall go? —A. Yes.

Q. Do you settle who shall go?—A. I make out a list, and submit it to the Minister for his approval.

Q. Of course these explorers require sub-explorers?—A. Yes.

SESSIONAL PAPER No. 29a

Q. Are these people generally appointed by the Minister or yourself?—A. Mostly by myself. I apply to the Universities of McGill and Queen's and Toronto, and I get undergraduates and send them out as assistants.

Q. How many expeditions do you usually send off?—A. About twenty-five.

Q. To all parts of the Dominion?—A. Yes.

Q. Are they confined pretty much to unexplored territory or do they include territory which is pretty well known?—A. We do both. We are doing more work now in the easterly and settled parts of the country than we used to do.

By Mr. Fyshe:

Q. That is principally for minerals, is it?—A. Yes, the geology and the natural resources of the country.

By the Chairman:

Q. It was elicited from Dr. Selwyn at the time of the last commission, fifteen years ago, that when the chief of an exploration party wanted a good boy who was going through the university, if he could not get him as assistant explorer, he took him as a canoe man. Is that done sometimes now?—A. Yes.

Q. Does not that create trouble with the ordinary canoe men and labourers?—A. It is liable to. It is not done as much as it used to be, because these boys, if they cannot get employment from us, can get it from some one else.

By Mr. Fyshe:

Q. How many men do you usually send on one expedition?—A. Generally about half a dozen on each party.

Q. Three or four being students?—A. No, generally one or two students. The others are canoe men, packers and so on.

By the Chairman:

Q. When your parties set out you give them advances?—A. Yes.

Q. Do you give them lump sums?—A. Not as a rule. We give them a certain portion of the money appropriated to them, and afterwards we send out an order on a bank somewhere.

Q. Do you take your vote and cut it up in lots, assigning so much for the Laurentian range, so much for the Hudson bay, so much for the Yukon, and so on?—A. Not quite. We have a form which each man fills in, showing the places to which he is going and how much he requires, and we allot to him that much.

Q. You give cash to some of them to pay canoe men and to buy supplies?—A. Yes.

Q. And that is accounted for at the end of the exploration?—A. Yes.

By Mr. Fyshe:

Q. I suppose all of them have to have Indians?—A. Indians or half-breeds.

By the Chairman:

Q. You have no trouble in accounting for these advances?—A. No.

Q. The troubles of the past are all over?—A. I think so, largely.

Q. An explorer gets no advantage when he is out on an exploration—he gets simply what he is out of pocket?—A. Yes.

Q. He gets no allowance?—A. He gets his living allowance, which he accounts for from day to day.

Q. There is no fixed sum?—A. There is no fixed sum—no per diem allowance.

Q. He has to show what he actually expended?—A. Yes. If he treats any one from whom he gets information, he has to pay for that himself. There should be some allowance for expenses in obtaining information.

Q. You had a dispute with the late Auditor General about some of your explorers giving plugs of tobacco to some Indians ?—A. Yes. Every man who goes out is more o.' less out of pocket every year.

Q. You say that the chief of an exploring party is as a rule out of pocket as the result of his explorations ?—A. Yes.

Q. Although he goes through a rugged part of the country and undergoes great hardships and perhaps dangers to life ?—A. Yes.

Q. And you think there should be some travelling allowance ?—A. There should be some scheme for allowing them something to obtain information. A man going into a small mining town has to spend some money around the hotels in order to get the ordinary information he requires, and there is no means by which that can be rec)uped to him.

Q. Is your survey overmanned ?—A. No, it is undermanned.

Q. Is that because the vote will not go far enough ?—A. We cannot get the men at the salaries paid.

Q. And the Geological Survey is suffering for the want of good men ?—A. Yes.

Q. What do you think would be a fair emolument for a young man just leaving the university to enter into your service as an explorer?—A. About $1,500 after his first appointment. At present we have to give them $1,200 in the probationary period.

By Mr. Fyshe :

Q. I suppose all the men you take in are college graduates ?—A. Yes, every one of them.

Q. An ordinary clerk would not do?—A. No, an ordinary clerk would not do at all. A man must have a scientific training.

By the Chairman :

Q. He must also have good physical strength ?—A. Yes.

Q. And good moral character ?—A. Yes.

Q. And be of the proper age ?—A. Yes, and proper education.

Q. And you think that after he has passed the probationary period he should be paid $1,500 ?—A. We have to do it now.

Q. With the mining development now going on all over the world, in the Yukon, in Cobalt, in South Africa, your men are continually passing from you ?—A. Yes.

Q. You find great difficulty in retaining them?—A. Yes.

Q. You think there should be a greater emolument attained to than $2,600 ?—A. Yes. They should go up to $3,500 at least. The yearly increase should be more than $50. It should be at least $100.

Q. You think that after the probationary period is passed, there should be an entrance of at least $1,500 and a maximum of at least $3,500, and a superannuation Act ?—A. Yes.

Q. Otherwise there would be no stability in your department ?—A. There will be no chance of stability unless we get something like that. With the present increase in mining, mine owners are beginning to appreciate the worth of college trained men. This spring I have lost three men from the staff.

Q. Where have they gone to ?—A. British Columbia and Cobalt. Mining in Canada is becoming better all the time.

Q. Do you yourself go on any explorations now ?—A. No. I go out inspecting and adjusting difficulties.

Q. But your position as director does not permit you to go into the field as an explorer ?—A. No.

Q. Dr. Selwyn in his evidence fifteen years ago, speaking of allowances to explorers, stated that in Australia when he was director, the Government allowed a lump sum ?—A. I do not know anything about that.

Q. Do you think a lump sum would be better than a travelling allowance ?—A. I think a travelling allowance would be the best.

Q. Have you many women in your employ ?—A. About a half a dozen.
Q. One of them, Mrs. Alexander, is a very capable woman ?—A. Yes, very capable.
Q. She assists Dr. Thorburn in the library ?—A. Yes.
Q. She has a high scientific knowledge ?—A. Yes.
Q. She is capable of directing attention to almost any book in the library from which any one wants to obtain information ?—A. Yes.

By Mr. Fyshe :

Q. She has been there for some time ?—A. I think for nearly twenty years.

By the Chairman:

Q. What do the other women in the Survey generally do ?—A. One is a stenographer for myself, another a stenographer in the accountant's branch, two are in the statistical branch, and two in the library.
Q. They have nothing to do with the scientific part of the work ?—A. No.
Q. They would not as a rule be able to rise to the higher positions ?—A. I do not think so.
Q. The stenographers could not take down the dictation of a report of a scientific character ?—A. I think my stenographer could.
Q. That would be an exception ?—A. We have another young lady stenographer for the editor, who is very good. The other women are ordinary clerks.

By Mr. Bazin:

Q. I see by the list of your department that there is the geologist, Mr. Dowling, whose salary is $1,800, and there is an assistant geologist, Mr. Brock, whose salary is $2,150 ?—A. Mr. Brock is not an assistant geologist any more. That is a mistake in the printing.

By the Chairman:

Q. You have only one who is a mining engineer ?—A. Yes. We are going to make him a geologist.
Q. Do these titles refer to the duties the different officers have to perform ?—A. Yes.

By Mr. Fyshe:

Q. Do you ever send an expedition down the Mackenize river ?—A. Yes. Mr. McConnell was down at the mouth of the Mackenzie river about ten years ago.
Q. When men go on expeditions like that, do you not give them extra pay ?—A. No, simply the ordinary pay.

By the Chairman:

Q. Your explorers as a rule are on the temporary staff ?—A. Yes. A number of them are classed as explorers, but they all like the title of geologists better.
Q. Do any of them explore ?—A. Yes, McConnell, McInnes, Chalmers, Dowling, Ingall, Brock, Wilson.
Q. The permanent staff discard the title of explorers ?—A. Yes.
Q. Most of the temporary staff are dubbed explorers and draughtsmen ?—A. Yes.
Q. Are any of the permanent staff draughtsmen ?—A. Yes, some of them are. Two called second-class clerks are draughtsmen.
Q. They are scientific men although they are called clerks ?—A. They are not technical men except as regards draughting.
Q. You have one photographer, I see—Topley ?—A. Yes.
Q. You share him with the Department of the Interior ?—A. Yes.
Q. Do you get a fair amount of attention from him ?—A. Yes.

7-8 EDWARD VII., A. 1908

GEOLOGICAL SURVÈY DEPARTMENT.

TEMPORARY STAFF.

Statement Shewing Salaries for 1905-06, Compared with 1891-92 or on First Employment.

No.	Name.	Classification.	Salary. 1905-06.	1891-92.	First Employment.
1	S. Herring..........	Taxidermist, 12 months.........	1,000 00	1,000 00	
2	Jane Alexander.	Assistant in library, 12 months...	821 25	523 50	
3	Bessie Urquhart ...	Assistant in Account's Branch, 12 m.	600 00	......	400 00, March, 1900.
4	C. F. King.	Museum assistant, 184 days........	460 00	......	2 00 per d. Jan., '02
5	May H. Barry	Copyist, 12 months	766 50	361 00	
6	Wilhelmina Sparks..	Clerk and writer, 12 months.	645 00	......	400 00, March, 1898.
7	Constance M. Alex-. ander..........	Clerk and writer, 12 "	475 00	....	400 00, October, 1903
8	Emily F. Goodman..	Stenographer and writer, 12 months	700 00	....	450 00, October, 1896
9	Marie C. Stewart....	" " "	575 00	....	400 00, November, '01
10	Jessie M. Loux......	Stenographer and writer, 1 month, 23 days....	72 57	......	500 00, May, 1906...
11	H. N. Topley.... ..	Photographer, 12 months...	300 00	498 75	
12	J. F. E. Johnston...	Explorer and draughtsman, 12 mos.	1,095 00	3 00 per d.	
13	P. H. Selwyn......	Secretary to Director, 12 months...	1,596 50	....	2 00 per d. Dec., '92
14	Jno. McLeish.......	Asst. Div. Min. Stat., 12 months..	1,368 75	.... .	1 50 per d. July, '97
15	W. H. Boyd........	Explorer and Draughtsman, 12 mos.	1,186 25	....	50 00 per m. March, 1900.
16	O. O. Sullivan	" " "	1,139 00	....	2 00 per d. April, '01.
17	W. H. Collins	Explorer, 8 months..............	800 00	.... ..	100 00 per m. June, '05.
18	D. D. Cairnes......	" 7 " 26 days...	786 76	....	100 60 per m., May, '05.
19	W. A. Johnston	" 8 " 30 "	896 77	....	100 00 per m. May, '05.
20	M. F. Connor.	Metallurgist, 12 months.	1,200 00	....	100 00 per m. Sept., '03.
21	G. A. Young.... .	Geologist and asst. petrographer ..	1,200 00	....	100 00 per m. May, '04.
22	F. H. Maclaren....	Draughtsman, 12 months	1,003 75	....	75 00 per m. June, '04.
23	P. Frereault.. ....'	" 363 days...........	1,089 00	......	2 50 per d. July, '01
24	F. O. Farrell.	" 365 days.	1,186 25	....	2 75 per d. Oct. '04
25	A. Dickson....... '	" 12 months..........	1,095 00	....	3 00 per d. July, '01
26	F. J. Nicolas.	Editor, 12 months....	1,500 00	....	125 00 per m. Dec., '04·
27	D. A. Esdale. ...	Carpenter, 274 days..	788 85	549 50	
28	Jno. Duggan.	Night watchman, 12 months. ...	675 25	457 50	
29	Nap. Gagne	Labourer, 12 months	693 50	457 50	
30	R. E. Lyons	" " 12 "	654 00	... .	1 25 per d. April, '01·
31	H Walters........	Fireman, 12 "	600 00	....	50 00 per m. Sept., '04·
32	J. H. Fortune.....	" 12 "	600 00	....	50 00 per m. Oct., '04
33	Nap. Seguin... .	" 12 "	600 00	.... .	50 00 per m. Jan., '05.
			28,169 95		

Ottawa, May 20, 1907.

GEOLOGICAL SURVEY DEPARTMENT.

PERMANENT STAFF.

Statement showing staff, classification, salaries, &c., for year ending June, 1892, and salaries of same officers for year ending June, 1906.

Name.	No.	Classification—1891-1892.	Salary. 1891-92.	Salary. 1905-06.	Remarks.
			$ cts.	$ cts.	
Selwyn, A. R. C. .	1	*Director and Deputy Head*	4,000 00		Superannuated.
	19	*Technical Officers.*			
Dawson, G. M.		Asst. Director and Chief Geologist.	2,250 00		Deceased.
Bell, Robt.		" "	2,250 00	2,400 00 / 3,000 00	To 1 April, 1906. / To 30 June, 1906.
Whiteaves, J. F.		Asst. Director, Palæontologist and Zoologist	2,250 00	2,650 00	
Hoffmann, G. C.		Asst. Director and Chemist	2,200 00	2,650 00	
Macoun, Jno.		Asst. Director and Botanist..	1,950 00	2,500 00	
Ells, R. W.		Geologist	1,800 00	2,400 00	
Fletcher, Hugh		"	1,800 00	2,400 00	
McConnell, R. G.		"	1,600 00	2,400 00	
Ingall, E. D.		Mining Engineer and Geologist	1,600 00	2,150 00	
Tyrrell, J. B.		Geologist	1,600 00		Resigned.
Low, A. P		"	1,350 00	2,100 00 / 3,500 00	To 31 March, 1906. / To 30 June, 1906.
Lambe, L. M.		Artist	1,350 00	1,950 00	
Chalmers, Robt.		Geologist	1,300 00	1,950 00	
Ferrier, W. F.		Lithologist	1,300 00		Resigned.
Faribault, E. R.		Asst. Geologist	1,200 00	1,950 00	
Ami, H. M.		Asst. Palæontologist	1,150 00	1,950 00	
McInnis, Wm		Geologist	1,200 00	1,950 00	
Giroux, N. J.		Asst. Geologist	1,100 00		Deceased.
Barlow, A. E.		"	1,100 00	1,900 00	
Barlow, Scott.	1	*Chief Clerk and Geographer*	1,800 00		Deceased.
Marshall, Jno.	1	*First Class Clerk and Accountant*	1,800 00	2,050 00	
	6	*Second Class Clerks.*			
Weston, T. C.		Second-Class Clerk	1,400 00		Superannuated.
Cochrane, A. S.		"	1,400 00		Deceased.
Willimott, C. W.		"	1,250 00	1,500 00	
Broadbent, R. L.		"	1,150 00	1,550 00	
Wait, F. G		"	1,162 50	1,800 00	
Brummell, H. P.		"	972 60		Resigned.
Richard, L. N.	1	*Third-Class Clerk*	1,000 00	1,300 00	
Thorburn, Jno.	1	*Librarian*	800 00	850 00	
Burke, Thos	1	*Housekeeper*	700 00		Deceased.
McKinnon, A. T.	1	*Messenger*	360 00	900 00	
	32		48,145 10		

7-8 EDWARD VII., A. 1908

GEOLOGICAL SURVEY DEPARTMENT.

PERMANENT STAFF.

Statement showing Staff, Classification, Salaries, &c., for Year ending June 30, 1906.

Name.	Number.	Classification.	Salary, 1905–06.
			$ cts.
Low, A. P.............	1	*Deputy Head and Director*, $2,100 to March 31.	2,450 00
	24	*Technical Officers.*	
Bell, Robert....	....	Assistant Director and Chief Geologist, $2,400 to March 31, $3,000 to June 30	2,550 00
Whiteaves, J. F..........		Assistant Director and Palæontologist	2,650 00
Hoffmann, G. C.............	....	„ „ and Chemist	2,650 00
Macoun, Jno.....	...	„ „ and Naturalist....	2,500 00
Ells, R. W..............	....	Geologist........	2,400 00
Fletcher, Hugh.	....	„	2,400 00
McConnell, R. G........		„	2,400 00
Ingall, E. D..		Mining Engineer and Geologist....	2,150 00
Lambe, L. M....	...	Vertebrate Palæontologist..	1,950 00
Chalmers, Robt..........		Geologist...	1,950 00
McInnes, Wm....		„	1,950 00
Ami, H. M.		Assistant Palæontologist.....	1,950 00
Faribault, E. R.	...	Geologist	1,950 00
Barlow, A. E.............		„	1,900 00
Macoun, J. M......		Assistant Botanist and Naturalist..........	1,850 00
Wait, F. G.		„ Chemist.....	1,800 00
Dowling, D. B		Geologist	1,750 00
Senecal, C. O....		Geographer and Chief Draughtsman...............	1,750 00
Johnston, R. A. A	...	Assistant Chemist...............	1,650 00
Keele, Joseph.............		Geologist	1,600 00
Brook, R. W	....	„ at $1,450 (5 mos. 5 days)..........	624 28
Wilson, W. J...........		„	1,300 00
Denis, Theo...	....	„	1,300 00
Camsell, Charles..........		„	1,150 00
Marshall, Jno.........	1	*Chief Clerk and Accountant*.................	2,050 00
	2	*First Class Clerks.*	
Broadbent, R. L..........	....	First Class Clerk.	1,550 00
Willimott, C. W........	....	„	1,500
	4	*Second Class Clerks.*	
Richard, L. N........	....	Second Class Clerk.	1,300
Prud'homme, O. E..	....	„	1,225
Robert, J. A...........	...	„	1,225
Lefebvre, J. S. H......	....	„	1,212
	2	*Junior Second Class Clerks.*	
McKinnon, A. T........	..	Junior Second Class Clerk...............	900
McGee, Jno. J., Jr.	....	„ „	850
Thorburn, Jno...	1	*Librarian*.................	850
Lyons, J. F.	1	*Caretaker*..........	800
	36		62,036

MEMO. ACCOMPANYING STATEMENT HANDED IN BY DIRECTOR, GEOLOGICAL SURVEY.

In 1891-2 the permanent staff consisted of 20 technical officers, 1 chief clerk, 1 first class, 6 second, 1 third, 1 librarian, 1 housekeeper, 1 messenger, total, 32; salaries paid, $48,145.10.

In 1905-6 the numbers were 25 technical officers, 1 chief, 2 first, 4 second, 2 junior second, 1 librarian, 1 caretaker, total 36; salaries paid, $62,036.78.

The temporary employees in 1891-2 numbered 25 and their wages amounted to $17,198.25. Twelve of the 25 were either science graduates of universities or had special qualifications for the technical work in which they were engaged.

In 1905-6 the temporary employees numbered 33 and wages paid totalled $28,169.95. Sixteen of those employees were engaged in technical or professional work.

The increase of salaries to permanent officers appointed under the Geological Survey Act, schedule A, section (b) of the Civil Service Act, by vote of parliament, are not statutory as are those appointed directly under the Civil Service Act. In most cases the usual increase has been $50, but in some special cases more.

The permanent and temporary clerks directly under the provisions of the Civil Service Act receive the usual statutory increase of $50 until their salaries reach the maximum of their respective classes.

The salaries of temporary technical clerks, draughtsmen and others having special qualifications have been increased from $50 up to $200 in some years as their length of service and ability have warranted such increases.

Promotions have, as a rule, been made from the staff employed, but the salaries are in no way adequate to the services rendered nor to those paid by outside corporations to men of equal standing and ability.

RETIRING ALLOWANCES.

Of the 36 on the permanent staff in 1905-6, 24 came under the provisions of the Superannuation Act, 11 contributed to the retirement fund, and the librarian, who was appointed when over age, is by order in council ineligible for Superannuation, not having been allowed to contribute to the fund.

RETIREMENT FUND.

This fund is most unsatisfactory and should be abolished. It is claimed much better returns can be had by the outside investment of abatements. The Superannuation Act should be revived for all permanent officers, as it would secure a moderate provision for old age or infirmity. It would be an incentive to young men to take lower salaries than they might receive for outside work.

May 23, 1907.

THE SENATE,
ROOM No. 2,
May 23, 1907.

HUGH FLEMING, Esq., B.A.,
Geological Survey,
Ottawa.

SIR,—Your communication, under date of May 16 was at the earlist moment, read before the Royal Civil Service Commission, and I have been instructed to inform you that it was highly appreciated by that body. It is, therefore, needless for me to assure you that at the hands of the commission your views so expressed shall receive the fullest consideration.

Respectfully yours,

Secretary Commission.

To the Canadian Civil Service Commission of 1907 :

GENTLEMEN :—

Taking advantage of the intimation to the public press that you would be pleased to receive communications from all interested parties in regard to matters requiring consideration in your inquiry into the condition, remuneration, &c., of civil servants, and as a former representative before the committee of 1892 and one of the witnesses called by a Committee on Geological Surveys in 1884, I beg to submit a short personal statement in advance of representations that are sure to be made by the various departments and by the Civil Service Association to which I am one of the delegates from the Geological Survey.

In 1892, the third commission appointed to investigate the conditions and needs of the Civil Service of Canada reported that there had been legislation concerning Civil Service reform about every year since Confederation, and that public opinion, specially directed to the subject by certain irregularities, had extorted a promise from the Government that the service should be conducted upon business methods.

The best efforts of the commissioners were given to arrive at correct conclusions and many improvements were suggested, some of which have been made ; yet it may be doubted whether the service has gained in efficiency since the publication of the report, and whether as they say of the Act of 1882, amendments have not rather trended in the direction of the relaxation of its provisions and the consequent prevention of its intention from being carried out.

The deputy heads and representative employees of every department were called before the commission to express their views on departmental organization, mangement and discipline, on the correction of abuses and irregularities, and the increase of the efficiency and economy of the service.

In their report the commissioners discuss at some length the constitution of the civil service, the duties of its officers, the cost of salaries and various other subjects. In the case of service of a professional character they found that from lack of organization and otherwise no definite scale of remuneration existed, and they submitted a scheme to overcome this defect. They also found numbers of persons doing the same work whose salaries differed by as wide a range as 300 per cent, of some only of whom it could be urged that the higher pay was the reward of experience, reliability and knowledge.

They noticed generally that the highest salaries are low as compared with those of the higher officers of railways, banks and other mercantile corporations, but that in the Civil Service the percentage of persons whose salaries ranged from $1,000 to $2,500 is much larger than that which obtains in other institutions, while the percentage of persons having salaries from $400 to $1,000 is much smaller.

In their recommendations the commissioners endeavoured to ensure that men doing the lower description of work shall be remunerated accordingly, while the higher range of salaries shall be reserved for those who have responsibilities of management, or whose services require a higher degree of education or professional attainments. They also fixed what in their opinion would be an equitable scale of salaries for the various classes of clerks and employees in the departments.

They referred to the experience of Great Britain in regard to the Civil Service, to the value of open competition in which there is no patronage and therefore no motive to increase establishments beyond the strength which is required for the work they have to do, but on the contrary, a very strong motive in the department themselves to keep the establishments down, so as to have the credit of economical estimates. Common justice and the exclusion of partisan tests in selecting and promoting civil servants are essential for securing those most useful. British statesmen have had patriotism and independence enough to act upon their own conviction of duty and have shown that competition has given bright men of learning, of strong physical

SESSIONAL PAPER No. 29a

system, high character and ·practical administrative capacity to the service of the country, and they quote with approval the words of a United States writer on the Civil 'Service as follows : ' The merit system, therefore, with its test of character and capacity and its claims of justice and principle against favouritism and partisanship has achieved a victory over patronage.'

Under the Canadian Civil Service it was found that political pressure had led to the departments being generally overmanned in the higher offices, promotions having taken place as a rule for other caus-s than the necessities of the service. often for the benefit of the officers rather than in the public interest. The Commissioners were strongly in favour of making the position of deputy heads more independent and of providing that they should hold office during good behaviour, and they pointed out the desirability of having in every department a recognized official to take the place of a deputy in case of emergency.

The recommendations of the committee of 1892 in a Bill drafted by them are :

(1) The appointment of a Civil Service Commission, such as was also proposed by the committee of 1881, to consist of a permanent chairman and four deputy heads, one of them a French Canadian.

(2) The adoption of the principle of appointment by open competition. It is essential that the members of such a Commission should be deputy heads with an intimate knowledge of the service necessary to arrive at just conclusions and to give confidence to the members of the service that all claims would receive consideration, be decided upon their merits, and thus tend to allay discontent.

The Commission was to closely inspect all the departments of the service, to properly distribute labour so as to avoid elementary work being done by high salaried clerks and the employment of more than the number of officers required to accomplish the work to be done, and the gradual elimination of incompetent or unnecessary clerks.

They were also to consider the hours of office work, the hours for luncheon, absence for vacation or for illness, fines for non-attendance, and the employment of temporary clerks.

It was believed that by the creation of such a Commission co-operation and *esprit de corps* would be secured and a zealous and united service ensured to the Government and the country for the conduct of public affairs. In the concluding words of the report : ' The public service at Ottawa will be better for the change. Intelligence and ·capacity will meet with their due reward, politics and favouritism will cease to dominate, the service will soon become attractive to many persons who now seek other avenues of employment, and in general the title of public servant will be an honour to be coveted. The doors to appointments and promotions in the service will open only to capacity and honesty, and no man or woman who aspires, as all have a right to aspire, to any such position, will have occasion to seek or use any influence less honourable than his or her own merit and fitness for office.'

So much for Utopia and what might have been. It is an argument as old as Plato's republic that every Government makes laws for its own advantage and when it has made them proclaims that to be just for the governed which is advantageous for themselves ; and it punishes the transgressor of this as one acting contrary both to law and justice. It has the power and what is the advantage of the more powerful, the same is just.

According to the present system the Civil Service belongs to the party in power and its members hold their positions by the favour or humanity of the victors at the polls. There is much to be said for this system, but its application has been found to produce discontent, half-hearted service and discouragement. Therefore in 1907 your committee is appointed to deal with the defective Civil Service Act and ' it is a matter of grave concern to the great body of civil servants, to whom it directly applies, and who alone understand its provisions that they should be properly heard before this commission,' one member of which at least, Mr. J. M. Courtney, trusted by both the

29a—16

Government and the civil servants, has already proved their friend and a strong advi cate of fair-play and justice.

Most of us have long felt that some such action as that suggested by Mr. Payr in regard to this Commission is necessary for the good of the public service; w would heartily welcome any action that will work to make promotions ' notwithstan. ing anything in the Civil Service Act' less frequent, and obtain for us the mark value of our work and experience. I trust that your committee will do everythis that can be done to influence public opinion and the patriotism of the Government obtain for us what has been recommended by other Commissions.

I have the honour to be, gentlemen,

Your obedient servant,

HUGH FLETCHER.

OTTAWA, May, 16, 1907.

The Staff of the Geological Survey,
    Dr. Ells, Chairman.

As a result of one or two written suggestions and a general idea of the desires the staff gained from personal conversations, your committee begs to submit the a companying memorial for presentation to the Civil Service Commission.

Should it meet with your approval either in its present or in an amended for we would suggest that it be handed to Mr. Low for his information and for transm. tal to the Civil Service Commission.

HUGH FLETCHER,
JOHN McLEISH,
        Committee.

Approved by the staff, May 28, 1907.

R. W. ELLS,
        Chairman of Committee.

MEMORIAL from the Technical Officers of the Geological Survey Department to t Civil Service Commission.

GENTLEMEN,—Taking advantage of your kind permission to present before yo honourable Commission information affecting the Civil Service, the Technical Offic of the Geological Survey desire to submit the following facts and suggestions on a f of the more important questions affecting the well-being of the staff, such as (1) a status of the technical officers; (2) methods of appointment and promotion; (3) a question of superannuation and retirement fund; (4) the inadequacy of the prese rate of remuneration paid to technical officers.

(1) There is at present no definite minimum or maximum salary nor any reas< able certainty of regular increase or promotion for the technical officers of this staff

It is the opinion of the staff that a more efficient service could be maintained a a greater certainty of attracting the best men to the staff secured were a definite ma mum salary (provided it is sufficiently high) held in view and provision made at 1 same time for a regular or increasing rate of advancement from the minimum upwa The rate of increase for this special class of service should be not less than one hur red dollars per annum, and possibly greater at the end of five or ten years.

(2) It is felt that the principle of making the pay commensurate with the servio rendered and of having all appointments and promotions based on ability, efficienc and character is the only one which will give satisfactory results, and that this prin ciple can best be attained by the removal of the whole Civil Service from the spher of political control and the abandonment by Members of Parliament of that much abused principle of local patronage.

SESSIONAL PAPER No. 29a

(3) It is felt that the abandonment by the Government of the principle of superannuation of civil servants, even though it had been much abused, was a backward step, and that some such principle of superannuation should be restored to the Civil Service. In fact, we would go even further and suggest the adoption of some principle akin to that of insurance endowment to provide that if an employee of the Government died in service, his family should receive a reasonable protection, or if he became a candidate for superannuation, he might have the privilege of accepting one of several options, such as an annuity, a stated sum, or other option that might be provided.

In this connection it is felt that the regulations governing the 'retirement fund' are much too drastic and arbitrary and that in the event of the unwillingness of the Government to restore the principle of superannuation, the regulations governing the retirement fund be so amended as to give to the beneficiaries of the fund the option of investing the moneys so deducted from their salaries in life insurance protection for the benefit of their families.

It is also felt that the rate of interest now allowed by the government on the retirement fund is too low and not commensurate with the value of money in the commercial world.

(4) With regard to the rate of remuneration paid to technical officers in this department, we may take it for granted that it is the desire of the Government to retain as far as possible the best men now on the staff and attract to the service good men from the outside, and technical graduates from our colleges.

To do this we feel that it is absolutely necessary that the present rates of pay be considerably increased.

In support of this opinion, we would call to your attention the large numbers of the experienced and capable members of the staff (see appendix) who during the past few years have resigned to accept more remunerative employment not only in private service but in other Gvoernment service, and we may say here that we do not believe it necessary on the part of the Government to meet the same level of salaries as is offered in private service in order to retain its employees. It is our opinion that a majority of the officers who have resigned in the past would have been glad to remain in the public service at salaries equivalent to from 50 to 75 per cent of those offered them to go into private employment.

This would be more especially true were the principle of superannuation restored and improved.

The Provincial Governments of British Columbia and Ontario, the Geological Survey of the United States, the Geological Survey of India all pay higher salaries for geological and affiliated work than does the Dominion of Canada. In fact, graduates from our scientific schools are now being offered salaries immediately on graduation higher than is paid in the Geological Survey Department to university men of ability who have been in the service of the government for 15 and 20 years, and who are now possessed of the experience which that length of service implies.

We append herewith a resolution adopted by the Government of India regarding the Indian Geological Survey. The first two paragraphs of this we think very appropriately describe the conditions affecting the Geological Survey of Canada.

These are some of the most important matters concerning our own department in particular and the Civil Service in general which we consider it advisable to bring to your attention,

No. 7092—7106-151.

GOVERNMENT OF INDIA—DEPARTMENT OF COMMERCE AND INDUSTRY—GEOLOGY AND MINERALS.

Resolution.

SIMLA, September 7, 1906.

The Government of India have recently had before them the question of the reorganization of the Geological Survey Department. Owing to the expansion of

29a—16½

mining enterprise in America, South Africa, Australia, and other countries, there is at present a large and growing demand for mining and geological experts. Men possessing a sound scientific education and with practical experience of mining and geological work command very high salaries. This has not been without effect on the Geological Survey Department, and it has become increasingly difficult to enlist candidates possessing a technical training. It has, in fact, become evident that the rates of pay in force are insufficient to attract the class of officers whom it is desired to secure, and that it is necessary to offer to geological officers salaries bearing a reasonable relation to the emoluments which they could obtain in the open market. The only alternative to an increase in the rates of pay would be to recruit officers, who have obtained a sound general education, but who have not received a special preparation for geological work. In that case it would be necessary to train them after their appointment to the department, a process which would not only result in a considerable loss of power, but is also open to objection inasmuch as there would be no guarantee at the time of their appointment that the candidates selected would develop the qualities and acquire the specialized knowledge which are essential to the satisfactory conduct of the work of the department. It was also found that the rates of pay were not liberal enough to retain officers after they had acquired sufficient experience to qualify them as mining and geological experts. Government were therefore threatened with the danger of losing the service of trained experts at a time when their services were absolutely indispensable.

2. Not only was a material increase in the pay of the various grades required, but also a considerable addition to the strength of the existing establishment. The rapid expansion of the economic side of the work is a new feature, and it is regarded as vitally important that all possible facilities should be given to assist the development upon a sound basis of mining industries in India. The necessity for the rapid completion of the geological survey of India has frequently been urged on the Government of India, who fully recognize the immediate scientific, and the ultimate practical, advantages of this work, but it was felt that the Geological Survey Department could not, with its existing strength, undertake the scientific work, for the performance of which it was primarily constituted, and at the same time devote that amount of attention which the interests of India now demand to purely economic inquiries.

3. Proposals for the reorganization of the department were, therefore, submitted to the Secretary of State, and have now received his approval. The following are the changes which have been made in its constitution:—

(1) Two short-term appointments of mining specialists have been abolished, and two new appointments have been added to the graded list in their place.

(2) Three new appointments have been added to the cadre to increase the strength of the department and to provide a reserve for leave vacancies.

(3) An ungraded post, to be held by a trained chemist, has been created, carrying a salary of Rs. 500 per mensem rising to Rs. 1,000 by annual increments of Rs. 50.

(4) The distinction between deputy superintendents and assistant superintendents has been abolished, and all graded officers below the rank of superintendent will be styled assistant superintendents, and will receive a monthly pay of Rs. 350, rising to Rs. 1,000 by annual increments of Rs. 30 during the first five years, and of Rs. 50 thereafter. One assistant superintendent, employed as palæontologist, will obtain, as at present, a monthly allowance of Rs. 150.

GEOLOGICAL SURVEY OF INDIA.

Annual Salaries paid previous to July, 1906.

—	Minimum.	Maximum.	Annual Increase.
	$ cts.	$ cts.	$ cts.
1 Director	5,832 00	6,998 00	223 28
3 Superintendents..	2,721 00	4,276 80	194 40
5 Deputy Superintendents.............................	1,944 00	2,721 00	155 52
5 Assistant Superintendents........................	1,360 86	1,944 00	116 64
2 Mining Specialists, not more than $3,838, not less than $2,721...			
1 Assistant Curator........................	972 00	1,360 80	

GEOLOGICAL SURVEY OF INDIA.

Annual Salaries paid since July, 1906.

—	Minimum.	Maximum.	Annual Increase.
	$ cts.	$ cts.	$ cts.
1 Director, $7,776, together with a special allowance to Mr. Holland of $1,944, making a total of $9,720....			
3 Superintendents...	3,888 00	5,443 20	311 04
15 Assistant Superintendents —			
First five years......................................	1,360 80	1,944 00	116 64
Thereafter................................	1,944 00	3,888 00	194 40
1 Chemist	1,944 00	3,888 00	194 40
1 Assistant Curator..................................	972 00	1,360 80	

(5) The scale of pay for superintendents has been fixed at Rs. 1,000 per mensem rising to Rs. 1,400 by annual increments of Rs. 80.

(6) The pay of the Director has been raised from Rs. 1,500—60—1,800 to Rs. 2,000 fixed. A personal allowance of Rs. 500 a month has been specially sanctioned for the present director, Mr. Holland, in addition to the pay of the appointment.

4. In view of the increase in the emoluments of the service, exchange compensation allowance will not be granted to future entrants into the department in addition to the rates of pay now sanctioned. As regards present incumbents, the allowance will be absorbed as soon as an officer begins to draw on the new scale higher emoluments than he would have obtained on the old scale including the allowance. Both the present director and his successors will, however, continue to draw it.

5. The revised scheme will come into force from July 1, 1906. The staff of the department as it stands after reorganization is contrasted below with the existing strength:—

	Rs.		Rs.
1 Director on.. ...	1,500—60—1,800	1 Director on.	2,000
3 Superintendents	700—50—1,100	3 Superintendents on	1,000—80—1,400
5 Deputy Superintendents on..	500—40— 700	15 Assistant Superintendents on Rs. 350— 30 — 500 for first five years and Rs. 500— 50—1,000 thereafter.	
5 Assistant Superintendents on..	350—30— 500		
2 Mining Specialists on salaries not exceeding Rs. 1,000 and not less than Rs. 700.			

	Rs.		Rs.
....		1 Chemist on..	500—50—1,000
1 Assistant Cura-		1 'Assistant Cur-	
tor on	250— 350	ator on.. ..	Rs. 250—350

6. The conditions of service in the department have been revised and are annexed to this resolution.

W. L. HARVEY,
Secretary to the Government of India.

APPENDIX.

CONDITIONS FOR INDIAN GEOLOGICAL SURVEY APPOINTMENTS.

1. The Geological Survey Department is at present constituted as follows:—

Monthly salary—Rs.

1 director	2.000
3 superintendents	1.000 rising by Rs. 80 to Rs. 1,400
15 assistant superintendents—	
For the first five years....	350 rising by Rs. 30 to Rs. 500
Thereafter..........	500 rising by Rs. 50 to Rs. 1,000
1 chemist..	500 rising by Rs. 50 to Rs. 1,000

A local allowance of Rs. 150 per mensem is granted to the officer doing the work of palæontologist at headquarters.

No allowance of the nature of exchange compensation will be given.

2. Appointments to the department are made by the Secretary of State for India. They will usually be made about July of each year, and the probable number of appointments will, if possible, be announced about two years in advance. The age of candidates should not exceed 25. Every candidate must be in sound bodily health, and will be required to satisfy the medical board at the India Office of his physical fitness in all respects to perform the duties of the Geological Survey, which involve considerable fatigue and exposure.

3. Besides a good general education, a sound education in geology is essential: a university degree and a knowledge of French or German will be regarded as important qualifications; and certificates of a high moral character will be required.

4. Candidates must also have had one or two years' practical training in mines, or in technical laboratories, as may be required by the Government of India.

5. First appointments are probationary for two years, at the end of which time the probationer, if found qualified, and continued in the department, will reckon his service for leave and pension from the date of arrival in India.

6. A first-class passage to India is given subject to the condition that its cost shall be refunded in the event of an officer resigning the service, on grounds other than certified ill-health, before the expiry of the period of probation. If, on the expiry of the period of probation, the officer's service is determined, or if he is compelled by certified ill-health to resign the service before such expiry, he will be provided with a free first-class passage back to England. Pay commences from date of arrival in India. Travelling allowances, regulated by the rules applicable to the department, are allowed at a rate calculated to cover actual expenses of tentage and locomotion.

7. Under ordinary circumstances, all assistants, unless they have special claims from previous training and experience elsewhere, will enter the department in the lowest class on a salary of Rs. 350 per mensem. This will increase annually at the rate of Rs. 30 per mensem for the first five years; thereafter at the rate of Rs. 50 per mensem until the limit of pay for the grade, viz., Rs. 1,000 per mensem, is reached; the first increase to be from the date on which the assistant shall be declared

SESSIONAL PAPER No. 29a

to have passed the ordinary examination in the language of the country by the first or lower standard, according to the general rules provided for such examinations.

8. This annual increase will, in all cases, be granted only on the certificate of the head of the department, that the assistants so recommended have proved fully deserving of the promotion by the intelligence and zeal with which their duties have been performed.

9. Promotion to the grade of superintendent will depend on qualification and merit and on the existence of vacancies in that grade. In the case of an officer who joined the department before the end of 1893, but not in the case of one who joined later, the following rule applies, viz., that he may, if especially qualified, count all service on the maximum pay of a grade toward increment in the salary of the next higher grade.

10. While local experience and training must always hold a very prominent place in estimating the position or the promotion of assistants, it must be distinctly understood that mere seniority of service, unaccompanied by proved ability and steady devotion to duty, gives no claim to promotion into the higher grades of the staff of the survey.

11. The leave, leave allowances, and pensions of officers of the department will be governed by the provisions of the civil service regulations applicable thereto. These regulations are liable to be modified by the Government of India from time to time.

OTTAWA, Thursday, June 13, 1907.

The Commission met at 2.30 o'clock, Mr. Courtney, Chairman, presiding.

Mr. FRANK PEDLEY, Deputy Superintendent General of Indian Affairs, called, sworn and examined.

By the Chairman :

. You are the Deputy Superintendent General of Indian Affairs ?—A. Yes.
. How long have you held that position ?—A. Since November 21, 1902.
What were you before that date ?—A. Superintendent of Immigration.
. You preceded Mr. Scott in that position?—A. Yes.
Q. How long were you Superintendent of Immigration ?—A. From September 1, 1897, until the date of my appointment to my present position.
Q. Had you been in the public service before that ?—A. No.
Q. I see that last year the expenditure under the control of your department was a little over $1,250,000 ?—A. Yes.
Q. You now have in the Indian trust fund to the credit of the several tribes a balance of $5,378,000, or you had at the time the statement was compiled?—A. Yes.
Q. How many agencies have you got outside of Ottawa?—A. I cannot tell you off-hand. We have a large number.
Q. And you have about 50 employees in the department inside ?—A. Between 50 and 60. We have a total staff in our service of about 1,100, including doctors and school teachers.
Q. What salary do you receive for administering this department ?—A. $4,000.
Q. What does the Indian population number throughout the Dominion ?—A. About 110,000.
Q. Is the Indian population increasing or decreasing ?—A. About holding its own ; it varies a little either way from year to year. We have from 15,000 to 20,000 Indians who are outside the regular jurisdiction of the department, outside of what we call treaty limits, so our figures as to the number are not absolutely correct.

By Mr. Fyshe :

Q. Have you anything to do with the other Indians at all ?—A. We render them relief when the necessity is brought to our attention.
Q. You have no continuous machinery for looking after them?—A. No.

By the Chairman :

Q. There are five chief clerks in the department ?—A. Yes.

By Mr. Fyshe :

Q. Are the Indians pretty healthy?—A. Yes, fairly so.

By the Chairman :

Q. Mr. Bray, what are his duties ?—A. He is the chief surveyor.
Q. He surveys the Indian lands ?—A. Yes, or arranges for them.
Q. Mr. McLean is the secretary of the department?—A. Yes.
Q. Mr. McLean is an officer of 30 odd years' standing?—A. About that, I think. He was appointed in 1876.

Q. What are Mr. Orr's duties?—A. He is clerk in charge of the Lands Branch.

Q. You promoted him from first-class clerk to chief clerk ?—A. Yes.

Q. What are Mr. Page's duties ?—A. He is acting as assistant accountant.

Q. When was he made assistant accountant?—A. I should say from one to two years ago.

Q. Mr. Scott is the accountant ?—A. Yes.

Q. He has been in the service since the year 1880 ?—A. Since 1879 or 1880, if my memory serves me right.

Q. And what is Mr. Stewart ?—A. He is the assistant secretary.

Q. He also has been a very long time in the employ of the government ?—A. He was appointed temporarily in 1878 and made permanent in 1879.

Q. Are the six chief clerks doing chief clerks' work or have any of them been doing the same work as they were before they were promoted ?—A. They are all doing about the same work that they were doing before they were promoted. Some of them have been promoted in my time and others before.

Q. Those promoted in your time are doing the same work as they were before promotion ?—A. Yes, practically.

Q. What was the reason of the promotion ?—A. In one or two cases vacancies occurred in the senior clerkships, and the promotions were made to fill those vacancies.

Q. Although the men were doing the same work ?—A. Yes, practically the same work.

Q. The character of the work has not increased in importance ?—A. Not in those special cases. Of course, I think I am safe in saying that the work of the department is increasing in a general way.

Q. Then you have seven first-class clerks ?—A. Yes.

Q. Are they immediately under the chief clerks ?—A. Yes, they are under the chief clerks where they are attached to the branches, but we have one or two officers, first-class clerks, who are not attached to any particular branch, as for instance, Mr. Ross. Of course, Mr. Ross looks after the translation and printing of any documents that are ordered by the department and takes charge of the annual report. He is a first-class clerk now but is not attached to any particular branch.

Q. Then you have twelve second-class clerks ?—A. Yes.

Q. And twenty-five junior second-class clerks ?—A. I presume so, if that is the number given in the Civil Service list.

Q. You have no third-class clerks ?—A. We have no third-class clerks.

Q. But you have nine temporary clerks ?—A. Yes.

Q. Those temporary clerks, with the exception of Graham and one messenger are all women ?—A. Yes.

Q. A large number of your junior second-class clerks are women ?—A. Quite a number. I should say, speaking from memory, one-half and probably more are women, but the Civil Service list will show that.

Q. Do you find now a falling off in the number of men applying to enter the service as third-class or junior second-class clerks ?—A. I could not say that there is a falling off, but the number of applicants for positions is greater among women than among men.

Q. Considerably greater ?—A. Yes.

Q. I suppose, as in the case of other departments you have lots of applications on file ?—A. Quite a number.

Q. Is the fact that the salary of a third-class clerk upon entering the service is only $500 detrimental to encouraging good men to come in ?—A. I am rather inclined to think that it is.

Q. On the other hand $500 is rather an encouragement to women to enter the service ?—A. I am not in a position to speak accurately as to that. The avenues of employment probably are not so numerous for women in this world, and they are willing to enter the service at $500 and take their chance in regard to increase of salary and promotion.

Q. Do not women in brokers' and lawyers' offices, as a rule, receive from $250 to $300 salary?—A. I cannot say as to the girls in brokers' offices, but as to lawyers' offices, the stenographers and typewriters of the other sex will earn from $4 to $8 and $10 and probably $12 a week.

Q. That is from $250 to $500, depending on their ability?—A. Of course I am speaking now of what I knew myself some eight or ten years ago. There may have been an advance in their remuneration since then.

Q. In view of the large number of women in the junior divisions of your department, when the time comes for the senior clerks to retire, how are you going to replace them from the junior members of the staff?—A. Under the law as it now stands we could only do it by promotion or by special resolution of the House or else the position to be filled is one of a technical or professional character.

Q. When Mr. Campbell, Mr. Kent, or any of the senior clerks retire, how are you going to replace them if you have nothing but women?—A. They will have to be replaced by women if no one else is available; you must get somebody to do the work.

Q. Do you find that women can do first-class work as a rule?—A. I find that in the classes occupied by women at present, generally speaking, the work is done satisfactorily.

Q. But in the higher classes, do you think they would be able to do the work as well as men?—A. We have one or two ladies in our department who are capable, I think, of doing the high-grade work.

Q. No doubt. All over the service there are exceptional women, but as a body do you think women will be able to take the higher positions?—A. I am not prepared to say offhand that they are not. My own view—it may be a prejudice—would be rather to have the superior positions filled by men.

Q. It is not prejudice, it is the result of observation?—A. It is the result, very largely, I think, of the experience that the superior positions have hitherto been filled by men and not by women.

By Mr. Fyshe:

Q. You are in favour of that?—A. I am not opposed to it. Of course the proper principle would be if a woman is capable of filling a position she should get it. I do not see why she should be discriminated against because she is a woman.

Q. But bearing in mind the control of the office and the maintenance of discipline, do you not think a woman is as well fitted for the position as a man?—A. I think the chances are in favour of the man.

By the Chairman:

Q. We have no prejudice against women as women, it is only for the general efficiency of the service that we are asking these questions?—A. When I used the word 'prejudiced' I used it not in the extreme sense. Our views have been moulded so largely by experience, that it becomes a fixed view that we prefer men to ladies in these cases.

Q. Do your temporary clerks pass the Civil Service examination?—A. Yes.

Q. And the junior second-class clerks also?—A. Yes, they have all passed, except in one or two cases, where we have professionals. The architect, Mr. Ogilvie, is a professional man.

Q. Mr. R. L. Ogilvie?—A. Yes.

Q. Is he in the second-class?—A. Yes.

Q. But the junior second-class clerks and the temporary clerks have passed the Civil Service examination?—A. Yes.

Q. Of course passing the Civil Service examination implies that the candidates are of the proper age, are healthy and of good moral conduct?—A. Yes.

Q. They are appointed on probation?—A. Yes, I think that is a matter of law.

Q. And at the end of the period you give a certificate that they are worthy of employment?—A. Yes, their engagement being confirmed they become permanent.

Q. You have recently had some promotions? There were promotions to two first-class clerks? Did the persons promoted pass the promotion examination under the Civil Service Act?—A. In one of the cases, the man had passed the Civil Service examination, and in the other, I think the passing of the examination was waived. The officer had been for a long time in the public service, was thoroughly efficient, and it was not considered necessary that he should pass the promotion examination.

Q. Was he a barrister, attorney, draughtsman or land surveyor?—A. No.

Q. Well how was the examination waived?—A. I am not quite sure. He may have had a special examination on the duties of office, but the ordinary promotion examination as to the three R's was waived.

Q. But in all matters relating to the department and to his knowledge of the department, the clerk passed the promotion examination?—A. I think I am safe in answering that in the affirmative. There is only one case, I think, where that may not be so, but even that man passed a special examination.

Q. You say the Indian population is about stationary?—A. Yes.

Q. Your staff has increased from 47 in 1892 to 66 in 1906, the staff chargeable to Civil Government? What is the cause of that increase?—A. Our work is increasing very much.

Q. What was the nature of the increase?—A. We conduct a great deal more work amongst the Indians than formerly; that necessitates an increase of work at the head office. We spend a lot of time and money in trying to bring these Indians into a better state of living and that means voluminous correspondence and detailed management.

Q. Have the Indians become in a sense civilized? That is to say, at the time treaties are made do they require extra care and extra thought until they become developed like the Six Nation Indians, when they are practically freed from control? Probably when they are in an undeveloped state they require more care than when they are developed?—A. Immediately following the treaty a certain care has to be exercised, or a certain kind of oversight. As they become more civilized and adopt working habits, and so on, the system of management changes. If you compare our expenditures you will find, I think, that our management expenses have increased but our expenses for relief and rationing expenses have decreased. In other words, our policy is leading to larger expenditures for management but to less expenditure for the keep of Indians.

Q. And in the generations to come, when the land gets settled and parts of the reserve are sold and formed into a land management fund, the expenses chargeable to the Federal Treasury will decrease?—A. That is the object we are looking forward to, when the Indian will be practically self-supporting. Of course, so long as the Indian lives in a tribal way and remains in the communal state, there will be more or less expenditure by the Government. If they became enfranchised, of course, and were placed in the same status as white men, our care for them would practically cease.

Q. When that time came, you would only have the agents on the reserves?—A. As soon as they became enfranchised the reserves would cease to be, and the agents would disappear.

By Mr. Fyshe:

Q. Do you think there is a prospect of their becoming self-supporting as citizens?—A. Yes, there is no doubt about it. A great many of them are self-supporting now.

Q. And they show capacity to take in civilized ideas?—A. Yes.

By the Chairman:

Q. Going back to the clerks chargeable to Civil Government, for one minute. All these junior second and third-class clerks are appointed by the Minister after passing the Civil Service Examination?—A. Yes.

7-8 EDWARD VII., A. 1908

Q. How do you find out when a new official is needed?—A. If it is a case of a vacancy, that is known as soon as the vacancy arises, or is about to arise. When you are going to add to the number of clerkships, that is generally done upon the representation of the officer in charge of a branch, or it may arise from the fact that the deputy himself, after a general survey of the work of the department, feels that one or two more clerks should be added. The recommendation is laid before the Minister and if he agrees the financial provision is made and the necessary steps taken to make the appointment.

Q. You examine into it yourself before you make a recommendation to the Minister for the appointment of a new clerk or the filling of a vacancy? You examine into the necessity also of filling up a vacancy?—A. Yes. As I have to be responsible to the Minister, for the recommendation, I must satisfy myself that I have good grounds for the faith that is in me.

Q. You send to the Treasury Board a statement as to the people you consider it desirable should have the annual increment?—A. Yes.

Q. In the case of promotions, did you ever look at the Civil Service Act?—A. Yes.

Q. In sections 46 and 47, it is stated in the one case that where an appointment has to be made the head of the department shall select, and in the other case the head of the department may reject? Should that not be on the advice of the deputy minister?—A. I would naturally think that in the case of a promotion the deputy minister should make a report or should give his opinion. He having, under the statute and under the practice, general charge of the department, subject, of course, to the direction of the Minister.

Q. As a matter of fact, in making promotions, you do submit the recommendations?—A. Yes.

Q. To make the matter clear, do you consider that it would be desirable to amend those two sections by adding the words 'on the advice of the deputy minister' or something to that effect?—A. As far as my experience goes the practice has been that the deputy is consulted. I do not know whether it would be wise to make the promotions depend absolutely upon the recommendation of a deputy minister.

Q. Well, we will be glad to hear your views as to that?—A. I think it would be wisdom on the part of the Minister to consult some one who has a practical knowledge of the working of the department in making a promotion.

By Mr. Fyshe:

Q. Do you not think that the deputy should have a keener sense of responsibility for the conduct of his department than the political head?—A. It is quite possible that he has a keener sense of responsibility.

Q. He must necessarily, if his heart is in his work, feel sure as to what should be done, and should be prepared to advise the political head to that effect?—A. And so he does, but the political head may relieve the deputy of the responsibility and assume it himself.

Q. Is that advisable?—A. I should say from the general run of cases it would not be advisable.

By the Chairman:

Q. In the matter of appointments no appointment can be made except on the report of the deputy minister, and the same with regard to the annual increment. Why, in the case of promotions, should the deputy minister be ignored?—A. I think it is advisable that he should be consulted.

By Mr. Fyshe:

Q. I will go further than that and say that the promotions will depend upon his initiative?—A. The deputy would initiate it. He would make a report to the head of the department that a vacancy has occurred and submit a recommendation to the Minister.

Q. The initiative should be taken by the deputy minister and he should feel that the responsibility rests on his shoulders and not on the political head?—A. That is correct, but whether it should be made a matter of law, so that the head of the department should not make a promotion unless the deputy consented, is a different thing.

By the Chairman:

Q. We might say 'on the report of the deputy head?'—A. So far as that section is concerned, it might possibly be amended so as to harmonize with the section providing for statutory increases.

Q. We will now come to another matter. You have no third-class clerks?—A. No.

Q. You are aware that all appointments are made at the minimum of the class concerned?—A. Yes.

Q. The salary of third class clerks ranges from $500 to $700 and that of junior second-class clerks from $800 to $1,100?—A. Yes.

Q. If there was a little latitude enabling appointments to be made above the minimum in the third-class clerks, do you think you would be able to appoint more third-class clerks, and less junior second-class clerks? Supposing, for example, you were able to appoint at $600 or $700?—A. Of course there would be the inducement of the increase you would be able to offer above the minimum. The question is whether the range is large enough to make it attractive, as between $500 and $700, for the class of applicants, or seekers, for employments in the Civil Service, who would not take the position at $500.

Q. That is just what I am coming to, too. Do you not think it would lead to economy if there was a little latitude allowed in regard to the salary of the first appointment?—A. Well, I am not quite sure how it works out from the standpoint of economy.

Q. It cannot be done now because you must appoint at the minimum?—A. Yes.

Q. You have 25 junior second-class clerks, but you have no second-class clerks? If you could appoint at $600 or $700 instead of $500, would you not have less women in the junior second-class clerkships?—A. It comes down to the question of whether the power of raising the minimum salary on appointment from $500 to $700 would be a sufficient inducement to bring in the men. I am not very sure on that point. I think the higher you can increase the salary above $500 the better chance you have of attracting the men. Of course the Government can create third-class clerkships if it wants to.

Q. You have eleven temporary clerks paid from the civil government contingencies?—A. Yes.

Q. With the exception of one messenger and a man called Graham, they are all women? Have they been there long?—A. I think the majority of them have been appointed in the past five years.

Q. You propose to make them permanent?—A. I suppose I am entitled to state to this Commission that I recommended that the temporary clerkships be converted into third-class clerkships, so that we could promote, but the matter was not disposed of by the Government in that way. Having in view the work of the Commission, I do not know whether that is a subject for publication. It is for the Commission themselves to say.

Q. What leave of absence do you give your staff?—A. Three weeks.

Q. You grant a little latitude if a man has done good work and has got a distance to go on his vacation?—A. Yes.

Q. You would give them another week or so?—A. I think the deputy has a certain amount of discretion.

Q. Naturally in the government of his office he would?—A. Yes.

Q. Have you an attendance book in the department?—A. We have.

Q. Is that kept by yourself?—A. That is not kept by myself, but it is revised by myself periodically.

Q. You do not initial the book daily?—A. No, that is done by the secretary of the department.

Q. How do the clerks sign?—A. They sign in the morning.

Q. That is all the law compels them to do?—A. Yes.

Q. They do not sign the attendance book going out and returning from luncheon. and going out in the evening?—A. I believe they could beat the department if they signed four times a day. I do not believe it is a protection to sign every hour or two hours.

Q. What are the office hours?—A. From half-past nine until four.

Q. In the session, is there any additional work?—A. No.

Q. Your officers, if there is any demand upon them, stay after office hours?—A. Generally the heads of branches remain until half-past four or five. The main object with me is to get the work done.

By Mr. Fyshe:

Q. I suppose none of the staff are apt to break down from nervous exhaustion?—A. They do occasionally break down from nervous exhaustion, not so much from the work as from its nature. There is nothing in the world that breaks a man down more than working in the Civil Service.

By the Chairman:

Q. What are the luncheon hours?—A. About an hour and a quarter.

Q. Is the department always open to the public?—A. The public have the right to go through the department.

Q. During the luncheon hour is the department entirely closed?—A. No, somebody is there.

Q. There is somebody there to keep in touch with the public?—A. Yes.

Q. Are all your offices in one building?—A. Yes.

Q. You have no outside offices?—A. No.

Q. Your department, when I visited it some years ago, had very valuable records, the minute-books of the Indian Commissioner at Albany at the beginning of the eighteenth century. Are those books there yet, or have they been sent to the Archives?—A. The records not required for the work of the department have, I think, during the past year been transmitted to the Archives, under an Order in Council that was passed some time ago.

Q. Your department has the Indian records since the conquest?—A. It has records dating back, not to the dawn of time, but pretty far back.

Q. Dating back to 1759, for instance?—A. Yes.

Q. And before the States became independent the Indian Commissioner at Albany reported here?—A. Yes.

Q. What have you done with the valuable treaties, the Wampum, Belts, signatures and things like that? Where are those kept?—A. The treaties, unless some of them have been sent to the Archives, are kept by the department in a vault.

Q. Would it not be better to send them down to the Archives? You would not have to refer to them?—A. Well, at this particular juncture, we are having our book of treaties reprinted, that is a whole set of documents that we are holding, until the work of rewriting and comparing is through. After that they can be sent to the Archives or anywhere the Government orders.

Q. You are acquainted, I suppose, with the Treasury Board minute, promulgated in 1879, about the use of political influence in connection with the appointments or promotions?—A. Yes.

Q. Are the recently appointed officials in your department aware of it?—A. It was passed in 1879, and I think revived within the past ten years. I heard about it when I came into the service, and I think that most of the officials know about it.

Q. Do you find that your staff in their desire for promotion and advancement pass you by and go to the political head? All people naturally want to get on, you know?— A. So far as my recollection serves, I think that most applicants for promotion have come to me direct, and they have been frank enough to ask me if I had any objections to their going to the Minister. I told them so.

Q. Are you under the Superannuation Act or the Retirement Fund?—A. Under the Superannuation Act.

Q. You were lucky enough to come in before the Act was abolished. What is your opinion regarding the abolition of that Act?—A. My opinion is that the superannuation system is susceptible of a good deal of modification for the benefit of the service.

By Mr. Fyshe:

Q. But it should not have been abolished unless a better system was substituted?— A. No doubt the Government substituted what it thought was better. I do not think the Superannuation Act should have been abolished if it turns out that the Act substituted is a worse one than the one the Government did away with.

By the Chairman :

Q. The present Act provides simply for the deduction of a man's own money ?— A. Yes.

Q. Is that a better system than the former one, do you think ?—A. I should say not for those who enter the service with the object of remaining in it for the rest of their natural lives, and until such time as they will be allowed to retire.

Q. Is it not desirable that persons entering the public service should be encouraged to remain ?—A. I should think so.

Q. If that is the case is it not desirable that some kind of Superannuation or Pension Act should be placed on the statute-book ?—A. I should think so.

Q. Then the abolition of the Superannuation Act tends to instability of the service ?—A. That would appear to be a reasonable deduction.

Q. Then you think it is desirable in some way or other to place on the statute-book a Superannuation Act and in some respects probably, to make it a Pension Act for others than the recipients ?—A. I think so.

Q. Say the widows and orphans of the civil servants, for instance?—A. Widows and others who depend upon the widows. I think the pension should not die with the wage-earner.

Q. Have you anything more to add with respect to the Civil Service Act ? In what way could that Act be amended or improved ?—A. There is this one thing about the Act which strikes me as rather unfortunate, at least so far as our department is concerned : We cannot appoint junior second-class clerkships now—we have to appoint to second class clerkships—and we cannot promote from the ranks of temporary clerks. We have several vacancies in the junior second-class clerkships and cannot fill them until we have third-class clerks appointed, or the Act is changed, or else do it by special Act of Parliament.

Q. Do you think the gradation of classes under the Civil Service Act is good for the Civil Service ? Do you pay any attention to the classes ?—A. I have thought that the classes might be reduced in number.

Q. Would your idea be to have a permanent high class and a lower copying class? You say you would reduce the number ?—A. The number of classes.

Q. Perhaps you had better exemplify what you mean ?—A. We now have chief clerks, first, second, junior second and third-class clerks, and temporary clerks—six classes.

Q. How would you reduce them ?—A. I should think chief clerks, and first and second-class clerks, with a minimum salary, would fill the bill.

By Mr. Fyshe :

Q. Do you mean that you could dispense with some of your staff if the others worked harder ?—A. No, I do not say that. The number of officials in the department would be regulated by its requirements, but the number of classes that these officials are composed of is a theoretical thing made up by the Government. They can make a dozen classes if they like, but there would not be any more officials than would be required for the work.

By the Chairman :

Q. Is your staff more than abundant for the work of the department ?—A. I think not. I think the staff is just about right. We try to get things so that the staff will do the work and do it well. Our department is kept up pretty well to the mark.

Q. Have you any persons on the inside service whose retention in office you consider undesirable, from bad habits or otherwise ?—A. I have no one in mind now that would come within that class.

Q. You have Indian agents scattered all over the Dominion ?—A. Yes.

Q. How are these Indian agents appointed ?—A. They are appointed in practice in the same way as those who are officials under the Civil Service Act are.

Q. Except that they pass no examination of any kind ?—A. Except they pass no examination, but the head of the department makes the appointment. The employees are summed up in the Civil Service list by provinces. You have the Ottawa list first and then the others.

Q. Take the case of the Indian agent at Sarnia, does the member for West Lambton send in the nomination ?—A. It just depends what Government is in power. The gentleman holding the patronage is asked to nominate a man to fill the position.

Q. And the same thing would happen at Belleville, Brantford and other places ?—A. Yes, all round.

Q. These agents receive public moneys from the sales of land and that kind of thing ?—A. Most of our agents, or practically all of them now, are paid a salary with no other remuneration.

Q. They receive public moneys ?—A. They handle public moneys for transmission to Ottawa ?

Q. Do they give bonds ?—A. They do.

Q. Bonds of guarantee companies or personal bonds ?—A. Both. That is to say, some give a personal bond and others give a guarantee company bond. I think the majority now give bonds of guarantee companies; I am only speaking from memory. It is not obligatory on the department to take guarantee company bonds or to reject them. If the agent gets a substantial security in the shape of an individual we will take him.

Q. Are those bonds kept in your department ?—A. They are passed upon by the Department of Justice and then they are kept by us.

By Mr. Bazin:

Q. How do you fix the salary of these agents ? I see that a Mr. Cameron is getting $1,500 ?—A. He is, or rather was, a superintendent. He died a short time ago.

By the Chairman:

Q. He was in charge of a large band, the Six Nation Indians ?—A. The largest single band in the Dominion, numbering 4,300.

By Mr. Bazin:

Q. It depends upon the number of the Indians and the size of the district ?—A. Some of the agents have a large number of bands.

Q. I see in Quebec very small salaries are paid, for instance, $150, $200, $300, $100. Is the payment of larger salaries to other agents due to the fact that they have a larger district?—A. It is due to that. The agents whose salaries you have quoted have very little work in comparison with some of our agencies which require the undivided attention of the agent from morning till night.

By the Chairman:

Q. Are these teachers appointed to the Indian schools qualified?—A. If we can get qualified teachers we take them in preference to those who are not qualified. I think most of them have some form of qualification.

By Mr. Fyshe:

Q. What is the qualification, that they should be able to speak the Indian language?—A. No, we do not teach the Indian language. We teach English, and in the province of Quebec, French. I think in most of the schools the English language is taught exclusively. That would be the only language other than the Indian that would be in evidence. Of course in the province of Quebec, where the French language is more commonly used, that language is taught, because you have to accommodate the teaching to the pupils.

Q. Are any scholars throughout the country making a study of these Indian languages?—A. There are some, but we do not hear of very many. There are some who give a little attention to these languages, but it is not very much in evidence in the department.

By the Chairman:

Q. The management of the Indians in Manitoba and the Northwest cost $855,000, made up chiefly of schools, $345,000; annuities, $141,000, and the general expenses, $170,000. Contributions for agricultural implements, seed and live stock, are rapidly falling away?—A. Those are contributions by the Government?

Q. Yes?—A. They vary from year to year.

Q. But the value of the agricultural implements supplied to all the Indians in Manitoba and the Northwest Territories amounted to only $6,000 last year?—A. You have to draw a line of distinction between what was given to the Indians as a stipulation of the treaty and what was given to the Indians as an assistance by the department.

By Mr. Fyshe:

Q. To keep them from starving?—A. Not to keep them from starving, but to enable them to work to a self-supporting condition.

Q. Do you give them implements as applied for?—A. No. We give them implements when we think the merits of the case would justify it. Then again, a good deal of the money that is spent in the purchase of implements and live stock is money belonging to the Indians themselves, realized from the sale of part of their lands.

By the Chairman:

Q. All that $855,000 was spent in Manitoba and the Northwest by the federal Government?—A. Yes.

By Mr. Fyshe:

Q. Is there any truth in the rumours in the newspapers that the Indians are trying to hold up the Grand Trunk Pacific in connection with the purchase of land for the western terminus?—A. I do not think so. We have no official notification to that effect. They are quite anxious to get the money and willing to take it when it arrives here.

Q. The money that was originally agreed upon?—A. Yes.

Q. It was stated by the newspapers that the Indians repudiated their agreement with the company and wanted double the money?—A. No.

29a—17

By the Chairman :

Q. How many farms have you now in Manitoba and the Northwest ?—A. I could not tell you.

Q. You have farmers in charge of each of these farms ?—A. We have what we call farm instructors.

Q. Are they appointed in the same way as the agents ?—A. There is a little more latitude allowed to the deputy heads and sometimes to the inspectors. Where they want a farm instructor for a month or two we tell them to go and appoint a new man. Running through all this is the restriction that these appointments should be made conformable to the views of the gentlemen who hold the patronage. That of course is a sort of cardinal principle which is observed.

Q. In Manitoba and the Northwest you expended out of the public treasury last year $150,000 in supplies for the destitute. Are the destitute Indians increasing or decreasing in number ?—A. They are decreasing.

Q. The Indians are becoming more self-supporting and do not take supplies ?— A. We are cutting down the rations by leaps and bounds. I fancy it was thought that feeding the Indians was cheaper than war.

Q. Then on the whole the Indians are undergoing a betterment in the Northwest ?—A. Very much so.

Q. I suppose the same thing is happening in British Columbia ?—A. The British Columbia Indian is of an entirely different stripe. There are no treaties with the Indians in that province.

Q. You apparently gave nothing to destitute Indians in British Columbia ?—A. Apparently very little. We do give a little relief.

Q. You call it relief ? I see there is a sum of $7,000 for that purpose. Do your Indians now wander about the Territories or are they becoming settled on reserves ? —A. Settled on reserves ; they wander about very little. Of course they visit each other occasionally.

Q. Do they cross the international border now and involve us in international trouble ?—A. No, they very seldom cross the international boundary.

Q. You will supply us with a number of the employees of your department in the outside service ?—A. Yes.

Q. Do you think the employees of your department should be brought in and made permanent ?—A. I have thought that matter over and I have been unable to discover why there should be such a line of distinction drawn between the so-called inside men and the so-called outside men. I think something should be done for the outside official who is giving just as valuable service as the inside official and who is devoting his life to the service. I think there ought to be some way of working it out so that a man of that class should be provided for.

By Mr. Fyshe :

Q. If there is any difference it should be as between those who give their whole time to the service and those who only give a part of their time ?—A. Yes.

By the Chairman :

Q. You have a certain number of inspectors continually travelling about ?—A. Yes.

Q. Do they receive as travelling expenses simply their out-of-pocket expenses ?— A. Their actual living and travelling expenses.

Q. They have no per diem allowance ?—A. No.

Q. Then presumably they lose money if they travel ?—A. That is what they say ; I do not know whether they do or not.

Q. You occasionally go to British Columbia and other provinces? You have been away once or twice?—A. Yes.

Q. Did you have a per diem allowance?—A. I had only one per diem allowance since I joined the service. I was money out of pocket when I was travelling.

Q. When you were travelling you were always money out of pocket?—A. I never could see any chance of getting rich by travelling.

Q. But the inspectors who do the inspecting?—A. There ought to be a check on the inspectors as well as the agents, I suppose.

Q. You would desire as a matter of policy, that your inspectors should be always on their rounds?—A. The inspector should be on the rounds sufficient to get a thorough knowledge of the work of his inspectorate. Of course, there are certain seasons in the year when travelling is practically a waste of time. As a general rule, however, the inspectors should be moving around sufficiently to thoroughly acquaint themselves with a condition of their inspectorates.

Q. It is no encouragement for an inspector to go around when he is losing money?—A. No.

Q. Do you think some arrangement should be made by which an inspector should be encouraged to do his duty?—A. I am still of the opinion that the responsibility very largely rests with the department as to the work the inspectors should do. It should demand from their inspectors a return from the different points of the inspectorate so that the department can be satisfied from the information which it gets that the work is being done.

Q. You are aware that for probably three-quarters of a century there has been built up an Indian land benefit fund?—A. Yes.

Q. Take the Batchewanas, Six Nation Indians and Chippewas, whenever land or timber is sold ten per cent of the purchase money is put aside for the expenses of management, and the balance is credited to the fund?—A. That ten per cent reduction applies to all lands now wherever sold.

Q. The balance now in the Indian land management fund is about $180,000?—A. Yes.

Q. And as the whole of the Indian reserves come upon a cash basis, the fund will be built up so that it will maintain probably the whole of the expenditures of the Indian department?—A. It will be reaching that way. It is supposable that at no distant date the Indian department will be self-supporting.

Q. The trust funds of the several bands which have been built up by sales of land and other things amount to pretty nearly $5,000,000 now?—A. Yes.

Q. It was built up long before confederation, and six per cent was allowed by agreement?—A. Yes.

Q. On half a million or so. That was capitalized at confederation, and five per cent was taken as the basis of agreement?—A. Yes.

Q. Since then the sums that accumulate get the savings bank rate of interest?—A. They get the government rate of interest.

Q. Three per cent. Out of these trust funds you pay the expenditure for the agents and schools connected with each band. Take the Batchewana Indians. There was an expenditure of $3,190 for the purpose?—A. Out of the management fund we pay certain expenses in Ontario and Quebec.

Q. You will do the same by and by when the reserves are sold in the Northwest, I suppose?—A. I fancy so. I fancy we are leading up to it, but we have not reached that stage yet.

Q. But in the older Provinces you pay out of the trust funds of the Indians the salaries of the agents, schools, &c.?—A. We pay the salaries of our agents in Ontario out of the land management fund. Take, for instance, the Six Nation Indians; they pay the running expense of the superintendency practically out of their own particular band funds.

Q. They have a capital of nearly a million dollars. They are settled in and around Brantford and have got a large available capital. Then when the Indians be-

29a—17½ .

7-8 EDWARD VII., A. 1908

come a civilized community and these lands are realized on as in the case of the Six Nations, there will be no charge to the federal treasury on behalf of the Indians?—A. Except the annuities under the treaties. That will apply then, but there will always be Indians on the outskirts of civilization that will be more or less of a charge on the government.

Q. These trust funds are continually increasing?—A. Yes.

Q. Certain of the tribes in the Northwest are already beginning to establish trust funds?—A. Yes. They surrendered their lands to the Crown to be sold. We sell the lands for the Indians and after making the usual deductions, fund the balance for their benefit.

By Mr. Fyshe :

Q. Have you got an exact record of everything?—A. Of everything. We keep an exact record of every Indian under treaty.

By the Chairman :

Q. And you keep an exact account of these several bands?—A. Yes, we have several thousand individual accounts.

Q. Do you know how many accounts there are under the Indian trust fund ? There are several pages of them in the Auditor General's Report?—A. We probate all their wills and administer all their estates; we are a regular surrogate court.

By Mr. Fyshe :

Q. Of course the Indians are the nation's wards?—A. They are the nation's wards in a sense. They claim, in some cases, to be allies not subjects.

By the Chairman

Q. The Auditor General's Report, besides giving a summary of the balances to the credit of each of the funds, sets forth particulars showing the capital account and interest account of each particular tribe. Take the Chippewas, for instance. Their capital amounts to about $40,000. They distribute as a matter of interest $2,378. That went partly towards the support of a medical officer and the schools? —A. Yes.

Q. That is the usage with all these trust funds, as a rule?—A. Yes.

Q. You were in the happy condition last year of having no correspondence with the Auditor General?—A. He has trouble enough with the white men; he does not want to encounter the Indians. We have had no supplementary estimates for our current year for a few years except this year, when we had to vote a sum in connection with the Babine Indian troubles, and one or two other small items. We run our department up to the nines.

Q. Your department now is becoming a matter of steady daily grind ?—A. I think we are the fourth largest department in the government service as regards expenditure.

Q. You forget the Department of Railways and Canals, the Public Works Department, the Marine and Fisheries Department, the Post Office Department and the Department of the Interior?—A. We handle about $6.000.000 to $7,000,000 every year.

By Mr. Fyshe :

Q. Do you ever visit the Indian bands yourself?—A. Yes.

Q. The more distant ones?—A. In British Columbia and Nova Scotia; I have visited the Indians in both extremes.

By the Chairman :

Q. Almost all the Indian bands now are under treaty?—A. The bands of Ontario, Manitoba, Saskatchewan and Alberta are all under treaty. In the maritime provinces, Quebec and British Columbia there are no treaties.

SESSIONAL PAPER No. 29a

Q. Well, have they certain reserves?—A. The reserves in the maritime provinces were set aside in the early days, before Confederation, and handed over to us in 1867.

By Mr. Fyshe :

Q. Are there any reserves in Nova Scotia?—A. Lots of them. Twenty-five or thirty in Nova Scotia. Some time ago I was down and dug one of them up which was lost and fined a lumberman $600 for trespassing on the property of our Indians up at Ship Harbour.

Q. Are the existing Indians in this country a mere fraction of their predecessors, say 100 or 200 years ago?—A. They about hold their own. I do not know what their numbers were in Nova Scotia a hundred years ago, but elsewhere they seem to be holding their own. I do not think the Indian population of this country was ever very large.

Q. You do not allow them to have whiskey?—A. That does not come into the form of relief we grant them. I fancy they get it all the same.

By the Chairman :

Q. You made a new treaty, did you not, with the British Columbia Indians?—A. The British Columbia Indians never entered into a treaty.

Q. I thought you were in British Columbia making a treaty with them?—A. No.

By Mr. Fyshe :

Q. Is there any advantage to the Indians in having a treaty ?—A. I think so. To this extent: Their rights are defined and you know where they are.

Q. That must involve an assumption of responsibility by the Canadian Government to some extent?—A. We have just as much responsibility in British Columbia, practically, as we have anywhere else.

Q. You assume it but you are not by law bound to do so?—A. We are bound by the constitution to look after these Indians.

By the Chairman:

Q. What I was trying to get at is this: In the development and evolution of the Dominion the Indians are becoming settled and treaties are being made. Is there anything unsettled in regard to the Indians in the Northwest and British Columbia or have all the tribes nearly come in under agreement?—A. In British Columbia all of the tribes have received their allotment of land practically.

Q. They get an allotment of land?—A. Yes, under an arrangement made by the federal and provincial Governments to which the Indians were not a party.

By Mr. Fyshe:

Q. What kind of lands were allotted to them?—A. They have, it is alleged, the finest land in British Columbia. They knew where to get the land all right and they selected the best of it.

Q. Timber land?—A. Timber land, grazing land, fruit land, farm land and fishing grounds. They have got the pick of the land in British Columbia; at least so say the white people who think some of this land should be thrown open for general use.

By the Chairman:

Q. The Indians in British Columbia then have been placed on lands selected by the two Governments, federal and provincial?—A. Yes.

Q. And in the Northwest, where the Dominion Government holds all of the lands, reserves have been created?—A. Reserves have been set aside under the treaty made between the Government and the Indians. The Indians themselves selected, or were satisfied with, the reserves set aside under the treaty.

7-8 EDWARD VII., A. 1908

Q. Are there any bands of Indians in Manitoba or the Northwest who have not reserves as yet?—A. There may be an occasional band that we escaped when the other reserves were set aside.

Q. But they are small in numbers?—A. They have been settled with, all of them, in accordance with the terms of the treaty.

Q. Practically all the bands in Manitoba and the Northwest have been settled on reserves?—A. Yes.

By Mr. Fyshe:

Q. Are those reserves excessive?—A. The reserves are set aside on the basis of a square mile for every family of five—128 acres per head. If they were to increase of course they might be short of room?—A. Yes, and they would ask for more land, but they have not asked for any of the land to be taken off where they have fallen away in numbers.

By the Chairman:

Q. In the older parts of Ontario, for instance, the Six Nation Indians have increased, but the land is sufficient?—A. Yes.

Q. No question has ever arisen about the insufficiency of land in the Indian reserves?—A. Only once or twice, I think.

Q. To a small extent?—A. A very small extent.

Q. There is still territory north of Saskatchewan and Alberta that is unorganized? Do you look after the Esquimaux?—A. We voted $500 last year in connection with the Esquimaux.

Q. Do you regard them as Indians?—A. Yes, to a certain extent.

Q. Have you got agents looking after the Esquimaux?—A. No. I should explain that, by the end of this year a treaty will be made with the Indians rounding off the two provinces of Alberta and Saskatchewan. The whole of Ontario has been brought under treaty and along the boundary line between Keewatin in Ontario, where the Indians intermingle, we made a treaty with them last year and set aside a reserve for them.

Q. Then practically almost all the Indians inhabiting the Dominion now have treaty rights or have lands set apart for their use?—A. Yes, or are recognized by the Government.

Q. Have you any other information that you think it would be desirable for the Commission to know? For instance, in connection with the work of your department so as to show its efficiency?—A. Nothing occurs to me just now.

By Mr. Fyshe:

Q. You are well satisfied with the administration of your department?—A. have no ground for complaint if the Government is satisfied.

Q. I mean as to the responsibility of the men in the department. You do not see how the department could be greatly improved, do you?—A. There might be possible here and there some matters of detail in which improvements could be made, but these arise in every large concern. Things are working very satisfactorily in the department and the officers appear to be anxious to do their work.

Q. Your administration of the Indians in Canada, I suppose, compares very favourably with the administration of the Indians in the United States?—A. I am not very familiar with the United States and would not like to venture an opinion. I have heard that the policy of the Canadian Government with reference to its Indians is superior to that of the United States. That is only hearsay, I have nothing to base an opinion upon.

Q. I suppose the Hudson Bay Company's officials still come into closer contact with the Indians than anybody else?—A. In the remote districts they come into pretty close contact with them. At the same time other fur traders are entering the northern territory and making an inroad on the Hudson Bay Company's ground.

Q. There is still a very extensive fur trade done north of Edmonton, is there?—A. The fur trade is carried on all the way from the St. Lawrence right through to the mouth of the Mackenzie river, all through that northern country. There is a lot of fur-trading done in Northern Ontario and Northern Quebec.

Q. There is fur trading also in Nova Scotia, New Brunswick and even in Prince Edward Island, and I should suppose there is a lot in Labrador?—A. Yes.

Witness discharged.

DEPARTMENT OF INDIAN AFFAIRS, CANADA,
OTTAWA, June 25, 1907.

DEAR SIR,—In compliance with your request, I beg to say that the number of Indian agencies is 97, and the number of outside officials as follows:—

Commissioners, superintendents, agents and other employees..	397
Physicians...	323
School teachers..	277
	997

Yours very truly,
(Signed)   FRANK PEDLEY,
Deputy Superintendent General of Indian Affairs.

J. M. COURTNEY, Esq., C.M.G.,
   Chairman, Civil Service Commission,
      Ottawa, Ont.

Return of Officers and Employees of the Department of Indian Affairs, for the year ended June 30, 1906.

1	Deputy minister......................	$ 4,000 00
6	Chief clerks..........................	11,583 32
7	First-class clerks.....................	9,717 85
12	Second-class clerks...................	14,588 17
25	Junior second-class clerks.............	21,579 44
9	Temporary clerks.....................	3,533 37
2	Private secretaries...................	600 00
3	Messengers...........................	1,569 11
1	Packer...............................	700 00
66		$67,871 26

Paid from Special Votes, 1906.

P. H. Bryce, medical inspector................	$1,000 00
G. L. Chitty, timber inspector.................	1,500 00
J. A. M. Macrae, inspector of agencies..........	1,800 00
E. A. Lord, clerk............................	305 46
H. Fabien, draughtsman......................	889 74
R. M. Ogilvie, architect......................	147 85
J. L. Reid, surveyor.........................	1,800 00
S. Swinford, clerk, accountant's branch.........	1,500 00
	$8,943 05

.7-8 EDWARD VII., A. 1908

Return of Officers and Employees of the Department of Indian Affairs for the Year ended June 30, 1892.

1 Deputy minister	$3,200 00
1 Chief clerk and accountant	2,400 00
6 First-class clerks	9,912 50
11 Second-class clerks	14,750 00
24 Third-class clerks	15,604 08
Solicitor (Deputy Minister of Justice)	400 00
Allowance for private secretary	600 00
3 Messengers	1,000 00
1 Packer	573 35
47	$48,439 93

Mr. JAMES A. J. McKENNA, sworn and examined.

By the Chairman :

Q. What is your position ?—A. Assistant Indian Commissioner for Manitoba and the Northwest and for that part of Ontario covered by Treaty No. 3.

Q. That relates to the Indians north of Lake Superior ?—A. Yes, and our jurisdiction extends northward as far as we can go.

Q. And how far west ?—A. To the boundary of British Columbia.

Q. Who is the Commissioner ?—A. The Hon. David Laird, who was at one time Minister of the Interior in the Mackenzie government, and afterwards Lieutenant-Governor of the Northwest.

Q. What salary do you get as assistant commissioner ?—A. $2,600.

Q. What salary does the Commissioner get ?—A. $3,200. That was the salary paid in Regina when there were perquisites attached to the office.

Q. I suppose that was equivalent to the salary of a deputy minister ?—A. Yes. The position was held by Mr. Dewdney, Mr. Hayter Reed and Mr. Forget. Messrs. Reed and Forget were assistant commissioners for a time.

Q. How long have you been in the service ?—A. I entered the service at Ottawa in February, 1886, as an extra clerk in the Department of Justice; I was afterwards made permanent with the Department of the Privy Council, and from there was transferred to the Department of Indian Affairs.

Q. You were Sir John Macdonald's assistant secretary ?—A. Yes, and I was previously employed in the Department of Justice in the preparation of the Riel papers. Before coming to Ottawa I was employed in the Accounting Department of the Prince Edward Island Railway.

Q. At what salary were you appointed in the Indian Department ?—A. When I was with Sir John Macdonald I was transferred from the Department of the Privy Council to the Indian Department. I received the pay of a third-class clerk and an allowance of $600 as private secretary. Sir John Macdonald administered the Indian Department for some time after relinquishing the ministry of the Interior, and finally it was transferred to Mr. White. After a time I was appointed a second-class clerk at practically the same salary that I was getting under the two heads.

Q. And after that you became a first-class clerk ?—A. Yes.

Q. When did you go to the west ?—A. I was appointed assistant Indian Commissioner on July 1, 1901. Before that date and since I have held special commissions to which attached extra remuneration.

Q. Did you become a chief clerk before you went to the west ?—A. No. Under Mr. Sifton as Minister of Interior, I received extra pay which gave me more than the equivalent of a chief clerk's pay.

SESSIONAL PAPER No. 29a

Q. Then you went out as assistant commissioner ?—A. Yes.

Q. You have been a commissioner in negotiating some Indian treaties ?—A. Yes, Sir. I was one of the commissioners who made Treaty No. 8 with the Indians in the Peace river and Athabaska countries ; last year as special commissioner I made Treaty No. 10 with the Indians in the country lying to the north of Prince Albert and east of Treaty No. 8; in 1900 I was chairman of the commission for the settlement of the half-breed claims, and in 1901 and subsequent years I was sole commissioner for the settlement of outstanding half-breed claims.

Q. What extent of land was settled by treaties Nos. 8 and 10 ?—A. I cannot give the exact figures just now. Treaty No. 8 covers a very large territory, including the country along the Peace and Athabaska rivers and along the shores of Great Slave lake, and extending to the height of land on the east. Treaty No. 10 extends from that height of land to Reindeer lake.

Q. Has any settlement gone on in these districts ?—A. Yes. There has been some settlement in the Peace river country. At the time of the treaty there was no settlement at Lesser Slave lake. Then settlement north of Edmonton along the Athabaska trail only extended some twenty-five miles, now settlement extends to Athabaska landing, where a good sized village has grown up. There were only traders and missionaries. But there is some settlement there now.

Q. When did you make Treaty No. 8 ?—A. In 1899.

Q. And since then settlers have gone in ?—A. Yes.

Q. When did you make Treaty No. 10?—A. Last year.

Q. I suppose it is too early for any settlers to go into the country north of that ? —A. Too early, and the country does not lend itself to settlement as readily as other parts of the west.

Q. Are there any Indian bands left with whom treaties have not been made ?—A. There are some along the shores of Hudson Bay and in the Mackenzie river country.

Q. Then the Indian question in the Northwest is practically settled ?—A. Yes. I should think that one more treaty, taking in the country still unsurrendered, which would be traversed by a railway to the Hudson Bay would pretty well cover what there is need of covering.

Q. The basis of these treaties consists of annuities to the chiefs and other members of the tribes ?—A. Yes, and the setting aside of reserves. In the Peace river country we made one change from the established practice. We allowed Indians to take their lands in severalty, if they desired, instead of as members of the band. I myself favoured the idea that we should also give them the opportunity of being dealt with as individuals in regard to money, but the administration was not prepared to go that far.

Q. Before that time the reserves were held in common ?—A. Yes ; there was no exception. .They had the alternative in this case of holding the reserve in common, but if an individual wanted to have his quota of land in severalty he could have it, with, of course, a non-alienable title.

Q. In addition to the annuities, do you allow them any agricultural implements ? —A. Yes.

Q. In proportion to the number of Indians?—A. In proportion to the number and having regard to the conditions.

Q. Are these implements given yearly ?—A. No. We give them periodically but not yearly. We do not follow any hard and fast rule in regard to them.

Q. You also give them seed ?—A. We give them seed and live stock when and where required.

Q. Is that done periodically ?—A. No, just according to the circumstances.

Q. Where do you get the live stock ?—A. We used to buy exclusively in the east. We now buy it almost exclusively in the west. All of the stockers or breeding heifers were bought this year in the west, as were the most of the bulls ; and I think the time has arrived when live stock can, with advantage, be purchased exclusively in the west, where conditions have so changed as to provide ample stock for our breeding purposes.

Q. If the west is raising its own live stock, why should meats be dearer in Winnipeg than here?—A. The cattle industry is now undergoing a change. The ranches are not on so large a scale as they were in the early days when the ranchers had such an immense territory that they could let their cattle roam at large. Now, they have to keep their herds within a certain defined size, and they consequently have stockers as as well as butcher's cattle to dispose of. I do not think there is much western beef sold here. The first-class beef sold here is, I fancy, Ontario stall-fed beef. When you get western beef in appreciable quantities it is only because old country prices have fallen, and it suits the dealers better to sell in Montreal than to ship the cattle to Liverpool. Rent, taxes and help are higher in Winnipeg than here, and these are factors that affect the price of meats.

Q. There is a small sum paid for the distribution of clothing triennially?—A. Yes, for the chiefs—a sort of uniform.

Q. Out of an expenditure of nearly $900,000 last year, $345,000 went for Indian schools?—A. Yes. Our schools are run on the per capita system. The Government built industrial schools throughout the country and for a time met the actual expenditure for maintenance. A report on the subject was made previous to the inauguration of the system by the late Nicholas Flood Davin. The schools when built were handed over to certain religious denominations to be conducted under their auspices, but we paid the salaries of the principals and teachers and met all expense. The clergyman at the head was a salaried officer. But some years ago, under the late administration, the per capita system was changed and the Government allowed so much per capita to the same people for running the schools, still of course retaining the ownership of the buildings.

Q. What salaries do you pay the teachers—A. We have day schools run in connection with churches. We pay the teacher about $300 a year, and his salary is augmented by the allowance he receives from his church. In my opinion, it is a very poor system. I think we should pay an adequate salary to a teacher and require him to confine his work to teaching, not having any extra duties as a missionary. I am speaking now of the day schools, and I do not desire to be taken as opposed to a proper and adequate provision being made for religious training. In our industrial and boarding schools, which are the chief and most effective agencies of Indian education, the state stands in *loco parentis* to the children in the fullest sense. The children are removed entirely from the care and guardianship of their parents and come directly and exclusively under state tutelage. For their ethical training it is essential that provision should be made. I know of only two ways in which it could be made. One way—and the only alternative way to that followed—would be for the state to create a sort of composite ethical system of its own. This, to say the least, would be a dangerous experiment. The other—the way approved by experience—is the employment of the means afforded for ethical training by the different churches which have done and are doing missionary work among the Indians. There are people who consider it an evidence of advanced thought to belittle the work of the missionaries; but those who have studied the Indian question seriously and at first hand find it difficult to adequately describe the civilizing influences of their devoted labours. I have seen the effects of these influences far in advance of the operation of our civil system, and can bear witness to their great benefit to the state. I am not wedded to the present per capita system. The rate was made rather low at the beginning. The officials who made it were, in my opinion, too largely influenced by the compelling requirements of economy, whereas the first consideration should have been the educational efficiency of the system. And the rate has not expanded in the ratio of the increase in the cost of living. As a consequence, the minds of the principals of the schools are so strained by the absorbing question of making ends met, that sufficient mental energy is not left for fruitful thought and work upon the complex problem of Indian education as its different phases are made manifest. The question of ways and means of maintenance puts out of first place the immensely more important one of best methods for transforming the Indian child into a self-supporting citizen—a wealth producer instead of a charge upon the common-

wealth. The financial limitation of the schools compel their managers to look to the immediate revenue-producing or money-saving side of the work of the pupils in the industrial departments of the schools rather than to the educative value and larger future results thereof.

Q. You furnish supplies to destitute Indians?—A. Yes.

Q. What is the distinction between the destitute Indian and another Indian?—A. It is a very difficult line to draw. Strictly speaking, the destitute would be the old and infirm who are unable to work at all and for whom we have to provide during the year. Then there are Indians who are able to help themselves during part of the year, but whom we help to some extent. There are others whom we have to help in seed time and harvest, so that they can get the means to exist for the rest of the year.

Q. Then there are general expenses?—A. The general expenses are largely salaries, office expenses and employees' rations.

Q. I see that for each agency there are charges for supplies for the destitute and charges for general expenses, the same person in many cases furnishing the supplies under the two different headings. Is that merely an accident?—A. No. We ration our officers, clerks and farmers on the different reserves.

Q. Then the general expenses include rations?—A. Yes.

Q. Although the same person receives money under both sub-heads, that is not done with any sinister purpose?—A. No. That is done in the ordinary analysis of the accounts, in order to charge the various items to the different branches of the service.

Q. I find that system running right through the accounts, and generally the proportion is about the same?—A. We estimate the rations for an agent and the farmers and clerks at each agency at a certain figure. We do not charge, for instance, the price of the tea and the price of the bacon which they actually get; but we take a certain fixed rate all through, based on the cost of the articles, and charge a certain amount to management for rations. We have nothing to do with that in Winnipeg; that is done here in Ottawa.

Q. Do you not certify the accounts?—A. No. At one time all the accounts came to the Commissioner's office and were passed on by him and were paid on his certificate; but in 1897 a new rule was adopted providing that accounts should come here. We do not now see the accounts at all, although we supply the estimates on which the expenditure is based. I am inclined to the view—a view which I have on other occasions expressed—that the supervision of expenditure is too centralized. In my opinion, the former system was the better. No matter how able and conscientious the staff of the accounts branch at headquarters may be, the lack of first-hand knowledge of conditions which change with the passing of time, militates against the effectiveness of the supervision of expenditure. The direct representations of agents, who are naturally influenced by personal considerations, are taken without the corrective consideration of the commissioner. Moreover, our ignorance under the present system of the progress of expenditure during a current year makes it extremely difficult for us to estimate closely for the requirements of an incoming year. The large field of expenditure from consolidated revenue for Indian purposes is the west, and there cannot be in the public interest too close or too well informed a supervision of it.

Q. Do you prepare the estimates of how much is wanted?—A. Yes.

Q. But the tenders are called for here?—A. Yes.

Q. You have nothing to do with that?—A. Nothing to do with that.

Q. What check have you on the supplies when they go out? Have you an invoice of them?—A. Yes.

Q. Have you anybody to check them?—A. Yes, we have a man to check them.

Q. Do you keep store accounts?—A. In each agency they keep an account of what goes to them and the distribution of it.

Q. At each agency there would be a record of so much bacon, so much tea, and everything else?—A. Yes.

Q. And a record of the issues?—A. Yes.

Q. And a stock book?—A. Yes.

Q. Do your inspectors inspect the stock?—A. Yes.

Q. I suppose there is no means of keeping down this great expenditure in Northwest?—A. I would not despair of that. The expense of managing has becc larger, but the expenditure for destitute Indians has lessened. An improved orga zation would make for reduction in the cost of management.

Q. It was hoped at one time that the Indians would become more or less s supporting?—A. Yes.

Q. Is there any tendency in that direction?—A. Yes, there is; but it is a v slow process. The Indians of Southern Alberta, the Blackfeet, the Piegans and Bloods—live in a country where until recently very little farming was done. T were exclusively and practically are still exclusively cattle raisers, and we had to f them beef all the time. We are now getting some of them on a self-supporting ba They turn in a certain number of cattle to be butchered and draw on these.

Q. Have you begun to sell any Indian lands?—A. Yes.

Q. To any great extent?—A. To some considerable extent.

Q. Do you sell under the old Indian land management fund, retaining ten cent?—A. Yes, which I think is not fair to the west. I made a report on that s ject some time ago. At one time that fund was, as you know, used as a sort of si hole. and to-day is charged with practically the whole expenditure on the Indi of Ontario and Quebec. Towards that fund Parliament has since 1892 voted sc $14,000 a year. Under an order in council and in virtue of a provision in Indian Act, ten per cent of the proceeds from the sales of any Indian lands in Northwest is deducted for management. My contention is that if we continue t system, we shall have the Indians of the Northwest contributing the money fi which the Indian services in Ontario and Quebec will be maintained, while Indians of the Northwest will continue apparently to be a charge on the pul exchequer. It is from the sale of lands in the Northwest that the future Ind revenue is to come. I suggest, therefore, that there should be a western managen fund so that as our revenues from the sale of land increases, we would reach the st at which the public would clearly see that the Indians of the west were not only coming self-supporting, but through the sales of their land were meeting in la measure from year to year the expenses of the management of their affairs.

Q. I suppose that the revenue derived from the trust funds is not considers as yet?—A. No. not very considerable in the west: but you can see that whate revenue comes into the Indian management fund from the west is lost sight of ir far as the public vision goes.

By Mr. Fyshe:

Q. Are the Indians maintaining their numbers?—A. Yes, fairly well. Then not a very marked increase or a very marked decrease. At one point there will an increase and at another point a decrease. In the early days I think the Inc population was overestimated owing to the great extent of territory they occup I think that is always the case with an aboriginal population whose habitat covel broad extent of territory. In looking back. you will find that our estimates of Indian population in a territory not covered by treaty a portion of which is i covered by treaty, were always in excess of the reality. The great cause of de among the Indians is tuberculosis—glandular tuberculosis.

Q. Do these Indians migrate in winter and go south?—A. No.

Q. Did they originally?—A. No. They lived pretty well within certain defi areas. Particular tribes were recognized as having particular spheres of influenc to say. They might go to a certain hunting ground in winter and to another in s mer. but not with the idea of seeking a mild climate.

By the Chairman:

Q. In the accounts of the Indian trust fund there are two bands which rather stand out in comparison with the others; that is, Sharphead's band, with the sum of $51,486, and White Bear's band, with a sum of $47,000?—A. Sharphead's band at one time occupied a reserve on the Battle river. They surrendered it and amalgamated with Paul's band, whose reserve is situated at White Whale lake, northwest of Edmonton. The agreement of amalgamation provided for equality of interest in the land of Paul's band in the moneys derived from the sale of the land which Sharphead's band surrendered. The fund would be more properly described as Paul's bands, which band has really absorbed what was Sharphead's band. The Moose Mountain agency formerly comprised reserves set aside for three bands: Pheasant Rump's, Striped Blanket's, and White Bear's. In 1901 the reserves of Pheasant Rump's and Striped Blanket's bands were surrendered; the three bands were amalgamated and located in White Bear's reserve, and the proceeds of the sale of the surrendered lands formed a common fund known as White Bear's.

Q. These sums represent sales of land?—A. Yes.

Q. That shows that the opening of the land for settlement has been productive to the Indians, and that they have begun to realize upon them?—A. Yes, there is no doubt about that.

Q. These bands are beginning to show very fair amount of balances to their credit?—A. Yes. I think that the Indian charge upon the public would be very much lessened by a systematic throwing open of reserves for settlement while at the same time protecting the Indians. If a reserve were subdivided among the Indians, each given a non-alienable title to his portion, and the balance surrendered, provision being made that the old people would not simply participate in the interest derived from the fund, but would be given an annuity based on their estimated term of life, it would be better for both the Indians and the public.

Q. Have you reported to that effect?—A. Yes.

Q. Do you find that the Indians who are tilling the land in proximity to white's begin to show a better idea of cultivation than they had before?—A. I think so. Of course, there are counter-balancing disadvantages in Indians being put sometimes too suddenly in proximity to whites.

Q. But still it improves their farming?—A. Yes.

Q. Practically, I suppose your idea is to bring the Indians to the same condition as the Six Nations near Brantford?—A. Yes, only I think the Six Nations would be in a better condition if at an early stage the land had been divided and allotted in severalty so that the Indian would feel that he was working on land which would be his and his children's. I think the community system has worked disadvantageously for the Six Nations. The raison d'être of the community system is the preservation of the land from alienation; but the United States, while securing such preservation for such period as there is considered desirable provides for the recognition of individuality by giving the Indians an unalienable title to their land in severalty.

Q. I see that Enoch's band has a fund to its credit of more than $126,000?—A. Yes, they sold a considerable portion of their land. The band's location is some thirty miles west of Edmonton.

Q. What is the upset price of the land?—A. We put it up at auction or tender at an upset price fixed after examination and which differs as localities and conditions differ.

Q. Do you do that periodically?—A. No, not on any periodical system. It may be represented to us that a certain tract of land should be thrown open to settlement, and if we are satisfied that it should be, and that it will not be prejudicial to the interest of the Indians so to do, we begin negotiations with the Indians, and if they agree, we have the land surveyed and valued, and it is put up for sale at auction or tender, at an upset price.

7-8 EDWARD VII., A. 1908

Q. Have you any suggestions to make in regard to the present practice as to the sale of lands?—A. No, except that I think it should be exclusively by public auction and that it would be better to have the payments extend over ten years instead of five years. The longer term tends to bring a better price for the lands, and the interest received would be greater than the interest obtainable on the funded money.

Q. How many Indian agents have you?—A. In Treaty 3, two; in Manitoba, five; in Saskatchewan, eleven, and in Alberta, eight. All the agents in Saskatchewan and Alberta have clerks and farm instructors—some one, some two and some three. Then, we have four inspectors in Saskatchewan and Alberta, and two covering Manitoba and a portion of Ontario. We have, so far, no agents in Treaty 8. One of the inspectors, whom I have reckoned as of Alberta and Saskatchewan, but whose headquarters are at Ottawa, goes over the country covered by Treaty 8 every summer and pays the annuities.

Q. How many officers have you at Winnipeg?—A. Eight, but in addition to these two surveyors are charged to our office, although they report direct to Ottawa, and when not in the field occupy offices at headquarters.

Q. You have two or three ladies there?—A. Two.

Q. They are stenographers?—A. Yes.

Q. You pay them how much?—A. One gets $600 and the other $660 a year.

Q. Did you find that you could not get young men to come into the service, or that it was easier to get women?—A. We had not the opportunity of trying. My own opinion is that the employment of women in the service has closed the avenues for young men and that we are not training young men for the higher positions in the service as we should do.

Q. The women, I presume, have the privileges of their sex and are appointed at higher salaries in the Government service than they could get outside?—A. I do not think that that would apply so much to Winnipeg as it does to places in the west, because salaries generally are higher in Winnipeg. But it does apply to the service as a whole.

Q. The difference of salaries of clerks in one position and another does not affect Manitoba so much as it does eastern Canada?—A. Oh, no. For instance, a good woman stenographer in a lawyer's office in Winnipeg will get from $50 to $75 a month, whereas in Montreal the same class of stenographer would start at about $30.

Q. How are your agents appointed?—A. Usually from outside. Occasionally a man is promoted.

Q. You have how many inspectors?—A. Six—for Alberta, Battleford, Lake Manitoba, Lake Winnipeg, Qu'Appelle and Treaty 8 inspectorates.

Q. These inspectors are always travelling?—A. They travel very extensively.

Q. Do you travel much?—A. A good deal.

Q. Your travelling is chiefly to Ottawa in connection with legislation?—A. Lately I have done special legislative work in connection with the Department of the Interior, and my work as Half-breed Claims Commissioner brought me here to dispose of reserved cases.

Q. Of course, you want your inspectors to inspect?—A. Yes.

Q. How often have they to go to an agency or a band?—A. We have no fixed time for their going, but if an agency has not been inspected within a reasonable time, we notify the inspector.

Q. Do you expect them to visit each agency once a year?—A. Yes.

Q. And each band?—A. Yes, each part of the agency. In some instances the reserves of an agency are scattered about.

Q. How do you provide for the travelling expenses of these inspectors?—A. They are paid their actual expenses.

Q. In many cases there are no hotels?—A. No, but we have a system by which if the inspector stays with the agent, the agent is allowed 75 cents a day, and camping outfits are provided where country has to be traversed which does not afford accommodation for travellers.

Q. Is there a certain amount of discomfort in connection with the travelling on these inspections?—A. Yes.

Q. If they were paid a trifle extra in the shape of a per diem allowance, you could send them out much oftener?—A. I think so.

Q. If the business of an inspector is to inspect, would it not be desirable to give something to induce them to inspect?—A. I am in favour of a per diem allowance. One difficulty of the present system is that a man has to devote a considerable part of his time to keeping track of his expenses, and if he fails to include the small items he is out of pocket.

Q. No inspector, I presume, ever makes anything on his bill of expenses?—A. I should think not. If an inspector stops with the agent or a friend and no charge is made, I imagine that the general experience is that a return has to be made in some way.

Q. You think it would rather add to efficiency if the inspectors had a per diem allowance?—A. Certainly. I think it would add to the efficiency of the whole of that portion of the service whose officers have to travel.

Q. How were these six inspectors appointed?—A. Mr. Markle was promoted; he was for many years agent at Birtle. Mr. Graham was promoted from the agency at Qu'Appelle. Mr. Chisholm was appointed from outside. Mr. Semmons has been a missionary. Mr. Swinford was promoted; he has been in the service a good many years as agent and clerk. Mr. Conroy came from the outside.

Q. Do these inspectors keep clerks?—A. Mr. Conroy has a clerk during his summer trip. Mr. Graham has a permanent clerk; he is the only one. He is charged also with the supervision of the Qu'Appelle agency, and is provided with a residence in the Qu'Appelle agency, where he was formerly agent. Although I do not at all intimate that his inspection of that agency is not correct, I suggested that another inspector should inspect that agency in which he is superintendent, and that he should inspect the Blackfeet agency where Mr. Markle lives.

Q. That is, you would not have them inspect agencies in which they have other duties?—A. No. For instance, I would not have a bank inspector inspect a branch in which he has a directory jurisdiction over the manager.

Q. How are the agents appointed?—A. Sometimes by promotion and sometimes from outside.

Q. When you know that an agency is vacant, do you write to Ottawa?—A. Yes, and we are notified that a certain person has been appointed.

Q. Is that the usual course?—A. Yes. Sometimes we may recommend that a farmer or clerk be promoted.

Q. But the appointment comes from Ottawa?—A. Yes.

Q. And it is to be supposed that political influence prevails in regard to the the appointment of Indian agents as in regard to other appointments?—A. We are not immune from it.

Q. You know the staffs of those agencies?—A. Each agent has a clerk and one or two or three farmers, as the case may be. Then there is an interpreter, who is a sort of handy man for the agent.

Q. The agents employ farm instructors?—A. Yes.

Q. Do they apply to you before a farm instructor is appointed?—A. They report the vacancy, but the appointment is made at Ottawa.

Q. As to that a member would have something to say?—A. Very likely.

Q. You are in accord with the other gentlemen, I presume, on the subject of superannuation?—A. Quite in accord. I think the efficiency of the service requires a superannuation system.

Q. You yourself are under the old system?—A. Yes.

Q. Do you find people leaving the Indian service now?—A. Since I went west an inspector has left to better himself. We lose farmers sometimes—not frequently an agent.

Q. These farmers play an important part as instructors?—A. Yes. They should be good men, and the longer they are in the service the better fitted they are for the positions.

Q. And you find that owing to the inducements outside being better, they leave the service—A. Yes. It is hard to keep a really good man.

Q. Do you think that some kind of superannuation should apply even to them?— A. I think so, because the superannuation tends to keep good men in the service, whereas without it there is nothing to anchor the good man. He drifts out, while the poor man remains. In fact many good men would have left the service but for the fact that they have been anchored to it by the superannuation system.

Q. Do you think that if there was a re-enactment of some kind of Pension Act, provision should also be made for widows and orphans?—A. I think there should be. That would attract people to the service and hold good men in the service.

Q. The present condition of affairs does not attract people, but in fact sends them out?—A. Yes. The fact that large corporations, in the interest of efficient and permanent service, have been voluntarily providing for pensions, is the best proof we can have of the advantage of the system.

Q. How do you find the condition of affairs as to the increased cost of living, affecting the agents, who live away from the large centres of life?—A. They are not so much affected by it, because they are provided with houses and fuel and rations. In certain cases in which such provision is not made we give the agents an allowance for rent. There are instances in which that is not done, and I suggested that all should be treated alike in that respect.

Q. So far as the Indian department is concerned, your memorial would apply especially to the officials in Winnipeg ?—A. Yes, and to those at other points for whom special allowances are not provided.

Q. Although you do not disagree with Mr. Smith with regard to the immigration agents ?—A. No. I think the salaries of agents and other employees should vary according to the character and importance of the agencies, so that a man might be promoted from a poorer agency to a better agency, and that as good men are required at all agencies the minimum salaries should be adequate.

' Q. You think a classification of salaries and duties could be made ?—A. I think so.

Q. May we ask you to prepare a memorandum on that point ?—A. I will try to do so.

Q. Have you anything else to suggest ?—A. I wish to direct attention particularly to the difference in the cost of living between the east and the west. That difference is made up mainly by house rent, fuel and servants' wages. The higher rental in Winnipeg is due to the higher land values and also to the greater cost of building. For instance, I have a letter from Kelly Brothers, Mitchell, Limited, large contractors in Winnipeg, which states that in five years the increases in wages have been from ten to twenty-five per cent ; plumbers, twenty per cent; painters, twenty per cent, and labourers, ten per cent. A letter from Mr. Aird, secretary treasurer of Havergal College, who has special means of knowing the increased cost of living, says that in the last four years there has been an increase of from forty to fifty per cent in the city of Winnipeg in the cost of the necessaries of life. The manager of the Tilden-Gurney Company writes that during the last five years it has been almost impossible to secure a home in Winnipeg for less than from $35 to $40 a month, that coal cost $10.50 a ton cash, and that firewood is at a price which puts it out of reach of the ordinary wage-earners. The manager of the Ames-Holden Company says that he believes that the average increased cost of living in Winnipeg is fully thirty-three and a third per cent higher than in Montreal. These men are not interested in over-stating the cost of living in Winnipeg because they have to pay increased salaries in consequence, and the wholesale man whose statements we present, are not interested in an over-statement, because they fix the prices of a good many of the necessaries of life. I would like to

, on behalf of the post office employees in Winnipeg and the Northwest, that they
ly concur in the position taken in the memorial put before you by the Toronto
rials ; but they claim that the fact should be taken into consideration that the cost
.iving in the west is thirty-three and a third per cent higher than the cost of living
the east, and that for that reason adequate extra remuneration should be provided
their case. The Bank of Commerce allows to men transferred from the east to the
rt, if unmarried, a special grant of $200 a year, and if married $400 a year, and
er banks make a special average allowance of $300 a year.

Q. Do you think that people appointed there at $400 or $500 a year cannot live
their salaries at all ?—A. They cannot properly live on them.

Q. What do they do ?—A. They get extra work outside. For instance, the secre-
y of the Western Civil Service Association made a statement at a meeting which I
ended, that if he were to do the work of secretary it would be necessary for him to
re up work which he was doing after hours and for which he was getting $30 a
onth.. He is a man who works in the Customs-house from 9 o'clock till 4, and yet
s to go outside and earn $30 a month by extra work.

Q. I suppose you gentlemen, like the members of the Civil Service down here,
ke oaths of office to give your full time to the service ?—A. Yes. You might wonder
w clerks in stores and offices manage to live in Winnipeg, in view of the fact that
r a small attic room they have to pay $14 a month and for the poorest and cheapest
ard $3.50 a week, that is $14, a month more. The only way they manage to exist is
r two to take a room and sleep in the same bed.

Q. Why do they stay ?—A. The employment is there for them and they are hoping
r advancement.

Q. In going on year after year, don't they see what the public service is—that
en if they get a little amelioration, there is nothing to induce them to continue ?—
. 'Hope springs eternal in the human breast.' Outside of the service men go into
ops or offices and get speedy advancement, as the avenues of advancement are more
merous than in the public service.

Q. Even if the public service were better paid, one would think that the principle
political appointments which underlies it would preclude good men from entering
e service ?—A. The essentials to a good service are permanence of employment, a
nsion system, and the incentive to study and work which only comes from a know-
dge that good service will be rewarded by advancement to the top. If you reserve
ur best positions in the service for outsiders, the interest of the others will become
ssened in proportion. Then, again, when a man comes from the outside to take
large of an organized department, it takes him years to familiarize himself with the
ork of the department, and in the meantime he has to depend on certain officials.
hey may not be the best informed or most efficient officials, so that the evil is in-
eased by the fact that the men upon whom he depends are as a reward advanced to
ore remunerative positions over the heads of more competent officials. There should
a no influence of any kind, political or otherwise.

Q. Did you ever know a man in Ottawa or in the Northwest to be transferred
om the Customs Department or the Railway Department to the Post Office or Inland
evenue Department ?—A. No.

Q. Did you ever hear of a railway mail clerk being advanced from that position ?
-A. No.

Q. Did you ever hear of a postman being advanced to a clerkship ?—A. No, nor
ave I ever heard that there was any search made in the service, if it was necessary to
rganize a branch, to ascertain whether a man could be got in one department to organ-
ze such a branch in another department.

Q. You have formed an association in Winnipeg and have, I suppose, talked mat-
ers over with each other; have you ever heard that men of inferior grades are doing
igher-grade work ?—A. Yes.

29a—18

Q. Are there in Winnipeg any postmen doing clerk's work and deprived of their uniforms and street car privileges?—A. I could not say of my own knowledge.

Q. Is there dread of the politician in Winnipeg, as everywhere else?—A. I would not like to say that. I would prefer to use the expression extraneous influence.

Q. Is there a dread of extraneous influence?—A. There is a dread of extraneous influences which militates against the efficiency of the service.

Q. Rather than apply for the assistance which it is desirable to have of a skilled character, the officials of the higher grades will put their heads together and do what they can to get over the difficulty?—A. I have not sufficient detailed knowledge of other departments to say.

Q. I was presuming that you had a very serious talk with each other?—A. We have discussed these matters, but I would not like to put it in that way as a matter of evidence.

Q. Has it been said that the Collector of Customs or the Collector of Inland Revenue, or the Postmaster will try to shift along as best he can rather than apply for extra assistance which might be put in of an inefficient character?—A. I would not like to commit myself on that.

Dr. Barrett.—I know that the collector of Inland Revenue in Winnipeg, when vacancy occurs, if he gets his eye on a desirable young man, tries to induce the Liberal Association to secure his appointment. He asks them to make it a personal matter not to appoint so-and-so, because he wants the other man. In that way he has sometimes succeeded in bringing in men who were less objectionable. But our bitterest feeling is in regard to paying men a pittance like $500 a year. I have no doubt that the Member for Winnipeg and the Liberal Association would often recommend good men for appointments if the remuneration were adequate. The president of the Young Men's Liberal Association said to me a few years ago: 'We can give you good men if you will only pay them; but we can only get a few and these of an inferior class to accept positions at $500 a year.' That is the difficulty—you would get much more efficient men there if the remuneration were better.

Mr. McKenna.—I think that with few exceptions the rule should be that appointments to the public service—to the outside as well as the inside service—should be made on examination. That examination should be such as to test the intelligence and qualifications of the candidate from a literary and mathematical standpoint. He should know something about the history of his country and its form of government. After his admission to the service, his promotions should depend on examinations designed to test his familiarity with the work of his particular branch of the service and further knowledge of our system of government and of departmental administration; but these examinations should not deal with literary matters, because a man who becomes most efficient in the service may have forgotten all about the rules of grammar, although able to write English perfectly.

The Chairman.—Was anything said at your meeting about Entrance examinations?

Mr. McKenna.—No. As a matter of fact, I was put on the executive of the association when I was absent from Winnipeg. At the meeting of the executive which I attended it was understood that the scope of the commission embraced only the question of salaries and retirement.

Dr. Barrett.—The great object in forming that association was to induce the commission to visit Winnipeg, so that they could see the conditions for themselves.

Mr. McKenna.—What I have said with regard to the service is the result of long experience in both the inside and outside service. I think the service should be made as professional as possible. After many years experience of the service, I would say without hesitation that I would be very sorry to have any one of my sons enter the service as at present constituted.

The CHAIRMAN.—If you have anything further to bring before us, we shall be glad to hear it.

Mr. MCKENNA.—I would submit that to secure and maintain the most efficient and economical Civil Service a permanent commission should be formed; that it should consist of three carefully selected men; that at least one of them should have had a large experience in the administration of an important department of the service; and that the other two should have had large experience in the management of extensive business concerns. I may venture to add that a well defined line could be drawn between the purely clerical and the administrative work of the service, opportunity being afforded through examinations such as I have already suggested, for advancement from the lower to the higher grade. There should be minimum and maximum salaries for each grade. Years of service should not in themselves be recognized as reason for advancement from the lower to the higher grade.

MEMORANDUM.

Time does not admit of more than an outline of my idea as to the organization of the outside service of the Indian department in the west.

The commissioner's office should be organized on the same lines as the inside service.

The agencies should be scheduled in the order of their size and importance. There should be three divisions in the agency service: Agents, farming instructors and clerks; interpreters are taken from the same class as are general helpers, and do not lend themselves to Civil Service classification.

There should be minimum and maximum salaries fixed for agencies. The minimum salary of agents should be $1,000; the maximum, $1,800. The minimum for farming instructors, $600; the maximum, $900; the minimum for clerks, $600; the maximum, $900.

I would not have the maximum paid at every agency merely because of length of service and irrespective of the volume of work and degree of responsibility. The agencies could be grouped and a scale of maximum pay fixed to accord with conditions. The maximum of $1,800 I would make payable only at the most important agencies.

Provision should be made for annual increments of—for clerks and farmers, $50 a year, and for agents, $75 a year, until the maximums fixed were reached. These increments should be contingent upon efficient service and the recommendation of the commissioner.

The organization should have these as basic principles: appointments and promotions regardless of extraneous influences and on test of merit, and participation in a pension system. An examination could be set for agents, farming instructors and clerks, both for entrance to the service and for promotion. Agents, clerks and farming instructors should be advanced on evidence of fitness from the smaller to the larger and more important agencies, and instructors and clerks advanced to the office of agents as opportunity offers.

To objections which may be made to the suggestion of examination for appointment as farming instructors, I would submit in reply that the training of Indians in husbandry can be much more effectually secured by educated farmers than by men who are rather farm labourers than agriculturists. In the Indian service the trained official is very necessary. It seems to me that as to farming instructors a workable arrangement could be made for having men drawn from the experimental farms and agricultural colleges, and that under an improved system it might be found that in the agricultural work of the Indian service men might be developed for larger fields of agricultural work in other branches of the service.

I may add that I have never been able to understand why the same large lines of classification could not be applied to the outside service, with the exception of the particular service referred to by Mr. J. Obed. Smith, as can be applied to the inside service.

If the public interests require the walling round by statutory enactments of the inside service, there can be no ground for assuming that the outside service can, without disadvantage to the commonwealth, be left without similar safeguards.

J. A. J. McKENNA.

OTTAWA, October 24, 1907.

INDIAN OFFICE, BRANTFORD, October 29, 1907.

THOMAS S. HOWE, Esq.,
    Secretary Civil Service Commission,
        Ottawa. ·

SIR,—I beg you to place the following memoranda before the Civil Service Commission in regard to the salaries payable to Indian agents and superintendents:—

1. The cost of living has increased from 25 to 40 per cent within the past ten years owing to the higher prices charged for food, clothing and rent.

On this point I beg to refer you to the evidence submitted to your Commission by the Customs and Postal clerks, which I submit is equally applicable to Indian agents.

2. Having to deal entirely with people of another race and language, and almost always through an interpreter, the work of an Indian agent is extremely harassing and requires an immense deal of tact and more than the average amount of patience. In this regard I submit that our duties are more onerous and require more administrative ability than those of men engaged in mere clerical duties, and should be correspondingly better remunerated.

3. The Indian Act, Chapter 81, R.S.C., 1906, contains the whole law (except the Criminal Code) applicable to Indians. This Act gives very great powers to an Indian agent. He has large semi-judicial powers. All appeals from the Indian Council are made to him. He acts as a justice of the peace in disposing of charges for breach of the liquor clauses of that Act. He acts as arbitrator between Indians and settles their disputes. He advises them on all fence line disputes and family quarrels. He keeps the land register and records all transfers of land, supervises all testamentary dispositions and with him are filed all wills. He prepares all agreements for Government leases of Indian lands to white men. He presides at all meetings of the Council of Chiefs, acts as their adviser and reports on all minutes of council to the Indian Department either for or against the various decisions.

4. He is also the adviser of the Department in regard to all matters affecting the interior economy of the reserve.

I beg also to submit to you the following memoranda as more particularly applicable to my own agency:—

(1) The Six Nations Reserve is the largest in Canada, having a population of 4,200, with a capital of $881,850.

(2) The council meets every month as Ohsweken, twelve miles from Brantford, which has no railway, telegraph or telephone communication with the outside world, and I have to attend each monthly council meeting. The council sometimes lasts two or three days and the minutes are consequently very voluminous, refer to a vast number of matters requiring considerable knowledge of the people and subjects considered, to report upon intelligently to the department.

(3) About 10,000 acres of the whole 43,696 acres are under Government leases to white men. Each lease requires an agreement between locatee and lessee, which I prepare. The collection of the rents, amounting to $3,471 in 1905-6, under these leases involves considerable work and responsibility and is done through this office.

SESSIONAL PAPER No. 29a

4. This reserve has a loaning system by which $20,000 of the band funds are set apart by the department for the purpose of assisting the Indians to build barns, fences and wells. These loans vary in amount from $25 to $300. The interest is payable half yearly by holding back the borrower's annuity money `and apportioning it on capital and interest. This item alone entails more work, anxiety and worry than all other matters in connection with our semi-annual payments of interest money, involving a collection and accounting of about $5,000 per annum in small payments varying from $3.50 to $35. Further, I have to see that all buildings under loans are insured and the premiums kept paid up. In addition to collecting the interest and principal on these loans the payments of the sums loaned are made through my office to the merchants and others who supply material and work for the erection of the barns, &c., on the orders of the borrowers.

5. Twice a year I have to distribute about $15,000 annuity money, two-thirds of which is payable in cash at Ohsweken, requiring three days residence there and guarded night and day by two constables. The responsibility attendant on handling such a large sum of money under such circumstances is great. The balance of the annuity has to be paid by cheque or express order, requiring heavy clerical work.

6. The hearing of appeals from the decision of council is a very responsible duty. As a general rule, the Indians employ Brantford counsel, and the appeals are fought out with all the keenness of a regular court of justice. Fine points of evidence are raised, agreements pro and con are heard and rulings given, then I transmit a viva voce copy of the evidence to the department with my recommendation. I am a barrister and solicitor of many years' standing, otherwise I would not feel qualified to perform this part of my duty. It is in reality the work of a judge, as questions of descent, limitations and actions, admissibility of evidence, title to land, wills, &c., are constantly coming up. Within the last six months I have heard 14 appeals.

7. There are 10 schools on this reserve, over which I must have an oversight, assisted by an inspector. I am chairman *ex officio* of the S. N. School Board, and call four or more meetings a year. All matters of education are dealt with through this office and require my personal supervision.

8. My predecessor in office was appointed in 1901 with a salary of $1,200. In 1905 this was increased to $1,400, and in 1906 to $1,500 per annum. His clerk received $900, and his successor, my present clerk, was appointed in 1904 at a salary of $600 per annum, and he still draws this salary. This, I submit, is not a fair nor reasonable salary for the work he does. He is an Indian and acts as interpreter in my office, and without his assistance, and his complete knowledge of all the Indians and their relationships one with the other, the work of the office and at the pay-table would be greatly retarded.

My stenographer, who is also of necessity an Indian, receives only $300 per annum, which, I submit, is not enough, considering the increased cost of living. Our correspondence is most voluminous, both with the department and with members of the reserve, besides having to typewrite numerous agreements, deeds and wills.

My salary is only $1,400, with $125 allowance for travelling expenses, out of which I have to pay $40 per year for an indemnity bond of $20,000.

9. I therefore beg to respectfully submit that you recommend that the salaries of this office be increased as follows:—

Superintendent, $2,000 and travelling allowance.
Clerk, $900.
Stenographer, $500.

in view of the above statement of some of my duties and for the reasons above mentioned.

I have the honour to be, sir,
Your obedient servant,
GORDON J. SMITH,
Superintendent Six Nations.

OTTAWA, WEDNESDAY, May 29, 1907.

The Royal Commission on the Civil Service met this morning at 10.30 o'clock.

Present:—Mr. J. M. COURTNEY, C.M.G., Chairman.
  Mr. THOMAS FYSHE, Montreal, and
  Mr. P. J. BAZIN, Quebec.

Mr. W. J. GERALD, sworn and examined.

By the Chairman:

Q. You are Deputy Minister of Inland Revenue?—A. Yes.
Q. How long have you been deputy minister?—A. Since 1901.
Q. How long have you been in the service of the department?—A. Since April, 1867.
Q. Then, you have been over forty years in the service?—A. Yes.
Q. You have gone through all the steps up to the deputy minister?—A. Yes. from the lowest to the highest.
Q. This (showing) is the memorandum you have sent in?—A. Yes.
Q. I see by it that your revenue has gone up from about $8,000,000 in 1892 to over $14,000,000 in 1906?—A: That is right.
Q. While the cost of collecting you have reduced from five per cent to three and six-tenths per cent?—A. Yes.
Q. You have an army of collectors and inspectors—about 470 outside officers?—A. We had, in 1906, 519 altogether, inside and outside.
Q. The number outside is about 470?—A. In 1906, 483 outside and 36 inside.
Q. To look after all these what are you paid?—A. $4,000 per annum.
Q. No extra emoluments of any kind?—A. Not of any character. I may point out, moreover that from 1870 to 1883 there was a commissioner and a deputy commissioner. Between 1883 and 1887 there was a commissioner only. From 1887 to 1901 there was a commissioner and assistant commissioner.
Q. You were the assistant commissioner?—A. I was the assistant commissioner. From 1901 to 1907, I have tried to do the work alone, but I must say that with the increased business it is beyond my power to do it properly.
Q. Then you think at present, with the extent of the revenue, that an assistant commissioner would be a desirable appointment?—A. Absolutely necessary.

By Mr. Fyshe:

Q. Don't you think there might be a conflict of responsibility?—A. There never has been any such conflict in the past.
Q. It would be difficult to define exactly the duties of the chief commissioner and the duties of the assistant?—A. No. There has never been any trouble of that character. The commissioner, of course, is the head of the department; but during his absence, or even when he is present in his office, certain classes of work are handed over by him to his assistant, and he is there for consultation, which is a very desirable thing.
Q. But you might achieve the same result by having an officer with a different title?—A. It works out in the same way no matter what the title is.

> *By the Chairman:*

Q. Whatever he might be designated, you think that with your growing revenue an officer next to yourself should be appointed?—A. I undoubtedly do, and more than that, he should be a man who is thoroughly acquainted with the outside work of our department, because that is where the revenue comes from.

> *By Mr. Bazin:*

Q. When you said that the percentage of cost of collecting the revenue had been reduced, there was at the same time an increase in the duties—in 1897, if I recollect rightly?—A. That was on raw leaf tobacco only.

Q. There was no increase in the duty on spirits?—A. In 1892 the duty on spirits was $1.'50; to-day it is $1.90. In 1892 there was no duty on raw leaf tobacco, but the duty on raw leaf tobacco to-day brings us in something over a million dollars a year.

> *By the Chairman:*

Q. You have a duty on an article on which there was no duty before, and you have increased work to collect that?—A. Yes, and the volume of business in every direction has increased.

Q. Taking the inside service first, you have not a very large department?—A. Not large in numbers.

Q. As a matter of fact, you have only 35 in all?—A. Yes.

Q. You have five chief clerks?—A. Yes.

Q. Is the number greater than the work requires?—A. I do not think it makes any difference what title a man goes by, he will do the work just the same as a first-class clerk as he will as a chief clerk.

Q. He gets more money?—A. Yes, he gets more money.

Q. Do the chief clerks do the same work as first-class clerks?—A. They do the same work as first-class clerks, and as they did when they were first-class clerks, except two men. The secretary of the department and the accountant of the department are chief clerks, and I think quite properly so.

Q. Now you have three additional chief clerks who are doing practically the same work as they did when they first-class clerks?—A. Identically the same. The assistant accountant was made chief clerk, the clerk at the head of the statistical branch was made a chief clerk, and the clerk having charge of all the weights and measures and the electric light work was also made a chief clerk.

Q. Then, you have four first-class clerks now as against six before, that is, a consequence of the reduction of the one class and the increase of the other?—A. Yes, because the first-class clerks were promoted to the position of chief clerks.

Q. The lower grades are pretty much the same as they were in 1892?—A. Yes, there is very little difference in them.

Q. When a man becomes a second-class clerk, does he do any different work from what he did when he was a third-class clerk?—A. Not any—the same work exactly.

> *By Mr. Fyshe:*

Q. I suppose the fundamental cause of that is that the work is pretty much the same?—A. No. There are some classes of work very much more important than others. For example, in the statistical branch we want good careful men to check every paper that comes in to the department—that is, the amounts and the rate of duty, and to see that they are properly computed.

Q. Is there a branch of your department in all the large cities?—A. Certainly.

Q. If there is a big distillery in a country place, how do you do?—A. It is necessary to have a staff there.

> *By the Chairman:*

Q. When a new clerk is wanted, do the chief clerks report to you that they want additional assistance?—A. Yes.

7-8 EDWARD VII., A. 1908

Q. And you examine into the matter yourself?—A. I examine into the necessity for the help they ask for.

Q. You do not appoint a new junior on account of political pressure from the outside to appoint a man?—A. I have nothing to do with the appointment.

Q. You ask for a clerk?—A. Yes, exactly.

Q. No clerk is forced upon you unless you ask for one?—A. No permanent clerk.

By Mr. Fyshe:

Q. The initiative in the appointment is not taken by you?—A. Yes. It is done at the request of a chief clerk.

Q. I mean in fixing the man?—A. Not in fixing the man.

By the Chairman:

Q. Have you found that the men appointed to the department have been men of good moral character and good health?—A. I think on the whole that can be answered in the affirmative.

Q. When a clerk is appointed, he is appointed on probation?—A. On probation for six months.

Q. Do you use that term to find out whether he is fit or not?—A. When a clerk is appointed on probation or in any other way, unless his conduct is very bad, he retains his position.

Q. You have to report as to his competency?—A. Yes, we do as to the outside service. I do not think that is done to the same extent as respects the inside.

Q. You have not had many appointments?—A. No, very few.

Q. In your Promotion examinations, when these first-class clerks, for instance, were made chief clerks, did you set the papers?—A. I only set the papers on duties of office as a rule. The other papers are set by the Civil Service Board. We deem that to be better.

Q. What does this mean—Section 45 of the Civil Service Act: ' No such examination shall be required for the re-employment or promotion of excise men who passed the departmental examinations for the special class in the excise service before the first day of July, 1882 '?—A. It simply means that special class excise men have passed the highest technical examination that can be set by the department.

Q. Over 25 years ago?—A. Yes, over 25 years ago.

Q. Might they not have got rusty by this time?—A. We did not put that provision in the Act.

Q. Is it desirable to retain it?—A. I can see no object at all in doing so. A man who has passed to-day is as good as a man who passed twenty-five years ago.

Q. You think that might be left out?—A. I would leave out the part as to the limit of time.

Q. You have a hand in the promotion of your officers?—A. I have to report on their conduct and efficiency.

Q. In sections 46 and 47 it is provided that the head of the department shall select the persons for promotion, or may reject the person promoted within the probationary period of six months. Should not that also be worked ' on the report of the deputy head '?—A. I think it should, because the head of the department cannot so well judge; he has not the same means of judging as his deputy.

Q. How long is it since you appointed a third-class clerk or a junior second?—A. I think we have appointed a third-class clerk within a year.

Q. A man or a woman?—A. A man.

Q. What did you appoint him at?—A. $500.

Q. Did you have any difficulty in getting a man at $500?—A. The only chance the man had was that when he passed the Promotion examination he would go up to a junior second.

Q. Then, he came in with the expectation that he would go up?—A. Yes, because he could not live on the salary of $500.

By Mr. Fyshe:

Q. How old is he?—A. Twenty-five years.

Q. What was he at before?—A. I think he was a country boy on a farm before he came here.

Q. Has he a fairly good education?—A. Fairly good.

By the Chairman:

Q. Where does he come from?—A. From Oxford.

By Mr. Basin:

Q. Does it not seem surprising that a man of that age who has been brought up on the farm should wish to take such a position?—A. I think it is; but there seems to be a great desire to get into the public service. I cannot understand it, but it exists.

By the Chairman:

Q. All clerks on their appointment begin at the minimum of their salary?—A. Yes.

Q. Would it be desirable that the minimum of the third class should be modified? —A. I think it should be increased. I think that any man who comes in, if fit to be a third-class clerk, should not begin at less than $700 or $800.

Q. So you think that the minimum of the third-class clerk might be increased?— A. I certainly do.

Q. Did you ever suspend any man in your department?—A. I cannot recall a case of suspending a man in the inside service. We have withheld increases, but I do not recollect a case of absolute suspension in the inside.

Q. Were these increases afterwards restored?—A. Yes, if the man's conduct justified it, and it did justify it. We found that the effect of stopping the increase was beneficial.

Q. I see you have no temporary clerks in your department?—A. We have no temporary clerks in the department paid out of the inside vote.

Q. What people have you in Ottawa that are not paid out of the inside vote?— A. We have at the present time in the department a Mr. Cavers.

Q. What is he working at?—A. He is doing ordinary work in the statistical branch.

Q. What vote do you pay him out of?—A. We have to pay him out of the outside vote, because we cannot admit him without an examination.

Q. Is he the only man in that position?—A. I think so.

Q. How many women have you?—A. Two.

Q. To what votes is their pay charged?—A. One to weights and measures and the other to preventive service. Mr. Cavers' pay is charged to our methylated spirits warehouse, although he is doing work in the statistical branch.

Q. You have charged to the methylated spirits vote the salary of a person who works entirely apart?—A. Yes.

Q. And to the outside preventive service other persons who work in the department?—A. Yes. I want to correct a previous statement. While one of the ladies I refer to does work in the building, she does not do work in connection with the inside service. She does work in connection with the office of the chief inspector of weights and measures, who is an outside employee.

Q. That would be justified?—A. Yes, that would be justified.

Q. Do you ever dismiss anybody in your inside service?—A. I have no recollection of any one having been dismissed in recent years.

7-8 EDWARD VII., A. 1908

Q. You have an attendance book?—A. Yes.

Q. Does everybody sign it?—A. Everybo 'y but the two chief clerks.

Q. Has that always been so?—A. For the last fifteen or twenty years.

Q. What are the office hours?—A. From half past nine until four o'clock; but many officials are there until five, half past five and six o'clock.

Q. How long have they for luncheon?—A. An hour.

Q. Do they all go for luncheon together?—A. No, they go at irregular periods.

Q. Then there is always somebody in the department?—A. Always.

Q. Are all your offices in the west block, or have you any in outside buildings?—A. All the inside service are in the west block.

Q. You have no objection to Mr. Fyshe and Mr. Bazin going over your department?—A. I shall be very glad indeed to show them over the department.

By Mr. Bazin:

Q. Don't you think it would be advisable to have longer hours—say from nine till five?—A. I think half past nine in the morning is early enough, but I think the hours might be extended to five in the afternoon.

Q. If the hours were from nine to five, don't you think everybody could go at five? Don't you think the work could be done better in that space of time?—A. The hour of nine o'clock is rather early to get people there, and in that case the majority of the clerks would sign below the line, which would be a sort of black mark against them, because we could not give them credit for punctuality. But half past nine is a reasonable hour to get there.

By the Chairman:

Q. Your employees are not paid for extra services?—A. Nobody gets any extra pay for extra services, no matter how much they work.

Q. The Treasury Board in 1879 passed an order to the effect that any attempt to obtain promotion by political influence would be tantamount to dismissal. Did you notice that?—A. We issued a circular on that subject to the whole of the outside service.

Q. What is your opinion with regard to the abolition of the Superannuation Act?—A. I think it is most desirable that the Act should be retained. It is an encouragemen to men to work faithfully.

Q. Do you think the abolition of the Act was a mistake?—A. I think so.

Q. Do you find your men leaving the service in the outside?—A. Yes. Men have left the service and have gone into the service of men who have licenses from us—men who know our work thoroughly and can be of service to the manufacturers, who pay them larger salaries than we can pay.

Q. The main revenue of the department is derived from the distilleries?—A. Yes, from spirits.

Q. Tell us what you do in a distillery from the beginning?—A. All grain that comes into a distillery is weighed by our officials, and we provide as a standard that the distiller must produce a gallon of proof spirits from every twenty and four-tenths pounds of grain. The whole process of manufacture from the time the grain comes in until the spirit is produced is carried on under the supervision of our officials. The rate of duty, $1.90 a gallon, is so high that we cannot trust anybody. After the grain is mashed and fermented, it is placed in the stills, where the alcoholic vapour is driven off, and from the time the beer or wash is placed in the still all the connections are sealed in order that no portion of the vapour can be condensed and conveyed to any other vessels than the closed spirit receivers where the quantity subject to duty is determined.

By Mr. Fyshe:

Q. Does that not involve a considerable Government staff at each distillery?—A. Yes, it takes a large staff.

Q. And all men of thoroughly reliable character?—A. The best men we can select out of our service.

Q. What would be the average salary of these men?—A. The chief man in charge gets. I think. $1,800 a year.

Q. He would not be there all the time?—A. Yes, practically every minute of the time. The chief officer would probably be there from nine o'clock or earlier until six.

Q. In other words he has to be there as long as the distillery is open?—A. It is always open, day and night. At Walker's distillery at Windsor, for example, we have fifteen or sixteen men watching every operation.

By the Chairman :

Q. In the distillery you follow the process from the time the grain is measured? —A. From the time it comes in until the spirit runs in the vessel at which we determine the quantity, subject to duty.

Q. You hold an account against the distillery for so many thousand pounds of grain?—A. Yes.

Q. And that goes all through the process of manufacturing?—A. Yes.

Q. And when the spirit is put in barrels, you follow these barrels?—A. If it is shipped in bond.

Q. Then it goes into a bonded warehouse?—A. Yes.

Q. Of which your employees have control?—A. Yes.

Q. Then, so far as spirits are concerned, you follow the process from the moment the grain is entered in the distillery until the spirits go to a bonded warehouse? —A. Yes.

By Mr. Fyshe:

Q. Suppose a mistake is made by the distiller and he spoils a batch of grain?—A. Then we require him to pay the duty on the spirit that should have been produced from it. The standard fixed by the law is a very liberal one.

By the Chairman :

Q. How many distilleries are there now in Canada?—A. Thirteen.

By Mr. Bazin :

Q. I suppose the spirit is all made in batches—they put in a certain quantity of grain and make a certain quantity of spirits from that grain?—A. It is a continuous operation.

Q. What means have you of checking the amount?—A. We have in the first place a stock book in which all the grain that comes into the distillery is debited to the distiller. Against that is credited the grain taken for use in the distillery, and we say that on that account he should produce from every twenty and four-tenth pounds of grain one gallon of spirits.

By the Chairman: .

Q. When the product comes out in bottles, with a stamp on each bottle, what do you do?—A. When the spirit is completely manufactured. it is taken from the closed spirit receivers and rectified. Then it is placed in storage tanks under lock and key, where it must remain for a period of two years, or it may be there indefinitely. Certain allowances are made on account of the length of time it is in storage.

Q. For evaporation?—A. Yes. exactly. If the distiller wants to bottle it, it is bottled in bond under the supervision of our officials, and the label over the capsule of the bottle is a guarantee of the age of the spirit. The date on it is the date of the manufacture of the spirit.

By Mr. Bazin :

Q. Of course, they reduce those spirits ?—A. Yes.

Q. That is done under the supervision of your officers ?—A. Yes. It is done in this way. We hand out to-day, for example, ten thousand gallons of spirits. They want to reduce that, and we hand it over to them to be reduced. After reducing it, they have to hand back to us ten thousand gallons. If there has been a loss in reducing, we require the distiller to pay the duty on it. Then it comes back in barrels at a reduced strength of say 25 under proof. It remains there until they want to sell it. Our collections are all on the basis of a gallon proof.

By the Chairman :

Q. Your officers follow it, whether in barrels or in bottles, until it gets back to the examining warehouse and the duty is paid ?—A. Yes.

By Mr. Fyshe:

Q. Do you find any cases of attempted smuggling ?—A. There has been no case of fraud in connection with the distilleries for so many years that I cannot recollect when a case of that kind did occur.

By the Chairman :

Q. In all these big distilleries, such as Gooderham & Worts, Walkers' and Seagrams, you have a large staff ?—A. Yes. It depends on the extent of the business. In some there are fifteen or sixteen, in others three or four.

Q. But there is always one ?—A. Yes, we do not trust or place the responsibility on any one man.

By Mr. Fishe :

Q. There could not be collusion between the distiller and the exciseman ?—A. There could not well be under these conditions.

Q. Is it not a fact that the distillers are extremely gracious to your chief men ?—A. I have never heard of it.

By the Chairman :

Q. These licensees are always ready to take a good man into their service, if they saw a good excise man ?—A. They might be.

Q. Do they ever do that ?—A. I do not know a case of that kind, as respects distilleries.

By Mr. Bazin :

Q. I do not suppose they would have much use for a man of that kind ?—A. The only use of a man of that kind would be to keep charge of the books you require them to keep. Their own clerks do that.

By Mr. Fyshe:

Q. Is there much skill required in making whiskey?—A. Like everything else, there is special skill required in the manufacture of whiskey. The manufacture of the yeast is the principal secret in all distilleries. As far as my memory serves me, each distiller is very jealous of the recipe for making his particular yeast, because the production of the spirits depends on proper fermentation. If the mash is not properly fermented and all the starch converted into sugar and the sugar into alcohol, a certain loss is suffered.

By the Chairman:

Q. In your outside service, you have inspectors, collectors, deputy collectors, accountants, special class excisemen, first, second and third-class excisemen, and probationary excisemen?—A. A probationary exciseman simply means a man who after six months will be a third-class exciseman.

Q. You pay your men annual increments?—A. Yes, fixed by Order in Council.

Q. They have sometimes duty pay?—A. Yes, they have duty pay.

Q. What do you mean by that?—A. That is a sum of money paid to officers who are on important surveys, and whose hours are longer on that account. We pay them additional rates running from $75 to $200 per annum. Many of these men have to be at the distillery before 7 o'clock in the morning, winter and summer, and stay there till six. On account of their serving these long hours, we give them from $75 to $200 a year in addition to their salaries.

Q. In following up this system, of course there is not always an exciseman at every point where a barrel of whiskey goes into use, and you sometimes employ collectors of customs?—A. In the collecting of revenue at small, unimportant points we utilize the services of the collectors of customs.

Q. What do you pay them?—A. There is a sliding scale. On collections up to $3,000 they are paid 5 per cent; on collections over $3,000 they are paid a fixed salary dependent on the amount of their collections, but in no case over $250 a year.

Q. Take Almonte, for instance, where you have no exciseman; on a barrel of whiskey consigned to a local grocer the revenue would be collected by the collector of customs?—A. The collector of customs would be appointed our official and paid a commission on the collections. We save by that system.

By Mr. Bazin:

Q. The bonds are used jointly for the Department of Customs and the Inland Revenue Department?—A. No, we do not permit that. If it is done, it is done contrary to our knowledge and contrary to our wish. We have separate bonds. It was permitted at one time, but we found it very unsatisfactory, as the responsibility rested on two departments. We do not want that. We provide that for excise purposes the owner must have a warehouse, separate and distinct, for which our own men will be responsible.

By the Chairman:

Q. You have a different system for beer ?—A. Yes.

Q. How do you do when the malt goes into the brewery?—A. We do not keep any control over beer, because there is no duty on it. We collect the tax on the malt used.

Q. When malt gets unfit for use, it is destroyed in the presence of two officers?—A. Yes.

Q. So that there will be no collusion?—A. So that there will be no collusion.

By Mr. Fyshe:

Q. Do you make them pay duty on that?—A. They paid the duty on the malt before its use, and the department gives the brewer credit for that. Then they may appeal to the Treasury Board, with whom it rests entirely to say whether the duty so paid will be given back or not.

By Mr. Bazin:

Q. Is it your experience that the refund is made?—A. The refund is made if the proof of destruction is absolute. We insist on the malt being burned or destroyed absolutely.

By the Chairman:

Q. Instead of following the process to the end in the brewery, you charge duty on the malt in the beginning?—A. Yes, but we make the brewer keep a record of all the malt used and the beer made from it.

Q. Coming to the tobacco part of the business, what is the process with regard to cigars?—A. The raw leaf comes in in bond, and it is locked up and delivered to the manufacturer as he requires it, and every ten days he pays duty on the quantity of leaf he takes out for use. Every twenty-two pounds of leaf is estimated to produce a thousand cigars. That is a liberal standard, and it is only a rare case in which a manufacturer does not come up to that standard.

By Mr. Fyshe:

Q. What is the duty on raw tobacco?—A. It is 10 cents per pound on unstemmed and 14 cents on stemmed. One of the reasons for that is that we want to encourage the stemming of leaf tobacco in our own country.

Q. The result is that they do the stemming here?—A. Yes, probably nine-tenths of it is done in our own country, although some bring in stemmed leaf.

By the Chairman:

Q. Then you follow the whole process from the introduction of the leaf until the product goes out in the shape of cigars?—A. Exactly, but it cannot be followed to the same extent as the process in the distillery. The reason for that is that in the manufacture of cigars they necessarily require to have the leaf to be made up at any time during the day, and nobody could keep a check on every pound of leaf used by a cigar maker; so we correct that by a standard production of twenty-two pounds to a thousand cigars.

Q. The same thing would apply to cigarettes?—A. Cigarettes are classed as tobacco.

Q. With the bottled whiskey and the cigars and the cigarettes come in your system of stamps?—A. Yes. Of course we do not call the labels on whiskey bottles stamps. They are designated as bottling labels as distinct from stamps.

Q. Are the labels printed at the British American Bank Note Company?—A. Yes.

Q. They have a contract for printing them?—A. All the contract they have is for printing bottling labels. The printing of the other stamps is done by the American Bank Note Company.

Q. All these stamps are paid for by the distillers?—A. The cost of all the stamps used on bottles of spirits is borne by the distillers. The labels on bottles cost a cent each. The labels on flasks cost one-fifth of a cent. The stamps in connection with tobacco and cigars are attached simply to show that the duty has been paid. The manufacturers do not buy the stamps. They pay the duty at whatever rate it may be and these stamps are put on as evidence that the duty has been paid.

By Mr. Bazin:

Q. The stamp is a receipt for the duty?—A. That is practically what it is.

By the Chairman:

Q. You have a preventive service?—A. We have.

Q. What are the duties of the preventive service?—A. The duties of a preventive officer are to go about the country and endeavour to check illicit distilling, the illicit manufacture of tobacco and cigars or even illicit importation of any goods which are subject to duties of excise.

By Mr. Fyshe:

Q. How many preventive officers have you?—A. I should say probably thirty.

Q. They are not generally known, I suppose?—A. They are not generally known. They are men in different parts of the country who secure information, and act upon it, under the direction of the local collector of inland revenue.

SESSIONAL PAPER No. 29a

By the Chairman:

Q. You have nothing to do with the cases which used to be pretty common, of spirits being brought up the St. Lawrence in schooners?—A. No, that is all under the Customs Department.

Q. We had evidence fifteen years ago that it was a practice to load up old rotten schooners with spirits, which could be got at sixty cents a gallon, and the selling price of which was three dollars a gallon, and land somewhere up the St. Lawrence, and the captain of the schooner would inform the department and have the cargo seized, and half the value of it would go to him as the informer, and in that way he made money out of the transaction?—A. I have heard of that being done, but I do not know anything about it personally, because it does not come under our department.

By Mr. Bazin:

Q. You have nothing to do with the sale of confiscated liquors, I suppose?—A. No. When we have liquors of that kind we do not desire to sell them. We prefer to turn them into the gutter.

Q. I have known of cases of liquor being seized, and being sold in the Custom-house, although there was no stamp on them to show that any duties had been paid. I think that was a method of helping a contraband business?—A. I think it is most objectionable.

By the Chairman:

Q. The manufacture of methylated spirits is a monopoly of the department?—A. Yes.

Q. You buy the alcohol from the distillers?—A. Yes.

Q. And you buy the wood naphtha?—A. Under contract given to the lowest tenderer.

By Mr. Fyshe:

Q. Where is the manufacture carried on?—A. At 519 Queen street, in Ottawa.

Q. Is it the only one in the Dominion?—A. The only one at the present time.

Q. How much is made?—A. About 80,000 or 90,000 proof gallons a year.

Q. What is the value?—A. The selling price in 1906 ranged from $1.19 to $1.50. At the present time we sell it at 70 cents and 80 cents a gallon—two grades.

Q. Why has the value fallen so much?—A. Because we are trying to give a cheaper spirit.

By the Chairman:

Q. At cost price?—A. To-day we are selling it at less than cost price.

By Mr. Fyshe:

Q. What is the object of that?—A. To encourage manufacturing. There is a demand all over the world for cheap, denatured alcohol, and the department is trying to furnish it.

Q. That is not used for automobiles?—A. It is not in this country, and I do not think it is in any other country. The price of it has not been reduced enough to meet the price of gasoline.

By the Chairman:

Q. You are trying to develop this industry to aid manufacturers?—A. Yes. Methylated spirit is simply a combination of wood alcohol and grain alcohol.

Q. The manufacture is only in the experimental stage yet?—A. Yes, to a certain extent.

By Mr. Fyshe:

Q. The difficulty, I suppose, is in watching the operations of the people—in the States anybody is authorized to make denatured alcohol?—A. I think so, under their law and under certain restrictions. The quantity of wood alcohol used in the United States per gallon is very small.

Q. If everybody makes it, the farmers and everbody else, there cannot be any possible revenue from it?—A. I think not.

Q. You have a monopoly of the manufacture in Canada?—A. Yes, we took it over in order to protect our spirit revenue, and we have been giving it at as low a price as it could ever be obtained for. To-day we are giving it at a price about half of what it could be obtained for when manufactured by outsiders.

Q. Then, you will not be able to cover your expenses?—A. I think we shall before the end of the year, because we are working on a new system of denaturing, which I think will enable us to meet the cost.

By Mr. Bazin:

Q. The object is to help the drug manufacturers and others, otherwise they would have to use wood alcohol?—A. Yes, any manufacturer in whose business denatured alcohol is essential.

Q. It is not potable ?—A. No. We supply varnish manufacturers under bonds given by them that they will use the denatured alcohol for a specific purpose and at some specified place, and under that bond they can obtain denatured alcohol of a higher grade than supplied for ordinary purposes.

By the Chairman:

Q. You have inspectors of weights and measures?—A. Yes.

Q. And you have a warden of standards?—A. We have what is practically a warden of standards. The deputy minister is the head of that branch.

Q. How is the standard fixed originally?—A. The standards we use are standards sent out by the British Government.

Q. A pound is a pound all over the British Empire?—A. Yes.

Q. And a gallon a gallon?—A. Yes, I think so.

By Mr. Fyshe:

Q. What is called an Imperial gallon?—A. The Imperial gallon is the only legal gallon here. In the United States the wine gallon is legal. The wine gallon contains 231 cubic inches, while the Imperial gallon contains 277·274 cubic inches—about one-fifth larger.

By the Chairman:

Q. To carry out this system you have inspectors all over the Dominion?—A. Yes, at various points.

Q. Do they go around and visit all stores and places where weights and measures are used?—A. Yes, every two years.

By Mr. Fyshe:

Q. Do they go into every shop?—A. They are supposed to. That is their duty. They are also to see that the manufacturers' scales and measures are submitted to verification.

Q. Are the farmers required to have proper scales and measures?—A. We do not go to farmers, only to dealers. The Act applies to scales used for the purposes of trade—the buying or selling or fixing the price of something. A farmer might have a scale for weighing his potatoes, but not for trade purposes; that would not be subject to inspection.

Q. It would not be official?—A. It would not be official, if it is not used for purposes of trade.

By the Chairman:

Q. Every two years the scales used for the purposes of trade are tested?—A. They are supposed to be.

Q. And you have a small army of inspectors and assistant inspectors constantly on the road?—A. Constantly on the road.

By Mr. Fyshe:

Q. Do you ever find a false scale?—A. Not very frequently, but occasionally.

By the Chairman:

Q. What happens then?—A. We have a case now proceeding in Montreal against a man charged with having a piece of lead under one of the pans of his scale. It is now before the Department of Justice. It is the first case we have had for some time, and we felt that it was of such a serious character that an example should be made of the man.

Q. The stamp has a date?—A. Yes, it has a letter which distinguishes it.

Q. You have also an inspection of gas and electric light?—A. Yes.

Q. And you have inspectors and assistant inspectors for that?—A. Yes. The inspectors of electric light are our officials connected with gas inspection.

By Mr. Fyshe :

Q. You have experts for that work ?—A. We have. We have a chief inspector for weights and measures, and we have an electrical engineer in charge of the gas and electric light branch.

Q. You have to pay them large salaries, I suppose ?—A. They are paid each $2,600 a year, which I do not think is a very excessive salary.

Q. Is it not a rather common thing to have defective wiring in connection with the electric light ?—A. We have nothing to do with the wiring—only the inspection of meters by which the consumer is charged for his supply of electricity. The wiring I think is subject to provincial laws.

By the Chairman :

Q. Do your inspectors go into private houses to inspect meters?—A. No, not unless consumers ask them to go and check their meter.

Q. Before the Ottawa Gas Company sends out its meters, are they all tested?—A. Yes, all tested and sealed up.

Q. Every gas company or electric light company has to have its meters tested before they go out ?—A. Yes, before going out, and every five years they have to be brought back for reinspection.

Q. Another very important matter over which you have jurisdiction is the adulteration of food ?—A. Yes.

Q. You have samples of cocoa, tea, coffee, spices and all other food products sent to you for analysis, to see that there is no adulteration ?—A. Yes. We do more than that. We have food inspectors who go and select the samples just as they are offered to the public for sale ; they go to the wholesale and retail stores and also to the factories where the articles are made, and collect samples which are sent here for examination.

By Mr. Fyshe :

Q. It is a very important duty?—A. A very important duty, and the Act is a very hard one to administer ; but I think it is doing a great deal of good.

Q. A great deal would depend on the conscientiousness of those men ?—A. Should we send an order to our food inspector in Montreal to collect a hundred samples of butter, he starts out and visits any store to get a sample.

29a—19

Q. He might take ten samples from one store ?—A. That is not done.

By Mr. Chairman :

Q. Does this apply to milk ?—A. Yes, to every article of food or drink and to drugs.

Q. Do your officers, for instance, go to Mr. Bazin's warehouse and take sam of Force or rolled oats?—A. Yes. They buy a package wherever they choose. T are not supposed to make themselves known at first, but just to make a purchase, after they have made the purchase they state : ' We require this for analytical poses,' and they divide the sample so obtained into three parts, leaving a part with man from whom they purchased, sealed and labelled, so that the person from w the article is obtained can protect himself.

Q. Are all these samples sent to Ottawa ?—A. The bulk of them come here. have some analysts outside, but we wish to centralize the work as far as possibl Ottawa, where we have trained analysts.

By Mr. Fyshe :

Q. Have you a district analyst in every town ?—A. No, we have one in Tor(one in Victoria, one in Montreal and one in Ottawa.

By Mr. Bazin :

Q. They do not analyse liquors ?—A. They do not unless a collection the is ordered.

Q. There is a complaint among the public that retail liquor dealers are ser very bad liquors, and there is no means of detecting them ?—A. I may mention i happened some years ago. There was a question raised in the House of Common Mr. Gallery, the member for Montreal, who stated that vile and poisonous spirits ' being sold in the city of Montreal. We had samples collected, some of them from lowest saloons in the city. Every one of these samples were sent here and exam either by the chief analyst himself or under his supervision and in not one sat was anything found more injurious than the alcohol itself. These are practi(the words the analyst used.

By the Chairman :

Q. You get a little revenue from acetic acid—is that vinegar?—A. No, the the acetic acid itself.

Q. You get it from Toronto and Montreal?—A. Yes.

Q. Only the two places ?—A. Yes, only the two places.

Q. Do you get it from factories ?—A. Yes. It is made from acetate of lime.

Q. What check have you there ?—A. The very moment the acetate of lime is into the vessels, we have a basis upon which to determine the quantity of acetic which should be produced.

Q. You have a revenue from bonded manufactures ?—A. Yes, that is on vine

Q. That is in the shape of licenses ?—A. Yes, and duty upon the vinegar duced.

Q. That has nothing to do with the manufacture ?—A. A license to manufac in bond is granted to the person who uses spirits free of duty in the manufactur an article in which the alcohol is destroyed. In the manufacture of vinegar the (hol is converted into acetic acid. In the manufacture of fulminate of mercury the alcohol is vaporized and passed off.

By Mr. Fyshe:

Q. In the manufacture of vinegar you collect the duty on the vinegar?—A.

Q. The manufacturer gets the alcohol free?—A. Yes, but an officer is in the tory from the time it opens until it closes, and all the compartments in which the version take place are under the supervision of our officers all the time.

SESSIONAL PAPER No. 29a

By the Chairman:

Q. What is McGill's salary charged against?—A. The adulteration of food.

Q. He is the assistant chief analyst, and will probably be chief analyst, and he is a Bachelor of Arts and a Bachelor of Science?—A. Yes, and a very clever man, one of the brightest men in the country.

Q. He was a science master in the Ottawa Collegiate Institute before he passed into the Government service?—A. Yes.

Q. What is he paid for analysing all these foods?—A. $2,300.

Q. He is wholly in the Government service?—A. Wholly.

Q. He gets nothing else in the way of emolument?—A. No, nothing. It is no salary at all for such a man.

By Mr. Fyshe:

Q. How old is he?—A. About 60. A man with the professional knowledge to enable him to handle the work he is doing ought to get at least $4,000.

Q. I do not see how you can get these men to remain?—A. The reason is this. When he came into the service he was about 40, and he expected to get an increase of salary some day, but he gradually grows old in the service, and cannot go out again into the business world.

By the Chairman:

Q. And in those days the cost of living was lower than it is to-day, and a man could get superannuation?—A. Yes.

Q. You have also to do with fertilizers?—A. We analyse fertilizers as we do food products, for the purpose of protecting the farmers.

Q. That work is carried on in a small way at present?—A. No, you would be surprised at the number of samples of fertilizers submitted every year.

Q. Is there a tendency on the part of the officers of the department, outside and inside, to go past the deputy to secure promotion or better pay?—A. I would not know that if they did it. I cannot tell.

Q. What is the highest position a man can obtain in your department?—A. Deputy minister.

Q. There is nothing beyond $4,000 a year?—A. Nothing at all.

Q. A city excise man has to have some idea of mensuration?—A. Yes. He has to pass an examination, and he cannot improve his standing unless he passes an examination on our technical subjects.

Q. What are the technical subjects?—A. Bookkeeping, Inland Revenue laws, arithmetic, mensuration, malt gauging computation of commodities in bulk, use of the hydrometer and saccharometer, malting and supervision of malt houses, tobacco and cigar manufacture and supervision of factories, stamping, marking, warehousing and removal of exciseable goods, petroleum inspection, distillation and supervision of distilleries, bonded manufactures, and testing of products. He has to pass an examination on all these subjects, and I can assure you that it is an examination that can by no means be classed as easy.

By Mr. Fyshe:

Q. And what wages do you give him when he has passed?—A. It depends entirely on the number of points he secures. If he gets three-fifths on a maximum of 1,500 he is entitled to a second-class certificate; if he gets four-fifths he is entitled to a first-class certificate. The salary of a probationary excise man is only $500 a year. After six months, if his conduct is good, he is permanently appointed at $600. After that he goes on at increments of five per cent a year until his salary reaches $850, unless by one of these examinations he has improved his standing. If he has improved his standing, he can get into the second-class, where the salary is from $850 to $1,000. From that he can go to the first-class, which runs from $1,000 to $1,200.

By the Chairman:

Q. One Promotion examination does not do for all; you have one pr
from second to first and another from third to second?—A. No. If a man
examination secures enough points, he is entitled to go on to the first class.
department never allows a man to jump a class. We keep him a year in the ne
and then promote him to the higher class.

Q. Then the knowledge required by an excise man is largely technical?—
largely technical.

By Mr. Fyshe:

Q. Do you find that your men are tempted with bribes?—A. I have not kno
single case of that kind in twenty years. I have no knowledge or information
of our officials being offered a bribe. I will tell you why I think that is rare. 1
run by the proprietor of an establishment is too great to cause him to put hir
the hands of an official. One of these distillery properties which we could seiz
be worth ten or twelve million dollars, and the proprietor is not likely to put
at the mercy of an officer.

By the Chairman:

Q. Do people in your outside service give bonds?—A. They give bonds.

By Mr. Fyshe:

Q. What kind of bonds?—A. The bonds of a guarantee company, appr
the Government.

Q. What companies do you patronize?—A. There are five or six; I can
the names just now. They are all Canadian or British companies.

By the Chairman:

Q. Have you throughout your department more officials than the departn
quires—a redundancy of officers?—A. I can hardly answer that; I do not
Reports we get from outside would indicate that we have not enough; but
quality were improved, I think the number need not be exceeded.

Q. Do you find that they come up to the standard when they enter?—A. S
some do not.

Q. If they do not pass that initial examination, they stay where they a:
Yes, they stay in the lower ranks unless they pass the examination. They can
any promotion.

Q. In your outside service is it like the inside service, that a man who h
promoted is doing the same kind of work year in and year out?—A. Very large
so in all branches of the service, because we will not put any man in charge
special survey unless he has passed that examination. We will not put a 1
charge of a distillery unless we know his character and work, and until he has
his fitness by passing the highest examination.

Q. Although a man be doing the same class of work after promotion, the
tion shows him to possess a higher standard of ability?—A. Yes, it shows that

Q. But taking all the outsiders, you think the standard might be improve
There is no doubt it could be improved, we could get better men if we selecter

By Mr. Fyshe:

Q. Is there a good spirit in the men?—A. Yes. I think on the whole that
said.

By the Chairman:

Q. What is the highest pay of an officer of the outside service?—A. $2,500.
is the salary of an inspector of a district.

Q. Looking at the future, is there any inducement for any brilliant boy to stay in the department?—A. No. There is every inducement, in my opinion, for him to go out. I think a young man is unwise to go into the Government service.

By Mr. Bazin:

Q. Still, you have always plenty of applications?—A. Always. If there is a vacancy, there are probably a hundred applicants for it.

By Mr. Fyshe:

Q. They all overestimate the advantages?—A. They all overestimate the advantages. There are no advantages.

Q. Except for people who have no energy worth speaking of or power of initiative or ambition to get on?—A. If a man is willing to go into a service and simply exist there, satisfied with $600 or $700 a year, and do his work in a mechanical way, he gets the place he wants, I presume.

Q. Of course, no one admits that he is that kind of a man?—A. I do not think he would acknowledge it himself.

By the Chairman:

Q. You have not many women in your department?—A. Not a great many.

Q. You have only seven or eight?—A. Eight, I think.

Q. Are there more women applying to enter the department now than men?—A. I will not say that there are more, but there are many applications from ladies to get into the department.

Q. It was said that the increased number of women applying for entrance to the departments arises from the fact that they are paid better at the beginning and have better prospects than bright young men?—A. I do not think that is the case. The women, as a rule, never rise to high positions. I fancy the highest, with few exceptions, would be to the junior second class.

Q. But they all enter at $500?—A. They all enter as third-class clerks at $500.

Q. In the outside world the emolument for women is nothing like $500?—A. Not as great as that.

Q. That is to say, a woman entering the public service enters at a higher salary proportionately than a man would, as compared with the opportunities in the outside world?—A. I fancy so. I have no means of knowing what they receive in commercial life.

Q. Last year the Auditor General had correspondence with you in regard to a refund of duty on raw leaf tobacco. Has that question been settled?—A. No, it has not.

Q. Has it been referred to the Department of Justice?—A. Yes. The Department of Justice has given an opinion that the Governor in Council had not the authority to pass the order granting the refund, and I had a draft Act prepared for the last session of Parliament to legalize those payments, making the Act retroactive. At the same time the Government had under contemplation a rearrangement of the manner of the collecting of duty on tobacco which in itself would have nullified the order referred to; but the session came to an end without the question being reached.

Q. Then, the Auditor General's contention was right?—A. Yes.

Q. Have you ceased the practice?—A. No, we have not. We follow the Order in Council.

Q. What does it amount to?—A. About $40,000 a year.

Q. You have to continue doing what according to the Department of Justice is illegal?—A. We have probably no absolute right to go on.

Q. It is the formal opinion of the Department of Justice that the Auditor General is right?—A. That the Governor in Council had no right to pass the order.

Q. When the inspectors go out on inspection duty they get their bare travelling expenses ?—A. Their actual expenses.

Q. There is no inducement for them to travel ?—A. No. It is an inconvenience. They would gladly escape the trip if they could.

By Mr. Fyshe :

Q. Have you any supervisors above them to see that they do their duty ?—A. They are the highest supervisors themselves.

Q. Nobody is over them ?—A. Nobody except the department. They report to the department.

By the Chairman :

Q. The Auditor General, finding that the inspectors' returns had not come in for some years, wrote to the department ?—A. Yes.

Q. Do you think it would be advisable to give the inspectors a per diem allowance to encourage them to travel and do their duty better ?—A. Yes, I think it would because I think they are all men who can be absolutely trusted.

By Mr. Fyshe :

Q. If they could not be trusted——?—A. They should not be where they are.

Q. In addition to that they would give vouchers and hotel bills to show that they had gone?—A. I will not ask any man in my department to produce a hotel bill. They have to swear that all the expenses in their account have been incurred on Government business, and if a man swears that, a man holding the rank of an inspector or collector, I will not ask him to produce vouchers.

By the Chairman :

Q. He simply sends in a sworn statement that he has been on inspection duty and that he is so much out of pocket ?—A. He sends in a statement showing the day he left home, the cost of a cab to the railway station if he took one, the railway fare, the cost of a cab in connection with any inspection at a distant point, and his various personal expenses in detail, and he swears that all was expended on Government business.

Q. It is only absolutely what he is out of pocket ?—A. Only what he is out of pocket.

Q. The inspector gets nothing but the wear and tear of his clothes for going away ?—A. That is all he gets, besides the experience of sleeping in cold rooms.

Q. Then there is no inducement for an inspector to do any more than he has to do ?—A. Except the pride that he would have in doing his work well.

Q. They do their duty, but get nothing except their out-of-pocket expenses ?—A. That is all they get.

Q. And that is no encouragement for them to do their duty ?—A. Not beyond the man's interest in the service.

By Mr. Fyshe :

Q. Do you find your inspectors competent and trustworthy people ?—A. We do. We believe we have a good lot of inspectors.

By the Chairman :

Q. In your system you get all these returns, and they go before the Auditor General ?—A. Yes.

Q. Another complaint he wrote to you about was that he had not received some distillery returns ?—A. My replies explain all these points.

Q. These matters have all been adjusted ?—A. Yes, and all these points explained to him, so that the subject has been dropped.

Q. How about the returns of excise collections ?—A. The returns of excise collections are remitted to the department daily or as soon as the amount reaches $100. Weights and measures collections—in fact all collections—are on the same basis. The collectors of inland revenue and weights, measures and gas, make returns every month showing the nature of all the transactions in their divisions during the month preceding. The same is the case in all the branches. The district inspectors send in a report that they have visited their district, examined the books, checked all the entries, and so on, and that every dollar has been remitted to the department. Then the inspector checks the bonding warehouse to see that the balance of excisable goods actually in bond agrees with the collector's books. His report is sent to Ottawa, and we check it with our books to see that it is all right.

Q. How is the money remitted ?—A. By a draft through a bank.

Q. Your department is one that receives no money at all ?—A. No actual money. Everything comes in in the way of bank drafts and is sent to the Department of Finance, which gives us credit for it, but we do not handle the money itself.

DEPARTMENT OF INLAND REVENUE,
DEPUTY MINISTER'S OFFICE,
OTTAWA, May 25, 1907.

T—pa. S. HOWE, Esq.,
Secretary Civil Service Commission,
Room No. 2, The Senate, Ottawa.

SIR,—I beg to acknowledge the receipt of your communication of the 18th inst., requesting to be furnished with memoranda showing the number of the staff of this department, permanent and extra, graded into classes, and the amount of salaries paid during the years ended June 30, 1892, and June 30, 1906; and also such other information as may in my judgment elucidate the increase of business in this department.

In accordance with your request, I am submitting a statement showing the departmental staff of this department in the years named with the salaries paid to each separate class of officials as well as the aggregate salaries so paid.

From this statement it will be observed that the number of the permanent staff has increased from 27 to 35, that the aggregate salaries, permanent and temporary officials, have increased from $39,073.85 to $48,181.99, and that between these two fiscal years the accrued revenue has increased from $8,076,526 in 1892 to $14,435,642 in 1906.

The total salaries of the departmental staff in 1892 for each one dollar of revenue accrued represented $\frac{48}{100}$ of one cent, and in 1906 $\frac{33}{100}$ of one cent.

The excise revenue in 1892 was $8,007,944, as compared with $14,267,064 in 1906. The cost of collecting the excise revenue in 1892 was 5 per cent, whereas in 1906 it was but 3$\frac{1}{2}$ per cent.

The weights and measures, gas, electricity and law stamp revenue in 1892 was $53,127, whereas in 1906 it amounted to $160,853.

In 1892 the weights and measures revenue was collected at a cost of 182 per cent, whereas in 1906 the cost was 125 per cent.

The collection of the gas and electricity revenue in 1892 cost 217 per cent, and in 1906 but 51 per cent.

I remain, sir,
Your obedient servant,
(Signed)   W. J. GERALD,
Deputy Minister.

7-8 EDWARD VII., A. 1908

STAFF OF THE INLAND REVENUE DEPARTMENT, 1892 AND 1906.

1892.		1906	
1 Commissioner..............	$ 3,200 00	1 Deputy Minister.............	$ 4,000 00
1 Asst. Comr....	3,000 00		
2 Chief Clerks	4,550 00	5 Chief Clerks..	11,049 88
6 1st Class Clerks...............	10,150 00	4 1st Class Clerks...	6,800 00
12 2nd Class Clerks	13,141 59	11 Sr. 2nd Class Clerks..........	14,738 34
1 Jr. 2nd Class Clerk...........	1,000 00	10 Jr. 2nd Class Clerks..........	8,375 00
2 3rd Class Clerks.......	1,728 51	3 3rd Class Clerks	173 14
2 Messengers............	912 50	2 Messengers............	1,310 00
Private Secretary...	600 00	Private Secretary........ ..	520 66
27	$ 38,282 60	35	$ 46,967 02
Temp. Clerks........... $391 29		Temp. Clerks.. ....$ 15 00	
Extra Messenger....... 399 96	791 25	2 Extra Messengers.... 1,199 97	
			1,214 97
	$ 39,073 85		$ 48,181
Revenue in 1892.....	8,076,526 00	Revenue in 1906......	14,435,642

OTTAWA, June 19, 1907.

Dr. ANTHONY FREELAND, Collector of Inland Revenue at Ottawa, called, sworn and examined.

By the Chairman:

Q. You are collector of Inland Revenue?—A. At Ottawa.

Q. How long have you been in the service?—A. I could not say; I think it was in 1901 I came in.

Q. You entered the service in 1901?—A. I think it was, I am not quite sure, sir.

Q. Did you come in as Collector?—A. I came in as Collector.

By Mr. Fyshe:

Q. Where?—A. Here in Ottawa.

By the Chairman:

Q. You are a doctor of medicine ?—A. I am.

Q. Might one ask how you came into the service?—A. You might. Mr. Costigan was my predecessor here, that is, Mr. Harry Costigan. He left, he resigned, and Mr. Stewart was looking around for a man, and there was some difficulty about it. Of course it was a political appointment in a way, and there was some difficulty in getting a proper man; they wanted a man who had passed the Civil Service examination or a man who had a degree, and I had both.

By Mr. Fyshe:

Q. Why had you both?—A. Because I had passed the Civil Service examination years ago, before I studied medicine, and as I had both qualifications, it made it easy for them.

By the Chairman :

Q. You passed the Civil Service examination, and although it was a political appointment, you were not appointed without examination ?—A. Oh, no, I have the Civil Service certificate.

Q. In your department the inspector of weights and measures and the preventive officers are appointed without examination?—A. I cannot say about the inspectors of weights and measures, but the deputy collectors and preventive officers are appointed without examination.

By Mr. Fyshe:

Q. Why is that?—A. Because it is a political necessity apparently. There is no reason to my mind why these appointments should be in the outside service. They should some of them be in the inside service, I think. They are good men, some of them.

By the Chairman :

Q. What is your salary here?—A. $1,800.

Q. What is the revenue derived in this division ?—A. Nearly $400,000 a year. $380,000 I think.

Q. Is there a distillery in your division ?—A. There is no distillery.

Q. Are there breweries ?—A. Three.

Q. Is there any tobacco factory ?—A. No, no tobacco factory, but there is a cigar factory.

Q. What is the strength of your office ?—A. Seven men.

Q. How are they graded ?—A. There is the deputy collector, Class A and two deputy collectors, Class B.

Q. You have a big district, I suppose ?—A. Oh, yes, an immense district; for instance, I have an outpost at Hudson bay and another at Ville Marie, Lake Timiskaming, near Cobalt.

Q. What staff have you besides the deputy collectors ?—A. I have two first class officers.

Q. First class excise men ?—A. First class excise men, one temporary man just put on a little while ago and I have two deputy collectors, Class B.

Q. Where are your offices ?—A. In the Woods building.

Q. In the Woods building ?—A. Yes, 30 Slater street.

Q. Have you any bonded warehouses ?—A. Yes.

Q. Where are they ?—A. They are situate in Ottawa with the exception of one at Ville Marie and one at Moose Factory, Hudson bay.

Q. Where are they situated in Ottawa ? Name some of the warehouses ?—A. For instance, Bate & Sons have one, the Ottawa Wine Vault Co. have one, Kennedy & Co., and others have them, I forget just how many there are.

Q. You have no scattered bonded warehouses all around like the Customs have ? —A. No, no Government bonded warehouses.

Q. Beyond the examination which you passed, the Civil Service Examination, and beyond your graduation at the university, had you any experience in mensuration and distilleries or anything of that kind ?—A. Yes.

Q. What experience had you ?—A. Well, I taught school and I had a special liking for mathematics and chemistry. In Kingston at the time of my examination I was first in chemistry and I always had a liking for mathematics, the higher branches of which I studied.

Q. In what class is your division, A or B ?—A. Well, they are not distinguished as classes A or B, but are divided into first, second or third classes. My division is in the third class.

Q. What is the revenue limit for your division ?—A. $500,000. As soon as I get up to $500,000, it is $400,000 now, I will get into class 2.

Q. What is the revenue limit for class 2 ?—A. From $500,000 to $1,000,000.

Q. Montreal, for instance, would be in class 1 ?—A. Yes.

Q. And some other division which has a revenue between $500,000 and $1,000,000, would be in class 2, and yours, being under $500,000 is in class 3 ?—A. Yes, but there are other classifications; the revenue is one element in determining the class. Another element is the amount of work done. For instance, some places, although they do not take in as much revenue as we do here, still they have more work to do ; they have more tobacco factories and distilleries. There is a small distillery, for instance, at Perth, and that gives them a higher classification than they would otherwise have, on the basis of the two elements.

Q. Have you any important manufactories here, for instance ?—A. No, we have the vinegar factory but that is not important, or not of very much importance.

Q. It is not what you would call an important factory ?—A. No, it is not.

Q. What is the limit of salary to collectors in class 3 ?—A. $1,800, I am at the maximum.

Q. You are at the maximum ?—A. Yes.

By Mr. Fyshe :

Q. What is the minimum ?—A. $1,600, and it rises to $1,800, but when I came in it was $1,400. The minimum has been raised since I came in at $1,400.

SESSIONAL PAPER No. 29a

By the Chairman:

Q. In some special cases, although they have not as large a revenue as your division produces the collector may get a salary equal to yours ?—A. Yes, if they are in charge of a distillery, for instance, or something of that nature.

Q. A deputy collector could not exceed you in salary ?—A. No, I think not ; $1,700 is the limit of the first class deputy, he could not exceed me.

Q. Then collectors are so graded that no assistant can get more than they do ?—A. No.

Q. You were appointed in 1901, you say ?—A. Yes, I think so.

Q. You came in under the present Retirement Act ?—A. Yes.

Q. That is to say, you are contributing five per cent of your own money for a retiring allowance ?—A. Yes, it is treating us in a childish manner, it is like making a boy put money into a savings bank.

Q. One of your predecessors, Mr. Martin Battle, was superannuated ?—A. Yes.

Q. What is your idea, looking at it from the outside service point of view, regarding the abolition of superannuation ?—A. I would prefer the Superannuation Act of course; they are not giving me anything now. I do not look upon the retirement allowance as anything at all, it is taken out of my salary. I ought to have a salary sufficient for me to live on and a salary out of which I could provide for my old age, but I have not, I have only a salary I can live on.

By Mr. Fyshe:

Q. You have the means of earning something outside, have not you ?—A. No, I was coroner for the city when I took this over, and I asked permission to continue that, but it would not be permitted. I could have made $500 or $600 at that, but it was cut right off.

By the Chairman:

Q. Keep on the superannuation question, if you please ?—A. I have made a note or two about superannuation, which will put it clearly. Here is another point I want to make about superannuation—superannuation is a guarantee of permanency to my mind, and the present system is not. Now take the deputy minister, supposing in our department he gets $4,000 a year, and under the old system of superannuation he would be superannuated when he put in his full term at $2,800. In order to supply his place it would cost the country $6,800, because they have to give him $2,800 superannuation and they have to give his successor $4,000, making the cost to the country, $6,800. Now, supposing there is a deputy minister who is under the present system, that is the retiring fund, it costs the country nothing, they just shove him out and a new man takes his salary, and the change costs the country nothing.

Q. It costs the country nothing directly, but they lose a great deal indirectly ?—A. The point I want to make is that there is no financial reason why they cannot dismiss a man at once, if they want to, for political reasons. Before, if they wanted to take action of this kind, those who made the suggestion were confronted with the position, if we do this, we will have to pay him $2,800, and we will have to pay the new man $4,000, and it will make it expensive. Under this system of the retiring fund, I maintain that the conditions are very materially changed, and that the financial objection which prevented such action under the old system will not exist. As soon as ever there is a change of government, political expediency will come into operation and they can dismiss a man at once and can advance the plea that it does not cost the country anything to make the change.

Q. And the man who goes out only gets back his own money ?—A. He only gets back his own money.

By Mr. Fyshe:

Q. It might work great injustice, but of course it does not follow that they will do it ?—A. Well, politicians, the men who do the work in the election, are sometimes very hungry for positions, and they will not stop at anything to get them. I do not say that the Government will do as they want them, but there is always a little danger. If a man has a superannuation to live on he feels independent about that.

By the Chairman:

Q. Coming back to the original question, do you think the abolition of the Superannuation Act was a mistake?—A. It was a mistake, yes.

Q. And no stability attaches to the service in consequence of that?—A. There is no stability in consequence, and not only that, it has been practically a lowering of the salary, because with the Superannuation Act I did not provide for my old age and my salary was enough to live on, but my old age was provided for. Now I only get the same salary, I have not the superannuation to fall back upon, but I have to provide for my retirement out of the same salary, so that it is practically a lowering of my salary.

By Mr. Fyshe:

Q. Undoubtedly, but you were not under the old Superannuation Act?—A. No, I am under the retiring allowance. They stopped $90 a year from my salary so that I am only getting $1,710 a year to live on in this country and educate my children.

By the Chairman:

Q. So that it would be just possible, supposing the pendulum swung back in another direction, that you might be asked to give way to some prominent man on the other side, and that you would go out and take your retirement allowance with you?—A. Yes.

Q. Of course, being in a way a political appointment, that would be within the bounds of possibility?—A. Within the bounds of possibility.

Q. You have no other emolument or fees in connection with your office?—A. No.

Q. And you have no outside practice now?—A. No outside practice now.

By Mr. Fyshe: •

Q. Don't you think you were foolish, doctor, in entering the service?—A. Yes, I was, I think so sometimes.

By the Chairman:

Q. Then the whole of your time is given to the service of the country?—A. Yes. I might say that I have passed several examinations since coming into the public service.

Q. And you have generally, since coming into the department, endeavoured to acquire all information in order that you may render yourself creditable to the department?—A. I do not like to speak about myself, but I wrote in a first-class examination and I passed, and I wrote on a special examination and came very near passing. The reason I did not pass was on account of not having any tobacco factory or distillery here. Theory is all very well but it will only take you a little distance, and I had not the actual experience that was necessary to pass.

Q. Supposing you had all the knowledge of all the spheres embraced in your department you can never become Collector of Inland Revenue at Montreal?—A. Well—

Q. Would not the same conditions apply to Montreal as exist here?—A. In what way?

Q. That the local people look after their patronage down there, you could not aspire to that position?—A. Oh, no, no.

Q. Having entered the service here, you are limited to Ottawa?—A. Yes, pretty much.

Q. And you have got to the top of the tree under present conditions?—A. Yes, under present conditions. Then we have to pay for guarantee bonds through a company. Formerly we had to get individuals to become security for us, but that has been changed and now the cost of the guarantee bonds is taken out of our salary, making another reduction of salary.

By Mr. Fyshe :

Q. What is the amount of the guarantee bond you give ?—A. I do not remember.
Q. Do you pay anything ?—A. Yes, it is stopped out of my salary every month, sixty cents per month.

By the Chairman :

Q. You deposit your money to the credit of the Receiver General every day ?—A. Yes, every day.
Q. You have a system of inspection in your department, have you not?—A. Yes.
Q. How often does the inspector come around to see you ?—A. Every three months, he is very regular, a good inspector, there is no better.
Q. Do you know when he is likely to come, or approximately ?—A. No, he comes without our knowing when to expect him.
Q. What does he do when he enters the place ? Does he take the keys from you ?—A. The first thing he does he goes to the books and checks them right off. That is the first thing. He goes to the cash book and checks the cash book with the orders. And then after checking the cash book with the orders, he checks the journal with the orders. Then he takes the balance off the journals and then goes around the warehouses, counts the packages and compares them with the balance he has in order to see that they are all right. Then he counts over the stamps to see that the stamps on hand and the stamps that have gone out make up our debit. You are debited with so many cigar stamps, for instance, and the stock you have left, with what has gone out, must equal that debit.
Q. There can be no method of emptying casks in the bonded warehouses and filling them up with water and defrauding the government in that way ?—A. No.

By Mr. Fyshe :

Q. In collecting your excise duties, do you collect the duty by selling the party stamps, or how ?—A. On tobacco and cigars we sell stamps, that is how it is collected, but the duty on whiskey is not collected that way. There is no stamp for whiskey at all. We have the barrels in bond and when they want a certain barrel they come and tell us the gauge marks and numbers of that barrel, how many gallons it contains and all that information.
Q. You have an officer to check that ?—A. We have an account of it in our books and the department have an account of it in their books and the merchants have an account of the marks on the barrel, &c.
Q. In collecting duty on cigars and tobacco do you see that the stamps are affixed?—A. No, the officer does, he sees that they are affixed, we give the stamps to the officer.
Q. He is an officer in your department ?—A. Yes.

By the Chairman :

Q. All the staff of your office have been appointed politically, of course ?—A. No, I cannot say they have been. I do not think the accountant was, he was in the service before being appointed accountant. He went in as a messenger and has worked himself up from the ground. His was not a political appointment. Mr. Laporte was not a political appointment, but I fancy all the others were, myself included.
Q. You say there are special classes ?—A. One of the deputy collectors is in class A and two deputy collectors are in class B.
Q. That is to say, out of a staff of seven, you have three deputy collectors ?—A. Yes.

7-8 EDWARD VII., A. 1908

Q. And they are exempted from any examination under the Act ?—A. Yes.

Q. Simply they were appointed by their friends to office ?—A. Yes.

Q. Have you found the deputy collectors well up to the mark ?—A. Well, one of them is. He is anxious to get along and do his duty, but the others are not. The others just want to draw their salary and get things as easy as they can.

Q. Are they at different places or are they all at Ottawa ?—A. They are all at Ottawa, the man at Moose Factory just gets percentage.

Q. If you had fewer deputy collectors, men who were always anxious to do their duty and hard work, you might do with less than three, I suppose ?—A. Oh yes, I could do with less than three deputy collectors. The deputy collectors in Class B do not in fact rank as deputy collectors. It is just a name to cover the payment of that salary. there is no stated salary for that class of deputies, so that they can be given pretty much what salary the department likes.

Q. Does it not come to this that political appointments are made to provide salaries for certain people, and if only people were appointed who were necessary to do the work there could be better remuneration paid to the other officers ?—A. I would not like to answer that question, I was a politician myself and I do not want as an old politician to put anything in the way of the Government helping its friends.

By Mr. Fyshe:

Q. You are an old politician ?—A. Yes, I interfered in politics a little; being an Irishman I cannot keep out of politics.

Q. Do you not think after being in the service for a few years, your ideas about the political way of doing things begin to change ?—A. Well, I tell you, I have seen some excellent men come in and I have seen some poor men. As far as I know men those that are rewarded by the higher appointments are generally good men. They are generally members of parliament who have been defeated, or business men or something of that nature, all good men and generally smart men. but when you come down to the lower grades the political appointments that are made are not good appointments at all, they are just ward heelers.

By the Chairman:

Q. These people that have been appointed in this way, are they amenable to discipline ?—A. Oh, yes.

Q. They do what they are told ?—A. Yes, they do what they are told.

Q. In seeking for extra remuneration in your office, do your subordinates pass you by and go to the department ?—A. No.

Q. They all go through you ?—A. Only once, they did that once, and I called them to account and it never happened again.

Q. It never happened again ?—A. No, in such case the department acts through me.

By Mr. Bazin:

Q. I see you have one man at $1,300 and the other two at $1,125 each ?—A. Yes. they are first-class officers those two men. Does it give the names there ?

Q. Yes, Fox and Slattery ?—A. Yes, they are first-class officers.

Q. What are they doing ?—A. Slattery is assisting the accountant at present.

Q. And he gets more salary than the accountant ?—A. Yes, the accountants are all wrong; they are not paid at all efficiently.

Q. What does the accountant in your office get ?—A. He gets $1,000 a year and handles $400,000 a year. The accountants are not sufficiently paid at all. They should get as much as a first-class officer at least.

By Mr. Fyshe:

Q. Are these accountants, as a rule, competent ?—A. Yes, my own is very competent.

SESSIONAL PAPER No. 29a

Q. Have they any special training as accountants, or do they rise in the service ? —A. This man had not; he rose from messenger and there could not be a better man. He is a thoroguh business man; he is there sharp at nine o'clock and would not leave until four, and I am very glad of it, because I am not so exact myself. He is a thoroughly good man.

Q. You place implicit confidence in him?—A. Oh, yes; place implicit confidence in him, I could not have a better, he is accurate and he understands the books; we have a complicated system of bookkeeping because it is not only. a straight keeping of books, but checks and counter checks have to be provided.

Q. I can see it is wearing?—A. He has to be more than an accountant, he has to be an actuary, or whatever you call those men who are experts in bookkeeping.

By Mr. Bazin:

Q. That other man there, McGuire, gets $1,300, what is he ?—A. He is a deputy collector, that is a political appointment, Class A.

Q. Bennett, Laporte and McGuire are deputy collectors?—A. Yes, you will see the other two are Class B.

Q. I see there is a big difference in salary?—A. Yes, they do not rank as deputy collectors except for the sake of giving them salary.

Q. Have you any lockers in your office ?—A. We do not call them lockers in our service, they have lockers in the Customs Department; it is excise officers in our department.

Q. Who are they?—A. Well, the deputy collectors, they all do the same work.

Q. They go around to where?—A. To the different places and deliver the goods.

Q. They get big salaries for that in Ottawa.

The CHAIRMAN.—And better in Montreal.

By Mr. Bazin:

Q. And much smaller in Quebec. I see what we call 'lockers' in Quebec, or men who go around the bonded warehouses and the merchants' places, they get $800, that is all?—A. No, Mr. McGuire attends to the bonded warehouse work like that and to the vinegar factory, and he has to be there pretty much all the time, because he has to test the vinegar going through it to see that there is no fraud practised on the Government. That takes up all his time. Mr. Bennett is employed in the cigar factory, and the other men have several factories. We have no preventive men here specially appointed, we have in a way, we have women paid in the preventive service, but they are in the department; I do not know what they are doing, but I pay them.

By the Chairman:

Q. Even if you had preventive officers, they would be appointed politically and without examination?—A. Yes, but what I want to draw your attention to is that our men do preventive service; whenever we get any information we send our men out. For instance, we sent up to the temperance county above here and seized a still; they thought apparently that a temperance county was a good place in which to make whiskey.

Q. All the officers in the outside service when they are appointed are started at the minimum?—A. Yes.

Q. What percentage is the annual increment—5 per cent?—A. I was appointed at $1,400, and I got $70 a year increase, and when I was getting that the minimum was increased to $1,600 and then I got $80 a year increase until I got to the maximum.

Q. But is this increase given perfunctorily whether a man is worth it or not ?—A. No, for instance, take Fox and Slattery, Slattery is getting $1,125 salary, he is up to his maximum, but Fox is not. There were marks against him and his salary was not increased.

Q. It is on the report of the officer, and in your division the report comes from you ?—A. From me.

Q. Then supposing you report against a man, are you overruled?—A. Well, no, I cannot say I am.

Q. Supposing you reported against McGuire?—A. It would be acted upon right at once.

Q. Is it not possible that junior officers might upset the report of their superior officer by using political influence?—A. I doubt it very much. I think any finding of delinquencies would be through myself, because to be frank with you, I have great sympathies with some men who have failings, especially with old men who drink. The young man who drinks I have no hesitation in reporting, because I think the best thing to do is to cut him out, in his own interest, and let him get better habits. But the man who is old and who has acquired the habit and cannot get rid of it entirely, I think it would be a great sin to report him. I told Mr. Bernier to his face once that I could not do that, because when an old man has acquired that habit it is hard to break. And then again an old man requires stimulation more or less.

By Mr. Fyshe:

Q. And it would have the same effect?—A. No, it would not. If there is anything wrong in my department about that I will take some responsibility on that score. Mr. Gerald is a very strict man and Mr. Bernier was also very strict in that matter.

By the Chairman:

Q. I suppose the work does not depend upon times and seasons, you have daily work all the year around in your department?—A. Oh, yes, there is hardly a time we are not busy.

Q. Is there any particular season when the work is harder?—A. Yes.

Q. How so?—A. At Christmas time there is a great increase in the work at Christmas and around the holidays.

By Mr. Bazin.

Q. And around Easter?—A. Yes, but at Christmas and New Years especially. That is the great season. I think on one day around Christmas we took in $8,000, that was in one day, just getting in goods.

By the Chairman:

Q. And sometimes on the eve of budget speeches?—A. Oh, yes.

Q. But except at Easter and Christmas and New Year's Day?—A. The work is pretty steady.

Q. What leave of absence do you take?—A. Three weeks.

Q. You go fishing occasionally, I suppose?—A. No, I haven't fished and I do not hunt either. There is too much work about it; I had the gout.

Q. Do the whole staff take three weeks?—A. Yes, all except one man, and that is that man Fox who does not take any holidays, but who loses the time off and on during the year.

Q. They do not go away all together, I suppose, you always keep enough on duty to carry on the work of the office?—A. Oh, yes, two is the largest number away at one time.

Q. Do you keep an attendance book?—A. No.

Q. You have no occasion, that does not apply to the outside service?—A. No.

Q. What are the office hours?—A. From nine to four, with one hour for dinner.

Q. That is to the public?—A. That is in the office. But we take in hours outside of that, and they have to pay extra for it. I will explain how that is. Supposing anything goes wrong in the vinegar factory, and they want a man to go down there on Sunday or any other time outside office hours, they have to pay us.

By Mr. Fyshe:

Q. Who pays you?—A. The person requiring our services will have to pay us extra. We will charge it to them; they will pay it to the Government, and it will come back to us.

SESSIONAL PAPER No. 29a

By the Chairman:

Q. Have you any suggestion with regard to the improvement of the outside service in the excise department ?—A. Well, I have. I was thinking perhaps—the idea I had in my mind is this, that men like first-class collectors and second-class collectors that are collecting over $1,000,000 and $500,000 respectively should be paid over what they are getting now. For instance, I see that a chief clerk in the inside service, Class A. will get $2,800, and Class B will get $2,500. I think that a collector, that I myself should get as much as a chief clerk. I am collecting about $400,000, with seven or eight men under me, and have great responsibility. I am getting $1,800, and a first-class clerk—I know some of them in the Post Office and they are getting $2,500 a year on a rating as chief clerk.

By Mr. Fyshe:

Q. That does not seem proportionate?—A. No, not proportionate to the amount of work and the responsibilities involved.

Q. They havn't as much responsibility as you have?—A. Not at all; no responsibility compared to what I have.

Q. Because the collector is certainly in a responsible position?—A. Yes.

Q. And he has to see that other people beneath him do their duty, and a first-class clerk is relieved even of that?—A. I have been trying to get some sort of classification by which to make a comparison between the inside service and the outside service, but it is extremely difficult to make the different grades correspond, and I think I cannot manage it. I was endeavouring to get them to correspond to make the chief clerk, Class A and B, the first-class clerk, the second-class clerk and the different grades in the two branches of the service correspond for purposes of comparison, but it cannot be done altogether. The deputy collector comes in there and is a disturbing influence.

By the Chairman:

Q. That is a political appointment. What other suggestions have you?

By Mr. Fyshe:

Q. In regard to the deputy collectorships, can't you get along without them?—A. Well, no, you see the deputy collector takes the position of the collector when he is away, and there is where it is a curious thing—the deputy collector, Class A, takes the place of the collector when the collector goes away anywhere on his holidays, or if he is called away anywhere. There is an anomaly there.

Q. Why should you be called away?—A. When he goes on holidays, for instance, and he has to go around visiting the different offices. For instance, I was to be up at Ville Marie visiting our office there; the inspector is there, and he telegraphed me and told me that I was wanted there, but I could not go as I had an appointment here to-day. The deputy collector, Class A, in that case, would take my place. But here is the anomaly about it: I pass an examination and am supposed to understand the work, he is a political appointment and does not know anything about it.

Q. The deputies or assistants should be eliminated, I think, there is no harm in having an officer under you who would take your place in your absence, but I do not think he should have the title of 'deputy,' or 'assistant.' He should have the title of 'first clerk' or 'accountant,' or whatever title you choose to give him; the title should convey the distinct measure of his responsibility. If you give him the title of assistant or deputy then there is the question as to the extent of his responsibility, whether it may or may not conflict with yours. I think every man's position should be as correctly defined as possible.

By the Chairman:

Q. You have other suggestions there?—A. Yes. I am not satisfied with my classification. I was going to suggest that in respect to first-class collectors, we will say,
was going to compare them with chief clerks, Grade A, and the second and third cla▒▒
collectors with chief clerks, Grade B, then the first and second class accountant, th▒▒
will mean that they are accounting from $500,000 to $1,000,000, and from $1,000,0▒▒
upwards, and special class officers, that is men who pass special class examinations ar▒▒
who rank as first class clerks get $1,900. Then first-class inland revenue officers, w▒▒
have to pass a very stiff examination, men that are getting $1,200, like Fox and Slatte▒▒
and all other accountants, should rank as second-class clerks and go up to $1,5▒▒▒
You see, the limit for them now is $1,200. Then, the other ones, all the rest in t▒▒
service below that, the men who Mr. Bazin calls lockers, &c., should get junior secon▒▒
class pay, from $800 to $1,100. That is as fair a classification as I can get to compa▒▒
it with the inside service.

By Mr. Fyshe

Q. I think you had better put those suggestions in your evidence.
The CHAIRMAN.—As an adjunct to your evidence. You will get this to revise a▒▒
any suggestions you desire to make you can do so?—A. I was giving the reasons w▒▒
we should be put on a level with the inside service. The work is more important th▒▒
that of the mass of the chief clerks, that is the collecting of this money and the loo▒▒
ing after it. Secondly, our examinations are the most difficult in the service and
would like you to send and get a copy of the examination paper.
Q. We have it?—A. I may say there was a general kick at the time I was passing
this special examination because of the extreme difficulty and length of the question.
There were twenty questions in mensuration each one of which would take from one
quarter to three-quarters of an hour to work out. It was not the difficulty of the
questions so much as it was the nature of the questions owing to the figures used. We
had four or five hours to do it in, but no person could sit down and do the work required in that time in an examination; that is a limit to endurance. We drew up a
protest which was signed by every man under examination and it was sent to the
department, and if the Commission wish to see that protest no doubt it is on file.
We are examined in the higher mathematics, we are examined in conic sections and
we have to know all about cubes and spheres; we are examined in hydrometry, which
takes in specific gravity and which if you go into thoroughly is a very difficult thing.
In order to understand malting, vinegar making, distilling, &c., you have to be a good
chemist. For instance, fermentation must be thoroughly understood. There is the
great scientific Tyndal who brought up this about fermentation and then there is our
friend the bacterial man Pasteur, that all comes under fermentation. The very same
fermentation that causes disease in the human system brings about the changes that
make the vinegar and alcohol. Therefore, as I have already pointed out, it is a most
responsible position, because a man could if he were so inclined, easily make a lot of
money by neglecting his duty. I think there was one man dismissed for being dishonest at one time, but he had made thousands of dollars before being found out.

By Mr. Fyshe:

Q. Was he an officer of the department?—A. Yes.
Q. Where was he engaged?—A. He was at a distillery.
Q. You mean he was a distillery examiner?—A. He was in charge of the distillery, and he was winking at things. I mention that of course to show the responsibility of the position.
Q. You are in the Department of Inland Revenue?—A. Yes. That is all, I
fancy, with respect to classifications.

SESSIONAL PAPER No. 29a

By the Chairman:

Q. Have you any other remarks to make ?—A. I have a few remarks to make about our examination. You see, in our branch of the service, the idea is to have officers as competent as possible, and I think there should be prescribed text books for them to study.

By Mr. Fyshe:

Q. Even after they are in the service ?—A. Yes, for the promotion examinations. A man comes in as a third class excise man and works his way up. After he comes in there there should be a text book provided for him to study on distilling, on malting, on vinegar making and all such things. There is an English work by Loftus that takes in all those things, mathematics and everything of that kind; a text book should be prescribed and the examinations should be limited to the text books authorized.

Q. To give him a chance of promotion?—A. Yes, sir. Another suggestion that I have to make is this, that papers you have written on at the examination—our papers are now collected and we are not allowed to see them again. That does not give the other man who is coming up for examination a chance. They do not know what they are going to be examined upon. When I went up for examination the only paper I saw was a paper which was published in the Inland Revenue Report. it was for 1876 and 1880, the examination papers for those two years were printed, but they have not been printed since that time.

Q. Why do you think they should have the privilege of seeing the other people's papers?—A. I do think that the papers set for the examination this year should be published and that the men who wrote on that examination should be allowed to take them away with them. The idea of the examination is not to pluck a man, or to keep him out. but to make the officer better fitted for his duties and so the candidates for examination should be allowed to know what they are to be examined upon, and it would assist them if the examination papers set for the previous year were accessible to them.

Q. Can the men who write not take away the papers with them?—A. No, they are not permitted, those papers are taken away from them and they are not allowed to see them afterwards.

Q. But you could keep a copy of them?—A. No, we do not have time to make a copy. anyway you are not allowed.

By the Chairman:

Q. Are the questions in the paper now of a catchy nature?—A. Yes, and not only of a catchy nature, but the work was extremely arduous as it was put in very ugly figures. I can show you one instance; I cannot just remember the exact figures, but it was something like this, just for illustration: There was a box, and the area of one side of it was 38·2 and another side of it was 1·564, and then this other side would be 1·236, or something like that, and the question was what each edge of that box would be.· It was all set out in three places of decimals which was not at all necessary in order to illustrate the principle, but it gives an immense amount of work to the parties writing on the examination.

By Mr. Fyshe:

Q. It makes the operation of figuring it out difficult?—A. It makes it very tedious, but it does not illustrate the principle any more than it would if the figures were fewer. That is the idea I wish to impress upon the Commission, that the multiplication of figures in that way is unnecessary and is not required to illustrate the principle.

Q. That is a very important distinction to make?—A. Yes, the questions set entailed a lot of absolutely unnecessary work and that affects a man materially when he has only a limited time.

29a—20½

By the Chairman:

Q. When a probation excise man is regularly appointed he begins at $600 a year
A. No, sir, $500.

Q. And when he passes after probation?—A. I think he goes up to $800.

Q. What chance has this man, you are talking about a probationary officer, e
to get beyond the $2,500, even if he could get that?—A. None, he can never get th
in Ottawa, he cannot do it; he has no chance whatever of doing that, and he has v
little chance of getting up to a first-class officer in this division here.

Q. Do you find now that there is a disinclination to enter the service in the lo\
grade?—A. Well, I could not say. I have not had any experience in that. I have o:
been in the department a few years, and this is the first vacancy since I was here.

Q. Is it not likely under the present development of the country with talent bei
bought up in all directions and with the slight chance of promotion, or doing bet
for one's self in the Government's service, that ability and enterprise would go el
where?—A. Yes. For instance, my son is in the Post Office Department; he had
B.A. degree, and he took the M.A. this morning over in Ottawa University. He
not going to stay in the service, he is in there now, but he is just there temporarily
get a little money ahead, that is all. As soon as he gets that, he will leave.

Q. You have not followed up the examination for entrance into the service,
suppose?—A. Well, no, I have not done that, sir.

Q. Do you know that out of 349 successful candidates at the last examinati
230 were women?—A. Well, of course that is a very difficult matter to deal with. F
instance, I have an old *Nineteenth Century Magazine*, printed in English, in whi
it advocates women getting into the service, that they could do the work as well
men, and that the men should get out and do the hard work and let the women do t
unproductive work; from an economic standpoint that would be all right.

Q. Is there any position in the outside service of the Inland Revenue Departme
to which it would be desirable to appoint women?—A. No, it would not.

Q. There is none at all?—A. None at all.

Q. What is going to be the condition of the public service in Canada when all t
records are kept by women?—A. I would not like to say.

Q. You were relieved then from the privilege of having ladies in your offi
—A. Oh, yes, I haven't them at all.

Q. Would it tend to the stability of the public service, do you think, if there v
an exclusive writer class, that is to say, a class for small pay men?—A. Yes, I think
would, I think it would be a good idea. I think there should be a special class for '
smaller pay men.

Q. Although there might not be much hope of getting out of it?—A. Well, a
man of ability will rise. There is one man of ability went into the Post Office Depi
ment as a letter carrier, now he is a second-class clerk ,and he can go on up higher.
think any man of ability can pass the examinations and go on, but there are men th
who, as soon as they get that position, will not qualify, they want to get the mo:
without doing the necessary labour.

Q. You think it might be beneficial to the service to have a writer class?—A. 1

Q. Have you ever thought of any limit for this writer class, a thousand a yea:
so?—A. Yes, I think that amount would do very nicely. I think there are men in
service that do copying, pure mechanical work, that a child in the third class in sch
could do just as well as they do it, they have no initiative, and they have gone on do
that work since they have been in the department. That class I would refer to as
writing class, but they have to bring up their families, they have to be honest and
dustrious, and they should get a thousand a year, but the men who have to do ini
tory work, who have to take the letters and answer them, they should get more.

By Mr. Fyshe:

Q. Yes, they require good judgment?—A. Yes, and they should get well paid
their services and they are worth more than the man who will not take responsibilit;

SESSIONAL PAPER No. 29a

Q. In addition to the writer class there would be the well-paid, highly-educated class?—A. Yes, there would be the elementary and the routine class, and the class who do original work.

Q. Do you think it would be desirable to abolish. political appointments in your department?—A. No, I do not. I think you get in some very good men through political appointments. I, myself, am a political appointment to begin with.

Q. You passed the examination though?—A. Yes, and Dr. Frankland, of Toronto, is a political appointment, he did not pass any examination, and he is an excellent officer.

By the Chairman:

Q. I would remind you, Doctor, that we are talking generally, not particularly? —A. I stand corrected. Well, there are a number of these men who are good officers, and that is one reason why I mentioned Mr. Frankland; he was a business man, and he wants to do away with a lot of red tape and do business on business lines. His was a political appointment, and I think the service has done well by getting him in.

Q. If you think political appointments should be retained, do you not think that the entire service, the outside service of the department, should be thrown into one and that there should be no disability such as there is at present, which would prevent your leaving Ottawa and going to Montreal?—A. I don't think that could ever be overcome, there will always be political pull.

By Mr. Fyshe:

Q. Should we not endeavour to get the best system, and if necessary, eliminate 'pull'?—A. The difficulty is the distinction which is drawn between the inside and the outside service, the deputy collector is used for a higher political appointment. The objection I would have is this: Why are these confined to the outside service, why are not the same principles applied to the inside service, the only ones in the inside service are the deputies.

By the Chairman :

Q. Would not that be extending the abuse rather than contracting it ?—A. Yes, but in the higher offices you will get better men.

Q. In your department the lower officials are political appointments—the deputy collectors?—A. Well, the deputy collector is a high appointment, he goes up to $1,500 a year.

Q. You had to pass an examination?—A. Yes.

Q. And the deputy collector has to go up by a system of promotion ?—A. Yes.

Q. Do you not think it should be reasonable that the special class of excise man in charge of some big distillery should have some hope of getting a collectorship ?— A. Well, he has. He has to pass examinations, and I think he has to have a pull.

By Mr. Bazin :

Q. It will depend upon his influence ?—A. Yes, he has to depend upon his influence, there is no doubt about it, influence counts.

By Mr. Fyshe :

Q. Which it should not ?—A. It should not, but it does and no doubt it will.

By the Chairman :

Q. Take the man in charge of Gooderham's or Walker's distillery, shouldn't he have a chance to get to the higher positions in the service?—A. Yes.

Q. At present he has not ?—A. Well, he has some chance.

7-8 EDWARD VII., A. 1908

Q. But the chance is so remote ?—A. Well, the chances are remote. I have a memo. with regard to this matter of the cost of living which I intended to deal with, but you have had so much about it already that I do not think it necessary to go into that.

Witness retired.

To the Chairman and Gentlemen of the Civil Service Commission,
Ottawa, Ont.

GENTLEMEN,—We the officers of Inland Revenue (Excise Branch), of the division of Montreal, respectfully submit :

That in the course of the last session of parliament we addressed to the Honourable Mr. Templeman a petition asking for an increase of salaries.

We have become aware, through the press, that we could communicate with you and, therefore, take the liberty to present, for your consideration, the principal reasons underlying our request; hoping that you will find them just and reasonable, and worthy of being recommended by you to whom it may concern.

1st. On account of the rapid and enormous increase in the cost of living in Montreal, the present salaries are incontrovertibly insufficient. The cost is still increasing on the principal items. It has been established by experts that, during the last ten years, the percentages of increase are as follows:—Rent, 50 per cent; provisions, 50 per cent; clothing, 25 per cent, and fuel, 22 per cent. •

Under the most economical conditions, far from being able to make provision for the future of our families (which is, undoubtedly, their right) we find great difficulty in meeting our legitimate current expenses.

2nd. When establishing a comparative scale of salaries some fifteen or twenty years ago, owing to the special and technical knowledge required by excise officers, a higher grade of salaries, than that paid to skilled workmen was granted ; but now it is, in some cases, inferior to that of an ordinary labourer. ·It seems only reasonable to ask that we should receive higher remuneration than the labourer, or skilled workman, who has no such responsibility as we have, nor has he to submit to such a high standard of examination.

3rd. Not wishing to exaggerate the importance of our position, we cannot let pass unnoticed, the high qualifications the department requires from us, and the great responsibilities pertaining to our position as excise officers. No doubt, Mr. W. J. Gerald, our deputy minister, will be pleased to supply you, on request, with copies of the last promotion and special class examinations, from which you will see the extensive knowledge we require of arithmetic, commercial and departmental accountantship, mensuration, computation of commodities in bulk, a complete knowledge of the laws and regulations of our department as applied to the practical working of the various establishments, and to possess a technical knowledge of the working of distilleries. breweries. malt houses, tobacco and cigar factories, and other places of business controlled by the department.

In the exercise of his duties, the excise officer is actually the assessor of the duty on all articles subject to excise. Incompetence or negligence cannot be tolerated, on account of the loss of revenue which may be occasioned thereby. He must acquaint the manufacturer with the laws and regulations governing his establishment, and efficiently protect the revenue in preventing all irregularities and fraud.

4th. We, in Montreal, collect yearly more than $6,000,000, which is greater than one third of the excise revenue of the whole Dominion. Some years ago the cost of collection in this division was 2 per cent, whereas to-day it is only nine-tenths of 1 per cent.

On account of the enormous volume of business transacted a continuous audit is proceeding in the office, and the outside surveys.

For these and other reasons, besides a general increase of salaries, we would add a few suggestions. which, if acceded to, would contribute to overcome our present difficulties.

1st. Seeing the importance of the division of Montreal, on account of the volume of business, as well as the revenue collected, we would urge that a special scale of salaries be made to apply to this division.

2nd. In the matter of promotions, we are of the opinion that, qualification being equal, the preference should be given according to seniority.

3rd. The augmentation of salaries from the minimum to the maximum be made at the rate of 10 per cent instead of 5 per cent as at present.

4th. That the staff, as in the case of some other departments, be paid bi-monthly, instead of monthly.

5th. That in lieu of the present retiring system, other provision, more satisfactory to us, be inaugurated; if a better system cannot be found let all be placed under the provisions of the old Superannuation Act.

6th. That it is desirable for the sake of uniformity in the classification of officers, and of equal justice to all, that the special class be not restricted as to numbers, and that any officer having passed the special class examination be paid the minimum salary of that class. At present, an officer, who has passed this examination, may have to wait ten years or more before being placed on the special class list and drawing the minimum salary.

Praying that our petition will receive your favourable consideration, and that we may be participants in the prosperity of this, our country,

Respectfully submitted by your humble servants.

MONTREAL, May 29, 1907.

A M. le Président et Messieurs
de la Commission royale *re* Service Civil,
Ottawa, Ont.

MESSIEURS,—L'humble requête des soussignés, Employés d'Accise de la cité de Montréal, expose respectueusement:—

Que dans le cours de la dernière session du Parlement, nous avons adressé à l'honorable M. Templeman une requête portant une augmentation de salaire;

Qu'informés, par la voie des journaux, que nous pouvions communiquer avec vous, nous prenons conséquemment la liberté de soumettre à votre considération les principales raisons motivant notre requête, espérant que vous les trouverez justes et raisonnables, et pourtant susceptibles d'être recommandées par vous à qui de droit:

1. Que vu l'augmentation rapide et énorme du coût de la vie à Montréal, les salaires actuels sont devenus pour nous incontestablement insuffisants.

Cette augmentation encore progressive des principaux item indispensables à la vie, d'après une statistique établie par des experts, pour les dix dernières années, se résume comme suit:—Loyer, 50 pour 100; aliments, 50 pour 100; vêtements, 25 pour 100; combustible, 22 pour 100.

Sous les conditions économiques actuelles, loin de faire la plus légère économie pour l'avenir, que nos familles sont en droit d'attendre de nous, nous avons peine, dans bien des cas, à rencontrer nos dépenses les plus légitimes;

2. Qu'en établissant un état comparatif des salaires en général il y a 15 ans, il était légalement reconnu, qu'en raison des connaissances techniques et spéciales nécessaires aux officiers d'Accise, leur salaire était supérieur à celui des ouvriers professionnels, tandis qu'aujourd'hui il est parfois inférieur au salaire d'un simple ouvrier; ceci naturellement nous est tout à fait préjudiciable;

3. Que sans vouloir exagérer l'importance de notre position, nous ne pouvons laisser passer inaperçues les qualifications que le département requiert de nous, et les lourdes responsabilités qui incombent à notre charge comme officiers d'Accise:

(a) Sur votre demande, notre Deptué-Ministre, M. Gerald, se fera un plaisir, nous n'en doutons pas, de vous soumettre copies des derniers examens de promotion et de classe spéciale, par lesquelles vous constaterez les connaissances approfondies que

7-8 EDWARD VII., A. 1908

nous devons avoir de l'arithmétique, comptabilité commerciale et départmentale, mensuration, jaugeage et mesurage de vaisseaux; de connaître la loi du Revenu parfaitement dans son application, et de posséder la science technique du malteur, brasseur, distillateur, manufacturiers de tabac et cigares et autres industriels dont la production est contrôlée par notre département;

(b) Dans l'exercice de ses fonctions, l'officier qualifié devient l'assesseur proprement dit des droits sur tous les articles sujets aux droits d'accise; l'incompétence ou négligence ne peuvent être tolérées, vu la perte de revenus que le département pourrait subir; il doit instruire les industriels des droits régissant leurs établissements; veiller à protéger efficacement les droits appartenant au département en empêchant ou prévenant toute irrégularité ou fraude possibles;

4. Que nous collectons à Montréal au delà de $6,000,000, soit plus que le tiers ($\frac{1}{3}$) du revenu de tout le Dominion; ce volume d'affaires nécessite une audition continuelle des livres de notre division.

Relativement à cette collection il y a quelques années, le coût en salaire était 2 pour 100; maintenant il n'en est plus que les $\frac{7}{10}$ de 1 pour 100.

A ces causes et pour nombre d'autres d'ordre inférieur, en outre d'une augmentation générale de salaires vivement sollicitée, nous intercalons dans cette requête quelques suggestions, qui contribueraient, si elles étaient prises en considération, à améliorer notre position présente:

1. Qu'étant donnée l'importance de la division de Montréal, tant au point de vue des affaires transigées, qu'au montant des droits perçus, qu'une échelle spéciale de salaires soit adoptée pour les employés de cette division;

2. Qu'en matière de promotion, quand il y aura qualification égale, la préférence soit accordée au plus ancien employé;

3. Que l'augmentation du salaire du minimum au maximum s'effectue à raison de 10 pour 100 au lieu de 5 pour 100;

4. Qu'à l'instar de plusieurs autres départements et pour nombre de raisons personnelles, nous soyons payés bi-mensuellement;

5. Qu'en lieu et place de la retenue de 5 pour 100 sur notre salaire, nous demandons, si un autre système de protection ne pouvait être établi en notre faveur, de nous accorder d'être mis sous le système de pension;

6. Qu'il serait désirable, pour l'uniformité de la classification des officiers, et de justice égale pour tous, que la classe spéciale comprenne tous les employés qui ont satisfait aux examens de cette dite classe, avec salaire correspondant.

Et nous ne cesserons de prier.

MONTRÉAL, 29 mai 1907.

Signed:—

G. H. BRABANT,
E. MILLIER,
G. E. PANNETON,
J. F. MILOT,
D. J. WALSH,
A. H. RENAUD,
D. J. KEARNEY,
FIS. VERNER,
ALF. ANDREWS,
I. DUMOUCHEL,
J. S. HAMMOND,
JOS. PREVOST,
EUG. FOREST,
A. P. BELAIR,
J. H. CREVIER,
L. H. MARIN,
D. P. GRAVELINE,
E. J. O'FLAHERTY,
J. O. BOUSQUET,
M. HUGHES,
I. E. A. DESAULNIERS,
F. J. A. TOUPIN,
W. CAVEN,
JNO. D. FOX,

T. M. LANE,
G. NORMANDIN,
C. P. CHAGNON,
GEO. THURBER,
H. J. S. CODD,
JAS. J. COSTIGAN,
J. A. LAMBERT,
L. J. McGUIRE,
C. P. MAINVILLE,
H. LONGTIN,
W. L. ROSS,
A. LEDOUX,
J. A. LESPERANCE,
THEO. DAVID,
WILLIAM RYAN,
J. J. COURTNEY,
WM. J. SCULLION,
HENRY G. S. DIXON,
JAMES DAVIDSON,
C. E. A. PATTERSON,
M. J. O'DONNELL,
D. I. KEARNEY,
J. A. HARWOOD.

MONTREAL, September 11, 1907.

To the Chairman and Gentlemen
of the Civil Service Commission,
Sitting in Montreal.

GENTLEMEN,—On May 29 last we, the officers of Inland Revenue, Montreal, addressed you a petition setting forth our views on what we desired for the betterment of our position as excise officers, permit us to add to said petition a few more remarks.

Montreal division passes about 20,000 entries annually, equal to 60,000 entries in some other divisions or customs, and about 20,000 requisitions ex-factory for stamps; collects over $6,000,000 and has 1 distillery, 4 malt-houses, 10 breweries, 25 tobacco factories, 33 cigar factories, 3 vinegar bonded factories, 2 acetic acid manufacturers, 3 bonded factories for perfumes, 3 bonded factories pharmaceutical preparations, 26 bonded warehouses, not to mention chemical stills and compounders, now this large number of licenses entails a great amount of work both for office work and supervision.

An excise officer who does his duty conscientiously renders himself, to say the least, disagreeable to the public, with whom he comes in contact.

As it is difficult to have competent clerks for office work in the excise office, Montreal, we believe it would be advisable to have a special scale of salaries made for this class of officers, and would suggest an extra allowance for such as are suitable for the work.

In the matter of salaries in general, while we would particularly urge a special scale for this division, we are of the opinion that a deputy collector, class A, should rank with a chief clerk, grade A, of the inside service; an accountant or special class officer in charge with a chief clerk, grade B; a special class officer between grade B and first-class clerk inside, first, second and third class excise officers with the same classes or their equivalents in the inside. We might say, in this connection, that, at present the accountant in Montreal is only in receipt of a salary equal to a second-class clerk in the inside.

When the Customs Montreal collected less revenue than the Excise Montreal now collects, the salary of the collector of Customs was $4,000 per annum, and it would not be too much to scale the salary of the collector of inland revenue to a similar salary as the collector of Customs was then in receipt of.

While we are of the opinion that it would be advisable to give salaries sufficient to compensate for 'duty pay,' yet if found inconvenient it might be well to give duty pay on factories according to a certain standard.

The Government should pay the cost of the guarantee bonds exacted from civil servants.

Under the provisions of the Superannuation Act, if an officer dies, his widow and family receive nothing from the superannuation fund, we would submit for consideration that an allowance be made the widow or children during widowhood or minority, as the case may be, to provide in a small way for the loss of the wage-earner.

We annex hereto a few statistics to show how the cost of living has increased in Montreal in recent years.

We have the honour to be, on behalf of the excise of Montreal,

Your humble servants,

(Signed)   J. A. TOUPIN,
J. O. BOUSQUET,
W. CAVEN,
JNO. D. FOX.

7-8 EDWARD VII., A. 1908

L'ASSOCIATION DES BOUCHERS DE MONTRÉAL.

MONTREAL, September 10, 1907.

I, the undersigned, believe that the proportion of increase of meats and vegetables has fully gone up from 20 to 30 per cent within recent years.

(Signed)   A. PREVOST,
Vice-President.

J. J. JOUBERT,
Ferme St. Michel.

MONTREAL, September 10, 1907.

To whom it may concern :

Having been asked for a report on the milk and butter trade, I hereby certify that within the last ten years the price of such commodities has fully grown up 25 per cent due to high price of fodder, &c., &c.

(Signed)   J. J. JOUBART.

U. H. DANDURAND,
Real Estate Broker.

MONTREAL, September 10, 1907.

To whom it may concern :

I, the undersigned, believe that the proportion of increase of rents in the city of Montreal have varied from 25 per cent to 60 per cent within the last ten years according to location.

(Signed)   W. F. GINGRAS,
For U. H. Dandurand.

EDOUARD GOHIER & CIE.,
Constructors and Real Estate Negotiators,
71 St. James Street.

MOCNTRÉAL, 10 septembre 1907.

Nous soussignés déclarons et croyons que la proportion d'augmentation des loyers dans la cité de Montréal, pour les dix dernières années peut s'évaluer de 60 à 75 pour 100 pour les maisons de 1ère classe et de 40 à 50 pour 100 pour les maisons de condition inférieure.

(Signed)   EDOUARD GOHIER & CIE.

LAPORTE, MARTIN & CIE.

MONTREAL, CAN., September 10, 1907.

To whom it may concern :

In reply to an enquiry about the advance in the prices of the necessaries of life. we wish to state that there is certainly an increase of fully 10 to 15 per cent in the price of general groceries, whilst in provisions the increase is certainly about 35 to 40 per cent.

We know as a fact that we have been forced to increase salaries to a very large percentage owing to said general increase in cost of life.

(Signed)   LAPORTE, MARTIN & CIE , Ltée.
Per L. V. Delorme, Sec. Treas.

HUDON & ORSALI,
Importateurs d'épiceries, thés, vins et liqueurs.

MONTREAL, September 10, 1907.

To whom it may concern:

On being asked to state our opinion about the advance in the prices of groceries. we state that on an average the advance is about 10 per cent, but on provisions it is at least 40 per cent. We had to increase the salaries of our employees about 20 per cent in the last three years. It is a well known fact that rents have advanced out of proportion to everything else.

(Signed)   HUDON & ORSALI,
Per Alexr. Orsali.

L. CHAPUT, FILS & CIE.

MONTREAL, September 11, 1907.

To whom it may concern.

We have received lately an inquiry about the advance in the cost of the necessaries of life, and beg to state there is a great increase of about 10 per cent in the proce of general groceries, and 35 per cent on provisions. In some instances we have been obliged to increase salaries on account of these advances.

Hoping this information will be useful, we remain,

Yours truly,

(Signed)   L. CHAPUT, FILS & CIE.,
Armand Chaput.

HUDON, HEBERT & CIE, LIMITÉE
Importateurs en gros d'épiceries, vins et liqueurs.

MONTRÉAL, 10 septembre 1907.

Mr. J. A TOUPIN,
Percepteur, Revenu de l'Intérieur,
Montréal.

MONSIEUR,—Relativement à la question que vous nous posez, au sujet des articles de consommation qui font l'objet de notre commerce, après étude, nous constatons que dans la dernière décade, il s'est produit, en moyenne, une hausse de 15 pour cent, et ceci au bas mot. Cette hausse s'applique aux articles de toute première nécessité, comme à d'autres qui sont en très grand usage. Nous espérons que cette information vous sera d'utilité pour le but que vous avez en vue.

Bien à vous,

(Signé)   HUDON, HEBERT & CIE., LIMITÉE,
Zéph. Hebert, gérant.

LACKAWANNA COAL CO.

MONTREAL,.September 10, 1907.

To whom it may concern:

We do not hesitate in certifying that the increase in the price of fuel within the last ten years has been fully 20 per cent.

(Signed)   LACKAWANNA COAL CO.,
L. M. LeBel.

DAOUST, LALONDE ET CIE.,
Chaussures et Claques.

MONTRÉAL, septembre 10 1907.

A tous ceuxque ceci pourra intéresser:

Nous constatons que dans la ligne de chaussures, il y a eu une augmentation depuis dix ans, d'au moins 20 à 25 pour 100.

Vos dévoués,

(Signé) DAOUST, LALONDE ET CIE.

RENAUD & CO., .
Jobbers in Hats and Men's Wear.

MONTREAL, September 10, 1907.

To whom it may concern:

This is to certify that within ten years the prices on gents' furnishing goods have advanced from 20 to 30 per cent.

(Signed) RENAUD & CO.,

P. L. Dubord, Manager.

L. C. DE TONNANCOUR,
Marchand tailleur.

MONTRÉAL, septembre 10 1907.

Ceci est pour certifier que dans notre commerce les effets sont augmentés de 25 pour 100 à 30 pour 100 depuis 10 ans.

Votre serviteur,

(Signé) L. C. DE TONNANCOUR.

ARSÈNE LAMY,
Grand magazin départemental.

MONTRÉAL, septembre 11 1907.

Je, soussigné, considère que depuis quelques années il y a eu une augmentation de 25 à 35 pour 100 dans le coût de la vie.

(Signé) ARSÈNE LAMY.

W. A. LAJEUNESSE & CO.,
Exporters' Agents, Commission Merchants, Butter, Cheese, Eggs, Poultry, &c.

MONTREAL, September 10, 1907.

Mr. Bousquet:

DEAR SIR,—To whom it may concern, this is to certify that the price on eggs, butter, cheese, &c., has gone up fully 40 per cent within the last ten years.

We are yours truthfully,

(Signed) W. A. LAJEUNESSE & CO.

SESSIONAL PAPER No. 29a

TRANSACTION OF STAMPS DURING ONE MONTH IN MONTREAL.

ISSUED.

—	No. of Stamp.	Lb.	Amounts.
			$ cts.
On Foreign Tobacco....	971,080	438,921	109,730 26
" Snuff........................	1,080	7,226	1,323 25
" Canadian......	139,122	38,239½	1,911 98
" Farmers' "Rolls"............	10,670	3,710	185 50
" Combination., ...	106,461	28,155½	1,407 79
Total Duty for one month	1,228,413	516,251	114,558 78

—	No. of Stamp.	Lbs.	Amounts.
			$ cts.
On Foreign Cigarettes.....	4,561,544	37,005,870	112,273 11
" Canadian "	1,900	19,000	28 50
" Combination "	2,700	19,000	28 50
Total Duty for one month	4,566,144	37,043,870	112,330 11

—	No. of Stamp.	Cigars.	Amounts.
			$ cts.
On Foreign Cigars..........	48,354	6,123,070	36,738 42
" Combination Cigars............ ..	1,290	77,000	231 00
Total Duty for one month	49,644	6,200,070	36,969 42

This will give for one year about.

Tobacco.....	14,740,956 Stamps.	6,195,012 lb.	1,374,705 36
Cigarettes..	54,793,728 "	444,526,440 Cigarettes.	1,347,961 32
Cigars...........	595,728 "	74,400,840 Cigars.	443,633 04
Grand total duty for about a year..		....	$3,166,299 72

7-8 EDWARD VII., A. 1908

BALANCE OF STAMPS ON HAND.

—	No. of Stamps.	Lb.	Amounts.
			$ cts.
Foreign Tobacco....	1,913,117	1,413,497	353,374 25
Snuff "	20,379	214,275	43,144 75
Canadian "	725,433	465,794	23,289 70
Mixed "	725,534	524,343	26,217 15
• Farmers' Rolls............	74,381	47,332⅔	2,366 64
Total Balance.................	3,458,844	2,665,241⅔	448,392 49

—	No. of Stamps.	Cigarettes.	Amounts.
			$ cts.
On Foreign Cigarettes.................	4,629,674	40,467,041	129,169 82
" Combination "	26,217	5,514,700	8,272 05
" Canadian "	61,680	1,268,640	1,902 96
Total Balance...................	4,717,571	47,250,381	139,344 83

—	No. of Stamps.	Cigars.	Amounts.
			$ cts.
On Foreign Cigars	345,592	24,008,438	144,105 00
" Combination Cigars	132,794	6,850 960	20,452 88
" Canadian "	13,483	1,675,300	5,025 90
" Sample.....................	3,319	82,975	497 85
Total Balance...............	495,188	32,617,673	170,081 63

GRAND TOTAL BALANCE ON HAND.

Tobacco........................	3,458,844 Stamps.	26,652,441⅔ lb.	$ 448,392 49
Cigarettes...................	4,717,571 "	47,250,381 Cigarettes	139,344 83
Cigars......................	495,188 "	32,617,673 Cigars.	170,081 63
Total amount on hand.......	....	....	$ 757,788 95

(Signed)   W. CAVEN,
D.C.I.R.

I am in charge of stamps since March 1, 1899, and I have a salary of $850. I have for assistant Mr. Leo Thurbur, with a salary of $630. I think the department should appoint me as ' Clerk Stamps ' with a medium salary.

Hoping that you will take this in consideration,

I remain, yours truly,

(Signed)   C. P. MAINVILLE.

MONTREAL, Sept. 9, 1907

The officers of the Inland Revenue Division of St. Hyacinthe beg to offer for the consideration of the Commission:

1st. In view of the admitted fact that the cost of living is constantly on the increase, that some sort of provision be made for the future in order to prevent a repetion of present conditions.

2nd. The fact that the officers of the Inland Revenue Department are not paid in accordance with the services they render is strongly borne out by comparing the cost of collection and protection of the revenue with the business of any mercantile establishment in Canada. If the officers employed in the department are not worth more than the salaries they are at present legally entitled to, they are not competent to discharge the duties they are entrusted with. Their comptency is admitted.

3rd. Considering the standards fixed by which the ability of officers is tested, the service has no attraction for the class of men required by the department, because of the low salaries paid. This is particularly true of the higher offices.

While a young man may start at a somewhat higher salary than in mercantile institutions, his merits have a chance of quickly placing him in a better position in such a business than he could command in the Revenue's service, no matter what capacity may be shown.

4th. That men who have been appointed as temporary officers and who by reason of age, &c., have not passed the Qualifying examination, but who have been found competent to discharge the duties assigned to them, should, on the recommendation of the collector and inspector, be placed on the permanent list at the expiration of five years.

5th. That special provisions should be made for officers engaged in the supervision of the manufacture of fulminate of mercury and such other articles, the manufacture of which is dangerous, by extra duty-pay or accident insurance.

6th. A uniform system of duty-pay for officers at distilleries or other surveys where duty-pay is given.

A uniform rate of salary to deputy collectors (Class B) doing practically the same work in outlying points in the same division.

7th. That the pension system formerly in force be restored or offered to officers in lieu of the present retiring allowance system.

8th. That some special provisions be made for the higher grades of distillery officers because of the fact that they are liable to be moved from one distillery to another. At present the transportation expenses alone are paid, and no allowance is made for the sundry expenses, which are very costly (such as breakage of furniture, readjustment of house fixtures, &c.). In addition to this, the interruption that takes place in the education of the children of such officers is an item which is the most costly of all.

All of which is respectfully submitted.

(Signed)   L. BENOIT,
Collector of Inland Revenue;
F. M. LANGELIER,
J. P. MORIN,
J. D. DUMAINE,
J. C. ROULEAU,
D. J. BRENNAN,
H. LAMOUREUX,
N. J. D. BERNARD.

MONTRÉAL, le 20 juin 1907.

HONORABLES MESSIEURS,—Les soussignés prient humblement votre honorable Commission de bien vouloir prendre en considération les allégués suivants:—

1. Qu'ils sont employés à titre d'officiers temporaires depuis huit, dix et vingt-quatre ans.

2. Que, comme tels, ils n'ont aucun droit ni aux vacances, ni aux augmentations annuelles, et ne reçoivent aucun salaire lorsqu'ils sont forcés de s'absenter par maladie.

3. Qu'en considération de leur long état de service et du fait qu'ils ont toujours remplis leurs devoirs à la satisfaction des officiers supérieurs de ce bureau, ils sollicitent la faveur:

1. Une augmentation de salaire;
2. D'être payés en temps de maladie;
3. D'avoir des vacances annuelles.

Il n'est pas hors de propos d'ajouter que cette catégorie d'employés a toujours joui de ces privilèges jusqu'en 1894, et que ce qui était possible dans ce temps peut le redevenir aujourd'hui.

Veuille croire. honorables messieurs, à nos sentiments les plus respectueux et à nos remerciements anticipés et sincères.

(Signed)   EDMOND BEAUCHAMP,
T. CUNNINGHAM,
J. MANNING,
D. R. HURTUBISE.

La Commission du Service Civil,
Montréal, Qué.

To the Chairman and Members of the Civil Service Commission,
Ottawa, Ont.

SIRS,—We, the assistant inspectors of weights and measures for the division of Montreal, take the liberty to submit for your consideration the following:—

Our present scale of salaries was established in 1878, and has remained unchanged since, although all other branches of the civil service have had readjustments.

New industries have been inaugurated in the city of Montreal as well as in the suburbs; railway and navigation traffic as well as general trade have been greatly increased and the population has more than doubled in the last thirty years, all of which have tended to increase the varieties of weights and measures and weighing instruments necessitated by the changed condition of business, thereby greatly increasing the labour of the officers.

In support of this statement permit us to quote a few statistics from the annual reports of weights and measures for the fiscal years 1896 and 1906. In 1896, with a total staff of nine officers, at a salary of $7,200, the collections for Montreal were $7,777.50. In 1906, with seven officers, receiving a salary of $5,573.16, the collections were $13,364.60, notwithstanding the fact that in 1902, sixteen counties were taken off this division and added to St. Hyacinthe.

To collect this sum of $13,364.60, it was necessary to test 59,370 weights, measures or weighing instruments, at an average of 22½ cents an inspection.

Although the Weights and Measures Act was, and is meant as a protection to the public primarily, the Montreal division has not been a tax on the Government, as it shows a surplus of receipts over expenditure every year since its inception.

Furthermore, the officers of this branch of the Inland Revenue, with one exception, do not participate in the superannuation or retirement funds as other Government employees.

On account of the continually increasing cost of living, let us state, it has become impossible for an assistant inspector of weights and measures in the city of Montreal to live honestly and not become indebted to merchants, let alone make provision for old age and our family's safeguard.

As you are aware, the Federal scale of salaries makes no exception as to the location of the officers, and we trust that your board will fully recognize the fact that the salaries paid in rural localities are altogether inadequate for those located in the chief commercial centres, as Montreal, where the cost of living is more than double that of outside districts, we therefore respectfully ask if it would not be possible to make a scale of salaries for large divisions (like Montreal) with a minimum of $800 and an annual increase of $50 up to a maximum of $1,200, the present staff of officers to receive the salary that their time of service would give them at this rate, as if the suggested rate had been in force when each one was first appointed.

With such a scale of salaries it would be possible for us to live as our position requires also to make provision for our families and old age, not as we are to-day.

Gentlemen of the Commission, we sincerely hope that you will give our petition favourable consideration and that we may not be the only ones not partaking in the general welfare of our country.

Respectfully your obedient servants,

(Signed)   J. A. DAOUST,
J. A. HEBERT,
D. COLLINS,
E. BAUDET,
T. H. BEAULNE,
H. C. HALL,
J. O. WILSON,
J.-Bte N. GALIPEAU.

To the Chairman and Members of the Civil Service Commission sitting at Montreal, September 11, 1907.

GENTLEMEN,—Below is a statement of the monthly expenses of W. L. Ross, temporary excise officer, for the last seven (7) years, who is a widower, having five (5) children, and as may be seen below cannot afford a servant.

Rent... $	15 00
Water..	1 00
Insurance..	0 75
Fuel and light...	7 00
Butcher..	10 00
Grocer...	20 00
Baker..	3 00
Clothing...	10 00
Milk...	2 40
Boots..	5 00
Schooling and books...	4 00
Doctor...	1 00
Drugs..	2 00
Church dues..	2 00
Guarantee bond..	0 24
Amusements..	....
Total.. $	83 39

I am in receipt of the small monthly salary of $41.66 (given to some temporary officers. (Others have less.)

As can readily be seen from above figures it is impossible for me to make both ends meet without some other source of income.

I pray the Commission to recommend that a salary sufficient to live on be granted and that if an officer has been found satisfactory in his allotted position for a given period that he be named permanent.

(Signed)   W. L. Ross, E.O.

MONTREAL. September 12, 1907.

29a—21

MONTREAL, September 12, 1907.

To the Chairman and Members,
    Civil Service Commission,
        Montreal.

GENTLEMEN,—I would pray you to take into consideration my case as a temporary excise officer.

I have been in the employ of the Inland Revenue for the last eleven years, at a salary of $500 per annum, during which time I have been at the factory of the American Tobacco Company, where I have fulfilled the duties of a second officer, and in the absence of the first officer, replaced him and believe I have given satisfaction.

I find it a hardship not to be named permanently, and obliged to work for the above mentioned small salary (less than a labourer). Because I find it difficult at my age to study and pass the required qualifying examination, although I am capable of fulfilling the position and performing the duties required of officers in receipt of much more salary than that given me.

I would respectfully ask you to make a recommendation covering persons situated as I have been whereby officers in the employ of the department for a certain number of years, and giving satisfaction in the position allotted to them, should be named permanent at an increased salary, and you will earn the gratitude of your obedient servant.

(Signed) MICHAEL HUGHES.

GAS AND ELECTRIC LIGHT INSPECTION SERVICE, CANADA.

MONTREAL, September 12, 1907.

To the Civil Service Commission,
    Montreal.

GENTLEMEN,—As you are now investigating the claims of the various departments of the outside Civil Service, I take the liberty of putting before you a few facts which will place you au fait in regard to our financial standing as to revenue and expenditure.

By referring back to returns of 1885 you will see that the receipt for that year in the district of Montreal amounted to $1,859 with an expenditure of $2,135 showing that it cost the department $276 more than they received, while in the year 1906 our receipts for gas and electric light insection in this district amounted to.... $11,050

With an expenditure of only..   3,818
                                                                      _____
Showing a surplus of.. ... .$ 7,232

Considering this vast increase, from a deficit of $275 dollars to a surplus of over seven thousand dollars, do you not think the department would be justified in allowing the officers of this office suitable remunerations in proportion to the increased work performed and increased cost of living.

Hoping you will favourably consider the above.

I have the honour to be, gentlemen,

Your obedient servant,

(Signed) A. AUBIN,
Inspector of Gas and Electric Light,
    and Consulting Gas Engineer.

MONTREAL, WEDNESDAY, September 11, 1907.

Mr. FRANCOIS-X. J. A. TOUPIN, Collector of Inland Revenue, Montreal, called, sworn and examined.

By the Chairman:

Q. You are collector of Inland Revenue here?—A. I am, sir.

(Memorial of the excise branch, division of Montreal read, also supplementary memorial from the staff.)

Q. How long have you been in the service?—A. Twenty-four years, and will take my twenty-fifth year next October.

Q. When did you become collector?—A. Four years ago last April.

Q. Have you always been in the Montreal division?—A. I was for the first two years in Toronto and about seven years afterwards I was a year in Quebec before returning to Montreal.

Q. In the Inland Revenue Department, unlike the Post Office and other departments, the officers are shifted about to some extent, you began in Toronto, came to Montreal, went to Quebec and then came back here?—A. Yes, sir.

Q. There is a certain amount of shifting around in the Inland Revenue Department?—A. There is.

Q. Mr. Crane, for instance, he is not a Berthierville man?—A. No, sir.

Q. He came from some part of Ontario, did he not? (Mr. Crane, yes, sir, I have been shifted ten times.)

Q. What distillery is there in operation in the Montreal district?—A. The Canada Sugar Refinery, of which Mr. E. W. Parker is the licensee.

Q. Do they distil whiskey and all that?—A. They distil alcohol.

Q. But there is no distillery like Walker's, Gooderham's or Seagram's in this division?—A. Well, they do not make any rye or anything of that kind. Anything in regard to whiskey, Mr. Fox can explain better than I can, he knows more about that.

Q. In the Montreal division there are no distilleries like that of Gooderham, Walker or Seagram that make absolutely nothing else but malt whiskey?—A. No, the whiskey here is made especially from molasses.

Q. Then the revenue derived here in Montreal is a good deal made up from duties paid on whiskey in bond shipped from other divisions?—A. Yes.

Q. Of course, I suppose tobacco is a good deal down here, but the spirits on which you collect a large amount of duty here are manufactured elsewhere as a rule?—A. Yes, but Mr. Fox can give you more information about the details.

The CHAIRMAN.—Perhaps I had better swear Mr. Fox now and then he can give us information upon points on which you are not posted.

(Mr. JOHN DAVID FOX, accountant, Inland Revenue Department, sworn.)

Mr. Fox.—Mr. Parker manufactures and there is taken for consumption around Montreal 50,000 out of 80,000 proof gallons monthly, so that the revenue on the produce of the distillery here in Montreal is collected part of it here, and some of the duty that should be collected here is transferred to other divisions to which the whiskey is sent in bond.

Q. Is it as broad as it is long, that what revenue you lose that way from collections made by other divisions for you is equalized by the amount you collect for other divisions in a similar manner?—A. I could not say that.

29a—21½

Q. It is immaterial, but when it is stated there is one distillery here, I wanted to know whether it is analogous to Walker's or Gooderham's or Seagram's?—A. In a way it is.

(Examination of Mr. TOUPIN resumed.)

Q. Are there any excise men employed at Parker's distillery?—A. Yes, there are three officers at Parker's.

Q. What staff have you in your division?—A. Forty-four, and out of that number one is located at St. Jérome, which is an out-office of this division, and I have also on my staff Mr. Costigan, who is inspecting food most of his time, so I may say I have forty-two regular officers, and there are eight temporary officers and one preventive officer.

Q. You have over fifty officers in your jurisdiction?—A. Fifty-one altogether.

Q. Do you include in that list gentlemen from Joliette and St. Jérome?—A. No, only the Montreal division.

Q. You include the one from St. Jérome, I think?—A. Yes, because it is included in the Montreal division.

Q. The fifty-one officers, with the exception of the one man at St. Jérome, are all employed in the city of Montreal here?—A. Yes, well there is a young lady employed in the office.

Q. You say you now have a revenue here of?—A. Over $6,000,000.

Q. You collect a revenue of over $6,000,000 here?—A. Yes, sir. Last year, of course the fiscal year was only nine months, and for that period we collected $4,511,986.

Q. Since March 31 is the revenue going on in the same proportion?—A. Yes, it is increasing all the time.

Q. And at the end of the twelve months' period it would be——?—A. Here are the figures; since April, for the last five months, that is the first five months of the present year, which shows a large surplus each month over the corresponding month.

Q. You need not read them, we will have them put in. Have you staff enough to carry on the work with the increased duties shown by that statement?—A. Hardly. In fact I have been asking for some new men from the department lately.

Q. Can you tell me what number you had on the staff fifteen years ago?—A. Well, fifteen years ago—48.

Q. You were around here then, I suppose?—A. I was, but, of course——

Q. Had you one half the staff you have now? The reason I ask that question is that the last Civil Service Commission sat in 1892, and we want to know what proportion the staff has increased in relation to the revenue, if we can get at that. If you are not prepared to tell us now you may furnish the information when revising your evidence, if you like?—A. Well, I might say that for the last four years the revenue has increased 50 per cent, because the first year I was collector the revenue was $4,004,000, and if last year had been up to June 30 instead of March 31, we would have collected $6,008,000, which is a 50 per cent increase. In 1892 we had a staff of forty-eight men and collected $2,154,000.

Q. What has been the increase in the staff for the last four years?—A. The increase in salaries?

Q. I am not talking about salary, but the increase in the number of the staff?—A. It has increased—I cannot say exactly. I might say that I have six new men, but there were two removed to another division.

Q. That brings it down to four?—A. And one died and another one has left.

Q. That brings it down to two?—A. Yes.

Q. Then, while the revenue has increased 50 per cent, the number of the staff has increased 4 per cent?—A. Yes, about that—well, with regard to temporary men, I have six temporary men.

Q. While the permanent staff has increased about 4 per cent you have six temporary men. The salaries paid to the several employees in the Inland Revenue Department outside service are all regulated by the Civil Service Act?—A. Yes.

Q. You cannot get more than is laid down there? There are no means within the grade of increasing the salaries as was recently done in the outside branch of the Customs service?—**A.** I did not know it was done in the Customs service.

Q. Do you not know that some of the lower people got additions to their salary?—**A.** Yes, I know they did get increases, but I do not know how they got it.

Q. Well, in the Inland Revenue a collector, according to the importance of his division gets from $500 to $2,400, and a deputy collector from $400 to $1,700, and a special class excise man from $1,400 to $1,800, and so forth?—**A.** Yes.

Q. These salaries depend upon the importance of the division, and when they are in between they are regulated by a certain fixed percentage of the revenue. In your memorandum you say you want the percentage increased. The ordinary exciseman gets 5 per cent added per year?—**A.** Yes.

Q. That is to say, that the employees in the Excise Department can get nothing beyond the percentage or beyond the limit laid down in the Act. What I was coming at is this, a tide waiter in the Customs can be paid anything between $800 and $1,200 a year; if he begins at $800 he is not limited to a fixed percentage in getting up to the $1,200, whereas if you appoint an exciseman he can only get an increase of 5 per cent per annum until he gets to his maximum?—**A.** Yes.

Q. Where you differ from the Customs Department is that in the Customs Department men may, by the will of the minister, in the lower grades, if they are within the limits of that grade, get an increase to their salary, while your people could not; is not that what you are driving at?—**A.** I do not know how it is in the Customs, but for us I know we cannot get more than the statutory increase.

Q. You cannot get beyond your percentages, or beyond the limit laid down in the Act?—**A.** No.

Q. You stated in your subsequent memorandum, I believe, as a justification for your request for an increase of salary that your Inland Revenue division at Montreal has now come to a stage that is equivalent to what was the Customs collections here when the Collector of Customs was paid $4,000 a year?—**A.** Yes.

Q. Following that train of reasoning, could not the Collector of Customs say, that being the case, 'my revenue has increased so much that $4,000 should not be the limit for my salary?'?—**A.** Well, I do not know. The Collector of Customs was paid $4,000 when collecting $6,000,000, I know the customs revenue has increased.

Q. I know, but when the Customs collection has increased to $17,000,000 or $18,000,000 and when the cost of living has increased, if $4,000 was an equivalent salary for $6,000,000 collection, could he not use the same argument as a justification for an increase in his salary?—**A.** I suppose he could.

Q. Do you not think that is rather trying to prove too much?—**A.** I do not know.

Q. You say that in this division you have 20,000 entries to clear each year, which is equal to about 60,000—how do you get at that equity? How do you arrive at the conclusion that 20,000 entries are equal to 60,000?

Mr. Fox.—Permit me to answer that—you see that in the Customs and some other divisions they permit only one ex-warehouse entry from each warehouse on an entry; that is, if a consignment of goods is warehoused then they only allow to take from one warehouse entry, when ex-warehousing, one entry on that. Now, in the Montreal division we permit one, three, five, seven, or ten, from as many entries ex-warehouse, as they choose, on that one ex-warehouse entry. They can make a separate ex-warehouse entry for each case or barrel in their warehouse, according to the orders they may have for goods on that same entry, so that we may have from one, or we may have from ten, twelve, or fourteen warehouse entries on that one ex-warehouse entry.

Q. But taking the average, you think it will equal three entries for each original entry?—**A.** I would say three, and that is a very low estimate.

Q. There are 20,000 separate and distinct entries in the Montreal division each year?—**A.** Yes.

Examination of Mr. Toupin resumed.

Q. Who is your inspector here, Mr. Toupin?—A. Mr. Lawlor.
Q. How often does he visit you as a matter of inspection?—A. About twice a year he makes a full visit of the whole of the factories, &c.
Q. Does he come unexpectedly?—A. Yes, sir.
Q. He does not give you notice that he is coming?—A. No. Of course, when he has started his inspection, every one knows he is here.
Q. And can guess about when he will reach them?—A. Yes.
Q. Have you a lot of balances carried forward in your books?—A. Yes, sir, some for over twenty years.
Q. Do you not think they had better be written off?—A. I think so.
Q. Have you ever made any report on the matter?—A. Mr. Lawlor has reported, when collector, and since he has been inspector.
Q. He was formerly collector and is now inspector?—A. Yes, sir, I know Mr. Lawlor has worked at that and has tried to have the balances written off.
Q. Where is Mr. Lawlor now, is he in Montreal?—A. I think so, I haven't seen him this morning, but I think he is here.
Q. Is his office in the same building as yours?—A. Yes, sir.
Q. Your office is on the river front?—A. Yes, sir.
Q. Is it distinct from the Custom-house?—A. Yes, sir.
Q. You have an office of your own?—A. Yes, it used to be the old Custom-house.
Q. When do you close your office to the public?—A. At 4 o'clock.
Q. How do you manage with the collections that come in after 3 o'clock?

Mr. Fox.—They are deposited in the safe until the following morning. The collections from our office are deposited once a day, ostensibly from 12 o'clock noon one day until 12 o'clock noon the next day, but in reality and practically it is from 4 o'clock one afternoon until 4 o'clock the next afternoon; then we make up our deposits the following morning and the money is deposited for the previous day.
Q. Have you always a day's revenue in the vaults?—A. At night time, yes, but most of the payments are made by cheque.
Q. Who has the custody of that vault?—A. The cashier has the combination, the collector, I believe, has the combination, and I personally know it, although the cashier is the only one that I know of who carries the keys. The money is kept in a safe in the vault at night.
Q. What hour in the day is the money paid into the bank?—A. During the forenoon, as soon as the deposit can be made up and checked and the entries verified, in order to see that it is right and there are no errors in it, then the deposit is sent to the bank.

Examination of Mr. Toupin resumed.

Q. In all this diversity of work, malt-houses, breweries, distilleries, tobacco factories, &c., there are distinct forms and returns?—A. Yes.
Q. How many excise men have you stationed in these factories and warehouses?—A. I could not tell you the number off-hand.
Q. Will you please supply that when you revise your evidence, give the number in charge of factories?—A. I have twenty-nine regular officers and six temporary officers.
Q. That is thirty-five out of fifty odd are employed in factories?—A. That is including the bonded warehouses and everything.
Q. You said just now that the staff is scarcely sufficient for the duties to be performed?—A. It is not.
Q. What steps have you taken to advise the department of that fact?—A. I have lately, about two or three weeks ago, informed the department. I was asked and I answered.
Q. Why did you not, when you saw the revenue increasing as it has been for several years past, during the last four years it has doubled, why did you not apply before?—A. I did apply before.

Q. You had applied before for assistance?—A. Yes, sir.

Q. Didn't they pay any attention to it?—A. I received a temporary man occasionally.

Q. Do you know how vacancies are filled up, on whose recommendation are appointments made?—A. I do not know.

Q. They are all Montreal men who come here?—A. Well, we have, every once in a while, some men sent here from some other place, but lately they are all men from Montreal.

Q. As a matter of fact, they are appointed by the members for Montreal as a part of their patronage, are they not?—A. That is what I understand.

Q. You do not come into direct communication with the members?—A. Not at all.

Q. You do not tell any members when there are vacancies?—A. No, I do not.

Q. You would rather dread such a thing for fear that you would have somebody pushed on you that you would not care about?—A. Yes, the thing has happened sometimes, and now my answer is—even if I do want some officer, I say I do not want any.

Q. Considering the opportunities now open to men of sterling character and enterprise in the Dominion, do you get as good men now entering the service as you used to?—A. No, not as good. I may say that lately we have nearly all temporary men coming there.

Q. And they are not up to your mark?—A. No, they are not.

Q. Have you remonstrated with the department for sending you inefficient men?—A. I have, sir.

Q. What did they say about that?—A. Well,——

Q. You do not want to antagonize the department, if you can help it, by saying that you want more men?—A. Well, I do not like to go too often.

Q. Especially when men are sent that are not as good as they were before?—A. Yes, and I notified the department to that effect.

Q. Are the men recently appointed men of good habits?—A. Well, they are all, I may say, of good habits.

Q. There have been no drunkards or anything of that sort sent to you?—A. No, sir.

Q. None of your men have come within the jurisdiction of the police at any time?—A. No, never.

Q. You have nothing like what has happened in the Post Office Department—occasionally there have been thefts by letter carriers—you have nothing of that?—A. No.

Q. And you have no drunkenness or bad conduct on the part of your men?—A. No, not that I know of.

Q. And you would know if there was anything of that kind?—A. A few years ago we had one or two, but they went through the gold cure, and since then they have been all right.

Q. I suppose that with all these warehouses, where there is a certain amount of 'good stuff' about, there is a temptation for excisemen at times? The warehouse man may broach a bottle occasionally, I suppose?—A. Yes, there is a good deal of temptation, I suppose.

Q. But all your men resist temptation, they do not succumb?—A. As far as I know; I never noticed anything wrong.

Q. But, at the same time, you think men recently appointed are not as good, or as efficient, as the men appointed in former years?—A. No, I do not think so.

Q. That, I suppose, arises from the fact that there are better openings for good men now in other walks of life?—A. That is the point, I think, the salaries are not high enough to get good men.

Q. Coming to the Superannuation matter for a minute, you think that if a Superannuation Act was enacted granting superannuation to the officers and their families, it would lead to greater stability in the service?—A. That is so, because there is nothing now, with few exceptions, for the officials to look forward to; nearly all the officers die in harness.

Q. There is no inducement to good men to come into the service now?—A. No, none whatever.

Q. There is a deduction made now from his salary, his own money, which is returned to him. A man who is appointed now contributes 5 per cent of his own money to the retirement fund, and if he goes out, it is returned to him?—A. Yes.

Q. There is no provision for the future practically?—A. No.

Q. If there was a provision for the future it would be an inducement for men to come into the service and remain there?—A. Yes.

Q. It would lend permanency to the service?—A. Yes.

Q. Do men leave the Excise office now? Are there many resignations?—A. No, there has only been one since I became collector, that is four years now.

Q. He bettered himself, I suppose; he was a good man?—A. Well——

Q. Of course, there are resignations for cause?—A. Yes, he went into some other business; he thought he would make more money attending to that business than by remaining in the Excise. There is also an old gentleman retiring on account of his years.

Q. That, of course, comes naturally; there are lots of us old gentlemen have to retire. What do you think yourself has been the increase in the cost of living in Montreal in the last four years?—A. The increase in the cost of living?

Q. Yes, we know that milk has gone up to 10 cents a quart, and all that kind of thing?—A. Yes—well, the rent has gone up 50 per cent at least.

Q. I suppose that all around, take it one way or the other, in the last fifteen years, owing to the increase in the price of commodities, the cost of living has grown by 40 per cent?—A. I would say 35 per cent and 50 per cent, with an average of 40 per cent.

Q. You complain that the salaries laid down by the statute governing the outside service in the Excise department were laid down in 1892, when the cost of living was so much less than it is now, and that owing to that increase in the cost of living they should be revised; that is the contention?—A. Yes.

Q. That the salaries should be revised?—A. Yes, according to the cost of living which has increased so greatly.

Q. And also, in your special case, because the importance of your work demands it?—A. Yes.

Q. Did you say how many bonded warehouses there are in your division?—A. Yes, twenty-six.

Q. Are there not more than that number of wholesale warehouses?

Mr. Fox.—Oh, yes, but they have not all bonded warehouses; some merchants store their goods in the public warehouses, such as the terminal warehouse. One license in that case covers a large number of grocers or merchants, as the case may be.

Q. What I was going to say is, that it struck me when Mr. Fyshe was reading the memorial from this department that twenty-six bonded warehouses would hardly cover the whole of the bonded warehouses in the city of Montreal, where Walker's, Gooderham's and Seagram's rye is stored?

Mr. Fox.—It covers that. You see the conditions in Montreal are different to those in other cities, here the public warehouses give facilities to the merchants who would otherwise require bonded warehouses of their own; they take advantage of the public warehouses and these twenty-six warehouses cover all the goods of the description you have named which are stored in Montreal.

Examination of Mr. Toupin resumed.

Q. What do you pay the men—how many men have you got at E. W. Parker's distillery?—A. Three.

Q. What do you pay them?—A. Do you mean what salaries do they receive?

Q. Yes?—A. Daniel J. Walsh, $1,600; James W· Snowden, $1,200, and Mr. Davidson—Mr. Walsh, $1,600 and duty pay.

Q. What would his duty pay be?—A. $200.

Q. Would it not pay the Canada Sugar Company to give that man a supplementary salary?—A. It certainly would if he were susceptible to it.

Q. They could be liable to that temptation if they were not high minded officers?—A. Oh yes, with great advantage to the manufacturer.

Q. Are those three men in that place checking each other?—A. One is in charge; he is responsible, and the other two are subordinate to the one who is in charge.

Q. There is a certain amount of refund of duty allowed for leakages, and stuff spoiled in manufacture and that kind of thing that has to be destroyed in the presence of two officers, such as malt turned sour or tobacco turned musty?—A. Yes, it is destroyed in the presence of two officers.

The CHAIRMAN.—I know that when secretary of the Treasury Board that rule was laid down, requiring that it should be destroyed in the presence of two officers.

Q. That is in, we will say, Sir William Macdonald's factory, a certain amount of tobacco turns musty and has to be destroyed, that is destroyed in the presence of two officers ?—A. In the presence of two officers; there are two officers there all the time.

Q. And in a case where the duty is refunded the stuff destroyed must be destroyed in the presence of two officers ?—A. Yes, sir.

Q. Could there be any fraud on the revenue in the alleged destruction of this stuff? Could tobacco said to be destroyed actually enter afterwards into manufacture?—A. Not likely.

Q. Does that depend also on the honesty and high-mindedness of the officers?—A. Well, like everything else, it rests, of course, on the law being carried out.

Q. It is not likely that such a thing could happen, but there might be temptation if the men were not high-minded?—A. Yes, if the two officers should agree.

Q. There might be collusion?—A. It would require the consent of two officers.

Q. Yes, I know, but with a large amount of tobacco alleged to be destroyed in that way it might be a temptation to a rascally manufacturer to buy up your officers, might it not? I do not mean to say that Sir William Macdonald would do such a thing; I used his name for purposes of illustration because he would be beyond suspicion?—A. Well, in fact, we have very little tobacco destroyed except in the case of fire; with that exception we have very little.

Q. You have some beer that is destroyed that turns sour?—A. But there is no duty on the beer.

Q. Yes, but the duty is paid on the malt used in the manufacture of beer?—A. Yes, duty is paid on the malt.

Q. And the malt occasionally gets musty?—A. It might, but it does not happen very often.

Q. Who are your maltsters here?—A. The Canada Malting Co., Ltd., A. J Dawes, Wm. Dow & Co. and John T. Molson.

Q. Do you send much beer out of this division to the other divisions?—A. It is not removed in bond; therefore, we have no means of knowing how it is disposed of. Once the duty is paid on the malt we have nothing more to do with it.

Q. It is not like whiskey?—A. No, it is not in bond.

Q. Do you sell many stamps down here?—A. Yes.

By Mr. Bazin :

Q. In a case where a brewery turns a batch of beer sour, do you refund the duty on the malt?—A. No.

Q. There is no refund whatever?—A. No.

Q. It is an entire loss to the brewer?—A. Yes.

Q. I know of a case lately in Quebec, in a brewery there, I was told there was a loss of about 15,000 gallons of beer, so there would not be any refund for the malt consumed in the manufacture of that beer on which the duty had been paid?—A. No; at least——

Mr. CAVEN, Deputy Collector, Montreal.—I think he gets an allowance on the amount of malt used in making that beer.

A. (Cont.) Well, that never came before my notice

By the Chairman :

Q. The duty is charged on the malt; there is so much malt allowed to be used in the production of so much beer. I understand that if the malt is found to be unfit for use that quantity of malt is destroyed in the presence of two officers of the department; if the malt, at the time of its destruction, has not paid duty and has not gone into consumption nothing more is said, but if it has paid duty and gone into consumption a refund is given for the quantity of malt that has been destroyed, or for the quantity that is equivalent to the quantity of beer destroyed.

Mr. FOX.—This is a statement by Mr. Mainville, a memorandum of the transactions in stamps during one month in the Montreal division. The issue on foreign tobacco was 971,080, representing 438,921 lb., the duty on which is $109,730.26; snuff, 1,080 stamps representing 7,225 lb., on which the duty is $1,333.25; Canadian tobacco, 139,122 stamps, representing 28,239½ lb., the duty on which is $1,911.98; farmers' tobacco twist, 10,670 stamps, 3,710 lb., the duty on which at 5c. is $185.50; combination tobacco, 106,461 stamps, representing 28,105½ lb., the duty on which is $1,470.79; making a total duty for one month of $114,558, representing 1,228,413 stamps—that is for tobacco. Then for foreign cigarettes——

By the Chairman :

Q. Never mind reading the statement; you may put that in. What amount of stamps have you in possession of the division here, as a rule; is it two months' supply?—A. We are supposed to keep three months' supply on hand, but the balance of stamps on hand is 3,458,884 stamps, representing a duty of $448,392.49.

Q. How are these stamps kept?—A. That is for tobacco and for cigarettes, we have 4,717,571 stamps, representing a duty of $139,344.83; of cigar stamps we have 495,188 stamps, representing a duty of $170,081.63. This makes the total duty represented by the stamps in possession $758,718.95. .

Q. You have that $758,000 worth of stamps in this division; how is that quantity of stamps stored? Are they in the vaults?—A. No, they are stored down stairs in cupboards.

Q. Has anybody access to them ?—A. There are two men who have access to them.

Q. Does the inspector check them when he is inspecting the office?—A. I believe he does, personally.

Q. Has it ever been represented to the department that this large amount of stamps has been stored in cupboards?

Mr. TOUPIN.—We would require a very large vault to store them.

Mr. FOX.—It would not be easy to store these stamps in vaults unless the vaults consisted of a large room.

Q. Yes, I understand that: but considering that this $758,000 .worth of stamps represents so much money and forms part of the revenue when it comes into the department, should there not be some security?—A. Possibly it would be advisable, although the stamps representing this amount are not actually so much money at all until we collect for them and they go into use in the factory.

Q. Granted that they are of no value except as bits of paper until they come into use when they do become valuable, but who has custody of these stamps?—A. There are two clerks, Mr. C. P. Mainville and Mr. George Thurber are at present in charge.

Q. Is it a joint custody?—A. I believe so, they are both responsible for the stamps.

Mr. Toupin.—Well, Mr. Mainville is the clerk who is responsible, of course, his assistant is also responsible to him.

(Examination of Mr. Toupin resumed.)

By the Chairman:

Q. When did Mr. Mainville enter the department?—A. Thirteen or fourteen years ago.

Q. He gets $900 a year?—A. $850.

Q. And he has the custody of $750,000 worth of stamps?—A. Yes, sir; I may say that I am very well satisfied with the way he keeps them.

Q. Does the inspector check the stamps when he comes around?—A. He did lately, about two months ago; the inspector is around the office in Montreal every six months, and it takes over a month to make the inspection of this division.

By Mr. Fyshe:

Q. Are the stamps checked periodically?—A. Well, of course they cannot check the stamps when they receive them as we receive them in large amounts.

By the Chairman:

Q. Are they sent down in sealed packets?—A. Yes, sir.

Q. With the denominations specified on the outside of the packets?—A. On the outside of packet.

Q. When you say that you have 10,000 cigarette stamps, that is according to the enumeration of the outside?—A. Yes.

Q. And you take it for granted that is accurate until there is a demand for them and the package is opened?—A. The officer in charge does not open the packages until there is a demand for its contents.   We have a cupboard for the stamps of every denomination, and if there is any shortage when they open the sealed package they are supposed to notify the inspector or me at once, because it would be impossible to check these stamps when they first come in.

By Mr. Fyshe:

Q. Is the supply of stamps periodically checked by the inspector counting the packages as they appear on the face? Is there any periodical inspection made at all? —A. As I say, the inspector makes an inspection every six months and checks all the stamps.

Q. Did he ever find anything wrong?—A. Not that I know of.

By the Chairman:

Q. Has Mr. Mainville always been in charge of the stamps?—A. For a good many years.

Q. Do you never shift the officers around?—A. The second officer, that is Mr. Mainville's assistant, has been changed, but Mr. Mainville has been at that work for about ten years.

Q. I suppose it is like everything else in the public service, once a man delivers letters, or once a man has control of stamps he is there until the end of the chapter, is he? You never shift your men around or change them about?—A. I do, but in that position, of course, Mr. Mainville has given satisfaction, he is a very good and a very steady man so we thought it better to leave him there.

WEDNESDAY, September 11, 1907.

The Commission resumed at 2.30 p.m.

The examination of Mr. TOUPIN, Collector Inland Revenue Department, Montreal, continued.

Mr. TOUPIN.—I wish to give some explanation about the evidence I gave here this morning, perhaps I did not understand the point you were making, Mr. Chairman. You were asking me about the class of the spirits distilled at the Canada Sugar Refinery Company's distillery, whether they were the same as those distilled by Mr. Walker or Mr. Gooderham. I said they shipped spirits, potable spirits the same as they do at any other distillery. The difference is they do not make any rye whiskey. For the rest they ship spirits, that is potable spirits the same as the others, but not in the same quantity perhaps, although they ship that kind of spirits all the same. There was another thing, when you were asking me if the officer might not be in collusion with the manufacturer, I understood it was specially with reference to the point regarding the destruction of duty paid articles.

By the Chairman :

Q. I meant generally in the discharge of their duties, and I was referring to officers in charge of a warehouse ?—A. In a general way ?

Q. In a general way ?—A. Of course, it is different if the officer should act in collusion with the manufacturer, it could very easily be done, for instance, take, say the cigar factory, the officer registers the tobacco standard, and he might, instead of making it one per centage, he could make it a good deal less if he wanted to, and, of course, there is the duty on the leaf, it is the same way with regard to that and it is also the same in connection with the malt houses, the officer weighs the malt produced and he could very easily make a difference in the weight.

Q. I thought as much, and I knew as much, I might say before I asked the question. Was there any other point that you desired to refer to ?—A. No, I have no more explanations to give.

Q. We were asking about the stamps before adjournment, do you know when those stamps were counted last by the inspector ?—A. It was in June last.

Q. Did he go thoroughly into the matter or did he simply count the number of packages ? Do you know what was done ?—A. I was not present but as far as I have seen I think the stamps are received there in packages, and you count the packages and take it for granted they are all right. Then when we want any particular denomination for delivery, the officer opens the packages wanted and counts the contents to see that it really contains the quantity stated on the packages; I think at least that is the way it is done. All untouched packages are taken as if the contents were all right as stated on the outside. All loose stamps are, of course, counted.

Q. You said that the average stock in hand was about three months' consumption, that is generally, you had about $758,000 worth of stamps ?—A. Yes, here is the statement for one month.

Q. What is the total in that month ?—A. $262,000 and the stock on hand is about three months' supply ; the instructions are to have about three months' supply on hand.

Q. I have known of instances in a bank where a man filled a bag of sovereigns with coppers and the bag would ostensibly contain gold. If three months' stock is kept in hand could not some packages remain there for a long time and be sealed up all right and apparently contains stamps yet contain none in reality. Do you use the stamps in the order of rotation ?

Mr. Fox.—The stamps are numbered in rotation and you must take them in rotation in their numerical order.

Q. Then it is only possible for that to happen within the three months.

Mr. Benoit.—The inspector checks the numbers of each series of stamps.

Q. Then there could be no dead package of stamps there ?

Mr. Fox.—There could be none that did not contain what it was represented on the outside of the package to contain without eventually being found out.

Examination of Mr. Toupin continued.

Q. Do you know whether any check of the stamps or stores is made by the Auditor General or any other of his officers ?—A. I understand they are kept in Ottawa I do not know by whom they are kept.

Q. How could that be done in Ottawa ? I mean to say is there any check by any officer of the public service, beyond the inspector, who checks your stamps here ?—A. Anybody coming to Montreal you mean ?

Q. Yes.—A. No, nobody comes to Montreal, except the local inspector.

By Mr. Fyshe:

Q. Does the local inspector check them ?—A. He does.

Q. How often ?—A. Every six months.

Q. Does he make a written report after his inspection ?—A. Yes, he makes his report to the department.

Mr. Benoit.—In a smaller division he checks the stamps over every three months.

Q. Does he make any report on that ?

Mr. Benoit.—Yes, he makes a report on that.

By the Chairman:

Q. You were saying, Mr. Toupin, in this general memorial that because an officer should do his duty conscientiously he renders himself more or less disagreeable to the public; why should that be the case?—A. Well, it is.

Q. But why should it be necessary if a man does his duty that he should render himself disagreeable to the public ?—A. I do not think it is necessary, but very often you see the public wants favours or they want to discuss the question with the officer, and if he does not consider it right, of course, they do not like it.

Q. That happens to everybody else who does his duty, besides an excise officer, I suppose ?—A. I suppose so.

Q. I quite agree with you that it is necessary to have competent clerks, and you have said before that the present salaries will not attract good men to come into the service?—A. That is my opinion.

Q. And you say that in order to retain men in the service you think the scale should be revised ?—A. It should, in my opinion.

Q. And then you have put down as your opinion and the opinion of your colleagues what you think should be the proper grading and remuneration?—A. Yes, exactly.

Q. Then there is another small change, you think the government should pay the cost of guarantee bonds ? In some departments that is done, is it not. Mr. Fox ?—A. In the Customs it is, I understand.

By Mr. Fyshe:

Q. I have an idea in my head about these fidelity bonds which, if carried out, will be, I think, very much better than that. It would not have the effect of charging it on the Government because then it would be considered just so much salary. But I think it would be possible to organize a fund among the staff, I have already done it myself in the case of two banks, by which this fund could guarantee all loss to the Government and the balance would be available to be returned to the officers when they retire from the service, who would receive the amount they had paid in, less their proportion of any losses incurred. The advantage of that would be that there would be less temptation to people to steal because they would, if they did any pilfering, not be stealing from the Government, but they would be taking, so to speak, their own money. Every employee would be under this scheme to some extent a detective against the others, because it would be to the interest of every employee to speak of anything that looked like drifting into fraud?—A. I quite understand that.

By the Chairman:

Q. You say in this memorial that you require an extensive knowledge of arithmetic and the computation of commodities, and so forth; have you any suggestion to make respecting change or improvement in the returns made to Ottawa or any modification in them?—A. I would refer that to Mr. Fox, who knows more about that than I do.

Mr. Fox.—I do not see any immediate necessity for any particular change.

Q. I will ask you, Mr. Fox, as accountant, whether you have any suggestion to make regarding any change or modification of the form of returns made to Ottawa?—A. I do not see any necessity for any change at present.

Q. And the bookkeeping is good?—A. Yes, it is a very good system.

Q. Who organized it?—A. I understand it was the late Mr. Miall, a very clever accountant.

Q. He was in the inside service?—A. He was responsible for the outside also.

Q. In addition you require to pass an examination as to technical knowledge of the work of malt houses, breweries and all that kind of thing, that is purely technical?—A. The knowledge of distilleries, breweries, malt houses and vinegar factories is purely technical, it is something you must learn apart from everything else.

Q. In the exercise of his duties the excise officer is actually the assessor on all articles subject to excise.' How is that?—A. Well. Mr. Toupin explained that a minute ago. He stated that the officer really establishes the quantity on which duties are paid, he determines the quantity of tobacco, raw leaf, malt or spirits. If this officer is not an honest man, or if he is in collusion with the manufacturer he could give them any quantity he wishes, and that is all they will have to pay duty to the Government on.

By Mr. Fyshe:

Q. What officer is that?—A. I am speaking of the different officers in charge of factories or distilleries. Any officer if he is in charge of a distillery, for instance, establishes the quantity on which the distillery pays duty and the officer in a tobacco factory does the same for the leaf and manufactured article.

Q. Is there no check?—A. He is the check, there is no other except the inspecting officers who visit periodically, at different times.

Q. How often does the visiting officer visit?—A. Mr. Caven will answer that himself.

Q. Do any of these men to your knowledge give any signs of becoming rich?—A. I have no knowledge of any excise officer being dishonest.

Q. I am merely asking you whether they give any signs of becoming rich?—A. No, as a class they are all poor men who are unfortunately not well paid, but they are honest.

Q. I should suppose that if he were weak-kneed merely he would have a chance to become rich. and I expect it would take the shape of keeping a horse and buggy or an automobile or yacht or anything of that kind?—A. No, none of the excise officers in Montreal keep a horse or automobile or yacht.

Q. 'A continual audit is proceeding in the office' what is the meaning of that ?— A. Entries after they are posted are checked through the different books before they are sent to Ottawa, that is an audit for the office on the inside and on the outside the manufacturer makes returns, the deputy collector takes a copy of that month's returns, visits the factories, checks up the books with that return and checks up to the time he visits there, he verifies everything and if there are any clerical errors or any mistakes in the shipping or anything of that kind he traces it back.

Q. And is the error corrected ?—A. Yes.

By the Chairman:

Q. That is all right so far as the thing is on record, but, of course, that does not touch the original decision of the man who says there is so much duty to pay on that ? —A. No, it does not touch that.

Q. There is no check on that at all ?—A. Yes, there is a check on that.

Q. How is there a check ?—A. Well, Mr. Caven will explain that, he is the deputy collector who makes the check outside.

Q. You are giving us in your memorandum a reason why you consider a special arrangement should be made to apply to the division of Montreal. We are going to Toronto, and there are special circumstances there, there is Gooderham's distillery and all that sort of thing there; we would like a little amplification of that. Why should Montreal have a special scale ?—A. The department has determined that there are several classes of divisions, first, second and third, &c., with a certain scale of salaries for each class according to the collections made in the divisions, plus the warehouse entries passed. Now the work in the division that collects $1,000,000 or thereabouts has no comparison with the work and responsibilities involved in the collection of a much larger amount, such as in the division of Montreal in particular, where the collection now amounts to $6,000,000. The officer in a division which is collecting $1,000,-000, the chief officer, that is the collector, will get the same salary as a collector in the city of Montreal who is collecting $6,000,000, and who may not have one minute to himself during his office hours, whereas the other man may have plenty of time to himself.

Q. What I wanted to make myself fully acquainted with was the grounds upon which you asked for this. We will be in Toronto the week after next, and Toronto has one of the largest distilleries in Canada, and they may say there 'considering we have one of the largest distilleries in Canada we ought to have a special scale for Toronto.' What is the Toronto collection, it is pretty nearly as much as yours, I suppose ?—A. No, we collect pretty nearly as much as the whole of Ontario.

Q. But Toronto, although it does not collect as much as your division, manufactures an immense amount of liquor, the duty on which is collected outside ?—A. Yes, it does, that is for spirits.

Q. What I want to get at, we want to be just all round—?—A. Certainly.

Q. I want to amplify this so that when we get to Toronto if this is brought up the question may be asked 'Why should Montreal officers be treated better than Toronto officers'?—A. My opinion is that if two men are equally competent and one has to work to the full limit of his capacity he should be allowed something extra for that.

Q. I am not quarrelling with the action of the Montreal staff, but I suppose the same thing would apply up there ?—A. We have no objection to Toronto being well treated at all, we want fair play for all our confreres in the business.

Q. You urge that this should be made specific, that a special scale of salary should be applied to this division. I suppose you mean it should apply to any other division of equal importance ?—A. That Montreal might be put in a special class which might apply to any other division of equal importance certainly.

Q. In the matter of promotion have there been any instances of people having been forced over the heads of their seniors ?—A. There have been some cases.

Q. Because you make a special point of dealing with that, you think all things being equal that promotion should be by seniority ?—A. A case I could mention was that some years ago there was a vacancy in the inspectorship, the then collector, Mr. Lawlor, was jumped over by a man now dead, who was a first-class officer, although Mr. Lawlor was a special class officer, that is a case in point.

Q. Are you dealing with that because instances have occurred where men have been shoved on, through politics, over the heads of others who were as well deserving and who were seniors in the service?—A. There must have been something like that in the mind when that memorial was written.

By Mr. Fyshe:

Q. Was that done through political influence?—A. It must have been, because necessarily all appointments are made by political influence.

By the Chairman:

Q. I think the question was asked in your memorial that the staff as in the case of other departments, should be paid bi-monthly. I do not know of any other department being paid bi-monthly?—A. The Montreal post office staff is paid bi-monthly.

Q. I do not think so?—A. If you wish to call in any of the clerks they will tell you so .

Q. The pay cheques come from Ottawa, do they not?—A. They come from Ottawa, but they are issued bi-monthly here, I do not know whether it is a local arrangement or not.

Q. How can cheques be issued bi-monthly because they are drawn at the end of the month?—A. Well, if you will kindly send for Mr. Callaghan, you will find that they are paid bi-monthly.

Q. I think that is a mistake. I know that the post office, like other departments, pay their employees at the end of the month.

By Mr. Fyshe:

Q. It would add to the labour and bi-monthly payments would be objectionable on that account?—A. That should not be a great objection if it would be for the convenience of the officers.

Q. The convenience would be more nominal than real, I think, it is not always an advantage to get money in your possession ?—A. It is very convenient.

By the Chairman:

Q. When is your monthly salary paid?—A. Three days before the end of the month, on the 28th or the 29th of the month the cheques generally reach here.

Q. You are not, like the inside service at Ottawa, paid on the 15th?—A. No, we are not.

Q. How, in the December month are you paid ? Before Christmas day?—A. Yes, sometimes.

Witness retired.

Mr. WILLIAM CAVEN, Deputy Collector Inland Revenue, Montreal, called, sworn and examined.

By the Chairman:

Q. You are the deputy collector here?—A. Yes, sir.

Q. Were you appointed under that political clause which gives exemption from examination?—A. No, sir.

Q. How long have you been in the service?—A. About twenty-six years.

SESSIONAL PAPER No. 29a

Q. You entered the service before that political clause came into existence, 1 think?—A. I was appointed in the Inland Revenue Department, I think I got my permanent appointment in 1882, after passing the Civil Service examination.

Q. You must have been an 'early bird,' the Civil Service Act was only instituted about that time?—A. That was the first examination.

Q. But you have been in the employ of the department since 1877?—A. Yes, when I was a boy I was in the Customs Department and was afterwards appointed in the Inland Revenue.

Q. Have you always been in Montreal?—A. No, sir, I was in Prince Edward Island, Toronto, British Columbia and Montreal.

Q. After being in Prince Edward Island, Toronto and British Columbia, you were sent here ?—A. Yes.

Q. Under Mr. Toupin, you had control of the office here?—A. Of the outside.

Q. You have nothing to do with this stamp question that we have been inquiring about?—A. No, sir, nothing at all.

Q. You examine the accounts of the people at the factories?—A. Yes, sir.

Q. Have you anything to suggest about those accounts?—A. No, I think they are all right.

Q. With your long experience of thirty years in the service, have you anything to suggest with reference to those accounts ?—A. I think they run along very well.

Q. There is nothing to lead you to think that anybody is derelict in their duty?—A. Oh, sometimes we come across an officer who is careless.

Q. What do you do then ?—A. I report him to Mr. Toupin or Mr. Lawlor.

Q. What happens in such a case as that? You report to headquarters and a little remonstrance will set him right, I suppose?—A. We warn him here.

Q. Have you ever come to a case where Mr. Toupin had to report a man to the department?—A. I do not think Mr. Toupin has, no.

Mr. TOUPIN.—I reported a good officer last week, because he went away without permit, that is the only case I have reported.

Q. Mr. Fyshe was suggesting that I should ask whether you have anything to do, or does it come within your purview to deal with the balances that remain ostensibly due to the department?—A. No, sir, I have nothing to do with that, those balances are on the ledgers in the office, they are not on the factory books.

Mr. Fox.—There are some spirits that were stolen some years ago, and permission has been asked to write them off, but the Treasury Board does not see fit from the evidence put before them to write off the balance.

Q. With reference to these gentlemen who are in charge of distilleries and factories, there is nothing in their conduct to lead you to the suspicion that they are living beyond their means, or anything in that way?—A. No, sir, I never noticed anything of that kind.

Q. You think there could be collusion between the officers and the manufacturers if the officers were disposed to be dishonest?—A. I think if the officer was disposed to be dishonest he could reap personal benefit by it.

By Mr. Fyshe:

Q. Do you not think that some of the extraordinary wealth of these distilleries seem to make is perhaps due to causes like that?—A. No, sir, I do not think so.

By the Chairman:

Q. What is your salary?—A. $1,700.

Q. That is the salary you have obtained after thirty years' service?—A. Yes, sir.

Q. What did you enter the service as?—A. As probationary officer.

Q. How many examinations have you passed?—A. Three.

Q. Step by step you have won your way?—A. Yes, sir.

29a—22

7-8 EDWARD VII., A. 1908

Q. And you have been all over the Dominion, practically?—A. From one end to the other, yes.

Q. You have nothing to do with the control of the stamps here ?—A. No, nothing at all.

Q. You simply attend to the outside work as you have told us ?—A. Yes, sir.

By Mr. Fyshe:

Q. You do the inspecting yourself?—A. Yes.

By the Chairman:

Q. Do you go around yourself and visit these factories?—A. Yes, every one of them.

Q. How often?—A. Once a month.

Q. Do the officers who are stationed there know when you are coming?—A. Oh, no.

Q. You go haphazard, promiscuously?—A. I go to any place I feel like going to.

Q. You might go to the Canada Sugar Company's factory this week, or you might go next?—A. Yes, I might.

Q. They have no information, the officers stationed there, when you might come around?—A. No.

Q. When you go out into one of these offices, do you look into the work from the beginning to the end?—A. Yes, sir.

By Mr. Fyshe:

Q. Mr. Lawlor is the chief inspector, is he not?—A. Yes, sir, and when he makes his inspection I accompany him both to the factories and to the warehouses in Montreal. I am doing the same work here every month that he does on his periodical in spection.

Q. You say you always go with him?—A. Yes.

Q. He is supposed to inspect about once a quarter?—A. Yes.

Q. And you always go with him?—A. Yes, that is when he is inspecting in Montreal.

Q. But you do not go outside with him?—A. No, not outside.

By the Chairman:

Q. That is to say you occupy a position like the inspector going into a bank, you are the bank officer, and with the inspector take charge for purposes of examination?—A. Yes, he goes around and makes his examination and I help him check.

Q. Have you any suggestion to make for the better governing of the service?—A. No, sir, I think the system we have in the factories is a very good check.

Q. Are the men now in charge of these factories, and their assistants as good as they used to be?—A. Sometimes they are, but sometimes we get men that do not seem to be as efficient.

Q. Have they as much intelligence?—A. Some of them would make good men, if they applied themselves.

Q. Have there been any resignations lately?—A. There was one a few months ago.

Q. He resigned to better himself, I suppose?—A. To better himself.

Q. Under the present conditions, with openings for good men throughout the Dominion, do you find good men entering the service to the extent they used to?—A. We have not been getting a very good class, although we had one man refuse to accept art appointment a little while ago, or rather he has not accepted it yet, owing to the small amount of salary offered.

By Mr. Fyshe:

Q. But you would have taken him into the department?—A. He was appointed.

SESSIONAL PAPER No. 29a

By the Chairman:

Q. He was absolutely appointed, and would not enter?—A. Yes, sir.

Q. What salaries have these men who have charge of distilleries, and who have practically to decide what a distilery should pay?—A. About $1,800.

Q. And they are responsible men?—A. Yes, sir, responsible men.

Q. How long would they have been in the service until they got such an appointment as that?—A. It depends upon their passing an examination; if they are not special class officers, they might be in the service all their lives and not get it.

Q. In addition to that, they must be of well-known reliable character?—A. Undoubtedly, and then they are trained for the work.

Q. Have you now enough men in charge of the factories and distilleries?—A. No, sir, we have not enough.

Q. Mr. Toupin has said that he has memorialized the department. I suppose you have notified Mr. Toupin that you require more men?—A. Yes, sir, I have told him we require more men.

Q. Would the inability to get good men arise from the fact that better openings are offered outside and that the salary is not big enough?—A. I should judge that to be the case from the last appointment to which I have referred.

Q. You think yourself qualified, I presume, for the position you occupy, going around looking after this outside work, you have all this knowledge, this detailed technical knowledge of the working of distilleries and breweries, malt-houses and factories, and also the knowledge of mensuration, &c.—you possess that in your own person?—A. Yes, I have passed all examinations.

Q. Departmental and Civil Service?—A. Yes, sir.

Q. And you get $1,700 a year?—A. Yes.

Witness retired.

Mr. J. O. Bousquet, First-class Exciseman, Montreal, called, sworn and examined.

By the Chairman:

Q. You are the gentleman who said this morning that you had been looking forward to this day?—A. Yes, sir, I have been looking forward to it for a long time.

Q. What is your position in the division?—A. Well, I am not yet classified, I think.

Q. You are in the list as a first-class exciseman?—A. Yes, but I have passed my special class examination; I should be put on the special class list, but I am only down as a first-class officer, although I have passed my special examination.

Q. You only entered the service in 1900?—A. That is seven years ago.

Q. What made you enter the service?—A. I did not know any better, I suppose; if I had known as much as I do now about it, I would not have gone into it, sure.

Q. What did you enter as?—A. As a probationary officer at $500 a year.

Q. And in seven years you have come to be a first-class exciseman at $1,200?—A. Yes, I have come up.

Q. What was your idea in coming into the service?—A. It was more of a personal affair, but like lots of others, I never knew what the salary was before I came in.

Q. You were thirty-two years of age when you entered the service?—A. Yes, sir.

Q. Were you married at that time?—A. Yes, sir.

Q. And with that brilliant prospect before you, you entered the public service at $500?—A. At that time I had something else I was working at, and this came to me as an addition, because I could do that as well, but if I had only known as much at that time as I learned afterwards, I would certainly not have gone into it, and would

29a—22½

have been better off. I was outside Montreal at that time, I was at Drummondvill and was doing other business.

Q. Considering that you are a highly intelligent man on the right side of fort; do you think your prospects are sufficient to induce you to remain in the service ?—*I* No, sir, I can tell you that this spring I came very nearly getting out of it.

Q. What are your duties as first class excise man ?—A. I am outside here takin control of cigar and tobacco factories.

Q. Whose factories ?—A. J. M. Fortier's.

Q. What amount of duty does Mr. Fortier pay during the year ?—A. Well, th produce of Fortier's factory is about 5,000,000 cigars a year, and on tobacco and cig arettes I suppose he pays just about as much duty as on cigars.

Q. Confining it now to cigars how much duty does he pay ?—A. There would t a duty of $6 per thousand.

Q. That is how much ?—A. That is $30,000 on cigars, besides the duty on lea on which he pays 10 cents per pound.

Q. Then in the course of a year he must pay $100,000 in duty ?—A. I suppos about $80,000 a year.

Q. Is there anybody else there with you ?—A. I have an assistant there, that i to say a temporary clerk. They always send a new man there to be trained.

Q. You act as schoolmaster ?—A. Yes, sir.

Q. And Mr. Caven pays you a visit ?—A. Every month.

Q. Do you know when he is likely to come around ?—A. No, because he alway keeps that secret, although we are looking for his visit and when he comes we are gla to have him come.

Q. He is a good fellow to you ?—A. He is a gentleman to us, we cannot expec less from him.

Q. Tell us do you think there can be any improvement in this outside work—i regard to these cigar factories, I suppose you have always been in Mr. Fortier's place —A. No, I have been in other places too.

Q. You have been to other factories ?—A. Yes.

Q. Have you any suggestion to make in regard to duties or inspection ?—A. N＊ I think the way it is carried on is all right.

Q. You are a first class excise man ?—A. Yes.

Q. And you have passed the examination for the special class ?—A. Yes, sir.

Q. And one of the causes of complaint in the department is that there are n＊ enough special class officers ?—A. No, there are not.

Q. The number is limited ?—A. Yes, sir.

Q. How many special class excise men are there in this division of Montreal ?– A. Only two.

Q. Then you think, to take this as a concrete instance, you think that in a b＝ division like Montreal with $6,000,000 of revenue the number of special class me provided for is not enough ?—A. No, sir.

Q. To what extent would you have the list increased ?—A. Well, I think that ＝ the industries of tobacco and cigars, taking a certain standard, that we should ha＝ here in Montreal four or five more at least that would come on the special class li＝ because we have industries here in tobacco and cigars that take as much of our tim＝ as any other place where they have special class men.

Q. In making this tobacco, cigars, cigarettes, all that kind of thing these stamp come very prominently into use ?—A. Yes, sir.

Q. How do you get hold of stamps ?—A. The stamps are bought by the man＝ facturer, and every morning we go around and check our stock, and if by error, ＊ otherwise, there should happen to be one stamp in the factory that should not be ther we detect it at once, by the way the books are kept. For every box of cigars they hav excised they must have one stamp, therefore, if the manufacturer in one day or or month produces a half a million cigars, and excises the same, and buys stamps, if h has one stamp less than the number of boxes he has excised the next morning we would detect it.

By Mr. Fyshe:

Q. Does not the inspector or excise officer put on the stamps ?—A. No, that is done by the manufacturer, but we check every stamp.

Q. Does the manufacturer buy a stock of stamps?—A. He buys from Mr. Toupin, and the books are so kept that they cannot buy more or less stamps than they had cigars, because every day they have to make a return of their production.

Q. Nothing goes out of the factory that is not properly stamped ?—A. We see to that, and we see that the stamps are properly cancelled, that is our duty to watch that, there is not a box of cigars the manufacturer produces that he can get out of the factory unless the stamps are properly cancelled.

Q. Then again, do you keep a record of the stamps, they are all numbered ?—A. Oh, yes.

Q. Do you keep a record of the number?—A. We do not, because it is kept in the office, in the stamp department.

By Mr. Bazin:

Q. But you would notice, for instance, stamps that have been stolen from the office?—A. Decidedly we can—well for one stamp—I would not say that they might not work that.

Q. But I mean in quantity ?—A. Well, the next morning we would at once detect it and we would say to the manufacturer ' you have too many stamps in the place where did you get then '; we do our examination every morning and supposing he has ten or fifteen stamps, or even if it is only one more than he should have we would detect it, but if he had only one stamp over it might be an error.

Q. Are you so thorough as to notice the different number ?—A. All the denominations—you see the books are so arranged that the manufacturer makes up his stock by all these denominations and we check his books and we have access to his private books if we think he is doing something that is not right, and therefore to my comprehension, the way we do it, there is not the slightest doubt he cannot do anything or move at all unless he moves in the right way.

By the Chairman:

Q. I do not want to be impertinent, Mr. Bousquet, but I suppose when entering the service, you had some political backing?—A. Decidedly, like all other people, I suppose.

Q. But since you have been in the service you have lived up to the traditions of the service, I presume you have not gone outside to get political help towards obtaining an increase of salary or promotion ?—A. No, sir, I have gone up from the bottom of the ladder.

Q. When you once got in you threw politics aside ?—A. I thought it was the best thing to do.

By Mr. Fyshe:

Q. What are the methods in force in the department, are they quite efficient ?—A. I think so, oh yes.

Q. You do not see anything that you could suggest an improvement in ?—A. Well, I was just going to say that—of course, I should make the raise in salary the capital point in this interview, but I would place second in order the question of classification. As you will see there by the memorial we are talking about the classifying of officers who have passed the special class examination and they are regarded everywhere as first-class officers. I should say that it is no inducement for an officer after he has

striven hard to pass a special class examination to be still kept as a first-class offic⁴
The way we are we have worked hard for years and years in order to be able to p⁴
that special class examination and now the result is that we are told the business of t·
department does not warrant us being put on the special class list and, therefore, ⁴
are not reaping any benefit from all our work. The special class list should not
limited and should be thrown open to every officer qualified for that class.

Q. Is that because they do not require as special class officers ?—A. It is becau
they have not any 'special class' open at the time.

Q. But is there special class work to be done ?—A. Decidedly. As I said a mome
ago in Montreal we should have four, five or a half dozen special class officers in tl·
service in order that those who have passed the special class examination should be ab.
to raise themselves up.

By the Chairman:

Q. Does it not come down to this as a general thing; the same fear pervades a
departments—the department is afraid of the politicians and afraid of extension f(
fear undesirable men should be pressed upon them ?—A. You should refer that to tl
head of the department.

Q. You state there are not sufficient special class excise men, the department h
been memorialized to extend the list; do you think that the inattention of the depar
ment to this request arises from the fact that the department might have pressure p
upon it to appoint men who are not sufficiently qualified ?—A. Well, I do not know.

Witness retired.

Dr. Louis Victor Benoit, Collector of Inland Revenue, St. Hyacinthe, Quebe
called, sworn and examined.

By the Chairman:

Q. You are the collector of inland revenue at St. Hyacinthe?—A. Yes, sir.

Q. When was St. Hyacinthe made a division?—A. That was long ago, before
was in the service.

Q. What class division is St. Hyacinthe?—A. We are in what is called the third
class division.

Q. Is it not of recent erection as a division?—A. No.

Q. What have you in St. Hyacinthe's division, you have Melcher's gin distillery
—A. No, that belongs to Joliette. We have a distillery, two vinegar factories, fiv
cigar factories, and eleven bonding warehouses. The division is a very extensive divi
sion; although we might not collect a very large amount of duty it is a very large divi
sion, because 'it comprises sixteen counties. All the counties between Montreal an
Quebec and the eastern townships on the south side of the St. Lawrence, belong t
St. Hyacinthe.

Q. You have not been long appointed?—A. I was appointed in 1901.

Q. By whom?—A. By the Honourable Mr. Bernier.

Q. Who was then the member for St. Hyacinthe?—A. Yes, sir.

Q. You were a doctor before that?—A. Yes, sir.

Q. Did you pass any examination?—A. I passed two examinations, the Qualif
ing and the first-class examination.

Q. Were you in the service at all before you were appointed?—A. No.

Q. Then you did not come up from the ranks?—A. No.

Q. In addition to being the collector of Inland Revenue, you are inspector of g
and gas meters?—A. Yes. I am the inspector of gas for the district of St. Hyacinth

Q. That would involve your travelling to some extent?—A. No, all that work is done in the office, that consists practically of the inspection of gas meters.

Q. These meters are all inspected by you at St. Hyacinthe?—A. They are inspected at St. Hyacinthe.

By Mr. Fyshe:

Q. Do you also inspect electric meters and electric lights?—A. No, there is a special inspector for that.

By Mr. Bazin:

Q. Are you inspector of weights and measures also?—A. No, there is a special man for that.

By the Chairman:

Q. In addition to excise, the only other office of emolument you hold is that of inspector of gas and gas meters?—A. Yes.

Q. There is a slight emolument attached to that additional office?—A. One hundred dollars a year.

Q. Is there any other place in the division that has gas outside of St. Hyacinthe? —A. No, I do not think so.

Q. Were you in practice before you entered the service?—A. Yes, sir.

Q. Had you any special opportunity of acquiring all this knowledge of distilleries, and tobacco and cigar factories?—A. No, I had to make a special study in order to pass the examination.

Q. I suppose you had a general knowledge of the work?—A. Not until I had to pass this examination.

Q. Did you go to a ' crammer '?—A. No, I worked on alone.

Q. How did the position come to be vacant? There was a superannuation, was there?—A. Mr. Boivin was collector and he was superannuated on his own application.

Q. How old was he at the time?—A. Fifty-nine.

Q. Was there any physical disability in his case?—A. Yes, he was physically incapable of doing the work.

Q. Then, of course, it came to Mr. Bernier's turn to make the appointment?—A. I was then in the division, I had been there for four months.

Q. And then you were appointed?—A. I was promoted, yes.

Q. Was there any dissatisfaction over your appointment?—A. I would rather let somebody else say as to that.

Q. I presume you have a salary of some $1,800?—A. $1,800, yes.

Q. Mr. Caven, who has been many years in the service, and is deputy collector at Montreal, has only $1,700, I think, is it not Mr. Caven?

Mr. CAVEN.—There is also a strange thing in connection with my appointment, and that is I was a special officer, and when I came into the office I lost $100 a year.

Q. Although everything I have heard about you since your appointment was to your credit, did not your appointment cause dissatisfaction in the service, Mr. Benoit? —A. I do not think so, because they could not very well take anybody outside the city of St. Hyacinthe for an appointment of that kind.

Q. That comes out of the eternal political sentiment?—A. Yes, that is the case unless there is some special reason against it, they had to take some one from St. Hyacinthe.

Q. And if some Montreal man were appointed in St. Hyacinthe, a St. Hyacinthe man would have to go to Montreal?—A. That appears to be how it goes.

Q. What is the collection of your division?—A. About $175,000, besides the duty accrued on spirits.

Q. What is the staff in your division?—A. I have quite a number of out offices, is a very large division. I have out offices at St. John, Sorel, Victoriaville, St. Césair Marieville, St. Anne and Farnham, these are all out offices.

By Mr. Fyshe:

Q. Where there are cigar factories?—A. Yes.

By the Chairman:

Q. How many offices have you?—A. Eight—I was forgetting one at Thetfoi Mines, in the county of Megantic.

Q. How are the moneys deposited?—A. In Sorel, St. John and Victoriaville the deposit direct at those places, and they send the certificates of deposit to the hea office at St. Hyacinthe. The other places are all small factories and they deposit the collections through St. Hyacinthe.

Q. In fact in some of the places you have mentioned there are no branch banki —A. No.

By Mr. Fyshe:

Q. You have quite a number of men under you?—A. I have thirteen men on th list and five temporary officers.

By the Chairman:

Q. That is rather an increase? How many temporary officers had you when yo began?—A. When I went into the service the division of St. Hyacinthe comprised onl St. Hyacinthe proper—Sorel, Victoriaville and St. John were annexed to St. Hyacinth afterwards; they were all separate divisions and collected and returned their mone separately, but they were all annexed to the St. Hyacinthe division. The collection i St. Hyacinthe at the time was $45,000, and last year it was $80,000.

Q. How many temporary men had you when you began?—A. Only three men, bu since then we have had a distillery which takes three men, a vinegar factory whic takes another man, and two other cigar factories added.

Q. These men are all of recent appointment; do you find them efficient?—A. can say I consider I have a very efficient staff.

Q. Is that personal regard to you or is St. Hyacinthe a cheap place to live in?—A No, I think they do their work properly.

Q. Do the officers at the outside offices get the same rate of pay as at St. Hya cinthe?—A. They are not paid very much, I can tell you.

Q. Are the lower grade men in your division paid the same as the men in th lower grade men in the division of Montreal?—A. If they are of the same classifica tion.

Q. What is the relative proportion of the cost of living at St. Hyacinthe as com pared with Montreal?—A. I really believe that outside the item of rent everything just as dear in St. Hyacinthe as in Montreal and the rent is very little below the ren in Montreal.

By Mr. Fyshe:

Q. I should think provisions were cheaper?—A. No, they are just as dear as i Montreal.

By the Chairman:

Q. Considering the many opportunities which exist even in St. Hyacinthe for me to better themselves, do you find any difficulty in getting good men?—A. I have no been wanting any men for a long while; I have all I want, I do not want any more.

Q. When was your last appointment made?—A. Four years ago.

Q. Are men leaving you at all, are they resigning?—A. No, they have all stayed with me.

Q. Are they paid remunerative salaries in proportion to the cost of living where they are employed?—A. The lower class of officers especially are certainly underpaid.

Q. They live in hopes of getting better salaries?—A. Oh, yes.

Q. You laid emphasis on 'the lower class of officers,' but with regard to the higher class of officers, the men in charge of factories and all that, are they paid remunerative salaries?—A. Well, of course, they are, but if you take into consideration the class of work they have to give us, because they are first class men, and I want first class work from them; I will not expect the same class of work from the temporary officer that I do from the first-class man——

Q. That is right enough?—A. And I think they should get well paid in consequence.

By Mr Fyshe:

Q. You have to send a government officer to the establishment of everybody who starts a cigar factory?—A. Yes, I do that work myself. I have to make a survey of the premises before I give a certificate for the license, and they can only get a license after getting the certificate of the surveying officer, and I generally do that work myself.

Q. Of course, you only want an officer where there is a store to keep the stock in bond?—A. No, the officer has to be there on duty at the factory, we have to have a man there to check the work anyway; if they do not put out a single cigar or a pound of tobacco in bond, we have to have men there to check the work during the current month anyway.

Q. But they could not get tobacco to work with unless they took it out of bond somewhere?—A. Cigars or tobacco made exclusively from Canadian domestic leaf, they would not have to take out of bond; that leaf does not go into bond or come through bond at all, and the manufactured product would not go through bond at all.

By the Chairman:

Q. Is any man in your division in charge of more than one factory?—A. I have one man in charge of two.

Q. Is there any difference in his pay, compared with that of the others?—A. No.

Q. These men who are employed at Thetford Mines and other places, do you think their salaries relatively are fair in proportion to the cost of living in those places?—A. I should think they are not.

Q. You think the advance in the price of commodities has reached these out-of-the-way places?—A. Yes; take Thetford Mines, it costs as much to live there as in Montreal now, you cannot get a house.

By Mr. Bazin:

Q. You have a resident officer there?—A. The officer we have there is sub-collector of Customs, and we pay him a commission, because that license has only been granted in the month of July, so we appointed the collector of Customs as our officer, on commission, which will probably give from $200 to $250 extra salary for that work.

Q. Who has opened the warehouse?—A. Mr. Lebranche.

Q. Is he not the hotelkeeper?—A. He is the merchant, hotelkeeper, real estate, and everything.

Q. Do you know, as a matter of fact, that the bonded warehouse is kept separate from his store and hotel?—A. Oh yes, before I granted the license I was there personally.

Q. Did he give a guarantee?—A. Of $2,000 in the guarantee company, which has been accepted by the department.

Q. And I suppose he has got some whiskey consigned to him in bond, and he could only open the door to take the whiskey out when some one is present?—A. He cannot open the door, our officer takes it out.

Q. I thought you said he was the officer?—A. Oh no, the officer is the sub-collector of Customs; Mr. Lebranche is the licensee.

By the Chairman:

Q. You were appointed in 1901?—A. Yes.

Q. You come under the benefits of the retirement fund?—A. Yes, I belong to that.

Q. That is to say, 5 per cent of your salary is deducted, and when you choose to come out of the service, you get your money back again?—A. Yes. I do not think they give quite as much interest as if we deposited the same amount in the bank.

Q. You could make more than 4 per cent on your money now?—A. Yes, because the bank pays more than that every three months.

Q. I doubt that statement, but still you could make more than 4 per cent out of your money. Do you not think it desirable to establish a superannuation fund?—A. Yes, or if it was practicable to have a combination of the two, it would be better yet.

Q. There is nothing in the world, except the dignity of the office, which stands in the way now of your resuming your old profession?—A. Nothing at all.

Q. And if you wanted to resume your profession to-morrow, you would get your money back again?—A. That is all I would get.

Q. But if you saw a prospect before you of bettering yourself, there is nothing to deter you from going out of the service?—A. Well, I am getting to be a little old now, and I do not want to make a change every day.

Q. How old are you now?—A. I am forty-six.

By Mr. Fyshe:

Q. Do you do any professional work now?—A. No, I cannot do so.

By the Chairman:

Q. You say you cannot do professional work now?—A. No.

Q Have you any means of adding to your living?—A. Nothing at all.

Q. What is Mr. Brennan in your office?—A. He is in charge of the distillery at St. Hyacinthe. We have some of our men who are sent sometimes on especially hazardous service, and I would like to say to the Commission that I think there should be provision made in such case for extra pay, or they should be given protection for insurance. I have one of my men who is called on two or three times a year to spend two or three weeks in the fulminate of mercury factory. He should be paid extra for that, or he should be protected by insurance paid for by the department.

Witness retired.

Mr. DAVID JOSEPH BRENNAN, special class excise man, St. Hyacinthe, P.Q., called sworn and examined.

By the Chairman :

Q. How long have you been in the service ?—A. Nearly seventeen years.

Q. Where were you stationed, what has been your career in the service ?—A. was appointed in the Windsor division, and was stationed at the Walkerville distillery on February 14, 1891, I was transferred to the Toronto division in 1894, to Hamilton on January 5, 1903, and March 1 last year found me at St. Hyacinthe.

Q. Which of those places do you like the best ?—A. It is really immaterial, have been moved around so often.

SESSIONAL PAPER No. 29a

Q. Have you a family ?—A. I have.

Q. How many changes and tribulations have you passed through with your family ?—A. From Toronto to Hamilton and from Hamilton to St. Hyacinthe.

Q. What is the compensation for removal expenses for sending your family down? —A. The cost of packing up, the actual cost of transportation, the cost of unpacking and one week's board for the family.

Q. One week's board for the family and the actual expenses out of pocket ?—A. Not the actual expenses out of pocket, but just the actual cost of transportation, packing, and unpacking ; whatever breakages occur I have to bear the loss of.

Q. What distillery is it at St. Hyacinthe ?—A. The St. Hyacinthe Distillery Company.

Q. When you were at Hamilton what were your duties there?—A. I was acting as special class warehouse man although for the first ten months I had not the qualification, I passed the examination in the fall of 1903.

Q. What warehouse were you at ?—A. The Royal Distillery.

Q. And were you stationed at Toronto?—A. I was at Gooderham & Worts for eight years.

Q. You had practical knowledge of the distillery work before you went to St. Hyacinthe ?—A. I had practical knowledge obtained at Walkerville, Toronto and Hamilton.

Q. Have you anybody with you in the distillery?—A. I have two officers with me at St. Hyacinthe.

Q. How do you manage to divide the work, day and night?—A. No, sir, the officers are on duty from 7 in the morning until 6 at night unless the work requires longer hours.

By Mr. Fyshe :

Q. They are paid extra if they work longer hours?—A. They are paid 50 cents per hour for the first two hours and 25 cents an hour for the extra time after that. That is for extra services which are not required very often.

By the Chairman :

Q. You get extra pay for extra hours ?—A. All distillery officers get a stated amount.

Q. Would that apply to tobacco factories ?—A. I cannot say. I think it does in some of the 'larger factories.

Q. What do they pay you now ?—A. $1,300 and $150 duty pay.

Q. How many years do you say you have been in the service ?—A. I have been in the service nearly seventeen years.

Q. How many examinations have you passed ?—A. I have passed all promotion as well as the special and qualifying examinations.

Q. Did you have any notice that you were to remove to St. Hyacinthe or were you simply ordered to go ?—A. I was notified by telegram on a Friday night to report on the Monday following.

Q. Was that a promotion then ?—A. Yes, sir.

Q. What did you get by going to St. Hyacinthe ?—A. I got to be officer in charge of a distillery.

Q. How much additional emolument did you get ?—A. The special class list was full when I went there so I was still a first class officer, but when I had been there about a month the special class list was enlarged to the extent of six, I being the first place on the list I reached the minimum which was $1,200.

Q. And you got $1,200 and duty pay ?—A. $150 for special duty.

Q. Is there any rule in the department that you could not get more than $1,200 ! —A. The minimum salary of the ordinary special class is $1,200.

Q. Does that depend upon the class of the division in which you are engaged ?—
A. No, sir.

Q. At St. Hyacinthe you would get the same as in Montreal for the same classification ?—A. The same as in Montreal.

Q. What are your juniors paid ?—A. They are both first class men and are all
right, and they get from $1,000 to $1,200.

Q. Then there is no very great distinction between your pay ?—A. No, sir.

Q. Have you anything else to tell us ?—A. Well, simply that I would like to speak
about my experience and to show you what that has been in the moving of my family
from one point to another. I am speaking more particularly now with regard to the
moving from the province of Ontario to the province of Quebec, and, of course, the
same would apply to any officer who was moved from the province of Quebec to the
province of Ontario. Take my own case, a man with a family of children going to
school, I had to take my children out of the school where English was taught in Ontario
and I came to St. Hyacinthe where French is taught to the same extent as English was
in the Ontario school.

Q. That is certainly a handicap ?—A. Yes, and the salary paid is not sufficient to
enable me to put my children in a college and the consequence is their time is actually
wasted because they have to go back into lower classes than that which they left in
Ontario. I am trying to keep my family at school, but this is a decided hardship.

By Mr. Fyshe:

Q. The Government pay all the expenses in bringing your family from Ontario to
Quebec ?—A. Only the actual travelling expenses, the cost of packing and unpacking
and a week's board for the family. When it is borne in mind that it requires every
month of every year of a boy's career at school to prepare for the future you can see
gentlemen that owing to the change from Ontario to Quebec schools my boy is not
getting that training in school at St. Hyacinthe, he is not making that progress that
he would have made had he remained in an Ontario school.

Q. Still he is learning French ?—A. As I said it required every hour of the boy's
career at school to prepare himself for the future and he is being handicapped by the
time lost in acquiring French which if he had remained in the Ontario school he would
have made progress in the essentials.

By the Chairman:

Q. How old is your boy now ?—A. He is ten years now and his Ontario course has
been interrupted and has had to commence again fresh in the St. Hyacinthe school,
and then again that course at St. Hyacinthe does not fit him for the career that he will
fill in Ontario, and when he goes back to Ontario he has to go back three or four years
with his juniors. The same thing would occur with a person going from Quebec to
Ontario.

Q. Is there no discretion in the removal of officers ?—A. Up to a very few years
ago there were no distilleries in the province of Quebec, and, therefore, there were no
officers there to take charge and it is owing to that fact that we have been sent down
from Ontario. As it is now there are officers in Quebec who are being fitted to take
charge of distilleries, but in the meantime we are suffering.

In connection with the extra pay, I would suggest that the duty pay of officers in
distilleries, since they are liable to be moved about so much, instead of being from $150
to $200 should be raised to three times the amount mentioned ($600) in order to provide for the educational expenses of the officer's children. As it is now I am losing
money every month that I am down here, my expenses having increased a great deal
more than my salary.

Q. That is owing to the fact of your transportation from one province to
another ?—A. The cost of living is, with the one exception of meat and vegetables, as

SESSIONAL PAPER No. 29a

ear as it was in the city of Hamilton; I pay as much house rent, more for coal, double or gas, and other things are equally dear.

Q. But I suppose you have more grounds to your house ?—A. I have just the mount of ground my house stands on, with probably 30 feet in depth at the back and the width of the house.

Q. I have no experience of St. Hyacinthe except passing through on the train, but thought it was a place of houses with large gardens?—A. The larger part of the people re living in tenements, four or five families to the house.

I would beg to suggest that in the event of a readjustment of the schedule of alaries, the officers will be so paid as to feel immediate relief, that is by giving a man who has reached the maximum of his class under the present conditions, the maximum nder the improved conditions and others accordingly.

Witness retired.

Mr. JOHN ECKFORD GOW, special class exciseman, Joliette, P.Q., called, sworn and examined.

By the Chairman:

Q. How long have you been in the service?—A. For nearly nineteen years. I was appointed in 1888.

Q. You are still a special class excise man?—A. Yes.

Q. What has been your career in the service?—A. I was appointed to the Stratford main office and from there I have been transferred to Palmerston, Waterloo, Ont., Guelph, Pelee Island, Prescott, Walkerville. I also served in Montreal for a few weeks.

Q. Is Joliette a division?—A. Yes, sir.

Q. Have you a collector there?—A. Yes, sir.

Q. What is the name of your collector?—A. Mr. Louis Victor Labelle.

Q. How long has he been collector?—A. I do not know; I think about four or five years.

Q. Was Mr. Labelle the first collector?—A. No, there was one there previous to that; I have forgotten his name—Mr. Leprohon, I think.

Q. How many are there on the staff at Joliette?—A. There are three at Joliette head office, but one is only a messenger.

Q. That is, there is yourself and Mr. Labelle and the messenger?—A. Excuse me, I am not at Joliette, I am the distillery officer at Berthierville, but I am attached to the Joliette division.

Q. In what class is the Joliette division?—A. The third class.

Q. What is the revenue of the Joliette division, do you know?—A. I cannot say.

Q. How many employees are there altogether in the division; can you tell that? —A. We have five in the town where I am, three in Joliette, and I think about two others at out stations; a number of them are mostly on commission or with very small salaries.

Q. At what distillery are you engaged?—A. At the Red Cross gin distillery.

Q. In all these removals that have taken place, you, like Mr. Brennan, have been compensated for your transportation expenses and a week's board?—A. Yes.

Q. Have you a family?—A. Yes.

Q. Are you any relation to the Hon. Peter Gow that was in the service?—A. No ?, he was a sort of second cousin of my father's.

Q. Why is it that you have been shifted about so much?—A. Well, for many years I was unmarried; I was a distillery officer, and I had passed the required examination and was eligible; I was shifted about much more before I was married than since.

Q. Have you a family now?—A. Yes.

Q. How long is it since you have been in your present location?—A. I am nearly three years there.

Q. And you suffer from the same disability in bringing your family from one province to the other as Mr. Brennan complains of with regard to your family having to begin their education over again?—A. Very much so; I do not know that it was any worse, but I certainly had troubles of my own.

Q. What do they pay you?—A. I am getting $1,500 and $150 duty pay.

Q. Do you find house rent reasonable down there?—A. Yes, sir.

Q. What is the cost of living at Berthierville compared to your former expenditures in Ontario?—A. I think I save a little more than I did when I was living at Windsor and working at Walkerville, which is a very dear town, and probably I save a little more here. I saved nothing the last two years at Windsor, but I do save something here.

By Mr. Fyshe:

Q. You think the cost of living is lower where you are now?—A. Yes, sir, it is a little lower, rent is lower, although it is made almost as high by the education fees. Might I say in reference to what the last witness has said about the difficulty in making the same progress in education here and the disability suffered in going back to Ontario from Quebec, that my little daughter has been sent to Windsor for an English education, I could not obtain it at all in Joliette, and although she could read and write French very well it was no use to her, and she was actually dropped one class.

By the Chairman:

Q. Yet Windsor is a frontier town with a lot of French there?—A. Yes.

Q. Are there many English people in Berthierville?—A. Seven families.

Q. Then, as we are told, man is a gregarious animal you suffer from loss of social intercourse?—A. Yes, we know all the seven families; I am Protestant, and of course——

Q. We are not going into that question at all, but you are naturally a stranger in a strange land down there?—A. Yes, it is no great hardship, of course.

Q. Then the reason of this removal is that the distilleries are of recent origin down there?—A. Yes sir.

Q. How many assistants have you with you down there?—A. Four.

Q. Is the business so extensive as to require five officers?—A. Yes, sir, we require them all.

Q. What are your hours there?—A. Well, we have men from seven to six, my own hours are from eight to six.

Q. And then the officers get extra pay if they work beyond the time?—A. Yes, sir.

Q. Does that amount to anything?—A. Well, we have a night officer, one officer working all night and these officers are paid $25 a month in addition to their salary.

Q. Do you shift that about?—A. Yes, sir.

Q. The man who is doing night work this month will not be doing it next month?—A. That is the arrangement.

Q. You shift them about continually?—A. Three officers do that work, we do this in order that they may share in the emoluments.

Q. Is there anything peculiar in connection with the Berthierville work that you would like to bring to our attention?—A. No, I do not think there is anything in regard to that office in particular. I might say about grading the officers in the distilleries that an officer does not necessarily get more money because he is in the large distillery. An officer appointed on the special class list remains on that list, and a certain one is appointed after me he generally ranks behind me in salary, although he might have harder work than I have, that is owing to seniority.

ESSIONAL PAPER No. 29a

Q. You have been here while the other gentlemen have been under examination?
-**A.** Yes.

Q. Have you anything to add at all to what they have said?—**A.** I have two or three items I would like to refer to. One of them is 'long service.' I think there should be some compensation for an officer with long service. We have men in our service who have been appointed at an age when perhaps it was not easy to pass the examination, and still they are there from twenty to twenty-five years and have given good service, and through that inability to pass the examinations the young school boy, the younger man outstrips the older man. If there was some little compensation for the older men, I do not mean a great deal, it may be $50 a year for every five years of service after twenty years, it would help to put the old men on a par with the younger.

Q. How many examinations have you passed—**A.** I have passed all that are required.

Q. What other suggestions have you?—**A.** With regard to superannuation, I wish to make the remark about that, that in the first place superannuation is based on the officer's salary which he received for three years past; I contend that it is altogether unjust that an officer may pay his percentage into the superannuation fund for thirty-five years and while still in the service he may die and his family receives no compensation; that is unjust, his family should receive something in consideration of that. In regard to the increase of salaries, I would like to say that if any recommendation is made to the government about salaries, I think there should be some clause by which the time of payment would be assured. For instance, the last increase was ranted in October, 1904, but we received no benefit until January, 1905, the Civil Service Act states that the annual increase may amount to five per cent, but it is not always advanced five per cent. In my own case, I was only advanced $50 on $1,400, and the objection is that at that rate it takes four years from the time that the Act becomes operative for me to receive the full benefit, whereas, had I received the full amount possible, i.e., five per cent each year I would have obtained the whole of the increase in three years. Then the next point is if the commission and the government recognize that there is a hardship and that we have grievances that we are not sufficiently paid and that the grievance exists now, that the remedy be applied, at once or at least that one-half of it be given now and that the other half be given in not more than two years, and further that the amount should be made sufficient to cover not only the estimated insufficiency that is earned now, but we should not have the circumstances occur again, and it should anticipate to some extent the probable increase which would take place perhaps in the cost of living before we receive the full benefit that is granted to us.

Q. You take it that commodities will continually advance in price and that there should be some elastic arrangement by which the salaries of Government officials should be raised accordingly?—**A.** It appears as if it would last for some time. I do not believe that our present buoyant condition of affairs will always last, and I think that there will be a turn, but it appears as if it will exist for some little time at all events, and it would be better to provide for it so that the officers would not suffer from receiving too low remuneration. I also want to plead for an additional raise for the lowest class officers. In my experience the third and even second-class officers are the men who suffer the greatest hardships in the matter of salary. I am speaking for them and not for myself in this case, but my experience is that generally the men who have to work from seven to six are mostly second and third-class officers and as the man rises higher in the service he goes later in the morning. I think these men should be placed in a comfortable position at least, in spite of the fact that they are only in the third-class, the basis of salary should be high enough for them to live comfortably.

By Mr. Fyshe :

Q. What is about the average for them now ?—**A.** There are not very many third class officers, but they must average from $750 to $800. Of course, we have other men who have not passed the Excise examinations and who are employed in out stations who are getting $200 a year or less.

By the Chairman :

Q. Have you sufficient officers in your district to carry on the work of the district ?—A. Speaking for the entire division I believe there is a lack of men in one or two of the out offices.

Q. Do you know whether your collector has reported asking for more men ?—A. I do, well I know that he reported at least that one man he has was not satisfactory, and I believe he asked for more.

Q. This man that is not satisfactory, where is he stationed?—A. I think it is St. Jacques. I may explain that that man is not an officer but he divides this duty with others, and he admitted his own unsatisfactory work but stated that he was giving work for all that he was paid, that he considered he was doing enough for the pay he got.

Q. Is he in charge of a factory ?—A. Yes.

Q. And the collector reported his inefficiency ?—A. He told me he had done so.

Q. And you can't get rid of him, and the man says he does as much as he is paid for ?—A. He apparently does not care very much whether he retains the job or not, but he is doing the work.

Q. You were saying that the lower grade men are not paid sufficient in your estimation. Do you have sufficient men entering the service now to fill the vacancies? Can you get good men now ?—A. I have no experience in that line at all.

Q. In other places we found that the uniform cry is that good men will not enter the service ?—A. It seems to me that is the only legitimate conclusion to arrive at.

By Mr. Fyshe :

Q. Do you find a disposition on the part of some of those men who are so poorly paid to slur their work?—A. No, sir.

Q. They are quite conscientious in the discharge of their duty, although continually grumbling at the insufficiency of the pay?—A. The insufficiency of the pay is very frequently the occasion for remark.

Q. What do you think should be the minimum pay for a young man in such service as you speak of?—A. Well, for the third class I think we should base it on the probability of a man having a family, and I think that in the average town a man should have at least $900, or perhaps $1,000; $900 is not, I think, too much.

Q. That would be nearly $3 per day, excluding Sundays?—A. Yes, I am saying that at haphazard, but I think that would not be anything too much in comparison with the work he is called upon to do.

Q. How would that compare with the pay of similar men in the old country?—A. I do not know; I presume it would be more.

Witness retired.

Mr. JOSEPH OLIER CHALUS, inspector of weights and measures, Montreal, called, sworn and examined.

(Memorial of weights and measures staff read.)

By the Chairman:

Q. You are the inspector here?—A. I am inspector of weights and measures for the Montreal division.

Q. How long have you been in the service?—A. Twenty-nine years.

SESSIONAL PAPER No. 29a

Q. You came in when the Act was first established?—A. A little after, I came in in 1878.

Q. And the Act was established some time before that?—A. About 1874.

Q. What was your first appointment?—A. Assistant inspector of weights and measures, Montreal.

Q. Then in the course of time you became inspector?—A. After three years I was appointed chief inspector.

Q. Then you have been inspector since 1881?—A. Yes.

Q. What is your salary?—A. $1,600.

Q. Is that the highest salary paid to an inspector of weights and measures?—A. To my knowledge it is, yes.

Q. You are the head, the top of everything else in the weights and measures branch?—A. Yes.

Q. What is your establishment in Montreal? How many officers have you?—A. I have eight assistants with me.

Q. Mr. Daoust and Mr. Boudet are two of your assistants?—A. Two of them, yes.

Q. What are the salaries paid your subordinates?—A. The maximum salary paid is $800, but they do not all get that.

Q. Tell me what are the duties in the weights and measures branch? Do you go around all the shops inspecting weights and measures?—A. First, we visit every place of business where scales, weights or measures are kept for trade, we call at every one of these places and verify all weights, scales and measures; all scales, weights and measures used in trade are tested. We also attend to the scale factories. No scale or instrument for weighing or measuring can be legally sold unless first verified, and we attend to the importers and manufacturers of these articles.

By Mr. Fyshe:

Q. You have a tremendous lot of work?—A. Yes.

By the Chairman:

Q. How many officers do you say you have in Montreal?—A. There are eight on the staff besides myself. We have the city of Montreal and suburbs and sixteen counties outside the city to attend to.

By Mr. Fyshe :

Q. You do not do that with eight men, surely?—A. Oh, yes; I have to.

Q. You don't say so?—A. Yes, I have to. The inspection in the country districts only takes place every two years. Some scales are verified every year and others every two years, but all scales in public elevators and scales used by the railways and all that description of scale are verified every year. ·The law is that the public scales have to be verified every year.

Q. Do you visit these stores periodically or do you go in any time when you think fit?—A. We visit them at any reasonable time during the day.

Q. And without notice?—A. Without notice, yes.

Q. When you send a man around is he specified as to a certain district he is to take?—A. Oh, yes, of course, I direct the staff.

Q. Does he keep a record of every visit to these establishments?—A. He has to send a lengthy report of every place visited and specify every thing he has inspected at each place.

Q. And you keep a record of that?—A. Yes.

Q. So that you can tell at any time when any place was last inspected and what the report was?—A. Oh, yes, we keep a day book and record everything.

By the Chairman:

Q. Your men make these inspections without any notice just when you think fit to send them?—A. Of course, I think that is the right way to reach it if there is anything dangerous. If there is anything that is not right, if they had notices they would hide it away.

Q. Do you meet with any opposition, take for instance, when your men go into a shop and demand that all the weights and measures should be brought to their notice? —A. As a rule we do not meet with any objection from the public, our officers generally are well received.

Q. Do you send one man or two to make an inspection?—A. One man goes at a time, he has his full equipment, he has his standards with him and has a carter to take him there.

Q. You drive up in a cart to the place?—A. Yes, sir.

Q. But when the cart drives up could not the storekeeper get rid of a lot of his weights and measures if he knew they were not right?—A. Well, of course, he may possibly do it—I am speaking now of our regular visit.

Q. Yes, supposing there is a deficiency in some of the measures or scales, could not those measures or scales be hidden away?—A. Certainly, I do not pretend to say that they could not.

By Mr. Bazin:

Q. As I understand the law, are they not liable to a penalty if they do not get all their weights and scales passed?—A. Certainly, because we are sending more than once and the second time the officer goes there, if he finds scales, or weights or measures that have not been verified, he has a right to remove them and have the man fined for using them.

By Mr. Fyshe:

Q. Is there any special mark on them to show that they have been verified?—A. Yes, there is the Government mark, and that mark is changed every two years on the two-years' scales and every year on the annual scale.

By the Chairman:

Q. In your twenty-nine years' experience you believe that all weights, scales and measures have been reached?—A. Yes, that is what we try at. We have sixteen counties outside the city of Montreal and suburbs to look after.

Q. That corresponds with the divisions of Montreal and St. Hyacinthe?—A. Formerly they had thirty-two counties in Montreal division, and since a few years they have formed a new division of St. Hyacinthe, with sixteen counties, so that we have the city of Montreal and its suburbs, with sixteen counties in our division.

Q. When the storekeeper's scales, weights and measures are being inspected is the fee paid at the same time?—A. Yes, sir.

Q. On the amount of work that is done?—A. And we issue the officer's certificates bearing stamps representing the amount of money received, and we deliver it to the owner of the scales.

Q. That money you pay into the credit of the Receiver General?—A. Yes.

Q. You have nothing to do with the Montreal division of excise here?—A. Nothing at all.

Q. You account direct to the department at Ottawa?—A. The chief inspector audits our books.

Q. Mr. Lawlor, in addition to inspecting the Montreal division of the Inland Rev. enue Department also inspects the weights and measures?—A. Certainly he counts our stamps and everything.

Q. How often does he inspect your office?—A. Every six months.

Q. Do you know when he is coming around?—A. He does not tell me beforehand when he is coming, but when he comes I will receive him well.

Q. Your revenue is derived from the sale of stamps?—A. Yes, we issue stamps for checking all the receipts.

Q. These stamps, are they kept in a vault or safe, or anything of that kind?—A. The department supplies the stamps for the inspectors of each division and keeps an account with him, and the inspector distributes these stamps to his assistants and keeps a separate account with each of them.

Q. To what extent do you keep a supply of stamps on hand? Have you about three months' supply?—A. There are seven varieties, namely, one-cent, two-cent, five-cent, ten-cent, fifteen-cent, twenty-cent, thirty-cent, fifty-cent, seventy-five cent, one dollar, one dollar fifty cents, two dollars, five dollars, and ten dollars, that is what we keep.

Q. How often do you ask for stamps?—A. As a rule about every three or four months.

Q. You have about three months' stock in hand?—A. Yes.

Q. What would be the value of the stock you have on hand?—A. It all depends upon the denomination of the stamps.

Q. As a rule, how many stamps do you keep on hand?—A. As a rule, I keep a larger amount of the small stamps than of the larger denomination.

By Mr. Bazin:

Q. Give us the amount in dollars?—A. Oh, the average value of the stamps would be about $4,000 or $5,000.

By the Chairman:

Q. Are those stamps kept in a fireproof vault?—A. In a fireproof safe.

Q. Who has the key of that?—A. It has a combination lock. We send in monthly reports showing how many stamps we have on hand and we have to produce the cash for the difference. If we issue so many stamps we must show a deposit equal to the amount of the stamps issued during the month.

Q. Have you always been in the Montreal division?—A. Yes, I was born in Montreal and have always lived in Montreal.

Q. You have grown up in the office here?—A. Yes.

Q. You have been here since 1878?—A. Yes.

Q. In Montreal itself, what has been the increase, you say that new industries have been inaugurated, how many more are these than when you first entered the service?—A. I might say that Montreal has been spreading a great deal within the last twenty years, at the time I joined the department it was a comparatively small city, and now even the commercial part of the city has spread a great deal, the population has almost doubled since I entered the service.

Q. You say that in 1896 the total staff was nine officers, and in 1906 you had seven officers, that is owing to the diminution in the number of counties comprising the district?—A. It is accounted for by the factory work, which has been increasing a great deal, the new scales will have to be verified.

By Mr. Fyshe:

Q. I should think the present staff does very much more work per day than the old staff?—A. Certainly and now our system is getting better, we master our duties better now than we used to, there is no question about that.

By the Chairman:

Q. Now, there is a greater tendency to verify the weights and measures at the factory, where they are constructed than in the shops?—A. They have no right to use them in the factory until they are stamped.

Q. Then the weight, or measure, or scale before it, is sent out to the merchant or storekeeper has to be verified by an officer?—A. Yes, our weights and measures law is very rigid, all the friction points, bearings, &c., must be of hardened steel, we demand that on every scale manufactured in the Dominion.

By Mr. Fyshe:

Q. You must be competent to judge whether they are of hardened steel or not?—A. We try them with a file, you see.

By the Chairman:

Q. It has led to this result that in 1896, or about that time, you went into more places than you do now, because you verify them at the factory instead of verifying them piece meal as much as you used to?—A. Yes.

Q. I see you tested nearly 60,000 weights and measures during last year?—A. Yes, of course, the Commission will understand that our receipts at first sight seem to be small on account of the price of verification of a weight or measure which is only 5 cents, so it takes a great many of them to make up a large amount, but the work is still there to be done, although it is not like the excise where they draw large amounts; we draw all small amounts, but we have the work to do.

By Mr. Fyshe:

Q. And you have to be just as conscientious?—A. Yes, but that accounts for the comparatively small receipts we have.

By the Chairman:

Q. What was your previous experience before entering the Government service?—A. In what way?

Q. Were you a mechanic?—A. I was a notary. I was a student when I left the country for two years; I went on an expedition to Rome and I was one of the Pontifical Zouaves for three years; that was in 1867.

Q. You came under the glamour of a soldier's life then?—A. Yes, and when I came back from my service there I had no disposition to study law, and I looked for a Government position and got a position in the service. That is the whole history of my life, and since I have been there I have had no reason to regret it.

By the Chairman:

Q. I wanted to find out whether you had anything in your previous career to qualify you to be inspector of weights and measures, that is the reason I asked you. You were thirty-two years old when you joined the service?—A. Yes, it was quite new to me.

Q. Does it take long to acquire that knowledge?—A. I put my mind to it; I tried to do honour to myself and I think I have done as much honour to the service as any other officer in the Dominion.

Q. Have you a sufficient number of officers to carry on the work of your office?—A. Yes, I think I can pull it through with the number of officers I have.

Q. You have not had any new appointments lately?—A. I had one yesterday to replace one of my officers who died last week. Yesterday morning I received the news that another man had been appointed to replace him.

Q. Do you know anything about the qualifications of this new man?—A. I could not say.

Q. Do you know what salary he was appointed at?—A. $500, but if I was permitted to say so, I think it is impossible for an officer to give good service on that salary.

Q. Do you think $500 is sufficient to get good men to enter the service?—A. I would not like to undertake to get good men for that.

Q. If it were a young man?—A. This is a man fifty-one years of age.

SESSIONAL PAPER No. 29a

Q. And what is he to get?—A. $500.

Q. Has he reported yet?—A. He reported himself this morning.

Q. Did you know anything about him before he was appointed?—A. Yes, he used to be a merchant and had some financial reverses.

By Mr. Fyshe:.

Q. Is he a respectable man?—A. Yes.

Q. A decent man?—A. Yes, I think he will make a good officer.

Q. He cannot live on that?—A. I do not see how he can live on that; he is a married man and has a wife and family, and I do not see how he can live on that money.

By the Chairman:

Q. He had to acquire a certain amount of political influence in order to get that position?—A. I understand he was appointed through political influence very likely.

By Mr. Fyshe:

Q. Is it a friendly thing to do to appoint a man at $500 a year?—A. Well, hardly; I think perhaps it is a poor service to him.

Q. If he is a competent man, when is he likely to get an increase?—A. That is what he is looking for; he told me he would not stay long at that figure.

By the Chairman:

Q. How old are you?—A. I am fifty-nine.

Q. Perhaps he may have the idea that you may be superannuated, but you could not be superannuated?—A. Not yet, not until I am sixty.

Q. Are you one of those who are on the superannuation?—A. Yes. He must have thought, I suppose, that through political influence he can secure a better salary in a short time.

Q. It is rather absurd to suppose that a man of fifty-one, married and with a family and with experience, should enter the public service at the rate of $500 a year. The Weights and Measures have never really formed a part, have never been scheduled under the Civil Service Act?—A. No.

Q. They have never had the advantages, such as they are, of superannuation?—A. Well, I have.

Q. That is a fluke. Are any other members of your staff on it?—A. Only Mr. Daoust and myself, because we were ten years appointed at the time of the passing of the Act.

Q. Except Mr. Daoust and yourself, nobody in the Weights and Measures Branch are under superannuation?—A. I had five or six other officers at the time who had paid for nine years into the fund, and the amount they paid in has been refunded to them, and they have been left without superannuation.

Q. It was found that there was nothing in the Civil Service Act to bring in the weights and measures inspectors?—A. No, but the weights and measures men, are not alone; the gas inspectors are in the same position as we are.

Q. I was going to say that in the course of time, in a few years, you, being one of the eligibles to be superannuated, may be retired?—A. Oh yes, I have paid into the old fund.

Q. You score now twenty-nine years' service?—A. Yes.

Q. And in another five or six years' service you will be up to your full maximum? Very likely, and when that time comes, I may be looking forward to that.

Q. The new gentleman may be looking forward to something like that happening? I do not know anything about that.

Q. It is not likely that a man would enter at $500 a year at that age without anticipating something?—A. To tell you frankly, I cannot understand it.

Q. Have you anything further to say?—A. Incidentally, I think it would be proper that the Commission should see about the amount that we are raising every year, and I will show you a copy of the last report of the Montreal division. We collected during that fiscal year $13,354.60. Now, I think—I do not desire to disparage any other division—but I think you should know that we collected the most revenue of any division in the whole Dominion. The Belleville division has collected $4,000; the Hamilton division, $7,000; the Toronto division, $7,700; the Windsor division, $10,559; then comes Montreal at the rate of $13,351. That shows that we have not been idle in Montreal, that we have done what is called fair duty.

Q. What does the Ottawa division collect?—A. Ottawa collected $4,574.

By Mr. Fyshe:

Q. Yours is actually a revenue-producing department?—A. Yes.

By the Chairman:

Q. Montreal has a surplus, has it?—A. Montreal's expenses amounted to $8,716, and the receipts were $13,000.

Q. You are a revenue-producing division?—A. Yes.

Q. But all divisions are not revenue-producing?—A. No, but Montreal is a revenue-producing one.

By Mr. Bazin:

Q. What does Quebec show?—A. The receipts are $3,934, and the expenditure $8,930.

Q. Does that include all the lower part of the St. Lawrence, Gaspé?—A. Yes.

Q. That is what makes the expenses so heavy?—A. And they have no scale factories in the city of Quebec to produce revenue.

Q. And the territory is so large it must be very expensive to cover it?—A. And the division is scattered very badly down the gulf, the officers have to spend so much in travelling to reach the small places where there are almost no scales. This is in contrast to the Montreal division, which is thickly populated.

By the Chairman:

Q. The whole province of Ontario is revenue producing, that is to say its total expenditure is $32,000 with a total revenue of $35,000 and in fact the province of Quebec has a total expenditure of $23,800 with receipts of $21,800, therefore, the record for the province of Ontario is not so very bad. You say you have a salary of $1,600?—A. Yes, sir.

Q. And you said you had the highest amount paid to any official?—A. Yes, sir.

Q. Has there been any scale laid down by the department of salaries to be paid officers of the Weights and Measures branch?—A. It is not to my knowledge that there has been any scale established for the Weights and Measures branch. We have always been left to the good pleasure of the Minister.

Q. As it is now you get a salary of $1,600 and you have been an inspector for over twenty-five years?—A. Yes, sir.

Q. What had you when you became inspector?—A. I was appointed inspector at the salary of $1,200, which was the salary my predecessor had.

Q. That was twenty-five years ago?—A. Oh, more than that.

Q. You were appointed collector when?—A. Three years after I was in the service.

By Mr. Fyshe:

Q. When you went into the service first you did not have $1,200?—A. I had $700.

Q. Then you got $1,200 when you were made an inspector in 1881, and twenty-seven years afterwards you get $1,600, that is to say your salary has increased from $1,200 to $1,600 in twenty-six years?—A. Yes.

Q. That is slow enough ?—A. That is not a very generous increase.

By the Chairman:

Q. Do you know, Mr. Chalus, whether any representations have been made to the department respecting the small salaries paid to the assistants ?—A. Petitions have been sent through me to the department calling attention to the small salaries paid in the department.

Q. You received an acknowledgment I suppose of the receipt of the petition ?—A. I did, but that is about all I got.

Witness retired.

Mr. J. O. CHALUS recalled.

By the Chairman:

Q. Do you find that you are getting efficient men now, Mr. Chalus ?—A. The greatest drawback we meet with is this that men are chosen from the ordinary people and are given to us as officers. They do not know the first thing practically about weights and measures or weighing machines; they have not the least idea of what constitutes a weighing machine and these men are shovelled into the service without any practical knowledge whatever.

By Mr. Fyshe:

Q. And you have to educate them ?—A. Yes. I believe that the department should have these men put on probation for one or two months under a practical man for their education before they come into the service at all, because our officers have no chance to learn their duty before entering the service. We have at the head of the Weights and Measures Department at Ottawa Mr. James Fife, our head inspector, he is a practical man and he could give them the practical training they would require for the service. Here, when they are shoved into the division, they have practically no chance to learn, but if they were given a course of training for one or two months they would acquire very necessary knowledge. If that could be embodied in your report gentlemen, I think it would be of advantage.

Witness retired.

Mr. JOSEPH A. DAOUST, Assistant Inspector Weights and Measures, Montreal, called, sworn and examined.

By the Chairman :

Q. How long have you been in the service?—A. Twenty-seven years.

By Mr. Fyshe :

Q. How old are you?—A. Sixty-two.
Q. You are not very gray for that?—A. Not yet.

By the Chairman :

Q. You now have a salary of $800?—A. Yes.
Q. How long have you been assistant inspector?—A. Twenty-seven years last June.
Q. What salary had you when you began?—A. $500.
Q. You were not appointed assistant inspector at first?—A. Yes, at $500.

7-8 EDWARD VII., A. 1908

Q. When did you get the next move up?—A. Two years afterwards I had $100 increase, and my last increase dates from October 1, 1886, that is my last increase from $700.

Q. As assistant inspector of weights and measures you have for twenty-one years been in the employment of the public at the same salary?—A. At the same salary.

Q. What is the highest salary paid to an assistant inspector of weights and measures?—A. I do not know of any one getting any more.

Q. You do not know of any one getting more than that?—A. Here in Montreal, I mean.

Q. What time do you begin the day's work?—A. Sometimes at 8.30, because I am making the inspection at the factory; office hours are 9 a.m. until 4.30, and some-sometimes 5 o'clock when it is needed.

Q. Do you take any time for luncheon?—A. Three-quarters of an hour or an hour.

Q. Practically all your working days are given up to the Government service?—A. Government service only.

Q. You are not supposed to be working on Sundays or anything like that?—A. No, sir.

Q. You work all the week and you have had no increase in salary for twenty-one years?—A. That is correct, sir.

By Mr. Fyshe :

Q. You have had an increase surely in twenty-one years?—A. No, not since that date, and my net salary is only $65 per month, because I belong to the superannuation fund. I have seven of my family, and I have to feed and clothe them out of that.

Q. Is that all the salary you have now?—A. Yes.

By the Chairman :

Q. Do you ever feel inclined to leave the service?—A. Not at my age.

Q. But have you not felt so during the years of your life since 1886?—A. No, I was always pleased to work, and did the work for my health.

Q. You get a good deal of outdoor work?—A. Yes, for ten years I was charged by Mr. Chalus to visit the city all around, and I went to the country for eight months too, and that agreed with my health.

By Mr. Fyshe :

Q. You live in the city?—A. Yes, sir.

Q. You can't own your own house?—A. No, sir, I can't, and my rent is increased pretty much during the last few years; it is $18 per month now, and twenty-five years ago I paid $13.

Q. For the same house?—A. Yes, I have been in the same house for twenty-five years and I have been noticed to pay $20 next year.

Q. Are you a married man?—A. Yes.

Q. Have you any children?—A. Yes, five.

Q. Do you live on air?—A. We are obliged to economize, and sometimes we have not much heart to live.

Q. I do not see how any man can live on that salary?—A. For a few years I have been keeping house with my mother-in-law and she had a little rent from another house, and that helped me for a time, but she is dead now, and it is very hard for me to live.

Q. You must have the secret of living cheap?—A. I have one son that earns money and he tries to give me help from what he earns.

By the Chairman:

Q. You were thirty-five years old when you came into the service?—A. I was quite thirty-five.

By Mr. Fyshe :

Q. What were you before that?—A. I was a lawyer, but I was sick, and the doctor ordered me to travel, and as my family had some political influence, and I was ordered to go out and inspect at the district of Terrebonne. After eight months Mr. Aikins became Minister and called me down to Montreal.

Q. Where were you born?—A. At St. Eustache, Two Mountains, and I came to Montreal as a student a year before Confederation took place.

By the Chairman :

Q. Practically you belong to a past age and your friends are all dead and gone now?—A. Many of them.

Q. And there is nobody to stand at your back?—A. No, sir.

By Mr. Fyshe :

Q. Do you feel able to have any political views?—A. No, I belong to the Civil Service; I have been in it for a long time and I will die in it.

By the Chairman :

Q. You came in in Mr. Baby's régime ?—A. Yes, sir.

Q. You go to the factories, do you ?—A. For a long time I visited the factory every day.

Q. Leaving aside the remuneration it is healthy work, is it not ?—A. Yes, it is healthy work, you have to stand up and move around and write a little in order to make your report to the office, but when I am through with the factory I help my confrères in the office writing.

Q. How many factories do you inspect ?—A. Mr. Fairbank's factory, they import also. The factories we have in Montreal are New Warren Scale Co., Fife Scale Co., A. Joncas Factory, Collier Scale Co. and Frotheringham as importers.

By Mr. Fyshe :

Q. Where is the head office of the weights and measures branch ?—A. On St. Gabriel street, opposite the Champs de Mars.

Q. Mr. Boudet is in the same position as yourself having $800 salary?—A. Yes.

Q. Do you know Mr. Daoust, whether any representation has been made to the Deputy Minister or the Minister with respect to the small salaries paid?—A. We have sent in a petition to Mr. Templeman and also to Mr. Brodeur.

Q. That is not done collectively ?—A. Collectively we sent in a petition to Mr. Brodeur and also to Mr. Bernier. Some years ago we started by sending a petition collectively to Mr. Bernier.

Witness retired.

Mr. ETIENNE BOUDET, assistant inspector Weights and measures, Montreal, called, sworn and examined.

By the Chairman :

Q. How many years have you served Mr. Boudet ?—A. Eight years.

Q. Are you satisfied with your lookout, Mr. Boudet ?—A. Well, I would be if I could make the two ends meet, but I can hardly do so.

Q. You have only been eight years in the service with no prospect of any retirement, did you not know that when you entered the service ?—A. I did not.

Q. You live in hope, do you ?—A. I live in hope.

Witnesses retired.

Mr. JEAN PASCAL MORIN, inspector of weights and measures, St. Hyacinthe, Que., called, sworn and examined.

By the Chairman :

Q. You are the inspector at St. Hyacinthe ?—A. Yes, sir.

Q. How long have you been in the service?—A. Seven years, I was one year in the excise, and then transferred to the weights and measures when they formed the division of St. Hyacinthe.

Q. You are the inspector ?—A. Yes, sir.

Q. What were you during the year that you were in the excise, were you an excise man ?—A. I was deputy collector under Dr. Benoit.

Q. What did they give you as deputy collector ?—A. $800.

Q. And then made you inspector of weights and measures at $900 ?—A. No, sir, at the same salary.

Q. When did you get the other $100 ?—A. I was raised twice, $50 each year.

Q. I suppose you came in under Mr. Bernier's auspices ?—A. Yes, sir.

Q. Are there any scale factories in St. Hyacinthe ?—A. No, sir, there are none in my division, but the Fairbanks Scale Company are to open a large scale factory in Sherbrooke before long which will make more work at the same time increase the revenue of the division.

Q. Now you go about from St. Hyacinthe to all the villages ?—A. Sometimes I am called myself, but I have three assistant inspectors to do the general work during the season.

Q. You have three assistant inspectors?—A. Three assistants.

Q. What are they paid ?—A. Two of them were paid $700 each and the other $650. A year ago last July one was raised $50 more, and I have just received a letter from the department last night, stating that the two others were raised $50 more on the next pay day.

Q. Then the assistant inspectors at St. Hyacinthe are paid how much ?—A. Two will be paid $750 and one $700.

Q. And the assistant inspectors in Montreal with long service like Mr. Daoust are paid $800?—A. Yes, sir.

Q. I do not think any of them are exorbitant salaries, but it seems to me there is a discrepancy between them. When was the St. Hyacinthe division started?—A. Six years ago.

Q. Before then it was the Montreal district?—A. Part of it was in Montreal and part of it in Three Rivers; I have nineteen counties in my division.

Q. And do your men travel over the division?—A. Yes, sir; about 5 or 6 months in the year, during the summer season.

Q. Do they get any addition for travelling expenses, beyond what they spend? If they go to any place in your division are they given a daily allowance, or are they paid their hotel bill?—A. They are paid all the necessary expenses when they are on duty.

Q. The Government pays their expenses but nothing more?—A. No, sir, nothing more.

Q. Is that an inducement to travel, if the man only gets what he spends, is there any inducement to go away from home?—A. I do not think there is, they hurry up their work, do all their writing at night in order to get through with their work and home as soon as they can. It is different in the Montreal division; they do the outside work during the summer months and they have the large city with all the factories for the winter work. In my division the work has to be done during the summer months, having no large cities and no factories where the men could work during the winter. The largest cities in this division are St. Hyacinthe and Sherbrooke, and the work is done with the rest during the summer.

By Mr. Fyshe:

Q. Where is that?—A. St. Hyacinthe.

Q. Where is there anything doing in the winter?—A. As I stated before, we have no large cities in that division, the largest being St. Hyacinthe and Sherbrooke, and the work is done in the early spring and summer.

Q. Your men who only work six months in the year get $750 a year, and those in Montreal who work all the year round get $800?—A. When these men are on the road, as I said before, their living and travelling expenses are paid for the 5 or 6 months they are out, but I have to pay my own expenses at home all the time.

Q. Do you mean to say that when you go out you have to pay your own expenses? —A. I do not go out much as I am all alone to attend the office work and the men on the road; when I am called out my expenses are paid. But I mean to say that my men, working five or six months in the year and having their living expenses paid during that time, when I work myself twelve months, being at the head of the division, having all the responsibility, paying my own living expenses—I think if those men get a salary of $750 a year, I am entitled at least to double their salary, but all I receive for all that is $200 more than they do, so I do not think it is quite just.

Q. How many men have you under you?—A. I had four sometimes, but only three at present.

Q. You get $900 per year?—A. I did until last month, then I was raised $50 more.

Q. And they get $750 and only work 6 months in the year?—A. Yes, sir.

Q. And there are always some on the road?—A. They are on the road until the inspection is completed in the division. I have some out now.

Q. Is any attempt being made on behalf of the weights and measures branch to bring to the attention of the department at Ottawa the small salaries being paid?—A. I am not aware that there has been.

Q. You are fully occupied with the duties of your office?—A. I can't do much outside, being alone. I have to be there to attend correspondence, and work that comes to the office. When my men are through on the road I have to get the list of the work ready for them the next season. I do not always follow the office hours, as I could not do all my work on time, I am sometimes in the office early in the morning, sometimes late at night, especially at the end of the month for the reports.

Q. Is Mr. Lawlor your immediate chief?—A. Mr. James Fyfe, of Ottawa, is our chief inspector, he makes the inspection of my books every six months.

Q. Mr. Fyfe, has he no influence with the government to increase the salary?—A. He is favourably disposed, but he cannot do much himself; he has always found my work satisfactory; I have friends who have influence at Ottawa, and I spoke to our deputy myself once or twice; all the augmentation I had lately is $50.

Q. For your subordinates?—A. For my subordinates and myself.

Q. Don't you think you would have done better outside the Government?—A. Yes, sir; and I was better off when I was in the excise, because my salary would go up with the division, the division having come up two classes since I was transferred from it. Those who were having a salary of $800 at the time I left are now getting $1,100. I went to the weights and measures branch to please Mr. Bernier, then Minister of Inland Revenue; he wanted me to take that place, being a kind of mechanic, and acquainted with both French and English languages, which was very much needed in that division. I expected that my salary would increase, but it has remained very near the same.

1

7-8 EDWARD VII., A. 1908

Q. Do you not think you are too easy going?—A. Well, I do my work, I do not find fault, but my assistants are much better off than I am; I have the responsibility of the division, the department depend on me. And when my assistants get through with their work, as I stated before, they go home until the next season, but I have to remain myself at the office the twelve months in the year with a salary of only $200 more than what they have.

Witness retired.

Mr. J. P. MORIN re-called.

By the Chairman:

Q. What is your experience in the matter of obtaining new men, Mr. Morin?—A. I had a new man put on, and really he did not know how to handle a hammer and tools to work with. I had to put him with another man to go around for a couple of months and teach him, and give him all the instructions possible; there was no place in the office to teach him.

Q. It is like a nurse being appointed who has never been in a hospital before?—A. Very much that way.

Witness retired.

Mr. M. HUGHES, Excise Officer, Montreal, called, sworn and examined.

By the Chairman:

Q. We had the gentlemen from the excise department here yesterday?—A. Yes, sir.

Q. Have you something particular to tell us?—A. Well, I was told I might state my case to you.

Q. Yours is a particular case, particular to yourself—I suppose you want to state your own case?—A. Yes, sir, I am temporarily employed.

Q. You are temporarily in the service of the excise department here?—A. Yes.

Q. How long have you been in the service?—A. Eleven years this month.

Q. Did you ever pass an examination?—A. I passed the Preliminary examination after being in the excise a couple of months.

Q. The Preliminary examination under the Civil Service Act, applies to messengers, packers and all that sort of thing?—A. Yes.

Q. How are you employed, what are your duties now?—A. I am employed in one of the biggest surveys in the Dominion since I have been in the service.

(Memorial prepared by witness read.)

Q. You have been eleven years in the service, you say?—A. Yes, Mr. Chairman.

Q. It was in 1896 you entered?—A. It was in 1896, this month, I went in.

Q. How did you come in then at that time?—A. Well, Mr. Chairman, it was the Hon. Mr. Prefontaine, who is now dead, placed me here in 1896.

Q. And he brought you in, although you passed no examination you were show in?—A. Yes, sir.

Q. What were you called when you came in, you could not be called an excise man?—A. Well, three months after I came into the excise I was placed, it was scarce three months, in Mr. J. M. Fortier's tobacco factory, then I went to the American bacco factory.

Q. But what were you placed in the pay-list as in 1896 when you passed no amination?—A. As a temporary clerk on the contingent account.

AL PAPER No. 29a

ou were not called labourer or anything of the kind?—A. No, sir.

ou say that your first employment was when they put you in the office here?—
old you, I went to Mr. Fortier's factory. I was assistant there to the officer
; after two or three months my collector, Mr. Lawlor, at that time, who is
ispector, sent me to the American tobacco factory, which is one of the second
rveys in Montreal, and I have been there ever since, with the exception that
i I have been sent to the Macdonald factory, that is a very big factory, to re-
officer there during vacation. But with these exceptions I have been con-
i duty at the American tobacco factory and during the absence of the officer
ed the duty in that big factory.

By Mr. Fyshe:

There is it situated?—A. On St. James street, it is a new building.

By the Chairman:

re there any other temporary men like you in this division?—A. I know of
Ross, in this division. We do not get to the office very often to learn what
in.

ou only know of one man like yourself who did not pass the examination and
n as a temporary employee?—A. I could not say whether Mr. Ross ever went
he examination, but I know I have gone to pretty nearly every one, and it cost
iry year to go to these examinations out of the limited salary that I had.

s a general rule there are no temporary employees like yourself that you
in this division?—A. There were twelve others employed during last month.

i it not desirable, in the interest of the public service, that all men, before en-
e excise department, should pass an examination?—A. For my case, Mr.
i, I must state that although I have not passed the required examination, the
g examination, as they call it, I daresay there is not a man that will pass the
examination that will keep the factory in better order than I do, and yet I
been able to pass the examination.

hat may be; to fail to pass the examination is no disgrace, but when there are
uld they not be observed?—A. I do not know what answer to give you, but
rd to the increase of salary I assure you that it was the promise that kept
i excise department at the small salary that I am receiving.

ir. Prefontaine being a good-natured, broad man, said 'come in and I will
ou are all right'?—A. Mr. Prefontaine said to me 'there is a clause whereby
i be created an officer in class B without examination,' so he held out that into me, that I could get a salary of $1,000 a year. which would be little enough
here.

By Mr. Fyshe:

e held that out to you as an inducement?—A. Yes, sir, the last time I met
intaine was in this room.

By Mr. Bazin:

e was simply a Member of Parliament at the time?—A. This was after his
ent to the Cabinet.

y Mr. Fyshe:

hat employment were you in before this?—A. I was in the employ of the
l corporation as an inspector.

ow old are you?—A. Forty-eight.

nd you have been eleven years here?—A. Yes sir.

By the Chairman:

Q. It seems to me you made a mistake in coming in the way you did.

By Mr. Fyshe:

Q. Have you any other means?—A. I have a little bit of revenue, otherwise I could never have existed.

By the Chairman:

Q. Why did not Mr. Prefontaine make you a preventive officer, in which case the examination could be evaded. You have butted into a place where examinations are held by law to be necessary, and you request that Parliament shall be asked to waive the law in your particular case?—A. I did not request, it was something that was held out to me.

Q. This is a request that you shall get out of the temporary into the permanent class. You want to be made permanent?—A. Yes sir.

Q. But you have not passed the examination?—A. No sir.

Q. And Parliament requires an examination to be passed?—A. Yes, sir.

Q. It amounts to this, in plain English, that the request you make is that by some means or other you shall be made permanent and the examination waived?—A. Yes.

Q. How can that be done?—A. I think, Mr. Chairman, by your recommendation, you are very well aware whether I am worthy. I will tell you, if you will pardon me, Mr. Chairman, I think when I am twelve months here and have given satisfaction to my superior officer I should either be discharged or appointed permanently. That is my opinion.

Q. That seems reasonable enough, but you know what Mr. Bumble said about the law, ' the law is an ass,' and if the law is as it is how can you get over it. I do think, Mr. Hughes, it is a rather hard case. but the Commission can do nothing more, I am sorry to say, than bring it to the attention of the Department.

By Mr. Fyshe:

Q. If you were made a permanent officer your salary would be increased?—A. I would expect it to be about double what I am getting. It ought to be.

Q. Would you still continue at the same work?—A. I suppose I would, it would depend upon the collector.

Q. Are there men doing the same class of work as you are doing, at a larger salary?—A. Yes, sir, I believe so; there are several. During the eleven years I have never had a word of reprimand said to me, and I have never absented myself without my collector being made aware of my absence.

Q. I am surprised that a man of your intelligence would not easily pass that examination?—A. Well sir, it is a very technical examination, and there are men holding very important positions who, if they tried it, would be thrown down on it. I understand the first time I went up on it I passed a very good examination, from conversing with others and learning the way they answered, and yet I went up again repeatedly and failed to pass. I was thirty-seven when I came into the excise, and eleven of the best years of my life are gone.

Witness retired.

Mr. J. B. A. LARUE. Quebec, sworn and examined.

By the Chairman:

Q. You are the deputy collector of Inland Revenue here ?—A. One of the deputy collectors; deputy collector, class B.

Q. When were you appointed?—A. On the third day of February, 1898.

Q. What salary had you on your appointment ?—A. I was appointed at $700 a year.

Q. What is your present salary ?—A. $1,000.

Q. Is that the limit?—A. I was appointed by Order in Council.

Q. You did not pass any examination?—A. Not for the Civil Service. I was a professional man.

Q. You being a deputy collector had not to pass an examination but appointed direct ?—A. Yes.

Q. The scale of salaries for deputy collectors, class B, is what?—A. The salary is at the discretion of the Minister in accordance with the importance and responsibility of the duties performed by the officer.

Q. What is the particular thing in the Order in Council appointing you to which you want to draw our attention ?—A. In 1898, according to the regulations, there was no class A or class B. Therefore I have always asked myself how I could have been appointed as class B, being appointed at the head office of the division.

Q. The Inland Revenue Department, for purposes of its own, grades the different divisions into class A, class B, class C, class D, and so on. Isn't that done in accordance with the importance and magnitude of the division ?—A. No. The divisions are classified as first class, second class, third class, in accordance with the amount of business done in each division.

Q. Deputy collectors are in four classes, their classification being coordinate with the division to which they are attached, and you were appointed as deputy collector, class B ?—A. Yes

Q. What is your salary now?—A. $1,000. My class as deputy collector has no reference at all to the division. In a division of the fourth class there might be a deputy collector in class A. I produce a circular issued by the Department of Inland Revenue which says: ' The term deputy collector as used throughout these regulations refers only to those officers bearing that title by virtue of an Order in Council, and being next in rank to the collector at the head office of the division. Deputy collectors of this character shall be known as class A. It does not include other deputy collectors, class B, whose salaries shall be determined by the Minister in accordance with the importance and responsibilities of the office.'

Q. Then the department has determined that you shall be in class B ?—A. I will explain. When I was appointed, I made representations to the department that being a deputy collector at the head office of the division, I should have a salary in accordance with the class of the division to which I was appointed. The division of Quebec was then a second-class division, and my salary should have been $1,200, to go up to $1,300. I was answered that being a deputy collector, class B, I was not entitled to that salary, but that my salary was at the discretion of the Minister. Then I fought the case. I said that according to the regulations existing when I was appointed, there was no specification of class A or class B. I fought the case so well that in 1903 the Hon. Mr. Bernier, who was then Minister, gave an order to amend that clause, and then instituted class A and class B.

Q. You are in precisely the same position now as you were at the time you were appointed ?—A. Exactly.

Q. You have had an increase of salary in that time ?—A. The Hon. Mr. Joly, in 1899, gave me an increase of $200, and this spring, after the death of my father, who was the collector, I got an increase of $100.

Q. The department. I presume, interpret their own regulations, and consider that that is the salary that you are entitled to ?—A. That depends on what representations are made.

Q. You think the department consider individual cases and apply a different rule to your case from what they do to others ?—A. No, of course not.

Q. But you consider, in your interpretation of the clause, that your salary should go up to $1,300 ?—A. I consider that I should have got at first the salary, I was entitled to, $1,200, and then I would have gone up to $1,300; and when two or three years ago there was a change and an increase of salary of $200 for the collectors and $200 for the deputy collectors, I should have got $1,700.

Q. You were appointed politically, without examination ?—A. I am appointed according to law.

Q. Well, you were appointed without an examination, that being the law.—A. Certainly.

Q. Have you ever passed an examination since you were appointed ?—A. No.

Q. Could you not, if you passed an examination, be an excise man or special class officer ? In other words, is it not in your own hands, if you pass an examination, to improve your position ?—A. My position could have been improved, but being a married man and having a family, I have not the time to study.

Q. Could not your position have been improved if you had taken the steps to improve it ?—A. I could have had $200 more.

Q. That is to say you came in under this political class without an examination, you prefer not to pass an examination, and you want to be specially treated, apart from the rules of the department—is not that the case ?—A. No. I have not the means to pay for professors to train me, and being a married man I have not the time to study.

Q. If you had trained as an exciseman, after having passed the usual examination and knowing what would be required of you, would you not have been able to have done your duties in quicker time?—A. I consider that I could not do my duties in shorter time if I had passed the examination.

Q. Do you know anything of mensuration?—A. I did when I left school.

Q. A knowledge of mensuration is an important qualification in the Inland Revenue Department?—A. Yes.

Q. You have only the knowledge you acquired when at school?—A. Not so much.

Q. In the ordinary duties of a deputy collector, a knowledge of mensuration forms a great part, does it not?—A. It depends on the duties allotted to him by the collector.

Q. A deputy collector is supposed to know something about mensuration, is he not?—A. Yes, he should.

Q. Your knowledge was acquired at school and is getting daily less?—A. Certainly.

Q. Do you know anything about the specific gravity of fluids?—A. Yes, I have been a druggist.

Q. What is your occupation in the office?—A. I am cashier.

Q. You know nothing about the supervision of a distillery?—A. No.

Q. Do you know anything about the supervision of tobacco or cigar manufactories? —A. Yes.

Q. How did you acquire that?—A. In my daily work, because every entry passes through my hands.

Q. You do not know about the practical supervision of the manufactory. You do not know how tobacco or cigars are manufactured?—A. I know how many pounds of tobacco are allowed for a thousand cigars, but have had no practical training.

Q. Do you know anything about malting or brewing?—A. Yes.

Q. How do you know that?—A. Because I am a druggist.

Q. Have you had any bonded manufactory to superintend?—A. No.

Q. Then practically it comes to this that either from want of time or other cause you are unable to get out of the grade of deputy collectors to which you were appointed without examination, and you want your position improved without having to pass the examination?—A. Yes.

Q. If there is anything else you wish to add, we shall be glad to have it?—A. I came here only to mention what I was doing, and I wanted to get an exchange of work in the office, because I have done more than my share.

Q. How can you get an exchange of work when you have not passed the examination?—A. I have to handle over $100,000 a year, check every paper and verify it, and take the responsibility of it.

Q. You say that you are doing the duties of bookkeeper or accountant?—A. Cashier.

Q. Are not examinations required for the clerical staff, the accountants and bookkeepers?—A. There are examinations for accountants.

Q. The only positions for which no examinations are required in the Inland Revenue Department are those of the inspector of weights and measures, deputy collectors and preventive officers; that is the law?—A. Yes.

Q. If you are doing the duty of an accountant or cashier, you must have been put at that work because in a way it was the most suitable for you, because you have not the knowledge of the ordinary excise business?—A. I had to do the duties that were allotted to me by my chief.

Q. It all narrows itself down to this, that you were appointed without examination, you say you have not the means nor the time to go up for an examination, and you have to be kept graded as you are now, and you want your position improved ?—A. Yes.

Witness retired.

Mr. CHARLES E. ROY, inspector of weights and measures at Quebec, and JOSEPH LEBEL, assistant inspector of weights and measures, were sworn.

Mr. ROY was examined:—

By the Chairman :

Q. You are the inspector of weights and measures here ?—A. Yes.

Q. What is the extent of this district?—A. It includes twenty-one counties and the city of Quebec. It extends on the south shore from Megantic to Gaspé and on the north shore from Portneuf to Labrador. The assistant inspectors have 700 miles to travel on both shores.

Q. How many assistant inspectors have you?—A. Nine.

Q. Are they all permanent?—A. All except two.

Q. Are those two of recent appointments?—A. Yes, since January last.

Q. What is your salary?—A. $1,400.

Q. When did you get $1,400?—A. In July of last year.

Q. What had you before that ?—A. I had $1,150. I was food inspector also, but this nomination has been cancelled since.

Q. How much did you get as food inspector?—A. $200.

Q. You got about $900 as inspector of weights and measures and $200 as inspector of food, and now you get $1,400 for the inspection of weights and measures ?—A. Yes.

Q. How much does Mr. Lebel get?

Mr. LEBEL.—$1,100.

Q. How much do the other inspectors get?

Mr. ROY.—Some $750, others $700, others $650 and two $400.

Q. These are the two temporaries?—A. Yes.

Q. Your people are away travelling all the time?—A. With the exception of December, January, February and March.

Q. Naturally, you do not travel in the worst months of the year if you can help it?—A. To save money to the Government, do we not.

Q. Is it entirely to save money to the Government, or because it is less comfortable for yourselves?—A. It is expensive to travel in the winter time.

29a—24

Q. It is also uncomfortable?—A. I had a statement the other day from an assistant inspector that it was preferable. I asked him why he did not travel in the winter. He told me it would be preferable, because in the hotels he would be more comfortable in winter than in summer.

Q. The assistant inspectors are only paid the actual cost of travelling; they do not get any daily allowance?—A. No.

Q. Then, of course, if they get no inducement to travel they do not travel more than the law compels them to do ?—A. Sure.

Q. How often are you obliged to inspect in a year?—A. Every two years.

Q. How often are you obliged to inspect a shop or warehouse?—A. The law provides for a biennial inspection for one kind of scales. For spring scales it should yearly.

Q. In some cases you must inspect annually, in other cases every two years ?— A. Yes.

Q. Then you do not, in excess of zeal for the public service, do more inspection than the law compels you to do?—A. Certainly not.

Q. Of course, in Quebec city, where there are no travelling expenses, you constantly drop in for inspections?—A. Yes, we inspect the whole year round.

Q. Then, being paid only your out of pocket expenses, and with twenty-five counties, and having to go to places where there is uncomfortable travelling, you naturally go only when the law compels you to?—A. Yes.

Q. You have a set of standard scales here ?—A. Yes.

Q. What do you do when one of your inspectors goes into an establishment?— A. The first thing to do is to ascertain the capacity of the scale.

Q. Do you stop the work ?—A. Yes, and they inspect as many scales as there are there and then make certificates. On the first inspection the scales are marked, then every two years a certificate is given. The idea of giving a certificate instead of marking the scales each time is so as not to destroy the scale.

Q. Are there any scale factories in Quebec ?—A. There is one.

Q. You visit that factory ?—A. Every day.

Q. And you stamp or give certificates for the scales that come out of it ?—A. Yes.

Q. Before they come out ?—A. Yes.

Q. Are there any scales brought in Quebec from outside ?—A. Yes.

Q. What do you do with these ? Are they sent in a kind of bond to you, or how do you manage them ?—A. Generally I am notified by the inspector at Montreal that such a scale has been sent from there.

By Mr. Fyshe :

Q. Could not some one import a scale from the Fairbanks Company direct ?—A. The Custom-house is obliged to advise the Department of Inland Revenue of any such importation.

By the Chairman :

Q. Take a place like Bic or Cacouna where there is no customs officer, is it not possible for the Fairbanks Company in the summer time, to send by the Intercolonial railway or by the boats, scales without their being inspected ?—A. The law provides for that.

Q. How ?—A. If a merchant receives a scale between the inspections, he has a right to keep it until the inspector passes. But generally I receive advice from the collector of Customs that such a scale has been sent to such a place.

Q. Are the scales stamped before they leave the Fairbanks Company in Montreal ? —A. The law provides that they must be stamped.

Q. No scales can be sent from the factory without being stamped ?—A. No.

Q. Then it would be impossible for scales to be sent from the factory to out of the way districts without being stamped ?—A. Yes. If such scales should arrive, I would report them to the department.

SESSIONAL PAPER No. 29a

Q. Have your duties been increased lately by the addition of other work besides the inspection of weights and measures ?—A. No.

Q. Are there more scales now in use owing to the increase of trade ?—A. A great many more.

Q. Has the number of assistant inspectors been increased ?—A. Since I have been inspector they have been increased by three.

Q. Is that increase in proportion to the increase of work ?—A. Yes.

Q. Have you enough assistant inspectors now to do the work ?—A. Yes.

Q. Then your work does not suffer from a deficiency in the staff ?—A. No.

Q. What were the salaries laid down to be paid to inspectors of weights and measures when the Act came into force ?—A. $1,200.

Q. And for an assistant inspector ?—A. It is the same as now.

Q. There has been no increase in the scale of salaries since the Act came into force ?—A. No.

Q. When did the Act come into force ?—A. In 1872.

Q. Then the Act has been in force 35 years, and in that time there has been no increase in the scale of salaries ?—A. There has not.

Q. Considering that in 35 years the prices of all commodities have advanced so considerably, I suppose you consider that the salaries of inspectors and assistant inspectors should be increased somewhat in proportion to the increased cost of living ? —A. Yes, that is what I am here for. At the inauguration of the service, it not only did not pay expenses, but the inspection of scales was voluntary. The people brought their scales to be inspected. Now it is compulsory, and I am at work from 9 till 5 every day. The correspondence is very large, and to follow all the assistant inspectors is a great work.

By Mr. Bazin :

Q. In some places it is said that your office has a deficit every year, while in other places there is a surplus. How do you explain that ?—A. Montreal has a very small territory ; all the factories are congregated together, and the counties of the district are small and all have railroads. In our district, take Beauce county, for instance, an inspector has to travel 660 miles to inspect that county. The counties of Gaspé, Bonaventure and Portneuf are also very large, and the expenses are correspondingly great. The district of Quebec is so large and so unpopulated that the expenses are very large. That is the only explanation that I can give.

Q. In fact, your territory requires more assistant inspectors than Montreal ?— A. Yes.

By the Chairman:

Q. Is there anything else you wish to say ?

Mr. LEBEL.—The only statement I would like to make is this, that the assistant inspectors should be put on the same footing as other civil servants. We are not classified, and we are left at a low salary without any prospect of an increase. I think we should be classified, so that when a man enters the service, he would be sure that after so many years' service he would be entitled to a certain increase of salary, whether he passed the Promotion examinations or not. We have no classification, but are left entirely to the good-will of the Government, and sometimes, if a man has no influence, he has to remain at a very low salary.

By Mr. Bazin:

Q. You are not speaking exclusively for yourself ?—A. No, for the class.

INLAND REVENUE, CANADA,
TROIS-RIVIÈRES, 16 sept. 1907.

M. C. S. RINFRET, M.D.,
Inspecteur du Revenu de l'intérieur,
Québec.

MONSIEUR,—J'ai l'honneur de vous transmettre l'humble requête des officiers *du* Revenu de l'intérieur de la division de Trois-Rivières, vous priant humblement de *la* présenter à messieurs les membres de la Commission du Service Civil et de bien *vou-* loir être notre interprète, dans cette circonstance.

Vous remerciant d'avance pour tout ce que vous ferez pour nous.

J'ai l'honneur d'être, monsieur l'inspecteur,

Votre très humble et dévoué serviteur,

(Signé) CHS. DUPONT-HEBERT,

Percepteur.

REVENUE DE L'INTÉRIEUR,
TROIS-RIVIÈRES, 16 sept. 1907.

A Messieurs de
La Commission du Service civil.

Le soussigné, Charles Dupont-Hébert, percepteur pour la division de Trois-Rivières, parlant tant en son propre nom qu'au nom de ses officiers, représente humblement que les salaires du service civil devraient être augmentés, pour les considérations suivantes, savoir:—

1° Augmentation considérable du coût de la vie.

La moyenne de cette augmentation, d'après calcul fait, sur ce que coûtait la vie il y a dix ans, et ce qu'elle coûte aujourd'hui, tant ici à Trois-Rivières que dans les autres centres, pour loyer, vêtement, nourriture, chauffage, écoles, etc., est de 30 à 40 pour 100.

2° Echelle actuelle de salaire insuffisante aujourd'hui même pour le nécessaire, ceci dit sans vouloir exagérer.

Nous ajouterons, si vous le permettez, comme suggestions qui, croyons-nous, mériteraient aussi votre considération :

1° Que l'augmentation du salaire du minimum au maximum s'effectue à raison de 10 pour 100 au lieu de 5 pour 100.

2° Que le privilège soit accordé à tout officier qui le désirerait d'être mis sous le système de pension.

3° Que pour chaque dix années additionnelles passées dans le service, une augmentation de 5 pour 100 soit allouée, à titre de gratification et d'encouragement, à celui-là qui se dépense au service du gouvernement.

4° Qu'une augmentation de salaire d'au moins 25 pour 100 devrait être accordée, avec privilège de bénéficier de la dite augmentation aussitôt accordée.

5° Qu'il ne nous paraît que juste qu'un officier, ayant contribué au fond de retraite durant trente années, ait le privilège de se retirer du service après ce terme d'office, et que les deux tiers du salaire maximum auquel il aurait droit, dans la classe à laquelle il appartient, lui soit payé mensuellement.

J'ai l'honneur d'être, messieurs,

Votre très humble et dévoué serviteur,

(Signé) CHS DUPONT-HEBERT,

Percepteur.

INLAND REVENUE, CANADA, DIVISION NO. 8,
QUEBEC, September 17, 1907.

To the Honourable Commissioners of the Civil Service:

I beg to offer a few remarks concerning the classification of the service.

I beg to be understood as speaking only of the Excise branch of the service. The work in the Excise Office being specially of a technical character, I submit that the officers appointed on probation without passing the Qualifying examination may be appointed as third-class officers under the following conditions, viz.:—

That they have been employed in the keeping of the books or the surveyance of the distilleries, tobacco or cigar factories, malt houses and bonded factories and have proved their ability and reliability in this kind of work when they have been so employed for a period of five years.

Five years after having been appointed, and after having given full satisfaction for a period of ten years, that they be entitled to the maximum salary of the third-class.

I beg to call the Honourable Commissioners' attention to a special case in the Quebec office.

We have here a bookkeeper who has been appointed 27 years ago. For the last 25 years he has always done the work of an accountant. He is a third-class officer. This man has, in my opinion, no superior in the other offices in Canada. His salary is $850 a year. I submit that in cases of this kind, when a man has for a period of 20 years or over been in charge of the books in a first-class division as an accountant, he may be dispensed of the Promotion examination by Order in Council based on a certificate as to his merits by the deputy minister of the Department.

I beg to say that outside of the restrictions just offered, I am in favour of the examinations as they now exist, and that I consider that they are the best way of testing the capacity of the officers.

Now, gentlemen, speaking of another matter in which I am personally interested, I beg to submit that the maximum salary of the district inspectors have not been increased at all since 1873. Since that time the cost of living has increased from 60 to 75 per cent. Speaking only for the Quebec division, the revenue has doubled, so have the work and responsibilities. I understand that it belongs to the deputy head of the department to give every information concerning the importance of this position and of its responsibilities; but I may be allowed to submit that the district inspector is the head of all the excise, weights and measures and gas and electric light offices in his district, and that it requires a good deal of attention and knowledge to fulfil his duty in a satisfactory manner.

Your obedient servant,
(Signed)   DR. C. RINFRET,
District Inspector.

INLAND REVENUE, CANADA, DIVISION NO. 8,
QUEBEC, September 18, 1907.

To the Honourable Commissioners of the Civil Service:

I beg to call the Honourable Commissioners' attention to another special case in our office.

Mr. Coleman was transferred from Montreal to be appointed here as surveyor of the tobacco and cigar factories. This position would belong to a special class officer; but in this instance the responsibilities were put on the shoulders of a first-class officer. Now I beg to offer as my own views of this matter that one or the other of the two following alternatives may be just: either to put there a special class officer, or if the department would choose to leave the responsibilities of this position to a first-class officer, to give him the salary of the special class.

Mr. Coleman is in every respect a first-rate officer, and he has filled the position for fifteen years to our entire satisfaction.

Your obedient servant,

(Signed)   DR. C. RINFRET,

District Inspector.

WEIGHTS AND MEASURES INSPECTION SERVICE, CANADA,

TROIS-RIVIÈRES, 16 septembre 1907.

Dr. C. RINFRET,
    Québec.

MONSIEUR,—En réponse à la votre en date du 9, je dois vous dire que j'accepte avec plaisir, les propositions que vous me faites de me représenter devant la commission, car je sais que vous êtes en état d'expliquer ma position aussi bien que moi, sino mieux, car nous en avons parlé ensemble plus d'une fois, et vous savez que le salai que j'ai n'est pas suffisant pour vivre à Trois-Rivières au prix que coûte la vie aujou d'hui, car depuis dix ans le coûte de la vie est monté tant qu'au loyer, etc., de 35 à pour cent, et le salaire est le même qu'il était il y a vingt ans. Vous serez assez b d'insister pour que l'augmentation soit ajoutée de suite au salaire.

Je vous inclus un petit mémoire que vous soumettrez si vous le jugez à propos
Je vous remercie des services que vous allez me rendre en cette circonstance croyez-moi,

Votre tout devoué,

(Signé)   A. T. GRAVEL,

Inspecteur, poids et mesures, division de Trois-Rivières.

INLAND REVENUE, CANADA,

WEIGHTS AND MEASURES INSPECTION SERVICE.

De 1887 à 1897 les revenus du bureau ont été de $9,859.82, et le salaire des t employés pour ces dix années a été de $22,000.

De 1897 à 1907, les revenus ont été de $13,225.80, et le salaire des deux offici car nous sommes que deux maintenant, a été de $15,000.

(Signé)   A. T. GRAVEL.

INLAND REVENUE, CANADA, DIVISION No. 8.

QUEBEC, September 17, 1907.

To the President and Members of the Royal Civil Service Commission.

GENTLEMEN,—The undersigned would humbly represent the following facts t the members of your Commission, and earnestly solicit a generous consideration of th same:—

That the cost of living, food, clothing, fuel, light, furniture and rent have increased 55 or 65 per cent in the past ten years.

That municipal taxes, the cost of education, the services of the liberal professions, rates of insurance and interest, have increased considerably during the same period.

That all the railway, telegraph and telephone companies; all large and small industrial and commercial establishments, have granted a reasonable increase to their employees.

SSIONAL PAPER No. 29a

That labourers who were receiving $1 a day are now being paid from $1.50 to $2 the same work.

The Inland Revenue emlpoyees, especially accountants, book-keepers, officers in .rge of manufactories require special qualifications, the acquisition of which enls considerable study and expense upon them.

That for a large number it is utterly impossible for them to live on their present iries, and provide the bare necessaries of life for their families.

Your petitioners would therefore pray that you kindly report in favour of an in'ease of salary in proportion to or based on the present high cost of living; and said increase be granted immediately instead of, by the small annual increments ve per cent usually allowed.

If the Government will grant this request, it will relieve the straightened circumces to which many have been reduced under the present system.

And your petitioners will ever pray.

(Signed)   THE EXCISE OFFICERS OF THE INLAND
REVENUE OFFICE,

Per D. ARCAND,
Collector.

QUEBEC, September 13, 1907.

the Gentlemen Members
of the Civil Service Commission,
Quebec.

GENTLEMEN,—I beg leave to submit humbly my actual position in the Civil Ser
. I was appointed first as messenger and caretaker of the weights and measures
·e on August 22, 1904, at a salary of $600, and on August 22, 1906, I was proed to the position of assistant inspector at the same salary, but on February last,
7, I received an increase of $50, as I fill both positions as messenger and caretaker
assistant inspector. My work is daily and very assiduous, and I have all the
>onsibility attached to both positions.

I am the supporter of two sisters, of whom one is a sick person, and I find that
present salary is insufficient to meet the daily expenses owing to the high costs
living, and would respectfully ask that my salary be raised so as to meet at the
of the year the budget of my expenses without incurring indebtedness.

The whole respectfully submitted.

(Signed)   PAUL PARENT,

Assistant Inspector of Weights and Measures of Quebec.

As caretaker, I would also submit that I have to attend to the heating of the
·e for nearly ten months in the year.

Dr. C. I. RINFRET, district inspector of Inland Revenue, sworn and examined:—

By the Chairman:

Q. Have you a memorandum you wish to submit?—A. I beg to submit the memodum which was prepared by the collector of Three Rivers. (Memorandum read
filed.) I submit another from Mr. Gravel (filed.) These gentlemen are asking
increases in their salaries, on the ground of the increase in the cost of living.
·y are also asking that the annual increases be ten per cent instead of five per
t of their salaries. They are asking for a special increase at once of five per cent
every one who has been on the service for ten years or over. They also ask that

7-8 EDWARD VII., A. 1909

any officer should have the right to take his superannuation and retire after 30 or 35 years' service. I also submit a memorandum prepared by myself (Memorandum read and filed.)

Q. You were appointed in 1899 ?—A. Yes.

Q. What district have you under your inspection ?—A. Quebec and Three Rivers.

Q. You have not Sherbrooke ?—A. No, it belongs to Montreal.

Q. You have a deputy collector at Montmagny ?—A. Not now. There was one last year.

Q. Have you one at Paspebiac ?—A. Yes.

Q. One at Rimouski ?—A. Yes.

Q. One at Rivière du Loup ?—A. Yes.

Q. One at St. Alexandre ?—A. Not now.   There is one at Gaspé and one at Chicoutimi. Gaspé is about 500 miles from here, and Chicoutimi is very far away also. I am the inspector of all these places outside of Three Rivers.

Q. That is to say, you have one collector and five or six deputy collectors in your district ?—A. Yes, two collectors and five or six deputy collectors, and I am obliged to go to Grand Mère and to Shawenigan. I travel between ten and twelve weeks every year, sometimes thirteen weeks.

Q. What are the boundaries of your district ?—A. From the upper side of the Three Rivers division to Gaspé, and on the north side Chicoutimi.

Q. Does this district require you to travel all the time ?—A. No. I have just said that I travel for ten or twelve weeks a year.

Q. Would it be desirable that you should travel any more ?—A. No.

Q. You get nothing for your travelling expenses beyond what you pay out ?—A. No.

Q. If you had, as in the old days, a daily allowance for travelling, to give you something for the wear and tear of clothes, &c., would not that be an inducement to travel oftener ?—A. I suppose so. I cannot say that I would travel any more, for the reason that I have no intention to rob the government.

Q. You choose the most comfortable time of the year to do your travelling, I suppose ?—A. No, any time in the year. I travel summer, winter, fall and spring. I make the trip never less than four times a year and always more to some places.

Q. It is not pleasant to go to Chicoutimi, about Christmas time ?—A. Oh no.

Q. Then if you had some inducement to travel, you might be induced to go more often to some of those places ?—A. Yes, but I never think of that. I am obliged to go to these places four times in a year in order to make my report to the department.

Q. But if there was something to make it desirable for you to go the fifth time, it would not strike you if you got nothing to induce you to go ?—A. Oh no, I never think of that.

Q. Don't you think it would be desirable to encourage frequent inspections, that the inspectors should get a per diem allowance instead of their out of pocket expenses ? —A. No, I do not think that. I think the payment of the actual expenses incurred while travelling for the government is the correct system.

Q. Have you an assistant inspector attached to your office ?—A. No.

Q. Your office is in the Inland Revenue building here ?—A. Yes. I beg to say that travelling is not the only work I have to do. Of course, I am in charge of the office here and the office at Three Rivers, not only for excise but also for weights and measures and gas and electric light inspection.

Q. What was the revenue in Quebec when you were appointed in 1899 ?—A. The revenue eight years ago was a little more than one-half the amount that it is now. Last year the revenue was $792,000. The revenue has nearly doubled, but there is now a source of revenue in the division which did not exist before, that is, a distillery. This is gives no special revenue to the division, but the responsibility for the officers is the same as if it did.

Q. Whose distillery is it ?—A. Mr. Robitaille's.

By Mr. Fyshe:

Q. I understood that that distillery was not working ?—A. It is in operation.

Q. Is it still in full blast ?—A. Yes. There was an interruption for a few weeks, at it is in full blast now.

By the Chairman:

Q. Then the work in the district has been increased by the addition of one distillery ?—A. Yes.

Q. There are breweries in this district ?—A. Yes.

Q. How many ?—A. Four—three at Quebec and one at Beauport, and another one ill start in a few weeks.

Q. Is that a larger number than there used to be ?—A. Yes. When I was appointed think there were only three.

Q. Has there been an increase in the production of cigars and tobacco ?—A. A big rease. It has more than doubled.

Q. Then, it comes to this, that the revenue has doubled and the work has doubled ? A. Yes, nearly so.

Q. At what salary were you appointed ?—A. My salary was put at $2,500. Mr. moine, who was in charge of the office before me received the same salary. A readtment of the salaries in the excise offices took place four years ago, but for some son or other the district inspectors were left aside; I do not know for what reason.

Q. You get the same salary as you did when you were appointed ?—A. Yes. I am making a claim on personal merits, but on the increased cost of living.

Q. While the revenue has doubled and the work has doubled, the salary of the in-ctor has not been increased in the last ten years ?—A. Exactly.

Q. Under the Civil Service Act the salaries of inspectors are graded from $1,600 to 500, so that you could not get an increase without an amendment to the Act of Parment ?—A. Exactly.

Q. In going about your district and inspecting the work, do you find the officials the Excise Department as efficient now as they were at the time you were appointed ? A. I am inclined to think that the organization is a little better than it was formely. course, we are always inclined to judge in our own favour, but my opinion would that.

Q. In view of the increased cost of living and the opportunities outside, do you l that people who want to enter your service are as good as those who used to enter ? A. Yes, about the same, I suppose.

Q. Do you find people leaving the service to better themselves ?—A. I do not member any case just now.

Q. You call attention to the case of your bookkeeper; who is he?—A. His name is les Lemoine, an old officer.

Q. He is now a third-class officer ?—A. Yes.

Q. I suppose he did not pass the examination ?—A. No, he never passed the ex-ination. He was appointed twenty-seven years ago, and in those times officers were t in the habit of passing the Promotion examination, especially in Quebec. This man ing kept at the books all the time, and never going to the factories or the distilleries, had no opportunity outside of the work he was doing, and it would be very hard for m to pass the examination.

By Mr. Bazin:

Q. He is a lawyer by profession ?—A. Yes, an advocate.

By the Chairman:

Q. He is between 50 and 60 now, and he keeps all the accounts of a revenue of 0,000 ?—A. Yes, 53. He occupies the position of an accountant.

Q. And he is graded as a third-class clerk, and at his age, although he has been doing his work satisfactorily, he has not passed the Promotion examination ?—A. No.

Q. You also mention Mr. Coleman's case as a special case. He went into the service of the department twenty-two years ago and is now a first-class exciseman?—A. Yes.

Q. He was transferred from Montreal to Quebec to take charge of the tobacco and cigar factories here?—A. Yes.

Q. That you consider to be the duty of a special class exciseman?—A. Yes.

Q. Has he passed the examination?—A. Yes, he has passed the first-class examination. He was transferred from Montreal to Quebec as a promotion. He has been here fourteen or fifteen years. He asks me very often to be allowed to go back to Montreal, for the reason that his family and the family of his wife are there. He claims that his position here is no longer a promotion. He receives duty pay in addition to his salary, but he says he would prefer to go back to Montreal and receive no duty pay. He has not passed the special class examination, but so far as his special business is concerned, he is a first-class man.

Q. Have you many cases of lower graded men like Mr. Coleman and Mr. Lemoine doing higher class duties?—A. No, there is no other case.

Q. You say in this memorandum that the officers appointed on probation should be appointed third-class officers under conditions?—A. Yes, sir.

Q. Under these conditions as recited here you think the officers passing the Qualifying examination should be appointed third-class officers?—A. In some special cases. Generally speaking I am not in favour of classifying an officer unless he has passed the examination; but I call your attention to special cases in the excise office. Of course, the work in the excise office is purely technical. Some merchants have been appointed on probation, and are doing the work of bookkeepers or surveyors in factories, for the reason that we have no other men to take their place. These are very good officers. I suppose that the men doing this kind of work of a technical character might be put on the list of permanent officers, and after having been so employed for a number of years, may be entitled to the maximum salary.

Q. You as an old and experienced public man may have in your mind certain points which we may have omitted to ask you about, and if you think it desirable furnish us with a supplementary memorandum we shall be very glad to have it?—I might have some remarks to make with regard to the promotion examinations some other matter; but while I was in politics I always felt that it was dangerous to replace an existing system with another. We see the faults of the system is existence but we cannot see the faults of the one with which we might replace it. I would have no objection to say something on the subject of Superannuation.

Q. Do you think it was advisable to abolish the Superannuation Act?—A. I am not in favour of the system of retirement which we have now. My opinion is that it is absolutely useless, giving no protection whatever to the officers.

Q. Are you of opinion that the enactment of a proper Superannuation Act, possibly with extensions to include the families of officers, and administered under proper regulations, would be beneficial to the service and to its stability?—A. I would not be in favour of going so far as to extend the system of Superannuation to the families of officers, as was done in the province of Quebec formerly. That system was put in operation for some years, and was abandoned as being too expensive. If I might be allowed to express my own opinion, I would propose to have a system of Superannuation entirely at the cost of the Government. Of course, the allowances might not be so large as they are now, the officers paying nothing into the superannuation fund, would have no right to expect to receive so much. But I think it is only just to give a certain superannuation to public officers, as they are not at all in the same position as other people. Take a business man, for instance. When he gets old, if he is not able to conduct his own business himself, the firm continues and he is still connected with the business. The same is true of farmers and many other people. But the public

ficer can do nothing at all when he is retired from the service of the Government.
The Government may remove him at any time it chooses to do so. When a man has
grown old in the service, and is no longer able to perform his duty, and is removed by
the Government, he should be allowed something to help him to live. Of course, it
would not be for me to suggest the amount.

Mr. D. ARCAND, sworn and examined:—

   By the Chairman:
   Q. How long have you been in the service?—A. Nearly seven months.
   Q. What is your position?—A. Collector of inland revenue.
   Q. How did you happen to become a Collector Did you pass the examination?—
~ No.
   Q. How did you happen to become a collector when the Civil Service Act requires
collector to pass an examination?—A. That is the law, but you know there is always
a exception to the rule. I am like a good many others. I suppose Sir Wilfrid Laurier
ut me there as a reward for services given to the party.
   Q. What salary do you get?—A. $2,000.
   Q. Was that the salary your predecessor got?—A. He was getting $2,400.
   Q. What is the limit of salary of a collector of excise?—A. I do not know. I was
lways told $2,400 was the limit.
   Q. Have you a very large staff here?—A. We have over thirty. If we include the
reventive officers and all, the number is 36 or 37.
   Q. Although you were given the position as a reward for party services, you are
a active officer, I suppose. You do not sit in your chair and read the papers, but look
fter the work of the division?—A. When I came into the office, I was not supposed
know everything; but I have been in business twenty-five years as a broker and real
tate agent. I required some instruction, but I think I am getting into the work.
   Q. You happen to be one of those men who, however appointed, have been in busi-
ss and are getting into way of the work?—A. Yes. I can say that I do my own
rrespondence, writing with my own hand to the department.
   Q. How old are you?—A. I am over 66. I do my own corespondence, in both
iglish and French, and keep my own accounts, and up to the present they seem to be
tisfied with my work.
   Q. When you came in did you think that $2,000 was sufficient, or did you come
with the expectation of getting an increase?—A. I did not ask for any salary. I
s told that I would get so much.
   Q. And you took the chances of getting an increase?—A. Yes.
   Q. But you consider that the position of collector of inland revenue in Quebec,
th the total revenue of $800,000, should demand a greater salary than $2,000 a year?
A. I am satisfied with what I am getting now. Of course, if the Government are
ased to increase my salary a little later on. I will have no objection.
   Q. You are submitting a memorandum on behalf of the staff?—A. Yes. I told
em that every one of them might come and speak for themselves. They said they
d not care to do that. They said they would write down a petition, and I could put
before the commission.
   Q. It is very gratifying that although you have been in the office only seven
onths, your staff have such confidence in you that they allow you to represent them?
-A. It looks like that.
   Q. You think that all these men, some of them doing high class work at low rates,
nd having the technical knowledge that is required of officers in the excise, are as a
ile paid insufficient salaries for the work they do?—A. Yes. It is hardly necessary for
e to insist upon an increase. You have the petition, which speaks for itself.
   Q. Are your officers generally efficient?—A. Yes.

Q. You have no officers with bad habits amongst them?—A. There was one exception, but the man has been dismissed.

Q. When you find a man with bad habits, do you report him at once?—A. I do not. I try to improve him. I gave this man advice and told him that if he did not improve I would report him.

By Mr. Fyshe:

Q. What salary was he getting?—A. A small salary of $500 or $600. When I saw that he did not improve, I reported him.

By the Chairman:

Q. How many officers have you at the distillery?—A. Four.

Q. What revenue do you derive from it?—A. There is no revenue from it yet. It will be two years before they can put out their product, and then they will pay duty.

Q. What salaries do you give the men that work at the distillery?—A. The head man has $1,750, the second $1,200 and the other two from $500 to $600, but they work at night and get extra pay for that.

Q. Are you paying these men sufficient to keep them out of the way of temptation from the distiller?—A. The first one occupies an important and responsible position I suppose he may be satisfied, but if he were getting a little more salary I do not suppose he would be sorry.

Q. Then, considering all things, and that it will take about two years before any revenue will be derived from the distillery, you think that the salaries at present paid to the men are sufficient so that they will not be subject to temptation?—A. I believe they are honest men, but I think the salaries are too low. I have such confidence in them that I believe that even if their salaries were lower, they would still be honest. But they have a right to get higher salaries like everybody else.

Q. Have you anything else to suggest?—A. I have nothing to ask beyond what in the petition. The cost of living has gone up so much in the last fifteen years that I think the salaries of all the officers should be increased according to their qualifications. Perhaps our best men could not pass an examination, but they are doing the work well.

Mr. NAZAIRE LEVASSEUR, sworn and examined:—

By the Chairman :

Q. You are the inspector of gas and electric light for this district?—A. Yes.

Q. You have been in that position since 1878?—A. Since October 2, 1878.

Q. That is over twenty-nine years?—A. Yes, twenty-nine years.

Q. What salary had you on appointment?—A. I was appointed at $1,000.

Q. What is your salary now?—A. $1,100 since a few months ago.

Q. That is to say, you were appointed twenty-nine years ago at $1,000 and only lately you have got another $100?—A. Yes.

Q. Have you a statement that you wish to submit?—A. Yes. (Memorandum read and filed.)

Q. What is the extent of the Quebec district?—A. It includes the city of Quebec, with two electric companies, Lévis Montmagny, Fraserville and Rimouski on the south shore. On the north shore, Raymond, in the county of Portneuf, Roberval, Lorette, the Lake St. John district, Chicoutimi and Murray Bay.

Q. On the north shore it extends to the Saguenay and on the south shore to Rimouski?—A. Yes.

Q. And how far west?—A. As far as Raymond in Portneuf county.

Q. Has it always been the same district?—A. I was nominated for the city of Quebec only.

SESSIONAL PAPER No. 29a

Q. You say in your memorial that the duties have been increased by the addition of the electric light?—A. Yes.

Q. Did not the people who now use the electric light use gas before?—A. Yes.

Q. Were your duties increased?—A. Yes. Since 1893, when the electric light system was installed, the duties of inspector have been trebled.

Q. Many people in Quebec now use gas in their cooking stoves?—A. Yes.

Q. What are your office hours?—A. From 9 a.m. to 4 p.m., but I am called to inspect meters at other times.

Q. How long does your day's work last altogether?—A. You can put the average at six hours all the year round.

Q. How many more hours of the day besides your office hours do you give to your work?—A. In the evening sometimes from 5 to 9 I make photometric experiments; that is to ascertain the power of the light. This may be done two or three times a month.

Q. How many hours a day do you spend in the public service?—A. Four nights every month on the average; I work four hours extra per night.

Q. You do your inspection of meters between 9 and 4?—A. Yes.

By Mr. Fyshe :

Q. Do you travel around?—A. Yes.

Q. What arrangement have you for travelling expenses?—A. When I send my account for expenses, I send vouchers.

By the Chairman :

Q. You are only paid what you spend?—A. Yes.

Q. Do you travel much in winter?—A. Probably three or four times during the winter.

Q. You do not as a rule go to Chicoutimi during the winter?—A. No.

Q. You do not travel willingly where there is any discomfort?—A. Oh, no.

Q. How often do you have to go to Chicoutimi during the year?—A. I have not been to Chicoutimi yet.

Q. There is no obligation upon you to go to these places?—A. No.

Q. You go when you choose?—A. When asked or written for.

Q. How long has Chicoutimi been in your district?—A. At least two years.

Q. And you have not been there?—A. No.

Q. Have you been at Murray Bay?—A. No.

Q. Have you been at Fraserville?—A. Yes.

Q. It is easier to reach?—A. Yes.

Q. You get nothing beyond what you spend?—A. No.

Q. And you go to the places easy to get at?—A. Yes.

Q. And you go to other places when you are asked to go?—A. Yes.

Q. Are you under the Superannuation Act?—A. Yes.

. Is there any difficulty in getting assistant inspectors now?—A. Oh, no.

. Have you a good assistant?—A. He is very obliging.

. Is he efficient?—A. Well, he helps me.

Q. How long has he been appointed?—A. Since July, 1906.

Q. Did you select him?—A. No.

Q. I suppose you know how he came to you?—A. No. He came to my office and reported one morning. He was unexpected.

Q. He passed no examination, I suppose?—A. I think he did. I cannot reply for him.

QUEBEC, September 18, 1907.

To the Members of the Civil Service Commission, in Session at Quebec, this Wed;
day, September 18, 1907.

GENTLEMEN,—I beg leave to respectfully submit to your most serious attent
the following recommendations respecting the gas and electric light inspection serv
in the Dominion of Canada :—

Divisions and subdivisions might be established as follows for the service :—

1. One inspector general in Ottawa, for the Dominion (already existing).

2. Inspection office per Province or other geographical division, in conformity wi
the map of the Dominion, under the superintendence of a district inspector, being &
thorized to make an annual or periodical tour of inspection of all the inspection offi
within the said Province or other geographical division, to superintend such repairs
improvements, as might be deemed opportune or necessary, with the approval of
inspector general, and report to the last named official. This might make it cc
pulsory, as regards the appointment of inspectors, to select persons having in t
respect technical and especially mechanical experience, and would no doubt enha-
the efficiency of the service.

3. Classification of the inspectors respecting salaries and powers, in proportion
the annual receipts and the extent of their respective districts.

Such classification might be made as follows :—

(1) Inspector general for the Dominion.

(2) District inspectors having charge of a province or any other equivalent ≘
graphical division, viz., including many districts.

(3) District inspectors having charge of many towns, &c.

The assistant inspectors are included in the above three classes.

In virtue of 64 Victoria, A. 1901, annex B, page 196, of the annual report of
Secretary of State (Civil Service list), the salary of the inspectors, with no desig
tion as to what service, is paid as follows :—

Inland Revenue inspectors, $1,600 to $2,500, with the general proviso of an
crease of $50 per annum as long as the maximum of the salary is not reached.

In spite of that, on the 2nd day of October, 1878, I was appointed inspector
gas at Quebec, with a salary of $1,000, and was entitled to the usual increase of
per annum. Accordingly, taking that salary of $1,000, as it is, I should receive x
about $2,350 per annum ; but taking it at $1,600, as it should have been according
the Act 64 Victoria, and giving the same a retroactive effect, I would now h
reached the maximum of the salary, about eight years ago.

A little over a year ago I was given an assistant inspector of gas and elec!
light, who is paid a salary of $300. That assistant is also food inspector at Que
and in the district, for which service he is paid another $300, and out of which he
to pay a guarantee of 30 cents per month for all the goods entrusted to his care by
Department of Island Revenue. He will have no pension. The sum of $600 a yea
about the salary of a messenger whose responsibility does not go beyond the erra;
he is ordered to do ; and, moreover, that same food inspector is not even provic
with an office where to store away, under proper conditions, the samples he is instruc'
to collect, and to attend to his bookkeeping and correspondence.

The increase of $50 per annum in any salary until the maximum salary is reach
is, in too many cases, illusive. It is exposed to favouritism and to political chang
more especially in the outside service. It is of no account, and there is no way f
self-delusion in that respect.

This being a settled fact, it is consequently very important in the interest of t!
stability and efficiency of the Civil Service, that the salaries, as a rule, be fixed on t!
highest minimum to couple with the average cost of living, which has increased !
from 40 to 60 per cent since the last ten years, and that, the members of the Ci;
Service, faithfully attending to the duties of their charge, shall be made sure th
some say after five, others after ten consecutive years of service, while I will fix

period at seven years, to be paid, according to their class, the fulness of their salary,
and that such an increase be automatic on the very day when it comes due, without
making it necessary to notify the authorities.

I beg leave to draw your attention to the fact that since the establishment of gas
inspection offices here and there in the Dominion, the electric light inspection was
added to the gas inspection service, this increasing with no compensation, the obligations and responsibilities of the inspectors, while on another side the receipts of the
inspection offices have been increased fourfold since about fifteen years at least in the
city and district of Quebec, where they will soon grow larger with the operations of
a new gas company.

Pursuant to the classification of the service which I have the honour to recommend, salaries should be remodelled as follows:—

1. Inspector general, salary to be paid by the Government.
2. Assistant inspectors, idem—

First, minimum........	$800
" maximum....	1,400
Second, minimum....	600
" maximum....	1,000

These inspectors would belong to a special class, as they would be not merely
inspectors, but also expert mechanics.

3. District inspectors—

Minimum salary....	$1,500
Maximum salary....	2,000
Assistant inspectors—	
Minimum salary....	800
Maximum salary..	1,000

I have the honour to be, gentlemen,
Your obedient servant,
(Signed)   N. LeVasseur,
Gas and E. L. Inspector.

Thomas Alexander, Esq.,   Winnipeg, August 31, 1907.
Collector of Inland Revenue,
London, Ontario.

Dear Sir,—We, the district inspector and collectors of the Manitoba District,
have before us the minutes and resolutions passed by a meeting of the inspector and
collectors of the Windsor district.

We have after careful consideration of the same, unanimously endorsed the resolutions passed at your meeting, and forward this letter to be used by you when you
appear before the Civil Service Commission next month.

We are using every means at our disposal to have the Commission visit Winnipeg, but in the event of them not doing so it is the intention to send a representative
from Winnipeg to appear before them in our behalf at some of their sessions in the
East.

Yours very truly,
(Signed)   Jno. K. Barrett,
District Inspector.
T. S. Gosnell,
Collector, Winnipeg Division.
Wm. M. Conklin,
Collector, Moosejaw Division.
X. Saucier,
Collector, Calgary Division.
G. A. Ironside,
Collector, Port Arthur Division.

A meeting of the collectors of Inland Revenue of the inspection distric
sor, was held at the Inland Revenue office, London, on August 19. Those pre
J. H. Kenning, inspector, Windsor.
Thos. Alexander, collector, London.
J. B. Powell, collector, Guelph, Ont.
George Rennie, collector, Stratford.
James McSween, collector, Windsor.
M. J. O'Donohue, collector, Brantford.
Mr. Kenning was elected chairman, and Mr. Alexander, secretary.

The chairman of the meeting explained that the object of the meeting v
sider the best means of placing before the Civil Service Commission the
officers in the Excise Branch of the Inland Revenue service, to an increase
After considerable discussion the following resolutions were unanimously

Resolved that, in view of the marked increase in the cost of living; th
bility attached to the duties to be performed; the severe and searching de
examinations, in addition to the regular Civil Service examinations that the
the Excise Branch are required to pass; the technical knowledge that they
to possess; the desirability of attracting first-class men to the service and th
the service to the dignity of a desirable profession, which is believed to hav
original intention of its organizers; and in order to place the service on a
would somewhat compare with that of commercial and monetary institutions
standing throughout the country; it is respectfully submitted that there sh
increase of at least thirty-three and one-third per cent (33⅓ per cent) made
sent schedule of salaries.

It is further resolved, that the gratuity of two months pay which is no
the heirs of deceased officers, is entirely inadequate and it is respectfully rec
that in case of an officer dying while in active service, fifty per cent (50 p
the superannuation allowance he would have been entitled to receive be paid
during her widowhood, and in case of an officer dying after he had been supe
a fair proportion of his superannuation allowance should be given his wid
her widowhood.

Mr. Collector Alexander was named as the representative to lay these i
fore the commission.

MEMORIAL OF THE CIVIL SERVICE, INLAND REVENUE BRANCH, WESTERN OI

To the Honourable the Royal Commissioners, appointed to inquire into m
    taining to the Civil Service of Canada.

GENTLEMEN,—We, the officers of the Excise branch of the outside servi
Revenue, in Western Ontario, respectfully ask for an increase in our salari
cause others are asking but because we wish to be able to supply our famili(
necessaries of life and keep them up to the standard required in their every
socially and otherwise. Without sufficient to maintain the position we occu
back and lose the respect of our fellowmen. We claim, and claim right!
honest toiler is worthy of every consideration.

We, as government officials, are deprived of certain civil rights and, be
to pursue other callings, we ask that justice be done us especially as the (
demands that all our time be given to the service, we, therefore, only ask for
and believing in the justice of our claim, we submit the following resolutio
tistics passed by the different divisions in Ontario and carried unanimous
division:—

Resolved, that in view of the marked increase in the cost of living, th
bility attached to the duties to be performed, these duties requiring officer
arbiters between the Government and the manufacturers. daily determining

and assessing the duty accruing thereon and adjusting quantities between manufacturers and purchasers; the severe and searching departmental examinations (in addition to the regular civil service examination) that the officers of the Excise branch are required to pass; the technical knowledge that they are obliged to possess; the desirability of attracting first-class men to the service and thus to maintain the service at its present high standard as a desirable profession, which is believed to have been the original intention of its organizers; and in order to place the service on a basis that would compare favourably with that of commercial and monetary institutions throughout the country; it is respectfully submitted that there should be an increase of at least enough to place us in the position we were in in 1900, and to enable us to live as comfortably, or in other words, give us a relative worth of the purchasing power of one dollar.

That we thoroughly endorse the memorial of the Civil Service Association of Ottawa wherein they take up the question of superannuation and retirement, believing their recommendation to be along the line of good Government.

In any increase of salary which your honourable body may see fit to recommend we trust that you will consider the outside service of sufficient importance to be dealt with as liberally as the character of the duties involved warrants, the staff having to deal directly with the general public, made up of manufacturers, merchants, and all classes of licensees, the doing of which requiring tact, judgment and a reasonably high order of intelligence and such increase to be paid *en bloc*, when properly authorized, instead of in annual five per cent increments, as has been the practice heretofore, so as to give immediate and substantial relief to the various officers.

We further recommend along the lines of reform:—

That a re-arrangement of the salaries of deputy collectors, class A, be made, whereby they will receive, as a maximum, the minimum of the collector under whom they serve.

That the class known as 'deputy collector, class B,' be permitted to rank, as regards salary, with excise officers as soon as they pass the required promotion examination. We mention this fact as 'class B' men only reach nine hundred per annum, while excisemen, of first-class rank, go to twelve hundred dollars per annum. At the same time it would be well to see no more appointments to this class.

That we would like to see a clause in the Act whereby appointments to the service be on probation at a salary of seven hundred dollars per annum to enable them to live until such time as they pass the promotion examination.

That we strongly recommend the preventive service be abolished, all officers being preventive officers in case of need.

That we do not approve of the abolition of the Promotion examinations but strongly adhere to the system now in vogue. The Deputy Minister of Inland Revenue will submit a set of papers which will go a long way to show the honourable the Commissioners the standard the excisemen have to attain.

That in large divisions where messengers are employed they receive, when appointed, not less than seven hundred dollars per annum and an increase each year of fifty dollars until they reach the maximum of eight hundred dollars. These messengers have to be responsible men carrying large sums of money and are at times called upon to do certain exciseman's work.

That we strongly recommend where it is necessary to employ stenographers they receive a salary of not less than fifty dollars per month and an increase of fifty dollars per year until such time as they reach a maximum of eight hundred dollars, and in the event of their passing the prescribed excise Promotion examinations and being assigned to the discharge of exciseman's duties, that they be paid such an aggregate salary as their length of service and the examination they passed would have properly and justly entitled them to had they been originally appointed as excise officers.

We had hoped to be able to present to you a memorandum respecting the efforts of this service to enforce such pure food laws as now exist or which may hereafter be

29a—25

7-8 EDWARD VII., A. 1908

passed and we desire to be able to introduce such memorandum at a later date, if so privileged.

That the gratuity of two months' pay which is now given to the heirs of deceased officers is entirely inadequate and it is respectfully recommended that in case of an officer dying while in active service, fifty per cent·(50%) of the superannuation allowance he would have been entitled to receive be paid his widow during her widowhood, and in case of an officer dying after he had been superannuated, a fair proportion of his superannuation allowance should be given his widow during her widowhood, or, in case of there being no widow, to his infant children if any.

That we recommend a conference of inspectors and collectors of Inland Revenue be held in Ottawa at least once in every three years to discuss matters with the department respecting law, regulations, &c.

That while under our present system of Government it may reasonably be expected that political appointments will obtain, considerable cause of friction might be avoided by consultation between those who have the patronage in hand and the collector· who would have to deal with such officers after appointment and the nature of the work to be done and the qualifications for such work thoroughly understood before recommendations for appointments are made; in this way an understanding might be arrived at whereby only those fitted for the positions would be selected.

TORONTO, September 26, 1907.

The Commission met at 10.30 a.m.   Present, Messrs. Courtney, chairman, she and Bazin.

Mr. H. R. FRANKLAND, Toronto, called and sworn and examined.

By the Chairman:

Q. I understand you have a memorial of some kind to present?—A. Yes, I now beg ave to submit this memorial.
(Statement read and filed as exhibit.)
Q. You are the collector of inland revenue here?—A. Yes.
Q. Did you enter the service as collector?—A. No, as deputy collector.
Q. Did you pass the Promotion examination?—A. No.
Q. How did you get over it?—A. The law does not require the deputy collector ʘ pass an examination.
Q. I mean how did you get over the Promotion examination required to become ollector?—A. I served six months as deputy collector.
Q. In this division the revenue is about $1,600,000 a year?—A. Our collections last ʏr amounted to about $1,600,000.
Q. That is from all sources?—A. All sources.
Q. You have Gooderham and Worts distillery here?—A. We have two distilleries re.
Q. What is the other?—A. The Canadian General Distillery.
Q. How many men have you at Gooderham and Worts distillery?—A. Nine.
Q. What is the revenue derived from Gooderham and Worts distillery?—A. About ⅃‚000 a month.
Q. You do not get all the revenue that originates here when you pass things in ʌd? The revenue is collected elsewhere?—A. The revenue is collected mostly in ʼntreal and Winnipeg so far as our division is concerned.
Q. But the thing is originated here and the manufacture takes place here?—A. B.
Q. If all the revenue was collected at the place of manufacture can you form any ɪmate of what the revenue of the Toronto division would be?—A. The revenue of the ʀonto division would be about $2,000,000 more than it is at the present time.
Q. That is to say the revenue of the Toronto division, if all the duties on the ʟnufactured products were collected here, would be about three and a half million llars?—A. Yes, and it might be four million dollars. I am under the mark when I ʏ two million dollars more. During the past ten years our cigar production has in-ᵉased 23,000,000 alone.
Q. How many maltsters have you in your division?—A. I think there are ten.
Q. Your division includes Barrie and the Soo, does it not?—A. Yes.
Q. In other places do you have deputy collectors?—A. They are the only two places ₁ere we have collectors.
Q. How far does this division extend geographically?—A. To James bay on the ʼrth and Pic river on the northwest, taking in the Simcoes on the west and the On-ʀios on the east to Lake Ontario on the south, Muskoka and Parry Sound districts.
Q. You gentlemen of the Inland Revenue Department have amalgamated to come ᵗore us?—A. We are from Prescott, virtually speaking, to Lake Superior.
Q. It is very good of you to unite in that way, because it permits the case to be ᴺdensed and saves us a good deal of trouble?—A. Mr. Kenning, the inspector, lives
29a—25½

in Windsor, Mr. Stratton belongs here, and Mr. Dingman belongs to the eastern part of the province. I have received a letter from Mr. Dingman stating that whatever was done——

Q. He would coincide with?—A. Yes.

Q. Besides the manufacturers of spirits and malt, how many tobacco manufacturers have you in this division?—A. There are four on the list, but, of course, there are only two that are worth calling tobacco manufacturers.

Q. Who are they?—A. W. A. McAlpine, he is the foreign tobacco manufacturer, and Mr. Iler, who manufactures Canadian combination tobacco. Mr. Bollard manufactures tobaco for his own use.

Q. How many cigar factories are there in your division?—A. I think twenty-two.

Q. Then this is a very important division?—A. I think it is the second important division in the Dominion.

Q. If I do not ask you questions exhaustively do not entertain the idea that we are neglecting your case because we have already heard representatives of the Inland Revenue Department?—A. I quite understand that, Sir.

Q. Before I left Ottawa, Mr. Gerald, the deputy minister of Inland Revenue, sent me a stack of examination papers which I have not yet been able to look at. Those are the papers——A. That we have reference to in our statement.

Q. Your examinations deal with such subjects as mensuration, computation, &c.?—A. Yes.

Q. You do not say anything, I suppose from motives of delicacy, about what you think should be done for collectors and inspectors. You have talked about the officers —the deputy collectors and the excise officers?—A. Yes.

Q. What do you think of the position of your colleagues and yourself?—A. I feel that the emolument the inspectors for Ontario—and they have inspectors throughout the country that are just as competent as those in this province—receive is not what they are worth by any means. In fact, if they were employees of mine personally I do not think that anything else than a 50 per cent increase would meet the requirements of their case at the present time. I think the same thing applies to the collectors.

Q. The Excise department governs the inspection of weights and measures?—A. Yes, the inspection.

Q. That is part of the duties of the Excise department?—A. Yes.

Q. There are also inspectors of gas and electric light?—A. Yes.

Q. And inspectors who look after the adulteration of food?—A. Yes.

Q. Under the Trade and Commerce Department there are inspectors of grain?—A. Yes.

Q. And inspectors of hides?—A. Yes.

Q. An Act was passed at the last session of parliament that was called for by the public, relating to the inspection of canned goods?—A. That is under the Department of Agriculture.

Q. So practically three departments are engaged in inspection duties?—A. Yes.

Q. Does it require a special training to look after the adulteration of food and the inspection of canned goods?—A. I think that it requires a man with a certain amount of tact and good judgment. He ought to be more than above suspicion and reproach, and a man who has been in some commercial calling.

Q. He could do both; I suppose?—A. He could do both.

Q. The same man might also inspect the grain?—A. Well, no, not the grain.

Q. But he could inspect the canned goods and look after the adulteration of food? —A. Yes, the same man could attend to both duties.

Q. What do you pay your men at Gooderham and Worts distillery, taking that as the test distillery?—A. The chief officer in charge receives a salary of $1,800 per year and $200 per year duty pay, $2,000 in all. The next officer in command is paid $1,400 a year and $200 duty pay. The other officers are first-class officers, with the exception of two. They receive $1,200 a year and $100 a year duty pay.

By Mr. Fyshe:

Q. What does duty pay mean?—A. Their hours are from 7 o'clock in the morning til 5 o'clock in the afternoon, or from 8 o'clock in the morning until 6 o'clock in the ternoon, and it is to encourage them to accept the position without a lot of grumbling at they are given duty pay, and, of course, there is extra time. In fact that means tra time. The officers' duty begins at 8 o'clock and ends at 5 o'clock in the afternoon.

By the Chairman:

Q. They get a lump sum for duty pay?—A. Yes.

Q. Whereas, their extra time is paid by the hour?—A. Their extra time is paid y the hour. It is paid by the manufacturer, not by the Government.

Q. The extra hours?—A. The extra hours.

Q. Does that not open the door to possible abuses?—A. No, it does not. Supposing hat Gooderham & Worts wanted one of our officers to remain until 8, or 9 or 10 'clock at night, they would have to pay him a certain sum for the first hour, and so uch less for the other hours. They will not pay $1 more than they have to.

Q. Do you know how much all your officers get in the shape of extras?—A. Everyhing comes to me and then goes to the department.

Q. The extra pay is collected by whom?—A. By myself, or at least by collector.

Q. Why should the lower paid officers get only $100?—A. The responsibility rests ith the two chief officers. They have to do all the checking; they are responsible to me.

Q. Supposing the beer in a brewery turns sour and is destroyed, that takes place in e presence of two officers?—A. Yes, in the presence of the officer in charge of that ewery and an officer detailed to that work by myself or by the collector.

Q. In a distillery is there any product that is destroyed because of turning bad? A. No.

Q. That takes place only in a brewery?—A. It is only in a brewery and a tobacco ctory.

Q. That product also is destroyed in the presence of two officers?—A. Yes.

Q. Coming back again to Gooderham and Worts, does the distillery work night and y?—A. No.

Q. It closes down at certain hours?—A. Yes.

Q. But while the distillery is at work your officers are there?—A. They are there.

Q. Do they live near the building?—A. Some of them do.

Q. At what hour have they to be there in the morning?—A. At 7 o'clock they open the doors.

Q. And they have the keys of the vats and all that kind of thing?—A. Yes.

Q. Have you anything to tell us in regard to the working of the distillery that eds to be elucidated?—A. No, I think not. Mr. Kenning is the Distillery Inspector.

Q. You consider that deputy collectors, class B, might be done away with?—A. s.

Q. Having one deputy collector class A?—A. I have two in my division. One es the inside work and the other does the inspection on the outside.

Q. There are two grades, class A and class B?—A. Yes.

Q. You think they might be amalgamated, and have no class B?—A. Have no ss B. We do not want any more, in fact I think it would be in the interest of the vice to have only one deputy collector.

Q. Do you not think the deputy collectors, appointed as they are now without amination, might be done away with altogether?—A. That, of course, is a matter argument.

Q. You came in through that door but now you are in, do you not think the door ght be closed?—A. I would not say that. I think my coming in has been of some cial advantage to the service.

Q. I have no doubt of that?—A. Of course, I have Mr. Stratton, my inspector, vouch for that.

Q. You, Mr. Frankland, unfortunately are under the Retirement Act, I suppose ?—A. Yes.

Q. You came in after the Superannuation Act was abolished ?—A. Yes.

·Q. I suppose, like all the witnesses that have come before us, you are of the opinion that it would be desirable to re-enact the Superannuation Act ?—A. I think so, in the interest of the widows and orphans.

Q. And in the interest of the stability of the service ?—A. Yes.

Q. In the case like that of Mr. Patteson, who has just died, after having contributed some thousands of dollars to the superannuation fund, you think it would be desirable that his family should have had the money ?—A. I think his widow should receive one-half of his pension. I suppose Mr. Patteson, like every other Government official, did not have too much of this world's goods.

Q. Do you not think it would be desirable to have the Pension Act include the widow and the orphan if it could be managed ?—A. I do think so or I would not have asked for that in the memorial which I have presented.

Q. You recommend that a conference between inspectors and collectors be held in Ottawa once every three years. You think that would be desirable ?—A. I do. So far as the excise service is concerned I think it is absolutely necessary for the good of the country.

By Mr. Fyshe :

Q. Would that be on account of possible differences of opinion ?—A. Differences of opinion.

By the Chairman:

Q. Differences of duty, I suppose ?—A. No, the duties are the same.

Q. There would be a difference of ideas, and at such a conference you could thresh the differences out together ?—A. I think it would be in the interest of the country that a conference such as we suggest in our memorial should be held so far as we are concerned.

Q. You suggest, in order to remove friction, that it would be desirable the collector should know something about the patronage ?—A. Yes.

Q. When you have vacancies here do you report to the department ?—A. I do.

Q. And Mr. Jones or Mr. Somebody else that you have never heard anything about until he enters the position is appointed ?—A. That is right.

Q. You know indirectly how he comes there ?—A. Yes, sir, no doubt about that.

Q. Are the young men leaving your service now ?—A. No. All my officers are through their examination. With the exceptions possibly of three or four they are all first class officers.

Q. Then they have not such a great inducement to leave the service ?—A. No. They are all up in years, but I suppose if they were young men it would be different.

Q. Like in the case of the post office, for instance, they would be leaving ?—A. There is no doubt about that.

Q. Looking around the service generally do you find that the men now entering are as efficient as they were some seven or eight years ago ?—A. I do. The staff of officers that have come into the service, so far as the Toronto division is concerned, are up to the required standard.

Q. When was the last appointment made here ?—A. We have not had an appointment here for five years.

Q. Since the great increase in the price of commodities you have not had any appointments ?—A. No, we have not had any appointments, and I might say for your information we lost a first class officer and have not had one man inquire for his position.

By Mr. Fyshe :

Q. Is that not curious ?—A. It is just because they are not desirous of coming into the service.

SESSIONAL PAPER No. 29a

By the Chairman :

Q. In view of the openings now available and the means of getting on in life do you say. from personal experience, that young men are not anxious to enter the service? · A. Three or four years ago I suppose I had an applicant every day. In the last three years I have not had one.

By Mr. Fyshe :

Q. What would a young man entering the lower ranks of the service be paid?— A. $600 to begin with, and as soon as he has passed the examination he would get $850 and go on to $1,200.

By the Chairman:

Q. Even with that, although there is a vacancy, you have not had an application?—A. I have not had an application.

Q. If after receiving this evidence you wish to supplement it in any way, we shall be very glad to receive from you an additional memorandum?—A. Thank you. We ask you for that privilege.

Witness retired.

Mr. W. C. STRATTON, Toronto, called and sworn and examined.

By the Chairman:

Q. Have you any memorial to present ?—A. No, sir. I joined in the one that has been presented to you.

Q. You are inspector of bonded factories?—A. I am district inspector of Inland Revenue for the Toronto district and bonded inspector for the Dominion.

Q. You act in a dual capacity like a good many other people ? You are the inspector for the district, but you are also inspector of bonded factories throughout the Dominion?—A. Correct.

Q. Will you kindly tell us what is understood by a bonded factory?—A. It is a factory where material is used upon which there was originally a duty. For instance, if spirits are used in these bonded factories, a small duty is charged on the product, but nothing on the spirits. In the case of vinegar it is 4c. a gallon. Spirits are used in the manufacture of perfumes and they are given at a reduced rate. In the manufacture of explosives where they are exported, and that is the case with nearly all the products, no duty is charged on the spirits at all; the duty is all foregone. The operations are all conducted with the object of preventing the spirits from going into use for potable purposes. That is the object of the control of bonded factories.

Q. How many bonded factories are there throughout the Dominion ?—A. I did not sum them up but there must be between thirty and fifty of one kind and another, and they are growing all the time. I received a fresh application this morning.

Q. Does the territory in which these bonded factories are located extend from the Atlantic to the Pacific ?—A. From St. John, N.B., as far west as Vancouver.

Q. Are you obliged to visit these factories periodically ?—A. I visit them about once a year.

Q. Is that the obligation?—A. No. I am supposed to use a certain discretion. I visit them not less than once a year.

Q. How often are you obliged to go around for inspection purposes to the several divisions?—A. I try to go around three times a year to each division.

Q. How long have you been inspector?—A. I have been inspector since 1900. Before that I was acting inspector. There is one thing I would like to explain. Mr. Frankland, as he has himself explained. entered the service as deputy collector. His succession so quickly to the collectorship was an accident. That is to say, the then inspector, Mr. Morrow, was taken ill in the year 1899, and he was ordered to become acting collector, and I was ordered to become acting inspector. Mr. Morrow retired, and we were appointed to our respective offices in 1900. That is how that thing came about so quickly.

Q. Do you recollect how long Mr. Morrow was inspector?—A. Really I do not know.

Q. How long have you been in the Excise service?—A. I was appointed in February, 1871. I have been in the service for thirty-six years.

Q. You know, as a matter of fact, I suppose that some years ago there was a per diem allowance granted to inspectors when they were travelling?—A. Yes.

Q. Now the inspectors are only allowed their actual expenditure?—A. Not that even.

Q. There are certain things you cannot charge for?—A. You are compelled to incur a certain outlay, but you cannot swear positively that the money was expended solely on behalf of the Government, that is unless you have got an elastic conscience.

Q. But a man with a conscience is out of pocket?—A. He is out of pocket, sometimes more, sometimes less.

Q. Then there is no inducement to travel on inspection duty beyond a sense of duty?—A. None whatever.

Q. Do you think it desirable to have a per diem allowance in order to permit of a little more freedom?—A. I would not like to recommend it.

Q. You would not?—A. When the system prevailed before I think it was abused. If it is honestly conducted, then it is the proper thing.

Q. You know that in the Imperial Service inspectors are given a per diem allowance?—A. I am not familiar with that.

Q. To the man who knows he would be out of pocket there is no inducement to travel?—A. There is no inducement to travel.

Q. Is your district a difficult one?—A. No, I have got the nicest district in the Dominion.

Q. You must be a happy man. You do not go far north beyond the reach of railway?—A. It is a very comfortable district to inspect.

Q. It is comfortable compared with the trip of a post office inspector going up the Gatineau or River Desert, two or three hundred miles away from trains?—A. I have not to go any farther north than the Soo. There is no place where I experience any discomfort.

Q. Well then, as a matter of fact, in your particular division not having any discomforts in travelling the service as it is conducted now with respect to travelling allowance does not bear hardly upon you?—A. No.

Q. Although in some cases it might bear very hard?—A. No doubt, but I do not know of any. I have not experienced such.

Q. Well, as I said to Mr. Frankland, if you desire to supplement your evidence in any way we will be very glad to receive information?—A. Of course, you will understand, Mr. Chairman, that I am also a district inspector for the weights and measures office and for the gas and electric light office. What you have been inquiring into now relates to the Excise branch of the Inland Revenue Department.

Q. You get no salary for that?—A. No.

Q. You are the inspector looking after the local inspectors in the district?—Supervising all the branches of the Inland Revenue service.

Q. I am very glad you told us that. How many branches of the weights and measures are there in your division?—A. There are two in my district, one in Toronto and one in Hamilton.

Q. And with respect to gas?—A. There is one in Toronto, one in Barrie, and one in Owen Sound.

Q. And Listowel?—A. No.

Q. London?—A. No, those are out offices.

The witness retired.

Mr. J. H. Kenning, Windsor, called, and sworn and examined.

By the Chairman:

Q. I see that in the Auditor General's Report you are called inspector of distilleries?—A. Yes.

Q. You inspect Walker's distillery at Windsor, and Gooderham and Worts' distillery here?—A. Yes.

Q. Does that mean that you are inspector of distilleries throughout the Dominion?—A. Yes.

Q. And also the others?—A. Yes.

Q. Are you constantly on your round?—A. Well, I am inspector of the district of Windsor which comprises five collectors' divisions, and I am constantly employed. Perhaps you may not be aware that inspectors have no office staff and that while they are away whatever correspondence comes to the office accumulates until they return. So that I am probably half the time away and half the time engaged in the office.

Q. Your headquarters are at Windsor?—A. Yes.

Q. How many distilleries are there throughout the Dominion?—A. Thirteen.

Q. How far do your travels extend?—A. Well, on the east the farthest place is Beauport, a suburb of Quebec.

By Mr. Fyshe:

Q. Is the distillery of Mr. Robitaille at Beauport in actual operation?—A. Yes, they commenced last year. I have been there twice since January 1.

By the Chairman:

Q. You commence at Beauport and go to the Pacific coast?—A. There is one in New Westminster, B.C.

Q. Then the district you travel over extends from Quebec to New Westminster?—A. Yes, when I became inspector I had conferences with the deputy minister respecting the frequency of visits. He thought that a couple of visits a year would suffice, and I have followed that plan up to the present time with the exception of New Westminster. That is a long journey and a expensive one and I have only been there once.

Q. You go there once a year?—A. I have not been once a year.

Q. How long have you been in office?—A. It is five years last March since I became inspector.

Q. Did you succeed Mr. Davis?—A. Yes. There was for a time no inspector of distilleries after Mr. Davis retired.

Q. Then the general idea is that you visit each distillery twice a year?—A. Yes, with the exception of the one at New Westminster.

Q. Is the output large at New Westminster?—A. No, it is small, but it is growing.

Q. Is it desirable that you should visit that distillery only once in five years?—A. That is a matter which rests with the deputy minister. I went out in 1905 and after I was there he said he thought it was not desirable for me to go out on account of the long distance and the expenditure necessary. I consulted him each succeeding year and he said, 'Oh, well, it is a long journey and pretty expensive and I don't think you need go as we have there a good officer in charge—I don't think you need undertake that journey.' Personally I was quite willing to go. The others I have visited regularly twice a year and sometimes more frequently.

Q. Your expenditure is not very great. I see that in the year 1905-6 for transportation and personal expenses your expenditure was only about $180?—A. Yes, quite so.

Q. Your transportation came to $106.65, and personal expenses $76?—A. Yes.

Q. Well, if you visited the distilleries twice a year that is not a very great outlay, you must travel economically?—A. Yes.

Q. How long do you stay generally at each distillery?—A. Generally a day, some-times longer.

Q. When you come from Windsor to inspect Gooderham and Worts' distillery, how long does it take you?—A. I do not stop more than a day.

Q. Do you see the absolute volume of spirits in the vats? Do you inspect thoroughly when you are at Gooderham and Worts' distillery?—A. With reference to that matter I may say that a thorough inspection would require the taking of stock, which I do not attempt to do. That is generally left to the district inspector. I have two distilleries in my own district, and in visiting them I take stock.

Q. Then in the case of the distilleries like Gooderham and Worts, outside your own district, it is a kind of supervision more than anything else?—A. Just that.

Q. The district inspector in this division would take stock at Gooderham and Worts?—A. I think so.

Q. You take stock at Walker's distillery?—A. Yes.

Q. How often do you take stock?—A. Once a year.

Q. Do they expect you when you come around?—A. No, they do not.

Q. Do you go in at any time and say 'I have come to take stock'?—A. Yes, they have no reason to expect me.

Q. No reason to think you are coming?—A. No.

Q. How long does it take to take stock at a distillery like Walker's?—A. It takes me about two weeks to inspect the division of Windsor and a week to take stock at Walker's. Of course, we do not actually weigh the packages, you know. We take stock of the packages and check with the ledgers.

Q. But you gauge what is in the vats, do you not?—A. We gauge an approximate number. As regards the vats we take stock of the amount checked up against each vat in the ledgers, and perhaps we will gauge one in ten.

Q. Do you make tests during the examination?—A. We make a test, yes.

Q. And you select indiscriminately the vats which you test?—A. Indiscriminately.

Q. You do not do as the bank inspector does when he goes into the branch bank? He counts all the cash and all the securities?—A. Speaking of that, we do not meddle with a collector's cash. We check the collections on the cash book from the time of the previous visit, and take an abstract from the books of the stock of various kinds in bond, and then go and see that the stock is in the warehouse.

By Mr. Fyshe:

Q. Do you make a practice of going over the books from the time of the previous visit?—A. I do.

Q. And you bring them up to date?—A. Bring them up to date.

Q. And see that things have been kept regularly in the interim?—A. And that the moneys collected have been deposited to the credit of the Receiver General.

The CHAIRMAN.—As I have said to your colleagues, we are very glad to meet you, and if you think you have not explained matters sufficiently we will be very glad to have more data.

The WITNESS.—There is one thing I would like to mention. You asked me how long I was inspector of distilleries, and I thought possibly you might have been mistaken as to my length of service. I have been in the service about forty years.

The CHAIRMAN.—I know you are an old officer, but I did not know whether you succeeded Mr. Davis or not?—A. There was an interregnum between Mr. Davis' retirement and my appointment.

Q. You went up through all the Excise branches?—A. Yes.

The witness retired.

. Thomas Alexander, London, called, sworn and examined.

By the Chairman :

You are collector of Inland Revenue at London?—A. Yes.

Have you got a statement with you ?—A. Yes.

itatement read and filed as exhibit.)

You have been over thirty years in the service ?—A. Thirty-seven years on ber 1.

Did you pass up through all the grades ?—A. Yes, sir. I was appointed at $500.

. What do you receive now ?—A. $2,400.

. Have you much business in the London division ? What is your revenue ?—A. been considered by the department to rank as first class.

. You are in class A ?—A. Class A.

. What is your revenue in London ?—A. About $425,000, that is the collections.

. You have Carling's Brewery in London ?—A. Yes.

. Who has the largest cigar factory ?—A. That is McNee's, it makes 6,000,000.

. Have you anything to add especially as regards London to what Mr. Frankland ie other gentlemen have said?—A. Of course, London is a large cigar making . Outside of Montreal it is the largest in Canada, making 36,000,000 cigars lly. Then we have an extensive district which includes the counties of Elgin, on and Middlesex, with out offices at St. Thomas, Sarnia, Petrolia and Strathroy.

. How many officers have you got at McNee's factory ?—A. One, and he attends bably two others.

. You say that McNee's factory turns out 6,000,000 of cigars in a year ?—A. ,000,000.

. Is this officer in constant attendance there ?—A. Not in constant attendance. dges from one to the other but loses no time coming or going.

. Are the factories all in the city of London ?—A. No, we have two in St. is and one in Aylmer.

. What check have you in the absence at St. Thomas of the officer that things)ing rightly at McNee's, for example ?—A. The officer in question is never

. Well, he is at other factories then ?—A. The only thing is he checks up and i the stock when he returns to the factory. At periodical times he counts up the checks the book, and checks off the different balances even to the empty boxes.

. During his absence there could be no means of getting in a lot of tobacco and it up before his return ?—A. No possible means.

. How many officers have you got at Carling's Brewery ?—A. One.

. Is he there all day long ?—A. Yes

. Does he look after Labatt's as well?—A. No, there is one at Labatt's too.

. Then you have two big breweries in London, Carling's and Labatt's ?—A. Yes.

. The officers are at the breweries all through the hours of working, are they ?— s, they are supposed to be there from 8 o'clock in the morning until 6 o'clock :ht.

. If there is only one officer at each place how do you manage when malt be- musty and has to be destroyed ? It must be destroyed in the presence of two s ?—A. There is an officer detailed by the collectors. Permit me to say that is rarely destroyed of itself. There is no duty on beer when made from malt the duty is on the malt contained in the beer. Beer sometimes becomes sour .sty, and is destroyed in the presence of two excise officers. The quantity de- d is carefully computed, and samples of the beer are taken and sent to the depart- at Ottawa, where it is analyzed, and the quantity of malt used in each gallon is ained. The refund of duty on the malt is calculated from this analysis.

Q. You send another officer there ?—A. Another officer is detailed by the collector and the two officers give a joint certificate.

Q. Then a refund is made?—A. A refund is made.

Q. You say your salary is $2,400?—A. Yes.

Q. Is that the limit of the class?—A. That is the limit.

Q. How long have you been collector at London?—A. Twenty-four years.

Q. What was the revenue in London twenty-four years ago? Do you recollect offhand?—A. No, I could not say just now.

Q. How long have you been receiving $2,400 a year?—A. Probably for about three years.

Q. What salary had you before that?—A. $2,200.

Q. How long did that date back?—A. That took place when the division was raised to class A.

Q. Do you know when that was?—A. I think it was about 1900.

Q. Then it comes to this: in seven years you have had an increase of $200 salary?—A. Yes.

Q. Although your revenue is what?—A. About $425,000.

Q. Well, Mr. Alexander, we are glad to have heard you, and as I have said to the other gentlemen, if you find there is anything you have left untouched you can forward a memorandum to us?—A. Can I say a word for Manitoba?

Q. Certainly?—A. If you will allow me I will be as concise as possible. They have asked me to speak for them and I have a letter here from Mr. T. S. Gosnell. He says in part: ' The members of the Civil Service are acting as one body here and are endeavouring to bring the members of the Civil Service Commission here so they may be enabled to see matters as they are, and if they are men who believe men should be paid in accordance with the work done and the responsibility of the office we have no fear but a further sum will be added to our salaries. I have been penalized from $800 to $500 for each year since 1877 I have lived in the West. I am free to say that no collector in Canada gets the compensation he should have, but the officers west of Port Arthur have a double grievance.'

By Mr. Fyshe:

Q. They have what?—A. They have a double grievance, he says. That is on account of the extra cost of living above what obtains in the rest of the Dominion. I think they have pretty good ground for their statement according to what is reported.

The witness retired.

Mr. J. B. POWELL, Guelph, called, sworn and examined.

By the Chairman:

Q. You are the collector of Inland Revenue at Guelph?—A. Yes.

Q. How long have you been in the service?—A. Thirty-four years.

Q. Guelph includes Galt, Preston, and Waterloo?—A. It includes the counties of Wellington and Waterloo.

Q. You have excise men, outside of Guelph, stationed at Berlin and Galt?—A. Yes, and at Preston and Waterloo, and then there are the officers at Seagram's distillery.

Q. Is there an inspector in your division?—A. Mr. Kenning is the inspector.

Q. Have you anything to say in addition to what has been stated by your confreres?—A. Yes, there are one or two points I wish to make reference to. For instance, in the matter of duty pay. There is one case especially, and that is Berlin,

SESSIONAL PAPER No. 29a

where the collections will average about $100,000 a year, which is a very large amount and more than some divisions collect. There is only one officer there who does his work very satisfactorily. The whole survey is of such importance that I think a case if that sort ought to be ranked under the heading of the duty paid servants.

Q. At present Mr. Spence is there, is he not?—A. Yes, Mr. Spence is there.

Q. He is only an excise man?—A. He is only an excise man.

Q. The revenue derived from Berlin is about $100,000?—A. It will be this year.

Q. What is the total revenue of the Guelph division, including the cities of Guelph and Berlin?—A. It is in the neighbourhood of between $650,000 and '00,000.

Q. Then latterly Berlin has been contributing one-sixth?—A. Berlin is a very important survey.

Q. It contributes about one-sixth of the whole collection?—A. One-sixth of the whole collection, that is leaving out the volume of business besides the bonded business.

Q. Is Guelph pretty centrally located for the division?—A. It is at one end. It is ally central, yes.

Q. It is as good to have the headquarters at Guelph as anywhere else?—A. Yes, certainly.

Q. You would not advocate any change?—A. Not at all. It is only fifteen miles 'om the other place.

Q. How many men have you in Seagram's distillery?—A. Six.

Q. What are the hours in that distillery?—A. Just the same as in the other distilleries.

Q. Have you got any breweries in your district?—A. I have six malt houses and even breweries now and I have eight cigar factories and three large bonded warehouses.

Q. Then yours is a pretty representative division with a big distillery and several breweries?—A. I think our division ranks about third in Ontario as far as collections are concerned.

Q. I suppose, just as in the case of Toronto, that if the collections on all the whiskey manufactured at Seagram's were made in your division the revenue would be considerably increased?—A. It would be very much larger.

Q. That is to say, Seagram's whiskey is to be found all over the Dominion?—A. s.

Q. And duties are collected wherever the whiskey is bonded?—A. In the other divisions to which it is removed.

Q. So that a statement of the revenue collected in a division does not absolutely represent the work that is carried on there?—A. Not at all. The total volume of business is really not represented by the collections by any means.

Q. That is to say in a consuming division there would be a larger proportion of revenue collected as regards manufacture than there would be in others?—A. Yes.

Q. For example, you send a lot to Sherbrooke?—A. Yes, we send a lot.

Q. And the collections there represent a lot of stuff that originated elsewhere?— · Precisely.

Q. Have you anything more to say?—A. I do not quite agree with Mr. Stratton as to the per diem allowance. The per diem allowance, I think, is a better system than the one which is now in force, and for this reason. Of course, we all know that the exigencies of travel entail expenditures which, as Mr. Stratton very truly says, cannot very well be put in. Especially is that the case with relieving officers who feel that the allowance for board during the time they are relieving does not by any means cover the personal expenses to which they are subjected.

Q. Yours is the only branch of the public service where officers are sent occasionly from one division to the other? A man in your divisions may be sent down to oronto or may be packed off to Sherbrooke?—A. Yes.

Q. And what is allowed them for removal expenses?—A. Transportation and personal expenses.

Q. And a week's board?—A. Yes and a week's board. That includes the removal of the furniture.

Q. And the family?—A. And the family.

Q. In no other branch of the public service are people taken out of the division as far as I know?—A. I do not think it is done anywhere else.

Q. And this occurs on rare occasions in the Excise Department, does it not? It does not often happen?—A. No, not nearly as frequently as it used to.

Q. When the Excise Department was growing and divisions were being formed, officers were continually being shifted about?—A. Yes, I think sometimes in some cases it would be beneficial to have more frequent changes.

Witness retired.

Mr. W. F. MILLER, Hamilton, called and sworn and examined.

By the Chairman:

Q. How long have you been in the service, Mr. Miller?—A. Thirty-four or thirty-five years. I was appointed in 1873.

Q. Have you always been in Hamilton?—A. No, sir.

Q. Where did you begin duty?—A. I commenced in Hamilton, and then went to Windsor, where I was for eleven or twelve years in Walker's distillery. After that I was for one year in Gooderham and Worts' distillery, Toronto, and since then I have been in Hamilton as collector.

Q. What salary do you get now?—A. $2,400.

Q. That is the limit?—A. Yes.

Q. Yours is division A, I suppose?—A. It is a first-class division.

Q. How long has it been first-class?—A. I think previous to 1890.

Q. You then had $2,200?—A. It worked up to that.

Q. And since 1890 your salary has been increased $200?—A. Yes.

Q. You are in the same position as the gentlemen who have already spoken?—A. Yes.

Q. Are there any distilleries in your division?—A. One.

Q. What distillery?—A. The Hamilton Distillery Company.

Q. There are vinegar factories in Hamilton, are there not?—A. Two.

Q. Is there rather a preponderance of vinegar factories in Hamilton as compared with the other divisions?—A. No, I think Toronto has more than we have. One of ours is a very large one.

Q. Which one is that?—A. That is the Imperial.

Q. Have you many bonded factories there?—A. We have three and a small one, the F. F. Dalley Company. They make some liniments out of spirits.

Q. You have only one outside place, Dundas?—A. Yes, Dundas.

Q. You are pretty compact. How far does the Hamilton division extend?—A. It takes in the city and county of Wentworth.

Q. Have you an inspector in your division?—A. Mr. Stratton is our inspector in the Toronto district.

Q. Have you got any general remarks you would like to make?—A. I would like to draw your attention to the subject of duty pay. After several years' close observation of that question, I think there should be a general revision of that pay, that every officer who puts in extra time in these distilleries should receive the same amount. I differ with my friend, the collector from Toronto, and I say the subordinate officers are the ones who do what may be called the drudgery or dirtier work. Permit me to make the following statement in regard to the question of duty pay (reads): 'Hours of attendance 7 a.m. to 6 p.m.

SESSIONAL PAPER No. 29a

Distilleries—

Toronto, 2 officers......................................	$200 each.
" 7 officers..	100 "
Walkerville, 1 officer................................	100
" 1 officer..	150
" 8 officers......................................	100 '
Waterloo, 1 officer....................................	200
" 1 officer..	150
" 3 officers......................................	100 '
Prescott, 1 officer....................................	200
" 1 officer..	150
" 2 officers......................................	100 '
Hamilton, 2 officers................................	150 '
" 2 officers......................................	100 '
Belleville, 2 officers................................	150 '
" 1 officer..	100
Perth, 2 officers....................................	100 '
Joliette, 2 officers..................................	150 '
" 2 officers......................................	100 '
Montreal, 1 officer..................................	200
" 1 officer..	100
St. Hyacinthe, 1 officer..............................	150
" 2 officers......................................	100 '
Quebec, 2 officers....................................	150 '
Vancouver, 1 officer..................................	200
" 1 officer..	100

Tobacco Factories—

Montreal, 1 officer..................................	200
" 1 officer..	150
" 1 officer..	100
Toronto, 1 officer....................................	200
Hamilton, 1 officer..................................	200

If Hamilton is a fair criterion for hours of attendance at tobacco factories, there is no comparison with distilleries, being much shorter. I further wish to emphasize the paragraph in memorial requesting that the maximum salary of deputy collectors be placed at the minimum of collectors.

By Mr. Fyshe:

Q. The subordinate officers do the heavier work?—A. The heavier work, and none of them receive as much as the leading officers. I cannot see, with respect to duty pay, why the whole staff receiving this money should not get the same amount.

Q. Do you not approve of subordinate officers receiving less?—A. I do not. I think the man who puts in the hours should get the money.

Q. Who does the actual work?—A. Yes, who does the actual work. There is a graded officer in charge, and then there is a warehouse man and his assistants. The man who goes to the distillery at 7 o'clock in the morning, no matter what his duties may be, he puts in as many hours as the other man, no matter whether he is the officer in charge or not, and I think the subordinate officer is as much entitled to the larger remuneration as the officials who are above him. Then the officers of some distilleries receive larger amounts than they do at others for the same service, which I do not th nk is just.

By the Chairman :

Q. Mr. Frankland based his opinion not on the equality of time but on the difference in the work. You differ with Mr. Frankland ?—A. I do differ because I think they are all entitled to the same pay.

Q. When doctors differ how is the poor layman to get along?—A. They sometimes die.

Q. Have you anything further to say ?—A. There is a question that should properly come before you and that is in reference to officers who have passed a special class examination and are not yet in that class.

Q. There is a limitation of the number ?—A. Twenty-four.

Q. All the clergy cannot be bishops you know ?—A. I think there are somewhere in the neighbourhood of thirty and they will be old men before the last man gets on. They think that there should be some recognition in the meantime for their having come up to that standard. I just wished to say this on their behalf.

Q. In the case of a lieutenant in the army who has passed an examination in colonel's duties, you would not give him the equivalent of a colonel's pay, would you! —A. I would not go that far, but I think they ought to receive something more than a first class officer.

Q. There should be something betwixt and between, like Mahomet's coffin ?—A. Yes, that is a very good way to put it.

Q. Now do you wish to add anything more ?—A. Nothing more than to generally state that the outside branch of the civil service, as is set forth in the memorial, is largely technical and thoroughly practical. The officers in a distillery are able to go into the mashing room or fermenting room and pass a fair judgment on the condition of the several fermenting vats. It is the same in tobacco and cigar factories. The officers having charge of them have to test a tobacco and reduce it to a standard by which the government assess their duties. It is a delicate little operation in which the revenue is largely affected either one way or the other.

Q. Have you a large staff at Hamilton ?—A. Eighteen.

Q. Have you had any vacancies lately?—A. Yes.

Q. Have you like Mr. Franklin experienced a difficulty in filling up vacancies ? A. No, I must say that the appointments that have been made in my division have been very satisfactory.

Q. How long ago was the last appointment ?—A. About three or four months ago.

Q. That is one appointment ?—A. Well, we have had two appointments within six months.

Q. Are the people likely to stay that are appointed ?—A. I think so.

Q. Hamilton is an enterprising place, is it not ?—A. At least they seem satisfied with their prospects. They see before them opportunities of increasing their standing by these Promotion examinations and they are satisfied to give the service a fair trial anyway.

Q. But if the special excise men are limited in number the Promotion examination does not give them a show ?—A. It does in this way. For instance, if a man has gone out of the probationary class and is in reality a third class officer. If he goes up for Promotion examination and he gets a first-class certificate he readily goes up.

Q. That is so?—A. The only class that labours under a difficulty after having passed the examination is that special class.

Q. That is the top, the first class ?—A. Yes.

Q. A young man may see himself fairly landed into the first class but not going beyond that ?—A. Not rapidly.

Q. Then with the new developments in the country do you think, from your observation, that men are glad to enter the Excise service with all these prospects?— A. If I was a young man I would not. There is one other point I wish to impress

SESSIONAL PAPER No. 29a

upon you : the appointment of what is usually known as temporary employees. These men come in now at $500.

Q. But their employment does not last long, does it?—A. Six months or so. It depends upon how soon they pass that Qualifying examination.

Q. Do you not think it is desirable they should pass some examination ?—A. I do.

Q. Six months is not a long time to wait ?—A. But the amount I think is entirely inadequate.

Q. Do you mean to say that the $600 is inadequate after passing the Qualifying examination and all that ?—A. I do, sir.

Q. Are there many men leaving your division ?—A. No, sir.

Q. They are staying there ?—A. Unfortunately when a man gets into the Civil service, no matter what branch, they generally stay.

Q. Well, your men as a rule are men that have been some time in the service ?—A. I have about five officers who have not been over four years.

Q. You know that in the process of fermentation the scum comes up to the top. Do you find there is a certain amount of inefficiency in your late appointments as compared with your former ones ?—A. Well. I have not had the opportunity——

Q. They do not show as yet whether they are efficient or inefficient?—A. I have not had the opportunity of observing.

The witness retired.

Mr. THOMAS ALEXANDER, recalled.

The WITNESS.—May I supplement the evidence I have already given? There is an important item in connection with the London division which has not yet been touched upon at all, and that is the protection to the public in connection with the manufacture of petroleum. Perhaps you are not aware that all the petroleum for illuminating purposes is made in the division of London and amounts to about 20,000,000 gallons a year. It is all made in that division and all inspected there; it undergoes a special inspection before leaving the refinery.

By Mr. Fyshe:

Q. There is no duty on it?—A. There is no duty on it but the work has to be done, though it does not show in the revenue for the division. We do not even get the benefit of the inspecting fees now. The inspecting fees have been thrown off and the duty is off so that the London division gets no credit so far as collections are concerned, though the work of inspection has to be done.

Q. Do you put any stamps on the petroleum or take any means to show that it has passed examination?—A. None whatever. The refiners have to make a requisition to an officer as to the quantity of oil and number of packages they require to be inspected and a record of these requisitions. after the inspection is made, is placed in the government books. Then the refiner has the record in his book of every shipment that made and the place to which it has been shipped. If a man only buys one barrel of oil it has to be recorded in the refiner's book and a sworn statement at the end of a month has to be made out by the refiner and inspected by the officer.

Q. Does this statement include a certificate to the effect that the oil has been all duly examined?—A. The statement certifies that the officers have examined and inspected its oil.

Q. And that the refiner has sold nothing but what has been examined?—A. Yes. If there was only a duty of five cents per gallon, it would yield a revenue of about 1,000,000 annually.

29a—26

Q. That would be better?—A. That would give, as far as the London division is concerned, a revenue of $1,000,000. As it is now the work is done, but London division gets no credit as far as collections are concerned.

By the Chairman:

Q. That is to say, looking at the revenue received on account of inland revenue as compared with the work done by these officers there is no record of what they have done in the inspection of petroleum?—A. Not at all.

Q. I am very glad you have brought up this matter of petroleum inspection, as we are investigating and trying to find out what officers in each branch of the service do? —A. I thought it was a matter that was overlooked.

Q. We want to get at what is really done in the several departments?—A. I thought I had better bring that before the commission.

By Mr. Fyshe:

Q. Does not the service collect anything at all from the refiners for this examination?—A. Simply $1 a year for a license.

Q. That is contributing a service to the refiners for nothing and a valuable service too?—A. Yes, and it is for the protection of the public.

Q. Well, in your opinion should they pay something?—A. I would not like to make the suggestion. Although there is no duty on this petroleum, it must be remembered that the officers have very unpleasant duties to perform getting among the barrels of oil. They destroy their clothes and a refinery is not a very pleasant place to be in all the time, yet the officers receive no extra remuneration for their services. Now, then if excise officers at distilleries enjoy what is called duty pay, I think the same emolument should be granted to officers on duty at refineries.

Q. You mean petroleum refineries?—A. Yes.

Q. The officers there get no duty pay?—A. They get no duty pay.

The witness retired.

Mr. J. H. KENNING, recalled.

The WITNESS.—There is a matter that I overlooked, although it appears to have been frequently brought to the surface and that is the quality of the officers that come in as new material to meet the needs of the service.

By the Chairman:

Q. That is what I have been trying to get at?—A. Yes.

Q. Well, go on?—A. In the division of Windsor where I live, the distillery has increased its capacity very much within the last few years, and there was a demand for a greater number of officers. We have there I think fourteen officers altogether, and some of the applicants for positions now are men who have not yet passed the Civil Service examination. As a consequence they come in at $500 a year.

Q. As temporary officers?—A. Yes, as temporary officers, and we have a good deal of difficulty in keeping them at that figure. Some of them have effected an exchange from our service to that of the Customs and the latter, although the salary is small at the beginning, is so constituted that at Windsor there is a good deal of overtime to be made by Customs officers in attending to boats and trains. The consequence is that most of the landing waiters at Windsor are able to earn from $600 and this with their overtime is augmented to about $900. The consequence is we have lost a couple of our men. They have had influence enough to get removed from our service to the Customs, and consequently we have been repeatedly put to the disadvantage of having to get other men. They, as a rule, are in the same position with respect to the Civil Service Examination. I could mention four or five men that we have got in the last four or five years, of whom only one had passed the Civil Service examination. We had a case of a young man in our service at Kingston who went through our examinations and passed the special class examination and almost immediately afterwards left to take up employment with a manufacturing firm on account of the better terms offered to him. It was a larger salary than we could give without his waiting to climb up. So you see there are influences that attract young men, and the effect is increasing. The reason that we have so few men who are qualified, who have passed the first examination, is that there are attractions for bright young men of some education across the border in the city of Detroit. Most of our bright young men go over there and they are not available to the Canadian Government service. I thought it would perhaps be as well to mention these points.

The CHAIRMAN.—Mr. Frankland and gentlemen, I thank you on behalf of the Commission for the information you have laid before us. As I already said, we are very glad to have met you, and if upon reflection you find that there is anything additional you wish to bring to our notice we shall be very glad to receive it.

Mr. ALEXANDER.—We thank the Commission very heartily for the very courteous and kind manner in which they have heard us.

Witness retired.

Mr. R. C. JAMIESON, Toronto, called and sworn and examined.

By the Chairman:

Q. How long have you been in the service?—A. Since July 1, 1877.

Q. You are chief officer in charge at Gooderham & Worts' distillery?—A. Not of Gooderham & Worts', of the general distillery, and second officer at Gooderham & Worts'. •

Q. What do you call the general distillery?—A. The general distillery is a distillery that got its license in July 20, 1906, for manufacturing spirits from syrup obtained from the refuse of beet roots.

By Mr. Fyshe:

Q. Whose company is it?—A. It is a company organized by the several distilleries, including Gooderham & Worts, Walker's and others.

Q. Gooderham & Worts' and Walker's are both interested in it?—A. Yes. The chief at Gooderham & Worts' distillery, Mr. Gerald, is in England at the present time, and before leaving he requested me to appear for him.

By the Chairman:

Q. Have you a memorial to present?—A. There was a memorial gotten up by the distillery officers and tobacco officers in the provinces of Ontario and Quebec. They got up this petition before they thought there would be concerted action on the part of the various officers in the respective divisions. This petition covers about the same ground—I will show it to you in a minute—as I think has been taken by the collectors whom you have just had before you. The petition is signed by forty-seven officers and the addition of the name of my chief, Mr. Gerald, would make forty-eight or about one-seventh of the total outside service of the Dominion. You have also a letter from Mr. Gerald dealing with the points touched on in the petition.

Q. You say in your petition that the work you perform in these distilleries is very often done amidst disagreeable surroundings?—A. I cannot say that in regard

29a—26½

to the distillery of Gooderham & Worts or the general distillery, but I have been informed that in some places the surroundings are not very pleasant. However, I cannot say that from my own knowledge.

Q. You are given to understand that with respect to other places?—A. I am given to understand that.

Q. But as to your own knowledge?—A. As far as I am concerned everything is in order in the distilleries in which I work.

Q. We have heard from the collectors that the hours of work are from eight until six?—A. Yes, sir.

Q. But you represent that in order to be at the distillery at the appointed hour you have to get up early in the morning?—A. Well, some of the officers have to go a long distance. You see a city like Toronto is very different from a small place.

Q. Possibly the officers might live in close proximity to the place they work in?—A. In Toronto they have to travel from one and a half to about two miles to get to their occupation and in the winter months they have to be up by at least half past five in the morning in order to reach the distillery at 7 o'clock. That is taking into account the vicissitudes of the weather, the stopping of street cars and so forth. You can easily understand that.

Q. Most of these points about the duty pay and other matters have already been fully gone over?—A. I do not want to touch on that question at all. I have a statement which I am handing in showing that the cost of supervision amounts to about three-tenths of one per cent. I have also prepared a statement showing the manufactures at the Gooderham & Worts distillery for six periods from July 1, 1901, to March 31, 1907, also a statement of the manufacturing of malt which we supervise and the malt which they manufacture for their own use, also a statement of the manufactures of the general distillery from July 1, 1906, to March 21, 1907, also a statement showing the number of officers employed during those years, the amounts of salary they receive, and the percentage that represents of the duty levied on the manufactured goods during those periods.

(Statement handed in and filed as exhibit.)

Q. You have been twenty years in the service?—A. Yes, sir.

Q. You are a special class excise man?—A. I am a special class excise man. Let me point out that in the period 1901-2 at Gooderham & Worts' distillery there was manufactured 838,297·65 proof gallons spirits and there were manufactured 605,100 lb. malt. The duty on the spirits was $1,592,765.54. The duty on malt was $9,076.50. The total duty together amounted to $1,601,842.04. In regard to salaries, the officers employed in that year numbered eight, and they got $9,500. That included the duty pay.

Q. The percentage of salaries in comparison with that of duty was 59/100ths of one per cent?—A. For the six periods I have mentioned the aggregate duty was $17,175,-053.23.

Q. One of the results of this statement is that the total duty has about doubled and the percentage of the salaries has about halved. It has gone from 59/100 to 27/100ths?—A. Yes, the average of the six years is 34/100ths. There is another statement that the bottling stamps nearly paid the whole cost of supervision.

Q. That is a detail that will not be washed out?—A. It is just as well to show it anyway.

Q. The statement about the bottling stamps does not enter into your salary?—A. I do not want to press the matter. The total salaries paid amounted to $59,413.

Q. About one-half could be covered by the bottling stamps?—A. Yes.

Q. Is there anything particular arising out of the work of these distilleries with which you are personally so well acquainted that you want to bring before our notice besides the discomfort experienced?—A. The only thing is in regard to the work done. A person not in the service might say so and so is at the distillery, but they do not y understand the work that has to be done. There is also a statement here showing the bookkeeping is a different system and the calculations——

Q. We know that?—A. You will understand that; you have been in the service. ı have heard about the superannuation also from the collectors.

Q. We know all about that?—A. Well, there is nothing more that I have to say in matter than what you fully understand.

Q. Our time is rather limited, but if you think that you have not explained matters ficiently or that we have not received sufficient information send us another state-nt?—A. I am pleased to learn, gentlemen, that you understand the business so well l that the collectors have explained matters so thoroughly. This has left me little ʉy because I tell you gentlemen I did not covet the job of appearing before the Com-sion although I was willing to answer all questions that you might put.

The witness retired.

the Civil Service Commission, Ottawa, Ontario:

The memorial of your petitioners of the Inland Revenue Service humbly showeth, ıt the salaries at present paid them are totally inadequate, owing to the increased t of living which is fully 50 per cent greater than when the present schedule was ꜩd.

Rents have increased from 50 to 100 per cent, and foods have advanced in many es to an equal extent. These increases have been going on for many years, with ʀy prospect of a continuation in the future.

Salaries in every walk of life have been increased in keeping with the increased t of living.

That the work and responsibilities of the officers are not understood or recognized they should be.

That the work pertaining to the collection of revenue is done by the outside service, t it is they alone who have the establishing of the charge for duty, that the work ı to be done very often amidst distinctly disagreeable surroundings and not in com-tably furnished offices, that the hours ordinarily are long, from 8 a.m. until 6 p.m. the survey of distilleries the officers are obliged to be on hand at 7 o'clock in the ⸗ning or the work cannot proceed. This fact may be better understood when you lize that means for six months during the year, the officers, in order to reach their rk at this hour, have to arise while it is yet as dark as midnight, breakfast byｦ ıficial light, go out into the storms, ⹁ften the first to break the road—still in dark-м. Married men often having to prepare their own breakfast, or as frequently ⸗urs, hurriedly roll up a lunch to eat after reaching the distillery. The unmarried ᴎn find it very difficult to secure boarding places when they require to have breakfast ꜩed at such an early hour. For this service they are allowed by the department cents per day extra, and this to men who are educated and trained as indeed they ꜩst be, otherwise they would be of no use for the work they are required to do. They ve the care of goods, the duty on which, in some cases, amounts to approximately ten llion dollars, and they have constantly under their care and for which they are re-onsible scores of packages of spirits, each one of which has practically to be given name and followed all through its course of blending, reducing, &c., until finally ꜱposed of by removal from the premises. This requires a great amount of clerical ⸗our and an intricate system of bookkeeping, that the responsibilities in connection th this work are very great, that it is unfair to place men in such positions of trust d perhaps of temptation, on salaries so low that they are financially embarrassed the eater part of their existence, that the sons of these men have not the same chances of ıding openings in business that many others have.

That the great bulk of the revenue is derived from distilleries, tobacco factories. ꜩar factories and malt houses.

That the cost of surveying these places does not exceed probably three-tenths of one per cent of the duty established and collected.

That in the case of distilleries the cost is almost nil, as the revenue derived from bottling stamps is almost sufficient to pay for officers' salaries.

That the Government's interest in distilleries is about three-fourths and that of the manufacturer one-fourth.

That the Government's share, less the small cost of supervision, is all clear profit, whilst the manufacturer has to pay the cost of all raw materials, the expense of the different processes, the cost of labour and all other incidentals necessary to place the goods on the market.

That in malt houses, tobacco factories and cigar factories, the interest of the Government is about one-half.

We respectfully ask for an increase in salaries sufficient to equalize the increased cost of living, and that such increase be not paid in increments of five per cent, but in a lump sum.

That for the purpose of superannuation, where an officer is in receipt of 'duty pay,' and which is virtually part of his salary, that his superannuation be based on these two amounts.

That the Superannuation Act be so changed, that in case of the death of an officer before superannuation, his heirs be entitled to an amount equal to the allowance that would have been paid him had he been superannuated for one year, and to such other relief as in the opinion of the Commission should be granted under the circumstances.

And your petitioners, as in duty bound, will ever pray, &c.

(Signed)   (Signed)

ROBT. C. JAMIESON,   GEO. TAYLOR,
W. T. GRAHAM,   A. EGENER,
A. COULTER,   N. MARTIN,
L. B. HURST,   JOHN E. GOW,
C. H. BISSELL,   J. B. WHITE,
WILLIAM BYRNE,   P. M. KEOGH,
GEO. S. KEELER,   G. A. BAYARD,
E. A. McPHERSON,   A. F. BRAIN,
A. JONES,   A. R. ADAM,
W. W. S. HOWARD,   JNO. BRENNAN,
B. J. DOYLE,   J. P. DAVELUY,
T. J. O'LEARY,   TIMOTHY RALSTON,
D. M. CAMERON,   H. OLIVIER,
W. H. GERALD,   N. J. D. BERNARD,
A. B. MACDONALD,   A. DESAULNIERS,
GEO. BOUTEILLER,   E. MILLIN,
GEO. H. McARTHUR,   WM. J. SCULLION,
F. D. CUMMIFORD,   M. HUGHES,
R. J. BERGERON,   N. J. D. BERNARD,
J. W. CAHILL,   DAVID MURRAY,
J. E. FALCONER,   W. DAWSON,
D. H. PETRIMOULX,   A. T. COWIE,
D. J. BRENNAN,   GEO. W. WOODWARD.
J. D. DUMAINE,

from July 1, 1901, to March 31, 1901, also the spirits manufactured by the General Distilling Co., from July 1, 1906, to March 31, 1907. This statement also shows the gross salaries including Duty Pay of the Officers employed in these Surveys, also Cost of bottling labels used in bottling spirits for the same periods.

Periods Date.	Manufacturer.	Spirits Manufactured. Proof Galls.	Malt Manufactured. Lb	Duty.	Total Duty.	Officers employed on Survey.	Gross Salaries of Officers including duty pay.	Percentage of salaries in comparison with account duty.	Cost of Bottling Labels actually used in Bottling Spirits.
				$ cts.	$ cts.		$ cts.		$ cts.
1901-1902	G. & W. Duty	83,629,765		1,592,765 54	1,601,842 04	8	9,500 00	·59 p.c.	2,411 25
1901-1902	G. & W. Malt House		605,100	9,076 50					
1902-1903	G. & W. Duty	87,352,738		1,659,701 93	1,666,279 28	8	9,583 72	·57 "	3,388 49
1902-1903	G. & W. Malt House		438,450	6,577 35					
1903-1904	G. & W. Duty	163,218,444		101,150 44	3,117,960 19	8	9,740 00	·31 "	4,216 99
1903-1904	G. & W. Malt House		1,120,650	16,809 75					
1904-1905	G. & W. Duty	191,574,300		3,686,111 70	3,665,763 10	8	10,380 91	·28 "	4,421 98
1904-1905	G. & W. Malt House		1,976,760	29,651 40					
1905-1906	G. & W. Duty	199,404,698		3,788,689 26	3,818,025 21	8 and 1 for 2 mos.	11,162 50	·29 "	6,544 24
1905-1906	G. & W. Malt House		1,965,730	39,335 95					
July 1, 1906, to March 31	General Duty	114,799,254		2,181,185 88	3,305,183 41	July 1, 1906, to March 31, 1907.	9,050 00	·27 "	5,906 72
1907	G. & W. Malt House	58,202,354	1,210,190	1,105,844 73 18,152 85		9			
					17,175,053 23		59,427 13	·34 p.c.	26,889 67

STATEMENT showing cost of supervision of Distillery, &c., and cost of Bottling Labels actually used in Bottling Spirits at the price charged by the Department to the Manufacturer.

Period Date.	Gross Salaries of officers including Duty Pay.	Cost of Bottling Labels actually used in Bottling Spirits.	Percentage that cost of Bottling Labels are to Salaries, &c.
	$ cts.	$ cts.	
1901-1902	9,500 00	2,411 25	25·38 p.c.
1902-1903	9,593 72	·3,388 49	35·31 p.c.
1903-1904	9,740 00	4,216 99	43·29 p.c.
1904-1905	10,380 91	4,421 88	42·59 p.c.
1905-1906	11,162 50	6,544 24	53·62 p.c.
July 1, 1906 to March 31, 1907	9,050 00	5,906 72	65·26 p.c.
	59,427 13	26,889 57	45·24 p.c.

Mr. DONALD MCPHERSON, Hamilton, called, sworn and examined.

By the Chairman :

Q. You are in charge of Tuckett's tobacco factory at Hamilton?—A. Yes, sir.

Q. How long have you been in the service ?—A. Thirty-five years on the first of March last.

Q. What is your present grade in the service ?—A. Special class excise man.

Q. What salary do you get ?—A. $1,500 and $200 duty pay.

Q. You could not get any more under the present arrangement?—A. No, sir, I believe I am $100 above what I ought to have.

Q. How long have you enjoyed that remuneration ?—A. Since 1892.

Q. Then in the last fifteen years you have got nothing ?—A. No increase.

Q. Have you brought a statement with you ?—A. I have a statement showing the accrued revenue at that establishment.

Q. How many of you are on duty in the factory ?—A. One only.

(Statement handed in and filed as exhibit.)

Q. This extends over a period of years ?—A. Five years.

Q. It is an average of about $600,000 a year ?—A. Exactly.

Q. You, yourself are there alone supervising that factory ?—A. Yes, supervising that factory.

Q. What are your daily hours there ?—A. My daily hours are fixed from 8 o'clock to 6 o'clock, but the peculiar system prevailing in that factory makes it much easier for me than is generally the case. I get away at between four to five o'clock.

Q. Do they cease manufacturing about 4 o'clock and go into their bookkeeping or how can you get away ?—A. It is not necessary for us to supervise the manufacture. It is merely taking care of the warehouse and seeing such raw material as are brought into it. They want to get at their own work and do not want to be bothered with us.

Q. They want to get at their own work and so you get released ?—A. I get released.

Q. That is rather exceptional ?—A. Very. In the factory of Sir Wm. Macdonald in Montreal the officers stay until 6 o'clock.

Q. Then you have been in other places besides Hamilton ?—A. I have been pretty well all over those two provinces.

Q. And you have been thirty-five years in the service ?—A. Yes, sir.

By Mr. Fyshe :

Q. You must have started pretty young ?—A. Sixteen years.

By the Chairman :

Q. Then like Mr. Gerald you have grown up with the service?—A. Yes, sir, actly. I would just explain that the duties of an officer in charge of the manufac- 'e of tobacco are intricate in this way: the law has established a standard pound of v leaf tobacco which must contain 90 per cent solid matter and 10 per cent moisture. 'w it is utterly impossible for it to come at exactly that stage so the officers have to ke tests and a slight variation in their work would be very considerable for or 'inst the government. The work, therefore, has to be done accurately. Then when nufactured tobacco is exported from the country the Government returns a rebate 12½ cents a pound from the actual raw leaf contained in it. Now it is necessary the officer to know how to demonstrate that because all tobaccos do not contain same percentage of raw leaf. Some contain fifty, others fifty-four, and others as h as ninety and ninety-three per cent.

By Mr. Fyshe :

Q. Do they not sometimes get rebates on what they have not paid duty on ?—A. 'o not understand just what you mean.

Q. I understand that in certain cases where they import tobacco for the manu- ture of cigars they cut out part of the tobacco ?—A. That is what they call cuttings. ey get a refund there but I am not as familiar with that end of the business as I 're not had much to do with that. My branch is the plug and cut tobacco. I simply nted to bring before you the onerous duties performed by an officer in charge of a 'acco factory so that we might demonstrate our work to be quite as responsible as ' distillery work.

The CHAIRMAN.—That is all right. I will say to you as I have said to other gen. men if you feel that you have not covered the ground thoroughly send us in a :morandum and we will be very glad to append it to your statement.

The witness retired.

'ATEMENT showing the amount of Excise Duty accruing at the Tobacco Manufactory of the Geo. E. Tuckett & Son Company, Limited, at Hamilton, from July 1, 1902, to June 30, 1907, each period of 12 months shown as an item.

Year 1902-1903.	Lbs	$	cts.
w Leaf Tobacco Duty Paid		142,021	56
nufactured Tobacco Warehoused			
Manufactory	1,017,027½	254,256	87
nufactured Tobacco Duty Paid			
Manufactory	198,916	49,727	00
arettes Warehoused Ex Factory	2,000	6	00
arettes Duty Paid Ex Factory	11,212,800	33,638	40
nufactured Tobacco Duty Paid			
Warehouse	316,964½	79,241	12
		558,890	95

Year 1903–1904.	Lb.	$ cts.
Raw Leaf Tobacco Duty Paid	....	160,512 16
Manufactured Tobacco Warehoused....	....	....
Ex Manufactory....	1,164,865½	291,216 37
Manufactured Tobacco Duty Paid	....	....
Ex Manufactory......	283,865½	70,966 38
Cigarettes Warehoused Ex Factory...........................	12,900	36 70
Cigarettes Duty Paid Ex Factory............................	8,222,700	24,668 10
Manufactured Tobacco Duty Paid........	....	....
Ex Warehouse...............	351,984	87,996 00
		635,397 71

Year 1904–1905.	Lb.	$ cts.
Raw Leaf Tobacco Duty Paid.....................	....	153,404 22
Manufactured Tobacco Warehoused...........................	....	....
Ex Manufactory........	1,079,782½	269,945 62
Manufactured Tobacco Duty Paid.....	....	....
Ex manufactory..	278,304½	89,576 13
Cigarettes Warehoused Ex Factory........	140,000	420 00
Cigarettes Duty Paid Ex Factory.......	6,420,400	19,261 290
Manufactured Tobacco Duty Paid...	....	....
Ex Warehouse.....	305,391	76,347 75
		588,954 92

Year 1905–1906.	Lb.	$ cts.
Raw Leaf Tobacco Duty Paid.........:.......	....	142,758 32
Manufactured Tobacco Warehoused.........	....	....
Ex Manufactury....	979,253	244,813 25
Manufactured Tobacco Duty Paid.......... ...	....	....
Ex Manufactory...................	328,354	82,088 50
Cigarettes Warehoused Ex Factory.....	25,500	76 50
Cigarettes Duty Paid Ex Factory...................... ..	5,909,600	17,728 80
Manufactured Tobacco Duty Paid.....	....	....
Ex Warehouse...............	281,216	70,304 00
		557,769 37

Year 1906–1907.	Lb.	$ cts.
Raw Leaf Tobacco Duty Paid	....	156,446 40
Manufactured Tobacco Warehoused.......................	....	....
Ex Manufactory...................	1,003,369½	250,847 37
Manufactured Tobacco Duty Paid...	....	....
Ex Manufactory.....................	379,085	94,771 25
Cigarettes Warehoused Ex Factory................	5,000	15 00
Cigarettes Duty Paid Ex Factory....	9,846,400	29,539 20
Manufactured Tobacco Duty Paid....	....	....
Ex Warehouse...............	247,618	61,904 50
		593,523 72

WALKERVILLE, October 24, 1907.

ıurable

ı Board of Civil Service Commissioners,
     Ottawa, Ont.

.ᴇᴍᴇɴ,—I notice by the paper that you have fixed the 31st instant as being
ıy upon which you would receive memoranda regarding the condition of the
'ice.

are a few points which have come particularly under my observation during
ᴇw years to which I beg leave to call your attention, when considering this
  having been connected with the service for the past thirty years, my obser-
e entirely from practical experience and more especially related to the dis-
nch of the Inland Revenue Service, being now the officer in charge of Messrs.
ılker & Son's distillery at Walkerville.

ᴇs myself there are twelve officers connected with the supervision of the dis-
ıh one of whom being responsible for, and having under his charge and care,
ılar department of the distillery at which he is located.

ıirits, as soon as manufactured, are charged for duty at the rate of one
  ⁹⁰⁄₁₀₀ dollar per proof gallon, and as there is being manufactured at this
ıbout three million gallons of spirits in a season, the amount of duty levied
ıtillery· in a year amounts to about five million seven hundred thousand
.ll spirits, as soon as manufactured, are prepared for warehouse for maturing
ıither in tanks, vats or barrels.   There are about four hundred tanks and
e premises, all of which are full most of the time, also nearly two hundred
ıarrels in use all the time.

ıock of spirits at present on the premises is over seven million gallons, every
ıhich is under the direct control of the officers at the distillery. ·

are about three hundred barrels of spirits shipped each day, and about one
ıases.   In a season's run about forty million pounds of grain are used.

. given you this information in order that you may have some comprehension
ıme of work that is necessary in the handling and control of this enormous
f spirits during the different stages through which it must pass before being
he market, and also to give you an idea of the responsibility placed upon the
  seeing that all spirits are properly accounted for, and it is only by the
ıligence and vigilance on the part of the officers that this result is accom-

ıajority of the officers at the distillery are qualified officers in the service,
ȿed some of the prescribed examinations, but I find that lately those securing
ıt are not of the younger class, but rather are men who have spent some
ıme other line with no special training, and I am informed by Members of
; from Essex that it is impossible to get young educated men to accept posi-
e service at the small initial salary offered, with the ordinary fair salary as
ɑ after years of study and training.   I cannot help but notice that the ordi-
ɴgmen around the distillery are in receipt of a larger wage than the last
ʀs appointed to the supervision of the distillery by the Government, and as
;ȿ will not have an opportunity of writing on a Promotion examination until
t least, they will not be in line for promotion for about two years from the
ıntered the service.

I am on the subject of comparing salaries of the workingmen with our
ᴇrs, I would like to call your attention to the great disparity between the
the employees of the Messrs. Walker and the officers of the Government in
sion of the distillery.   One of their salaried employees is in receipt of a
fteen thousand dollars per year.   The other employees are in receipt of from
t thousand dollars per year.   Shipping and correspondence clerks and book-
ım sixteen hundred to twenty-five hundred dollars per year.

Taking all these matters into consideration I think that the initial salary of officers appointed to the Inland Revenue service should be increased and also the maximum of each grade in the service should be increased in order that some attraction may be held out as an inducement of securing young capable men for the service.

A point I would particularly like to emphasize is the fact that two of our officers have lately resigned from the Inland Revenue service to enter the Customs Department, and another is awaiting the opportunity as they have found upon investigation that the examinations prescribed by the Inland Revenue Department call for a higher standard of education than that required by the Customs Department.

If I can be of any service to you towards furnishing further information, or if you desire specific particulars of any of the statements I have made I shall be pleased to hear from you.

As to the increased cost of living in the last few years, no doubt you have had abundance of evidence along this line; we notice the increase here particularly where without exception the advance has been from thirty to fifty per cent, at the same time salaries in all other lines have from absolute necessity been increased.

It is not anticipated that a rate per cent of increase applicable to all ranks of the service would be justifiable from the standpoint of the Commission, but if I were allowed to suggest a manner of increase, a graduated scale appeals most to me, the higher percentages being alloted to the classes receiving the minimum pay at the present time and a descending scale applicable to the higher grades.

I will append to this letter a list of the officers at the distillery, showing salary and length of time in the service.

Your obedient servant,

G. A. BOUTEILLER,

Officer in charge,

Hiram Walker & Sons, Limited, Distillery.

LIST of Inland Revenue Officers engaged in the supervision of Messrs. Hiram Walker & Sons' Distillery at Walkerville, Ont.

—	Time of Service.	Annual Salary.
George Bouteiller, Chief Officer	30 years.	$ 1,800
George H. McArthur, Asst. Chief Officer	6 "	1,250
John Brennan, Accountant	21 "	1,400
A. F. Brain	12 "	1,200
Robert Thomas	16 "	1,200
G. A. Bayard	18 "	1,200
J. E. Falconer	31 "	850
J. W. Cahill	20 "	850
A. R. Adam	7 "	680
P. M. Keogh, Deputy Collector Class " B "	28 "	1,000
R. J. Bergeron	1 "	600
F. D. Cummiford	6 months.	500
D. H. Petrimoulx	6 "	500

Mr. WILBUR HENDERSON, Toronto, called, sworn and examined.

By the Chairman:

Q. You are a deputy collector, class A?—A. I am.

Q. You have been twenty-four years in the service?—A. Twenty-four years on the 8th last March.

Witness submitted a memorial which was read and filed as exhibit.

*SIONAL PAPER No. 29a

Q. There are about five deputy collectors concerned in this matter?—A. Yes, five.

Q. The trouble arises in this way, that the number of special class excise men is :ed?—A. Yes, the number is now thirty.

Q. You cannot get into the charmed circle of thirty until somebody dies or retires? The deputy collectors are not brought in.

Q. Although they have passed the special examination?—A. When it became my to be put on the special list I was a deputy collector. Deputy collectors cannot get ils special class list even if they have passed the special class examination.

By Mr Fyshe:

Q. Why?—A. Because they are debarred.

Q. Is there any special reason for debarring them?—A. Deputy collectors are sup- d to be in rank for the collectorship, which he does not always get.

Q. But being enrolled in the special class list would not debar him from succeed- :o the collectorship?—A. No, but you are struck off the list.

By the Chairman:

Q. Is it not the fact that deputy collectors can be appointed without examination? They can and are.

Q. Deputy collectors, preventive officers and inspectors are the three classes of le in your service who are appointed politically and without examination?—A. 'entive officers, deputy collectors and inspectors? Well, I could not say all.

Q. The preventive officers and the deputy collectors in the Inland Revenue service be appointed without examination and are?—A. Deputy collectors, class B, sir. I in class A.

Q. Is class A a promotion after examination from class B?—A. No, sir.

Q. Then after serving in class B, without an examination you can get into class -A. I could.

Q. And that is done?—A. They appoint them straight without their having been lass B.

Q. Then the deputy collectors being appointed without examination and the excise being appointed after examination, the idea is that the special class excise men l be recruited from the excise men who do not come in politically?—A. From those pass the examination. Well, I passed the special class examination.

Q. But as deputy collector you were originally passed without examination?—A. lased every examination in the service.

Q. After you had come in?—A. I passed the Qualifying examination before I was)inted an exciseman. I passed my first-class examination. Then I was appointed -class exciseman. Afterwards I passed the special class examination and was ap- ited assistant accountant, and subsequently I was appointed deputy collector, class So I was appointed to nothing I had not passed the examination in.

Q. You are a deputy collector, class A?—A. I am.

Q. Are you not available for further examination?—A. I am not. I have passed he examinations, but I would refer you to what this memorial draws attention to a certain class of officers are getting more salaries than deputy collectors.

Q. Let us commence at the beginning. Deputy collectors are exempt, under the l Service Act, from examination?—A. Yes.

Q. You are one of the few deputy collectors who began at the bottom and worked : way up after passing the necessary examination?—A. I am.

Q. There are about five deputy collectors in the same position?—A. There are.

Q. How did they come to make you a deputy collector instead of your passing ugh the grades of excise men?—A. I was an excise man.

Q. How did they come to make you a deputy collector when those positions are rved for political appointments?—A. Well, I got the appointment.

Q. The deputy collectors came in originally without examination?—A. Not all of them.

Q. There are five that have not come in without examination?—A. There are five that have not.

Q. With the exception of the five the others have all come in without examination?—A. I cannot answer for the Government, sir.

Q. How did you yourself come to be made a deputy collector when that class is reserved for political appointments?—A. The chief inspector, Mr. Godson, heard that somebody else was going to be appointed and he came and said to me: 'I hear they are going to make an appointment. You go to work and get this appointment yourself.'

Q. I wish you had said this at the beginning?—A. Your questions did not lead to it.

Q. Then you were made a deputy collector because the inspector had a dread of the politician?—A. Well, I do not know as to that.

Q. He said to you 'Come and we will make you a deputy collector, because we do not want another man to come in'?—A. That is practically it.

By Mr. Fyshe:

Q. You were a political appointment?—A. You may call it so if you choose.

The CHAIRMAN.—No, because he had passed all the examinations.

The WITNESS.—We people want our salaries to be in proportion to our duties and our standing in the service. The deputy collector in my position is the next man to the collector, but there is another officer in the division below me who receives more salary than I do.

By Mr. Fyshe:

Q. Who is that?—A. A special class excise man. He receives $300 more than I do.

Q. Yes, but is he not a specialist?—A. He is no more a specialist than I am. I am a specialist in all branches or surveys, while he will only be conversant with the particular survey that he has charge of.

By the Chairman:

Q. He has passed the examination and has got into the favoured list?—A. He is in the favoured list, but I have to go over his work. I have to check his statements and all that, and whenever the collector is out or goes away I have to act in his place.

By Mr. Fyshe:

Q. You are this man's superior officer?—A. I am his superior officer. Yet I have an officer under me receiving more salary than I am paid.

By the Chairman:

Q. Do not all the men that pass from excise men to special class excise men get into the list when vacancies occur?—A. Yes, they get into the list.

Q. What I want to know is this: if you had not been side tracked into this deputy collectorship you would no doubt by this time have been on the special class list?—A. Decidedly so. Then, too, I claim that a deputy collector should rank higher than a special class excise man, and be paid more in proportion to his duties and responsibilities.

The witness retired.

TORONTO, September 21, 1907.

To the Honourable
    The Board of Civil Service Commission.

GENTLEMEN,—Believing you are prepared to receive suggestions in your difficult work of reforming the Civil Service, we presume to lay before you a grievance of

puty collectors Class A, who hold special class certificates, and who, thereby, show
ecial fitness for the duties pertaining to their respective offices.

At present, such deputy collectors are receiving a less salary than that received
special class officers at certain surveys, apart from the additional salary received by
ch special class officers under the regulations, while by such regulations the deputy
llectors holding special class certificates are debarred from being appointed to such
)re lucrative positions.

We maintain that officers holding special class certificates in the service, should,
in other walks in life, have such special fitness recognized by increased remuneration
·r their co-labourers, not holding such higher grade of certificate.

This principle was formerly recognized by the departments, but of recent years, it
ms to have been ignored and the deputy collectors holding special class certificates
·e received no special recognition.

We feel that all deputy collectors who have given such time to study and such
˖ial attention to all the details of their duties as to enable them to pass the pre-
bed examination for special class certificates should be classified as such.

We have the honour to be, gentlemen,

Your obedient servants,

(Signed) W. HENDERSON,

WALTER A. THRASHER,

Signed on behalf of deputy collectors, Special Class A.

Mr. W. J. HAYWARD, London, called, sworn and examined.

By the Chairman:

Q. You are inspector of weights and measures?—A. Yes, for the Windsor division.

Q. Where are your headquarters?—A. At London.

Q. What is the extent of your division?—A. It comprises eleven counties. It runs
n about Brantford west and north up to the Georgian Bay.

Q. Have you any other duties to discharge besides the inspection of weights and
ᴸsures?—A. No.

Q. You have nothing to do with gas?—A. No.

Q. What is your salary now?—A. $1,600.

Q. How long have you had the $1,600?—A. One year last July.

Q. And what salary had you before that?—A. $1,500.

Q. How long were you at $1,500?—A. Two years.

Q. And then before that you had $1,400?—A. $1,400 before that.

Q. How long did you remain at $1,400?—A. I think three or four years, I almost
ᵍet.

Q. You entered the service in 1879?—A. Yes.

Q. Twenty-eight years ago?—A. Twenty-eight years ago.

Q. What was your salary when you entered the service?—A. $1,000.

Q. In twenty-eight years you have received $600 increase?—A. Yes.

Q. The greater part of it has been obtained comparatively recently?—A. Yes.

Q Are you continually on the road?—A Not since I have been moved to London.
ℓ two divisions of Windsor and London were amalgamated about ten years ago, and
ᵖas removed from Windsor to London. Since then my duties have been principally
ce duties, but I have attended to the factories in London myself. I have no resi-
ᴸt assistant there.

Q. You also have sub-inspectors at St. Thomas and Brantford, have you not?—A.
, at Aylmer, Brantford and Chatham. Another one lives about thirty miles from
ᴸdon; he does the London city work.

Q. Are there any scale factories in your division?—A. Yes, there is a small one in London, one in Aylmer, and one in Chatham.

Q. Where is Fairbanks' place?—A. It is not in our branch. That is in Toronto.

Q. You stamp the scales in the factories before they go out?—A. Certainly.

Q. And then you go around to the different establishments. How often do you do that?—A. Whenever we are called upon, that is in the factories.

Q. And with respect to the shops and general warehouses?—A. Every two years we inspect certain scales, such as coal scales and grain elevator scales. The inspection of them is done annually.

Q. Who is Mr. Hughes?—A. He lives in Chatham.

Q. He is an assistant inspector?—A. Yes.

Q. Who is Mr Liddle?—A. Mr. Liddle is a recent appointment. He lives in Aylmer.

Q. Mr. Hughes does the chief part of the travelling, does he?—A. No, not so much. Mr. Coughill and Mr. Thomas do the chief part of the travelling for each of the separate counties.

Q. You simply get your out of pocket expenses when travelling, do you not?—A. Yes, that is all.

Q. I suppose some of these places that require to be inspected are not very comfortable?—A. Indeed they are not.

Q. When you were first appointed there was a per diem allowance for travelling was there not?—A. No, there never was.

Q. Not in the weights and measures branch?—A. No.

Q. Do you think it would be an inducement to go out more frequently on inspection duty if the present system of paying expenses were done away with and a per diem allowance adopted in its place?—A. I do not think it would be.

Q. I suppose you lose money on your travelling expenses, do you not?—A. I do not think we lose a great deal.

Q. And you experience a certain amount of discomfort?—A. Yes.

Q. Would you not perform inspection duty more often and more vigorously if you had a per diem allowance instead of the present system?—A. I do not think so. I was eighteen years on the road working as assistant inspector and I have had a good deal of experience as far as the discomforts of travelling are concerned.

Q. Have you any memorial to present?—A. Yes. With the assistance of Mr. Freeland, the inspector at Hamilton, we got up a paper which contains a very full statement of what we would like to present to you. I now produce that statement.

Statement read and filed as exhibit.

By the Chairman:

Q. As I have already said we have met your colleagues at other places. Whatever evidence you have to bring forward here should be in relation to local circumstances which may differ from those in other cities. I suppose there is not much difference between Toronto and Montreal in regard to the cost of commodities?—A. Except in regard to rent. There is a little difference in regard to rent.

Q. Now you have dealt with the question of travelling. Gentlemen in your position frequently have to drive through the country, over bad roads and through mud and snow and have to put up with many discomforts. You have set down the disadvantages of the occupation very strenuously. In view of all the circumstances, do you think the present system of simply paying out of pocket expenses is good enough?—A. I think as far as travelling expenses are concerned the contingent account is sufficient to pay what they incur and they give a fair account of what they have expended.

Q. You have gone into the question of the department being self-sustaining. Carrying that out to its logical conclusion you would think, I suppose, that the Customs officers should take all the Customs revenue. You base your ground for increased pay upon the fact that the weights and measures branch, conjointly with the

NAL PAPER No. 29a

electric light branch, more than pays its way. But you would not argue that
toms officers should divide the whole Customs revenue among them because
a surplus, would you ?—A. Not at all.
Why should you not base your claim upon the work you have been doing
han the revenue you receive ?—A. I thought I put it pretty strongly what our
rere.
But you branch off into the question of the revenue that is derived ?—A. Well,
a great many of the weights and measures officers also inspect gas and electric

I may say that the Commission are very much impressed by the facts in regard
rannuation and the system of gratuities. We have heard statements on those
i so universally that there is no occasion to go into them now. Have you any-
lore you would like to say to us ?—A. Not very much. Of course, it is no
ering into the question as to the increased cost of living except that we cor-
i what has been said in that regard by other branches of the service and we
be treated on the same basis as may be granted to them. I would like to say
lf of the assistant inspectors that they should have some classification. At pre-
y are not classified and we think they should rank as high at any rate as junior
:lass clerks. We have some very good officers—although like other branches of
rice we have some poor ones too—and we think that the assistant inspectors
:ought into closer contact with the public should be men of good education and
siness tact and should have a practical knowledge of the mechanism of scales.
have not got these attributes they are not fit to be assistant inspectors. If they
:ss them they should receive better compensation in future than they have in

? witness retired.

R. J. MILLIGAN, Toronto, called and sworn, and examined.

:ness produced a memorial on behalf of the inspector and assistant inspectors
its and measures, Toronto division, which was read and filed as exhibit.

By the Chairman :
You are an assistant inspector?—A. I am assistant inspector of weights and
:s.
How long have you been in the service?—A. Twenty-one years less a month

What salary do you get ?—A. I get $800.
How long have you been receiving that amount ?—A. About four years.
What did you receive before that ?—A. $750. Originally it was $500 and went
650 and then to $700, next to $750 and now I am getting $800.
Since your appointment twenty-one years ago you have jumped from $500 to
-A. Yes, I have jumped from $500.
Taking it chronologically ?—A. It is a long time though. Considering the
[have had to perform I should think that if I were receiving about $1,600 I
ie about paid.
In twenty-one years you have only had an increase of salary of $300 ?—A. Yes.
You have heard what Mr. Hayward has said ?—A. I have.
Do you agree with what he says ?—A. Yes, I agree. _
Have you had much trouble in your work ?—A. A great many years ago but
ily. My work has been largely confined to office work during the last few
id factory work. I have had to oversee our office during the last few years and
—27

I also do factory work. I never did travel regularly ; I have taken periodical trips that is all.

Q. I see that during last year you only got $17 travelling expenses, so practically you had but little travelling?—A. I had very little.

Q. Do you agree with Mr. Hayward in his approval of the present method of paying travelling expenses?—A. I do. Of course, board is getting higher all the time, and that will increase travelling expenses. But there is one thing I cannot see, and that is why the assistant inspector of weights and measures should have all the vouchers. I think his word is as good as an hotelkeeper.

Q. Do you not think it would be better if you were paid a certain sum each day while you were on inspection duty?—A. I think so, yes. It is a great waste of time having to wait for two vouchers for a fifty-cent meal. Then, there is your time making out your vouchers and keeping track of it in your subsidiary contingent account. If the assistant inspector got so much a day for expenses, he would be better off.

Q. With a reasonable amount allowed him, he would not be out of pocket?—A. Not with a reasonable amount. As it is now, a man is considerably out of pocket.

Q. And that happens with gentlemen who are enjoying a salary of only $800?—A. My car fare costs me now more than I can afford. It has got to be quite an item.

Q. How much do you pay for rent?—A. Thirty dollars a month. If it were not for my family living with me, I could not support it.

Q. How many children have you?—A. Three at home, and a son and daughter away. Were it not for them, I could not live.

Q. How old are you?—A. I will be seventy years old next month.

Q. You are nine months older than I am?—A. And I was born in Toronto, on York Street.

Q. And lived here all the days of your life?—A. Very much, except for some time in Chicago.

Q. A man of your intelligence and vigour, why did you stay in the service?—A. Simply because I came into the service when I was about forty-eight and, like Micawber, I was waiting for something to turn up.

Q. Something did turn up, but it turned up in the wrong way?—A. I felt very much like throwing the office up five or six times, but I was simply waiting for a good time to come.

Q. Well, I hope the clouds will break?—A. I was going to say this about the difference in the receipts and expenditure. They are gradually getting closer together but the fees that were paid for inspection when I went into the service have dropped 50 to 66⅔ per cent in a great many instances. That would make a great divergence in the expenses in comparison with the revenue.

The witness retired.

Mr. A. T. FREED, Hamilton, called, sworn and examined.

By the Chairman:

Q. How long have you been in the service, Mr. Freed?—A. Between thirteen and fourteen years.

Q. You were a public man before you went in?—A. I was a newspaper man.

Q. What salary are you getting?—A. $1,600.

Q. When you were appointed, what was your salary?—A. $1,400.

Q. Then, in the thirteen years you have only had an increase of $200?—A. Yes.

Q. You are at the maximum as far as the present scale of salaries go?—A. As I understand.

Q. What do you think of the expense of living in Hamilton, as compared with Toronto and Ottawa?—A. I am not in a position to compare Hamilton with Toronto

SESSIONAL PAPER No. 29a

or Ottawa. I think the average cost of living is about 50 per cent higher than it was ten or twelve years ago.

Q. That agrees with the statements made in the other places?—A. I should think that is a fair estimate.

Q. That is to say, that for each of the three first years the scale was about the same, but in the last ten years the increase has been about 50 per cent?—A. I think about that, taking house rent and clothing, food, and other supplies.

Q. How old are you?—A. I shall be seventy-two next month.

Q. You surely did not enter the service with the idea that it was anything in the way of a sinecure?—A. Not altogether, but it was easier than the work I was doing.

Q. Do you travel at all?—A. I do not travel on inspection duty.

Q. You go around in Hamilton, I suppose, seeing the factories and warehouses? —A. When it is necessary to look into things. I have one man in each factory. I have one assistant in the office and three men on the road.

Q. How many factories are there in Hamilton?—A. Two. The Gurney Scale Company and the factory of Burrows, Stewart and Milne.

By Mr. Fyshe:

Q. Do they make weights?—A. All sorts of scales except the fine finished scales.

By the Chairman:

Q. Are there scales sent all over the Dominion?—A. Yes, all over the Dominion. They are the largest manufacturers, I understand, in the Dominion.

Q. Your sphere of usefulness is centered in Hamilton alone?—A. No, I have supervision of seven counties extending from the Niagara frontier to the northern part of Wellington county.

Q. But you have no outside officer. All your officers live in Hamilton?—A. One of them temporarily lives in Wellington county, but I try to keep them centered in Hamilton.

Q. You are not like some of the previous witnesses who have officers at Brantford and other places?—A. No, I have no outlying offices.

Q. You are a man of observation who has been closely identified with public affairs and you have been a leader writer. Have you anything special to say based on our own experience?—A. With your permission I would like to add one or two points to what has been already said.

Q. Certainly?—A. The service in which the outside men, the men who travel, are engaged is to a large extent a dangerous service. For instance, in my own division I have one man who contracted a severe cold. It developed into pneumonia and he died. Another man, a few weeks after that froze his fingers while engaged in inspection duties and was laid up for nearly three months. Another man whilst inspecting a scale in an elevator struck his knee in a dark passage and was laid up for about six weeks.

By Mr. Fyshe:

Q. Did they lose their pay while they were laid up?—A. No, their pay continued. Now the assistant inspectors have to drive in all sorts of weather and are exposed to all sorts of dangers. They have to get down under large scales and get dirt on their clothes and wear their clothes out very quickly. And with all due deference to Mr. Hayward it is an expensive thing travelling. The men must spend more money on the road than they can possibly get back. They must declare that all the money they have spent has been spent in the service of the Government. They are not allowed to put any other items in their account, and if they did the inspector would throw out anything expended in the way of entertainment. We all know that a man cannot travel without spending money. Now the paragraph respecting the service not being self-sustaining was put into Mr. Hayward's report by myself. My reason for putting it there was

29a—27½

this: a short time ago the officers in my division waited upon the then Minister of Inland Revenue, Mr. Brodeur, I think, and told him that they thought they were entitled to an increase of salary. He said they could not get an increase, and he could not hold out any hope of that until the service was made self-sustaining. That was why I inserted that paragraph in the memorial. You asked Mr. Milligan why he remained in the service at inadequate pay. A man who has been in the service for a good many years has lost his grip upon his former profession and he probably could not get back to the old position he held. I could not go back to journalism and make a fair living at it, although I think I am perfectly competent to discharge my present duties. I think that is the reason why men stay in the service. I would strongly urge the restoration of the superannuation system not only in the interests of the officers themselves, but because ministers and deputy ministers are human and they do not like to drive a man out of the service to starve when he has not been allowed to make provision for his old age. A man at the maximum salary given to assistant inspectors cannot provide for his old age on the salary of $800 a year. This is all I wish to say. I entirely approve of every word in the memorial handed in by Mr. Hayward.

By the Chairman:

Q. I might say, Mr. Freed, that in a paper I read at Ottawa before the Canadian Club I advocated the restoration of the Superannuation Act, in fact to extend it if possible so that it might include the widows and orphans of deceased civil servants. It has universally been recommended by the witnesses who have appeared before us that some system of superannuation should be devised?—A. I am not here to speak for myself or the inspectors—we will gratefully take whatever you can see fit to grant us —but we want to speak especially for the assistants who are very much underpaid.

The CHAIRMAN.—Mr. Freed, you are an old newspaper man and you understand these things thoroughly. Our time is rather short and if you think we have omitted any matters or you are under the impression that your evidence needs to be supplemented we shall be glad to receive further information from you.

The witness retired.

INLAND REVENUE, CANADA, WEIGHTS AND MEASURES INSPECTION SERVICE,
TORONTO, September 25, 1907.

To the Board of
    Civil Service Commissioners.

SIRS,—The inspectors and assistant inspectors of the Weights and Measures Service respectfully request your consideration of the following matters:—

1. The scale of salaries was fixed many years ago. Since that time salaries in every other branch of the public service have been advanced, some by yearly statutory increases, some by general benevolent consideration for the public servants. The weights and measures officers alone have been neglected. They have gradually increased the revenue, until, instead of being one-half as great as the expenditure, it now meets three-fourths of the outlay. But the officers who have attained this result have received no consideration; the rates of salaries paid them are those established a quarter of a century ago.

Granting, for the sake of argument, that the salaries were fair salaries when they were fixed, it is manifest that they are not fair salaries now. The cost of living has increased since that time fully 50 per cent. Clothing, rents, provisions, and almost every article necessary to life and comfort, have risen greatly in price; all ordinary salaries and wages have been correspondingly raised. The mechanic who then received $10 a week now gets $15; the labourer who then worked for $1 a day now gets $1.50 to $2. But the assistant inspectors of weights and measures are held down to the salaries paid a quarter of a century ago. They have not shared in the

SESSIONAL PAPER No. 29a

eneral prosperity of the country; on the contrary, that very prosperity, by increasing he cost of living, has made them worse off than they were before.

These officers are hard working men. They are required to work nine hours a ay in summer, and seven hours in winter. In summer they do not confine them-elves to the nine hours. But in order to get the best value out of hired horses and ehicles and make long days, they, while doing country work, work twelve and thir-een hours a day, and have one or two hours' clerical work to do besides and no extra ay for this. They must drive over country roads, through mud or snow, in sum-ner's heat and winter's cold. They must put up with such accommodation as they an find at country houses of entertainment. Their work is hard. For weeks to-:ether when handling iron standards they handle from ten to fifteen tons of weights er day.

Perhaps there is no class of civil servants who come into such close contact with he public the assistant inspectors of weights and measures. They must be intelli-rent men with some tact and good temper. They are required to have a good prac-ical knowledge of scales, and to keep intricate accounts. They are chargeable with heir stamps, and if they make any mistakes they must bear the loss. They are re-luired to give bonds, which shows the Government's appreciation of the responsibility f their positions. And these hard worked men, these skilled mechanics, these ex-»ert clerks, begin with a salary of $500 a year, and may hope after eight or ten or ifteen years to reach a maximum of $800.

They are not even permitted to make provision for their declining years. It rill hardly be asserted that a man with a family can put aside much from a salary uch as has been mentioned; and these deserving officers are denied the benefits of he superannuation system. Those who had been less than ten years on the list were ummarily cut off. The sums they had paid into the fund were returned to them; ut after keeping their money for seven or eight or nine years, the Government did 10t allow them one penny for the interest on it. The thing is not of great importance, ut it illustrates the spirit which has actuated the department in dealing with these fficers.

It is not creditable to the country, that while the revenues are expanding, some f the public servants are so poorly paid that they cannot live in comfort, and can-10t at all provide for their declining years.

Whenever the assistant inspectors of weights and measures have made applica-ion for an increase of salary, the reply has invariably been that this service is not elf-sustaining and until it is, we cannot accede to your request. It never was in-ended that this service should be self-sustaining. It is a preventive service. The Veights and Measures Act for the Dominion of Canada has two objects in view:— t is intended to assure the dealer who uses scales or measures of any kind that they re correct; and to protect the purchasing public against intentional or unintentional rror in the articles by which the purchases are measured. The general public, the urchasing public, has a greater interest in the weights and measures service than 1e dealer has. It receives a greater benefit from it; therefore, it is but reasonable ask that the public shall bear at least a part of the cost of its operation. This ew was held when the measure was introduced, and it was consistently held until ithin a few years. Mr. Brunel, to whom the country is mainly indebted for the orking out of the plan at first, in his report for 1880, said:—' I think it very likely 1at, under the present tariff' (of fees) 'the cost will generally be more than double 1e revenue.' In 1883, Mr. Miall, the then Commissioner, reported receipts of $28,-)0 and expenditures of $56,000; and to that statement he appended the following mment:—' It is hardly expected that this service can be made entirely self-sus-ining, neither is it desirable to render it so.' 'The benefits accrue not alone to ·aders, but to the entire community, which in fairness should be chargeable with proportion of the cost.'

If it be contended now that it ought to be made to pay its way, that end ought to be reached by increasing the fees, not by keeping the employees of the Government at inadequate wages. Does not the Government practically say to the officers of this service:—' We have fixed the fees to be collected at such low rates that the system cannot be self-supporting; therefore we shall not pay you the salaries which in all fairness you ought to have? We will do you an injustice because we have not changed our minds, and intend to reach an end which we did not propose to reach when the service was established.'

The inspection of weights and measures, gas and electric light may fairly be considered one service; they are grouped together in one report; and to some extent they are self-supporting. For the year ending June 30, 1906, the receipts and expenditures on account of these services were as follows:—

	Receipts.	Expenditures.
Weights and measures	$ 72,979.43	$ 91,518.87
Gas inspection	41,439.25	29,063.26
Electric light	35,099.75	8,117.76
	$149,518.43	$128,699.89

So that taking the three inspections together, there is a modest surplus now and not a deficit.

The assistant inspectors are of opinion that they are entitled to a minimum salary of $800 to be raised by an annual increase of $100 up to a maximum salary of $1,200.

The assistant inspectors in the Northwest Territories submit that the cost of living is much more than in Ontario.

It is respectfully submitted that there should be an increase of at least thirty-three and one-third per cent (33⅓%) made to the present schedule of salaries.

It is further submitted—That the gratuity of one or two months pay which is now given to the heirs of deceased officers, is entirely inadequate and it is respectfully recommended and requested that in case of an officer dying while in active service, fifty per cent (50%) of the superannuation allowance he would have been entitled to receive, be paid his widow during her widowhood; and in case of an officer dying after he has been superannuated, a fair proportion of his superannuation allowance should be given his widow during her widowhood.

The inspectors respectfully request that upon application and before appointment of candidates for the position of assistant inspectors, that in addition to his primary examination before the Civil Service examiners, that he should serve three months in a scale factory to get an expert knowledge of his duties.

(Signed) W. G. HAYWARD,
Inspector Works, Windsor Division

TORONTO, ONTARIO, September 25, 1907.

To the Honourable Members of the Civil Service Commission.

GENTLEMEN,—I, Robert J. Milligan, have the honour to appear before your honourable Commission as the appointed representative of the officers of the weights and measures division of Toronto, respecting the memorial annexed.

The division comprises the city of Toronto and counties of York, Ontario, Peel, Grey, Simcoe, Muskoka and Dufferin.

We respectfully base our request for an increase of salary upon the following claims:—

1. That the weights and measures is the most unpopular branch of the Civil Service, for the reason that we collect inspection fees, which are, in most cases, paid very unwillingly. The fees are all returned to the department.

SESSIONAL PAPER No. 29a

2. That the greater part of the inspection work is laborious and, at least, one-third of our time is taken up with exacting clerical work connected therewith.

3. That the wages of artisans and the salaries of those engaged in mercantile pur-suits have been steadily advanced.

4. That the salaries (fixed by Order in Council), we receive at present are the same that were being paid more than thirty years ago, notwithstanding the facts that the cost of living, rent, &c., have increased from at least fifty to one hundred per cent.

We respectfully submit the following increases:—

Inspectors, from $1,500 to $2,000.

Assistant inspectors from $800 to $1,400.

Commencing at the minimum an advance of $50 a year be paid until the maxi-num is reached, and that the time of officers now in the service be counted and paid t the above rate.

We thank you for your courtesy in giving us an opportunity to appear before ou and state our case, and trust that you will give it your best consideration.

We remain, gentlemen, your obedient servants,

> (Sgd.)   D. KELLY, *Inspector.*
> ROBERT J. MILLIGAN, *Assistant Inspector.*
> ROBERT J. WRIGHT, *Assistant Inspector.*
> J. C. SMITH, *Assistant Inspector.*
> JAMES MURDOCH, *Assistant Inspector.*
> A. LYONS, *Assistant Inspector.*
> J. L. CRUIKSHANK, *Assistant Inspector.*

Mr. D. McPHEE, Hamilton, called, sworn, and examined.

(Witness presented a memorial which was read and filed as exhibit   .)

By the Chairman :

Q. We have heard Mr. Lavasseur, of Quebec, and other officials in your depart-ment, so that we have already before us the grounds upon which you base your repre-sentations, and we have acquired a certain amount of knowledge regarding the mat-ter.   This statement has not been circulated generally, has it?—A. It has been sent to the inspectors in the east. I sent one copy to Quebec, Montreal, Halifax, St. John and Ottawa.

Q. I do not think Mr. Levasseur presented one of these?—A. I do not know that he would.   I have sent him one accompanied by a letter desiring to know if he wished to make any changes or suggestions.

Q. How long ago was that?—A. About a week ago.

Q. We left Quebec last Friday, so that Mr. Levasseur had not received it before your departure. Now we come to the first thing. It is suggested that a certain class shall constitute the gas and electric light inspecting branch. There are only about twenty-five inspectors, are there not, who devote their whole time to this branch?—A. I am not quite sure of the exact number, but it is somewhere in that neighbourhood.

Q. It is suggested to have four grades or classifications in a staff of twenty-five?—A. Two grades of inspectors and two grades of assistants.

Q. Well, out of twenty-five employees is that not too many grades?—A. The object, of course, in making that suggestion is that the staff should be graded accord-ing to the amount of money they collect.

Q. Would it not be better, with all due respect, to base your claim upon the amount of work done rather than the amount of money collected?—A. Well, the one represents the other.

Q. Not necessarily. Lots of work, for instance, is done about the canal where there are no fees collected?—A. In this case there are fees collected.

Q. I am only suggesting to you it might be a better argument to rest your case on the amount of work you do. However, leaving that aside, it seems to be a large number of grades for the small number of employees. I suppose you have well thought out the proposed maximum and minimum salaries?—A. Yes, we have. Of course, we do not know whether it will meet with your approval. We have thought the matter over carefully.

Q. This is a general recommendation?—A. Yes. In the meantime, we have no regular system. I would not have put that in the statement if we had.

By Mr. Fyshe :

Q. I suppose you have been brought up in connection with the gas business?—A. Yes. I have been at the business for fifty-four years.

Q. Inspecting gas?—A. Inspecting gas since 1876, but I have been connected with the business since I was between fifteen and sixteen years old.

By the Chairman :

Q. Under the present system of inspection there are no grades at all?—A. No, there are no grades.

Q. You propose this as a substitute for what is practically chaos now?—A. That is the idea.

Q. You say that classification is necessary by reason of the fact that to be efficient, gas and electric light inspectors, technical, mechanical and clerical knowledge is required. I suppose you understand all about illuminants and all that sort of thing a certain amount of mechanical knowledge is necessary in dealing with motors?—A. Yes, and a knowledge of the instruments.

Q. What instruments are there ?—A. The meter prover is the instrument that meters are proved by. Then there is the photometer for testing the strength of the lights, and we also test for sulphuretted hydrogen. and in some offices they test for ammonia and sulphur.

Q. You say that when vacancies occur by death or resignation the vacancies should be filled by promotion of the assistant inspector or the transfer of another inspector Are there many vacancies occurring now ?—A. No, I think not.

Q. Do you find your men going out of the service to other employment?—A. No, we do not find that.

Q. The number of officers is rather small. It is not like the Post Office where there are many men continually leaving ?—A. We have not many officers.

Q. Have you had any vacancies lately ?—A. There was a couple of appointments in Toronto. The last appointment in my district I think was over a year and a half ago.

Q. Was a good man appointed ?—A. Yes. He is receiving $600 a year and is dissatisfied.

Q. The appointee to the latest vacancy in your division is not satisfied with the salary he is receiving? How are the vacancies filled? You suggest that they should be filled by promotion ?—A. I rather think they are filled very much by the executive of the Reform Association.

Q. They are filled politically ? What do you mean when you say that gas and electric inspection be conterminous ?—A. An explanation of that will be this : I can give you a short illustration of it in my own words. Mr. Nash who is the inspector for the London division, tests the gas and gas meters in Woodstock. I test the electric heaters in the same place. I test the electric meters in Ingersoll and he tests the gas in the same town. You see how the thing crosses?

Q. Then your recommendation amounts to this that the same inspector should perform both services in the same place ?—A. That is the idea. My district has been defined by circular.

(Circular produced and read.)

Q. That is a recent circular is it not ?—A. It was issued on the 7th.

Q. That is three weeks ago. The trouble now arises, and it has brought forth this, is that two inspectors do work in the same place. In fact there is overlapping? —A. Yes, overlapping.

Q. One inspector will test the gas in Woodstock and the other, the electric lights? —A. Exactly. There is one thing I would like to explain, if you would allow me, in reference to the electric business when it was introduced. I think I am the only one who can give that explanation. I was called to Ottawa at that time by the late Commissioner, Mr. Miall, for the purpose of being consulted respecting the increase of fees on gas meters and gas inspections so that it would pay two-thirds of expenses. After I got through with that Mr. Miall asked me if I had thought over this question of the introduction of electric light inspection. I said I had given it some consideration. He said 'I would like to get your ideas on that question because it will be put in force shortly. I would like to hear what you have to say.' This was before Mr. Higman, the present chief electrician, was appointed. Being on the subject of the increase of fees I suggested to Mr. Miall that it should be put into the hands of the gas inspectors because they were now acquainted with the inspection of meters and also the testing of the strength of light, and that no salary be paid them until the gas and electric light branch became self-supporting. He said: 'That is a very good idea.' He did not say whether he would adopt it or not but merely got my ideas. However, the thing was put into force on the lines that I had expressed to Mr. Miall at that time. However, when it became self-supporting the department did not pay the officers for this work. The result is that the electric light companies will very shortly be petitioning the Government to reduce the fees not knowing, as a matter of fact, that the officers have not been paid for electric light inspection. That is how the surplus arises. I think the only officers that are paid are Mr. Higman, the chief electrician, and perhaps an assistant or two. They are the only officers who are paid for that service. I suppose I am the only man in the department who knew how the system was introduced and I think it was found on suggestions that I had made to the late Mr. Miall.

Q. When it was considered desirable or necessary by force of events that electric light should be inspected you were summond to Ottawa and conferred with the Commissioner ?—A. On the gas question.

Q. And the result of your conference was that a scale of fees for electric lights was adopted ?—A. Not a scale of fees for electric meters. The question of fees was not discussed but merely putting the inspection into the hands of the gas inspector who should be paid nothing extra for that work until such times as the two branches became self-supporting. I said to him 'If you put this inspection into the hands of special officials, appoint special men for electric light inspection, it would be worse than the gas so far as becoming self-supporting is concerned. My ideas was that the two branches should be placed under the one inspector and that no additional salary should be paid until they became self-supporting.

Q. You thought in fact that it would be better that the inspector of gas should take on the extra duty rather than that new officers should be appointed ?—A. On account of the fact that otherwise the thing would not pay.

Q. Have you anything else to say?—A. Dr. Johnston and Mr. Nash are here. We have differed a little in our ideas, although in my letter I say that the officers concerned, with the exception of Mr. Roche, inspector of the Ottawa district, have all assented. At that time I supposed Dr. Johnston and Mr. Nash would agree with the petition that I had got up. However, they seem to differ from me and I think it would be better for them to present their own petition and give the reasons why they differ.

The witness retired.

Mr. A. F. NASH, London, called and sworn and examined.

By the Chairman:

Q. Have you got a memorial to present?—A. Yes. Memorial read and filed as exhibit.

Q. You and Dr. Johnston are associated in this?—A. Yes.

Q. Well, as far as I can understand, you recommend the creation of three grades of inspectors and assistant inspectors?—A. We have divided them into three grades, thinking, as Mr. McPhie has said, that the amount of work done is shown to a large extent by the revenue returned and also that the service could be improved by classifying them.

Q. The three grades of inspectors would be paid $2,400, $2,000 and $1,600. The salaries of assistant inspectors would run from $800 to $1,200?—A. Yes.

Q. All three of you agree that only properly qualified men should be appointed and that in case of vacancies, appointments should be by promotion?—A. That is the idea. Of course, then an assistant inspector would have to be a properly qualified man.

Q. There is one recommendation in your memorial which does not appear in the other: The inspectors shall be required to give their undivided attention to the work and not in receipt of salaries from other sources?—A. Yes.

Q. Are there inspectors enjoying other emoluments besides what they derive from gas inspection?—A. The inspectors that are referred to there are, I think, Inland Revenue officials.

Q. Some of the emoluments are from Customs and some from other sources?—A. Yes. I would like to explain, if I might, how the system of inspection works out in practice. Take Woodstock, for example. I am inspector of London, but a short time ago Woodstock was in my inspection district. I received a communication from the department advising me of the appointment of a gas inspector for the Woodstock district and ordering me to instruct him in his duties. I instructed him and started the office for him. I gave him what instructions he has received and went to Woodstock on two different occasions for the purpose. Now it works in practice this way: He was an Inland Revenue official of the town. Necessarily a man of that kind cannot know a great deal about gas inspection. The gas company know that. They are aware how much he might possibly know in view of the fact that he has only recently been appointed. Now the gas inspection service is intended as a check on the gas companies and a protection to the consumer, and I think that the man who is inspecting the gas should understand the work. If it is to be a farce, all right, but we do not understand that to be the intention of the Act.

Q. Under the present system the twenty-six gentlemen in whose interests Mr. McPhie presented a letter, are supplementing their incomes to the extent of $100 to $300, in places, I presume, where the business is not sufficient for a full inspection?—A. I do not think that altogether.

Q. Well, we will say that all the twenty-six people get a supplemental allowance of $300, whereas the salaries they would receive under your system would range from $800 to $1,200?—A. No.

Q. If they gave their whole time, would they not get salaries equal to $800 $1,200?—A. If this recommendation were carried out. For example, I have the electric inspection of three Inland Revenue districts, Windsor, London and Stratford. I cover all that territory. In my district there are three different gas inspectors. If this recommendation were carried out so that the boundaries would be coterminal, these men would not be any longer gas inspectors. That is simply as regards the London district. I am satisfied that it would not cost as much to do that work as it does now. I am inclined to think that the work would be better done and the revenue increased.

Q. That may be so, but the main question is, that now there are, say, twenty-six people, Customs officials, inspectors of weights and measures, and Excise officers, who

· drawing emoluments of from $100 to $300 for doing this gas inspection work, ether it be done good or bad?—A. I am not certain as to that. That is a statement :annot swear to. That is stated by Mr. McPhie.

Q. I have no doubt that it is the case. Well, if these twenty-six men were all to $300 a year, that would be $7,800. They do not all get $300 extra, and so the total ght not be more than $5,000. If you appointed the twenty-six men as assistant pectors, or appointed twenty-six assistant inspectors, under your scale of salaries, ιging from $800 to $1,200, the cost would be enormously multiplied. Of course, the tem you recommend might be more efficient, I am not saying anything about that? Λ. You are perfectly right, if the present conditions are as you state. In my own ·ision, however, I do not think there would be another assistant appointed; it would t be necessary. I am not prepared to say that such would be the case in all the dis- cts. I do not think that there would be another assistant appointed, it would not be :essary. I am not prepared to say that such would be the case in all the districts. Io not think there would be more than two or three additional gas inspectors ap- inted as exclusively gas inspectors in the whole Dominion.

Q. And these twenty-six officers, if two or three additional gas inspectors were pointed, could be done away with?—A. They would be Inland Revenue officers, awing their income from that source.

Q. Or Customs officials?—A. Or Customs officials.

By Mr. Fyshe:

Q. When inspecting electric lights, do you go into all the private houses?—A. No, r. We take what we call voltage tests at different points in the city. We have a ɔrtable instrument we carry with us.

Q. Do you test the main wires?—A. Where they enter the buildings. We take ʒhat we call the voltage tests at the points where the wires enter the building, to find ·ut what the service is like at that point.

Q. But you do not test the wires at the private houses?—A. Yes, if we are re- uired to make a special test. I might test these wires in a private dwelling or a ublic building; it would not make any difference. In making tests of that kind, I ould usually go into private houses, because the testing is done at a time when pos- bly the stores are not open.

Q. In a residential district, where there are possibly several miles of houses, there ə at certain places what are called transformers to bring the current down?—A. In ə alternating system they have transformers.

Q. Do you ever test those transformers?—A. That is what we do test.

Q. I am told sometimes that if anything goes wrong with them and the full lume of the current is on, the houses will be set on fire from the transformers?—A. the secondary wires should get the primary voltage, undoubtedly there would be ɯnage done, although there are fuses placed in these lines to protect from a discharge that kind. It would be melted out, and, of course, the line would be open; but if ə transformers are in proper condition, if they are working as they should, there is · possibility of direct contact, because the wires do not come together.

By the Chairman:

Q. Supposing in a private house a series of short circuits occur, and all that kind : thing, and the householder goes to the electric light people, and they say, 'Your lring is dangerous, and we will not guarantee it. We do not think your insurance ould carry the defective wiring.' What happens then? Does the inspector go ʋund?—A. It is really out of the jurisdiction of the Government inspector to test e electric light wires in the buildings. The electric light people are not responsible. the wiring is defective, it is really the fault of the inspector of the underwriters, ιo should inspect that wiring and see that it is all right. You cannot go through this building and tell whether the wiring is properly put in or not after the wires are concealed.

Q. I know a house where short circuiting began and continued, and they applied to a company in Ottawa, and the company said it was dangerous, and the insurance people said the same thing, and the house was rewired. I want to know where the inspector comes in there?—A. I do not think the Government inspector of electric lights comes in, not in that case.

Q. You say that the senior gas inspector, in order to superintend the construction and placing of apparatus in a new gas inspection office and keep the same in repair, should be allowed the sum of $500 per annum in addition to his ordinary salary. That is to say, you recommend, besides the creation of these grades, that there should be a senior inspector, who should also be charged with the construction and placing of apparatus in the new gas inspection offices?—A. It is at present the practice of the department to hold one man responsible for the placing of the apparatus.

Q. Who is that?—A. Mr. McPhie. That is for placing these provers and opening up new inspection offices.

Q. Then, if a new inspection office were opened, say at Woodstock, Mr. McPhie would be sent there?—A. Mr. McPhie is the man. I do not say that I do not know something about gas provers, because I was in the gas business for twenty years before I was appointed an inspector, but the department holds Mr. McPhie responsible. All I have to do is to to write to the department to complain that my prover or any of my instruments needs repairing.

Q. We are talking of new districts being created and the construction and placing of apparatus in new gas inspection offices. There are only about twenty gas inspection offices upon the list. Supposing a new gas inspection office is opened at any point it would be Mr. McPhie's duty to construct and install the apparatus there?—A. I might say that I want a new office opened at Petrolia for the reason that they are commencing to supply gas and have been supplying gas since January, but we have no inspection office there. I cannot, as gas inspector, test the gas at Petrolia because we have no office there.

By Mr. Fyshe:

Q. Do they not know where to find you?—A. We should find them. We should go to the gas company and test their gas, they do not have to find us; they are not worried about that. It is a gas inspector's duty to see they are supplying proper gas and that there is a prover for testing the meters.

By the Chairman:

Q. We are wandering from the question. You are speaking in your memorandum about new offices and you have stated that when a new office is created Mr. McPhie, the senior gas inspector, goes there and directs the construction and placing of apparatus?—A. I would think so. Of course, the matter is outside my district.

Q. I am not talking about your district or any other man's district but of the fact that on the creation of a new gas inspection office the department requires the senior gas inspector, that is Mr. McPhie, to superintend the construction and installation of apparatus?—A. Yes, that is Mr. McPhie, he has been doing that work, and is at present doing that work.

Q. Then you suggest that in order to carry that out an additional salary should be granted of say $500 a year?—A. That is the recommendation.

Q. How many offices are opened during the year?—A. Mr. McPhie can tell better than I can.

Mr. McPhie.—I have no record of it. While it is new offices that are mentioned in the memorial it is not, simply new offices.

The Chairman.—Then the memorial is badly worded.

Mr. McPhie.—At present we make repairs of old instruments. I have two prov-
from Ottawa now under repair at Hamilton. It is my duty to see that these are
perly repaired and returned to Ottawa or wherever they are required in good order,
I I have got to so report to the Department of Inland Revenue.

The **Chairman.**—What Dr. Johnston and Mr. Nash mean by the recommendation
this: that the senior gas inspector superintend and direct the construction and
cing of new apparatus in the new gas inspection offices and also keep the same in
od repair in the offices now in existence.

Mr. Nash.—Is that not in the memorial? If not it was overlooked. I am cer-
n I had the expression in the original draft, 'and to keep the same in repair.'

By the Chairman:

Q. The memorial speaks of new offices?—A. Not only that but the old offices.

Q. The expression you use is 'new offices and keep the same in repair'?—A. I
ully thought I had stated what I meant to say in the memorial.

Q. Limiting the matter to new offices and only opening up one or two offices a/
ar, your proposition would be to give an additional $500?—A. I do not want to take
more of your valuable time and I hope I have made my meaning clear.

Q. The recommendation in your memorial then applies to the keeping in repair
the apparatus in the old offices as well as the installation of apparatus in the new
as?—A. Certainly. He is responsible to the department for the care of those instruments.

Q. That is what I wanted to make clear?—A. And it is only to recommend that
r inspectors called upon to do that should have an extra allowance.

The **Chairman.**—We are very much obliged to your for your testimony. A copy
rour evidence will be sent to you and if you want to supplement it you will have an
ortunity of doing so.

Dr. **Johnston** was called and presented a memorial, which was read and filed as
ibit.

By the Chairman: .

Q. The statement you make amounts to this: Do you think that as the officer is
rking overtime and the gas company pays the fees some extra remuneration should
given to him?—A. That is it.

Mr. Nash.—It is hardly necessary for me to say that there should be something
lnite in the way of promotion. If this were done a deserving officer would look
ward with some assurance to the fact that there was some future for him.

The witness retired.

GAS AND ELECTRIC INSPECTION SERVICE.

the Honourable
The Royal Civil Service Commission.

Gentlemen,—On behalf of the gas and electric light inspection service, we beg to
sent our petition containing suggestions, which we hope you will consider reason-
e and which outline some of the changes that are desired by this service.

While the increased cost of living necessarily makes the salary question the
in issue, we would like to convey the idea that this petition is not altogether of
nercenary spirit, but that the proper grading and classification herein outlined is
equal importance.

This petition has been approved by the undersigned although it does not repre-
t the unanimous opinion of all the inspectors.

7-8 EDWARD VII., A. 1908

We suggest the following classes shall constitute the department of gas and electric light:—

(1) Chief inspector.
(2) Inspector of gas and electricity, and district superintendent of construction.
(3) Inspector of gas and electricity.
(4) Assistant inspector of gas and electricity.

The chief inspector should be the head of the service of gas and electricity in Canada.

The inspectors of gas and electricity and district superintendent of construction shall be the inspectors in their respective districts and also have control of the construction and erecting of the government apparatus in a district set apart by the department. There should be three such inspectors in Canada, one to have Quebec and the maritime provinces, one to have the proivnce of Ontario and another to have Manitoba and the western provinces.

Inspectors of gas and electricity shall be the inspectors in their respective districts only.

There should be two classes of inspectors: inspectors over first-class districts and inspectors over second-class districts.

First-class inspectors are inspectors in districts whose annual revenue exceeds $5,000.

Second-class inspectors are inspectors in districts whose annual revenue is less than $5,000. Districts having exceptional large territory should have special provision as to its class.

The salaries of the different classes should be $2,500. Inspectors of gas and electricity and district superintendent of construction.

First-class inspectors, minimum, $1,600; maximum, $2,200.
Second-class inspectors, minimum, $1,400; maximum, $2,000.
First-class assistant inspectors, minimum, $800; maximum, $1,400.
Second-class assistant inspectors, minimum, $800; maximum, $1,200.

The salary of a first-class inspector should begin at $1,600 with annual increases of 5 per cent until he reaches the maximum salary of $2,200.

The salary of a second-class inspector should begin at $1,400, with an annual increase of 5 per cent until he reaches the maximum salary of $2,000.

The salary of an assistant in a first-class district should begin at $800 with an increase of $100, after two years' service, and an annual increase of $100 until he reaches the maximum salary of $1,400 in seven years.

A classification for a minimum and maximum salary with a fixed number of years to reach the maximum is necessary to stop the continual interviewing of different Members of Parliament by the officers in their behalf for increase.

That classification is necessary by reason of the fact that to be an efficient gas and electric light inspector technical, mechanical and clerical knowledge is required.

The department of gas and electric light, which is not supposed to be a revenue deriving one, had for the year 1905-6 a surplus of $38,000, and it is therefore no burden on the general taxpayer, and as there are not more than twenty-one officers who would be affected by the new arrangement of salary the department should be quite able to stand any increases that might be made.

When the different gas inspectors were given the service of electric light inspection in 1896 at the then present salaries, it was understood that when the service produced a sufficient surplus, they were to be recompensed for the extra work, but, up to the present, this has not been done.

That appointments to the office of assistant gas inspectors should be only men who can qualify for the position and pass a preliminary examination as well as the special examination recently introduced by the chief inspector on electricity. This shall not affect the position or status of any officer already in the service.

ESSIONAL PAPER No. 29a

That when vacancies occur either by death or resignation of the gas and electric ght inspection, the vacancies will be filled by the promotion of an assistant inspector r by the transfer of another inspector from some other district, the same to be made y the direction of the Department of Inland Revenue.

That the boundaries of gas and electric inspection districts be co-terminal, that is, he inspectors of all electric districts be also inspectors of all gas companies in their espective districts, and the salaries paid should be charged equally to the gas and lectric inspection.

It is to be understood that if the Commission sees fit to adopt the different clauses nd salaries put forth in this petition that the increases are to be retroactive and calulated from the time that the different officers entered the service.

We would also suggest that the gratuity of two months' pay which is now given to ie heirs of deceased officers is entirely inadequate, and it is respectfully recommended lat in case of an officer dying while in active service fifty per cent of the superannuaon allowance he would be entitled to receive be paid his widow during her widow-)od, and in case of an officer dying after he had been superannuated a fair proporon of his superannuation allowance be given his widow during her widowhood.

As an evidence of the increased cost of living we call your attention to what the fferent banking institutions consider the least an employee of theirs could properly 'e on. They now prohibit any clerk in their employ from marrying till he receives salary of $1,500 per year.

We beg to submit a few extracts from the departmental blue-book showing the eat increase of receipts during the last ten years.

Years.	Receipts.	Expenditure.	Surplus.
7	$ 24,167 00	$ 23,126 30	$ 1,040 70
*3	76,539 00	38,917 48	37,621 52

Years.	Revenue.	Expenditure.
9-1900	$ 25,523 50	$ 26,424 48
0-1	37,536 57	28,247 20
1-2	45,663 05	33,328 48
2-3	49,054 55	36,006 47
3-4	50,218 75	33,426 15
4-5	62,561 37	34,774 02
5-6	76,539 00	38,917 48

We remain, gentlemen,
Your obedient servant,
(Signed)   D. McPHIE, *G. I.*

TORONTO, September 23, 1907.

he Honourable Civil Service Commission.

GENTLEMEN,—In addition to the petition presented by the inspectors and assistant spectors of gas and electricity. I would beg to call your attention to the case of an sistant in my office who has done and is yet doing work beyond the legal hours re: iired by the department. According to the Act, chapter 101, sec. 31, a test of the illuminating power of gas has to be taken between the hours of seven and ten o'clock in the afternoon, in summer, and five to eight o'clock in afternoon, in winter. This night test is asked for by the gas company of this city, and for some time I have had one of my senior assistants make this test bi-weekly. The time from the officer's residence and return, with the test carefully made, entails fully two hours' work. For this extra time at night the inspector never received any remuneration, outside of street car fare. I would strongly recommend to your honourable body that some provision be made for payment for the overtime required in addition to the officer's regular salary.

I may add that the gas company pays twelve dollars weekly, as fees, for this test to the department for the certificate.

I have the honour to be, gentlemen,

Your obedient servant,

(Signed) J. K. JOHNSTONE,

Inspector of Gas, &c.

To the Honourable Civil Service Commission :

GENTLEMEN,—I am in receipt of a letter representing the feelings of those officials whose whole time is not devoted to the gas inspection service, asking that they shall share proportionately any increases that the Commission may see fit to recommend.

There are about twenty-six of this class of officials in the Dominion, three being in the Customs service, eleven in the excise service and twelve are weights and measures inspectors. Their salaries range from one hundred to three hundred dollars per annum for the extra work of gas inspection.

I have the honour to be, gentlemen,

Your obedient servant,

(Signed)   D. McPHIE, G.I.

GAS AND ELECTRIC INSPECTION SERVICE.

To the Honourable the Royal Civil Service Commission :

GENTLEMEN,—We, the undersigned inspectors of gas and electricity believing that the service would be greatly benefited by a change in the regulations as constituted at present, respectfully request that you take into consideration the following :—

In the year 1896 when the Electric Light Inspection Act was brought into force, the gas inspectors became also the inspectors of electric light, and the net revenue from that service having amounted to $25,245.53 for the year ending June 30, 190 is evidence that the work of the inspectors has greatly increased, but notwithstanding as yet, no salaries are paid for doing the work which, in our opinion, is not only an injustice but has also resulted in united action being taken by the electric light companies to obtain a reduction in the fees.

We also are of the opinion that in order to obtain the best results and to the end that the salaries paid should bear some relation to the work performed it is most desirable that the different inspection districts be classified on the basis of the amount of revenue produced during the fiscal year, and would suggest three classes :

First class.—All divisions producing a net revenue of $10,000 or more during any fiscal year.

Second class.—Districts producing $5,000 and less than $10,000.

Third class.—Districts producing less than $5,000.

In view of the fact that it is conceded that the cost of the necessities of life have largely increased, we think the following salaries to be fully justified. Salaries of ctors of gas and electricity, in the first class, to be $2,400, salaries of inspectors in ;cond class to be $2,000, and salaries of inspectors in the third class to be $1,600. 3alaries of assistant inspectors to be $800 the first year, to be increased fifty dollars .r for two years and subsequent increases to be one hundred dollars a year until reach a maximum of twelve hundred dollars.

\n assistant inspector may, on the recommendation of his inspector, and having d an examination by the chief electrical engineer as to his proficiency, acquire osition of first-class assistant inspector and, in such case, shall receive a yearly ase of one hundred dollars per year until he shall have reached a maximum of n hundred dollars, time of service to be computed from date of appointment.

Ve would recommend that only properly qualified men be appointed as assistant ctors, which would be determined by examination made by the chief electrical ieer.

:n case of vacancies made by death or resignation of gas and electrical inspectors acancies should be filled by the promotion of assistant inspector or by the trans- f another inspector from some other district, the same to be made by the direction e Department of Inland Revenue.

[hat the boundaries of gas and electrical inspection districts be co-terminal, that ie inspectors of all electric districts be also the inspectors of all gas companies eir respective districts.

'hat the inspectors should be required to give their undivided attention to the and not to be in receipt of salary from other sources.

Ve would also suggest that the salaries paid should be charged equally to the nd electric inspection.

\s it has been found necessary by the department to require the senior gas :tor to superintend and direct the construction and placing of apparatus in new ispection offices and to keep the same in repair, we would recommend that such :tor be allowed the sum of $500 per annum in addition to his regular salary.

t is further suggested that the gratuity of two months' pay, which is now given ? heirs of deceased officers is entirely inadequate, and it is respectfully recom- ed that in case of the decease of an officer while in active service, 50 per cent ? superannuation allowance he would have been entitled to receive be paid his r during her widowhood, and in case of the decease of an officer after superan- on, fair proportion of his superannuation allowance should be given his widow g her widowhood.

We have the honour to be, respectfully yours,

(Sgd.)   J. K. JOHNSTONE, *Gas Inspector, &c., Toronto.*

A. F. NASH, *Gas Inspector, London.*

OTTAWA, September 23, 1907.

.e *Chairman and Members of the Civil Service Commission.*

!ENTLEMEN,—I have been requested, to join in two petitions addressed to your irable body in connection with the above branch of the Civil Service, but as of said petitions have presumed to deal with much more than the question of es and with matters which appear to me to be questions of policy, I have been :d to return said petitions unsigned.

f, however, your honourable body deem it advisable to go beyond the question aries, in your research and report with respect to this branch of the Civil Ser- [would respectfully submit that the revenue produced from inspections during iscal year is not the standard by which the services of gas and electric light :tors should be gauged. but rather by the competency and efficiency of the offi- ind more particularly for the reason that in this branch of the service technical

7-8 EDWARD VII., A. 1908

and practical knowledge and competency in the adjustment and use of the machinery employed is of the greatest consequence.

In addition to the above, length of service and performance of duty should be considered in any readjustment of the salary question.

Officials in this service should be paid salaries sufficient to maintain them, and should not devote any of their time to work outside the duties of their respective positions.

Inspectors in the several divisions should be paid a uniform salary, as the duties to be performed by them under the Gas and Electric Light Inspection Act do not vary in so far as inspectors are concerned.

I have the honour to be, sirs,

Yours most respectfully,

H. G. ROCHE,

Gas and Electric Light Inspector.

OTTAWA, October 23, 1907.

The Royal Commission on the Civil Service met this morning at 10.30 o'clock.

Present:—Mr. J. M. COURTNEY, C.M.G., Chairman.
Mr. THOMAS FYSHE, Montreal, and
Mr. P. J. BAZIN.

Dr. BARRETT, Winnipeg, called, sworn and examined.

By the Chairman:

Q. What is your position?—A. I am inspector of Inland Revenue for the district Manitoba.

Q. How long have you been in the service?—A. I have been thirty-four years v. I entered the service on September 5, 1873.

Q. Before you went to Manitoba what position did you occupy in the governnt service?—A. I was special class excise officer up to 1879. In that year I was ointed deputy collector at St. Catharines, Ontario.

Q. And then afterwards?—A. In 1885 when the position of district inspector ame vacant in Winnipeg I was appointed to it. I was appointed on May 1, 1885.

Q. And since then you have been made inspector of malt houses and breweries? A. Yes.

Q. That appointment was made about three or four years ago? You are one of men in the service that have gone up from point to point to the position of district pector?—A. I went up from third-class officer at $600 a year to my present ition.

Q. We have had the pleasure of reading your statement and we will come to the t point dealt with which is the increased cost of living. Have you got any memoada with you?—A. I have got several statements here which Mr. McKenna handed this morning from the chief officers of banks and other institutions in Winnipeg.

Q. Have those been condensed in any shape or form?—A. They are very brief tements. Here is a copy of the memorial we filed with you.

Statements presented and filed.

Q. Briefly what do you put the difference between the cost of living in Winnipeg compared with the cost at Ottawa or Montreal at?—A. Putting it at a very convative figure, I consider it is 33½ per cent higher in Winnipeg. You will find a cument by Mr. Aird, the manager of the Bank of Commerce, Winnipeg, among the pers I have handed in, in which he states that he is connected with Havergal Colre and the cost of living, general supplies have increased from 45 per cent to 50 r cent in the last three years.

Q. We have held sittings at Ottawa, Montreal, Quebec, and Toronto, and what u want to emphasize is the increased cost of living as compared with these cities? A. Certainly.

Q. I see at the bottom of your memorial you give the cost of living at Ottawa d Winnipeg?—A. Of course, we had no data on which to base anything else except t produced here. The figures given in our memorial are taken from the memorials pared by the Ottawa Civil Service Association.

Q. Well, generally speaking, Ottawa, Montreal and Toronto are pretty much of nuchness?—A. I think they are, although perhaps the cost of living in Ottawa is rhtly higher than at the other two cities.

29a—28½

7-8 EDWARD VII., A. 1908

Q. It may be a little higher, but the difference is not so great as it would be between Ottawa and Winnipeg, for example?—A. Certainly not.

Q. You have produced a statement showing the cost of fuel and clothing, but you have not summarized the increased cost of living with respect to other supplies. You take, rentals, taxes, coal and clothing. You say the cost in Winnipeg would be 33½ greater in that city than in Ottawa. Then you come down to the beef and other food products, but you have not given us the statement of any household showing the annual expenditure as compared with what it would be at Ottawa?—A. Here is the statement, and I consider it a very moderate one, of an officer in my department at Winnipeg who receives the munificent salary of $630 a year. The statement shows the very cheapest rate at which he finds it possible to live.

Statement read and filed.

Q. According to this the man's expenses amount to $100 a month?—A. That is his actual expenses were over $100, and his salary is $630. He has an allowance of $125.

Q. Reference is made to a provisional allowance. There is a provisional allowance for officers in the west, is there not?—A. Yes, for some classes of officers.

Q. What is the range of the allowance?—A. In our department any officer drawing less than $1,000 was receiving an allowance of $50 a year up to the end of the last fiscal year. In the weights and measures branch the officer received $100 a year, but in the excise branch he was only paid $50. That allowance has now been raised to $125 a year for all officers whose salary is under $1,000 per annum. Those officers receiving $1,000 and over do not get any allowance whatever.

By Mr. Fyshe:

Q. What was the idea of that provisional allowance?—A. The idea was this: We urged upon the Government the necessity of supplementing the salary of these people because they were actually starving. They were in the position, they could not get credit and they could not live on the salary they were receiving.

Q. Why should they call it a provisional allowance?—A. Because the Civil Service Act fixes the salaries of our officers and the only way the Government could supplement those salaries was to give a provisional allowance. That is why they call it a provisional allowance.

By the Chairman:

Q. Of course, the provisional allowance being in excess of the salaries fixed by the Civil Service Act the Government had to take a special vote for the purpose?—A. They had to take a special vote just for that purpose.

Q. And you say the provisional allowance has been limited in your department to officers receiving a salary of less than $1,000 a year?—A. Yes.

Q. An officer in receipt of $1,100 a year would not get any allowance?—A. The man who had $1,000 a year would not get anything. We have in our staff in Winnipeg to-day men who are getting $950 salary. They draw $125 provisional allowance, so that they are actually better off than the man who is only getting a fixed salary of $1,000.

Q. These men do not want their annual increment, I suppose?—A. Not while that condition of things lasts.

Q. How long has this provisional allowance been granted?—A. When I first went to Winnipeg, there was a provisional allowance granted. The system has been going on, I think, from 1882. It was started in 1882 and continued until 1887, a period of five years.

Q. And then what happened?—A. Then it was struck off completely, as far as our department was concerned.

Q. Go on please?—A. When I went up to Winnipeg first, I got an allowance of $1 a day in consideration of the extra cost of living. I am under oath now, and I

:sitivaly swear that the cost of living to-day in Winnipeg is at least 30 per cent higher
than when I got that provisional allowance.

By Mr. Fyshe:

Q. How do you account for that?—A. At that time rents, provisions and clothing
are lower. We were going through a season of depression. After the boom burst in
82, things became very depressed there, and living was much cheaper. I could then
y eggs for 10 cents a dozen in Winnipeg, which was cheaper than you could have
ught them for in Toronto or Montréal. Butter I could buy for 15 cents a pound.
her commodities that we required for the household were very much cheaper than
y are now. We were granted a provisional allowance. I was allowed 20 per cent of
salary. You see, the allowance was graded according to salary. A man whose
ary was $600 or under $1,000 received 40 per cent of a bonus, based on his salary.
a salary of from $1,000 to $1,500 the officer received 25 per cent; from $1,500
$2,000, 20 per cent; over $2,000, 12½ per cent. That was the basis on which the
visional allowance was given at that time; it was based on the salary of the officer.

Q. I should think that any increase in the cost of living that has occurred since
st be common to all Canada, and not peculiar especially to the Northwest?—A. We
prepared to admit that the cost of living all over Canada has increased very mater-
y, but we claim that the cost of living in Winnipeg and west of that city is at
st 30 per cent greater to-day than it is in Toronto, Ottawa, or Montreal. There is
question about it at all; we have documents and figures to prove the statement.

Q. It is difficult to understand that, except in the matter of house rents and fuel?—
Take the item of fuel alone. We have to pay $11 a ton for coal. Last year we burned
l for eight months at $11 a ton, and, owing to the severity of the weather, we had to
n it for a much longer time than, say, in Montreal. There is a large item in itself.
en, wood in the last three years in Winnipeg has almost doubled in price. Wood
ich formerly cost us only $4.50 a cord is selling to-day for $9.50 a cord. It is the
ne in every other line. Take the item of servants' wages. We cannot get a servant
Winnipeg to-day, and even a very poor one at that, for less than $25 a month. We
a washerwoman to-day $2 per day and grant street car fare going and coming. When
rst went to Winnipeg we could get a sewing girl for $1 a day. We cannot get a sew.
girl to enter the house to-day, except as a great compliment. She would come
und about 9 o'clock in the morning and leave at 6 o'clock and charge us from $2 to
0 a day—in fact, she can get almost any price she pleases. She can place any value
likes on her services, and if we need her, we have to pay the money.

Q. Then, you say the provisional allowance according to salary was cut off at the
e of the collapse of the boom?—A. It was cut off in 1887 because of the representa-
us of some of the Members of Parliament from the west. We have one of those
nbers at our board this day. The allowance caused adverse criticism in the west,
it was represented that things were no dearer in Winnipeg and the west at that
e when they were down here. Hence, when the vote came up in Parliament, we
to suffer the consequence of it being struck off.

Q. Then for a while after the collapse of the boom the civil servant in Winnipeg
a really good time?—A. He had a very good time.

Q. How long did that halcyon period last?—A. I went to Winnipeg in 1885 and
asted until June, 1887.

Q. Just about two years?—A. Yes, two years.

Q. A brief two years of happiness?—A. Two years of comparative ease, as far as
ncial matters went.

Q. When was the provisional allowance re-established?—A. I think it was estab-
ed about three years ago; I would not be positive as to that.

By Mr. Fyshe:

Q. But only in the case of those civil servants whose salaries were——A. Whose salaries were less than $1,000. That is how it was in our department. Of course in other departments it was different.

By the Chairman:

Q. The examination is about your own department just now. When Mr. Smith comes forward, we will talk to him about the increase in the population. I suppose the population of Winnipeg is spreading all over the prairie now?—A. During the recent boom in Winnipeg they were selling land at a distance of from seven to eight miles from the centre of the city, and they found people to buy it.

By Mr. Fyshe:

Q. That is town lots?—A. Town lots. Certainly those lots will never be of any use whatever until the city of Winnipeg has a population of one-half or three-quarters of a million of souls.

By the Chairman:

Q. How far do the street cars run?—A. There is a street car running out to St. Charles. That is the farthest point, I think.

Q. How far is that from the centre of the city?—A. I should judge that would be about five miles from the city hall.

Q. You were talking about the increase in the cost of living resulting from rent and fuel. Of course, the cost of fuel goes without saying. As to rents is there not a tendency to equalization owing to the space covered by the city of Winnipeg?—A. There are no houses for rent in Winnipeg scarcely now. What has caused the almost doubling of rent within the last few years in Winnipeg is the rise in property and the sudden influx of immigration so that people need houses and would give any price almost for them; they simply have to have houses. Let me instance the case of our collector. He rented a house for which he was paying $22.50 five years ago. Since this tidal wave of immigration came in to Winnipeg people began offering his landlord $30 a month for the house he occupied. The rent was raised to $30, afterwards to $40, and now he is paying $50 for a house that rented for only $22.50 five years ago.

By Mr. Fyshe:

Q. Per month?—A. Per month.

By the Chairman:

Q. Comparing that house with a house in Ottawa, what kind of a dwelling would it be like?—A. It is a frame house, semi-detached; there are two houses under the one roof. It contains a small sitting-room, a dining-room, a kitchen, two bed-rooms and a bath-room. It is a very small house and I do not believe it would cost in Ottawa more than—well, I really could not say; I do not know what the rentals are here. I do know this, however, that in other Ontario towns such a house would cost only from $12.50 to $15 a month.

Q. Perhaps in Ottawa such a house might cost $25?—A. I doubt it, Mr. Courtney. It was only five years ago that the tenant was paying $22.50 and that was supposed to be a large rental at that time.

Q. You state in your memorial that the rent of a house bringing $25 in Ottawa would be in Winnipeg $40?—A. We took those figures from the memorial presented to you here.

Q. You took the figures from the memorial of the Ottawa Civil Service Association and based your increase on your local knowledge. You say the rent of an Ontario house would be $12.50 as against $50 in Winnipeg. that is four times as much. In your memorial, however, you place the rent in the east at $25 as against $40 in Winnipeg, or 60 per cent more?—A. Yes.

Ɋ. I want to get at the absolute fact in regard to the rent?—A. In our statement are very careful to keep well within the mark.

Ɋ. Then you consider that 60 per cent is within the limits?—A. I do, sir, as re-ı rentals. It is easily that.

Ɋ. Why should the price of provisions be higher in Winnipeg than in Ottawa? have supplies of beef, pork, and mutton in the west?—A. That is one of the most ilar things. It is almost inexplicable because we are a food producing country the beef that you buy here from your butcher for 15 cents a pound comes largely the west. We pay in Winnipeg 20 cents and 22 cents a pound for the same beef you can purchase in Ottawa for 15 cents a pound. I do not know what is the n for this disparity unless it is the existence of a beef combine. They say that a thing exists in the west. However, those are the facts.

Q. I cannot make out why that should be so. What is the distance between Win-ɾ ɑnd Ottawa?—A. 1,400 miles.

Q. Why should people send beef 1,400 miles and sell it at 15 cents a pound when can get 22 cents a pound for the meat on the spot?—A. Of course, the Winnipeg ɾet is a limited one. They produce more beef in the west than they consume.

Q. Then Winnipeg should be a cheap centre?—A. It should.

By Mr. Fyshe:

Q. I think it is understandable because of the fact that there is not a thoroughly ılished retail trade?—A. I was speaking to my butcher in Winnipeg. A commis-was appointed there to look into the alleged beef combine and I said to him, 'Why ꞉ you appear before that commission?' He said, 'If I appeared before that com-ion I might as well put up my shutters. I would be told by the beef supply, by ꞉old storage—Gordon, Ironsides and the others—that they had no goods that would me, and I might just as well go out of business entirely.' That was his explana-of it. But I have no doubt whatever there is a beef combine in Winnipeg.

By the Chairman:

Q. What is the population of Winnipeg now?—A. It is variously estimated at 95,000 to 110,000. I think 100,000 would be a good estimate.

Q. That is 30 per cent more population than there is in Ottawa. Yet with a popu-n of 100,000 people those supplying meat send it 1,400 miles to get a cheaper price they could sell the meat for on the spot?—A. Yes, if they send it here.

Q. You were telling us a while ago that we have the same meat here?—A. I know ship meats to Toronto, Ottawa and Montreal.

Q. You can see there is a discrepancy. If meat is shipped down here and sold at a lb., why can you not buy it in Winnipeg on the spot for the same price?—A. I oᵗ explain it, but the facts are as I have stated.

Q. I do not think we need go into the question of fuel. Your winter lasts ight months and coal costs you $11 a ton. Furthermore, it comes a longer distance is the case with coal supplies in the east. Neither need we go into the labour ꞉ion because I have no doubt the facts are as you state. Now is there anything respect to your own department that you would like to tell us. We have already the pleasure of meeting representatives of the Inland Revenue Department in wa, Montreal, Quebec and Toronto, but if there is anything of a local nature that ɑesire to bring to our attention we will be glad to hear it?—A. Do you mean as to ıdministration of the department?

Q. As to anything. With respect to appointments or anything you care to tell us? I think the Civil Service to-day is suffering from two things: first, politics, and ıdly, that we have in the service a certain number of drones and worthless fellows e only object is to draw their salary in peɾfect indifference as to whether they do hing for it or not. Those are the two things that the Civil Service, in my opinion, o suffer most from.

By Mr. Fyshe:

Q. And the same influence that keeps incompetent people in the service is also visible, I suppose, in the fact that really deserving people are not promoted?—A. Yes.

By the Chairman:

Q. I was about to ask you to kindly amplify your first statement as to politics?—A. I can give you an instance in my own department. The collector of Inland Revenue at Port Arthur has been retired. The division has been increased largely by the addition of Kenora and Rainy River and it is necessary that we should have a man of experience as collector there. It is absolutely necessary in the interests of the service, first, because the office is far removed from the inspector's office, and secondly, the territory covered is very large. Now what are they doing? I recommended that a competent man be appointed to that position and as I had no one in the west I could nominate—our staff being pretty well depleted by recent promotions—I suggested that a man from the east be sent there. The politicians say ' No, we will have no eastern man up here. We have got enough ability here in the west and we are not going to have an eastern man sent in.' As an alternative I begged of them to put in an officer who has been in the service for about two years. Under ordinary circumstances I would not recommend such a man for the position at all, but he is better than an outsider. I do not know what they are going to do, but I suppose they will do just as they please and the service will have to suffer.

Q. How long has the position been vacant?—A. Since October 1 this year. I inspected the division last June and the collector then wrote me a letter asking to be retired immediately. I begged of him not to ask for retirement before the 1st October last so he amended his letter in that way. I at once wrote to the department making this recommendation at the beginning of July. The department has had three months to prepare and no appointment has been made yet.

By Mr. Fyshe:

Q. The politicians then objected to any outsider coming in?—A. The Member for the constituency says ' No, I will not allow any one outside of my constituency to go in there.'

Q. That is very bad?—A. That is one instance of what the Civil Service is up against everywhere.

By the Chairman:

Q. Do you know what staff there is in the collector's office at Winnipeg?—A. There is in the office a collector, a deputy collector and an accountant. We have five probationers who are only temporary officers.

Q. They are called temporary excise men?—A. Temporary excise men. We have five or six of them.

Q. And you have got two or three messengers?—A. We have one messenger.

Q. Are the officers of your department in the Northwest resigning?—A. Yes. Some of the probationers that are appointed at $500 a year take the position for a month or two, and some for a year or two, and then they get an offer of something better and they leave.

Q. There is nothing to look forward to and they go out as soon as they can?—A. There is nothing to look forward to. They just take the position as a stop-gap.

Q. How do you find out when an officer is wanted in the division?—A. We know from the increased duties. The collector is the head of the staff in Winnipeg and he reports to me that he wants another officer.

Q. And then you write to Ottawa?—A. Then I write to the department at Ottawa and ask for an appointment.

Q. And then the department approves and gives you a name?—A. If the appoint-
mt is approved the Minister, I suppose, or some one acting for him——

Q. Gives you a name?—A. Gets a name. That name is generally given by the
beral Association of Winnipeg.

Q. By the association?—A. Yes.

Q. Not by the Member?—A. When the Conservatives were in power they did the
me thing. I am not discriminating one way or another. The service suffered just
much then as we are suffering to-day.

Q. You have been in the west since 1885, twenty-two years. Did you have a
tter class of men desirous of entering the service in 1885 than you have to-day?—
Yes, we had a better class of men coming into the service. At that time we gen-
lly got men who had passed the Civil Service examination. They were only pro-
tioners for six months, and then their salary was increased to $600 a year. Living
en was not as acutely high as it is to-day. The result is those men went up and
ok their Promotion examinations and some of them were appointed at $500. The
countant, for instance——

Q. That is Mr. Hawkins?—A. No, Mr. Long is our accountant. Mr. Hawkins
.s accountant of the Brantford division, and on coming up to us retained his rank
thout filling the duties of the office.

Q. So Mr. Long is your accountant?—A. Mr. Long is our accountant. He came
to the service five years ago, and is getting a salary of $1,500 now. He went up and
ok the necessary examination. He was a university graduate and an industrious
llow, and went in to get rank and position in the service, and he has won it simply
his own application.

Q. Can he get a salary of more than $1,500 a year?—A. That is the highest salary
can get in the position as it is graded at present.

Q. Then you say there are not such a good class of men entering the service as
ere were twenty-five years ago when you were promoted?—A. Decidedly not.

Q. And they do not remain in the service, you say?—A. They do not stay; they
ive us as soon as they can get something better. I attribute that to the ridicu-
isly low salary at which they are appointed. In the Customs service the lowest
lary given a man is $800. In our department the only salary an officer can come in
is $500.

Q. But do not men leave the Customs service as well as your own?—A. I am not
a position to answer that. Colonel Scott, the collector at Winnipeg, who is here,
better able to do that.

Q. Do you think that the abolition of the Superannuation Act had anything to
with destroying the stability of the service?—A. I do certainly. I think that the
iperannuation Act was a great lever in getting good men and keeping them.

Q. Do you think it desirable that some form of a Pension Act should be restored
the statute book?—A. I certainly do.

Q. Do you think it would be as well to include in a Pension Act some provision
r widows and orphans?—A. Yes. That is one of the things we incorporate in our
emorial. We know that is done in commercial institutions. I know of one particu-
: case in the Merchants Bank. There was a Mr. Miller, who was manager of the
innipeg branch. He was afterwards removed to Toronto and superannuated. He
ceived a superannuation allowance of half his salary, and there was a provision that
he predeceased his wife she would get half the allowance while she remained a
dow.

By Mr. Fyshe:

Q. I organized that pension fund myself!—A. I think it is most equitable and
st. That is what we want to see incorporated in a Superanuation Act in your ser-
ce. I would say that if a man serves the Government for twenty years and dies
harness he should be entitled to two-fifths of the amount he would have received

7-8 EDWARD VII., A. 1908

had he been superannuated at the time of his death. Then we claim that one-fifth of his salary should be paid to his widow during her widowhood.

By the Chairman:

Q. If you were to die to-morrow, notwithstanding all the deductions made from your salary for the purposes of superannuation nothing would go to your family?—A. I will have been thirty-five years in the service next September, and my family would not get one cent.

Q. Under the Retirement Fund, five per cent is compulsorily deducted off salary?—A. That is the most cruel thing in the whole business. They give a man $500 a year, and then keep off five per cent, when he is starving, to save for him.

Q. And then when he breaks down his own money is returned to him?—A. When he quits the service they give him that. It is a very fine class of paternalism, but we do not appreciate it at all.

Q. The rate of interest does not compare in any way with what you would get if you invested your own money?—A. No; but the trouble in the west is to have any money to invest.

Q. There was another point you mentioned as being one of the evils of the Civil Service?—A. That is as to the drones?

Q. There is no incentive in the way of getting on in the service to cause a man to do anything more than the bare work he is called upon to do?—A. In our service, if it was administered according to the regulations, there would be, but unfortunately politics comes in and overrides those regulations.

Q. So a man feels, as long as he shuffles through his day's work he is as well off one way as the other?—A. I suppose that may have been the cause of a lot of the trouble, but I should think that a man who accepts the position and the responsibilities attached thereto should try to do his duty.

Q. That is the ideal man. Do you find there has been political pressure in favour of the promotion of officers in your department?—A. I find that the political influence is against the promotion of officers and in favour of the bringing in of outsiders; that is what I am objecting to.

Q. A vacancy occurs at a certain point and there are officers occupying subordinate positions who might be promoted. However, political pressure is brought to bear either to appoint a new man or promote some favourite?—A. Yes, and sometimes the favourite is——

Q. Is the most incompetent?—A. Is the most incompetent man they could get to promote.

Q. Then the worthy man does not feel that there is any certainty of his getting promotion, work as hard as he likes?—A. It is largely that way. If we could arrange the service so as to make two distinct classes, the administrative class and the mere clerical class, it might be better. That would result in our getting the right class of men into the administrative work and we could get along with the drones and the clerical class. That would probably form a combination that would be in the best interests of the country.

By Mr. Fyshe:

Q. But do you not think if such a plan were adopted the tendency would be to keep the clerical men from getting beyond the class they were in?—A. No, I should not think so. If they did their work especially well and it came to the knowledge of the superior officers and they are competent for promotion to higher positions, they could, on the recommendation of their chief, be promoted to a higher class as occasion would arise.

Q. It seems to me that, as the service is constituted, there is nobody in any department who is on the lookout to have good deserving men promoted, and on the other

there is nobody in a department whose business it is to see that incompetent men
ıt out?—A. Once a man is appointed it is a most difficult thing to remove him.
}. Why should it be?—A. Because every man has his friends, and if I were to re-
end a man for dismissal because of incompetency his friends would charge me
partiality and say that I was inimical to him. They would get up a hundred ex-
to show that I was not treating that man fairly, and they would use their politi-
fluence to baulk me in the endeavour to increase the efficiency of the service.
fore, I would only incur the enmity of that officer without doing any good to the
e.

By the Chairman:

}. Have you not got departmental examinations?—A. Yes.
}. Occasionally, by a fluke, by luck or something else, you do advance a good man
ı did in Mr. Long's case?—A. Yes.
}. If these departmental examinations are properly administered, you can get
ıromoted from the lower grades?—A. Certainly, any man in the service that will
can go up to the Promotion examinations. The only objection I have to the Pro-
n examination is the manner in which it is conducted.
}. May one ask for an amplification of that statement?—A. In our service they
·e a man to pass an examination that is very technical. It is an examination
thematics, an examination in book-keeping, an examination in the conduct of
·ies, an examination that applies to his general work. Questions are prepared
ıme of these questions are taken from old and obsolete books. The fact of the
r is these questions are prepared by a certain class of our inspectors. They go
:o the old books they themselves studied fifty years ago instead of publishing the
ons and giving the officers some status by which to study. Now, in the univer-
and colleges when a man has to go up and pass an examination, whether in medi-
arts, or anything else, the books that he is to be examined under are prescribed.
is no book prescribed in our examination at all; there is nothing to guide the
date for examination as to the work he has to do except the questions prepared.
they will not allow the questions to be published. Those questions should be
: property after the examination is over; they should be published by the Board
ríl Service Examiners. They do not do so at present because the Inland Revenue
·tment asks them not to do so, and they give as the excuse this absurd reason:
ground over which the questions range is so limited that we do not want the ques-
to be published so that we can use them again on some other occasion.'
}. You consider that the departmental examinations are good if certain modifica-
were made?—A. Yes, they are very good.
}. And occasionally a man like Mr. Long, who succeeds in passing over the hur-
does get on?—A. Yes.
}. But promotions you say are given to the just and the unjust alike?—A. I
l correct myself in this regard; an officer in our service may enter at $500 a year
y passing these examinations there is a certain salary attached to it. He may go
$500 to $1,200 by the mere fact of passing the examinations independent of any
ıal influence of any kind. But when a vacancy occurs in the higher service, when
ınt a collector, a deputy collector, or a special officer, there is where the politician
. in, and he says: 'I want my friend appointed to that position.'
}. Deputy collectors are allowed to be appointed without examination under the
Service Act?—A. Deputy collectors in our branch of the service, but a deputy.
tor is the only political appointment under the Civil Service Act.
}. And when a deputy collectorship becomes vacant instead of one of these able
ʋho have passed all the necessary examinations being eligible for the position out-
ıen are brought in?—A. Generally they are, although in Winnipeg quite recently
cceeded in having a man promoted.
}. Is there anything further you would like to say?—A. There is one thing.
ring to deputy collectors sometimes the appointment is made from the service.

We have in Winnipeg a deputy collector who has passed the highest examinations in our service and it is claimed there are several such deputies in the public service. They claim they should receive a minimum salary equal to the minimum at which the collector is appointed. That is a collector in a first-class division is appointed at $2,200 and he goes up by annual increments until he reaches $2,400.

Q. What would be the salary of a deputy collector in such a division?—A. The minimum is $1,500 and the maximum $1,700. What they claim, in justice to themselves, is that they should be appointed at a salary equal to the maximum salary of the collector of a second class division, $1,800 and that they should go up by annual increments until they reach $2,200, which is the minimum salary of their superior officer. I think that is especially due to deputy collectors who have passed all examinations.

Q. The Inland Revenue Department has a certain system of annual increments for the outside service?—A. Yes.

Q. Do you wish to say anything else?—A. I have here a statement from the mail clerks of western Canada. It is addressed to me and I was asked to submit it to the Commission. The statement deals with the peculiar grievances of the railway mail clerks in the west.

Q. You have no particular knowledge of the conditions under which that service is operated?—A. No, I have not.

Statement handed in and filed.

The WITNESS.—Here is an editorial published in the Winnipeg *Free Press* after we had formed our association there. If the editorial is not already on file, I desire to hand it in.

Q. The editorial you refer to is already on file. Do you desire to say anything else?—A. I have two pathetic letters addressed to the Civil Service Commission by unfortunate fellows who are getting a salary of only $400 a year, or somewhere in that neighbourhood in which they indicate their grievances. They have asked me to place the statements in your hands.

Q. The writers are both in the Post Office Department?—A. Yes, they are both in the Post Office Department.

Letters handed in and filed.

The witness retired.

WINNIPEG, October 9, 1907.

DEAR SIRS,—In compliance with your request re my actual expenses for living in Winnipeg, I beg leave to say that I herewith attach a list of the costs of my housekeeping and verily believe the same to be a careful estimate, if anything under my actual expenses, as I do not allow for any luxuries such as tobacco, &c.

I was appointed into the Inland Revenue Department service May 1, 1903, having been a civil servant four years previous to that in the Winnipeg post office.

I am now receiving a salary of $630 per annum, and lately have received an additional $125 per annum for provisional allowance.

I am a married man with three children, ages 2, 4 and 6 years.

You will be surprised at the lowness of my rent (for Winnipeg), but when I say that I am living about two miles from the office, and the prairie is at my back door, it will explain this.

In reference to the fuel, I use one ton of coal, $10.50 and one cord of wood, cut and split $11.50 = $22 for 6 months, the remaining six months of the year I consider $6 per month, thus averaging during the twelve months $14 per month.

In respect to clothing, I have taken as close an estimate as possible and think $250 per annum for clothing boots, underwear, &c., is the lowest average yearly expense for the family and myself.

You will wonder how I manage when my disbursements are greater than my income from the Inland Revenue Department. The only explanation I can give to this is, that I have to work at side lines when off duty to make both ends meet.

MONTHLY INCOME AND EXPENSES.

me ⅙ of salary at $630		$ 52 50
me ⅙ of Provisional allowance $125		10 41
action for Retirement and Guarantee—		
Fund	$ 2 87	
Rent	25 00	
Electric Light	2 90	
Water	1 00	
Fuel	14 00	
Groceries	18 00	
Meat and Vegetables	11 00	
Milk	2 00	
Bread	3 35	
Clothing, Boots, &c	20 00	
Deficiency per month		37 21
	$100 12.	$ 100 12

OTTAWA, October 16, 1907.

ORMOND HIGMAN, sworn and examined, submitted a memorial, which was read and

By the Chairman :

Q. You are chief electrical engineer in the Department of Inland Revenue ?—Yes.
Q. You have been there since 1894 ?—A. 1894 was the year of my appointment, I was called on by the Minister of Inland Revenue in September, 1892, to draft Act and the regulations.
Q. Have you any other offices besides that of chief electrical engineer ?—A. Yes. minister four Acts—the Act respecting the Units of Electrical Measure, the Act acting the Inspection of Electricity, the Act to regulate the Exportation of Electrical Power and certain liquids and gases, and the Act respecting the, Inspection of and Gas meters.
Q. You have nothing to do with the weights and measures now ?—A. Not at ent. For some time I was considered the chief of that branch, as will appear from following letter written by Mr. Miall :

'INLAND REVENUE DEPARTMENT.
'OTTAWA, May 5, 1897.
·JOHN G. BOURINOT, K.C.M.G., LL.D.,
'Clerk of the House of Commons,
'Ottawa.

'SIR,—I have the honour to request that you will be good enough to allow Mr. Higman, chief of the weights and measures branch of this department, to have ession of the departmental standards of weights and lengths (standards B) in r that they may be compared with the Dominion standards as required by the ghts and Measures Act.
'The department will guarantee that these standards will be returned to you in same order as received within a few days.

'I have the honour to be, sir,
'Your obedient servant,
'(Signed) EDW. MIALL,
'*Commissioner.*'

Q. You have nothing to do at the present moment with weights and measures ?—A. Not at the present moment, but I had for six or eight years. I did most of the technical work of the branch.

Q. Has the Act which was passed last session come into force yet ?—A. Yes, it came into force when assented to by the Governor General.

Q. It did not come into force by proclamation ?—A. The Act of 1894 did, but this was practically a re-enactment of the old Act.

Q. This Act consolidated the previous Acts, and came into force on the date on which it was assented to, that is April 27 ?—A. Yes.

Q. You have been appointed by order in council the chief electrical engineer ?—A. Yes.

Q. Have the inspectors been appointed yet ?—A. Not reappointed. As I understand it, their positions were not interfered with by the re-enactment.

Q. It is provided that everybody shall be required to pass a Qualifying examination to be held by a board of three examiners ; has that examination been held ?—A. We have not been called upon to hold an examination yet. Two men have been brought into the service since ; they have been employed, but not appointed.

Q. That is to say, the provisions of the Act to appoint two examiners to act with yourself have not yet been complied with ?—A. Not yet.

Q. All the old inspectors who were in existence prior to the passing of this Act retain their offices ex officio ?—A. Yes

Q. How many inspectors have you got outside ?—A. Thirty-five.

Q. Are they paid by salaries or by fees ?—A. In all cases by salary.

Q. What salary do you pay the inspectors ?—A. They range from $500 to $1,800.

Q. What is your own salary ?—A. $2,600.

Q. You had a practical experience before you entered the Government service ?—A. Yes, an experience of thirty years.

Q. What was your employment before you entered the service ?—A. I commenced my electrical service in England in 1864, in the electrical telegraph service there. After two years telegraphic service, I resigned and took a two years' course in chemistry in London. I then came to Canada and was continuously for twenty years chief of the operators staff and electrician for the Montreal Telegraph Company at Ottawa, also inspector of electric light for the Underwriters Association. In September, 1892, I was called on by the Government to inaugurate the elctrical inspection work in connection with the Inland Revenue Department. From the age of fourteen until now I have been continuously engaged in electrical work.

Q. How many districts have you where your inspectors are placed ?—A. I think there are sixteen districts. The whole of Canada, excepting the Yukon, is divided into districts.

Q. Are these inspectors expected to visit places periodically ?—A. Yes, they have to visit every electric lighting plant within their district once at least in every year, and as often as may be required to test meters and the electrical pressure—that is the voltage of the supply.

Q. For instance, what is the district of Mr. Roche, the inspector at Ottawa ?—A. It takes in the counties of Carleton, Lanark, Renfrew and Pontiac.

Q. Then, during the year Mr. Roche would have to visit Aylmer, Pembroke, Renfrew, Arnprior and Almonte—wherever electric light is used ?—A. Yes.

Q. And in addition, if a private consumer of electric light wanted his meter inspected Mr. Roche would have to do it ?—A. Yes. Mr. Roche or one of his officers. Usually the inspectors map out a week's work where meters need inspection, and in this way ensure sufficient work to cover the expenses of the trip.

Q. Do your inspectors go when they are told, or do they choose their own time of inspecting ?—A. They have to go when they are required. An electric lighting company may get in a dozen or two of new meters which they require to have inspected before they are put into use, and the inspector will go as soon as possible after receiving notification.

SSIONAL PAPER No. 29a

Q. Then Mr. Roche would not, as a rule, choose his own time for travelling—might be sent out in the middle of winter?—A. Yes.

Q. The inspector when travelling receives his bare travelling expenses?—A. Yes.

Q. I presume that in the outlying small places there would be no electric light—up the Gatineau, for instance?—A. There is none up the Gatineau.

Q. Then the visits of your inspectors would be to places where decent accommoon could be had?—A. Sometimes it is not very decent. My experience has been : the accommodation in some places which we have to visit is very rough indeed. : generally I think it is fair.

Q. Do you think it would act as an inducement to the inspectors to be con-itly on the road if they were paid a per diem allowance instead of their bare out-iocket expenses?—A. There might be a tendency in that direction.

Q. I presume that no man is fully compensated for what he spends while he is y from his head office, as there must be certain charges which he cannot render lccount of?—A. My own experience is—and I am a moderate living man—that I lot cover my expenses.

Q. And probably in the best interests of the public service you think it might n inducement to the inspectors to render more frequent inspections if they were n a per diem allowance instead of their absolute out-of-pocket expenses?—A. I k the service would be greatly improved under a per diem allowance. Under the ent system officers do not care to leave headquarters.

Q. How is the revenue derived from electrical inspection—by fees?—A. Yes.

Q. Can you tell us how much was derived from the electrical inspection last t?—A. In the neighbourhood of $35,000.

Q. What was the expenditure?—A. About $8,000. So that there was a surplus ibout $25,000 roughly.

Q. $8,000 would not cover the salaries of the inspectors?—A. The salaries of most he inspectors are charged to gas inspection.

Q. We will put it another way—gas inspection is under your control?—A. Yes.

Q. What was the revenue derived from gas inspection last year?—A. I have not exact figures. The revenue from the combined services of gas inspection and the iection of electricity was about $58,000 for the nine months ending March 31.

Q. What are your inspectors paid as a rule?—A. Some of the assistants have i getting as low as $500, while one of the inspectors of districts is getting as high :1,800.

Q. Which one is that?—A. Mr. McPhie, of Hamilton. There are two districts e important from a revenue standpoint than the Hamilton district—Toronto and itreal. The inspectors in those districts are paid only $1,600.

Q. I think Mr. Johnstone, of Toronto, got $1,700 last year?—A. Possibly.

Q. When was this scale of salaries laid down?—A. I do not think there has ever i any definite scale of classification.

Q. Has there been any general increase in the salaries?—A. No.

Q. They are pretty much the same as they were ten or fifteen years ago?—A. , pretty much the same.

Q. You said that it was the intention to classify the inspectors; have you any gestion as to their classification?—A. I think the memorandum that was presented Toronto by Mr. Johnstone embodied a fair classification, both as regards revenue salaries.

Q. Would you prepare a little memorandum on that subject?—A. I shall be very i to do so. I would point out that under the new law we require a higher standard our inspectors and assistants. They have now to pass a pretty stiff examination, a college training will be necessary to meet our requirements. In fact, the electric iting companies are insisting that we provide better men, and I think that the iimum of $800 is about the lowest figure that we can hope to procure such men for.

Q. After all, there is not much for an assistant inspector to look forward to?—No, except the position of inspector of a district.

Q. Is it not more than probable that a graduate of a college who has his diploma in electricity would be secured by some outside concern making him a higher offer?—A. I admit that there is a difficulty there. We might find it difficult to retain such men in our service, we certainly could not hope to retain them at present rates of remuneration.

Q. With such development as is now going on, do you think that if a graduate did enter the Government service, the chances are that he would stay there long?—A. We have to face this difficulty. We must not overlook the fact, however, that our universities are turning out hundreds of these young men every year, and they cannot all find first-class employment, so that we may be able to get some of these men in our service and get them to remain with us, if we treat them fairly well.

Q. At the present moment is the supply greater than the demand?—A. I think it is nearing that point.

Q. So that by and by it may be the case that a graduate of a university in electrical engineering may find it difficult to secure employment?—A. Precisely.

Q. In your memorandum you speak of creating new offices. Have you any suggestion to make as to new offices being created?—A. No; I simply had reference to a petition presented to your Commission at Toronto, in favour of creating a position of superintendent of construction, with a salary of $2,400.

Q. Who presented that?—A. Mr. McPhie. We have no construction, and we need no such officer. It is true, we have occasionally an office to fit up electrically or for gas inspection, but it does not require a man appointed specifically to superintend that work.

Q. Then, the only suggestion so far for the creation of a new office was this suggestion of Mr. McPhie?—A. Yes.

Q. And that, you think, is undesirable?—A. Yes. I have here a memorandum which I prepared some years ago for the organization of a bureau for standards, but unfortunately the matter never went through.

(Memorandum read and filed.)

Q. Then, your idea, following this memorandum, is a consolidation of the weights and measures, the gas and the electricity Acts?—A. Yes. I may explain that the gas and electricity inspection is here taken up from the standpoint of weights and measures. Section 3 of the Electrical Units Act says: 'The units of electrical measure described in this Act, or such standard apparatus as is necessary to produce them shall be deposited in the Department of Inland Revenue and shall form part of the system of standards of measure and weight established by the Weights and Measures Act.' Here the electrical standards are placed in the weights and measures system and we can only hope to carry out the gas and electrical inspection from the weights and measures standpoint. Therefore, I say that we should combine them and make one service of them.

Q. For efficient administration and due regard to economy. you think a consolidation of the weights and measures and gas and electric inspection should take place?—A. Yes. I may say that all the officials required are in existence now; there would be no additional cost.

By Mr. Fyshe:

Q. Would this suggested reorganization take these services from the control of the Inland Revenue Department?—A. Not necessarily; but I do think that the present arrangement is an anomaly. For instance, the work of the electrical expert is revised by one who, admittedly, knows nothing technically about electricity.

By the Chairman:

Q. Your idea is that the consolidation should take place, that a superintendent of standards should be appointed, and that the bureau or branch would be under the Minister of Inland Revenue as before?—A. Yes.

Q. Have you anything else to suggest to us?—A. I do not care to advance any-
ıg with reference to my personal status.

Q. You are now getting $2,600 you say?—A. Yes.

Q. How long have you had that?—A. About three years.

Q. What had you before that?—A. I was started in 1894 with $1,500.

Q. What was the number of inspection districts in 1894?—A. Practically the
ıe as now. The whole country from coast to coast was divided into districts which
e remained practically the same. Owing to the influx of population in the North-
t new districts will have to be made there.

Q. Can you tell us the number of inspections that were made in 1894 compared
h the number made at present?—A. I cannot give the number of inspections, but
ın state the matter in another way. The revenue in the first year of the inspection
ı $5,000; last year it was some $35,000, showing a seven-fold increase in the work.

Q. Have the fees always been the same?—A. Always the same.

Q. When was the first increase in your salary?—A. In 1896. Further increases
·e been made from time to time until my salary reached the present figure in
4. In the matter of salary I consider that the Government should have begun
ɔre it has apparently left off. I am in the enjoyment of no superannuation privil-
s, and I trust that if the Superannuation Act is brought in I may be allowed to par-
pate in the benefits of the Act.

Q. How old are you?—A. 56.

Q. What are your hours of work?—A. They are all kinds of hours. I never
.re myself. My work often goes far into the night. When I have been away from
ne I have worked as late as midnight or two o'clock in the morning in order to get
ɔugh, and return, because my offices are closed when I am away from Ottawa. I
lertook the introduction and administration of the Electrical Inspection Act with-
; any assistance. It was very hard work then, and it is harder now with these four
ts to administer. I often find myself taxed to the utmost for the simple reason
ıt I have not got proper assistance. The fact would scarcely be credited that I
·e often to pay a typewriter out of my own private purse to do the departmental
rk. I am allowed no clerical assistance by the department. I have to spend hours
handwriting my letters and doing other office work that an amanuensis at a com-
·atively small salary could do.

By Mr. Fyshe:

Q. Whom do you recognize is your head?—A. The deputy minister.

By the Chairman:

Q. You are a great deal absent from Ottawa, are you?—A. Yes, necessarily.

Q. A great deal of your work is done outside, installing new inspectors?—A.
ı, and supervising their work. For the most part they are not technically trained,
l they need a good deal of help.

Q. Have you any idea how much of the year you spend out of Ottawa and how
ch in Ottawa?—A. I suppose that altogether I spend nearly three months of the
r at outside work.

Q. And during the nine months of the year that you are here you are at your
·k all the day long?—A. Yes.

Q. Do you ever take any holidays for yourself?—A. Not very often. I have never
ɛn the full three weeks in any one year since I have been in the service, and I
not think my vacations will average one week in the year. I may get an odd day
ı and again, but I have not taken regular holidays.

Q. You have no assistant at all now?—A. I have one who has been appointed
hin the last month, promoted from the Toronto office and made Dominion in-

29a—29

spector. In future I shall not need to leave the department so much as I have hitherto done.

Q. You will be able to spend more time in Ottawa?—A. Yes.

Q. You have no clerical assistance at all?—A. No, I have no clerical assistance, and my correspondence has got to be quite considerable.

Q. When this system of inspection of weights and measures, gas and electricity began, there was no Department of Trade and Commerce?—A. No.

Q. There was no department to which it might be attached except the Department of Inland Revenue?—A. No.

Q. In the beginning of the weights and measures system in Canada, where was the standard of a pound weight obtained?—A. From the Imperial authorities.

Q. It was taken from the standard kept in the Tower of London?—A. Yes, Canada was furnished with copies of the standards there.

Q. And they were tested and proved?—A. Yes.

Q. And from them the standards in use in Canada were evolved?—A. Yes.

Q. Sir Henri Joly de Lotbinière was formerly Minister of Inland Revenue?—A. Yes.

Q. From his examination and experience as such he came to the conclusion that a metric system in Canada would be desirable?—A. Yes.

Q. And he has publicly expressed that belief?—A. Yes, on many occasions.

Q. Did he publish a pamphlet on the subject?—A. I think he did.

ELECTRICAL STANDARDS LABORATORY,

OTTAWA, November 4, 1907.

To the Royal Civil Service Commission of Canada:

The undersigned begs most respectfully to submit the following brief memorandum in respect of the classification and reorganization of the inspection services of the Inland Revenue Department:—

As the work of inspection of gas and electricity is performed largely by the same set of officers, all candidates for positions in these services should be required to take the Qualifying examination in electricity prescribed by section 11 of the Electricity Inspection Act, 1907. Candidates for positions as inspectors of weights and measures should undergo the Civil Service Qualifying examination with some special features added, such as mensuration and the construction and testing of weighing machines generally.

In view of the fact that the inspection of gas and electricity in Canada is a part of the weights and measures system, the writer is of the opinion that the three branches of the service could, with great advantage, be administered as a distinctive department of government by a single chief officer. The department might be known as the Bureau of Standards and should be presided over by a technically trained man preferably a graduate in applied science with a thorough practical, as well as theoretical knowledge of electricity. Two technical experts are suggested for positions as chief inspectors, one for eastern Canada and the other for the west. These chief inspectors would supervise the work of all three branches. Such a reorganization as is here outlined could be established without adding anything to the present cost of administration and would result in a very decided improvement in the service.

The undersigned would also recommend that the inspection districts of all three branches be made co-terminous, that is, having the same territorial boundaries; that the districts be classified in accordance with their revenue earning capacities and that the salaries of inspectors and assistant inspectors be arranged proportionately thereto, the minimum in any case being not less than $800 per annum.

Respectfully submitted,

ORMOND HIGMAN,

Chief Electrical and Gas Engineer.

OTTAWA, THURSDAY, June 13, 1907.

The Royal Commission on the Civil Service met this morning at 10.30 o'clock.

Present:—Mr. J. M. COURTNEY, C.M.G., Chairman.
Mr. THOMAS FYSHE, Montreal, and
Mr. P. J. BAZIN, Quebec.

Mr. W. W. CORY, called, sworn and examined.

By the Chairman:

Q. You are Deputy Minister of the Interior?—A. Yes.

Q. A most important department, apparently. Your expenses last year were over $3,000,000?—A. Yes.

Q. And your revenue was about $1,800,000?—A. Yes.

Q. And there are apparently employed in your department and charged to Civil Government about 150 clerks?—A. Yes.

Q. And you have also charged to other votes about 400 clerks who are spread over various buildings in Ottawa?—A. The department employs about 590 clerks.

Q. You were asked to produce certain statements? You now produce them?—A. Yes.

(Statements produced and filed.)

Q. You, as deputy minister, are charged, among other things, with the administration and development of the whole of the Northwest and with the promotion of immigration?—A. Yes.

Q. What salary do you receive?—A. I am receiving $3,700.

By Mr. Bazin:

· Q. I suppose your salary ultimately will be $4,000?—A. That is the maximum.

By the Chairman:

Q. How long have you been in the service?—A. Since 1901.

Q. Where were you employed before that time?—A. I was for eleven years in the service of the province of Manitoba. I was in the Attorney General's department.

Q. Have you been called to the bar?—A. I served my articles and passed my examinations, but was never called to the bar.

Q. You have in the department about eight chief clerks?—A. Yes, about that number.

Q. Whose salaries are charged to Civil Government?—A. Yes. We asked for three more last year but we did not get them.

Q. Mr. Beddoe keeps the accounts of the whole of the services under your administration. He is the accountant?—A. Yes, he is the accountant.

Q. And Mr. Campbell is the head of the timber and mines branch?—A. He is superintendent of forestry now. Mr. B. L. York took Mr. Campbell's place in the timber and grazing branch. We have separated what was known as the timber and mines branch. Mr. Rowatt is now at the head of the mines branch and Mr. York is in charge of the timber and grazing branch.

29a—29½

Q. Mr. Campbell was appointed to succeed Mr. Stewart?—A. Yes, as superintendent of forestry.

Q. Has he been transferred to the outside service?—A. Yes, to the outside service.

Q. Has Mr. Stewart left the Government service?—A. Yes, he has left the service.

Q. Having had better opportunities outside the government service?—A. Yes, he is receiving a better salary.

By Mr. Fyshe:

Q. The custom of men leaving the Government service to better themselves is becoming quite common in Ottawa?—A. It is quite common with us.

By the Chairman:

Q. Who is Mr. J. A. Coté, in the Interior Department?—A. He is my secretary.

Q. And Mr. Narcisse Omer Coté? Is he head of a branch?—A. He is the head of the patents branch.

Q. He succeeded Mr. Goodeve?—A. Yes, Mr. Goodeve.

Q. Mr. Coté has been a long time in the service?—A. 27 or 28 years.

Q. The probability is that if he enjoyed better health he would accept an outside position also?—A. Yes, it is quite possible.

Q. Mr. Henry is in charge of the registration branch?—A. He was until a year ago when his health failed. He is now in the outside service.

Q. Has he been transferred?—A. We have not transferred him; we have made no change. He still holds his position, although another man is performing the duties, but he is engaged in outside work, which agrees with him much better.

Q. Then Mr. Keyes is the secretary of the department?—A. Yes, the secretary of the department.

Q. He is in charge of the correspondence?—A. Yes, we have a large amount of correspondence.

Q. And Mr. Rothwell is law clerk to the department?—A. Yes, law clerk.

Q. He has been a long time in the Government service?—A. Yes.

Q. In your absence, Mr. Rothwell acts as deputy?—A. Yes.

Q. Mr. Ryley, who at one time was in charge of the timber and mines branch of your department, left the Government service to accept a position with the Grand Trunk Pacific Railway Company?—A. Yes, as land commissioner.

Q. What salary did he enjoy in the Government service?—A. I think about $2,500 or $2,700.

Q. And he is now in receipt of $5,000?—A. Something like that.

Q. In addition to the chief clerks, you have what are called technical clerks?—A. Yes.

Q. What does Mr. Biggar do?—A. He is under the chief astronomer; he is a surveyor and astronomer.

Q. Mr. Deville is the surveyor general? How long has he been in that position?—A. I think, about twenty-three or twenty-four years.

Q. You have seen Mr. Deville's letter to the Minister of the Interior, on the subject of salary?—A. Yes, I have seen it.

Q. Mr. Deville says that after a service of twenty-four or twenty-five years he is only receiving a salary of $2,800?—A. I obtained an increase of $200 for him. Since the last of May he has been receiving $3,000. I tried to get his salary advanced to $3,500, but I did not succeed.

Q. Is Mr. Deville an engineer?—A. Yes, he is a very high-class man.

Q. I know that, but has he been an engineer?—A. He is an engineer.

Dr. Deville, I understand, graduated with much distinction from the French Naval School. and was subsequently engaged upon hydrographic surveys for the French government in the islands of the Pacific and other parts of the world. He came to Canada in the seventies, and was first employed by the Government of Quebec as astronomer, surveyor and inspector of surveys. He has had considerable experience in the field. He entered the service of the Department of the Interior as inspector of surveys, and succeeded Mr. Russell as Surveyor General in 1885.

By Mr. Bazin:

Q. The salary paid to him seems to be a very poor one?—A. It is.

By the Chairman:

Q. You have Dr. King, the chief astronomer, in connection with your department?—A. Yes.

Q. He is employed, by virtue of his office, in connection with international boundary commissions?—A. Yes, he has been our boundary commissioner and is now engaged in the delimitation of the international boundary line between Canada and the United States.

Q. And Dr. Klotz is an astronomer?—A. He is an astronomer.

Q. Has he also something to do with delimiting the international boundary?—A. I do not think he has very much to do with the international boundary, but he went to Australia in connection with some scientific work.

Q. Take Mr. McArthur, what is his technical position?—A. He is one of the surveyors in our permanent staff. He is the chief surveyor we have had, under Dr. King, in charge of the surveys in connection with the international boundary line over the Rocky mountains. He is completing that, and will now take up the prairie section almost immediately.

Q. Among the technical officers of the department is Mr. White, the geographer?—A. Yes.

Q. He is the man that prepared the fine atlas that was issued by the department a short time ago?—A. Yes.

Q. The Department of Militia also prepares maps?—A. I think so.

Q. And the Department of Public Works also?—A. Yes.

Q. The Geological Survey likewise prepares maps?—A. Yes.

Q. Also the Railway Department, the Marine and Fisheries Department and the Post Office Department, they also prepare maps?—A. Yes.

Q. Would it not be desirable, in view of Mr. White's technical knowledge, to concentrate the preparation of maps in one bureau under his direction?—A. We keep Mr. White constantly employed in our department in the preparation of maps, and, unless his staff were very largely increased, it would be impossible for him to undertake work such as you suggest.

Q. But the staffs of the other departments would be correspondingly decreased?—A. Yes.

Q. There is nothing in the nature of the work to prevent geological features, or railway lines, or lighthouses being shown on the same map?—A. No. In fact, the Department of Agriculture and a number of other departments use our plates. We have engraved copper plates, that are always in the Toronto Lithographic Company's hands, and other departments ask for the use of them in order to run off their maps. They put on what special features they desire on the black and white map. We are far better equipped than any other department for getting out maps, general, special or any kind of map that is desired.

Q. Considering the magnitude of your department, do you think you have too many chief clerks and technical clerks?—A. No, I do not think we have enough.

Q. I am talking, of course, about this inside service?—A. My reply has reference to the inside service.

Q. You have 17 first-class clerks?—A. Yes, 17.

7-8 EDWARD VII., A. 1908

Q. Do they perform distinctive duties?—A. Yes, they are all heads of branches.

Q. Then, you have 25 second-class clerks?—A. Yes.

Q. Forty-seven junior second-class clerks?—A. Yes.

Q. About 29 third-class clerks, and only 2 messengers who are permanent?—A. We have only 2 permanent messengers.

Q. And you have only 7 temporary clerks? Coming to the third-class clerks, with two exceptions they are all women?—A. Yes, I think so.

Q. Is there now a difficulty in getting the men to enter the public service in the lower ranks?—A. There is difficulty in getting desirable men. We cannot get a desirable man to enter as a third-class clerk.

By Mr. Fyshe:

Q. At $500?—A. At $500.

By the Chairman:

Q. But you have scores of applications for positions from women?—A. Yes, many hundreds.

Q. More than you can employ?—A. Yes, we do not attempt to engage all that apply. We have hundreds of such applications, and we cannot deal with them at all.

Q. Is that not largely due to the fact that persons appointed begin at $500 a year? —A. The women are willing to come in at any moment.

Q. They cannot get less salary than $500?—A. We do not engage them at less than $500, but women are quite willing to come in at that figure. A certain class of men are willing to enter service at $500; but no sooner are they there, than they make complaint and say they cannot live on the salary.

By Mr. Fyshe:

Q. Do they get out, then, as soon as they can?—A. No, but they worry the life out of us to get more salary.

By the Chairman:

Q. The women have a tendency now to press forward into the class above?—A. Yes, they are very anxious to do that.

Q. Take your own department. Would it be a good idea to have a limitation of the salary of women to say $1,000 a year?—A. That has been my view all the way through, that women should not go past the salary of a junior second-class clerk.

By Mr. Fyshe:

Q. But do you not think an arbitrary limitation of that kind is apt to work badly? —A. No.

Q. A matter that is arbitrarily fixed does not take in all possible conditions?—A. As far as our service is concerned, I am quite satisfied that $1,000 is all that any woman can earn.

Q. There are some very able women?—A. There are some very able women, but by the time a woman passes through the third-class and has reached the top of the second class, she has arrived at the place in our service where, in my opinion, she is performing as useful duties as are usually assigned to women, and is, therefore, drawing as much salary as she earns.

Q. Do you not think that some women, like a great number of men, keep growing mentally right along?—A. They do. But women I have always looked upon as different to men; you cannot put a woman at the same class of work that you could put a man at.

Q. You could not appoint them to the control or management of an office?—A. No. Now, in the case of a $1,000 salary, you could get a bright young man with the hope and chance of promotion. When girls enter first at the age of seventeen or eighteen, or it may be from eighteen to twenty-three or twenty-four, they are inspired with the idea either of getting married or of something happening that they can get out of the service. They do not usually take the same interest in their duties that a man does who feels that it is his life's work and he is going to remain at it.

Q. With women it is only an alternative?—A. Only an alternative. When a woman has been in the service for ten or fifteen years, in the majority of cases, while she may do the work assigned to her carefully and well, she does so to a certain extent in a perfunctory manner. I do not find that women give as useful service as men, except as stenographers and junior clerks.

Q. You have been talking of women generally?—A. Of course, there are special cases.

Q. Now and again there are cases?—A. We have some excellent women in our service.

Q. Then, if you had an exceptionally good woman, and promoted her, political pressure would be resorted to to advance other women?—A. We find the difficulty that once you promote a woman, if you raise her from one class to another, pressure, both from inside and outside the service, and not necessarily political, is brought to promote other women from the subordinate ranks.

Q. That is very natural?—A. It is quite natural. We have some women in the department at present in the senior second class, and that fact, together with the natural desire for more pay and promotion, has resulted in many applications from other women servants for like treatment.

By the Chairman:

Q. A lot of people are appointed at the minimum salary of $500 ?—A. Yes.

Q. Supposing that the minimum salary in the third class of $500 was abolished, and you were able to appoint clerks at $600 or $650, would it not stop the pressure being made for the appointment of junior second-class clerks?—A. That might stop the pressure, but I think where you have a desirable young man, a salary of $800 is little enough for him to start on.

Q. How do you ascertain, in an enormous department like yours, the need for the appointment of new clerks?—A. That need I would learn from the reports of the heads of the various branches of the department. They report to me when they are in need of another stenographer or clerk, as the case may be. Then I make inquiry and find out whether or not the need is pressing, and if it is, another clerk is supplied.

Q. Of course, the nominations are all political?—A. Very largely, but not entirely. With us, we have put on a number of officials without political recommendation.

Q. All these third-class and junior second-class clerks have passed the examination ?—A. They cannot become a junior second-class clerk or a third-class clerk without passing the examination.

Q. That presumes the proper age and proper health and good moral conduct?— A. Yes, exactly.

Q. They are appointed on probation ?—A. Yes, always, so far as extra clerks are concerned.

Q. And you give your certificates, after a certain period of time, that their services are satisfactory?—A. Yes.

Q. Coming back to the women, do you find that they claim all the privileges of their sex and the benefits extended to men?—A. Yes. These appointments are very largely from amongst people who have been perhaps five or six years in the service: persons that we take on as temporary clerks on probation.

By Mr. Fyshe:

Q. After examination?—A. They cannot become clerks until they do pass their examination. Many of them, of course, passed the Civil Service examination before

7-8 EDWARD VII., A. 1908

they enter. Upon my recommendation, as to whether they are efficient or not, they are given clerkships.

By the Chairman:

Q. Then, having been examined, and the period of probation having expired, when it comes to promotion they all undergo a further examination?—A. A Promotion examination.

Q. You set certain papers?—A. Yes, on duties of office.

Q. Do you limit your Promotion examinations to two classes of subjects, or do you allow the Civil Service Examiners a free hand?—A. They have a free hand. The candidates simply come up and take the ordinary Promotion examinations, unless it happens to be a special examination. Then, I understand, there is a provision in the Act whereby they can be promoted on the duties of office paper only.

Q. Under sections 46 and 47 of the Civil Service Act, in the case of all promotions, except as otherwise provided, the head of the department has to select, and the head of the department has to reject. Should that not be on the report of the deputy head?—A. I should imagine so.

Q. You have always had to report on a promotion ?—A. Always.

Q. Have any transfers been made to your department from other branches of the public service?—A. We have had a few since I have been there.

Q. Have transfers been made at the instance of the clerks themselves, for their own comfort or benefit, or for the benefit of the department?—A. Perhaps both. First of all, I fancy, we have to know that a clerk desires the transfer before we take any action, and if he is a suitable man and we know him to be such we agree to the transfer. We have had two or three transfers from our department to another department. For instance, Mr. Lewis went to the Trade and Commerce Department, and quite recently Mr. Drake was transferred from the Northwest Mounted Police Department to our Forestry service.

Q. These were special cases?—A. These were special cases. There was another transfer quite recently. Mr. Hobart was transferred from the Interior Department to the Department of Indian Affairs.

Q. But in that case the same minister is at the head of the department?—A. Yes, the same minister.

Q. Have you ever had cases where you had to suspend clerks?—A. Yes.

Q. Were the clerks reinstated afterwards?—A. Yes.

Q. They purged themselves of their wrong-doing, I suppose?—A. To a certain extent.

Q. Of course they lost their pay during the period of suspension?—A. Yes.

Q. Have they had any increments since?—A. I think so. One did; the other was at the head of his class.

Q. They would be deserving of the increments?—A. Yes.

Q. You would not issue a perfunctory report in such cases?—A. No.

Q. You have only in the department now, as a matter of fact, seven temporary clerks. Is it your policy now to have few temporary clerks?—A. We have a very large number of temporary clerks.

Q. But I mean charged to Civil Government?—A. We do not desire to have temporary clerks if we can avoid it.

Q. What is the leave of absence granted to the officers of your department?—A. Three weeks annual leave and special sick leave on a medical certificate.

Q. Did you ever take leave yourself?—A. I have never had any leave since I have been in the department.

Q. How many years is that now?—A. Over six.

Q. And you say you never had any leave?—A. That is I never went off for leave. I have been away from the department, but always transacted public business. I have never gone away for a week or two weeks as a holiday.

Q. Do you think that is right either to yourself or to the department?—A. I do
not think it is, but I have been so situated that I could not get away. I think in the
case of such a large department it is only fair to the department and to myself that I
should take a holiday.

Q. How about attendance books in a large department like yours, with so many
branches and employing over 500 people?—A. We have attendance books in every
branch of our service. I think the employees sign twice a day—when they come in
in the morning and when they come in in the afternoon. We do not require them to
sign when they leave because we do not allow our clerks out until 4.30. A large
number of them remain until five or six o'clock; others leave very promptly at half-
past four.

Q. Are these attendance books brought in to you?—A. They are under the control of the secretary.

Q. What are the luncheon hours?—A. From half-past twelve to two o'clock.

Q. That is, a series go out at half-past twelve and another series at one?—A. All
out together. Our department is closed at half-past twelve. .

Q. During the session of Parliament when members are free between one and
two o'clock is your department entirely shut up?—A. It is to all intents and purposes,
but heads of branches always arrange to have one or two clerks on hand during
luncheon hour, so that the offices are always open.

Q. Then the department is always open to the public in one way or the other?—
In one way or the other.

Q. Of course during the session some of the officials have to go up to the House
Commons during the evening?—A. Quite frequently.

Q. During the evidence of Mr. Burgess, the then Deputy Minister of Interior,
some fifteen years ago, he talked of the state of the records in the department. He
said that the surveys, maps, plans, and all that kind of thing were in a very dangerous and unprotected state?—A. The survey records are now all down in the Woods
building.

Q. Are they secure from fire?—A. The building is supposed to be fireproof, and
they are in steel cases.

Q. The cost of your survey from first to last amounts to some millions of dollars
I suppose?—A. We estimate about $750,000 a year.

Q. And these maps are pretty secure?—A. I think so.

Q. They are not unprotected as in the old time?—A. Not as in the old time.

Q. Where are your offices, containing the 500 odd employees situated?—A. It is
quite a task to say where they are. We have the land patents branch, the land commissioner's branch, and the offices of the Minister and myself in the Langevin block.
The immigration branch is located in the Canadian building on Slater street, near the
canal. The Surveyor General has a building on Metcalfe street. That official also
has a branch in the Imperial building and our stationery office is in the same structure.

By Mr. Fyshe :

Q. That is very awkward ?—A. Yes, it is very awkward.

Q. Can you not all get into the same building?—A. We have tried repeatedly, but
cannot get the accommodation.

Q. Can you not get an appropriation sufficient to erect a building in which the
staffs of the whole department could be accommodated ?—A. We have not been able
to as yet. Then, the timber and grazing branch is also in the Canadian building.
The survey records are in the Woods building, and also the school lands and ordnance
branches.

By the Chairman :

Q. How can you properly control your staff ? You cannot perambulate all day
going from one building to the other ?—A. No, it would be impossible for me to do

it. Of course we have our chief clerks in charge of the several branches and we have telephonic communication. Then, we have a system by which all the letters coming from the various branches, except the immigration branch, have to be signed by the secretary of the department, Mr. Keyes. A messenger each morning brings the letters that have been dictated the previous day to the secretary and he signs them and another messenger takes the letters back.

Q. That must lead to a great deal of delay ?—A. Very considerable delay.

By Mr. Fyshe :

Q. Is the secretary fully acquainted with the particulars of the correspondence in the several branches ?—A. He is not acquainted with the particulars but we require the chief clerk of the branch to initial the press copy of the letters.

Q. So that the secretary's signature is to a large extent formal ?—A. Quite formal.

Q. Having to sign so many letters he would be apt to do it rather mechanically ?—A. Quite true, but he sees that each letter bears the initials of the chief clerk of the branch.

Q. Do you not think it is rather objectionable to have secretary of the department appending his signature just as if he were a machine? Would it not be better to thrust the responsibility upon the department for the letters written ?—A. They do it in that way through the secretary. The department is responsible through the secretary for the letters that go out. We hold the chief clerk responsible through the secretary for letters that go out. We hold the chief clerk responsible for his initials on each letter that goes from his branch.

Q. You might save a lot of trouble by having a stamp ?—A. Yes.

By the Chairman :

Q. In your department you have stamps to sign your letters ?—A. Not the originals. We never sign any original documents with the stamp. That is simply for the press copies that remain on the file.

Q. And not used in signing these letters ?—A. They are all signed by the secretary or the assistant secretary.

Q. Anything from yourself would be signed by you ?—A. Personal letters I sign; letters to Ministers, Members and that sort of thing.

Q. In this large department of yours do you find the health of the clerks suffering through over-crowding ?—A. Yes, we had a great deal of difficulty with that. We have had something like twenty to twenty-five stenographers in one room, with all the machines going at the same time, sitting as close to each other as they can sit. We are using for such purposes the top story of the Langevin block which was never intended for offices. It is very difficult to get ventilation and the place is very hot in the summer. However, we are helpless in the matter. We had to get the work done. All the employees were in the Langevin block at first, and they have been forced out from time to time in order to give breathing room for those that had to remain close to the Minister.

By Mr. Fyshe :

Q. That certainly is very awkward?—A. It is very awkward and very unsatisfactory.

Q. Do you think your department with such a number of clerks is over-manned ?—A. No. I do not think so. I have a summarized statement here showing the rate per cent of the increase in work also in the staff, in each of the branches of the Department of the Interior since the year 1900. This statement is as follows:—

Branch.	Staff in 1900.	Staff in 1906.	Rate, per cent of Increase in Staff.	Rate, per cent of Increase in Work.	Remarks.
Minister.	3	4	33	50	
ry.	2	4	100	400	(Correspondence included.)
nt Secretary.	2	4	100	400	
erk.					No report.
y.	2	8	300	492	
ce.					66 p.c. decrease in staff, 12 p.c. decrease in work.
in Council				15	No increase in staff. 15 p.c. increase in work.
Branch	3	6	100	500	
pher	6	20	233	300	
l.	25	58	132	216	Increase in Letters Patent.
				463	Increase in homestead entries.
Records.	6	12	100	800	
Branch.	34	90	165	450	
ation.	21	56	166	340	
ation	15	39	160	600	
on Lands	10	38	280	428	
y and Swamp Lands				100	Did not exist in 1900. Increased 100 p.c. in 3 years.
Lands	5	10	100	300	
tant.	14	16	14	125	
and Grazing.	18	22	22	75	
Rowatt).		13			New branch.
f Mines (Haanel)			137		Increase of work not given.
; Room	5	8	60	277	
tory	14	44	300	550	

By Mr. Fyshe:

. Your methods of doing work, I suppose, are as simple and economical as possi-
-A. I think they are.
. Is any unnecessary work done ?—A. Not that I am aware of.
. Is there any duplication of work ?—A. There is no duplication. That is a
we are very careful about.
. Has there been a regular system devised for the registration of the work?—
s, we have a very careful system of registration. I should say that every week a
is made to me from every branch as to the amount of work done. Then, reports
ade as to attendance, sick leave, absences, and all that sort of thing.
. I suppose the increased immigration gives your department much additional
—A. That is one of the sources of our increased work. As the new arrivals come
l take up land, they immediately open correspondence with the department, and
rk is increased in that way.

By the Chairman:

. Coming to the general effect of the Civil Service Act, do you think the grada-
f classes under the Act is a desirable system ? I mean the gradation of
into first, second, and third classes?—A. I think we should have classification.
. You think the classification, as laid down in the Civil Service Act, might be
red?—A. I do not think there is anything the matter with the classes.

By Mr. Fyshe:

. There is not a strict correspondence between the different classes and the dif-
kinds of work, is there?—A. It is quite impossible in a department to get every

man at the work of his class; for instance, a second-class clerk doing a second-class clerk's work. A second-class clerk may be doing the work of a first-class clerk. Very often that is the case, because we have not enough first-class clerks to do the work of that class.

By the Chairman:

Q. Then, in your opinion, promotion is not quick enough?—A. Not quick enough.

Q. With practically a new department, which is developing fast, the men in the several classes are doing work which belongs to a higher class?—A. Yes, I am satisfied of that.

Q. Then, the general effect of the Civil Service Act is economical, as far as your department is concerned?—A. Yes, it is economical, as far as our department is concerned.

Q. You are not one of the officials to whom the superannuation abatement applies?—A. No.

Q. You are under the Retirement Act?—A. Yes, under the Retirement Act.

Q. That is to say, you contribute to a retirement fund out of your own money? —A. Out of my own money, and I get that money back with interest.

Q. What do you think has been the effect on the public service of the abolition of the Superannuation Act?—A. I do not know how it affects the Civil Service, but it affects the individual.

Q. How does it affect the individual?—A. I think, prejudicially, and the service the same way.

Q. It does not add stability to the service?—A. No.

By Mr. Fyshe:

Q. Was there any organized protest against the abolition of the Superannuation Act?—A. Not that I am aware of. There is one objection I have to the Superannuation Act, as it affects those to whom it applies: That is, a man may die in harness after thirty-five or forty years of service, during which he has paid into the fund, and yet his family would not get one cent. We have had several such cases in our own department.

Q. It was only half an Act?—A. Take the case of Mr. Ryley, who paid for twenty-four years into the superannuation fund. He left the service and did not get a farthing from the fund, nor did his family.

Q. How was that?—A. Because he resigned.

Q. How much percentage of his salary did he pay?—A. Two per cent. Then, there was the case of Mr. Goodeve who paid, I think, into the superannuation fund for thirty-five years.

By the Chairman:

Q. He died suddenly?—A. He died suddenly. He was like working in the office to-day and died at night; his wife never got a farthing.

Q. A recent notorious case is that of the late Mr. Thos. MacFarlane. This day week he was living and on the eve of superannuation and six months' leave of absence. He died suddenly, and notwithstanding his contributions to the fund for many years, his widow receives nothing?—A. Such cases, I think, constitute a very serious objection to the Superannuation Act.

Q. Then you think something better than the Superannuation Act, perhaps in the nature of a pension, would be desirable?—A. I think it is absolutely desirable.

Q. You know, as a matter of fact, that since the Superannuation Act has been abolished a system of pensions for the militia has been adopted?—A. I understand so.

Q. And pensions are now granted to the warriors?—A. Yes.

Q. And to their widows and orphans?—A. Yes.

Q. The Northwest Mounted Police officers also are now entitled to pensions?—
ʟ I understand so.

Q. So that in the Northwest you find mounted police inspectors who receive
ᴘensions working side by side with your agents who get no pensions? Does that not
ᵣeate a little envy?—A. I should imagine it would create envy. Then I understand
ᴛhe officials on the Intercolonial Railway are also provided with pensions.

Q. They are a grade lower down?—A. But they are something better than the
ᴇst of us.

Q. Now we come to your outside service. You have about 400 people here in
'ttawa that are not charged to civil government but to other votes?—A. Yes.

Q. Are these people appointed notwithstanding anything to the contrary in the
ɪvil Service Act?—A. No, I think we have special votes. We simply appoint them.

Q. They have all passed the Civil Service Examination?—A. Oh, no; many of
ᵉm have passed, but it is not necessary in their case.

Q. In the school lands branch I see that Mr. Checkley is chief clerk. He was
ᴛᴀferred as a first-class·clerk from the department?—A. Yes.

Q. What do you call school lands particularly?—A. They are lands set apart by
Dominion government as an endowment to the schools in the provinces of Mani-
a, Saskatchewan and Alberta. There are two sections in every township, sections
and 29, set aside for the purpose of endowing schools in those provinces.

By Mr. Fyshe:

Q. The lands are not given away to the provinces?—A. No, they are held by the
'ᴍinion. We sell them for the benefit of the schools in the provinces I have men-
ᴛᴇd.

Q. They are for the benefit of the provincial schools?—A. For the benefit of the
ᴏvincial schools.

By the Chairman:

Q. The school lands are sold by public auction?—A. By public auction.

Q. And the interest of the school lands funds goes to the provinces you have
entioned?—A. Yes. We have inspectors that are sent out to inspect the school lands
ᴅd value them; that is, place a minimum or what may be termed an upset price upon
ᴇm. We accept nothing less than the inspector's valuation.

By Mr. Fyshe:

Q. Prices vary so much and are changing all the time?—A. Quite true, but our
ᴤpectors take that into consideration. We have a minimum price of $7 an acre.
e do not allow the inspectors to value the school lands at less than $7 an acre, but
ᵉy may value the lands at $5,000 if conditions justify it. Then we will not sell the
ᴅd at less than the $5,000. That must be the first bid, and of course we accept any-
ᴉng over that.

By the Chairman:

Q. Then those lands are sold openly and in public, and the provinces get the
ᴤerest on the money realized?—A. Yes, they get the interest on the money.

By Mr. Fyshe:

Q. Practically the Federal government acts as trustee?—A. Yes, as trustee, and
: cost of administering the lands is charged up pro rata against the three provinces
against the interest of the funds of the three provinces.

By the Chairman:

Q. You have a raft of people charged to immigration?—A. Yes.

Q. This branch is under the control of a superintendent and inspector?—A. Yes.

Q. Where is the immigration branch located?—A. In the Canadian building.

Q. All under one roof?—A. All under one roof.

Q. Is the number of employees disproportionate to the wants of the service?—A. No, I think not. Our superintendent is a very cautious man.

Q. What was he before he came into the service?—A. Originally, I think, he was in the service of the Canadian Pacific Railway Company in Manitoba many years ago. Then he was in the service of the Manitoba Government. He has always been in the immigration service, whatever Government or corporation he has been employed by.

. Q. Do you give bonuses now in aid of immigration?—A. Yes, in the case of British people.

Q. And what about immigrants from the continent of Europe?—A. There are bonuses given in the case of people from certain continental countries.

Q. Is the North Atlantic Trading Company still in existence?—A. Not that I am aware of.

Q. That business is all settled up?—A. The company is not doing any business with us now.

Q. You have travelling agents who go out with the immigrants as they arrive?—A. Yes.

Q. From the time the immigrant lands at Quebec or Halifax until he is placed on the land he is under the charge of some person or other?—A. Somebody has the charge of him.

By Mr. Fyshe:

Q. Are there many complaints from the incoming immigrants about the way they are treated?—A. No, very rarely. We seldom get complaints from the incoming people; they are very well satisfied.

Q. And how about the foreign arrivals?—A. We have foreign interpreters who take charge of the foreign element. The foreign arrivals are placed in charge of people who can speak their own language.

By the Chairman:

Q. Some of your travelling agents were spotted making charges for luncheons and sleeping berths that they never paid?—A. Yes, I understand so.

Q. They were dismissed, I suppose?—A. They were dismissed.

Q. Is care taken in the choice of these travelling agents?—A. I think there is as much care as you can take in matters of that kind. Certain parties are applicants and we make the best choice we can of those that apply for positions. Many of them are old railway men familiar with travelling on trains and that sort of thing.

Q. Do your inspectors and travelling agents get anything more allowed to them than bare out-of-pocket expenses?—A. Nothing but their actual and necessary travelling expenses. They get $4 a day while on the train and their actual disbursements.

Q. Then they get a per diem allowance?—A. Just while they are working.

By Mr. Fyshe:

Q. That is the regular pay?—A. That is the regular pay, $4 a day. In addition they receive their actual necessary travelling expenses.

By the Chairman:

Q. Do you not think that if there was an allowance for travelling expenses an official might entertain a little?—A. I think that our chief officers should have a per diem allowance when travelling.

By Mr. Fyshe:

Q. It would be better than the present system?—A. Much better.

By the Chairman:

Q. An inspector going out on duty is out of pocket, I presume?—A. There is no doubt about it.

Q. And considering that you are opening up a vast territory, it is politic to have inspectors continually on the move?—A. Yes, we must keep them constantly on the move.

Q. Then, as a matter of fact, the inspectors who are constantly on the move are losing money while travelling?—A. That is my impression. I am told that, and from my own experience I judge it to be correct.

By Mr. Fyshe:

Q. The tendency is to deter them from doing what they might otherwise do, because it means a loss of money?—A. Yes, a loss of money.

By the Chairman:

Q. What do you call detention hospitals?—A. A detention-hospital is a hospital where immigrants otherwise desirable, are detained while temporarily disabled. We have hospitals at Halifax, Quebec, Vancouver and Victoria.

Q. You have also one at St. John?—A. Yes, there is one at St. John. We have a detention hospital at every port of entry.

Q. When a steamship comes up the River St. Lawrence it should undergo quarantine at Grosse Isle for infectious and other diseases?—A. Yes, at Grosse Isle, but merely for small-pox.

Q. And for diphtheria?—A. No, I do not think the steamships are detained for diphtheria.

Q. Then when the steamship arrives at Quebec it is met by Dr. Page?—A. Dr. Page is our officer.

Q. He has to pass the immigrants there?—A. Yes, but he has three assistants.

Q. He told those who were present at the last tuberculosis convention in this city that he had to frequently pass last year as many as 3,000 immigrants a day?—A. Yes.

Q. I suppose, this year, with the increase in immigration, the number will amount to more than 3,000 a day?—A. Yes, I think they have passed as high as 5,000 immigrants a day this year.

Q. How, in the name of heaven, can a medical officer pass 5,000 immigrants a day?—A. We have three inspectors before whom the immigrants come. First of all, the second-cabin passengers are examined on the steamship. Their eyes are examined, and when anything out of the ordinary is apparent, the immigrant is asked to stand aside. Then he undergoes a more minute examination afterwards. A large percentage of the immigrants, however, really do not require examination. The third-class passengers are brought into a large room and pass along before the inspectors and are treated exactly in the same way. The inspectors turn the eyelids of the immigrants up to see that their eyes are clean, examine their heads to see that their scalp is clean, look at their teeth, and all that sort of thing. If the immigrant has any physical deformity or disability, he is sent into a room to be examined more minutely. If he is found to be suffering from disease, he is taken to the detention hospital, and the transportation company pays the cost of his treatment until he is cured and allowed to go forward.

By Mr. Fyshe:

Q. The inspectors cannot examine the immigrants for such diseases as tuberculosis? —A. No. If the inspectors suspect that an immigrant is suffering from tuberculosis, they will ask him to stand aside. If there are indications of any disease, the inspector asks the immigrant to stand aside. The same system of inspection is in force in New York, and I have seen them pass immigrants there at the rate of 7,000 or 8,000 a day

By the Chairman:

Q. Dr. Page mentioned that a lunatic had slipped through the hands of the inspectors last year?—A. Well, I believe one lunatic did.

Q. Is it possible to pass 5,000 people in a day?—A. I think it is possible.

By Mr. Fyshe:

Q. Is it possible for one man to do that?—A. Oh no, we have three inspectors.

Q. That is something over 1,600 persons for each inspector?—A. Yes, but you see
they pass along quickly, and, as I said, a great many do not require minute examination.

Q. If there were a hundred an hour, or two a minute, it would take about 15 or
18 hours?—A. The inspectors work long hours, but while they may have 5,000 people
to pass to-day, tomorrow there may be none.

By the Chairman:

Q. If the inspectors fail to get through with the inspection of the immigrants they
would keep them until next day?—A. The inspectors pass the immigrants very
quickly.

Q. Do you think it would be desirable to amalgamate the public health branch
and your inspection of immigrants branch?—A. Do you mean amalgamate the quarantine branch with our inspection branch?

Q. Yes?—A. I do not know as to that. They do not do that in the States. Over
there the quarantine work is under the state officers, and the inspection of immigrants
is carried out by the federal officers. They keep the two branches separate and
distinct.

By Mr. Fyshe:

Q. Do they manage the inspection of immigrants as you do through the Department of the Interior?—A. The inspection of immigrants is handled through the Department of Labour. That department has control of the admission or rejection of
immigrants, and they charge each immigrant admitted so much per head.   The
United States makes a large revenue out of the immigrant arrivals, over and above
the actual cost of examining and deporting. Every person entering in at the United
States is charged $2 a head.

By Mr. Bazin:

Q. Does Canada charge anything for the admission of immigrants?—A. No.

By Mr. Fyshe:

Q. The United States used to charge immigrants $1?—A. The charge is $2 now,
and they are proposing to raise the amount to $5. I am not sure that that has not
been done.

Q. That is rather a new departure, is it not?—A. A head tax has been exacted in
the United States for some time, but we have not made any change. We are anxious
to get desirable people.

Q. In the United States they used to levy $1 a head on people coming from
Canada?—A. Yes.

Q. I have paid it myself?—A. They are not exacting it now from Canadians.

Q. I do not mean to say the charge was made when crossing to the United States
by railway, but going from Nova Scotia by boat?—A. Quite so.

By the Chairman:

Q. Of course in such a service as that of immigration there is a large expenditure
for the printing of pamphlets and leaflets?—A. Yes.

Q. I see you spent last year for printing and advertising over $112,000?—A. Yes.

Q. Is that expenditure under the control or audit of the King's Printer?—A. No.

Q. What steps do you take to see that only the proper amount is charged?—A. When we are getting out a pamphlet we take it to certain firms and ask for prices. Then the quality of the work must be satisfactory, and there must be expedition in turning the pamphlet out. When we are issuing a pamphlet we want it printed quickly and we want the work done well.

By Mr. Fyshe:

Q. Do you get your pamphlets printed by independent firms?—A. By independent firms.

Q. Why do you not get them printed at the Printing Bureau?—A. One reason is that in urgent cases it is found more expeditious to have the work done outside.

By the Chairman:

Q. I see that a great many newspapers have a share of the patronage?—A. Not so much in printing pamphlets. In the case of the ordinary plain pamphlet, a newspaper can get it out much cheaper.

Q. There are certain newspapers that have a certain share of the work?—A. Yes, we have had work done by newspapers.

Q. Do you take care that the proper price only is charged?—A. We get our work done as cheaply as it is possible for us to do and get it done well.

By Mr. Fyshe:

Q. Is it done only by people who belong to the proper political faith?—A. That may be, possibly.

By the Chairman:

Q. Would it not be desirable to have this large expenditure audited by the King's Printer?—A. It might not.

Q. He audits all the work of this kind done for the Intercolonial Railway?—A. Does he?

Q. Oh, yes.—A. Well, I do not see any particular objection.

Q. It would at all events have this benefit that whilst the newspapers were doing printing for the Government, the public would be shown that the expert only allowed the proper price to be paid?—A. Yes, there is something in that.

Q. In the United States for the same purposes you expended $90,000 last year?—A. That was largely for maps and high class pamphlets.

Q. That went to Rand & McNally and Lord & Thomas?—A. The money paid to Rand & McNally was for maps, geographies and atlases. They can do a class of work that we cannot get done in Canada at all for any money. They have a very nice wall map which they frame for us and get out for possibly fifty cents each. In Canada you could not get such a thing done for five times the amount. Messrs. Rand & McNally have the wax process.

By Mr. Fyshe:

Q. Is it true that they cannot get up in the United States maps equal to those which are produced in England and on the continent of Europe?—A. We have not had very much to do with maps in the old country. We do not handle them, and I have not seen very much of them, but they may be able to produce maps much cheaper in the old country than here.

Q. It is not that they are so much cheaper but they seem to be infinitely better?—A. They may be better, but the maps we get in the United States are very good for our purpose, and they show everything up to date. They are the class of matter that the

29a—30

people want. There is nothing like a map or an atlas to attract people's attention; we find they are the most satisfactory class of matter we issue.

Q. I should think the difficulty about the Northwest would be to get maps that are recent enough?—A. We get all our information for our maps from our geographer and he obtains it from the surveys branch and from other sources. Our maps are therefore up to date and turned out at the lowest rate.

By the Chairman:

Q. I see that you spent $30,000 in London for printing and advertising?—A. Yes.

Q. This chiefly went to Streets? The firm is well-known?—A. That is largely for newspaper advertising.

By Mr. Fyshe:

Q. Do you advertise all over the country?—A. In almost every paper. Through Lord & Thomas in the United States and through Streets in London.

Q. McKim's agency in Montreal is quite an extensive one?—A. We do our advertising in Canada direct with the newspapers. We can get just as good a price as an advertising agency can, but in the States it is not possible to get into touch with the individual newspaper people. Therefore we do our advertising through Lord & Thomas in the United States, and through Streets in England.

By the Chairman:

Q. How many offices do you think you have in the outside service of your department?—A. I can get that information.

Q. I see from the Auditor General's report that you have two batches of immigration offices in Manitoba and the Northwest?—A. These are largely people at the Winnipeg office. They have an office very much the same as we have here for the care and distribution of immigrants. The offices at various other points are for the same purpose. The agents travel with the people they take out and there are places where they stop for a week or so until the immigrants are located.

Q. You have travelling agencies and caretakers and interpreters, and you furnish the immigrants with every information?—A. Yes.

Q. A Galician or a Doukhobor by merely looking at a man would know he was in the service of the Dominion government?—A. The immigration officer wears a cap with a distinctive mark on it.

Q. Is the Dominion astronomical observatory where a staff of people are employed under the control of the Department of the Interior?—A. Yes. Part of the staff of the Dominion astronomical observatory are on the civil list and part on the list of extra employees.

Q. They are stationed at the observatory which is located on the Experimental Farm?—A. Yes.

Q. The observatory answers the same purpose in Canada that Greenwich observatory answers in England?—A. Yes.

Q. It is the centre of latitude and longitude for the Dominion?—A. Yes, the centre.

Q. Then you have staffs attached to the boundary surveys?—A. Yes, those are all technical officers.

Q. Occasionally there is a solar eclipse—say once in ten years—and you send out a staff of astronomers to take observations?—A. There has been one eclipse since I have been in Ottawa.

Q. And the observations were made somewhere on the Labrador coast?—A. At Hamilton inlet, I believe.

Q. In the case of the surveys some of the staff are paid salaries?—A. Yes, we send some of our surveyors direct from the head office.

Q. And some go out under contract?—A. Yes.

Q. When the last Civil Service Commission sat some of these contractors were in lefault ?—A. In what way ?

Q. They had advances under their contracts and never accounted for them ?—A. I was not aware of that fact, there is nothing of that kind now.

Q. Under the contract now, the contractors when they come back have to make returns ?—A. Yes, they make returns.

Q. In the Auditor General's report you will notice several instances dating from 880 where the accounts are kept open; no account has ever been rendered. Latterly he contractors seem to have accounted as they came back. You will find the items to 'hich I allude at page L—58 of the Auditor General's report ?—A. Things are done etter now.

Q. When you send men out on surveys, do you give them cash ?—A. We give lem letters of credit cheques.

Q. I suppose the banks are available almost everywhere ?—A. Take a party oing north of Edmonton. They would get their cash in that city or they would de->sit their cheques, say in the Montreal bank or the Merchants bank in Edmonton, nd then simply draw against it from time to time and the banks honour the cheques.

By Mr. Fyshe :

Q. You keep sending out these survey parties all along ?—A. Yes, every spring ı the early part of April, we usually start sending our surveyors out.

Q. And they return about September or October ?—A. No, not much before the rst of December. Some of them would remain out all winter where the district is 'ooded.

By the Chairman:

Q. Coming back to the subject of the survey contracts that are unaccounted for, ould it not be better to have them closed up ? Perhaps you had better make a note l it and give it your attention. No doubt many of these men have died ?—A. I will ıake inquiry about it. Of course these things were long before my time.

Q. There is no discredit upon the department now because it was before your me. Many of the accounts date back to 1880, 1881, 1882. If the people have died, ıd the surveys were performed, you had better wipe the accounts out or make in-ıiries ?—A. I will attend to it.

Q. Do you take securities for these contracts ?—A. We take a personal bond for ıuble the amount of the contract.

Q. In your time have there been any defaulters ?—A. No, there has not been any ·fault.

Q. Or any case of not accounting ?—A. No case of non-accounting, but there ıs one case where we advanced money to a man who did not pay his workmen. We ıd some difficulty over that, but otherwise I think everything has been straight-rward. The case referred to occurred just a year before I came in, but I knew ıout it.

Q. Would it not be much better to take bonds in a guarantee company ?—A. I n much in favour of that. Guarantee company bonds are much preferable.

Q. Before we leave the matter of surveys, what is the grant of land to an immi-·ant at present ?—A. 160 acres.

Q. Must a landholder in the Northwest be a British subject ?—A. Not when he kes up a homestead, but he must be a British subject before he gets his patent.

Q. In the case of the settlers coming in from the United States, when they get ıeir patents they must become British subjects ?—A. That is why we make our term ıree years. It takes three years for a man to become naturalized if he comes into ıis country to reside. Therefore we make our homestead conditions extend over ıree years before he can get his patent, so that a man can qualify as a British sub-ct at the same time that he completes his homestead duties.

29a—30½

By Mr. Fyshe:

Q. He can go on occupying the land?—A. Any one can take up a quarter-section of land and occupy it, and continue to perform his homestead duties, but before a foreigner gets his patent he must be naturalized.

By the Chairman:

Q. If an immigrant wants another section of land how does he obtain it? Is there an upset price?—A. We do not sell land now. All our lands are held for homestead entry. Additional land beyond the 160 acres must be acquired from somebody else, a private corporation or an individual; it cannot be bought from the Government.

By Mr. Bazin:

Q. Then in the case of the children of a settler, they could not get land alongside his own?—A. He could, if his son had passed the age of 17. We sometimes hold lands for young men who are in their 18th year, so that they may have an opportunity of remaining near their parents.

By the Chairman:

Q. Then if a man goes out with three or four sons over 18 years of age, they can settle around him?—A. They can take up the four quarters of an even section if the land is available.

By Mr. Fyshe:

Q. If they are under age?—A. They must be 18 years of age or over, and they can live with their father and do their duties and residence in that way.

By the Chairman:

Q. The free grant lands are the only ones you deal with?—A. We only deal with free grant land, with the exception that under the Irrigation Act of 1898 it is provided that where a man will undertake to bring water on semi-arid land and irrigate a fourth of it, we will sell the land to it at $3 an acre. In certain districts the land is semi-arid, and will not produce wheat without water. A man can file plans with the commissioner of immigration at Calgary, and make application for what land he requires, a quarter-section, a half-section or a section. He must, however, irrigate at least twenty-five per cent of the land he requires. Then we will sell to him at $3 an acre.

By Mr. Fyshe:

Q. Including the irrigated part?—A. Including the irrigated part, yes.

By the Chairman:

Q. How does a surveyor, working under contract, obtain his contract?—A. He simply applies to the surveyor general.

Q. And the surveyor general lets the contract?—A. The surveyor general reports to us how many contractors he requires, and out of a list of surveyors, we select the men the surveyor general thinks most suitable for the work.

Q. May we ask whether politics enter into the selection?—A. We do not know what the politics of the man may be. He may reside in a certain district, and the member may recommend him for employment, but we do not necessarily employ that man. I suppose that if two men are equally qualified, the man who is recommended is usually employed.

By Mr. Fyshe:

Q. I should think that at the present time, when there is such a craze for mining discoveries, that a lot of fellows would like to get money advanced by the Government to go out and prospect the land for their own advantage?—A. We select the land that the man has to survey, and we make him an advance of perhaps $1,500 on a $6,000 contract. Then he has to send in, I think monthly, a return of the amount of work that has actually been performed. The man is not entitled to go outside of that district to do any work; we would not pay him for any work done outside of the area actually assigned to him.

Q. Do you make it necessary that he should spend some of his own money?—A. We give him enough to start with. We give him perhaps $1,500 and then on progress estimates showing the work that has been done, we make other payments, but we always keep back not less than 10 per cent until the whole thing is completed, and the plan accepted by the surveyor general.

By Mr. Basin:

Q. Are these contracts usually made at a certain price per mile or acre?—A. That depends upon the nature of the country. The country is classified into prairie land, hilly country and country that is extensively timbered.

Q. You would only know that after the survey had been done?—A. We know whether the district is wooded or whether it is not. Then the surveyor is paid on the way his lines are shown, and we have inspectors who go around and see that the work is done as it is required to be done. . .

By the Chairman:

Q. What is the process adopted in selling timber limits?—A. The process adopted is shortly this: A man goes out and prospects and applies to us to have put up a certain area of timber, indicating it by township, range or other marks that can be plainly set out on the map. Then we get a report on that from our agents of Dominion lands, to find out whether there is any demand for that timber from the settler residing in the district or whether there is any reason why it should not be put to public competition. If the agent reports everything correct we advertise in the local newspapers that this area of timber will be tendered for on a certain date at the head office of the department. Then the man who pays the highest bonus in cash is the man who is awarded the timber berth.

By Mr. Fyshe:

Q. Are there not abuses perpetrated by scheming speculators getting hold of large tracts of timber lands?—A. We limit the area. No one can get more than 50 miles at a time.

Q. Still that is a large amount?—A. Yes, it is a large amount.

Q. I dare say you have noticed that there have been great abuses of the kind in the United States? President Roosevelt has taken the matter up and is trying to stop it?—A. There is this difficulty. If you refuse to put up any more timber those people that have acquired lumber berths simply have gold mines. They then control the output of lumber locally. The individual settlers would be the first to cry out if you stopped putting up any more timber at competition.

Q. You do not sell these lands outright?—A. We do not sell the lands at all, simply the timber on the lands.

Q. Is that preferable to simply selling stumpage?—A. We charge a ground rental, and so much a thousand feet, and the successful tenderer pays us a bonus over and above the settled charges.

Q. That is what they are put up to tender for?—A. That is what they are put up to tender for. Every one knows what the specific charges are. They know what we require per thousand on the manufactured lumber, and they know what the ground rental is.

Q. That would be the equivalent of the stumpage?—A. The equivalent of the stumpage, I suppose, is the rate per thousand that they have to pay on the manufactured article.

7-8 EDWARD VII., A. 1908

Q. What do they pay?—A. I think it is 50 cents or $1.50 per thousand—I am not sure which—for the lumber manufactured. They have to make sworn returns and we have inspectors who go around and check up their books and their operations in the winter time. The sale of the timber gives them no right to the land; any one can go in on our timber berths and prospect for minerals.

Q. Yes, but I am speaking of the timber lands?—A. The successful tenderer does not get the lands, he has no right to the occupation of the lands at all. Once the timber is removed from the land, we can open it for homestead entry, or make any other disposition of it we choose.

By Mr. Bazin:

Q. The right to cut the timber is sold just for a certain number of years?—A. For one year, but it is renewable. There are certain conditions attached: They have to make returns and pay their rental. As a matter of discretion, the right is renewed until the timber is removed from the land.

Q. Is it liable to be confiscated, if not renewed every year?—A. We have the right to do it if we wish, but I have never heard of it being done.

By the Chairman:

Q. You have a system for the protection of timber limits which was introduced by your former superintendent, Mr. Stewart? The rangers are continually patrolling and looking over the timber limits owned by the Government?—A. We have certain of what are called forest reserves, in which large tracts of timber lands are set apart. The men to whom you refer are looking after these reserves, and they also attend to the fire-guarding of the timber areas.

Q. Is every precaution taken to see that the full value of the timber limits goes into the public treasury?—A. There is no doubt about that. Every farthing that comes from the sale of timber goes immediately to the Receiver General.

Q. But does the full value of the timber limits go to the Receiver General?—A. We do not know that. We do not go out and estimate the timber on the berths, nor do we guarantee that there is a stick of timber on the land. It is for the various competitors to take that risk. They pay their money, and if there is timber on the land, they get it back; if there is no timber, they lose their money.

By Mr. Fyshe:

Q. Do you not run this risk: in an out-of-the-way place, where only a few people know what is on the land, a group of men can put their heads together, form a combine and get the timber from the Government at a mere fraction of what it was worth?—A. We cannot protect ourselves against that.

Q. But possibly such might be the case?—A. We do not put up timber in out-of-the-way places. We are now restricting ourselves to areas that the people know something about. An advertisement is issued by the King's Printer, calling for tenders. A copy of this advertisement is sent by the department to every one in Canada and a great many in the United States who are known to be interested in timber.

Q. You assume these men will be all independent bidders?—A. They largely are.

Q. The first thing for the seeker after a bargain would be to find out who are likely to bid, and make a little pool and get the thing for a mere nothing?—A. We had that same difficulty when selling lands at public auction; people did the same thing.

Q. It seems to me that the department should send an officer to inspect that land and put a solid value on it?—A. The expense would be away outside of the value to us.

Q. You would not lose half as much as by selling lands below their proper value?—A. The difficulty is that our lands are separated and scattered over such a large area the cost would be a great deal more than it was worth.

Q. Supposing the lands are in an out-of-the-way place, those interested in them will make it their business to go, whatever the cost may be. You may be sure they will go and examine the lands.—A. Some do, but we have had hundreds of cases where people have bought timber berths they never saw and never had any men on.

Q. They are reckless speculators, then?—A. That is certainly what they are.

Q. If such men suffered loss, they would throw their hands up and tell you they could not pay?—A. Yes, but we would have their money.

Q. Is every possible precaution taken to get for the public treasury the full value of the timber limits that are sold?—A. We take every precaution. We advertise the sale in the most public manner possible and sell the timber to none but the highest bidders. The man who puts in his accepted cheque for $10 more than the next bidder, is the man who gets the timber.

Q. Do you fix a limit?—A. No. As I may say we do not know whether there is a sliver of timber on that land.

Q. What is the good of having such extensive machinery in connection with your department if you cannot get from the surveys a more exact knowledge of timber lands you are trying to sell?—A. The timber areas are not in the surveyed areas.

Q. Should they not be?—A. We could not do that. A river, for example, runs for 200 miles into a country where no surveys have been made, and perhaps none will be made for twenty years. A man comes along and says: 'I want to erect a mill so that I can run lumber down the river to the settlement.' If there is no objection we put it up by auction and if he pays more than any body else who bids he gets the timber. If he does not he does not secure the timber.

Q. You do send experts sometimes away up to the Arctic Circle and beyond?—A. That is true.

Q. If you can do that, you can surely send men to explore property that you may have to put up at auction?—A. We can do that, but it never has been done.

Q. It seems to me to be a rational thing that you should make some efforts to ascertain the value of what is offered for sale?—A. That is a question whether we should or should not do that. We have never done so.

Q. It opens the door for a large amount of perhaps not fraud but possible heavy loss to the country?—A. In many of the heavily timbered districts that might happen—in British Columbia, for instance—but in our northwestern country the timber is not of a valuable character. It neither grows tall nor thickly.

Q. Do you mean in the Northwest?—A. Yes, it is very largely scattered timber.

Q. That is not so in British Columbia?—A. No, in British Columbia the timber is more valuable. We get four or five times, probably ten times, the bonus on British Columbia berths that we do on the others.

Q. Perhaps you do not get enough. I know men who have gone out there and made fortunes through getting possession of timber lands?—A. Quite true, they went out and invested their money when nobody else would.

Q. Possibly they had no money?—A. They must have got money somewhere; the banks must have advanced money to them, or somebody else, because you cannot buy timber for nothing.

By the Chairman:

Q. You have a lithographic office in your department?—A. That is in connection with the Surveyor General's branch.

Q. Lithographic work is of course done in the Bureau?—A. It is, to a certain extent. We use ours entirely for township plans. We get out what are called township plans of every township that is surveyed showing the various sections, the road allowances and the several physical features.

Q. You think it would not be possible to amalgamate that with the Bureau?—A. It would not be practicable for us.

Q. Would it not be better to put that work under the geographical branch?—A. No.

Q. You think the work is better done by having it done as it is at present?—A. We find it to work very much better as it is.

Q. I see you have a raft of people working in the land commissioner's office?—A. Yes.

Q. Who are they?—A. They are the people who look after the homestead entries. The patents branch is a branch of the land commissioner's office, and those who deal directly with homestead pre-emptions and other matters are connected with the same office.

Q. You have several agencies in the Northwest?—A. Yes, there are 16 agencies.

Q. Have any of the agents ever become defaulters?—A. Not to my knowledge.

Q. I think in the old days there were one or two?—A. Possibly. In one sub-agency at Macleod there was a man who defaulted, but we make a rule of not paying a sub-agent his money unless he makes his returns. This man has not made his returns for several months, but we had more money belonging to him than he had belonging to us.

Q. You had some discussion with the Auditor General about that?—A. Yes, I think so. We now take bonds with guarantee companies for all our agents and sub-agents.

Q. All the agents for the sale of land now give guarantee bonds?—A. Yes.

By Mr. Fyshe :

Q. Is that system general throughout the service ?—A. I am speaking of our officials that handle money. All our officials that handle money, in the Yukon, in the assay office at Vancouver, and throughout the Northwest are bonded by guarantee company bonds.

Q. In which company ?—A. We have got the Ocean and Accident and the British America.

By the Chairman :

Q. They are either British or Canadian companies ?—A. Yes.

By Mr. Fyshe :

Q. Do you largely use the guarantee fund in North America?—A. We do not use any American companies at all.

Q. What is the annual premium they charge?—A. We have some as low as 30 cents a thousand.

Q. The yearly charge used to be one-half per cent ?—A. We have got it at less than that.

Q. Some of them pay the half I suppose ?—A. I do not know. We have some very heavy bonds. For instance we have $90,000 on our assay office people. Then we have about $70,000 on officials in the Yukon Territory.

Q. Would the rate be low or high ?—A. We pay 30 cents on the Vancouver people.

Q. I suppose the people employed as a rule, are exceptional in character ?—A. We have never had any difficulty.

Q. You have never had any claims against the guarantee company?—A. No, we never have had any claims.

Q. Does the Government pay the premiums?—A. The Government pays the premium.

By the Chairman :

Q. Then except in the case of the Macleod subagency where you held more money than was due from the agents, there have been no defaulters in your time?—A. There have been no defaulters in my time.

Q. There is a complete system of check now on the returns ?—A. Yes, we have an absolute system of check.

Q. You divide your Dominion lands expenditure into capital and income ?—A. Yes.

Q. The capital, I suppose, is expenditure on new and entirely undeveloped land?—A. Entirely. The appropriation for our surveyor general is voted as a capital expenditure.

Q. It is the initial step towards bringing new lands under survey ?—A. Yes.

Q. Then the income is in connection with lands that have been surveyed ?—A. Yes, that is the administration of lands that have been surveyed.

Q. Have you any Government expenditures now in the Northwest Territories since the two new provinces have been created ?—A. I think there is a vote of $6,000 which is under the control of Lt. Col. White, Controller of the Northwest Mounted Police, as commissioner.

- Q. I suppose there are schools outside of Alberta and Saskatchewan ?—A. A few, not many.

By Mr. Fyshe :

Q. Have you any in Keewatin ?—A. Yes, I fancy there are one or two in Keewatin and one or two in the far northern regions—church schools.

By the Chairman :

· Q. Now we come to the Government of the Yukon. Is the staff there being reduced ?—A. Yes, we have been reducing the staff there very materially for some time.

Q. Are the living allowances the same as they were at the beginning ?—A. No.

Q. You are revising the living allowances ?—A. We revised the allowances about two years ago. Formerly there was a straight living allowance of $1,800 a year or $150 a month. It has now been cut down to $125 for a married man and $100 for a single man.

Q. I suppose as the country comes into closer touch with the outside world the living allowance will be again revised ?—A. Yes.

Q. Do you know what it was in the beggining ?—A. $150 a month.

Q. That was not in the beginning ?—A. I think that in the beginning there was no living allowance at all. It was not known what the conditions were. As soon as the people went into the Yukon they began to clamour for some allowances. They had a mess-house and they were furnished with food, but they found it very unsatisfactory.

Q. Your men have to get leave of absence in the Yukon every two or three years? —A. Yes.

Q. The climate is such that they cannot stay there very many years ?—A. I would not like to stay there very long.

Q. The climate there gets on their nerves ?—A. A great many people break down from nervous trouble.

Q. Do you give the officials a liberal travelling allowance when they come out? —A. We do not give them any travelling allowance now at all. If a man has not been out of the Yukon for three years he is entitled to nine weeks holidays with pay. He gets his pay and living allowance during that time, but if he stays longer than nine weeks he receives no salary or living allowance.

Q. You have also an expenditure in connection with Banff and Field?—A. Those are the national parks.

Q. You have, at each place, a superintendent?—A. Yes, at Banff and at Field.

Q. And you have an assistant superintendent at Banff?—A. Yes.

Q. Are there any lands sold in the national parks ?—A. We do not sell any lands in the parks; we simply lease them.

Q. The management of the Banff Springs Hotel, did they acquire a freehold?— A. No, a leasehold.

Q. A lease for a term of years?—A. 41 years.

Q. Are there conditions about building cottages or anything?—A. Yes.

Q. I see that you still have a kind of partial supervision over the affairs of the Yukon Local Council?—A. We make them a grant of $125,000, I think, and then $100,000 for roads and bridges, $225,000 in all. They administer that money in any way they choose, and I understand their accounts are audited by the Auditor General.

By Mr. Fyshe:

Q. They have quite an extensive Government up there now?—A. Six appointed members and five elected members, besides the Commissioner.

Q. That constitutes the council?—A. That constitutes the council, and the Commissioner presides.

Q. Is the population increasing in the Yukon?—A. I think not.

Q. The production of gold is going down?—A. It has been going down during the last six years.

Q. That is the way with all these alluvial gold diggings?—A. Dredging operations are now being undertaken in a larger way.

Q. They have not discovered any quartz in the Yukon?—A. Not to amount to anything.

By the Chairman:

Q. According to the Auditor General's Report, page L—137, there was a practice growing up recently among your agents of using the revenue to meet the contingencies of their office?—A. I do not know what that was in particular reference to. That is not generally the case; we are very strict with our officers.

Q. The end of it was that the Secretary of the Department (Mr. Keyes), sent a circular to each of the agents stating that the practice was irregular and had to be stopped?—A. Yes, we have had no complaints since.

Q. The gross receipts received by the Dominion lands agents are now deposited in the bank which the Finance Department points out has to receive public money?—A. Yes.

By Mr. Fyshe:

Q. And drafts are made for the expenses?—A. Yes.

By the Chairman:

Q. Coming to the question of the employment of all these batches of people in the outside service in Ottawa. Do you not think it would be better to include them in the department and make them subject to the Civil Service Act?—A. Yes, I think so.

By Mr. Fyshe:

Q. You think there is no good reason why they should not be?—A. I never could see any reason.

By the Chairman:

Q. As it stands now, charging the salaries and expenditures to votes here and there, it results in a lack of understanding in the public mind as to the number of persons employed?—A. Quite true.

Q. Naturally you would want to show the administration and the working of your department under one head?—A. Yes.

Q. Have you any suggestion to make about the classification of these men?—A. No, I think they all could very well be brought under the present classification.

By Mr. Fyshe:

Q. But classification practically means merely classification according to the time the employees have been in the service?—A. Not altogether, in a way it does. Of course there are numbers of men employed in the outside service in the head office that we could not begin to bring into the service at Ottawa and start them at $500 a year. We would have to have an elastic arrangement whereby we could give such men the minimum salary of a second-class clerk, which is $1,200, and then give them a rise from year to year.

By the Chairman:

Q. Would you consider it desirable to amalgamate all these branches of the department at Ottawa into one administrative body?—A. When appointed to my present position, I set out to find the reason why there was a distinction and have never been able to discover it yet.

Q. As a matter of fact, your department is only about thirty years old?—A. Yes.

Q. The present condition of things is a matter of evolution? The department began in a small way and spead its tentacles out everywhere?—A. Yes.

By Mr. Fyshe:

Q. Is it not a matter of fact that this condition of affairs has arisen from political influence in order to avoid the restrictions of the Civil Service Act? Is there much pressure to appoint people to positions coming under these votes?—A. I would not consider there was very much pressure. We have constant applications in which the applicants are recommended possibly by this man or that man, it may be a clergyman or somebody of that sort. Still we do not regard that as special.

Q. You ignore it?—A. We do not ignore it but listen, and possibly when we want a clerk, I will ask for several of these young men to come up before me, and then by talking to them find out what their experience has been and what their educational attainments are, and then make the best selection.

By the Chairman:

Q. Do you think you have more people employed in these outside branches than the service requires?—A. No, I do not think so.

Q. Have you ever paid any attention to the English Civil Service?—A. No, I never have.

Q. Do you think if there was an independent Civil Service Commission, that had nothing to do with politics to examine candidates and make appointments, it would be better than the present system?—A. No, I am not clear on that; I am not sure whether it would be better or not. Political appointments may not sometimes be of the best, but on the other hand, scholarly attainments are not always the prime qualifications for an efficient clerk. We have had experience of men with high scholarly attainments, but who did not appear to have the energy nor the ambition of these other men who have come into the service in a lower grade

By Mr. Fyshe:

Q. You are speaking now on educational grounds?—A. No, I am speaking generally. In many of these so-called political appointments, a man necessarily has to have a certain amount of energy and push before he can come forward sufficiently to be recommended politically, and frequently these men turn out to be excellent officials. You can get a man who may pass a rigid examination——

Q. These examinations are not conclusive?—A. Not conclusive at all.

By the Chairman:

Q. With a strict system of probation—as in the English public service, where a probationer may be rejected and the next good man is taken—and proper selection, do you think an independent commission would be better?—A. It would materially change the conditions if there was a strict period of probation and applicants were accepted or rejected on their merits.

By Mr. Fyshe:

Q. But, is it not, as a matter of practical management, almost impossible to weed out men, once they have entered the service, for six months, even after competition?—A. We do not keep a man usually that long if he is not competent.

Q. If you find he is not satisfactory you positively discharge him or send him to another department?—A. We have frequently dispensed with the services of men that were not satisfactory.

Q. Are they not apt to raise a political howl then?—A. Complaints are made, but we have never taken back a man we have laid off.

By Mr. Bazin:

Q. Before you take the man on probation, you have a good idea of what he can do?—A. Of course the man may come from western Ontario and be an absolute stranger to me. But in the case of residents in the city, I bring them in and talk with them. I could not do that in the case of men who come from a distance. I put them on for a month or two months, and if not satisfactory let them go.

By the Chairman:

Q. Your department being connected with the Northwest, all your ministers for some time past have come from Western Canada?—A. Yes.

Q. And their constituencies are a long distance off?—A. Yes, they are a long distance off.

Q. Then politics would not enter so much into appointments to your department as it would where the Minister lives nearer Ottawa?—A. We have not, I think, in our department, in Mr. Sifton's time or in Mr. Oliver's time—those are the only two Ministers I have any knowledge of—had a dozen western men appointed to the department here.

Q. I do not think you had either in the time of Mr. Dewdney or Mr. Daly?—A. Where the Minister might have an opportunity of making appointments, would be in the western end of the service, in the agencies and inspectorships and similar offices.

Q. But in the case of the 500 odd employees of the department in Ottawa, politics has not entered so much into the appointments as it might in other departments?—A. No, I think not.

Q. Have you any other remarks to offer?—A. So far as efficiency is concerned, I think we have a very efficient staff, and we are well satisfied with our men. The great difficulty that we will experience hereafter will be in getting men to take the place of those who must necessarily disappear in a short time. There are so many women who have come into the department. The women come in for less salary than we can get men for, and now we have not got efficient and well-qualified men to take the higher positions.

By Mr. Fyshe:

Q. You are firmly convinced that women can only rise to a certain level, and are not available beyond that?—A. As a rule, that is my view. Nearly all our women are stenographers and patent writers, but outside of that, they do not do clerical work.

Q. That seems very likely?—A. This difficulty is the one we have to face now.

By Mr. Bazin:

Q. Unless you arrange the salary?—A. We have got to admit men at a higher scale of salary than we can at present.

By Mr. Fyshe:

Q. That is an argument against taking in useless women?—A. Yes, that is true.

By the Chairman:

Q. But even then, if you admitted men at a higher salary, the duties performed would not justify you in continuing an increase of salary, unless the men showed great ability?—A. No.

Q. Your department is only credited with 17 first-class clerks and 10 chief clerks, so there is no opportunity of getting up?—A. We have not enough first-class clerks, second-class clerks, or chiefs.

By Mr. Fyshe:

Q. Could you not arrange to meet the difficulty you spoke of by transferring clerks from some other department, when vacancies occur?—A. The other departments do not like that. They are having just the same difficulties as we are, and it is not a very nice thing to offer a man a better salary than he is getting in another department in order to secure him for our department. The greatest difficulty is with our technical officers. The surveyor general loses perhaps anywhere from 20 to 30 men a year; he cannot keep them. When young men pass their Dominion lands final examination and become Dominion land surveyors, we perhaps pay them $1,200 or $1,300 a year. Then some railway company, or some corporation will offer to double their salary, and away they go.

Q. It seems very ridiculous to pay technical men $1,200 a year, when you employ girls at the same salary?—A. That is what I say. Of course, you have to have a beginning. We take in graduates in engineering or in a scientific course, at $75 a month. The man remains at that salary for two years. Then, if he proves to be efficient, he is given the salary of $1,200, which is increased $50 a year until a maximum of $1,500 is reached.

Q. That is, if he is taken into the Civil Service?—A. We have a special Act covering the surveyor general's branch, and the salary of these young men is increased $50 a year until the maximum of $1,500 is reached. It takes a man six years to obtain that maximum. In the meantime somebody comes along and offers him $1,800 or $2,000, and we cannot keep him. We are constantly training batches of young men, and when a man gets used to the work, then he goes.

By Mr. Bazin:

Q. Do you not think a certain latitude should be allowed to the deputy minister in the matter of fixing the salary? For instance, you may have the right man in the right place, but you cannot give him, under the statute, more than a certain salary. Would it not be better, if you had the power, knowing he was a valuable man, to give him $300, $400 or $500 increase, as the case may be?—A. I could have retained several good men, if I had been able to do that.

By Mr. Fyshe:

Q. There is no way by which you can fully cover that difficulty?—A. No, you cannot cover it fully.

Q. It would be absurd to say that the Government should compete on even terms with these corporations?—A. We cannot do that.

Q. Because every now and again a special man is wanted for a special business, and it would never do for you to adjust the whole business of the Government on that basis?—A. We cannot do that.

Q. It is not possible?—A. No, it is not possible.

Q. You have to make up your mind to lose some men? The only question is whether you can adjust things so as to retain some of the most capable?—A. That is the only thing we can hope for.

Witness discharged.

Commission rose.

7-8 EDWARD VII., A. 1908

DEPARTMENT OF THE INTERIOR, CANADA,
OTTAWA, June 11, 1907.

THOMAS S. HOWE, Esq.,
    Secretary, Civil Service Commission.
        Room 2, the Senate, Ottawa.

DEAR SIR,—In compliance with the request contained in your letter to me of the
18th ultimo, I beg to transmit you herewith statements in detail showing the number
of officials employed by this department at Ottawa, and the sums paid to each during
the fiscal years ending June 30, 1892, and June 30, 1906, respectively.

Yours truly,

W. W. CORY,
Deputy Minister.

DEPARTMENT OF THE INTERIOR, FISCAL YEAR 1905-6.

STATEMENT showing in detail the number of officials employed at Ottawa, and sums
paid to each during the fiscal year ending June 30, 1906.

SUMMARY.

(A) Civil Government Salaries.

1 deputy head...............................	$ 3,550 00
7 chief clerks................................	16,055 02
6 technical officers..........................	13,972 94
18 first-class clerks..........................	27,427 94
25 second-class clerks........................	33,920 70
47 junior second-class clerks.................	43,962 68
29 third-class clerks.........................	18,076 60
2 messengers................................	1,283 30
Private secretary...........................	600 00

134 permanent clerks......................... $158,848 49

(B) Civil Government Contingencies.

7 temporary clerks.........................   4,172 96

141   Total civil government....................... $163,021 45

MISCELLANEOUS VOTES.

(C.) Immigration.

3 permanent officers of the outside service ..$ 6,600 00
43 temporary clerks.................... 25,857 80
                                        ———————— $30,457 80

(D.) Dominion Lands Income.

8 permanent officers of the outside service..$17,002 68
100 temporary clerks.................... 53,253 62
                                        ————————   70,256 30

(E.) Dominion Lands Capital.

120 temporary employees....................   100,205 53

(F.) Dominion Astronomical Observatory.

10 permanent officers of the outside service........ $ 13,226 62

(G.) Boundary Surveys.

24 temporary employees.................... 21,290 00

(H.) Dominion Lands Income—Protection of Timber.

1 permanent officer ....$ 2,833 32
4 temporary employees............. 3,632 50
                                      6,465 82

(I.) Mines Branch.

1 temporary messenger 512 50

(J.) Ordnance Lands.

1 temporary clerk....................... 561 00

(K.) School Lands Funds.

1 permanent officer.............$2,050 00
7 temporary employees............ 4,005 61
                                  6,055 61

323	Total miscellaneous	249,031 18
464	Grand total....................	$412,052 63

DEPARTMENT OF THE INTERIOR, FISCAL YEAR 1905-6.

STATEMENT showing in detail the number of officials employed at Ottawa and sums paid to each during the fiscal year ending June 30, 1906.

(A.) Civil Government Salaries.

1 Deputy Head—
W. W. Cory..$ 3,550 00

7 Chief Clerks—
1. T. G. Rothwell, law clerk.............................. 2,700 00
2. P. G. Keyes, secretary................................. 2,700 00
3. C. H. Beddoe, accountant.............................. 2,350 00
4. K. J. Henry, registration.............................. 2,250 00
5. N. O. Coté, lands patents *vice* Mr. Goodeve............. 2,025 00
6. R. H. Campbell, timber and mines *vice* G. U. Ryley......... 1,108 33
7. J. A. Coté, secretary to deputy minister *vice* N. O. Coté...... 163 44
Wm. Goodeve, salary $2,500 (died March 31, 1906)........... 1,874 97
G. U. Ryley, salary $2,650 (resigned October 31, 1905)......... 883 28
                                  $16,055 02

6 Technical Officers—
1. E. Deville, surveyor general.............................$ 2,600 00
2. W. F. King, chief astronomer—
Salary for 12 months.......................$2,500 00
Less 86 days on Waterways Commission........... 577 06
                          1,922 94
3. O. J. Klotz, astronomer............................... 2,400 00
4. C. A. Bigger, surveyor................................ 2,300 00
5. J. J. McArthur, surveyor 2,300 00
6. James White, geographer.............................. 2,250 00
                                  $13,972 94

17 First-class Clerks—

1. P. B. Symes..	..	$ 1,900 00
2. A. H. Whitcher..		1,900 00
3. L. O. Pereira..		1,900 00
4. L. M. Fortier..		1,800 00
5. W. S. Gliddon..		1,662 50
6. H. H. Rowatt..		1,650 00
7. M. Prady..		1,600 00
8. O. J. Steers..		1,575 00
9. A. Chisholm..		1,550 00
10. P. Marchand..		1,550 00
11. G. D. Pope..		1,550 00

12. P. Robertson—Salary, 12 months.. ..$1,550 00
         Arrears, 1904-1905.. .. 48 35
           ————— 1 598 35

13. George Bell	1,537 50
14. C. C. Pelletier..	1,500 00
15. W. S. Surtees (from October 1, 1905)..	1,125 00
16. J. M. Roberts (from May 31, 1906) *vice* J. A. Coté..	129 03
17. B. L. York (from January 1, 1906) *vice* R. H. Campbell..	750 00
R. H. Campbell (promoted January 1, 1906)..	687 50
J. A. Coté (promoted May 31, 1906)..	1,462 37

                          $27,427 25

25 Second-class Clerks—

1. J. S. Brough..	$ 1,500 00
2. W. F. Boardman..	1,500 00
3. F. Nelson..	1,500 00
4. G. H. Newcomb..	1,500 00
5. G. A. Sparkes..	1,500 00
6. Brown Wallis..	1,500 00
7. H. N. Topley..	1,450 00
8. James Dunet..	1,350 00
9. J. N. Ferguson..	1,350 00
10. Jos. P. Dunne..	1,325 00
11. C. W. Badgley..	1,300 00
12. F. O. Capreol..	1,300 00
13. F. W. C Ouming..	1,300 00
14. Robt. Dunlop..	1,300 00
15. J. S. Eagleson..	1,300 00
16. F. Loyer..	1,300 00
17. H. Sherwood..	1,300 00
18. S. J. Willoughby..	1,300 00
19. Edward Connelly..	1,275 00
20. H. H. Turner..	1,275 00
21. J. D. Bollard..	1,250 00
22. G. W. Paterson..	1,250 00
23. B. H. Wright..	1,200 00
24. A. A. Pinard *vice* B. L. York, from January 1, 1906..	600 00
25. G. Lemieux *vice* J. M. Roberts, from May 31, 1906..	103 23
J. M. Roberts (promoted May 31, 1906)..	1,129 97
B. L. York (promoted January 1, 1906)..	650 00
W. S. Surtees (promoted October 1, 1905..	312 50

                          $33,920 70

47 Junior Second-class Clerks—

1. E. Belleau..	$ 1,100 00
2. O. H. Lambart..	1,100 00
3. P. V. Low..	1,100 00
4. F. C. Macdonald..	1,100 00
5. Miss M. May..	1,100 00
6. T. W. E. Sowter..	1,097 00
7. Miss A. B. Yielding	1,097 00
8. Mrs. J. Ricard..	1,050 00
9. Miss M. Barber..	1,050 00
10. G. P. Pereira..	1,050 00
11. Miss L. Coleman..	1,000 00
12. Miss M. Shaw..	950 00
13. Beresford Scott..	925 00
14. J. G. Mitts..	925 00
15. Miss S. M. Guthrie..	912 50
16. Miss M. D. Munro..	512 50

PAPER No. 29a

cond-class Clerks—*Con.*

Ackland..	$ 900 00
A. H. Beauchesne..	900 00
M. Caldwell	900 00
omas Davidson	900 00
ss R. G. Ellis..	900 00
mond Fortier..	900 00
H. Hutton..	900 00
R. Morissett..	900 00
J. McIsaac..	900 00
E. Ryan..	900 00
Swinburn..	900 00
E. Turton..	900 00
E. Wood..	900 00
ss A. G. E. Crawford..	887 50
n. Bailey..	875 00
B. Duhamel..	875 00
W. Hobart..	875 00
P. Morris..	875 00
ss S. Rolph..	875 00
A. Browne..	862 50
L. Masson..	850 00
H. Byshe..	825 00
ss G. Hawley..	825 00
W. Hodgins..	800 00
C. Roger..	800 00
ss E. N. H. Mercer—Salary for 12 months.. ....$825 00	
Less deducted for absence.. .. .. 67 80	
	757 20
Addison, salary, 11 mos. at $800 per annum..	733 34
ss E. Dunlop, salary from September 20, 1905, at 800..	624 44
ss I. Dunlop, salary from September 20, 1905, at 800..	624 44
M. Larkin..	624 44
ss M. B. Williams..	624 44
Lemieux, salary 1,100, promoted May 31, 1906, clerkship not filled.	1,005 38
A. Pinard, salary $1,050, promoted Jan. 1, 1906, clerkship not filled	525 00
	$43,962 68

class Clerks—

ss M. Martin..	$ 670 00
ss M. Casey..	650 00
ss M. A. Earls..	650 00
s. A. MacMaster..	650 00
s. L. L. Norton..	650 00
ss M. D. Schofield..	650 00
ss M. L. Semple	650 00
ss L. Hilliard..	620 00
ss L. May..	620 00
ss J. Prindiville..	620 00
ss E. Shiels..	620 00
ss J. G. Stewart..	620-00
ss W. Ainsborough..	612 50
ss M. E. Burnett..	612 50
ss E. Dewar..	600 00
ss O. Hawley..	600 00
ss V. E. Johnston..	600 00
ss M. Johnston..	600 00
s. M. E. Mulhall..	600 00
ss V. McGill..	600 00
ss A. J. Phoenix..	600 00
ss M. Robinson..	600 00
ss M. McK. Scott	600 00
s. F. E. Waine..	600 00
ss E. M. Haldane..	587 50
ss G. B. Campbell, from July 22, 1905, to June 30, 1906..$600 00	
Paid from Capital Account for 21 days. 33 87	
	566 13
H. Allen..	550 00
ss H. Seed, from Oct. 1, 1905, to June 30, 1906, at.. .. ..$600 00	
Paid for 3 months from Dominion Lands.. .. 137 49	
	450 00

29. Miss E. Loudon, resigned March 31, 1906, salary $620.. .. ..$		464 94
R. Addison, salary, $700, promoted Aug. 1, 1905..		58 33
Miss E. Dunlop, salary, $550, promoted Sept 20, 1905..		120 69
Miss I. Dunlop, salary, $600, promoted Sept. 20, 1905..		131 66
J. M. Larkin, salary, $550, promoted Sept. 20, 1905..		120 69
Miss M. B. Williams, salary, $600, promoted Sept 20, 1905..		131 66

$13,076 60

2 messengers—

1. Joseph Beaudoin, died April 8, 1906, salary $700.. .. ..$		533 30
A. Pegg..		700 00

$1,233 30

J. B. Harkin, private secretary, salary estimated under Department
　of Indian Affairs.. .. ..$ 600 00

(B.) Civil Government Contingencies.

Miss M. Richardson.. .. .. $		612 50
Miss A. Murphy..		612 50
Miss M. Stalker..		597 96
Miss H. R. Burns..		587 50
Miss G. Leprohon..		587 50
Miss E. L. Shattuck..		587 50
Miss B. McCullough..		587 50

$4,172 96

(C.) Immigration.

3 permanent officers—

W. D. Scott, superintendent..		$2,800 00
G. B. Smart, inspector of British immigrant children..		1,600 00
P. H. Bryce, medical inspector..		2,200 00

$6,600 00

43 temporary employees—

1. E. B. Robertson, asst. superintendent.. .. ..$		1,500 00
2. R. Fraser, statistician		1,200 00
3. R. W. Hillyard, asst. inspector immigrant children..		1,200 00
4. D. McGillicuddy, compiler, 11 mos. at $100..		1,100 00
5. F. C. Blair, clerk..		900 00
6. W. Thompson, clerk..		900 00
7. A. C. Ecclestone, clerk..		800 00
8. D. W. Johnston, clerk, 12 mos., less 6 days at $800..		787 10
9. A. Ackerlindh, clerk, 6 m., 24 d. at $100 ; 5 mos. 7 d. paid from Capital Account, $522.58..		677 42
10. James Back, clerk..		650 00
11. Miss E. Esdale, clerk..		612 50
12. Miss J. Hopkirk, clerk..		612 50
13. Miss G. Kinsella, clerk..		612 50
14. Mrs. F. S. Shotwell, clerk..		612 50
15. P. I. Turgeon, clerk..		600 00
16. W. Perron, clerk..		600 00
17. Miss E. V. Gillies, clerk		600 00
18. Miss H. M. Gould, clerk..		600 00
19. J. O. Cowan, shipping clerk, 9¾ mos. at $60..		580 00
20. W. Traversy, clerk..		550 00
21. Miss M. E Reynolds, clerk..		550 00
22. Miss M. Thomson, clerk..		550 00
23. John Curley, clerk..		550 00
24. Miss E. F. Rossé clerk..		537 50
25. Mrs. S. M. Geddes, clerk..		500 00
26. A. J. Havey, clerk..		499 18
27. Miss E. Stackhouse, clerk..		495 00
28. Miss M. Martin, clerk, salary $500, less 6½ days..		491 10
29 Miss N. O'Reilly, clerk, 7 mos. at $500, 3 mos. at $550..		475 24
30. J. H. Stanford, clerk, 3 mos. at $900, 3 mos. at $1,000..		474 99
31. M. A. Cook, clerk, 5 mos. at $90..		450 00

Temporary employees—*Con.*

32. Miss B. Bedard, clerk, 9 m., 29 d. at $500..................$	415	25
33. Miss J. Lang, clerk, 9 m., 26 d. at $500......................	411	08
34. Miss E. Haskett, clerk, 8 m., 27 d. at $500	369	62
35. John Satchell, clerk, 5 mos. at $53.95 (deceased)............	269	75
36. N. W. Cragg, clerk, 4 mos. at $800 per annum; paid balance of year from Dominion Lands, $354.13.........................	266	66
37. J. S. Fraser, clerk, 6 mos. at $500......................	249	98
38. Miss E. Cavanagh, clerk, 5 m. 20 d. at $500..............	235	22
39. R. Valiquette, messenger, appointed May 23, 1906, at $500....	45	69
40. Miss E. G. Richardson, clerk, 2 m. 12 d. at $500............	100	79
41. Alex. Gillis, clerk, appointed May 28, 1906, at $50 per month..	56	45
42. L. J. Kehoe, clerk, appointed April 20, 1906, at $60 per month....	142	00
43. Mrs. C. M. Knight, clerk, appointed June 11, 1906, at $500 per annum...	27	78
	$23,857	80

(D.) Dominion Lands Income.

8 permanent officers—

1. J. W. Greenway, commissioner.......................$	3,200	00
2. Dr. E. Haanel, superintendent of mines................	3,000	00
3. R. E. Young, supt. railway and swamp lands............	2,725	00
4. T. R. Burpee, deputy commissioner...................	2,550	00
5. F. F. Dixon, chief clerk..........................	1,925	00
6. E. Nystrom, asst. superintendent of mines..............	1,700	00
7. H. Fitzsimons, asst. supt. railway and swamp lands (apptd. Feb. 6, 1906, at $1,500 pr annum; paid from Capital Account to Feb. 5, 1906, at $1,200 per annum, $717.85................	602	68
8. A. J. Fraser, clerk	1,300	00
	$17,002	68

100 temporary employees—

1. B. F. Haanel, clerk, mines branch...................$	1,500	00
2. Wm. Lamb, clerk, Dominion lands branch..............	1,200	00
3. S. Maber, clerk, Dominion lands branch..............	1,200	00
4. C. F. Spence, clerk, Dominion lands branch............	1,200	00
5. E. Trudel, clerk, 11 mos. at $1,200................	1,100	00
6. J. L. Johnston, clerk, 8 mos. at $1,000, 4 mos at $1,050..	1,016	70
7. A. Kemeys-Tynte, clerk..........................	1,000	00
8. A. Pelton, clerk...............................	1,000	00
9. A. S. Robertson, clerk..........................	1,000	00
10. P. Laflamme, clerk............................	900	00
11. C. Mair, jr., clerk............................	900	00
12. O. Lafleur, clerk, 3 mos. at $720, 9 mos. $840........	810	00
13. J. L. Rombough, clerk..........................	800	00
14. John Mason, clerk.............................	732	00
15. A. E. Smith, clerk, 5 mos. at $500, 7 mos. at $720.....	628	33
16. G. J. Taylor, clerk............................	625	00
17. Miss K. Parlow, clerk..........................	625	00
18. Miss F. M. Joyce, clerk........................	625	00
19. D. P. Purcell, messenger........................	625	00
20. Miss L. K. Wright, clerk, 9 mos. at $600, 3 mos. at $650..	612	50
21. Miss E. Rowland, clerk, 9 mos. at $600, 3 mos. at $650..	612	50
22. B. J. Doherty, clerk, 9 mos. at $600, 3 mos at $650.....	612	50
23. Miss N. K. Derensy, clerk, 9 mos. at $600, 3 mos. at $650..	612	50
24. Miss M. McDougall, clerk, 9 mos. at $600, 3 mos. at $650..	612	50
25. Miss M. Campbell, clerk, 9 mos. at $600, 3 mos. at $650..	612	50
26. Miss M. G. Lawson, clerk........................	600	00
27. S. E. Hand, clerk.............................	600	00
28. Jos. Keating, messenger........................	600	00
29. Miss E. McLaurin, clerk........................	600	00
30. Miss C. McStravick, clerk.......................	600	00
31. Miss I. Ritchie, clerk..........................	600	00
32. Miss F. Sharpe, clerk..........................	600	00
33. J. J. Shea, messenger..........................	600	00
34. Miss M. Tremblay, clerk........................	600	00
35. Miss E. Wood, clerk...........................	600	00
36. Miss F. Bridgeman, clerk........................	587	50
37. Mrs. M. Rutherford, clerk.......................	587	50

Temporary employees—*Con.*

38. Wm. Haggerty, clerk.. .. ..$	587	50
39. Miss J. Orme, clerk..	587	50
40. Geo. Beeson, clerk..	575	00
41. H. C. Coones, clerk..	575	00
42. John Eyles, clerk..	575	00
43. Miss E. M. Lawson, clerk, less 2 days deducted..	572	04
44. C. A. Hunt, clerk..	562	50
45. Miss F. H. Burgess, clerk, less 6 days deducted..	563	63
46. Miss A. Duhamel, clerk..	550	00
47. B. R. Eastman, clerk..	550	00
48. G. H. D. Gibson, clerk..	550	00
49. Miss M. T. Kealey, clerk..	550	00
50. Miss M. A. Kennedy..	550	00
51. Miss E. MacRitchie, clerk..	550	00
52. Miss S. R. Preston, clerk., ...	537	50
53. Miss H. P. Johnson, clerk, 'ess ! d y deducted..	536	84
54. Miss T. Cook, clerk, less 1 day deducted..	536	02
55. H. Buckham, clerk, 8 m., 28 d. at $720..	534	19
56. Miss A. Baudry, clerk, less 9 days deducted..	528	05
57. Miss J. M. Ahearn, clerk..	534	68
58. C. H. Bennett, clerk, less 1½ days deducted.. .. ..·..	537	82
59. A. K. Cohoon, clerk..	525	00
60. F. J. Mitchell, clerk..	525	00
61. J. S. Morrison, clerk, 7 m., 3 d. at $900..	532	26
62. Miss L. Putman, clerk, employed 10 mos..	504	16
63. Miss H. Williams, clerk..	512	50
64. Miss S. Wood, clerk..	521	50
65. Miss W. E. Leslie, clerk..	512	50
66. Miss M. Cameron, clerk..	512	50
67. Miss H. Bennett, clerk, less 1 day deducted.. .. .. ..—..	511	10
68. Miss R.Belliveau, clerk, less 1 day deducted..	511	10
69. R. C. Henry, clerk..	500	00
70. Miss A. J. MacCuaig, clerk..	500	00
71. Miss I. Moore, clerk..	500	00
72. Miss G. McDougall, clerk..	500	00
73. B. St. George, clerk, 11 m., 22 d. at $500..	487	90
74. F. C. McGee, clerk, 4 mos. at $1,200.. .. ..·..	400	00
75. Alex. McCracken, clerk, 10 mos. at $500.	416	66
76. T. Morin, clerk, 8 m., 26 d. at $500, 3 m. at $550..	505	16
77. J. E. Featherston, clerk. 11 m., 14 d. at $500..	477	13
78. A. Allen, clerk, 10 m., 20 d. at $500..	446	52
79. O. Charron, clerk, 11 m., 24 d. at $500..	490	58
80. D. F. Blyth, clerk, 5 m., 14 d. at $800..	366	88
81. Miss A. C. Nolan, clerk, 4¼ m., at $500..	201	70
82. J. J. Higgerty, clerk, 7 m., 4 d. at $500..	297	21
83. Miss F. B. Beatty clerk, 5 m., 3 d. at $500..	210	96
84. C. F. Bell, clerk, 3 m., 17 d. at $600..	175	69
85. H. L. Fulford, messenger, 2¾ mos. at $500..	111	10
86. Miss E. Hayes, clerk, 4⁴⁄ mos. at $500..	199	64
87. J. Laflamme, clerk, 2 m , 28 d. at $500..	122	20
88. G. F. Landerkin, clerk, 1 m., 30 d. at $1,000..	163	97
89. Miss A. R. Montgomery, clerk, 3 m., 19 d. at $500..	150	54
90. E. P. J. McCabe, clerk, 2 m., 8 d. at $900..	165	16
91. Miss Clara Ross, clerk, 4 m., 5 d. at $500..	181	54
92. Miss A. Traveller, clerk, 3 m., 17 d. at $500..	147	84
93. John Anderson, clerk, 16 days at $500..	26	67
94. L. G. Brennan, clerk, 1 m., 27 d. at $500..	73	84
95. R. G. Douglos, clerk, 18 d. at $600..	30	00
96. E. Gamache, clerk, 1 m., 16 d. at $500..	63	17
97. Miss B. Jeffers, clerk, 24 d. at $500..	33	33
98. Miss N. Lefurgey, clerk, 24 d. at $500..	33	33
99. A. Ryan, clerk, 1 m., 18 d. at $720..	94	84
100. W. Tubman, clerk..	42	14
	$53,253	62

(E.) Topographical Surveys Branch.—Chargeable to Dominion Lands Capital.

Surveyors—

1. P. R. A. Belanger, 2 m., 18 d. at $1,800.. .. ..$	388	21
2. E. W. Hubbell, 3 m., 10 d. at $1,800..	495	96
3. J. A. Pel'eau..	1,500	00

SESSIONAL PAPER No. 29a

Correspondence and accounts—
- 4. R. H. Hunter, accountant, 8 mos. at $1,500, 4 mos. at $1,550.. .. .. $ 1,516 66
- 5. Miss M. F. Percival, typist, 5 m., 27 d. at $500, 6 m. at $550.. .. .. 520 95
- 6. F. T. Ellis, messenger.. .. .. 550 00
- 7. M. J. Cullen, typist, 9 m., 24 d. at $500.. .. .. 402 73

Draughting office—
- 8. Thos. Shanks, asst. chief draughtsman, 10 mos. at $1,850, 2 mos. at $1,900.. .. .. 1,858 33

Draughting office—First division—
- 9. G. H. Watt, in charge of division, 8 mos. at $1,500, 4 mos. at $1,550. 1,516 66
- 10. John Sylvain, draughtsman, 10 mos. at $1,200, 2 mos. at $1,250.. .. 1,208 33
- 11. Carl Engler, draughtsman, 8 mos. at $1,500, 4 mos. at $1,550.. .. .. 1,516 66
- 12. T. E. Brown, draughtsman, 10 mos. at $1,200, 2 mos. at $1,250.. .. 1,208 33
- 13. T. H. Clunn, draughtsman, 11 mos. at $1,200, 1 m. at $1,250.. .. .. 1,204 16
- 14. F. H. Mackie, draughtsman, 3 m. 15 d. at $950, 3 mos. at $1,200.. .. 575 80
- 15. G. B. Dodge, draughtsman, 9½ mos. at $1,200.. .. .. 933 33
- 16. H. A. MacKenzie, draughtsman, 11 m. 29 d. at $900.. .. .. 897 53
- 17. M. B. Weekes, draughtsman, 11 m., 24 d. at $900.. .. .. 885 43
- 18. W. E. Weld, draughtsman, 9 m., 25 d. at $900.. .. .. 737 33

Draughting office—Second division—
- 19. E. H. Phillips, in charge of division, 8 m. at $1,500, 4 m. at $1,550.. 1,516 66
- 20. F. D. Henderson, draughtsman, 8 m., 19 d. at $1,200, 1 m. at $1,250.. 967 49
- 21. H. L. Seymour, draughtsman, ... 1,200 00
- 22. John Empey, draughtsman, 11 m., 26 d. at $1,200.. .. .. 1,186 66
- 23. H. G. Barber, draughtsman, 6 m., 14 d. at $1,200 .. .. 645 16
- 24. T. S. Nash, draughtsman, 5 m., 16 d. at $1,200.. .. .. 651 61
- 25. A. G. Stacey, draughtsman, 6 mos. at $1,200, 2 mos. at $1,250.. .. .. 808 33
- 26. F. G. Durnford, draughtsman, 9 m., 27 d. at $1,200, 2 m. at $1,250.. 1,198 54
- 27. J. C. Baker, draughtsman, 2 m., 23 d. at $900.. .. .. :. 198 30
- 28. W. D. McClennan, draughtsman, 2 m., 26 d. at $900.. .. .. 890 23
- 29. E. L. Burgess, draughtsman.. .. .. 1,200 00
- 30. J. E. Umbach, draughtsman, 11 m. at $1,200, 1 d. at $1,250.. .. .. 1,204 16
- 31. A. Roger, draughtsman, 4 m., 27 d. at $900.. .. .. 365 81
- 32. S. M. Hill, draughtsman, 10 m. at $900, 2 m. at $1,200.. .. .. .. 950 00
- 33. F. W. Rice, draughtsman, 10 m., 7 d. at $900.. .. .. 719 43
- 34. F. A. Moore, draughtsman, 4 mos. at $900.. .. .. 300 00
- 37. R. B. Owens, draughtsman, 9 m., 17 d. at $900.. .. .. 717 50
- 36. E. M. Dennis, draughtsman, 7 m., 19 d. at $900, 1 m. at $1,200.. .. 673 14
- 37. R. P. Owens, draughtsman, 9 m., 17 d. at $900.. .. .. 717 50
- 38. A. J. Elder, draughtsman, 6 m., 2 d. at $900.. .. .. 454 84
- 39. G. McMillan, draughtsman, 3 m. at $950, 7 m., 14 d. at $1,200.. .. .. 977 36
- 40. J. E. Morrier, draughtsman, 6 m., 21 d. at $600.. .. .. 333 87
- 41. A. S. Cram, draughtsman, 11 m., 26 d. at $900.. .. .. 890 08
- 42. W. Crawford, draughtsman, 7 m., 19 d. at $900.. .. .. 572 82
- 43. A. L. Cumming, draughtsman, 11 m., 5 d. at $900.. .. .. 837 98
- 44. T. A. Davies, draughtsman, 4 m., 16 d. at $900, 4 m. at $1,200.. .. 738 70
- 45. W. Elwell, draughtsman, 8 m., 11 d. at $900.. .. .. 626 83

Draughting Office—Third division—
- 46. E. L. Rowan-Legge, in charge of division, 8 mos. at $1,500, 4 mos. at $1,550.. .. .. 1,515 66
- 47. H. Lawe, draughtsman, 9 mos. at $1,250, 3 mos. at $1,300.. .. .. .. 1,262 50
- 48. E. T. B. Gillmore, draughtsman, 11 m., 22 d. at $1,500.. .. .. 1,466 66
- 49. P. A. Carson, draughtsman, 10 mos. at $1,200, 1 m., 4 d. at $1,250.. 1,118 04
- 50. C. C. Smith, draughtsman, 10 mos. at $1,200, 2 mos. at $1,250.. .. .. 1,208 33
- 51. R. W. Morley, draughtsman.. .. .. 900 00
- 52. E. E. Wilson, draughtsman, 9 m., 23 d. at $900.. .. .. 720 00
- 53. W. C. Gillis, draughtsman, 1 m., 22 d. at $720.. .. .. 102 58
- 54. G. A. Grey, draughtsman, 3 m., 8 d. at $500.. .. .. 134 87
- 55. J. P. McCormich, draughtsman, 3 mos. at $540.. .. .. 135 00
- 56. W. L. McIlquham, draughtsman.. .. .. 900 00
- 57. E. R. Williams, draughtsman, 1 m., 23 d. at $500.. .. .. 72 56

Draughting Office—Fourth division—
- 58. W. T. Green, in charge of division, 2 m., 25 d. at $1,200, 2 mos. at $1,250.. .. .. 588 97
- 59. W. J. Graham, draughtsman, 28 d. at $1,250.. .. .. 94 08
- 60. J. R. O'Connell, draughtsman, 10 mos. at $1,200, 2 mos. at $1,250.. 1,208 33
- 61. J. E. May, draughtsman, 9 mos. at $1,200, 3 mos. at $1,250.. .. .. 1,212 50
- 62. W. J. Moule, draughtsman.. .. .. 900 00
- 63. J. D. Helmer, draughtsman, 7 mos. at $500, 5 mos. at $550.. .. .. 520 83
- 64. B. Archambault, draughtsman, 7 mos. at $500, 5 mos. at $550.. .. 520 83
- 65. A. Groulx, draughtsman.. .. .. 500 00
- 66. H. V. Finnie, draughtsman, 2 m., 26 d. at $900.. .. .. 215 32
- 67. D. F. Robertson, draughtsman, 2⅔ mos. at $900.. .. .. 200 00
- 68. C. H. Taggart, draughtsman, 10 mos. at $500, 2 mos. at $550.. .. 506 98

7-8 EDWARD VII., A. 1908

Draughting Office—Fifth division—
69. Jacob Smith, in charge of division.. .. ..$ 1,850 00
70. J. B. Lepage, draughtsman, 4 mos. at $1,200, 7 m., 25 d. at $1,300..   1,248 58
71. P. A. Begin, draughtsman, 10 mos. at $1,400, 2 mos. at $1,450.. ...   1,406 32
72. A. E. Blanchet, draughtsman, 10 mos. at $1,200, 2 mos. at $1,250..   1,208 33
73. T. E. S. Davies, draughtsman, 1 m., 18 d. at $900.. .. ..   118 54
74. V. Perrin, draughtsman, 1 m., 18 d. at $900.. .. .. ., ...   150 00
75. A. D. Orsonnens, draughtsman, 4 mos. at $900, 4 mos. at $1,200..   700 00

Photographic office—
76. H. K. Carruthers, photographer, 10 mos. at $1,200, 2 mos. at $1,250.   1,208 33
77. Jno. Woodruff, asst. photographer, 10 mos. at $830, 2 mos. at $1,000 ·   858 30
78. W. E. Morgan, asst. photographer, 12 mos., less 1 day, at $720..   718 06
79. H. E. Whitcomb, asst. photographer, 10 mos. at $556.20, 61 days at
    $2.. .. ..   585 50
80. A. Devlin, asst. photographer, 5 mos. at $360, 7 mos. at $500.. ..   441 66
81. A. Kilmartin, asst. photographer, 7 mos. at $500, 5 mos. at $550..   520 83

Lithographic and Printing Office—
82. A. Moody, foreman, 52 weeks at $21.. .. ..   1,092 00
83. C. R. Thicke, engraver, 52 weeks 1 day at $18.. .. ..   939 00
84. H. S. Thicke, printer, $16 per week.. .. ..   803 99
85. James Bergin, printer, $14 per week.. .. ..   684 80
86. H. J. Higgerty, printer, $12 per week.. .. ..   612 17
87. E. Villeneuve, draughtsman, $9.60 per week.. .. ..   481 60
88. Wa. Bergin, draughtsman, 10 mos. at $500, 2 mos. at $550.. .. ..   508 32

Geographer's office—
89. E. Chalifour, draughtsman, 9 mos. at $1,550, 3 mos. at $1,600.. ..   1,562 50
90. H. E. Baine, draughtsman, 9 mos. at $1,450, 3 mos. at $1,500.. ..   1,462 50
91. H. Taché, draughtsman, 3 mos. at $1,000, 9 mos at $1,080.. .. ..   1,060 00
92. M. W. Sharon, draughtsman, 3 mos. at $930, 9 mos. at $1,080.. ..   1,042 50
93. H. M. Blatchley, draughtsman, 11 mos. at $900, 1 m. at $950.. .. ..   904 16
94. J. S. Gagnon, draughtsman, 11 m., 25 d. at $800.. .. ..   788 05
95. G. E. Dumouchel, draughtsman, 8 mos. at $830, 4 mos. at $880.. ..   846 66
96. M. Darrach, draughtsman, 9 m., 18 d. at $720, 2 m. at $770.. .. ..   701 22
97. James Bennie, draughtsman, 9 mos. at $770, 3 mos. at $820.. .. ..   782 50
98. C. G. Wood, draughtsman, 8 mos. at $770, 4 mos. at $820.. .. ..   786 67
99. J. R. Craig, draughtsman, 8 mos. at $770, 4 mos. at $820.. .. ..   786 67
100. H. W. Wilson, draughtsman, 11 mos. at $720, 1 m. at $770.. .. ..   724 16
101. J. P. McElligott, draughtsman, 7 mos. at $450, 5 mos. at $500.. ..   470 83
102. A. Anderson, draughtsman, 6 m., 27 d. at $1,080.. .. ..   613 38
103. S. Chandler, draughtsman.. .. ..   500 00

Patent branch—
104. N. B. Sheppard, draughtsman. 10 mos. at $1,500, 2 mos. at $1,550..   1,508 32
105. J. Langlois, draughtsman, 10 mos. at $1,200, 2 mos. at $1,250 ....   1,208 32

Timber and mines branch—
106. S. M. Genest, draughtsman, 10 mos. at $1,400, 2 mos. at $1,450..   1,408 33
107. J. H. Reiffenstein, draughtsman, 10 mos. at $1,400, 2 mos. at $1,450.   1,408 33
108. G. S. Proctor, draughtsman, 11 m., 27 d. at $1,050.. .. ..   1,041 53
109. H. W. Humphreys, draughtsman.. .. .. ;.. .. ..   500 00

Survey records branch—
110. P. W. Currie, draughtsman, 10 mos. at $1,500, 2 mos. at $1,550..   1,508 33
111. E. Lecourt, draughtsman, 11 mos. at $1,300, 1 m. at $1,350.. .. ..   1,304 16
112. C. T. Routh, draughtsman.. .. ..   600 00
113. T. W. Smith, 361 days at $1.75.. .. ..   631 75
114. A. Ashton, draughtsman, 11 m., 24 d. at $900.. .. ..   885 48

Railway and swamp lands—
115. J. B. Challies, draughtsman, 11 mos. at $1,200, 1 m. at $1,250.. ..   1,204 16
116. M. F. Cochrane, draughtsman.. .. ..   900 00
117. F. C. Lynch, draughtsman, 2 m., 4 d. at $600.. .. ..   106 67
118. R. T. Moore, draughtsman, 9 m., 29 d. at $540, 2 mos. at $590.. ..   546 82
119. J. M. Mudie, draughtsman, 9 m., 10 d. at $900.. .. ..   696 76
120. W. N. Oswald, draughtsman, 1 m., 24 d. at $500.. .. ..   73 91

                                                            $100,205 53

(F.) Dominion Astronomical Observatory.—(Permanents of the Outside Service.)

1. J. S. Plaskett, astronomer.. .. ..$ 2,000 00
2. J. Macara, chief computer.. .. .. 1,800 00
3. L. Gauthier, keeper of records.. .. .. 1,800 00
4. W. Simpson, secretary.: 1,500 00
5. R. M. Stewart, supt. of time service.. .. .. 1,200 00
6. F. W. O. Werry, observer, 7¾ mos. at $1,550.. .. .. 1,001 07
7. F. A. McDiarmaid, observer.. .. .. 1,050 00
8. W. M. Tobey, observer.. .. .. 1,050 00
9. T. D. Wallace, photographer.. .. .. 1,030 00
10. J. H. Labbe, clerk, $800 per annum.. .. .. 795 55

$13,226 62

(G.) Boundary Surveys.

1. G. W. White-Fraser, surveyor, April 15, 1905, to June 30, 1906, at $1,800... .. ..$ 2,180 00
2. A. J. Brabazon, surveyor, April 5, 1905, to June 30, 1906, at $1,700.. 2,106 09
3. Howell Biggar, surveyor.. .. .. 1,500 00
4. J. D. Craig, surveyor, May 2, 1905, to June 30, 1906, at $1,100.. .. .. 1,280 36
5. W. F. Rats, surveyor, April 15, 1905, to June 30, 1906, at $1,050.. .. 1,271 66
6. J. D. McLennan, asst. surveyor, salary $1,200 per annum.. .. .. .. 1,003 23
7. S. S. McDiarmid, surveyors' asst., 2 m., 11 d. at $950, 12 mos. at $1,050 1,250 53
8. W. F. Nelles, surveyors' asst., 364 days at $2.50.. .. .. 1,092 00
9. W. Treadgold, surveyors' asst., May 1, 1905, to June 20, 1906, at $900 1,025 00
10. N. J. Ogilvie, surveyors' asst., 14 m., 29 d. at $1,000.. .. .. 1,247 30
11. Ed. Treau de Coeli, surveyors' asst.. .. .. 900 00
12. A. Gillespie, surveyors' asst., $2 per day.. .. .. 897 00
13. D. V. Ritchie, surveyors' asst., 244 days at $1, 212 days at $2 . .. 668 00
14. J. M. Bates, surveyors' asst., 11 m., 28 d. at $2 per day.. .. .. 895 16
15. D. Robertson, telegrapher.. .. .. 1,000 00
16. A. Steadworthy, asst. photographer, $2 per day.. .. .. 728 00
17. W. V. Poapst, computer, 5 m., 16 d. at $900.. .. .. 413 71
18. W. P. Near, computer, salary $2 per day.. .. .. 184 00
19. A. H. Swinburn, computer, salary $1.50 per day.. .. .. 228 00
20. A. Arcand, clerk, salary $500 per annum.. .. .. 325 46
21. B. F. Howe, clerk, 36½ days at $1.50.. .. .. 54 75
22. F. Lambart, clerk, 214 days at $2.. .. .. 428 00
23. H. S. Mussell, clerk, 74½ days at $1.50.. .. .. 111 75
24. Geo. S. Spratt, messenger.. .. .. 500 00

$21,290 00

(H.) Dominion Lands Income—Protection of Timber.

Permanent officer—
1. E. Stewart, superintendent, 4 mos. at $2,500, 8 mos. at $3,000.. .. $2,833 32

Temporary employees—
1. N. M. Ross, asst. superintendent.. .. .. 1,400 00
2. R. D. Craig, inspector.. .. .. 1,200 00
3. H. C. Wallin, inspector.. .. .. 900 00
4. Guy Boyce, clerk.. .. .. 132 50

$6,465 82

(I.) Mines Branch.

1. A. F. Purcell, messenger, 9 mos. at $500, 3 mos. at $550.. .. .. .. $ 512 50

(J.) Ordnance Lands.

1. Miss E. Joliffe, clerk, 9 mos. at $550, 3 mos. at $600.. .. .. $ 561 00

(K.) School Lands Funds.

Permanent officer—
1. F. G. Checkley, chief clerk.. .. .. **$2,050 00**

Temporary employees—
1. W. T. Rollins, clerk 1,200 00
2. Miss F. Aylen, clerk, 9 mos. at $600, 3 mos. at $650.. .. .. 612 50
3. Miss L. Bradley, clerk, 9 mos. at $600, 3 mos. at $650.. .. .. 612 50
4. D. H. McDonald, clerk, 9 mos. at $600, 3 mos. at $650.. .. .. 612 50
5. Miss A. Swinburn, clerk.. .. .. 600 00
6. A. A. Traversy, messenger, salary $500 per annum.. .. .. 348 11
7. A. L. Geddes, clerk, salary $600 per annum.. .. .. 20 00

$6,055 61

DEPARTMENT OF THE INTERIOR, FISCAL YEAR 1891-1892.

STATEMENT showing in detail the number of officials employed at Ottawa and sums paid to each during the fiscal year ending June 30, 1892.

SUMMARY.

(A.) Civil Government Salaries.

1 deputy head.. .. ..$ 2,933 34
4 chief clerks.. .. .. 3,822 91
2 special technical officers.. .. .. 3,700 00
11 first-class clerks.. .. .. 17,547 80
15 second-class clerks.. .. .. 18,195 39
47 third-class clerks.. .. .. 31,625 95
5 messengers.. .. .. 2,058 27

85 $84,883 66

MISCELLANEOUS VOTES.

(B.) Dominion Lands Capital.

40 temporary employees.. .. ..$30,847 25

(C.) Dominion Lands Income.

1 permanent clerk.. .. ..$1,200 00
16 temporary employees.. .. .. 5,167 45
                                                           ——————— 6,367 45

(D.) School Lands Funds.

1 permanent clerk.. .. .. 1,400 00

(E.) Immigration.

2 temporary clerks.. .. .. 191 50

60 $38,806 20

145   Grand total.. .. ..$123,689 86

DEPARTMENT OF THE INTERIOR, FISCAL YEAR 1891-1892.

STATEMENT showing in detail the number of officials employed at Ottawa and sums paid to each during the fiscal year ending June 30, 1892.

(A.) Civil Government Salaries.

1 deputy head—

    A. M. Burgess, 8 mos. at $2,800, 4 mos. at $3,200.. .. ..$ 2,933 34

4 chief clerks—

    1. John R. Hall, secretary, 11 mo. at $2,800.. .. ..$ 2,66 71
    2. W. M. Goodeve, patents, 5½ mos. at $2,100, 5½ mos. at $2,150.. .. 1,947 90
    3. J. A. Pinard, accountant, 11 mos. at $2,100.. .. .. 1,925 00
    4. Ed. Deville, surveyor general, 11 mos. at $2,600.. .. .. 2,383 30

                                         $ 8,822 91

2 special technical officers—

    1. J. Johnston, geographer.. .. ..$ 1,850 00
    2. W. F. King, astronomer.. .. .. 1,850 00

                                         $ 3,700 00

11 first-class clerks—

    1. K. J. Henry, 11 mos. at $1,800.. .. ..$ 1,650 00
    2. Wm. Mills.. .. .. 1,800 00
    3. F. Clayton.. .. .. 1,800 00
    4. L. C. Pereira, 11 mos. at $1,800.. .. .. 1,650 00
    5. G. U. Ryley, 11 mos. at $1,800.. .. .. 1,650 00
    6. A. H. Whitcher.. .. .. 1,750 00
    7. H. Kinloch, 5½ mos. at $1,700, 5½ mos. at $1,750.. .. .. .. 1,581 20
    8. C. H. Beddoe, 11 mos. at $1,700.. .. .. 1,558 30
    9. T. G. Rothwell, 11 mos. at $1,500.. .. .. 1,375 00
    10. N. O. Coté, 11 mos. at $1,400.. .. .. 1,283 30
    11. P. P. Symes.. .. .. 1,450 00

                                         $17,547 80

15 Second-class clerks—

    1. N. Tetu, 11 mos. at $1,400.. .. ..
    2. C. C. Rogers, 11 mos. at $1,400.. .. .. 1,283 30
    3. A. Grignard.. .. .. 1,400 00
    4. Brown Wallis.. .. .. 1,400 00
    5. A. Chisholm, 11 mos. at $1,400.. .. ..$ 1,283 30
        Allowance for private secretary.. .. .. 600 00

                                     1,883 30
    6. P. G. Keyes, 6 mos. at $1,350, 6 mos. at $1,400.. .. .. 1,375 00
    7. George Bell, 11 mos. at $1,300.. .. .. 1,191 71
    8. J. S. Brough, 11 mos. at $1,200.. .. .. 1,100 00
    9. R .Rauscher.. .. .. 1,200 00
    10. W. S. Gliddon, 11 mos. at $1,150.. .. .. 1,054 21
    11. G. A. Sparkes.. .. .. 1,150 00
    12. H. E. Hume, salary $1,100, less $26.70.. .. .. 1,073 30
    13. Frank Nelson, July 1-14, $12.50, Oct. 17 to June 30, at $1,100.. .. .. 834 63
    14. Martin Brady.. .. .. 1,200 00
    15. F. H. C. Cox, 8 mos. at $1,150.. .. .. 766 64

                                         $18,195 39

47 third-class clerks—

    1. Henry Sherwood.. .. ..$ 1,000 00
    2. Bradish Billings.. .. .. 1,000 00
    3. J. L. Etoile, 115 mos. at $1,000.. .. .. 916 71
    4. E. B. Genest.. .. .. 1,000 00
    5. G. W. Paterson.. .. .. 1,000 00
    6. S. T. Lacasse, 10 mos., 20 d. at $1,000.. .. .. 886 16
    7. D. Dunn.. .. .. 1,000 00
    8. T. W. E. Sowter, 11 mos. at $1,000.. .. .. 916 71
    9. H. B. D. Bruce, 11 mos. at $1,000.. .. .. 916 71
    10. C. J. Steers, 11 mos. at $1,000.. .. .. 916 71
    11. H. H. Turner, 11 mos. at $950.. .. .. 883 32
    12. F. C. Capreol, 8 mos. at $900, 3 mos. at $950.. .. .. 837 49

7-8 EDWARD VII., A. 1908

13. C. C. Pelletier.. .. ..$	900 00
14. O. H. Lambart..	900 00
15. F. Loyer, 11 mos. at $850..	779 21
16. Eug. Belleau, 11 mos. at $850..	779 21
17. P. V. Low, 12 mos., $820, and arrears $50.34..	880 34
18. Mrs. M. P. Lee..	800 00
19. J. A. Coté, 5½ mos. at $750, 5½ mos. at $800..	710 40
20. Walter Hatch, 9 mos. at $750, 3 mos. at $800..	762 50
21. H. H. Rowatt, 11 mos. at $750..	687 50
22. Geo. D. Pope..	750 00
23. F. W. C. Cuming, 6 mos. at $700, 6 mos at $750..	725 00
24. P. Robertson, 8 mos. at $700, 3 mos at $750..	654 20
25. A. F. Grant..	660 00
26. J. S. Eagleson, 11 mos. at $650..	595 80
27. Jos. P. Dunne, 6 mos. at $600, 6 mos. at $650..	625 00
28. S. J. Willoughby, 5½ mos. at $600, 5½ mos. at $650..	572 90
29. C. W. Badgley, 5½ mos. at $600, 5½ mos. at $650.. .. '	572 90
30. B. L. York, 5½ mos. at $600, 5½ mos. at $650..	572 90
31. R. H. Campbell..	550 00
32. Mrs. J. Ricard..	547 00
33. Miss A. B. Yielding, Sept. 21, 1891, to June 30, 1892, at $547..	425 41
34. G. Lemieux..	500 00
35. F. C. Macdonald..	500 00
36. Mrs. C. Ridley..	500 00
37. A. A. Pinard, Feb. 9 to June 30, 1892, at $500..	196 81
38. Miss M. May..	450 00
39. Mrs. M. E. Bell..	450 00
40. F. E. Stuart..	450 00
41. Edward Connelly, 11 mos. at $450..	412 49
42. Miss L. Coleman, July 21, 1901, to June 30, 1892, at $450..	425 81
43. G. P. Pereira, October 14, 1891, to June 30, 1892, at $450..	321 77
44. P. M. Duffy, 6 mos. at $400, 6 mos. at $450..	425 00
45. Miss M. Barber..	400 00
46. Miss M. Shaw..	400 00
47. John Curley..	400 00
R. G. Bourne, resigned, 2 mos., 3 days at $400..	69 99
	$31,625 95

5 messengers—

James Dunnet, 11 mos. at $500.. .. ..$	456 27
A. Swinburn, 11 mos. at $500..	458 27
Alf. Pegg..	500 00
Robert Dunlop..	500 00
E. E. Turton, Feb. 9, 1892; to June 30, 1892, at $300..	141 73
	$ 2,058 27

(B.) Dominion Lands, Capital.

Temporary clerks—

J. S. Dennis, 357 days at $5..	1,785 00
Jacob Smith, 365½ days at $4..	1,462 00
W. McL. Mainguy, 6 mos. at $95.41, 6 mos. at $100, less 1½ days..	1,167 52
L. Gauthier, 6 mos. at $80, 6 mos. at $84.36..	987 36
N. B. Sheppard, 6 mos. at $80.20, 6 mos. at $84.36, less 4 days..	976 79
J. A. Belleau, 6 mos. at $80.20, 6 mos. at $84.36..	987 36
E. Chalifour, 6 mos. at $80.20, 6 mos. at $84.36, less 8 days..	964 32
E. L. Rowan-Legg, 6 mos. at $72.60, 6 mos. at $84.36, less 2 days.. ..	936 14
J. Macara, 6 mos. at $69.16, 6 mos. at $84.36, and 2 plans, $35..	956 12
A. Bristow, 6 mos. at $69.16, 5 mos. at $84.36, less 1 day..	834 04
J. M. O'Hanly, 6 mos. at $69.16, 6 mos. at $84.36..	921 12
J. I. Dufresne, 184 days at $2.50, 6 mos. at $100, and examining Dominion land surveyors, $105..	1,165 00
J. B. Lepage, 6 mos. at $69.16, 6 mos. at $73.32, less 5 days..	842 83
J. H. Reiffenstein, 6 mos. at $65, 6 mos. at $73.32, less ½ day..	838 70
S. M. Genest, 6 mos. at $53.95, 6 mos. at $69.16, less 8 days..	720 22
P. A. Begin, 6 mos. at $53.95, 6 mos. at $69.16..	738 66
W. S. Surtees, 6 mos. at $53.95, 181 days at $2..	685 70
E. W. Hubbell, 285 days at $2..	570 00
E. T. B. Gillmore, 6 mos. at $49.79, 6 mos. at $53.95, less 6 days,.	599 80
J. Woodruff, 184 days at $1.50, 6 mos. at $49.79..	574 74
Percy Turner, 6 mos. at $19.50, 5 mos., 25 days at $20	233 67

SESSIONAL PAPER No. 29a

Temporary employees—*Con.*

H. N. Topley, photographer.. .. ..$	800 00
C. R. Thicke, engraver, 308½ days at $2..	617 00
A. Pouliot, draughtsman, salary $14 per week..	708 23
J. Ridgway, draughtsman, salary $4.50 per week..	240 80
R. A. Baldwin, draughtsman, 30 weeks at $4.50, 23 weeks at $4.60.. ..	239 27
A. Moody, litho. printer, 52 weeks, 1 day at $19..	991 18
E. Sievers, litho. printer, 52 weeks, 4 days at $16..	842 68
J. Foran, litho. printer, 53 weeks at $16..	848 00
J. Cherry, litho. printer, 49 weeks at $12, 4 weeks at $13..	639 00
J. R. Allan, sur. asst., 190 days at $2..	380 00
P. R. A. Belanger, D.L.S., 2 mos., 4 days at $125 per month..	266 67
Thos. Fawcett, D.L.S., 2 mos., 6 days at $150 per month..	330 00
W. S. Drewry, D.L.S., 143 days at $6, 2 mos., 2 days at $125..	1,116 33
James Gibbons, surv. asst., 140 days at $2..	280 00
R. H. Hunter, clerk, 365 days at $2..	730 00
Otto J. Klotz, D.L.S., 2 mos., 2 days at $2..	310 00
J. J. McArthur, D.L.S., 196 days at $6, 2 mos., 2 days at $125..	1,434 33
Wm. Ogilvie, D.L.S., 80 days at $7, 2 mos., 2 days at $150..	870 00
A. St. Cyr, D.L.S., 2 mos., 4 days at $125..	266 67
	$30,547 25

(C.) Dominion Lands, Income.

Permanent clerk—

George Newcombe, agent.. .. ..$ 1,200 00	

Temporary employees—

Henry Ackland, messenger, 3 mos., 29 days at $25.. .. .. $	98 39
Miss I. Coleman, clerk, 20 days at $400 per annum, prior to being made permanent..	21 50
Miss M. A. Earle, clerk..	400 00
A. Houdet, clerk, 21 days at $1.75..	36 54
Ralph Jones, clerk, 114 days at $2..	228 00
John Judge, clerk..	400 00
Mrs. A. MacMaster, clerk, salary $400, less 8 days..	391 29
D. Macnamara, clerk..	400 00
Mrs. L. Norton, clerk, 12 mos., less 4 days at $400..	395 52
Wm. Peart, clerk, 1 m., 12 days at $395..	45 66
*G. P. Pereira, clerk, 7 mos., 13 days at $400, prior to being made permanent..	113 97
*A. A. Pinard, clerk, 7 mos., 8 days at $400, prior to being made permanent..	239 17
E. Lecourt, clerk, 266 days at $1.50, 6 mos. at $49.79..	548 37
Miss F. Pope, clerk, 5 mos. at $400..	166 44
John Mason, carpenter..	732 00
A. St. Cyr, clerk, 2 mos., 4 days at $125..	266 67
John Satchell, clerk..	400 00
*E. E. Turton, messenger, 4 mos., 4 days at $25, 3 mos., 8 days at $30, prior to being made permanent..	195 00
Miss A. P. Yielding, clerk, 2 mos., 20 days at $400..	88 88
	$ 5,167 45

(D.) School Lands Funds.

F. S. Checkley, clerk.. .. .. $1,400 00.	

(E.) Immigration.

Transferred to Department of Agriculture—

J. D. Bollard, clerk, 2 mos. at $50.. .. ..$	100 00
Miss R. G. Mills, clerk, 61 days at $1.50..	91 50
	$ 191 50

---

* Name already included in Civil Government salaries.

7-8 EDWARD VII., A. 1908

DEPARTMENT OF THE INTERIOR,
OTTAWA, October 23, 1907.

The Secretary,
    Civil Service Commission,
        Ottawa.

DEAR SIR,—I wish to lay before the Civil Service Commissioners, for their consideration, the following suggestions:—

1st. Re *Leave of Absence.*

Instead of the present rule of giving three weeks annual holiday to all employees,
regardless of length of service, I would suggest a graded scale as follows:

Two weeks during first five years' service, after five years' service, three weeks,
after ten years' service, four weeks; after twenty years' service, five weeks.

It is not necessary for me to say anything in favour of the contention that three
weeks annual vacation is not sufficient for officials of advancing years and long service.

This suggestion is borrowed from the English Civil Service Act, which provides
that in the lower grades of service twelve working days shall be the annual holiday,
and after five years eighteen days. In the higher grades 36 working days, and after
ten years, 48 working days.

2nd. A suggestion borrowed from the Civil Service Act of the United States,
which provides that not more than two members of the same family be employed in
the service at the same time.

                        I have the honour to remain;
                            Yours faithfully,
                                FRANK NELSON.

                                        OTTAWA, June 20, 1907.

Mr. N. B. SHEPPARD, sworn and examined.

By the Chairman:

Q. You are a clerk in the lands patent branch of the Department of the Interior?
—A. Yes.

Q. You wrote this letter to the Commission (showing)?—A. Yes.

Q. The purport of that letter is that you wish to be placed on the permanent staff
of the department?—A. It is partly that; principally for an increase of salary.

Q. You are now getting $1,550 as a temporary employee, and you wish to be made
permanent and to get $2,000?—A. Yes.

Q. There are apparently many other draughtsmen in the same class in that branch?
—A. Not in that branch; in the topographical surveys branch.

Q. Do you desire that all the draughtsmen in the topographical surveys office
should be made permanent?—A. I think that is the general impression among them.

Q. Are you writing this letter simply on your own behalf or as a representative
of yourself and others?—A. On my own behalf.

Q. But you think the other people are in the same position as yourself?—A. I
know some of them are.

Q. There are in the Auditor General's Report a list of four pages of people classed as draughtsmen in the surveys branch of the Department of the Interior employed temporarily?—A. I daresay.

Q. How were you appointed?—A. I made application in 1883.

Q. To whom?—A. To the member of parliament for Yamaska, I think.

Q. Who was that?—A. Mr. Vanasse.

Q. You made application for a Government appointment?—A. Yes.

Q. Were you a Dominion land surveyor?—A. No.

Q. A Provincial land surveyor?—A. No. I followed the profession of surveying for several years before I came to the department. I have been in the surveys branch ever since.

Q. Have you been in Ottawa all the time, or have you gone into the field?—A. Since 1883 I have been in Ottawa.

Q. Did you ever, since you have been in the service, go into the field?—A. Yes, just slightly.

Q. What vacancy do you refer to in this letter?—A. The vacancy caused by the resignation of the clerk who had the position I am holding at present.

Q. What was his name?—A. E. W. Hubbell.

Q. He is a Dominion land surveyor?—A. Yes.

Q. He goes into the field every year?—A. Lately.

Q. What was his position in the department?—A. They did not give it any definite name. He took charge of looking after the descriptions of the land patents.

Q. Was he a Dominion land surveyor when he did that duty?—A. Yes.

Q. He was always a Dominion land surveyor, from the time he entered the department?—A. No.

Q. Was he always a Dominion land surveyor when he looked after these descriptions?—A. Yes.

Q. Then, you wish to be appointed to a place held all the time by a Dominion land surveyor, although you are not a Dominion land surveyor yourself?—A. I am there.

Q. You are looking after the descriptions of land patents?—A. Yes.

Q. That position was held by Mr. Hubbell?—A. Yes.

Q. When he held that position, he was a Dominion land surveyor?—A. Yes.

Q. You are not a Dominion land surveyor?—A. No.

Q. Is it desirable that the position you occupy should be held by a Dominion land surveyor?—A. I do not think so.

Q. What are your technical qualifications for this position?—A. My experience in surveying, my technical knowledge of surveying, and my experience in the department.

Q. Are you a senior amongst all these draughtsmen?—A. Yes.

Q. You are the senior draughtsman?—A. Yes, one of the seniors by service.

Q. In the Auditor General's report they are all described as draughtsmen in the surveys branch?—A. Possibly so.

Q. Are you the only person technically described as a draughtsman who does superior work there—work of a description the other so-called draughtsmen do not perform?—A. I do not know who makes descriptions in that office now, because I am no longer in it—have not been for years.

Q. What are you doing now?—A. I am preparing descriptions in the Dominion land patents branch.

Q. That is not draughtsman's work?—A. No, you cannot call that drafting, but I do a great deal besides that.

Q. Is there any other person in the department preparing descriptions of Dominion land patents?—A. Yes.

Q. Are there more than one besides yourself?—A. Yes, in a different branch.

Q. In other branches of the department there are people doing analogous work to yours?—A. I suppose I might say there are, in connection with descriptions of railway lands.

Q. What are the patents you are preparing?—A. Homesteads, sales, special grants—in fact, all patents, with the exception of railway lands.

Q. Who prepares the descriptions of the school lands?—A. I do.

Q. Then, the only descriptions that are not prepared by yourself are the descriptions of railway lands?—A. Yes, and they pass through my hands.

Q. Who is your immediate chief?—A. Mr. N. O. Côté.

Q. He is described as chief clerk of patents?—A. Yes.

Q. He succeeded Mr. Goodeve?—A. Yes.

Q. Do you report directly to him?—A. Yes.

Q. There is no intermediate between you and Mr. Côté?—A. No.

Q. Are you one amongst many who report to him direct, or are you the chief of all these others?—A. I have nothing to do with the others; I am in charge of a sub-branch.

Q. There must be about a hundred draughtsmen in the surveys branch; do they report through you, or do they report to Mr. Côté direct?—A. I have nothing to do with them, and they have nothing to do with me. Allow me to explain. The topographical surveys branch is under the control of the surveyor general. All technical men came through the surveyor general's office, and I was one of them. I was transferred from the surveyor general's office to take charge of the fiats and the descriptions in connection with the patents in the head office. I have nothing whatever to do with any draughtsman in the surveyor general's branch, with the exception of supplying information that may be required for that branch from me. I have charge of a sub-branch in our own branch of the department.

Q. Do any of these other men detailed in the Auditor General's report, report to Mr. Coté?—A. No.

Q. You are the only man who reports to Mr. Côté?—A. Yes, of those draughtsmen.

Q. In your petition you request that steps should be taken to give you $2,000 a year and make you permanent? In listening to the petition, are we to infer that there are others in the same category who should also be appointed permanent and at the same salary?—A. I certainly think that those who have been in the service as long or nearly as long as myself should be in the same category as myself.

Q. What are the qualifications required in a Dominion land surveyor?—A. Ability to survey Dominion lands.

Q. In making out these descriptions, is there a great deal of technical knowledge required which a Dominion land surveyor necessarily possesses?—A. Yes, certainly.

Q. Is it detrimental that a man making out descriptions of these lands has not passed as a Dominion land surveyor?—A. No, it is not detrimental in any way.

Q. Then how do you reconcile the two statements, that it is desirable on the one hand that he should possess the qualifications of a Dominion land surveyor, and that he need not be a Dominion land surveyor?—A. A man may well possess the qualifications of a Dominion land surveyor who has not been a Dominion land surveyor.

Q. Would it not be better that a man making out these descriptions should have passed the examination of a Dominion land surveyor?—A. That is a matter of opinion. I can say that I have done just as good work as my predecessor, if not better; and moreover, if any particular descriptions were required at the time he held the office, they were sent to me to do at the time I was in the surveyor general's office.

Q. What do you mean by any particular descriptions?—A. If there were peculiarities which might perhaps require a little studying. I do not say that it was because he was not able to do them, but the fact remains that I did them.

Q. What is Mr. Hubbell getting now?—A. I could not say.

Q. He is surveying on contract ?—A. I could not say. I think he is engaged by the day.

Q. He takes out parties under his control ?—A. Yes.

Q. Did you ever conduct a party in the field ?—A. Yes.

Q. In what way ?—A. As an articled student under my uncle.

Q. Did you have sole charge of the party ?—A. Yes.

Q. Was that survey in the province of Quebec ?—A. Yes.

Q. Was it a survey as important relatively as a survey of new unsurveyed territory in the Northwest ?—A. Is was a cadastral survey.

Q. That is for dividing the seigniories?—A. It is for the cadastration of the lots for the purpose of registration and legal process.

Q. Is there any other fact you think you should tell us that would in your opinion justify an increase of your salary and putting you on the permanent force ?—A. I might state, as I think I mentioned in my letter, that at the time I made the application I asked that I be given the same salary as the officer who had just vacated the place—that I was not looking for the place particularly, as I had a very good position in the Surveyor General's office but not sufficient salary; and the only answer I got to that was to report for duty.

Q. Through whom ?—A. The Deputy Minister at the time.

Q. You did not get it through Mr. Deville or Mr. Coté?—A. No.

Q. It went through the regular course of the department, and the Deputy Minister wrote you an answer ?—A. My application was to the Deputy Minister, and I got the answer from him.

Q. What are your office hours ?—A. From 9.30 to 4.30.

Q. Do you ever get any holidays ?—A. Three weeks.

Q. Do you sign an attendance book ?—A. Yes.

Q. Whose attendance book do you sign?—A. The attendance book of the Land Patents branch.

Q. That is Mr. Coté's ?—A. Yes.

Q. How many people are employed in the Land Patents branch?—A. Perhaps 70 or 80. I may be mistaken though.

Q. Do you think these 70 or 80 people in the Land Patents branch should be appointed permanently ?—A. I think the greater portion of them are appointed permanently.

Q. Then some of the officials in the Land Patents branch are permanent and some are not ?—A. I have never inquired much into their personal matters, but I know for a fact that four are not.

Q. Are there only about half a dozen or so of the officials in the Land Patents branch that are not permanent ?—A. As far as I know.

Q. Do you think those half dozen or so should be appointed permanently ?—A. I think so.

Q. In a big department like the Department of the Interior, where there are about 150 permanent and about 400 non-permanent officials, do you think it would be desirable that a greater number of the non-permanents should be appointed to permanent positions ?—A. I think so, because it has been found that those who were not permanent made their best endeavours to obtain work outside, and almost immediately left after being appointed.

Q. There are several officials who left the department in 1883; there were about 40 members in your branch. Of those 40 there are 6 left?—A. Since I have been there, there have been added to the staff probably 80, and some 50 have gone in the way of deaths and leaving.

Q. But there is a constant shifting?—A. A constant shifting in the Surveyor General's branch.

Q. Are all the appointments made like yours, through the influence of Members of Parliament?—A. I could not say.

Q. Yours was made through the influence of the Member for your district?—A. Probably. I simply asked him if I could get employment in the department; that is all I said; and I got notice to report at Ottawa.

Q. You do not know how the other members of the temporary staff got their appointments?—A. I believe some of them got them through a circular which was sent to certain colleges and universities throughout the country asking them to lay before their students the proposition that they enter the Government service under certain conditions.

Q. What salaries do draughtsmen in the Topographical Surveys branch get on appointment?—A. Different salaries.

Q. What is the minimum salary at present?—A. I do not know.

Q. Are they appointed at $400 or $500?—A. Probably at $75 a month up.

Q. Are they graduates of universities?—A. Some.

Q. Are those who are not graduates of universities Provincial or Dominion land surveyors?—A. Some of them.

Q. Are some of those described as draughtsmen persons that never were in the field, never obtained a graduation certificate from a university, and never passed the examination of Dominion land surveyors?—A. Yes.

Q. And these people are called draughtsmen?—A. Yes.

Q. Do you happen to know whether these people who did not pass the examination of Dominion land surveyors and have never been in the field have had any experience at all?—A. Some I know have not had any experience outside of what they have gained in the office.

Q. They came in fresh from school or somewhere else and were dubbed draughtsmen, though without experience?—A. I expect so.

Q. And were paid at the rate of $75 a month?—A. I will not say as to those who were paid $75 a month. When I entered the department we were paid from $30 to $45 a month.

Q. Are there people now there who are dubbed draughtsmen paid at the rate of $45 or $50 a month who have had no experience?—A. As I understand, those who have been appointed within the last two or three years or so are supposed to be graduates of some technical school or university.

Q. What increments do they receive? Suppose they begin at $900 per annum, how much is the first increment?—A. I do not know what they are getting now as a rule, but I understand some litttle time ago that an increase of $50 a year was granted to some of them. As I say, I have no interest in the Topographical Surveys branch other than that I am still on its pay-list.

Q. In looking over the list I see that some draughtsmen are paid at the rate of $900 a year, others at the rate of $500 a year, others at the rate of $1,500 a year, some at the rate of $300 a year and others at the rate of $720 a year. Is there any standard or any system adopted in the Surveys branch of the Department of the Interior regulating the salaries of draughtsmen?—A. I am not sufficiently conversant with it to say except that I think any increases that have been given to them have been based on their term of service and their qualifications.

By Mr. Bazin:

Q. On whose recommendation would that be done?—A. The Surveyor General's.

By the Chairman:

Q. Here is a draughtsman paid for a month and a fraction at the rate of $300 a year, and next to him is a draughtsman getting $1,200 a year. Do they do the same duties?—A. Probably not.

By Mr. Fyshe:

Q. Surely it is incredible that a draughtsman of any standing should be worth only $300 a year?—A. The term draughtsman is a general term used in the branch.

SIONAL PAPER No. 29a

not know why; but they are virtually draughtsmen; they could be called on to raughting if necessary.

Q. What do they draught?—A. Township plans.

Q. Merely outlining certain areas?—A. No, not at all. The probability is that ι at the very low salaries are those employed in the lithographing branch of the ch.

Q. That should involve some technical skill, shouldn't it?—A. Certainly; it does. l depends on the actual work. There are those who manipulate the machine.

Q. The chances are that a man getting $300 a year is doing the most ordinary of mechanical work?—A. It is quite possible that he may be doing draughting. ɔw for a fact that there were those who did not get any more than that who did good draughting work there.

Q. Why should they remain?—A. Because they were not in a position to leave. eat many of them did not remain. As soon as they got something better they

I might state that one man that I know, who was getting I think $300 a year ιe department some few years ago, is now getting a salary of $1,500 or more a outside.

2. What is he employed at?—A. Surveying and draughting.

2. For whom—for the railroads?—A. I think it is a coal company, but am not

2. Can he look forward to steady employment at that?—A. Oh, yes.

2. He is a regular officer of the company?—A. Yes.

By the Chairman:

2. At the bottom of page 9 of the Auditor General's Report, E. W. Hubbell, whom rucceeded, is called a surveyor, and he is the only man designated as such. Was ork distinct above all others while he was in the employ of the Surveyor-General's :h?—A. No.

2. Are you doing the work he did while he was paid as a surveyor?—A. Yes.

2. He was there for three months and a half, from January 1 to April 15, 1906. t was he doing for the other nine months of the year ending June 30, 1906?—A. ɾas probably out in the field.

2. But was paid out of the Topographical Surveys business?—A. Yes. You asked ust now if I was doing the same work as he did when he was getting $1,800 a year. s, but not the work that the amount you mention is charged against. He was ng $1,800 for the same work I am doing now.

Q. Do you find it difficult to get young men to enter the service now?—A. I think ecause though they come in, they leave very quickly.

By Mr. Fyshe :

Q. You must be getting them all the time then?—A. Yes.

By the Chairman:

Q. Is it want of proper status that prevents them coming into the service?—A. I y so.

Q. And want of proper emolument?—A. Yes.

Q. And want of proper prospects?—A. Yes.

2. What did you get when you first came into the service?—A. $45 a month.

Q. In what year did you come in?—A. In 1883.

Q. And after twenty-four years of service you obtain the munificent salary of ¡0?—A. Yes. There has been no regular increase.

2. It is simply haphazard?—A. Haphazard.

Q. It depends, I suppose, a good deal on the good will of the man to whom you ·t?—A. Possibly. I do not know.

7-8 EDWARD VII., A. 1908

Q. It is hardly to be supposed that with 400 temporary employees, the deputy could know much about each?—A. Oh, no.

Q. He must depend on the report of the person immediately above you?—A. I could not say.

Q. If you wish to amplify your evidence when you revise it, we shall be very glad to have you do it. Have you anything else to tell us now that you think of?—A. I think there should be some difference made in the classification of those clerks who have been there for a long time from those who have been recently appointed.

Q. You think there should be a difference between the old employee and the new employee?—A. Certainly. There are employees who have been there for twenty-four years who, though not professional men, are much more capable for a certain work than those who are professional men. A good number of the employees of the Topographical Surveys branch are, I understand, Dominion land surveyors, but they are Dominion land surveyors of very recent standing; but there are other men who have had practical experience of the office work for twenty-four years. I might add that while I was in the Surveyor General's Branch I took the place of the head clerk, Mr. Symes, when he was away.

Q. Then Mr. P. B. Symes is the buffer between you and Mr. Coté?—A. He has nothing to do with Mr. Coté.

Q. You say you took his place?—A. When I was in the Surveyor General's branch.

Q. You are not now in the Surveyor General's branch?—A. No, I have not been for four years.

Q. Then we infer that that list of draughtsmen is rather a confused statement, some being under Mr. Coté and some under Mr. Deville, and that is not a proper classification ?—A. The only draughtsmen under Mr. Coté would be Mr. Langlois and myself.

Q. When was Mr. Langlois appointed?—A. About 1890, I think.

Q. How long has Mr. Reiffenstein been there?—A. He came in, I think, in 1886, because in 1885 he was out in the field surveying.

Q. Have you written anything else to the commission besides this letter?—A. I signed a joint memorandum with three others who are about on the same footing as myself.

Q. Who were the others ?—A. Mr. Rowan-Legg, Mr. Gillmore and Mr. Bégin.

Q. This is the memorandum you refer to (showing)?—A. Yes. I would like to state that in addition to the actual preparation of the descriptions there is a great deal of other work involved, and I have a great deal of correspondence to look after and carry on in connection with my work. I have under me at present four clerks, and the work has increased to such an extent that the staff is not really sufficient.

Q. You want additional assistance ?—A. Yes.

Q. Is that want universal in your branch, do you think ? Does the Topographical Surveys branch want additional assistance?—A. I do not know anything about their requirements.

Q. Then, this list in the Auditor General's Report is rather confusing—it mixes up the Topographical Surveys branch and the Survey General's branch ?—A. Yes, two or three branches. There are names on that list of persons employed in the Timber and Forests branch, the Land Patents branch and others.

LAND PATENTS BRANCH,
DEPARTMENT OF THE INTERIOR,
OTTAWA, May 29, 1907.

T. S. HOWE, Esq.,
    Secretary Civil Service Commission,
       Room 2, Senate, Ottawa.

SIR,—I respectfully beg to lay before the Commission a statement of my status in the service and request that the same be taken into consideration with a view of bettering my position, both as to classification and salary.

ESSIONAL PAPER No. 29a

I entered the service in 1883 in the Technical or Topographical branch of the epartment of the Interior and was continually employed in that branch up till April, '08.

The clerks of that branch have from time to time tried to better themselves iancially, but with very indifferent success.

During the early part of the year 1903 the position of technical officer in charge the preparation of the descriptions for the patents of land having become vacant, ie chief clerk of the Land Patents branch applied to me for information as to whom) could get to fill the place, knowing that I, in my position in the technical branch, as fully conversant with such matters and could advise him of some one. On my iggesting that perhaps I might take the place if it would give me an increase of lary, he said he would be very glad to have me.

The clerk who filled the position before me had a salary of $1,800 per annum. I)plied for the position and salary but did not obtain the latter; since that time the ork has doubled in amount, and I can verify the statement when I say that I do as)od work and a great deal more than my predecessor, yet I am receiving only $1,550. uring all these long years of service, viz.: 24, I have never been made permanent id therefore have nothing to look forward to in the future, should anything arise in ie way of sickness or any such thing that might incapacitate me for further service. contend that in view of my long service, the technical qualifications which I possess id the great increase in the cost of living that I should rank as a first-class clerk, id should be in receipt of a salary of $2,000 per annum.

The work I am called upon to do requires special knowledge and is of a very sponsible character, and I am well assured that the chief clerk of the branch will ar out my statements as to my capabilities for the position.

I would, therefore, request that I be recommended for a permanency at $2,000 per num.

I have the honour to be, sir,

Your obedient servant,

(Signed)   N. B. SHEPPARD.

OTTAWA, FRIDAY, June 21, 1907.

The Royal Commission on the Civil Service met this morning at 10.30 o'clock.

Present:—Mr. J. M. COURTNEY, C.M.G., Chairman.
Mr. THOMAS FYSHE, Montreal, and
Mr. P. J. BAZIN, Quebec.

Mr. P. A. BÉGIN, called, sworn and examined.

By the Chairman :

Q. You are in the Department of the Interior ?—A- Yes, sir.
Q. You have written on behalf of four gentlemen there, technical officers ?—A. Yes.
Q. Mr. Sheppard was here yesterday ?—A. Yes, he told me he was here yesterday.
Q. He went off independently of you other three, apparently ?—A. Yes; well, he did not know we had taken the matter up.
Q. You and the other gentlemen are not permanent ?—A. No.
(Letter dated June 10 read.)
Q. You are paid out of what they call the Topographical Surveys branch ?—A. Yes.
Q. Who is your chief ?—A. Captain Deville, the surveyor general.
Q. Mr. Sheppard is under Mr. Coté ?—A. Yes.
Q. Under whom does Mr. Rowan-Legg serve ?—A. Under Captain Deville.
Q. And does Mr. Gillmore serve under the same man ?—A. The same man.
Q. Are you a Dominion land surveyor?—A. No, I am not.
Q. Are you a Provincial land surveyor?—A. No.
Q. Are you a graduate of any university?—A. No.
Q. Mr. Gillmore was a graduate of the Military College, I think ?—A. I think so.
Q. Was Mr. Rowan-Legg ?—A. No.
Q. You are called draughtsmen here ?—A. We are called draughtsmen.
Q. Are all the draughtsmen employed as draughtsmen, or are they only copying blue prints ?—A. Some draughtsmen are only copying prints, but these are real draughtsmen; they make all kinds of maps and compiling, any kind of work for a map.
Q. You chiefly base your application to us on your long service ?—A. No, long service, technical qualifications and great increase in cost of living.
Q. On length of service rather more than on technical qualifications ?—A. No, sir, for all of above reasons.
Q. You consider that having gone into the service as far back as that, if you had been permanent from the beginning, you would have been first-class clerke now ?—A. I think so.
Q. You also request that if superannuation is again put on the statute-book, you should have the advantages of it ?—A. Yes.
Q. From the date of your first appointment ?—A. Yes.
Q. That is, that your back service should count ?—A. Yes.

By Mr. Fyshe:

Q. Being in the outside service, you would not have been under the superannuation fund as it existed before?—A. No.

Q. Nor even the retirement fund?—A. No.

By the Chairman :

Q. He was obliged to pass as a civil servant; Mr. Gillmore, as a graduate of the Military College, was exempt?—A. Well, as draughtsmen, we were exempt.

Q. You have been examined since ?—A. Yes.

Q. When you entered the Civil Service, you passed the Civil Service examination? —A. Yes.

Q. And Mr. Gillmore was a graduate of the Military College?—A. Yes.

Q. Did Mr. Rowan-Legg pass any examination ?—A. Yes, Civil Service examination.

Q. Since you entered the service, the three of you have passed examinations as draughtsmen?—A. Yes.

Q. Then, although you were not surveyors at the beginning, you have passed examinations since as draughtsmen?—A. We passed the Civil Service examination.

Q. Do you ever go out in the field, all of you people?—A. I have never been in the field.

Q. Your occupation is simply when the survey is made by the field staff, you make the draughtings from them?—A. Yes.

Q. Your chief is Mr. Deville ?—A. Yes.

Q. Who is the surveyor general?—A. Mr. Deville.

Q. You are one of four who signed this memorial. Do you think all those draughtsmen charged to the topographical surveys branch should also be included?— A. Some of them can take the name, but all such who have been employed are not really draughtsmen.

By Mr. Fyshe:

Q. What are they doing?—A. Copying maps.

Q. But they are not real draughtsmen?—A. No.

By the Chairman:

Q. Although classified as draughtmen here, some of them are not draughtsmen? —A. No.

Q. Then you do not suggest that the whole of these gentlemen who are called draughtsmen should be made draughtsmen, as you are?—A. It would not be satisfactory to the old clerks to put all the new men on the same footing.

Q. Many of these gentlemen who are called draughtsmen have passed no examination at all?—A. No departmental examination.

. Q. How were you employed originally yourself?—A. They called for a few draughtsmen, and I made application to the Deputy Minister and got the position.

Q. What part of the Dominion do you come from?—A. Point Lévis.

Q. I suppose some Member or other backed your application?—A. No.

Q. You came up yourself?—A. Yes.

Q. Were you through Laval University?—A. No.

Q. You would be well known, and after proper inquiries had been made by the Deputy Minister, probably he ascertained what your qualifications were, he appointed you, is that it?—A. Yes, sir.

Q. You owed nothing to political yourself influences yourself?—A. No, sir.

Q. Those so-called draughtsmen that have passed no examination, have they been appointed by political influence?—A. Some of them have.

Q. How about the others?—A. They were recommended by the surveyor general himself; they came in from the colleges.

Q. Then a man may come in there and be called a draughtsman and know nothing about draughting?—A. No.

7-8 EDWARD VII., A. 1908

Q. Simply by a certain amount of political influence they get an appointment. Have you any more examinations to pass?—A. No.

Q. You have passed all the examinations that will be required of you?—A. Yes.

Q. How many have you passed?—A. Only one.

Q. Under the Board of Dominion Land Surveyors, I suppose?—A. No.

Q. I think you said you first passed the Civil Service examination?—A. Yes.

Q. And then you passed the examination in the department for draughtsman?— A. Well, we are considered after several years' service in the department that we are really draughtsmen.

Q. I thought you said you had passed an examination?—A. That is it, before the surveyor general.

Q. That is what I wanted to get at. After you passed the Civil Service Qualifying examination there was a departmental examination under the surveyor general? —A. Not a departmental examination, but a cursory examination of my work by the surveyor general.

Q. Then you did not pass any examination of the Dominion land surveyors in order to become a Dominion land surveyor?—A. No, sir.

Q. The examination by the surveyor general was an examination to show that you were fitted for the position you occupied in the department?—A. Yes, sir.

By Mr. Fyshe:

Q. Who is surveyor general?
The CHAIRMAN.—Mr. Deville, a very capable man.

By the Chairman:

Q. Do you know how many years Mr. Deville has been there?—A. About twenty-eight years, I think.

Q. He has been there a very long time?—A. Yes.

By Mr. Bazin:

Q. Twenty-six years?—A. Yes.

By the Chairman:

Q. Well, Mr. Bégin, Mr. Sheppard was so fully examined yesterday that I do not know we have much more to ask you, unless Mr. Bazin desires to ask you some questions.
Mr. BAZIN.—No, it would all be on the same lines as the evidence we heard yesterday.

By the Chairman:

Q. Except that Mr. Sheppard is in the Lands Patent Branch and you are in the Survey branch?—A. Yes.

By Mr. Fyshe:

Q. Where are your offices?—A. At the corner of Metcalfe and Slater.

Q. Are the draughtsmen all together?—A. No.

By the Chairman:

Q. But the surveys are all there?—A. Only the surveyor general and staff are there.

Q. It is at the corner of Metcalfe and Slater?—A. Yes.

Q. All those people that are employed in what is called the Topographical Surveys branch are there?—A. No, some are in other places.

By Mr. Fyshe:

Q. Have you any fixed ideas as to what might be an improvement in the service?
—A. Well, about the old clerks, I think I said all I have to say in my letter. I do not think it is necessary to repeat that again, about the old clerks being made permanent, with first-class standing and with income according.

Q. That paper is only signed by four names?—A. Yes.

By the Chairman:

Q. This witness does not know anything outside of his own little circle. You are limited to the surveyor general's department?—A. Yes, it is quite different with the other branches.

By Mr. Fyshe:

Q. Do you think that the lower paid officers are justly treated, that they are fairly treated?—A. Well, some of them are getting $75 a month and they are in the service only a couple of years.

Q. You think perhaps they are overpaid?—A. No, they are not overpaid.

Q. None of them are overpaid?—A. I do not think there are any overpaid.

Q. Then the department does not err on the side of extravagance?—A. No, it does not.

Q. Have you work for all the men in the department, sufficient work for all the men?—A. Oh, yes, there is more work than we can do.

By the Chairman:

Q. What are your office hours?—A. From 9.30 to 4.30.

Q. There is an attendance book of course?—A. Oh, yes.

By Mr. Fyshe :

Q. You get one hour for lunch?—A. One and a half hours for lunch.

By the Chairman :

Q. Do you sign when going out for lunch?—A. We sign in the morning and at two o'clock on returning from lunch.

By Mr. Fyshe :

Q. Do you like the service?—A. Yes.

Q. Does the staff generally like the service?—A. Oh, yes, the staff generally like the service very much.

Q. You are not a race of grumblers?—A. No, sir.

Witness retired.

DEPARTMENT OF THE INTERIOR,

OTTAWA, June 10, 1907.

T. S. HOWE, Esq.,
    Secretary Civil Service Commission,
        Room 2, Senate, Ottawa.

SIR,—We the undersigned technical officers of the Department of the Interior beg to lay before the Civil Service Commission the following facts in respect to our standing and financial position in the department.

We have been employed continuously in the department for a long time, ranging from eighteen to twenty-five years as beneath.

E. L. Rowan-Legg, twenty-five years; N. B. Sheppard, twenty-four years; P. A Bégin, twenty-four years; E. T. B. Gillmore, eighteen years.

. During all this term we have never been made permanent and have therefore nothing to look forward to, should we in the future, through any cause be incapacitated from further service.

The work we are employed on is purely of a technical character calling for special qualifications.

We are assured that our work has been well and honestly performed and is appreciated by the heads of the branches.

We further submit that we are insufficiently recompensed for the work we are called upon to do and in view of our long service, the increased cost of living and our special qualifications that we should be appointed to the permanent staff with the rank of first-class clerks, and that in the event of superannuation the same should be based on our first appointment to the service as temporary clerks.

We respectfully invite inquiry as to our capabilities collectively and individually, and request that this application be given your favourable consideration.

We have the honour to be, sir,

Your obedient servants,

(Signed)   N. B. SHEPPARD,
E. T. B. GILMORE,
E. L. ROWAN-LEGG,
P. A. BEGIN.

QUEBEC, September 18, 1907.

Mr. PATRICK DOYLE, sworn and examined.

By the Chairman:

Q. You are the immigration agent here?—A. Yes.

Q. How long have you been agent?—A. For over fifteen years.

Q. What salary do you get now?—A. $1,800.

Q. What did you get when you were appointed?—A. $1,400 up to April 1, last.

Q. You have an interpreter in your office?—A. Yes.

Q. How many clerks have you?—A. I submit a memorandum showing the staff.

Q. You have an interpreter, two or three guardians, engineers, matrons and a medical officer?—A. Yes. There are twenty-one altogether on the staff.

Q. You yourself have been thirty-eight years in the service?—A. Over thirty-eight years.

Q. What were you before you became agent?—A. I was a clerk, then assistant agent, and then agent.

Q. Who was your predecessor?—A. Mr. Stafford.

Q. The assistant agent is a new appointment?—A. Yes, from April 1, last.

Q. He is a doctor?—A. Yes.

Q. Was he appointed because he was a doctor?—A. Not at all. He does not make use of his capacity as a doctor.

Q. Then you have four clerks?—A. Yes.

Q. Mr. Stein has been 34 years in the service?—A. Yes.

Q. And Mr. Stafford fifteen years?—A. Yes.

Q. Mr. Morrisset eight years?—A. Yes.

Q. Mr. Beaulieu a year and a half, Mr. Byrne, a year and a half and Mr. O'Connell, a year and a half?—A. Yes.

SESSIONAL PAPER No. 29a

Q. They are paid each $2.50 a day?—A. Yes.

Q. All the year round?—A. Yes.

Q. Then you have Mr. Anderson, who has been thirty-nine years in the service?
—A. Yes, he is interpreter.

. He was appointed at $400 and has now $800?—A. Yes.

. That is, in 39 years, he has gone from $400 to $800?—A. Yes.

. Then you have a caretaker?—A. Yes.

. You have an engineer and landing master of eighteen years' service?—A. Yes.

. What engines does he look after?—A. A steam engine for pumping water.

. An assistant engineer and one messenger?—A. Yes.

Q. Two matrons, one of whom has been there twenty years and the other six
years?—A. Yes.

Q. And six guardians?—A. Yes.

Q. When you entered the service, thirty-eight years ago, how many immigrants
arrived in the port?—A. I suppose 15,000 or 16,000 in the season. It would fluctuate.

Q. From 1869 to 1897 there was very little increase in the number arriving yearly?
—A. Very little. It would go up in one year and down in another.

Q. From 1869 to 1898 the number of immigrants arriving yearly varied from
15,000 to 20,000?—A. Yes.

Q. From 1898 onwards there has been a steady increase until in 1906 there were
112,000, and this year up to September 15 there have been 115,000?—A. Yes, and
there will be probably 20,000 more before the end of the season.

Q. Then you believe that 135,000 will be the number to arrive this season?—
A. Yes.

Q. That is, in nine years the number of immigrants arriving at the port of Quebec
has increased over six-fold?—A. Yes.

Q. How do you manage to cope with so many?—A. We are at work night and day
and on Sundays. As a rule ships come in on Sundays.

Q. After navigation closes do you have many immigrants passing through?—
A. No.

Q. Then, for eight months in the year you live a very strenuous life?—A. Yes,
from about April 25 to the end of November.

Q. And have no Sundays?—A. No.

Q. Then for about for months in the year you hibernate?—A. No. So much work
accumulates that in the winter we have plenty to do. We have to put our papers into
proper shape.

Q. In the ten years since this big influx began, you seem to have had only three or
four additional clerks?—A. Only three—my assistant and two clerks.

Q. With nearly the same machinery you are doing six times the work you did
ten years ago?—A. Yes.

Q. Have you any fixed office hours?—A. No.

Q. You are down when a steamer arrives?—A. Yes. A telephone message often
comes at night that a ship will arrive early the next morning.

Q. All the steerage immigrants are landed at Quebec, are they not?—A. Yes.

Q. How long are they kept in Quebec?—A. It depends on the nationalities. It
takes a long time to get the foreigners through—about a hundred an hour. They
cannot go till each person claims his own baggage, and it takes perhaps ten or twelve
hours before a ship load of a thousand can be got through.

Q. How many extra trains are put on?—A. Two for each ship.

Q. What is the largest number of immigrants that have arrived in a ship?—A.
2,200.

Q. What ship was that?—A. One of the Antwerp boats, the *Montezuma*, I think.

Q. You have various nationalities coming here?—A. Yes.

Q. Does your interpreter know all the different languages?—A. Oh, no.

Q. With all these different nationalities, how can you manage with only one interpreter?—A. The Canadian Pacific Railway Company, the Grand Trunk Company and the steamships all have interpreters. The Canadian Pacific Railway Company has stationary interpreters, so has the Grand Trunk Company. All the interpreters come together, and if one does not understand the language of any particular immigrant, another does. There is one interpreter there who speaks twelve languages.

Q. Has every steamship line an interpreter?—A. Yes, and the railroads as well; so that there are seven or eight interpreters in the building all the time the immigrants are there.

Q. You say that during the season of navigation you are rung up by telephone and informed when a ship is about to arrive ?—A. We generally know, and we watch out for it, or we are notified that a ship has passed Father Point and will arrive at 4 or 5 o'clock in the morning.

Q. Are you personally on the wharf when every vessel of immigrants arrives ?—A. It would be almost impossible for one man to be there always. Since Dr. Lavoie has been appointed my assistant, we have made arrangements between ourselves for one or the other to be there.

Q. So that either you or Dr. Lavoie are always there to meet whatever batch of immigrants come, at the time of their arrival?—A. Yes, and the whole staff also.

Q. From Thursday night until Sunday there is a continuous arrival of steamers; are the whole staff there all the time ?—A. No, they relieve each other.

Q. Does the staff there at night one week do the day work the next week ?—A. Yes, they relieve each other.

Q. What sleeping accommodation have you in the shed for the immigrants ?—A. For the females only.

Q. How many beds do you make up ?—A. There are fourteen rooms with some double beds in each room.

Q. How many beds in each room ?—A. We have single rooms and double rooms.

Q. Every care is taken for sanitation and cleanliness ?—A. Yes. The doctors are too particular as to that.

Q. Every attempt is made to make the immigrants comfortable on their arrival ?—A. Yes.

Q. Do you give them meals ?—A. If any of them are stranded waiting for tickets or expecting their friends, we allow them to stay in the building, and the ship pays their expenses until they get letters or money or their friends meet them.

Q. You take care of them ?—A. The instructions to the matrons are to see that no person in the building is allowed to be hungry. The ship has to provide for them.

Q. All this goes on for eight months in the year ?—A. Yes.

Q. In the remaining four months you are cleaning and repairing and getting your reports ready ?—A. Yes. Each immigrant who arrives has to pass an inspection. We have to question every immigrant who arrives.

Q. I suppose there is a form of questions—as to whether they are going to settle in the country and all that ?—A. Yes, and their professions and trades.

Q. And whether they are single or married and whether they are going to remain in the country—following the form adopted in the United States ?—A. Exactly. They are very nearly alike. And if we find any one physically defective or likely to become a public charge, we put that one aside and report the case to Ottawa, or in extreme cases deport the immigrant.

Q. Who composes the board of inquiry?—A. The clerks. It is amongst ourselves.

Q. You occupy an important position in connection with getting good and contented settlers in the country ?—A. Yes.

Q. The lowest salary paid to any other agent of a Government department in Quebec is $2,200 ?—A. Yes. There are six federal officers in Quebec, of whom two are paid $2,200 each, one $2,500, and another $3,000.

Q. You consider that your long and valuable experience entitles you to something more than you are receiving ?—A. I think so. I think I should be paid, at any rate, as much as the lowest of the others. There have been three immigration agents here since 1825. Mr. Buchanan served from 1825 to 1862, Mr. Stafford from 1862 to 1892, and I from that time. Mr. Buchanan had $2,400 at a time when there were only a few sailing ships arriving at Quebec.

Q. He was an Imperial appointment?—A. Yes.

Q. Do you know what Mr. Stafford got when he died ?—A. $1,700.

Q. He never was superannuated ?—A. No.

Q. Are you a contributor to the superannuation fund ?—A. Yes.

Q. The later appointments are not?—A. No. There are three in my department who contribute.

Q. From your long experience, do you think you are getting as good a class of men into the service now as clerks as you used to get?—A. I have got good clerks.

By Mr. Fyshe:

Q. Are you getting as good clerks as thirty years ago?—A. They are equally good clerks.

By the Chairman:

Q. The clerks who come from Ottawa to help you in the summer time go back to Ottawa in the winter?—A. They are Quebecers, appointed from Quebec, but in the winter they go to Ottawa.

Q. Do any of the clerks pass an examination to come into the service?—A. I do not know.

Q. When the stress of work became so great that you found you were obliged to get more assistants how did you set to work to get them?—A. I told the superintendent, Mr. Scott, when he came here.

Q. Then I presume he made his report to the department?—A. I have no doubt he recommended it.

Q. Did you select Mr. Beaulieu, for instance?—A. No. The department appointed him on the recommendation of Mr. Scott, who, while on his annual visit, said, you want more assistance. Then he was sent to us.

Q. It is absolutely necessary for you to have uniforms?—A. Yes, we were forced to get them.

Q. On the caps are there the words, 'Immigration agent'?—A. Each one has his own title.

Q. So that an immigrant, if at a loss for information, can pick you out?—A. Before the immigrants land we line up from the vessel into the building, and then the place is fenced and no outsiders are allowed in. In case of bad weather the immigrants pass through a covered passageway, and when they land on the wharf the guards are around them to direct them safely into the building.

Q. When the immigrants come off the ship, do they bring their baggage with them?—A. Only their hand baggage.

Q. Does the customs officer inspect this baggage in your shed?—A. Yes, or on the platform. The heavy baggage is taken on the ship and brought on lorries to our building by the railway companies where it is spread out, and each one claims his own baggage and has it inspected by the customs officers.

Q. Is there any difficulty about the baggage?—A. Not usually.

Q. Would it not simplify matters if the steamship companies issued checks?—A. They do. Every one gets a check.

Q. When the immigrants have finally passed all the bars and are ready to go into the train, are they sorted out—those for Winnipeg, Toronto and other places? —A. The cars are backed down in front of our building, and each is labelled, for

Montreal, for Toronto or for Winnipeg, as the case may be, and the interpreters and guards keep the people back until the car for Montreal is loaded, and then the one for Toronto, and then the one for Winnipeg, and so on.

Q. So that a man ignorant of the English language cannot get astray?—A. No. Each one is labelled after he has passed his examination.

Q. Then every sympathy is shown by the staff at the immigration sheds towards the immigrant when he arrives?—A. Yes, every sympathy. If any railroad or steamship official insults or says a rough word to one, I can order the company to discharge him.

Q. Is there anything else you would like to tell us, as how, for instance, the immigrants are protected in changing money?—A. We have an office in the building for a broker, Mr. MacNider, who is appointed by the Government to change foreign moneys into Canadian money. No outsider is allowed in the building to change a penny belonging to an immigrant. The immigrants must get their moneys changed at this broker's office, and he is responsible for every mistake that occurs.

Q. You guard the immigrant in every way?—A. Yes. Last summer, at the time so many were arriving, I called the Provincial Police to assist me. On Sunday, when a steamer comes in, there will be two or three thousand people come down, but we keep out the general public.

Q. Do photographers come down to take photographs of groups of immigrants? —A. Very often.

Q. Are the immigrants as good a class as they used to be?—A. There is no comparison. Those arriving now are much superior to those arriving formerly.

Q. Have you any idea as to whether many paupers are sent out?—A. There are a few societies sending out people, but they are people who are able and willing to work. Though they have not much money they will not become paupers. These societies have agents at different points to look after the people they send out, and these agents are obliged to report to the Government if anything goes wrong.

By Mr. Fyshe:

Q. There is a larger number of English-speaking immigrants arriving?—A. Oh, yes. They are always in the majority.

Q. There are not as many Irish as there used to be?—A. Very few Irish are coming. As a rule, the Irish that are coming are going to their friends; very few of them are seeking employment. Some of the Irish who are living in Liverpool are coming.

Q. Do all these immigrants, as a rule, settle in the country?—A. Out of the 115,-000 who have arrived this summer, there have not been 11,000 for the United States. The balance have settled in Canada.

Q. In former years it was different?—A. It was the other way altogether. They used to try to deceive the Government by saying that they were were going to Toronto, while their destination was the United States.

By the Chairman:

Q. Are there many people coming to the sheds to secure labourers?—A. Yes, contractors. We cannot supply the labour market.

Q. Is good care taken that the interests of the immigrants are protected, and that the contractor does not make a bargain detrimental to them?—A. The contractors come and tell them how much they are willing to give them a day, and they take the men off to where they want them.

Q. Is due care taken, when an immigrant enters into a contract with a farmer or a contractor, that his interests are looked after?—A. Oh yes. If a farmer wants to take a man, we make a price for him, and the immigrant can return to us at any time for protection, if he is not well treated.

Q. Has it ever been brought to your notice that farmers at the end of the term of employment refuse to make payment to the immigrant?—A. I have never heard of it.

Q. That farmers come here and hire immigrants as labourers, and then, at the end of the season, for some reason, tell them that there is nothing coming to them?—A. I have never heard of that in our district.

Q. Or in the Eastern Townships district?—A. No. There is an agent here from the Eastern Townships, Mr. Brewster, and he looks sharply after the interests of the immigrants.

Q. How long has he been appointed?—A. He has been here since last summer.

EMPLOYEES OF THE IMMIGRATION OFFICE, QUEBEC.

P. Doyle, agent, 38 years' service; salary, $1,000; 15 years as agent, salary, $1,400; present salary, $1,800, since April 1, 1907.

Dr. J. P. Lavoie, assistant agent since April last; salary, $1,400.

L. Stein, chief clerk, 34 years' service; present salary, $1,400, for last ten years.

J. P. Stafford, clerk, 15 years' service; salary since entering service, $2.50 per day up to May, 1907, now $1,000 per annum.

G. Beaulieu, clerk, 1½ years' service; $900 per annum.

S. Morrisset, clerk, 8 years' service; entered at $1.25 per day; present, $2 per day.

J. Byrne, E. T. O'Connell, clerks, 1½ years' service; salary, $2 per day.

Wm. Anderson, 39 years' service, as interpreter; salary, $400; raised to $620; present, $800, since 4 years.

E. Valin, caretaker, 9 years' service; $700 per annum.

S. Hayden, engineer and landing master, 18 years' service; salary, $800.

J. Huck, assistant engineer, 3 years; salary, $50 per month.

E. Drouin, messenger, 4 years' service; salary, $50 per month.

Mrs. E. Cameil, matron, 20 years' service; lodgings; salary, $50 per month.

Mrs. M. C. du Tremblay, 6 years service; lodgings; salary $40 per month.

E. Galarneau, guardian, 10 years..............	$1 50 per day.
J. Fitzgerald, guardian, 14 years.............	1 50 "
J. Rochette, guardian, 10 years..............	1 50 "
G. Martel, guardian, 5 years................	1 50
R. Charest, guardian, 5 years................	1 50
N. Poulin, Quebec and Lévis, guardian, 3 years..	1 75 "

1907.

GOVERNMENT DEPARTMENTS IN QUEBEC CITY.

Customs.—J. B. Forsyth, collector, salary $3,000.

Inland Revenue.—C. J. Rinfret, collector, salary $2,500.

Marine and Fisheries.—J. U. Gregory, agent, salary $2,200.

Post Office.—E. J. Paquet, postmaster, salary $2,200.

Immigration.—P. Doyle, agent, salary $1,400 up to April 1, 1907, now $1,800.

Port of Quebec, 1907—Immigration.

Arrivals	Immigrants.
1897..	20,495
1898..	19,246
1899..	29,422
1900..	40,840
1901..	31,704
1902..	41,000
1903..	58,124
1904..	62,446
1906..	83,368
1907, up to September 16..................	115,036
To arrive to end season..............	20,000
	135,036

Up to 1906 average number of steamers was 106.
1906 and 1907, number of steamers was 205.

QUEBEC, September 18, 1907.

EDMOND VALIN and P. CHAREST, sworn and examined.

By the Chairman:

Q. Mr. Valin, you are a guardian of immigration?
Mr. VALIN.—The chief guardian.
Q. And Mr. Charest is a guardian?
Mr. CHAREST.—Yes.
Q. How long have you been appointed, Mr. Valin?
Mr. VALIN.—Eight years.
Q. How long has Mr. Charest been appointed?
Mr. CHAREST.—Five years.
Q. What do you get, Mr. Valin?
Mr. VALIN.—$700.
Q. What do you get, Mr. Charest?
Mr. CHAREST.—$1.50 a day.
Q. That is $547.50 a year. In addition to that, you are both allowed uniforms and caps?
Mr. VALIN.—Yes.
Q. The same allowance to both?—A. Yes.
Mr. VALIN.—Yes.
Q. What is your complaint?
Mr. VALIN.—I have five men under me who are each getting $1.50 a day for the whole year. I am getting $700 a year. I complain that my salary is too low. I have been employed for eight years at the same salary, and, considering the increased cost of living we think our salaries should be increased. I think I am the only one in the Dominion who is a chief guardian.
Q. How old are you?
Mr. VALIN.—Fifty-seven.
Q. How old are you, Mr. Charest?
Mr. CHAREST.—Fifty-nine.

○

QUEBEC, September 18, 1907.

Dr. J. P. LAVOIE, sworn and examined.

By the Chairman:

Q. You have recently been appointed?—A. I have been appointed only since April 1, this year.

Q. What is your salary?—A. $1,400.

Q. That is six months ago. You surely have not acquired a grievance in that time, have you?—A. Maybe I have.

Q. Tell us what you want?—A. I only appear here to give you any information I can, but I do not think I can give you a great deal. All I can tell you is what I have been doing.

QUEBEC, September 18, 1907.

L. STEIN and J. P. STAFFORD, sworn and examined.

By the Chairman:

Q. We had a visit from Mr. Doyle this morning, and what have you to tell us in addition?

Mr. STAFFORD.—We were told to come here, but if Mr. Doyle has explained everything, we cannot do more.

Mr. STEIN.—I am chief clerk, and the Civil Service Act says that the minimum salary of a chief clerk shall be $2,000, or something like that. I do not ask for $2,000. My predecessor, Mr. Doré, about forty years ago, had $1,900 for the same position I have now, and the agent, Mr. Buchanan, had $2,400. At that time there were two steamers a week arriving here, and the immigration was about 6,000 in the season, whereas now it is 140,000.

By Mr. Bazin:

Q. What is your salary now?

Mr. STEIN.—$1,400.

Q. You are only called a clerk in the Auditor General's report?—A. In the Civil Service List I am called chief clerk, and my appointment is that of chief clerk. I have my appointment by Order in Council, signed by the Governor General. I have always been a chief clerk since 1874.

Q. How long have you been there?—A. Thirty-four years in May next.

Q. What were you appointed at when you entered the service?—A. $1,000.

Q. You think, because chief clerks in the departments at Ottawa, in charge of the several branches of the departments, have salaries going to $2,400, you should get the same? That is your contention?—A. No.

Q. Then what do you expect?—A. I expect to have more than I am getting as a chief clerk in the department.

Q. What do you expect as a chief clerk?—A. I am expecting $1,800.

Q. As a minimum, or do you expect to go beyond $1,800?—A. Yes, according to the increase of the other salaries in the office. Since ten years I think I have had the same salary as Mr. Doyle. Of course, Mr. Doyle has not the salary attached to his position, but he got an increase lately, and I think I should have an increase too. Everything has increased.

Q. Then it comes to this, that because you are chief clerk in the office here, you think you should have the equivalent of the salary of a chief clerk at Ottawa?—A. Yes.

Q. Mr. Stafford, what do you get ?

Mr. STAFFORD.—$1,000 this year.

Q. How long have you occupied your position ?—A. Fourteen years. I am not on the list.

Q. What did you come in at ?—A. $900, and remained at $900 until last May.

Q. What do you get now ?—A. $1,000.

Q. And you think you should be graded at what ?—A. I do not know that I could be graded at anything. I claim to be an expert on immigration. I know the business from one end to the other.

Q. What do you think you should get ?—A. I would not pretend to say ; but I can say this much, that I have travelled over the whole of Canada and the United States and the greater part of Europe, and I claim to be an expert on the immigration business; so that if the Government think I am worth anything, they can give it to me.

By Mr. Fyshe :

Q. Do you speak several languages ?—A. No, I speak but two languages, but I am posted on immigration matters. I was connected with passenger business previous to my entry into the service. Of course, I have not asked to come here.

By the Chairman :

Q. Who asked you to come here ?—A. Mr. Doyle asked us to come.

Q. You think, like all others in the public service, that owing to the increased cost of living, and in your case the responsible nature of your duties, your salary should be increased ?—A. Yes. If there is to be an increase all around, I expect to be increased like the others. We rely on your good judgment in the matter.

Mr. STEIN.—Ten or fifteen years ago we could live a great deal better on $1,000 a year than we can now on $1,500. I am paying $35 a month now for the same house I used to get for $14 a month.

Mr. BAZIN (to Mr. Stafford).—You do not say what salary you expect.

Mr. STAFFORD.—I will tell you why. We were told by our superintendent last spring, when he came here, not to say anything about salaries, because any man who said anything about salaries might as well send in his resignation.

Mr. FYSHE.—It is a different matter with us. If you have any grievance you are authorized to state it to us.

Mr. STAFFORD.—My grievance is this : If I am considered a good employee, and I think I am, because there is not a scratch of a pen against me at Ottawa, should I be kept at $900 for so many years ?

OTTAWA, October 23, 1907.

Mr. J. OBED SMITH, Winnipeg, called, sworn and examined.

By the Chairman :

Q. What is your title, Mr. Smith ?—A. Commissioner of Immigration, Winnipeg.

Q. How long have you been in the service ?—A. About seven years. Prior to that time I was in the service of the Manitoba government for eight years.

Q. Had your former position anything to do with immigration ?—A. No, nothing to do with immigration.

Q. What is your salary ?—A. $3,000.

Q. You are Immigration Commmissioner for Manitoba and the Northwest Territories ?—A. All west of Lake Superior.

Q. We have had the evidence of the officials at Quebec respecting the medical examination and the care that is taken of the immigrant. After the immigrant leaves Quebec and enters the train for Winnipeg who accompanies him ?—A. As a rule one of the travelling agents of the department who boards the train at Ottawa and goes as far as Winnipeg.

Q. Between Quebec and Ottawa is there nobody with these immigrants?—A. I do not think so.

Q. Then at Ottawa somebody boards the train, one of these travelling agents ?—A. Yes.

Q. Dr. Page told us at Quebec that this year they have passed as many as 5,000 immigrants in a day and in the reports I was reading to-day of the medical association the statement is made that consumptives and diseased persons are continually turning up and have to be deported. Is there a medical man attached to the train besides the travelling agents?—A. Not attached to the train. We have in Winnipeg a medical inspector whose duties comprise the examination of immigrants in the buildings there and he also goes two or three hundred miles on the immigrant trains thereby picking up an occasional sick person whom we place in our hospital at Winnipeg.

Q. Have you a detention hospital at Winnipeg?—A. We have a hospital as part of our equipment in Winnipeg.

Q. What is called the detention hospital?—A. Well, we use it for other purposes also.

Q. The immigrant has first to pass quarantine at Grosse Isle?—A. Yes.

Q. For the detection of smallpox or diseases of that kind?—A. Yes.

Q. Then he has to pass the medical inspector at Quebec? He is also met on the train by another doctor and has to pass a medical examination at Winnipeg?—A. Yes.

Q. Well, is that a hasty or a very careful examination?—A. It is necessarily somewhat hasty, but if you would allow me I would like to explain the system. The first inspection really takes place at the gangway of the steamer before she leaves Liverpool.

Q. It is supposed to take place?—A. It is rather perfunctory I admit, but I have seen men turned back even there. The second step is the examination on board the steamer by the ship's surgeon who has to verify under oath that the immigrants are free from disease. Then comes the medical examination at Quebec and on the train.

Q. Let us go back to the ship's surgeon. There is generally one surgeon, with probably an assistant, and there are frequently 2,000 or 3.000 immigrants on board?

29a—33

—A. Not on our steamers but there are on some of the vessels going to United States ports.

Q. There are as many as on a ship like the *Empress of Britain* or the *Victorian*?
—A. Yes, there would be close on to 2,000 passengers.

Q. And the voyage is made in a week?—A. Yes, in a week.

Q. That is to say in a small community, for instance a place like Aylmer, there will be half a dozen surgeons?—A. Yes.

Q. Whereas, on a steamship during a voyage lasting a week a doctor and an assistant are supposed to be looking after the health of 2,000 people?—A. I think it is manifestly plain to everybody that it is a physical impossibility to make such an examination as you and I would like.

Q. A ship's doctor has to certify that as far as he knows they are free from disease?—A. In effect it is so.

Q. Then the third stage, as I have stated, is the medical examination by Dr. Page?—A. Yes.

Q. Then the fourth stage is the medical examination when the immigrants are on their way to Winnipeg during a journey of 300 or 400 miles?—A. Pardon me. Of course the doctor, the moment he boards the train, finds out from the man who is travelling with the immigrants if any one is sick. That is something. I might say this: we depend very largely, of course, upon the deportation clauses of our Act, because a man might appear to be physically well for six days in the week but the seventh day after having passed all the medical officers he might tumble to pieces. Of course, we cannot tell. We depend very largely on our deportation clauses to detect those who have passed all these former stages.

Q. Do you not find that minor diseases, like measles, break out on the immigrant trains?—A. There is seldom a train arrives during the rush season that we do not have a case of measles on. We have a special ward for this disease in our hospital. Sometimes last season there were as many as twenty-three or twenty-five in that ward at once.

Q. The disease would be caught on board ship would it not?—A. Yes, or caught from another child on the train.

Q. The disease might not be so apparent and might escape discovery during the successive medical examinations until the sufferer was on the train bound for Winnipeg?—A. Until the disease exhibits itself on the face or neck nobody might be aware of it.

Q. And you have probably had twenty-three or twenty-five cases?—A. At one time.

Q. Out of one ship?—A. Yes, that might happen. Probably by the time the immigrants got to Winnipeg the disease had spread very rapidly.

Q. That is to say women would have young children sitting in their laps and the disease would spread from one to the other?—A. There is such close contact in the trains the wonder is that we do not have more infectious diseases.

Q. Then there is rather a more careful inspection in Winnipeg, I take it, than there can be at Quebec?—A. Well, I imagine——

Q. We are not finding fault with Dr. Page at all. He has to do his work in a great hurry?—A. The medical man at Quebec is pushed on by the transportation companies and by the people themselves. They do not want to stay there.

Q. We have had the pleasure of meeting Dr. Page?—A. He is a very good man, I think.

Q. And naturally he is pushed on?—A. By the transportation companies and by the immigrants themselves.

Q. And, of course, he has to pass a lot of immigrants in the time?—A. Yes.

Q. Naturally enough the medical man at Winnipeg having a little more leisure can examine the cases better?—A. I will give you an instance of how the system works. A side light sometimes gives you information better than you can get it in any other way. I will mention this side light just to show you how impossible it is for our officers to absolutely prevent a man going into Canada who positively makes up his mind he will go. Sometime ago I had advices from a society in England that they were sending out a young man, and they thought that on account of his condition he ought to go to southern Alberta, which to me was an indication that the man had lung trouble or supposed lung trouble. I immediately wired to Dr. Page to examine this man specifically, because I feared it was a case of tuberculosis. Apparently he did so. We go on the assumption that if our officers do not report otherwise the work has been done. In our peculiar class of business we cannot follow hundreds and thousands of people day after day and year after year. However vigilant we are we must be content with something less than that. However, I had a presumption that the man had got into the country somewhere and because of the fact that southern Alberta was mentioned as the probable district in which he would reside, I wrote to our agent at Lethbridge, 'Hunt up this man and see if he is in your district. If he is sick take him to the hospital and have him cared for and keep an eye on him.' Our agent did not find the man for six or seven days afterwards. Then he reported that he had found him on a ranch about eleven miles away apparently all right. Two days afterwards he was brought to Lethbridge hospital sick by the man with whom he was working. Four days after that I had a report from Dr. De Veber that this man was suffering from galloping consumption and could not recover and could not be moved. The ultimate result was that in twenty-two days after being passed at Quebec the man was buried at Lethbridge. Now what are the facts of that case? When I was at Quebec last I went to see Dr. Page and brought this matter up. I said to the doctor, 'How was it possible for this man to escape when he was in such an advanced state that he died in twenty-two days afterwards?' The doctor turned to the record and showed that there had been a microscopical examination of the sputum, as well as a careful examination in other respects. The supposed consumptive had passed an excellent examination. All the way down there was absolutely no trace in the man's appearance, or in his record, of consumption.

By Mr. Fyshe:

Q. Then the consumptive must have been personated by somebody?—A. He was personated undoubtedly. No doubt he was told, 'If there is any suspicion as to your health, you will be refused admission.' Doubtless he went to a fellow passenger and said 'I will be John Brown and you will oblige me by being Thomas Smith.' Yet twenty-two days afterwards he was dead and buried.

By the Chairman:

Q. That is an extreme case?—A. It is an extreme case. Yet you see how it is possible to evade every examination.

Q. Then after your doctor examines the immigrant upon his arrival in Quebec, what happens to him supposing he is all right?—A. It depends entirely upon the class of man he is, whether married or single, and where he is going.

Q. Supposing it is a married man from a rural district?—A. We always have more places than we have men to supply. Winter or summer we make it our business to keep posted, and our agencies throughout the west are very extensive. In that way we are able to find places for all who desire to go to work on a farm at any time of the year.

Q. Then you would consign him to one of your colonization agents?—A. Or to one of our interpreters or other officials. Might I explain that our service in the west is very different from what it used to be. The immigration service is based upon the colonization idea at first. But we have gradually developed our business to such an extent that we have not less than three or four hundred officials now in the employ of the Immigration Department in the west. Some are engaged as interpreters, some as travelling inspectors—because we patrol many thousand miles of territory—and some are land guides who will meet the immigrant on the train and take him out and put him on the right land, even if it be twenty miles away. So you see our officials consist of medical officers, immigration agents, travelling inspectors, land guides, interpreters, caretakers of immigration halls and other men that are required in order to this business. You are dealing with individuals that you may never see again. You are dealing with different men to-day from those you saw yesterday and every person has different ideas and the circumstances are also different. We find our business very complex in that way. The system of the Government is to allow no person to suffer because it is manifestly absurd for the country to spend so many dollars in getting people for Canada if we do not take care of them afterwards. I feel that I have got a very wide latitude and a very wide responsibility. We do not want anybody to give our country a bad name and we take the best care of them that we can. The service naturally requires a lot of men that you do not find trace of anywhere in the Civil Service List. If you, Mr. Chairman, looked up the list you would not find more than six or eight of our entire staff whose names appear there. Many of them are paid very fair salaries, and others are paid less than they are worth. But our officers can hardly be classed in the same category as the officers in other branches of the public service. That is a point I desire especially to emphasize.

By Mr. Fyshe:

Q. But is the employment of these men not shown in the details of the office?—
A. Yes, it is shown, but they are all men subject to dismissal at a day's notice.

By the Chairman:

Q. Let us go back to the case of the immigrants. Supposing he has been passed by the medical officer in Winnipeg, and you send him to a farmer at Yorkton. Does the caretaker or agent at Yorkton see him on the land or procure him employment?—
A. Yes. In a good many cases we have the application of a farmer direct to us, and in order to make sure that the newcomer to the west will not get astray and lose his place, we direct him to our local agent. If we have no agent, we have a voluntary correspondent at each station to whom this man can go and ascertain, say, that Bill Taylor's farm is six miles away, and how to reach it. If the farm is a long distance off, the immigrant will be told: 'Stay here, and Bill Taylor will probably be in to-morrow to get you.'

Q. Then, after a man is placed on a farm, or takes up land on his own account, do you or your officers look after him for a certain time to see that he does not suffer from being a newcomer?—A. As to that, I must refer back to my original statement, where I pointed out that where we have no complaints, we assume everything is all right. Because, you see, we could not possibly begin to look after all these people individually. There are, however, exceptional circumstances, where it becomes not only a question of business on the part of the Government, but a matter of common humanity to take further action. That is very often necessary where men are located hundreds of miles from a railway. Last winter, for instance, we had to patrol the middle of Saskatchewan, 175 miles from the nearest railway. We had men out there in the stormy period for fourteen days, doing their best to discover anybody who was in distress. In some cases we had to team cord-wood for seventy-five miles, and provisions also. In one case, we had to bring a whole family into Battleford and place them in the hospital or our immigration building. It is a great tribute to the energy of our agents that very few deaths resulted from last winter's storms.

By Mr. Fyshe:

Q. Those people must feel very kindly towards the Government who took such pains?—A. I presume they do. However, it is the business end of it that we look after.

SESSIONAL PAPER No. 29a

By the Chairman:

Q. Do you ever find a farmer will take an immigrant and keep him all the season until the crops are gathered, and then turn him out without any money?—A. If he does that, it is the immigrant's own fault.

Q. But I have heard of such things?—A. Yes, but they are very exceptional. I make that statement because there is a law in force up there for the easy collection of wages, and we tell our agents to inform the immigrants when they go out there: 'If you have any trouble about your wages, go to the nearest justice of the peace and make a complaint that you cannot get your wages.' He will say: 'Bring that farmer before me.' When the farmer is before him, he will say: 'Why don't you pay this man?' The answer may be, because of so-and-so. The justice of the peace may then decide: 'You will pay this man within twenty-four hours, or I will issue a distress warrant on your goods.'

Q. Do these men, when they are placed on farms, live with the farmers?—A. They always live with the farmer. Sometimes it is not very nice, I admit.

Q. They could not do better in that case?—A. No.

Q. Are your agents instructed to be courteous and considerate to these newcomers?—A. Yes, there is no question about that. Any violation of this well-understood rule would meet with instant dismissal.

Q. Then, the immigrant is made to feel at home once he gets into the Northwest?—A. We have that reputation.

Q. So far, we have been talking about immigrants from Britain or the United States, but there are many arrivals from continental Europe, such as Galicians and Doukhobors. Have you a system under which interpreters are provided for these foreigners?—A. Yes.

Q. Do these interpreters go with the foreign immigrants from Winnipeg and place them on their lands?—A. No, we have people out there who meet them at the nearest railway station. I might say that, owing to the rapid development of the west, it has not become necessary in later years to adopt what is commonly called the system of colonization. The department is opposed practically to that kind of segregation of people. Moreover, there are so many different points through the west that are get-atable by railway, or otherwise, that we prefer, they having once gone through our hands in Winnipeg, to pass them on to the nearest agent and allow them to be mixed up with other settlers. Furthermore, as fast and as often as we can, our interpreters and our travelling men go and visit the newcomers in these various localities. Our officers drive amongst them and ascertain if there is anything wrong. If a man does not fit in one place, he may be removed to another. I might just give you an example of what we are doing in one case. Some men homesteaded on a timber reserve in southern Manitoba. This was against the regulations and against the policy of the department, because of the danger from fire, if nothing else, arising out of people living in the reserve. This is an instance of how the Government cares for the newcomers through our branch. They decided to settle these families elsewhere, because they could not give them entry on the lands in this reserve. I have made the necessary arrangements with our agents for their settlement in the Swan River district, in northwestern Manitoba. We are paying railway fare from Turtle Mountain, southern Manitoba, to northwestern Manitoba, for all these families, and taking their stuff up free. Our men will take them up with teams and tents, and put them on homesteads, which they can have, and will see that they do not starve. Furthermore, in that particular case we are going to advance them enough money to put up their houses, taking as security a lien upon the homestead for the cost thereof.

Q. Then the policy of the department just now is not to form communities, but rather to mix the new arrivals among the existing settlers?—A. Exactly, like the plums in a pudding, all over.

Q. Do these immigrants bring money in with them as a rule?—A. They bring in more now than they ever did, and they are a better class of people.

Q. Do you endeavour to impress upon them the desirability of depositing their money in banks?—A. Yes. Sometimes we take the money ourselves and deposit it to our own trust account until the immigrants decide where they are going to locate. Then we pass it over to the bank at the nearest point.

Q. What do you call your trust account?—A. Sometimes we have money sent to us to purchase tickets for people in the old country to come over. Such people we carefully pass along from one to the other until they reach their destination. Sometimes we bring families over—children whose father and mother are here, or wives whose husbands are in Winnipeg or other western points.

Q. Do they sometimes give you money to take care of yourself?—A. Yes. They do not feel safe with it themselves and they hand it over to us.

Q. What is the aggregate amount of this trust fund you have at your disposal? —A. I could not tell you the exact amount. There is generally a balance of $3,000 or $4,000. There are other items which throw a light upon this question. There are quite a percentage of young Englishmen sent out to the west whose parents bless them before they go, and probably send £10 to me besides. The chief ambition of the young man is to get hold of the £10. He does not get it from me unless he needs it very badly. That is where part of the trust fund comes from.

Q. You act as a kind of paternal despot, so to speak? You look after the men as well as you can?—A. Yes.

Q. You keep their money and all that kind of thing?—A. No, I do not keep their money.

Q. You take care of their money?—A. Yes, I take care of their money.

Q. You take their money in that sense? That is what I mean?—A. I understand now exactly what you mean.

Q. You have been getting a very good class of immigrants lately?—A. Yes, very good.

Q. And are they getting on?—A. Yes. Let me speak of an instance that came to my notice the other day A man was grumbling about western Canada, and said he was going home. He said lots were doing the same. I said, 'How many?' 'Oh,' he replied, 'lots of them.' I asked, 'do you know six?' His answer was, 'yes.' 'Do you know ten?' 'Yes.' 'Do you know twenty-five?' 'Yes, I know twenty-five.' 'Well, do you know 100?' 'No.' 'Well, do you think there would be a thousand altogether that are going back?' 'Oh, no.' Well, gentlemen, even if a thousand were to go back what percentage would that be out of over 300,000 immigrants we have coming into Canada this year—less than one-third of one per cent. Can you show me an institution, public or otherwise, dealing with individuals from all parts of Europe and America of all nationalities and all circumstances, poor and rich, worthy and unworthy, who will lose less than one-third of one per cent in twelve months?

Q. What is the cost of a ticket from Winnipeg to Liverpool?—A. For an immigrant to go back?

Q. Yes, by steerage?—A. About $62.

Q. I suppose you find that certain of the immigrants who have settled in the west go back and visit their former homes every three or four years?—A. Yes. We find that is one of the greatest features that we have to help in our immigration. We believe in what is called 'induced' immigration. In Great Britain we have large city offices and the people are urged to come out. The work that is done in that way cannot be gainsaid. Other nations within the British empire believe Canada has got the right end of the stick so far as immigration is concerned. They are coming to us for pointers; in fact I had the chairman of one of their boards in Australia in my office the other day. I have also had a representative of one of the South African Governments come to my office for information about immigration. That shows the results of our direct emigration work. We aim at satisfying newcomers who will 'induce' others to follow.

Q. Some of the settlers in the west go back to their former homes in foreign countries occasionally?—A. You spoke about men returning to their former homes. In a month or two months what happens every year in Winnipeg will be observed. This will throw a side light upon the conditions of labour here as compared with the wages paid. Scores of stonemasons, bricklayers and stonecutters, &c., will be leaving.

By Mr. Fyshe:

Q. Because they are out of employment?—A. Because their work has closed down for the winter. They have been receiving 60 to 65 cents an hour for their work. Those men make and save enough in three weeks to pay their passage to England and back.

By the Chairman:

Q. And they will go over for the Christmas holidays?—A. They say, 'We can go over there on three weeks' pay, live for nothing and come back in the spring.' We cannot do that in the Civil Service.

Q. How many men are employed in the immigration service in Manitoba and the Northwest? They are all under your control, I suppose?—A. I think there are between 300 and 400.

Q. What is the lowest pay?—A. The lowest is $2. Twenty cents an hour is what the men get who clean our buildings. The street sweepers get more from the city.

By Mr. Fyshe:

Q. Your officers can do other work, I suppose, or do they work for you all the time?—A. The salaried officer does no other work.

By the Chairman:

Q. His time is fully occupied?—A. Fully occupied. We must not, Mr. Chairman, lose sight of this fact; our service has become an extensive one. Eight years ago the immigrants to the west was 31,000. Last year it was about 216,000.

Q. And this year it is increasing still more?—A. These figures apply to the west. For the whole of Canada the immigration will be 300,000, in my opinion. However, I do wish to amplify especially regarding the immigration service. I do not know of any other service composed of men that can by no means be brought under the Civil Service Act; they are all temporary employees. If the need for temporarily engaging a man arises we have not got the opportunity of writing to Ottawa about it because the people who need to be looked after are coming through.

By Mr. Fyshe:

Q. You engage the man instantly?—A. We engage him instantly. Sometimes at Ottawa they disapprove of my appointments. I cannot help that—that is my misfortune—but as a rule we have to meet exigencies that arise immediately.

Q. You cannot correspond about it?—A. No, we have no time to correspond about it.

By the Chairman:

Q. Do you supply your men with distinctive uniforms?—A. All the men who travel have uniforms with brass buttons and official caps.

Q. Winter and summer uniforms?—A. Yes, it takes two suits a year to keep them respectable. The uniforms are supplied only to those officers that meet or travel on a passenger on every train. We do not jump at the figures and say, 'There were so many got in yesterday.' Every train that comes into Winnipeg from the east, from the south, or from the west, is boarded by one of our officers in uniform who catechises every person and must find out if the immigrant is coming into Canada to remain permanently and coming for the first time. If so, he is an immigrant. If not, he is classed as a tourist, and so recorded, but not in the immigrant records.

Q. Are these questions ever resented?—A. Once in a while. That is where a man has to be trained to do his work thoroughly.

Q. The officer is not told to mind his own business?—A. Sometimes the passengers tell him to do that, but it depends upon how they are approached by the officer. There are two ways of doing a thing and sometimes three. We find sometimes that our men who are new at the service are turned down, but they soon get used to the work. It is not an easy thing to ask a man to give his name, where he is going, and what he is going to do. If some of the passengers resent it, you can hardly blame them; I think I would resent it myself.

By Mr. Fyshe:

Q. They think it too much like playing the detective on them?—A. It is a very curious thing, but an Englishman especially when he is going to some other part of the British empire, considers he ought to be entitled to do as he pleases and no one should ask him about it.

By the Chairman:

Q. Do you find many pauper immigrants are sent out?—A. No, very few. On that point I might say we do not mind a man being poor if he is healthy and able to work. Under such circumstances, we will not see him starve. If a man is in bad luck and is doing his best and needs provisions for his family, we will give them to him. If he needs wood for his family we will give it to him. I think it is poor business not to do so.

Q. The boards of guardians of some unions in Great Britain still send out pauper immigrants, do they not?—A. We very seldom get them, because it costs too much money to send them far west. I do not think there is a great deal of that kind of thing done now.

Q. I noticed a contribution in connection with settling of pauper children in Canada of seven hundred odd dollars?—A. I can explain to you how that is. There are certain boards of guardians in England who are allowed to emigrate children to Canada. But there is an over-riding Imperial statute which provides for the details of an inspection once a year by an official of the Government. Sometimes it takes place twice. All these children coming out are subject to that inspection which I understand the Canadian Government will not pay for and they bill the Imperial Government or the local authority with that cost. The procedure is very simple. Our officer has his list of children. He takes a rig and drives to the farm where the child is located. At the farm they do not know when he is coming. His instructions are to interrogate the child apart from anybody. He looks at the child, and perhaps this is what transpires: 'Have you not got any better boots than that?' 'Yes, I have a pair for Sunday.' 'Well, I will go up to your room and see your clothes. Now, where do you sleep?' So and so is the reply. 'How do they treat you? Do you go to school, go to Sunday school, go to church? Are they nice people? All these are questions that a man experienced in the business can find a way to secure a ready answer to. If the officer is satisfied the child is fairly treated he is allowed to remain. If not he puts the child in the buggy with him and takes him right away.

Q. Have you any Barnardo children in the west?—A. Yes, there are a lot of such children out west, but they can always find places for them.

By Mr. Fyshe:

Q. Does your department attend to that?—A. Yes, to the inspection.

Q. Has the inspector the power to do what you state?—A. Yes, he has the power to take the child right away.

Q. You must have an army of men doing that?—A. Not very many men. You see there is the whole year to do it in. There are two or three men that do that work in the west.

ESSIONAL PAPER No. 29a

By the Chairman:

Q. Do you think your officers should come under the general memorial presented?
A. I think they should. That is my plea before the Commission to-day. The
ttside temporary man has nobody to fight his battles in parliament.

Q. Of course, in this comparison between Winnipeg and Ottawa you are making
lowance for the men at Edmonton, Rosthern and Saskatoon?—A. The conditions
e similar as far as the increased cost of living is concerned.

Q. The same price is paid for fuel and all that sort of thing?—A. Yes.

Q. They are nearer the point of production, are they not? They get their bread,
itter, meat, and all that kind of thing cheaper?—A. Yes, but they are farther away
om the factories that manufacture clothing, boots and shoes.

Q. Then you consider that your outside agents have the same grievance as the
ficials in Winnipeg?—A. Yes, exactly the same.

Q. And the officers of the outside service in your department are not classified
nder the Civil Service Act at all?—A. No. We have very large buildings in Winni-
g and sometimes 2,000 people sleep there in one night. We have about sixty different
nployees there, and I think myself and another are the only two officials on the Civil
ervice List. Therefore, it is for the great bulk of officers outside I am appealing for
-day.

. Q. We have had Mr. Cory, the Deputy Minister of Interior, before us, and I
iink there are 300 temporary employees and only 200 permanent employees?—A. Yes.

Q. Have you any statement you desire to hand in?—A. I have some notes here
iat I would like to dictate, if you please. We estimate that west of Lake Superior
iere are over 2,000 officials, paid by the Dominion Government, that are embraced
ithin the association which we represent. There is just one other point that I want
make. Some figures have already been given to you in connection with the increase
salaries paid in the west by bankers and others. I have here some figures which I
ceived from railway companies, but they declined, for public reasons, to give any
tters. However, I am under oath, and I know these figures are true, because I have
en them in their books. This is the percentage of increase in wages paid to various
asses of railway employees during the last three years (reads).

'Machinists, 26 per cent; boiler makers, 26 per cent; blacksmiths, 24 per cent;
elpers, 25 per cent; moulders, 13 per cent.'

I would like to bracket these together and say that in addition the companies state
iat this class of employee is receiving from them in the west 30 per cent more than
ey would pay in the east for the same work. That is what they call the mechanical
ranch of the service. Now here are figures for the operating branch of the service
reads):

'Locomotive engineers, 14 per cent; firemen, 12 per cent; hostlers, 16 per cent;
nductors, 15 per cent; baggage men, 15 per cent; trackmen, 15 per cent; yard men,
3 per cent; agents and operators, 15 to 45 per cent; maintenance of way men, 14
er cent.'

Bracketing the latter classes together as operating employees, the companies state
ey are paying for that class of work 15 per cent more in the west than they are
aying for the same work in the east. There are a great many other points, but I do
ot wish to take up too much of your time. I desire to emphasize Dr. Barrett's state-
ient as to the cost of living in Winnipeg, and I assume that Winnipeg is representa-
ve of the west. I feel quite safe in saying that he is conservative in his statement
; to the increase in the cost of living in Winnipeg over that of Toronto, Montreal,
r Ottawa. It is a matter for regret that there is no provisional allowance for the
nmigration officers, who, as it happens, are not in the Civil Service List. We do
el that this additional allowance ought to be awarded to immigration officers, in
mmon with the members of other branches of the service, and no doubt the fact will
recognized when you come to present your report to the House of Commons. The

provisional allowance was granted in the first place because it was recognized that the cost of living was very much greater in the west than in the east. And that brings me to this point, that whereas wages in all other classes of work, not only in the west, but all over Canada, have been increased, the salaries of civil servants have been largely stationary. This is the fact, although, so far as the west is concerned it is recognized that it costs there so much more to live. I think also that Dr. Barrett was somewhat conservative in his estimate of the population of Winnipeg. I am quite satisfied that we have to-day within the limits of that city a population of 117,000 people. As to the population of the west, estimating very closely from our own figures, the new arrivals, I would say that we have to-day west of Lake Superior a population of at least 1,000,000 people. That is very different from what it was some years ago. The other statements as to superannuation made by Dr. Barrett we quite agree with. I think there is no one but will admit that when a man gives the best time of his life to the public service he is entitled to some consideration, or at least a salary which will enable him to put by something against the rainy day which is coming.

By Mr. Fyshe:

Q. The mass of men will not save, and I think it is the duty of the Government to establish a superannuation fund in any case?—A. The existing retirement allowance is something which I do not think commends itself to very many people. I refused it myself, because I thought I could do better with the 5 per cent deduction than the Government could themselves.

By the Chairman:

Q. We were talking about political influence coming into play. Practically, your immigration staff has been appointed within the last seven or eight years?—A. Yes, the appointments have been made upon a system built up in that time.

Q. May one ask, has politics played a conspicuous part in the appointment of agents, caretakers, and interpreters?—A. Not a conspicuous part in my service, because we have got to have men who are skilled. It is no use asking a man whether he is a Grit or Tory, if he cannot speak German, for instance.

Q. I suppose the Doukhobor is not influenced by Grit or Tory?—A. I do not think he has any idea of it at all.

Q. He would be appointed because he was the best interpreter?—A. Yes.

Q. And knew more of English than the other man?—A. We have to get men in our service who are qualified. They would class as experts in a good many examinations.

Q. Then, in order to get the best results you possibly can, in order to develop and populate the Northwest, the immigration staff has been selected with a view rather more to efficiency than to political proclivities?—A. I think so. I will go further and say this, Mr. Chairman: The bulk of the men in the immigration service in western Canada are the men who have gone in and farmed the land, and because they have done that, they are the people we look to to guiding other people in the same way. When the original Barr colony of 2,000 people came out to the west a few years ago, we sent to them two or three Englishmen who had settled in the west and acquired the necessary experience of the country. These men moved from one farm to the other, instructing the newcomers where to put their houses, how to cultivate the land, and so on. And so I say that politics would not cut much figure in our branch of the service, as we must have the men who are especially qualified.

Q. So that you have less politics in your department than there is perhaps in others?—A. Less politics in our department.

Q. Have you anything more to say?—A. Nothing further, but I will be glad to answer any questions that you gentlemen may put to me.

The witness retired.

The Commission adjourned until the afternoon at 2.30.

The Commission resumed at 2.30 p.m.

Mr. J. OBED SMITH.—As I learn that the scope of the Commission is wider than I supposed it to be this morning, I would request permission to make a brief explanation in regard to the immigration branch of the service. It is known to you, Mr. Chairman, that for years vast sums of money have been paid out on account of immigration which were not always directly traceable to the service for the year in which they were paid. That was because of the peculiar nature of the service. We were dealing with one year on estimates based on the service of the previous year, while our business increased so rapidly from year to year that those estimates necessarily fell short of the requirements. The western country is developing and has developed so fast in the last few years, that it is almost impossible for us to keep pace with the requirements of the service, and therefore, some of the recommendations of our officers in the west are not viewed by the public in the same way as we view them, because they are not so cognizant as we are of the rapidity with which this work in the west has been increasing. Our plea would therefore be that the members of the Government who are particularly acquainted with the affairs in the west do not expect us to be able to say from one day to another just how much we shall require to carry on our portion of the public service. What is required to-day may be totally insufficient for the needs of next week, and we have to meet emergencies which arise from day to day by expenditures for which there may be no authority except the bulk appropriation or the Minister's discretion. The point I wish to make is, that we ought to be in a position to offer to men of the class required for our particular service a sufficient wage to induce them to take up that work. It is peculiarly a service in which a man may be required at a certain point in the one year, but in the following year the immigration may have passed that point and be active at a new station or along a new line of railway, while the man at the other point may be left high and dry without anything to do. We are constantly closing up old offices from which the tide of immigration has passed and opening up new offices where it has begun to swell. Therefore, these temporary officials should be paid well, because we can only keep them for a short time, and because they must be men possessing peculiar qualifications. While the immigration branch of the service is in this position, I fancy that there is no branch of the service in the west that does not feel the same extraordinary condition of affairs. The country is developing so rapidly that it is almost impossible for us to keep pace with it, and I ask the kindly consideration of this Commission for all branches of the public service in the west. May I, at the same time, express our sincere thanks to the Commission for giving us this opportunity to represent the views of the members of the Civil Service in the west, and on their behalf we desire to express to the Commission our appreciation of the kindly manner in which our representations have been received.

The CHAIRMAN.—The Commission appreciate what you have said. We are sorry that it was beyond our power to go to Winnipeg. The main point, I fancy, which you suggest to the Commission is that conditions in the west are so different from conditions in the east that special consideration should be extended to you.

Mr. J. OBED SMITH.—There are included in our association a number of other branches of the public service whose interests we feel should not be entirely ignored in our statements. While we are not prepared to make any specific representations in regard to them, Dr. Barrett asks me to state that the association includes all branches of the public service in the west, taking in weights and measures officials, post office clerks, railway mail clerks, officials of the Assistant Receiver General's office, the Dominion Land offices, with their agencies throughout the west, and the Department of

Public Works, consisting of two branches, that of the Construction of Buildings and that of Engineering. In fact, the association includes every class of civil servant drawing pay from the Dominion Government in western Canada. The memorial was endorsed by a large meeting of the association, attended by nearly 300 members, all voicing the same sentiments and having the same desires that we have expressed to the Commission. The great desire of the association was that the Cmmmission might come to Winnipeg and see the unique position of the west in regard to salaries and expenses; and members of the Board of Trade of Winnipeg and other public spirited men volunteered to go before the Commission and support the statements contained in our memorial. But we have had great pleasure in coming here, and we appreciate the kind manner in which we have been received by the Commission. Might I suggest that the Commission procure a copy of the report of the last meeting of the Grand Trunk Railway Company, held at London, at which Sir Charles Rivers-Wilson made the statement that the company would be obliged to form a superannuation or pension fund, without which they could not hope to retain the best officers in their employ.

The CHAIRMAN.—We have practically had before us the outside service in Ottawa, in Toronto, in Montreal and in Quebec; and before you gentlemen came here we had been made acquainted with practically all the desires of the various departments of the outside service, except as regards the difference in the cost of living as between the east and the west. It has been exceedingly fortunate that Mr. McKenna and Mr. Obed Smith have been selected in the delegation to come here, because they have been able to give us useful information in regard to the outside work of the Immigration Department and the Indian Department.

Mr. J. OBED SMITH.—Mr. Chairman, I was very glad to hear you state to-day that you were particularly interested in the care and attention paid to new arrivals in the country. I will say, on behalf of myself and my staff, that these new arrivals feel when they come here that they are among friends, because of the desire of the officials to carry out the policy of the Government, which is to spend money to make these new settlers comfortable and prosperous. We impress upon the settler that where they are fairly successful, they can afford to bear a reverse in one particular season; but when a man comes in and loses his first year's crop, he loses all, and the question has arisen, why should not the Government let him have a temporary loan, taking as its security a lien on his homestead. This would require a great deal of care, because applications would come from people who had no right to assistance of that kind, and we would have to be watchful to see that the deserving ones were supplied and the undeserving ones rejected. I am quite satisfied that people in the east have no idea of the multifarious duties thrown on the Immigration branch. The truth is that the officials in that branch as in other branches of the public service are thoroughly in earnest in their work. We believe in the west and in the ultimate destiny of Canada, and our guiding star is that the newcomers cannot withstand the domination of the British tongue or our Canadian institutions, no matter where they come from.

The Commision adjourned.

OTTAWA, Thursday, May 30, 1907.

The Commission met at 2.30 o'clock, Mr. Courtney, chairman, presiding.

Mr. E. L. NEWCOMBE, Deputy Minister of Justice, called, sworn and examined.

By the Chairman :

Q. You were asked to produce a statement. You now do so ?—A. Yes. (Statement produced and filed.)

Q. You are Deputy Minister of Justice ?—A. Yes.

Q. How long have you held that position ?—A. Since the spring of 1893.

Q. What salary do you get ?—A. $6,000 per annum.

Q. That is more than is paid to the average deputy ?—A. Yes.

Q. How long is it since your salary was increased to $6,000 ?—A. Since the 1st uly last.

Q. Have you made a synopsis of the duties of your office ?—A. I did not bring iything to hand in, but, of course, the duties of the minister, which are largely my uties also, are prescribed by the Department of Justice Act, chap. 1 of the statutes. have the statutes here and the duties are enumerated. Shall I read them ?

Q. Yes, certainly.—A. (Reads) :

' The Minister of Justice shall,

' (a) Be the official legal adviser of the Governor General and the legal member f His Majesty's Privy Council for Canada ;

' (b) See that the administration of public affairs is in accordance with law ;

' (c) Have the superintendence of all matters connected with the administration f justice in Canada not within the jurisdiction of the Governments of the Provinces;

'(d) Advise upon the legislative acts and proceedings of each of the legislatures f the Provinces of Canada and generally advise the Crown, upon all matters of law eferred to him by the Crown ;

' (e) Have the superintendence of the penitentiaries and the prison system of lanada ;

' (f) Be charged generally with such other duties as are at any time assigned by he Governor in Council to the Minister of Justice.'

Then the Minister of Justice is also *ex officio* Attorney General and the duties f the Attorney General are defined as follows :—

' The Attorney General of Canada shall :

' (a) Be entrusted with the powers and charged with the duties which belong to he office of the Attorney General of England by law or usage so far as those powers nd duties are applicable to Canada; and also with the powers and duties which by he laws of the several Provinces belonged to the office of the Attorney General of each 'rovince up to the time when the British North America Act of 1867 came into effect o far as those laws under the provisions of the said Act are to be administered and arried into effect by the Government of Canada ;

' (b) Advise the heads of the several departments of the Government upon all iatters of importance connected with said departments:

' (c) Be charged with the settlement and approval of all instruments issued under he Great Seal of Canada ;

' (d) Have the regulation and conduct of all litigations for or against the Crown r any public department in respect of any subject within the authority or jurisdiction f Canada ;

' (e) Be charged generally with such other duties as are at any time assigned by the Governor in Council to the Attorney General of Canada.'

Q. Your department, in point of fact, is the legal adviser in all matters ?—A. Yes.

Q. Your immediate predecessor became a judge of the Supreme Court ?—A. Yes.

Q. And his predecessor became judge of the Exchequer Court ?—A. Yes.

Q. It is part of your duty to read over all the Acts passed by the several local legislatures ?—A. Yes.

Q. That has to be done within a certain period of time for the purpose of disallowance, if necessary ?—A. It must be done within a year from the date of receiving the legislation.

Q. And you advise also as to the legality of commissions issued under the Great Seal ?—A. We draft all the commissions.

Q. The Civil Service Commission was drafted in your department ?—A. Yes.

Q. You prepare all contracts entered into by the several departments which you are asked to put into legal form I suppose ?—A. We draft them all or revise the drafts prepared in the department.

Q. We had before us this morning the Deputy Minister of Militia and Defence, and we were asking him some questions about the Ross rifle contract. Was that contract drafted in the Department of Justice ?—A. I do not know where it was drafted, but we had a great many conferences over it. It was, I think, drafted preliminarily by Sir Charles Ross' solicitor.

Q. He had a solicitor acting for him ?—A. Yes.

Q. In drafting these contracts, if it should appear they contained something that might be detrimental to the interests of Canada, would it be your duty to go on with the drafting or call the attention of the department concerned to the matter ?—A. I would call the attention of the Minister, or the officer from whom I was taking instructions, to any situation of that sort and ask him whether that was intended. As to the substance of the contract, I would not interfere with the policy, but would endeavour to see that any deficiencies that suggested themselves to me or any supposed provisions that I thought would not work with adequate security to the Government, were called to his attention. Then, that being considered, I would take the policy of the contract from him and give effect to his intentions.

Q. You have nothing to do with the policy of the Government ?—A. No, so far as concerns the business of the other departments.

By Mr. Fyshe:

Q. I suppose there is such a thing in the Government service as cultivating a habit of doubt or suspicion about everything ?—A. As far as I am concerned I have no suspicion. I point out to the Government, or the Minister or officer who is instructing me, what I suppose to be reasonable or what may work unreasonably, but the policy in regard to that is a matter for him to consider and settle.

By the Chairman:

Q. You have the superintendence of matters connected with the administration of justice under this Act ?—A. Yes.

Q. Capital cases, before the decision of the judge is carried into effect, are reviewed in your department ?—A. Yes. The evidence is all transmitted and carefully considered. All cases of clemency are considered in the department—all cases of applications by a convict for remission of sentence—but not necessarily upon the evidence taken at the trial except in capital cases. There the whole volume of the evidence is transmitted. It is of course a question of life and death and has to be very carefully considered. The essential parts of the evidence are abstracted and a report prepared, which is considered by the Governor in Council.

By Mr. Fyshe:

Q. You would not be called upon to pass upon all the cases presented for leniency ?—A. Yes, all of those cases.

By the Chairman:

Q. After you have reviewed the evidence in capital cases, the Governor in Council decides?—A. Whether the law is to take its course or not.

Q. Or whether a reprieve shall be granted?—A. That is right.

Q. The only cases coming from the judges that you review from the beginning are the capital cases?—A. Yes, they have to be reviewed whether any application is made or not.

By Mr. Fyshe:

Q. Do you do that in all criminal cases?—A. No, in all capital cases.

Q. Before the sentence is executed?—A. Before the sentence is executed, whether any application is made or not.

Q. You are a sort of court of appeal then, or a court of review?—A. Not exactly. We exercise the jurisdiction which the home office does in England.

Q. You could not upset a sentence, could you?—A. We can remit the sentence. I mean to say His Excellency can, upon the advice of the Minister of Justice.

Q. What is the origination of that custom or institutiton, because it would seem to indicate a lack of confidence in the judges?—A. It follows practically the system of the Home Office in England.

By the Chairman:

Q. I was going to ask you that. The Home Secretary reviews all the evidence in capital cases in England?—A. Yes.

By Mr. Fyshe:

Q. I did not know it was the custom of England to review capital cases in that way?—A. You see it is a question of life or death.

The CHAIRMAN.—It is only done in capital cases.

Mr. FYSHE.—But it would still indicate to me a certain lack of confidence.

By the Chairman:

Q. In capital cases, the judge dons the black cap and decides that the execution shall take place at a certain place, say, within ten days?—A. The execution is usually in Canada, fixed for a period more remote than that; it is often several months. During the interval the case in England goes to the Home Secretary and in this country to the Department of Justice. We review the evidence and see whether there is any reasonable doubt or grounds for clemency.

By Mr. Bazin:

Q. If you find there is doubt you can prevent the sentence from being executed, I suppose? Supposing a man is sentenced to be hanged, and upon reviewing all the testimony you find there is no justification for the sentence, I suppose you can prevent it from going into effect?—A. Yes. His Excellency's prerogative is unlimited in respect to clemency, either to remit absolutely or conditionally, or to suspend or otherwise, as he may be advised. A judge, of course, has no alternative. It is the duty of the jury to pass upon the evidence as to whether the prisoner is guilty or not guilty. Having found the prisoner guilty of murder, the judge has no alternative but to sentence the prisoner to be hanged. Of course there are various degrees in these cases, and some instances where a prisoner has been found guilty and sentenced to death are manifestly cases where mercy should be extended—where the ultimate penalty of the law should not be enforced.

By the Chairman:

Q. In fact in England when the jury suggests a measure of clemency, the judge says he will remit their recommendation to the proper quarter for consideration?—A. Yes.

7-8 EDWARD VII., A. 1908

Q. That is frequently the case, I should judge, from the reports of trials?—A. And it is occasionally the case that the judge on his own initiative recommends to the Home Secretary or the Minister of Justice, that the extreme penalty of the law should not be carried out. A judge has no power of mercy.

Q. It goes without saying that the initiation in the appointments of judges is in your department?—A. Yes, they are appointed on the recommendation of the Minister of Justice.

By Mr. Fyshe:

Q. Does the initiative come from you, as deputy, or from the Minister?—A. For the appointment of a judge?

Q. Yes?—A. That, of course, is a political matter. The Minister tells me that he proposes to appoint so and so to fill a vacancy. Thereupon I have a report to Council prepared which he signs and lays before his colleagues.

Mr. FYSHE.—Of course the judicial appointments are very important—I suppose none more so in the country. It is a pity if politics should be mixed up with it at all.

By the Chairman:

Q. That is done in England, practically?—A. The Lord Chancellor names the judges.

By Mr. Fyshe:

Q. Even that does not prove it is the best system?—A. I do not mean to say that the appointments are made on political grounds. What I mean to say is that the recommendations for the appointments emanate from the political side of the department.

Mr. FYSHE.—Exactly, but I am drawing the inference that probably politics does interfere, and I am not wrong in doing so, for everybody knows it.

By the Chairman :

Q. The Department of Justice also has control of the penitentiaries ? How many are there now ?—A. There is Dorchester, St. Vincent de Paul, Kingston, Stony Mountain, Alberta and New Westminster.

Q. To carry out the administration of the penitentiaries you have a branch in the department ?—A. Yes.

Q. With two inspectors ?—A. Two inspectors.

Q. A chief clerk ?—A. No.

Q. A first-class clerk ?—A. Two.

Q. A second-class clerk ?—A. Yes.

Q. A junior second-class clerk ?—A. Yes.

Q. A parole officer ?—A. Yes.

Q. And an architect ?—A. Yes.

Q. The parole officer is a new appointment is it not ?—A. Yes, within three years or so.

Q. In the Civil Service List you do not return the record of your penitentiary officials ?—A. I do not know why that is, but I can send you a statement.

Q. Can you tell us offhand how many officials are employed in the penitentiaries? —A. I cannot tell you exactly. Roughly speaking, the number is about 300, but that may be fifty more or less. However, I can give the information accurately.

Q. And in each penitentiary there is a warden and an assistant warden ?—A. A warden and a deputy warden.

Q. And guards ?—A. A chief keeper, guards and trade instructors.

Q. Take St. Vincent de Paul Penitentiary for instance. When vacancies occur among the guards, how are appointments made ?—A. They are made by the Minister.

Q. Would the Member of Parliament for the constituency have something to do with the appointments?—A. I think he could. I rather think the Minister proceeds largely on that, but I am not prepared to give a definite answer.

Q. In a place like Kingston, for instance, where there are so many employed, I suppose that is the biggest of the penitentiaries?—A. That is the largest.

Q. If the Member were consulted that would be a great piece of political patronage?—A. No doubt.

Q. You would think that a penitentiary belonged to the entire Province and not to the localities in which it is situated?—A. It does belong to the entire province.

Q. And therefore should be exempt from the system of local patronage?—A. I would suppose so.

The CHAIRMAN.—I have always taken that view, in regard to the offices of the Assistant Receivers General.

By Mr. Fyshe :

Q. How are the convicted criminals distributed?—A. The judge sentences each convict to the penitentiary for the district in which he is tried. Each penitentiary is declared to be a penitentiary for a certain part of Canada. The limits are defined by statute or proclamation. Then in case of overcrowding we transfer by executive act from one penitentiary to another.

By the Chairman :

Q. A criminal only goes to the penitentiary if he has a certain sentence?—A. Of not less than two years.

Q. If he has a sentence for six weeks or a month he goes to the local jail?—A. Yes.

Q. Following the terms of the Act you have also the regulation and conduct of all the litigation for or against the Crown?—A. Yes.

Q. That is to say, if the Crown gets into a conflict with contractors over extras or anything of that sort and the case comes before the court you have the conduct of the matter?—A. Yes.

Q. Frequently such cases lead you from court to court until the Judicial Committee of the Privy Council is reached?—A. Yes, such cases occur every year.

Q. Every year you have found it necessary yourself to go over to argue before the Judicial Committee of the Privy Council?—A. Yes, recently.

Q. Are you going over this year?—A. I expect to go.

Q. What are the cases coming up before the Judicial Committee of the Privy Council this summer, illustrating the work of the department?—A. There is that case of Martineau and the Bank of Montreal. There is a case about level crossings in Toronto ; a case about the jurisdiction or authority of the Railway Act—I mean as to whether certain sections are *ultra vires* or not ; and probably another question of accounts between Ontario and the Dominion, and some smaller matters.

Q. The question in the Martineau case is whether the Government or the Bank of Montreal is liable?—A. Yes.

Q. The contention is that the Bank of Montreal ought to have detected the forgeries and dishonoured the drafts?—A. The question is whether the bank can recover back from the Government the moneys which it paid on these forged cheques.

By Mr. Fyshe:

Q. What was the defence of the Bank of Montreal?—A. They raised various points. One was that the Government were negligent in not finding out that the system of forgery was going on.

Q. How has the case been decided here?—A. In favour of the Government.

Q. In every court?—A. Yes.

Q. Was it before the Supreme Court?—A. Yes.

29a—34

7-8 EDWARD VII., A. 1908

By the Chairman:

Q. In cases that come up where there is a conflict between any of the Provinces and the Dominion and the matter goes to court, you have to follow it up?—A. Yes.

Q. Owing to the extension of the business of the Dominion cases of litigation constantly come up?—A. We have the control of all the litigation of the country, and in view of the business which the Government is undertaking it is certainly very varied and very extensive.

By Mr. Fyshe:

Q. And it is growing more so?—A. It is growing more so. For instance, there are the cases arising out of railways. All business arising out of the Intercolonial Railway, questions of accidents involving negligence, questions of carriers' contracts, bills of lading and construction contracts—where works are going on. A large addition will be made to that sort of thing in connection with the Transcontinental Railway which is just beginning. Then in connection with the canals, there are questions of negligence about their management and operation—large questions. It is only recently we had a case in which over a hundred thousand dollars—I am not sure but that it was nearly two hundred thousand dollars—was involved. It was a large amount claimed against the Government by reason of the stranding of a vessel in the ship channel of the St. Lawrence, which the Government had dredged and deepened, but had not made perfect, in consequence of which it was alleged the steamer *Arabis* stranded in the channel. The Government was sued for a large sum, and the case went as far as the Privy Council.

Q. Some of these cases are got up in order to obstruct and annoy?—A. They are got up with the idea of getting something out of the Government if they can; by law if they can, if not sometimes by way of politics or settlement. Then in regard to navigation and shipping. The country owns a great deal of shipping. We have questions also with regard to the protection of the fisheries, both as to domestic and foreign vessels. Then there is the dredging of channels, buoys, lighthouses, &c. I have a claim which came in the other day for the loss of a vessel caused by reason of the alleged negligence of the lighthouse keeper in not keeping the lights burning, or something of that sort.

Q. Did that occur down the River St. Lawrence?—A. No, up at the Soo. Then in the Customs there is a very large amount of litigation in regard to smuggling—customs frauds—there are some very large cases of the kind. It was not long ago we had a case which I managed in which we recovered $20,000 of penalties and duties, which had been the result of systematic undervaluation for many years. These cases are rather difficult to fathom and consume time.

Q. Is there any effort made to keep such cases from being made public?—A. No, not at all.

Mr. FYSHE.—It seems to me they ought to be well advertised.

The CHAIRMAN.—They are. All the courts are open, and the decisions given are reported.

The WITNESS.—These high court cases are not reported as police court cases are. There is nothing about them to attract the public, for instance, as there is in the case going on at Fredericton; that will be reported in every paper in the country. If we had a smuggling case in Montreal you would not perhaps see anything about it in the papers. If you went into the court room you might see nobody there except the lawyers and the witnesses concerned. Such cases do not attract the public notice as do police court cases.

By the Chairman:

Q. You might proceed with your enumeration of duties. The Customs Department was the last you mentioned?—A. The Inland Revenue Department has a good many prosecutions. As a rule they do not run into such complicated transactions as the Customs Department, but there are a good many minor prosecutions.

Q. That is for illicit distillation and that sort of thing?—A. Yes, all that sort of thing. Then there is the Militia Department. That department gave comparatively little trouble in the past, but the business has got to be very large now. It has become very much enlarged since the department has taken over the services formerly administered by the Imperial authorities.

Q. There was the buying of property at Petawawa and other places. for example? —A. We have recently acquired a large tract of land there. Then there is the acquisition of land for rifle ranges and drill hall sites, contracts for rifles, stores handed out which are made away with and have to be recovered, and besides that a great many questions referred to us for opinion. Their business is differentiating, spreading out now and making very great progress. Then, of course, with regard to public works there is a considerable amount of litigation, and a great many contracts, questions over the construction of buildings, and so on.

By Mr. Fyshe:

Q. In such cases is it customary to go to law, or do you sometimes compromise with the parties?—A. We compromise, of course, in proper cases. In the first place, the question comes before me. The Government cannot be sued without its consent; it has that immunity which an individual does not have, and therefore we always have the opportunity to consider a case, and if we have no defence, or a very doubtful defence, either to pay or make a prudent compromise before going into litigation. So all these questions are submitted in the first place and considered, as far as we can consider them, in a somewhat judicial spirit, for the purpose of ascertaining whether or not the claim is one which should be paid or compromised or resisted; and having determined, as we do in many of these cases, that the claim should be resisted, then the fiat goes out and the case takes its ordinary precedure through the courts. Therefore, all these cases that I am speaking of now involve not merely litigation, but consideration in the way of advising before the actual time of the suit. A great deal of our advising is to the Interior Department in the management of their Dominion lands—sales, patents, titles and so on. Formerly there was no mining business of any importance. Recently the Government have established a Mines branch to deal with the mining business of the country.

By the Chairman:

Q. And the business is growing?—A. It keeps growing, and it has given us a great deal of work. It is only a few years ago that we had large cases before the Judicial Committee of the Privy Council, after having gone through all the courts in Canada, in regard to Yukon royalties. The Department of Agriculture furnishes its contribution in the way of patent cases, copyrights, quarantine, and so on. The Trade and Commerce Department also has a number of contributions.

Q. Dealing with mail subsidies?—A. Yes, the mail subsidies; and then there is the enforcement of the Inspection Act, which gives rise to considerable business of a minor character. The State Department is not concerned in litigation, but necessitates a great deal of drafting of commissions and forms, and so on. In the Finance Department there are a great many Treasury Board and Civil Service references, and matters dealing with insurance, and sometimes litigation. In that connection I have only to refer to the disputes between this Government and that of the Governments of Ontario and Quebec on financial matters.

Q. You have left out a very important department in your resumé; you have not mentioned the Indian Department?—A. That is the next department I was going to refer to. The Indian Department furnishes questions of accounts between it and the various Indian bands, which go back to time immemorial as to the status of Indians

29a—34½

7-8 EDWARD VII., A. 1908

and treaty rights. We are at present in litigation with the province of Ontario over questions arising in the Indian Department involving a million of dollars, or some such amount.

Q. When a band of Indians conclude a treaty with the Government and a reserve is set aside for them, do you give advice?   You are called in to draw the documents, I suppose?—A. Not as a rule.

Q. There was the treaty executed last year or the year before in British Columbia? —A. I do not remember drafting any treaty with the Indians. I think those are negotiated on the spot and put into a more or less rough state by the commissioner. They are not very artistic documents anyway, those Indian treaties.

Q. They involve a great deal of area if not of prospective money rights?—A. They do and you cannot tell how much value there is in them at the time.

Q. In fact it was an Indian treaty that caused the trouble with Ontario about the disputed territory?—A. Yes.

By Mr. Fyshe:

Q. Are you having anything to do just now with the negotiations that are supposed to be going on for the settlement of troubles beween Canada and the United States as to the boundaries and waterways?—A. We advise with regard to that. We have references from the Governor in Council with regard to that.

By the Chairman:

Q. Your duties are simply of an advisory character in such cases?—A. Yes, so far.

Q. Now, in the carrying out of this work which you have enumerated——A. Before you put that question, might I say another word or two. There is the question of expropriation and titles which I have not grouped under any department because they relate more or less to all the departments. It is a very large subject involving the consideration of titles and compensation. Last year we had 250 titles of lands to pass. As to those the majority would be agreed for, as far as the compensation is concerned, but a very large percentage of them are not, and we have to go to law to determine how much is to be paid. That is a branch in which we usually meet with extravagant claims.

By Mr. Fyshe:

Q. Is that settled by the Exchequer Court?—A. Yes. Then with regard to litigation pending I should suppose that we have at least 200 law suits on hand in one stage of progress or another. I see by a statement given to me that Mr. Gisborne says that in his docket for 1906 there were 122 cases, Mr. Chisholm had 22 and Mr. Pownall would have a larger number than that.

By the Chairman:

Q. Occasionally the Crown, as in the case of the Bank of Yarmouth, has instituted criminal proceedings against the late manager?—A. Yes.

Q. You have to employ local counsel in many cases?—A. In distant places nearly always.

Q. And in addition to these duties you have just enumerated, you have to get reports from the local counsel in such cases?—A. Yes.

Q. Are there many cases in which local counsel are employed?—A. There are a good many, taking the provinces all over.

Q. Now we will come to the staff in your department. You now have 24 officers as against 20 in 1891-2? That, of course, is not a large increase. Your chief clerks have increased from two to four. One of your chief clerks, Mr. Power, has amongst other duties, to review the capital cases to which you have referred ?—A. Yes, capital cases, and remission cases generally.

Q. A member of your staff is Mr. Fraser, who is a most capable man?—A. Yes.

Q. What questions do you refer to him?—A. Principally questions relating to Dominion lands and Indian affairs and contractor's claims.

Q. He is one of the most capable men in my own experience in the public service?—A. He is.

Q. Who are the other chief clerks now?—A. Mr. Gisborne is a chief clerk and Mr. Côté, who was recently promoted.

Q. Are these four men barristers?—A. Not Mr. Côté.

Q. But the other men have been called to the bar?—A. Yes.

Q. What do the chief clerks attain to?—A. In salary?

Q. Yes?—A. Mr. Power and Mr. Fraser each get $2,800.

Q. And Mr. Gisborne gets $2,250?—A. I should say there are five chief clerks now, because Mr. Côté has been promoted and Mr. Leslie is a chief clerk.

Q. Mr. Leslie has been confidential officer to every Deputy Minister of Justice?— .. He is the oldest officer in the department.

Q. He knows the traditions of the department?—A. Yes. He has been secretary of each succeeding deputy. He is getting along, and last year I thought it right to recommend him for a chief clerkship.

Q. Now take a man like Mr. Fraser, whose work is beyond all question. Do you think he is really adequately remunerated at $2,800 per annum?—A. Not at all.

By Mr. Fyshe:

Q. Whose fault is that? Is that the fault of the law?—A. It is the fault of the law in a large sense because the limit is there. We had to get special legislation to give him $400 more than $2,400. The latter amount is the maximum limit to which his class takes him.

Q. What is his title?—A. Chief clerk.

Q. He is a trained lawyer, I suppose?—A. Yes.

By the Chairman:

Q. He is a university man and a trained lawyer?—A. Yes.

By Mr. Fyshe:

Q. You could not get a man, I presume, of his experience and efficiency for any such price if you went into the market for him?—A. No.

By the Chairman:

Q. He has over thirty years' service, I see?—A. He has been there a long time.

Q. Since September 30, 1876?—A. Of course on that I would like to say that the Civil Service Act——

Q. I was coming to the Civil Service Act later. Although you have five chief clerks, considering the importance of the duties you do not think your department is over-manned?—A. It is not over-manned, it is under-manned.

Q. You do not think that five chief clerks out of twenty-four in your special department are too great in proportion?—A. I do not regard the name of chief clerk ; all in my department. It is a mere name for the purpose of carrying a larger salary under the Civil Service Act.

Q. And all your chief clerks, although you disregard the name, do work of a highly important character?—A. They do.

Q. Of the highest importance?—A. Of course Mr. Power, Mr. Fraser and Mr. Gisborne are all concerned in various branches of this work which I have endeavoured to describe. Mr. Côté, although not a lawyer, was a student at law for a couple of years or so. He came into the department a long time ago, and undertook the care of the criminal remission register in connection with Mr. Power, and he drafts the preliminary report upon all these cases. He gets information from the judges and the jails, and considers that as a preliminary matter. His duties are therefore quasi professional, and he has been there a long time.

Q. You had seven first-class clerks and you have now six, as Mr. Leslie has become a chief clerk?—A. That would be Mr. Côté, I suppose. The statement from which you are quoting would refer to Mr. Leslie as chief clerk and to Mr. Côté as a first-class clerk.

Q. The latter having now become a chief clerk?—A. Yes.

Q. So that if the number of chief clerks was increased to five the number of first-class clerks would be reduced to six?—A. That would be so.

Q. Then of your first-class clerks Mr. Chisholm and Mr. Pownall are of the legal profession?—A. Mr. Chisholm is a barrister, Mr. Pownall is a solicitor.

Q. Mr. Pownall is a solicitor of the English courts?—A. He is an English solicitor.

Q. Is there a distinction in duties between what we technically call chief clerks and first-class clerks in your department?—A. No.

Q. Although there is no distinction would the more important cases go to the chief clerks?—A. No, not necessarily. Each one of these officers has what I may call a specialty, and unless you can call a land case of greater importance than a shipping case, for example, Mr. Fraser's duties so far as concerns the class of work are not higher than those of Mr. Gisborne.

Q. Is it probably on account of length of service—Mr. Leslie having gone into the service in 1872 and Mr. Côté in 1883—to some extent that these officers have been promoted?—A. Yes, so far as Mr. Leslie is concerned, and the same for Mr. Côté. And further, because I thought, having regard to the length of service, the age that they had attained, and the duties performed, that they were not adequately remunerated by the maximum of a first-class clerk.

Q. So you made them chief clerks?—A. Yes.

Q. You do not consider they are overpaid by their being promoted from first-class clerks to chief clerks?—A. No.

Q. You do not regard the ordinary classification of the Civil Service in your office?—A. I do not regard it as applicable to our department.

Q. Although technically——?—A. It applies.

Q. You were one of the members of the commission that revised the Dominion Statutes?—A. Yes.

Q. Did it fall to your lot to revise the Civil Service Act?—A. Yes.

Q. Then you can tell us a great deal about the Civil Service Act. By the way, when a vacancy occurs in your department—there are not often vacancies occurring—do you take a person into your department from the list of candidates that have passed the Civil Service examination?—A. No, I do not think we do. I mean to say, as a matter of fact, I do not remember that we ever did.

Q. How many extra clerks have you got in your department? I see their number is put down as three?—A. It says three, does it?

Q. Yes?—A. Mr. Morris is one, Miss Pillar is one, and Miss Lindsay would be another. I think probably Miss McAmmond was counted at that time.

Q. Miss Lindsay is in the Penitentiaries branch?—A. Yes.

Q. Has she been transferred?—A. No, she is still in that branch.

Q. You disregarded the Civil Service Act in taking them in? They did not pass the examination?—A. I am not sure about Miss McAmmond. She had never passed the examination, but she was there doing work for a short time only. Miss Pillar came in and passed the examination before she got her appointment. She did some work in the department temporarily and got her appointment as soon as the time for the examination came along.

Q. None of these permanent or temporary clerks were appointed by yourself? They came into the department on application from one of the chief clerks, who was in want of assistance, I suppose?—A. Yes. Of course, our department is not a large one.

Q. You would see yourself that assistance was needed before any one came in?—A. Yes.

Q. You don't meet with political pressure to shove people in if you do not want them?—A. That does not bother me very much. I think we keep control of our department in that respect pretty well.

Q. What I was trying to get at was this: If the person is taken in after examination, or if they came in without going through the examination, I presume they would be fitted to carry on the duties?—A. Yes.

Q. You have not had any who were shoved in from political pressure?—A. No, we have had no one shoved in from political pressure.

Q. They are healthy and moral and their conduct is good, I suppose?—A. Yes, the service is satisfactory.

Q. All your clerks are appointed on probation, of course?—A. Yes.

Q. Then you report as to their competency?—A. Yes.

Q. Have you frequently had officers brought in on account of their technical and professional qualifications?—A. No.

Q. The men in the department have gradually grown up with it, Mr. Fraser, Mr. Power, and other members of the staff?—A. Yes.

Q. In the examination of Dr. Coulter the other day he was asked as to one of the clauses in the Act, I think it was section 44, and he said he could not understand at all what it was for. When you revised the Act, did you consult the other departments concerned?—A. No, I do not think I did. I think I submitted it to the Finance Minister, but not to any of the others.

By Mr. Basin:

Q. Section 44 relates to railway mail clerks, and clerks employed in post offices?—A. Yes, that they shall not be required to pass the Promotion examination. That is a mere statement of the law, it was taken from the previous Act, and it is easy enough to understand. I do not know the motive of it.

By the Chairman:

Q. Section 46 of the Act reads: 'Except as herein otherwise provided, when any vacancy occurs in one of the higher classes, in either division, the head of the department shall select from the list of successful candidates, for promotion, the person whom he considers best fitted for the office,' &c. Section 47 provides that every promotion so made shall be subject to a probation of six months. Do you not think that it would be advisable to have that with the concurrence of the deputy head?—A. Yes, I think it would be an advantage.

Q. You never have any transfers of clerks from your department to another department or from another department to yours?—A. No, except in the way of a minister's secretary occasionally.

Q. But I mean of the ordinary clerks employed in the business of the department?—A. No. Of course I would like to say in regard to that that so far as my own experience goes, in the few appointments that have been made in my time there has never been any difference between the Minister and myself. We have always been able to work very harmoniously with regard to that.

Q. The Minister of Justice is always a strong man? Section 53 of the Act relates to the salary of the Deputy Minister of Justice?—A. Yes.

Q. Under that section the maximum salary you are to get is $5,000 a year?—A. Yes.

Q. But Parliament in its wisdom has granted you another thousand dollars?—A. Yes, and it is not enough.

Q. To get beyond that would require a special vote of parliament?—A. Yes.

Q. Now that the revision of the statutes is over you have no other emolument than your salary?—A. That is all. I would like to say this with regard to that: As you may see from the imperfect statement that I have already made, our department is doing beyond question the largest legal business in the whole of the Dominion. We are not only doing that business and carrying on that litigation, but we are doing it with a very large measure of success. That being so, if you take the salary list and see what it has cost to the country to carry out all that sort of thing, you will find it bears no manner of proportion to the income of men who are successfully engaged in outside practice. Their work as a rule does not compare in magnitude with what we are doing.

Q. If you were dishonest you would greatly increase your emoluments. It would not be done by anybody in your department that I know of, but still it could be done! —A. I have not considered that project.

Q. It is impossible to get the men you want for the departments at $500, is it not? Some of the deputies have told us that it was getting difficult to secure third-class clerks when they would have to come in at a minimum of that amount?—A. Well, in our department the only class of people we would want at that rate would be typewriters and stenographers, and there are any number of them to be had.

Q. You mean women?—A. Yes, women.

Q. Not men?—A. No, probably not.

Q. In the Finance Department it is said they have to strain the law when they want a man and give him $700 to begin with. For this purpose they have to take a special vote of parliament?—A. Yes.

Q. Do you not think in a case like that there ought to be a little elasticity in the Act?—A. Yes. If you ask me about that, I think the classification of the Civil Service Act is altogether wrong. I think the classification ought to be with regard to duties, and the $50 a year automatic increase I do not approve of. I would class the service according to duties, and I do not think it would be a difficult thing to do. Take for instance the ordinary class of typewriter and stenographer. There should be a minimum and maximum salary for work of that class. If the minimum salary for such an employee were, say, $500, and the maximum, say, $1,000, or whatever is right, the salary should be regulated within these limits according to the value of the clerk.

By Mr. Fyshe:

Q. And the judgment of the Deputy Minister?—A. Certainly. I mean to say it would go no doubt on the deputy's recommendation. You may have a vacancy for a typewriter and a stenographer, and you may take on trial one that you find out to be a first-rate workman. You are paying that employee $500, and within the year you discover he has made his services very valuable, and that he ought to get $700 or $800. It should not be necessary to get special legislation to provide for that increase. It should merely be necessary to say to Parliament, 'we have an officer here who is now getting $500 but is earning $800, we want the money to increase his salary by $300.' It is quite possible you may have an officer in the department who is earning a certain salary and cannot earn any more. Why should it be that he must go on automatically getting $50 a year increase until he is in receipt of $400 or $500 more than he earns?

By Mr. Fyshe :

Q. It seems to me that you cannot frame rules that would adapt themselves to the people in every class?—A. Perhaps there may be cases you cannot provide for, but I suppose it is admitted that you must have some sort of regulation with regard to the employment and payment of the Civil Service. And then I say that they should be framed as nearly as may be according to those which a business man carrying on large operations for himself would frame. He would not say 'I am going to have a first-class clerk, a second and a third-class clerk, to start at the minimum and go forward each year with $50 increases no matter what they earn.

Mr. FYSHE.--No business man would do it.

By the Chairman :

Q. To carry out that ideal of administration it would be necessary to have a permanent commission to inquire into every man's worth periodically.—A. I do not know about that.

Q. We will take, for instance, the Post Office Department where there are nearly 3,000 permanent employees ?—A. Supposing the Deputy Postmaster General is satisfied that an officer in his department who is getting $500 a year ought to get $800. Supposing the officer is working in the class the salaries of which are from $500 to $1,200, why would not the public interests be safeguarded by providing, for instance, that on the certificate of the Deputy Minister, the Minister or the Governor in Council may authorize the increase if there be a parliamentary appropriation for it ?

The CHAIRMAN.—In the particular case of the Post Office Department there would be probably 100 men in the same class. Now would it be advisable that the Deputy Postmaster General should select one out of the 100 and leave the 99 untouched ? Would it not be better to have some outside authority ?

Mr. FYSHE.—They would have to take the word of the deputy.

The CHAIRMAN.—A commission for example. They would inquire into the work of each of the candidates.

The WITNESS.—In order to do that satisfactorily, they would have to be in the position of deputy minister of each department.

Q. They would examine just like an inspector does into the work of a department ?—A. Yes, but they cannot be experts in any of these departments.

Q. They cannot be experts but I am taking the Civil Service as we find it, and as it will always be, and with the trend of public opinion if a man were treated in that way in the Post Office Department the life of the Deputy Postmaster General would not be worth living. The newspapers would get hold of it, he would be accused of favouritism, and he would be criticised from one end of the country to the other ?—A. The manager of a bank would not want an outside commission.

Q. But the manager of a bank acts without reference to the public at all ?—A. I do not see why a deputy should shirk the responsibility. I think the best incentive to good service is the idea that a man stands well with his deputy chief, which he can only do by performing his duties faithfully and well, he is going to get rewarded for that, as he would if the deputy were the owner of the business.

Mr. FYSHE.—That is the right view, I think.

THE CHAIRMAN.—I do not say that it is not the ideal view, but would it not be better for the deputy to bring these circumstances before an independent commission and let them inquire into it and take the onus of the thing ? .

By Mr. Fyshe :

Q. You would have to let the deputy make the suggestion and follow it unless there was good reason for doing otherwise. Do you not think so?—A. I should think so.

By the Chairman :

Q. You were speaking about the classification and the increases. Have you finished your remark in regard to that ?—A. I think I made the point I had in mind with regard to that.

Q. There are six penitentiaries and you have two inspectors of penitentiaries. Do the inspectors only get their out-of-pocket expenses when they leave Ottawa ?—A. That is all.

Q. They are married men with homes in Ottawa. ?—A. Yes.

Q. Is it to their interests to go, in the dead of winter, to Dorchester or New Westminster and only get what they are out of pocket ?—A. No.

Q. How often do they go to the penitentiaries? Do they go periodically ?—A. Yes, periodically.

Q. So many times a year ?—A. I do not know that the more remote penitentiaries are visited more than once a year unless occasion requires. Mr. Dawson is absent the greater part of the time I think visiting the penitentiaries. Mr. Stewart does not go very often now. He rather looks after the work in the head office.

Q. After the returns that come in ?—A. Yes. The accountant also has to visit the penitentiaries for the purpose of auditing and examining the accounts.

Q. The pentitentiary inspectors like all other inspectors are really out of pocket by doing their duty in the public service ?—A. Every man who travels loses money by it.

Mr. Fyshe.—What do the inspectors get as salary ?

The Chairman.—The two inspectors get $2,800.

Q. Would it not be better, as is the custom in England with the post office inspectors, to pay per diem allowances, or rather more travelling expenses and less salary, so as to encourage them to be frequently on the road rather than forcing them to make journeys which are a loss to them ?—A. I am not prepared to answer that, I have not thought about it, but I should think there should be some provision to recoup officers in one way or another for expenses which are necessarily incurred and cannot be charged up.

Q. A per diem allowance or something of that sort ?—A. Something of that sort.

Q. There should be some encouragement for an inspector to inspect ?—A. Yes, certainly.

Q. You have a pentitentiary in Alberta, you said ?—A. At Edmonton.

Q. It is not, I suppose, pleasant travelling to go to Edmonton in the winter ?—A. No.

Q. But still it is advisable that the inspectors should visit the institutions ?—A. Yes, no doubt. I have a statement with me of facts relating to the Penitentiary branch which the inspectors have prepared at my request, to bring before the Commission. I will hand the statement in if it is permissible.

(Statement handed in and filed.)

Q. This statement is about the preparation of estimates calling for tenders, works of construction, appointment of guards, audit of accounts, volume of correspondence, the number of the staff and the salary of inspector. I see that in 1892 the salary of the inspector was $3,200, with the franking privilege, and a reasonable liberal per diem allowance when travelling. So the inspector at that time, 15 years ago, has a per diem allowance ?—A. Apparently according to that statement.

Q. The system of payment for travelling is such that no official can travel as a business man would travel without serious personal loss ?—A. That is so.

Q. What leave of absence do you give to the clerks in the department ?—A. The three weeks granted by statute.

Q. But you are generous, I suppose ?—A. Yes, circumstances may affect that.

Q. That is the measure of administration which ought to be omitted from the statute-book and left with the deputy ?—A. I should think so.

Q. What are the hours in your department for luncheon ?—A. I have never had occasion to define that. The attendance is good in our department and there are not a great many clerks. If any clerk or officer were delinquent in attendance I would know it very soon.

Q. Is your department always open to the public, at all hours during the working day ?—A. From nine o'clock until six.

Q. There is always somebody there?—A. I am always there, unless at court.

Q. There is generally somebody there, to answer questions if the public should come in?—A. Yes. The members of the staff are there from 9.30 to 4 certainly.

Q. What do you call your office hours? I suppose in a professional department you are not bound down in that respect?—A. If you ask one of the staff he would tell you from 9.30 to 4. My own office hours are from 9 until 6 as a rule, and the hours of the staff vary as occasion requires.

Q. During the session with constant legal questions coming up in the House, and all that sort of thing, your chief men have no office hours. They are always at work? —A. Yes.

Q. Do you keep any records now in the Department of Justice, any historical records?—A. In charge of anybody, do you mean?

Q. Have you in the vaults of the Department of Justice any historical records that ought to be under the care of the archives?—A. Not that I am aware of; I do not know.

Q. Who controls the records in the department?—A. They are in Mr. Narraway's charge.

Q. And they are so systematized that you can always find a reference, I suppose? —A. We can of recent years, but if we go back it is very difficult. We are very cramped for want of space, and there is no place for filing away papers.

Q. You have not destroyed any of the records, I suppose?—A. They are not intended to be destroyed.

Q. They could not be destroyed, I suppose?—A. They could not be wilfully destroyed, but they are no doubt effaced and more or less destroyed by the fact that we have no proper place to keep them in.

Q. Many of the documents, for example those relating to the case of the disputed territory, are of historical and permanent interest, and it would be desirable at some time or other to turn a lot of these records, which must be of immense value, over to the archives?—A. Probably. I should think so.

Q. All your offices are in the East block?—A. Except the offices of the Dominion Police.

Q. With that exception?—A. Yes.

Q. You have no objection to Mr. Bazin and Mr. Fyshe visiting you some day?— A. I would be delighted to have them come.

Q. Now, we come to the big question of superannuation. You were one of the officers who came in before the Act was abolished?—A. Yes.

Q. You know that the Act was abolished in 1897?—A. Yes.

Q. You know that the Militia Department has obtained a Militia Pensions Act, which gives the warriors a pension and upon their death a pension to the widows and daughters?—A. Yes.

Q. The same thing applies to the mounted police, who also got an Act passed?— A. Yes.

Q. Since the Superannuation Act was abolished?—A. Yes. I am not sure that the railway employees did not also.

Q. The railway employees of the Intercolonial got an Act last session?—A. I think so.

Q. So virtually, there is a growing tendency to place a certain class of public officials on the pension list, but not the great army of civil servants. What is your opinion of the abolition of the Civil Service Act?—A. I say it was altogether wrong. I think that for many reasons there should be reasonable provision for retiring annuities for the service. In the first place the salaries of the good men are small, and no matter what increase may result from the recommendations of this Commission they will continue to be small as compared to what can be earned outside for similar work. But if coupled with that there is a fair and reasonable provision for a retiring allowance upon which a man can live in the declining years of his life, that is an induce-

7-8 EDWARD VII., A. 1908

ment to many a good man. Many men have more or less dread of what is going to happen in their last years, and I think a retiring allowance is a good inducement to bring good men into the service. Furthermore, it is a means which can be invoked for getting rid of a man when he becomes inefficient. As it is now, as long as a man is able to hobble around, and get to his office and sign the attendance book, he will do so. You know that in spite of due economy he has had to expend every dollar he has made; he has been a good public servant according to his capacity; and yet if he is retired from the service, with his earning power spent, as it is he has nothing perhaps to keep him out of the poor-house. Now, it is very hard for any Deputy Minister to recommend that such a man should be retired. He is retired with a few hundred dollars that have accumulated in the retirement fund—that have been paid out of his salary—with interest.

By Mr. Fyshe:

Q. It is all his own money anyway?—A. Yes, all his own money.

By the Chairman:

Q. You think the abolition of the Superannuation Act was an utter mistake?—A. I think so.

Q. And the sooner it is restored the better?—A. On some heads.

By Mr. Fyshe:

Q. What were the Members thinking about?—A. It was a Government measure.

Q. It was such an important measure that I cannot imagine it being mentioned in the House without attracting the attention and consideration of everybody. To have a measure like that shuffled through as fast as if it were of no account is incredible?—A. I am not familiar with the debates, which of course appear in the *Hansard*.

By the Chairman :

Q. You agree with all the other deputies that have come before in the statement. that the sooner the Act is restored the better, and that without it there is no stability in the service?—A. I have no doubt that reasonable provision should be made for retiring annuities.

Q. Have you been losing any men from your department ? Have any men desired to come in but would not on account of the abolition of the Superannuation Act ?—A. No, because we have brought no one in. We have not had a case, likely to meet with that sort of objection.

Q. Since the Superannuation Act has been abolished the judges have had their pensions modified, in addition to the granting of pensions to the militia warriors and the mounted police?—A. The pensions have been enlarged.

Q. In certain cases a judge can go out on his full pay?—A. Yes.

Q. Before he could only go out on——A. Two-thirds.

Q. So that every department of the public service except the Civil Service itself has had its privileges, as far as pensions are concerned, increased ?—A. I think that is so.

Q. You were saying just now that you had revised the Civil Service Act and that you had no particular regard for the classification under the Act. It was mentioned to you that the Deputy Postmaster General said he did not understand one clause. From your experience of the revision of the Act are many of the sections incongruous or opposed to each other?—A. No, I think that the Act is pretty consistent now. I deny that there is a single section in it that any man cannot understand if he applies himself to it with reasonable care. I think the sections work *consistently* enough, but of course as to the quality of the Act that is a different thing.

Q. We want to get you as an expert to give us an opinion as to the quality of the Act. In what way do you think it could be improved. Do you know the Civil Service Act is the first thing referred to the Commission ?—A. Well, it is like the Indian's gun. it needs a new lock, stock and barrel.

Q. You see our commission empowered us to inquire into the general operation of the Civil Service Act, the classification, which you have given us an opinion about and the salaries ?—A. The operation of the Act in that one particular is the principle that I object to. You take a man at a minimum salary and you have to give him $50 a year increase whether he earns it or not. If you withhold the increase from him, it implies censure. You do not want to censure him when he is doing the best he can and earning all he is worth, but still if the increase goes on you may ultimately give him much more than he is worth.

Q. You would not have a minimum ?—A. Have a minimum if you like, or not.

By Mr. Fyshe :

Q. There should be a maximum ?—A. I suppose we must have a maximum. At all events if you classify according to duties, it seems to me it would not be hard to say what the satisfactory performance of certain duties per annum should be worth at a maximum.

Q. Well, of course with more or less mechanical duties that would be an easy matter ?—A. That is what I am speaking of now. They are more or less mechanical duties. You take the case of the docket keeper, the man who enters papers in a docket and files them away, he must be careful, methodical and accurate.

Q. But no great amount of brain power is needed?—A. No. It is not hard to say that that man could get not more than so much. Well, then, doubtless you could say the same thing with regard to the typewriters and stenographers, copyists, draughtsmen, &c., and very likely each department could name classes within which the bulk of its employees would fall. Then there are in addition to that of course, officers with general or technical qualifications which it is impossible to classify. There is no limit now under the Act as to salary attaching to those qualifications.

By the Chairman :

Q. They are really what we call chief clerks, specialists.—A. A deputy's salary is limited there but not the salary of the man coming in with special qualifications.

Q. The engineer may come in at $10,000 a year ?—A. Yes.

Q. Before the revision of statutes, the provisions of the Civil Service Act were scattered among various Acts and it was very difficult to find out what its provisions really were ?—A. Very difficult and there was considerable inaccuracy by reason of the effect of the publication by the State Department. They have not given effect to all the amendments. I have had my attention called to the fact that they had been acting under statutes repealed some years ago. It was not surprising that that should happen because the thing was mixed up and so confused among various Acts, and it was very difficult for the State Department to bring out a consolidation of the Civil Service Act after it had been amended so many times.

Q. Some of the sections are not consistent and are opposed to each other, I presume?—A. I do not think so.

Q. You revised it yourself?—A. I did, I spent a good deal of the time over it.

Q. You say there are no incongruities in the Act?—A. I do not think so. Under our commission we were to revise the law as it stood, and to give effect to the apparent intention. In all the Acts that I dealt with I endeavoured to do that, so that when I turned out this Act, I thought I had accomplished the purpose, and I have no reason to think otherwise at present.

By Mr. Fyshe:

Q. You have no objection to some of the alterations we suggest, have you?—A. Not at all, I am not committed at all to the policy.

By the Chairman:

Q. As the expert who revised this particular Civil Service Act, have you anything to suggest in the way of improvement or alteration or modification? We come to you as the expert, you know?—A. You mean as to the substance of the Act?

The CHAIRMAN.—If you do not like to answer that question off-hand, we would like you to prepare a little memo. as to the improvements of the Act, if you have time.

The WITNESS.—I will tell you one thing that occurs to me now, and that is about temporary employees. I do not think there should be any restriction in the case of temporary employees, so far as concerns examinations. Set a limit as to salary, if you like, but if I have a pressure of work on hand and want to get the person who is most qualified to come to the department and spend a week, or six months if you like, there should be no statutory obstacle to that. As it is now, you have to resort to a sort of subterfuge in order to carry that out. You may not be able to find any one at the moment who has passed the Civil Service examination, or perhaps those that you can find are not qualified for the work, and you have to take in somebody else; and then you have to arrange in some way that the account for salary shall be passed without a certificate that the recipient has passed the examination. That is contrived in various ways, I believe, in different departments.

Q. We would like to get a memorandum from you as to what modifications you think it desirable to have in the Act? Your suggestions would probably infringe on the other departments, but we are going to work at the other departments along the same lines, and as your suggestions would be based on common sense, we may as well have them, if it would not be too much trouble?—A. Of course, I have not considered the Civil Service Act so much with regard to other departments, but simply with regard to my own.

Q. You made the valuable suggestion about temporary clerks?—A. That is a stumbling block.

Q. There may be in your department other things which you may regard as stumbling blocks?—A. I should think our powers ought to be enlarged in regard to the employment of such professional assistance as we need. In the case of the Geological Survey Department, they have special legislation.

Q. That has been abolished by the new Mines Act?—A. Well, they had at all events special legislation. There should be power, either defined by the Act or delegated whereby such a department as mine might be, so far as professional services are concerned, exempt and placed on an establishment list that may be framed by the Governor in Council, on the recommendation of the Minister or deputy or something of that kind.

Q. Does it not come to this, that no two departments are alike? Each department has got its own environment and its own duties, and own specialties?—A. No doubt.

Q. There is no doubt whatever about it. Would it not be advisable, as in England, to have the special Civil Service Commission to regulate and take charge of the public service, having a special examination for each particular position, not a general examination for the Finance, Post Office or Justice Departments, but having a special examination suited to the particular department, and having a list of the best candidates, it may be, sent to the several departments on probation?—A. I dare say that would work. I am not familiar with the working of the English system in regard to that; I have not studied it at all.

Q. The Chancellor of the Exchequer does not appoint a man to the Treasury. When they need a man the Secretary of the Treasury writes to the secretary of the Civil service Commission, and they send a person over.—A. And this Civil Service Commission is non-political, is it?

Q. Non-political. They employ examiners and sub-examiners.—A. If a Minister, for instance, wanted to get his son into the department——

Q. He could not do it. There is no patronage in Great Britain at all?—A. Supposing I wanted to take another lawyer into the department, I would not have to go to the Civil Service Commission for that?

Q. There is no Department of Justice in England. There is an Attorney General's Department, but I would not like to say what happens in that case. That is provided for, I have no doubt, as in the Foreign Office, where there are specialists?— A. There are appointments there. They have the Treasury 'devil' and Treasury solicitors there. They are appointed by the Government, and they correspond largely to the professional officers of my department.

Q. But these officers from the Attorney General's office would come from the Civil Service Commission?—A. Of course it would be very convenient indeed if it could be arranged for. If, for example, I wanted a man to take charge of the docket and file papers connected with cases, and keep the records and so on, and could refer to a body of experts saying, 'I am in need of a good man with these qualifications, I want a good man and I can afford to pay him so much,' and if I could get a man in that way to fill the bill it would be splendid.

Q. Take that typical case: You have said to them that you want such a man. They would publicly advertise that on such and such a date there would be an examination for a docket clerk in the Attorney General's office. They would set the papers and a certain number of candidates would pass. They would send to the department the man who got the highest marks. If the man proved inefficient, or some defects of character developed, and the department rejected him, the Commission would send a second man, and so on, until a good man was found. Politics are entirely eliminated. —A. It sounds good.

Q. It eliminates favouritism or jealousy on the part of a deputy, and in the long run it seems to me is calculated to procure the best results.—A. I should like to say a word or two more in regard to the work.

Q. Yes, certainly?—A. As to references for opinions from other departments. In 1904, there were 1,132, and that number has increased to about 1,800 per annum.

By Mr. Fyshe:

Q. That involves a good deal of examination in every case?—A. Yes, a great deal. But not in every case, because many of these references are not difficult to answer. But there are a great many of course where there are large files and papers to be examined and very complicated transactions to be unravelled.

Q. Do not some give you a lot of gratuitous trouble?—A. Of course some of the deputies refer more than others, but still I am always glad to have a reference, for as a rule it saves me trouble afterwards. We sometimes get into complications by reason of a reference not having been made, and very often a comparatively simple reference at the beginning will save a lot of trouble at the end.

Q. Would you have to attend to each one of these personally?—A. I sign all the letters.

Q. You are responsible then?—A. I am responsible in this sense: I refer the matter to the officer who is specially qualified to deal with it, and according to the subject and the officer to whom I refer it, I am more or less satisfied to take his statement of the facts and of the law unless I consider it questionable upon the face of his letter, without looking into the whole thing myself, because if I had to do that myself in every case I could not do it.

Q. The number you give would be three or four a day?—A. Yes.

Q. That is a lot of business?—A. We have an immense amount of business. I have references in the department which have been six months before me.

By the Chairman:

Q. I want to get from you what the work of the department is?—A. Another thing is with regard to legislation. It is not our business departmentally to draft legislation. That is the duty of the law clerk of the House of Commons and his staff. But it sometimes happens that a Minister will come in and really insist that we take charge of a particular measure, or prepare amendments or consider a Bill that has been already drafted. So we have during the session a great deal of that extra work put upon us.

Q. When I was in the Department of Finance, I would go around and consult you regarding the Bank Act and the Bounties Act?—A. Yes.

By Mr. Fyshe:

Q. I suppose the idea is to know that it does not conflict with something else?— —A. Yes, in part. Then of course with regard to the judges' leave of absence and payments. I may say that the accounting branch of our department has had a great deal put upon it through the changes in the law with regard to official travelling allowances and probably issues three times as many cheques now as were issued three years ago. Then there is the adminstration of justice in the Yukon territory, which is a considerable burden, and the applications for extradition and the return of fugitive offenders. Those have to be passed upon by us, and there were 52 in 1906.

By the Chairman:

Q. One a week?—A. Just one a week. Of course every new departure of the Government involved additional work for us, such as the purchase of the Ross rifle, and the deportation of immigrants, which has arisen in the last year or two. The development of the Northwest with the increase in population, also causes a steady increase in our work from year to year. As to remissions, there were of such cases in 1904, 770 and in 1906 there were 949. Those are new cases. In addition to that there are old cases to be reconsidered every little while, and it is estimated that there are from 1,200 to 1,500 coming before us in one way or another each year. We have also the Dominion police and the Supreme Court and Exchequer Court staffs; they fall under the administration of justice. All payments of supplies for the Dominion police are made from our letter of credit, and there is a secret service of the Dominion police and the Customs Department which for some reason or other was put upon us. Then there is the matter of disallowance of Provincial legislation. That, of course, is increasing. There is evidence of legislative activity both in the provinces and in the Dominion. Two new provinces were recently added to the Dominion and last year I had 4,856 pages of additional legislation to read and report on.

Q. Do you read all this yourself?—A. I do that myself.

By Mr. Fyshe:

Q. You did not disallow all of them, did you?—A. No, I had to report upon all the measures as to whether they should be disallowed.

Q. How many were disallowed?—A. I could not tell you off-hand; not a great many.

Q. How is it possible that such a thing could occur as took place at Emerson, where a municipality undertook to get a local Act compelling its creditors to come to a compromise?—A. Well, that is a thing that is permitted to the Provincial legislatures. We do not as a rule interfere with legislation of that kind, if it is within their jurisdiction, even if it does injustice. There are a great many questions of legislative authority that arise under these statutes.

Q. How is it possible that any Provincial authority should have power to say to the creditors of a municipality ' you must accept so and so or get nothing'?—A. That is the omnipotent power of the legislature.

Q. That is a perfect outrage; the Dominion Government itself would not do it. It is one of the great weaknesses of our Provincial legislation. You cannot do that in the United States?—A. Because they have a written constitution there.

Mr. FYSHE.—Because they are sensible, that is all.

By the Chairman:

Q. The 4,856 pages you read would have to be gone over very carefully, because there is always the attempt to get further powers than the British North America Act would seem to allow to the provinces?—A. Yes, always a disposition to legislate right up to the border line, or a little beyond, and that is a thing that passes into a precedent if it is not checked.

Q. On the other hand, the provinces complain that the Dominion is perpetually infringing their rights?—A. But they think they have rights beyond what are given to them as a rule. There is very little *ultra vires* legislation of the Dominion.

Q. You would like to think the matter over, and if you have any suggestions or modifications of the Civil Service Act to propose, we would be glad to receive them?—A. I will do so.

Witness discharged.

OTTAWA, May 23, 1907.

(Enclosure.)

The Secretary,
    The Civil Service Commission,
        Ottawa.

SIR,—Referring to your letter of 20th instant, I have the honour to inclose a statement with regard to this department such as I understand you desire.

I have the honour to be, sir,
    Your obedient servant,
        (Signed)   E. L. NEWCOMBE,
            Deputy Minister of Justice.

7-8 EDWARD VII., A. 1908

DEPARTMENT OF JUSTICE.

STATEMENT showing number of staff and amount of salaries paid during fiscal years 1891-2 and 1905-6.

	Number.		Salaries.	
	1891-2.	1905-6.	1891-2.	1905-6.
Department Proper.			$ cts.	$ cts
Deputy Minister	1	1	4,000 00	4,000 00
Chief Clerks	2	4	4,275 00	9,500 00
1st Class Clerks	3	7	5,275 00	12,075 00
2nd Class Clerks	4	2	5,312 50	2,550 00
Junior 2nd Class Clerks	0	3	....	2,600 00
3rd Class Clerks	2	0	1,900 00	....
Messengers	2	2	663 33	1,340 00
Extra Clerks	3	3	1,856 35	1,466 64
Extra Messengers	3	2	677 58	1,250 00
Allowance to Private Secretary to Minister	...	...	600 00	600 00
Allowance to Private Secretary to Solicitor General	...	...	...	554 88
Totals, Department Proper	20	24	24,559 76	35,936 52
Penitentiary Branch.				
Inspectors	1	2	3,200 00	5,600 00
Chief Clerks (6 months)	0	1	....	975 00
1st Class Clerks	1	1	1,800 00	1,600 00
2nd Class Clerks	1	1	1,071 44	1,500 00
Junior 2nd Class Clerks	0	1	....	850 00
Parole Officer	0	1	....	2,000 00
Architect	0	1	....	1,249 97
Totals, Penitentiary Branch	3	8	6,071 44	13,774 97
Dominion Police.				
Commissioner	1	1	1,850 00	3,000 00
2nd Class Clerk	0	1	....	1,200 00
Extra Clerks (38 days)	2	0	19 00	....
Totals, Dominion Police	3	2	1,869 00	4,200 00

OFFICE OF INSPECTOR OF PENITENTIARIES,
OTTAWA, May 29, 1907.

Memorandum for the Deputy Minister,

· Re *Penitentiary Branch.*

(1) Previous to 1895 estimates were prepared at the penitentiaries. They are now prepared by the inspectors.

(2) Previous to 1895 tenders were prepared, advertised for, opened, checked and scheduled by each warden. This work is now done by the inspectors at Ottawa.

(3) Previous to 1895 (partially) and previous to 1890 (absolutely) all work of construction and reconstruction of the various penitentiaries was done on plans and estimates prepared by the officers of the Department of Public Works, and carried out under their supervision. Since 1895 these works have been done entirely, under the supervision of the inspectors and the prison architect, by convict labour. At the re-

quest of the inspectors the architect recently compiled a statement showing the value of work actually performed in this connection during the past seven years. The value of these works based on data used in the preparation of estimates by the officials of the Department of Public Works and by outside architects, amounts to $697,250, while the actual expenditure amounted to but $209,487. The saving in expenditure effected by the present system and the utilization of convict labour was therefore $487,763 during the past seven years.

The data upon which this statement was prepared was carefully examined by a practical contractor who expressed the opinion that the value of the structural work was decidedly understated and that therefore the saving was to that extent under-estimated. The supervision and consultations with the architect regarding the details of these works, from day to day, involve additional and responsible duties not previously performed by the inspector.

(4) About fifty per cent of the purchases required for the institutions cannot be anticipated in time to be placed on contract, or can be purchased to better advantage on the open market, and since 1895 detailed lists of articles as required are submitted to the inspectors and revised by them before authority for purchase is granted. This involves care and also correspondence with manufacturers and dealers in order to ascertain where purchases can be made to the best advantage. This work was formerly left to the wardens.

(5) Previous to 1895 the appointment of guards, &c., was made by the wardens who conducted all correspondence with applicants. All appointments are now made by the Minister, and the necessary correspondence regarding applications, physical examinations, &c., is conducted by the inspectors.

(6) Until 1902 all accounts were audited and paid at the penitentiaries and no books were kept or accounting done in the Ottawa office. Since that date all accounts are audited and paid at Ottawa, and the bookkeeping for all the institutions, in connection with expenditure, is done by the accountants under the supervision of the inspectors who sign all cheques and returns. The cheques issued in 1905-6 numbered 6,575, amounting to nearly half a million dollars, which will give an approximate estimate of the journal and ledger entries, the other labour involved in the centralized system as well as the necessary registered transmission of cheques.

(7) The volume of correspondence has increased from 900 letters sent out in 1894 to 3,100 sent out in 1906, the latter is without reference to the larger number of inclosures, addressed, registered and sent out by the accountants in connection with the payment of accounts.

(8) The staff in 1894 consisted of an inspector and auditor and a secretary. It now consists of two inspectors, three accountants, a parole officer, an architect and a typist.

(9) In 1894 the salary of the inspector was $3,200, with the franking privilege and a reasonably liberal per diem allowance while travelling. Nearly all those who were then receiving that salary (throughout the service) have had their salaries increased to $4,000. The present salaries of the inspectors is $2,800. The franking privilege has been taken away, notwithstanding the large increase in the volume of mail matter, and the system of payment for travel is such that no official can travel, as business men usually travel, without serious personal loss.

OTTAWA, FRIDAY, May 31, 1907.

The Royal Commission on the Civil Service met this morning at 10.30 o'clock.

Present:—Mr. J. M. COURTNEY, C.M.G., Chairman.
Mr. THOMAS FYSHE, Montreal, and
Mr. P. J. BAZIN, Quebec.

Lt.-Col. A. P. SHERWOOD. sworn and examined.

By the Chairman:
. You were a witness before the Civil Service Commission in 1892?—A. Yes.
. You are still Commissioner and Superintendent of Dominion Police?—A. Yes.
Q. That is in charge of the Department of Justice?—A. Yes.
Q. How long have you been Commissioner of Dominion Police?—A. Twenty-two
years as commissioner. I was three years as superintendent before that.
. You have charge of the Dominion buildings here?—A. Yes.
Q. Both the interior and exterior?—A. Yes.
Q. You have also something to do with the safety of distinguished strangers,
when they pass through Canada, such as the Prince of Wales and Prince Fushimi?—
A. Yes.
Q. You look after their safety and welfare?—A. Yes.
Q. What is your salary now?—A. $3,000.
Q. How many men have you in your force?—A. Forty-eight.
Q. Is there a kind of gradation for them?—A. Yes.
Q. Just tell us the gradations?—A. Two inspectors, one in the police branch and
one in the secret service branch; four sergeants, twelve first-class constables, nine
second-class, seven third-class, and the balance are fourth-class.
Q. What buildings do you guard now?—A. All the buildings, the East Block,
the West Block, the Langevin Block, the Museum, the Printing Bureau, the Supreme
Court, the Woods Building, the Canadian Building, the House of Commons and the
Senate, Rideau Hall, the City Post Office, the Archives Building, Militia Stores,
Fishery Building and Art Gallery.
Q. Rideau Hall only when the Governor is here?—A. No, all the time.
Q. You have in charge all the buildings in this inclosure, and the Langevin
Block?—A. Yes, and all the leased buildings.
Q. How do you arrange about the men—do you divide them into watches?—A.
Yes.
Q. How many watches a day are there?—A. It is somewhat of a mixed service,
and it is hard to explain it. We have to keep the doors, and we cannot keep the men
on too long at a time. What we aim at is to give them about eight hours only a day,
that is, three men to cover the twenty-four hours. There is a perpetual service.
Q. The buildings are open to the public, and the public have free access to them?
—A. Yes, from 8.30 a.m. till 6 or 6.15 p.m.
Q. The public can wander freely through the House of Commons corridors or
through any of the other buildings from half-past eight in the morning till about six
o'clock in the evening?—A. Exactly.

By Mr. Fyshe:

Q. Have you any trouble from loafers?—A. We have trouble from petty thieving.
We do not have much trouble from loafers as such, but beggars, book agents and can-

vassers give occasional annoyance, and must necessarily interfere with public business, There are so many places of access that the policeman does not see them always, and it is only in case of his going around and accidentally running across them that he prohibits them from soliciting.

By the Chairman:

Q. From six o'clock in the evening till half-past eight in the morning the doors are shut?—A. Yes.

Q. And nobody, clerk or otherwise, can go in without a pass?—A. No.

Q. For instance, a clerk in the Finance Department, if he goes back to work in the evening, has to get a pass from the Deputy Minister?—A. Yes.

Q. These passes are renewed annually?—A. There is what is called a permanent pass list, embracing the chief officials. Then, there are periodical passes, either for a day or a week, issued for special work. These passes are issued by the Deputies. There is a book kept in which the exact time every one enters and leaves is recorded.

By Mr. Fyshe:

Q. Who keeps that record?—A. The officer in charge enters it in his book, and the sergeant takes it from that and enters it in a book that is kept in his office, so that we can tell at any time who was in the building.

By the Chairman:

Q. From six o'clock at night till half-past eight the next morning you know of every official in the public service who was in the building?—A. Yes.

Q. But from half-past eight in the morning until six o'clock at night a clerk can go in and out of these rooms without reference to the police or anybody else?—A. Yes, anybody can. I think that has largely to do with the great number of petty thefts that are reported.

Q. Have you had any experience of the public offices in London?—A. I have not as to their method.

Q. You were in England, in charge of the Bisley team, two or three years ago?—A. Yes, in 1903.

Q. When you were in England at that time, did you visit any of the public offices?—A. I visited the War Office.

Q. When you went there, you had to send in a card?—A. Yes.

Q. You could not get past the door?—A. No.

Q. There was an official at the door, a messenger or a caretaker, who did not let you pass?—A. Yes.

Q. You have been frequently at Washington in the course of your duties?—A. Yes, very often.

Q. The practice at Washington, you stated in your last evidence, was that the public were admitted in the mornings?—A. Yes, up to two o'clock, I think.

Q. But although the public are admitted in the morning, they cannot enter any of the offices?—A. Not inside where the clerks are.

Q. Then, in the offices at Washington the doors only open from one side?—A. Yes.

Q. So that even when the offices are open, the public cannot get into any of the rooms?—A. No.

Q. After two o'clock what happens?—A. The public are excluded. Of course, if they want to see anybody in particular, they stop at the door and send a card to the chief clerk, who will authorize them or not as he sees fit.

Q. Since you gave your evidence in 1892, in order that the messengers should not be sent about absenting themselves from their offices, a mail service has been instituted by the Dominion police?—A. That was in operation then, but it has been extended since.

Q. The last time you gave evidence you sent in five or six papers showing the rules and regulations of the Treasury Department, Washington, relating to the watch, to entrance into the buildings, to passes and all that sort of thing?—A. Yes, they are still in vogue.

Q. Have they been modified or extended?—A. I think they are practically the same to-day as they were then.

Q. Of course, the police are not spies, but it is notorious that clerks can go in and out of the offices without reference to the police or anybody else in office hours?—A. Certainly.

Q. If there were a system that the offices were not open to the public, would not the clerks probably remain more in their rooms than they do now?—A. Naturally they would have to pass the policeman or whoever was in charge of the door, and he could keep a register.

Q. But now, in the present system of open doors and free entrance, they can go and come whenever they like?—A. Certainly.

By Mr. Fyshe:

Q. When you speak of petty thefts, you do not mean thefts by any of the junior members of the staff—you mean by outsiders?—A. I do not know whom. It is pretty hard to say.

Q. You sometimes follow them up?—A. We sometimes do, but it is almost impossible to do anything when we hear of it a day after it is done. The parties do not go in and out of the door where a policeman is, and even if they did he has no authority to stop them. In Washington anybody going out with a parcel is checked. One cannot take a parcel out of a public building unless it is initialled by a chief clerk.

Q. Would it not be well to have such an arrangement here?—A. I think it would. I think it is highly proper to throw all possible safeguards around the protection of these buildings.

By the Chairman:

Q. In your last evidence you stated that instead of closing the buildings at six o'clock you thought it would be preferable to close them when the staff left, from four till half-past four?—A. I think so still. I might say that while we close some doors at that hour, others are not closed because it is convenient for a Minister to use a certain door. But as long as that door is open——

By Mr. Fyshe:

Q. You might as well have them all open?—A. Yes.

By the Chairman:

Q. Take the Privy Council door?—A. That is left open till after six o'clock, because during the session some of the Ministers are out till the House closes. Although others are closed at six o'clock, that will be left open until 6.20. The same is true of the Customs Department and other departments. There is no authority to say that the doors must be closed.

Q. You think some authority should be given to yourself or some one else in regard to closing the doors?—A. Yes, and I think there ought to be a sort of commission to regulate these buildings.

Q. You say the doors are open at half-past eight in the morning?—A. Yes.

Q. That is to enable the charwomen to go in and and clean the offices?—A. No. The charwomen are admitted before that, at half-past six, and they are supposed to be out at 8.30. The clerks are supposed to be able to go in and occupy their offices at 8.30.

Q. You have a list of the charwomen given to you?—A. Yes.

Q. The charwomen are not under your control?—A. They are not. They mostly leave their keys with the policemen at the door, and they have to go there and get them.

Q. That is to say, nobody can get into the offices until the police open the doors? —A. That is right.

Q. The charwoman comes at half-past six, gets the keys from the officer at the door and when done cleaning her set of offices she locks the doors and returns the keys to the constable at the door; the clerks begin to arrive at 8.30, and the constable on duty opens the doors at that hour. That is the system?—A. Yes.

By Mr. Fyshe:

Q. Then the officer does not feel the necessity of watching people while the doors are open?—A. They would not allow a drunken man in the building if he came to their door.

By the Chairman:

Q. Many of the officers in the public service are in their offices after six?—A. Certainly.

Q. What do you do with them?—A. When they go out they are marked out.

Q. In addition to this work and the work of looking after distinguished strangers, you have work in criminal cases, such as offences against the currency?—A. Yes, offences against the currency and all sorts of post office offences.

Q. For instance, if it is found that the Bank of Nova Scotia has a forged note, you endeavour to look after it?—A. Certainly, because it might lead to an infraction against our own currency. The Government currency is in ones and twos, and being the most largely circulated it is more often operated upon.

Q. You also act in cases of extradition; that is to say, when news reaches here that an accused person is coming across in an ocean steamer?—A. Yes, we look after fugitive offenders and arrest them wherever they may be found.

Q. You have also certain duties to perform in connection with the secret service?—A. Yes.

Q. If you find that it is desirable to get information, it is left to your discretion to buy that information?—A. Yes.

By Mr. Fyshe:

Q. Have you a special detective force?—A. I have an inspector who is a detective. I have authority to employ detectives wherever they may be usefully employed, but for the most part I take my own uniformed men off and detail them for the duty. For instance, just this week there was a case of falsely branding fruit. It came to the knowledge of the department that Canadian fruit which was branded on this side by a fruit inspector as grade 2 or grade 3 reached the old country as a grade higher, and of course commanded a better price. We have just completed a case this week against an exporter on two charges. I merely mention this because the infraction of any law of the federal Government is dealt with by my officers.

Q. You have not a large enough staff for that?—A. We do the best we can. We do not deal with it unless we are asked to by the department concerned.

By the Chairman:

Q. You are all times at the service of any of the Federal departments whenever a case arises, such as a case against the Currency Act or against the Fruit Marks Act?— A. Yes; or the prevention of the illegal sale of intoxicants to Indians, or post office burglaries.

Q. You attend to these duties with about forty-five people?—A. Yes.

Q. In your own office the only clerical assistance you have is one clerk?—A. Yes. I have also duties in connection with the Ticket of Leave Act.

By Mr. Fyshe:

Q. Is not that ticket of leave system somewhat abused?—A. I do not think so. I think it is working very well. There have been cases which one might call abuse, but I think on the whole it is doing very well. The percentage of people who have fallen back is quite small.

By the Chairman:

Q. Have you any other duties which you wish to mention?—A. No, I think you have covered the ground.

Q. What do you pay your constables?—A. For the first six months, $1.50; for the next two years and six months, $1.80; for the next seven years, $2.05, and after ten years, $2.15.

Q. Does that include Sunday?—A. Yes. The sergeants receive $2.40.

Q. Are the sergeants generally promoted from the lower ranks?—A. Yes, always. The inspectors receive at present from $3.25 to $3.40.

Q. Do you require the men to be of good moral character and good habits, and physically strong?—A. The best. They require to be of the very best physical condition, because they have a very trying service. They have in the winter time to go from a temperature of 70 sometimes to 40 below. They have to patrol around these buildings, and they have to stand in draughts at the doorways.   •

By Mr. Fyshe:

Q. Where do you get your men?—A. We pick them up and train them. They are mostly Canadians.

By the Chairman:

Q. You have a large hand in the selection of these men yourself?—A. Yes.

Q. Politics has entered very little into it?—A. Very little.

Q. Despite all, you find that they leave you occasionally?—A. Oh, yes.

Q. Your chief inspector in the secret service is leaving you to become chief constable of Vancouver?—A. Yes. Another man resigned about the same time to go into business where the opportunities were better.

Q. Besides the opportunities of going into business the municipalities are glad to get hold of your men?—A. Yes.

Q. And there is a constant inducement held out to men to leave the service, the men being of good moral character and good physical condition, and suited to the work?—A. Yes.

By Mr. Fyshe:

Q. Do you find that embarrasses you?—A. I can get men.

Q. When you attach them to the service you do not make it too hard for them to remain?—A. They have to do their duty. We try to treat the men fairly.   -

By the Chairman:

Q. It is a uniformed force?—A. Yes.

Q. And with certain hours?—A. With certain hours.

Q. Take the case of Chamberlain who is becoming the chief constable of Vancouver—was there any future for him in the service beyond what he had attained to if he had remained?—A. Not very much.

By Mr. Fyshe:

Q. How old is he?—A. Forty-two or forty-three, I think. He has been twenty-two years in the service.

Q. A good man?—A. There is no better.

By the Chairman :

Q. There is no pension for your men ?—A. No pension. Of course, they would not go if there was a pension.

Q. This man had been twenty-two years with you, and he has shown his worth in, many ways ?—A. An excellent man.

Q. Known to all the departments ?—A. Known all over Canada. He had an intimate knowledge of the police officials and could go anywhere and get information.

By Mr. Fyshe :

Q. Was his case covered by superannuation?—A. No. They are the only permanent branch that is not provided for with a pension in some form.

By the Chairman :

Q. No doubt Mr. Chamberlain would have remained in the service if there had had been a pension ?—A. He told me he would have remained if he was certain that a Pension Act would come into force—he would never have thought of leaving.

Q. When a man breaks down in your force the practice has been, without any law, to get a special vote of parliament to give him a month's pay for each year of his service ?—A. Yes, up to ten years, and half a month's pay for each year after ten years—the contrary of what one would think was right. One would think that after ten years a man should get double what he did for the first ten years.

Q. Then if Chamberlain had remained in the service and he had received a paralytic stroke and became incapacitated, all that would have been done for him, and it would have necessitated a vote of parliament, would have been to give him sixteen months pay ?—A. Yes.

By Mr. Fyshe :

Q. What salary was he getting ?—A. $3.25 a day. I have a statement showing the men who have resigned or have died. For instance, an excellent man after twenty odd years of service, a man named Barber, died last year, leaving a wife and child, and his widow got only two months pay, which had to be voted by Parliament. Sergeant James Hughes died on the street, just at Rideau Hall gate, and all that was voted in his case was two months pay after a service of about thirty years. Stringer, who died in active service, got no gratuity. Murphy resigned in October, and was voted $752.55 after twenty or twenty-five years service. Morrison resigned and got $767.65, and lived for years after this money had been expended. William Timbers, resigned through ill-health in 1896 and received $604.46. James Codd resigned through ill-health in 1887 and received $360.79. Angus McCuaig resigned through ill-health in 1906 and received $1,111.73. Joseph E. Minard resigned through ill-health in 1897, died seven days after he resigned, received nil, John H. Phillips resigned through ill-health in 1885, received nil. Richard Brown died in the service received nil. Alex Prudhomme resigned through ill-health in 1896, received $439.25. James Stuart died in the service, received nil. Matthew Heron resigned through ill-health in 1899, received $250.95. W. J. H. Ross died while on active service in South Africa, received nil. T. G. Charlebois resigned through ill-health in 1906, received $556.97. Jos. L. Vanasse resigned through ill-health in 1907, received nil. P. M. Schmitz resigned through ill-health in 1887, received $178.27. Arvais Thibault resigned through ill-health in 1884, received $152.08.

Q. It is wrong to give a retiring allowance to these men because they are not accustomed to handling money ?—A. You have hit it exactly.

Q. The only proper thing is to give them a pension ?—A. Yes. It is not a large force, and it would not cost the country very much.

By Mr. Bazin :

Q. Does it require any special ability to become a sergeant in the Dominion Police?—A. No. When a man shows an aptitude for command, he will get more respect from the men than one who does not, and I can pick him out.

By the Chairman :

Q. Whenever you are called away to Quebec or anywhere else Chamberlain was here to act in your place ?—A. He looked after the secret service work—the confidential work.

Q. During his twenty-two years of service he had been in every part of the Dominion ?—A. Yes. He was on all the important cases for years.

By Mr. Bazin :

Q. Has he been replaced ?—A. No. He is still in the service, but he is now on leave.

By Mr. Fishe :

Q. Does it require a peculiar type of man to develop into a competent detective ! —A. Yes, it does. Very many men think they are adapted to it, but they are not. It requires a man to know when to speak and when to be silent, and always to be affable and when necessary to be firm.

By the Chairman :

Q. During the night your men patrol all the buildings from top to bottom ?—A. Yes. The buildings are provided with clocks, keys being stationed at the dangerous points in case of fire, so that the men must go to those points.

Q. So that the building through the night is patrolled by the police on duty, and as far as possible they try to prevent the danger of fire ?—A. Yes.

Q. Still, in the upper parts of the buildings there is a certain amount of danger! —A. Oh, yes. The buildings are very vulnerable in that respect.

Q. And from your knowledge of the buildings there are very valuable records contained in them ?—A. There seems to be.

Q. Especially piled away in the upper parts of the buildings ?—A. Yes.

Q. Do you know whether the surveys of the Northwest Territories, in the Department of the Interior, are still in the upper part of the building ?—A. I could not say that.

Q. One of your duties is to prevent the outbreak of fire in the buildings ?—A. Yes, and my men have charge of all the fire appliances.

Q. Wasn't there a fire in the Public Works building ?—A. Yes, in the daytime. It broke out at four in the afternoon, while the clerks were at work.

Q. Do you mean to say that you have fire apparatus which your force controls ?— A. Babcock machines and other fire extinguishers, and the hydrant stands. They keep them in order and ready for use all the time.

By Mr. Fyshe:

Q. And test them occasionally ?—A. Yes, and record the date that they are tested. Of course, the practice is to get the city fire department to the place immediately, in case of any fire being discovered.

Q. Where do you get your water supply ?—A. Direct from the city.

Q. Where does the city get it ?—A. From the Ottawa river, above the falls.

By the Chairman:

Q. Do you have constant drill of your men ?—A. Oh, yes, squad drill and drill with arms.

Q. And fire drill ?—A. I would not say that it is fire drill. They are instructed in the use of the fire apparatus. It is very simple. All it requires is for one man to take hold of it, and another man to turn on the water.

Q. Perhaps you would like to submit to the Commission a memorandum containing any other suggestions you wish to make ?—A. I will do that, if you will allow me.

Q. From your position, you know practically all the Civil Service?—A. Yes, I know almost everybody.

Q. If any evening Mr. Fyshe and Mr. Bazin would like to see how the buildings are guarded, you would have no objection?—A. I would be very glad to take them around at any time.

By Mr. Bazin:

Q. You say you have the choice of your men. Do you admit them on probation? —A. Yes. They do not go directly on. They are all taken for six months on probation.

Q. Do you ever have to reject or dismiss any?—A. Oh, yes.

By the Chairman:

Q. You have a system of reprimands, if they are late in reporting for duty?—A. Yes.

Q. And you occasionally dismiss?—A. Yes, for serious offences, or for constant repetition of petty offences.

Q. An accumulation of petty offences will lead to dismissal?—A. Yes.

Q. When a man is reprimanded, you fine him a day's pay?—A. Yes, and sometimes five or ten days' pay. It depends on the offence.

Q. I see by your book that a man forgot to punch the patrol clock, for which he was reprimanded?—A. Yes.

Q. A little time afterwards he absented himself without leave; a little time after that he was found sitting on the stairs, lolling about while on duty. That was reported to you?—A. Yes.

Q. This man resigned?—A. Yes, he resigned on account of ill-health. There is nothing very serious there.

Q. You keep a strict tab on them, even for using discourteous language or reporting themselves late, or sitting down and loitering?—A. Yes.

Q. Like any other disciplined force?—A. Exactly.

Q. I see you found one man making false entries in the memorandum book and fined him five days pay?—A. That is where a man on outside duty was allowed to come into the building and remain longer than necessary, the door duty man marking him out at the usual time, whereas he was found by the sergeant, when paying his visits, still inside. Infractions of this nature are always dealt with severely, as upon the strict carrying out of orders in this respect depends the efficiency of the supervision.

Q. The slightest infraction of duty leads to a reprimand, and as the infraction grows more important, it leads to loss of pay, and may lead to dismissal?—A. Exactly.

OTTAWA, June 13, 1907.

Constable GEORGE W. KENNEDY, called, sworn and examined.

By the Chairman:

Q. You are one of the Dominion Police?—A. Yes, sir.

Q. How long have you been that?—A. It will be ten years next February.

Q. What is your rank in the Dominion Police, what does this stripe indicate?— A. That is the badge of duty, sir.

Q. The force is divided into grades, is it not?—A. Yes, sir, there is the inspector, and there are four sergeants.

Q. Are you a sergeant?—A. No, sir.

Q. You are simply a constable?—A. Yes, sir.

Q. What pay did you get when you entered the service?—A. $1.25 per day.

Q. What is your pay now?—A. $2.05.

Q. Have you got your budget since the time you entered the service, your budget of expenses showing what you paid out?—A. Well, I have it for the year you will see— (book produced). I have a wife and four children.

Q. This is from May, 1906, to May, 1907, showing the living expenses for one year for your family, consisting of a wife and four children, and it totals up $715.54; your salary was $748.25, leaving a balance of $30.71, from which you had to provide clothing for your family and yourself?—A. Yes.

Q. Have you a similar statement of living expenses for some ten years back?—A. This is my book; I went back for one year exactly, and the total of my monthly account with the butcher comes to $72.01, one cent over $6 per month. I just went over it to see what it was for a year back, and that is what it really comes to.

Q. This is at the present moment, but have you an account of your expenditure when you went into the service, ten years ago?—A. No, sir, I have not. I have given you just what I have got, what it costs me to live at the present time.

Q. How do your expenses stand, as compared with what they were ten years ago, when you went into the service, how many children had you then?—A. Three.

Q. That is, you have only had one child since?—A. Yes.

Q. How much did it cost you to live in the year you went into the service?—A. I haven't an account for that year.

Q. Do you not see that there are no means of making a comparison to show how much things have increased and what your salary should be, unless we have something to go upon?—A. The way I looked upon it was that this is an account of my expenditure to-day and of my salary, and the two could be compared.

Q. I know that, but your chief writes that you wanted to come here and show us your expenditure now, as compared with previous years. What you have given us is very good, but what one wants to know is how far your expenditure has increased in the ten years you have been in the service. Did you keep books at that time?—A. No, sir, I did not; but what I have given you is an accurate statement of my receipts and my bills. I never thought you would require my expenditures ten years back.

Q. But your chief writes to the Commission that ' at least two of my men keep an accurate account of what they expend, and I would like to have one of them called.'

By Mr. Fyshe:

Q. Your expenditures have increased?—A. I know that when I first came here you could get a bag of potatoes for fifty cents, and it is double that price now.

By the Chairman:

Q. Was the $1.25 a day salary you got ten years ago sufficient to maintain yourself, your wife and three children?—A. I could do it better than I can to-day on my present salary.

Q. Can you make up from your past records a statement of your living expenses for a year ten years ago?—A. I am very doubtful if I could give you as good a statement as I have given you of last year, because as time goes on you lose track of your bills and the various items of expenditure.

Q. Yes, but there is this statement of your chief, in which he says that two of his men keep accurate accounts of their living expenses. We know the cost of living to-day, but what we want to get at is, what was the cost ten years ago, for the purpose of making a comparison. Would you mind trying to compile a statement of what your expenditure was ten years ago?—A. I could try and find out, but I cannot give you as good a statement as I have given you for last year.

By Mr. Fyshe :

Q. Perhaps some of your friends may be able to assist you?—A. My wife may be
le to hunt up some of the bills.

By the Chairman:

Q. What is the name of the other member of the force who keeps an account of his
penditure?—A. Constable Charron.

By Mr. Fyshe:

Q. How old are you?—A. I am thirty-nine.

Q. You have been ten years in the service?—A. Yes, sir, I have been at this sort
duty all my life; I have done nothing else.

By the Chairman :

Q. What did you do before you came here ?—A. I came here from the Kingston
ty force and I was keeper in Rockwood Asylum for insane before that.

By Mr. Fyshe :

Q. Where do you come from ?—A. Guelph, Ont., is my home, my people live at
uelph.

By the Chairman :

Q. Then if you broke down in health, what provisions does the Government make
r you?—A. On the recommendation of our Commissioner we would get a month's
lary for every year up to the first ten years and half a month's salary for the re-
ainder.

Q. That is to say if you retire from the service?—A. No, no, you have to be in-
lided to get that, if you retire you get nothing.

Q. And if you are invalided and the Commissioner reports favourably there has
be a vote of Parliament before you get it paid?—A. Yes.

Q. Now if you died, supposing you dropped down as did that man—what is the
ime of that man who dropped down ?—A. Sergeant Hughes, sir.

Q. If you dropped down dead on the road from Rideau Hall as that man did
)u get nothing ?—A. His family got two months' pay, and that man served over
iirty years.

Q. You get no pension if you leave, though ?—A. No, sir.

Q. The Mounted Police get pensions ?—A. Yes, sir.

Q. And the members of the permanent force also ?—A. Yes, sir.

Q. And you consider that your duties would entitle you to have a pension as well
i members of the Mounted Police and permanent force ?—A. I think so, sir, and more
) because our duties are far more irregular than are those of the Mounted Police or
ie soldiers. There are no two days in the week we get our meals or our sleep at the
ime time.

By Mr. Fyshe :

Q. Is that so ?—A. That is so, sir. I was on duty last night from six p.m. until
velve midnight, and from twelve noon until six p.m. to-day. I get all night in bed
)-night. I have to go on at seven to-morrow morning until twelve noon and from
velve midnight until seven a.m.

Q. Can't you do things more regularly?—A. I suppose it could be arranged, but
would require three or four more men to get a regular system, in order to put us on
ne post or beat for two weeks, say, it does not matter whether it would be at night or
iy.

Q. It would not be fair to put a man permanently on the same beat ?—A. No,
e have to change ; but if you got one or two weeks on the same duty you will get

your sleep and meals regularly. If you cannot get your sleep regularly you cannot derive the benefit from it you should.

By the Chairman :

Q. Will you endeavour to get that information with reference to your former expenditure for us as well as you can ?—A. I will, sir.

Witness retired.

STATEMENT OF P. C. KENNEDY.

LIVING expenses for year commencing July 1, 1899, ending June 30, 1900. Family consisting of self, wife and three children.

House rent, $7 per month.. .. ..$ 84 00	
Groceries, including milk and bread for year.. .. .. 196 87	
Wood for year.. .. .. 20 00	
Boots, 6 pair (children), 75 cents per pair.. .. .. 4 50	
Meat, $4 per month.. .. .. 48 00	
Doctor and medicine for year 15 71	
Paper, 25 cents per month.. .. .. 3 00	
Privy vaults, cleaned once a year.. .. .. 1 40	
Water and snow for year.. .. .. 6 42	
	$379 90
Salary for year.... .. ..$456 25	
Expenditure.. .. .. 379 90	
Balance... .. ..$ 76 35	

The balance, $76.35, is to provide clothing and other articles always necessary for a home.

(Signed) GEO. W. KENNEDY.

STATEMENT OF P. C. KENNEDY.

LIVING expenses for one year for family consisting of self, wife and four children. 1906-7.

House rent, $15 per month.. .. ..$180 00	
Meat, $6 per month.. .. .. 72 00	
Bread, $5 per month.. .. .. 60 00	
Coal and wood, cost for one year 56 00	
Vegetables and fruit, $5 per month.. .. .. 60 00	
Butter, 3 lbs. per week at 25 cents per lb 39 00	
Milk, 1 quart per day, 6 cents per quart.. .. .. 21 90	
Boots, 10 pairs per year, average $1.50 per pair.. .. .. 15 00	
do repairs for year.. .. .. 7 00	
Medicine and doctor for year 29 00	
Electric light, $1 per month.. .. .. 12 00	
Insurance, $2.67 per month.. .. .. 32 04	
Groceries, $2.50 per week.. .. .. 130 00	
Paper, 30 cents per month.. .. .. 3 60	
	$717 54
Salary for year.. .. ..$748 25	
Expenditure.. .. .. 717 54	
Balance.. .. ..$ 30 71	

With a balance of $30.71 I have to provide clothing for family and self as well as other articles which is always necessary for a home.

(Signed) GEO. W. KENNEDY.

OTTAWA, THURSDAY, November 7, 1907.

The Commission met at 2 p.m.

Present: Messrs. Courtney (Chairman), Fyshe and Bazin.

A deputation appeared representing the officials of the Kingston penitentiary, and consisting of Rev. Father McDonald, Roman Catholic Chaplain; R. A. Caughey, Assistant Superintendent of the binder twine factory; C. S. Wheeler, guard; M. P. Reid, keeper; P. M. Beaupre, instructor.

Mr. R. A. CAUGHEY, sworn and examined.

By the Chairman :

Q. Have you a memorial ?—A. Yes. (Memorial read and filed.)

Q. You are the assistant superintendent of binder twine?—A. Yes.

Q. What salary do you get ?—A. $800.

Q. That is equivalent to the salary of a trade instructor ?—A. Yes.

Q. In the first line of your memorial you say : ' The members of the staff request an all round increase of salaries.' Were not the salaries readjusted two years ago according to the circumstances of the case ?—A. Yes, they were readjusted according to what were supposed to be the circumstances of the case ; but, while no official objection was taken by the staff to the increase then given, many of them felt that the increase was not sufficient, but they accepted it.

Q. Then, two years ago, whether the increase was sufficient or not, a new scale was laid down ?—A. Yes.

Q. It was an increase on the former scale ?—A. Yes.

Q. On what do you base your desire for another increase of salaries within two years of the last increase ?—A. There has been an increase in the cost of living, especially in house rent.

Q. In two years?—A. Yes. There has been an increase in rent in Kingston in the past year of twenty per cent.

Q. Is the population of Kingston increasing?—A. Some; there is not a boom.

Q. What was the scale of increase two years ago compared with the former scale ?—A. For instance, the salary of a guard was increased from $500 to $600.

By Mr. Fyshe:

Q. Were all the others increased in the same proportion?—A. Some were, but some were not increased at all.

By the Chairman:

Q. The salaries of the higher officers, such as the warden, the deputy warden and the chaplains, were not increased?—A. No, and the chief keeper.

Q. The salaries of the guards and keepers were increased about twenty per cent?—A. Yes. The salaries of the guards and keepers were all increased, but only part of the other staff.

Q. So that there was a twenty per cent increase in the salaries of the majority of the officials two years ago?—A. Yes, the majority.

Q. Was not the increase in the population of Kingston in the last decade only about 150 people?—A. Yes, about that.

7-8 EDWARD VII., A. 1908

Q. Then how do you say that house rents have increased there in the last two years?—A. I do not know whether it is due to manipulation on the part of the landlords, but the fact remains that rents have increased.

Q. I was under the impression that Kingston was a cheap place to live in?—A. It may be in theory, but in practice I think it is as dear as any other place.

Q. It may be in regard to supplies, but I thought that house rents in Kingston were about half what they are in Ottawa?—A. I do not think so.

Q. May I ask what rent you pay for your house?—A. My house is not in the city of Kingston. It is in the village of Portsmouth.

Q. Is the penitentiary in the city of Kingston?—A. No, it is in the village of Portsmouth, immediately on the outskirts of the city.

Q. You are living at Portsmouth, which is practically to Kingston what Hull is to Ottawa?—A. Yes.

Q. What rent do you pay?—A. I have a special arrangement which makes my rent very low until next year, when I expect to have to make a new arrangement. My rent is only $5 a month, but I do not think there is a member of this Commission who would care to live in the house I live in under the circumstances. It has no water, no electric light, no sewage, no fire protection.

Q. Is it in Alwington avenue?—A. No. It is on the other side of the prison, the west side. I am not as favourably situated as those who live on Alwington avenue.

Q. May I ask what percentage does your landlord propose to increase your rent next year?—A. I do not know.

Q. You anticipate an increase?—A. Yes.

Q. The prices of provisions, I suppose, are about the same in Kingston as they are in Ottawa?—A. Yes, I think so.

Q. What are your hours? You have no shift like a guard, I suppose?—A. I have not yet been permitted to have the hours of an ordinary instructor. I have the hours of an ordinary guard or keeper, although I have endeavoured to have them changed.

Q. What are the ordinary hours of a guard or keeper?—A. According to the new Act, they should begin at 7 o'clock in the morning from October 15, but we continued until about a week ago to come at 6.30, but since then we have been coming at 6.15.

Q. What are the hours of closing?—A. The gong sounds at fifteen minutes to 5 for the close of the prison, and the officers are entitled to leave their posts and go home at 5.30. That happens during the short hours now.

Q. That is to say, you have about ten and a half hours duty a day?—A. Yes, and in summer time eleven and a half hours.

Q. Is there any going out for lunch?—A. At noon some of the staff go, but quite a number have to remain on duty. An officer who is detailed for dining hall duty is on from the time he begins in the morning till he goes off at night, because when he goes in with his gang for dinner he has to take up a post to see that they pass properly.

Q. All the guards and keepers are not on duty in the dining hall?—A. No.

Q. What are the ordinary guard's hours of work?—A. He has an hour off for dinner.

Q. Then he has eleven and a half hours duty less an hour for meals?—A. Yes.'

Q. Is that every day?—A. Every day during the summer season. On all these points I am not the best posted man here. I am allowed the privilege of going home for dinner every day at noon.

Q. I want to know what are your hours of work. They are ten and a half hours a day in the summer?—A. Yes, they are my hours.

Q. Have you a uniform?—A. Yes.

Q. You have a winter and a summer uniform?—A. Yes.

Q. There are no perquisites now allowed to the minor officials; for instance, do you occupy any place free of rent?—A. No.

Q. Do you get any supplies out of the garden?—A. Nothing whatever, except what I pay for.

Q. But you pay for them at cost price, do you not?—A. No, the market price.

Q. Do you not get anything at cost price from the penitentiary—for instance, if you wanted a bit of furniture?—A. Anything manufactured in the prison we get at cost price with ten per cent added.

Q. Mr. Moylan said before the Commission in 1892: 'We have our own tailor shop and our own shoe shop for the manufacture of clothing for the prison. The Minister of Justice has extended to the officers of the prison the privilege of getting at penitentiary prices whatever is made.' Is that still in force?—A. Yes.

Q. You get nothing from the produce of the soil?—A. No, except at market prices.

Q. Then it amounts to this, that you get your salaries and your uniforms free, and certain things at market prices?—A. Yes, if we wish to take them.

Mr. BEAUPRE.—Outsiders have the same privilege.

Q. (To the witness). You get clothing and shoes if you wish at cost price?—A. Yes, with ten per cent added. Everybody gets the same.

Q. The man outside the prison could not get clothing and boots from the prison at cost price with ten per cent added?—A. Yes, a few do through the medium of an officer.

Q. Do the 15,000 people in Kingston get their clothing and boots at the Kingston Penitentiary?—A. One or two may, but that is all; is not that so, Father McDonald?

Rev. Mr. McDONALD.—Yes, some do—the officers' friends.

Q. (To Mr. Caughey). Then, the officers get their salaries, which were increased about twenty per cent two years ago, their uniforms free, and their boots and shoes if they wish to take them at cost of manufacture plus ten per cent?—A. They get boots and shoes free as well as uniforms.

Q. How did you get your appointment?—A. From the Minister of Justice.

Q. The Minister of Justice had not a personal acquaintance with you; who originated the appointment?—A. I wrote an official application to him.

Q. Who did you send it through?—A. The warden.

Q. Did the warden know you?—A. Yes.

Q. Were you introduced to the warden by anybody?—A. I was on the staff as a guard.

Q. Then this vacancy occurring the warden recommended you, and you got the appointment?—A. Yes.

Q. How long were you as a guard before you became assistant superintendent of binder twine?—A. I was on the staff since August 1903.

Q. How did you get appointed to the lower position in August, 1903?—A. Through a regular application.

Q. Did the warden appoint you?—A. My notice of appointment came from the warden.

Q. Did you apply to the warden?—A. No, direct to the Minister, I think. I was an outsider when I was appointed as a guard.

Q. The Act says: 'The Governor in Council may appoint, for any penitentiary, a warden and a deputy warden, who shall hold their offices during pleasure. The Minister may appoint, or authorize the appointment of such other officers as may be necessary for the proper administration and police of any penitentiary.' How did you come to get your appointment in 1903? The Minister of Justice did not know you; did some political friend make the recommendation?—A. I asked two or three political friends in Napanee to recommend me.

Q. To recommend you to the warden?—A. Yes.

Q. And the warden sent down the recommendation?—A. I suppose he did.

Q. Originally you got political friends to back up your application to the warden?—A. Yes.

Q. Is that the general practice in the appointment of guards?—A. I do not know.

Q. In the old time I think the warden appointed the guards?

29a—36

Mr. BEAUPRE.—Yes.

Q. Has that practice been changed lately?

Mr. BEAUPRE.—Yes.

Q. How long ago has that been changed?

Mr. BEAUPRE.—By the last Act.

Q. Then since 1906, the old practice of the warden appointing the guards has been changed, and since then the guards have been appointed by the department at Ottawa?

Mr. BEAUPRE.—Yes.

Q. How many prisoners are there in the Kingston Penitentiary?

Mr. CAUGHEY.—About 460.

Q. How many of them are under twenty years of age?—A. I do not know.

Q. I suppose you did not read an article in the Ottawa *Citizen* this morning pointing out that one of the gravest condition of affairs in Canada is the number of juvenile offenders in the penitentiaries?—A. I did not read that.

Q. Father McDonald, what is the proportion of juvenile offenders in the penitentiary?

Father McDONALD.—The number is very large, compared with the number of seniors or adults, and larger than it should be, and I notice that the number is increasing. Boys are there of from fifteen to sixteen years of age, sent there for most petty and trifling offences. The last report, that of 1906, gives the total number of prisoners under twenty years of age as 156, out of a total of 1,423 in all the penitentiaries of the Dominion; that is about 11 per cent.

Q. (To Mr. Caughey.) In your memorial you call attention to the disabilities under which the guard suffers in the way of danger to his life. Has there been any instance in the last few years of a guard being killed in the exercise of his duty?—A. Not that I remember.

Q. Yet you think the danger is always apparent?—A. The danger is apparent.

Q. How many guards and keepers are there in the penitentiary?—A. About 57.

Q. How many of these are on during the day and how many at night?—A. There are 10 guards and a chief night watchman on duty at night.

Q. That is to say, 11 are on duty at night, as against 46 in the daytime?—A. Yes.

Q. Are the guards shifted around week and week about?—A. There is a permanent night staff now. Part of the staff is permanent, and they are trying to make it all permanent. They are not shifted.

Q. Is that the present policy of the department?—A. Yes, under the new Act.

Q. Of course, all the prisoners are out of their cells in the daytime?—A. Nearly all.

Q. Except those that are sick?—A. Except those that are sick or insane.

Q. How many are insane?—A. Between thirty and thirty-five.

Q. I thought there was a provision that the insane prisoners went to Rockwood?

Rev. Mr. McDONALD.—Not the criminal insane; the public protested against it.

Q. Are these criminal insane generally of homicidal mania?

Mr. CAUGHEY.—Yes, generally.

Q. In the last few years has there been any concerted riot or attack by the prisoners on the guards?—A. Yes.

Q. How long ago?—A. In November, 1904, I was attacked myself, with another officer, on the road by four men. Two attacked me, and two attacked him.

Q. Where were you then?—A. I was working on the road just back of the prison wall.

Q. You had a rifle, I suppose?—A. No. The guard with me had a rifle. I had a revolver.

Q. I thought the guards on the outside and on the walls had firearms?—A. So they have; but I was working in the capacity of an instructor, showing the men how

' make the road, and it is not safe for a man in close proximity to the prisoners to urry anything except a revolver.

Q. You have this constant danger always hanging over your heads?—A. Yes.

Q. Has there been any attack on an officer, except this case, that you can recollect ι the last few years?—A. Yes. In the spring of 1903, Guard Kenny was attacked ι the binder twine factory by a convict, who made a slash at him with a knife, touch-ιg his face and making a slight abrasion. The assistant matron was also attacked ιd cut over the shoulder—that was before my time.

Q. Then, your plea for consideration is based, not only on the long hours and the se in the cost of living, but on the danger of your occupation?—A. Yes.

Q. We will now come to the question of gratuities; a system of gratuities is laid ιwn by the Act?—A. Will you permit Mr. Beaupré, who is much my senior and is ιtter posted on the matter of gratuities than I am, to answer to that.

Q. What are the Sunday hours?—A. The bell for opening the prison rings at 7.45 m. Then, the prisoners get their breakfast and go to the chapel, and are usually out ιtween 10 and 10.30.

Q. Are all the 46 guards and keepers on duty on Sunday?—A. Not all of them.

Q. How many are on Sunday duty?—A. Perhaps 10 less than on week days.

Q. That is, about 36 are on Sunday duty?—A. Yes.

Q. What becomes of the prisoners when they come out of chapel?—A. They go to ,eir cells. They are all supposed to attend chapel.

Q. They have no other duties on Sunday?—A. No, except those in the kitchen.

Q. How do they spend the hours of Sunday when they are not in chapel? Is liter-ure given to them?—A. Yes, reading.

Q. Can they write their letters on Sunday?—A. Yes.

Q. Do guards look after the letters coming to the prisoners?—A. The warden's erk does.

Q. The guards are off every fourth Sunday?

Mr. WHEELER.—Yes, about every fourth Sunday. We have 39 Sundays out of 52.

Q. What is the curtailment of perquisites you draw attention to in your memorial, hat aditional perquisites had you in the old time that are now curtailed?—A. That a question on which Mr. Beaupré would perhaps be able to give you more definite ιformation than I can.

Q. Mr. Moylan, formerly inspector of penitentiaries, who was before the Civil ervice Commission in 1892, was asked this question : 'You state that the wardens ppoint the guards, but you recommend that the guards in future should be appointed ι some other manner, such as being recruited from the Dominion Police or the [ounted Police ? We want some improvement, and the idea struck me the other even-ιg in considering that question.' If the wardens in the old time appointed the guards ithout any political pressure, while the guards are now appointed by the department, would seem that there is more room for improvement now than there was in 1892?

Mr. BEAUPRÉ.—I am in a position to state that the warden did not have the sole ppointment, even as far back as 1885. He was subject to the recommendation of the ιliticians.

Q. Then as well as now?

Mr. BEAUPRÉ.—Yes, I know it, because I nearly lost my job.

Q. Mr. Moylan was also asked this question : 'There is no political influence rought to bear upon the wardens—they are left free ?—A. Of course I only know it ·om hearsay, that politicians endeavour to get some of their candidates appointed to ιe penitentiary service; but as a rule, under the instructions of the department, and ith his own sense of responsibility, the warden will not accept any such candidate ιless he be morally convinced of his suitability for the position to which he is to be ιpointed.'

29a—36½

Mr. Caughey.—That refers to the past, prior to the present arrangement. Of course, he admits that there is a possibility of political influence.

Q. He says, ' I only know it from hearsay,' but the warden, being responsible, will not accept any candidate unless he is morally convinced of his suitability for the position. How are matters in that respect now ?—A. I think the warden has power yet to reject a man who is not suitable. An officer is on three months' probation, and if he is not suitable the warden will not recommend him to be permanently appointed.

Q. Mr. Moylan was further asked: ' But a Member of Parliament cannot recommend with any more authority than any other individual ?——No.

' That is, there is no pressure exercised upon the wardens by the Minister to appoint any one that a politician recommends ?——No. On the contrary, the instructions to all the wardens are that they shall use their own judgment in their appointments.

' The Minister gives them a free hand to appoint their own officers——Yes.

' It never happens that the Minister himself recommends any one to be appointed by the warden ?——No.'

Mr. Beaupré.—I can name two officers in the Kingston Penitentiary who came there in 1885 on a recommendation from Sir John Macdonald to appoint them on the staff.

Q. (To Mr. Caughey.) When you were appointed did you undergo any medical examination as a test for health ?—A. Yes.

Q. And for eye sight ?—A. Yes. I was examined by a regularly qualified physician.

Q. Not by the doctor in the penitentiary ?—A. No.

Q. There is a doctor in the penitentiary ?—A. There is a surgeon there.

Q. You were examined outside ?—A. I was.

Q. Is it the rule to examine by outside doctors ?—A. No.

Q. The penitentiary physician generally examines the guards that are appointed ? —A. Yes.

Q. Are the guards drilled steadily ?—A. Yes, quite regularly.

Q. What kind of drill is it?—A. Military movements and the handling of arms.

Q. Are there any old soldiers or military men among the guards ?—A. Yes, young soldiers—young volunteers.

Q. Is there a standard of height ?—A. Yes, 5 feet 9 inches.

Q. And a standard of measurement around the chest ?—A. Yes, and a standard of weight—I am not sure what it is.

Q. Has the number of the staff of the penitentiary increased in the past few years?—A. No, it has remained about the same. The personnel have been about 460 for four or five years.

Q. When the prison gets full, do you send convicts to the St. Vincent de Paul Penitentiary?—A. No, but they send them to us.

Q. How many prisoners will the Kingston Penitentiary contain?

Mr. Reid.—If they are doubled up it could accommodate 800 or 900.

Q. Are there any annual increases in the salaries of guards ?—A. No.

Q. Are they always appointed at $600 ?—A. They are appointed at a lesser salary while they are temporary guards.

Q. When they become permanent guards they get the $600?—A. Yes.

Q. And after they are appointed at $600 they remain at $600?—A. Yes.

Q. Do any of your guards leave to go into other service—are there many resignations?—A. Some.

Q. What do they generally become?—A. They sometimes go back to their former occupations.

By Mr. Fyshe:

Q. Do the guards live very far from the prison?—A. A few blocks away. Some of them who own property in the city live about a mile away.

SESSIONAL PAPER No. 29a

By the Chairman:

Q. In the winter, even those living a mile away, in order to be at the prison at 7.30 have to get up and dress in the dark?—A. They certainly have. Even to go from where I live, I have to get up in the dark.

Q. Have the guards and yourself any leave of absence in the year?—A. Yes.

Q. How much?—A. Two weeks.

Q. Who gives you the leave?—A. The warden.

Q. Is it so arranged that there shall be a sufficient number of the staff left?—A. Oh, yes.

Q. Do you draw lots or ballot for the leave of absence?—A. We ballot for it, but even then the warden will not let a man go if he thinks the safety of the prison requires him to remain.

Q. Are you still manufacturing binder twine in the prison?—A. Yes. Just now we are repairing the machinery.

Q. You sell the binder twine to the public?—A. To the farmers.

Q. Do you sell it chiefly in the immediate neighbourhood, or do you ship it out? —A. Most of our shipments in past seasons have been to the Northwest.

By Mr. Fyshe:

Q. Do you sell to traders as well as to farmers?—A. Not that I know of—only to farmers and to farmers' clubs.

By the Chairman:

Q. Who is Mr. Keene, of Edmonton?—A. I do not know.

Q. Who is Mr. Edwards, of Strathcona?

Mr. CAUGHEY.—I do not know. I have nothing to do with the shipping, only with the manufacturing and the machinery. The superintendent looks after the shipping.

Q. Have you anything else in your own particular line to tell us?—A. No, unless perhaps that my own department is being run to-day at less cost than it was ten or twelve years ago. It is being run to-day by a superintendent, an assistant superintendent and a guard, whereas there used to be four officers, and the total cost now is $2,600, whereas it used to be $3,200 or $3,400.

Q. I suppose you know nothing about the purchase of the manilla?—A. Not sufficient to give you the data.

Mr. P. M. BEAUPRE called, sworn and examined.

By the Chairman:

Q. You are a trade instructor at Kingston Penitentiary?—A. Yes.

Q. You are not the chief trade instructor?—A. No, sir.

Q. There is only one chief trade instructor at Kingston?—A. Yes, only one chief instructor.

Q. That official gets $1,000 a year?—A. Yes.

Q. The ordinary trade instructor gets $800 a year?—A. Yes.

Q. That is your salary, I presume?—A. Yes.

Q. How many instructors have you got at Kingston?—A. Eight, I think.

Q. According to the Auditor General's Report there is Mr. Burns, chief instructor, and the following instructors: Mr. Cowan, baker; Mr. McCaugherty, farmer; Mr. Walter, blacksmith; Mr. Beaupré, quarryman, and Mr. Lawlor, stonecutter. They are employed all the year round. Then there are some employed for broken periods—Mr. McCarthy, assistant farmer; Mr. Paynter, shoemaker; Mr. Young, mason; Mr. Tweddell?—A. Yes.

Q. Are they employed all the year round?—A. They have been since their appointment.

7-8 EDWARD VII., A. 1908

Q. The list I have read makes nine instructors?—A. Since that report was published Mr. Cowan has been moved to the west. He is now steward and baker in the Alberta Penitentiary.

Q. Is there no baker in the Kingston Penitentiary now?—A. Not now. The steward has to look after the baking.

Q. Then there are eight trade instructors receiving $800 a year each?—A. Yes, sir.

Q. Mr. Caughey stated that you could tell us more about the working of the system of gratuities?—A. It is very simple, sir. The Act explains it.

Q. Under the Act if you desire any change in the matter of gratuities, an amendment would have to be brought in. You are aware of that?—A. Yes.

Q. The gratuities are laid down under the Act?—A. Yes.

Q. The gratuities are arrived at in this way: if a retirement takes place, a gratuity may be given, calculated at the rate of a half month's salary for each year of service up to five years, and a month's salary for each year of service in excess of five years, based on the salary that such officer was in receipt of at the time of his retirement. How many years have you been in the Kingston Penitentiary?—A. Twenty-two years and ten months.

Q. Then, if you are getting a salary of $800 a year, that is $66.66 a month. Upon retirement you would receive half a month's pay for each of the first five years, and after that a month's pay for each subsequent year of service?—A. Yes.

Q. Then, $1,366.66 is what you would receive as gratuity?—A. That is the exact figure, sir.

Q. What suggestions do you make in regard to the system of gratuities?—A. We think, sir, that an officer should get at retirement what he is entitled to, and in case of sudden death, or anything like that, his family or dependents should receive the gratuity. That is the only point we wish to make in connection with the gratuity.

Q. Is there not something in the Act providing for increase of gratuity in the event of the officer receiving a gun-shot wound or some injury that disables him. For example, subsection 2 of section 35 of the Act respecting Penitentiaries provides as follows:—' Such retiring allowance may be increased by one-half the amount thereof if the infirmity which compels such officer to retire from the service is occasioned by any injury received by him in the performance of his duty without fault or negligence on his part, &c. So that, if you were permanently disabled in your right arm, for instance, by a gun-shot wound, one-half would be added to the gratuity?—A. As the Government see fit.

Q. Well, the Act lays it down?—A. Yes.

Q. In such a case you would get about $2,050. Now, how do you think the Act should be amended?—A. You stopped at the critical portion of it.

Q. Well, go on?—A. You would have reached the point, if you had continued reading the subsection. It goes on to say, or rather the subsection following does, 'If any officer dies in the service leaving a widow——

Q. I was coming to that, but I wanted to ascertain your views about the gratuity to the man himself before taking up the case of the widow. Have you anything to say as to the desirability of amending the Act relating to the gratuity to the officer?—A. No, sir, that seems satisfactory.

Q. Then, we come to the next clause: ' If any officer dies in the service leaving a widow or any person who in his lifetime was dependent on him, a gratuity may be paid to such widow, if any, and if not, to any person or persons in the lifetime of such officer dependent on him,' &c. The gratuity is not to exceed the amount of salary of such officer for the two months next preceding his death, if he was appointed by the Governor in Council or for the three months preceding his death, if he was appointed by the Minister or the warden?—A. That is the point.

Q. Then if you died in harness, the widow would only get two months' pay?—A. That is the weak point of that clause.

Q. Or in certain events the widow might get three months' pay?—A. Just the limit.

Q. Subsection 4 provides that such gratuity may be increased by one-half the amount thereof, if the death of such officer has been occasioned by any injury received by him in the performance of his duty, without fault or negligence on his part, at the hands of any convict, or in preventing an escape or rescue, or in suppressing a revolt? —A. Yes. Take it at my age, for instance——

Q. I am talking about the gratuities for widows. If you were shot or disabled, and certified to it, you could get your own gratuity increased by one-half, and if you were shot and died from the effects of the injury, your widow might get her gratuity increased?—A. Yes, to four and a half months.

Q. Four and a half months or three months?—A. There is another weak point in connection with the gratuity.

Q. Tell us what amendment you think should be made to the Act in connection with the gratuity to the widow?—A. We think that when an officer dies in the service or in harness, his widow or any others dependent upon him should receive the gratuity that he would be entitled to.

Q. Then, your idea is, that the gratuity which the officer might have received if he were alive, should be given to the widow, or other dependents, if he dies?—A. Exactly.

Mr. FYSHE.—That seems only just.

Mr. RED.—That is after twenty-three years' service in Mr. Beaupré's case.

By the Chairman:

Q. You think that if you were to die to-morrow, your widow should receive the same gratuity that you would have got had you retired, disabled, yourself?—A. Precisely. Furthermore, if I retire from the service on account of ill-health, I should get my gratuity because I have rendered faithful service to the department. In some cases they have refused to allow officers to retire. If they do retire, it is at their own risk, and they are not allowed their gratuity. In connection with the last clause of the Act just referred to, we have known cases where the cheque actually arrived at the penitentiary, but the officer had died between the time of his resignation and the arrival of the cheque, and the cheque was returned to the department. If that is not a hardship, I do not know what is. I know a case where a guard died who had something like $2,000 coming to him. His wife had not $50 to pay the undertaker's expenses, and all she got was three months' pay. In that case the cheque was a few hours late in arriving. Another case was that of Mr. Elsmere.

Q. You are paid monthly?—A. Yes.

Q. This is November 7. If you were to die to-morrow would the full pay for November be given to your widow?—A. Excuse me for seeming a little frivolous, but I have had not had any such experience. The pay ceases and the case is handed over to the department to deal with. That is what has happened in the past. Excuse me for seeming a little frivolous.

Q. That is all right. Here in Ottawa the pay for the month of November would go to the widow?—A. It is not so in cases at the penitentiary. I know of instances where the pay has ceased upon the death of the officer. The department was then notified and they made arrangements as to gratuity or allowance such as seemed fit to them to give.

Q. You say a cheque came to the penitentiary after the man was dead. When do you get your cheques?—A. On the last day of the month.

Q. When did the man die in the case that you say the cheque arrived late?—A. That was a cheque for the amount of the man's gratuity.

Q. Then after the gratuity had been allowed to the man, he having died before receiving it, the cheque was returned and the widow did not get anything?—A. She did not.

Mr. FYSHE.—Supposing the cheque had been delayed through the neglect of the department at Ottawa?

By the Chairman:

Q. The matter might have been delayed a week when the man was hovering between life and death?—A. I must say that the department has been prompt in forwarding cheques but in former years—the years I have been referring to for purposes of comparison—they were very slow about it. It would be a week or two weeks, sometimes before the cheque would arrive at Kingston, and in the meantime the officer died, and his family were without the money.

Q. You are au fait in regard to the gratuities. Are there any other points you desire to bring to our notice?—A. No, sir, nothing in particular.

Q. Take the gratuity to the widow of an officer to the amount of his salary for the three months next preceding his death, if he was appointed by the Minister or warden. Who does that apply to?—A. I would infer from the wording of the subsection that it would be either the one or the other.

Q. That applies to officers who were living at the time the Act was passed who had been appointed by the warden?—A. I presume so.

Q. Since this Act has been passed the warden does not make any appointments at all?—A. The Act does not allow this.

Mr. REID.—At the time that came into force the Minister appointed certain officers and the warden appointed the guards.

By the Chairman:

Q. That is what I am coming to. Somebody said here that the warden did not appoint guards previous to this Act coming into force?—A. In some cases he did, but in other cases he appointed subject to recommendation the same as in the case of Mr. Caughey.

Q. Supposing I were to write to the warden and say, 'I know a good man who has been an English soldier. Could you not do something for him?' It would be entirely within the warden's discretion to make that appointment, would it not?—A. At the present time?

Q. Yes?—A. No, he has not got the power of appointing guards now.

Q. You are an old officer, have you always been instructor?—A. No, sir.

Q. How long have you been an instructor?—A. Two years and some months.

Q. Before that you were always a guard?—A. Not, keeper.

Q. You were always a keeper?—A. No, sir; part of the time keeper, and part of the time guard.

Q. You were always a guard or keeper in your twenty-one years' service until you became a trade instructor?—A. Yes, sir. My first appointment was on January 10, 1885, and I served fourteen years and seven months as a guard. On August 1, 1899, I was appointed keeper and served in that capacity five years and eight months. On March, 27, 1905, I was appointed instructor, and I have been in that position now for two years and ten months.

Q. You have filled the offices of guard, keeper and trade instructor. Looking at the matter as an outsider, is the discipline in the penitentiary as good now as it was in the olden time?—A. Yes, and in many respects better.

Q. Although the political system is in full vogue?—A. I do not know what would cause a difference. In many respects the discipline is better now.

Q. How often do the inspectors go around to see you?—A. At various times. Perhaps three or four times a year, sometimes oftener; it depends how matters are running there.

Q. Do both of the inspectors visit you or only one?—A. We have had both in the last year.

Q. Do they come together or separately?—A. Separately generally.

Q. Who generally visits you, Mr. Stewart or Mr. Dawson ?—A. Mr. Dawson comes oftener than Mr. Stewart.

Q. Mr. Dawson is a new appointment ?—A. Yes.

Q. Do you think there are enough guards for the population of the penitentiary? —A. I would not care to express an opinion on it.

Q. Have you anything else to tell us, Mr. Beaupré ?—A. No, sir, I do not know of anything further.

The witness retired.

Mr. M. P. REID, called, sworn and examined.

By the Chairman :

Q. What is the difference between a keeper and a guard ?—A. The keepers do the locking and the guards do the watching over the convicts. The keepers are generally detailed in charge of the shops also.

Q. Does the keeper lock the convict in his cell at night?—A. He does and also counts all the prisoners.

Q. And in the morning the keepers unlock the cells and let the convicts out ?— A. Yes, they unlock the cells.

Q. What other duties do the keepers perform ?—A. Those are their duties.

Q. What other duties do the keepers perform between the hours occupied by the duties you have enumerated ?—A. They are in charge of the shops and gangs.

Q. Then they are the officers that are brought a good deal into contact with the convicts ?—A. Yes, and they are responsible for the men. They are amongst them all the time.

Q. Are you on duty at night ?—A. No, I am in charge of the north gate.

Q. Do you lock up the prisoners in their cells ?—A. I have not done so these last two years. I am responsible for what goes in and out the prison and I am also in charge of the armoury.

Q. There is a limitation of the number of the people entering the penitentiary is there not ?—A. Yes, sir.

Q. How does the ordinary person who wants to see the penitentiary obtain a pass? —A. They have a system that no visitors are allowed. That is the rule. But suppose you have a friend coming to Kingston and you are personally acquainted with the warden. This friend comes to you and asks for a letter of introduction to the warden from you. Well, if the warden has confidence enough in you to know that you would not give the visitor a letter unless he was all right they would simply show him a portion of the prison. They would not allow the prisoner into any of the shops at all but simply show him the outside of the buildings and the cells and the churches. He would be given a bird's eye view in fact.

Q. Visitors would not get close to the prisoners ?—A. No, they do not come into touch with them.

Q. They could not pass any tobacco or things of that kind to the prisoner ?—A. No. They might try it but the officer in charge would be responsible and if visitors were caught at such a thing they would be punished. Of course, the officers on the watch to guard against anything of that kind.

Q. How long have you been in the penitentiary ?—A. Ten years on the 15th of next month.

Q. Is the keeping of the gate considered more important than the ordinary duty of locking and unlocking the cells?—A. Yes, it is considered a responsible position.

Q. You have to look after the ingress and egress of all parties ?—A. Yes, sir. If a prisoner happens to dress himself in another suit and gets by the gate I am up against it. That is all.

7-8 EDWARD VII., A. 1908

Q. You are always on the *qui vive* to see that no prisoners escape ?—A. Yes, sir.

Q. Occasionally a man does escape ?—A. Very seldom.

Q. When a convict does escape is it by climbing the wall or running through the gateway ?—A. Not through the gateway.

Q. Well, how does a convict escape ? I think I read a case where a convict got out and took a boat and got off ?—A. That was a case of a convict cutting the bars of his cell and getting out and climbing over the wall.

Q. Then convicts have climbed the wall ?—A. That was done at night.

By Mr. Fyshe :

Q. How could the convict get over the wall ?—A. He could scale the wall with a rope. By assistance in some shape or form he obtains possession of a rope and gets over the wall.

Q. How would he fasten the rope ?—A. I can give you an instance, to make a long story short, of the only escape we have had in that way, I suppose, for a great number of years. We had a man in the penitentiary who, after several weeks' work, used the shank of a boot and made a small saw out of it. By means of this saw he sawed through the bars a space large enough to crawl out. He worked at this at night for several weeks. When any of the officers would be around the convict would put back the bar and fasten it up with some black stuff. When the officer would leave the convict, knowing that he would not be back possibly for another hour, went to work again. He kept on sawing in that way until he had a hole large enough to get out. He then worked on the outside bars on the same plan. Then he took some cords and made a rope and lowered himself into the yard. That rope he threw over the wall, making a hook out of the handle of a pail. When the rope was thrown over the wall it caught in the coping, which enabled him to scale the wall and get away.

By the Chairman :

Q. How long did the operation go on ?--A. Three or four weeks, according to his own statement.

By Mr. Fyshe :

Q. Did he succeed in getting away?—A. He did, but he was landed back again in a short time.

Rev. FATHER McDONALD.—It should be mentioned here that the convict in question was an inmate of the asylum and therefore, the surveillance over him was not as strict in a sense.

By the Chairman :

Q. I was coming to that. If a man works at night at bars of his own cell how can he be fit to do any work in the daytime?—A. In this case he was not called upon to do any work. This man got a boat to cross from one shore to the other. There happened to be a vessel unloading coal and he took the boat and crossed to the other side.

By Mr. Fyshe :

Q. If the bars in the window of that man's cell had been made of steel he could not have sawn them?—A. They were old bars that had been in for years that he worked on. The bars now being put in are made of steel.

By the Chairman :

Q. Have you anything to say as regards the payment of keepers suffering from any disability?—A. Our position is just the same as theirs.

Q. Is there anything with respect to your own duties, that we have not yet heard, that you would like to say?—A. No, there is nothing. If you wish to hear it I have a separate statement to present to you.

Q. Oh, certainly?—A. It is on behalf of one of the officers. He is a good servant, and I cannot express myself too strongly in his behalf.

By Mr. Fyshe :

Q. The statement is signed by M. J. Kennedy?—A. Yes, he is a messenger in the penitentiary.

(Statement read and filed.)

• Q. Is this man not in the service now?—A. Yes, he is in the service now.

By the Chairman :

Q. Why did they take his quarters from him?—A. He lived at the west gate. We have a north gate and a west gate.

Q. I suppose the quarters he occupied were wanted?—A. No, the house was tumbling down.

By Mr Fyshe :

Q. They should have compensated him for that?—A. Yes. That is why I have presented this separate statement in his behalf. I also wish to state that this man was one of the very few that did not receive an increase of pay under the last Act that went through. Why that was I am at a loss to know, because there is no better servant in the penitentary than that man.

Q. You say he is a good man?—A. He is a splendid fellow.

By the Chairman :

Q. Is there only one messenger?—A. Only one messenger, and he is on deck every day. He is at the call of the penitentiary at all hours.

Q. Your salary is $700?—A. Yes, $700.

The witness retired.

Mr. M. P. REID, recalled.

By the Chairman:

Q. How old are you?—A. I am thirty-six years of age.

Q. How does it happen that you became a keeper so early in life while Mr. Wheeler despite his age is still a guard?—A. There was a new position created. In the first place I was guard and gatekeeper. Then I was given charge of the armoury and received $50 a year for that, making my salary $550—$500 as guard and $50 for looking after the armoury. The position of gatekeeper and armourer was created under the last Bill. They appointed me to it, making me responsible for the arms and for everything going in and out of the prison. In that way they made my position more responsible.

Q. Then in the ordinary course of things a keeper would naturally be older than a guard?—A. Yes, it depends upon length of service.

Q. And as the keepers go off the guards get promotion in point of seniority?—A. Yes.

Q. Then promotion from guard to keeper means an additional $100 a year, and upon retirement an increased gratuity based upon salary?—A. Yes, sir.

The witness retired.

Mr. C. WHEELER, called, sworn and examined.

By the Chairman:

Q. How long have you been employed at the Kingston Penitentiary?—A. Fifteen and a quarter years.

Q. The old scale of pay for guards was $500, was it not?—A. Yes, sir.

Q. When you were appointed were you appointed as guard?—A. Yes, sir.

Q. Then you were appointed at $500?—A. No, $400.

Q. That was as temporary guard?—A. No, I was a full guard. I only received $400 for the first two years because I was appointed after the 1st July. If I had been appointed in June I would only have been one year at $400.

Q. You were appointed after the beginning of the fiscal year?—A. Yes, sir.

Q. Then you got a raise from $400 to $500?—A. I got a raise from $400 to $430. We had a small increase that year, and next year our pay was raised to $460.

Q. Then you got $500?—A. No. $490, and then $500.

Q. Now you get $600?—A. Now I get $600.

. You are one of the men that go on duty at 6.30 in the morning?—A. Yes.

. And in winter at 7?—A. Yes.

Q. You are supplied with uniforms like the rest of the officers?—A. Yes.

Q. How many uniforms do you get a year?—A. Two. A coat and pants and shoes, but no vest.

Q. But the coat buttons over?—A. It buttons up close.

. You get caps, I suppose?—A. Yes.

. Do you not get overcoats besides the two suits?—A. Every fourth winter.

. Do you get fur caps?—A. Yes, sir.

Q. How often do you get a fur cap?—A. We get a fur cap when it is necessary.

Q. How many pairs of boots do you get a year?—A. Two pairs.

Q. Are you supplied with heavy boots for winter and lighter boots for the summer?—A. We get lighter boots in the summer, but there is not much difference.

Q. Then beyond your uniform you get nothing in the way of extras?—A. No, sir.

Q. You get your salary and your uniform?—A. Just salary and uniform.

Q. There is no such thing as getting extra time, for instance, in the penitentiary?—A. No, sir.

Q. If by chance there was an emeute or a fire, or a rising of convicts, and you were employed after your ordinary day's work, would there be any pay for overtime?—A. No, sir.

Q. Has it occasionally happened that you have been on duty beyond the fixed hours?—A. Yes. For instance, whenever there is a guard suspended we have to take up his duty. That is we have to be there at night in his place.

Rev. Fatther McDONALD.—Or if a guard is sick.

Q. How did you work it out that in July last one man worked 382 hours and 385 hours in August, making 767 hours in two months?—A. Some men are twenty-four hours on duty. A man would be on as long as thirty-six hours.

Q. But in the computation of 767 hours Sunday is included?—A. Yes, Sunday is included.

Q. That would be about thirteen hours a day?—A. It would not be thirteen hours a day, would it?

Q. Pretty nearly thirteen hours. How could you manage that?—A. We were twenty-four hours on duty part of the time. I suppose that is how we managed it.

Q. Do you mean to say that during this time some men were on duty for twenty-four hours?—A. We are there on duty but we sleep part of the time.

Q. Then twenty-four hours on duty means you were in the penitentiary, and not at your home? During part of that time you might have been in the guard-room asleep?—A. Yes.

Q. Just like a soldier who is on duty in the guard-room, he is allowed to sleep there part of the time?—A. Yes, sir.

Q. So that when you speak of a man being 767 hours on duty, you do not mean that he was absolutely walking about or looking after the convicts all the time, but was in the guard-room?

Rev. Father McDONALD.—On duty and ready to be called.

Q. That is all right enough. Have you always been a guard?—A. Yes, sir, always a guard.

Q. The next step for the guard is that of keeper, I suppose?—A. Yes, sir.

Q. When one of the keepers retires or dies, is a guard generally promoted to the vacancy?—A. Yes, sir.

Q. Are you pretty nearly at the top of the list of guards?—A. Pretty close to it.

Q. How old are you, if one may ask?—A. I am fifty-five years of age.

Q. Then, the probability is you will be a keeper in a very short time and getting another hundred dollars a year?—A. I cannot tell about that.

By Mr. Fyshe:

Q. Have you to retire at any specified date?—A. It used to be the case. They claim now there is no age limit, but there used to be.

Q. Then, you would be kept on as long as you were fit?—A. Yes, sir.

Q. Have you anything else to tell us, Mr. Wheeler?—A. Well, the farm instructor wished me to mention his case.

Q. He is in the same category as Mr. Beaupré—A. Yes.

Q. What is the particular point you wish to bring to our attention?—A. At the time he got his appointment, he was allowed the use of a house and light.

Q. Who is the gentleman you are talking about?—A. Mr. McCaugherty.

Q. Has he no house now?—A. Yes, he has a house. They gave him an increase of $100 in salary, but charged him $100 rent for the house.

Q. Then, practically, he had no increase at all?—A. No increase at all.

Q. Before that he had a house free of rent?—A. Yes, free of rent before that.

Q. And they gave him an increase of salary according to the schedule of the Act, and charged him $100 for house rent?—A. Yes, sir.

Q. Do you know of any reason for that?—A. I do not.

Q. Have any of the other trade instructors houses free of rent?—A. The hospital overseer is the only one.

Q. They have rooms in the hospital, I suppose?—A. They have rooms in the hospital. The overseer lives there. They gave him an increase of $100 in salary and charged him $50 for rent.

Rev. Father McDONALD.—The reason for that is that all perquisites were cut off by the new Act.

Q. Is there anything else you wish to say?—A. Not that I know of.

The witness retired.

Rev. Father McDONALD, called, sworn and examined.

Witness presented a statement, which was read and filed.

By the Chairman:

Q. How long have you been at the Kingston Penitentiary?—A. Almost nine years. I was appointed in March, 1899.

Q. You are constantly in attendance at the penitentiary?—A. Yes.

Q. You have no other duties, except that of chaplain in the penitentiary?—A. Yes, I attend to the families of the guards.

Q. Well, practically, that is in connection with the penitentiary staff?—A. No, it is independent of the penitentiary staff.

Q. Do the families of the Roman Catholic guards attend the same religious services?—A. No, they have a church of their own.

Q. Outside of the prison?—A. Yes.

Q. You have no parochial duties?—A. Yes, in that way.

Q. You are not a parish priest?—A. Yes, I am supposed to be the parish priest of these people.

Q. You are not the parish priest of Portsmouth?—A. Yes, it is very largely composed of the families of guards, numbering about thirty-five families.

Q. One of the recommendations made by the late Inspector Moylan to the Civil Service Commission in 1892 was: 'The constant daily presence of the chaplains among the prisoners for the purpose of giving advice, instruction, and exhortation, not only at stated times, but whenever occasion for the exercise of these functions arise.' Has that been carried out?—A. Yes.

Q. What are your hours in the penitentiary?—A. I am there almost every day in the week.

Q. What time do you go in the morning?—A. I go in the morning between 9 and 10 o'clock, and sometimes between 10 and 11 o'clock. I go again in the afternoon.

By Mr. Fyshe:

Q. Your presence is obligatory, is it not?—A. In a strict sense of the word it is not. Then again it is.

Q. You have made it a practice to attend?—A. Yes.

By the Chairman:

Q. For the higher officers there are no fixed hours of duty?—A. No.

Q. But you are required to be there all the time?—A. I am there morning and afternoon and very often at night. I have to respond at any hour at all for a sick call or such like.

Q. Is there any attempt at isolation of the youthful convicts from the hardened criminals?—A. No, except in this way; if there be a discreet man in the shop in which the young boys are placed, they are generally put side by side with him to remove them as far as possible from the bad element. In this way a little provision has been made as far as they can provide it.

Q. But there is no utter isolation?—A. No.

Q. A hardened criminal may be in the next cell to a youthful prisoner?—A. Yes.

Q. And one of the great responsibilities that weighs upon you is that of endeavouring to reform the convicts?—A. The youth particularly.

Q. You stated earlier in the present sitting that 150 of the prison population in Kingston Penitentiaary were under thirty years of age?—A. That was the total for all the penitentiaries.

Q. Do you know how many prisoners in Kingston penitentiary are under twenty years of age?—A. I could not say just now.

Q. Would it be from fifteen to twenty per cent?—A. I see by the last report that it is only eleven per cent of the whole.

Q. But still the percentage is so large that it gives you a great deal of anxiety?—A. Yes, and it is larger than it has been in former years.

Q. That percentage of increase in youthful criminals is still going ahead?—A. Yes.

Q. Do you think there is anything that could check this growth of crime amongst the younger members of society?—A. I think that the judges are not discreet enough in that respect.

SESSIONAL PAPER No. 29a

Q. In what way?—A. In this way; that they jump too quickly at conclusions and in order to rid a place of this element they foist them upon the penitentiaries. They think it is better to get them out of the road without considering the consequences that will accrue therefrom.

By Mr. Fyshe:

Q. Have you considered the work of that Chicago judge of whom perhaps you have heard?—A. Yes, I have. I have sent for his pamphlets and placed them in the hands of our local magistrate. You mean, I suppose, Judge Lindsay, of Denver, Colorado.

Q. The judge I speak of is in Chicago?—A. Judge Lindsay was the originator of the juvenile court system.

Q. He is not the one I refer to?—A. I think the plan is the same at all events.

By the Chairman:

Q. The ticket of leave system is in force now throughout Canada?—A. Yes.

Q. It was not in force in 1892?—A. No.

Q. Do you know whether the introduction of that system has been beneficial?—A. Yes. We have only had two or three, possibly four, convicts who have returned to the penitentiary since it has been in vogue.

Q. Does a convict at Kingston Penitentiary get any share of his earnings at all? —A. No.

Q. Does a convict when he is released get no money that he may have earned?— A. Only sufficient money to send him back to the place from whence he was committed.

Q. Do you think it is desirable in order to encourage him to lead a better life, that he should have a share of what he has earned placed to his credit?—A. I do.

By Mr. Fyshe:

Q. You would not give him the whole of his earnings?—A. No, but I would give him something as an encouargement when he leaves the penitentiary. I have known parties that have expressed a desire upon their release to go elsewhere than to the place from whence they came, but they would not be given sufficient money for that purpose.

By the Chairman:

Q. No man in such a position wants to go back to the place he was brought up as a boy?—A. Not unless he was devoid of shame.

Mr. REID.—In many cases they go back to the same place and return to us again.

Q. Mr. Moylan in 1892 suggested the multiplication of trades and industries?—A. I think it would be good.

Q. Among the 460 convicts you have got in Kingston Pentitentiary, some of them must previously have been tailors, shoemakers and such like?—A. Yes, and a large percentage of the convicts are sent to the industries to learn a trade.

Q. Which they will drop the moment they are released?—A. Possibly they may.

Q. There is a way of getting around it, I suppose? For instance, what is Mr. McGill doing?—A. He is in the accountant's office. Mr. McGill and Mr. Duncan are both there.

By Mr. Fyshe:

Q. Where does Mr. Duncan come from?—A. He was the manager of a bank in the neighbourhood of Toronto. Mr. Rowley was manager of the Atlas Loan Company at St. Thomas. For a time Mr. Banwell, formerly of the Crown Bank, Toronto, was also in the office, but his health failed him and he has been transfered to outdoor work in the quarry.

Q. What does the work in the office amount to ?—A. The convicts there help the accountant to keep the books in connection with the binder twine manufacture and the general running of the penitentiary.

By the Chairman : .

Q. You would have more clerks in the office than they want ?—A. Exactly.

Q. Because you have not trades enough to go around you are obliged to put the convicts in the office ?—A. Yes. There is considerable office work in connection with the manufacture of binder twine.

By Mr. Fyshe :

Q. You ought to put some of these accountants at the shoemaking trade ?—A. It is discretionary with them sometimes. It is not obligatory always to put them in the accountant's office. Still if they happen to be appointed to the position they must accept or suffer the consequences of refusal.

By the Chairman :

Q. Another of Mr. Moylan's recommendations was that there should be a separate prison, wholly reformatory in its character and management, for persons convicted for the first time of any serious crime, between the ages of sixteen and thirty. Has that recommendation ever been carried out?—A. Never.

Q. I suppose you agree with that theory?—A. Yes, it was, I believe, suggested by our present warden in one of his reports—the possibility of its being done—but, of course, it would entail a great deal of expense.

Mr. WHEELER.—I believe they started to build a penitentiary somewhat on those lines at Alexandria.

Rev. Father McDONALD.—That was a reformatory.

By the Chairman :

•   Q. Although it might have been contemplated at one time the idea has never been carried out ?—A. Never.

Q. Do you not think it would be desirable for the people concerned ?—A. It would.

Q. It need not necessarily be very elaborate to begin with ?—A. No.

Q. A prison of a reformatory character might be instituted with advantage to the community ?—A. And it will meet with the general approval of the officers from the warden down. A matter of daily conversation at the penitentiary is the regret at having to witness the evidence that is there given of young boys being found continually with hardened criminals of all classes.

Q. Mr. Moylan, when before the Commission in 1892, stated that owing to structural defects in the penitentiaries, the isolation of bad and habitual criminals from comparative neophytes in crime had not been hitherto practicable. Do those structural defects still exist ?—A. There is a prison of isolation where they can isolate hardened criminals when they deem them deserving of such punishment. At the present time there are no such men in isolation from the fact that their behaviour has been such that they are not deemed deserving of such treatment.

Q. When before the Commission in 1892 Mr. Moylan was asked about the chaplains and their duties. You say that you have other duties in connection with the families of Roman Catholic guards. Is that generally the case with all the chaplains ?—A. I could not say.

Q. Has the Protestant chaplain any other duties ?—A. No.

Q. He gives all his time to the penitentiary and to the convicts?—A. Yes, but no more time than I do. The chapel, in connection with the church at Portsmouth, has a famous name. It is called ' The Church of the Good Thief.' It was erected in the days of Sir John Thompson for the purpose of accommodating the people of ertsmouth who were principally the families of guards, otherwise they would be liged to walk miles into the city to attend church on Sunday.

Q. Yes, I recollect that now ?—A. The Protestant chaplain is of the Anglican rsuasion and in Portsmouth there is an Anglican church attended to by an Anglican inister.

Q. Who is the Protestant chaplain?—A. Rev. A. W. Cook.

Q. Mr. Cook has no parish outside ?—A. No.

Q. The chaplains are still unprovided with houses?—A. They are still unprovided ith houses.

Q. Would it not be better, in order to have the chaplains there constantly, to prode them with residences within the penitentiary?—A. That rests with the Governent I presume.

Q. I know that, but what is your own idea ?—A. I do not know that there would anything, in a sense, gained by it, except that it would be more economical for us.

By Mr. Fyshe :

Q If you were acting as parish priest it would not be convenient for you ?—A. is only five minutes walk from my house to the penitentiary.

By the Chairman :

Q. In 1892 Mr. Moylan was asked : 'Do you think it advisable that the chaplains ould have houses and remain near at hand'? His reply was 'I do, just as they have t the Mountjoy prison at Dublin, which is conducted on the Crofton system. The ntinual presence of the chaplains at the prisons is of great advantage'?—A. We are nly within five minutes walk of the penitentiary.

Q. That might be by accident. You might be a mile or two miles off ?—A. That where we reside.

Q. But supposing your residence were a mile or two miles away I am taking it a rule ?—A. Precisely. Of course, there are some so situated, the chaplains elsehere I suppose. That is the case at Dorchester and Stony Mountain I believe.

Q. The salaries of the chaplains are unequal?—A. Yes.

Q. At Kingston Pentitentiary you get $1,200 each?—A. Yes.

Q. You have always got that amount?—A. Yes.

Q. What do the chaplains get at Dorchester Pentitentiary?—A. $1,000. The atholic chaplain got $600, and the Protestant chaplain more than that. I do not now why they discriminated between the two, but they were both raised to $1,000.

By Mr. Fyshe:

Q. It is probably because there were more Protestants than Catholics amongst the nvicts?—A. Or it may have been from the fact that the Protestant chaplain was earer the penitentiary and attended more frequently. There might have been some cal reasons.

By the Chairman:

Q. At St. Vincent de Paul Penitentiary, the two chaplains get $1,200 each?— Yes.

Q. You have got no increase in salary?—A. No.

Q. At the other penitentiaries the salaries of the chaplains have been increased om $800 to $1,000?—A. The salary of the chaplain of the Alberta Penitentiary egan at $1,000, although there were only thirty or forty prisoners, all told, of all deominations. If I mistake not, the question was asked in the House: 'What about e chaplains in Kingston and St. Vincent de Paul Penitentiaries, that have not had eir salaries raised?' And the answer to that was to the effect that no complaints ere made. Well, we were not aware of the fact that the salaries of chaplains in any enitentiaries were going to be raised and therefore, could not make complaint.

29a—37

7-8 EDWARD VII., A. 1908

Q. How many hours a day do you devote to your duties?—A. It varies.

Q. How many hours, as a general rule?—A. Sometimes two hours, sometimes three hours, sometimes only an hour and a half. On Sundays——

Q. I was going to ask about Sundays?—A. I go there in the morning at a quarter to nine, and sometimes it is ten o'clock or after ten o'clock before I leave. I go back again at half-past one and remain until three or half-past three. Then I am at the penitentiary on Saturdays for the purpose of hearing confessions and preparing the prisoners for communion. I go at twelve o'clock on Saturday and remain there until 2.30. It was nearly four o'clock when I left, last Saturday.

Q. Are there any week-day services?—A. Not now; they have been dispensed with.

Q. You occasionally take a holiday, I suppose?—A. I have never taken a holiday since I have been there.

Q. But all the chaplains are not in that condition, I suppose? Some of them take holidays?—A. Perhaps they may, but I have never taken them.

Q. Have you not sanction, if you went on a holiday, to appoint a substitute?—A. I never was told that.

Q. Mr. Moylan stated: 'The chaplains have had the sanction of the board which had formerly the control over the penitentiaries, to appoint suitable substitutes to read the morning prayers, such as the deputy warden or the chief keeper, which custom has been continued to the present time'?—A. They have dispensed with that for many years.

Q. How long has Mr. Cook been chaplain?—A. I do not know. I suppose since Mr. Cartwright resigned.

Q. He resigned not long ago?—A. He was there thirty years.

Q. I know, but he resigned recently?—A. Mr. Cook was appointed at his resignation.

Q. Has he ever taken a holiday?—A. No, sir, not to my knowledge.

Mr. REID.—Mr. Cook was appointed on November 1, 1903.

Q. Has Mr. Cook in the four years never had a holiday?—A. No, I do not think so.

Q. You are to-day in good health, but some time you may be ill. What would happen then? Would the spiritual machinery dry up?—A. No, I would have a substitute, but fortunately I have not been ill.

Q. Do you give any time during the week to catechetical exercises?—A. Yes, to candidates in preparation for the sacrament of confirmation. I have seven or eight convicts under my tutelage for that purpose, and teach them catechism twice a week in preparation for the reception of this sacrament.

Q. Where does Mr. Cook live?—A. In the village of Portsmouth. He lives in the old residence that Mr. Cartwright occupied.

Q. How far is that from the penitentiary?—A. About five minutes' walk.

Q. You made an observation earlier in your examination about Dorchester Penitentiary. Do the chaplains of the other penitentiaries live close to the institutions?—A. I think the chaplain of Dorchester does not.

Q. The Catholic chaplain lived six miles away, it was stated in 1892?—A. I presume it is a fact yet. I could not say as to that.

Q. Have any of the chaplains parochial duties outside as well as yourself?—A. I think the priest at Dorchester may perform parochial duties in a sense, too.

Q. Do you know how they make the services at the penitentiaries fit in with the services of their own churches?—A. The services in each chapel? Is that what you mean?

Q. Mr. Moylan was asked: 'How do they fit in their services at the penitentiaries with their services in their churches?' Practically, at Kingston, you give your whole time, one way or the other?—A. Yes.

Q. Have you anything to suggest as to the reformation of criminals, beyond what mentioned?—A No.

Q. You have nothing in the way of a memorandum as to what you think would ɪ for the better government of prisons?—A. No.

Q. Or better inducements to a prisoner to lead a better life?—A. No. I might ːrhaps mention that I take exception to the retirement fund as at present con- ituted because we are labouring under a disadvantage and have not even the same ɪvantage that a guard has got.

Q. Mr. Cartwright, the former Protestant chaplain, was superannuated?—A. Yes.

Q. Who was your predecessor as Catholic chaplain?—A. Father James Vincent eville.

Q. Did he die?—A. He died.

Q. Mr. Cartwright was superannuated, and you have been appointed since the uperannuation Act was abolished?—A. Yes.

Q. You give 5 per cent of your salary, or $60 a year, to the retirement fund? ·A. Yes.

Q. And when you retire?—A. I get my money back, that is all.

Q. You are not like the guards and keepers? You do not have a gratuity built ɔ for you?—A. Precisely.

Q. You come under the retirement fund?—A. Yes.

Q. And the warden the same?—A. Yes.

Q. Do you not think, in the interest of the officials generally, it would be desir- ɪle to have some form of a pension that would apply not only to the officer himself ɪt to those dependent upon him?—A. Yes, I heartily approve of it and so does the arden himself also, because he has told me of his great dissatisfaction at the idea of ːing treated in that fashion. I had a talk with the inspector about it.

Q. With Mr. Stewart?—A. No, Mr. Dawson. He happened to be there one day hen we were discussing the question.

Q. You, from the circumstances of the case, have nobody dependent upon you?— . That is so.

Q. Then it would seem that you have got no increase in salary?—A. Yes, that so.

Q. Except at St. Vincent de Paul and Kingston, the penitentiary chaplains have ɪd their salaries raised 25 per cent?—A. Yes.

Q. Your salary is the same as Mr. Cartwright had when he was appointed, in the ʋenties?—A. Exactly.

Q. The chaplains of the penitentiaries, unlike the ministers outside, have nothing . the shape of special offertories at Christmas?—A. Yes, I get that.

Q. From the families of the guards?—A. Yes.

Q. If you did not minister to the guards' families, but were simply restricted to ɛ penitentiary duties, like Mr. Cook, there would be no addition to your emolument . all?—A. I would get nothing.

Q. There you differ from ministers of the gospel outside?—A. Yes.

Q. They get something in addition to their stipend?—A. Yes. I might mention ᴀt the revenue that accrues to me from the families of guards goes in outlay for the aintenance of the church and such like.

Q. How many families are there?—A. About thirty-five.

Q. They are the families of guards who have no money beyond their salaries?— . No.

Q. It just pays——?—A. The running expenses of the church.

The CHAIRMAN.—Well, Father, we are very much obliged to yourself and the embers of your deputation for coming to lay your views before us.

Rev. Father McDONALD.—We are sincerely grateful to you for the very kind and ᴈntlemanly way in which you have treated us and the magnanimous manner in which ʋu received our proposition to wait upon you here.

29a—37½

The CHAIRMAN.—It was absolutely impossible for us to visit Kingston, in view of the fact that Parliament meets in three weeks, and our report m@t be ready to lay before it at an early date.

Rev. Father McDONALD —We heartily appreciate your kindness, and are more than grateful to you.

The witness retired.

TO THE CIVIL SERVICE COMMISSION.

REPRESENTATIONS OF THE STAFF OF SUBORDINATE OFFICERS OF THE KINGSTON PENITENTIARY.

The staff of subordinate officers of the Kingston Penitentiary respectfully submit the following:—

1. The members of the staff request an all around increase in salaries. They ask, at least, an augmentation of one hundred dollars per annum for each one. And, in view of the circumstances of their case, they consider that even that amount is below what would be required to fairly meet their abnormally increased expense of living. In order not to intrude a too lengthy document on the Commission, they merely draw attention to the numerous and repeated representations made by all other branches of the service on this important point. Kingston, no more than any other part of Canada, has not escaped the exceptional increase in the cost of living, and the members of this staff feel the stress in a most particular manner. Further on this point need not be said, as we understand that this, being so generally recognized, has been the main reason of the existence of this Commission.

Before coming to the second point of this requisition, the members of the staff wish to briefly draw attention to the fact that their service is one apart, in many ways, and should be so considered; it differs in many respects from other branches of the Civil Service. Firstly, because each time that one of the staff goes on duty he takes his life in his hands; he is as much exposed to death or severe accident as is the soldier in active service; he never can tell, when he leaves his home in the morning, if ever he will return to it alive; he is constantly on the breach doing duty for the country; and he has to deal with the hardest and most dangerous class of men in Canada—for Kingston contains the very worst of the criminals as well as maniacs. This will be brought out in other words when dealing with the question of hours of work and comparisons of pay.

2. In regard to the question of gratuity, we may first state that according to present rule one-half month's pay, for the first five years of service and one month's pay for each following year, constitutes the gratuity that is allowed on retirement. And here it may be noted that no man fitted for service, no matter how good his reasons for resignation may be, will have his resignation accepted, unless he thereby forfeits his claim to the gratuity. Now, if an officer of the staff should die suddenly, even on duty, or should be killed by a convict, his family has no claim to his gratuity —save three months' pay, which is a trifle. The desire is that this be so changed that in the case of the member of the staff dying or being so killed his family may receive the full gratuity that he could have claimed on regular retirement.

3. As to the question of the hours during which the prison is open there is, to say the least, ground-work for a very beneficial improvement. During six months of the year the hours are from 6.30 a.m. to 6 p.m., and during the other six months from 7 a.m. to 5.30 p.m., or any hour fixed by warden. Thus during the short days the officer has to come on sometimes before daylight, and occasionally it is dark when the doors close. Surely a ten hours' day should suffice. From 7 a.m. to 5 p.m. on week days is, in the estimation of all concerned, a sufficiently long time for open hours. Not unfrequently men have to rise very early and get to their post of duty, merely

to sit down and await the daylight before their services are required. This point is merely expressed in its rough outlines, for much can be said in regard to it.

4. On account of the hours of attendance, during the day time, on Sundays, being much longer than is generally believed by outsiders to the service, and as the greater part of the forenoon and of the afternoon of that day of rest is taken up with attendance to duty, we would suggest that some means be devised whereby such hours could be shortened: either by having the services earlier, or by allowing the staff, in place of those hours, a part holiday on Saturday (as is the case in many like institutions), or by any other means that might suggest themselves to the proper authorities.

5. The pay received by the members of the staff is entirely out of proportion to the hours of work. In all other institutions there is some regulation as to regular rest from work; but this staff has to be on duty frequently 24 and sometimes 36 hours at a time. Taking the average work by one example we find that in July last one man worked 382 hours, and in August 385 hours, making 767 hours in two months. He receives $50 per month, or $100 for his two months; this gives him a little over 13 cents per hour. And he has worked night and day, and ever and always exposed :o the chances of death by accident. Just imagine a man in this perpetual life of danger, with the ever-increasing cost of living for his family, and the fear of their lestitution, should he fall at his post, receiving not more than $1.30 per day. Stress need not be laid on this point; we are confident that the special features of the serrice are apparent to the Commission. While Dorchester Penitentiary has but 211, Manitoba 190, British Columbia 139, and Alberta 30 or 40 convicts, Kingston has 460. St. Vincent de Paul has 410, but Kingston receives the worst of the criminals, and even those that are considered too dangerous for other institutions.

There are different minor grievances that we might mention, but we do not wish to over-load the documents that the Commission has to deal with, nor unduly encroach upon its time, nor do we desire to make and move or raise any issues that might tend to unpleasant feelings in any quarters. We simply place this skeleton of our case before the Commission, fully confident of the careful and just consideration that it will receive.

P. M. BEAUPRE,
Instructor.
R. A. CAUGHEY.
Asst. Supt. Binder Twine.
M. P. REID, *Keeper.*
C. S. WHEELER, *Guard.*

REPRESENTATIONS OF THE CHAPLAINS OF THE KINGSTON PENITENTIARY.

To the Civil Service Commission :

Rev. M. McDonald, Roman Catholic Chaplain, and Rev. A. W. Cooke, Protestant Chaplain, of the Kingston Penitentiary, respectfuly submit the following :—

That their salaries of $1,200 each, per annum, are not in accord with either the services rendered or the needs of the present under existing circumstances, nor are they at all proportionate to those of clergymen occupying like positions in other institutions.

Both the Protestant and Roman Catholic chaplains of the herein mentioned penitentiaries have had their salaries raised from $600 and $800 to $1,000, that is to say, Dorchester, Manitoba, British Columbia and Alberta.

In Dorchester they have to do duty for 211 prisoners; in Manitoba, for 190; in British Columbia, for 139; and in Alberta, for about 40; while in Kingston the chaplains have to serve the spiritual interests of 460, and possibly more prisoners. Some thirty odd years ago the salary of the chaplain, which has not changed since, was not considered excessive, but was looked upon as fair and adequate. If so, in view of the changed conditions of living to-day, surely it becomes, by very force of circumstances, totally insufficient.

In all walks of life the necessity of increased salaries has become recognized and that in a practical manner—the only proper and satisfactory manner possible, which is a proportionate augmentation. Merchants, farmers, traders, judges, lawyers, doctors, parliamentarians, are all receiving either higher prices for goods and produce, or more wages for work, or increased salaries and indemnities. The receipts of the country have increased in all departments and as the cost of living has also increased, it is but just and fair that the individual citizen should reap some benefit from the universal prosperity and not be allowed to drift into a poorer condition in the midst of increasing plenty.

The chaplains of the Kingston Penitentiary, while desirous of placing their case as briefly as possible before the Commission, do not wish to either preach a sermon on obligations nor intrude any suggestions ; but they wish to draw attention to the fact that, as a rule, the world is inclined to the idea that ministers of the gospel should not worry about money matters, but live upon a spiritual diet and the free air of heaven. In common with all ministers of the gospel, the chaplains of the penitentiary, feel the effects of the increased expense in living. Were the Government in a stress and short of revenue none would more ready than the chaplains to accept patriotically their humble share of the burden and forego any increase ; but with an overflowing treasury and an unparalled prosperity in the land, it is another matter.

One word about the special work of the penitentiary chaplain. Unlike other ministers of the gospel, he is called upon to preach to, to advise with, to guide and to assist the very worst class of men. He must perform his ministrations in a place where the feet of the murderer, the robber, the libertine, and the hardened criminal of every class have left their footprints in the dust. It is his duty to deal with the dark and lurid side of life, without even a stray ray of the brighter and better side falling across his pathway. It is his duty to reform criminals and to seek, by every means in his power, to so convert those he has to serve that when they go out they may be less of a menace to society. In a word, it is a public duty that he performs, not only for the spiritual good of the souls, but for the greater good and safety of socity and the country.

We need not dwell upon the obvious fact that the clergymen, occupying a public position, should, at least, be compensated sufficiently to permit him to live, not in luxury, but as a gentleman. Not inferior, any way, to gentlemen of other professions.

In placing this our requisition before the Commission and asking a proportionate increase in salary to that accorded to others, we take the liberty of quoting the words of Rev. S. W. Chapman, D.D., chaplain of the Illinois State Penitenitary, for we feel that they are appropriate in our case. He says:

'Who and what is a prison chaplain? A minister of Jesus Christ called to minister to men in confinement, who must have all the qualifications of a successful pastor of a congregation. He must understand men, must be filled with the missionary spirit, and should invariably be chosen from the ranks of the best ministers. Such a man, when found, should be amply compensated, and after years of faithful service, pensioned. A chaplain who faithfully preaches the gospel and does conscientious work is the highest disciplinary force in a prison.'

To the Civil Service Commissioners,
            Ottawa, Ont.

KINGSTON, ONT., November 11, 1907.

Mr. J. M. COURTNEY.

DEAR SIR,—The Rev. Father Macdonald, my fellow chaplain, sent me a copy of *the memorial* which he had the honour to present to the Commission last week, in

SESSIONAL PAPER No. 29a

Ottawa. The memorial states the case of the chaplains clearly and well, and I agree with it and endorse it.

In regard to the Sunday services, I am strongly convinced that it would be ·a very serious mistake, a decidedly backward movement, to do away with one of them— the afternoon service. Surely two hours out of seven days are not too much time to spend in the worship of God, especially if the place and all the sad circumstances of the situation are considered.

The Sunday services are, indeed, to the great majority of the prisoners, the oasis, *i.e.*, rest and refreshment, in the dreary desert of prison life. And to abolish one of them would be a grievous wrong, and that for many more reasons which I could give, and I am speaking from an experience of more than twenty years of penitentiary life. For I visited this prison and took occasional services there for the space of sixteen or seventeen years, for the former chaplain, my old friend, the Rev. C. E. Cartwright, before I was appointed his successor, four years ago. I trust no changes will be made in the services.

In regard to the number of youths under my care, under twenty years of age, it grieves me to have it say that there are thirty-two. What to do with them, how to deal with them, are the most serious and difficult problems.

This part of my work so depressed and troubled me, that in order to help these lads as far as I possibly can, I have arranged that the seven youngest, of whom the youngest is a little fellow of the age of 14, should sit together in church, away from the old criminals; and I also hold, in addition to my other classes, a weekly class of religious instruction for these 32 youths. I feel it has already done, and will continue to do, much good.

The presence here of so many youths is to me the saddest feature of prison life. Indeed, I have it in my mind to write a letter on the matter to the Minister of Justice, pointing out to him the crying demand of righteousness that these boys should be kept from the other prisoners as much as possible.

I ask you, sir, not to consider this a private letter. You may make it a part of the memorial, if you think fit to do so.

Yours truly,

A. W. COOKE.

KINGSTON PENITENTIARY, November 1, 1907.

GENTLEMEN,—I have been in the service since I was fifteen years of age, being appointed teamster April 1, 1872, at $156 per annum, receiving several small raises in salary, the largest being $400 per annum, when on May 1, 1884, I was appointed messenger at $600 per annum, with free quarters, light and fuel, which was taken from me in 1897, and nothing given me in lieu thereof. I am now the father of nine children, and it takes great manœuvering to keep out of debt, and the fact is, that sometimes I cannot do that.

Hoping your honourable body will do what lies in your power to secure me an increase in salary.

I have the honour to be, gentlemen,

Your obedient servant,

M. J. KENNEDY,

Messenger, K.P.

7-8 EDWARD VII., A. 1908

KINGSTON PENITENTIARY,
J. M. COURTNEY, Esq.,   KINGSTON, ONT., November 6, 1907.
Chairman of Civil Service Commission,
    193 Sparks Street, Sparks Chambers, Ottawa, Ont.

SIR,—I have the honour to respectfully ask the consideration, by your Commission, of the facts in connection with my case, under the present retiring fund law, and will be very grateful if you can do anything to assist me in regard to same.

I have been an officer of this institution for almost fifteen years, and during the past four years have been accountant and clerk of industries.

Prior to my appointment to said position I was chief keeper and clerk of industries, and enjoyed a salary of $1,400 per annum and was having $116.66 added to my retiring gratuity allowance each year.

Upon my promotion to the position I now hold, March 1, 1903, I lost this $116.66 gratuity, and instead of drawing a salary of $1,400, as heretofore, I drew only $1,330, thus losing a gratuity of $116.66 and also $70 in cash each year.

I am satisfied you will agree with me in saying that this was an injustice to me, and it is this matter I would beg of your Commission to consider and try to have redressed.

If I may be permitted to make a suggestion, I would ask that if possible, I be placed back on a gratuity fund as I was, and that the money deducted from my salary be refunded to me, the Government keeping the interest.

This I consider, would be a fair arrangement and would compensate me for the injustice I suffered under the retiring gratuity law.

I have the honour to be, gentlemen,
                          Your obedient servant,
                                W. S. HUGHES,
                          Accountant and Clerk of Industries.

DEPUTY WARDEN'S OFFICE,
        KINGSTON PENITENTIARY,
            KINGSTON, ONT., November 13, 1907.

Memo of D. O'Leary, Deputy Warden of Kingston Penitentiary, to the
            Civil Service Commission, Ottawa.

With the hope of not being too late to yet bring to the notice of the Commission a few facts bearing upon my case as Deputy Warden of Kingston Penitentiary, I beg to submit the following for your kind consideration:—

1st. That since my appointment as deputy warden, some ten years ago, very substantial increases in salaries have been granted to warden—from $2,000 to $2,600; surgeon, from $1,800 to $2,400; accountant, from $1,400 to $1,700, not to mention anything of increases of salaries granted to several other officers holding good positions in said penitentiary, yet the salary of the deputy warden is still found to be what it was some thirty years ago, $1,500.

2nd. My predecessors in office, and myself, were allowed the privilege of cultivating, with the aid of convict labour, a certain parcel of land inside the prison walls for gardening purposes for private use. But I regret to say that within the past year this privilege has been denied me, thus compelling me at great inconvenience to go some two miles away from the prison to procure my table supplies.

In view of this condition of things, I feel it is not unreasonable on my part to ask that said salary of $1,500 should be increased to $1,800, more especially when it is borne in mind that the entire responsibility for the safe-guarding of the very large convict population of our penitentiary, and the entire prison discipline of same rests upon the deputy warden's shoulders.

Trusting that this may meet with your favourable consideration, I remain, sirs,
                          Yours respectfully,
                                D. O'LEARY.

OTTAWA, May 22, 1907.

Dr. S. E. DAWSON, sworn and examined.

By the Chairman:

Q. You are the King's Printer?—A. Yes.

Q. How long have you been in that position?—A. Since November, 1891.

Q. You are one of the Deputy Heads who were in existence at the time of the last Civil Service Commission?—A. I think so.

Q. The staff, I see, has been increased in that period from 51 to 58?—A. Yes.

Q. That is altogether, temporaries and permanents?—A. Yes.

Q. The expenditure of the department has increased in that period from $42,000 to about $60,000?—A. For salaries, yes.

Q. I see you have made the general average of your department $1,000?—A. Yes.

Q. The total amount of business done by the department has about doubled?— A. Yes.

Q. It has increased from $574,000 to $1,107,000?—A. Yes.

Q. The advertising in the newspapers which you audit, has increased from $24,000 to $107,000?—A. Yes.

Q. And the outside work, that is to say, printing for the Intercolonial, which is more conveniently done near at hand, but which you audit, is about $80,000 a year? —A. Yes.

Q. What do they pay you for all that?—A. $4,000.

Q. You have no other remuneration?—A. No.

Q. Your permanent staff has increased only from 25 to 30; in that number how many chief clerks are there?—A. There are three chief clerks now—the heads of the three branches.

Q. That is, the chief clerk in the printing, the chief clerk in the stationery and the accountant?—A. Yes.

Q. Then you have one first-class clerk?—A. One first-class clerk.

Q. And 12 second-class clerks?—A. Fourteen second-class clerks, 11 junior second-class clerks, and the messengers and one caretaker.

Q. Your office being isolated, you have to have a caretaker?—A. Oh, yes.

Q. Were the third-class clerks promoted to second-class?—A. Some were, but many of the older clerks are dead or retired. Many of the present clerks came in from the temporary class as second-class or junior second-class clerks.

Q. You have eight temporaries?—A. Yes.

Q. How do you get the temporaries?—A. By simple appointment.

Q. You find from the chiefs' branches that they want temporaries?—A. Yes, and then I apply in the usual way to the Minister.

Q. Do you look into the matter to see whether temporaries are necessary?—A. Oh, yes.

Q. And then the Minister sends you a temporary?—A. Yes.

Q. Of course the temporary has passed the Civil Service examination?—A. Generally, unless he is technical.

Q. You have not a temporary clerk who is a technical man?—A. Oh, yes. Four of them at least are technical men. They have to come in either as technical men or must pass the Civil Service examination before promotion.

Q. Did you really desire the technical men?—A. Yes, I needed them.

Q. Then all these appointments have been made at your instance, though made by the Minister?—A. They have all been made at my instance.

7-8 EDWARD VII., A. 1908

Q. Have you a redundant number of clerks?—A. No.

Q. You have no more than sufficient for the purposes of the Bureau?—A. No.

Q. You need in the Bureau from the very fact of distribution, a greater number of packers than are usually found in the service?—A. Yes, because nearly all the distribution for the Government is done there.

Q. And you also have to employ carters?—A. Yes. There are not as many packers in our department as there are in the Post Office Department.

Q. This, of course, does not comprise ordinary printers?—A. No, not the operatives. This is the managing staff. There are 509 operatives in the manufacturing department.

By Mr. Fyshe:

Q. Is there not a good deal of unnecessary printing?—A. I think so.

Q. Consisting mostly of what?—A. I think the reports are unnecessarily bulky, and there is a good deal of printing ordered by the House, over which I have no control. I must print what is sent to me. For instance, there are eight *Hansards* printed—three for the House of Commons, and five for the Senate, English and French.

By the Chairman:

Q. Do these 509 include all that are employed in the printing and bindery and everywhere?—A. Yes, and all miscellaneous hands.

Q. What proportion of that number are women?—A. 124 out of the 509.

Q. I suppose they are employed at the lighter work—they are not printers?—A. No, they are not printers. They are employed in the bindery. They do the folding and stitching, the sewing of blank books, the collating of books, paging, perforating, gathering, &c.

Q. For all those 509 there is no examination required to be passed?—A. No.

Q. How do you get them?—A. I get them on recommendation.

Q. You ask your Minister for printers?—A. There are always more printers offering than I can take. I do not require to ask for them. They are all around, and I can get them when I want them.

Q. Are they pressed upon you?—A. Well, I need not take them without I wish.

Q. Of course, it is rather difficult at times to refuse a Minister?—A. Sometimes it is.

Q. You might have operatives forced upon you from a country newspaper supporting the party?—A. Well, I might have a good deal of pressure occasionally to put a man on.

Q. Are there not a number of Members of Parliament and Senators connected with the daily press of the country?—A. There are not a great many.

Q. Do they try to use the patronage of the Bureau?—A. It is not from there that the patronage chiefly comes. The patronage, as I understand it, in political institutions, is with the local members and the associations.

Q. But yours is a department of the Government, and you have nothing more to do with the Members for Ottawa than with the Members for Quebec?—A. But the local Member exercises the patronage of the department in the place, and there are, of course, influences from outside also.

Q. The department tells them that this place belongs to the whole country and not to Ottawa alone?—A. That is a moot point, which is argued on both sides. It is a difficult question to answer, because it is very much disputed.

Q. In practice, have a great number of the operatives in the Bureau been employed through the influence of the Members for Ottawa?—A. I think a good many have been employed through their recommendations. Others have been employed through the recommendation of other Members.

Q. But the Members for Ottawa incline to the view that the Printing Bureau is *part of their patronage*?—A. Yes.

Q. And of course, if you have 500 operatives, there would be an immense political influence attached to the employment of these?—A. Yes, but when 'they come in they remain there permanently, and it is only the vacancies that they touch, but when there is a vacancy they think they should be consulted as to how it is filled.

By Mr. Fyshe:

Q. How are these operatives paid, compared with those in private printing establishments?—A. They are paid the highest rate current in the market—the trade union rates, for instance, that are paid in Toronto, not more. The statute fixes the Toronto and Montreal rate as a standard, and Toronto being the higher is adopted.

Q. The wages are regulated by their association?—A. They are regulated by treaties between the employers and the trade unions. They agree upon an established rate for a certain number of years.

Q. What regulates the higher officers of your department?—A. The Civil Service Act.

By the Chairman:

Q. Are the hours of work of the operatives the same as those of the ordinary printing establishments of the country?—A. No, the hours are shorter; they are eight hours. They are now nine hours in Toronto, but there the printers are making a great effort this year, and I am inclined to think they will succeed for the eight-hour day.

Q. That is to say, in the Bureau the operatives come under the trades union limit as regards salaries, but not as regards hours?—A. No, the hours are shorter.

By Mr. Bazin:

Q. Are they paid by the hour or by the day?—A. The rate is fixed by the week, but they are really paid by the hour, for if they stay away an hour they lose it.

Q. If the operatives are worth 25 cents an hour in Toronto, are they paid 25 cents an hour here?—A. Yes, but they are paid by the week, divided into 48 hours, not 54.

By the Chairman:

Q. They are practically paid the same rate for the eight hours work as a man in Toronto gets for nine hours work?—A. Yes.

Q. You say you have 509 operatives now?—A. Yes.

Q. In a session of Parliament when the work is at its highest, how many do you have?—A. Well, we have not any more, but we then work night and day and extra hours; because we have not room to put more men. If I could get more room, I would put more men on; but the room being limited, I have to work the men I have extra hours, for which we have to pay an extra percentage. The rate after the regular hours is one and a third or one and a half.

Q. Then your operatives have the two privileges—the trades union privilege and the Government privilege?—A. They work shorter hours. They do not call that a privilege, because they think eight hours is the normal period of work. They have won the eight hours all over the United States.

By Mr. Fyshe:

Q. I do not see how they can call it a normal rate when it is an hour shorter than elsewhere?—A. That is their way of looking at it.

Q. When the session is over and the reports are brought down to Parliament, and you come back to the normal work at the Bureau until the session is opened again, do you reduce your staff?—A. There has been no occasion for reducing the staff for eight years past, because the amount of work is greater than the staff can compass. The overflow goes outside.

Q. What work do you keep in arrears?—A. I do not keep purposely any work in arrears. For ten years back there has always been enough work, it has increased so much, only there is not the same drive after the session and less work goes outside. We stop the extra hours and the night staff and work regular hours. There has not been a lay-off in the printing bureau for eight years.

By the Chairman:

Q. The staff is a constant staff?—A. Not theoretically or legally, but practically.

Q. Do your clerks have the usual leave of absence prescribed by the Civil Service Act?—A. Yes.

Q. Do the operatives have leave of absence?—A. No, the foremen have.

Q. If an operative is absent, his pay is deducted?—A. Yes, if he is absent an hour, he loses that hour.

Q. Is that rule enforced?—A. Oh, yes. I have to sign a statement that the hours of work have all been served.

Q. Do you have a kind of attendance book for the operators?—A. No, but we have a check taker, who takes all the time. The time is kept exactly.

Q. The ordinary clerks sign the ordinary attendance book, I suppose?—A. Yes.

Q. What are the office hours of the staff?—A. From 10 o'clock in the morning until 4.30 in the afternoon.

Q. Do they go for lunch?—A. Yes.

Q. What time do you allow for lunch?—A. Theoretically an hour, but practically more. They cannot get back in an hour.

Q. Their homes being distant from the department, they require a little longer time?—A. That is the trouble. It is a long way for them to go home and back.

Q. You have no objection to Mr. Fyshe and Mr. Bazin going over the Bureau?— A. I wish they would. It would give me a great deal of pleasure.

Q. Your employees on the fixed staff have been there for sometime?—A. Oh, yes. A good many of them have been there for many years.

Q. Do you recollect whether the Superannuation Act applies to all the permanents? —A. No, not after 1895.

Q. Do you find a difficulty in getting juniors for your fixed staff as a result of the abolition of the superannuation?—A. I have difficulty always in getting capable persons. I have to take a raw untrained youth and put him in the lowest place.

Q. What is your opinion about the abolition of the Superannuation Act?—A. I think it has been mischievous to the Civil Service. It will prevent bringing men of capacity into the service. I do not see how you can get capable men to enter the service if there is no provision made for their retirement. At the present time all the nations of Europe, you may say, are striving to bring into operation old age pension systems for all their people. All large institutions are instituting superannuation funds, and the Government of Canada is almost alone in having none. I do not see how you are going to keep up the service at all.

Q. Have you had any resignations in your fixed permanent staff on account of the lack of prospect?—A. I do not remember any.

Q. Do you ever suspend any of the operatives for misconduct?—A. I have had to do that sometimes. I have suspended them for drunkenness, and for going out before their time. It is not very easy to keep up discipline in a large establishment of that kind. Lately a number of them were suspended for going out too soon

By Mr. Fyshe:

Q. If they are looked after by this time keeper, does he not dock them?—A. But they may go off before the whistle sounds.

By the Chairman:

Q. Do they work up to the time the whistle goes?—A. They work up to five minutes of the time. They are allowed five minutes to wash their hands and clean up.

Q. Do you find that they are reinstated after being suspended?—A. I find they *have a tendency to get reinstated.*

Q. When they come back, it is with a distinct warning that a repetition of the offence will lead to dismissal?—A. Oh, yes.

Q. Can you ever carry that out?—A. I have in some cases.

By Mr. Bazin :

Q. That is for misconduct, I suppose?—A. I find it difficult to answer some of these questions. If a man were a very pronounced drunkard, I would get rid of him. But they have a tendency to get back somehow or other.

By the Chairman :

Q. Do you often have a promotion examination?—A. Oh, yes. There was one the other day.

Q. Who sets the papers?—A. I set the papers.

Q. Are the full number of papers of the Civil Service set?—A. I only set the papers for duties of office.

Q. You allow the Civil Service examiners to set the others?—A. They set them.

By Mr. Fyshe :

Q. In case of the promotion of any of the officers of your establishment, do you examine them for promotion?—A. Yes, they must have passed a promotion examination in their duties.

Q. The promotions are made on your initiative, are they?—A. Yes, I always recommend the promotions.

By the Chairman :

Q. Are the promotions in a way perfunctory? Are the first-class clerks doing the work of ordinary junior seconds, or have the first-class clerks distinctive duties?—A. In my department the first-class clerks are all doing first-class work.

Q. Then the grades are proper grades?—A. I think so.

Q. Do your operatives get increases of pay? Do they claim that they have the Civil Service privilege of getting annual increments?—A. No.

Q. They simply get the operative prices?—A. The operative prices—the rates paid in Toronto or Montreal. That is fixed by statute. (R.S., cap. 80, sec. 18, ss. 2.)

By Mr. Fyshe :

Q. There is no provision for gradual increase?—A. There is no provision for gradual increase; but they get the current rates as settled by trades unions, so that there is no question of any increase by regular increment.

Q. And I suppose that rate of wages would not fluctuate very much?—A. It has increased from $12 to $15 a week from 1892 till 1906.

Q. Is that increased rate now the steady rate?—A. It has been the steady rate for three years. The trades unions in Toronto are meeting the employers now to make a new arrangement, and if they get a further raise in Toronto, there will be a raise in the Bureau.

Q. What is the ordinary plea in these cases?—A. The plea is the increased cost of living and the increased profits of trade. There is no lack of a plea.

Q. And you regard the increased cost of living as a pretty valid reason, don't you? —A. I think it is a valid reason.

Q. Is that increase, in your opinion, natural or artificial—that is to say, is it general all over the world, or is it caused by any peculiarity existing in Canada?—A. It is a general increase all over the world, I take it. There seems to be a general rise of the labour unions all over the world to better their conditions, and their conditions are better than they were twenty years ago, and I think they should be.

Q. You do not consider that the conditions existing in Canada have much to do with it?—A. No, because these conditions do not exist everywhere. There is an increase in England as well.

Q. Still, the cost of living in England is very much less than it is here?—A. I do not know what the cost of living in England is, but I know that there is a general movement on the part of operatives all over the world towards an increased rate of pay. Fortunes are larger, there is more luxury, and you cannot have the labouring classes left behind.

Q. The operative classes are becoming more alive to the situation—that has probably a good deal to do with it?—A. Yes, the growth of education. They want more comforts. The demands of civilization are greater. In short, the labouring man is entitled to a certain proportion of the general advancement of comfort and luxury in the whole nation. Take the increase from $12 to $15 a week for the operatives in the Bureau from 1892 to 1906. I do not think that is an extravagant increase—twenty-five per cent.

By the Chairman :

Q. Do you think if the Bureau ceased to exist and the Government reverted to the old system of contract, that the work would be done better or cheaper?—A. The work would not be done better or cheaper or so quickly.

Q. If you are paying for an eight-hour day what the printers in Toronto are paying for nine hours, how can the work be done cheaper?—A. I have explained that fully in several of my reports. A great deal of the work of the Government is twice printing for one setting up. We make stereotype plates, and we use these over and over again, and we have standing headings. In that way there is only one charge for composition and the cost is kept down. Again, the Bureau is so large and the amount of material is so great that the men do not have to wait for material.

By Mr. Fyshe:

Q. Is the average printer in your establishment quite equal to the printers employed in outside establishments?—A. Printers differ very much. They are better for the work than outside men, for the reason that they understand the work better. For instance, a man who has set a job for twenty years will do the work more quickly. I have, of course, a good many men who are not so good as others.

Q. Is it not a fact, that the average printer is necessarily a man of superior intelligence?—A. Yes, I think he is.

By the Chairman:

Q. In the old time there was a lithographing service in the Department of the Interior?—A. Yes.

Q. Is that in existence now?—A. Oh, yes.

Q. Why is that?—A. They seem to require it. I think they do require it. It has been increasing.

Q. What do they lithograph there?—A. Maps of surveys, which they want very quickly, and which they can, they say, do more quickly and better than they can get them outside. My impression is that they can.

Q. Although this is not part of the Bureau, you think it is justified?—A. I think it is justified. You would have to about double the Bureau in size to put in a lithographing establishment that would cover all Government needs.

Q. There are maps being prepared in the Department of the Interior, in the Geological Survey, in the Post Office Department, in the Militia Department, in the Marine and Fisheries Department, and in the Department of Railways and Canals?—A. Yes.

Q. A very fine atlas has been recently published by the Department of the Interior which has received great commendation?—A. Yes.

Q. Would it not be desirable to gather together all these officers engaged in mapping in the separate departments?—A. I think it would be conducive to economy and efficiency. That is done in England. But the change would be a very radical one. In England they have an immense establishment—the Ordnance Survey—and all the departments use the Ordnance Survey maps, and they make them on different scales to suit every requirement, enlarging or diminishing them by photography. There is a very large establishment at Southampton for doing this work.

By Mr. Fyshe:

Q. You do a great deal of outside work, such as the printing of currency and stamps?—A. No, the department does not do that. I have nothing to with the printing of stamps or currency. That is done by the Finance Department or the Post Office Department or the Inland Revenue Department. They do it through the American Bank Note Agency.

By the Chairman:

Q. You inspect the bills for lithography?—A. Yes, all the bills for work done outside pass through our audit.

Q. You make all the purchases of stationery?—A. Yes.

By Mr. Fyshe:

Q. Where do you get your supplies of stationery?—A. From the manufacturer in every instance.

Q. Do you import any?—A. Yes, we import a good deal. Most of the paper we use is made in the country, but we import a great deal from England and some from the United States.

Q. Most of the writing paper?—A. Printing paper is the great bulk of what we use, and that is all made in the country.

Q. When you import, do you go through the form of paying the duties?—A. We do now, but formerly we did not. Since the last Customs Act was passed, we pay the duties when we import, and the departments are charged. The Government gets it back through the Custom-house.

Q. Is there any competition between the native manufacturer and the English in the paper which you import?—A. Where we can get Canadian paper which will answer the purpose, we prefer to buy it in Canada.

Q. If it is more expensive?—A. If it answers the purpose, we buy it in Canada.

Q. Even if it is more expensive?—A. Practically, there is no such a question as that, because it is not more expensive. The English paper, when you pay the duty on it, is more costly.

Q. But the Government does not pay the duty?—A. The English paper really does not compete much with the Canadian paper, and the Canadian paper has improved so much of late years that it is gradually superseding English paper, even in the manufacture of blank books. They are making very good paper in Canada now.

By the Chairman :

Q. You buy wherever you can get it the cheapest as a rule ?—A. As a rule. We do not put the English paper in competition with the Canadian paper. If we find that the paper in Canada answers the purpose at a reasonable price we buy that paper.

Q. The ordinary foolscap paper comes from Aberdeen, does it not ?—A. I think not. If a department says it needs English paper of a particular kind, we buy that without saying a word; but the high class papers now used most extensively in the service are made by Canadian mills.

By Mr. Fyshe :

Q. What is that made of (showing paper) ?—A. Pure linen rags.

Q. It is not mixed with wood pulp ?—A. Not high class writing papers. The printing papers are. But wood pulp for printing papers has now superseded rags nearly altogether.

Q. What is the reason of that ?—A. Because it is so much cheaper.

Q. It will not last as long ?—A. It depends. You have to consider two kinds of pulp. If the pulp is boiled by the soda or sulphite process, thoroughly cooked and cleaned, it will last a very long time; but if it is simply ground wood, we do not use it in the Bureau at all, it is rejected.

Q. The question has arisen how the libraries of the world were going to be preserved ?—A. That is, with paper made of ground wood.

Q. No paper will last ?—A. It may last a thousand years if properly made. I can show you a book made in 1642 in which the writing is as black and the binding as good as it ever was.

By the Chairman :

Q. When a department sends you anything to be printed, you return the manuscript with the proofs ?—A. The manuscript is returned with the proofs.

Q. You keep no records in the Bureau ?—A. Oh, yes. What kind of a record do you mean ?

Q. The official records of the country—the archives ?—A. No, we do not keep those ; but we keep the records of our department. For instance, I can tell you when any copy came in and when the printing went out.

Q. Then the national records of the country are going steadily to the archives now ?—A. Steadily to the archives.

Q. Your place is absolutely fire-proof, as far as things can be ?—A. Yes. It is better than it was. I do not think it is absolutely fire-proof. We are gradually replacing the wood shelving with steel shelving. When that is done it will be pretty nearly fire-proof.

Q. Your stores are audited annually by the Auditor General ?—A. Yes.

Q. In that respect it differs from most of the other departments—that is laid down in the Act ?—A. I think so. He goes over the stock and verifies it.

Q. Is there any other suggestion you would like to make ?—A. I feel very strongly about the necessity of a retiring allowance. Another point: I think where an expert is appointed in middle age or at an advanced period of life, it is quite proper to add a certain number of years to his service. That is provided for in the Superannuation Act, but it is never carried out.

By Mr. Fyshe :

Q. On what grounds ?—A. Because he brings to the service without cost a life's training in that branch of business. My point is that when a man passes 30 or 40 years of age and is brought into the Government service as an expert in any particular business or for the special work for which he has been elsewhere trained, it is right, as it is allowable, on his retiring to add ten years to his service. Then, the whole question of patronage is a trouble at the bottom of the Civil Service; but although it is a very important question it is one concerning which one cannot say much. Another difficulty met with lately is that a temporary clerk cannot be put into the service at the rank of a second-class clerk, no matter how capable he is. He must begin again at the bottom and enter at $500 a year. That seems to me to be wrong.

By the Chairman :

Q. You would like the temporary clerk to come in at the salary he is getting ? —A. Yes, and with the grade of that salary. I have a case before me of a man who cannot be promoted without being examined, and he cannot be examined because he has not been promoted. We cannot examine him because he is not in the Civil Service, and I cannot put him in the Civil Service because he has not been examined. In this case the man is an exceedingly capable man, and I am blocked in that way. It is necessary now to take youths into the service. I can get all kinds of people that I do not want, but I cannot get the right kind of a person to come in at $500 a year.

Q. In your temporary staff are there many women?—A. None. Another point : I would like, if it were possible, to have an examination for all the operatives brought into the Printing Bureau. I would like compositors to be examined by practical men, and binders by the foreman or other experts. I would like to have a committee of experts to examine every one of these men. It would obviate a good deal of mischief from political patronage.

DEPARTMENT OF PUBLIC PRINTING AND STATIONERY.

OTTAWA, May 18, 1907.

SIR,—In answer to your request, asking for a memorandum showing the number of the staff of my department, and such other information as may in my judgment elucidate the increase of business, I beg to hand you a succinct statement of the transactions for the fiscal years ending June 30, 1892, and June 30, 1906, respectively:

APPROPRIATIONS.	NUMBER OF CLERKS.		SALARIES.	
	1891-2.	1905-6.	1891-2.	1905-6.
			$	$
Permanent staff..	25	30	29,147 50	41,000 00
Franchise	2	2	1,652 40	2,423 43
Contingencies, messengers	4	2	820 00	1,220 00
Miscellaneous—				
Clerks	10	8	6,246 67	5,912 50
Packers	5	10	2,185 00	5,880 00
Messengers	2	3	540 00	1,491 00
Carters	3	3	2,160 00	2,160 00
Totals	51	58	42,751 57	60,086 93
General average			838 26	1,035 98
Total amount deposited to the credit of the Honourable the Receiver General..			574,222 31	1,107,517 80
Advertising in newspapers. (Audited by King's Printer).			24,819 54	107,812 56
Outside work. (Intercolonial printing, audited by the King's Printer.)			....	79,228 93
Grand totals			641,793 42	1,354,646 22

OTTAWA, June 19, 1907.

Evidence of Mr. R. BELANGER, proof-reader, Printing Bureau (Revised).

Mr. R. BELANGER, proof-reader at Public Printing Bureau, called, sworn and examined.

By the Chairman :

Q. You are proof-reader down at the Bureau?—A. Yes, sir.

Q. And your salary is $18 ?—A. Per week.

29a—38

Q. You complain that you are asked to read the proof sheets, while the printers get $20 per week?—A. Yes, sir; the machine men, during session, get as much as $44 and $45 a fortnight.

Q. And the proofreaders for the House of Commons receive from $1,500 to $1,600?—A. Yes, sir.

Q. What do the proof-readers get in ordinary business establishments?—A. About the outside establishments, there are many of them in Canada, but I do not think there are any constituted as the Printing Bureau is, because in private establishments the author is generally responsible for all he gets printed. The proofs are sent down to him, he reads them and signs them for the press, while for the Government work it is not the same thing. We require to have qualifications for our work, and the fact is that in the outside establishments the proof-readers are mostly girls and the employers pay them $6 or $7 or $10 per week. They do not assume any responsibility, while in our case we are responsible for the departmental reports, several of which are not sent back to the departments for correction or revision.

By Mr. Fyshe :

Q. You are in the printing department?—A. Yes. As far as the salary is concerned, if you will permit me, Mr. Chairman, I will take that document of ours which has been submitted to you—here is where the difficulty lies—in the Printing Bureau there is a practical branch composed of the printers, pressmen and bookbinders. These are protected by their unions and the Printing Bureau cannot pay them less than the minimum fixed by the union. There are several other branches, like the Stationery branch, that are protected by the Civil Service Act, while we, the proofreaders, have nothing behind us, we have nothing at our back .

Q. You have neither the union nor the Civil Service Act?—A. Neither a union nor the Civil Service Act; we stand aside, that is my first point in the document. We want to be classified in some way.

Q. Under the Civil Service Act?—A. I think we should be included in the clerical staff. I think we are nothing else but a clerical class, and being such we should be included under the Civil Service Act, should we not ?

Q. You think your work is as important as the work of those already under the Civil Service Act?—A. Just so. Now, as to the importance of our work: In the outside establishments the author sends in his work which is set by the compositor, and it is sent back to the author, who reads the proof and returns it to the printing office; it is sent back to him and he signs the proof for the press, his imprimatur is put on it; in the case of the Government work it is not the same. The departments send in their reports, the House of Commons sends in its copy, the *Hansard*, and we read the proofs, we have the whole of that to do, and we are entirely responsible for it.

Q. There is no check beyond you?—A. No, sir.

Q. So that if anything comes up wrong, of course they are down on you for it?—A. We are responsible for it, we have to sign for the press, we have to read the first and last proof, and are responsible.

Q. Does it pass through more than one hand in the final proof-reading?—A. The final proofreading ?

Q. I mean when it comes into your hand, after it has been looked over I suppose by the party making the speech, or sending the document ?—A. Yes.

Q. Then it comes into your hands to be looked over before being finally printed ?—A. Certainly.

Q. Does it go through the hands of only one of your staff or of two or more ?—A. It goes through the hands of three or four.

Q. But why of three or four?—A. Well, you know the work must be subdivided to be finished.

SESSIONAL PAPER No. 29a

By the Chairman:

Q. Take that page (indicating report) you read the proof of that page ?—A. We read the first proof, it is sent back to the department.

Q. Who reads the second proof ?—A. The department reads it.

Q. When it comes back?—A. In page form and then it comes back to our department here and we go over it once again.

Q. Will it be the same man who went over the first one ?—A. No, not generally, another man goes over it and reads it, and if it is French he compares it with the English, and then we sign it for the press or for stereotyping or anything like that. We are entirely responsible. If I put my signature on a forme. that is 16 pages, as is generally done, I am entirely responsible for that. If it is to be reprinted, I may be held responsible for the reprint.

Now. gentlemen, I got a letter last week from the Public Printer in Washington. I had, in a letter, asked him to inform me what salaries they are giving to their proof-readers down there, and I have the letter here in reply. The salary is about $1,500, or a little less than that. They do not ask or require the same qualifications from their proof-readers down there as they do here. I am willing to give you a few instances if I am not taking too much of your time.

The CHAIRMAN.—Go on.

A. Gentlemen, take a French Canadian for instance. I am supposed to know English and just now am reading the Revised Statutes, or revised version. I am not only proof-reading them, I am really editing them, and in what way? Because I read the French version of the Revised Statutes, and I have the English version beside me, and I compare every line, every paragraph, every reference with the English, and the fact is that although it comes from a lawyer, from the Justice Department, from men well qualified to do the work, in the translation I find in nearly every page serious errors, wrong references, &c. Well, I have to correct those errors and I do that. Many of the men down there in the Printing Bureau have to know the two languages. Down in Washington all they have to know is English in order that they may follow the copy and read the proof, that is all they have to do. When we read important matter, statutes or anything like that, we have to take the French and compare it with the English. Some years ago, take for instance the Auditor General's Report, there was no translation, there was no one in the department that was authorized to do the translation of that report, so the English copy came down to the Printing Bureau, it was set there in English, and after it was printed in English they began the French edition. They put men to work on it there who were printers and compositors, but who knew nothing about translation, and they translated it from the English as best they could. Of course the report was composed of different items, which made it a simple matter enough, but still when it came into our office we had to correct all the errors in translation made by the compositors.

Q. You had to make it in good French?—A. Yes.

Q. In other words, you were simply doing the work of translators?—A. Yes, some got indignant over that, because it was not their work, so they asked for supplementary pay for that work, because it was really the translators' work. We did not get the extra pay, but the work was taken away from us and give to a special man, and of course, he had no kick coming. But for other reports, the Trade and Commerce, Trade and Navigation, which are composed of tables and headings, and which are mostly figures there is no translation for them until it comes to the Bureau, where we proof-readers have to supply the translation for them. That is the compositors set them to the best of their knowledge, and when the proofs come to us we have to correct them and we are responsible for their accuracy.

Q. That is you are responsible for putting it into good French?—A. For putting it into good French. and it is all along like that.

Q. What salary do they give you?—A. $18 per week.

29a—38½

Q. You are all paid by the week?—A. All paid by the hour and each fortnight.

By Mr. Fyshe:

Q. Do all of you get the same pay?—A. Yes, sir, we all get the same.

By the Chairman:

Q. All who signed this memorial get the same pay?—A. Yes, sir.

By Mr. Fyshe:

Q. How long have you been there?—A. Ten years. There are men who have been there twenty years, there is Mr. Harwood and Mr. Ami, and they are getting $22 a week. Speaking of their case, it is really a shame, because I think there is little work done there without either the King's Printer or the Superintendent consulting one or the other of these gentlemen.

Q. How old are they?—A. Mr. Harwood is 64 years of age, and Mr. Ami is 50.

By the Chairman:

Q. Of course it is necessary for the proof-readers to be men of education?—A. I will leave you gentlemen to judge of that. Take the case of the Revised Statutes, where a man has to read English on the one side and French on the other and really ⌐ edit the work. I was down to see Mr. Newcombe two weeks ago. He wished to get out the Statutes in time to satisfy the Members for the next session. I gave him the means of doing so, and we are helping him in every way. We are doing the whole work over at the Bureau. I give you this as an illustration of the class of work we have to do down there. Whenever we have asked for an increase of salary we have had this Printing Bureau Act quoted to us in answer to our question.

By Mr. Fyshe:

Q. What does that provide?—A. That the rate paid at the Printing Bureau shall be the same as that paid in other cities, that is in Toronto and Montreal and other cities.

Q. That does not cover the proofreaders?—A. No, we thought not, but they said it did. So that you will see, gentlemen, in our case it is not so much a question of increase as it is a question of classification. What we would most require of you, gentlemen, would be that you put us under the Civil Service Act, whether it be in the technical class or any other class, so that we would have something to refer to. There would be this to it that would be advantageous: if we are put under the Civil Service Act there will be a chance for our chiefs to classify their men and to see that the good men in there, who are doing their duty, are put in the proper class. For instance, with regard to the statutory increases the chief will have a chance every year to recommend the statutory increases, and the men who are really doing their duty will get an increase or they will be promoted when the opportunity offers, or when they get to the maximum of their class. Whereas, to-day as it stands, they cannot but put the whole of the staff there on an even footing.

By the Chairman:

Q. Then it comes down to this that your request is that the proofreaders be made a class under the Civil Service Act with increased remuneration, that is the chief thing you are asking for?—A. Yes.

Q. Of course you have no objection whatever to having your memorial included in the appendix to our report, as it will be?—A. That will be quite satisfactory. There is another matter I would like to refer to, if you will permit me. You take our chief, Mr. Harwood, who has been in the service for nearly thirty years. I do not think there is a better translator in Canada. I make no exceptions. I have been his assistant for ten years, his understudy. He is translating the official *Gazette*, and I think there is nothing in the world that is worse to translate than that; you have to give the sense and to give the words; the translation is most difficult. Now, Mr. Harwood has been translating for the *Canada Gazette* for over thirty years, I think.

By Mr. Fyshe:

Q. Is there no check on his translation?—A. None at all, because no one would dare to check his translation. He has been there for thirty years, and I do not think there is another man in the Dominion, a French-Canadian, who can quite replace him unless he has made a special study of the work. I was put in there as his understudy by Dr. Dawson. I was just coming out of college. I was not appointed by political influence. Dr. Dawson told me he wanted a man who had had a classical education, who knew the French and the English languages, and he wanted him to go in there so that when Mr. Harwood, who was getting up in years, left, there would be some one to succeed him. I am qualified to translate the official *Gazette*. I must say that Mr. Harwood receives special pay for the translation of the *Gazette*. But I mention this to show how the men in that office are qualified.

Q. You do not think you are getting enough?—A. Not at all.

Q. Who translates the Geological report, that is a highly technical report?—A. That is done by one of the newspaper gentlemen who is here during the session.

Q. It is not done by one of your staff?—A. No. To illustrate your question with reference to the living wage, I have been obliged to live in a certain position, being in the employ of the Government. I have been educated to certain things, I have been obliged to take extra work, to translate technical reports for other departments. That report of Dr. Haanel on the Electric Smelting of Metals is one of these. I translated that for him and he was very well satisfied with the translation. I have to do this work in addition to my regular work at the Bureau, in order to obtain an addition to my salary. I translated the last Forestry report for Mr. Campbell, and many other reports. Several of my colleagues have to do whatever extra work they can get outside, translation, indexing, &c., to make a reasonable salary. The English proof-readers are very efficient men. Except a couple, they have been long in the service, all over ten years. During the sessions of Parliament (night work) they are responsible for the correction of the daily *Hansard* and of the Orders and Minutes of the Senate and House of Commons. There is no check on them for this work. No one else reads it or sees it. It is arduous work, which they must do whether the sittings of the House are short or long. They sometimes have to remain working until late in the morning to prepare those publications for press. Now, as to overtime. The printers, pressmen, binders are paid for every minute of work done after hours. They get pay and a half or double pay for such work. We, on the other hand, are supposed to do all the work, and if it keeps us after hours, we get no extra remuneration. During the sessions of Parliament two or three men are obliged to work every Saturday afternoon and every Sunday to keep up with the work. They do not get a cent for that extra work, which is supposed to compensate for the two weeks' holidays given to us, but I cannot see how these can be counted as holidays if we are obliged to pay for them by extra work. In all the departments the employees are given three weeks' holidays and are not supposed to work more than the regular hours to compensate for this.

By the Chairman:

Q. Mr. Bazin and Mr. Fyshe are going over the Bureau, and of course they will look over the conditions?—A. Just to illustrate what I was saying, of course comparisons are not always right. But take the Superintendent's office. There are clerks in there who are being paid $20 and $22 a week who do nothing else but keep the time and enter in the book the numbers of the requisitions. And they are paid $3 or $4 or $5 a week more than we are.

By Mr. Fyshe:

Q. That is in the office of the Superintendent of Printing?—A. Yes, sir, there are timekeepers, who keep the time of the men, and who see to the requisitions and the correspondence. I am not saying they are too liberally recompensed for their work. But if we compare our work with theirs, we must say that we are indeed underpaid. And why do they get a reasonable salary? Because they are classified under the Civil Service Act.

Q. For no other reason?—A. No.

Witness retired.

OTTAWA, May 27, 1907.

The Secretary, Civil Service Commission :

SIR,—Any communication relative to the enclosed statement may be sent to

R. BELANGER,

Proof-readers' Room, Printing Bureau.

OTTAWA, May 27, 1907.

The Civil Service Commission, Ottawa :

SIRS,—Our object in appearing before you is to invite your attention to some of the disabilities we are under as proof-readers in the Government Printing Bureau, and to ask for redress.

Our position is an anomalous one. The Department of Public Printing and Stationery is divided into two branches, viz., the clerical branch, including the civil servants, and the practical branch, including printers, pressmen, &c. The proof-readers are not classed with either branch; we are not union men with power to insist upon consideration, and we have not the advantage of permanency enjoyed by those members of the Civil Service in the department.

Under those circumstances, we are compelled to come to you to ask that we may be put upon a proper basis as a branch of the department, the first requisite of which is a rate of pay commensurate with services rendered. The present rate of pay to proof-readers is, we submit, altogether inadequate. We are paid at present $18 per week, and we have been given to understand that we have reached our limit.

Fifteen years ago that rate might have been thought reasonable—to-day it is not. This has been called the 'growing time,' and certainly the expansion of the Government departments keep pace with the demands of the country. All of this increase of public business which it is necessary to put upon record passes through our hands, and while 'times are good,' living in the capital is not by any means cheaper. The contrary is the case.

There are no means of comparison by which a fair rate of pay can be arrived at in our case, and the reason is obvious. We have had the scale of pay given to Toronto proof-readers cited to us in answer to our expressed dissatisfaction. But there is no analogy between the cases. We are required to have a far wider range of knowledge than newspaper proof-readers. It is necessary for us to keep abreast of political happenings. Our work in connection with departmental reports calls for a varied acquaintance with scientific and technical subjects. We are often called upon to use our own judgment and discretion in the matter of incomplete or erroneous copy, and for these and other reasons our work is on a higher plane than that of outside proof-readers.

During the recent long sessions of Parliament we have been reading and are responsible for *Hansard* and committee reports which are set up by printers who receive $20 per week, while we are paid $18. The discrepancy does not seem reasonable to us.

ʀ point to which we would direct your attention is that proof-readers for the
of Commons receive $1,500 to $1,600 per annum for the session's work. All of
atter is again read by the Bureau proof-readers before being signed and finally
to the printer. Among these gentlemen are: Messrs. Quéry, $1,600, Briand,
; Gascon, $1,500; Charlier, $1,500; and Boyce, $1,200.

ᵻere are in the different offices of the Printing Bureau young clerks employed as
epers or bookkeepers and filling positions that demand no special ability, who
higher wages than the proof-readers. We do not say that their salary is too
ıut if we compare their work with ours, we must conclude that. we have been
neglected.

may be noted here that a few years ago all departmental reports were sent to
ᵻartments for proof-reading before going to the printers. . A great number of the
ı are now read in the Bureau only and signed for there. The translation is also
n the Bureau, when necessary, by proof-readers who are also competent trans-

is not the least of our complaints that our pay is inadequate. We are re-
at times to work overtime and after the usual hours. Compositors and press-
lo likewise, but compositors and pressmen being union men demand and receive
vages for such extra work. We have never received any extra or overtime pay.
ɔ sum up, the proof-readers' pay is in no wise commmensurate with the require-
of the position. The first of these is high qualifications, since the King's
ʳr will accept as proof-readers none other but men who have made classical
ᵻ, or who are pastmasters of the printing craft. Then they are required to do all
ırk, working overtime evenings, holidays and Sundays, without extra pay. Lastly,
ᵻave the entire responsibility for the correctness of departmental and parliamen-
ıublications, since their imprimatur is the only one accepted by the Government
s. And withal they are paid very little more, and often less, than mere com-
ᵣs.

ᵻur request is that the proof-readers of the Printing Bureau be made a class or
led in one of the existing classes of the Civil Service, with increased remunera-
We would then enjoy the privileges of the other clerical staffs of the public ser-
vhich are governed and protected by the Civil Service Act, in the matter of sal-
in every other matter.

ʜese are the principal points we would submit for your consideration. Confident
ı justice of our request and hoping that you will see fit to give us redress, ve
ʀs,

Your humble servants,

The Proof-readers of the Printing Bureau.

(Signed)   R. BELANGER.
R. AIME TISON.
W. J. KANE.
WM. A. TAYLOR.
H. G. LETCH.
J. W. PATTERSON.
GEO. G. MERCURE.
CHARLES J. BETTEZ.
R. HOOD.
M. J. BRENNAN.
L. MALONEY.

OTTAWA, Wednesday, October 16, 1907.

The Royal Commission on the Civil Service met this morning at 10.30 o'clock.

Present:—Mr. J. M. COURTNEY, C.M.G., Chairman.

Mr. THOMAS FYSHE, Montreal, and

Mr. P. J. BAZIN, Quebec.

A deputation from the Foremen's Association of the Government Printing Bureau, composed of J. C. Shipman, John Munro and W. C. Allan appeared and submitted a memorial, which was read and filed.

Mr. J. C. SHIPMAN, sworn and examined.

By the Chairman:

Q. How long have you been in the Bureau?—A. Practically since its inception continuously, that is, for eighteen years.

Q. It was established on July 1, 1889?—A. Yes, and I started to work on August 1, 1889.

Q. Are all the foremen in the same position?—A. They are practically in the same position, so far as length of service is concerned. There is one who has not been there that long. He was appointed on the death of the previous foreman.

Q. Are all the foremen selected from the operatives?—A. All except the one I have just mentioned.

Q. Then, as a rule, the foremen have gone through the lower grades before they became foremen?—A. Yes, in every instance.

Q. How are they made foremen—at the will of the King's Printer?—A. Yes, the King's Printer has the appointment of all.

Q. You have all been selected, I presume, without any outside influence?—A. Yes. Some of the foremen came from the contractors, and are still acting. For instance, Mr. Allan, the foreman of the bindery, was with the contractors for the binding.

Q. Then some of the foremen came as foremen from the contractors, and others have been selected from the operatives by the King's Printer without any outside influence?—A. Yes, without any outside influence. Of course, the King's Printer and the Superintendent of Printing consult together.

Q. But no outside influence have been employed in giving these positions?—A. No. Speaking personally, in my case, there was no outside influence whatever, and I believe the same thing applies to all the other foremen.

Q. The gist of the memorial is that you think you should be made Civil Service clerks?—A. Yes. The idea is that we should have some permanence. As the matter now stands, we have been working there for the last eighteen years, and we are in the position of temporary employees—that is, if it pleases the King's Printer.

Q. You have read the Printing and Stationery Act, I presume?—A. Yes.

Q. The 17th section says: 'The Superintendent of Printing may, with the approval of the King's Printer, employ such apprentices, journeymen, workmen, skilled hands or other, as are necessary to perform the work of the establishment, and may remove the same. The provisions of the Civil Service Act shall not apply to the persons so employed by him.'?—A. Yes.

Q. Not being a lawyer, I would not like to lay down anything *ex cathedra*, but I imagine that to carry out the proposal of your memorial would require an amendment to an Act of Parliament?—A. I presume it would. At the same time, there are others, such as clerks, employed by him, who are finally made permanent.

Q. The clerks would not come in as apprentices, journeymen, or skilled hands? —A. No, unless you could call them workmen. So far as I can see, that section would require to be amended.

Q. Have you anything else to add to the memorial?—A. In our endeavour to find out exactly how the foremen in commercial establishments were treated, we sent communications to all the leading firms. The printing firms are very close, and it is almost impossible to get information from them. But we did get answers from a number of firms, and they showed that in Toronto the average number of operatives under each foreman was 22 and in Ottawa the average number was 20, whereas in the Bureau the average to each foreman is 45, which is a little more than double the average in the outside offices.

By Mr. Fyshe:

Q. Is the work and responsibility of the foreman increased in proportion to the number of employees under him?—A. Yes. In my own room, for instance, the linotype room, the number has more than doubled since 1900.

By the Chairman:

Q. But outside of the session of Parliament, is not your staff a fluctuating staff; that is, does it not go up and down in proportion to the amount of public business?— A. No. During the session of Parliament we put on a night staff; but after the session the volume of work coming into the Bureau is so great that we are able to keep the men employed right along.

Q. Then the only difference is that during the session you have a night staff?— A. Yes.

Q. What are the hours of the foreman?—A. 48 hours a week, or 8 hours a day.

By Mr. Fyshe:

Q. Do you keep the hours rigidly?—A. Yes, very rigidly, particularly during the session of Parliament, when the hours at times are excessive, and it is necessary for the foremen to work very much overtime in order to meet the requirements of both Houses. I kept track of my overtime last session, and it amounted to the equivalent of over eight weeks.

Q. Do you get pay for that overtime?—A. No. In lieu of overtime we receive two weeks' holidays.

Q. If you have any short time it is deducted from your holidays, and if you have enough short time to wipe out your holidays you would get no holidays whatever?— A. We would get no holidays whatever.

Q. Is that rule maintained rigidly?—A. Yes.

Q. Who attends to that?—A. The Superintendent of Printing. We have to enter the time when we come in the morning, the time when we go out at noon, the time when we come back, and the time when we go out in the evening. Since I have been foreman, for eight years, I have been off only twice outside of my holidays, and both times it was on account of sickness at home.

Q. Is the rule the same in regard to all the workmen?—A. No, the workmen are paid for overtime.

Q. Is the same track kept rigidly of their coming and going?—A. Yes, and if a workman is five minutes late he loses an hour.

Q. And the attendance book is the sole evidence of this?—A. No. It would take the operatives too long to sign an attendance book. There is a check system, under which the checks are numbered, each man having his own number. He takes the check from a box and puts it into a receptacle, from which it is taken away five minutes afterwards.

Q. You have a timekeeper?—A. Yes.

Q. And he looks after all that?—A. Yes.

By the Chairman:

Q. When your eight hours' day's work is up, who takes charge of the linotype room—it runs night and day, doesn't it?—A. Yes, during the session.

Q. Who takes charge of it at night?—A. Mr. Cross, who is the night foreman during the session, and after the session he becomes the assistant foreman.

Q. Is that rule confined to your room, or is it general?—A. That is confined to my room. There is only a night staff in the linotype room and in the press room.

Q. Is there the same condition of affairs in the press room?—A. No. The press room staff is small at night, and they merely put one of the pressmen in charge and give him a little more remuneration. He is not classed as a foreman and does not get foreman's wages.

Q. You get a fortnight's vacation, and if you exceed the fortnight your pay suffers deduction?—A. Yes.

Q. Whatever extent of overtime you may have put in during the year?—A. Yes, it does not count. In support of our memorial, I wish to submit the following letters which we have received from some of the employing printers in Ottawa:—

'THE "JOURNAL,"
'OTTAWA, ONT., September 23, 1907.

'J. C. SHIPMAN, Esq.,
'272 Stewart Street,
'City.

'DEAR SIR,—With regard to our recent conversation, I would like to make it clear that as an employing printer I am heartily in favour of the Government placing the foremen of the departments at the Printing Bureau on any basis whatever of compensation.

'The recent contention of the master printers against an increase in wages of Bureau linotype operators was based on the belief that the operators enjoy the full statutory rate fixed by parliament, which is already higher than the Ottawa union rate, and that any increase in the scale, besides being illegal, would by tending to force up the union scale soon affect the private employers of Ottawa unfairly, in view of our competition with other cities.

'This objection the master printers do not apply to the foremen of departments, who are skilled experts, and to whom we do not, in our employ, apply considerations of union rates.

'I think I represent the feeling of the employing printers generally in saying that we have no objection to the Government paying any scale of compensation it pleases to foremen of departments.

'I am, yours truly,
'(Signed)   P. D. ROSS,
'*President, Employing Printers' Association.*'

'THE MORTIMER CO., LIMITED,
'OTTAWA, September 19, 1907.

'JOHN C. SHIPMAN, Esq.,
'Ottawa.

'DEAR SIR,—Our foremen are part of the executive management, and as such are not classed same as employees under them, nor are they paid by any scale. The salary is fixed according to size of department they look after and the amount of responsibility.

' The rate of pay runs from $25 to $35 per week, and as certain departments increase in size these salaries will be increased accordingly, providing those in charge keep up with the progress.

' Your truly,

' (Sgd.)   THE MORTIMER CO., LTD.,

' A. E. MORTIMER, *General Manager.*'

' THE ROLLA CRAIN Co, LTD.,

' OTTAWA, September 16, 1907.

' J. C. SHIPMAN,

  ' Secretary, Foremen's Association,

    ' Ottawa.

' DEAR SIR,—Your letter of the 11th instant received.

' In reply we beg to say that we enclose herewith schedule filled out as required, and would further say that all foremen are paid a salary and are not classed with the ordinary workmen.

' They are really treated the same as our office staff, and two weeks' holidays are given them with pay.

' They do not receive overtime, but at the same time they have nothing deducted for lost time, for sickness or otherwise.

' Trusting this is the information you desire, we remain,

' Yours truly,

' (Sgd.)   THE ROLLA L. CRAIN CO., LTD.,

' ROLLA L. CRAIN, *Managing Director.*'

' OTTAWA " FREE PRESS," OTTAWA, September 11, 1907.

' Mr. J. C. SHIPMAN,

  ' 272 Stewart Street.

' DEAR SIR,—You ask me what would be the attitude of the employing printers to the application of the foremen at the Government Printing Bureau for an increase of salary.

' So far as this office is concerned, we regard foremen as members of the executive staff, and in fixing their wages, no consideration whatever is given to the rate of wages paid to the men placed in their charge.

' For particular office reasons one foreman may be worth a good deal more than another.

' I would regard any interference by the employing printers in the matter of wages paid to Government Printing Bureau foremen as unwarranted.

' The amount paid to foremen at the Bureau does not affect us in the slightest.

' Yours faithfully,

' (Sgd.)   E. NORMAN SMITH,

' *Managing Director.*'

Q. How long has this scale of $25 a week to the foremen been in force?—A. Since the 1st of June, 1904.

Q. What was it before that?—A. $22. I think in 1891 we received an increase to $20 a week.

· Q. Then, since 1891, shortly after the establishment of the Bureau, your remuneration has gone up from $20 to $25 a week?—A. Yes.

Q. And $25 has been the rate during the last three years?—A. Yes. In connection with the number of operatives we have to look after, we have figured out the rate which the foremen cost per operative. We have found that to be in Toronto $1.10 a week, in Ottawa commercial offices $1.05 per week, and in the Government Printing Bureau 55 cents a week per operative.

Q. Have you anything else to say?—A. The work in the Bureau has increased about sixty per cent in the last six years, in the amount charged for it.

By Mr. Fyshe :

Q. Have the employees increased in the same proportion?—A. No. They have increased to a certain extent, but not in proportion.

By the Chairman :

Q. Before that time a number of operatives were taken on temporarily during the session, but they have since gradually become permanent?—A. Yes. During the last six years that has been largely done away with.

Q. That is to say, the floating element has become permanent?—A. Yes, a portion of it, since the linotype machines have been employed to the extent that they are. During the session the surplus of work is covered by putting on a night staff.

Q. What becomes of the night staff after the session?—A. They are distributed throughout the Bureau and put at other work.

Q. They work at night during the session and at day during the recess?—A. Yes.

By Mr. Bazin

Q. So that during the whole year round you employ the same number of men?—A. Yes, practically.

Q. Except that during the session you use some for night work?—A. Yes. It was the introduction of the linotype machines which enabled us to do that.

By the Chairman:

Q. Then the introduction of the linotype machine has saved the suspensions?—A. Yes.

Q. Have you anything further to tell us?—A. No, except to compare the Bureau here with the Government Printing Bureau in Washington—as we call this the Washington of the North. In the Bureau in Washington the foremen receive forty per cent of the Public Printer's salary, that is, $2,000. The Public Printer receives $4,500.

Q. He is the equivalent of the King's Printer?—A. Yes. We receive thirty-two per cent of the salary of the King's Printer.

Q. That is your salary is about $1,300 a year and his is $4,000?—A. Yes. These figures are taken from the report of 1906; I could not get the report of 1907. We think that in view of the way foremen are treated in commercial offices, we might very well be treated as an executive staff and be placed on a permanent basis. We think that in view of the responsible duties we have to perform that after eighteen years of service we are entitled to some consideration along that line. I might say that our case was presented to the management of the Bureau, and they looked favourably on it, although I do not suppose they feel like recommending it unless we convince the powers that be of the advisability of it.

Q. Have you approached the Secretary of State on the subject?—A. No.

Q. Have you ever approached the King's Printer with a view to obtaining an amendment to the Act?—A. Yes. We approached him last April on this question and again within the last couple of weeks.

Q. You do not know what he may do, as Parliament has not been in session since you approached him?—A. No.

Q. He can do nothing before the coming session?—A. No. He knows that we are approaching you. His suggestion to us was to convince other people of the advisability of it before he would recommend it. He is perfectly willing that it should take place.

SESSIONAL PAPER No. 29a

In fact, there are advantages which would accrue to him, in the proposal, which he appreciates; but we have yet to convince the Secretary of State.

Q. What are the advantages which you think would accrue to him?—A. He could answer that better than I could. Of course, we would have a better standing before the operatives and could handle them better.

Q. It would be a matter of discipline?—A. Yes, there would be better discipine for one thing.

Q. At present you are first among equals?—A. Yes, that is the way it stands. The King's Printer said that there were many advantages that he could see in our proposal. What they were he did not tell us, but it was such a departure that he did not feel like recommending it unless we convinced other people as well. We have not approached the Secretary of State yet, but we intend doing so.

JOHN MUNRO, sworn and examined.

By the Chairman:

Q. You are the foreman of the press room at the Government Printing Bureau? —A. Yes.

Q. How long have you been there?—A. Six years on August 1 last.

Q. Have you all that time been foreman?—A. Yes.

Q. Where did you come from?—A. From Winnipeg.

Q. Were you a foreman printer in Winnipeg?—A. Yes.

Q. You have been a printer all the days of your working life?—A. Since my school days.

Q. Have you anything to tell us supplementary to Mr. Shipman's evidence?—A. First, in fuller answer to your question as to where I came from, I was receiving in Winnipeg at that time the same salary that I am receiving to-day.

Q. May one suggest that Winnipeg was a more expensive place to live in than Ottawa, and that your salary was really an increase though it was the same amount? —A. I will scarcely admit that was the case six years ago. I was disappointed from my lack of knowledge of positions here. I anticipated a larger salary and greater privileges. As a matter of fact, when I came I found that it was $22, so that I was practically losing the difference.

Q. Now the salary has come up to an equivalent?—A. It has come up in the meantime to an equivalent. I endeavoured at that time to secure the equivalent, and I asked the manager of the establishment I worked for in Winnipeg if he would give me evidence of what he had been paying, and this is the letter he wrote to me in 1902, a year after I came here:—

THE TRIBUNE PUBLISHING CO.,
WINNIPEG, MAN., October 21, 1902.

Mr. JOHN MUNRO,
Foreman and Pressman,
Government Printing Bureau,
Ottawa, Ont.

DEAR SIR,—Replying to your favour of the 17th inst., I have no hesitation in saying that when we brought you on as pressman from New York and gave you a salary of $25 per week, I offered you a contract for one, two or three years, at your option, if you had remained in our employ as foreman of our press room.

You voluntarily, however, relinquished the situation and went east to accept your present situation.

Wishing you success in all your undertakings, I remain,
Yours truly,
(Signed)   D. L. McINTYRE,
Manager.

Q. What is meant there by contract?—A. We were to sign papers for one, two or three years, and they were to guarantee my situation for that period.

Q. What else have you to say?—A. As regards the press room particularly, I have to look after at the present moment 27 presses and 3 other machines, accessories to presses. The number of employees at present in the press room is 57.

Q. How many of these are women?—A. There are 9 girl feeders, 23 boy feeders, 18 pressmen, 5 general help, 1 assistant foreman, one foreman; the wages ranging from $5.50 to $25 a week. The wages paid in the press room in 1905-6 in round numbers amounted to $33,000, while the amount charged in the departmental accounts for press work is about $40,000. The difference is represented by incidental expenses, such as printing inks, general repairs, wear and tear of machinery, oils, and so forth. There is no attempt on my part to have anything short or anything over, only to cover the necessary running expenses of the room. In the following year, the nine months year, the wages came to $29,000 and the charges were about $33,000. In the six months of the present year, ending September 30, the wages in the press room, come to about $18,000, and the charges will hold about the same average as the previous years, though I have not gone into them with the same detail.

Q. That is rather less than in the year before?—A. Yes, and this explanation is necessary for it: The figures cover the first half of the fiscal year commencing on April 1, and in it we had only two or three weeks of the session. At the end of the session we shut down on the night staff and on overtime and on everything else. In the management of the press room I have endeavoured to give the full executive power that is necessary, and I consider that I have saved the Government, in my official capacity, some thousands of dollars—first, in this specific matter, by putting an attachment on one of the presses which prints envelopes. Formerly, when we printed them we put them into the press in packages of twenty-fives, but they came out, not in packages of twenty-fives, but all confused. By putting this attachment on the press, I got them to come out in counted packages of twenty-fives. By that means I saved the foreman of the bindery the operation of handling these envelopes in counting them.

By Mr. Fyshe:

Q. Did you patent that attachment?—A. I have had it patented, but unfortunately, as I am a Government employee, there is no money value in it for me at present as regards the Government work. It is working for the Government for nothing.

Q. By that means you have considerably increased the value of your services to the Government?—A. I consider so, to the extent of five cents per thousand envelopes, which that one operation cost. It also saves the delay of time in delivering the envelopes from the press room to the bindery and from the bindery to the delivery room, as they now go direct from the press room to the delivery room.

By the Chairman:

Q. Is your patent in use in outside printing office?—A. I have just secured the patent in the United States, as that is where the field for it is. We have not done anything with it in Canada.

Q. So far as your inventive powers have gone, you have benefited the country by giving it the use of your patent free of charge?—A. The Government has had the use of it for the past two years.

Q. There would be no objection, legal or otherwise, to your getting the benefit of the patent in the United States?—A. Not at all.

Q. You have spoken of the amount of wages and the charges for ink, oils, and all that; do you buy these oils and inks?—A. Yes.

Q. $4,000 are spent in odds and ends?—A. In the full year it would probably average about $5,000.

Q. Is there not an officer who purchases supplies, is that left to be done by each foreman?—A. In my own case, inks, oils, roller composition, benzine and coal oil, pieces from the press builders or renewals and repairs to presses, are bought on my requisition. I have an order book with a stub to it, and I make out my requisition of what I wish, and in most cases I write the name of the firm to which that order is going. If it is out of the city, the clerk orders it, and puts it through the letter book, after he makes a duplicate order, which is the official order signed by the Superintendent of Printing. So that practically I am responsible in ordering.

Q. If it is bought in the city, you indicate the name of the firm which supplies the article; and even if it is bought outside of the city, you suggest the name of the firm from whom it can be bought?—A. As a rule, both ways.

Q. But the order itself, after you fill up the requisition, passes from the clerk to the Superintendent of Printing?—A. Yes.

Q. And he orders?—A. He approves of it and signs it.

Q. And he writes to the firm that supplies the article and gives the order?—A. Yes, from his office.

By Mr. Bazin:

Q. Is this for supplies bought outside the city, or is it also for those bought in the city?—A. We buy all that is possible in the city.

Q. What I mean is, does the order go through the same process when you buy in the city?—A. Yes, it goes through the same routine for a city order as for an outside order, only a letter is not mailed to the party receiving the order.

By the Chairman:

Q. Do all the foremen do the same thing?

Mr. SHIPMAN.—Pretty much the same. In the linotype firm we have only one firm to buy from.

Q. Is it possible that this method of buying supplies may lead to a certain amount of graft? None of you, so far as you know, receive any benefit from these orders?

Mr. MUNRO.—I receive no benefit in one form or another. I might say that coming to this situation six years ago, I was entirely unfamiliar with any of the usages of Governmental rule.

Q. Have you been enlightened?—A. I was quite humble to receive advice from the authorities about me. When I had an order to give out, I would inquire who were the people formerly patronized, and as a rule I followed the old course without very much regard to personal feelings, and have followed it pretty constantly right along.

By Mr. Fyshe:

Q. You did what was done before?—A. As a rule. When I found anything unsatisfactory in my opinion, I would discard it and take the next choice.

By the Chairman:

Q. Is there anything else you wish to say ?—A. We have in the press room a variety of subjects. There is the paper.

Q. You do not buy the paper?—A. I have nothing to do with the paper except to check it and see that I have received exactly what the order calls for, and to give the best workmanlike results. I would like to emphasize the point in the memorial, that we would like to be recognized as an executive staff. I have been accustomed to be recognized in that capacity. I hope I have not been deteriorating in the six years that I have been in the Government service.

Q. I suppose there is a certain stability in Government work that there is not outside?—A. Yes, there is a certain stability, but how to name it might be rather indefinite. At the same time, I think that every one of the present foremen, and probably our successors, would be pretty well satisfied if they were assured of permanent standing, with a first-class salary and the status that would necessarily go with it, in walking shoulder to shoulder with the clerk or the official in the same building with us, who at the present moment may or may not consider that we are simply mechanical operatives lacking the full calibre of the clerk or the officer.

The CHAIRMAN.—Has Mr. Allan anything to add?

Mr. ALLAN.—No, Mr. Shipman and Mr. Munro have covered the ground.

MEMORIAL OF THE FOREMEN'S ASSOCIATION

(GOVERNMENT PRINTING BUREAU.)

To the Honourable the Commissioners appointed to inquire into matters pertaining to the Civil Service of Canada:

GENTLEMEN,—Your petitioners, the Foremen's Association of the Government Printing Bureau, number ten persons, governing a working staff of over 450 people. All this working staff, foremen included, are subject to dismissal at an hour's notice.

All alike are equally governed by the same rules and privileges, excepting that the workpeople are paid for all overtime and deducted for lost time, while the foremen receive two weeks' vacation in lieu of overtime, and deduction made for all lost time over that.

Most of the foremen have been employed in the Bureau since its inception, over eighteen years ago, and are yet in the positions of temporary employees. After such a length of service for the Government, by reason of being out of touch with the commercial life of the printing and allied trades, we would be placed at a disadvantage in securing similar positions in our calling.

A striking illustration is here given of one foreman retiring with the infirmities of age after having served 15 years with the contractors, and continuing in the Government Printing Bureau service for 16 years additional. Another foreman, through illness, was compelled to retire from duty after long years of faithful service, and he and his family were kept from actual want by subscriptions taken among the men over whom, while in health, he presided as foreman.

And still another foreman, yet on active duty, but frail with age and faithful service, has served 15 years with the contractors and to date has been 18 years with the Government Printing Bureau.

No real reward or superannuation is provided for such faithful and lengthy service.

The foremen, acting as an executive staff, deem that some greater return could well be made to them, and submit that they should be placed on the permanent Civil Service staff of at least first-class standing, with superannuation consideration. Apart from a sentimental viewpoint, the following summaries may further strengthen our endeavours for permanent appointment:—

1. The United States Government printing office at Washington is governed by the Civil Service Commission. The foremen receive $2,000 per year, with 30 days' vacation, sick leave, and no deduction for ordinary lost time.

2. A partial census of Toronto printing offices show the foremen there to be receiving an average of $20 to $30 per week, and in some instances an additional bonus. They also receive a two weeks' vacation, and no deduction for ordinary lost time.

3. Foremen of printing offices in Ottawa receive from $20 to $30 per week, and similar treatment to those of Toronto as regards vacation and other privileges.

Comparatively, the Toronto and Ottawa printing offices do not nearly equal in size and volume of output the Government Printing Bureau establishment.

SESSIONAL PAPER No. 29a

4. The ten foremen in the Government Printing Bureau receive $25 per week, and deductions are made for lost time exceeding two weeks' vacation allowance. With a total of over 450 operatives and a weekly pay-roll of not less than $6,000, machinery valued at $400,000, the individual oversight and executive duties of a foreman are exacting of a faithfulness which a commercial printer will readily appraise.

While the outside employing printers always look askance at any wage increases of the Government Printing Bureau employees, we are pleased to show that we have the sympathy and endorsement of these same employers.

In seeking this permanent appointment, we have endeavoured to show the onerous position of a foreman—being the executive medium between employer and employee— and, in the present case, between the King's Printer and Superintendent of Printing and the operatives. In all past arrangements of scales of wages stipulated for by the operatives themselves—the foremen have not been considered by them, but have been allotted increases at the discretion of our two superiors.

P. M. DRAPER,
W. C. ALLAN,
C. W. CLOSE,
J. BYRNE,
F. ROGER,
J. C. SHIPMAN,
JOHN MUNRO,
I. COTE,
E. CARTER,
L. A. BELLEAU,

OTTAWA, October 16, 1907.

A deputation appeared representing the pressmen of the Government Printing Bureau, and consisting of Messrs. J. G. Trowbridge. E. J. Pearce and A. J. Landen.

J. G. TROWBRIDGE, sworn and examined.

By the Chairman :

Q. You are all pressmen ?—A. Yes. •

Q. How long have you been in the service of the Bureau ?—A. Since its organization.

Q. Have you always been a pressman ?—A. Yes.

Q. What wages do you get now ?—A. $16.50 a week.

Q. When you began what were the wages of the pressmen?—A. $11.

Q. How did the increase from $11 to $16.50 come about ? When did you get your first increase ?—A. Some two years after the organization of the Printing Bureau we were increased to $13 a week.

Q. That was in 1891 when Mr. Senecal was there ?—A. Yes.

Q. When was your next increase ?—A. I could not give the year exactly.

Q. What did it go to ?—A. $14.50.

Q. Was there another increase between $14.50 and $16.50?—A. No.

Q. When did you get the $16.50 ?—A. About three years ago.

Q. How many pressmen are there in the Bureau ?—A. Twenty-five.

Q. All the twenty-five think alike, and you are the spokesman ?—A. Yes.

Q. I suppose you come to impress on the Commission your views as to an increase of wages ?—A. Chiefly.

Q. What are the wages paid to pressmen in Montreal and Toronto ?—A. As to Montreal I could not say. In Toronto the union rate of wages is $16.50 a week.

,7-8 EDWARD VII., A. 1908

Q. Does the union go to Montreal ?—A. There is a union there, but I think it is not very well organized, and a good many of the offices are not under the control of the union at all.

Q. In Montreal would the rate of wages be more than $16.50 ?—A. No, I think it would be less.

Q. Are you a member of the Ottawa union ?—A. Yes, the Ottawa Printing Pressmen's Union.

Q. Have you read the Public Printing and Stationery Act by which you are governed ?—A. Yes.

Q. Do you know that it provides that ' No increase of any such rate of wages shall be made so as to raise the rate above that which is at the time of such increase paid for similar work in the cities of Montreal and Toronto ?—A. Yes, we have heard of that.

Q. Then, if $16.50 is the rate in Toronto, and not more than that is the rate in Montreal, how can you get an increase unless you get the Act amended or repealed ? —A. We have thought of that, but we thought the Commission were appointed for that particular purpose.

Q. The Commission have investigating powers, but cannot repea' an Act of Parliament.—A. No, but we understood that the Commission could make a recommendation to that end.

By Mr. Fyshe :

Q. Do you think you have harder work or greater responsibilities than the ordinary men in outside offices ?—A. No, but the conditions in Toronto are different from the conditions in Ottawa. In Ottawa the commercial offices are paying a higher rate of wages than the Government is paying in the Printing Bureau. The Mortimer Company is paying $18, $19 and $20 a week. One man is getting $15, but he is what is called a platen pressman, not a cylinder pressman. In the Government Printing Bureau we are all cylinder pressmen with one exception. The Rolla Crain Company are paying $17 a week and the *Free Press* Company are paying over $18; the Ottawa Printing Company are paying $17 a week. And this, I may say, is outside of any influence which the union has brought to bear on these companies. The scale in Ottawa is only $15 a week, but the conditions of the trade are such that the employers find themselves compelled to pay these higher rates of wages in order to get men.

By the Chairman :

Q. One would think that in such a case, you would be leaving the Government service and going into the service of these other people ?—A. There are only a limited number employed by them. We could not all be employed.

Q. Practically your work goes on all the year round ?—A. Yes.

Q. The work of these other companies depends on the amount of business coming in ?—A. I do not know any time in recent years when they have had a slack time and require to suspend any of their men. They have employment all the time, and sometimes overtime.

Q. Do you get anything extra for overtime ?—A. Yes, we get a time and a third for overtime.

Q. What do the men in the outside offices get ?—A. A time and a third.

Q. The rules in the Bureau are the same as in the outside offices ?—A. Yes.

Q. What are your hours of work per week ?—A. 48 hours per week.

Q. During the session of Parliament do any of you work at night ?—A. Yes.

Q. How do you manage that ?—A. We have three men working all night, and they are paid $20.65 a week.

Q. Outside of the session they go back to day work ?—A. Yes.

SESSIONAL PAPER No. 29a

Q. Is the work of a pressman engaged on a cylinder press harder than the work of a platen pressman?—A. No, but usually a platen pressman is not a journeyman pressman. He has not finished his trade. He is really not a competent pressman.

Q. Then, a man attached to a cylinder press, like those in the Bureau, must be a finished mechanic?—A. Yes.

Q. You have no special holidays except Sundays and such days as Thanksgiving Day?—A. Yes, all the statutory holidays.

Q. If you are late, the hour in which you come late is deducted?—A. Yes.

Q. You put in your check, and if it is five or ten minutes late, you lose an hour?—A. We cannot get our check, and the timekeeper checks off the hour. We report to the foreman and he signs the book.

Q. Where are the presses situated?—A. On the ground floor.

Q. You have no trouble about elevators?—A. No.

Q. Where do the elevators go—from your room up?—A. From our room on our side, and from the basement on the other side.

Q. All your work, after it is pressed, is sent upstairs?—A. Yes.

Q. And gradually gets into the binding department?—A. Yes.

Q. It goes through the process of folding and stitching, and then gets into the binding department?—A. Yes.

Q. Your main object in coming here, is, I presume, to recommend the Commission to look into the question of your wages, and see whether an increase could be made?—A. That, and if it is feasible, that we be granted a vacation like all other Government employees. We have to work all the year round or else lose our time.

Q. Do the pressmen in any of the outside offices in Ottawa have a vacation?—A. No.

Q. That is to say, if they are not there, they lose their day's work?—A. Exactly.

Q. Your idea is that being in the public service you should get holidays?—A. Yes.

Q. What does the union say about holidays?—A. The union has not said anything about the matter.

Q. Do the pressmen in Montreal and Toronto get holidays?—A. I believe not.

Q. Then, if holidays were given to pressmen in the Government Printing Bureau, you would be in a rather unique position, receiving a benefit which other pressmen throughout Canada do not receive?—A. So far as the pressmen of Canada are concerned, we would be in a unique position; but all the Government employees in the Government Printing Bureau at Washington receive holidays. They are in a unique position in that respect.

Q. What are their hours at Washington?—A. 48 hours a week.

Q. Have you ever sent a memorial to the King's Printer regarding your wages?—A. Not since we received our last increase.

Q. That was three years ago?—A. Yes.

Q. Don't you think it would be better to send a memorial to the King's Printer and ask him to submit it to the Secretary of State?—A. No, sir, I do not think it would work to our advantage at all, because he quotes the Act of Parliament and says he cannot go beyond that.

Q. But don't you think it would be as well to send a memorial to the King's Printer asking that he submit to the Secretary of State the question of the advisability of bringing in an amendment to the Act of Parliament?—A. We have not considered the matter from that point of view at all.

E. J. PEARCE, sworn, stated :

The Act which you refer to provides that the minimum shall be paid, but it does not state the minimum and it does not debar the King's Printer or those in authority

7-8 EDWARD VII., A. 1908

from paying whatever wages they wish. The scale is not adhered to because there are some men getting $18 and some getting $20. They may be classed as in special positions.

The CHAIRMAN.—The Act provides that no increase in the rate of wages shall be made so as to raise the rate above that which is at the time of such increase paid for similar work in the cities of Montreal and Toronto.

Mr. PEARCE.—Then you do not construe that to mean that there is any possible chance of the Government paying any more than is being paid in Toronto. Everything here is very dear, and our wages have not gone up in the last three years in proportion to the advance in outside offices.

The CHAIRMAN.—If the rate in Montreal and Toronto is $16.50, that fixes the standard, and I do not see how the rate here could be raised above that without an amendment to the Act of Parliament.

Mr. PEARCE.—$16.50 is the minimum rate.

The CHAIRMAN.—Is there a graduated rate in Toronto ?

Mr. PEARCE.—$16.50 is the minimum rate, but there are many offices paying $25 or $30 in special cases.

The CHAIRMAN.—But you would not say that the special cases fix the standard rate!

Mr. PEARCE.—No.

Mr. LARDEN.—The rate in Ottawa is $15, but a great many offices are paying more than that. The employers in Toronto cannot pay less than $16.50 but a great many are paying more.

Mr. PEARCE.—The Act either has to be amended or the Government has to show a sympathetic spirit and pay in the Bureau at least the wages that are paid in outside offices. I was going to ask the Commission if you can see your way to recommend that the Act be amended.

The CHAIRMAN.—You consider that the Act should be amended on the ground that living is higher in Ottawa than in Montreal or Toronto ?

Mr. PEARCE.—Yes, on the ground that it is not fair to compare the cost of living in Montreal or Toronto with the cost of living in Ottawa.

Mr. FYSHE.—Do you think the increased cost of living is a permanent condition or merely temporary ?

Mr. PEARCE.—I have never lived in Toronto, but I have the words of those who have lived in both Toronto and Ottawa, and they say that Ottawa is the dearer city to live in. So that the cost of living in Montreal or Toronto is not a fair guide to the cost of living in Ottawa. Consequently I think that if the Act were amended to take in Ottawa and Toronto, it would be much fairer and the rate of wages would be higher.

The CHAIRMAN.—Then your people would approve of the Act being amended by substituting the rate paid in the printing offices of Ottawa instead of the rate paid in the printing offices of Montreal and Toronto ?

Mr. PEARCE.—Under present conditions I certainly would.

By the Chairman :

Q. Mr. Pearce, I will ask you another question : These sections appear not to have been in the original Act at all, but to have been inserted in an Act passed there years ago ?—A. Yes.

Q. What was the reason for putting in that limitation ?—A. I think it was on account of an agreement which was reached in Toronto on a revision of the last scale of wages there, and the Act was amended at that time so as to put the wages in the Printing Bureau on a par with those in Toronto. At the present time I think the agreement existing in Toronto governs the Printing Bureau far more than the Act, because at any time that we approach the officers of the Printing Bureau in regard to wages, the Toronto agreement is brought forward.

The CHAIRMAN.—When this Act was brought in, it was just previous to the last general election, when there was no want of consideration for those employed in the public service.

Mr. TROWBRIDGE.—I think I can explain the reason for the insertion of that amendment to the Act. At that time the unions were making an effort to get an increase of pay, and the authorities thought the unions were demanding increases too often, and they established a rule whereby they would always be governed and the unions in this city would have practically nothing to say as to what the rate of wages should be.

The CHAIRMAN.—Concurrently with that Act there was a rise in wages at the Bureau of $1 or $1.50 a week, and subsequently, within a few months, there was a general election, so that one would naturally suppose that there was not an unkind reference to the employees of the Bureau in introducing this into the Act.

Mr. PEARCE.—No.

The CHAIRMAN.—Now, having had three years' experience of it, you wish it to be modified?

Mr. PEARCE.—We contended from the very beginning that Montreal was not a fair city on which to base the rate of our wages. Our contention is, that Montreal is a poorly oragnized city, and consequently there is any kind of wages paid there, and a comparison is not fair to us. There is one other alternative which I think would solve the whole question. To my mind, the Government would do away with all these difficulties, if they would make the employees in the Printing Bureau permanent and treat them in the same way as the Civil Service, granting statutory increases. Then, they could devise other ways of controlling the employees. I think they will find that more feasible than the present system.

The CHAIRMAN.—Even that would require an amendment to the Act.

Mr. PEARCE.—I know that, but I am offering it as a solution.

Mr. TROWBRIDGE.—Will you allow me to say a few words on behalf of the feeders?

The CHAIRMAN.—What is a feeder?

Mr. TROWBRIDGE.—He is a man who feeds paper into a press. There are 25 or 26 feeders, of whom about half are married, and some have families, and they are receiving only $10.50 a week. It takes a man at least a year to become an expert feeder. I have never seen any who would become a good feeder in less time. Some of the presses run at the rate of 2,100 an hour, and a man of considerable ability is required to feed a press at that rate. The sheets must be fed straight, so as to register.

The CHAIRMAN.—Suppose some of the sheets get twisted and the press is stopped, is there a deduction from the feeder's pay?

Mr. TROWBRIDGE.—No. There are not more than one or two sheets spoiled, and there is a percentage allowed in the paper to cover that. My reason for bringing up the case of these men is, that their pay is altogether inadequate to bring up a family on at the present time. Then, the girls who feed the presses receive only $5.50 a week, although some of them have been there since the inauguration of the Bureau. They are not doing exactly the same work as the feeders, who help the pressmen to lift the formes, and so on.

Q. Girls sit on stools and feed the presses?—A. They do not sit; they have to stand all the time.

By Mr. Fyshe:

Q. What kind of girls are they, as a rule—working people?—A. Yes. Most of them have to keep themselves and pay their board. Most of them are over 25 or 30 years of age.

Q. Have they a fairly good education?—A. Yes, they can read and write and figure, but I do not suppose they are capable of doing anything but what they are at. They are all good, intelligent girls.

By the Chairman:

Q. Do they get any holidays?—A. No.

Q. And if they take a day or two off, they lose their wages?—A. They lose their time.

By Mr. Fyshe:

Q. How many of these girls have you in the department?—A. We have eight in our branch. There are over a hundred altogether employed in the Bureau.

By the Chairman:

Q. They have formed themselves into an association?—A. Yes, a sick benefit association.

Q. When Lady Aberdeen was here, she got the girls to form this association?—A. Yes.

Q. Is there any girl paid more than $5.50 a week?—A. I think some in the bindery are paid $6. The foreladies receive more.

Q. How much do the foreladies get?—A. I could not say.

Q. How many of them are there?—A. Three, I think. I think they get $10 a week.

Q. The highest a woman can attain to in the Bureau is $10 a week?—A. Yes.

Q. Is there any other class of employees you would like to mention?—A. I think not. I would be very glad if you would take the cases of these girls and the feeders into your consideration at least. I do not want to belittle our case, but I feel that they really need an increase more than we do.

Q. What do feeders in outside places here get?—A. I do not know.

Mr. LARDEN.—The press girls are classed with the bindery girls, and they are paid at the same rate.

The CHAIRMAN.—Do you think there should be a difference between the rate paid to the press girls and the rate paid to the bindery girls?

Mr. LARDEN.—Certainly.

Mr. PEARCE.—The press girls have to stand up all day and keep up with the machines, while the bindery girls can sit all day and do their work more leisurely.

OTTAWA, October 16, 1907.

A deputation appeared representing the Printers, Bookbinders and Finishers employed at the Government Printing Bureau and consisting of Messrs. James Firth, C. E. Clendinnen, Hugh Carling, A. E. Boyer, J. W. Turley, D. Ladurantaye, and submitted a memorial from the Printing Bureau Employees Protective Association, which was read and filed.

JAMES FIRTH, sworn and examined.

By the Chairman:

Q. You are a deputation from the printers, bookbinders and finishers?—A. Yes.

Q. You are the spokesman of the deputation?—A. Yes.

Q. How long have you been in the Bureau?—A. I went to the Bureau when it was started, in 1889, but I was away for a period.

Q. Most of these gentlemen have been in it for some years?—A. Yes, most of them have been in it for that period.

SESSIONAL PAPER No. 29a

Q. What do you say the remuneration at present is for printers?—A. $15 a week.

Q. Has it always been $15 a week?—A. No.

Q. When was it raised to that figure?—A. Three years ago.

Q. What was it before that?—A. $13.50; then it was raised to $14; then a year ago last June it was raised to $15. In other words, during thirteen years it has only been increased from $11 to $15.

Q. What is the rate of wages in outside establishments—taking this city first, because after all, the standard of living is the same?—A. The minimum scale in this city for hand work is $14 a week.

Q. What is the maximum scale?—A. I could not tell you exactly the scale for piece work; that is confined to newspaper offices. As a rule, the wages paid in Montreal and Toronto are higher than here.

Q. What are your hours?—A. Eight hours a day; that is 48 hours a week. We work eight and a half hours a day except Saturday.

Q. What is the time scale in the city offices in Ottawa?—A. 48 hours a week.

Q. Is that the union scale?—A. Yes.

Q. Then printers in the Bureau have the same hours as printers outside of the Bureau in Ottawa—48 hours a week?—A. Yes.

Q. Do you go through the front doorway?—A. No, we all go through the rear doorway.

Q. There is a book near the front doorway, where I saw a person writing his name?—A. That is for foremen.

Q. The foremen go through the front doorway?—A. Yes.

Q. And the operatives all go through the back doorway?—A. Yes.

Q. Where are the elevators?—A. There are two on the binders' side and two on the printers' side.

Q. What are the elevators used for?—A. They carry both passengers and freight; not the women.

Q. If they carry passengers, why should not the women be carried up on them as well as the men?—A. Certainly they could, if the women got that privilege; but the elevators are reserved for foremen and visitors.

Q. Are the women distributed generally throughout the building?—A. Yes, but principally on the side that the bindery is on. The printers and pressmen are confined principally to the other side.

Q. There must be some reason for the present arrangements in regard to going up and down in the elevators?—A. We do not think it is right that the women should not be allowed to go up in the elevators. In outside establishments, women in particular are not obliged to climb stairs, littered with every kind of refuse, to the top of the building. After they get there, if a fire took place, there would be no means of escape, because there is not a fire escape on the building.

Q. Is not the building built entirely of brick and cement?—A. Yes, so far as the building is concerned; but there is nothing to prevent a fire breaking out on any flat. The elevator shafts in the right and left wings act as funnels, and there would be no check to a fire if it took place on any flat.

Q. What do you mean by tradesmen in your memorial? A tradesman, to my mind, is a man who engages in a trade?—A. Yes, a bookbinder or a pressman or a finisher or an operative. But there are a large number of men in the Printing Bureau who are not tradesmen, such as those who run elevators, feed presses, or wheel trucks. While they have to be classed as labourers, they require a certain amount of skill, and they have a certain amount of responsibility. But as they are not classed as tradesmen, they do not get the wages they should. They have no organization.

Q. Then the term tradesman in the printing world applies to a person who has learned a trade, not to a person engaged in trade?—A. Yes, a person who has learned a trade.

Q. And the class of employees to whom you refer are the men who feed the presses, wheel the trucks, and run the elevators?—A. Yes.

Q. They receive $10 a week?—A. Yes, that is about the average.

Q. Do you get any holidays at all ?—A. We get the legal holidays, such as Thanksgiving Day, Christmas Day, New Year's Day and so forth.

Q. But you do not get any other holidays ?—A. No.

Q. If you are absent through sickness, do you get paid ?—A. No. We are simply paid by the hour, and if we are late we are docked an hour. We have checks, and when we go in, we take our check and place it in the box, and then our time goes on. If we want to go off or are called away by sickness or anything else, we sign the book when we leave, and our time is stopped from that time. We are simply paid for the hours we work.

Q. Then, instead of getting $15 a week, you think a flat scale of $20 a week should be paid ?—A. Yes, because of the reason we cite that there are two classes of labour who receive more than we do.

Q. If you were paid $20 a week, would not that be in excess of the scale paid to men doing the same work in outside printing establishments in Ottawa ?—A. Strictly speaking it would not, because there is hardly a firm in the city of Toronto or in Ottawa that adheres to that scale. They are paying all sorts of wages according to the supply of the labour market and the work that they are doing ; but the rule of the union is that they cannot pay lower wages than $15 a week, but they can pay as much more as they like. That is one of the things that would have to be changed by Parliament, because according to the King's Printer he cannot go above that figure; it would be for Parliament to erase that clause in the Act and place them on a scale of wages suitable to a Government institution.

Q. The Public Printing and Stationery Act provides that 'No increase of any such rate of wages shall be made so as to raise the rate above that which is, at the time of such increase, paid for similar work in the cities of Montreal and Toronto.' That is the standard ?—A. Yes.

Q. Comparing the rate paid in Montreal and Toronto, would not a flat rate of $20 a week be beyond the rate of wages paid in those cities ?—A. Not in comparison with the cost of living in the city of Ottawa. $20 a week in Ottawa would be about equivalent to $19 in those cities, because the cost of living in them is much less.

By Mr. Fyshe :

Q. Do you consider that an established fact?—A. Yes, we consider that the city of Ottawa is on the average about the dearest of any city in Canada.

By the Chairman :

Q. As the Act lays down that the rate of wages shall be the rate paid in Montreal and Toronto, any change in that rate would require an amendment to an Act of Parliament ?—A. If that were a stumbling block to the Government and they could not pay what they liked, that would have to be erased from the Act.

Q. Then the Act would have to be amended ?—A. That is what the King's Printer says—that he cannot go above that rate.

Q. Have you memorialized the King's Printer on this subject?—A. Yes.

Q. Have you asked him to forward your memorial to the Secretary of State ?—A. Yes, we were before the Secretary of State.

Q. When ?—A. About a month ago.

Q. Have you suggested to him that the Act of Parliament should be amended ?—A. Yes. We told him that it was in his jurisdiction to have the Act amended.

C. E. CLENDINNEN, sworn and examined. ,

By the Chairman :

Q. You are the secretary of the Printing Bureau Employees Protective Association ?—A. Yes.

Q. You say there are some employees in the bindery who have only received an increase of $1 a week since 1896 ? how many are in that position ?—A. Seven or eight.

Q. What did they get in 1896 ?—A. They got $14 a week.

Q. What do they get now ?—A. $15.

Q. You say that the same rate of wages for similar work was paid in Montreal twenty-five years ago ?—A. Yes. Finishers, who are a special class, were paid $15 a week in Montreal twenty-five years ago.

Q. Are these seven or eight employees in the bindery who have only had an increase of $1 a week since 1896, finishers ?—A. Three or four of them are.

Q. What is the rate paid to finishers throughout the country ?—A. A finisher is always supposed to get $2 or $3 a week more than those in any other branch of the trade. In Ottawa they are paid $18, and in Toronto from $15 to $18 or $20—it depends on the man's ability.

Q. Does the same thing prevail in Montreal ?—A. I do not know much about Montreal. I think they are paid there about $16 or $17.

Q. In Montreal or Toronto, you think they are paid more than they are now in the Bureau ?—A. Yes.

Q. How long have you been in the Bureau ?—A. Seventeen years.

Q. Have you always been in the bindery ?—A. Yes.

Q. What did you have when you began in the bindery —A. $13.

Q. And now you get $15 ?—A. Yes.

Q. Did you get the increase of $2 at one time ?—A. No. I had an increase of $1 in 1893, I think, and another $1 in 1896.

Q. Then you have not have had any increase for eleven years ?—A. No.

Q. How many people are employed in the bindery ?—A. I suppose 40 or 45.

Q. Are many of them women ?—A. There are five girls in the room with us, feeding ruling machines.

Q. When a book comes to you stitched, it is first gummed at the back ? --A The binder takes the book from the girls after it is sewed, and glues up the back, rounds the back, puts it in the press and covers it, and then it comes to the hands of the finishers, who puts the gold work on it, embellishes it on the sides and back, and letters it.

Q. Are the mouldings on the back part of the work of the finisher ?—A. Yes.

Q. Then the finisher has scarcely anything to do with the mechanical work other than putting the adornments on ?—A. Yes.

Q. Are many people in the Bureau doing finishing work ?—A. Five.

Q. The average blue-book doesn't require finishing ?—A. No, we never touch those; but there are a great many books for the Library.

Q. What are the duties of an ordinary binder ?—A. He takes the book as it comes sewed and glues up the back, then rounds it, puts the boards on it, puts it in a press and presses it, and when it is fairly pressed, takes it out and puts the leathers on it.

Q. What is the difference between the trade of an ordinary binder and that of a finisher ?—A. In most cases a finisher gets from $1 to $2 a week more than a binder, but not at the Printing Bureau.

Q. There each binder and finisher is paid $15 a week ?—A. Yes.

Q. You consider that there should be some difference between the pay of a finisher and that of an ordinary binder ?—A. I consider that a finisher should have more because he requires more intelligence. He does finer work, just as a job printer does finer work than an ordinary compositor.

Q. Where is the bindery ?—A. On the fourth flat.

Q. How many flats are there ?—A. Five.

Q. What is on the top flat ?—A. There are girls on the top flat just now.

Q. What do they do ?—A. They fold and stitch books.

Q. These are the preliminary steps towards the binding?—A. Yes.

Q. How many girls are employed in that way?—A. I should think there are almost a hundred girls in the bindery altogether, but they are not all on one flat.

Q. Are there more girls than men on the top flat?—A. Yes.

Q. As secretary you had a hand in drawing up this memorial?—A. Yes.

Q. And I suppose these are your observations, showing the disadvantages under which the women labour?—A. I got my information from the women themselves.

Q. I presume that you saw that the information was correct?—A. Yes.

Q. What would you suggest in the way of amelioration?—A. I think that in any public institution such as that the girls ought to be allowed to use the elevators. It is a great hardship for girls to have to climb five flights of stairs two or three times a day; and I do not think there is any other building where the employees are forced to go in and out through the rear entrance. In all the departmental buildings all the employees go through the same entrance as the Minister. But the need of using the elevator is, I think, the chief cause of complaint.

Q. Have the women and the men the same hours of work?—A. Yes. The women are allowed to leave five minutes before the men.

Q. Have you anything else to tell us?—A. No, I do not think so.

Q. Practically you represent the binders and the finishers?—A. There are binders here, but I practically represent them.

To the Royal Commission appointed to inquire into matters pertaining to the various branches of the Government Service:

GENTLEMEN,—We, the delegates representing the Printing Bureau Employees' Protective Association, desire to place our grievances before your honourable body. We might explain that our association is composed of all classes of mechanics, skilled and unskilled, and female labour. We deem it unnecessary to mention in detail the present increased cost of living in Ottawa, as the fact is pretty generally known, and for this reason alone we consider we are entitled to an increase in wages.

We desire to submit various reasons for your consideration: According to an Order in Council passed in 1903 the rates of wages in the cities of Montreal and Toronto were, for the future, to be taken as a standard not to be exceeded; the conditions existing then, both here and in those cities above-mentioned, were reasonable, but they are far different now, and whilst the Act calls for a minimum rate of $15 per week, which wages we receive, the rate paid in outside offices is far in excess of that amount. We would also call your attention to the difference in prices paid to the hand compositor and the machine operator, whilst the later receives a greater remuneration, the class of work done by the former is yet of a far more technical nature.

There are some employees in the bindery who have only received an increase of $1 a week since 1896, eleven years of the greatest prosperity this country has ever known, notwithstanding the fact that the same rate of wages for similar work was paid in printing establishments in Montreal twenty-five years ago.

In regard to the female employees, we contend that they are not receiving sufficient compensation for the arduous duties which they perform, and are forced to enter the Bureau through the rear entrance, and are not allowed the use of elevators, but are compelled to ascend and descend five and six flights of stairs; the girls who work on the top floor are in great danger of fire, there being no fire escapes, and the gate on the front stairs being kept locked all day. We would humbly request that you should take into your favourable consideration the case of certain employees who are not enumerated as tradesmen, although their work requires a certain amount of technicality, who receive the paltry sum of $10 per week. As the majority of Government employees receive two or three weeks' holidays, although their hours of labour are not as long as ours or their work as arduous, we respectfully request to be placed on the same footing.

In view of the above-mentioned facts and conditions existing in the Bureau, we would request that a flat scale of at least $20 per week be granted to all mechanics a said Bureau, and a corresponding percentage of increase be granted to the several lasses of employees mentioned in this memorial.

Your petitioners as in duty bound will ever pray.

     (Sgd.) JOSEPH FIRTH, *President.*

        O. A. E. CLENDINNEN, *Secretary.*

OTTAWA, October 16, 1907.

OTTAWA, Wednesday, June 5, 1907.

Mr. W. L. MACKENZIE KING, C.M.G., called, sworn and examined.

By the Chairman:

Q. You are Deputy Minister of Labour?—A. Yes.

Q. You are a graduate of Toronto University?—A. Yes. I have degrees in arts and law from the University of Toronto, and also a master's degree in arts from Harvard.

Q. Did you go to Harvard University immediately after you left the University of Toronto?—A. I went to the University of Chicago for a year as Fellow in Political Economy, and took a post-graduate course there. Subsequently I went to Harvard.

Q. Afterwards you completed your post-graduate course at Harvard, where you also got a degree?—A. I held a resident fellowship for a time and in 1899 I received the degree of master of arts from Harvard and passed the examinations for degree of doctor of philosophy. The university gave me a travelling fellowship. My intention was to return to the university. I received the appointment of instructor in political economy at Harvard in the spring of 1900, but resigned that position to accept my present position under the Canadian Government.

Mr. FYSHE,—You got a pretty thorough training.

By the Chairman:

Q. Did you travel in Europe while holding that travelling scholarship?—A. I spent a year in Europe studying industrial conditions.

Q. Afterwards you returned to Canada?—A. When I was in Italy I received a cable from Sir William Mulock informing me of the Government's intention to establish the Labour Department, and asking me if I would accept the position of editor of the *Labour Gazette*. I did not accept at the outset because of my desire to continue academic work. When I reached London, a few weeks after, I changed my mind, having had interviews with different parties in the interval, and an intimation from Harvard which led me to believe that my acceptance of this position would not prejudice me in the matter of taking up university teaching should I decide to do so later.

By Mr. Fyshe:

Q. It was not merely the editorship of the *Labour Gazette* that was offered you, was it?—A. That was the position that was mentioned in the first instance, but Sir William Mulock subsequently intimated that the department would be established on a regular basis and that I would probably have the direction of it.

By the Chairman:

Q. The department was established by Act of Parliament?—A. Yes, in 1900.

Q. Was the department placed under one Minister, or can the Minister act under the direction of the Governor in Council?—A. By direction of the Governor in Council, any Member of the Government may be selected as the Minister of the department.

Q. The Department of Labour being an entirely new creation, you had something to do with the choice of your assistants?—A. Yes, I was allowed rather a free hand in the choice of one or two, who were to be immediately connected with myself.

Q. Did you choose university graduates?—A. I chose the late Mr. Henry Harper, with whom I had been a fellow student at the University of Toronto, as the associate editor of the *Gazette*. He lost his life in an endeavour to save Miss Blair from drowning, and after his death I selected as his successor Mr. Coats, who was also a graduate of Toronto University. Mr. Edgar, who is in the department, is likewise a university graduate. He was also appointed on my recommendation. There are, of course, other members of the staff with whose appointments I have had nothing to do.

Q. Having a new department, did you deem it desirable to follow the working of the Civil Service Act and create the staff into first and second-class clerks?—A. In the main we followed the requirements of the Act. Of course in connection with our department the work of some of the officers is technical in its nature. Take for example, as the work of the fair wages officers. They are special officers, in a way, but it was thought advisable to grade them with the others.

Q. Knowing that it is a new department and there was nothing to entangle you in the past, you thought it desirable to follow the gradation adopted in the other departments?—A. I thought it would be desirable to have the members of the staff graded. If the grading is based on merit with some recognition for length of service, it helps, I think, to preserve discipline, unless it is based on merit, it operates against it.

Q. You were asked to prepare a memorandum. You now produce that memorandum?—A. Yes. (Statement produced and filed).

Q. Would you mind producing a copy of the *Labour Gazette*?—A. The *Gazette* is published each month, and at the end of the year the 12 numbers are bound in the form of a volume. This is last month's *Labour Gazette* (producing copy), and this is last year's volume (producing volume).

By Mr. Fyshe:

Q. This is an official publication?—A. Yes, an official publication.

Q. This is a new idea as a Government publication, is it not?—A. No, the English Government publishes a *Labour Gazette* also; the Governments of several other countries publish statistical periodicals similar in their nature.

Q. Since when have the British Government published a *Labour Gazette*?—A. The first number was in May, 1893, 14 years ago.

By the Chairman:

Q. The Board of Trade publishes it?—A. Yes. The United States Government publishes a bulletin of labour. The Government in several of the States also publish labour bulletins.

By Mr. Fyshe:

Q. Does it take purview of the whole labour world?—A. No, we confine our investigations and statistical records largely to Canada, so far as outside countries are noticed, it is only by way of reviewing their statistical publications or noting happenings which may throw light on conditions in Canada. It would be impossible for us to attempt much outside of the Dominion without having a very much larger staff.

By the Chairman:

Q. Have you any extra employees among your staff?—A. We have two young ladies who assist in typewriting, and during part of each month we find it necessary to get extra help to assist in mailing the *Gazette*.

Q. I do not see any temporary employees enumerated in the Civil Service List. There are a few here mentioned in connection with mailing the *Labour Gazette*?—A. They would be the ones, I think.

Mr. FYSHE.—I suppose the publication of the *Labour Gazette* adds very materially to the duties of the printing department.

The CHAIRMAN.—The printing costs $16,000 a year.

By the Chairman:

Q. I suppose all the members of your staff have passed the Civil Service examination excepting the graduates of the university?—A. I think not. Some of the junior clerks have, but we have clerks whose duties are special in a sense—the fair wage officers, for example. Their duties require them to investigate wage conditions and disputes between employers and their men, where the Government is interested in the carrying out of a contract on which they may be engaged. It was thought advisable to get men who would do that kind of work with efficiency, to secure persons familiar in a way with the labour world, and also possessing the right kind of judgment and ability. A Civil Service examination would be no test, or at best only a poor test as to these qualifications.

Q. And you procure them notwithstanding anything to the contrary in the Civil Service Act?—A. Quite so.

Q. Were they selected for political purposes or for the efficiency of the department?—A. I do not think that political purposes were the first consideration. I think in most cases they were chosen with regard to the manner in which they would carry on the work. For example, this year one of the fair wage officers, Mr. D. J. O'Donohue, died in January. We had to make a new appointment, and the Minister consulted with me in reference to possible candidates. I had already, having had to do with the *Labour Gazette*, become familiar with the way in which our several correspondents had done their work. Of that number no one seemed to have been more efficient that Mr. McNiven, who was in Victoria, B.C. The department had had occasion to call upon him at different times to prepare special reports, and he had always done his work very efficiently. He had proven himself reliable, trustworthy and able. I wanted him solely on account of his efficiency and because I thought he was a man who would be likely to fill the position with satisfaction, and the Minister accepted my recommendation. There have been one or two appointments in which, I think, personal or political considerations may have entered too largely.

Q. Are all these officers stationed at Ottawa?—A. They are all stationed in Ottawa.

Q. You are frequently absent from the city?—A. Too frequently, I am sorry to say.

Q. Who acts at the head of the office when you are away?—A. At the present time, Mr. F. A. Acland. His name does not appear on the Civil Service List you have.

Q. What position does he hold?—A. Mr. Acland is secretary of the department. Three years ago an appropriation of $1,900 was voted for a secretary of the department. The Minister left me, in a way, with choice of the person to fill that office, but I could not find any one willing to accept at that salary whom I cared to recommend. It seemed to me that it was too responsible a position with which to entrust any one who was not a person of considerable experience, tact and judgment. I knew of no one better qualified for the position than Mr. Acland, under whom I served some twelve years ago, at which time he was the News Editor of the *Globe* in Toronto. With all the other members of the *Globe* staff I had the highest admiration for Mr. Acland's ability and exceptional capacity for administrative work, as well as for his intimate knowledge of men and affairs. I tried time and again to get him to consent to enter the service, but it was too large a sacrifice for him to make. Rather than appoint any one who was not efficient I allowed the appropriation to lapse for two years, and finally I told the Minister that it was quite impossible for me to keep up with the work without having some one who was thoroughly reliable in the position of secretary. I told the Minister it would be necessary to increase the appropriation. The amount was augmented to $2,600, and Mr. Acland then came into the department at a sacrifice of $400.

By Mr Fyshe :

Q. Were you not ashamed of yourself to try and influence him to that extent?—A. I was, and I would have hesitated to do it if I had not known that once he was in the department he would demonstrate his efficiency to such an extent that the Government would see the injustice of placing him financially in the position he was in prior to entering the service.

By the Chairman :

Q. What is your own salary?—A. $4,000.

Q. That is the normal salary of a deputy head?—A. Yes.

Q. Have you had any offers to leave the service since you entered?—A. I have had repeated offers.

Q. At a greater salary than you now receive?—A. Considerably more than I am receiving at the present time.

Q. Are you staying in the service under a strong sense of public duty rather than with the idea of any benefit accruing to yourself?—A. If it were a matter of dollars and cents I would have left the service several years ago, but there are opportunities in the service which I believe more than compensate for the financial sacrifice.

By Mr. Fyshe :

Q. It is something new to hear sentiments of that kind?—A. There are other men in the department in the same position. Mr. Acland, the secretary, is an instance in point.

By the Chairman :

Q. And it is the same with some of the other gentlemen, I suppose?—A. Yes, my own feeling is this: that in regard to the positions in the service the men who are really qualified to fill responsible offices and to do effective work for the country are not paid salaries at all adequate compared, for example, with what they might receive from private corporations.

Q. As a matter of fact, is it not notorious, at the present moment—do we not see it in every newspaper we pick up—that capable young men are leaving the Government service in the west and others are leaving here?—A. I know it is so in our service. Mr. Ruel, of the Department of Railways and Canals; Mr. Bain, of the Department of Customs; Dr. Reginald Daly, of the Geological Survey, are all instances in point.

Q. And the Civil Service now, owing to the abolition of the Superannuation Act, has not that stability which it used to have?—A. I think superannuation an element of stability.

Q. None of the members of your staff are under the Superannuation Act, having all been appointed since that Act was abolished?—A. There is one clerk, Mr. Ardouin.

Q. He was transferred from the Post Office Department?—A. Yes.

Q. With that one exception all your officers are under the new Retirement Fund? —A. Yes.

By Mr. Fyshe :

Q. Who is the Minister of your department?—A. Mr. Lemieux. He is also the Postmaster General.

By the Chairman :

Q. In carrying on the business of the department you have a certain number of correspondents at various points in the Dominion to whom you pay an honorarium of $100 a year?—A. We have about 45 correspondents in all, one in each of the cities of Canada, and in certain industrial districts. They send monthly returns.

Q. What do these correspondents do?—A. They are required to furnish a monthly report on the industrial and labour conditions in their city or district, and to supply the department throughout the month with information in regard to threatened or existing strikes or lockouts, important changes in rates, wages, accounts of industrial accidents, or matters of that kind.

Q. I suppose the department was created in response to an agitation on the part of the public?—A. I think so, and I think also the fact that the Governments of other countries had departments that were devoting special attention to industrial conditions and that Canada was a most important country industrially made it appear advisable for the Government to pay special attention to matters affecting the industrial classes.

Mr. FYSHE.—It strikes me as something so altogether extraordinary, that the Government, as a Government, would get so interested in this great labour problem as to specially organize a department to look after it, and immediately before, abolish what it had already done in the way of this Superannuation Fund providing for old officers.

By the Chairman:

Q. To come back to the work of the department, are the reports of the correspondents of the *Labour Gazette*, all stereotyped?—A. No. You will see their character from the *Labour Gazette*. Correspondents are supplied with forms on which they report. For example, there is a communication from Hamilton and district. Mr. Landers is our correspondent there. He reports on the general condition of the labour market, and any special feature of interest in local industries, and the condition of affairs in the particular trades. We try to follow a general system in the reports, and we use them as a basis of an industrial review of conditions during the month. For example, here is an article 'General Summary of Industrial and Labour Conditions.' The reports of our correspondents are in part the basis of this article, and also any matters that are brought to our attention through the press or in other ways.

By Mr. Fyshe:

Q. Is this article signed?—A. No, this information was prepared in the department.

Q. The department is responsible for it?—A. Yes.

By the Chairman:

Q. And you compile these articles from the returns?—A. They are compiled from a variety of sources.

Q. Do you have a hand in the appointment of these men?—A. No, they are appointed by the Minister on the recommendation generally of the local Member.

By Mr. Fyshe:

Q. It is perhaps a little too soon to be able to form an exhaustive opinion upon it, but it naturally occurs to me to ask whether all this labour pays for the worry and trouble. Is the machinery really paying for itself?—A. I think, Mr. Fyshe, that the department has been the direct means of saving to the country hundreds of thousands of dollars which, but for its existence, would have been occasioned by industrial disturbances. Losses of many kinds have been saved by virtue of having this department. I think if it came down to a matter of dollars the department would be found to have paid for itself several hundreds of times over.

Q. That is just what I wanted to know, because if the department did prevent great strikes and all that sort of thing money would be saved?—A. It has both prevented and been the means of terminating many serious industrial conflicts.

Q. You cannot always depend upon that, I suppose?—A. I think one may count, looking back upon the experience of the last six or seven years upon the department

ing year by year of increasing service to the country by way of preventing industrial isturbances and helping to reduce the loss that would be occasioned on account of 1em.

Q. At any rate it cannot but help having the effect of keeping before the public ll the conditions of labour, and if anything goes wrong it would naturally come out? -A. Quite so. More than that, we gather information here which is of vast service > Parliament in any legislation which it contemplates. I might illustrate. Last year 1e Government put through an important measure, the Industrial Disputes Investiga- ion Act, but for the information which we had gathered in the department during he preceding six years there would not have been a Member of the House who would ave given authoritative statistics such as could have served to exemplify the need >r such a law in regard to the industries to which it relates.

By the Chairman:

Q. As soon as we get through with the staff and expenditure then we will take up 1e entire labour question. . These correspondents send in their reports and the *Labour !azette* is based on them to a certain extent and published?—A. In part. The reports >rm only a small part of the information we gather.

Q. That forms the chief part of the expenditure. I suppose you have people :anning the papers, and all that sort of thing?—A. We have a great deal of corre- >ondence. For example, if we hear of a threatened or expected strike we immediately rite the parties and secure an authoritative statement. We seek to verify all in- >rmation from whatever source received.

Q. And the only other important outlay, for the whole outlay altogether is only >out $27,000, is the absolute printing of the *Gazette?*—A. There are the travelling cpenses of the different officers.

Q. That is only a few hundred dollars ?—A. Most of the expenditure of the de- artment up to date has been incurred in the publication of the *Labour Gazette.*

Q. Against that, although it is not so very important, you get a revenue every ear from the sales of the *Gazette* ?—A. Yes, but the amount is small.

Q. It is over $1,300 ?—A. Yes.

Q. There is one thing that strikes me in connection with the expenditure. I have ot the highest regard for the gentleman in question, Mr. Johnston, and I think he is ell worth the money, but is it not rather detrimental to the public service to give ctra emoluments to an officer ?—A. The point to which you refer is the payment to Ir. Johnston, accountant of the Post Office Department, for work done in the Labour)epartment. I think we shall have to appoint our own accountant. The arrange- ient in question was made at the outset for the purpose of saving the cost of engag- ig a special accountant when there was not very much accounting to do.

Q. With all due respect, I think it was a mistake. Mr. Johnston is the chief >ccountant of the Post Office Department, a very important department—I do not ant to detract from that ; but as far as the quality of the work goes it is nothing ke as onerous as that of the accountant who has to keep the accounts for millions f dollars of outlay. Now, Mr. Johnston receives an extra emolument of $500 a year rer the other man with the more onerous duties. While I have no objection what- rer to Mr. Johnston it is rather a bad practice ?—A. I do not think there is a more ficient officer than Mr. Johnston in the service.

By Mr. Fyshe :

Q. That is $500 extra pay?—A. Yes. I agree entirely with Mr. Courtney that it ould add more to the efficiency of the service if we had our own accountant.

Q. It would cost more ?—A. It would cost more, but I think it would promote 1e efficiency of the service, and would be better in other ways. We for a time have translator also who was appointed in the same way but I think the effect of the

29a—40

arrangement in his case was that the man was overworked and practically suffered permanent injury in consequence of doing too much.

By the Chairman :

Q. A man cannot be the chief accountant of the Post Office Department and also accountant of the Department of Labour without one department or the other suffering?—A. It is apt to work an injustice to one or the other.

Q. Or if he is a conscientious man his health must suffer ?—A. Possibly.

Q. The practice is one calculated to cause great discontent amongst the chief officers of the public service doing similar work ?—A. I can hardly speak as to other officers' services, but so far as the Department of Labour is concerned, I think it would improve the efficiency of our work if all our officers were quite independent of those of another department.

By Mr. Fyshe :

Q. Could you not divide this work among the other officers of your department and apportion the money among them ?—A. No. We will have to appoint our own accountant. We have already far too much work for the staff we have.

By the Chairman :

Q. As you are developing you require men of your own?—A. Certainly we do.

By Mr. Fyshe :

Q. You could get a competent accountant I suppose for $1,500 a year ?—A. I think we ought to, yes. Of course the only explanation of this arrangement is that during the first year or two of the department's existence, it was thought better to have an experienced accountant from one of the other departments.

Q. Especially if you did not want the whole time of any one man ?—A. But our work has grown very much since then and I think we can find plenty of work for an accountant to do.

By Mr. Bazin :

Q. Does this accountant come to your department during the working hours of the Post Office Department ?—A. He does a great deal of our work after hours and he does part of it during the day. It depends upon what the occasion necessitates. It means not only continued extra work for him but often leads to members of our staff being obliged to wait after hours and check up the work with him.

By the Chairman:

Q. In fact, the thing is a mistake?—A. As an expedient it is all right, but the time is past.

Q. You have paid a certain amount of attention to the question of pensions for Government officials?—A. I have given the matter some thought.

Q. Have any of your staff left since they were appointed in 1900?—A. Only a messenger, I think.

Q. He bettered himself by going, I presume?—A. No, he wanted to come back again, but he was never a valuable member of the staff. The reason that he left the department at the time he did was on account of ill-health. He thought he would have to go and live in the south, and then he came back and would like to have been reinstated, but that was not done.

Q. You know the Superannuation Act was abolished?—A. Yes.

Q. In the case of all the officers of your department, excepting one, a deduction is made from the salaries to build up a retirement fund?—A. Yes.

Q. It is your own money, and it is kept at four per cent interest?—A. Yes.

Q. Would it not be better in the general interest of the public service if some kind of a pension fund was created, or the Superannuation Act was re-enacted? Would it not give greater stability to the service?—A. I think it would. It would influence a man to remain permanently in the service. That should be the motive at the outset. I am inclined to think most here would be better satisfied with a pension arrangement.

Q. You have only one third-class clerk?—A. At the present time.

Q. He was appointed at $700?—A. No, I think he was appointed originally at $500, and he was there four years. This was the messenger that I refer to, who resigned.

Q. And you appointed him a third-class clerk?—A. This man was originally paid $500.

Q. As a messenger?—A. As a messenger. This was Lapointe. He was in the department from the time it was first established. He had only been four years in the department when he left. We have appointed a new man in his place.

Q. But he is called a third-class clerk?—A. He had been appointed as a third-class clerk, but did the work of a messenger; I should have explained that. His work was that of a messenger with some extra clerical duties.

Q. Can you get capable men such as you want to enter the service at $500 a year?—A. It all depends what the man is wanted for. There are two ways in which work can be done. I think if you want to get a clerk that can be relied upon to do work efficiently and to your satisfaction, it will be difficult to secure him for $500.

Q. You employ some few women in mailing the *Labour Gazette*?—A. And doing typewriting and the like.

Q. They are temporary employees only?—A. Quite so. We have found it necessary to keep two of them on pretty continuously. The work has been such as to necessitate that.

Q. I suppose, as in the case of every other department, pressure is brought to employ women?—A. I do not think there has been any particular pressure put upon us in that direction. As a matter of fact, for some of the clerical work I would as soon have women as well.

Q. $500 is a greater emolument than women get as a rule in outside employment?—A. I think possibly the remuneration in the service for women is on the whole greater than it would be outside. I will say this, though: We have one young lady in the department who has been doing temporary work. I think her services should be more highly paid than they are at present in the Labour Department.

Q. There are very exceptional women. There is Mrs. Alexander in the Geological Survey. She is a most exceptional woman?—A. Quite so.

Q. Take the case of ordinary women: 200 passed the last Civil Service examination in November. If appointed, they would be paid $500 on the average, which is greater than they would receive outside of the Government service?—A. If I were to judge from most of the young ladies, we have had in the department, serving as temporary clerks who have passed the Civil Service examination, I would say they were not worth $500. We have had them come in and do a little work and found they were not to be relied upon, and that it was necessary to get some one else. It is very difficult to get work done efficiently, I find.

By Mr. Fyshe:

Q. I suppose the class of women who want to get into the service have not received a very good education?—A. The class of women we want to get are employed somewhere else, and the ones that are the most anxious to get in, in a good many cases are those who have the greatest difficulty in getting employment elsewhere.

By the Chairman:

Q. This is the seventh year of the department's existence?—A. Yes.

29a—40½

Q. You began to publish the *Labour Gazette* from the beginning?—A. Yes, from the first.

Q. The next step was the adoption of the fair wages resolution in the House of Commons, or was that passed previous to the creation of the department?—A. Yes, that was passed before the department was created.

Q. That was the initial step?—A. Yes, it really was.

Q. That resolution provided for the insertion of a fair wages clause in contracts executed by the Government?—A. It applied to any work being executed as a Government contract.

Q. In the beginning I suppose that was permissive?—A. Perhaps I might explain just how the matter originated. Some four years before the department was established I happened to be investigating the subject of the sweating system, and found out that the Government clothing contracts were being made up in large measure in sweatshops. I knew Sir William Mulock, Mr. Mulock he was at the time, and went to his house and spoke to him about it. I said to him that I thought as Postmaster General he could help to remedy that evil. He readily and heartily acquiesced. He then asked me if I would prepare a report for the Government on the way in which the Government clothing contracts were being carried on, and I did so. In that report certain recommendations were made. When the report was presented to Parliament, Sir William Mulock introduced the resolution providing that all Government contracts in the future should contain a clause that would prevent sweating in the carrying out of these contracts. He inserted this clause in all contracts given by the Post Office Department, and his example was followed by the Militia Department. Subsequently the measure was extended to the other departments of the Government, the Public Works Department the Railways and Canals Department and the Marine and Fisheries Department. In carrying out the provisions of this resolution it became necessary to appoint special officers whose duty it is to go to the locality where the work is to be carried on, and ascertain what are the current and fair wages in the district, and prepare a schedule, which schedule appears in the contract awarded to the successful tenderer. After the Department of Labour was created it became its duty to see that these schedules were complied with.

By Mr. Fyshe:

Q. That was rather to ensure that the wages paid should be a little in excess of market prices?—A. No, I do not think so. I think what it does ensure is that part of the money which the Government expends on that account goes into the hands of the people who do the work, which without this arrangement would probably go into the pocket of the contractor. I might explain it in this way: The department in no way endeavours to fix an artificial rate. We simply consult with the contractors and workmen and fix what we believe to be the current rate in the district. That is not the maximum rate that a contractor may pay his men, but it is the minimum rate below which he is not allowed to go. When the Government invites tenders all contractors know on what basis they are obliged to tender. The effect is that a contractor who is dealing in a fair way with his men is not put at a disadvantage in tendering for the Government contract.

Q. With the contractor who was prepared to sweat his labour?—A. Quite so. I do not think it involves extra cost to the Government, but it does ensure a greater part of the Government money going into the hands of the people who help to do the work.

Q. In other words, it is a protection to the labouring classes?—A. We have found that in one or two cases the contractors were not paying the wages that we had fixed in the schedules. The employees complained to our department, and we brought the matter to the attention of the department which had awarded the contract, and they immediately asked us to investigate and report. I suppose that our department has

SESSIONAL PAPER No. 29a

investigated some eighty claims of that kind, and several hundreds of dollars have as
a consequence been paid over by other departments of the Government to the workingmen, to which amounts they were entitled in virtue of the rate fixed in the schedule.

Q. Is there not a more summary way of doing business than that? Should they
not be notified from your department direct that they must pay the right wages?—A.
That is what is done. The department does notify them, but it first holds an investigation to see whether the complaint is correct. Our officers interview both sides
and then the department notifies the contractor that unless he makes good the amount
that was outstanding, the department awarding the contract will send us the cheque
to pay the labourers and will deduct it from what is due on the progress estimates.

By the Chairman:

Q. And as a matter of fact the several departments have repeatedly paid the
labourers themselves and deducted the amount from the sums due on the contract?—
A. They have, as a matter of fact, on several occasions.

Q. Continuing the evolution of the department, there have been a number of
special investigations into industrial conditions?—A. Yes, quite a number.

Q. That was probably the next step in the evolution of the department?—A.
Naturally as the department and its work became known throughout the country, we
began to receive requests for information from different persons in Canada and outside of Canada and grievances of one kind and another were brought to our attention
by the industrial classes. I have mentioned in my written statement to the Commission
the case of a number of Italians that were brought into the city of Montreal three
years ago. An Italian leader there, a foreman who became later an employment agent,
named Cordasco had himself crowned King and published an Italian newspaper in
Montreal with an account of his coronation. This paper was sent over to Italy and
numbers of copies distributed there, and by his supplying the people there with letter
paper stamped with the Royal Arms of Italy and addressed to him in Canada he was
able to convey the impression to a great mass of Italians that all they had to do to
secure work in Canada was to come to this country and live under royal protection.
He had arrangements with one of the railways whereby he was to supply them with
labour and got a commission for supplying the railway with men, and also commissions from the Italian labourers for giving them a job.

By Mr. Fyshe:

Q. It seems to me we could learn something in the way of graft from the Italians?
—A. This was a unique form. The result of this was that several hundreds of Italians
were landed in the city of Montreal without any one to care for them or to supply them
with work. Our department was naturally appealed to to look into this matter, and
we made a somewhat careful and full investigation, which resulted in legislation being
passed by the Dominion Government providing against fraudulent representations of
that sort being made in future. That is only one example.

By the Chairman:

Q. Continuing further the history of this labour legislation, some of the Provincial Governments became interested, and British Columbia, for instance, appointed
a Royal Commission?—A. No, with reference to labour troubles in British Columbia
the commission was appointed by our own department. Perhaps I should say that the
Conciliation Act, which provides for the intervention by an officer of the department
in industrial disputes was taken advantage of to a considerable extent by companies
both in the east and in the west.

By Mr. Fyshe:

Q. I notice that in Montreal you were called upon the other day?—A. Yes, but
that is under the Act of last session. In 1903, when practically all the coal mines in

western British Columbia were tied up, and the Canadian Pacific Railway as well, because the men were on strike, the Dominion Government appointed a Royal Commission. I was appointed secretary of that Commission. The Commission were enabled to unearth in British Columbia a situation that revealed where this whole matter had originated from. A full account was set forth in this report, and it may be interesting to you gentlemen to know that the men who are on trial in Boise City now for the alleged murder of Governor Stunenburg were the men who were shown to be partly instrumental in bringing about strikes in British Columbia.

Q. That is very striking?—A. Well, the effect of that Commission established by our department was to get those men out of the coal mines in our Canadian West. They had been in all the coal mines in British Columbia prior to that, but the Commission revealed their methods and the result was that the working men themselves withdrew their affiliation and the Western Federation of Miners have no longer anything to do with the coal mines in this country.

Mr. FYSHE.—That was very productive. I should suppose the department is doing good work.

By the Chairman :

Q. Another Royal Commission was appointed to investigate disputes between the Bell Telephone Company and their employees ?—A. That Commission was appointed this year.

By Mr. Fyshe :

Q. That was at Toronto ? You were the chairman ?—A. Yes, at Toronto. There have been one or two others.

By the Chairman :

Q. Then after these Commissions had sat and reported the next piece of legislation was the Act of last session was it not?—A. There was an Act in 1903, the Railway Labour Disputes Act.

Q. You did not notice that in your memorandum ?—A. I must have overlooked it. The Act of 1903 related to threatened or expected strikes on railways. It contained provisions, whereby, in the event of a threatened strike on a railway, the Government could appoint a Board to inquire into the trouble and report upon it.

By Mr. Fyshe :

Q. They could not stop the strike in the meantime ?—A. They could not stop the strike in the meantime nor could they enforce the award. Publicity was felt to be the first step necessary. We had a most important inquiry under that Act. The telegraphers in the employ of the Grand Trunk Company threatened to strike on the whole system of that company in 1904. Our department established a Board under this Act and an inquiry took place before it with the result that an award was made which was subsequently adopted in part by the Grand Trunk Company. Not a day's work was lost, no strike took place, but there certainly would have been a strike but for this legislation. Before creating the Board the Minister required the officer representing the Telegraphers Union to bring into the department the ballots which had been taken on the question of whether or not there should be a strike, and it was shown clearly to the Minister that ninety per cent of the men on the system had voted for a strike and that it was authorized. Having that information the Minister then granted this Board, an inquiry was held, and the strike was averted.

Q. What was the result ?—A. The result was, as I have said, a slight increase in wages was conceded the men and they did not go out at all, there was no interruption on the railway whatever.

Q. The tendency, I suppose, is for the big corporations to act concurrently with you ?—A. It would depend, I think, largely on their sense of the fairness with which

.e inquiry is conducted. I am inclined to think that in most of the inquiries which
.e department will be called upon to make, as in the case of most of the inquiries
hich the department has made, the corporations on the one hand and the labour
nions on the other will fall in largely with the decision reached.

By the Chairman :

Q. Then continuing the several investigations, you also had at the commence-
ent of this year an inquiry into the strike of the employees of the Crow's Nest Pass
oal Company ?—A. Yes. Perhaps I should lead up to that, by mentioning that a
ep further in advance on the legislation of 1903 was the passing during the last
ssion of Parliament of what is known as the Industrial Disputes Investigation Act.

Q. That followed the Crow's Nest strike, did it not ?—A. It was passed just
fore the strike took place. It followed the Lethbridge strike. The trouble in the
row's Nest Pass district was brewing while this legislation was before Parliament
d the Act was passed almost simultaneously with the occurrence of the troubles.

Q. Did the Act become law then ?—A. It had just become law.

Q. Had the Governor General given his assent to the Act?—A. He had given his
sent but we had not been able to obtain copies of the Act from the King's Printer and
ie parties in the west were for the most part entirely ignorant of its provision.

Q. Please relate the circumstances of the Crow's Nest Pass strike ?—A. This re-
tes to it. This new Act goes one step further than the Act of 1903. It makes it
egal in certain classes of industries for a body of men to strike or for a corporation
declare a lock-out until there has been an investigation.

By Mr. Fyshe :

Q. By whom ?—A. By a Board appointed by the department. Each party to a dis-
ite is allowed to name a member of the Board, and the two are to agree upon a third
ember. If they fail to agree the Government appoints a third member.

Q. That ensures deliberation, which is a great thing?—A. That ensures delibera-
on. After the investigation has taken place, if the parties do not wish to accept the
vard that is made they are free then to do what they please. The trouble in the
row's Nest was rather an acute one. There were seven companies who formed the
'estern Coal Operators' Association. They were trying to arrange a contract with
ie members of the several unions belonging to the United Mine Workers of America,
imbering some 3,000. The two parties had a conference at Calgary which lasted
early a month, but were unable to reach an agreement. The men then applied to the
ipartment, through their leaders, for the appointment of a Board under this Act,
'e had supplied them with information in regard to the Act, and they made the regu-
r application for the appointment of a Board.

Q. What was the dispute between them?—A. It was a dispute over the question of
ages, hours and general conditions. The operators were trying to arrive at a contract
govern conditions for the next few years, the old contracts being about to expire.
he companies forming part of the Western Coal Operators' Association thought that
ie employees had not made application for the appointment of a Board in the regular
ay, so they undertook to make application also. The Act requires, where any per-
ns make application, that they must notify the other side, and the operators in noti-
ing the men, told them that there would be a reduction in wages at the end of thirty
iys, and posted notices at the pit head of the mines informing the miners of this
ct. The men, not knowing that notices of this kind were required by the Act, took
iis to mean a defiance on the part of the operators, and without the consent of their
aders quit work. Really under the Act they were liable for having violated the law.
he leaders, however, never sanctioned a strike, they would not even give five cents of
rike benefit to the men while they were out. We immediately took steps to establish
Board under the new Act, and the Government sent me out to Fernie. When I

reached Fernie I called a meeting of the employees and explained the Act to them, and they decided unanimously to return to work pending an investigation. However, the district in which the troubles existed extended over an area of two or three hundred square miles, and the employees at the outlying camps where there had been no chance to explain the Act to them, decided to remain out until there was a settlement. I did what I could under the Conciliation Act to bring the parties together, and we reached an agreement just the day that the Board arrived to investigate. The fact that the Board was there ready to inquire into the dispute brought each of parties I think very much to their senses, and they were enabled in that way to adjust their difficulties.

Q. It is all settled now for the present?—A. An agreement has been reached for two years. This is only one case of some six or eight that have occurred within the last few months under that Act. To-day's press reports a case on Vancouver Island where the men were brought before the magistrate for having violated the Act by having gone out without applying for the appointment of a Board to investigate the dispute in the first instance. The men stated that they did not know the provisions of the law, and the magistrate gave them time to see if they could adjust matters. The result was that they did, and the men are back again at work. The best instance of the working of the new Act was afforded a week or two ago in the case of the dispute between the Grand Trunk Railway Company and the machinists in their employ. The latter have had difficulties with the Company for some time past, and applied to the department for a Board to endeavour to adjust the differences. They named as their representative on the Board Mr. J. G. O'Donoghue, solicitor for the Trades and Labour Congress of Canada, and the company named Mr. Wallace Nesbitt.

Q. Is Mr. O'Donoghue an American?—A. No, he is a lawyer in Toronto. The Minister of Labour appointed as third member Prof. Shortt, of Queen's University. He was chairman of the Board. The Board met at Montreal and heard evidence for three days, with the result that they were able to arrange a settlement which was entirely satisfactory to the machinists and to the Grand Trunk Railway Company.

Q. That is very good?—A. And an agreement was reached covering a term. There has not been a loss of five minutes' work on the Grand Trunk Railway in consequence of that dispute, not a man has lost five cents in the way of wages, and the matter has been adjusted to the entire satisfaction of both sides.

Q. I think that is splendid?—A. But for this law those men would probably have been on strike. Then to-day we have a Board sitting at Springhill inquiring into the troubles in the coal mine there. The men applied for the appointment of a Board and the Board at the present time is taking evidence. Mining is going on and there is no interruption to the industry. A Board has also been appointed to look into the situation of the longshoremen at Montreal with a view to trying to adjust matters, so that there will not be fresh trouble again this summer or next year.

By the Chairman:

Q. Are the labour unions of Canada largely directed in the United States?—A. A good many are affiliated with International unions. They are local unions having affiliation with International organizations. They, however, manage their own affairs here for the most part.

By Mr. Fyshe:

Q. I was just going to ask you in this connection have the Americans adopted anything like your method in order to deal with labour disputes?—A. They have not enacted legislation precisely similar that I know of, but the President in his last message to Congress recommended similar legislation. Congress has not yet passed such a law.

By the Chairman:

Q. On the other side of the line would it not be a matter for each State to deal with rather than the Federal power?—A. I think that in regard to certain classes of sputes—for example, on railways, anything affecting interstate commerce—that ongress might enact such a law, but otherwise the power would lie with the several tates.

Q. The operation of the Standard Oil Company, for instance, in Pennsylvania ould have to be dealt with by the State ?—A. I think so in a case of that sort.

Q. Coming to the general question as regards labour in Canada, are they largely rected, influenced and governed by the labour unions in the United States?—A. That I have seen and learned as the result of experience would lead me to believe iat the influence of the United States on labour conditions in Canada is very much taggerated. I am inclined to think that our unions control their own affairs to a iry much greater extent than the public credit them with doing. Still there have en notorious instances of interference from the United States. The case that I ive cited about the closing of the mines in British Columbia and the tying up of ie railways was shown to have been part of a general plan engineered in Denver, olorado, and in Butte, Montana.

By Mr. Fyshe:

Q. That was not the case in the Crow's Nest Pass trouble, was it?—A. In the row's Nest Pass trouble I do not think the Americans were in any way responsible. s a matter of fact, Mr. Sherman, who had been the leader of the men and has been peatedly denounced in the papers as a Yankee agitator, is an Englishman who has en in this country only four years, and has been to the United States only for an casional trip. There has been, I think, a deliberate effort to prejudice the public painst some of the labour organizations by the insinuation that they are controlled itirely from the United States.

Q. It would seem from what you say that the Labour Department has had the fect of convincing the workers and the employers as well that it is an honest disinrested machinery by which industrial troubles can be settled?—A. I think, Mr. yshe, that each year the two sides have come to have more confidence in the imparality of the department.

Q. Of course it depends a great deal on the tact and judgment with which these erations are carried out?—A. Labour matters are sensitive problems, and have to dealt with with some care.

By the Chairman:

Q. Mr. Butler, in giving his evidence this morning spoke of the retirement fund r the 9,000 employees on the Intercolonial Railway, the Government contributing ie-half and the employees the other half. Have you seen in your investigations that ere is any such attempt made by big companies employing labour or big corporaons?—A. I think some of the principal corporations are adopting that policy. I ight cite as an instance which comes to my mind. Only a few days ago Mr. achado, of the American Bank Note Company, told me that his concern was condering a pension arrangement for the employees, and asked me if I could supply m with some data from the department. A good many of the large corporations are lopting something in the nature of a pension scheme for their employees.

Q. Do you know whether the railway companies are doing anything in that line? A. I think they are.

By Mr. Fyshe:

Q. I am rather inclined to the opinion that a law should be passed providing that corporations shall have a charter without a condition in it that before paying more an 4 per cent to its shareholders an efficient pension fund shall be established for all iployees and their dependents—not only for the employees, but for the widows and ildren?—A. I think if corporations would follow a suggestion of that kind it would fectively aid in reducing the possibility of labour troubles.

By the Chairman:

Q. All the work of the Labour Department, up to the present moment, has been carried on or developed under an increasing era of prosperity in Canada?—A. Yes, it has.

Q. Supposing the tide turned a little in the other direction. How far will the department show its usefulness then?—A. I think from the fact that we have at hand the machinery whereby we can gather accurate and satisfactory information and convey to the mass of people, the educational side of the work of the department should be as great in such a period as it is at present. In the same way in dealing with industrial disputes as they arise, we will be able to throw light on the situation, without which, a period of depression would, I think be harder to explain to the industrial classes and be less easily understood by them.

Q. Of course the prices of commodities in a period of depression would decrease?—A. I would say in that connection that I had hoped our department would be able to lay before this Commission a statistical table showing the movement of the cost of living. I regard, as one of the most important parts of our work the gathering of statistical information which will show the movement of wages and the movement of prices; the extent to which they are related and parallel each other.

Q. Just as the labour bureau has done in the United States?—A. Quite so. We have a great deal of information on wages. The staff that we have is quite inadequate, however, to do, in regard to prices, the work which we have done in the compilation of statistics on wages. We should do both, in order that each might receive its full value.

Mr. FYSHE.—In both England and the United States for years and years there have been people at work compiling figures with regard to the price of everything. I forget the authority in England which does this, but it is published in the *Economist*.

The CHAIRMAN.—The Statistical Society does it there.

Mr. FYSHE.—I think it is very trustworthy information.

The WITNESS.—And the Board of Trade in England does work of that kind. In the United States the Department of Labour and Commerce has done a great deal, also several of the State Bureaus. We have, in the six years in which the *Labour Gazette* has been published, kept the most complete record of wages and prices to be found in the Dominion, you will find no other single source which will be of greater service to you in that connection.

By the Chairman:

Q. If depression occurs or a set back the department would be able to cope with the difficulties which might arise then?—A. I do not know whether it will be able to cope with them, but I think the department will be able to prevent error and misunderstanding which, but for its existence, would arise.

Q. I think that the department will develop and grow considerably, and you will want to increase the staff all the time?—A. The present indications are such that it is hard to say where the growth will stop. Take the last session of parliament. Mr. Monk introduced a Bill having to do with the subject of co-operation. That is a most important subject, and if we are to judge from the growth of co-operation in other countries the growth of the system in Canada will, as years go on, be very considerable. The Bill which Mr. Monk introduced and which the Government had undertaken to take over at the next session, throws the whole onus of the work, whatever that work may be, in connection with the measure upon our department.

Mr. FYSHE.—What is the main object of this proposed legislation?

The CHAIRMAN.—It is inchoate now.

The WITNESS.—I do not know that I should say much about the measure, as it is still a subject of debate. I cited the fact merely to show that from one session to another the Department of Labour is likely to have extra duties thrown upon it, and the fact that industrial and social conditions generally are becoming more and more political questions seems to me to establish the fact that the Department of Labour is going to grow just as inevitably as the problems with which it has to deal.

By the Chairman :

Q. And at the present moment your staff is fully occupied ?—A. The staff is not adequate for the work we are doing. I have to admit moreover that work is being done in the department in a way that I am not at all satisfied with. I simply have not time to see how some of it is being carried on.

By Mr. Fyshe :

Q. Where is your office?—A. Over the Molson's Bank. We have two floors above the Molson's Bank and a floor above the Great North Western Telegraph office.

Q. When did you graduate in Toronto ?—A. In arts, 1895; in law, a year later.

By the Chairman :

Q. Have you kept an attendance book in your department ?—A. Yes.

Q. Do the officers all sign it ?—A. With one or two exceptions.

Q. And it is under your supervision ?—A. Yes.

Q. What leave of absence do you give your officers during the year ?—A. Three weeks. I might say that as far as my own holidays are concerned there have been years when I have had no vacation whatever. Almost every year some work has turned up which has prevented me from having a full vacation.

Q. Is that just to yourself?—A. I do not think it is just to myself. Still, I feel that I would not be doing just to the department if I did not stay with the work. Let me say in conclusion : There is a great need for men of training and education who can be trusted with responsibilities. There are too many clerks, not enough efficient officers. The greatest need in the Civil Service is increased efficiency, and that must be paid for.

Q. You know that Dr. Coulter broke down from over work ?—A. Yes, he did.

Q. And that other men in the Civil Service have broken down ?—A. Yes.

Q. If you would like to add anything to supplement your oral testimony we shall be glad to receive it ?—A. Thank you, I may avail myself of the opportunity.

Witness discharged.

DEPARTMENT OF LABOUR, CANADA,
OTTAWA, June 5, 1907.

SIR,—In reply to your communication of the 29th inst., I beg to inclose a statement showing the number of the staff of the Department of Labour, permanent and extra graded into classes, and the amount of salaries paid during the year ended June 30, 1906.

As to information elucidating the increase of business in this department, I would say the department is about to complete the seventh year of its existence. During that period the work of the department has steadily increased, in the first place, in consequence of its existence and purpose becoming better known, not only throughout Canada but to a degree in other countries of the world, and secondly, on account of the enactment by parliament of legislation imposing additional duties upon it.

The *Labour Gazette*, the official journal of the department, which appears monthly, and is published in both English and French, has increased in size from a volume of

599 pages in 1900 to 1,394 pages in 1906. As centres of population have, increased in size throughout the Dominion, additional correspondents have been added to the staff of correspondents of the *Gazette*, that number being 45 at the present time. The increase in the number of correspondents has greatly increased the work connected with the publication of the *Labour Gazette*. The increase in the circulation of the *Gazette* is shown by the following figures, will also indicate the increase in the amount of work involved both in the circulation and distribution branches of the department.

Year.	Annual Subscriptions.	Free and Exchange Distribution.	Total Circulation.
1900–1..........	4,394	2,158	6,912
1901–2..........	5,648	2,722	8,370
1902–3..........	7,748	3,046	10,794
1903–4	7,361	3,553	10,914
1904–5..........	6,645	3,717	10,362
1905–6..........	7,547	3,987	11,534

The intervention of the department in industrial disputes under the Conciliation Act, 1900, has become increasingly important as the services of the department in this connection have become more generally known. The work is such that the services of one or two special officers charged solely with the carrying out of the requirements of the Act in the public interest is not more than the situation at present requires, whereas the work has been carried on for the most part as incidental to the duties of the Deputy Head of the department, a situation which creates embarrassment in the efficient carrying on of the administrative work of the department.

The carrying out of the Fair Wages Resolution of the House of Commons, passed in March, 1900, which provides for the insertion of fair wage conditions in contracts for work being executed for the Government, has steadily increased. Not only have the number of contracts awarded by some of the departments considerably increased, but departments of the Government which had, during the first two or three years, inserted only a clause governing labour conditions, now call upon the department for detailed schedules of rates of wages to be inserted in such contracts. The correspondence of this branch has also considerably increased.

The number of special investigations into industrial conditions in the Dominion has increased from year to year. No special provision has been made for the carrying on of work of this kind. The department has endeavoured to meet the situation with its present staff as the occasion arose. The investigations conducted at Montreal in 1904 into the manner in which Italian labourers were induced to come to Canada by false representations and the investigation conducted in Winnipeg in 1905 into the manner in which British printers were also induced to come to this country under false representations, each of which investigations resulted in the enactment of legislation by the Canadian as well as the British Parliament, to obviate a repetition of the fraudulent practices exposed, are instances in point.

The appointment of a Royal Commission to inquire into industrial disputes in the province of British Columbia in 1903, of the Royal Commissions to inquire into the employment of aliens on the Grand Trunk Pacific Railway surveys, and in connection with the Père Marquette Railway the appointment of a Royal Commission to inquire into a dispute between the Bell Telephone Company and its operators, on all of which Commissions members of the staff were employed, are other instances in point. Not only was the actual time of members of the staff taken from their regular duties because of the special duties involved in connection with the work of these Commissions, but additional work of a delicate and somewhat complicated nature was occasioned by the situations out of which the creation of these Commissions arose, and the correspondence incidental to these situations, the work of the Commissions and the subsequent publication and distribution of the reports.

The preparation of comparative statistical tables on strikes and lockouts, industrial accidents and other economic phenomena illustrative of the industrial situation of the Dominion, is a work which has assumed increasing proportions each year. Considering that statistical information of this sort, carefully compiled, is a most essential part of the data which a legislator should have at hand in the framing of laws governing such matters, it is to be regretted that the inadequacy of the present staff of the department does not permit of the work being conducted on a scale either extensive or thorough enough to serve, with the degree of accuracy it should, the end for which it is intended. There are, moreover, a number of subects which are being considered by Parliament, and which have a direct bearing on the economic and industrial conditions of the country, with which the Department of Labour should be concerned in furnishing reliable data. The capacity of the staff being at the present time over-taxed, this work has to be neglected entirely.

A library is an essential part of a Department of Labour. An effort has been made to gather together in our department the publications of trade and labour organizations and other publications which have a direct bearing upon industrial and labour conditions in Canada. An effort has also been made to keep the public informed, through the medium of the *Labour Gazette*, of important industrial and labour reports appearing in other countries. A detailed subject catalogue, to which immedate reference may be made on any question concerning which the department may be called upon to investigate or report, is essential to efficiency. At the present time, the department has only one clerk charged with these duties, and they are performed in addition to other work, which he is also assigned. The result is that not only the department but the public suffer in a manner which is none the less real, because it is not apparent.

The correspondence of the department, particularly such as has to do with the replying to requests for information from Governments in different parts of the world, from public bodies, societies and organizations in Canada and other countries, as well as from individuals, is assuming proportions which necessitates an immediate addition to the staff, and this of a class of clerks who are qualified by ability and training to not only conduct correspondence in a proper manner, but to carry on such research as may be necessary in obtaining the information required.

The filing of correspondence has in the past been assigned to members of the staff who have been doing the stenographic work of the department. The volume of correspondence has so increased that it has now quite surpassed their capacity to properly cope with it, and as a result embarrassment is experienced almost daily in consequence of correspondence not being properly filed or sufficiently indexed. Immediate relief is necessary in this branch of the department's work, if Government business is to be carried on in the same manner in which a private corporation would expect to have it performed.

The enactment by Parliament at the last session of the Industrial Disputes Investigation Act has given a sudden and most exceptional increase to the work of the department. The discretion and care required to be exercised in connection with the carrying on of the correspondence necessary to the efficient administration of this law, and the number and amount of details which it is necessary to consider, it is impossible to over-estimate, while the amount of clerical labour which the additional work entails is quite sufficient, judging from the experience of the past two months, to require the services of at least two additional clerks. Parliament has voted a sum of $10,000 for the carrying on of this work, a sum which will prove inadequate, judging by present indications, but no provision has been made for an increase in the number of the staff.

In conclusion, I would say that I have not attempted to give in any detail a statement of the increase of work in this department, but have simply endeavoured to in-

7-8 EDWARD VII., A. 1908

dicate facts which will doubtless be only too apparent to the members of the Commission. There is at the present time not a single member of the staff who is not engaged in doing the work of two or three different kinds and whose whole time might to the advantage of the department and the country, be devoted to any one of them. As an illustration: several members of the staff spend a portion of each day in scanning the papers received from all parts of the Dominion, with a view to noting any threatened or existing strikes or lockouts, changes in wages, industrial accidents or other matters concerning which it is necessary for the department to correspond, with a view to obtaining an accurate statistical record of the industrial happenings of the month. The same or other members of the staff may be called upon to give part of their time to reading proof of the *Labour Gazette* during the days in which the copy is received from the printers. The typewriting which is required in connection with one branch has, at times, to be distributed among all of the stenographers in the department, the work being of a nature demanding immediate attention. All of this creates an inevitable amount of confusion and operates against efficiency.

I might add, further, that during the past winter my secretary and I have spent on an average at least three or four nights every week in the office, working until between ten and twelve o'clock at night, in addition to having been in the department until between five and six in the afternoon, and this on Saturdays as well as other days of the week, and that not infrequently other members of the staff have worked in the department several evenings during the month, and on Sundays occasionally, while some of them rarely left the office until nearly six in the afternoon. At the present time there is a volume of work in the department which should be overtaken, but with the present staff that is going to be impossible.

I have the honour to be, sir,
Your obedient servant,

(Signed)   W. L. MACKENZIE KING,
Deputy Minister of Labour.

THOS. S. HOWE, Esq.,
Secretary, Civil Service Commission,
Room 2, the Senate, Ottawa.

STAFF OF DEPARTMENT OF LABOUR, JUNE 30, 1906.

1 Deputy Minister of Labour and Editor of *Labour Gazette*..	$ 4,000
*2 First-class clerks, 1 at $1,700, 1 at $1,600	3,300
5 Second-class clerks, 3 at $1,500, 2 at $1,300.........	7,100
2 Junior second-class clerks, 1 at $950, 1 at $800......	1,750
1 Third-class clerk......................................	500
	$16,650

Extra Assistance.

1 Messenger...	500
1 Accountant..	500
1 French translator.....................................	500
2 Temporary assistants, at $500.........................	1,000
45 Correspondents to *Labour Gazette* (outside), at $100 each.	4,500
1 Legal correspondent...................................	300
	$7,300

*An additional chief clerk, secretary, has been since appointed at a salary of $3,600.

OTTAWA, FRIDAY, June 13, 1907.

The Royal Commission on the Civil Service met this morning at 10.30 o'clock.

Present:—Mr. J. M. COURTNEY, C.M.G., Chairman.

Mr. THOMAS FYSHE, Montreal and

Mr. P. J. BAZIN, Quebec.

Lieutenant-Colonel F. F. GOURDEAU, sworn and examined.

By the Chairman :

Q. You are the Deputy Minister of Marine and Fisheries?—A. Yes.

Q. How long have you been in the service?—A. Over 40 years.

Q. You have ceased to pay superannuation abatement?—A. Yes, some ten years ago.

Q. What is your salary?—A. $4,000.

Q. If you were retired now, you would get an annual allowance of $2,800 a year? —A. Yes.

Q. Practically you are working for $1,200 a year?—A. Yes.

Q. And your staying in the service only makes a difference to you of $100 per month?—A. Yes.

Q. Your department spent last year under your direction something over $6,000,-000?—A. Yes. Our expenditure in 1905-6 was $5,785,522.67.

Q. That is the amount of the appropriations, not the expenditure?—A. Yes.

Q. The expenditure was over $6,000,000?—A. Yes.

Q. You have in your department chief clerks and technical officers?—A. Yes.

Q. What are Mr. Halkett's duties?—A. He has charge of the correspondence.

Q. Have you a secretary in your department?—A. No.

Q. Practically he is the secretary?—A. No.

By Mr. Fyshe:

Q. Do you require a secretary?—A. Yes, or an assistant deputy minister.

By the Chairman:

Q. What is Mr. Kent?—A. He has charge of the fishing bounties.

Q. What is Mr. Magee?—A. He has retired.

Q. What is Mr. Owen?—A. The accountant of the department.

Q. What is Mr. Cameron Stanton?—A. He has the general supervision of the work of the department, because we have no secretary, but he ranks higher than Mr. J. B. Halkett. He is the officer in charge in my absence.

Q. What is Mr. Venning?—A. Assistant Commissioner of Fisheries.

Q. He has had something to do with international questions, such as the Behring Sea fisheries?—A. Yes.

Q. He has been to Washington and to England?—A. Yes, and he was sent specially by the English Government on a warship to the Pribyloff islands to study the seal question as British agent as agreed with Russia in 1893.

Q. Have you promoted any one to succeed Mr. Magee?—A. No. That will be done on the return of the Minister.

Q. You have also eight technical officers?—A. Yes.

Q. One of these is Mr. Frederick Anderson?—A. Yes. He is in the hydrographic survey on Mr. W. Stewart's staff.

Q. His work is chiefly outside?—A. He has control of a division on Lake Superior. The work is done in the summer and he comes here in winter and transcribes his notes.

Q. Mr. W. P. Anderson?—A. He is chief enginer of the department.

Q. Mr. Bell Dawson?—A. He is in charge of tidal survey.

Q. He is away all summer?—A. Yes. He has a ship under his charge.

By Mr. Fyshe:

Q. He is in Ottawa in winter?—A. Yes. The transcribing of his reports he does himself and staff. He is one of the busiest clerks in the department.

By the Chairman:

Q. What does Mr. Basil Fraser do ?—A. He is assistant chief engineer.

Q. Mr. James F. Fraser?—A. He has charge of all the lighting and the aids to navigation. His title is commissioner of lights, and he has a seat on the Lighthouse Board.

Q. Who compose the Lighthouse Board?—A. Hugh Allan, Captain Troup, the representative of the C.P.R. Fleet of British Columbia; Colonel Anderson, J. F. Fraser, Commander Spain, and I act as chairman of the board. We want to get the opinions of outsiders as to the aids to navigation, and we can call on any outsider to attend a meeting of the board on any particular case if considered necessary.

Q. Don't you find that having a board or council, it greatly tends to increase the expenditure?—A. In what way?

Q. Everybody making suggestions, and you are all too ready to adopt them?—A. No, it is quite the contrary. It has saved the Minister from pressure which he would have had to accede to if this board had not been there to say that what was proposed was not absolutely required.

Q. Then the Lighthouse Board acts as a buffer between the Minister and the applicants?—A. Yes.

Q. The Minister is answerable to Parliament for the expenditure of his department?—A. Yes.

Q. Would it not also serve in the opposite capacity of adding to the expenditure by carrying out the opinions of the members?—A. No. When the board sits and decides on any question, a report of its decision is prepared by the secretary of the board and submitted to the Minister.

Q. Who is the secretary of the board?—A. Mr. Clement, who succeeds Mr. W. C. Gordon, the late secretary.

Q. What is Mr. J. M. O'Hanly?—A. He is in Colonel Anderson's branch. He has charge of preparing the notices to mariners. All the different aids to navigation are laid off in triangular lines, and he must be a technical man to be able to verify these triangulations and prepare the notices sent to the Admiralty in England and all over the world.

Q. Then you have Mr. Prince, the commissioner of fisheries?—A. Yes.

Q. He was a professor at St. Andrew's University before he was appointed?—A. Yes.

Q. But he is continually going about the country looking after the development and the productiveness of the fisheries?—A. Yes, and he is the controlling man of the biological branch.

By Mr. Fyshe:

Q. Has he been long in the service?—A. About twelve or fifteen years. He is a very good officer.

By the Chairman:

Q. Who is Mr. W. J. Stewart?—A. He is the chief hydrographer for Canada.

Q. While Mr. Anderson has a district, Mr. W. J. Stewart has the whole of Can-

—A. Anderson is under Stewart, and there was an anomaly in that branch. We Commander Miles, who works under Mr. Stewart, and who received until lately a year more than Mr. Stewart.

Ͽ. When was Capt. Miles appointed ?—A. The hydrographic work is a particular kind ιgineering work; it requires particular studies, and Mr. Stewart, who is at the of that service, got the highest marks ever obtained at the Royal Military College, we took him on here. He worked under Commander Boulton, and when Com-ler Boulton was recalled to England, he stated that we could not find a better man ngland than young Stewart, and he has been in charge of the service ever since. s one of the best officers in the department.

Q. The salary of Commander Miles is charged to an outside vote?—A. Yes, the ographic vote.

Q. You are paying him at the rate of $2,920 per annum?—A. Yes.

Q. The chief clerks and the technical clerks are all doing distinct work ?—A.

Ͽ. Could they be lessened in number?—A. No.

Ͽ. Last year you had 16 first-class clerks?—A. Yes. We provided for that num-n the estimates, but there is some flaw in the Civil Service Act which prevents Minister appointing them at that rate for sometime, and we took a number of · 16 from those clerks paid as extras.

Ͽ. You have fourteen who are paid out of the Civil Government vote?—A. Yes.

Ͽ. Are they all doing first-class work?—A. Yes, doing distinctive and good work, ɔnly promoted to that class because they were fit for it.

Ͽ. You have nine second-class clerks?—A. Yes. They are all good.

Ͽ. And twelve junior second-class?—A. Yes. There is only one man among them is indifferent.

Ͽ. You have four third-class clerks?—A. No. Some of them have left the ser-

Ͽ. You have only one extra clerk and a messenger paid out of Civil Government ngencies?—A. Yes.

Ͽ. The extra clerk is Madame Lamouche?—A. Yes. She has been employed in lepartment over twenty-five years.

Ͽ. Why don't you make her permanent?—A. She is now.

Ͽ. Then practically you have only two messengers paid out of Civil Government ngencies?—A. Yes.

Q. Does your having so large a number of first-class clerks and so small a num-ıf junior second-class clerks arise from the fact that you cannot get good men to · the service as third-class clerks?—A. Yes, we have lost some because of the l salary. If a man has a good education and is a good clerk, I think it is abso-y out of the question to secure his services for less than $800 a year.

Q. The salary of a third-class clerk runs from $500 to $700, and you cannot get young men to enter at these rates?—A. No.

Q. At what minimum do you think you could get fair men to enter the service—ϧ00 or $700?—A. No, I do not think so. I think $800 is the lowest salary you ld offer a man who has some education and some ambition to get on.

By Mr. Fyshe:

Q. That must have changed a good deal within the last few years, because it used ys to be an easy matter for banks to get young men for much less than that?—A. because in a bank if a boy is intelligent or smart, he can look forward to getting n five or six years; but in the Civil Service even a good clerk will increase very y. In his first five or six years at the present salary, he will get into debt in ː to live decently, and he will have to live to good age before he is out of debt.

By the Chairman:

Q. You have two women on your staff?—A. Yes.

Q. Madame Lamouche and Mrs. Thomas?—A. Yes.

Q. You prefer to keep women as temporaries?—A. No, but in the employment of women there is this disadvantage: Though they may know as much as the men clerks, you cannot utilize them in the same way. You cannot confide outside business necessitating travelling, and they cannot transact certain business which would be done by a man having their knowledge.

Q. Would you suggest as a matter of fact that there should be a limit of pay for women?—A. Yes, second class.

Q. You have forty odd people employed as extra clerks?—Engineers, draughtsmen, preparing fishing bounty checks, &c., all paid from appropriations other than Civil Government?—A. Yes. The fishing bounty business takes between twenty-eight and thirty-two clerks. There are over 20,000 checks to be made out in a limited time. Every application for a bounty has to be strictly examined. The vessels are paid by the tonnage and the fishermen so much per man, provided a certain quantity of fish is taken.

Q. Coming back to the Civil Government staff, all these junior second-class clerks, second-class, and so on, pass the Civil Service examination?—A. Yes.

Q. Passed the Civil Service examination?—A. Which does not mean very much.

Q. It presumes that they are of the proper age, in good health and of strict moral character?—A. Yes.

Q. They are appointed on probation?—A. Yes.

Q. And after a time you give a certificate that they are fitted for employment in the department?—A. Yes.

Q. What leave of absence do you give your clerks?—A. Three weeks.

Q. Anything more than that?—A. No, and if a man is absent without leave, I dock his pay.

Q. Do you ever suspend any of your inside officers?—A. Yes.

Q. For what reason?—A. Absence owing to intemperance.

Q. Do you reinstate them?—A. The Minister reinstates them.

Q. After they have purged themselves?—A. Yes. If they are bad enough I insist on their taking the gold cure or leave the department.

Q. What are the luncheon hours?—A. Between 12 and 2, and no branch of the service are allowed to leave their rooms all at once. There must be always one answerable for the duties of that branch, and we have a sheet of paper attached to each branch showing the clerks who have been chosen between 12 and 1 and those between 1 and 2 for lunch.

Q. Then the department is always open to the public?—A. Yes.

Q. In what state are the records of your department in? Are they kept carefully? —A. They are perfectly kept.

Q. Are there any historical records in your department?—A. No.

Q. You have no occasion to turn over any to the Archives?—A. No.

Q. Your department only began at Confederation?—A. Yes.

Q. It corresponds somewhat to the Board of Trade of England?—A. The origin of the department was the Trinity House at Quebec.

Q. What became of the records of the Trinity House at Quebec?—A. They are in the possession of the Harbour Commissioners of Quebec.

Q. A great many of these records have reference to the navigation of the River St. Lawrence in the time of the early voyageurs?—A. No. We lost a lot of very valuable records when the Western Block was burnt.

By Mr. Fyshe:

Q. Does not that show that there should be a proper place to keep all the records? —A. Yes.

By the Chairman:

Q. Do you think the Harbour Commissioners at Quebec have any historical re- ords ?—A. No, because we are looking up some old matter connected with the earlier ilotage, the Minister thinking that it would be better to transfer any of these records) the Archives, and Mr. Woods, the secretary, advised us that they have nothing of he kind. They have the records of ships coming in, which would be of no value.

Q. Where is your department placed?—A. Part in the Western Block.

Q. Are there any of your officials in other parts of the city?—A. Yes.

Q. How many officers have you outside of your departmental officers ?—A. We ave the Hydrographic Branch, in the Corry Building, the Fishery Branch, the In- pector of Lights and the Tidal Survey, in the Woods Building.

Q. Mr. Bazin and Mr. Fyshe will require to visit these offices and the department? —A. Certainly. I shall be delighted to accompany them at any time.

Q. Do you prepare any maps in your department?—A. Yes. They have just as ood a reputation and standing as the Admiralty maps in England. They are accepted y the Admiralty.

By Mr. Fyshe:

Q. Who is principally employed in making them?—A. The staff under Mr. Stew- rt, of the Hydrographic Survey.

By the Chairman:

Q. Do you know that maps are prepared in the various departments?—A. Yes.

Q. And that there is a geographer of the Dominion?—A. Yes.

Q. And that an atlas of the Dominion has been recently published?—A. Yes.

Q. One of the maps in that atlas shows where each lighthouse in the Dominion is ituated?—A. I have not seen it.

Q. You do not know whether the ground work for that map came from your de- artment?—A. If I saw it I could tell you.

Q. Don't you think it would be better to concentrate all this mapping in one ureau, as is done in England?—A. The hydrographic work is absolutely distinct in England. No other department interferes with it.

Q. Do not the ordnance people?—A. They have nothing whatever to do with it.

Q. Who prepares the charts in England—the Admiralty?—A. Yes.

Q. You are aware that a Treasury Board Minute was promulgated in 1879 regard- ng the use of political influence on the part of public employees?—A. Yes.

Q. Are the officials of your department aware of that?—A. Yes.

Q. Do they ever in seeking to obtain extra emoluments or to better themselves in ny way, pass you by and go direct to the Minister?—A. Yes.

Q. The Minister always refers to you?—A. Yes.

Q. What happens to them when you find out that they have neglected to go through he proper channel?—A. Sometimes it takes them a long time to get there.

Q. Does it lead to a struggle between yourself and the clerk?—A. No. The Minis- er is always very particular in getting my recommendation.

Q. Then, by using political influence they do not gain much?—A. It does not help hem very much—not a good clerk, and in the case of a bad clerk the Minister will not ay any attention to it.

Q. You stated that for ten years you had ceased to contribute any superannuation batement?—A. Yes, sir.

Q. If you were to die to-morrow?—A. My family would not get a cent.

Q. Since 1897 there has been no Superannuation Act?—A. No.

Q. What is your opinion about the abolition of that Act?—A. I do not think it ins fair to those coming in; but the Government should do as the Provincial govern- nents, give an annuity to the widow of the family. In my case, and in other similar

29a—41½

cases. I think they ought at any rate to pay the money we have paid in for superannuation with accrued interest.

Q. Then you think it is desirable to re-enact some kind of Pension Act, and probably enlarge it so as to include a pension scheme to widows?—A. I think it would be fair to the employees.

Q. Looking at the civil service in general and your own department in particular, have you any suggestions to make as to gradation of classes or anything else?—A. I think every department, at least every large receiving and paying department, should have an assistant deputy.

By Mr. Fyshe:

Q. I have very definite ideas about that—I think it tends to make the line of re-sponsibility between the two quite uncertain. I have derived that from my experience in banking?—A. A bank is not the same thing at all as a large Government department. A bank deals with the receiving of money and the paying out of money, interest, exchange, loans, and that is all. That is a small matter, wherras in a Government department there may be twenty-seven different services, each of which service is a specialty in itself; and if you have not a secretary or an assistant deputy who will make himself acquainted with these different services, in the absence of the deputy for two or three weeks, the department will suffer.

Q. But if anything goes wrong, don't you think there is a possibility of each one throwing the blame on the other?—A. It is impossible.

Q. Again, will not an assistant always be clamouring for more money on account of his superior position?—A. He cannot clamour for more money if there is a stated amount attached to his position. In one branch of our department we have cases in connection with the registration of ships, pilotage administration of the different Provinces, &c., &c., &c., and unless an officer will make a special study of that, he is absolutely at sea. We have eminent lawyers coming to us for information on such matters which they do not understand themselves, simply because these officers make this work a special study.

By the Chairman:

Q. In 1892 you had 37 employees charged to Civil Government as against about 53 in 1906?—A. Yes.

Q. You had 10 temporaries in 1892 as against 43 in 1906?—A. Yes.

Q. Does the increased business in the department in fifteen years justify the increase in the staff?—A. Yes. There was an increase of 450 per cent.

Q. In what way?—A. In every branch.

Q. An increase in correspondence?—A. Yes. There were 9,000 letters written fifteen years ago, and there were 35,000 last year. That is apart of the Minister's correspondence and my own. There is not a day passes in which I do not dictate fifteen or twenty letters both in French and English.

Q. These forty odd people employed at headquarters, notwithstanding anything in the Civil Service Act, have passed no examination?—A. The clerks in that long list are attached to the different branches. For instance, Colonel Anderson has to have architects, engineers and draughtsmen. All these people need not be in the Civil Service.

Q. At present they pass no examination?—A. Yes, by the chief engineer.

Q. That forty odd people include architects, draughtsmen, typewriters and others?—A. Yes. Amongst those are the sixteen that we are transferring to the regular staff.

Q. Have those sixteen passed the examination?—A. Yes.

Q. Then you consider it desirable not to have these people employed notwithstanding the Civil Service Act, but to include them in the department?—A. Yes. They should be under the Civil Government. We would then know exactly what it costs to run the department.

Q. In your outside service have you any idea how many men you have employed?

in all branches under the control of your department?—A. Two thousand, perhaps more.

Q. None of them come under the Civil Servcie Act?—A. No.

Q. You have a large quantity of stores on hand?—A. Yes.

Q. Where are the stores kept? Are they scattered all over the Dominion?—A. At Prescott, Quebec, Halifax, Charlottetown, Victoria, B.C., Ottawa.

Q. Are there store books kept as to issue and receipt ?—A. Yes, in every case there are store books kept, and there is stock-taking once a year. That is done in every agency, but the only agencies with good buildings for that purpose are at Sorel, Quebec, Halifax and Prescott. That is done as well as in any business house in Canada.

Q. You have store books in which are kept accounts of the receipts and discharges? —A. Yes. For instance, if a foreman at Sorel has to make repairs to a small boat, he makes a requisition for what is required—so much wood, so much nails, so much copper or whatever it may be. That is sent to the supply man. He examines the requisitions and checks them. The list goes to the storekeeper and it is checked again, and charges are made to an account for that service, so that at the end of the year they take stock the same as any business house. If you gentlemen of the Commission will accept my invitation, I will take you from Montreal to Sorel in the *Lady Grey*, and you can visit our place there and see how the work is carried on.

Q. The same thing would apply to Prescott, I presume?—A. Yes, and I invite you to visit our place there also.

Q. Is there an annual audit?—A. Yes.

Q. Who makes the audit?—A. Alfred Roy.

By Mr. Fyshe:

Q. Are those stores ever inspected specially?—A. Yes.

By the Chairman:

Q. There is no compulsory audit by the Auditor General?—A. No.

Q. The Auditor General has never audited them?—A. He has been there three or four times to audit and he is quite satisfied with everything.

Q. How do you get your supplies?—A. By tender.

Q. In all cases?—A. In all cases.

Q. Is the lowest tender accepted?—A. Yes.

Q. Do you advertise for tenders?—A. Yes.

Q. What deposits do you require?—A. Ten per cent.

Q. What do you do with these?—A. We send them to the Department of Finance.

Q. In all cases?—A. In all cases.

Q. You stated just now that you had some professional men in the department— .they are accountants?—A. Yes.

Q. What did the Minister call them in for?—A. There had been an onslaught on the department, and the confidence of many people in the department was shaken. They found, I think, two duplicate payments for some few dollars in each case, and they were making such a fuss about it that the Minister, on the recommendation of Mr. Butler, the Deputy Minister of Railways and Canals, who said that these same auditors had done good work in his own department, engaged them to go over all the accounts of our department for the preceding year. They did so, and I am glad to say they did not find anything wrong. They initiated a few more books and a more modern way of entering accounts, by the loose leaf system; but the book-keeping in the department was found to be perfectly sound.

Q. Who are these professional accountants?—A. I do not know them. One was named Mr. Falconer.

Q. The result was to make some modifications in the book-keeping?—A. No. They opened a new set of books from the 1st of July to the 30th of June, balanced the books, and found absolutely nothing wrong.

Q. They found the system correct?—A. Yes.

Q. Was it any part of their functions to see whether the expenditure was extravagant or otherwise?—A. No.

Q. It was only to see whether the system adopted was the proper system?—A. Yes. Their salaries were from $75 a day down.

Q. How many were there?—A. Quite a number. Those at the top notch were paid at the rate of $75 a day.

Q. You were intending to have a scale of salaries applicable to the lighthouse-keepers?—A. Yes. We had a long conference with all the agents during last winter and a schedule has been prepared and will be submitted to the Minister on his return. The present salaries are small.

Q. They have been haphazard?—A. I would not like to say that, but they have been the same for some forty or fifty years. There are some men in New Brunswick who are raising a family as light-keepers on a salary of $120 a year.

Q. Are not those small salaries paid in places where there is simply a pole?—A. No

Q. Do you require their entire duties in these places?—A. Yes.

Q. Do they have houses in some cases?—A. In some cases.

Q. And they have supplies of wood and coal?—A. Not everywhere.

Q. You are about to lay down a scale of salaries?—A. Yes. We have divided the lighthouse-keepers into seven different classes—those of the first order, where they have whistling apparatus and a complete set of machinery for working it, and the lowest order is where there is simply a pole light, for which we allow them as little as $25 a year.

Q. Where are the supplies for the steamers purchased?—A. At headquarters.

Q. You have agents at several places?—A. Yes.

Q. How many agents have you got?—A. We have Mr. Gregory at Quebec, Mr. Parsons at Halifax, Mr. Lord in Prince Edward Island, Mr. Harding in New Brunswick. Captain James Gaudin in British Columbia, Mr. Boucher in Montreal. These are all constituted agents representing the Minister.

Q. They secure the supplies for the steamers?—A. No, the supplies are purchased from Ottawa.

Q. What steamers are placed at Quebec?—A. The *Montcalm,* the *Druid* and the *Constance,* and other boats we are obliged to charter.

Q. Does Mr. Gregory purchase anything for these boats beyond meats and vegetables?—A. I have endeavoured, and succeeded, in three cases, to give the victualling of the officers and men to the captains of the boats, and in each case I have been able to save about several thousand dollars a year. It is very hard to get the others into that system, for local and other reasons.

By Mr. Fyshe:

Q. Is Captain Spain at the head of a branch of your department?—A. He is inspector of steamers and commissioner of wrecks.

By the Chairman:

Q. You are now trying to inaugurate a system whereby the captains will victual the crews?—A. Yes, that is the best system.

Q. If the captain feeds the men on bad stuff and tries to make too much money out of it, the crew would leave him?—A. No. We have prepared with regard to the food designated daily rations, submitted by Commander Spain and approved of by the Minister, and they have to give the crews exactly the same kind of food.

Q. Is there any test?—A. They are inspected continually by Commander Spain.

Q. How are other supplies purchased—coal oil, for instance?—A. By tender. The agent is told to go to certain persons to purchase. He has no right or power to purchase or carry on any transactions with the public unless with the approval and sanction of the Minister.

Q. Are the persons from whom the purchases are made the lowest tenderers?—A. Yes. We wish to make the purchases from people belonging to the party in power,

.nd we ask the Member for the district to give us the names of six or seven grocers or
·ther tradesmen, and we write to them and ask them for their prices, and we make the
·urchases from the man who offers us the lowest prices.

Q. Might not those grocers enter into a combination?—A. I think not.

By Mr. Fyshe:

Q. Those tenderers all belong to one political party?—A. Yes.

Q. That is hardly fair, is it?—A. I think that is right.

By the Chairman:

Q. Even though a grocer belonging to the opposition party sold him tea at ten
ents a pound cheaper?—A. He would not be such a fool as to sell his tea cheaper be-
·ause he is on the other side.

Q. Suppose these other six or seven men to whom you send a circular should
·nite?—A. We would know it right off. These matters are under consideration prob-
.bly for a couple of weeks before the seasons begins, and the clerk who looks after that,
·as all the prices published in the grocers' papers, and if a man is selling cheese to the
·epartment at too high a price, he will draw my attention to the fact, and I will bring
·t to the attention of the Minister, and the Minister will cut him off the list at once.
·ll the prices paid by our department are marked prices.

Q. Could not an agent order a larger quantity when a smaller quantity would
·o?—A. No. We never keep any goods in stock. The steward goes to the captain and
·ays: I want this week so many pounds of tea, so many pounds of sugar, &c. The
·aptain signs the requisition and that goes to the agent, and when the goods are deliv·
·red they are verified by the steward, and if they are of inferior quality they are sent
·ack.

Q. You have check upon check, and there is no reason to believe that an excessive
·uantity is charged for?—A. No.

Q. Or that an inferior article is supplied?—A. No.

By Mr. Fyshe:

Q. Don't you think it would be fairer, in asking for tenders for the supply of
·oods, to include traders of the opposite political creed?—A. I do not think so.

Q. You are acting for the country, not for the party?—A. The other party, when
·hey come into power, will do the same thing.

Q. Would it not be a good idea to have it compulsory to do so?—A. I do not
·hink so, not in places where there are fifteen or twenty grocers of the same political
·olour.

By Mr. Bazin:

Q. Don't you think the prices are so low that there is not enough margin to make
·uch difference?—A. It does not amount to a row of pins.

By the Chairman:

Q. In the session of 1905 your department was vigorously assailed for expenditure
·o persons named Brooks and Merwin?—A. Yes.

Q. It was shown by the evidence of a Mr. Wilson that Mr. Merwin charged the
·epartment, for instance, $960 for something that he got for $600?—A. Yes, in three
·ases.

Q. As far as I recollect, Mr. Merwin was a middleman?—A. Yes.

Q. And he got in once case a profit of 180 per cent?—A. Yes, on a pump.

Q. I see by last year's Auditor General's Report that in the construction of lights
·n general account you paid Merwin $64,000, and on submarine signal apparatus you
·aid him $42,000. What steps are you taking after that investigation to find out that
·ese are the lowest prices at which the articles can be obtained?—A. The unfortunate
·hing was that the officer who purchased in these cases did so on the authority of the
·en acting minister. That has ceased; it is not done now.

Q. These payments in the year 1905-6 were likewise?—A. Yes, on the personal responsibility of an official of the department.

Q. Do you mind stating who the gentleman was?—A. Mr. J. F. Fraser. I may say that those are isolated cases for which the deputy minister is not in any way accountable.

· Q. With this example before you, were any steps taken to thoroughly scrutinize Mr. Merwin's bills?—A, Yes. Every possible means were taken, and there is not a dollar overpaid in those amounts.

Q. Mr. Strubbe was also up for investigation?—A. Yes.

Q. He was paid $11,000 for cement?—A. Yes.

Q. He supplied that cement at $2.20 and $2.30 a barrel?—A. Yes.

Q. In the same year the Department of Railways and Canals paid the Owen Sound Portland Cement Company for apparently the same thing $1.85 a barrel. Was there any attempt to cut down Strubbe's account?—A. No. There was a regular arrangement made with him, and recommended by the chief engineer of the department. There was a difference in weight which made the price equal.

Q. That was also Mr. Fraser, I suppose?—A. No, the chief engineer.

Q. Do you get supplies from Mr. Strubbe now?—A. No. He says we have treated him badly.

· Q. Do you get supplies from Mr. Coughlin?—A. Yes.

Q. He is only a middleman, is he not?—A. He employs some 200 men in Montreal.

Q. Is he a manufacturer?—A. Yes, he manufactures chains and other iron supplies.

Q. You get articles from him in the way of his business?—A, Yes. We ask for tenders from two or three men, and if he happens to be the lowest, we give him the order.

Q. You do not go to him as a middleman to buy things that he does not deal in?—A. No.

Q. He refunded $1,100?—A. Yes.

Q. Then you have not given him orders this year in order that he might make up the $1,100 ?—A. No. We had unfairly deducted some $600 from that particular account.

Q. You have also made large payments to the Canadian Fog Signal Company of Toronto ?—A. Yes.

Q. Who are they?—A. I do not know anything about them. That is under Colonel Anderson. That company controls that particular fog signal, and we have to get it from them, and all the arrangements are recommended and approved by Colonel Anderson, a man of the highest integrity, in whom the department has every confidence.

Q. They have works, have they ?—A. Yes.

Q. Did you call for tenders from the Canadian Fog Signal Company ?—A. He called for tenders for some part of machinery, but what was under patent we could not.

Q. Do they give any security for carrying out their contract?—A. We order these fog alarms as we require them, and if they do not deliver them we do not pay for them.

Q. There is no security ?—A. No.

Q. Colonel Anderson is in charge ?—A. Yes, and he sees that they are delivered. If they are not, we do not pay for them.

Q. Mr. Wilson, of Ottawa, supplies the automatic gas and whistling buoys ?—A. Yes.

Q. And he was paid by your department in 1905-06 $336,000 ?—A. Yes.

Q. Did he supply the buoys that blew up at Kingston?—A. No. They belonged to the Department of Railways and Canals. They were old buoys and transferred to our department.

Q. Did not a buoy also blow up at Parry Sound?—A. That was one of the old buoys.

Q. Did not one also blow up down below Quebec ?—A. I never heard of it.

Q. Have any accidents happened to any of the new buoys supplied by Willson?—A. No.

Q. Is not the filling up of these buoys with acetylene gas a very dangerous occupation ?—A. I do not think so—not any more than lighting a gas stove.

Q. The country has to pay rather heavily for the damages at Kingston. It paid $38,000 for loss of life caused by the explosion of the gas buoy?—A. Yes.

By Mr. Fyshe :

Q. Who supplied those buoys?—A. They were old buoys. There was something the matter with them—a fissure in them.

Q. Who made them ?—A. They were brought from England I think.

By the Chairman :

Q. Should not they have been tested by some one before the gas was put into them ?—A. That was in the inception of that kind of buoy, and there was a very high pressure in them. The buoy now furnished by Willson is a low pressure buoy, and there is no more danger in charging them than there is in working any gas plant. He is getting orders for the same buoy from England, France, Austria and Germany.

By Mr. Fyshe :

Q. Has Willson practically a monopoly of it ?—A. Yes.

By the Chairman

Q. Has it been ascertained whether there was a Brooks in that firm of Brooks & Company, or whether Merwin was Brooks & Company ?—A. I do not know. We had no interest in finding that out as long as we got the goods. We called for tenders from the actual firms in England which he represented, but they will not deal directly with us. They say : Go to our agent in Canada and he will sell to you. If we were dissatisfied with him we would have to write to England and they would have to change their agent.

Q. Are you in the habit of asking for considerable supplementary estimates ?—A. When they are required.

Q. What is the process adopted in the department in preparing the estimates for submission to Council ?—A. We call on the different agents to send us their estimates. First of all the inspector visits all the lighthouses of his district ; he takes a note at every lighthouse of every repair or article that is required and these details are sent to us, and we prepare our estimates based on the actual expenditure which we know should take place in the year following.

Q. When you have a Supply granted by Parliament do your officers try to live within that supply ?—A. Yes, under the present Minister. There is an order which has been adhered to. First of all, an account is received. That has to go to the clerk who looks after the estimates. If it corresponds with the estimate, he attaches his initial to it. Then it goes to the accountant, who checks it. If it is an expenditure for a new boat or lighthouse it has to stand until next year.

Q. You are trying to keep within the estimates of the year?—A. Yes. The present Minister said he would hold the accountant responsible if anything was paid for that was not estimated for, he would take strict measures to prevent a recurrence of that.

Q. The present Minister has taken steps to keep the expenditure of the department within the appropriations ?—A. Absolutely, and is particular in exacting a monthly statement showing how the appropriations stand.

Q. There was a certain amount of laxity previous to his assumption of office ?—A. It was a continuation of what had been the practice under every Government. When they had to spend money they spent it.

Q. But in the development of the country the supplementary estimates increased every year ?—A. Yes, and at the end of the year very often the officials would let matters stand until the beginning of the next fiscal year and pay for them in that year, although they belonged to the year previous. The present Minister squared off all such matters last year. He got from the accountant a statement with regard to every agency, and insisted that not a single dollar was to be paid this year that should be charged to last fiscal year. The overlapping of our services amounted to $200,000 or $300,000 in the aggregate, but it was a continuation for years of what had been the case ever since I have been in the department.

Q. In some instances in your department the salaries of quasi permanent officials are charged to special services ; for instance, Mr. Demers, the chairman of the Examining Board for Masters and Mates, is charged to the account of investigation into wrecks ?—A. No, to the right vote—Masters and Mates.

Q. He got $300 for investigating into wrecks ?—A. Yes, and that was paid out of investigations into wrecks.

Q. Are you paying any of your officials out of more than one vote ?—A. There may be.

Q. Captain Spain is the commander of the Fishing Inspecting Fleet ?—A. Yes, of the Marine Service which comprises 36 vessels, and Wreck Commissioner.

Q. He gets $2,400 a year ?—A. Yes, and is allowed $5 a day for travelling expenses.

Q. His travelling expenses come to $3,000 or $4,000 a year ?—A. I do not think so. In his travelling expenses are charged the payments for a number of witnesses, and that swells his account. He has the bills of witnesses and other expenses amounting to perhaps $600 in one case. We are trying to divide that up properly, so that it will show more clearly.

Q. What is the investigation into wrecks ?—A. He is the officer in charge of that, and nobody can attend to it better.

Q. What branch is the investigation into wrecks in?—A. It is an investigation into steamship casualties.

Q. But it belongs to some branch. Are his travelling expenses charged to several votes ? He is sometimes concerned in investigation into wrecks and sometimes in other matters?—A. Yes. Every officer of the department who absents himself from the office has first to make application for an advance. In his application he states the purpose for which he is leaving, the time he leaves, how long it will take him to do the work and we base the amount of advance on the probable time of absence and the service that he is about to perform. So that there is never any excessive amount of advance given to any officer for travelling expenses, and we do not give him any further advance until he accounts for the previous trip.

Q. Do they account when they return ?—A. Yes. That is one of the strict rules of the department.

Q. You mentioned in your list of agents that Mr. Boucher is agent in Montreal?—A. Yes.

Q. Is he also engineer in charge of the care of buoys in the St. Lawrence ship channel ?—A. Yes.

Q. Does he board the men ?—A. He boards the men of the *Shamrock*.

Q. You have in addition to Colonel Anderson and his assistants here several resident engineers and foremen engaged in the construction of lights?—A. Yes. This year we have to build, I suppose, thirty-five or forty different lighthouses in different Provinces—in British Columbia, Nova Scotia, New Brunswick, Prince Edward Island, Quebec and Ontario. Colonel Anderson is obliged to organize parties in the different places so that the work will go on simultaneously. We never engage any one in that work unless Colonel Anderson is satisfied with his qualifications and approves of him.

Q. Who appoints all the resident engineers ?—A. The Minister on the recommendation of Colonel Anderson.

Q. *Politics* does not enter in ?—A. No. We want an engineer or an architect

· a man who can look after the men on the work. There is no political pressure for ̣at. The Minister approves, but the recommendation must come from the chief ̣gineer. Colonel Anderson will not accept any man who is not able to do his work.

Q. One of those resident engineers is A. E. Beauchemin ?—A. Yes, a very good ̣an.

Q. He has nothing to do with the Beauchemin & Company of Sorel ?—A. No. hey are perhaps related, but that is all. He is such a good man to control men that [r. Cowie has secured him for superintending some very important dredging below ̣uebec.

Q. You established Marconi stations ?—A. Yes.

Q. Have you many of them ?—A. I think we have seventeen altogether.

Q. Are you establishing more ?—A. Yes, in British Columbia.

By Mr. Fyshe:

Q. Has your department everything to do with the Marconi wireless telegraph ?— . Yes, everything.

Q. Has Marconi got exclusive rights ?—A. Not at all. Nobody can establish system of that kind without getting the license from the Minister of Marine and ̣aheries.

Q. Hasn't he practically got control of Sable Island ?—A. Yes. We let him ̣ve a station there because it is useful for us.

Q. I understand that the National Signal Company of the United States ap- ̣ied for the right to put up a signal station on Sable Island and were refused ?—A. ̣o.

Q. It would not interfere with the Marconi business ?—A. No. They have per- ̣cted the system to such an extent that the tuning of one instrument will not inter- ̣re with the tuning of another.

Q. Don't you think it unfair that the other people did not have a chance ?—A. ̣o· We do not want that island to be peopled. There is a law that nobody can go on ̣at island without the permission of the Minister. That is an old English statute nder the Admiralty.

Q. I understand from this National Signal Company that they can communicate ̣r distances far greater than Marconi ?—A. I do not think so.

Q. They have actually communicated across the Atlantic ?—A. So has Marconi.

Q. Is it the policy of your Government to refuse such facilities as you have given ̣ Marconi to any competing companies ?—A. Each case is submitted separately and considered on its merits. We have no decided set rules about refusing people.

By the Chairman :

Q. You still continue to get supplies from Chance Bros. ?—A. Yes. There are only vo firms, Chance Bros. and Barbier Fils, and we get prices from both, and take the ̣ods at the lowest price.

Q. Chance Bros. are the oldest firm for supplying lighthouse supplies in exis- ̣nce ?—A. Yes.

Q. They are beyond doubt ?—A. Beyond doubt. They publish their list of prices ̣arbier Fils do the same thing, and in each case we take the lowest price.

Q. Chance Bros. have been supplying the department ever since it has been a ̣partment ?—A. Yes.

Q. Your meteorological service costs——A. About $75,000.

Q. You have a very small establishment in the central office at Toronto ?—A. ̣es ; they are divided up.

Q. Have you taken any steps in regard to a revision of their salaries ?—A. Yes ; ̣e Minister is at it now.

Q. I may say that one officer has written that after having been thirty years in ̣e service his salary is now only $1,400 a year ?—A. Yes. The Minister is revising ̣at service as well as the lighthouse service. There are technical men there who re- ̣ive very small salaries.

Q. Your hydrographic surveys cost $168,000 last year ?—A. Yes.

Q. Captain Irving Miles, the engineer in charge on the Atlantic coast, was a captain of the Royal Navy ?—A. We borrowed him from the Admiralty. He is a supplementary lieutenant.

Q. He gets £600 a year ?—A. Yes. He would not come for less.

Q. He gets half pay in addition ?—A. No.

Q. Has he full control ?—A. No, under Mr. Stewart's directions. He is working in the St. Lawrence at Tadousac. He has control of his ship and the men under him, but subject to the approval and inspection of Mr. Stewart.

Q. He has two steamers under him. *La Canadienne* and the *Gulnare* ?—A. One steamer, *La Canadienne*.

Q. The supplies for these steamers are purchased in the usual way, like those for the other steamers ?—A. Yes, by asking for tenders. Nobody on our ships has the right to purchase.

Q. In the last few years you have had a very important service committed to your charge, the St. Lawrence ship channel ?—A. Yes.

Q. On that service in 1905-06 you spent something over $1,000,000 ?—A. Yes, under Mr. Cowie, the chief engineer.

Q. The Sorel establishment is in connection with that service ?—A. The dredges and all our vessels of that district are looked after and repaired there.

Q. Some of the largest works are the permanent piers at Lake St. Peter ?—A. That is done under Colonel Anderson's branch.

Q. Did not one of the piers tumble down ?—A. No. It was moved by the ice.

Q. One of the piers slid into the water through the effect of ice ?—A. No, it merely canted a little.

Q. Was that from any defect in the, construction ?—A. The piles were rammed down forty feet in the mud. We have to devise some means to steady them and make them more permanent. We might not have another such ice shove for fifty years, but the department is examining as to the cause of these blocks having been so damaged by the ice.

Q. The wages at the Sorel ship yard last year amounted to $250,000 ?—A. Yes.

Q. Have you any unnecessary people employed there ?—A. No.

Q. What control have you of those men ?—A. They are under absolute control.

Q. Who is in charge of that ship yard ?—A. Mr. Desbarats, an exceedingly clever officer and he has things in absolute order.

By Mr. Fyshe :

Q. Do they build vessels there?—A. They build dredges as well as they can be built in any part of the world. They do everything. They build steamers and all kinds of works, and there is perfect control of the men—the time they work and everything that is purchased in the way of material and supplies.

Q. Is it closed in the winter ?—A. No. There are two or three hundred men employed in winter.

By the Chairman :

Q. How many men do they employ in the height of the season ?—A. Five or six hundred.

Q. Then the number varies from five or six hundred in the summer down to two or three hundred in the winter ?—A. Yes.

Q. Are there men kept on who ought not to be for political reasons or otherwise ?—A. Never.

Q. The ship yard is not overmanned ?—A. No, never.

Q. No unnecessary expense is incurred there ?—A. No.

By Mr. Bazin :

Q. There is an item in the Auditor General's Report of wages at Sorel Ship Yard,

$248,000, and there is another item for the construction of a new dredge. Are the wages of every one of the workingmen included there ?—A. Yes.

Q. Then how is it that there is a charge for the construction of a new dredge ?—A. Because that is under another appropriation. We work for the Department of Public Works, the Ship Channel, the Department of Marine and the Hydrographic Survey in the repairing of vessels and building of boats and the expenditure is apportioned. That is why we employ hundreds of men.

By the Chairman :

Q. You have also thirteen or fourteen ships engaged in|the fisheries protection ?—A. Yes.

Q. Your expenditure in the fisheries protection service was about $250,000 ?—A. Yes.

Q. There are not too many steamers ?—A. No. We are building two more for British Columbia.

By Mr. Fyshe :

Q. Don't you think that is more than the value of all the fish that could be stolen by the Yankees ?—A. That does not represent one-twentieth of the fish that is taken in the lower Provinces. It is estimated that in British Columbia waters alone about $4,000,000 worth of fish are illegally caught by Yankees.

By the Chairman :

Q. In this service you have of course your crews of officers and men ?—A. Yes,

Q. And the supplies are brought through the agents in the same way as in other cases ?—A. Yes. Everything is carried on in the same way.

Q. Of course, all the people who supply these steamers are people of the proper political faith ?—A. Yes.

Q. They could not get the orders otherwise ?—A. None others need apply.

Q. Your department has also gone into cold storage for bait and the conservation and development of the deep sea fisheries ?—A. Yes.

Q. Where are your bait freezers ?—A. Different places.

Q. You have a freezer at Canso ?—A. Yes, one at Canso, and one at Halifax, with about forty small fishermen's bait freezers at various points on the Atlantic coast of Canada.

Q. And one at Halifax?—A. Yes. We have also one in the Baie des Chaleurs and one at Souris.

Q. Who are the Halifax Cold Freezers Company ?—A. I forget their names at the moment.

Q. The amounts mentioned at page P—197 of the Auditor General's Report have at any rate been paid as contributions for the freezers at the several places ?—A. Yes.

By Mr. Fyshe :

Q. Do you pay in proportion to the quantity put through the small freezers ?—A. They have first to erect themselves into a company and get the sanction of the local Government. Then they come to us, and we pay one-half the cost of building and a bonus for the first five years.

By the Chairman :

Q. In addition to this cold storage business you have tried to develop a herring curing scheme ?—A. Yes. We have an expert named Mr. Cowie from Scotland, with curers.

Q. Did he come from Scotland ?—A. Yes.

Q. Where is he established ?—A. He moves about in the lower Provinces. Last year he was in Baie des Chaleurs division. I do not know where he is going this year.

By Mr. Fyshe :

Q. Are the people going on with that method and extending it ?—A. Yes.

Q. Are they increasing the fresh fish trade between Nova Scotia and the upper Provinces ?—A. We are at that now. We have $50,000 or $60,000 in the estimates to facilitate the transfer of fish in refrigerators, so that we shall not buy our fish from Boston and other American places, but from our own fishermen.

By the Chairman :

Q. You are also trying to convert the dog fish into a useful animal ?—A. Yes. This is in its initial stage. Although we use the dog fish as a fertilizer and extract oil from it, I believe more money could be made by sparing that fish and selling it in the Japan market.

Q. Then this cold storage business and the dog fish business are in their inception? —A. Yes, we are just working them up.

Q. And you have given these grants for educational purposes ?—A. Yes.

Q. For the development and curing of the herring and the utilization of the dog-fish ?—A. Yes.

Q. You have had some correspondence with the Auditor General about the forms of certificates issued by the department—sometimes they are according to agreement, sometimes fair and just, sometimes according to contract ?—A. Yes.

Q. Have you come to an understanding with him ?—A. Yes.

Q. There is no conflict between the department and the Auditor General ?—A. Not at all. Everything is going very pleasantly. We get a great deal of help and advice from the Auditor General, which we are always very happy to follow.

Q. There was also a correspondence with him as to coal from Archer & Company ? —A. That is stopped. We call for tenders and get coal from the mines.

By Mr. Fyshe :

Q. Who are Archer & Company ?—A. A merchant in Quebec. It was more for the satisfaction of seeing his name as selling to the Government. There was only a small percentage in it for him.

By the Chairman :

Q. Archer sold the coal to the Government in the first place and bought it back in dust afterwards ?—A. No. We bought coal unscreened, and when we examined it some of it was in a rather dusty state and we could not use it. The engineers refused to burn it. We sold that to Archer and he mixed it with good coal so that we could use it, and we purchased it back. It was absolutely right ; there was nothing wrong in it.

Q. Is Archer a regular coal dealer ?—A. Yes, a regular coal dealer in Quebec.

Q. What kind of control have you now over the cheque books ?—A. Absolute control.

Q. A Mr. Corcoran, a messenger. stole cheque books ?—A. Yes.

Q. He filled up two or three blanks and forged the signatures for three or four hundred dollars ?—A. Yes.

Q. He bolted, did he not ?—A. Yes. I do not know what became of him. We did not lose anything.

Q. The Bank of Montreal had to refund ?—A. Any bank that will cash a cheque such as that messenger forged deserves to lose three times the amount. The signature has not the least resemblance to mine. It was a very poor forgery.

Q. You are taking better care of the cheque books now ?—A. Yes. All that has been rectified since that happened. Now the cheque books are all kept in a safe, which is locked up at night and unlocked in the morning in the presence of two officials. Every precaution has been taken.

Q. How have you and the Auditor General settled the question respecting the revenues derived from the wharfs ?—A. That is a vexed question which we cannot settle.

Q. It is chiefly with regard to the Richelieu boats, is it not?—A. No. The question with regard to the Richelieu Company was not understood. I am speaking of the general principle. The Government builds a lot of wharfs in different parts of the country, and so long as they are not transferred to the Department of Marine they do not come under the Act, but when they are transferred to the department, vessels using them have to pay top wharfage and side wharfage according to the tonnage of the vessel. Top wharfage is paid according to whatever goes over the wharf. Then we appoint a wharfinger, and the trouble begins. We thought it better to hand over the wharfs to the municipalities provided they would guarantee the repairs. They refused. We rented a wharf to the municipality of St. Nicolet above Quebec for a number of years. We collected the rent, but we had some difficulty. Then we had a number of wharfingers who failed to collect from the Richelieu and Ontario Navigation Company. So we made up an average of what the company paid for several years and we settled on an annual payment authorized by Order in Council. We allow the wharfinger twenty-five per cent of the returns and the balance we paid to the Receiver General.

Q. Does the wharfinger get any other pay from the Government?—A. No. We have other wharfs that yield a large revenue, such as the Sault Ste. Marie wharf.

By the Chairman :

Q. Have you or any other officer of the department ever received anything in connection with any expenditures incurred by the department?—A. In what way?

Q. Any commission or gift?—A. No. The men are so independent of the officials that it is outside of common sense to think that a man would go to an official and ask him for information because every transaction of the department has to go before three or four officers. How could an officer ask a man for a commission when his business has to pass through the engineer, and submittted by me to the Minister for his approval. Besides everything is bought by tender, and they are opened in presence of the Minister who decides on the lowest tender on the recommendation of the Chief Engineer.

Q. If any additional matter strikes you we shall be glad if you will prepare a memorandum?—A. Certainly.

A.G.T.
Refer to No. 28,258. ·

OTTAWA, June 4, 1907.

SIR,—I have to acknowledge the receipt of your letter of the 18th ultimo asking for a statement showing the number of the staff of this Department, permanent and extra graded into classes, and the amount of salaries paid during the years ended June 30, 1892, and June 30, 1906 ; and also a memorandum showing Special Votes such as Extra Clerks, Engineers, Tidal Surveys, Registration of Shipping, Draughtsmen, &c., during the same period. In reply I enclose you the statements asked for.

I am, Sir, your obedient servant,

(Signed) F. GOURDEAU,
Deputy Minister of Marine and Fisheries.

· Enc.

THOS. S. HOWE, Esq.,
Secretary Civil Service Commission,
Room No. 2, The Senate.

7-8 EDWARD VII., A. 190

STATEMENT SHOWING STAFF OF MARINE DEPARTMENT, 1892.

1 Deputy Head..........................	$3,200 00
1 Nautical Adviser.......................	2,400 00
4 Chief Clerks..........................	9,300 00
4 1st Class Clerks.......................	6,350 00
6 2nd Class Clerks.......................	7,437 50
5 3rd Class Clerks.......................	4,180 00
Allowance Private Secretary..............	600 00
2 Messengers...........................	1,000 00

23                                    $34,467 50

FISHERIES DEPARTMENT, 1892.

1 Deputy Head..................	$3,200 00	
1 Chief Clerk..................	2,400 00	
1 1st Class Clerk..............	1,500 00	
Supp. to promote F. H. Cunningham....	100 00	
6 2nd Class Clerks.............	7,400 00	
4 3rd Class Clerks.............	3,025 00	
1 Messenger...................	300 00	
		17,925 00

37

                                    $52,392 50

DEPARTMENT OF MARINE AND FISHERIES, 1905--6.

1 Deputy Head........................	$ 4,000 00
6 Chief Clerks.......................	13,200 00
8 Technical Officers.................	18,149 99
16 1st Class Clerks..................	21,591 22
9 2nd Class Clerks...................	11,100 00
12 Junior 2nd Class Clerks...........	11,025 00
4 3rd Class Clerks...................	2,487 50
1 Messenger..........................	700 00

· 57 $82,253 71

STATEMENT SHOWING SPECIAL VOTES OUT OF WHICH CLERKS ARE PAID IN 1892 AND 1905-06

1891-92.

Civil Government Contingencies..............	4 Clerks.
Salaries of Lightkeepers...................	1 "
Steamboat Inspection......................	1 "
Construction of Lights....................	4

10

1905-6.

Civil Government Contingencies.. . . . . 1 Clerk.
                                          2 Messengers.
Extra Clerks at Ottawa.. . . . . 26 Clerks.
Tidal Service.. . . . . 2 "
Schools of Navigation.. . . . . 2 "
Registration of Shipping.. 1
Administration of Pilotage.. 1
Examination Masters and Mates.. 1
Ship Channel.. 3
Steamboat Inspection.. 1
Salaries, Lightkeepers.. 1
Fisheries Protection Service.. 1
Fish Breeding.. 1
                                          —
                                         43

OTTAWA, JUNE 19, 1907.

The Royal Commission on the Civil Service met this morning at 10.30 o'clock.

Present :—Mr. J. M. COURTNEY, C.M.G., Chairman.
        Mr. THOMAS FYSHE, Montreal, and
        Mr. P. J. BAZIN, Quebec.

Mr. BRUNO ST. PIERRE, of the Marine and Fisheries Department, called, sworn and examined.

By the Chairman :

Q. You are a clerk in the Marine and Fisheries Department?—A. Yes.
Q. What is your salary now?—A. $600.
Q. How long have you been in the department?—A. I have been in the department since January 29th or 30th, 1905.
Q. How many years?—A. Two and a half.
Q. What were you appointed at?—A. As temporary clerk.
Q. At what salary, $500?—A. $600.
A. At $600?—A. Yes.
Q. So that in two and a half years you got an increase of $50?—A. I did not get an increase. I state in my memorial that I was appointed at $600, and that I was recently appointed as third class clerk at the same salary, less 5 per cent for the retirement fund.
Q. That goes without saying, the payment to the retirement fund. What is your present salary?—A. The same salary.
Q. When were you appointed third class clerk?—A. On May 6th.
Q. 1906?—A. 1907.
Q. You have only just been appointed ?—A. Yes.
Q. Who brought you into the department?—A. Mr. Préfontaine.
Q. How many years' experience had you before that? Before you came into the department?—A. As what? Stenographer and typewriter operator?
Q. Tell us your past career?—A. I had ten years' experience as stenographer, typewriter operator, book-keeper and telegraph operator.
Q. Where?—A. In Montreal, St. Eugene, Vankleek Hill, Ottawa, St. Scholastique, and I have been official reporter. I have been in public life from youth.
Q. Your complaint is that you were appointed third class clerk without any reference to yourself?—A. Yes, without any reference to myself, and even more, it was not even communicated to me (the order for my appointment); I was told by the Chief Clerk that I had been appointed third grade clerk and I asked him if he would communicate to me the report from Council, and he replied, 'No,' although he had it in his hand at the time. I think that, as I was about the only one interested, I should have been allowed to take communication of this report
Q. Who was it had this report?—A. Mr. Halkett, but I presume he was acting under instructions.
Q. You made application to be appointed a first class clerk?—A. A first class clerk.
Q. Instead of a third class clerk?—A. Yes.
Q. But to have made you a first class clerk would have required a special vote of Parliament?—A. Yes, but I have in my possession a copy of the Act of 1903 and *since then* the Belcourt law amended the Civil Service law, and I could not be ap-

pointed a second class clerk without a qualifying examination. When I first came to the service, I would not come under any consideration; the late Hon. Mr. Préfontaine wanted me to enter the service and act as assistant secretary to the International Waterways Commission. I stayed at a salary of $50 a month as temporary clerk, I was considered a first class stenographer and typewriter operator, and was doing work for everybody, all kinds of work, and I expected to get a permanent appointment in the higher grade. Leading men in the department would come to me and I would do work for one and the other all the time. I can write from 100 to 200 letters a day, being an expert typewriter and a stenographer as well. When I write from 60 letters upwards a day, I conclude it is a very good day's work and I am doing very much more than anybody else is doing in that class of work.

By Mr. Fyshe:

Q. What do you say your salary is?—A. $50 per month.

Q. How long have you had that?—A. Two and a half years.

Q. Has there been any increase at all?—A. No, I have been appointed a third grade clerk, and I wanted to get appointed as first class clerk with reference to which the Minister wrote me two or three letters. I acted as assistant secretary to Hon. Mr. Préfontaine, the Minister, and when he left for Europe, he promised me he would give me what I was certainly entitled to, but he died in Europe, so that I had to wait. Then Hon. Mr. Brodeur came into the department, and he had to find out all about me, he did not know me, he is one who considers all matters very carefully before doing anything. I did not insist very strongly on his settling this question before he went to Europe as I thought when I had waited before, I could wait again. During his absence, there was no question of making me a third class clerk, Hon. Mr. Templeman on the report of the Deputy Minister, very obligingly made me a third class clerk and I have now to pass three examinations before I can get to the first class.

By the Chairman:

Q. Your complaint is that, in the absence of the Minister, the Acting Minister, on the report of the Deputy, made you a third class clerk, when you expected to get a first-class clerkship?—A. Yes.

Q. Mr. St. Pierre, this evidence will be published, and I do not know whether you want all that you are saying or all that you have stated in your petition to be published, I do not desire that you should labour under any misapprehension. You will have an opportunity of revising your evidence and you may excise anything in your evidence or in your petition that you do not desire to have published, otherwise your petition, as sent in, will form part of the appendix to our report. With reference to the 10th paragraph of this petition, do you know the name of the man you refer to?—A. I do not know the name.

Q. Do you know what position he has been appointed to?—A. I do not know what position he has been appointed to, because I do not suppose there is any written appointment, it is just a verbal appointment.

Q. You do not know whether he is temporary or permanent?—A. I know he is not permanent, he cannot be.

Q. How do you know that an appointment has not been made, you do not keep the records of the department?—A. I do not keep the records of the department, but I certainly know that he has been appointed.

Q. What are your duties in the department?—A. I am employed as secretary to the Chief Examiner of Masters and Mates, the Superintendent of Marine Schools and the Superintendent of Government Wireless Stations.

Q. You know nothing about reports to Council?—A. Which?

Q. In your own branch?—A. In the branch that I am employed I do know.

29a—42½

Q. You do not know anything about reports to Council, for instance in the Accountant's branch?—A. No.

* Q. You do not know anything at all with reference to this man, this stable man, who has been appointed, for instance. You have seen a man about the department and you make the allegation that he is there receiving public moneys?—A. Yes, I do; I see him every day.

Q. You do not know his name?—A. I do not know his name, but that does not amount to much; he is there.

Q. Well, again I say, this will be published and you had better consider the effect which the publication will have upon yourself?—A. It is all right, I will take the responsibility for it. If you want any more information with reference to the man, I can secure the name and give it to you.

141 ALBERT ST., OTTAWA, CAN., May 25, 1907.

SIR,—Please find enclosed an individual petition, which is a general statement of facts of the doings of our different departments, which you will be so kind as to bring to the attention of the Commission in due course.

Yours faithfully,

(Signed) BRUNO ST. PIERRE,
Third Grade Clerk.

The Secretary C. S. Commission,
House of Commons, City.

To the Commissioners,
The Royal Commission,
Civil Service of Canada.

The undersigned, a member of the Civil Service of Canada and a resident of the City of Ottawa, has the honour to submit for your consideration the following :

1o. That I have ten years' experience as a telegraph operator, book-keeper, stenographer and typewriter operator, in both languages.

2o. That I have acquired valuable experience in the above capacity, in the mercantile, political, professional and municipal world of both provinces.

3o. That on January 30, 1905, on the strength of a promise of a higher appointment, in accordance with my qualifications, I entered the Civil Service as a temporaary clerk in the employ of the Department of Marine and Fisheries.

4o. That I have successfully passed, at the annual examinataions of the year 1905, the qualifying and optional examinations of the Civil Service.

5o. That, as far as I have been repeatedly told and from what can be ascertained from the official files of the Department of Marine and Fisheries and others, my work was highly appreciated and very satisfactory in every respect.

6o. That lately I have filed my application for a vacant position of first-class clerk in this Department, and was promised recognition at the hands of those concerned.

7o. That on May 6, 1907, without my knowledge and consent and in the absence of the present Minister of Marine and Fisheries, an Order in Council was passed appointing me a third grade clerk, at the same salary as heretofore.

8o. That it is to be recommended that all members of the Civil Service should be treated as 'free men' and consulted with reference to any recommendation to Council which may affect their status in the service.

9o. That those who have passed the optional examinations are entitled to more consideration than the ordinary office hand, as they are invariably more useful and competent.

10o. Furthermore, after two and a half years of valuable service and expert work I am remunerated on the same basis as a newly appointed 'former stable-man,' and must suffer, for the moment, the prejudice of the unjust treatment of the questionable competency of a high-handed class of officials.

All of which is respectfully submitted.

(Signed) BRUNO ST. PIERRE,
Third Grade Clerk.

OTTAWA, CAN., May 25, 1907.

MONTREAL, September 12, 1907.

The Royal Commission on the Civil Service met this morning at 10.30 o'clock.

Mr. CHARLES A. LEBEL, Assistant Agent of the Marine and Fisheries Department, Montreal, called, sworn and examined.

By the Chairman :

Q. You are Mr. LeBel, the Assistant Agent here ?—A. Yes sir.

Q. When was the Montreal Agency established?—A. In 1903.

Q. Who was the Minister then?—A. The late Hon. Mr. Préfontaine.

Q. When he became Minister he established an agency in Montreal ?—A. He did sir.

Q Mr. Boucher is the agent ?—A. I represent Mr. Boucher here, because his duties are mostly outside, he is a technical officer, the engineer of the Department, and his duties call him out on the river a great deal and he could not come with any satisfaction because he might be called away at any moment. He has to keep his eyes open for the buoys.

Q. You are his assistant ?—A. I do the inside work.

Q. Are there any other people in the agency besides Mr. Boucher and yourself ?— A. The Montreal agency comprises our agency proper, the agent, the assistant agent, who is myself, and the assistant engineer of the buoy service, and we have a messenger and a typewriter in the office. Besides that there is the pilotage office, which comes under the Department of Marine and Fisheries, and they look after the pilotage of the river.

Q. That is under Capt. J. J. Riley ?—A. Yes.

Q. But he has nothing to do with your agency ?—A. We have to do with him, because all the accounts of the Montreal Pilotage Office pass through our agency. Then there is the Inspector of Steamboats, Mr. Laurie, and Mr. Arpin and the Inspector of Live Stock, Mr. Delorme and Mr. O'Grady, we have less to do with those two branches than with the Pilotage Office. Capt. Riley is this morning attending an investigation into a collision that took place.

Q. You say that agency was established here ; from what other agency were the duties taken over ?—A. From the agencies of Quebec and Ottawa.

Q. Did the Quebec agency formerly do all the duties from Ottawa to the gulf ?— A. Yes, sir, all the duties of this part of the Montreal district as far down as Quebec. Now our agency and the buoy service goes as far as Platon, thirty miles above Quebec.

Q. Then your agency here as far as the Marine and Fisheries Department is concerned independent of the pilot office and all that is an entirely new creation ?— A. Yes sir.

Q. Taken from the Quebec agency ?—A. That is so sir. It was the Quebec agency used to look after this part of the work.

Q. The Quebec Agency used to look after that, and now a new agency has been established here in the time of Mr. Préfontaine to do this work ?—A. Yes. You understand that the work has increased since the agency was established, and that a great part of this work was done directly in Ottawa and a part from Quebec.

Q. The fact is a certain amount of decentralization has taken place and a certain amount of work devolving on the department is now done at Montreal ?—A. Yes.

Q. A certain part of the work which was done at Ottawa is now done at Montreal, and a certain part of the Quebec work was taken from the Quebec agency also and transferred to this agency ?—A. Yes sir.

Q. Where are your offices ?—A. At 223 Commissioner Street, right near the water's edge.

Q. Are there any branches of the Marine Department not there?—A. We are all under the same roof, these branches I have named, but we do not occupy the same apartments.

By Mr. Fyshe :

Q. Where is your building ?—A. The Boyer building, at the corner of the Place Royal and Commissioner Street.

Q. Have you the entire house?—A. No, sir, we lease the greater part of the building, and besides the offices we have to provide for the commissioners court which sits there, and occupies nearly a flat, and in connection with our work, during the winter we have the engineer's draughting office there where the plans are made of the new work or changes made on the river during the summer. This work is done during the winter by Mr. Boucher and his assistant, Mr. Chatigny, who is the Assistant Buoy Engineer on the river, looking after the buoys which are displaced or out and have to be replaced in their proper position or relighted.

By the Chairman :

Q. To come back to the original question in consequence of the changes necessary owing to the changed conditions and one thing and another a certain amount of the Quebec work, work formerly done at the Quebec agency, and a certain amount of work formerly done by the department at Ottawa was decentralized, and given to the 'Montreal agency which was a new creation ?—A. Yes.

Q. Were you and Mr. Boucher previously in the Department or in the public service ?—A. Mr. Boucher was in the department, he is a technical man, twelve years before that. He was first in the employ of the Montreal Sand Cement Company and then he went into the department as engineer.

Q. When did he go there?—A. His work was as buoy engineer; he was engineer for the contractor—the work was formerly done by contract—from 1889 to 1897 and he went into the Department in 1898 as buoy engineer for Mr. John Cane, of Quebec. In this time some of the buoys were placed by contract. Mr. Boucher is now the agent of the Marine and Fisheries Department and the buoy engineer of the Montreal district, and he has also the inspection of lights for the Montreal district.

Q. What is the Montreal district now ?—A. Our district runs down as far as Platon, thirty miles above Quebec, and up as far as Montreal.

By Mr. Fyshe :

Q. Mr. Boucher has made a specialty of buoy work?—A. Yes, his work all along has been on the river looking after buoys; the putting down and taking up of the buoys is quite a work of importance and responsibility.

Q. It is work that has to be done very carefully ?—A. Yes, and he has to be always on the alert to see that they are maintained in position.

By the Chairman :

Q. Practically the office and the staff were constituted in 1903 ?—A. Yes, because Mr. Boucher was nominally appointed then. There was no office until after Mr. Préfontaine was appointed Minister and took charge of the Department. After Mr. Préfontaine took charge he rented part of the Boyer block for the Marine and Fisheries Department.

Q. In fact, we have heard in the Public Accounts Committee concerning the charges for furniture for the Boyer block ?—A. Yes, there was an investigation.

Q. Practically it was only three years ago that the salaries of Mr. Boucher and yourself were settled ?—A. Yes, four years ago.

Q. Then although the salaries may be insufficient for the work done, as to which

I am not judging, you cannot say anything as to a comparison between the salaries now and fifteen years ago ?—A. All we can say is that there is a great difference in the price of living.

Q. But that would not affect you if you were both appointed three years ago. If you were satisfied with the salary to which you were appointed three years ago the difference in the cost of living now and at that time is not so great ?—A. That all depends ; circumstances may force us at the time to take a salary at the commencement which we would not care to remain at.

Q. You think that at the commencement of your career three years ago the salaries were insufficient for the responsibilities and the duties ?—A. Because we expected to be increased from year to year.

Q. Were you led to expect an increase from year to year ?—A. Yes, sir. I wish to explain that we did not make any complaints or send any letters to Ottawa, but we were advised to wait for this Commission and we were waiting for the Minister's return. There is not a letter in the office at Ottawa about our complaining or asking for the raise of salary of late.

Q. One of the matters referred to the Commission is that of the salaries paid to members of the public service. Of course, in the old established branches like the Montreal post office, for instance, which goes back for a long time the circumstances would be different from that like an agency which was created only three years ago ?—A. Well, I admit that, but supposing at the beginning of our career or at the beginning of the career of any department like the Montreal post office and custom house, it would be young men beginning at eighteen or twenty-one years of age who would enter the Civil Service as a career, but when in the establishment of an agency like this men of experience at forty-five or fifty years of age are employed there is a very great difference.

Q. No doubt upon that, but you were content to come in at the salaries paid you four years ago ?—A. At that time, because we, as all other men, have more or less ambition to better our posittion, and I do not see that any one could be blamed for that.

By Mr. Bazin. :

Q. What was the salary at the time of the appointment ?—A. The salary of Mr. Boucher when he was appointed was $1,500.

By the Chairman:

Q. And he is now getting ?—A. $1,800.
Q. And your salary at the time of appointment was ?—A. $800.
Q. And you are now getting ? ?—A. $1,100.
Q. And you have obtained that increase of $300 in three years?—A. In four years.

By Mr. Fyshe:

Q. And you do other work?—A. What do you mean by other work?
Q. I presume you might have an opportunity of doing other work?—A. No, sir, my time is taken up from 9 o'clock in the morning until 5 every day, and I have had but one week's vacation since I have been in the office. I will tell you the difficulty, Mr. Boucher and his assistant engineer for the buoy service are continually outside during the season of navigation, and I have to be inside to answer everybody who comes in the office, that being the agency for the department in Montreal we are supposed to be there all the time and to be in continual communication with the large shipping interests and the public here. If the Shipping Federation wants information about anything in connection with the department it is to us they come. Our telephone is practically never idle, especially in the spring and fall of the year; if they want to know of the movements of any of the vessels in the service of the Government, or to forward any communications to the department it is to us they come.

:t is not merely a business routine, but a man must have some initiative of his own
io as to be able to satisfy all these people.

By the Chairman :

Q. The late Minister, knowing the requirements of Montreal, and being in Mont-
eal, thought it desirable that the agency should be opened?—A. Yes, sir.

Q. And an agent, appointed at $1,500 three years ago is now getting $1,800?—A.
Yes, four years ago.

Q. And you were appointed three years ago at $800, and you now get $1,100?
—A. Yes, sir, since last year, I was appointed four years ago.

Q. You keep a record of the arrival and departure of vessels here?—A. All that
s kept in the Pilotage Office.

Q. But you have control of the buoy service?—A. Altogether.

Q. These are the buoys which are filled with this new illuminant, the acetylene
;as?—A. Yes, sir.

Q. How many buoys are there in the Montreal district?—A. We have 348 buoys.

Q. But how many of these use the new illuminant?—A. I think there are 59, I
:ould not give you the exact answer.

Q. Have you had any accidents in filling these buoys?—A. I am glad to say that
n our agency we have never had any accidents in filling the buoys, and there is not
i week passes that we have not some to fill. Last week in one of the very worst
>laces in the river at Cap Charles two of our acetylene gas buoys had to be refilled.
It is a very dangerous operation and it takes skilled men.

Q. There have been accidents at some places below Quebec?—A. Yes, sir.

Q. And at Kingston?—A. Yes, and here at Lachine last year.

Q. Is Lachine in your jurisdiction?—A. No, sir, we finish here.

Q. Is it not a fact that the men are rather scary now about filling those buoys?—
A. Yes.

Q. Do you find it rather difficult to get men to undertake this dangerous operation?—A. We have not found any difficulty in getting men to do it, because I know
our engineers are so very careful of themselves and for the safety of the men and
of the Government property besides.

Q. Does that imply that there may have been, unwittingly and without design,
carelessness in those cases where there have been explosions?—A. I would be very
sorry to say that; accidents may happen at any time even when the best of care is
exercised.

Q. These other accidents happened from some defect in the buoy?—A. So it was
said, but we never got the exact report of those accidents.

Q. Are these buoys tested for capacity and pressure before being put down?—A.
Yes, sir.

Q. The intention is that these buoys are constantly kept lighted during the summer?—A. Sometimes a buoy will go out and it is our duty to immediately send the
boat to have it relighted.

Q. Does it go out because of the rough water on the river?—A. There is a good
deal of carelessness on the river, barges coming up loaded with sand and wood think
little of running up against one of the buoys and putting it out of position. It is
not so much the putting out of the lights of the buoy that has to be watched as it is
the putting of the buoys out of position. It may be placed in the middle of a
channel sometimes which makes it dangerous to navigation.

Q. When the lights go out you take care before the buoy is reloaded that an examination shall be made to ascertain that there is no stuff still in it?—A. Oh, yes,
the engineer attends to that.

Q. All due care is taken for the safety of the men employed in the operation?—
A. Yes, as far as we can. At the end of the season the engineer always opens it to
see if there is any defect. Supposing there has been a buoy defective during the
season and it has to be reloaded, that buoy will be reopened, and examined at the

end of the season to ascertain the cause of the defect. But if the buoy gives satisfaction all the way through they do not do that because it is not necessary and it is a
very long process.

By Mr. Fyshe:

Q. How long have you had these acetylene lighted buoys?—A. Since three or four
years, they have been increasing every year. The first year there were only a very
few and the second year there were a few more, and this year there are many more.
For instance, when the Shipping Federation, Montreal, considers it necessary to have
another gas buoy put down in the river, they notify the department at Ottawa and
give their reason for it. That is submitted to the Chief Engineer, and if the Chief
Engineer considers it is necessary then the buoy is put in position.

Q. How long does this stuff that is put into the buoy last?—A. It is supposed
to last ninety days.

Q. They fill it up?—A. Oh, yes, and it is supposed to last ninety days, but if the
machinery of the buoy is defective it will not last that long and that sometimes happens, because these things are not perfect yet.

Q. They have to be examined all the time?—A. Yes, they have to be watched.

By the Chairman:

Q. You say that an application for a new buoy is submitted to the Chief Engineer. Who is the Chief Engineer looking after the buoys?—A. For instance, supposing that there is to be an innovation made, we have to refer it to Ottawa to Col.
Gourdeau and he generally refers it to the Chief Engineer.

Q. Who is head of the buoy service?—A. The Chief Engineer of the buoy service
of the Montreal District is Mr. Boucher.

Q. And what does Mr. Fraser do in this connection?—A. Mr. J. F. Fraser!

Q. Yes?—A. He looks after the upper part of the river.

Q. He looks after the buoys in the other districts?—A. Yes, at Prescott.

Q. Who supplies this carbide calcium for this light?—A. It is supplied from
Ottawa.

Q. From Wilson's?—A. Yes, the Ottawa Carbide Company.

Q. That is under contract?—A. Yes, that is a contract made in Ottawa. We
have nothing to do with that contract. They apply to us to know the quantity we
require and we tell them.

Q. Has representation ever been made to Ottawa of the dangerous nature of
the service in connection with the buoys? Does the department fully realize the
danger of the service?—A. We fully realize that if the buoys are not handled with
proper care there is danger, but we know nothing further than that; there has been no
complaint made about any buoys between here and Quebec.

Q. Do you give instructions to your men on your boats when they fill up these
buoys to be careful?—A. Yes.

Q. Are there any printed regulations dealing with the matter?—A. Yes, and further than that there are none of those buoys filled up except when the engineer or
assistant is there.

Q. What is the connection between your office and the ship channel, or is there any
connection?—A. Yes, there is a connection. We have not anything to do directly
with the ship channel, but we have received instructions from the engineer of the ship
channel whenever we have to put down a new buoy or to remove a buoy for dredging
purposes.

Q. Have you anything to do with the expenditure of dredging the ship channel?—A. Not on account of the dredging, but we have everything to do with the construction that has been going on between Quebec and Montreal, that is part of our
work.

Q. Have you anything to do with the construction of the piers at Sorel?—A. Yes.

Q. Was there not an accident there?—A. I beg your pardon!

ESSIONAL PAPER No. 29a

Q. Was that pier under your jurisdiction ?—A. It was on the lake. The piers ere built by the departments for construction. You are aware that there is an office ı Sorel and the superintendent of the works and the resident engineer reside there.

Q. Wasn't there a pier in Lake St. Peter or was it in Lake St. Louis?—A. It was ake St. Peter.

Q. That came to grief?—A. Yes, it canted.

Q. Has there been any inquiry as to the breakage or canting of this pier?—A. he only information there is on the subject is that it was canted by the moving ice. ; is said that the pier was not solid enough to resist the ice coming down the lake in ıe spring.

Q. That would seem to indicate there was some defect in the engineering?—A. Yes, was said that the bottom of the lake is too soft and to put down a foundation strong ıough to resist the movement of the ice in the spring would require a very large rpenditure.

Q. Would it not be better to go to the extra expense and make the foundation ıre ?—A. I prefer to leave that to the engineers of the department to answer as I m not competent to answer that question. The piers were built according to the lans.

Q. You say you have nothing to do with the dredging. I suppose you get sup-lies for the dredging vessels do you not ?—A. No, that is in Mr. Cowie's hands, the redging vessels look after their own supplies.

Q. How are the men fed on those dredging vessels ? Do you know anything about ıat ?—A. Mr. Cowie looks after that.

Q. Does not Mr. Boucher generally get paid so much per day for feeding the ıople on board his vessels and scows ?—A. Yes, there is an understanding betwuun ıe department and Mr. Boucher with regard to the two steamers in the Government nploy directly for the buoy service, the *Shamrock* and the *Acetylene*, the last named ractically does all the filling up of the buoys, the material and the staff is all on ıard. There was an understanding with the department that Mr. Boucher feeds ıe sailors and officers on both boats.

Q. For which he gets 75 cents per day ?—A. 60 cents.

Q. Does he get any more for the officers than for the men, or is that the uniform ıte ?—A. I think he gets 60 cents for the officers and 50 cents for the men.

Q. Do you know how many people there are in these steamers and scows that Mr. oucher feeds ?—A. The regular crew of the *Shamrock* numbers fifteen and that of ıe *Alcetylene* nine.

Q. That is twenty-four men. How many months are these boats in commission?— . Allow me—sometimes in bad weather they may have to engage extra hands ıaking cedar buoys and anything like that.

Q. There are twenty-four permanent men?—A. I cannot say to the exact number. would not like to be positive about the exact number.

Q. How long are these vessels in commission ?—A. They have been in commis-on ever since I have been there.

Q. When do they go into commission? When the ice breaks up ?—A. They are ıpposed to be under steam about the 1st of April.

Q. And when do they come back to Sorel for the winter ?—A. As soon as navigu-on has closed when they are forced back by the ice, they come back so late that one ? our steamers got caught in the ice last year.

Q. That is for about seven months Mr. Boucher feeds these men ?—A. Yes.

Q. Is there any other arrangement that Mr. Boucher has with the department to ı any other work for which he gets pay like this?—A. He has no extra pay except is salary and what he makes—and I do not know if he makes any profit at all—in ıis way.

Q. There is nothing else ?—A. Nothing else that I am aware of, and I think if ıere was anything else I would be aware of it.

By Mr. Fyshe :

Q. These two special boats are under his control all the time ?—A. All the time, he is the engineer of the buoy service.

Q. Practically he lives on one of these boats ?—A. He has to be here more or less, one or two days, in the week because he has to certify to everything. Then anything passing through the office I submit to him; it is necessary before it goes to Ottawa that the engineer's and agent's signature should be on it. He is in the office as I say for two or three days in the week except in the spring, he is fully a month in the spring of the year putting down the buoys and then in the fall of the year, the last month of the year he is practically out of the office all the time taking the buoys up. Every week during the season of navigation he is supposed to go down and make an inspection of the buoys and lights. Every week, so that he has to take two or three days for that purpose.

By the Chairman :

Q. What are the sizes of these vessels ?—A. They are not very large.

Q. They are tugs, I suppose ?—A. Yes, large tugs ; the *Acetylene* is more like a scow with engine and boiler.

Q. How fast can they travel ?—A. The *Shamrock's* speed is twelve knots.

Q. They have good engines, I suppose ?—A. Yes, they are safe boats, but too slow and too small for the service ; we are promised new boats for next year.

Q. You are getting another one built ?—A. Well, there has been one recommended.

Q. The work of construction has not commenced yet ?—A. Plans have been made and I think the order has been given to build it this winter in Sorel. I wish to draw your attention to the fact that apart from the Buoy service the Montreal agency also looks after all expenditures made on the construction of work. Last year $250,000 were spent on this work between Montreal and Quebec.

Q. That is for the construction of new lights and piers ?—A. Yes and repairs to wharfs at Sorel.

Q. How many new lights were there built during last year ?—A. There were not only new lights built, but old lighthouses were repaired and replaced by new ones. I suppose this last year there must have been seven or eight lights put up, either put up or rebuilt in places where old lights were. Sometimes the Shipping Federation or the Mariners do not find the light in the proper place, and in such cases it was our duty to either take down the old lights or build a new one.

Q. Are these new lights built of concrete ?—A. Some of them are built of concrete.

Q. I have just come from Metis where solid blocks of cement are used; is that the plan adopted always by the department ?—A. That plan is not always followed, We have just commenced to build two new lights near the guard pier there.

Q. These new lights that replace the old ones, are they higher or larger than the old ones ?—A. It just depends upon the situation of the light. We only put a light after an inspection has been made by the chief enginer, and they are built according to his plans and on the recommendation, generally, of the Shipping Federation.

Q. How many wharfs have you built ?—A. There is the Government wharf at Sorel, which has been repaired.

Q. I thought that was the Public Works wharf ?—A. Yes, but there is a wharf there especially for the Marine Department, and we have to look after that.

Q. Is there any other wharf besides the Sorel wharf ?—A. No.

Q. How many piers did you build last year ?—A. I am not sure of the number.

Q. Were they built under contract ?—A. No, they were built by the Marine Department.

Q. By day labour ?—A. By day labour.

Q. How much money was spent, a quarter of a million ?—A. In round figures it amounted to $250,000. In the agency there we keep the accounts for construction, the buoy service accounts are kept separate, there is an appropriation by the Government every year for each of these. Of course, we do not control the disbursement of the money, which is controlled by the department on the report of the chief engineer.

Q. In construction, you are not talking about the ship channel or dredging, but for wharfs, piers, lighthouses, &c., about one-quarter of a million dollars was spent last year?—A. Yes, in round figures.

Q. That is under the management of the agency here?—A. Yes, every account went through their hands, and we had to look after it. Of course, the timekeepers and the clerks doing the work at Sorel receive the accounts and the bills, and they send us everything, and nothing leaves our office without being examined by Mr. Boucher and myself and all accounts are certified by Mr. Boucher.

Q. This work you have just stated was chiefly done by day labour, there were no contracts?—A. There is a contract for the broken stone, but for the building of these works it is all done by day labour.

Q. That is the broken stone that goes into the work is under contract?—A. Yes.

Q. But for the actual work of building, the construction is done by day labour?—A. Yes.

Q. Who appoints a timekeeper?—A. It is a political appointment, that is generally done by the Member of the county wherever the work is in progress. We have nothing to do with that.

Q. Has there ever been any idea that the pay lists have been padded?—A. I am not in a position to answer that question.

Q. The timekeeper being appointed by the Member for the district, the timekeeper would naturally try and put as many friends as he could on the work, I suppose?—A. I suppose that could have been done, but officially or personally I know nothing at all about it. They send their accounts certified by the superintendent and the resident engineer and we examine to see if they are correct, we make out the statements and send them to Otttawa certified as correct. What we look after is to see that the orders for every purchase account correspond with the accounts produced.

Q. We will just deal with the time-keepers first. The time-keeper reports to the superintendent engineer does he, this pay list?—A. Yes, that is for construction the pay lists are made out every fortnight, twice a month.

Q. And does the time-keeper sign them?—A. No, the local office at Sorel where the superintendent of works has his office and the resident engineer, and there is a clerk there in the office receives the time books from the time-keeper and the pay lists are made from his time books.

By Mr. Fyshe :

Q. In building these piers, or lighthouses, or whatever it may be, is there a competent man superintending the work apart from the time-keeper?—A. Oh my, yes, the time-keeper has nothing at all to do with the work, he simply keeps the men's time. Those who look after the works are the engineers and the superintendent of works.

By the Chairman :

Q. The timekeeper, when the lists are made up twice a month, sends them to Sorel, to the office at Sorel, that is Mr. Desbarat's office?—A. No, not for construction, we have a branch office there which is under the control of the resident engineer, Mr. O. Arcand, who looks after the construction work and Mr. Chas. Bazinet, superintendent of works.

Q. And he certifies the timekeeper's pay list?—A. The timekeepers do not make out the pay list.

Q. Have they any personal knowledge, would they be on the works to know that the proper or improper time is charged?—A. They have control of the works and have to be there to see that everything is going on all right.

Q. What I was coming at is this, practically the timekeeper's statement as to the amount of work performed is final. Nobody else can know absolutely the amount of work performed but the timekeeper. The other men are going backwards and forwards, are they not?—A. I do not know what answer you expect from me to that question, but what I know personally, and what I know in my official capacity, is that the superintendent knows, or should know, every man that is on the work, and when he goes there he sees these men are at work.

Q. But he is not there steadily?—A. He is not there constantly. I wish to call your attention to this that the works we did last year were far more important than the work going on at the present day and that the superintendent that was there last year is not there this year.

Q. You have changed your superintendent?—A. The change was made by Ottawa.

Q. Who was the superintendent last year?—A. Mr. Roy.

Q. What is he doing now?—A. He is in the Quebec district where Mr. Gregory is agent.

Q. He has been changed. Well, now it comes to this that the superintendent knows every man on the works, that is what you said just now?—A. Well, my contention is that the superintendent should know that every man is at his work, even if he does not see him, because they are supposed to report to him if a man that is engaged on the work is not there.

Q. That is all right?—A. Because that is the only check we can have.

Q. What we are coming to is that the timekeeper makes the pay list and the superintendent signs this pay list in his office, and from what I gather, Mr. Lebel, the superintendent ought to know, and does know every man who is on the work?—A. If he does not he should, because he has to go to the works and superintend them, he has to visit the works. But, as I said before, the timekeeper has nothing to do with the making out of the pay lists.

Q. Is there any chance of men being paid for this work of construction by day labour that have not performed their duties? In other words, are there any men paid there for nothing at all?—A. That I could not answer, because it has not come to my knowledge; you will understand that my work is completely here, I cannot leave my office, I have never been in Sorel but once since in office here, and that statement will show how difficult it would be for me to answer that question.

Q. After the pay lists are certified by the superintendent, what is the next state?—A. As a matter of fact the pay list is not made out by the timekeeper, he has a little book for each work in which he keeps the time, that book is examined every time the engineer or superintendent goes around and he finds out that the men whose names are in that book are at work; he checks it, and puts his initials at the bottom of each page. At the end of every fifteen days these books are sent to the Sorel office, and the clerk there, under the guidance of the engineer and superintendent, makes out the pay list and sends it to our office.

Q. After that where does the pay list go to?—A. It comes to me at the office of the Montreal agency.

Q. Then we will put it this way, the time-keeper keeps the books?—A. Yes, the time books only.

Q. In which the names of the men who are employed on the works are recorded?—A. Yes.

Q. The superintendent goes around and he checks these books and initials each page?—A. Yes, I suppose he should do so.

Q. And the books then are sent up to Sorel and the clerk, from this little book, makes up a pay list?—A. Yes.

Q. And then this pay list comes to you for action?—A. Yes.

Q. Is it not possible that with all this process many men may be paid, or may be put on the list there through political necessity and one thing and another that do not perform any work at all?—A. Well, I am under oath and I tell you that personally I know nothing about that, but I suppose such a thing could be done, but it is not to my knowledge that it has ever been done here.

Q. It has not been done this year?—A. I am sure that it has not been done this ear.

Q. We have gained now a very important admission?—A. I do not know what you re trying to get at, they may know more about it at Ottawa than we know of here, ecause although, we, Mr. Boucher and I, do all the work of the department, we might e the last ones to know when anything goes wrong if we are not informed of the fact y those in direct control, and personally I have never received any such information nd we do not get any credit for it when everything goes right.

Q. That is usually the case in the public service. Besides the agency business, he buoy business, and looking after this work of construction, what other duty has he agency here?—A. As I tell you, all accounts and pay-lists come to our office for construction work, although the labour has been done far away from our office, we repare the pay-lists and accounts, make out four copies and the statements and we lave four vouchers for every account, besides I have the ledger to keep where all the entries, accounts and cheques are entered.

By Mr. Fyshe:

Q. There is plenty of red tape?—A. We have to do it.

By the Chairman:

Q. This is for audit purposes?—A. We check them all over again to see that they ire correct, compare the accounts with the statements and with the purchasing orders to see that everything is correct. Of course, it may be that sometimes we make a mistake in a figure, which may happen to the best accountants, and why should it not happen to myself. We send two copies to Ottawa and keep two for reference in our office. Every voucher is numbered so that when anything is referred to we can go and put our hand on any record in the office.

Q. You get cheques from Ottawa to make disbursements?—A. Yes, Sir, with the pay-list it is different, we make out the pay-list in the name of Mr. Boucher because he is agent of the department, and all the cheques for the pay-list and construction come in his name, and when these cheques arrive he goes down or sends down the money to pay the men or sees that they are paid.

By Mr. Fyshe:

Q. He signs the cheques?—A. No, he receives the cheques payable to his order.

Q. How does he pay the men?—A. He gets the cheque from Ottawa, cashes it, and pays the men. Besides that Mr. Boucher receives a small amount from Uttawa for advances and when the pay-lists and statements are made out every fortnight, tho money is advanced so that the men will not have to wait, and when the cheques come back he places those cheques in the bank in his name.

By the Chairman:

Q. Is there a great expenditure for supply here about which you were talking just now?—A. What I mean is that when supplies are required for the men on board the boats, we have two or three vessels or more in commission, there is the *Vercheres* and two other vessels, they are allowed to buy what is necessary and these accounts come to our office for approval.

· Q. How many of these vessels are there?—A. There are the *Shamrock* and the *Acetylene* for the buoy service, and then for construction we have the *Vercheres*, that is the boat that is used by the resident engineer Mr. O. Arcand at Sorel, and then we have the *Hosanna* and we have the *Alpha*, these last boats are for construction.

Q. Are there any other vessels besides these and the two in the buoy service?—A. Not here in the Montreal district.

Q. Do you charter any vessels?—A. Only one this year, but last year on account of the importance of the work done there were some other boats chartered for the construction work. Just now we have the *Dandy* which is for very important work.

Q. When you take a charter of these vessels does the charter party include the feeding of the men?—A. It is just according to how the contract is made out. Sometimes we pay so much a month for the vessel and they pay all expenses.

Q. And sometimes you feed the crew?—A. Yes.

Q. There are two vessels you have entirely under your control for which you purchase supplies?—A. Yes.

Q. Are those supplies purchased by tender?—A. I am speaking of Mr. Boucher's supplies.

Q. I am not talking about those but the three others?—A. There is the *Vercheres* which is in commission under the resident engineer at Sorel, he is the local engineer who superintends the work under the direction of Mr. B. H. Fraser.

Q. Does he purchase these supplies by tender?—A. Mr. Arcand feeds all his crew on the *Vercheres* and there is a man by the name of Arthur Charland who got the contract this year for feeding the men for all the works that are done on construction. Last year it was Mr. Roy who did the same work.

Q. That was the gentleman who has gone to Quebec?—A. Yes, Sir, and this year it is Mr. Charland who feeds the men on board the boats and the men on the works. Since some time, we discharged the *Alpha* as being too small for the work she had to do.

Q. There are certain other supplies that are constantly being wanted, chains, &c. —A. Yes.

Q. Are those supplies called for by tenders?—A. There are some of them called for by tender. Now, the chains for a buoy service, as you are aware, are rather expensive and it is very important that it should be the very best chain. When wanted, prices are called for, I know that B. J. Coughlin down here, supplies a good deal, and Lewis Bros. and Caverhill, Learmont & Co. are the ones who generally supply them.

Q. And they are called in for open competition?—A. I could not say there is a competition in this for supplying that chain, they have to quote prices and the prices have to be sent to Ottawa and approved before we buy any chain from any of them.

Q. Who is to know that the prices are market prices, you are not an expert?—A. Well, the engineer is, and we have the market prices here, we know anyway what the chain is worth.

Q. There are other people in the trade besides Coughlin, Lewis and Caverhill Learmont; they are all respectable people I know, but would it not be more business like to call for prices by public tender?—A. It might be. We have no contract with these firms, but when we want any chain we are instructed to buy from these people.

By Mr. Fyshe:

Q. Are you instructed not to buy from ordinary men?—A. Except in cases of emergency. Suppose the *Shamrock* comes in and wants a chain, we are permitted to purchase from those who have the patronage.

Q. The matter has come to this then, that there are certain two or three firms who have the patronage to whom you can go and get these things?—A. That is generally the case.

By the Chairman:

Q. When supplies are wanted, that are known of beforehand, who instructs you to buy them?—A. Ottawa.

Q. Do they instruct you where to get them?—A. Yes, when the purchase is of any consequence or for a fairly large amount.

Q. Are there any tenders taken?—A. If there was a very large quantity required there would only be a tender asked, but sometimes we are purchasing some articles that we would only want once or twice in the season.

Q. And you are told who to buy from and what prices to pay?—A. We have to give the price to Ottawa.

Q. They do not specify the price at Ottawa?—A. In some cases it is specified, for stance, when we buy cedars, of which we buy a great deal for buoys, and everybody bo is in the business knows what is the price of cedar. We will say we want to pur-ase so many cedars and as we want them very straight and sound, we have to pay ie market price for this cedar and sometimes more, as they are very difficult to get in ie spring of the year. We have to go to lumber dealers such as Sir Henri Joly de otbinière to buy round cedars where we cannot get them near Montreal. We also iy cedars from Mr. H. Bourgouin, of Montreal. These are the only parties who irnish them, such as we require for the buoy service.

Q. And the prices, of course, are well known?—A. Oh, they are square prices, id if we pay more than the fixed prices, they would inquire at Ottawa why we did so.

Q. Ottawa does not trust you, in the ordinary course of buying supplies, to go ound and take tenders and buy the lowest?—A. We have nothing to do with that, a have to follow our instructions from the department, and I do not know of any ason why they should not trust us.

Q. Are there any other supplies besides those which you have mentioned?—A. here are supplies for the agency.

Q. Oh, that is very little?—A. We get them mostly from Ottawa, and, of course, hen moving into the new building new furniture had to be bought.

Q. The only supplies required for the purpose of construction are chiefly cedar id chains?—A. That is the main thing, and hardware supplies for the buoy service.

Q. And cedar for the buoy service?—A. Yes, these are the main things and other rticles of smaller value. We have also to supply at times for 'Aids to Navigation' ssides construction work and the buoy service, we have also to look after 'Aids to avigation' for which there is an appropriation, that is for lighthouses, lanterns for id lighthouses, or buying or leasing a piece of land for a new lighthouse, buying boats or the lighthouse keepers, or some necessary articles if a lightkeeper has run short of 1 or if anything has gone wrong with his light, there is a small appropriation for that.

Q. Have you anything to do with getting the oil that is used in the light-ouses?—A. That is all shipped from Quebec. It is said that next year we will look fter our own lighthouses, we look after five lighthouses here at present.

Q. Are there separate contracts made for each division for the purchase of oil, or i there one contract to supply oil from the Gulf to Lake Superior?—A. I could not nswer that, that is beyond me. All the oil asked of us comes from the Quebec gency.

Q. You have no contracts in this division for oil?—A. No.

Q. Is there anything else? The salaries are all fixed?—A. Yes, but increases are xpected in our agency.

Q. Then there is oil for the lights, cedar and chain and the feeding and other iings, we have covered all that, is there any other expenditure that you control?—A. 'othing of any importance. Of course, there are incidental expenses sometimes that e cannot foresee. Any accidents that may happen and we have to go and purchase ie articles required for any service. We are supposed to make out an order for rerything we buy, and those orders are sent to Ottawa with the account.

Q. Who examines the accounts in Ottawa?—A. It is all done by Mr. Owen, the ccountant, and his assistants.

Q. Are your accounts criticized pretty much in Ottawa?—A. No, very slightly, iey are criticized if there are any mistakes, I suppose.

Q. Have you ever had any criticism as to the cost of goods that you have paid o much?—A. It may have happened that we were asked why we had made such and ich a purchase of coal from certain dealers, but the prices were not criticized.

Q. I asked you about that just now whether there was any other articles that you irchased?—A. Well, it slipped my memory, we have to buy coal for our boats and ie price of coal is generally the standard price.

By Mr. Fyshe:

Q. What kind of coal do your purchase?—A. Steam and hard coal.

By the Chairman:

Q. Do you call for tenders, public tenders?—A. Yes, at Sorel, at the Government ship yards at Sorel, they give a big contract for coal every year for supplying their boats, and our boats get supplied there when they are in Sorel. But sometimes when our steamers engaged on the buoy service are on the lake or down the river and need coal, in order not to lose time they do not come back to Sorel for coal, but they go and coal at Three Rivers, or if, when they come to the Government ship yards the wharfs are taken up by other vessels, they will go and buy coal from other parties at the same price that we charged for at the Government ship yards and thus save time.

Q. For emergency say, at Three Rivers, you would pay the same price as if the coal was bought at Sorel?—A. Yes.

Q. How many tons of coal do your steamers use during the year?—A. Coal and carbide, are some of the principal expenditures in the buoy service, that includes all. Without examining the books I cannot say how many tons of coal we buy in a year.

Q. That nearly all goes to Mr. Willson, does it not?—A. Oh. no, we get carbide from the Carbide Company, Ottawa, and the expenditure on carbide is only a part of the appropriation for we use a great deal of coal.

Q. Then, $35,000 worth of coal is used, is that called for by public tender or does the department indicate where you are to get the coal?—A. I did not say that $35,000 was spent for coal, but that the whole buoy service last year cost us about that.

Q. The greater amount of the $35,000 paid for the buoy service last year was for coal. Was that coal called for by public tenders or did the department at Ottawa indicate from whom you were to buy the coal?—A. We buy the coal from those who have the patronage of the department, or we get it from the Government ship yards at Sorel.

Q. Just like the iron chain?—A. Yes, on the same principle.

Q. Who are the people who have the patronage?—A. At Sorel we have got coal from Martin and Lavallée. The patronage as much as possible is divided between two or three for coal.

Q. That is from Ottawa, those are the instructions you get?—A. You understand that the Member for the place divides up the patronage as well as he can among his friends, but we do not pay any dearer for the coal. In Three Rivers, it is a firm by the name of Leprohon & Son, and there may be another man there who is on the patronage list, who supplies coal when required by our boats.

Q. All these names are indicated from Ottawa?—A. All these names are on the patronage list.

Q. And are put there on the nomination of the Members for the district?—A. I do not swear to that.

Q. You say you cannot say?—A. I cannot say that. We receive instructions but we do not know by whose influence such names are put on the patronage list.

Q. Is there any other big item of expenditure?—A. I have given you the main items.

By Mr. Fyshe:

Q. You say you are limited in buying things for the service to those people who are on the patronage list?—A. Yes.

Q. Is it a clear advantage to those people?—A. Well, they get the order, but they do not get any more for their goods than if we went to any other man.

Q. Are you sure of that?—A. Well, the prices are all quoted.

Q. But is the quality always what it should be?—A. I am not a judge of coal, but I guess if the coal was not good we would soon hear about it from the men on the boats.

Q. There are great differences in coal you know?—A. I know there are. Take the item that the chairman has mentioned, take cedars now, they must be of the very best quality or we cannot use them. All the wood that we buy for buoy purposes is

SESSIONAL PAPER No. 29a

inspected by an inspector, and the engineer would not put a bad piece of cedar in the water.

Q. You say that you only pay the well known prices for these goods, but as regards the difference in the quality of goods, I say the quality is of as much importance as the price. They might shunt off on you coal that is of altogether inferior in quality?—A. I do not think that, because our engineers on board the boats would complain that the coal was working badly.

Q. What about the possibility of collusion between the coal men and the engineers?—A. Well, I can vouch that there is no collusion between the engineer of our agency and the local merchants. I know that if they did not supply the quality of coal required and the stipulated quantity as agreed upon, complaints would be made. I do not know of any collusion as far as the Montreal agency is concerned; I suppose it could be done, but to my knowledge it has never existed here.

There is matter I wish to bring before the notice of the Commission, it is the question of the position of the buoy engineer, Mr. Boucher; I am not here to plead my own case only, but I come in the interests of the officers of the Montreal agency. Engineers who are doing important works as he is, get far larger salaries than he gets. For the work he is doing the minimum salary should be $2,400; he is a technical man and a very capable man of long experience.

By the Chairman:

Q. He gets $1,800 now?—A. Yes, and the maximum should be $3,000.

Q. He began at $1,500?—A. Yes, he began lower than that in other employ, but then he was much younger. I want to just call your attention to the fact that he does a good deal of work and not only does he do a great deal of work, but it is a position of great responsibility. If anything goes wrong in the river, either in lights or in the buoys, which is very important to navigation, a great deal of damage would be done if proper care was not exercised to prevent serious accidents. If a buoy has gone astray, and if a large steamship happens along just as that time, it may cause a bad accident and heavy loss. We have to keep these buoys always in perfect order and always lighted, and we have to keep a steamer always under steam and ready to go and put these buoys back in their proper places, if they are misplaced, or to relight them if the light is cut. Not only that, but apart from the special duties of the engineer in charge we have to keep the marine companies posted on the position of every buoy between this city and Quebec. Often it has been necessary to give information at night for the morning papers, to have the positions of the buoys published for the benefit of the shipping interests. The shipping people expect a great deal from us, and we do all we can to assist them. I want to draw your attention to the importance of the agency here. It may be looked upon as a sinecure, but I can assure you that when there are accounts amounting to almost $400,000 passing through the office during the year there is no sinecure for those in charge.

Q. We do not look upon it as a sinecure, but it being a new office we ask questions about it, because we wanted to learn all there was about it?—A. I was not supposed to look after the books at first, there was an accountant there, and was removed to Ottawa.

Q. What was his name?—A. Mr. Alfred Roy.

Q. Is that the Mr. Roy that is now in Quebec, or is there another Mr. Roy?—A. This is another man, he used to get $1,700, he was an accountant, but all the work that is performed in our office is done practically by Mr. Boucher and myself.

By Mr. Fyshe:

Q. You formerly had an accountant and now you have none?—A. No, we have no accountant now; we have not asked for one. Mr. Chatigny, the assistant engineer of the buoy service, is only getting $1,200. For his services and the important work he does, he should get $1,500 as a minimum and $2,000 as a maximum salary, and the salary of the assistant agent, who since the removal of Mr. Roy, has to do all the

29a—43½

7-8 EDWARD VII., A. 1908

accountant's work, he should be entitled to $1,500 as a minimum salary. Miss Drolet, who does mostly all the typewriting of the several branches of the agency here, ought to have an increase as she only gets now a salary of $400 per annum. The messenger is only getting $500 per year, and has been in the agency since its establishment in Montreal. He acts as messenger for all branches of the department here, excepting the Montreal Pilotage office, which have their own messenger.

The witness retired.

MONTREAL, September 12, 1907.

Mr. WILLIAM LAURIE, of the Board of Steamship Inspectors, Marine and Fisheries epartment, Montreal, called, sworn and examined.

By the Chairman:

. You are the inspector of steamboats for this division?—A. Yes, sir.

. You were appointed in 1894?—A. Yes, sir.

. What were you before then, may one ask?—A. I was engineer.

. You were employed at outside work?—A. I was engineer on steamboats.

Q. You were not in the service of the Government?—A. No, sir, that was the :st time I entered the service in 1894.

Q. How did you get into the service?—A. Well, Mr. Burgess, the former steam->at inspector, my predecessor was in the Allan line with me. We were both engineers ι the Allan line, and when he decided to resign he recommended me for the position ıd was very anxious for me to take it. So I made application to the department for ιe position and they sent me to Toronto to be examined. I passed my examination ıere all right and it was Mr. Smith who was deputy minister at the time, but two eeks after I got back I received a letter from Mr. Smith asking me if I would accept salary of $1,000, which was offered by the Government. I wrote and told them I ould accept no such responsible position at that salary, and I had mentioned in my)plication I would not accept anything except what Mr. Burgess, the former inspector ıd.

Q. What was that?—A. $1,200.

Q. And for some years you were on the Allan line before entering the service?—A. es, sir.

Q. For how long?—A. For six years.

Q. You were chief engineer on one of their boats?—A. Yes, sir.

Q. What boat were you on?—A. I was on the *Rocket* and the *Merritt.*

Q. And Mr. Burgess, your predecessor, when he retired from the public service, commended you to Mr. Smith, who was then the deputy minister that you would be ι efficient successor?—A. Yes, sir.

Q. And Mr. Smith, looking into the question, being a Scotchman, and finding that)u had some knowledge of machinery and all that sort of thing, persuaded the Minis-r to appoint you?—A. No, he did not persuade the Minister. I tell you I refused ιe position at $1,000 and I did not expect the Government were going down on their ıees and ask me to accept the position. So they looked for a long time and they took ι Englishman named Cliff who was walking around the streets of Montreal, but he d so much rascality in condemning boilers and getting commission on them that 'ter they had him for eighteen months they had to dismiss him, and Sir Charles ibbert Tupper, the Minister of Marine at the time, telegraphed me asking if I would :cept the position of steamboat inspector at Montreal. I had never heard any thing)out this man Cliff or what he was doing, but I wired back that I would accept the)sition at the salary I had first asked. Mr. Smith told Sir Charles Tupper that I ould not accept the position at less than $1,200, and Sir Charles said, ' Give it to m, it is worth it,' and I was appointed.

Q. That was in 1894?—A. Yes.

Q. What is your present salary?—A. $1,500.

Q. When did you get the increase?—A. In Mr. Préfontaine's time, about three :ars ago.

Q. That is to say they increased your salary from $1,200 to $1,500?—A. Yes.

Q. All the inspectors get paid $1,500 I see, except the chairman?—A. Yes, sir.

Q. Where does Mr. Adams live?—A. In Ottawa, he is chairman of the board.

Q. Does the Board of Steamboat Inspectors often meet as a board?—A. Not very often, but we had a meeting about two months ago here in Montreal.

Q. Do you make regulations when you meet?—A. Yes, sir.

Q. Are those regulations approved by the Minister, or are they your own regulations?—A. Generally they have to be approved by the Minister.

Q. In addition to being a member of the board, you are the inspector of this division?—A. Yes, sir.

Q. How far does your jurisdiction go?—A. From Newport at the other end of Lake Magog up to Sudbury. This includes all boats on Lake Nipissing, Kippewa, Timiskaming and Quinze, all the Ottawa river down to Montreal, all the ocean steamers that come in here and that require inspection. I have about twenty-five ocean steamers this year.

Q. How far down the river do you go?—A. I only go as far down as Boucherville.

Q. And from there to Sudbury?—A. And to Newport, 108 miles south, taking in all Lake Magog, Lake Massiwippi and St. Johns. I inspect the machinery, there is another inspector for the hull and equipment.

Q. How many boats do you inspect during the year?—A. Generally from 130 to 150. These boats have to be inspected every year.

Q. Are there not more than 150 steam vessels in your division?—A. There are over 200 boats in this division.

Q. What about the others?—A. I have an assistant, he is the tackle inspector as well, he has to inspect all the tackle along the wharfs for loading and unloading these ocean steamers. They appointed an inspector for that purpose; there were so many injured and killed through carelessness and using bad ropes, slings and that sort of thing.

By Mr. Fyshe:

Q. Do you inspect ocean going vessels too?—A. All foreign registered ships trading between Canadian ports. That includes all those coal boats running between here and Sydney.

Q. And the Allan boats running between here and Glasgow?—A. They are not trading between Canadian ports.

Q. Your jurisdiction is with Canadian bottoms trading between Canadian ports?—A. And foreign ships trading between Canadian ports.

Q. That is to say, if the *Virginian* was simply trading between Sydney and Montreal, you would have to inspect her?—A. Yes, sir.

Q. But as she trades now between Liverpool and Montreal, you do not inspect her?—A. It is only within the last couple of years that law has been in force, owing to ship owners on the upper lakes getting vessels built on the other side and getting them registered there, so that we had no control of them. They got them registered there expressly to avoid our inspection law here, so that is why this law was introduced here.

Q. And that added to your work?—A. That gave us a great deal of extra work, especially with the coal boats, as they have to be inspected here.

Q. Was it considered a drawback to come under your inspection?—A. With these upper lake men it was, that is why this law was introduced and put into force in order to get at the boats up there, and in getting at those boats up there they brought in all these Norwegian ships that are trading between here and Sydney so that most of those boats come under my jurisdiction here.

Q. What fees do you charge for inspection?—A. There is no charge whatever, the fees were done away with about three years ago.

By the Chairman:

Q. I think it only amounted to about $20,000 anyway?—A. They had it up to $30,000, I think.

ESSIONAL PAPER No. 29a

By Mr. Fyshe:

Q. Do you give them a certificate?—A. We have to give them one if they pass ispection all right, and once we issue a certificate, then the inspector is responsible.

By the Chairman:

Q. That certificate is framed and put up in some prominent position?—A. On the iat.

Q. But this amended act came into force after your salary was increased?—A. It ime into force afterwards.

Q. With this new duty that has been imposed upon you, have you received no com-insating advantage in respect to an increase of salary?—A. No, sir.

Q. Your work in winter must be inconsiderable?—A. We are always kept busy, e have to go over all the plans of whatever new work is being built in the shops; we ive to go over those plans and correct them, and then there are always engineers, iite a number of them, coming up for examination, we have to examine them, that part of our duty. All these engineers who are running on the boats have to be tamined.

Q. In addition to examining the steamboats, you examine the engineers who run iem?—A. Yes, we do that in the winter as far as possible.

Q. Is there anything else you do besides inspecting the steamboats and examining ie engineers?—A. We have to look after all boilers and machinery built for the boats i the shops and see that they are built according to law. We go over the plans and e that everything is according to law.

Q. What shipbuilding yards are there that you have to inspect?—A. It is not the iipbuilding yards, but the machine shops. There are three here and one in Ottawa, have four or five to look after.

Q. And you regulate your work so that you are doing one thing in the summer me and the other in the winter?—A. Yes, sir.

Q. But your work keeps you busy all the year round?—A. Yes, I have often to avel at night and work during the day in order to get through with my work.

Q. And your work extends from Sudbury to Newport and down here to Montreal? -A. Yes.

Q. And you were appointed in 1894 in Sir Hibbert Tupper's time?—A. Yes.

Q. Do you pay anything towards the superannuation?—A No, sir, that is just ie trouble, I do not get superannuation. The same year as I was appointed super-inuation was done away with.

Q. Your predecessor, Mr. Burgess, was superannuated?—A. He was troubled with iart disease and died six months after he gave up.

Q. But he got a pension?—A. He only drew it for six months.

Q. In former days long ago, Mr. Riley was chairman, was he not?—A. Yes, sir.

Q. I know he was retired, and in former days the inspectors of steamboats when tiring drew annual allowances?—A. Yes, sir.

Q. You were appointed a little before the regulation was changed, so you did not intribute anything to the superannuation fund?—A. It was done away with just the iar I was appointed.

Q. Do you contribute anything towards the retirement fund?—A. No, sir.

Q. In addition to the increased emoluments you would like to be placed under the stem of pension?--A. I would just as soon have an increase of salary. The trouble that here in Montreal this is the most expensive city I believe in the Dominion to ve in. All the inspectors get the same salary and some of them are living in places here it does not cost one-half or two-thirds what it costs to live here, and I consider iat I am the poorest paid inspector in the whole service.

By Mr. Fyshe:

Q. What other inspectors are there?—A. There are about twenty-one inspectors together. There are two in Toronto, one in Collingwood, one in Kingston, two in

Montreal, one in Quebec, one in St. John, one in Halifax, two in British Columbia, and one in Winnipeg.

Q. Do they all get $1,500 a year?—A. There are a couple, two or three who do not, my assistant gets $1,300 and the inspector at Winnipeg gets $1,300, and all the rest get $1,500.

Q. Of course you take some exception to there being no superannuation fund?— A. Yes, it means that if I do not make a little money now I will be left out in the cold when I am unable to work.

By the Chairman:

Q. You are in your sixty-third year now?—A. Yes, I am sixty-two.

Q. And looking forward to the future you would like to see some pension system established?—A. I would like to see something ahead of me.

Q. What would you think is a practical fair remuneration for the service you are rendering, in your estimation, considering that you travel. You have had years of experience in the Allan line ?—A. I think we should get at least $1,800, but $2,000 to $2,500 would be a very fair salary and quite low enough to be paid for such work.

By Mr. Fyshe:

Q. What do men who are doing duty like that which you are performing get in the old country ?—A. I could not tell you, but the American inspectors get from $2,000 to $2,500 a year. I do not know anything about the old country.

Q. What do the inspectors at the Fairfield Works get for their work?—A. Some of them get big pay there, but I really could not tell you what their pay is. The American inspectors, we are quite often in touch with them, we meet them very often, and I know what their salary is, but I do not wish to speak about things I do not know anything about. I know the Americans are paid from $2,000 to $2,500, and I consider them a poor class of men in comparison with the class of men we have as inspectors.

Q. You do not know what Harland and Wolff or any of those big firms pay?— A. No, I do not know, but I know one thing, that there are lots of engineers holding small positions here that are getting as big salaries as I am, men whom I have to examine, that have not learned their business yet.

Q. What is the biggest tonnage of any steamboat that you have to examine?— A. 7,500 tons.

Q. That would be a boat trading from Sydney here?—A. Yes.

Q. One of the Black Diamond line?—A. We have that line, but most of them are Norwegian ships, and some of them are very large; I inspected one this summer over 7,500 tons.

Q. These boats that trade between Sydney and Montreal are chiefly owned by the Dominion Coal Co., are they not?—A. They are chartered by the Dominion Coal Co., the Intercolonial Coal Co. and the Inverness Coal Co.; there are quite a number of different companies that have these vessels chartered.

Q. This engineer of that 7,500-ton ship, what would he get?—A. They generally get about $100 per month and their keep.

Q. And you have to provide yourself with everything out of your $1,500?—A. Yes, and, of course, the inspection work is not like anything else, you have to destroy a lot of clothing, because you have to crawl into all kinds of places. On one trip you will destroy a suit of clothes; we have to go down into the boiler and into the hulls to examine the boilers.

Q. You have to do your work conscientiously ?—A. Yes, if a man makes up his mind to do his work conscientiously I tell you he has a lot of trouble and hard work.

By the Chairman:

Q. I do not recall, in all my long term of public service, that any criticism of any kind has even been made respecting the work of the steamboat inspection ?—A. No, sir.

Q. You do your work quietly, honestly, unostentatiously?—A. Yes, sir.

Q. And the proof of that fact is that there are no complaints?—A. That I have never had a complaint from the department since I have been in the service.

Q. And as a rule your colleagues are the same?—A. Yes, and I am certain that the Deputy Minister, Col. Gordeau, certainly would recommend an increase of salary to steamboat inspectors.

Witness retired.

STEAMBOAT INSPECTOR'S OFFICE,
MONTREAL, Sept. 23, 1907.

Chairman and Members of the Civil Service Commission,
Ottawa.

GENTLEMEN,—I hope you will pardon me for writing you a few lines in reference to my position as steamboat inspector for the district of Montreal.

Owing to the limited time and not being prepared to give you full particulars during the interview that you were so kind to grant me, I thought you would not consider it out of place, if I gave you a few more particulars in regard to the requirements to fill the position.

In the first place before being appointed, we have to pass a very severe examination on the construction of boilers and engines, calculations and designing, in fact a man requires to be a first-class engineer, boiler maker, arithmetician and draughtsman, or in other words a consulting engineer, and for the province of Quebec be able to speak the two languages.

I was appointed in the year 1894, at a salary of $1,200 with the understanding that the salary would be increased from year to year, but I got no increase for about ten years, then I was raised to $1,500 which did not improve my position owing to the increased cost of living and the extra work. $1,200 thirteen years ago was better than $1,500 to-day. About four years ago I was offered a position in New York at $3,000 per annum to start with, I went to Ottawa immediately to consult with Mr. Magee who practically was at the head of our department at that time, and he advised me to remain, that I would get a good salary later, and on my own part I thought it would be like commencing life over again to move to New York. This, with the expectation of getting more salary, I decided to remain. Then again the department strictly forbids an inspector doing any outside work in any capacity, where there is any remuneration, and some of them have been severely reprimanded for this offence.

Therefore, I consider a man who has served four or five years apprenticeship for nothing and worked hard and made many sacrifices to get to the top of his profession, and be obliged to live in the city of Montreal, he should be paid a reasonable salary at least $2,500.

I am gentlemen,
Yours most respectfully,

WM. LAURIE,
Steamboat Inspector.

MONTREAL, September 12, 1907.

Capt. JAMES RILEY, Marine and Fisheries Department, called, sworn and examined.

By the Chairman:

Q. You were a captain at one time?—A. Yes.

Q. That is your title ' Captain Riley '?—A. Yes.

Q. What marine experience had you?—A. I went to sea in 1856 in February, and I sailed up to August 1878 and then I became engaged in the marine insurance business, and so remained until four years ago when I retired from business and took a Government position.

By Mr. Fyshe:

Q. What is your occupation?—A. I have retired now.

By the Chairman:

Q. What is your position in the public service?—A. Superintendent of pilots, examiner of masters and mates and director of the Nautical College.

Q. I did not know there was such an institution?—A. I am acting under an Order in Council, I have received a letter from the department.

Q. You are superintendent of pilots?—A. And examiner of masters and mates.

Q. And director of the Nautical College also?—A. Yes.

Q. Your pilotage jurisdiction extends from here to Quebec?—A. Yes, sir.

Q. You are superintendent of pilots for the division?—A. That is it.

Q. Are you chairman of the masters and mates board?—A. No, I am examiner for this district.

Q. Is there a board?—A. No, sir, there is no board here, I report all my papers to the chief examiner at Ottawa.

Q. Who is he?—A. Capt. Demers.

Q. I see that you have no salary as examiner of masters and mates?—A. No, sir, I do not get any salary as examiner.

Q. What salary do you get for the pilotage?—A. $1,600 a year.

Q. And for this Nautical College?—A. I do not get any salary for that. I lecture each year, give thirty-two lectures. I lectured last year in the Monument National, and before that I delivered the lectures in my own office.

Q. This office of superintendent of pilotage, is that a recent appointment?—A. The Government took over the pilotage in the early spring of '94. I was the first superintendent in this district.

Q. Have you any assistants?—A. I have one assistant and a messenger.

Q. And you look after the pilotage funds too, don't you, in a way?—A. In this way that I keep a record of the superannuated pilots. I apply for their pensions, and send their pensions out and they send receipts back, and I forward the receipts to the Finance Department, who have to do with them, being the custodian of the funds and investing them to the best advantage.

Q. The pilots were taken away from the jurisdiction of the Harbour Commissioners and brought under the control of the Government?—A. Yes.

Q. And you became superintendent of the pilots?—A. Yes, sir.

Q. The pilots, when under the control of the Harbour Commissioners, accumulated a fund out of which they are, as they become old, superannuated?—A. That is it.

Q. The fund amounts to about $60,000, as far as I can recollect?—A. In September, 1904, the Harbour Commissioners turned over to the Finance Department, $55,643.52, for the pension fund, and $1,419.79 for pilots' expense account. At the end of last year there was $63,999.75 to the credit of the pilots' pension fund.

Q. It was in all about $60,000, I believe?—A. Yes, sir. It will be more than that as the seasons go on, because we are increasing the profits very largely; that is if the fund is wisely administered. The pilots contribute five per cent of their earnings, and their earnings are creeping up year by year.

By Mr. Fyshe:

Q. Is there any other source of revenue to this fund?—A. Nothing except accrued interest from the investments.

Q. The shipping interests do not contribute anything?—A. No, sir; the shipping interests are taxed for the pilotage of this jurisdiction. Last year the amount was very close on $75,000.

Q. That is a very large amount; is not that too large?—A. It depends upon the draught of the ship.

Q. Do you not think there are some abuses under this pilotage system? Don't you think it would be fair to allow the Allan or any other firm to keep their own pilots?—A. They do that. In the spring of the year—we have fifty branch pilots—and in the spring of the year each line applies for their own men by name, and these men are appointed to that line for the whole season. Those that are not selected for the special service are called 'tour de role men,' who take their turn as required. Some of the branch pilots earn close upon $3,000, while some of the others are as low as $240.

Q. How many pilots have you now?—A. We have fifty men called branch pilots, three apprentices and thirty-three pensioners.

Q. I suppose a pilot is only admitted after examination and after attaining a certain age?—A. They can only enter at sixteen. They have to come to me with their parents' consent, and send a certificate of physical ability from the family physician, an abstract from the parish register showing their birth, and a special certificate showing their fitness in sight and hearing, before they are examined by me. I examine them; they must talk English and French, and I examine them myself on sight and hearing. When there is a vacancy they come on as apprentices, and they must serve as apprentices for five years. Ten men of the senior apprentices are selected in rotation to form what is called the 'ten select list,' and these men have to go in the big ships with branch pilots, and learn to handle the big vessels. In these five years they have been on any boat they can get, but after that they have to go on large vessels and learn the difference between managing large vessels and small ones. When there are likely to be vacancies in the branch pilot's list, the men who have served more than five years meet the board of examiners, with myself as chairman, and they are examined. After they have passed they still continue on the role of selected apprentices, and they are not branched until there are vacancies in the regular role of fifty.

By Mr. Bazin:

Q. That is the limit, fifty, I suppose?—A. Yes, at the present time, but the Minister has the power to increase it. That leaves specially engaged in line work, all but about ten men.

By the Chairman :

Q. How do you account, after all this severe system of examination, for the stranding of the *Bavarian* or other occurrences such as we read about?—A. The *Bavarian* was not stranded in my jurisdiction, and it was a case of gross carelessness and the ship that went ashore on Red Island Reef was another piece of gross carelessness for which the captain is as much responsible as the pilot, because having the pilot on board does not relieve the captain of responsibility ; in fact within the last eighteen months a man has had his certificate cancelled for allowing the pilot to run his ship ashore.

Q. An investigation is held into a stranding such as the *Bavarian* ?—A. Every case of stranding is investigated now, and I am called upon to take part in many cases and to act as assessor, I am not paid for it. Five weeks ago I was sent to St. Johns as assistant to the Wreck Commissioner to investigate the stranding of a schooner called the *Wandrian*.

Q. After a disaster an investigation is held ?—A. Yes sir.

Q. If the investigation throws the blame partly on the pilot, what happens then, are their certificates suspended ?—A. We find it more beneficial to find them. To suspend them means to put them out of work for the time being and it is far more efficacious and beneficial to the service if we touch their pocket and at the same time they are kept at work. In the meantime, they are punished, and if they are regular line pilots they are dismissed from the line and become tour de role men and they are thus punished doubly.

Q. These men might come down from $3,000 a year to $250 ?—A. That would happen in this jurisdiction, but not in Quebec, because they are socialists there, they divide their earnings.

Q. If a disaster occurred to a line vessel in your jurisdiction the pilot in charge might drop from $3,000 to $250 ?—A. Yes sir, so you see that it is a punishment of no small amount.

Q. In the case of gross carelessness would the pilot be dismissed at all ?—A. Yes sir, in the case of drunkenness or gross incapacity we have dismissed them; we have unfortunately had to dismiss two of our members. It is far better to discipline the educated men you have than to try to get new ones.

Q. Are they ever reinstated ?—A. I have never known of a case, because we bear with them so long that they are past saving when we dismiss them.

Q. You are continually at work Captain, are you not ? If not examining the pilots then you are on these investigations into wrecks, and in the winter time you have these lectures to deliver ?—A. Yes, and as a matter of fact I have passed fourteen candidates within the past two weeks for master's certificates. I am continually at work.

Q. And for all this work they give you $1,600 ?—A. That is what I started with and that is what I get still.

Q. Do you give the same lecture over and over again ?—A. No sir, I do not, I vary the lectures according to the audience. I gave some extra lectures last year on the devioscope, some of the masters who were on shore asked that I should do so as they were much interested.

Q. Is only one examination required before a master gets a certificate ?—A. A man must first get a certificate as mate before he can pass for master.

Q. How long does he have to serve as mate before he gets a master's certificate ? —A. He must be actually in service as mate for twelve calendar months.

Q. He must pass two examinations then before he becomes master ?—A. Yes.

Q. And $1,600 was the salary given you at appointment ?—A. Yes sir.

Q. And there has been no increase since ?—A. None at all.

Q. You are not a contributor to the retirement fund ?—A. No sir, not at all.

Q. You naturally consider it desirable in the interest of the public service that some pension fund be established ?—A. I should think it would be advisable for the service generally and for the men.

Q. When you entered the service, having an established business and, I presume, having some means it was not a consideration in going into the service the non-existence of a pension fund ?—A. No sir.

Q. You are rather academic about the pension fund ?—A. Yes.

Q. Although you think that for the betterment of the Government service it might be a good thing ?—A. I think it would be a very good thing for the service that a pension fund should be established although personally at my age it is an academic matter.

Q. Do you know any officer in any other country who performs the same class of duty as you do ?—A. No sir, none.

Q. In any other country the examiner of masters and mates would be distinct, I presume?—A. Entirely apart.

Q. And the superintendent of the pilotage?—A. Entirely apart.

Q. And the lecturer in the Nautical College?—A. Entirely apart.

Q. Do you know anything about the control of the Deal pilots coming down the channel?—A. Particularly, no; generally, yes.

Q. There must be an examination of the Deal pilots, I suppose?—A. I think the Trinity Board have the Deal pilots in their charge.

Q. Of course, the Trinity Board looks after the lighthouses?—A. Yes, and the buoyage and pilotage.

Q. It is rather a personal matter, but what do you consider should be a proper emolument for the various services you perform?—A. Well, I would think £500 a year, that is $2,500 a year—that is my own personal opinion. I left a position of $6,000 a year to retire from business.

By Mr. Fyshe:

Q. I suppose, in cases of wreck investigations and such like, you are thrown into a good deal of communication with Commander Spain?—A. He calls upon me frequently to sit as an assessor.

By the Chairman:

Q. You are a colleague of his, nothing more?—A. Yes; I have been presiding all morning at an investigation into a collision, involving a breach of the navigation laws.

Q. You have not experience as a lawyer?—A. No, but I could not fail to pick up something about navigation laws in my experience; I was chairman of the Arbitration Committee of the Board of Marine Underwriters.

By Mr. Fyshe:

Q. You studied marine insurance?—A. I am an expert in that.

Q. You are pretty well equipped to perform the duties of your position?—A. Well, after fifty-one years one should be pretty well equipped or he should die. There is one thing I should like to mention, that is the case of my assistant. He came in over four years ago at $75 per month. he keeps all the books, he does what typewriting there is to be done, he draws out all the Trinity due bills for every ship that comes into our office, he prepares a form which goes through our books for every ship inward and outward, and for every pilot that comes inward or outward, no ship can clear the Custom-house without getting the Trinity bill showing the amount due from the pilotage for the pension fund. There is a very large amount of routine work. This man came in four and a half years ago, and he got $75 when he came in; he has not had the slightest increase since, everybody in the department has had an increase except this poor man who has had none, and he does not know why he has been left out, he has twelve children.

Q. What is his name?—A. J. O. Michaud. He has had no increase, but everybody else has got three or four increases in that time.

Q. He does the best he can, I suppose?—A. He is a very efficient man, and I know that three years ago Mr. Préfontaine promised him a rise of $300 a year. He has twelve children to maintain.

Witness retired.

QUEBEC, THURSDAY, September 19, 1907.

The Royal Commission on the Civil Service met this morning at 10.30 o'clock.

Present:—Mr. J. M. COURTNEY, C.M.G., Chairman

    Mr. THOMAS FYSHE, Montreal, and

    Mr. P. J. BAZIN, Quebec.

Mr. JOHN URIAH GREGORY, I.S.O., sworn and examined:—

By the Chairman:

Q. I see that you are of the mature age of 77?—A. That is all.

Q. And you have been 43 years in the public service?—A. I have been 44 years.

Q. Is your salary still at $2,200?—A. Yes. My salary has not been increased for twenty odd years, while the expenses of my agency have augmented from less than $200,000 to over three quarters of a million dollars.

Q. That is to say, you disburse three-quarters of a million dollars a year in the agency?—A. Yes, very nearly.

Q. Then it comes practically to this, that you are serving your country for $660 a year after 43 years' service?—A. Yes.

Q. That is the difference between your salary and what you would get if you went out?—A. Yes.

Q. How many people are employed in one way or another under your agency? —A. In my office there are 15 or 18, around the premises there are about 100 workmen, and I have to look after all the lighthouse keepers from Montreal to the Atlantic ocean, including the Baie des Chaleurs, the Island of Anticosti and the Straits of Belle Isle through inspectors under me.

Q. And I suppose a certain number of Dominion steamers?—A. Yes—the *Druid*, the *Montcalm*, the *Champlain* and the *Eureka*, and I look after the repairs and outfitting of any steamers that turn up, including four light-ships and the signal service.

Q. With the light-keepers and the labourers and the crews of steamers, and other employees, you must have five or six hundred people under your direction?—A. Yes, fully.

Q. How far does your agency extend now?—A. I take in all the lights from Montreal to the Gulf, about 1,200 miles. Then I have Lake Memphremagog to look after. Then, I have nearly all the Government wharfs in this district under my supervision.

Q. You have a marine hospital here?—A. No. The marine hospital was abolished and sold, but I have to look after the payment for sick mariners. I am also shipping master at Quebec. I also represent the British Government in regard to anything connected with seamen at this port.

Q. You look after hydrographic surveys?—A. No.

Q. Have you any medical men under your charge?—A. No.

Q. You pay the doctors?—A. Yes. There is a fixed rate of 90 cents a day.

Q. In the *Arctic* there was a doctor?—A. Yes.

Q. There are no doctors in the other steamers?—A. No.

Q. Have you any other Dominion steamers to look after besides those you have named?—A. I have the *Princess* also.

Q. Have you the *Lady Grey?*—A. No.

Q. How do you get the supplies for these steamers, such as coal?—A. It is bought by contract from the mines in Nova Scotia.

SESSIONAL PAPER No. 29a

Q. Is that after advertisement and public tender?—A. I cannot say. The best coal is chosen. I believe there is a certain amount of competition. I know that it is bought at the lowest rate. We get ours from the Nova Scotia Coal and Steel Company.

Q. Eight or ten years ago you did not get the coal from that company?—A. No. We bought from dealers on the spot.

Q. You bought largely from Archer & Company?—A. We bought from large dealers, not specially from Archer.

Q. Now you buy direct from the coal companies?—A. The department at Ottawa contracts with the coal company, and the company delivers the coal to us here on the wharf at so much a ton.

Q. The pile of coal on the wharf is brought from Nova Scotia?—A. Yes, and is put on the wharf at a certain rate.

Q. What coal company does this come from?—A. The Nova Scotia Steel and Coal Company.

Q. In addition to coal there is bought a good deal of hardware such as chains and anchors?—A. Yes.

Q. From whom do you get these?—A. When we buy new chains and anchors or any other heavy materials, we call for tenders.

Q. Who is F. X. Drolet?—A. The owner of the only machine shop of any importance in the city of Quebec—a large and well equipped establishment.

Q. How much did you pay to Drolet last year?—A. I could not say. We paid a great deal. It varies according to the amount of damage done to the machinery of our vessels. We have an ice breaker that smashes into the ice, and her machinery may be jarred more in one year than in another. The plates of her screws cost from $275 to $300 each. I had to buy six of them the other day.

By Mr. Fyshe:

Q. In cases of that kind I suppose you cannot take tenders?—A. We do. We know what the plates cost in Scotland, and we buy them as cheaply here. We get a price from Drolet and a price from other people, and if his price is not higher than the others, we give him the preference, because he has an establishment on the ground and the fitting has to be so well done that it is an advantage to the service to have it done here.

By the Chairman:

Q. Under the heading of maintenance of lights you paid to Drolet last year $23,000?—A. Yes. We pay him $50,000 in some years. Under the maintenance of lights is included an immense amount of fine machinery, such as revolving lights and revolving gear of different descriptions, which may require very careful work.

Q. Then you buy all these things from Drolet without tender?—A. We give him the work to do. There is nobody else in this city to do the work.

Q. How do you satisfy yourself that the amounts paid to him are the proper amounts?—A. As a general thing we fix the prices before we give the order. Then we have a superintendent who comes from Halifax to superintend the work; his name is Schmidt. Mr. Samson also inspects a great deal of our steamboat work as it progresses. These men certify that the work has actually been done, that the prices are fair and that the work was necessary.

By Mr. Fyshe:

Q. This man who comes from Nova Scotia—A. He is a general inspector. Before we undertake any work, he inspects the whole thing and estimates what it will cost.

Q. Is he a skilled engineer?—A. Oh, yes, a skilful man. He is a Scotch mechanical engineer.

7-8 EDWARD VII., A. 1908

By The Chairman:

Q. I suppose Drolet has what may be called heavy hardware and leather belting? —A. No. Occasionally he may furnish belting for some machinery which he has put up to complete his job; but the belting is bought from the Mechanics Supply Company, who are especially in that line.

Q. The Martineau Company last year supplied over $3,000 worth of small goods? —A. Yes.

Q. Were those at retail prices?—A. No, they were at wholesale prices—at prices fixed before we bought them. Every year I send out a circular to the different dealers who are friends of the administration—never anybody else since I have been here, whatever party in power.

By Mr. Fyshe:

Q. Is that not objectionable?—A. That is for the Government to answer. I have nothing to do with the Government policy. That has always been the case under any administration, Liberal or Conservative, and if it is not done I hear of it. Hardware, paints and oils are all bought by tender.

By The Chairman:

Q. But not by calling for public tenders?—A. No. We have never called for public tenders since I have been here. We get prices from seven or eight different men in the same trade, friends of the administration.

Q. Do you divide the purchases among them?—A. Yes

Q. If you do not go outside, could they not form a combine with their price lists? —A. It does not look like it from the way they reproach me for buying more from one than from another. I do not think they do. One might think it natural that they would do so, but in reality they do not.

Q. Coming to provisions, last year Louis Mercier & Co. supplied over $1,200 worth. Are they wholesale grocers?—A. No.

Q. These are groceries and provisions for the ships?—A. Yes. To the best of my recollection we have thirteen or fourteen firms for the supply of these things, and they all charge the same price. We do not buy large quantities of these goods and do not store any of them. We tried once to store them, and they were stolen. Then, our captains board their men at so much a day on our principal boats, and they buy these provisions for themselves.

Q. Is there any possibility of the captain catering for more seamen than are on the ship?—A. No.

Q. How do you check that? You know how many men there are, but can you know how many extra men you will take on board?—A. Every man is named to me before I approve of his engagement.

Q. Is it not possible to pad the list?—A. I suppose so, if I were blind, but I am not. For instance, there are ten sailors allowed to the *Druid*, and there is no eleventh ever put in, without approval.

Q. But when the *Druid* goes to any of the gulf ports, and the captain wants labourers, those labourers are boarded also, are they not?—A. No, there is nothing of that kind.

Q. The practice is not the same as with the dredge vessels?—A. Not at all.

Q. Where do you get the oil for the lights?—A. By contract; that is done in Ottawa—oils, paints, chimneys, wicks, brooms, buckets. If we have some small articles to get here, we get tenders, and divide up the orders, giving a little to each.

Q. Do you keep store books here?—A. Yes.

Q. Have they ever been inspected by any officer of the Audit Office?—A. Yes. several times. They have gone all over our stores, and we have books showing what we have taken in and where everything has gone to.

Q. You were examined in connection with the supplies for the steamer *Arctic*?— Yes.

SESSIONAL PAPER No. 29a

Q. Had you anything to do with calling for those supplies?—A. Nothing.

Q. You simply received the supplies and put them on board ?—A. I did not receive them and put them on board. I know they were received with the exception of the cigars. Another man got the tobacco.

Q. Your place is on Champlain Street ?—A. Yes. I have the signal service under my control also.

Q. I have observed on your wharf a lot of things looking like inverted pears ?—A. Yes. They are buoys of different sizes made in our shops. One reason why we do not keep on hand a stock of iron goods is that you can never tell what kind we may want most of. We do not want to keep anything except buoys. When we want iron we get it at the lowest rate as we want it, and charge it immediately to the service to which it goes. One man may have had a bill of $23,000, but item after item of that has been charged to a different service, so that he can tell what each lighthouse and each steamer costs to keep a year, but the whole amount is put to the debit of Mr. Drolet or whoever it may be.

Q. I think you said that these buoys were made here ?—A. Yes, made in our shops.

Q. Then you have a casting foundry in your shops ?—A. We have large forge and boiler shops. We make our own boilers and own boats—our gasolene launches.

Q. These are simple buoys not the acetylene buoys ?—A. We do not make the acetylene buoys. These are the conical buoys.

Q. Has there been any explosion of buoys in this district ?—A. No, we have not had any so far.

Q. There have been explosions at Parry Sound and at Prescott?—A. Yes. Our captains are afraid of the risk of these buoys.

Q. Are these acetylene buoys ordered elsewhere ?—A. I do not know anything about the order.

Q. How many of these acetylene buoys have you in stock?—A. I think there are 16 or '18. The buoys get out of order, and our captains will not load them while in the water, but will take down a buoy that is already loaded and put it in the place of one that is out. They bring that back, and after it is well dried it is loaded.

Q. The buoys on the wharf are practically reserve buoys ?—A. Yes.

Q. You are not in the habit of ordering any of these buoys in advance ?—A. No. They have been sent to us by the inspector by the department's orders.

Q. I see that Mr. Willson was paid in the year 1905-6 for these buoys $336,000. How many have you in your district under your agency ?—A. About twenty of the acetylene.

Q. He has three descriptions of buoys—automatic gas buoy, a whistling buoy, the automatic gas buoy of the new patttern and the automatic beacon buoys with tower ?—A. Yes.

Q. Are you replacing any of the old buoys with these automatic buoys ?—A. We are replacing the Pintsch gas buoys with the acetylene; the light from the acetylene is superior to any other—there is no question about that.

Q. How many Pintsch gas buoys have you ?—A. About ten.

Q. How many of these new buoys have been laid down ?—A. About twenty in my district altogether.

Q. Then practically there are ten new gas buoys?—A. Yes; but as they are asked for by the Shipping Federation we replace them.

Q. How do you arrive at the fact that a gas buoy should be laid down ?—A. The Shipping Federation of Montreal represent most of these demands to the department at Ottawa. Then, the Richelieu Company, for instance, making the Saguenay trip, have occasionally asked for one where they find their increasing trade makes it necessary. That is brought before me, and after consultation with my navigators and pilots, I suggest it to the department. Sometimes I oppose it. There may be a buoy

29a—44

asked for where my captains and myself come to the conclusion that it is not absolutely necessary.

Q. How many gallons of acetylene have you stored in your store house ?—A. To the best of my recollection we have twenty tons of the carbide stored now.

Q. It is a very dangerous thing to have in proximity to your stores ?—A. I think so. They say that nothing can injure it but water. It is all in iron cans ; but there is no doubt that if one of these were knocked about and broken up and water touched it, everything would go.

Q. Have you anything to do with the hydrographic survey?—A. No further than to be generally useful to them whenever they want me.

Q. The *Gulnare* is stationed here is she not ?—A. No, we have not anything to do with her. We have the *Canadienne* which is doing work below here. That is the only one I know anything about.

Q. I asked you that because I see in the Auditor General's report several references to purchases made in Quebec for the *Gulnare* and some in Sorel and so on?—A. She moves around from one place to another.

Q. Is Captain Miles, who is paid £600 a year, in the Royal Navy ?—A. Yes, he is in the Royal Navy. The Royal Navy pays him part of his salary.

Q. There is an arrangement with the Imperial Government to have his services?—A. I understand so.

Q. He is answerable for the purchases?—A. Yes. I have nothing to do with them.

Q. Have you anything to do with the Fishery protection service?—A. No, further than repairing the boat.

What is the boat?—A. The *Princess*.

Q. The same remarks that you have made generally with regard to the fitting out of the *Druid* and the other boats which you have in your branch of the service would apply to the *Princess* I suppose; that is, when supplies are wanted you go to the people whose names are on the patronage list?—A. Yes, the Commander does.

Q. Then practically three quarters of a million dollars of disbursements that you expend are chiefly on the maintenance and construction of lights and on the Dominion steamers?—A. Yes.

Q. We would be very glad to know if you would like to add anything in a memorandum?—A. I would like to add this. The cost of labourers has gone up from less than ten cents an hour to twenty-five cents, and even thirty-five cents an hour. You cannot get a labourer to work for you for $2 a day for nine hours. The wages of carpenters, blacksmiths and other mechanics have gone up from $1.00 or $1.50 to $3 and $4 a day, while the agent has had no increase. I have had no increase in twenty-three years while I am responsible for an expenditure of three quarters of a million, where I used to be responsible for less than $200,000.

Q. Has there been any relative increase in the remuneration paid to the officers of the Dominion steamers?—A. Yes, their pay has been very considerably increased and that of the men also. That matter has been left largely in my hands. We pay the highest current rates going. As to the workingmen, they are ruled by their unions and will not work for less than they demand. Another matter I wish to refer to is this. Many of our lighthouse keepers are paid less now than they were thirty years ago, but most of them are paid about the same. The light house keeper at Bird Rock had $1,500 a year. Now he is paid $1,300. I have written more than one letter recently to the department. One of our lighthouse keepers threw up his job because he could not live on his salary ; that was the Belle Isle lighthouse keeper. Then, these men were formerly able to get the help of young people for $100 a year and their board but they now cannot get them for $300 a year and their board. These men have the fog alarm to run night and day and the light to keep up, they may have sickness or death in their families and may have to take a boat to go ashore, and they must have someone to leave behind. The lighthouse keepers generally need an assistant and sometimes two or three. Our Department is taking into consideration the questiou of augmenting the rates of pay of all the lighthouse keepers and classifying them through the agents and inspectors for that purpose.

Q. When you want extra men at your stores, do you ask the Member to give you the names?—A. The Member takes good care to give me a list. I have about 300 names from Mr. Powers, and nearly a hundred from Mr. Lachance. In that respect I have no difficulty in getting names.

Q. You say that the wages of labourers, seamen, officers on board the Dominion steamers, have been increased and the rates of pay to the lighthouse keepers are being revised. The only people so far who have not had an advance in their salaries are the clerical staffs and the different agencies?—A. Yes, particularly the agent. However, I do not complain, because I have been very well treated.

QUEBEC, September 20, 1907.

Mr. J. U. GREGORY, I.S.O., appeared and made the following statement:—

I forgot yesterday to touch upon the question of superannuation or pensions. I am greatly inclined to believe that a pension to the lighthouse keeper is a necessity and it would probably enable the department to get better men and men who would stay with us longer. I have just to-day received a letter from the lighthouse keeper of West Point, Anticosti, a well-educated man, superintendent of the telegraph system, and a man who in the winter acts as an adviser to Mr. Meunier, the owner of the island. He has written to me to-day that he cannot live on his present salary. He cannot get a man as an assistant at anything near what he formerly could. He is getting no more salary than his father did forty years ago. This matter has been before the Minister, and it is put off from year to year.

The CHAIRMAN.—The Minister himself cannot say that a lighthouse keeper shall be superannuated. It would be necessary to re-enact the Superannuation Act.

Mr. GREGORY—This man cannot keep his situation on his present pay, because his help eats up the whole salary. Labourers who got ten cents an hour twenty years ago are to-day getting all the way from twenty to thirty-five cents, and labourers on ships get thirty-seven and a half cents per hour, and double pay for night work.

Q. What is the name of that lighthouse keeper?—A. Alfred Malouin. The lighthouse keeper at Belle Isle, who succeeded his father as lighthouse keeper, has had to resign because he could not live on his salary.

Q. And of course the life of a lighthouse keeper is subject to peril, and even if he escapes the peril, he is in a more unfortunate position than the majority of people, through the stress of weather, especially in exposed places like Anticosti?—A. Oh, yes. A lighthouse keeper needs an able assistant, because he may fall ill. The man recently appointed at Heath Point, Anticosti, cannot get a man to help him under $300 a year and board. That man himself gets only $600 a year. He has to have an assistant intelligent enough to telegraph and to signal passing vessels. So that it is no ordinary people we require for these positions. When you come to the question of superannuation, it seems to be no more than right that men placed in the most Godforsaken positions, where vessels are forbidden by the lights to come to, should be able after a certain number of years to retire on a pension. It is cruel to keep these men all their lives ekeing out a living with hardly enough to exist on. We have made out a schedule of salaries that we think would be fair and just for these men. That schedule is before our Minister but has not yet been adopted. In the meantime our people suffer. Two or three of the best men we have recently resigned for want of sufficient pay to live and pay an assistant, and more will follow.

29a—44½

7-8 EDWARD VII., A. 1908

Q. Do you know whether these light keepers at the Bird Rocks or at Anticosti, if they want to insure their lives, have to pay extra hazardous premiums?—A. Yes, and in some cases the companies will not insure them. The first two men at the Bird Rocks lighthouse went out of their minds from the monotony of the life. The second man went to kill some seals on the ice and was carried away and was never heard of afterwards. The third man there was blown to atoms in firing off the gun. The fourth man who went there had his hand dreadfully injured from the premature discharge of his gun, so much injured that he became a cripple. This man was getting less pay by $200 than the first man. Reliable and excellent men in these positions are absolutely necessary for the safety of navigation in the St. Lawrence. I think furthermore, that if a lighthouse keeper should be taken away, his widow should be paid half his superannuation at least. A man at Baie St. Paul had to resign on account of illness, and he received the small pension of $200 a year. His widow came to me yesterday and applied for aid. She received no pension, although, like a great many other women at lighthouses, she had done a great deal of the work of the lighthouse herself. I would therefore suggest that the widow get half the pension as long as she lives after the death of her husband.

TORONTO, September 26, 1907.

MR. F. F. PAYNE, called, and sworn, and examined.

By the Chairman:

Q. You are Secretary of Meteorological Service?—A. Yes.

Q. How long have you been there?—A. Thirty years, but not as Secretary.

Q. You were there in Professor Kingston's time?—A. Yes.

Q. And in that of Mr. Carpmael?—A. Yes, I have seen both of them die.

Q. How old are you?—A. I have just completed fifty-one.

Q. I see there are two Messrs. Payne?—A. The other is my brother.

Q. What is your present salary?—A. $1,350.

Q. After how many years service?—A. After thirty years' service.

Q. What salary did you enter the service at?—A. I can show it to you in this memorial.

Memorial produced and filed as Exhibit.

Q. What are the signatures attached to the memorial?—A. Those are the signatures of the men who got the memorial up.

Q. One gentleman was appointed fifty-one years ago?—A. He is an old man now.

Q. What was his salary when first appointed?—A. $180. He came in as quite a young man, as a boy in fact. The grant for the service in those days was very small.

Q. Has the director any residential privileges?—A. Not now. He had until about two years ago.

Q. Then nobody at the central office has any other emolument outside his salary?
—A. Excepting those whom you see there.

Q. That is something for house rent but with this exception, nobody receives any emolument outside his salary?—A. None whatever.

By Mr. Fyshe:

Q. Your work is of a rather scientific character?—A. Yes.

By the Chairman:

Q. The seven principal officers have all served thirty years and over?—A. Yes, I produce some of the work we have to get up. Our work is simply hardly known in Ottawa. We have to prepare daily weather charts.

Q. Your principal expenditure is in the telegraph service?—A. Yes.

Q. The expenditure is about $100,000 a year?—A. Not in telegraph.

Q. I mean the expenditure altogether?—A. $110,000 is our grant this year.

Q. But the two telegraph offices during that year got some where over $27,000?
—A. Yes.

Q. So at least a quarter of the money spent in the service goes to the telegraph companies for the circulating of the weather forcasts?—A. And the collection of data on which we base our forecasts.

Q. You have a very small establishment at the central office?—A. It is very small, but this summer we were allowed to take in three young men, students from the university, for the summer and that has been a great help to us.

Q. They have gone back to the university; they have not graduated?—A. Yes, the students go back immediately.

Q. They were there during the rush in the weather?—A. Yes. That is one thing I think might be discouraged. We would sooner have permanent officers if we could get them.

Q. Your service, I presume, requires some knowledge of mathematics and astronomy? The qualifications of the officers are highly scientific?—A. Yes.

Q. Your Director, Assistant Director and Climatologists, I presume, are university graduates ?—A. No, they are not.

Q. Professor Kingston comes from Cambridge ?—A. I do not think he ever took his degree; I am not sure. Professor Carpmael was the fifth wrangler at Cambridge.

Q. The former Director was a wrangler at Cambridge ?—A. Yes.

Q. And the qualifications for the positions in the observatory are wholly scientific? —A. Yes, decidedly so.

Q. Are there many complaints now of wrong forecasts ?—A. Yes, lots of them. It has not become a perfect science by any means.

Q. Are the forecasts or predictions generally verified ?—A. About eighty-two per per cent.

Q. That is as much as you can expect ?—A. That is the percentage at present. We are hoping to do better.

Q. Have you a full equipment of scientific instruments ?—A. Yes, we use the very best instruments and we are very well equipped.

Q. Latterly the country has been generous, except in the matter of salaries, in fitting up and equipping the institution ?—A. Yes. Of course, we are continually increasing our expenditure. For instance, there is a starting of new stations as the country is opened up. The people in the Northwest are always asking for new stations, especially in the wheat growing country, and the stations are pretty close to one another.

By Mr. Fyshe :

Q. Where is your observatory located ?—A. In the Queen's Park. It is a small building, but the plans for another structure are in the hands of the architect. It will be placed a little to the north of the present building. I now beg to produce some of the statistical work that we have compiled.

By the Chairman :

Q. I think that was sent down to us at Ottawa and we already have a copy?— A. Yes, I think so.

By Mr. Fyshe :

Q. How often do you publish editions ?—A. Those are published once a month and these every day. A monthly weather review is also published.

Q. What do you show in the way of forecasts of the weather ?—A. Here is a copy of the forecast we issue. It is issued every morning and has to be printed in a great hurry and sent out to different parts of Ontario. Then, of course, it appears in all the newspapers. We issue two forecasts. We issue a forecast which appears in the daily newspapers and we issue forecasts in the morning which go on these charts and are telegraphed to a few places. We exchange reports with the United States and it is on these reports that the chart I produced is based.

By the Chairman :

Q. The country has a well equipped observatory now ?—A. The observatory itself is in a very bad condition at present.

Q. You want a new building ?—A. Yes, we want a new building.

Q. And in the matter of instruments how are you situated ?—A. In the matter of instruments the equipment is very good. We have the best instruments.

Q. And the country is paying for additional stations all the time ?—A. As they are required.

Q. The great desideratum is the lack of appreciation of the officers at the central observatory ?—A. Yes.

Q. You consider you should be placed in a better position, more in accordance with the important duties you perform ?—A. Yes.

Q. You consider that the Director's position should be equivalent to that of a deputy head ?—A. I think so. I think it would be better for the service.

Q. And you men of old standing who have been for thirty years or more in the public service should have better recognition than you now enjoy?—A. Yes, I think so.

By Mr. Fyshe :

Q. There does not appear to be any appreciation of scientific work in this country ? —A. It is a very useful work which is performed by the Meteorological Service.

By the Chairman :

Q. The trouble is that somehow or other the great majority of people in the world do not appreciate what you do ?—A. There are similar services in every country and I do not think they do appreciate it. As I stated in the memorial we endeavour to predict the weather for the general public and the hardest thing to do is to predict rain. To predict temperature and storms is very much easier and that is very important to mariners and the business community.

Q. In connection with the harvesting of the crops and other undertakings your predictions are of immense value ?—A. Yes.

Q. You express the hope that the staff will be put in a better position and that the country should in some way recognize the work of your service ?—A. Yes, in a monetary point of view and also in regard to superannuation.

The CHAIRMAN : I think, Mr. Payne, you have gone very fully into all the matters touched upon in the memorandum submitted by you. It is a very able document and will be appended to your evidence. If, in thinking matters over during the next two or three weeks, you find there is anything else to explain we will be very glad to receive from you a supplementary memorandum.

Witness produced other statements which were read and filed.

The CHAIRMAN.—We are very glad to have these.

The WITNESS.—I had a letter from the Director, written in April, in which he said he had spoken to the Department and had recommended me for an increase.

Witness retired.

METEOROLOGICAL OFFICE,
TORONTO September 26, 1907.

Gentlemen,—I would respectfully request that you will allow me to bring to your notice a long standing grievance affecting my own interests.

Upon the appointment of the present director of the Meteorological Service in 1894 the salaries of the four senior officers were as follows :$1,216 ; $1,216 ; $1,216 : $800, the last being my own.

Although the work of each officer, excepting that of the director, has not changed 1894 the salaries of the four senior officers were as follows: $1,216; $1,216; $1,216; the latter being my own and the bulk of the appropriations for recent increases has usually gone to the first two officers.

Whilst I am informed by the director that he has repeatedly recommended to the department considerably better remuneration for my services the department has not accepted his recommendations. This of course is exceedingly discouraging more especially as the salary of the recently appointed assistant director was enormously increased immediately ·before and after he was allowed that rank.

The work of the secretary is not the same as that carried on by an officer of the same rank in business for besides the dictation of practically all letters sent out, chiefly on his own initiative and many of which are technical ; also general secretarial work, he has the care of all accounts, besides his share of the scientific work of the service.

In the United States Weather Bureau the salary of the secretary is as large as that of any other officer excepting the chief. I think in all fairness that the disparity existing in the salaries mentioned should not be continued and I crave your further inquiry into this matter.

I am, gentlemen,

Yours respectfully,

(Signed) F. F. PAYNE.

MEMORIAL OF THE METEOROLOGICAL SERVICE.

To the Honourable the Royal Civil Service Commissioners :—

Gentlemen,—Upon the receipt of your kind invitation to send a delegate to your meeting to be held in Toronto on September 20, to confer with you upon matters affecting the general interests of the members of the Meteorological Service of Canada a meeting of the staff of the central office was called and it was then decided *firstly* to accept your invitation and to express to you your gratitude for allowing them this opportunity of bringing before you their views in this matter, *secondly* to present to you through their delegate, Mr. F. F. Payne, in as concise a form as possible a short history of the Service, its work, aims and present condition together with comparative salary lists and the various suggestions in their order as they were put forward and agreed to at this meeting.

The Toronto Magnetic and Meteorological Observatory was established by the British Government in 1840 and was taken over by the Provincial Government in 1853 and by the Federal Government in 1866, its work at this time being the recording of magnetic and meteorological observations. A few years later other less important stations chiefly in charge of voluntary observers were started in different portions of Canada the reports from these stations being sent to Toronto by mail and used chiefly in studying the climate of Canada. These stations gradually increased and the importance of them necessitated the inauguration of a meteorological service, similar to that in many other countries, and Toronto became the centre of this Service. In 1872 the usefulness of weather forecasts, having been fully acknowledged by the Governments of several different countries, including the United States, an attempt in this direction was made at the central office, the forecasts being based as at present on the reports received by telegraph from different portions of Canada and the United States. The number of these reports were altogether insufficient and it was not until 1876 that regular forecasts and storm warnings were issued. From this date the improvement in the forecasts and the growth of the service was rapid, additional grants by the Government being also frequently required.

The usefulness of the work of the service does not consist wholly of forecasting rain or sunshine for the benefit of the general public as many suppose, but chiefly in the issue of storm warnings to mariners in which much greater success can be attained. In addition to these are the forecasts of changes of temperature which are of great importance to the agricultural and business community. Many special warnings and forecasts are issued to those inquiring for them and during the winter months all railways are directly informed of approaching heavy snow storms or high winds which are likely to cause much drifting. Almost as important as the forecasts are the climatological statistics gathered from 511 stations in all parts of the country and many requests have been received during the past few years for such -information by'intending immigrants. The number of inquiries for statistics required in the settlement of legal disputes is also very 'large and is continually increasing. The preparation of these statistics for immediate use and for the annual reports, weather reviews, monthly and daily weather charts and more particularly the issue of the various daily 'forecasts requires special care and training and we would submit that the services of those who have been trained in the work should be retained if possible by offering adequate remuneration.

The magnetic observations for which a separate grant of $3,200 per annum is allowed may be considered as Canada's contribution to a great international work the full importance of which will only be proved after many years collection of data and study of the earth's magnetic forces, the instruments for the purpose used requiring most careful manipulation and the observations recorded requiring highly scientific training to deduce from them the results to be obtained.

At present the service is labouring under a great disadvantage, the want of proper offices and record rooms preventing the work being carried on as well as it might be, and we would urge that the new building which is to be erected as a central office may not be further delayed.

·The officials of the central office may be classified as follows:—Director, assistant director, secretary, special officers, observers, computers, telegraph operators and clerks, and of the 184 outside stations as observers and storm signal agents. The former devote their whole time to the work of the service, whilst the latter'only give a portion of their time, excepting at Victoria, B.C., Quebec and St. John, where the same conditions prevail as at the central office.

For many years the members of the staff of the central office have urged their claim to recognition in the civil service and the enjoyment of the privileges which it allows, but without result and we would now ask you to consider whether this cannot be granted. Since it is the pleasure of the Government that the central office of the service shall continue in Toronto the staff of this department of the public service naturally ask why they should be debarred from privileges which the scientific institutions in Ottawa enjoy.

In bringing to your notice the small salaries allowed the members of the meteorological service and in asking for more liberal remuneration for our services, we do so not only on the plea that the greatly increased cost of living, which is patent to every one, makes it quite impossible for us to hold a position in the community commensurate with our official status; but also on the ground that, although this service is one of the chief scientific institutions in the country, the members of which require special training and their work continues both day and night and on Sunday, they have not received the same liberal treatment. If, however, this cannot be done may we not ask that increases to our salaries may be allowed on the basis of the increased cost of living of the past ten years? This increase as political economists and others have proved is in Toronto quite 35 per cent. 'We are well aware of the. difficulty before you of determining the amount of any increase that should be allowed in the different departments, but we feel some diffidence in making suggestions on this point and would only venture to mention that in our opinion the position of the small salaried man is probably harder that that of those who are in receipt of larger salaries and due consideration might be given those who did not share in the recent increases allowed. In the weather bureau of the United States the scale of salaries obtaining is considerably higher than in the meteorological service of Canada in spite of the fact that a specialist in that bureau has only to carry on the work in his own department whilst in the smaller Canadian service the duties of each individual are more varied. At one moment he may be worrying over a difficult weather prediction and the next moment disputing with an agent on a question of business. With the growth of the country the duties and anxieties of the members of the central office

7-8 EDWARD VII., A. 1908

increases, and we feel that this fact is hardly realized or earlier recognition would have been made. The salaries allowed at the outside stations can hardly be considered in the same way as at the central office as they only form a portion of the observers income earned by him for a portion of his time, excepting 'at the three stations already mentioned where it is the whole income of the observer.

Equally important with the question of better remuneration is that of superannuation, and if anything in this direction could be done we should be exceedingly grateful. Although some of the members of the service entered long before the new Civil Service Act of 1898 came into force we were not allowed the privilege of subscribing to the superannuation fund, nor have we been allowed the privileges of this last Act. Thus after thirty years' service or more, with nothing saved, for it was impossible to do so, we can only contemplate the spending of our old age without rest in the same daily round. If we may be permitted to do so we would ask that a proper retiring allowance may be allowed to each member of the service, and we would further ask that some form of pension may also be given to those dependent upon him in the event of his death. Without being asked to do so we would not suggest a scale of superannuation, and we rest confident in your judgment in this matter.

Your memorialists would ask permission to suggest that the Director of the Meteorological Service should be given the rank of a deputy head, as we are of the opinion that this would be beneficial to the service. We would also ask that the employment of outside influence for the benefit of any member of the service may be discouraged and that promotion may depend upon merit and seniority alone.

In conclusion we wish you God speed in the hard task you have undertaken and we beg to assure you that however little you may be able to improve our present condition we shall be extremely grateful to you for it.

Signed :

H. PAYNE,	A. J. O'CONNOR,	W. F. DAVISON,
FRANK L. BLAKE,	CHAS. ROSS,	W. A. BANNON,
JAS. YOUNG,	WM. CANE.	CHAS. E. TWEEDIE,
F. O'DONNELL,	F. F. PAYNE,	ROSS Mc'A. CAMERON,
		D. O'HALLORAN,

Name.	Rank.	Date of Appointment.	Length of Service.	Salary when Appointed.	Present Salary.	Average rate of Annual Increase.	Remarks.
			Years	$ cts.	$ cts.	$ cts.	
R. F. Stupart	Director	1872	35	180 00	3,000 00	80 57	
B. C. Webber	Assistant Director	1873	34	400 00	2,400 00	58 82	
F. F. Payne	Secretary	1877	30	350 00	1,350 00	33 12	
H. V. Payne	Clematologist	1875	32	390 00	1,454 00	33 33	
W. F. Davison	Observer and Computer	1853	50	400 00	1,550 00	23 00	
Wm. Menzies	Observer (Magnetic Observatory)	1870	37	425 00	1,370 00	25 54	Receives $180 additional for house rent.
James Young	Photographer	1874	33	400 00	1,300 00	27 27	
F. L. Blake	Astronomical Assistant.	1882	25	600 00	1,200 00	24 00	
W. A. Bannon	Librarian	1890	17	750 00	1,000 00	14 71	
D. O'Halloran	Telegraph Operator	1881	26	450 00	850 00	15 38	
Charles Ross	"	1893	14	480 00	925 00	32 17	
Charles E. Tweedie	Observer and Computer	1891	16	180 00	1,100 00	57 50	
Wm. D. Allan	Assistant Forecaster,&c.	1899	8	300 00	918 00	77 25	Receives $120 additional for night work.
Ross Mc. A. Cameron.	Computer	1887	20	150 00	750 00	30 00	
Harold A. Small	"	1889	18	144 00	750 00	33 67	
Frank O'Donnell	"	1900	7	400 00	750 00	50 00	"
W. E. W. Jackson	Assistant Forecaster,&c.	1904	3	600 00	650 00	16 66	"
A. J. Connor	Computer	1907	0	800 00	800 00		
Wm. Cane	Mechanical Assistant.	1887	20	704 23	900 00	9 79	
John Hurst	Caretaker	1897	10	400 00	750 00	35 00	

OTTAWA, May 30, 1907.

COLONEL EUGENE FISET, called and sworn and examined.

By the Chairman :

Q. You are the Deputy Minister of Militia and Defence ?—A. Yes, I am the Deputy Minister.

Q. How long have you occupied that position?—A. For the past four months.

Q. Previous to that time you were in charge of the Army Medical Corps ?—A. Yes.

Q. Director ?—A. Director General of Medical Services.

Q. Although you are Deputy Minister of Militia you were seconded ?—A. Yes.

Q. Lent to the department ?—A. Yes.

Q. You have not lost your army rank ?—A. No.

Q. You were in South Africa ?—A. Yes.

Q. And you received the D.S.O. for your services there ?—A. Yes.

Q. You saw active service there ?—A. Yes.

Q. And you have had some experience of warlike operations ?—A. Yes.

Q. What salary do you get as Deputy Minister ?—A. I am getting $3,500 now.

Q. That is during your first year as Deputy Minister ?—A. Yes.

Q. The salary rises to $4,000 ?—A. Yes.

Q. The report which I held in my hand is the report of the Militia Council ?—A. Yes.

Q. And this statement is a memorandum submitted by you ?—A. Yes. It is a memorandum of suggestions and proposals for your consideration, accompanied by a comparative statement respecting the pay in the higher appointments of the military and civil staff.

Q. In presenting the report of the Militia Council to the Governor General to be laid before Parliament the Minister of Militia and Defence says : 'The undersigned has the honour to present to Your Excellency the report of the Militia Council, such report being that of the Department of Militia and Defence ?—A. Well practically speaking it is.

Q. Has the Militia Council absorbed the Department of Militia or is the department a distinct entity?—A. The object of the creation of the Militia Council was to absorb the department, but in practice it is not the fact.

Q. But the law sanctioned that object ?—A. Yes.

Q. The defensive forces of the country are administered by a military Board and are not under the control of the civil authority ?—A. That is it. No, I beg your pardon. You must remember that by the constitution of the Militia Council the president is the Minister of Militia and the Vice President is his deputy.

Q. So there are two civil members besides the Accountant ?—A. Yes.

Q. And there are four military members ?—A. Yes.

Q. In point of numbers they outnumber you ?—A. Yes.

Q. Leaving that part of the subject for the present, you have chargeable to Civil Government a staff of 40 members?—A. Yes.

Q. In that list of 40 members you have five chief clerks, and nine first class clerks ?—A. Yes.

Q. Is that not an inordinate number of chief clerks and first class clerks to the total ?—A. We cannot help it. The administration of the Militia Department affects not only the civil branch but the military branch as well. One of these chief clerks at the present time has to administer part of the Adjutant Genreal's branch. Another chief clerk acts as Director of contracts and fills one of the most important positions in the Militia Department. His appointment is of a semi-military nature. Another of these chief clerks is the Accountant of the department.

Q. That is entirely Civil?—A. No it is not. The Accountant at the present time is Paymaster General as well? He is filling a semi-military position that could be filled by a military officer. If it was an officer who was filling the same position as the Accountant of the Militia Department he would be receiving $4,000 a year. Because, however, the Accountant is a Civil clerk he is given only $2,800 a year.

Q. As Paymaster he gets $1,200 additional, is that it?—A. No, not a cent.

Q. The reason I asked the question is as to the proportion of higher officials this: That in the Post Office Department with a staff of nearly 400 employees they have only ten chief clerks and seventeen first-class clerks?—A. That appears to be a piece of misadministration.

Q. Well, the work is done very effectively. The Department carries over 300,000,000 letters a year.—A. I know that, but still if you look at the distribution of our Department as it stands to-day I do not think you could do with a less number of chief clerks than we have there; it is impossible.

Q. You have increased the Civil Government staff in fifteen years from 30 to 40, I see?—A. Yes, it is all on account of the new creations.

Q. And the expenditure of the Department last year was $5,573,000?—A. Yes.

Q. The expenditure has gone up from about $2,000,000 to nearly $6,000,000 in fifteen years?—A. Yes, it has increased.

Q. It is continually increasing—A. Yes, but you must bear in mind that the increase has taken place more especially during the last two years since we have taken over Esquimalt and Halifax which cost us $2,500,000. That is the amount which it costs for the administration of the two stations.

Mr. FYSHE.—I hope Canadians are beginning to see how much England spent in Canada now.

By the Chairman:

Q. How many extra clerks have you got chargeable to Civil Government?—A. We have six.

Q. How is an extra clerk appointed, does the chief of one of the branches ask for a man or a woman?—A. I do not know what the practice was in the past but since I have taken charge of the department I have subdivided it into practically five different branches under a chief clerk and they are responsible for special details and a special part of the administration of the Department. Whenever a recommendation is made by the chief clerk if I consider the grounds good and sufficient I recommend it to the Minister and an Order-in-Council is passed.

Q. Pressure does not come from outside?—A. Sometimes it does more especially for the lower ranks.

Q. Do you have extra, or temporary, clerks appointed without your wanting them?—A. No, sir, not yet. I have refused them.

Q. But there has been pressure?—A. Yes, I have 17 on the list.

Q. And you have refused to appoint any more?—A. Every one of them.

By Mr. Fyshe:

Q. Have they been all strongly recommended?—A. Their applications are strongly supported.

Q. They have to pass the preliminary examination?—A. Oh, yes, every one of them has to. I have employed a few clerks since I have occupied my present position, such as lady typists and clerks who have all the qualifications needed. Not only are they required to pass the civil service examination, but a departmental examination as well. They must be able to write at least 120 words in shorthand and write on the typewriter at least 80 words. Not one clerk has been appointed to the Militia Department unless he or she has passed our own examination outside that of the civil service.

SESSIONAL PAPER No. 29a

Q. You do not have any objection to military examinations, I suppose?—A. This is only the civil list I am talking about.

By the Chairman

Q. Have you appointed nobody since you have been deputy minister?—A. Yes, I have appointed five temporary clerks, during the session especially.

Q. Are they continuously employed?—A. We had to get them because our staff was shorthanded and we were very badly handicapped, especially during the holding of the camps. Some of them may be discharged before the end of the year.

Q. And in addition to the civil service examination clerks appointed have to pass a departmental examination?—A. A most strict departmental examination and we choose the best independent of any recommendation.

Q. Are there many women appointed?—A. There was only one man appointed. The others, I think, were women.

Q. You cannot get men to enter, can you?—A. Yes, we can. We have lots of applications, but most of them have not got the qualifications we need.

By Mr. Fyshe:

Q. What is the minimum salary?—A. The minimum salary is $500.

Q. And these women suit your purpose?—A. Perfectly well, because we need typists more than anything else, and shorthand writers.

By the Chairman

Q. In the third-class junior clerks and seconds, are there any women?—A. Yes, there are two of them. One is in charge of the lady typists and supervises the whole of the work being done in that branch. Another one has been private secretary to the Minister for a very long time.

Q. It has not been necessary for you to appoint any of these extra clerks permanently?—A. No. We have had three permanencies given to junior clerks in accordance with the promotions carried out in the department. Those people had been in the department at least two years.

Q. Had they been reported on for efficiency?—A. Yes, and they passed the examination on duties also.

Q. Have you more employees in the Militia Department than are necessary?— A. No, I do not think so. I consider we have barely enough.

Q. Latterly a first-class clerk of over forty years' service was superannuated?—A. Yes.

Q. The department gave him about two days' notice?—A. Yes.

Mr. FYSHE—Did they discharge him?

The CHAIRMAN—No, they superannuated him.

The WITNESS—Do you mean that we did that?

By the Chairman:

Q. No, the department.—A. I beg your pardon. I will tell you how it happened. It is true the man to whom you refer was superannuated, but the recommendation went to the Minister three months before the man was notified that he had to go on the superannuation list. Unfortunately through a mistake of one of the clerks of the department the file, through going to the central registry, was pigeon-holed and the accountant was not notified. Hence there was a failure to notify the clerk concerned. When the session of Parliament was over and the money for this man's superannuation was voted he had to go, but it was decided to employ him for three months more on the extra list giving him the difference between his superannuation and the salary he formerly enjoyed in order to compensate him for what he had lost.

Q. That is to say——A. He got practically his three months' notice.

7-8 EDWARD VII., A. 1908

Q. That is to say it was arranged that this man who had been over forty years in the service should be superannuated?—A. Yes.

Q. But through some oversight the man himself was not told he was going to be superannuated?—A. That is the whole thing.

Q. And he did not know of it until it was practically accomplished?—A. Yes.

Q. And in order to give him some compensation, as a solatium, you had to employ him for three months at the difference between his former pay and the superannuation allowance?—A. That is it exactly.

Q. Could you not have given him the holiday?—A. He did get three months' holidays at practically full pay.

Q. But he had served for 40 years?—A. Yes.

Q. Do you think, after all is said and done, that giving a man with over 40 years' service three months' holidays at the end of his career was treating him generously?—A. Certainly not, but this was done before I took the position of Deputy Minister and happened through a mistake. He was given three months' leave of absence by the Minister, but by an oversight was not notified.

Q. This man had never had any bad habits?—A. Never.

By Mr. Fyshe :

Q. What was his name?—A. Aumond.

By the Chairman :

Q. Mr. Aumond did his work thoroughly well?—A. Thoroughly well.

Q. He was a faithful officer?—A. He could not be better.

Q. And yet that man after more than 40 years' service was turned out into a cold world.

Mr. FYSHE.—I call that brutal.

A. As explained, the incident happened through a mistake in not giving Mr. Aumond due notice.

By the Chairman :

Q. He was turned out into the cold world on seven-tenths of his salary and has since had to give up his house?—A. Yes ; it is pretty hard on a man, I agree with you there, but you must not forget that he had been notified three years in succession that he was to be superannuated.

Q. That may be?—A. That I am aware of.

By Mr. Fyshe :

Q. That only made it worse, hanging the sword of Damocles over his head?—A. There was pressure brought and it was decided to keep him on.

Mr. FYSHE.—You would not treat an old horse like that.

By the Chairman :

Q. Since this man's superannuation you have not lessened the number of first class clerks? You promoted a man in his place, I suppose?—A. Certainly. As a matter of fact, his successor was not promoted until three months afterwards.

Q. Do you think the fact that you employed Mr. Aumond temporarily would make up the difference?—A. Yes. It was the only thing that could be done to compensate him for not receiving due notice.

Q. His first-class clerkship was taken from him and you have promoted another man?—A. Yes, after the expiration of three months.

Q. Could you not have given Mr. Aumond that three months?—A. I would have done it, and I think the Minister would have done it also, but he was away in England. I think he would have given three months' leave without a moment's hesitation.

By Mr. Fyshe :

Q. Did this case come specially before the Minister ?—A. The Minister authorized three months leave of absence when he left, but through an oversight of one of the clerks in the Department Mr. Aumond was not notified of the fact three months in advance. When the time came the poor fellow was superannuated without sufficient notice. When I saw that I told the accountant, 'you will employ this man for three months longer. He will come to the department once a week and you can put him on the pay list.' Mr. Aumond did that and practically never did any work. That action was taken of my own accord.

By the Chairman :

Q. Have there been frequent promotions in the department among the staff chargeable to civil government ?—A. There have been frequent promotions, but none since I have been there with the exception of one clerk who replaced Mr. Aumond.

Q. Colonel Benoit, Director of Stores, was retired ?—A. Yes.

Q. And there was another Director of Stores appointed in his place ?—A. Yes. ,

Q. Was there a promotion examination on that occasion ?—A. The man appointed to succeed Colonel Benoit was a lawyer and a B.A. and was exempt from the promotion examination.

Q. Do you know whether examinations are held when promotions are made ?—A. In every case. I might say you will find very few cases of men who have been appointed from the outside without examination, especially to fill second and third-class clerkships.

Q. It is all the other way ?—A. Yes.

Q. Going from the inside to the outside ?—A. Yes, practically speaking.

Q. All these men in the several classes get their annual increment of $50 ?—A. Yes.

Q. You certify to these increments?—A. Yes.

Q. Is that done perfunctorily?—A. No, there is one case in which the increase has not been given this year because the clerk had not deserved it.

Q. What leave of absence do you give your officers ?—A. Three weeks per annum.

Q. Are you generous sometimes ?—A. I have caused to be promulgated an Order in Council lately, in accordance with the Civil Service Act which provides for a three weeks' holiday and fifteen days sick leave during the year. The rule has never been applied before but I have applied it ; I could not help doing so.

Q. You have an attendance book, I suppose ?—A. Yes.

Q. Do all the officers in the inside service sign it ?—A. Every one of them.

Q. What is your luncheon hour ?—A. From twelve to one in some cases and in others from one till two.

Q. Is the department ever empty altogether during working hours?—A. Never.

Q. There is somebody there to meet the public at all times ?—A. Yes.

Q. What are the officers' hours ?—A. That does not come under my jurisdiction.

Q. Well, in the civil branch ?—A. We start usually at half past nine—the chief clerks come at nine—and some leave again for luncheon at twelve and some at one, and then begin again at half-past two, and quit for the day at five. Sometimes during the session it is half-past five or six most of the time.

Q. You had some years ago, I know very valuable records in your department connected with the war of 1812 ?—A. Yes.

Q. Are those records still in the department do you know ?—A. As far as I am aware, part of them are in the department and part in the military library.

Q. Have any been transferred to the archives ?—A. I think so, but I am not sure.

Q. Then the archives are now in possession of the records relating to the war of 1812? and similar documents?—A. I could not specify in particular. In regard to the greater part of the documents I have made inquiries lately, and the information

I had from the library clerk was that nearly everything had been transferred to the archives.

By Mr. Fyshe :

Q. Are they contained in fire-proof vaults?—A. I do not know anything about the custody of papers in the archives.

By the Chairman :

Q. In the Militia Department maps of a strategical character are prepared ?—A. Yes.

Q. Would it not be desirable, as in England, where the preparation of maps is all done under the Ordnance Store Corps, that all the maps should be compiled in one place?—A. That is exactly what we are trying to do. The chief of staff met practically all the men in charge of the surveys of the different departments and an exhaustive report was submittted to the Minister in Council last year. I am afraid, however, that some of the men who have charge of mapping in other departments disagreed on the consolidation and I do not think we will arrive at any practical result for the present. It would, however, be the best thing that could happen.

Mr. FYSHE.—The only objection to that seems to me that the system will delay the completion of the maps.

THE CHAIRMAN.—They do not find that to be the case in England for that objection has been got rid of. The Ordnance Corps in the preparation of maps carry out the configurations of the country geologically, and place on the maps the postal routes, mile stones and all that kind of thing.

THE WITNESS.—The actual proposal is that a department of mapping should be formed here in the Canadian service and be divided into sub-branches—the military branch taking the military surveys—but all the reports should be congregated and be embodied in an annual report, submitted to the heads of these different branches through Canada. Then we will have a compilation of maps not only from the military point of view but for other purposes in Canada.

Q. Your officers are outside the departmental buildings on Parliament Hill?—A. Yes.

Q. They are all concentrated in the one block?—A. Yes, every one.

Q. What is the name of the building you occupy?—A. The Woods building.

Q. That is on Slater street?—A. Yes.

Q. You have no objection to Mr. Bazin and Mr. Fyshe going over the offices?—A. No, we will receive them with the greatest of pleasure.

Q. You know there is a Treasury Board minute of 1879 forbidding the use of political influence in the civil service?—A. Yes.

Q. Are your officers, as a rule, aware of that?—A. I think most of them are.

Q. Do you not think it would be desirable to promulgate it again?—A. Yes, I think it would be. It has already been done in my own department.

Q. I am still talking about your department. Are you suffering from the abolition of the Superannuation Act?—A. A great deal. As a matter of fact I do not believe in the present system. In regard to the classification of the chief clerks or the increases it does not seem to me that they are adapted to suit the needs of the service at all. The system is not elastic enough and is too restrictive in some ways. I have prepared a memorandum embodying my views on these questions.

Q. You will leave that memorandum with us?—A. Yes, I will leave it with you. In my opinion it is impossible to ensure any continuity in the work of the department unless the deputy minister or his representative is present at all meetings of the Militia Council—is thoroughly aware of all correspondence, data and facts brought forward and acts on these different proposals that come up in council, in perfect accordance with the views of the deputy head and this result will not be obtained unless an assistant deputy minister who would be at the same time secretary of the Militia

ouncil—is appointed. I do consider such an appointment as an absolute necessity.
would like also to call your attention to the fact that there are branches of the de-
irtment which are administered by technical officers. We have for example a direc-
r of contracts. He deals with all the contracts entered into by the inside military
id civil branches and the outside service which run up into large figures. He has to
udy the markets, obtain quotations and competitive prices, and he has the largest
ities to perform of any officer that I know of in my service.

By Mr. Fyshe:'

Q. What do you call that officer?—A. The director of contracts. Well, this offi-
ir is only paid $2,500 a year; he has reached the maximum of his class.

Q. What special training has he had, has he been in engineering work?—A. No,
ı is a lawyer and has been a bank accountant. He has been for nearly ten years in
ıe Militia Department and has made a special study of his duties. I have no hesita-
on in saying he is one of the best men we have.

By the Chairman:

Q. He was a bank accountant, was he not?—A. Yes, he was.

By Mr. Fyshe

Q. What is his name?—A. Mr. Brown. He has only had four years' experience as
rector of contracts, but nevertheless if you could see the change that has been ac-
ımplished since he first took the position, you would be surprised, although he has
ıen handicapped in a good many ways in the past.

Q. How old a man is he?—A. He is only 33 or 34.

Q. That is very young?—A. That is very young, but he has the ability.

Q. He has been a militia man, I suppose?—A. No, he was private secretary to Sir
rederick Borden.

Q. How did he get into the department?—A. He was private secretary, but he had
ade special study of the work he is now doing at that time.

Q. He came from Nova Scotia?—A. Yes.

By the Chairman:

Q. Do you know where he lived before he came to Ottawa?—A. He lived in Can-
ng, he was accountant of a bank there.

Q. Accountant of the Halifax bank?—A. Yes.

Q. Reverting again to the abolition of the superannuation system, as far as re-
ırds the civil service, you say you regard that as a mistake?—A. As a mistake, and
ore than that. I have a few suggestions to make. With respect to the classification
would classify and pay technical officers as such. Next would come the chief clerks
id first-class and second-class clerks; but the lower grades, I mean below second-
ass clerks down to messengers, should be treated only as temporary clerks. I am of
)inion that these employees should be enabled to leave the service at any time they
ke, and should only be considered as permanent employees when they had reached the
ınk of second-class clerk.

Q. That is practically coming to the English idea that there should be a per-
anent upper class and a large writer class.—A. That is it because otherwise you
ınnot get proficiency. I have been very carefully studying the whole of our admin-
tration, and there is no other conclusion I can arrive at but that.

By Mr. Fyshe:

Q. How about giving them a retiring allowance?—A. I would apply the Super-
ınuation System with a pension for the highest class.

Q. But what about the other classes?—A. Those people should be given the same
ivileges that are now enjoyed under the Retirement Act under which they are re-

29a—45

quired to pay five per cent to a Retirement Fund. Should they find that their promotion is too slow or that they cannot obtain the necessary qualifications to be promoted to second class clerks, or, if for any other reason they want to leave the service, I would give them back the money they have paid into the Retirement Fund plus interest; that would be so much to the good. On the other hand if they get to be promoted to second class clerks, they should be allowed to count the money they have paid into the Retirement Fund towards their Pension Fund, under the Superannuation System.

Q. Is this retirement allowance composed principally or wholly of the sums the officers themselves pay?—A. Practically speaking.

Q. And interest?—A. Interest at four per cent.

Q. That is simply playing at the thing?—A. It is of no use whatever. It does not afford any protection to the family and there is nothing in it.

Q. That is robbing a man and then returning the money and making a virtue of it?—A. If you want to make the Civil Service efficient no appointment should be made, except in the case of a technical officer or a Deputy Minister, or any appointment of that character requiring special qualifications at a larger salary than $500 a year. We could then bring young men in and train them for the special work we want them to do, or lend them to different branches of the service where they might become proficient. That is similar to the system adopted in the banks.

By the Chairman:

Q. When the Civil Service Commission sat in 1892, fifteen years ago, there were twelve military districts as now?—A. Except that now, there are four military commands.

Q. We will come to that later. Canada, like Great Britain is divided into military districts. The only difference since 1892 is that some of those districts have been grouped into commands?—A. Yes.

Q. There are four of these comamnds, are there not?—A. Yes.

Q. Two in Ontario, one in Quebec and one in the Maritime Provinces?—A. Yes.

Q. The military districts in western Canada have not yet come to a stage that they can be grouped in commands?—A. They have been formed into military districts now.

Q. They were in districts before?—A. I know, but they were not organized as districts. They have been organized only since the last two months.

Q. There is first the eastern Ontario command, comprising military districts Nos. 3 and 4?—A. Yes.

Q. In addition to the commandant there are what you call D.O.C.'s in each district?—A. Yes.

Q. The D.O.C. is the district officer commanding?—A. Yes.

Q. The Quebec command consists of three districts, Nos. 5, 6 and 7?—A. Yes.

Q. With three district officers commanding?—A. No, with two,—5 and 6 are grouped in one district.

Q. The Maritime Provinces command comprises districts Nos. 8, 9 and 12?—A. Yes.

Q. With three officers commanding?—A. Yes, one of them though is at the same time officer commanding command.

Q. Military district No. 10, consisting of the provinces of Manitoba, Alberta and Saskatchewan is not under a district officer commanding but under Col. Evans?—A. There was no district officer commanding formerly. He was the officer commanding the permanent force there and administering the district, but two months ago he was appointed district officer commanding. Col. Steele has been appointed district officer, commanding for Saskatchewan.

Q. Then there is Military District No. 11?—A. Yes.

Q. Comprising British Columbia and the Yukon Territory?—A. There is only one command there and it is under the charge of Col. Holmes.

Q. In 1892 you had, as now, the cartridge factory at Quebec ?—A. Yes. Except that we employed then 50 hands at the factory and we are now employing nearly 500.

Q. You had then, as now, infantry schools at London and Toronto ?—A. Just the same as there are now.

Q. And schools at St. Johns, Que., and Fredericton ?—A. Yes.

Q. Are there any more infantry schools now ?—A. Yes, at Halifax, Winnipeg and Esquimalt.

Q. You had then a cavalry school at Quebec ?—A. Yes.

Q. Is there another cavalry school now ?—A. No, the cavalry school is now at St. Johns, P.Q.

Q. You then had mounted infantry school at Winnipeg ?—A. It is the same now.

Q. And you had ' C ' Battery at Victoria ?—A. The designation of artillery units has been altered lately and I think we have only garrison artillery now at Esquimalt.

Q. You had a Royal Military College in 1892 as now ?—A. Yes.

Q. Then excepting the accretion of men in the cartridge factory, and adding another school or two, there has been no extension of the militia force ?—A. Oh, yes, you must remember that we have added schools at Halifax and Esquimalt and at Ottawa, and additions have been made at Quebec, and the schools have been doubled practically speaking all over the country in order to supply the needs of the militia.

Q. Fifteen years ago you gave the militia twelve days' training ?—A. Yes.

Q. And to-day you train the militia for twelve days ?—A. Yes.

Q. According to the last annual reports, there were something under 40,000 men drilled last year ?—A. Trained.

Q. In the twelve days ?—A. Yes, but I think that is not counting the city regiments.

Q. But the city regiments at that time underwent the same training that they do now ?—A. The number of days training is the same, except that the manner of trainings is different. They train at headquarters instead of training in camp.

Q. That may be. In addition you have established a kind of Aldershot at Petewawa ?—A. Yes.

Q. Has anything else been established ?—A. In addition at each camp we have practically a school of training for every branch of the service, where officers can qualify. That increases a good deal the proportion of officers going to camp, and of course also increases our appropriation as far as drill purposes is concerned during the year. Then there has been a school of musketry formed at Rockcliffe close to Ottawa which has added a great deal to our expenditure. At that school there are on an average from 50 to 100 officers and non-commissioned officers trained for three months. Then Petewawa, this will be the first year we have had a concentration training camp for the whole of the militia.

By Mr. Fyshe:

Q. And for artillery as well ?—A. Yes, sir, every branch of the service and will have over 1,200 of the permanent force there at the same time.

Q. Can you accommodate them all ?—A. We can accommodate 10,000 men there.

Q. I mean as to the needs of the commissariat ?—A. We have the commissariat organized and buildings and everything else ready for them.

Q. It will be expensive, will it not ?—A. No, all the buildings are up at a cost of about $50,000. We have erected some fifty huts, which includes recreation rooms and everything else.

By the Chairman:

Q. In addition to the camp at Petewawa you have still the district camps ?—A. Yes, but you must remember the camps are held now every year, whereas in the year you mention they were only held every three years, and the troops of two or three dis-

29a—45½

tricts grouped together, in the one camp instead of having the one camp for each district.

Q. No two camps now held at the same time ?—A. No.

Q. Is that to enable the inspector general to visit each camp separately ?—A. Not only the inspector general but each officer in charge of a special service, like the Army Medical Corps service, the artillery, and so on.

By Mr. Fyshe:

Q. You still have at the head of the service a British military man of some distinction, I suppose ?—A. Yes, the chief of the general staff.

By the Chairman:

Q. Has anything else been established during the fifteen years besides what you have recounted ?—A. Guns have been bought, forts are being built.

Q. In 1892 the military staff consisted of one major-general commanding the militia, one adjutant-general, one inspector of artillery, an A.D.C., and a clerk ?—A. Let me tell you also that in those days, if you want to probe the matter thoroughly, there was no Ordnance Corps, there was no Army Service Corps, there was no Army Medical Corps, no pay corps, but few units of artillery and infantry. Practically speaking, we had units of a permanent force of 800 men scattered all over the country which could be administered just as well by a colonel as a general.

By Mr. Fyshe:

Q. They were unorganized ?—A. They were organized, but we had few of them.

By the Chairman:

Q. But you had batteries of artillery ?—A. Yes, a few of them.

Q. The Militia Council is composed of the President, who is Minister of Militia ? —A. Yes, the Minister of Militia.

Q. And the vice-president is yourself ?—A. Yes.

Q. Then there is the chief of the general staff ?—A. Who is General Lake.

Q. His office, in a sense, resembles the former major-general commanding ?—A. No, sir. The chief of the general staff is responsible for the actual training of the militia and the permanent force. He gives the syllabus for the training, and he tells us how to carry on that training. He is the officer advising the department for the training of the militia. But the officer that reports on the actual training of the troops is the inspector general.

Q. Is the chief of the general staff simply an advisory officer ?—A. He is a member of the Militia Council, and advises the council on questions of training and organization. Training means the organization of every branch of the service, and he is the head of all the branches in that respect.

Q. He makes suggestions to you in his advisory capacity ?—A. Yes.

Q. Does he suggest the purchase of the field artillery ?—A. In concurrence with the master general of ordnance, yes. For every branch of the service there is an officer responsible at headquarters. There is a master general of ordnance responsible for the artillery, an adjutant general responsible for the infantry, and a quartermaster general who recommends the clothing for the troops.

Q. Take the first military member ? what are his duties besides those of an advisory character ? Is he the fountain head and beginning of things in the Militia Council ?—A. Not necessarily. Each member is independent and responsible for his own branch. The duty of the chief of the general staff, when a proposal has been brought to Council is to advise the Minister or the Council.

Q. He is paid a salary of $6,000 a year ?—A. Yes.

Q. The other members of the Militia Council are paid $4,000 ?—A. Yes, $4,000.

Q. Why is he paid half as much again if he is only an advisory officer ?—A. Well,

SESSIONAL PAPER No. 29a

it is on his advice that the whole militia force is run. He ranks as a General and is receiving the same sum that he would receive in England less perhaps $1,000.

Q. He was appointed for a certain number of years ?—A. Yes, for four years.

Q. He is the link between the Canadian militia and the defences of the Empire ? —A. He is not supposed to be.

Q. But he comes from the War office ?—A. He was seconded for duty from the Imperial service.

Q. He has been lent by the War Office for four years ?—A. Yes.

Q. And in the ordinary course of events, judging from the past, he will be succeeded by another man from the War Office ?—A. I do not think so.

Q. The whole of his training has been in the Imperial service ?—A. Altogether.

By Mr. Bazin :.

Q. What is the officer's name ?—A. General Lake.

By the Chairman :

Q. To assist the chief of the general staff you have a director of operations and staff duties?—A. Yes.

Q. And an assistant director of surveys ?—A. Yes.

Q. And three staff lieutenants ?—A. Yes, but you must remember that that statement is rather crude as it stands. These officers are all performing special and difficult duties, and I may add that all these officers are qualified for their respective positions. Of course this staff constitutes a skeleton for the organization of the Canadian militia in accordance with the home staff organization.

Q. That is just what I was coming at. These men represent English ideas and English training ?—A. Yes, in so far as they are applicable to the Canadian militia.

Q. And the chief of staff is carrying out the organization in the English way ?— A. Certainly, so it should be as far as practicable.

Q. I do not talk of course as an expert ?—A. You cannot expect the chief of the general staff with the numerous requests made of him every day of the year from so many branches of the service to be without assistance. In addition to being an eminent officer of the department and the responsible member of the Militia Council, he is the man who advises his colleagues on the Council, and, in fact, is the spirit of that body. The Director of Operations and Staff Duties is a practical staff college man who works out the details for the Chief of the Staff to submit to Council. Then there is the Assistant Director of Intelligence, that is a separate branch altogether. He is a junior officer, but is technically qualified.

Q. In addition to the Chief of the General Staff, who is an officer of the Imperial forces, there is the Director of Operations and Staff Duties, who is an Imperial officer also ?—A. He is also, but his assistant is a Canadian.

Q. The second military member of the Militia Council is the Adjutant General ? —A. Yes.

Q. That officer was lately made Inspector General ?—A. Yes, within the last two or three months.

Q. He is assisted by a Deputy Adjutant General ?—A. Yes.

Q. There is also an Assistant Adjutant General for Musketry ?—A. Yes.

Q. And an assistant Deputy Adjutant General ?—A. Yes.

Q. And a Director General of Medical Stores ?—A. Of Medical Services. He is under the Adjutant General only for gradation. The Adjutant General represents on the Militia Council all the different branches of the above mentioned services.

Q. There is in the Militia Department an officer specially employed ?—A. That is Colonel Smith. He is President of the Pension Board and President of the Claims Board.

Q. What are the duties of the Adjutant General ?—A. He has the most responsible position in the whole department. I mean to say everything goes to the

Adjutant General. He is in charge of the whole discipline of the Force from one end of Canada to the other.

By Mr. Fyshe:

Q. What is the name of the present Adjutant General?—A. Col. Lessard.

By Mr. Bazin:

Q. He is a good man from Quebec?—A. Yes, a very good man.

By the Chairman:

Q. There are four military members out of the seven composing the Militia Council and the third is Col. Macdonald, the Quartermaster General?—A. He is in charge of the stores of Canada from one end of Canada to the other.

Q. That is to say saddles, clothing and such like?—A. Saddles, clothing, blankets, uniforms, rifles, guns and everything of that kind.

Q. Has he got charge of the field artillery?—A. Yes.

Q. Everything goes to him as a matter of stores?—A. Yes.

Q. He has to assist him a director of clothing and equipment?—A. Yes.

Q. And a director of transport and supplies?—A. That is it exactly. There are two different branches. The director of transport and supplies is in charge of the railway and transport. He is under the branch of the quartermaster general, who represents him before the Militia Council.

Q. And the quartermaster general has charge of all stores?—A. All stores.

Q. Including great guns?—A. Yes, everything.

Q. An inventory is kept of all these stores?—A. Yes.

Q. How much do you spend on stores now?—A. We spend this year $400,000.

Q. Does that include the capital account?—A. No, it does not.

Q. You have a capital account for powder and shot?—A. The capital account is a special vote which we got four years ago for the buying of heavy ordnance.

Q. That amounted to $1,300,000?—A. Yes. That capital account was for other purposes besides the purchase of stores.

Q. It will cease in a year or two?—A. Yes.

Q. Your normal purchases amount, for stores, to about $500,000?—A. About that. That is only for a limited period of time. It will not always be that way.

Q. That is the present current expenditure on stores?—A. Yes.

Q. And there is an extraordinary expenditure, which will end in a year or two, amounting to $1,300,000?—A. Not for stores only. That capital account provides for the construction of rifle ranges and there is about $390,000 a year coming out of capital account for the payment of small arms and heavy ordnance and ammunition. The vote ceases in 1908 and we will not need it after that.

By Mr. Bazin:

Q. The vote of $1,300,000 a year on capital account was for what purpose?—A. To create a reserve of stores, to build rifle ranges, to purchase land more especially at the Petewawa concentration camp and to pay for purchases of the small arms and heavy ordnance.

By the Chairman:

Q. Do you keep an inventory of the stores?—A. Yes.

Q. Do you know, roughly, the value of the stores held in stock by the department throughout the country?—A. Do you mean the whole?

Q. Yes?—A. No, I cannot say.

Q. Since you became deputy minister, you have caused an inventory of the stores to be made?—A. Yes, a general inventory of the stores from one end of Canada to the other.

Q. How often do you endeavour to have an inventory made?—A. The inventory in future will be continuous.

By Mr. Fyshe:

Q. That is every year?—A. Yes. At every local store there is a ledger where stock issues and receipts are entered and compared at the end of each month. An abstract showing issues and receipts is sent to the headquarters monthly and there is a general inventory of each of the local stores made every year.

Q. That also should be checked?—A. That is checked here at headquarters.

Q. I mean there should be a special inspection?—A. There is a local special inspection. There is a board that inspects and checks off stores every year, and then at the end of every five years we will have a general stocktaking made all over Canada, in order to balance the account. It costs us to have such an inspection of stores made from $10,000 to $15,000. It has cost this year over $10,000, but I think it is worth while.

Q. I think it is worth it?—A. It is certainly worth the money.

By the Chairman:

Q. What do you mean by a Board of Inspection?—A. The board is composed of three officers detailed by the officer commanding the garrison, independent officers not belonging to the stores. They go around and inspect the stores.

By Mr. Fyshe:

Q. They are an inspecting board?—A. Really a stocktaking board.

By the Chairman:

Q. That is equivalent to an audit of stores?—A. Yes.

By Mr. Bazin:

Q. I suppose that inspection is also made as to the quality of the article?—A. Yes, certainly.

Q. As to the quality of uniforms for any stores?—A. Yes.

Q. To see if the quality is there?—A. To see if the quality is there, and that the stores are good. If the stores are condemned by the board they are burned, or sold at auction.

By the Chairman:

Q. These boards are composed of officers of the militia?—A. Yes, of officers of the militia.

Q. They are not members of the permanent corps?—A. Some of them are, but most of them are not.

By Mr. Fyshe:

Q. Are the stores kept in such a way that each article is placed in a separate compartment, and when account is taken everything delivered on special order can be deducted from the balance of the total on hand?—A. Yes.

Q. So on inspection the total shows that the books agree exactly with what is in store?—A. The system adopted is as follows: There is a tally board outside each cupboard, each box and each room. Then there is a general tally board on each floor enumerating the stores contained in the boxes, rooms or cupboards, and showing the issues and receipts. An inventory of the books shows exactly the same qualities as are contained on the tally board of the issues and receipts. At the end of each month a report showing the issues and receipts of stores is forwarded from each local store to headquarters. The contents are entered in the ledger kept in the Audit Branch of the Militia Department. In regard to the purchase of stores a system of requisitions has been adopted. The requisition comes from the officer responsible for the purchase of stores. It comes to the Deputy Minister for approval, who approves or refuses it. If approved, it then goes to the audit branch of the accountant's office, and the accountant gives it an audit number, which is checked against the appropriation, and the

7-8 EDWARD VII., A. 1908

requisition is then returned to the officer returned. The authority for that payment is the approval of the Deputy Minister and the audit number marked on the requisition by the accountant.

Q. The goods are bought and stored and charged up in the year?—A. Charged up against each allotted appropriation for the different services authorized for the year.

By the Chairman:

Q. You say the stores go into the warehouse and are checked by boards at stated periods?—A. Yes.

Q. And the quality is also checked?—A. Yes.

Q. What check is there at the beginning that the quality of the stores is good? —A. When the goods are delivered into the store they go into the inspection room at the Militia Department. We have qualified inspectors for each branch of the service who are there all the year around examining these goods and seeing that they are according to the pattern submitted, both for quality and material. All goods have to pass inspection and some are rejected and some accepted. Those goods that are accepted by the inspectors are brought into the stores and counted by the officer in charge and allotted to each special cupboard, box and room, and entered both in the ledger and on tally boards. Every month the receipts of stores and the issues made are kept track of, and then at the end of the month his report, which is based on the tally boards, and his books, is sent to headquarters, where it is tabulated. Then once a year this officer compares his tally boards with his ledger and books and takes a general inventory of his stock.

By Mr. Fyshe:

Q. That system is almost perfect ?—A. Not perfect, but certainly good.

By the Chairman :

Q. Has the Auditor General any check in any way ?—A. If the Auditor General comes down to the department our system is such, that I could show him at any moment what stores there are and what has been expended every day of the year.

Q. And the balance you have on hand ?—A. Everything. You must remember that outside of what we call the actual stores, there are also stores in charge of each unit, like batteries of artillery and companies of infantry.

By Mr. Fyshe :

Q. The same principle is applied to them ?—A. Yes, in exactly the same way.

By the Chairman :

Q. You were saying just now that when stores are wanted requisitions are made ?— A. Yes.

Q. Those requisitions are made to the Director General of Stores I suppose ?— A. Not if it is a requisition for expenditure. There are two kinds of requisitions.

Q. I mean for stores ?—A. The requisition comes from the officer commanding the unit.

Q. The stores are under the control of the Director General of Stores. We are keeping still to the directors?—A. The requisition from the officer that wants the article goes to the officer commanding the district who approves of it and passes it on to the officer in command of the ordnance stores at local headquarters.

Q. In 1892, when Col. Panet was examined, he was asked a question like this : 'Supposing Tommy Atkins of a militia regiment has his cap blown off and it went into the river. How is he to get a new cap ?'—A. Yes.

Q. Col. Panet said that the man had to go to the captain of his company and state what he wanted. Then the captain made a requisition and it was sent in to the deputy Adjutant General who forwarded it to the Adjutant General and that officer either recommended or refused the recommendation. If approved the requisition went from the Adjutant General to the Director of Stores and from the Director of Stores to the Deputy Minister of Militia, and then from there in succession to the Adjutant General, to the Deputy Adjutant General to the Colonel of the regiment, and then to the captain, and then the private would get the needed article. Is that system of requisition still going on?—A. Not exactly. You must remember one thing, this is in peace time, and the militia are in training for only 12 days. On active service there is always a certain amount of spare clothing allotted to every regiment, and that clothing accompanies the troops on the march. In the 12 days' drill it is different ; there are in camp, quartermasters in charge of district stores, and the requisition comes straight from the quartermaster of the regiment.

By Mr. Fyshe :

Q. You have temporary stores there?—A. Certainly permanent stores in each district.

By the Chairman :

Q. You have done away with all the former red tape ?—A. As far as possible.

Q. When you talk of requisitions, I want to know whether the same system exists as far as expenditure is concerned?—A. No. I may tell you that if a requisition for an expenditure entailing $25 or $30 comes from the D.O.C. to me, I have to approve of it finally. If we allowed people to incur expenditure indiscriminately we would expend money quickly.

Q. There is also another military member of the Militia Council called the master general of the ordnance?—A. He is responsible for the whole of the artillery.

Q. To assist him he has a director of artillery?—A. Yes.

By Mr. Fyshe:

Q. What is the name of the master general of ordnance?—A. Colonel Cotton.

By the Chairman:

Q. There is also a director of engineering services?—A. Yes.

Q. And you have also at headquarters, Colonel Rivers?—A. Yes, he is specially employed.

Q. At Quebec there is an inspector of small arms?—A. Yes. The master general of ordnance is not only responsible for the whole artillery but also of the engineering service. He is also responsible for the administration of the cartridge factory at Quebec, and for the administration of the Ross rifle factory as far as inspection is concerned.

Q. Everything relating to engineers, artillery, field guns or rifles?—A. He is in charge of everything except the expenditure.

Q. Supposing the master general of ordnance said that 15,000 rifles were required? —A. He would bring the matter before the Militia Council.

Q. Then the chief of the general staff would advise on that, would he?—A. He might.

Q. But I thought he had to, that he was the advisory officer?—A. If he considers the thing is right, he will support it, but it rests with the Minister finally to approve of it.

Q. If the four military members of the Militia Council supported an order for 60,000 rifles, 100,000 saddles, or 500,000 tunics, that order would still be under the control of the Minister and yourself?—A. Certainly.

Q. Before it could be carried out?—A. Certainly.

Q. Then you have more control than appeared at first?—A. The Minister has the full control of the whole department, more especially with regard to expenditures; the members of the Militia Council are only his advisers.

Q. In addition to the four military members of the Militia Council there are

three civil members—the minister, yourself, and the accountant of the department?
—A. Yes, the accountant of the department is filling a semi-military position. He is
accountant and paymaster general at the same time. Since 1906 a Pay Corps has
been organized, and one pay officer appointed for each command. When the appropriations are voted by parliament, officers commanding districts are informed that they
are entitled to such and such appropriation. They have not got the right to make
that expenditure, but they recommend expenditures within their appropriations.

Q. And the accountant at headquarters is called paymaster?—A. No, paymaster
general.

Q. Not paymaster general of militia, that would imply by name, at all events,
that he was the general paymaster of all the services in Canada?—A. No, accountant
and paymaster general for the Canadian militia.

Q. Before 1892 there were paymasters in the service?—A. Yes. The paymasters
at that time were regimental paymasters.

Q. There were also district paymasters then?—A. Yes.

Q. Colonel Herbert came before the commission in 1892, and in answer to a
question respecting district paymasters said: 'I confess I do not see the object of
having district paymasters in these days, when the transmission of money can be so
easily made by means of a cheque. I see no reason why a cheque should not be sent
directly from the deputy minister to the person who requires it, without the intermediary of a third person.' The system of district paymasters was accordingly abolished?—A. Yes.

Q. It is now reinstated?—A. Oh, no.

Q. Wait a minute. It has only been reinstated within the last twelve months?—
A. Yes.

Q. Before that time demands from the several districts came to the department
for so much expenditure, and the cheques were made out?—A. Yes. The accounts
came to headquarters and the cheque issued from Ottawa.

By Mr. Fyshe:

Q. Was the account audited before the money was paid?—A. Yes.

By the Chairman:

Q. Every account for expenditure incurred came to Ottawa in detail and the payments were made from here?—A. Yes.

By the Chairman:

Q. Perhaps the details still come to you?—A. No.

Q. Instead of the details of expenditure coming to you, you grant this man $3,000
and that man $5,000, and so on all over the country. You give little dabs of cash
everywhere. How many district paymasters have you got?—A. There are eleven.

Q. And the district paymasters also give dabs of money to the several people outside?—A. The pay officer issues all cheques as payment of accounts that before this
date had to be audited and paid for at headquarters, which are now handled and
settled at local headquarters. We have appointed an officer of the permanent corps to
each of the commands as pay officer. He deals not only with the permanent force,
but with the whole of the acting militia. Before this the Deputy Minister of Militia
and Defence had on the average between two hundred and three hundred cheques to
sign every day, and he could not possibly do that and keep up with his other work.

By the Chairman:

Q. I know the deputy minister could not do it, but the clerks in the department
might?—A. But he would not have had the same control.

By Mr. Fyshe:

Q. The thing is to pay the money to the people to whom it is due. You do not save money by shipping it to somebody else?—A. Yes, I know. But there is another thing to be borne in mind. When you have a district paymaster who knows everything about all allowances in lieu of clothing, detailed authorized expenditure, &c., it saves numerous inquiries being made at headquarters and any amount of correspondence respecting technical details that we have to answer and be responsible for. The paymaster is now responsible and he advises the militia in his own district. He advises the officers commanding the district in all financial matters, and in some ways the department has already saved money by it.

Q. Could he not do all that without handling money?—A. He does not in reality handle the money; but outside of his other duties makes payments.

By the Chairman:

Q. The department at Ottawa limits the sum?—A. Yes.

Q. That is what you call handling the money?—A. We cannot help that. That is only a small part of his duty. His usefulness comes in in advising the officer commanding regarding what scale of pay, what scale of expenditure, or what scale of allowances is authorized. It is in this way that this officer's services are valuable.

Mr. FYSHE.—He·can do that without handling a dollar.

By the Chairman:

Q. The accountant of the department, whom you also call Paymaster General, gives this money to the District Paymaster?—A. Yes.

Q. In order to assist him to give this money to the District Paymasters, there is an assistant paymaster here? Col. Ward?—A. Yes.

Q. What does he do?—A. Col. Ward purely and simply administers the Army Pay Corps. He is, practically speaking, the Officer Commanding the Army Pay Corps. The accountant is in charge of the financial matters that come before the department—he is the minister's financial adviser.

Q. We will come to it in another way?—A. And I may tell you another thing; this pay corps is also following exactly and closely on the organization of the imperial service. You cannot help that either.

By Mr. Fyshe:

Q. You should not follow unless you are quite sure you cannot do it better?—A. It is a good system.

By the Chairman:

Q. According to the report of the Militia Council, you control about 40,000 militia?—A. Yes, sir, the active militia.

Q. Who drill 12 days a year?—A. Yes, 12 days a year.

Q. You have about 500 people employed in the cartridge factory?—A. Yes.

Q. You have to carry on all this work by means of a Militia Council, which is partly composed of directors of various services, and according to the Militia List there is a gradation class of about 240 officers?—A. Yes, about that number.

Q. That is to say you have about 240 officers to administer the militia of the country?—A. Yes, permanent force and active militia.

Q. It is boasted by the department, I believe, that the expenditure for defence purposes is only about four shillings per head?—A. It is rather a small sum.

Q. And we pride ourselves on having such a system that it is infinitely cheaper than the armies of Europe. Perhaps four shillings per head might, under circumstances, be extremely dear?—A. I do not think so. I do not think we can do it for less as far as the administration is concerned.

Q. Have you not now a permanent corps and a headquarter staff that would suffice for at least 100,000 men?—A. Yes.

7-8 EDWARD VII., A. 1908

By Mr. Fyshe:

Q. Your organization is capable of handling what number?—A. Of handling 100,000 men.

Q. And the force only numbers 40,000 men?—A. You might say 50,000. I think it will be 50,000 this year.

Q. Is it because this is an irreducible minimum?—A. No, but we have to train officers for special service. The staffs that have been organized will give the results when action is necessary.

Q. The organization you have is practically the minimum organization?—A. Yes.

By the Chairman:

Q. I suppose with economical administration—I am not saying anything against the administration—all this paraphernalia and the headquarters staff and the gradation list might do for 250,000 men?—A. It might do for 100,000 men.

By Mr. Fyshe:

Q. I should think half a dozen clerks would pay all the armies in the world?—A. You forget that they are scattered a good deal all over the country. There are eleven altogether.

By the Chairman:

Q. What do they do?—A. They handle the pay-lists in each district and they pay the whole of the militia during the camp. They replace the paymasters that we formerly had in camp. Then they act as paymasters and financial advisers all the year around for all expenditure connected with the commands. Furthermore they give instructions to the different paymasters of each regiment during the camp. It is not only the question of handling the cheques but they teach the regimental paymasters how to prepare their pay sheets, &c.

By Mr. Fyshe:

Q. How often do they pay the men?—A. They pay the men at the end of the camp.

Q. In camp is it permissible for a soldier to go to his paymaster and say 'I want $5'?—A. Oh, no, he cannot do that. There is just the one cheque issued.

Q. Then why could not these cheques be issued from the head offices?—A. The head office could not issue cheques for a camp.

By the Chairman:

Q. If there are 5,000 men in training for twelve days, they want to be paid before they go home?—A. Yes, right on the spot. The regimental paymasters have to be instructed how to prepare their pay-lists and how much each man is entitled to; they do not know it.

By Mr. Fyshe:

Q. What training do they want?—A. They have to be shown what is to be done. You must remember that against each man's services is checked the worth of the uniform he has received. These officers are not only paymasters but accountants at the same time.

By the Chairman:

Q. I want to ask you about the Canadian Army Pay Corps. I see by your description that there are accountants engaged in instructional work. I see from the Militia list that you have graded them in a military way. There are two majors and six captains?—A. Four majors and seven captains.

Q. Is the uniform arranged yet?—A. Yes.

Q. I see they have not got the colour of the uniform or the colour of the facings in the Militia List. When did this corps spring into existence?—A. I think it was a year ago.

Q. They were only gazetted in January, 1907?—A. They were established last year and placed in the Militia List in January.

Q. This corps has not been created for the purpose of giving eight men rank or status or additional salary?—A. No, sir.

Q. Are the Army Pay Corps accountants?—A. They have all been trained in the Accountant's Branch.

Q. They are engaged in instructional work?—A. Yes.

Q. If they are engaged in instructional work they must be qualified auditors?—A. They are.

By Mr. Fyshe:

Q. The members of the Army Pay Corps, you say, are qualified as accountants? —A. Yes.

Q. Had they experience before they joined?—A. Yes, they had to pass army examinations. One of those officers had qualified in the Army Pay Corps in England.

Q. How many are there?—A. There will be 11 when the corps is completed.

By the Chairman:

Q. Now we come to another thing. In addition to this headquarters staff and the gradation list of 240 persons, which includes the headquarters staff, there are warrant officers?—A. Yes, but the rank of warrant officer is purely honorary. It is given to non-commissioned officers who have been in the army for a number of years.

By Mr. Fyshe:

Q. What are they?—A. The warrant officer is a non-commissioned officer with a warrant. He is the highest grade among the non-commissioned officers.

By the Chairman:

Q. Some of these people have consolidated pay, that is pay with allowances?— A. Yes.

Q. The allowances, I presume, are in lieu of barrack accommodation?—A. Yes.

Q. The fundamental idea is that they are more like officials?—A. Yes.

Q. The Militia Pension Act is applicable to all these people?—A. Yes.

Q. All these warriors have pensions when they go out of the service?—A. They have pensions after they have served fifteen years for the men, and twenty years for the officers.

Q. In addition, if any of these officers die the widows become entitled to pensions? —A. If the officer has served twenty years.

By Mr. Fyshe:

Q. What amount of pension is given?—A. There is a stated scale. For lieutenant colonel it is $500, for majors, $400; for captains, $300, and for lieutenants, $200.

Q. Is that for the widow?—A. That is for the widows.

By the Chairman:

Q. Then if they leave daughters after a certain period of service they also receive a pension?—A. They receive a pension up to the age of 21.

Q. Then the fundamental idea is that if these people went to war they would get pensions for themselves and for their widows and daughters?—A. Yes.

Q. Take one of these officers enjoying pay and allowances, would his pension abatement be on the full pay or only on the pay itself?—A. Five per cent on his pay.

Q. Not on the allowances?—A. No.

7-8 EDWARD VII., A. 1908

By Mr. Fyshe:

Q. You mean that he contributes that toward the pension fund?—A. To the pension fund.

By the Chairman:

Q. But the pension is to be for himself, or his wife and his daughters?—A. Remember that in the Imperial service the officers get exactly the same pension without paying a cent towards it.

Q. And in the Imperial service the civil servants do not pay a cent towards their superannuation?—A. That is what should be done here.

Q. Those officers receiving $4,000 get $3,200 as pay?—A. $3,200 pay.

Q. And $800 as allowance?—A. $500 as allowance.

. Then they pay towards their pension on the $3,200 only?—A. Yes.

. If they go out the pensions are based on the $4,000?—A. Yes.

Q. General Aylmer had $6,000?—A. Yes.

Q. Did he pay on the whole $6,000?—A. No, sir. For the last two years he paid on a basis of $4,200. As to that, however, I am not quite sure.

Q. And $1,800 was the allowance?—A. I think there was only $1,200 allowance.

Q. When he retired the other day he had a retiring allowance of $4,200?—A. Yes.

Q. Based on the whole $6,000?—A. Yes.

Q. Nobody has ever got such an allowance in any other branch of the service?—A. No.

Q. This Pension Act has been placed on the Statute book since the Superannuation Act was abolished?—A. Yes.

Q. In the beginning of your examination you stated that you were formerly the head of the Army Medical corps?—A. Yes.

Q. And you were seconded?—A. Yes, in order to become deputy minister.

Q. Was that not in order that you should not lose your pension?—A. Certainly. There had to be a special Act of Parliament passed in order to permit of paying me a pension. I have paid for five years into the pension fund and by the transfer to a deputy ministership I would otherwise have lost the whole of the money so paid because I was not entitled to receive a pension upon being transferred to the civil service.

Q. It has been stated over and over again that the permanent corps amounts to 2,300?—A. There are 2,800.

Q. You find it very difficult to get men to join the permanent corps?—A. Yes.

Q. The average Canadian won't do the soldiering?—A. No, not at the salary.

Q. The average Canadian with his love of freedom and outdoor life won't become a soldier and do drill and look after stables?—A. At certain seasons of the year they would but not all the year around. When there is no work to be done anywhere else they will come to us with great pleasure.

By Mr. Fyshe :

Q. Are you much troubled in the service with desertions?—A. Yes, sir, a good deal.

By the Chairman :

Q. You have not been able to recruit the force up to its authorized strength of 5,000 and have latterly had to get time-expired men from England?—A. Yes, that was its strength to begin with, but we have cut it down to 3,000.

Q. And not being able to recruit up to 3,000 in Canada, you have enlisted time-expired men in England?—A. Yes.

Q. That has only been done latterly?—A. Yes, we got 300 men lately.

Q. From what regiment?—A. I think the most of them belonged to the Inniskillings, but I am not sure.

Q. The authorities in England held out every inducement to men to join the army, and can hardly get them ?—A. In some cases they do and in others they do not.

Q. Do you mean to say you have got the best ?—A. We got the pick.

Q. How is that ?—A. Because we sent an officer to England to recruit, who knew his business. I think we have the best of the lot. Most of the men we have enlisted are technically qualified.

Q. You think they are good men?—A. They are good. We have not had a single desertion yet, and they have been nearly two months in the country. We sent an officer to England, who had been a major in the same regiment. Probably that is one of the reasons why those men came over for three years.

Q. They will remain in the force for how long ?—A. They will remain for the three years they have sworn for.

By Mr. Bazin :

Q. Was the pay any inducement ?—A. No, it is not any inducement for them.

Q. Is the pay higher here for soldiers than in England ?—A. It is 25 cents higher than in England, but our allowances are not as good ; we cannot afford it.

By Mr. Fyshe :

Q. What is the age of these men?—A. It varies between 30 and 40 years.

By the Chairman :

Q. After they do their drill and employment in the stables, how do they pass their time?—A. There are lectures in the afternoon. They have to perform their drill and other obligatory duties, and about three or four o'clock in the afternoon they have their recreation.

Q. At Petewawa, what sort of amusement is there for the men ?—A. They have there the loveliest bathing place a man could dream of, and there is baseball and all kinds of amusements. There are lovely spots to visit, and good fishing.

By Mr. Bazin:

Q. Is it far from here?—A. It is only 150 miles.

By Mr. Fyshe:

Q. They say it is an ideal place ?—A. It is lovely. The bathing there is very fine.

By the Chairman:

Q. There is no canteen?—A. There is a dry canteen.

Q. I see by the report of the Militia Council that you began on the first day of January, 1906, with 2,050 men, and on June 30 there were 2,267?—A. The west has been organized. Some part of that increase has been due to the organization in the west.

Q. During that period you have 348 deserters?—A. Yes.

Q. That is to say, in six months one man in six deserted?—A. Yes.

Q. In the year previous, up to December 31, 1905, about one man in three deserted?—A. About it.

Q. Take St. Johns, for instance. At three o'clock in the afternoon when work is over the soldier has got his own time, has he?—A. Oh, no. It all depends upon what has to be done. In St. Johns you are taking a special case. The cavalry are stationed there, and they have special duties at five o'clock in the afternoon. The only recreation they have is between the hours of two, three and four. If they go out at night they go on passes.

Q. They can leave the barracks between two and three o'clock?—A. Yes.

Q. And where they are stationed it is about an hour from the frontier?—A. I cannot say positively.

7-8 EDWARD VII., A. 1908

Q. But trains frequently pass?—A. Yes.

Q. And before the soldier's time is up he may be gone?—A. Yes, but we cannot help that.

By Mr. Fyshe:

Q. But you have to make vigorous efforts to trace them?—A. Sometimes.

By the Chairman:

Q. I read a lecture delivered by Col. Merritt, and he explained that for the expenditure made by Canada, 250,000 men might be drilled and made into an effective force of militia if the Swiss idea were adopted?—A. But you could not get the men. In Switzerland they do not receive pay, but only rations, and it is, I think, compulsory service. We could feed at least five times the number we are training now for the same amount of money.

By Mr. Fyshe:

Q. It is not a fair comparison?—A. Not at all. If they have compulsory service there and we have none here. Most of the time we cannot get men to go to camp unless they have had three years' service and are able to draw $1 a day pay.

By the Chairman:

Q. There have been observations made to the effect that an undue proportion of the expenditure is made on the permanent corps and headquarters staff to the detriment of militia training?—A. That is the opinion of the officers who do not belong to the permanent force and permanent staff. If you take the administration of each unit of the permanent force the number of officers is not excessive. Perhaps there is a feeling in favour of reducing the staff as far as the commands in each district and headquarters staff are concerned, but I do not think you could reduce it.

Q. To encourage the formation of the active militia is what you want to do?—A. Yes.

Q. And yet the officer who gives his time and attention to the militia service when he gets his new uniform from England has to pay duty on it?—A. Yes, full duty.

Q. How many military tailors are there in Canada?—A. Strictly speaking, I think there are only six or seven.

By Mr. Fyshe:

Q. Where are they located?—A. One in Montreal, one in Ottawa, one in Toronto and another in Kingston. I think there is one also in Quebec. Then at Halifax they have so-called army tailors.

Q. Take the Governor General's Foot Guards, for example, that regiment is maintained largely for ceremonial purposes, and the uniform is expensive. A man becomes an officer, and he does not get anything out of it—it is just for the love of the thing—yet he has to buy his uniform in England and pay duty on it?—A. That is not our fault. We have tried our best to get uniforms admitted free of duty.

Q. The duty has only been imposed in the last two years?—A. As far as we are concerned, we are not responsible for it. We have protested against it, but we are even obliged to pay duty on the guns we import.

Q. That is out of one pocket into the other?—A. We tried to get $170,000 put in the estimates this year to compensate the officers for the duty they were paying, but it was refused in Council.

Q. You estimate that the officers of the militia would be out $170,000?—A. Practically speaking, that is what I figured it at.

Q. That is the officers of the militia in Canada have to pay $170,000 more than they did about two years ago?—A. That sum does not include merely uniforms, but represents rifles in some cases, bugles, uniforms for the corps, and so on. I thought

SESSIONAL PAPER No. 29a

hat $170,000 would cover what was needed to compensate them for what they had xpended. I tried to get the amount through, but it was cut down.

Q. How do you expect men in the ordinary circumstances of life who have little 10ney to spend, to join the militia now?—A. Uniforms will have to be made in the 2untry.

Q. No militia officer 'makes anything by it when he buys his own uniform?—A. 'o officer from the militia force or permanent force.

Q. He is out of pocket all the time. I mean every officer of the militia. In the se of the permanent force it is his living?—A. Yes, he is out of pocket all the time.

Q. It is probably within our purview, as we have to make inquiry into the efficiency the service. I was going to ask a question about the Ross rifles. Did any other 'untry have a Ross rifle?—A. No, sir.

Q. Has there ever been a Ross rifle perfected yet?—A. I cannot express an opinion 1 that because I do not know.

Q. Is there a Ross rifle in existence except the few we have had made?—A. We ave 28,000 Ross rifles.

Q. When the manufacture of a Ross rifle was begun was there a pattern or a tandard rifle?—A. Yes, there was one.

Q. The newspapers say the Ross rifle is contracted to be delivered at $25 a rifle? —A. Yes.

Q. The Imperial army use the Lee-Enfield?—A. Yes.

Q. The Lee-Enfield cost about £2 10s.?—A. That is the price, no doubt, at the resent date, but you could not get that rifle five years ago at that price. Ten per ent more had to be allowed for the cost of manufacture.

By Mr. Fyshe:

Q. Why?—A. Because it is always the case that when the Government is buying new rifle the manufacturer is allowed so much per cent in excess of the price in order help in the process of manufacturing.

By the Chairman:

Q. But adding that ten per cent and making the allowance supposing the Lee-1field cost £3 ?—A. The Lee-Enfield would have cost us $25 when we were buying it.

By Mr. Fyshe:

Q. I see the Lee-Enfield cost $17?—A. $17 on the other side.

By the Chairman:

Q. It is £2 10s.?—A. You must remember the Lee-Enfield has been manufactured fteen years, and the process of manufacture has been all paid for, so that the manu-1cturers can afford to turn out rifles at nearly half the cost.

By Mr. Fyshe:

Q. A buyer who goes into the market need not bother his head about that?—A. I now, but we could not do that. We tried to get the Lee-Enfield rifle three years ago, uring the South African war. We wanted to have the Lee-Enfield, but we could not et it.

By the Chairman:

Q. We did in the case of the troops who went to South Africa?—A. Yes.

By Mr. Fyshe:

Q. Was it patriotism that produced the Ross rifle factory?—A. No, sir, it was usiness.

29a—46

By the Chairman:

Q. We pay $25 for the Ross rifle?—A. Yes.

Q. There was no standard rifle at the beginning?—A. I know nothing about it.

Q. You have had how many delivered up to date?—A. We have 27,000 delivered up to now.

Q. Of Mark I. or Mark II.?—A. 9,000 of Mark I. and 18,000 of Mark II.

Q. The 9,000 are condemned practically?—A. I cannot say condemned.

Q. Well, there is some defect about them?—A. There are some defects to be remedied.

Q. Are the defects going to be remedied?—A. I think so.

Q. The terms of the contract, according to what is stated in the press, are that you pay 75 per cent on the value of the work in the orders given to them?—A. Yes.

Q. That is to say you pay $18.75 as the work proceeds?—A. Yes.

Q. According to the newspapers, orders were given for 52,000 Ross rifles?—A. Altogether.

Q. And you have got 27,000 delivered?—A. Yes.

Q. Has 75 per cent been paid on the whole 52,000?—A. No, 75 per cent on 42,000.

Q. For how many the last order?—A. 10,000.

Q. 27,000 rifles have been delivered and paid for in full, I suppose?—A. Yes.

Q. And upon 15,000 more they have been paid 75 per cent?—A. Practically speaking, we have paid for the Ross rifle $359,000 altogether in excess, or in other words, we are entitled to the delivery of 15,000 more rifles before they should be entitled to any progress estimates.

Q. Before any further money shall be paid?—A. Yes.

By Mr. Fyshe:

Q. Do you intend going on opening up fresh contracts with them?—A. No, sir, not until the present orders are completed.

By the Chairman:

Q. You have paid for the value of 15,000 rifles apparently, which have not been delivered to you?—A. Yes.

Q. You have at the Ross rifle factory in Quebec an inspector of small arms?—A. Yes.

Q. Is it on his certificate that the payments have been made?—A. The payments have been made on the certificate of a chartered accountant and the inspector of small arms.

Q. Is the chartered accountant an officer of the militia department?—A. No.

Q. Is he an officer of the Ross Rifle company?—A. No, he is an independent man, chosen by both.

By Mr. Fyshe:

Q. How is the chartered accountant called in?—A. I do not know how we are proceeding. That is exactly what I have been inquiring into.

Q. What has a chartered accountant got to do with checking the Ross rifles?—A. I cannot say.

By the Chairman:

Q. Who drafted the contract? Where was it drafted?—A. There were about ten drafts made.

Q. By whom?—A. By the Justice department, I think.

Q. It was drafted on instructions by the department, I presume?—A. I suppose so, I do not know.

Q. And looking at the articles in the press, it would seem that the more orders

ESSIONAL PAPER No. 29a

ey get the slower they were to make delivery. They get orders that they never de-
rered?—A. The press says so.

Q. Where does the small arms inspector come in?—A. The inspector of small arms
rtifies to the accounts submitted, showing amounts expended for labour, superin-
ndence and materials which is also certified to by the chartered accountant.

By Mr. Fyshe :

Q. It is a question of ascertaining what percentage of the price charged has been
pended in labour ?—A. Yes.

Q. Where was the temptation to the Government or the Militia Department to
sist in starting a factory to make Ross rifles, when they have got the whole world to
lect their rifles from?—A. I do not know.

By the Chairman :

Q. It was with the idea that this rifle should be manufactured in Canada ?—
. Yes.

Q. Surely, if the Boers could get all the rifles they wanted, we could do the same,
ıd their rifle was an inferior weapon ?—A. I think it is a good rifle.

Q. The Boers bought the Mauser because they could not get English rifles?—
. The Lee-Enfield is preferable, but still the Mauser is a first class rifle, as far as
ılidity is concerned. I know that is so, by the results.

Q. Was the Boer service one of conscription ? Was it compulsory ?—A. I think

Q. Every Boer was a soldier ?—A. Yes. They were just formed into local com-
andoes, and those commandoes were exercised nearly every day. It was a patriotic
my more or less.

Q. The loss sustained by the Martineau defalcations which are now being threshed
ıt in the courts was over $75,000 ?—A. Yes.

Q. The defalcations did not extend over two years ? The man was employed in
ctober 1901, and practically in January, 1903, the thing was discovered ?—A. Yes.

Q. The thing was discovered because the balances of the letter of credit instead
ʼ being on the right side of the account, were between $50,000 and $60,000 on the
rong side. Martineau was employed in the accountant's branch ?—A. Yes.

Q. He made himself so supremely useful that he seemed to have command of the
tuation ?—A. Practically speaking.

Q. He got cheque books and everything else?—A. Yes.

Q. And forged the signature of the deputy and accountant?—A. Yes.

Q. Practically discovery was made because the clerk in the office woke up one
ıorning and found that the account rendered by the Bank of Montreal showed a
ılance on the wrong side?—A. I do not know.

Q. This man awoke his superior officer to a knowledge that there was a screw
ose and he went to the Bank of Montreal and it was deemed advisable to consult the
:inister. The Minister sent for Col. Sherwood chief of Dominion Police, and the cul-
rit was arrested going on board the train?—A. Yes.

Q. And $10,000 was found on his person?—A. Yes.

Q. He had lost in about fifteen months the sum of $60,000?—A. Speculating
ı stocks, I think.

Q. He opened four bank accounts I believe?—A. Yes.

Q. He gave his name in one place as Charles B. Côté, and in another instance
gned his own name?—A. Yes.

Q. He gave an address on a street where if they had looked at the directory they
ould have found there was no such address?—A. The bankers allowed an account
ɔ be opened on account of an official cheque that Martineau had with him, without
ıking who he was or anything else, as far as we know.

29a—46½

ROYAL COMMISSION ON THE CIVIL SERVICE

20a—46½

By Mr. Fyshe:

Q. Is the man in the penitentiary?—A. Yes, he is still there.

Q. And as the result of an inquiry the whole system has changed?—A. Yes.

Q. In Martineau's time the cheque books were in the stationery department where you kept your forms and anybody could take them?—A. Now the body of each cheque is numbered and the abstract is numbered also.

By Mr. Fyshe:

Q. Were they not numbered before?—A. No, they were not.

Q. That was a defect. Under my system in the Bank of Nova Scotia every cheque was numbered.

By the Chairman:

Q. Now your cheque books are all locked up and secured?—A. Yes.

Q. And you follow the rules laid down by the Treasury Board?—A. Yes, entirely.

By Mr. Bazin:

Q. Is Martineau under the Superannuation Act?—A. No, he was dismissed.

By the Chairman:

Q. We will be glad to receive from you any further suggestions in addition to those embodied in the statement which you have submitted?—A. Of course in that statement I have not gone into the details of the civil service, but you will find there my views as to what I think should be done. The statement simply embodies my opinions and nothing else.

Q. Do you think there are more permanent officers employed in the Militia Department than there should be?—A. Well, it all depends upon how you look at it. If you want to organize an army of some kind you must absolutely have the staff. The staff you now have may be a little too large for the outside service but if the militia force is going to grow as it is growing you must maintain the staff.

Q. As you progress the present staff will be sufficient? It will not be increased! —A. It will not be increased; it has not since the reorganization.

Q. Still you have created the Army Pay Corps?—A. Yes, but that was on the programme two years ago.

Q. Is there anything not on the programme that has been created?—A. No, nothing.

Q. If there are any other matters you would like to lay before us we shall be glad to receive a memorandum from you?

OTTAWA, May 31, 1907.

Colonel E. FISET, D.S.O., re-called and examined.

By the Chairman:

Q. During the two or three years before I left the Finance Department, the Militia Department having overrun the appropriations granted by parliament, sent in very heavy supplementary estimates?—A. Yes.

Q. The department did not pay strict attention to the appropriations that were granted and gave authority to expend beyond the amount appropriated by parliament? —A. But still, in those cases, I think the deputy minister always got authority from the *Auditor* General to make the expenditures.

Q. He could not get authority from the Auditor General?—A. Not exactly author-
ty, but we notified the Auditor General that we had overdrawn our account.

Q. How did that happen? Was that on account of the orders given by the department without considering the amount voted by parliament?—A. Not exactly.

Q. What I want to know is, did the department, regardless of the votes of parliament, give authority to expend money in one way or another?—A. I am afraid that
the expenditure was incurred without the department being aware that it had incurred
uch heavy expenditure. It was in connection with the work of training or the pur-
hase of heavy ordnance, and we did not know at the time what amount was involved,
nd when the bills came due we found that they were much larger than we had anti-
ipated.

Q. You are taking steps to rectify that?—A. I am.

Q. How are you framing your estimates now?—A. The estimates in future will be
repared by districts—district by district, command by command, and unit by unit,
nd every item will be fully covered from beginning to end. The estimates will have
) be submitted each year before October 1, to be compiled at headquarters, and after
eing compiled submitted to council. If we find on looking into the prices that we
annot go to the expense involved in any item, we will cut it down so as to submit the
stimates to parliament in accordance with our view. I think we have a system by
hich we shall be able to get along not only within our appropriations but at less than
ur appropriations.

Q. Having got the official estimate of each district and each command, you cer-
inly would not increase it beyond what they ask for?—A. No.

Q. And these estimates would be subject to revision when they came in?—A.
es.

Q. And they might be cut down?—A. Yes, I will tell you why. If these com-
ands ask for such equipment as will complete their establishment, we might not be
ble to give them the whole of it in one year, but we might be able to distribute it
ver a certain number of years, and in that way cut down our estimates.

Q. This (showing) is a statement showing how the estimtes have been compiled?
-A. Yes. (Statement put in).

Q. When you get these estimates in and know what the commands and the dis-
icts call for, there will be so many tents, so many saddles, so much of this thing and
int thing—will you call for tenders?—A. Always. We have always done so.

Q. Are the lowest tenders accepted?—A. In every case.

Q. Is security deposited with the tender when it is accepted?—A. Yes, ten per
nt.

Q. What is done with that security?—A. It is turned over to the Receiver
eneral.

Q. In the case of the Ross rifle contract, was there any security deposited?—A.
do not know.

Q. You have read the agreement with the Ross Rifle Company?—A. I have.

Q. Was there any clause in the agreement requiring security to be given for the
rrying out of the contract?—A. No.

Q. So that the Ross Rifle Company could not be called upon under their contract
put up any security?—A. No, but I must say that I do not think the Militia Dep rt-
ent would be entirely to blame for this, because the contract was approved by the
overnor General in Council.

By Mr. Fyshe:

Q. If such a wide variation from proper practice took place in that case, could
not take place in other cases? (No answer.)

By the Chairman:

Q. That was the special and only instance?—A. That is the only instance I know of. It is a contract to deliver one special rifle, the only rifle manufactured by the company.

Q. Since your previous examination, I met two officers connected with two city corps, and they tell me that it is very difficult now to get officers to join the city corps? —A. Yes, I am aware of that.

Q. That in consequence of the customs duty of 35 per cent which has to be paid on officers' clothing, it is extremely difficult now to get officers to join the city corps? —A. Yes.

Q. The result is that it is extremely difficult to officer the city corps?—A. It is, unless the officers can have their uniforms made in Canada. Of course, they will have to pay duty on the cloth, which increases the cost of the uniform.

Q. In the Governor General's Foot Guards, for instance, it would add to the initial cost of an officer about $150?—A. If he imports his uniform from England.

Q. The consequence of this will be that vacancies in the officers of city corps will have to be filled by rich men?—A. Practically speaking, it will be so.

Q. It is not surely the desire of the department to exclude worthy men who cannot afford to join the corps?—A. Oh, no, far from it. I may add that the Minister at the last session had provided $170,000 in our estimates in order to cover the duties on uniforms for our officers, but it was not carried out.

Q. It is coming to this, that a small and aristocratic and rich class will in the future, in consequence of this enlarged expenditure, be the class that will officer the regiment?—A. I am not prepared to say that. I do not know that it will have that consequence, but it will look like it unless the department takes some action in the matter. I think it is bound either to increase the allowances to officers for uniforms or have that arrangement altered. I hope we shall provide in our regulations next year for giving each officer an increased allowance for the purchase of his uniform. That is the system I have advocated.

Q. Have you any further statement to make?—A. Yesterday afternoon you asked some questions about the pay corps. I submit a paper giving the instructions for the organization of a pay corps in Canada in connection with the militia. It shows the duties of each paymaster, the duties he has to carry out in camp, and the instructions he has to give to others. I have found that the formation of that pay corps has saved the department in the cost of administration ten times the amount of salaries we are paying to those people, by the care they are exercising over the pay-lists, over the issue of uniforms, clothing, ammunition, and so on.

Q. One would gather from the fact that you save money, that previous to that there must have been money wasted?—A. No; but previous to this we have had no such control over the expenditure as we have now, and the more careful the administration the better the results.

Q. When you make a payment to any of the contractors doing business with the department, does the paymaster issue the cheque or is it a direct cheque?—A. It is always issued from headquarters here.

Q. Then the payments made by the paymaster are limited?—A. They are limited so far as the details of the administration are concerned. Large payments are always made from headquarters.

Q. You have an expenditure of about $6,000,000?—A. Yes.

Q. What part of that amount do the paymasters control?—A. They control perhaps $2,000,000 altogether.

DEPARTMENT OF MILITIA AND DEFENCE,
OTTAWA, May 31, 1907.

THOS. HOWE, Esq.,
Secretary, Civil Service Commission,
Ottawa.

SIR,—I have the honour to inclose herewith the draft of a militia order which is about to be issued in connection with the preparation of the estimates for 1908-9, to which I made reference in my evidence before the Civil Service Commission this morning.

With reference to the papers which I handed to you yesterday after I gave my evidence, there was a copy of a memorandum showing the strength of the staff of this department on June 30, 1882, and June 30, 1906. As I had already forwarded to you a copy of the statement, I shall be much obliged if you will detach the copy from the papers I handed in yesterday, and return it to me.

I have the honour to be, sir,
Your obedient servant,

EUG. FISET, *Colonel*,
Deputy Minister of Militia and Defence.

Estimates, 1908-9.

The attention of officers commanding commands and officers commanding districts is invited to articles 31 to 34, part III, Financial Instructions.

These estimates are to be carefully prepared during September, and forwarded to headquarters not later than October 1. In framing them, officers commanding commands, &c., will have regard to economy and include those items only, which are actually necessary for the various militia services. At the same time they will be careful to include everything that may be required for the proper conduct of the work and for the maintenance of the militia in their respective commands. The allotment of funds to the various commands, &c., will be based on these estimates, and any applications for expenditure in respect of items, &c.. which have been omitted therefrom will remain unprovided for. As soon as the estimates are voted by parliament, officers commanding commands, &c., will be notified of the amounts allotted for their expenditure.

In framing the estimates, the following is to be noted:—

Pay A.—District Staff.

This is to include officers of the staff holding permanent appointments as such. Officers of the permanent force attached to the staff, such as the district engineer officer, the senior army service corps officer, the principal medical officer, the command paymaster, &c., &c., are to be included in pay B, permanent force. Officers of the active militia, however, such as a principal medical officer attached to the staff, are to be provided for under this head.

Pay B.—Permanent Force.

All the permanent force are to be provided for under this head, military staff clerks included.

At Halifax and Esquimalt, civilians employed at the ordnance stores, in the offices of the Royal Canadian Engineers, Permanent Army Service Corps, &c., are to be considered as belonging to the permanent force.

The pay of each officer, with all allowances drawn on the pay-sheets is to be shown in detail. The total amount required to pay non-commissioned officers and men of each company or corps, at the time the estimates are being prepared, is to be given, and, in addition, an estimate in detail of the amount required to pay any authorized increase of the force in the district or command. .

A copy of the latest parade state is to be attached.

Pay D.—Allowances.

These are to be shown in detail for each regiment and corps, the estimate for the drill instruction allowances to be based on the assumption that the full number authorized for training will turn out. For care of arms allowance, regard will be had to those corps not authorized to draw the full allowance, as per articles 286-288, Pay and Allowance Regulations.

Pay E.—Guards of Honour, Salutes, &c.

This is to provide for pay of guards of honour, escorts, salutes; also for pay of officers of the active militia on board, or on any special duty not provided for elsewhere.

Annual Drill.

This estimate is to be made in three parts, viz.: Pay, supplies for the camps, and transport to and from the camps.

The total pay of each corps at its authorized strength for training is to be computed, the artillery 16 days, the other arms 12 days, also total efficiency pay at 40 cents per diem, which may be taken as the average rate. Opposite these figures is to be shown the actual pay at the last training; in each case the total efficiency pay and total ordinary pay to be shown separately for each corps. There is to be appended to this a statement showing, for each corps, the numbers of officers, non-commissioned officers, rank and file, and horses trained the previous year. In computing the pay for corps training in camp, the various allowances drawn on the pay-sheets are to be included.

The estimates for Petawawa camp will be made at headquarters.

The estimates for supplies for camps may be based on the cost of the previous year.

Transport is to be reckoned at 2 cents per mile for officers, and 1½ cents per mile for non-commissioned officers and men, between all points east of Port Arthur. West of that, 3 cents and 2 cents, respectively.

Salaries and Wages.

A list of all caretakers, watchmen, and other civilian employees, with their respective rates of pay, is to be shown; also, the probable requirements for additional employees, new appointments, &c., &c.

Military Properties. Care and Maintenance.

This is to provide for rents, fuel, light, water, telephones and sundry expenses, in connection with the care and maintenance of drill halls, armouries, rifle ranges and other military properties, barracks and fortifications excepted. A list of the various buildings, &c., is to be submitted, with an estimate for each.

Military Properties—Construction and Repairs.

The ordinary and necessary repairs to all military buildings, rifle ranges, fortifications, &c., are to be provided for under this head. Any proposals for new buildings, rifle ranges, &c., are to be submitted separately.

Clothing and Necessaries.

A statement, in detail, showing the number or quantity of the various articles required for both the active militia and permanent force is to be made up. Each corps will submit its requirements to the district officer commanding during July. The district officer commanding, having examined these and compared them with his books, will pass them to the senior ordnance officer of the district for compilation. Having complied them, the latter will show, opposite each article, the number that is likely to be available in the district stores at the beginning of the fiscal year—April 1, 1908—and transmit the estimates to the district officer commanding, who will, in turn, forward it to the officer commanding the command.

The prices will be fixed at headquarters, and the estimates completed there.

Military Stores.

The estimate for these will be compiled in the same manner as for clothing and necessaries. Special stores for the artillery and the departmental services are to be shown separately; the former will be made up in the armament office for the command, for each district, and submitted to the officer commanding the district, who will require the senior ordnance officer to show the number of the various articles in store.

Provisions, Supplies and Remounts.

This is to provide for fuel, food, light, forage, medicines and other incidental expenses in connection with the quartering and subsistence of the permanent force.

It is also to include purchase of remounts to the extent of 10 per cent of the establishment.

A careful statement of the cost of supplying the permanent force in the district, during the previous twelve months, is to be made up. From this, the average cost per man for food, fuel, light, medicines, and incidental expenses can be arrived at, and in the same way the average cost for maintenance of a horse.

Grant to Rifle Associations and Bands.

This is to provide for grants to rifle associations and bands, as per regulations governing same.

A list of rifle associations drawing the grant is to be made up, showing the probable amount for each, to which should be added a sum sufficient to pay any new associations likely to be formed.

The same method will be followed in making up the estimates for bands.

Transport, Freight and Contingencies.

Estimates for these will be made at headquarters.

Suggestions and proposals for consideration of the Civil Service Commission, with a comparative statement, respecting the pay in the higher appointments of the Military and Civil Staff, Department of Militia and Defence.

CLASSIFICATION—GENERAL PRINCIPLE.

To provide for an efficient and economical public service, continuity in the work is an absolute necessity. To ensure continuity, officers who attain the higher ranks should expect to make the service their vocation for life, or until retirement, and they should be sufficiently well paid to enable them to live like gentlemen and to bring up educate their families as such. Upon retirement, they should be pensioned, and there should be a pensionary provision for their families in the event of their death.

If the higher ranks are filled by capable and efficient officers, there is no great necessity for permanency in the lower ranks.

CLASSIFICATION.

The following, it is submitted, would be a good classification:—
Higher ranks.—Deputy minister, assistant deputy minister (for the larger departments), technical or grade 'A' officers, chief clerks, 1st class clerks, 2nd class clerks.

Lower ranks.—Temporary permanent clerks, temporary clerks, messengers.

Temporary permanent clerks would take the place of the junior second class and third class clerkships. They should be appointed during good behaviour, but need not necessarily accept appointment with a view to making the service their vocation for life. While serving in this class they would have to show their fitness for appointment to higher rank. There would, therefore, be a constant incentive to good work, and the clerk, who found his level so low that he would not have good chances for reaching higher rank, would get out.

Temporary clerks and messengers should be appointed by order in council ,as might as required.

PAY.

For the temporary permanent and temporary clerks, the pay, on appointment, should be $500 per annum, as at present, which is ample for a young man just starting life, which class should be encouraged to enter the service, rather than men who have tried other employment and failed.

Clerks should not be brought in at any other rate of pay than the minimum of the lowest rank—$500.

For the temporary permanent clerks there should be a retirement fund, but in the event of their attaining higher rank, their former service should reckon towards pension. A temporary clerk should be eligible for appointment as a temporary permanent clerk, at the rate of pay of which he is in receipt, but he should not be appointed direct to higher rank. The minimum pay of a higher class clerk should be $1,200 per annum.

[The following scale of pay, showing minimum and maximum for each class, the annual increase, and whether serving under pension or retirement fund, is submitted:—

Rank.	Maximum Pay.	Minimum Pay.	Annual Increases.	Pension or Retirement Fund.
	$	$	$	
Deputy minister..	6,000	6,000	....	Pension.
Assistant deputy minister...... ...	3,000	3,600	....	"
Technical or grade "A" officer......	2,800	3,000	100	"
Chief clerk...............	2,200	2,700	100	"
1st class clerk	1,700	2,100	100	"
2nd "	1,200	1,600	100	"
Temporary permanent clerk..........	300	1,000	50	Retirement.
			6 yrs., then $100.	
Temporary clerk..	500	1,000	" "	
Messenger..	400	700	$50 per annum.	

THEORETICAL ORGANIZATION.

There should be a theoretical organization for each department, which should be fixed, in the first place, after careful investigation of the work, by an independent commission, and changed, only on the recommendation of a permanent Civil Service Commission.

From an economical standpoint, a theoretical organization is ideal, but it would not provide that elasticity necessary to advance deserving clerks, who, through no fault of their own, have not had opportunities for promotion. To overcome this, some such arrangement as promoting a higher rank clerk, after a certain numbers of years' service at the maximum of his class, to be supernumerary of the next higher rank, and, while borne as such, to receive increases of half the usual amount only, until absorbed into the establishment, should be provided.

There should be no such thing as making a temporary permanent clerk or temporary clerk or supernumerary of the second class.

Examinations.

There should be a pretty stiff examination to qualify for first appointment. For every subsequent step in rank there should be an examination to qualify therefor in ' duties of office ' only. This paper should be made much harder than is customary throughout the service now, and it should be on the duties to be performed by the individual in the event of his promotion, rather than on the duties that he is actually performing at the time of his examination.

Organization of Department of Militia and Defence.

Deputy Minister.—It is submitted that the position of deputy minister of a department, such as that of Militia and Defence, is a very important one. He is vice-president of the Militia Council, and the permanent head of a department which has a very large outside service, and which spends annually some $6,000,000.

For the reasons set forth in the comparative statement hereto attached, it is submitted that his pay should be the same as that of the chief of the general staff, viz., $6,000 per annum.

Assistant Deputy Minister.—The deputy minister should have an assistant, who should perform, as part of his duties, the duties of the Secretary of the Militia Council.

The assistant deputy minister should have charge, under the deputy minister, of the interior economy of the department. He should sign routine correspondence, and in other ways act for the deputy minister in all routine matters, and, in the absence of the deputy minister, he should be the acting deputy.

He would be charged with the receipt, registration, distribution and custody of all official letters and telegrams received in the department.

He should prepare the official correspondence with other departments of state, and with the outside public, for the signature of the deputy minister; also reports to the Privy Council.

The preparation of papers for the decision of the Militia Council, insuring that all necessary information accompanies them, and that all the departments concerned have been duly consulted; notifying all the branches concerned of the decisions arrived at, recording the decisions in the files, reporting the proceedings of council, the printing thereof, &c., would be part of his duties.

The chief clerk for printing, stationery and contingencies, the chief clerk for correspondence, the central registration office, which is now in charge of a first-class clerk, but which should soon, if the department keeps on developing as it has during the past few years, have a chief clerk in charge, and the lady typists staff, who are available for duty for all the branches of the department, would be under his direct supervision.

The pay of the assistant deputy minister should be $3,600.

Accountant and Paymaster General.—The pay of the accountant and paymaster general should be considered on its merits, and apart from the duties of the accountant in any other department of the public service. He is a member of the Militia Council, and is responsible to the council, the same as any other member, for the efficiency of his branch.

. 7-8 EDWARD VII., A. 1908

His duties are such that he might be an officer of the permanent force, or a civilian employee. If he were on the military staff, his pay would be that of the other military members of the Militia Council, viz., $4,000 per annum, and it is, therefore, submitted, that he should be given that rate of pay.

The duties of this officer, and particulars respecting the pay of officers holding similar appointments in the British army, will be found in the comparative statement hereto attached.

Director of Contracts.—The duties of the director of contracts are:—

All work appertaining to the purchase of clothing, necessaries, equipment, fuel, barrack and other stores, and all other supplies, services and works, including those demanded on service requisitions from the Dominion Arsenal, Royal Military College, permanent force, and the militia generally; the calling for and scheduling of all tenders, the preparation of all contracts and the checking of claims relating thereto.

His duties are of such a responsible and important nature that it is submitted he should be rated as a technical officer, with pay for that rank.

As regards the chief clerks, and clerks below that rank, generally, their status and pay should be in accord with those of like rank in the other departments, i.e., there is nothing singular in their cases that calls for special consideration.

MILITIA DEPARTMENT—MEMORANDUM RESPECTING SALARIES—COMPARATIVE STATEMENT.

Military Division.

Chief of general staff	$6,000
Adjutant-General	4,000
Quartermaster-General	4,000
Master-General of the ordnance	4,000
Directors	3,200

Civil Division.

Deputy minister	4,000
Accountant and paymaster-general	2,800
Chief clerks	2,500

The above are the maximum rates in each case.

The purpose of this memo. is to show that the rates of salary in the civil division are too low.

It is submitted that the salary of the deputy minister should be equal to that of the chief of the general staff; that the salary of the accountant and paymaster general should be equal to that of the lesser paid military members ($4,000), and that the salary of a chief clerk 'Grade "A"' should be equal to that of a director $3,200).

It cannot be contended that the military staff are too highly paid. Army officers are continually being brought into the Canadian service, and these cannot be obtained unless they are paid as highly as in the army, consequently, the pay of regimental officers of the permanent force has to be quite as high as army rates, otherwise there would be the anomaly of Canadian officers of equal rank, standing and qualifications to those borrowed from the army, serving with them in the same force and yet drawing a lower rate of pay—a condition of things that would not be tolerated.

The pay of a regimental commanding officer (lieutenant-colonel), varies according to the arm of the service. The total remuneration to an infantry or cavalry lieutenant-colonel in command is atbout $3,000. The Colonel Commandant R.C.A., Quebec, receives $3,800, and the Officer commanding the R.C.E., about the same. The Commanding Engineer officer at Halifax received $4,500 when the garrison there was occupied by Imperial troops and paid by the British Government.

The higher regimental positions are, therefore, almost, and perhaps quite as good financially as the staff positions at headquarters, consequently it would not do to reduce the rates of pay for the latter. On the contrary, they should be raised, as an officer of the general staff should receive a higher rate of pay than a regimental officer.

If the military staff of the department is inadequately paid, the civil staff is still worse off. It is generally agreed that the position of deputy minister for a department like this should carry more pay than it does. An under secretary of state in the Australian civil service receives £1,000 p.a. and the departments there are not as large as in the Canadian service.

In England the Under Secretary of State for War receives £2,000 p.a., but the department is a much larger one than this, and, for that reason, a comparison cannot be fairly made between the two heads, but the Under Secretary of State for War has three assistants, one of whom receives $6,000 per annum, and the other two $5,000 each. Surely a deputy minister fills a position as responsible as an assistant under secretary in the War Office, and should receive as much salary.

For the benefit of those who are not acquainted with the departmental arrangements, it may be explained here that the department is divided into branches, as follows :—

(1.) Deputy Minister.
(2.) Chief of General Staff.
(3.) Adjutant General.
(4.) Quartermaster General.
(5.) Master General of the Ordnance.
(6.) Accountant and Paymaster General.

The deputy ministetr, in addition to any special work, has the supervision of the department generally.

The heads of these branches, with the Minister, form the Militia Council.

The accountant and paymaster general, who is the finance member of the Militia Council, is paid as chief clerk at $2,800 per annum. His duties, which are defined by Order in Council—Vide G. O. 31 of 1907, are as follows :—

(1.) Control and disbursement of militia funds.

(2.) Preparation of accounts and financial statements for the Auditor General, and financial adjustments with other departments.

(3.) Audit of all militia expenditure.

(4.) Advice on financial matters to the other branches of the department.

(5.) Preparation, in concert with the other branches concerned, of the annual estimates for militia services.

(6.) Watching the progress of militia expenditure under the various appropriations and reviewing proposals for new expenditure.

(7.) Administration of the Militia Pay department and of the Imperial Pension office.

(8.) Matters relating to pay and allowance (in money) of the militia and decisions as to the proper rates under the regulations.

(9.) Financial review of conracts entered into by the department.

(10.) Computation, in concert with the Pension board, of pensions claimed under Militia Pensions Act, 1901, and payment of pensioners.

(11.) Audit of stores account.

(12.) Preparation of special financial statements and returns of a statistical nature.

His salary is $1,200 less than the lowest paid military members of the Militia Council and $400 less than the pay of the director, and yet he has one of the largest branches in the department to superintend and direct.

Referring, as was done in the deputy minister's case, to the salaries paid in the War Office, the army estimates show the following:—

	Per annum.
1 Director of army accounts, £1,200..	6,000
1 Director of finance £1,200..	6,000
1 Director of army accounts, £1,200..	6,000
4 Principals (chiefs) £850 to £1,000, $4,250 to $5,000.	

The head of the financial branch has, therefore, 2 directors and 4 principals or chiefs under him, the latter at £850 to £1,000 each. These are civil employees. It is submitted that the salary of the head of the finance branch of the Militia Department should be equal to that of a principal or chief clerk in the War Office. The secretary of the Militia Council, at present in receipt of $2,800 p.a., and the director of contracts, $2,500 p.a., are both filling positions of large responsibility and are hard working officials. They should be placed on the same footing as directors in the military branches who receive $3,200 p.a. The former in the absence of the deputy, acts for him. The latter has the responsibility in connection with contracts, which is a heavy one.

DEPARTMENT OF MILITIA AND DEFENCE
1905-6.

1 Deputy Minister..		$ 4,000 00
5 Chief Clerks.. .. 9		11,550 00
9 First Class Clerks..		14,862 50
8 Second Class Clerks..		9,775 00
8 Junior Second Class Clerks		5,979 66
6 Third Class Clerks..		2,265 61
3 Messengers..		2,100 00
Allowance for Private Secretary..		600 00
Allowance for Secretary, Militia Council..		300 00
Extra Clerks..		3,282 50

40	Total Civil Service..	$ 54,715 27

1 Chief General Staff..		$ 6,000 00
1 Inspector General..		6,000 00
1 Adjutant General..		4,000 00
1 Quartermaster General..		4,000 0
1 Master General of Ordnance..		4,000 00
1 Director General Medical Services..		3,400 00
1 Assistant Adjutant General..		2,800 00
1 Assistant Adjutant General for Musketry..		3,200 00
1 Deputy Assistant Adjutant General for Musketry..		2,000 00
5 Directors at $3,200 each..		16,000 00
2 Assistant Directors at $2,400 each..		4,800 00
1 Intelligence Staff Officer..		2,165 00
1 Intelligence Staff Officer..		1,500 00
4 Staff Lieutenants..		3,600 00
1 Officer specially employed..		2,555 00
6 Military Staff Clerks..		5,500 00
30 Extra Clerks, Typists, &c., paid out of Outside Votes..		11,117 84

59		$ 82,637 84
	Total..	137,353 11

Certified correct,
Signed. J. W. BORDEN,
A. & P.M.G.

MILITIA AND DEFENCE.
1902.

1 Deputy Minister..		$ 3,200 00
3 Chief Clerks ($1,850) ($2,400) ($3,0000)..		7,250 00
6 First Class Clerks..		11,000 00
11 Second Class Clerks..		14,500 00
6 Third Class Clerks..		5,450 00
3 Messengers..		1,500 00
Private Secretary—Allowance..		600 00

30		$ 43,500 00
	Paid for extra clerks..	1,169 00

	Total Civil Service..	$ 44,669 00

MILITARY BRANCH.

1 Major General..		$ 4,000 00
1 Adjutant General..		3,200 00
1 Inspector of Artillery..		2,757 50
1 A. D. C..		1,000 00
1 Clerk—extra..		758 00

5		$ 11,715 50

OTTAWA, Thursday, September 5, 1907.

The Commission met at 10.30 a.m. Present :—Messrs. Courtney, Chairman, Fyshe and Bazin.

MAJOR GENERAL LAKE, sworn and examined:—

By the Chairman:

Q. You are chief of the general staff?—A. Yes.

Q When were your appointed ?—A. On November 10, 1904.

. For what length of time does the appointment run ?—A. Four years.

. Then your time will expire next year?—A. Yes.

. You were here in General Herbert's time?—A. I was.

. And with General Gascoigne?—A. I was.

. How long did you stay then?—A. For five years.

Q. You are personally closely allied with Canada?—A. I am closely connected by family.

Q. What has been your service in the English army?—A. About thirty-four years. I was a regimental officer for the first twelve years of my service, and since then I have been almost continuously on the staff.

Q. In what capacity lately?—A. I was called from India to be assistant quartermaster general for mobilization services and defence at the War Office on the breaking out of the Boer war. I held that appointment until March, 1904, when I became chief staff officer of the Second Army Corps in England, from which post I came to Canada.

Q. Then you have had both active duties and duties in connection with the staff? —A. Yes.

Q. What branch of the service do you belong to?—A. The infantry.

Q. In Canada there are thirteen military districts?—A. There are.

Q. That is the same number that was in existence in 1892?—A. One more.

Q. The system of dividing the country into military districts is similar to the English system?—A. Yes.

Q. Latterly these districts have been grouped into commands ?—A. Yes.

Q. That is following the English system?—A. Yes.

Q. How many commands are there now in Canada?—A. At present there are four commands and three independent districts in the west, which are not yet grouped together.

Q. These commands are a new development here?—A. They are a new development since I came.

Q. What do you call the chief officer in a command?—A. The officer commanding.

Q. How long is his term of office?—A. There is some uncertainty in regard to the tenure of military appointments in Canada. Theoretically five years is the time, but there is some uncertainty about it in practice.

Q. How is an officer commanding selected?—A. According to his general efficiency, seniority and experience in the service.

Q. Have you a selection board ?—A. The Militia Council acts in that capacity. The Adjutant General is responsible for all appointments and promotions. In making recommendations he generally consults with me in regard to staff appointments, and in certain cases the other military members of the Militia Council as well. The recommendations of the Militia Council go to the Governor General in Council. All gazettes require to have the approval of the Governor General in Council.

Q. The Governor in Council is aware of them obliquely, but they do not go to them for action?—A. They actually go to them for action. The procedure is that a submission to Council is drawn up in the ordinary way, submitting a gazette for His Excellency's approval in Council. When it receives that approval it automatically goes on to the Secretary of State for publication in the Canada *Gazette*.

Q. In the districts forming commands there is an officer in command called the District Officer Commanding—the D.O.C.?—A. Yes.

Q. The former title was Deputy Adjutant General?—A. Yes.

Q. For instance, Colonel Hodgins is in command of one district in eastern Ontario?—A. Yes.

Q. How do you regulate the flow of promotions, for evidently these officers commanding hold for a fixed period of time?—A. We look through the list of officers eligible and suitable for promotion and select from that list by merit and seniority.

Q. How are the original appointments made at the bottom these permanent staffs?—A. They are made generally on the application of the person concerned and the recommendation of the officer commanding the command or the district as the case may be. Those recommendations pass on their receipt to the Secretary of the Militia Council, who in the ordinary course of business, sends them to the Adjutant General to be dealt with. We also have the list of officers of the permanent corps. We compare the list of applications and the list of officers in the permanent corps, and from those two together the selection is made. Perhaps I might say that the attempt is made to combine the active militia applicants and the permanent force men so as to have a proper proportion of each.

Q. In those cases is there any examination previous to the appointment of a junior officer to the permanent corps?—A. In the permanent corps each officer has to qualify by examination for the ranks he holds. He is not allowed to hold the rank until he is qualified.

Q. Is the examination subsequent or previous to the appointment?—A. There have been one or two cases of appointment first and qualification afterwards. I think I only know of two such cases since I have been in Canada. In every other case the officer has had to qualify before appointment. In the active militia there are often men qualified for the rank they hold in the militia, but not for the rank they would hold on the permanent staff. If one of these men is selected, he is required to qualify himself by passing the necessary examination before permanent appointment.

Q. In the mother country appointments to the army come through the military college at Sandhurst and the military college at Woolwich?—A. Yes, or through the militia or one of the chartered universities.

Q. Before appointments are made examinations are held under the auspices of the Civil Service Commission?—A. Yes, and in the case of a candidate from the militia the literary part of the examination is carried out by the Civil Service Commission.

Q. Then it would follow that the officer in the imperial service, from the very commencement, from matriculation and graduation, is subject to examination?—A. Yes.

Q. And is subject to examination for subsequent promotions all through his career?—A. Yes.

Q. Strictly and unswerving examinations?—A. Yes.

Q. There is no escape?—A. Not that I am aware of.

Q. In Canada when an officer and a candidate gets into the permanent corps and a vacancy occurs, and a candidate has to be promoted, does he pass an examination?—A. Now and since I came here, he passes exactly the same examinations as are passed by the officers of the imperial army.

Q. Do you get the examination papers from England?—A. Yes, and we send them to England marked by numbers, not by names, and they are passed upon by the same examiners as the others. The only modification is that when there are questions asked applicable only to British conditions the Canadian supervising board has a right to substitute similar questions applicable to Canadian conditions.

ESSIONAL PAPER No. 29a

Q. The commands have under their jurisdiction not only the permanent corps, it also the authorized militia regiments in their districts?—A. Yes.

Q. What is the pay of an officer commanding?—A. The pay of an officer comanding is $4,000 a year.

Q. Does that include the allowances ?—A. The pay and allowances are included.

Q. That is the same as the pay of the three other professional members of the ilitia Council ?—A. Yes.

Q. The permanent corps are made up of cavalry, infantry and artillery?—A. And gineers, army service corps, army medical corps, ordnance store corps and army pay rps.

Q. What is the proportion of officers to men in the permanent corps?—A. In e combatant corps about one to twenty-three.

Q. Is the proportion of officers to men in the permanent corps greater or less in anada than it is in the mother country?—A. Nearly the same. In the mother couny it is about one to twenty-four.

Q. There is nothing in Canada equivalent to the staff college in England?:A. No. 'e send two officers from here to the staff college when candidates present themselves, it we have not a college of our own.

Q. You have nothing equivalent to the cavalry school, the school of gunnery, ie ordnance school, the school of military engineering, the school of mounted inintry, the school of musketry, the school of signalling, or the Royal Military College · Military Academy?—A. Yes, we have. The Royal Canadian Dragoons have a school ? cavalry. Every unit of the Royal Canadian Artillery is a school of artillery in itilf; but in addition we have the school of gunnery recently introduced, which teaches hat the school of gunnery in England teaches. We have a school of musketry. We ·e developing a school of military engineering with headquarters at Halifax. We ave a signalling corps to carry out the work of the school of signalling, and of course e have the Royal Military College, which corresponds to Sandhurst and Woolwich imbined.

Q. In the mother country there are several grades of manufactured clothing, ıade at the army manufacturing establishments?—A. Yes.

Q. The only manufacturing establishment we have in Canada is for the manuıcture of cartridges?—A. The only Government factory we have is the arsenal at juebec.

Q. That was established prior to 1892?—A. Yes.

Q. Except for turning out more cartridges, the same thing is in existence now ıat was in existence in 1892?—A. Its scope has been broadened. ·It can now manuıcture artillery ammunition of various kinds for the militia and to some extent gun arriages. It also undertakes part of the scientific teaching of the school of gunnery -that part which relates to chemical analysis and machinery.

Q. Coming to the active militia, there were about 36,000 officers and men trained p to the 31st December in 1906, according to the last report?—A. 39,000 odd received welve days' training and about 1,500 more received rather less.

Q. The drilling of the militia is done at different camps?—A. Yes, or at local eadquarters.

Q. For how long a time do they drill?—A. The artillery drill for sixteen days, nd the rest of the service for twelve days. It depends upon the amount voted by arliament.

Q. What is the amount voted by parliament for that purpose?—A. The amount oted for the annual drill was $850,000. Of course, there are other votes which are lso largely drawn upon for the expenses of that drill.

Q. How many camps are there in the militia?—A. Ten, in the east, in addition ɔ various camps in the west.

Q. When is the first camp formed?—A. About the end of the first week in June.

29a—47

Q. When is the last camp held?—A. As a rule, all except the camps of military district No. 9 are held between the end of the first week in June and the end of the second week in July. The camp of military district No. 9 is held in September.

Q. When do the militia begin training preparatory to the camps?—A. The rural militia practically do no training preparatory to camp. The amount done is so very small that it may be ignored. The city corps train as suits them best according to their local convenience, in the winter and the spring.

Q. In Ottawa, for instance, when do the 43rd and the Governor General's Foot Guards begin training?—A. Their drills begin as soon as the drill hall is warm enough to be used, probably in April; but the military instruction of officers and n. c. officers wi'! begin much earlier.

Q. Then practically the rural corps, except for the annual drill, are never called · her?—A. Practically it comes to that.

.Q. And the city corps have occasional drills and lectures for about four months! —A. Some of them go on right through the summer. The drill and training of some city corps will not be ended until Thanksgiving Day. They spread out through the year, giving the equivalent of twelve days' training and drill. They often give more than the equivalent.

Q. Then throughout the winter practically there are no militia under training at all?—A. No, except at the schools of instruction of the permanent corps.

Q. When do you open the camp at Petawawa?—A. It depends on the convenience of the militia who are going there. This year we opened it on the 1st of June and it will close about the 7th of September.

Q. How many men have you congregated together at one time?—A. The largest number has been about 3,000.

Q. Do you mix cavalry and artillery and infantry together there?—A. We have this year for the first time. We have had practically the whole permanent corps together for from six weeks to two months in camp. There have been from 1,800 to 1,400 men there.

Q. Does the active militia train there with them?—A. Yes, some. Military district No. 4 trained there this year, during that time, raising the number in camp to about 3,000 men. We hope to have other districts in other years. The financial question and the expense of transport govern that.

Q. What is the relative proportion of officers and non-commissioned officers to men in the English militia and the Canadian militia respectively?—A. About one officer to thirty-five men and one to twelve respectively. The English militia have no cavalry or field artillery, so these proportions apply to the infantry only.

Q. What is the pay of a lieutenant-colonel in the Canadian militia?—A. He gets $5 a day.

Q. What does a lieutenant get?—A. $2 a day on appointment.

Q. What do the men get while in camp?—A. The privates vary to some extent. A man in his first year's service gets so much, and in his second and other years he gets higher efficiency pay as well.

Q. You pay for results to some extent?—A. Yes.

Q. A man coming from a rural corps with no efficiency pay gets how much?—A. 50 cents a day.

Q. Considering that you cannot get labouring men for less than $1.50 a day, is that pay sufficient to enable you to increase the militia?—A. I think the militia are paid too small a sum under present conditions. At the same time the efficiency pay which we administer under very liberal rules does operate to raise that sum so much so that in 1906 we had 4,000 more men in camp than had ever been in camp before This year we have not quite maintained that, but we think we shall be only about 1,000 men short of that number.

Q. You think having the efficiency pay has resulted in increasing the number of men to a certain extent?—A. Undoubtedly it has.

Q. If the rural militia are trained only during time of camp, there would not be

uch efficiency pay, one would suppose, going to the men of the rural corps?—A. The
ficiency pay was instituted, I think, as a means of assuring that a man would be-
ve himself well in camp and try to do his best to learn.

Q. That is to say it is more good conduct pay than efficiency pay?—A. It is more
an that. This last year we introduced a system by which a man has to make a
rtain score at rifle practice and non-commissioned officers had to be certified as effi-
ent at their respective duties before being allowed to draw efficiency pay.

Q. What body chooses the uniforms for the militia? For instance, when a
w regiment is raised somewhere between this and Montreal, who would choose its
uniform?—A. The general rule is that according to the arm of the service the uniform
the same as that in the British service. The regiment is allowed to make proposals
r special badges or distinctive marks. The uniform question is dealt with by the
djutant General and the Quartermaster General together. They make up their
inds what they think is right, and then obtain the approval of the Minister in
ouncil.

Q. Is it a fact that the uniforms of the officers are so costly as to discourage the
rmation of regiments of militia—the men, I suppose, get their uniforms free?—A.
he men get their uniforms free.

Q. But the officers have to pay for their uniforms?—A. Yes. That is a most
fficult question. Every attempt that I have ever known to be made to reduce the
st of uniforms has been strenuously resisted by the officers concerned.

Q. Would it encourage the man of moderate means to become an officer if the
st of the uniform was reduced?—A. Possibly. As a matter of fact, the cost of the
ligatory uniform for camp is so small that it is not an excessive charge, but the
gulations allow other articles to be worn, and the regimental feeling generally, in
e city corps at any rate, insists on their being purchased with the result that the
niforms may become rather a costly item.

Q. In addition to the cost of the uniform, when anything belonging to an officer's
utfit is imported into Canada he has to pay the duty on it?—A. Yes, he does now.

Q. So that in addition to the cost of his uniform, a new officer appointed to a
giment has to pay this duty?—A. Yes, and that duty would possibly amount to more
an his pay for the year.

Q. In that state of the case how is it possible to enlarge the number of officers?—
. Apparently the officers are to be found.

Q. Are they not now apparently coming from the class of millionaires?—A. No
oubt this tends to exclude all but fairly rich men; but the obligatory part of their
niform is not expensive; the voluntary part is.

Q. What do you call the voluntary part of an officer's uniform?—A. An officer
only required, as regards upper garments, to appear in camp in his serge or patrol
cket, which is an inexpensive garment; there is hardly any gold lace about it. But
e regiment has also a full dress tunic, and a young gentleman joining a city corps,
ough not obliged to get it, usually does get it.

Q. The purpose of all this annual drill is chiefly, I suppose, to obtain efficiency in
ooting?—A. General efficiency, including good shooting.

Q. But the chief end and aim is to turn out a nation of sharpshooters?—A. To
rn out a nation of soldiers.

Q. That would necessarily involve efficiency in rifle shooting?—A. Yes, but I
ould not say merely a nation of sharpshooters. There are many other things that
ave to be taught—discipline, organization, power of manœuvre, &c., &c.

Q. After a time, the next process is the formation of a camp here under the
uspices of the Dominion Rifle Association to select a team to go to Bisley—that would
llow from the annual training, I presume?—A. I could hardly say that. It is in a
ay an independent effort to give a stimulus to rifle shooting throughout the country
ther than to stimulate it in the active militia only.

Q. All these men who come here to the camp of the Dominion Rifle Association
29a—47½

are attached to one corps or another, are they not?—A. Not at all. A considerable majority of them are. The larger numbers are from the city corps.

Q. Is there any attempt at decentralization in this matter of selecting men for the Bisley team—having competition in other districts besides Ottawa?—A. As far as I know, the different rifle associations work together, and the best shots as a rule come to Ottawa, and there is, I think, a rule that the highest scores in a certain number of matches entitle the makers to be chosen for the Bisley team.

Q. As a matter of fact, when the Bisley team is made up is there not always a large proportion of men from Ottawa who are used to the ground who become members of it?—A. That is just possible. It is a matter of which I cannot speak from personal knowledge, but I am told that it does not often occur.

Q. A man may go on the Bisley team year after year for twenty years in succession?—A. You will find men at Hamilton and Toronto who go on it as often as those from Ottawa.

Q. A certain set of men in Canada practically monopolize the Bisley team?—A. I don't know. That is a matter the department does not touch. The grant is made to the Dominion Rifle Association, and it selects and arranges for the team.

Q. One of the principal schemes of the department is the formation of rifle associations throughout the country?—A. Yes.

Q. Their main object is shooting?—A. Yes.

Q. From these rifle associations do the best shots come to Ottawa to the August and September matches?—A. Presumably.

Q. Is there any allowance made for their travelling expenses up here?—A. Not by the Militia Department.

Q. A man from Halifax, who may be the best shot in the Dominion, if he has not the funds to enable him to come to Ottawa to compete, would be barred out?—A. He might be. I understand that the associations have some arrangements made with the view of helping men in their transport, but these are made unofficially.

Q. But there is no allowance to enable good shots to come to Ottawa to compete? A. No public allowance.

Q. You used to have armourers to look after arms. Are they in existence still? —A. Yes.

Q. And throughout the country drill halls are used?—A. Yes.

Q. You have lately made most praiseworthy endeavours to promote rifle shooting in the public schools by the formation of cadet corps. How many boys are now formed into cadet corps?—A. About 11,000 are authorized, and perhaps 7,000 are enrolled.

Q. The government of the militia is laid down in the Act of 1904?—A. Yes.

Q. In looking through that Act I find that there is no reference whatever made to the deputy minister of the department on the civil side?—A. I presume that the deputy minister is included in the minister, he is mentioned in article 6.

Q. The Civil Service Act says that there shall be a deputy head of each department, and the Interpretation Act includes the deputy with the minister, practically as you say, but there has always been in every other department of the public service that I am aware of, provision that there shall be a deputy head of the department, with certain duties assigned to him; but there seems to be no duties assigned to the deputy head of the Militia Department in the Militia Act?—A. No military duties, of course.

Q. And no civil duties?—A. The Militia Act would hardly deal with civil duties, would it, when they are already prescribed in another Act?

Q. Would it not deal with the expenditure of public moneys, for instance?—A. It is a matter I do not profess to have an opinion upon. But the Militia Act of 1904, so far as mention of the deputy minister is concerned, is just the same as the Act of 1886.

Q. The Militia Act of 1904 seems to be partly a consolidation and partly a new departure from the old Militia Act?—A. Yes.

Q. A new feature of the Act of 1904 is the provision to establish a Militia Council? —A. It is rather the permission to establish a Militia Council. Equally under the

ESSIONAL PAPER No. 29a

ct you might have a general officer commanding, in that case you would not have a ouncil.

Q. At any rate the result of the Militia Act of 1904 has been the creation of the 'ilitia Council?—A. Exactly.

Q. And that is a new feature of the Act?—A. Yes.

Q. The Militia Council is made up of several members?—A. Yes. ·

Q. The Minister is the president, the Deputy Minister, the vice-president and the hers members, the Chief of the General Staff, the Adjutant-General, the Quarter-aster General, the Master-General of the Ordnance and the Accountant and Pay-aster General?—A. Yes.

Q. In the imperial service there is also what is called an Army Council?—A. Yes.

Q. That is also made up of seven members?—A. Yes, on which this one is odelled.

Q. There are four military members in each case, and the same titles are borne ʳ the military members in Canada as are borne by the military members in England, ɪt the Army Council appears to differ from the Militia Council in this respect, that ɔne of the officers of the War Office are members of the Army Council. It is com-ɔsed of four military members with the Parliamentary Under Secretary of State, ɪd the Financial Secretary of the War Office, who is a member of parliament: that ío say, there is parliamentary control?—A. The political and military elements are ike in each case, for the parliamentary Under Secretary and the Financial Secre-ry are both officers of the War Office.

Q. But the Militia Council practically has the military features without the poli-cal features?—A. It has the minister.

Q. But the Army Council practically excludes the War Office, while you have in-uded the department?—A. You must remember that the financial member of the rmy Council is essentially an officer of the department, as is also the civil member, ιe parliamentary Under Secretary.

Q. He is accountable to parliament?—A. He is accountable through the War ffice, but not separately to parliament.

Q. The financial member of the Army Council is a Member of Parliament and :countable to parliament?—A. I should say accountable only to his own chief, the ᵉcretary of State. The order in council clearly states that 'The Finance Member of ιe Army Council is to be responsible to the Secretary of State for the finance of the rmy.'

Q. But practically the difference between the Army Council and the Militia Coun-l is that the Army Council is made up of political and military members, while the :ilitia Council is made up of military members and members of the department?—
. Yes, but I do not quite follow you in the difference, since the political members of ιe Army Council are primarily War Office officials.

Q. It appears to me that the parliamentary control is directly maintained in the rmy Council, while in the Militia Council, with the exception of the minister, who ight not always be present, there is no political representative, though provision is ade, I understand, that in the absence of the minister, who may be away for months , a time, the deputy head of the department presides?—A. Yes.

Q. So that for months the political element may be absent from the Militia Coun-l, while the political element is an essential feature of the Army Council?—A. There this to be remembered that under the constitution of the Militia Council no matter ιvolving new principle can be decided without reference to the political head; also ιat by the letters patent appointing the Army Council any three of its members can cercise all its powers.

Q. There is also a council for imperial defence of the whole empire, over which ιe Prime Minister presides, and other members of which are the Chancellor of the xchequer, the Secretary of State for War, the First Lord of the Admiralty, and Sir rederick Borden and certain professional members?—A. Yes. It is a sub-committee : the imperial cabinet with certain professional members.

7-8 EDWARD VII., A. 1908

Q. With Sir Frederick Borden representing the colonial defence?—A. I fancy that he was summoned merely as an associate member, so to speak, one who attended only when matters affecting his own country were under discussion. I think that members of other colonial administrations are similarly associated with the committee when questions relating to their own colonies are considered.

Q. It would appear as if the members of the department, like the deputy head and the accountant, were numerically inferior to the professional element in the Militia Council?—A. Numerically, yes.

Q. They might be outvoted?—A. Yes, except that the decision always rests with the minister.

Q. Would it not be desirable to keep them entirely distinct?—A. I think not. I think their advice is very desirable.

Q. In the other country the two things are kept entirely distinct. I do not at all agree. The parliamentary Under Secretary of State and the financial secretary are both primarily War Office officials. I am uncertain as to the exact position of the secretary in the War Office in regard to voting power. Practically, I think he does not vote, but he exercises a great deal of influence.

Q. There is and always will be, I suppose, a tendency to remove as far as possible the expenditure on the army and militia from the control of and supervision of the Public Accounts Committee, for instance?—A. I thought that the expenditure was most closely examined into.

Q. But it is not desired to separate them on the ground that these high matters of defence should be too closely criticized?—A. I think not. What is desired by the military authorities in England is the freedom to expend the money provided in the estimates approved by parliament, with complete audit afterwards and responsibility to the Public Accounts Committee. I do not think there has been any tendency to withdraw the reviewing of the expenditure from the Public Accounts Committee. The desire has been to avoid the necessity of referring the details of the military expenditure already approved and provided for in the estimates to the central War Office again for authority on the ground that the parliamentary authority implied by the passing of the estimates was sufficient. That, I think, is the attitude in England.

Q. There was an army scandal in connection with South Africa and a Royal Commission was appointed to examine into it?—A. There was.

Q. I read an article the other day in *Truth,* headed 'The control of the purse strings,' in which it was asserted flatly that, there was a tendency on the part of high officials connected with the army to remove the examination of the expenditure from the public accounts committee. Of course, that has nothing to do with us in Canada; you would not follow the same line of conduct here?—A. What I have gathered is that there is a feeling in parliament that in matters of military expenditure the general officers commanding are in much better position to exercise economy than are the officials of the War Office. The only people who know where economies can be effected are the generals commanding. On two or three occasions members of parliament in high position, have expressed the opinion that the most economical expenditures of public money have been by the generals commanding, from the fact that they alone know the exact points where economies can be safely effected. Of course *Truth* may be right and it may be wrong.

Q. You have under you certain subordinates such as the director of operations and staff duties?—A. Yes.

Q. Also an assistant director of operations and staff duties?—A. Yes.

Q. An assistant director of intelligence?—A. Yes.

Q. With some staff lieutenants?—A. Yes, for work on the survey.

Q. The adjutant-general has under him a deputy adjutant-general, and assistant adjutant-general for musketry a deputy assistant adjutant-general for musketry, a director general of medical services, and an officer specially employed?—A. Yes.

Q. The quartermaster general has a director of clothing and equipment and a director of transport and supplies. The master general of the ordnance has a director of artillery, a director of engineer services, an assistant director of engineer services and an officer specially employed. That is following again the system laid down in the Army Council?—A. Yes.

Q. They have nearly the same titles as the several directors assistants over there? —A. Yes, only on a much smaller scale.

Q. When the 43rd regiment is ordered to Petawawa, and it has to get its transport, how is the correspondence carried on? Do they first write to the district officer commanding—A. The district officer commanding is the man who orders the regiment to go. The giving of that order implies that he has received the necessary authority and he would issue the transport requisition.

Q. From whom does he ask for authority?—A. The Militia Council.

Q. Does he correspond directly with the Militia Council?—A. It would be an exceptional arrangement which required the written authority of the Militia Council. Usually it would be conveyed by general order.

Q. How does the request for authority get to the director of transport and supplies?—A. It goes to the secretary of the Militia Council, who passes it in the ordinary course without comment to the director of transport and supplies for consideration and action.

Q. How is the action of the director of transport and supplies communicated to the colonel commanding the 43rd? Does it first go to the quartermaster-general and then to the officer commanding the eastern Ontario command, and then to the colonel of the regiment—A. If it were a case requiring special authority, the director of transport and supplies would take the orders of the quartermaster-general whose subordinate he is, who would give or obtain a decision. If it were a matter of policy which had already been decided upon by the Militia Council, the director of transport and supplies would be aware of that, and would give whatever sanction or make whatever arrangements were necessary outside of the command.

Q. Is there not a certain amount of unnecessary correspondence and reference taking place between the several branches of the militia?—A. In certain cases there no doubt may be, but I think it is usually counterbalanced by the advantages which it confers.

Q. In the inquiry by the last Civil Service Commission, Colonel Panet, who was then Deputy Minister of Militia, was asked this question: 'If Tommy Atkin's forage cap were blown into the Ottawa river, how would he get another'? His answer was that 'Tommy Atkins would communicate with his captain, who would communicate with his colonel, who would communicate with the quartermaster to ascertain if there was a cap in store, if there was he would communicate the fact to his colonel, who would send a requisition for a cap to the district officer commanding, who after giving his approval to it would refer it to the Minister of Militia and Defence, who would authorize a cap to issue. It would then be sent to the deputy minister for action, who would send it to the quartermaster general for issue, and then it would go back through all the same channels again. Is that process still continued?—A. There is now no general officer commanding and the system has greatly changed. I fancy that there is little more circumlocution than in any railway company or other large concern which furnishes clothing free to its employees. You must first have some person in position to decide whether an article of clothing should be replaced free at the public expense, or whether the man should be made to pay for a new one himself. If it is to be replaced free the order must evidently go from the person charged with deciding the point to the store which issues it. I quite agree that it was ridiculous that the general officer commanding, or even an officer junior to him, should not have been authorized to decide whether the man should pay for his cap or get a new one out of the public stores. It is not my business to say how far the the matter would now be settled locally. I think it would probably be settled by the officer holding the command or the D.O.C.

Q. Even then it would go through five or six of these processes?—A. I do not see how that can be helped. Some one has to decide whether the man should be given a hat free or not, and some one has to be authorized to issue it.

Q. General Herbert was very strong on the unnecessary details attending requisitions, and he laid down for the benefit of the Civil Service Commission some forms which he thought might simplify the business?—A. I might here mention one difference made by the institution of the Militia Council, and it is very important. Whereas previously the general officer commanding was practically responsible for everything in the militia on the military side, the institution of the Council was definitely intended to replace that system by making every member of the Council responsible to the minister for one branch of the work, and the question of clothing supply belongs entirely to the quartermaster general, as the care of buildings belongs to the master general of the ordnance. I, therefore, cannot fully answer your question.

Q. In addition to the Militia Council there is an officer called the inspector general?—A. There is.

Q. With regard to the militia, I presume that he occupies the same position as the Auditor General does with regard to general public expenditures, that is to say, he inspects the several camps, points out defects, and reports?—A. Yes, but he has no financial responsibility.

Q. Is he practically an independent officer?—A. He is absolutely independent. He is supposed to inspect and report on certain lines. You will find his duties laid down in the order in council; but he cannot do what I understand the Auditor General can do, refuse certain credits. He has only the power of reporting to the Council.

Q. He is in a way a subordinate of the Council; that is, he is independent and yet has to report to them?—A. He is an independent officer reporting to them, though in no way their subordinate. He is, of course, responsible to the Minister.

Q. When there is a camp, you generally visit it yourself?—A. Yes, as responsible for training.

Q. And there is there an officer commanding?—A. Yes.

Q. Does the inspector general also visit the camp?—A. The inspector general is supposed to visit them all.

Q. Are you and the inspector general there at the same time?—A. Inasmuch as the camps all take place practically at the same period of the year, it is impossible for one man to visit them all, and we generally arrange between ourselves that I shall inspect for the inspector general certain camps in the ordinary course of my watching the training, and that he shall tell me what he observes at those which he visits.

Q. I saw recently in the London *Times* an article which stated that the presence of the inspector general, of the chief of the general staff and of the general officer commanding in chief at Aldershot at the Essex manœuvres in 1904 led to such confusion of authority that we have been practically unable to hold great manœuvres ever since. Do you and the inspector general and the officer commanding the camp happen to be all present together at any of these manœuvres?—A. The English manœuvres are different from these camps. I and the inspector general never go to a camp together. It is physically impossible for each of us to see them all. We arrange to divide up the duties. What I endeavour to see is that the course of training for which the commandant of the camp is responsible is carried out according to the wishes of the Council, and incidentally I make the inspection which the inspector general would make if he were able to be there. Similarly he looks at the training and tells me whether our wishes with regard to that are carried out.

Q. In addition to the officer commanding the camp either you or the inspector general are present?—A. Yes.

Q. On these occasions who would take command?—A. The officer commanding.

Q. You would not replace him?—A. If there were any questions of military service distinct from the camp work the senior officer must take command by law; but when we visit a camp, we treat ourselves merely as visitors to see and report for the information of Council.

Q. There would be no conflict of authority?—A. There is none.

Q. The inspector general has to assist him, besides a staff officer, an inspector of cavalry, an inspector of artillery, an assistant inspector of artillery?—A. These are officers who are employed at their own special work throughout the year, and merely give him the technical information regarding the details of their arm which is required for inspection purposes, but which he may not possess himself. They are all employed otherwise throughout the year except during the camps.

Q. There is a gradation list of officers of the staff and the permanent force. The permanent force at present consists of about 3,000 men?—A. Their fixed establishment is about 3,000. Their actual strength is considerably below that.

Q. I have counted up this gradation list as far as I could, and I find that it is made up of 220 officers?—A. Very likely.

Q. That includes the headquarters staff and the permanent corps. It does not include the officers attached to the Military College?—A. I think not.

Q. Then there are 220 officers to look after a permanent corps of under 3,000 men, and the headquarters staff?—A. No, to look after the militia force of nearly 60,000 men, and they include the headquarters, command and district staff.

Q. And to look after a militia force who are trained in summer only?—A. But whose administration involves work throughout the year, and who are instructed at the military schools in winter.

Q. Then there are 220 officers employed to look after a permanent force of 3,000 men, a militia of 60,000 and the headquarters staff?—A. Yes. You will remember that these 220 officers include the headquarters, command and district staffs, and the instructors of the militia.

Q. In addition to this, there is a system which seems 'a very wise one, of Imperial officers being interchanged and coming to Canada on colonial employment—there are about twenty officers from the Imperial service now employed in Canada?—A. About that.

Q. Are these twenty officers included in the gradation list of staff?—A. Yes. The officers were lent to this extent from the Imperial service because we had largely to increase our permanent force when we took over the garrisons at Halifax and Esquimalt. We had not sufficient experienced officers to fill all ranks, and we had to borrow trained officers temporarily for the purpose. I take it that eventually the number employed will be very largely reduced. It will be probably something like five or six.

Q. In the development of the militia system new branches are constantly created, such as a Paymaster's Corps, an Army Medical Service Corps, and so on?—A. Yes, missing departments are organized.

Q. How are these new branches created ? For instance, who suggests that there should be an Army Pay Corps?—A. Those branches come into existence from the fact that without them we could not maintain an army in the field for a week. We are trying to arrange that the systems of peace administration and of war administration should be the same, and we are gradually organizing those individuals who previously carried out those duties under a civilian system, into such military bodies that they shall be able and liable to go into the field as soldiers should occasion require it. For instance, there have always been people who performed the functions of a paymaster for a district or a command. Formerly they were practically civilians. We are gradually forming from them a military body doing the same duties, but doing them under military discipline and in the same way as they would have to perform them if we found it necessary to put a force into the field.

Q. For instance, you have an Ordnance Stores Corps?—A. Yes.

Q. They are uniformed men?—A. Yes.

Q. They were organized in July, 1903?—A. Yes, I believe so.

Q. They have twelve sections and they have three lieutenant-colonels, seven majors, eight captains, eight lieutenants and four quartermasters of ordnance. Are they the old storekeepers?—A. They are with certain additions.

Q. They do the storekeeper's duties?—A. Yes, and other new duties.

Q. Why was it thought desirable to have this process of evolution, making the storekeepers into an ordnance stores corps?—A. For this reason, that otherwise you could not put them into the field. So far as they were civil servants they were independent of the officers whose troops they had to uniform and equip. They were solely responsible to the civil authority at Ottawa for everything they did. The result was that when stores were wanted, say at Toronto, the application had to be made by the officer commanding to the local storekeeper at Toronto as to an outside authority, who referred it to Ottawa, whence it was sent back again. The idea of the Ordnance Stores Corps now is that they are a military body organized to work in the field, really performing much the same duties as they did before, only as a military body under discipline rather than a civil body, and with a much wider scope of work.

Q. You rather go on the idea that a country able to govern itself should be able to defend itself, and that in times of peace these arrangements should be made for any emergency that may arise?—A. Yes. I think the organization of the army should be as much as possible the same in time of peace as in time of war, so that when emergency arises it could pass from the one condition to the other with as little dislocation of system as possible.

Q. Besides the Ordnance Stores Corps you have the Army Service Corps?—A. Yes.

Q. That is for transport and supplies?—A. Yes.

Q. That is to say, when camps are formed, they have to look after the mobilization of the troops?—A. The transportation, feeding and housing.

Q. Have they any other duties outside of the time of camps?—A. Oh, yes.

Q. I suppose in connection with the garrisons at Halifax and Esquimalt?—A. Yes, in connection with all the permanent stations. They also deal with a large number of questions which arise for some months before and after the camps; for instance, arrangements as to transport with the railway companies, contracts for food and supplies, purchase of remounts, &c., &c.

Q. That goes on all the year round?—A. That goes on, more or less, all the year round.

Q. And requires this staff all the year round?—A. I think so. The staff is largely a temporary staff, paid only for the number of days they work during the year.

Q. You have lately organized a Signalling Corps?—A. Yes.

Q. You have three command signallers and eight district signallers?—A. Yes.

Q. Signalling is, I suppose. an outdoor work?—A. Yes.

Q. Are they disbanded during the winter season?—A. They are paid for the period of the camp training only. They belong to the active militia.

Q. They are paid for the days they work only?—A. For twelve days' work only.

Q. When they come here for the school of signalling, they are paid for the time they are here?—A. Yes.

Q. For what purpose is the Corps of Guides organized?—A. They are intended to be a corps whose business it is to know thoroughly the roads and the conditions of the part of the country they belong to. They are trained for reconnaissance work and scouting.

Q. Are they employed all the year round?—A. No, they are often employed, but are paid only in the camps. There is one sergeant-major of the corps employed permanently.

Q. General Herbert was asked this question before the last Commission: 'As respects paymasters in the district staffs?' He said: 'I confess I do not see the object of having district paymasters in these days when the transmission of money can be made so easily by means of a cheque. I see no reason why the cheque could not be sent directly from the deputy minister to the person who requires it, without the intermediary of a third person.' I suppose that whatever opinion Sir Ivor Herbert gave should inspire respect?—A. I am a great admirer of him, but, if he is correctly reported. on that point I disagree with him. I cannot imagine the deputy minister in time of war sending a cheque to every man in the field.

ESSIONAL PAPER No. 29a

Q. The Canadian Army Pay Corps is the outcome of the paymasters' business to me extent?—A. Yes.

Q. We have had shown by the Auditor General instances like the following: ayments were due to tradesmen in Ottawa, and the cheque covering these payments as sent from the department to the paymaster of the district at Kingston, and he ansmitted it back to Ottawa, where the payment was made to the tradesman. Does)t that seem rather a round-about way of doing things?—A. It does. But supposing ie order to the tradesman in Ottawa was given from Kingston, would not the payent be made by the man who gave the order?

Q. I do not know who gave the order. The payment was made here, locally, rough the office of the D.O.C. The cheques were sent from here to Kingston, and idorsed back to Ottawa, and paid here at Ottawa?—A. I can quite understand that ι that particular case, where the headquarters of the command are at Kingston, there .ay have been a going backward and forward; but I think it right that the official r whom the order was given should make the payment.

Q. That would not apply to the paymaster; he would not give the order?—A. .y point of view is this: Suppose you have a camp for which supplies are required, 1d the contract is made by the officer in charge of supplies in that particular command. he accounts are submitted by him when the services are performed, and he has to rtify them before their payment can be authorized. He does not handle the money. ? the paymaster has a credit at the bank, and the necessary authority, he pays the)counts on his certificate. But if not, the accounts go to the central authority, who inds a cheque down, so that the man who gives the order knows that the bill is paid.

Q. The chief place for the duties of the paymaster is Halifax, I presume?—A. I iould think so.

Q. Are you aware that the paymaster sent to Halifax was a worn out officer in the rvice of the department, who died a few months after he was sent?—A. Yes. I now that he died, but he was not worn-out when he was sent, though he was old. :e had exceptional qualifications, and I concurred in the selection.

Q. If the system was necessary or desirable, would it not be desirable to send an)le man in the prime of life to the chief point to carry it out?—A. Yes, assuming iat a competent official was available.

Q. Was not one of the effects of sending this officer as paymaster to Halifax that ? became a member of the military branch of the department and came under military)ntrol rather than civil?—A. I do not know; I do not think so. There was no Army ay Corps at the time.

Q. When he went down he ceased to be an officer of the department on the civil de and became an officer on the military side. entitled to draw a pension?—A. That news to me.

Q. And that pension is continued to his widow?—A. He did not leave a widow.

Q. At all events, this man, who was worn-out in the service, was sent to Halifax, ie principal point, to inaugurate a new system?—A. I understand that he was the ıly man competent for the work they had available to send.*

_____ ___ __   _____

* The circumstances of this case were as follows: The British troops at Halifax were ι be paid by the Canadian Government at Imperial rates of pay and under the Imperial ıgulations. It was thought desirable to send for this job a paymaster (Lieut.-Col. Guy) ho had been in the Imperial service and knew their system, rather than an inexperi-ıced civil officer.

I deem it right to append to the evidence a statement of the facts upon which the uestions relating to the Paymaster at Halifax were based.

When, in 1902, I was a member of the Commission appointed to inquire into the !artineau defalcations, while examining the work of the Accountant's Branch of the !ilitia Department I found that one of the officers in that branch (Lieut.-Col. Guy) ppeared to be very dazed and enfeebled and quite unfit for duty. I suggested his iperannuation, but it was intimated to me that on account of his short term of ser-

Q. These paymasters do not make all the expenditures of the department—for instance, a payment made on account of Ross rifles or to Woods', of Ottawa, for tents?—A. I suppose not. These are contracts made at headquarters.

Q. You have a system of pensions to officers of the permanent staff and to officers and men of the permanent militia ?—A. Yes.

Q. That came into force in 1901, before your time ?—A. Yes.

Q. You are aware, I suppose, that the Superannuation Act applying to members of the Civil Service was abolished ?—A. Yes.

Q. But after the abolition of that Act, an act was passed to enable officers of the permanent staff and officers and men of the permanent militia to obtain pensions which are based on their salaries ?—A. Yes, on their pay and allowances.

Q. They are not based on salaries and allowances?—A. Yes, the pension is based on pay and allowances .

Q. The deduction is on pay only ?—A. Yes.

Q. The pension is based on length of service?—A. Yes.

Q. The highest pension will be seven-tenths?—A. Yes.

Q. Is there a fixed age for retirement ?—A. Yes.

Q. Lord Aylmer, who was 65 last February, went out under that fixed age period ?—A. I am not aware that he did. He went out under the Order in Council, which put a term to his appointment when he was appointed.

Q. Was that an order of the Militia Council or an order of the Governor in Council ?—A. An order of the Governor in Council.

Q. You say there is a fixed age for retirement ?—A. Except in the case of colonels appointed before a given date, of whom Lord Aylmer was one.

Q. But when he was appointed inspector general, that was waived ?—A. That was waived, and a fixed term was laid down for his appointment.

Q. You have in the branch of the adjutant general. an officer, specially employed, who was born in the year 1837?—A. Yes.

Q. It is his duty, amongst other things, to compile the militia list ?—A. I do not think he does as a matter of fact. I think another man does it, but he is not in my branch.

Q. He was specially employed there ?—A. I would like to say about that appointment that Colonel Smith is only temporarily employed. I do not consider him on the active officers' list. He was retired long ago. As I understand it, he does not get an officer's pay. He gets a certain daily salary, and is to all intents and purposes a civil employee, but I may be wrong.*

_____

vice his retiring allowance would be small, and that it would not be generous at that time to retire him. To my astonishment, when the system of paymasters was set on foot, Lieut.-Col. Guy was made Paymaster at Halifax. This was on the 1st July, 1905. The salary of Lieut.-Col. Guy was increased from $1,650 to $2,400 per annum, and, in addition he was brought under the provisions of the Militia Pensions Act. From the outset Lieut.-Col. Guy had to procure assistance to do the work, and he obtained help from an official of the Halifax post office. As the post office official could not demand two salaries, in a short time he was appointed assistant paymaster and certified the accounts. A year after Lieut.-Col. Guy went to Halifax, and when the Militia Pension Act permitted it, he was retired. Had he remained in Ottawa under the Superannuation Act Lieut.-Col. Guy would, on retirement, have received about $650 per annum. As it was, by an addition of 1¼ years military service he was retired on $1,450 per annum. Lieut.-Col. Guy died about a year after his retirement, being predeceased by his wife a very short time before his death. Such are the facts, and I feel certain that General Lake was not fully aware of the case when Lieut.-Col. Guy was sent to Halifax.

J. M. COURTNEY.

* The above answer is incorrect I find that Lt.-Col Smith was recalled from the Retired List and appointed " Military Secretary " by Maj General Lord Dundonald. When his appointment came to an end, he was specially retained under the circumstances mentioned In answer 229.

SESSIONAL PAPER No. 29a

Q. If Lord Aylmer went out at the age of 65, why is this man, who is over 70 still retained?—A. I cannot answer that. It was long before I came, but I under stand that they required an officer of some military experience to examine military law and pension question, which this ex-officer was quite capable of doing, and that he was granted a certain daily salary. He has no pension, I believe.

Q. As a matter of fact, officers eligible for pensions go out at a fixed age?— A. They are supposed to. That is gradually being carried into force.

Q. A man like Lord Aylmer did not want it, because he had served his full term, but suppose he had served only twenty years at the age of sixty-five, could he have any terms of years added to his pension?—A. I think not.

Q. What pension is payable to the widow?—A. The Act provides: ' The pension to a widow shall be as follows: The widow of a colonel, $500; of a lieutenant-colonel, $450; of a major, $350; of a captain, $250; of a lieutenant or second lieutenant, $200; of a warrant officer, $100.'

Q. Whether he serves two years or twenty-five?—A. He must have completed twenty years' service.

Q. But the sum would be the same whether he had served twenty years or thirty-five years?—A. Yes.

Q. How was Lord Aylmer's retirement put into effect?—A. It went to the Governor in Council.

Q. Do all militia pensions go before the Governor in Council?—A. I believe so.

Q. I see that tenders for supplies are to be addressed to the Secretary of the Militia Council?—A. Yes.

Q. Do these tenders go before the Militia Council?—A. I ought to explain that the secretary of the Militia Council is merely the business name under which all letters are addressed to the department. He is *ex officio* in charge of the central registry, which distributes the correspondence received to the different branches which deal with it.

Q. He is the secretary of the department, as well as the secretary of the Militia Council?—A. He is both, but his duties as secretary to the Militia Council are in addition to his duties as secretary to the department.

Q. Then, the secretary of the Militia Council receives all the correspondence coming to the department and distributes it?—A. Yes.

Q. That would include tenders?—A. That includes tenders.

Q. That does not necessarily imply that the tenders go to the Militia Council for adjudication?—A. As a matter of fact, they do not go to the Militia Council.

Q. When tenders are called for supplies, such as tents or other equipment, the practice in Canada is, I suppose, as it is in England, to have a sealed pattern?—A. A sealed pattern or specifications.

Q. It was stated the other day that the Australian Government are supplied with Lee-Enfield rifles at 37 shillings?—A. I should doubt it very much, unless the rifles are obsolete.

Q. The Militia Council, I presume, has nothing to do with the Ross rifle contract? —A. As such, nothing that I know of.

Q. The English arm is the Lee-Enfield?—A. The ' Improved Lee-Enfield.'

Q. It has gone to Mark No. 9?—A. Possibly.

Q. Was there such a thing as the Ross rifle when the contract was entered into? —A. I really know very little about the contract. I have no doubt there was, but I really do not know.

Q. The cost of the Ross rifle to the country is $25 each, payable 75 per cent as the work of construction proceeds, and it is inspected, I believe, by an officer of small arms attached to your branch?—A. Not of my branch.

Q. Attached to one of the branches of the Militia Council?—A. Yes. I cannot speak as to the payments, for I know little about it.

Q. There are continual changes made in military arms?—A. Yes.

Q. You do not know whether the Ross rifle is a pattern going on for a length of time and allowing of improvements?—A. It is constantly being improved. The various marks in a rifle mean improvements applied to that pattern of arm as time goes on.

By Mr. Fyshe:

Q. Have you made a report on the Ross rifle?—A. No.

By the Chairman:

Q. Has any communication come from the Militia Council in reference to it?—A. Do I understand you to ask if I, personally have made any report to the Militia Council on the Ross rifle? I made a report on certain points which I observed at some of the camps, but I have not made a general report on the Ross rifle.

Q. As a matter of fact, the contracts were entered into by the civil branch of the department, the minister and the deputy?—A. I presume so.

Q. There have only been two reports of the Militia Council published as yet?—A. Yes, those for 1905 and 1906.

Q. In the report for 1905 there was a part devoted to the clerical staff of the department?—A. Yes.

Q. In the report for 1906 no reference seems to be made to the clerical staff at all. Why was that?—A. The report is drawn up something like this. Each member of the council drafts that part of the report which affects his own branch. Then the reports from the different branches are all submitted to the council as a whole, a sufficient number of copies being made for each member to have a copy. They are all combined by the deputy minister and myself in one report, which is printed, and, as a rule, the council accepts what we submit.

Q. Then in this last report there is practically no report from the deputy minister?—A. Yes, there was a report from him, which is embodied, but probably not on that point.

Q. There was no report on the efficiency or sufficiency of the clerical staff of the department?—A. If you say there is not, I accept your statement, but I do not remember. I might explain that it was just after Colonel Pinault's death that the report was drawn up and possibly his successor hardly felt justified in making any reference to that subject.

Q. In the first report of the Council the duties of the different members are set forth?—A. Yes.

Q. The minister authorizes and the deputy minister administers the non-effective votes?—A. Yes.

Q. What do you call non-effective votes?—A. All votes such as pensions—that is, moneys paid for personal services not actively rendered.

Q. Does that imply that the deputy minister of the civil branch of the department has nothing to do with the other votes, the effective votes?—A. No, he controls all expenditure on behalf of the minister, but he specially and solely deals with the business affecting the non-effective votes.

Q. In England non-effective votes are administered through the Director General of Army Finance, and whether by inadvertence or not, this apparent limitation of non-effective votes to the deputy minister crept in here?—A. It was supposed that it was a military officer's business to deal with questions affecting personal active services, equipment, and so on, and non-effective services were recognized as matters that specially required close watching, and the deputy minister is particularly charged with watching them. It is the administration, and not the payment. The payment is carried out by the accountant, by cheque signed by the deputy minister, who, of course, is charged by the law absolutely with all financial action. That was the allotment by the minister of the various duties of the staff.

Q. If the deputy minister has control of all financial matters, why should it be specially notified that he had control of non-effective votes?—A. May I point out that you use the word 'control,' while the word in the order in council is 'administration'

SESSIONAL PAPER No. 29a

of these votes. The order details the arrangement of the business in the department. It was for the public convenience that each member of the department should know who dealt with any particular question, and it was, therefore, considered advisable to lay it down to whom a paper on that particular question should be addressed.

Q. Then, coming to the effective votes, I suppose the Ross rifle would be included in the effective votes?—A. I suppose so, but I am not sure.

Q. Take the pay of men at Halifax, there is nothing to show under whose control that is?—A. The control of the pay is entirely a question of the audit of military accounts.

Q. That is not mentioned there?—A. I am not certain.

Q. With regard to the non-effective votes, they were distinctly laid down as being part of the duty of the deputy minister of the department, and, although the law declares that all expenditures shall be under the control of the Minister, and, therefore, under the control of his deputy, there is a distinction made between non-effective votes and effective votes?—A. I should imagine that it is more a case of omission than commission, but do you not again confuse 'administration' with 'control'?

Q. As a matter of good government, I think the distinction is unnecessary ; although the non-effective votes are placed there under his charge, he has, also, under the minister, charge of all votes?—A. I do not know. I scarcely suppose that, for example, military pay would be under his authority, in his capacity as a member of the Council.

Q. Would it not have happened in this way? In the British Army List the Director General of Army Finance is an Assistant Under Secretary of State, Sir Fleetwood Wilson, so that all the financial operations of the British Army Council were under the finance member of the Council, who was a member of the Government, but the exclusively non-effective votes were under the Director General of Army Finance?—A. I am not quite certain that this list, which you quote, is the same as it was at the time the Militia Council organization was drawn up. It was drawn up on the War Office List, non-effective votes are administered by the civil member of the Army Council. Our system is as close a copy of that system as could be well made, subject to the modifications which under instructions were introduced.

Q. You stated just now that the strength of the permanent corps was laid down at 3,000?—A. Yes, the present fixed establishment was laid down at 3,000.

Q. It is not quite 3,000?—A. No, the actual strength is considerably under.

Q. You have had some difficulty in recruiting?—A. Yes.

Q. You have had to go to England to get time expired men?—A. No, men of corps about to be reduced.

Q. Do you think that will lead to good results?—A. So far they have done admirably.

Q. They have only just come, have they?—A. They have been here now for seven months.

Q. You find great difficulty in recruiting in Canada?—A. A good deal.

Q. Is not the Canadian temperament rather against the Tommy Atkins mode of life?—A. I think that the matter is governed mainly by money considerations.

Q. What do you pay a private in the permanent corps?—A. Fifty cents a day during the first term of service, more afterwards.

Q. With his rations and clothes ?—A. Yes.

Q. Are there married quarters ?—A. A certain proportion are allowed to be married ; about twelve per cent, all told.

Q. In your first report the strength of the permanent corps on December 31, 1904, was stated to be 959, and in your second report, it was stated to be on December 31, 1905, 2,058; that is to say, there was a difference of 1,100 minus 1, or the mean between them would be about 1,500. The desertions that year were 492, about one in three ?—A. Yes, you may put it so, though it is rather misleading.

Q. In the second year, the strength on December 31, 1905, was 2,058, and on June 30, 1906, it was 2,267, or a mean of 2,160. The desertions in the six months were 348, one in six, while they were one in three for the year. · Is not that an enormous proportion of desertions ?—A. It is an enormous proportion.

Q. How do you account for it ? Do they take an oath of office ?—A. They take an oath of allegiance. I think there is a general disregard for an oath in that class, and I think that the facilities offered to deserters by the demand of all employers for labour helps desertion.

Q. Is there an impatience of restraint ?—A. There is perhaps more than in England, but not very much more, I think.

Q. Is there a certain discontent in the ranks ?—A. If you ask me for the reason, I think the establishments are too small in these little stations and poor barracks, and the men have to remain so long there without any chance or prospect of a change, while the work is hard and somewhat dull, that they simply get disgusted and go. Government, too, does not always keep faith with them. In the British army they have changes of station from time to time, with a chance of seeing foreign countries, they have the excitement of occasional expeditions, and all these things go to make a man more contented, and they have much larger units and less work in proportion.

Q. Is there a good deal of marching, forming fours and that sort of thing ?— A. Their drill is supposed to comprise the whole of military training, except where we cannot give them the more advanced portions for want of ground space.

Q. Does not their training then become perfunctory ?—A. To a certain extent.

Q. Are the officers expected to see after their comfort ? A. They are intended to do so, but some do not seem to understand it very well.

Q. Do they not desert to some extent on account of the neglect of the officers ?— A. Possibly in some cases, although I do not think that it is the case to an appreciable extent.

Q. What amusement is provided for these men ?—A. It is difficult for me to say. They have a recreation room and a reading room well provided for, and their canteens are generally clean, cheap, and, I believe, well conducted. But too few officers take part in the men's sports out of hours or try to encourage sports. Some of them do so constantly, but others do not. I think it is a part of the Canadian temperament that they do not care about outdoor games and field sports as the British officers do.

Q. When Parliament grants an appropriation for new barracks the plans are submitted to the Militia Council, are they not ?—A. Yes, and sometimes altered by the Public Works department after the council has approved.

Q. There is a standard barracks in England. the cost being so much per man, I believe ?—A. There is a standard barracks with a standard of cost—I cannot tell you exactly what it is.

Q. Has not the tendency in Canada been rather to provide palatial accommodation for the officers and rather inferior accommodation for the men ?—A. We have not done any barrack building for many years, probably twenty. There are certainly none that can be called palatial. You should see the Tete de Pont barracks at Kingston, especially the officers' block. They are wretchedly bad.

Q. Were there not plans for barracks at Sherbrooke and Toronto ?—A. There are plans for new barracks at Toronto not yet commenced. but palatial is hardly a correct description. The difference in accommodation is that in Canada you supply quarters for married officers, which is not done in England except in a very few ranks.

Q. The militia list is prepared under the adjutant general ?—A. Yes.

Q. In looking over the list for October. 1906, I find among the field officers the name of Hon. Louis R. Masson, who has been dead twenty years, and the name of Major Wicksteed, who died four or five months ago ?—A. If you consider that this list is drawn up and supervised by one officer who has many other duties as well, you will see that there is a good deal of work involved in keeping it up to date. I quite agree that there are mistakes in the list, but it is faultless as compared with the militia list of a few years ago. I cannot see how these mistakes can be entirely avoided unless the officer is advised of the death of the men. How else is he to know.

Q. I find the following in the Toronto News in regard to the militia list: ' On page 47 we learn that Major G. A. Lodge was born in 1869, and became a second lieutenant in 1882 at the early age of 13. Two years later (in 1884) he had attained the rank of lieutenant, before he had completed his sixteenth year. Page 55 reveals the fact that Lieutenant Fitzpatrick was born on August 17, 1846, and that on the 1st of July, 1903, he became a lieutenant at the unusual age of 57. At 61 he is still a lieutenant, while certain elastic regulations fix the age limit of that rank at 40 years. Page 39, gradation list, headquarters staff, furnishes a pleasant instance of military longevity. Lieutenant Colonel H. Smith was born on August 1, 1837, and is consequently embarked upon his seventy-first year by remaining an officer of the headquarters staff. From the same staff Colonel Lord Aylmer was retired a few months ago because he had reached the age limit.' There are mistakes even now?—A. These are not mistakes in the list, except in Lieutenant Colonel Smith's case.

Q. There have been a series of articles on the papers in regard to rifle shooting by candidates for the Bisley team, setting forth that the present system does not tend to encourage rifle shooting?—A. That is a matter of personal opinion. You might do better, perhaps, but I would be sorry to say that it does not encourage rifle shooting. I think it does.

Q. An article in the Ottawa *Citizen* on rifle shooting says: ' These remarks may be taken exception to as regards city regiments, which as a rule shoot much better than rural corps, but in reality the principle is not affected. City corps do not go into camp, therefore the men do not lose their time, and are content to fund their pay for the benefit of the corps. Portions of this money together with prizes which the officers contribute from their private funds are used to encourage rifle shooting, and their standard of marksmanship is raised in that way, and in accordance with that good old stereotyped phrase so prevalent in our militia affairs, " without expense to the public." But the rural corps which form the bulk of our militia go into camp and have to pay their men, so that there is no regimental fund.' Would it not be desirable to have some slight appropriation to encourage rifle shooting?—A. Yes. We attempted that last year and did it to a certain extent, and this year we are doing it by making the efficiency pay dependent upon it. I think it will be found that the standard of shooting in the city corps has through it improved even more largely than in the rural corps. The former always produced a number of very good shots, but always had an enormous number of very bad ones as well.

Q. In these camps how many of the twelve days are devoted to rifle shooting and how many to the goose step, forming fours and that sort of thing?—A. I suppose twice as much to rifle shooting as to the goose step and elementary work. It is difficult to say exactly how much, because it depends so much on the range accommodation. Rifle shooting goes on to the utmost extent during the whole period of camp. At Petawawa, where there is ample rifle accommodation, I daresay that every man spends twice as much time at rifle shooting as he does at the elementary portion of his drill.

Q. In the Ottawa *Journal* the other day it was stated: ' The truth probably is that the vast majority of our militia are bad shots. We venture to think that on the average not one volunteer in ten could hit a man at 200 yards once in half a dozen shots, or hit a barn at 600 yards. Nor will this ever be cured by leaving rifle practice by the militia in its present haphazard condition.' Is there a certain amount of truth in that, do you think?—A. I think it was true some time ago. This year we have made the efficiency pay depend on the man being able to make an average of outers at both 100 and 200 yards. It is not a high standard, but it is the first time they have ever had a standard. The shooting is no doubt bad, but it is steadily improving.

Q. In an article in the Ottawa *Citizen* on the artillery competition between the British and Canadian artillery team, after stating that the Canadians won, the article says: ' It is not to be inferred that because the British artillery men drilled so admirably they could not shoot, but it is permissible to point out that the Canadians who did not drill nearly as well nor look so smart, shot better.' Is the inference to be drawn from that that there is an over development of drill and an undevelopment of encouragement in shooting?—A. The inference from that is the opposite.

Q. But would not the inference be that improvement in shooting could be obtained by paying less attention to drill?—A. That is perhaps the inference intended to be drawn, but which of the competitors is referred to? The British team won the field artillery competition and many individual prizes.

Q. Is there a proposal now being made that the field artillery brigades should each be furnished with a permanent adjutant?—A. It has been mooted, but I think the name permanent adjutant has been misunderstood. I think it has been taken to mean an officer of the permanent corps appointed as an adjutant, whereas the intention of the proposal was to pay the adjutant of the brigade, who is not a permanent officer but an officer of the active militia, a small allowance for being adjutant throughout the year.

Q. Then, in this criticism it is suggested that 'if this is the case it merely means the creation of a dozen or more billets and an expenditure of $25,000 or $30,000 a year that is quite unnecessary.'?—A. As I say, the man who wrote that article has heard a rumour, but has not understood what he was writing about.

Q. As the duty of the Corps of Guides is laid down to include reconnaissance and finding out the routes and paths throughout the country, there is in consequence a certain amount of mapping done in the department?—A. Not as a consequence, but there is mapping for military purposes done in the department.

Q. Do you think that as in the Ordnance Corps of England, one central bureau should do all the mapping for the different departments?—A. Yes. I have very strongly advocated that, and have drawn attention to the fact that there does not exist in Canada any topographical survey or any real trigonometrical basis on which it could be formed. We have recently had a conference on the subject, and I have pointed out that the only two civilized countries that have not a Surveys Department are Canada and Turkey.

Q. The result of the whole matter is this, that the expenditure on the militia has increased in fifteen years three times—from $2,000,000 to practically $6,000,000?—A. Yes.

Q. The headquarters staff which in 1892 was made up of the General Officer Commanding, the Quartermaster General, the Adjutant General, and the Adjutant General of Artillery, has increased to about 40 ?—A. 27, I think.

Q. The population of Canada of men between the ages of 20 and 40 is in round numbers a million; we have 39,000 of drilled militia who are drilled at the utmost for six months in the year.; the rifle shooting although improving, is still defective. The Swiss, according to Colonel Merritt's paper, with the expenditure of the same amount of moneys, drilled and rendered effective a militia of 250,000 men. Could we not attain better results for the expenditure we have made?—A. Undoubtedly, though I hardly think that parts of your question are an accurate statement of the conditions. I think that if the Swiss system were possible in Canada we could obtain enormously improved results, for the expenditure of the same amount of money, but Switzerland* has universal service, and we have not. Therein lies the whole difference. With reference to the increase of the staff at headquarters, a large proportion of it is made up by officers who at the previous date were performing exactly the same class of duties as civilians as they are now doing as military officers, and also by officers performing duties which at the previous date were not performed at all. In those days the militia as a whole could not have kept the field for a week.

Q. I will put to you a question which was put to General Herbert: There is an impression abroad that there is too much paraphernalia in the shape of officials. Is that correct?—A. The impression is not correct, in my opinion, now.

Q. There are 39,000 men drilled in the last year. Does that represent the total

---

*Note.—Switzerland has recently increased her expenditure considerably.

SESSIONAL PAPER No. 29a

militia?—A. The 41,000 (not 39,000) represents the total number drilled in the country—not the total establishment.

Q. The 39,000 or 40,000 men who were drilled last year were of all ages, I suppose, from 20 to 60?—A. Not a large number of very old men, and a considerable number of men under 20.

Q. The population of Canada of men beween 20 years of age and 40 years is, roughly speaking, a million; 40,000 if they were all between the ages of 20 and 40, would represent only four per cent. Don't you think that a system that would call out such a small proportion of men would need revising?—A. It is merely a question of money—of providing the pay for them.

Q. Do you think that if you had the money you could increase the number of militia?—A. I do.

Q. What proportion does the cost of the training and drill of the militia bear to the total cost of the department?—A. That is a question that it is nearly impossible to answer.

Q. The drill and training of the militia cost last year between $800,000 and $900,000?—A. The nominal vote was that.

Q. Did you exceed it?—A. Yes, but what I mean is that the vote was for a certain portion only of the cost of training. That does not include such things as clothing, arms, instructors, stores, and so on. It is very difficult to arrive at the whole cost of the training.

Q. Suppose that the whole cost of the training came to a million and a half, that would be not one-third of the total cost of the militia. Could not a saving be effected in the other branches of the department to increase the number of militia under training?—A. Not to a large extent with good results. I am far from saying that you could not improve the administration and economize in various directions without real loss of efficiency. But speaking in general terms, you could not economize largely in other directions and devote the money to the training of the militia. But I think your estimate of the cost of training is still under the mark.

Q. An article was published in one of the service magazines on the idea that because Canada, after confederation, with a population of three or four millions, had a militia expenditure of $1,000,000 when there was a revenue of $13,000,000. therefore, when the revenue increased to $100,000,000, it would be justifiable to expend $8,000,000 on the militia. Was there not an article to that effect in one of the service magazines? —A. I think there was, but I am not sure that it bore the construction you give it.

Q. You did not write the article?—A. No. You refer to an article in the Nelson Centennial number of the *United Service Magazine*, I presume.

Q. Is it not a fact that amongst statisticans all conclusions as to expenditure and debt are made oh a per capita basis, and that if the population increased the expenditure should increase without reference to the revenue?—A. My argument would be that the expenditure should depend on the necessity for it, and on your ability to pay.

Q. Not on revenue or population?—A. No, on the necessity of the case and the ability to find the money.

Q. You would not argue that because the revenue of the country has increased seven times the expenditure on the militia should increase seven times?—A. My view as to expenditure is, that it should be, like insurance, decided by the risk against which you wish to insure and the extent to which you are prepared to insure yourself.

Q. Do you happen to know how many men were drilled about the time the Militia Act was first introduced, in 1870 or thereabouts?—A. No. I know that in 1898 rather less than 20,000 were drilled.

Q. In 1892 the expenditure was only about $2,000,000?—A. Yes.

Q. If you doubled the number the expenditure should be only $4.000,000 instead of $6,000,000?—A. You must remember that we have taken over the expenditure at Halifax and Esquimalt, and we have undertaken the rearmament of the militia with modern rifles and modern guns. It always seemed to me that at least for ten or

29a—48½

fifteen years after 1870 you were living on your capital, that is, on the stores left by the Imperial troops, to a great extent, and a good deal of the expenditure since has been necessarily in order to catch up. In 1892 you had Snider rifles, muzzle loading field guns and no departmental services. Comparison between then and now is scarcely possible.

Q. Is there not now rather an over inclination to lay in sub-target guns, Sutherland rifle sights and Ross rifles—to over do it rather than under do it?—A. I think it is necessary to have an up-to-date modern rifle, whether it be the Ross rifle or the Lee-Enfield. I think you must have a rifle which is, in the opinion of the general public at least, equal to the rifle with which your foe may be armed. I believe the expenditure on certain things, such as the sub-target gun, is justified by its results on the shooting of the militia.

Q. Granted that it is desirable to have up-to-date methods, is there not an inclination, instead of ordering fifty sub-target guns, to order a thousand? Is there not an inclination to over do it?—A. Speaking for the Militia Council, I should say that we watch very closely not to order any thing more than we positively need. We know the amount available for our purposes is limited, and we endeavour not to expend any thing that we think could be avoided.

Q. Then the restraint lies in the amount of the vote?—A. Largely.

Q. If you could persuade Parliament to increase the vote, the Militia Department would gaily spend it?—A. I presume that we should say this: If Parliament accepts the Government policy and votes more money for military purposes, it presumably wants that money expended upon making its weapons of defence as strong and efficient as possible. At present we order artillery for exactly the number of militia we have available. If Parliament told us, as it has done, that it thinks an army of double the strength should be legislated for, and gave us the money to fit out that army, we should do it. But as it is we try to expend the money that Parliament approves, upon our estimates, without wasting any part of it at all.

Q. The Parliament of Canada has never been ungenerous in dealing with the militia?—A. I do not think it has always clearly known what it was voting for.

Q. But whatever has been asked has been readily granted?—A. Do you distinguish between Parliament and the Government.

Q. After the estimates have passed the Government and been laid on the Table, there, have been very few criticisms as to the amount granted for the militia ?—A. I should say that Parliament has always granted to the militia what the Government of the day, representing the majority, has asked for.

Q. How many high power Maxim guns have been ordered?—A. None that I know of.

Q. What are those big guns you have had from England?—A. There were, I think, half a dozen high power Maxim guns ordered. I did not believe in the policy of it, and I got permission to countermand the order. The firm agreed to do that, and turned the money over to one of our other orders for field guns of the ordinary pattern.

Q. How much were these heavy guns to cost?—A. I do not know.

Q. Only half a dozen were supplied?—A. None were supplied. The order was cancelled and the money devoted to the 18-pounder guns we then had under order.

Q. What is the cost of the 18-pounder gun?—A. About $5,250.

Q What is the cost of a battery fully equipped ?—A. Four guns with a full complement of ammunition wagons, but no ammunition, would cost about $50,000.

Q. How many batteries do you propose to fully equip?—A. The number of batteries now authorized, which is, I think, 26.

Q. What is the allowance to a cavalry man for a horse going into camp?—A. One dollar a day.

Q. Assuming that a regiment of cavalry was sent to Petawawa and a horse is killed by accident, what allowance would the Government make for the horse?—A. $100.

Q. Is it possible to get a horse in Canada to-day for $100?—A. Not in certain irts of the country.

Q. Where there is a cavalry regiment you cannot, as a rule, get a horse for $100? ·A. My opinion is that the present indemnity is too low. It is about to be increased.

The Commission adjourned.

QUEBEC, September 20, 1907.

Mr. JOSEPH LAROCHELLE, sworn and examined.

By the Chairman :

Q. You are attached to the Dominion arsenal?—A. Yes.

Q. That is what is called the cartridge factory?—A. Yes.

Q. There is a superintendent there, Colonel Gaudet ?—A. Yes.

Q. And an assistant superintendent, Captain Panet?—A. Yes.

Q. And an accountant, Mr. Dupre?—A. Yes.

Q. And yourself as paymaster?—A. Yes.

Q. And Mr. Denechaud as clerk?—A. Yes.

Q. Have you any other employees?—A. There is another clerk since July last.

Q. How many labourers are employed in the factory?—A. About 370.

Q. Your duty as paymaster is to pay the accounts of the factory and the wages of ie men?—A. Yes.

Q. Where do you get your cheques to do that?—A. From Colonel Gaudet; he signs ie cheques.

Q. Are you one of the army pay clerks?—A. No.

Q. You are simply paying the wages of the 370 men and the accounts of the ace?—A. Yes.

Q. The cartridges manufactured in the factory are packed in boxes?—A. Yes.

Q. How many does a box contain ?—A. 1,000.

Q. How many boxes do you turn out in a week?—A. We can turn out about 240,-)0 cartridges in a week.

Q. Does that turn out go on all the year round?—A. Yes.

Q. Where do you send these cartridges?—A. To the citadel.

Q. Are they stored there in the bomb-proof building — A. Yes.

Q. Are they sent there every day?—A. No, every month.

Q. Then, you have sometimes about a million cartridges on hand at the arsenal? ·A. Yes.

Q. Isn't that rather dangerous?—A. No. Of course they are not loaded.

Q. Do the militia of Canada use as much as 240,000 in a week?—A. They are iking for that number.

Q. Do you send everything to the citadel?—A. Yes, to the ordnance stores.

Q. Do you know how far the stock has been increased or decreased there?—A. I)uld not say.

Q. You have nothing to do with the cartridges after they once leave the factory nd go to the citadel?—A. No, nothing at all.

Q. You come here on behalf of the clerical staff at the factory?—A. Yes.

Q. You were appointed in 1902, five years ago?—A. Yes.

Q. What were you appointed at?—A. I was appointed as stenographer and type-riter.

Q. At what salary?—A. At $1.50 a day.

Q. When did you get your $800?—A. Two years ago, in July last.

7-8 EDWARD VII., A. 1908

Q. Did you go from $1.50 a day to $800?—A. No. I first went to $2.05 a day. Then in July, 1905, I was appointed at $800 a year.

. Mr. Dupre was appointed twenty-five years ago?—A. Yes.

. Was that when the factory was established?—A. Yes.

. What salary had he when he was appointed?—A. $1 a day.

Q. And now, after twenty-five years' service, he gets $800 a year?—A. Yes.

Q. Are the duties so great as to require an accountant and a paymaster?—A. Oh, yes.

Q. What account books are kept in the factory?—A. We keep a ledger only.

Q. You have only the one side of it to keep, the accounts of the materials received; the other side is simply a discharge of so much per day going to the citadel? —A. Yes.

Q. Would it not be possible for the accountant to do your work?—A. It would be impossible.

Q. What are your office hours?—A. From half-past nine till twelve, and from half-past one till five.

Q. Who looks after the work at night? I suppose the work goes on all the time? —A. Not at night.

Q. Is the factory entirely closed at night?—A. Yes. Sometimes we require a few men to repair.

Q. You have no night gang to do any work at all?—A. No.

Q. Then all the men employed there are day labourers?—A. Yes, sir.

Q. What do you pay the day labourers?—A. $7.50 a week, or $1.25 a day.

By Mr. Bazin:

Q. Is that the average wage?—A. There are some paid higher. We have some labourers at $8.75 a week, and we have three or four young labourers at $6.85.

By the Chairman:

Q. You have a large number employed at what is called piece-work?—A. Yes.

Q. Are they employed pretty nearly all the year round?—A. Yes, all the year round.

Q. There are from 70 to 80 employed by the week?—A. Yes, about that.

Q. And about 250 employed on piece-work?—A. Yes.

Q. How much do you pay for this piece-work?—A. It is according to the piece-work done. Some are making tools, and there are a lot of boys running machines. There are a certain number of operations, and we pay according to the operation.

Q. Your duty as paymaster is amongst other things to pay for this piece-work? —A. Yes.

Q. Does the accountant make up what is payable to each man?—A. No, some timekeeper.

Q. How do you find out that 250 people are wanted there at piece-work and about 80 by the week?—A. I could not say.

Q. When an election comes on, are a greater number of men put at work in the factory?—A. No, not one more.

Q. Do you employ about the same number every year?—A. Yes.

Q. Some are employed a short time and some a long time?—A. Of course, when they are not fit to work, they are dispensed with.

Q. Would it not be better to have a smaller number of people employed the year round than to employ a number of persons for a week or a fortnight only as you are doing now?—A. Of course it would; but we cannot keep these young fellows at work if they do not want to work. They come and work for two or three weeks or a month or two months and then leave, and we have to employ others to take their places.

Q. Do you employ the same number at piece-work winter and summer?—A. Yes.

Q. A lot of these people seem to run in families. For example, I find seven or eight Fortiers, seven or eight Belangers, six Greniers, six Lachances, twelve Morris-

SESSIONAL PAPER No. 29a

setts, six Pelletiers, nine Robitailles, seven or eight Tremblays, about twelve Trepanniers. How do you explain that?—A. I cannot explain it.

By Mr. Fyshe:

Q. How much does an ordinary workman make?—A. The women are paid by day work.

Q. Are the men paid by piece work?—A. Yes, pretty nearly all the men.

Q. If a man works on piece work and works steadily, how much will he make a week?—A. From $15 to $17 a week.

By the Chairman:

Q. Do the timekeepers keep the time of the people who do piecework?—A. It is kept by the time card.

Q. Are all these people good labourers?—A. Oh, yes.

Q. It looks as if there were a number of people selected from different families and put in as a matter of favouritism?—A. Oh, no, the superintendent is very particular about that.

Q. You come here, I suppose, like everybody else, to say that you think you are insufficiently paid?—A. Yes, that is the principal thing.

Q. What do you think would be the proper payment for the clerical staff to which you belong?—A. I could not say.

Q. Take your own case. You are now getting $800; in five years you have gone from $2.05 to $800 a year. What do you think you should be paid, looking at the increased cost of living?—A. Not less than $1,000.

Q. That means practically that you think the salaries of the clerical staff should be increased 25 per cent?—A. I do not think that would be too much.

QUEBEC, September 17, 1907.

To the President of the Civil Service Commission,
Quebec.

We, the undersigned whose occupation, salary and date of appointment at the Dominion arsenal, are stated opposite our respective names, beg humbly to state our salary is very low, considering our functions, responsibilities and work, the more so that the cost of living has greatly increased since some ten years and wish furthermore to expose that we have not in this lapse of time benefited of a proportionate rise of pay as have generally the mechanics, machinists and foremen.

Name.	Occupation.	Date of Appointment.	Salary per annum.
			$
Alfred Dupré.................	Accountant.........	November, 1882.....	850
J. LaRochelle.................	Paymaster....	October, 1902.......	800
Ch. Denechaud...............	Clerk...........	July, 1897.........	750

Hoping that you may deem it an act of justice to use your generous influence in our behalf, we beg to subscribe ourselves.

(Signed.) ALFRED DUPRE.
J. LaROCHELLE.
CH. DENECHAUD.

The annexed has been forwarded to the Commission by the civilian members of the staff of the Royal Military College, Kingston, Ont, as stated by request of the Department of Militia.

7-8 EDWARD VII., A. 1908

From the Civilian Members of the Superior Staff, R.M.C., to the Commandant R.M.C. of Canada.

September 30, 1907.

Sir,—We, the undersigned civilian members of the Superior staff of the Royal Military College, have the honour to request you to submit for the consideration of the Honourable the Minister of Militia, the following proposal for the superannuation of such members of the said staff as may, in future, become disabled for the performance of their duties in a manner consistent with necessary efficiency.

In submitting this scheme we trust it may be recognized that the condition which obtain in the treatment of the civil and militia services are not analogous to those under which we serve, inasmuch as the initial appointments to either of these services may take place, and usually do take place at a comparatively early age, and time is thus given for a pension scheme to mature materially before its application is necessary. The appointment of a member of the R.M.C. staff presupposes a professional experience in similar fields, as a preparation for the duties and work of a professorship, and age, with its ripened judgment and experience is an essential qualification for the position of head of a department.

We, therefore, submit that, under the circumstances, our cases with respect to pension may be considered fairly parallel to those of members of the judicial bench, and that the principle of retirement accepted for them might, in justice to us, be adapted to suit our circumstances, and we beg to be allowed in accordance with what is here set forth, to respectfully suggest the following scheme, viz.:—

'A civilian member of the Superior staff of the Royal Military College may be retired to promote the efficiency of the staff, under the following conditions:—

'(a.) If he has reached the age of fifty years and the duration of his service has been ten years or more, he shall receive an annuity for life of fifty per cent of the annual salary which he was enjoying at the time of his retirement, with an additional two per cent of such salary for each year's service over and above ten, but the maximum annuity shall not exceed seventy per cent of salary at time of retirement.

(b) If he is under fifty years of age on retirement with at least ten years service, he shall receive an annuity as before described less two per cent of salary for each year he is under fifty.

(c) If the duration of his service has been less than ten years, he shall receive for eaach year's srvice a gratuity of one-tenth of his annual salary at time of retirement.

(d) In cases of voluntary retirement with the approval of the Government, the gratuity will be as previously stated herein, but the annuity will be subject to a reduction of twenty per cent if the retiring member of the staff has not reached the age of fifty.

(e) Annuities shall be payable in monthly instalments clear of all taxes and deductions, whatsoever, imposed under any Act of the Parliament of Canada.

(f) Service on the staff of the Royal Military College shall be allowed to count towards pension of an officer under the Militia Pension Act in the event of transfer to the permanent force.'

We respectfully submit that by some such amendment to the Royal Military College Act the analogy between it and the Judges' Act might be rendered complete.

We have the honour to be, sir,
Your obedient servants,

Iva E. Martin.	Alex. Laird.
J. B. Cochrane.	J. M. Lanos.
W. R. Butler.	H. J. Dawson.

A further addition has been submitted, as follows:—

Any widow of a professor to whom she has been married at least ten years before his death, shall receive one-half of the allowance which would have gone to her husband.

OTTAWA, FRIDAY, May 31, 1907.

The Royal Commission on the Civil Service met this morning at 10.30 o'clock.

Present:—Mr. J. M. COURTNEY, C.M.G., Chairman.

Mr. THOMAS FYSHE, Montreal, and

Mr. P. J. BAZIN, Quebec.

Lieut.-Col. FREDERICK WHITE, C.M.G., called. sworn and examined.

By the Chairman:

Q. You are the Comptroller of the Northwest Mounted Police?—A. Yes.

Q. How long have you been Comptroller?—A. Since July, 1880.

Q. Latterly you have had added to your duties that of Commissioner of the Northwest Territories?—A. Yes.

Q. That is to say, the part that has not been formed into Provinces?—A. The unorganized territories; about two-thirds of the area of Canada, including Ungava.

By Mr. Fyshe:

Q. Have you many men scattered around in Ungava?—A. We have no men in Ungava as yet. We have some in Hudson Bay.

By the Chairman:

Q. What is you salary now?—A. $4,000 as Comptroller of the Mounted Police, and $1,000 as Commissioner of the Northwest Territories.

Q. Your service dates back to 1869?—A. Yes, to January, 1869.

Q. That is, you have been over 38 years in the public service?—A. Yes.

Q. In the first part of your service you were private secretary to Sir John Macdonald?—A. Not at first; I was for a time a clerk in the Department of Justice, and later on became his private secretary.

Q. You were examined before the last Civil Service Commission, in 1892?—A. Yes.

Q. You have now the same chief clerk as you had then?—A. Yes.

Q. Mr. Fortescue?—A. Yes.

Q. And the same first class clerk?—A. Yes and the accountant as well.

Q. You have three second class clerks?—A. Yes.

Q. The only addition to your staff since 1892 is one second class clerk, Mr. Drake? —A. Yes, he has recently been transferred to another department.

Q. And three junior seconds?—A. Three junior seconds.

Q. You have no women at all in your department?—A. None at all.

Q. In addition you have in Ottawa attached to your staff about half a dozen men engaged in packing and so forth whom you call constables?—A. Yes, non-commissioned officers or constables; one of them ranks as an officer. They are members of the outside service, but they do work at Ottawa which can be done more economically here than in the Northwest, and avoids duplication of labour.

Q. What kind of work are they engaged in?—A. Checking and classifying expenditure, packing and the distribution of clothing and other supplies, and a great deal of routine.

Q. Your first class clerk and accountant is now 77 years of age?—A. Yes. His retirement has been under discussion for some time; he has now asked to be retired

7-8 EDWARD VII., A. 1908

on the 1st January next, and the recommendation will be submitted to Sir Wilfrid Laurier on his return to Canada.

Q. You rank as a deputy head?—A. Yes.

Q. By an Act of Parliament?—A. Yes.

Q. And you are placed under the control of the Prime Minister of the day?—A. Yes.

Q. I suppose you have kept Mr. Fisher, the accountant, who is 77 years of age, for some years beyond the time when he might have been retired?—A. Mr. Fisher has been ripe for superannuation for years, but owing to old associations, I did not wish to press it upon him.

By Mr. Fyshe :

Q. Has he been efficient for the last ten years?—A. He has not been up to full work. He has suffered from internal troubles. When you have worked with a man for thirty years you do not feel like pressing him to retire.

By the Chairman :

Q. If the Superannuation Act had not been abolished, could not your department have been made more effective?—A. Undoubtedly.

Q. Everybody who has given evidence before us has declared that the abolition of the Superannuation Act was a mistake, in their opinion. Do you agree with that ?—A. I do, undoubtedly.

Q. In the Mounted Police you have a commissioner two assistant commissioners, superintendents, inspectors, surgeons, assistant surgeons, and veterinary surgeons. Do you have assistant inspectors?—A. No.

Q. How many are on the roll of the Mounted Police now?—A. Nominally 800, but 765 is, I think, the actual strength of the outside force at present. What I am aiming at is to have the old staff pass out in the next four or five years. My chief accountant is 77, my chief clerk is over 60, I am over 60, and the other clerks I principally depend upon are over 45. I think that those who built up the force are the best fitted to wind it up.

Q. The men on the force are engaged for a certain term of years ?—A. Yes, for five years.

Q. With the development of the Northwest there are many opportunities for a constable after his term has expired to go out and better himself ?—A. Yes, and they do it. That is one of our difficulties. Men go into the force simply until they can do something better. Four or five of the members of the new Provincial legislatures in the Northwest are men who were constables in the Mounted Police. You will also find mayors of towns, and some of the best men in the country.

Q. Do you offer them any inducement to re-enlist after five years?—A. Not the slightest. They may re-enlist for one year or three years. We have men in the force who have served for twenty-five years. If they can get a chance to better themselves, we are only too glad to see them go out.

By Mr. Fyshe:

Q. Are any of them married?—A. Many of them are married, but we restrict them as much as possible in that respect. The married men form a small colony outside of the barracks, where they are allowed their rations instead of drawing them in barracks in the mess.

By the Chairman:

Q. In order to secure continuity and length of service you have procured from Parliament an Act to give your officers pensions on retirement?—A. Yes, they have a pension.

Q. When did that Act come into force?—A. In 1902. Previously our officers were under the Superannuation Act. We also have a Pension Act for the non-commissioned officers and constables.

Q. The Officers Pension Act has been put on the statute book since the Superannuation Act was abolished?—A. Yes. We substituted the Pension Act for the Superannuation Act. Out of 52 officers 49 adopted the pension, and two or three remained under the Superannuation Act.

Q. The officers of the force who contributed to the superannuation fund had the privilege of election to either of the two systems?—A. Yes.

Q. Those who came in latterly came in under the new pension system?—A. Yes.

Q. Do you find any difficulties in getting officers now?—A. Oh, no. The difficulty is in resisting applications.

Q. Your Pension Act led the way to the Militia Department getting a Pension Act?—A. First of all, we got a Pension Act. Later on Sir Frederick Borden got a Pension Act for the militia, including both officers and men. We then succeeded in getting a Pension Bill for our officers on the same lines as the militia.

Q. Your Act provides that in case of the death of an officer, his pension goes to his widow?—A. Yes, in a reduced amount, and the children get a proportion also—I think up to the age of 18 for boys and the age of 21 for girls.

Q. What is the pension to a constable who serves only five years?—A. A constable gets nothing for five years. The non-commissioned officers and constables contribute nothing to the fund. The officers contribute five per cent of their salaries. In the case of a constable the pension amounts to one-fiftieth for every year of service up to twenty years, and after that it is increased so that twenty-eight years' service will give a man two-thirds of his pay. For instance, if a man attains the rank of a staff-sergeant, and his pay is $1.50 per day, he gets $1 a day pension after twenty-eight years' service. But if a man has been twenty years in the service he can only claim twenty-fiftieths.

Q. But practically your men go out at the end of the term of five years?—A. Many do..

Q. But with the openings in the Northwest, even the pension system is no inducement to them to remain?—A. Not much. Up to ten years ago the average term of service of men in the mounted police was from twelve to fifteen years, while to-day the average service, if you include the non-commissioned officers, is not five years. A man who has been in the police force is in demand by commercial companies, and every man can buy his discharge.

By Mr. Fyshe:

Q. I suppose some of them take up land?—A. They do take up land, and become the best kind of settlers and prominent men in their districts. In the legislature of the two Provinces to-day there are about eight members who served in the ranks of the mounted police. We also have representatives in the Senate and House of Commons.

Q. They are disciplined men?—A. Yes, and they know the ways of the country.

By the Chairman:

Q. According to last year's statement you spent in your department over a million dollars?—A. Yes.

Q. You still have about the same number of police in the Territories and the Provinces of Alberta and Saskatchewan that you used to have?—A. We have reduced the number. In the two new Provinces we have about fifty men less.

Q. As the Provinces have only started into existence and the municipalities are only about being organized, until they can have their own constabulary, you are still to some extent keeping your police there, and the Provinces are paying something towards their expenses?—A. Yes. Our arrangement is that we shall have 500 men in the old organized Northwest, which is now Alberta and Saskatchewan. We had 500

7-8 EDWARD VII., A. 1908

men there when the two new Provinces were created, and to have removed them at that time would have caused a great deal of disturbance; because, apart from being a police force, the mounted police have always been a general utility force in the country, doing work for every department of the public service. Under the arrangement with the two Provinces I have estimated that their proportion would be $150,000, and the police are to continue to perform police duty in these two Provinces for a period of five years from the 1st September, 1905, each Province contributing to the Dominion revenue $75,000 a year from the 1st July, 1906. I estimate that $150,000 is about one-third of the cost. We have an average of 200 prisoners in our guard-rooms. Last year over 1,500 prisoners passed through the police guard-rooms in the two Provinces. At Calgary to-day we have about 48 prisoners, at Edmonton about 30, at McLeod between 30 and 40. As soon as the Provinces can get their appropriations and build gaols they will take over these prisoners.

Another matter which affects my department very materially and the appropriation for it, has been the amount of work we have had to do for other departments. For this we have rendered accounts and got repayments. Last year we got from other departments for these services about $120,000. That $120,000 probably represented 3,000 vouchers. For instance a prisoner has to be brought from the place of committal to the penitentiary; a lunatic has to be brought to the asylum in the same way. Then there is work done for the Department of Agriculture. We have 16 veterinary surgeons employed in that work, and we have to be repaid for that. I am negotiating an arrangement by which our work will be reduced to the extent of about 2,000 vouchers in the Northwest alone, resulting in a saving of labour and cross entries. We are in that stage of winding up our work.

Q. As the Northwest becomes settled and the municipalities are formed, the Mounted Police will cease to exist ?—A. That is what I believe, within the next five years.

Q. But as certain parts of the area of Canada are still territorial, that will not happen in your time or mine ?—A. But it will not require the same number of men. For the next twenty-five years there will still be work for the police in the north, but it will be a different force. It will be more of a detective force. It will not be mounted police. For instance, we have men stationed at the mouth of the Mackenzie river, and we have them at Fort Churchill, on Hudson Bay. In the far north, north of the 30th parallel, there will be work for police for the next twenty-five years, but my estimate is that 100 men will be sufficient, and that the 500 men in the older territories will disappear in the next four or five years, the work they do being assumed by local jurisdiction. Our 16 veterinary surgeons have been doing all the quarantine work for the Department of Agriculture. The Department of Agriculture promised to take that work over on July 1.

By Mr. Fyshe :

Q. At these outlying points, where you have only a few men, I suppose they get more or less assistance from the Hudson's Bay company if they want it ?—A. Only what they pay for. The moment the Government sends a man in, the Hudson's Bay company drop everything. The Hudson's Bay company have been in the habit of supplying the natives to go out hunting, not so much from philanthropic as from business motives, because they depended on the natives for skins, but the moment the Government put a flag up, the Hudson's Bay company tell the natives who want assistance to go to the Government.

By the Chairman:

Q. You expect that in the next four or five years the police who are now stationed within the area occupied by the Local Governments will disappear ?—A. I think they ought to.

Q. And probably will ?—A. Yes. There is only one question about it. The

SESSIONAL PAPER No. 29a

Dominion Government has retained control of the land, the immigration and the Indians, and the provinces claim that, therefore, the Dominion Government is to a certain extent responsible for preserving law and order. That is their argument. We have the same argument in British Columbia. We sent police into British Columbia, and the British Columbia Government refused to pay the bill, because they said that the Indians were wards of the Dominion. That point may come up. The land matter will solve itself.

Q. At present the Local Governments contribute to the Mounted Police Department $150,000 a year?—A. Yes. I may say that our estimates of this year showed a reduction of $415,000. We cut down the general expenses by $265,000, and the Provinces contributed $150,000, making a reduction of $415,000.

Q. Are your officers paid any allowances?—A. No, except in the far north.

Q. When an inspector becomes incapacitated and retires under the Pension Act does he get such a proportion of his pay and the value of his privileges, such as living in barracks?—A. Yes. There is an order in council fixing the amount for each grade which is to be added to the pay for pension purposes.

Q. When he is retired he is paid a retiring pension on the basis of his pay and the value of his privileges?—A. Yes.

Q. We shall ask you to supplement your statement with a memorandum on anything it would be desirable for us to note?—A. I shall be very glad if you will allow me to do that.

Q. You have no objection to Mr. Fyshe and Mr. Bazin going to your office and seeing the returns sent in by the Mounted Police?—A. I shall be very glad indeed at any time, and I shall be most pleased to show what our work is and our system.

Q. You have, I believe, a system whereby you know at any moment, by the last return sent in, where every constable is situated?—A. Yes, within a month, except in the Hudson Bay district, where it may be six months. We have monthly returns by which we know the number of men at each station. We have 120 detachments of men divided into twos and threes.

Q. Subject to the delays in the mails consequent on the territory being so far distant, you know in your office where every constable and every officer of the Mounted Police is?—A. Yes.

By Mr. Fyshe:

Q. Have you not rather impressed the Americans with the efficiency of your system in that large territory?—A. I have a little personal vanity that our work is appreciated. The mystery of it to our neighbors south of the line is our prompt administration of justice.

By the Chairman:

Q. In this expenditure of a million dollars in your department, over $400,000 went to the pay of the force?—A. Yes.

Q. The chief part of the rest went to pay for forage, fuel and light. The forage is, of course, procured on the spot?—A. Yes, most of it, except in the Yukon, where we have to send it in.

Q. What do you call subsistence?—A. Subsistence covers food and all kinds of provisions. In many cases we have men living at hotels; the average cost of their board is about $18 per month, and we grant them what we call subsistence money. In the same way we make grants for forage for horses. A man has to pay from $12 to $15, and sometimes $18 per month for the board of his horse. We make allowances of that kind. Frequently there are married men at detachments. You cannot expect a man to remain unmarried on the force for twenty-five years, and we try to give our married men places where they have a little home of their own, and instead of issuing provisions to them, as to the men in barracks, we allow them $18 or $20 a month, and they feed themselves.

Q. And your men have to be clothed in uniforms?—A. Yes.

Q. Who supplies that as a rule?—A. It is supplied by contract.

Q. The lowest tender accepted?—A. We call for tenders about every three or four years. I am busy now with contracts. Thirty-two tenders came in about a month ago, and just before Sir Wilfrid Laurier left he approved of my recommendation awarding contracts for forty-two articles to the lowest tenderer. In one of the other cases it was awarded to one of two who were equal. One was an Ottawa man and the other was a Quebec man. It was a case of mocassins, and as they had to be made in Quebec, the contract was awarded to the Quebec man. In the other case the tenders were even, and we gave the benefit to the old contractor.

Q. Practically your rule is to take the lowest tender?—A. Yes.

Q. And you get security for the execution of the contract?—A. Yes, five per cent.

Q. Which is deposited with the Finance Department?—A. Yes, in every case.

Q. The same rule would apply to saddles, I suppose?—A. We have not bought saddles for years, but I may say that the same applies in the Northwest to even the filling of icehouses or the cutting of a stack of hay. We always demand a deposit, and if a man does not fulfil his contract the deposit is forfeited. The only exception to that was an Order in Council which was passed about a month ago returning a deposit of $18 to the widow of a contractor.

Q. Do you find any political pressure exercised by your officers to get promotion? —A. Oh, yes, when an election is coming on. We cannot help that under our political system.

Q. Have you any standard or examination by which you make an inspector a superintendent?—A. No. As a rule an inspector is not promoted until he has been in that office ten or fifteen years, and we have confidential reports from the commissioner on the capabilities of the officers, which to my mind, are far better than any competitive examination.

Q. Do all the men who have been promoted prove to be efficient?—A. We have some disappointments like everybody else; but on the whole we have a very efficient lot of men. There are a lot of old men like myself who have been in the service for many years.

Q. According to this list, the oldest commissioned officer in the force seems to be about 58. Have you any fixed age at which an inspector is retired?—A. No. It is simply a matter of efficiency.

Q. As it happens, among the commissioned officers of the mounted police in the Northwest, no officer at present is of the age of 60?—A. No.

Q. When a man gets to be over the age of 60, and is gradually becoming incapacitated from taking active exercise and riding about, have you any means of retiring him?—A. Yes, we can retire him under the Pension Act.

Q. You have not a fixed retiring age of 65, as in the British army?—A. No. we have not. We can retire a man at any time to promote efficiency.

Q. All your offices here are in one place?—A. Yes.

Q. Where are your storekeepers stationed?—A. In a building on Wellington street, just below the Bank of Montreal.

Q. That is where you keep your stores?—A. Yes.

Q. Your official staff is all in one building?—A. Yes.

Q. In the Western block?—A. Yes.

Q. You have no offices outside?—A. No. We have simply that building where we receive clothing, stamp it and re-issue it.

Q. Have you an audit of your stores?—A. We have in the west a semi-annual stock-taking. Here we simply receive and check the goods. In the west the stock-taking used to be quarterly, but now it is on the 1st July and 1st January in each year. There is a board, at every post, appointed to examine the stores. It is composed of three officers, and if there are not three officers at any post, a non-commissioned officer takes the place of an officer. They examine every article in store, and anything that is used up, such as old brooms, pots and pans, is recommended for condemnation, and is destroyed. Having agreed to that, an officer is detailed to see that everything is destroyed. No man can get a broom even unless he brings back the old one. We get a certificate from a responsible officer that he personally saw everything which was condemned destroyed in such a way that it could not be used again.

Q. You have no stock-taking by the Auditor General?—A. No, we have never reached that.

Q. What is the total value of your stores?—A. I think that to-day the stores for the whole force would not be worth more than $100,000. We have nothing in store except clothing. We have a form which shows everything that is in use, another showing what is in store that is new, and in every barrack room there is a board showing what belongs to that room. Our system of checking is about as complete as we can make it.

Q. How long has your department been in force?—A. It commenced in 1873.

Q. It has existed from the Hudson Bay period until the civil government period in the Northwest?—A. We began at Fort Garry before any treaty had been made with any of the Indians.

Q. The mounted police have seen the evolution of the Northwest Territories from an unoccupied prairie to a country of settled government?—A. Yes.

Q. Your force is a migratory force, always on the move?—A. It is always on the move.

Q. When on the move do they get any allowance beyond their bare out of pocket expenses?—A. No.

Q. How far does a man go on this patrol duty?—A. At Yorkton he has a radius of fifty miles. North of that a man has a radius of a hundred miles.

Q. When he goes out in this way is he paid his expenses merely?—A. What he produces receipts for.

Q. He must of necessity do this patrol work?—A. That is his work.

Q. And that is one of the inducements to enter the service?—A. That is one.

Q. Would it not tend to encourage him to go frequently over the road if he had a little allowance for that?—A. I would like very much if we could do something like that.

Q. We have learned from other witnesses that inspectors who go on trips are out of pocket as a rule, and it is only a sense of obligation that makes them do their work?—A. There is no question about that, and they incur liabilities. The men must travel and they pay a good deal more than they receive for expenses.

Q. Do the men in your department sign the attendance book?—A. Yes.

Q. The office hours in a small department like yours, I suppose, are not laid down by a fixed rule, but the men work when there is work to be done?—A. They work from half past nine until the work is done.

ROYAL NORTHWEST MOUNTED POLICE.
OFFICE OF THE COMPTROLLER,
OTTAWA, May 27, 1907.

SIR,—In reply to your letter of 18th inst., I send you, herewith, a statement which I think gives the information called for. If not, I shall be very glad to supplement it.

I have the honour to be, sir,
Your obedient servant,

F. WHITE,
THOS. S. HOWE, Esq.,   *Comptroller.*
    Secretary, Civil Service Commission,
        The Senate, Room No. 2,
            Ottawa.

7-8 EDWARD VII., A. 1908

ROYAL NORTHWEST MOUNTED POLICE, OTTAWA.

INSIDE SERVICE VOTE.

Name.	1891—1892.		1905—1906.		Salaries 1905-6, if Statutory Increases had not been stopped for two years.
	Rank.	Salary.	Rank.	Salary.	
		$ cts.		$ cts.	
Fred. White......	Comptroller	3,200 00	Comptroller	4,000 00	$ 4,000.00.
L. Fortescue	1st Class Clerk...	1,800 00	Chief Clerk. ...	2,350 00	2,450.00.
A. Fisher...	2nd " ...	1,400 00	1st Class Clerk ...	1,900 00.	1,900.00.
L. duPlessis......	3rd " ...	900 00	2nd " ...	1,450 00,	1,475.00.
R. M. Gallwey....	3rd " ...	900 00.	2nd "	1,350 00	1,350.00.
R. S. Bishop.. . .	3rd " ...	700 00	2nd "	1,300 00	1,300.00.
E. H. Hinchey....	Messenger........	420 00			
E. F. Drake			2nd "	1,275 00	Recently transferred to
A. V. Joyce......			Jr. 2nd " ...	800 00	Dept. of Interior.
W. Gravel.... ..			Jr. 2nd " ...	837 50	
	Total salaries.	9,320 00		15,262 50	

No amounts were paid for salaries or wages from contingency vote.

AMOUNTS PAID FROM OUTSIDE SERVICE VOTE.

Name.	1891—1892.		1905—1906.		
	Rank.	Salary.	Rank.	Pay and Allowance	
		Salary.		$ cts.	
George Stevens....	Staff Sergeant ..	1,129 10	Inspector....	1,583 33	
C. J. Pearson.....	"	1,044 71	Staff Sergeant	1,314 00	
C. R. W. Stuart..	Sergeant...... ...	573 13	"	1,186 25	
E. F. Drake	"	788 87	....		Transferred to inside service, as shown above.
L. Deslauriers	Constable	577 16	Sergeant.........	638 75	
W. F. Slaney.....	Packer and Messenger.	457 50	Packer and Messenger.	700 00	
M. G. Nagle	Packer..		Packer.......	645 00	
F. Bissonnette. ..	"	370 00	"	645 00	
R. F. Harris ...	Constable...... .	274 50	....	....	Transferred to Dept. of Justice.
E. Payne........	"	273 76	....	....	Transferred to Dept. of Customs.
W. O'Brien. ...	Packer..		Packer...	456 25	
Jno. Stevens.....	....		Constable...	591 40	Recently appointed to inside service.
		5,488 73		7,759 98